REMEMBERED PAST

REMEMBERED PAST

*John Lukacs
on History, Historians,
and Historical Knowledge*

A READER

edited by

Mark G. Malvasi and Jeffrey O. Nelson

ISI Books
Wilmington, Delaware

Library of Congress Cataloging-in-Publication Data:

Lukacs, John, 1924–

   Remembered past : John Lukacs on history, historians, and historical knowledge : a reader / John Lukacs ; edited with an introduction by Mark G. Malvasi and Jeffrey O. Nelson. — 1st ed. — Wilmington, Del. : ISI Books, 2004.

      p. ; cm.

   Includes bibliographical references, and a complete bibliography of Lukacs's writings through 2003.

      ISBN: 1-932236-27-9
      1-932236-28-7 (pbk.)

      1. History, Modern—20th century. 2. History—Philosophy. 3. Civilization, Modern. 4. Historians. 5. Lukacs, John, 1924– 6. Essays. I. Title.

D415 .L84 2004   2004102734
909.82—dc22   0409

ISI Books
Intercollegiate Studies Institute
P.O. Box 4431
Wilmington, DE 19807-0431
www.isibooks.org

Book design by Kara Beer

Manufactured in the United States of America

Contents

❄ ❄ ❄

III. Dissenting Opinions
(Or: A Few Other Prosaists)

❁ ❁ ❁

IV. Places and Times

❁ ❁ ❁

V. Some Twentieth-Century Questions

�֎ �֎ �֎

VI. Reading, Writing, and Teaching History

✖ ✖ ✖

Bibliography of the Published Writings of John Lukacs, 1947–2003 ✻ 783

Notes ✻ 833

Index ✻ 895

Preface

Wherever man has lived, wherever he has left some feeble imprint of his life and his intelligence, there is history. ❈ Fustel de Coulanges

In history, as in nature, the processes of death and birth are eternally in step with one another. Old forms of thought die out while, at the same time and on the same soil, a new crop begins to bloom. ❈ Johan Huizinga

This anthology presents the work of an original mind, a historian acutely sensitive to the conditions that shaped life in the twentieth century and the modern age: John Lukacs. Born in Budapest in 1924, Lukacs came to the United States in 1946 to escape the Communist takeover of his homeland. His life has spanned much of the history of the century about which he has so movingly written. As the author of *The Duel* and *Five Days in London, May 1940*, Lukacs is one of the most popular historians of World War II; as the author of *Historical Consciousness*, a study of the nature of historical thought, Lukacs remains almost unknown. *Remembered Past* seeks to call attention to this unjustly neglected aspect of Lukacs's work. The diverse essays and reviews that compose this volume situate his corpus in the unfolding narrative of historical thinking.

Human life is intensely, unalterably historical. "*Man . . . has no nature,*" wrote the Spanish philosopher José Ortega y Gasset. "*[W]hat he has is . . . history. . . . Man . . . finds that he has no nature other than what he has himself done.*"[1] Even the body originates in the past, a unique variant of ancestral genetic components. So completely does the past infuse being that man has come to have "no proper place in what is new."[2] The restive discontent with custom and tradition and the impetuous embrace of novelty and fashion signal not progress but an illness that may yet prove fatal: the inability or unwillingness to accept human limits and to live within our means on our inheritance. "The error of the old doctrine of progress," Ortega declared, "lay in affirming a priori that man progresses toward the better."[3] Time alone will tell. Without reconciling the ephemeral present with the enduring past, we will know neither peace nor rest. That much is certain. The accomplishments as well as the failures of history are ours to bear and to pass on. Civilization, and perhaps existence itself, depends on the effort to answer the unanswered questions of the past and to undertake anew the tasks that previous generations left incomplete. To forget the past is thus to invite moral catastrophe and spiritual ruin, for it means to lose contact with the self, with reality, and with all that is human.

Of utmost importance, according to John Lukacs, is the continuing need to rethink the significance of the past itself, to expose the past to "multiple jeopardy."[4] Yet Lukacs demurs to answer the epistemological question of what constitutes historical knowledge. He knows that historians cannot offer statements of definitive historical truth. On the contrary, Lukacs has concerned himself with the reduction of untruth by explaining the conditions of thought and identifying the limitations of knowledge. Modern men, as Lukacs puts it, have become "historians by nature." Their understandings of self and world emerge and take shape in relation to the past. He concurs with the nineteenth-century German historian and philosopher Wilhelm Dilthey that men know themselves through their history, and that they understand their history at least as much from the inside out as from the outside in. Similarly, insofar as the link between life and the past is indissoluble, Lukacs agrees with Benedetto Croce that all history is contemporary history, that all history is the remembered past—the imprecise, unsystematic, and partial knowledge that some human beings have of other human beings.[5]

The intellectual revolution that brought history to the forefront of consciousness began in the seventeenth century and, Lukacs argues, coincided with the rise of science and the adoption of the scientific method. Together, history and science reflected the growing secularization of thought that followed the Protestant Reformation and the ensuing wars of religion. In time, the ideological conflict between Protestants and Catholics, which resulted in the slaughter of hundreds of thousands in the name of God, debased religion, subverted theology, and inspired a mistrust—among all but the most zealous and enthusiastic—of any system proclaiming to embody truths beyond those that observation and evidence could verify. Conscientious and thoughtful men accepted nothing on faith. For the educated classes, history and science filled a void (as, perhaps, witchcraft did for the masses), introducing alternative methods of ordering and interpreting experience.

But, though they share common antecedents, history and science have diverged in their purposes. Science, Lukacs maintains, involves the exploration of nature, while history, as Giambattista Vico first observed in *Scienza nuova*, comprises man's knowledge of man. History, for Lukacs, is a form of thought. Science may be studied historically; the history of a science is science. History, by contrast, because it deals with the exceptional, the indeterminate, and the unpredictable, cannot be studied scientifically. Attempts to reconcile history and science, or, more precisely, to subordinate history to science and to subject the investigation of the past to objective and universal laws, has led historians into error and confusion. Nevertheless, well into the twentieth century, historians continued to associate their discipline with science, social science, and the prestige that both enjoyed. For example, in *What Is History?* E. H. Carr concluded that "scientists, social scientists, and historians are all engaged in different branches of the same study: the study of man and his environment, of the effects of man on his environment and of his environment on man. The object of the study is the same: to increase man's understanding of, and mastery over, his environment."[6] The nature and purpose of history, Lukacs replies, are not so pragmatic, so utilitarian, or so grandiose. History does not work. Unlike scientists, historians cannot manipulate data to change the world or to predict the future. Their intent is, or ought to be, not to increase the "quantity of knowledge" but to deepen the "quality of understanding."[7]

Yet, in some respects, the conception of history as science and, later, as social science marked an intellectual advance. During the eighteenth century, principally in Western Europe, history flourished as literature. Only in the nineteenth century did history sever its connections with literature and emerge as an independent form of inquiry governed by its own methods and objectives, which the German philologist Leopold von Ranke articulated. Historians, Ranke insisted, must try to write history as it actually happened or as it actually was (*"Ich will nur sagen wie es eigentlich gewesen ist"*). Unlike many of his successors, Ranke never intended that historians accumulate a multitude of facts to produce an exact transcript of the past to which, as Lord Acton hoped, all could assent. Such a project was as undesirable as it was impossible. "Those historians are . . . mistaken," Ranke protested, "who consider history simply an immense aggregate of particular facts, which it behooves one to commit to memory."[8] By themselves, facts revealed nothing. Only a systematic and critical evaluation of original documents enabled historians to organize the facts in meaningful ways, to expose the unity of disparate events, and to adduce the truth.

Ranke's innovative approach encouraged the study of the past in its own terms and not merely as a narrative expression of established authority, orthodox principle, or dogmatic system, whether literary, theological, or philosophical. He remained confident that whatever the shortcomings of his own work he could show "humanity, as it is, explicable or inexplicable: the life of the individual, of generations, and of nations, and at times the hand of God above them."[9] Far from making a science of history, Ranke's determination to reconstruct the past "as it was" cast history adrift from its philosophical moorings and left it vulnerable to diverse and competing political interpretations. Ranke's twentieth-century disciple, Friedrich Meinecke, ascertained the epistemological weakness that afflicted Ranke's thinking and continues to burden historicism. The study of history, Meinecke admitted, tended to make all values impermanent, arbitrary, and relative. Since no belief is, or can be, absolute, universal, and timeless, those inclined to do so can use the past to justify and promote their cause. Current academic pretensions notwithstanding, the effort to transform history into a neutral, objective science arose in part from the desire to insulate the study of the past from the ideological disputes and upheavals of the nineteenth century. In that ideologically charged atmosphere, gifted historians could not resist the temptation to indulge in partisan activity or to put historical scholarship at the service of political ambition. In France, their number included Augustin Thierry, François Guizot, Jules Michelet, and Jean Jaurès; in Germany, Johann Gustav Droysen and Helmut von Treischke; in Great Britain, Thomas Babington Macaulay and Thomas Carlyle; in the United States, George Bancroft. Most notable, of course, were Karl Marx and Friedrich Engels.

By the second half of the nineteenth century, then, the majority of historians had begun to associate history with the natural sciences. So pervasive was this conviction that in his inaugural lecture as Regius Professor of Modern History at Cambridge, delivered in 1902, J. B. Bury could assert that "history has really been enthroned and ensphered among the sciences; but the particular nature of her influence, her time-honoured association with literature, and other circumstances, have acted as a sort of cloud, half concealing from men's eyes her new position in the heavens."[10] Under the influence of positivism, the learned English amateur historian Henry Thomas Buckle aspired to discern uniform and unchanging patterns of human existence, just as scientists had purportedly fathomed the design of nature and the configuration of the universe. Historians, Buckle contended, had not only to make the past intelligible, but also to make events predictable. Only their indolence and incompetence had thus far delayed the creation of a true science of history.

Lukacs dismisses this persistent representation of history as science and social science, refusing, as he writes, to force "history into the Procrustean bed of the scientific method."[11] His views are more consonant with those of Croce, Dilthey, and Droysen, each of whom emphasized understanding (*verstehen*) at the expense of precision or accuracy of knowledge and accepted the unavoidably personal involvement of the historian with his subject. In addition, Lukacs suggests that an understanding of the past cannot be confined to "what actually happened." The potential is as important to historians as the actual, for, as Lukacs remarks, "human inclinations, even when they do not mature into definite acts, are essentially potential signs of actualities."[12] In this respect, Lukacs echoes the French social theorist Raymond Aron, who explained that "we speak of understanding when *knowledge shows a meaning which, immanent to the reality, has been or could have been thought by those who lived and realized it.*"[13] Historians do not reconstruct, reproduce, or re-experience the complex reality of the past "as it actually happened," summoning it again to life. Rather, they re-imagine its meaning and rethink its significance. The study of the past is an act of creative re-cognition in which historians contemplate the potential inherent in the actual and reexamine different and changing ways of feeling, perceiving, remembering, and thinking. About history there must forever be an element of contingency, indeterminacy, and doubt, since human communication even between contemporaries is always imperfect and since history is the continual reinterpretation of the past for the present.

History, though, constitutes more than ruminations occurring in the minds of historians. It is, in Lukacs's preferred formulation, the "remembered past," potentially encompassing the entirety of human experience beyond the information that documents record. Among other implications, understanding history as the remembered past "represents the beginning of an awareness of the limitations of the scientific method . . . , the recognition that Descartes' division of the universe into 'subjects' and 'objects' no longer makes sense."[14] To Descartes, no problem was beyond solution; no invincible secrets, no indomitable mysteries confounded the rational mind. The universe was transparent. Ideas about reality were objectively intelligible and mathematically certain. Nothing was ambiguous. Subject and object were radically separate and distinct, as were spirit and body, mind and matter. Quantitative deduction emancipated the intellect from error and superstition, rendering human beings at last "the masters and possessors of nature."[15]

Repudiating, or rather superceding, Descartes' methods and categories, Lukacs maintains that historical consciousness is neither subjective nor objective but personal and participant. The unequivocal and absolute separation of subject and object, the misapprehension that historical truth exists outside the mind, leads to, and is in fact predicated upon, a kind of determinism: the assurance that historians of varying educations, abilities, temperaments, nationalities, cultures, and perspectives will reach identical conclusions about the past. Neither are historical judgments subjective. Lukcas is no solipsist. Personal and participant knowledge is not the equivalent of individual and private knowledge. Human beings are not isolated, solitary creatures whose ideas are wholly inaccessible. They live in relation to, and in relationships with, other human beings. Nor is knowledge of the human—fragmentary, selective, and inaccurate though it may be—ever general, abstract, and bloodless. During the Modern Age man's knowledge of man may have turned introspective, but at the same time it came to be historical.

As consciousness evolved, reality became inseparable from mind, that is, from thinking about reality—and, Lukacs adds, from thinking about thinking. The language of reality is thus not scientific, mathematical, or geometric any more than it is merely psychological. The language of reality is, instead, personal, participant, and historical. "We have been geometricians not only through chance," Lukacs believes, "but through history, and we are now near the end of a phase of history when the *esprit de la géometrie* and the mathematical concept of reality seemed the best (and, increasingly, the only) approach to truth. But now as the antinomies of idealism and realism, of objective and subjective knowledge prove to be inadequate, we may find anew the potential for an idealistic and realistic view of life."[16] To eliminate such dualisms, Lukacs has stressed the essential importance of the human. He has no wish to substitute the intellectual order of science for the intelligible disorder of history. Unlike Enlightenment thinkers who enshrined the objective laws of reason and postmodernist critics who disavowed any reality beyond the subjective constructs of mind, Lukacs has restored man to the center of the universe.

Lukacs's humanism does not engender an exultant vision of mankind and a triumphant philosophy of history that reveal design, intention, and purpose. Quite the contrary: Lukacs espouses a chastened historical philosophy that recognizes the historical dimension of both existence and consciousness. No simple narrative from which to derive heroic examples or moral lessons, history is a form of thought integral to the nature and being of humanity. Historical knowledge is inseparable from personal knowledge. To "*know thyself,*" Lukacs asserts, "must also mean *know thy history.*"[17] Knowing thyself, however, requires an appreciation of the limitations of knowledge or, perhaps better, of the human conditions of knowledge—an appreciation that Lukacs regards as salutary and enriching rather than malignant and impoverishing. A heightened consciousness of the self and history, and of the self in history, abrogates the expectations of heaven on earth that accompanied faith in scientific, technological, and material progress. Sir Francis Bacon's aphorism "knowledge is power" seems vain and arrogant to Lukacs and, for all its presumption and immodesty, naïve, superficial, and reckless as well. "Only humility and submission . . . can produce a worthy man," wrote Montaigne. Men endowed with the mature and contrite sense that their knowledge and understanding are circumscribed by the very nature of their being do not aspire to utter definitive statements, do not pretend to speak for all time, and do not incline to dream of utopia (or of the apocalypse).

Developments in modern physics sustain Lukacs's assault on the scientific worldview. Far from confirming the operation of the universe according to a set of mathematical laws, the physicists who contributed to quantum theory demolished the ideas of scientific objectivity, immutability, and certainty. They abandoned constricting definitions, illusory facts, and mechanical causality in favor of potentiality, mutability, and flux. They substituted relations for absolutes. Quantum physics led to the acceptance of relativity, indeterminacy, and degrees of truth. Lukacs clarified the epistemological implications:

> Quantum physics does not allow a completely objective description of nature. To describe "as it really happened"—the famous desideratum of historical description (or, perhaps, more than description: definition) stated by the great German historian Ranke more than 150 years ago—is an unfulfillable desideratum in the world of matter too. . . . The very knowledge (or, let us say, the cognition) of physicists about subatomic events—that is, about the very basic elements of matter— . . . corresponds, and impressively, to the inevitable limitations of our historical knowledge: that is, of the knowledge of human beings about human beings.[18]

This change came about from the recognition that science, like history, is a product of the human mind and reflects what the German physicist Werner Heisenberg referred to as the "interplay" between man and nature. "It is thus that the recognition of the human condition of science, and of the historicity of science . . . ," Lukacs confirms, "may mark the way toward the next phase in the evolution of human consciousness, in the Western world at least."[19] Science historicized is science humanized. If humans did not exist, there would be no science, no mathematics, no history. We can no more escape participation in the knowledge of our environment than we can escape participation in the knowledge of our past.

The evolution of consciousness, moreover, betrayed the absence, or at least the inaccessibility, of eternal truth. It is for Lukacs the very fallibility and impotence of human knowledge and invention that places mankind again at the center of the universe. Human knowledge is no longer subordinate to the categories of natural science, which depend on classification and homogeneity. In history, as in life, uniqueness matters and exceptions count. "Nature preceded man," Lukacs writes, "but man preceded the science of nature; indeed, he created the science of nature. This, of course, is a historical recognition."[20] Copernicus, Kepler, Galileo, Descartes, and Newton destroyed the geocentric and anthropocentric cosmos, reducing the earth to "hardly more (indeed, even less) than a speck of dust on the edge of an enormous dustbin of the universe, with the solar system itself being nothing more than one tiniest whirl among innumerable galaxies."[21] The reunion of the observer and the thing observed effected by twentieth-century physics annulled the Copernican Revolution, reinstating human thought to its former primacy. Men may have only their own imperfect and incomplete knowledge of the past, the world, and themselves—a knowledge that they cannot transcend—but they nonetheless know that they know. Their consciousness augments their existence and gives it meaning. The "unique complexity" of human beings, Lukacs affirms, "is in itself an argument for our central situation."[22]

Yet human capacities invariably reveal human weaknesses. The resplendence of the imagination, the vigor of the mind remain insufficient to illuminate the mysteries of existence. No human being can have full, accurate, and perfect understanding, or even knowledge, of the self, the world, the universe, the past, another person. Such liabilities are the challenge and the genius of humanity. "Thought constitutes the greatness of man," reflected Pascal. "[I]f the universe were to crush him, man would still be more noble than that which killed him, because he knows that he dies and the advantage which the universe has over him; the universe knows nothing of this."[23] Men stand at the center of his universe, which does not and cannot exist apart from mind. "We did not *create* the universe," Lukacs writes. "But the universe is our *invention;* and, as are all human and mental inventions, time-bound, relative, and potentially fallible."[24] It is, hence, the quality of thought and the acuity of understanding, rather than the quantity of knowledge and the degree of certainty, that are important. Artless knowledge, even when factually accurate, may prove sterile, impersonal, abstract, and unreal. Evocative understanding, which the Dutch historian Johan Huizinga described as "historical sensation," inevitably connects men with the reality that arises from their experience and awakens in their consciousness.[25]

If Lukacs repudiates the illusion of scientific objectivity, he is equally skeptical of idealist determinism. For idealists such as R. G. Collingwood, history was the history of thought. "All history," Collingwood professed, "is the re-enactment of past thought in the historian's ... mind."[26] But historians themselves, in Collingwood's analysis, are the products (and the hostages) of their own times, moral convictions, political commitments, and individual biographies. They see the past and the present differently according to their different backgrounds, capacities, cultures, and so forth. They cannot do otherwise. The historian must "write with all honesty in the perspective his own irreducible values set for him," alleged H. Stuart Hughes. "A conservative cannot help writing as a conservative, and a radical as a radical. . . ."[27] Historical idealists were mistaken, Lukacs posits, because they failed to liberate themselves from the scientific worldview they elsewhere repudiated. They shared with the advocates of scientific objectivity antiquated concepts of mechanical causality and human nature derived from Cartesian geometry and Newtonian physics, and so "went wrong because, like the objectivists, they were thinking in terms of direct causes, of men as products."[28]

Idealists, Lukacs charges, unwittingly disavowed free will and human agency, thereby permitting men to avoid responsibility not only for their deeds but also for their thoughts and words. Although he emphasizes the primacy of mind over matter and registers the intrusion of mind into the structure of events, Lukacs discerns at the same time that "what matters is not what ideas do to men but what men do to their ideas."[29] No idea exists outside the mind and separate from the words in which, the circumstances under which, and the purposes for which, the thinker expresses it.

The task for historians, as for all men, is the pursuit of truth, which is itself a historical preoccupation. Elusive but not ephemeral, truth changes through time. "That something is not true for all time," wrote Ortega y Gasset, "does not mean that it may not have its moment of truth."[30] Lukacs's idea of truth corresponds to the Judeo-Christian view of the human condition, according to which man, although made in the image of God, is nevertheless a finite creature predisposed to error and sin. Evil is at the heart of the human will and personality; it originates in and with man himself. "We are not Gods," Lukacs proclaims, "but historical beings, and the fallible descendants of Adam."[31] Insufficient unto themselves, men cannot comprehend the full meaning of their existence. Immersed in nature and in history, they are at the same time acutely conscious of their struggle to transcend the constraints imposed upon them. In so doing, they are tempted to raise themselves above their proper station. Usurping the role of God, men distort their relation to the divine and the eternal. "*Sicut eritis dei,*"

Satan promised: You shall be as God. Soon, though almost invariably too late to save themselves from folly, men discover the barrenness of such pretensions. The rational ordering and interpretation of historical experience fail to elucidate the whole. "And here," Lukacs confesses, "our knowledge, our understanding, our very imagination stops . . . , because in the entire universe the meaning of God may be the only meaning that exists independent of our consciousness."[32] Truth endures—else why pursue it?—but, Lukacs concludes, "pure truth" belongs to God alone, the changeless source of man's variable being.

From the Christian perspective, the tension between time and eternity threatens life with meaninglessness. History may reach its end before reaching its fulfillment. Men cannot solve the most fundamental problem of human existence in history, and all attempts to do so have brought disaster in their wake. Yet, as Marc Bloch pointed out, "Christianity is a religion of historians. . . . The destiny of humankind, placed between the Fall and the Judgment, appears to its eyes as a long adventure, of which each life, each individual pilgrimage, is in its turn a reflection. It is in time and, therefore, in history that the great drama of Sin and Redemption, the central axis of all Christian thought, is unfolded."[33] According to Christian theology, God partially and episodically reveals Himself in history through Christ. For this reason, Lukacs states that the Incarnation, "the coming of Christ to this earth may have been? no, . . . it *was*, the *central* event of the universe; . . . the greatest, the most consequential event in the entire universe has occurred here, on this earth."[34] Unlike its Eastern counterpart, Western Christianity, while hardly neglecting the divinity of Christ, has accentuated his humanity. Lukacs observes, for example, that among Eastern Orthodox Christians, Easter, which celebrates the divinity of Christ, is a far more elaborate and solemn holiday than Christmas. Of greater moment to Western Christians, Protestant and Catholic alike, is the day on which Christ entered the world and history as a human being.

Redemption from history is necessary. Lukacs, however, regrets the emergence and popularity of an excessive, indiscriminate, and unconditional spiritualism that extends from a belief in mystical religions to a belief in extraterrestrial phenomena. The bankruptcy of "post-capitalist and post-bourgeois materialism" has created a moral and intellectual vacuum characteristic of the end of an age. The appeal of spiritualism in the West proceeds from the desire to fill this void, to overcome the antagonistic finite perspectives that negate comprehension of the eternal. Mystics abrogate consciousness by elevating it above the flux of temporal events and merging it with the infinite. This urgent but pitiful quest for an undifferentiated, timeless reality, of which the historical world is merely a corrupt emanation, is, in Lukacs's judgment, an especially ominous variety of spiritual determinism, "whose shadows have begun to creep over our world."[35] Lukacs, by contrast, reaffirms the Judeo-Christian doctrine of free will. It is imperative that men exercise the freedom to think and act as autonomous beings. Only thus can they answer some of the questions that they have about themselves. "Our ideas," Lukacs avows, "are the results of our choices. Yes, our choices are influenced (and sometimes even produced) by our times and by the world around us; but the consequences of our ideas . . . are seldom direct or simple or unequivocal."[36] Lukacs abhors determinism in all its forms, whether scientific or idealist, material or spiritual, for he equates it with the intellectual dishonesty, indolence, and stagnation that combine to breed the perilous and ultimately destructive willingness to believe without thinking and to live with untruth.

Realism and idealism are not antithetical. Representations of the past cannot be purely abstract, fantastic, or metaphoric; and they must adjoin imagination and reality or else they are lifeless. The idealist must also be a realist who sets out in pursuit of truth, or at least in the dim hope of eliminating untruth. The study of the past must retain its intimacy with life, with the mystery of being and the miracle of existence. Historians, though, lack the capacity to tell the whole truth, and no amount of research, however scrupulously pursued, will enable them ever to do so. The study of history requires much more than the careful sifting of evidence and the meticulous arrangement of facts, which then more or less speak for themselves. Nor is it sufficient merely to equate causes with effects. History demands of the historian skillful acts of interpretation that, as Lukacs states, do not and cannot validate "perfect truth but the pursuit of truth through a reduction of ignorance."[37]

Objectivity is not a criterion of truth. Historical consciousness, which to Lukacs is at once more difficult and more important to attain than scientific knowledge, implicates, engages, and occupies the whole personality. Human beings are not isolated individuals tangled in a web of subjectivity, but unique persons able to communicate their personal visions of truth, their "personal way of seeing and saying," in which others might share. "The recognition of the objectivist illusion," Lukacs maintains, "does not reduce, it rather enhances, the general validity of personal knowledge. . . . If . . . by historical 'relativity' we mean not only the historicity of every form of human cognition but also of every form of human expression, it should be obvious that this idea of relativity is neither a feeble nor a senseless one; for this 'relativity' of *truths* means not the absence but the potential richness, not the nullity but the multiplicity of *truth*."[38] That the knowledge, understanding, and significance of history are personal and participatory does not release historians from their obligation to truth. The more consciously they recognize their personal involvement with their subject, the more wisely they may govern their prejudices, aspirations, and sensibilities. For writing history, at last, is a moral act, and the greatness of the work is inseparable from the character of the mind that conceived it. Who a man is may, after all, be more important than what he knows.

Independence is the hallmark of Lukacs's mind and character, from whence arise both the originality of his thought and the obscurity of his reputation. *Le style c'est l'homme,* wrote the Comte de Buffon. Unlike many professional academics who now think it obligatory as well as advantageous to incarnate ideas that are fashionable, Lukacs has never tailored his scholarship to fit established (and thus temporarily respectable) intellectual or political categories. He is, instead, a skeptic, a reactionary, defying the "heavy accumulation of accepted ideas and of institutionalized ways of thinking" that occur at the end of an age.[39] He derides such constructs as:

> Human Rights Amendments and "Star Wars"; Sex Education and the Intelligence Community (whatever *that* is); World Government and Making the World Safe for Democracy; Abstract Art and the Gross National Product; Nuclear Power and Genetic Engineering; Quarks and Black Holes; Ecumenicism and The Science of Economics; Cybernetics and National Security; Computer Intelligence and Opinion Research; Psychohistory and Quantification, and so on, and so on.[40]

Unconventional though he may be, Lukacs is no cantankerous eccentric airing his private aversions. He is a historian, his standards and judgments about the present drawn from the potentially inexhaustible wisdom of the past.

There is a depth and gravity to Lukacs's finest writing that is rare in any time and nearly unmatched in ours. Humane and compassionate, evocative and profound, witty and sad, his meditations on history and human nature reflect the conditions of life and the fate of man during the short twentieth century and the long decline of the Modern Age. Toward the end of his elegiac *A Thread of Years,* Lukacs admits "it's all over . . . for most of the world that I . . . cherish." Even with "the sad decline of civilization," however, ". . . a few remnant memories of beautiful things and of decency and goodness" survive.[41] Life is still sweet and still worth living. Lukacs refuses to succumb to self-pity or despair, which on more than one occasion he has dismissed not only as sinful but also as useless.

Lukacs does not merely lament the passing of a civilization but aims, if possible, to revitalize it or to find its equivalent, though he is far from sanguine about the prospects. His anxious expectations notwithstanding, Lukacs is no disciple of Oswald Spengler, no prophet of doom contemplating the inevitable "sinking" (*Untergang*) of the West. A vestige of civilization and its traditions may yet survive, Lukacs writes, "at least in some small part due to [Winston] Churchill in 1940. At worst, he helped to give us ... fifty years. Fifty years before the rise of new kinds of barbarism ... , before the clouds of a new Dark Age may darken the lives of our children and grand-children."[42] Lukacs has aligned himself with Churchill, the writer, the historian, and the man of letters, the conservative guardian of tradition, the reactionary agent of a civilization founded not on birth but on breeding. To live in an age of dissolution and crisis entails special responsibilities; chief among them may simply be the unwavering refusal to capitulate, the stubborn will to press on. With somber fortitude, Lukacs continues to remind us of a world, very different from our own, that rested on the cultivation of manners and morals, on a luxuriant interior life, on the ideal of the gentleman, and on a sense of place and permanence. By calling to mind that lost and discarded world, Lukacs, like Churchill, may have afforded us a little time to rethink the world that we have made, time to face ourselves, time to slow the descent into the monstrous and inhuman Dark Age that now approaches, and time, perhaps, to rekindle the lamps of civilization in the West that, one by one, have begun to flicker and go out.

Regrettably, few historians have more than a passing acquaintance with John Lukacs's historical philosophy. The fate of Lukacs's books, particularly his masterful *Historical Consciousness*, arises in part from the intellectual stagnation that Tocqueville recognized as characteristic of a fading democratic age. Lukacs's most unorthodox and original works do not conform to prevailing suppositions and categories, and, as a result, are either misunderstood or ignored.

The inflation of scholarship and the bureaucratization of thought have contributed to the inattention from which such volumes as *Historical Consciousness* suffer. Even the most assiduous historians cannot hope to read all the books and essays published on a subject in which they proclaim expertise. Those works that do not receive adequate publicity, that do not add an élan to footnotes and bibliographies, often remain unknown, and so unread. The reasons for such lapses are even more complex and disheartening. As Lukcas points out, during this so-called Age of Information no one reads much anymore because few share the inclination to read. "We have now entire slews of professional experts who read little while they write much, for the sake of firming up their professional status," he observes. "In this respect, too, we may see the devolution of democracy into bureaucracy...."[43] Malice is not the source of this appalling ignorance. It emerges instead from the inability, and perhaps the growing unwillingness, to contemplate ideas that do not correspond with established, institutionalized, and accepted norms and systems. Little professional advantage or reputation accrues to scholars who dare criticize approved methods, impugn cherished theories, and question authorized conclusions. Those who adopt unpopular values and assumptions become immediately suspect, their work regarded as illegitimate, disreputable, and worst of all, insignificant.

The present collection aims to offer some redress, not only in the interest of doing justice to an incomparable writer, but also in the hope of sustaining his lifelong quest for truth, or, more humbly, reaffirming his determination, as much moral as intellectual, to reduce untruth. Lukacs's *œuvre* of more than twenty books and hundreds of articles encompasses the history of the Modern, or as he prefers, the Bourgeois Age, focusing chiefly on the political, ideological, intellectual, and military struggles of the twentieth century, the men and women who stood at the center of those conflicts, and the attendant decline of a civilization and a way of life. Integral to that project has been Lukacs's effort to "think about thinking," specifically to clarify and interpret the emergence of historical consciousness during the five hundred years that constitute "modern" history. No endeavor is more important to understanding ourselves and our world—especially as the institutions, ideas, values, and experiences that made up the life of that era recede and disappear.

Gathering many of Lukacs's assorted writings on history, *Remembered Past* serves at once as an introduction to and a compendium of this essential aspect of Lukacs's thought. The reviews, essays, commentaries, and excerpts that appear in the following pages address the nature of historical consciousness; challenge the suppositions and practices of the history profession; evaluate the contributions of historians and other writers who have used, and often abused, history; evoke the spirit of certain places in relation to their past; reconsider important events and figures of the twentieth century; and conclude, appropriately, with a discussion of teaching and writing. A bibliography of Lukacs's writings appears here for the first time and rounds out a volume that we hope will be of particular value to general and academic audiences seeking a more thorough encounter with this seminal thinker. In this book, readers will not only discover the joy of encountering a vigorous mind, but may also learn, as Lukacs has long affirmed, that reality lies within historical consciousness, which is nothing less than the consciousness of ourselves.

❦ *Mark G. Malvasi and Jeffrey O. Nelson*
December 2004

Acknowledgments ❊❊❊

WE wish to acknowledge foremost the gracious encouragement, advice, assistance, and hospitality of John Lukacs in conceiving and preparing this volume. If the appellation scholar and gentleman applies to any of our contemporaries, it applies to Dr. Lukacs. Both of us have long been indebted to him for his writings, but this volume has also given us the added gift—and it is a treasured one—of his friendship. It is our hope that this book suitably honors the high quality of his professional contributions to thinking and writing about history.

We also want to thank Jeremy Beer, Nancy Halsey, Eileen Duke, Doug Schneider, Kara Beer, and Sam Torode for their thoughtful criticism, constructive advice, and often heroic efforts to organize and produce such a long and complicated book. Their professionalism and dedication is admirable and appreciated. We also want to thank Helen Lukacs for her bibliographic labors. Her grandfather is honored by, and proud of, her contribution. We know because he often sang her praises.

Of course, we must acknowledge the journals and publishers who have given permission to reprint many of the pieces included in this collection.

Chapters 12, 17, 26, and 31 are reprinted by permission of the *New Republic*. Chapters 45, 46, 47, 49, and 50 are reprinted by permission of the University of Missouri Press. Chapters 27 and 56 first appeared in the *National Interest* and are reprinted by permission. Chapter 13 first appeared in *Commonweal*, © 1969 Commonweal Foundation. It too is reprinted here by permission (for subscriptions: www.commonwealmagazine.org).

Yale University Press has provided special permission to reprint here chapters 1, 30, 57, 58, and 64. Chapter 41 first appeared in *Harper's* and is copyright © 2002-Dec. by *Harper's Magazine*. It is also reproduced here by special permission.

Chapter 16 is © 1977 by National Review, Inc., 215 Lexington Avenue,

New York, NY 10016. It is reprinted here from *National Review* by permission.

Chapter 2 is © 1994 by Transaction Publishers and is reprinted by permission of the publisher.

Finally, we dedicate this work to the memory of John Lukacs's early colleague, patron, and friend—the late Fordham University historian Ross J. S. Hoffman (1902–79). Hoffman's picture hangs in Lukacs's personal library near the master files that contain original copies of his voluminous writings. We can not help but think that since his death Ross Hoffman has sent a ghost or two to watch over his dear friend.

❦ *Mark G. Malvasi and Jeffrey O. Nelson*
February 2005

I.

THE PROBLEM OF

HISTORICAL KNOWLEDGE

"*Historical thinking has entered our very blood,*" wrote the Dutch historian *Johan Huizinga in 1934. The growth of historical consciousness, according to the German historian Friedrich Meinecke, was "the greatest spiritual revolution Western thought has undergone." John Lukacs has clarified the implications of Huizinga's and Meinecke's insights: "We are all historians by nature," Lukacs writes, "while we are scientists only by choice."*

Historical consciousness, Lukacs suggests, is more extensive and more important than the professional concerns of academic historians. History is the "remembered past," encompassing far more than documents record. It is concerned with all manner of human activity, though memory is always limited, incomplete, fragmentary, and personal. Yet, Lukacs focuses on the quality rather than the quantity of memory, and on understanding rather than accuracy. As time goes on, we may remember fewer details about a particular incident or event, but our understanding of its significance may deepen. "I can write only from memory," explained the Russian playwright Anton Chekhov. "I never write directly from life. The subject must pass through the sieve of my memory, so that only what is important . . . remains." Historical thinking applies to any and every human experience and endeavor. We may describe and understand a person, a society, or a nation not merely through their material and spiritual, their physical and psychological qualities, but primarily through their history. Human existence is historical existence, and during the last five hundred years we have gradually awakened to that condition and its significance.

Since historical knowledge is anthropomorphic, since it is the knowledge that some human beings have of other human beings, Lukacs posits a convergence between history and science in the recognition that science, too, is a human enterprise. "Even in science," declared the German physicist Werner Heisenberg, "the object of research is no longer nature itself, but man's investigation of nature." For Lukacs, awareness of "the human condition of science, and of the historicity of science . . . may mark the way toward the next phase in the evolution of human consciousness." As the following essays reveal, it is not through the application of the scientific method that we come to understand ourselves and our world, but through memory and history, which are invariably personal and participant. Although the study of history yields no absolute, definitive, and incontrovertible truths, "the remembrance of things past" gives purpose and meaning to life.

1

The Presence of Historical Thinking
(2002)

When I say that "I am a historian," what does this statement mean? What do people understand by it? Three hundred years ago they would have been unaccustomed to such a designation. Now their first, and most probable, association is: it is this man's occupation. Or, more precisely: it is his professional affiliation. "A historian"—so he is probably employed in some institution of higher education.[1]

I do not wish to object to such a professional designation of myself: but it is not entirely to my taste. Yes, early in my life I chose to become a professional historian, to acquire a necessary degree of certification to enable me to seek such employment, to teach in a higher institution of learning, to be admitted into the guild of professional historians, to be recognized as such. All of this has been of course preceded—and succeeded—by something deeper: by an interest in history, but also by my developing sense of a vocation. Interest, inclination, vocation: three overlapping but distinct phases. The consciousness of such a distinction may appear only in retrospect. But that there is a difference, though of course not necessarily an opposition, between a vocation and a professional identification or certification, ought to be obvious.

A sense of vocation, though perhaps rare, is not necessarily good. Fanatics have such a sense; obsessive minds may have such a sense. At the same time a sense of vocation ought to involve at least some self-searching. Very early in my life and in my professional career I began to be interested not only in certain matters of the past about which I wished to know more and more; not only in certain periods of the past, but also in certain problems of their history; in problems of our historical knowledge. The motives of such questioning are almost always mixed and not easily ascertainable. They may not be separable from personal disillusionments and disappoint-

From *At the End of an Age* (New Haven, CT: Yale University Press), 47–83.

ments (in my case from the pretended objectivism in the writings and from the gray ice on the faces of certain professional historians); but, as in everything else, one may know one's purposes better than one's motives. In my life, this led me, perhaps at an unduly early stage of my "professional" career, to think and read and gather material and plan for a work dealing with problems about our very knowledge of history itself, questions including a few novel and radical propositions. They are there in *Historical Consciousness,* a book that took me—with various interruptions—almost thirteen years to complete. It was during my work on the first, often convoluted, draft of *Historical Consciousness* that, sometime in the late summer of 1958, I suddenly found that I might have arrived at what seemed to me an intellectual discovery of considerable magnitude. In any event, that was a crucial stage in my intellectual pilgrimage and in my historical vocation.

This is a personal record. Yet it is not autobiographical. I cannot but cite a great Hungarian Catholic poet, János Pilinszky, who wrote how he had been inspired to recognize this condition by reading St. Augustine and Simone Weil: "There are the personal, the non-personal, and the collective areas of life. One cannot reach the non-personal except from what is personal; from the collective, never. Something must become personal first; after that one may go forward to what is no longer personal."

❋ ❋ ❋

ALL living beings have their own evolution and their own life span. But human beings are the only living beings who know that they live while they live—who know, and not only instinctively feel, that they are going to die. Other living beings have an often extraordinary and accurate sense of time. But we have a sense of our history, which amounts to something else. Scientific knowledge, dependent as it is on a scientific method, is by its nature open to question. The existence of historical knowledge, the inevitable presence of the past in our minds, is not. We are all historians by nature, while we are scientists only by choice.

Modern scientific thinking appeared about three or four hundred years ago, together with a then-new view of the globe and of the universe. It meant the methodical investigation of nature, and eventually the manipulation of a kind of knowledge which, once applied, changed the world and our lives in unimaginable ways. Eventually Science came to mean (mostly, though not exclusively) the Science of Nature: our knowledge of things and of organisms other than ourselves. At the same time, about three or four hundred years ago, there occurred another evolution, first in Western Europe: a passage from a kind of historical thinking that had existed for a long time to a kind of historical consciousness that was a relatively new phenomenon. Of these two developments the importance of the first, of Science, has of course been recognized—with every reason, given its successive and successful applications; the second, hardly at all. Yet it may be argued that the second, involving man's knowledge of man, may have been— perhaps more and more evidently now—as important, if not more important, than the first.

❋ ❋ ❋

SHAKESPEARE in *Henry V*: "There is a history in all men's lives." This poetic phrase has a wider meaning in the democratic age, issuing from a recognition that every person is a historical person (and that every source is a historical source).[2] This is—or rather, should be—obvious. No less obvious is one result of the democratic development of the world. This has been the widening of the nineteenth-century practice of largely political history toward social history, from the history of governments to the history of the governed. (Alas, so many of the proponents and practitioners of the latter have been treating history as a kind of retrospective sociology.) Together with this widening there also have been attempts to deepen the scope and sharpen the focus of historical research. (Alas, so many of the so-called postmodern theoreticians of history have been writing analyses of texts and of statistics employing large quantities of words or numbers in the service of small amounts of thought.)

There is the past; there is the remembered past; there is the recorded past. The past is very large, and it gets larger every minute: we do not and cannot know all of it. Its remnant evidences help: but they, too, are protean and cannot be collected and recorded in their entirety. Thus history is more than the recorded past; it consists of the recorded and the recordable and the remembered past. The past in our minds *is* memory. Human beings cannot create, or even imagine, anything that is entirely new. (The Greek word for "truth," *aletheia,* also means "not forgetting.") "There is not a vestige of real creativity *de novo* in us," C. S. Lewis once wrote. No one can even imagine an entirely new color; or an entirely new animal; or even a third sex. At best (or worst) one can imagine a new combination of already existing—that is, known to us—colors, or monsters, or sexes. There is a startling and corresponding recognition of this condition in Goethe's *Theory of Colors.* In the preface of that extraordinary and difficult work he wrote that "strictly speaking, it is useless to attempt to express the nature of a thing abstractly. . . . We should try in vain to describe a man's character, but let his acts be collected and an idea of the character will be presented to us." And: "As we before expressed the opinion that the history of an individual displays his character, so it may here be well affirmed that the

5

history of science is science itself."[3] This is a prophetic foretelling of Heisenberg and Bohr, who more than one hundred years later were compelled to conclude that the history of quantum theory *is* quantum theory; or that the best way to teach quantum theory is to teach its historical evolution. William James wrote: "You can give humanistic value to almost anything by teaching it historically. Geology, economics, mechanics, are humanities when taught by reference to the successive achievements of the geniuses to whom these sciences owe their being. Not taught thus, literature remains grammar, art a catalogue, history a list of dates, and natural science a sheet of formulas and weights and measures."[4]

In sum, the history of anything amounts to that thing itself. History is not a social science but an unavoidable form of thought. That "we live forward but we can only think backward" is true not only of the present (which is always a fleeting illusion) but of our entire view of the future: for even when we think of the future we do this by *remembering* it. But history cannot tell us anything about the future with certainty. Intelligent research, together with a stab of psychological understanding, may enable us to reconstruct something from the past; still, it cannot help us predict the future. There are many reasons for this unpredictability (for believing Christians let me say that providence is one); but another (God-ordained) element is that no two human beings have ever been exactly the same. History is real; but it cannot be made to "work," because of its unpredictability. A curious paradox is that while science is abstract, it can be made to work. Abraham Lincoln (or one's grandmother) *really* existed; there was and will be no one exactly like him or like her. But the material elements of Science never exist in perfect or unalloyed form. H_2O is a most useful definition of water; yet of a liquid that, in reality, does not and cannot absolutely exist: we may find, or produce, a distillation of 99.99 percent H_2O but not of 100 percent "purity." Yet because of mechanical causality, scientific knowledge can be put to practical use: to a nearly incredible extent of precision and of predictability it can be made to "work."

One reason for this paradox is the essential difference between mechanical and other historical causalities; that what happens is inseparable from what people think happens. Inseparable: but not identical, and also not enduring. People may be wrong in thinking what happens, and they may have been wrong in thinking what happened. A man thinks that the motor stopped because of the failure of the water pump, whereas it was the oil pump. When he then learns that the real source of the trouble was the oil pump, his realization of the source of the trouble means an increase in the quantity and in the extent of his knowledge. But when it comes to a human event, a later realization that what had happened was not what we thought happened usually involves an increase of the *quality* of our knowledge, together with a decrease of the quantity in our memory. (Something happens to us today, something bothersome, whereof we can remember the smallest details. A few years later we recall that day, having forgotten many of its details; yet we may say to ourselves: "Why was I so upset about that then?" Or: "Why had I not noticed that then?" The quantity of our knowledge of the details of that day has waned; but the quality of our knowledge—and understanding—of what had happened may have increased.)

Human understanding is a matter of quality, not of quantity. At times it is a (sudden, rather than gradual) synthesis of accumulated knowledge. But this happens not often. The purpose of understanding differs from the scientific purpose of certainty, and of accuracy. We also know that human understanding of other human beings is always, and necessarily, imperfect. There are odd and illogical elements in its functioning. One of them is that understanding may precede knowledge, instead of being simply consequent to it. Another is that understanding, too, depends on memory. We often think that a failure, or defect, of memory amounts to an insufficiency of knowledge. Yet there, too, there is some kind of understanding at the bottom of the trouble, since we both understand and know what we wish to recall, except that we cannot yet bring those words or names or numbers up to the surface of our mind clearly. Another example is the inevitable dependence of understanding on comparison and contrast. That contrast is an inevitable element of color, indeed, of the very act of seeing. An early proponent of this inevitable condition was the Renaissance painter, poet, philosopher, musician, architect Alberti. Critical of the categorical "definitions" of philosophers, Leone Battista Alberti wrote *On Painting*. "All knowledge of large, small; long, short; high, low; broad, narrow; clear, dark; light and shadow and every similar attribute is obtained by comparison. . . . All things are known by comparison, for comparison contains within itself a power which immediately demonstrates. . . ."[5] And just as our act of seeing depends on contrast, our knowledge of the present depends on our knowledge of the past.

This dependence of understanding on contrast and comparison does not necessarily mean the relativity of all human knowledge. "But where would we be if we could speak only of things we know with certainty?" asked the sixteenth-century French historian Henri Voisin de La Popelinière—who nonetheless proposed the necessity of advancing to a "complete" history, including much besides the recorded acts and discourses of rulers.[6] Four hundred years later the solitary Russian thinker Mikhail Bakhtin wrote that neither human understanding nor creative thinking is the result of a synthesis. "On the contrary, it consists in the intensification of one's own *distinctness* from others; it consists in fully exploiting the privilege of one's own unique place outside other human beings." This is not solipsism, not subjectivism, and not even relativism. "This outsidedness must be preserved if solidarity with others is to be fruitful.... Our empathy with others [must be] completed with elements of our own perspective. Sympathetic understanding is not a mirroring, but a fundamentally and essentially new valuation, a utilization of my own architectonic position in being outside another's inner place."[7] Outside, yes: but with the intention to understand the other one, to participate, even if to a necessarily incomplete extent. Of course: love is always the love of *another*.[8]

But perhaps the most important element of historical thinking is the understanding that our knowledge of history (indeed, our entire knowledge of the past; indeed, even our personal memory) is not and cannot be restricted to "what actually happened," since potentiality is inherent in actuality. This is true of "great" historical events as well as of intimate human situations, because human inclinations, even when they do not mature into definite acts, are essentially potential signs of actualities. As Johan Huizinga wrote: "The sociologist, etc., deals with his material as if the outcome were given in the known facts: he simply searches for the way in which the result was already determined in the facts. The historian, on the other hand, must always maintain towards his subject an indeterminist point of view. He must constantly put himself at a point in the past at which the known factors still seem to permit different outcomes. If he speaks of Salamis, then it must be as if the Persians might still win...."[9]

The relationship of potentiality and actuality correspond to the difference—again, a qualitative as much as a quantitative difference—between what is significant and what is important. Here is the essential difference between historical and legal evidence—or between historical and legal thinking. Law (at least in a state governed by a constitution) can deal only with actuality, not with potentiality. "The law is a coarse net; and truth is a slippery fish." Yes: but the purpose of law has nothing to do with truth; it is the establishment of justice. Truth and justice are not the same things, even though the pursuit of truth and the pursuit of justice may, on occasion, overlap. But besides the question (or, rather, the obvious primacy) of truth over justice, there are other important differences between historical and legal evidences and thinking. One is that law, after all—inevitably and necessarily—is a closed system, within its own definite rules and regulations. For instance, it does not and should not allow multiple jeopardy: a case, when and if properly tried, is decided once and for all. History (and our memory) is open and never closed; it specializes in multiple jeopardy: its subjects and people are rethought over and over again, and not even necessarily on the basis of newly found evidence. There may be five hundred biographies of Lincoln, but there is hardly reason to doubt that sooner or later there will be a 501st one with something new in its contents, and not necessarily because of new materials that its author has found, but because of a new viewpoint. Another great difference—I am again referring principally to Anglo-American law—is the one between motives and purposes. These two are regrettably confused because of the vocabulary and the practices of twentieth-century psychology and thought, the attribution of motive having become a pestilential intellectual habit.[10] But we must distinguish between the two. Motives come from the past; purposes involve the pull of the future. At its best, Anglo-American law will admit only a "motive" which has been, in one way or another, expressed; in other words, an actuality, not a potentiality. (As Dr. Johnson said: "Intentions must be gathered from acts.") At its worst, unexpressed motives are sometimes attributed and accepted in some courts on the basis of psychological characterization or other dubious "expertise." A proper comprehension of the essential difference between motives and purposes is an essential condition of the pursuit and of the protection of justice and of truth—and of all historical thinking and speaking and writing.

Historical thinking accords with the recognition that human knowledge is neither objective nor subjective but personal and participant. Consciousness (*conscientia*) is participant knowledge. Nearly four hundred years ago Descartes argued, in his *Discourse on Method,* that the study of history was wasteful because we cannot acquire any accurate or certain knowledge of the human past, as we can of mathematics and of the world of nature. Yet another century after Descartes, Vico "said just the opposite. His claim was that the principles of human society, the 'civil world' as he calls it, are actually more certain than the principles governing the natural world, because civil society is a human creation"[11]—to which let me add that "the natural world," too, is inseparable from our knowledge of it—for us.

❉ ❉ ❉

THE professionalization of history—or in other words: the certification of historianship—has brought about great, widespread, and fruitful results during the past two hundred years, and especially during the nineteenth century. Still ... some of the finest historians of the past two hundred years did not have professional degrees. (You can be a poet without having a PhD in Poetry, and, yes, you can be a historian without having a PhD in History.) A problem for most professional historians is that their certification and their craft and their methods are still bound to the practices (and often to the philosophy) of historianship established in the nineteenth century, even though during the twentieth century great changes occurred in the structures of states and societies, together with changes in what I call the structure of events. Except here and there, most historians have been unwilling or unable to adjust the requirements of their craft to these changes. This is understandable (even when it is less justifiable) because of personal reasons, ranging from the conformism of an intellectual bureaucrat to the respectable seriousness of a traditional craftsman. Many of us have met many a "historian" whose main interest seems to be not the study of history but his historianship, meaning his standing within the profession—a failure in character. Yet we have also met many other historians whose interest and work in history is impervious to fads—small triumphs of character. More important: many of the methods and practices of research and management of sources established by the great historians of the nineteenth century are still valid. But before I turn to some of the problems with "sources," let me make bold to suggest something that more and more professional historians uneasily sense, even though they may be reluctant to state it: that behind the problem of "sources" looms the obvious recognition that documents do not by themselves "make" history; rather, it is history that makes documents. For history is, and always was, something more than a study of records; and just as actuality must, by necessity, include at least a recognition of the element of potentiality, if history is the memory of mankind (which it is), then it is something more than the recorded past; it must include something of the remembered past, too.

That a new structure of society involves new perspectives Tocqueville saw almost 180 years ago. He saw the forest from the trees with an astonishingly clear and acute eye. There is a small chapter, consisting of forty-eight sentences, in the second volume of *Democracy in America,* "Some Characteristics of Historians in Democratic Times," that ought to be read and re-read by every historian. (And Tocqueville also practiced what he preached: these generalizations in *Democracy in America* [which was not a history] became, here and there, incarnated in his own history writing twenty years later, in *The Old Regime and the French Revolution.*) The great clear insight of Alexis the Forester was his recognition that above and beyond the Ancient-Middle-Modern periodization of history in the West rose the present transformation of entire societies into democracies: the passage from the aristocratic to the democratic age; from peoples ruled by minorities to peoples ruled by majorities (even though that is not entirely identical with peoples ruling *themselves*). And it is because of this evolving democratization of the world that some of the problems of modern historical research—and writing—have arisen. I can only sum up some of them inadequately and briefly.

There is the problem of the quantity of materials with which the historian must deal. The nineteenth-century ideal—in many ways, still current—was that of definiteness and completion, meaning the filling of particular gaps in history (more precisely: in our professional historical knowledge) properly and perfectly, in accordance with the accepted norms and methods of the profession. There was (and there still is) merit in this ideal of history being something like the building of a vast and impressive cathedral, to which its professional workmen contribute by adding small pillars here and there, including the filling of small gaps with one brick, if needed, as for example with dissertations or monographs of minor scope. Yet we must keep in mind that no cathedral is ever completed; that repairs and restructurings are needed from to time to time; that the very surroundings of the cathedral change; and that every generation will see the cathedral in new and different ways. And perhaps even more important is the condition that even a great cathedral does not a city make; that with the onset of democracy we have, by necessity, extended the scope of history, so far as its themes and topics go, to the lives (and records) of all kinds of people; so far as its "methods"[12] go, beyond the official archives. History *does* depend on records, but it is not merely a matter of records. And the quantity (and the scope) of materials with which the modern historian deals is greater than ever before. The ideal that, at least concerning a small topic, the historian can—and must—have read everything written about it, exhausting all of the "sources," in many cases is no longer possible, or even reasonably expectable. And then there is the other problem, related to quantity. Democracy, almost invariably, leads to inflation: inflation in the number of people, inflation of papers, inflation of bureaucracy, inflation of records. One hundred years ago it was at least approximately (though not completely) possible for a historian to have read almost all the papers and documentary evidence written to and by and about a political or literary figure. This is no longer so. A "definite" history is necessarily an exaggeration; and an "orthodox" history is necessarily a contradiction in terms.

This oceanic rise in the quantity of potentially useful materials for the historian is of course inseparable from the problem of their quality. (When there is more and more of something, it is worth less and less.) But that is not all. The quality of every document, of every record, indeed of every kind of human expression, depends on its authenticity. With the oceanic tide of documents—the combined results of spreading democracy, spreading technology, spreading bureaucracy—the authenticity of "sources" with which the historian must deal decreases; in some cases it even disappears. The nineteenth-century canonical rule regarding historical evidence, the essential distinction between "primary" (that is, direct) and "secondary" (that is, successive and indirect) sources is being washed away. Through telephone, teletype, fax, e-mail, and so on, many statements are unreconstructable, unrecorded, disappearing fast. We also have important documents—for example, letters by presidents (and not only speeches by speechwriters and other expressions)—that were not only not written but not even dictated or read by them or signed by their own hand. There are records of twentieth-century presidential cabinet sessions that are less authentic than a postcard from one's grandmother found in an old drawer: no matter how mundane are the few words on that postcard, its authenticity exists because of that spiky handwriting, the old stamp and postmark, the yellowed cardboard, its musty smell.

This drastic mutation in the very essence of historical records has its special dangers. The recently fashionable practice of social history does not confront them, at least as long as it is sociological rather than sociographical, which is, alas, often the case.[13] The bringing up of records and statistics of all kinds from distant pasts presents another kind of danger: as far as the records go, the danger is not so much their authenticity as their incompleteness; as far as statistics go, the danger exists in the difficulty—at times, impossibility—of ascertaining their correctness. Sooner or later a historian with an independent mind ought to compose a guidebook: "New Problems of Historical Research," a list of warnings about new particular problems. I can mention only a general one. Many of the present "schools" of social history depend on the concept of Economic Man, from the—at times veiled—"scientific" belief that the basic realities of human existence and of historic life and development are material, whereof the mores and morals and thoughts and beliefs of most people are the superstructures. My belief, from an early time in my life, has been the opposite: that (perhaps especially in the democratic age and in democratic societies) the most important matter is what people think and believe—and that the entire material organization of society, ranging from superficial fashions to their material acquisitions and to their institutions—are the consequences thereof.

At the beginning of the twenty-first century, at the very end of the Modern Age, many professional historians seem to agree that historical "objectivity" and historical "determinism" are no longer sacrosanct, indeed, that they are questionable. Yet for many of them this means little more than the mere nodding of heads otherwise preoccupied, since they keep writing and teaching as if history were still determined. The fad for "psychohistory" in the 1960s, the "postmodern" definitions of conditions of "discourse," and the recent tendency among French historians to write about "mentalités" seldom amount, alas, to more than an uneasy feeling of progress along the dusty shoulders of a great roadway on which many stones had broken through the old rutted surface, making the marching a bit uncomfortable (not to speak of the heavy motorized traffic on it). A learned Hungarian thinker and unequaled master of literary history, Antal Szerb (he was murdered in 1944, in the same year as the great French historian Marc Bloch), wrote in his *Introduction to the History of Hungarian Literature* (1934) two prophetic and radiant sentences: "The new science of psychology is still in its infancy, so much so that for an auxiliary science it is nearly useless. In that field the writer of literary history remains alone, bereft of assistance; what he may try could be, at best, an attempt toward a new kind of knowledge that would consist of the study of the historical developments of spiritual and mental structures; perhaps one day that will be called spiritual history—that is, once it appears." Two sentences worth more than many of the volumes nowadays laboriously composed by proponents of psychohistory or of sociological history.

One very random illustration of the disinclination of otherwise well-meaning and thorough and serious historians to consider the personal and participant conditions—and responsibilities—of knowledge I recently found in an otherwise excellent large book by Heinz Huerten, *Deutsche Katholiken, 1918–1945,* which goes beyond the necessarily narrow framework of ecclesiastical history. In his chapter "The German Catholic Church and the Murder of the Jews," in which Huerten introduces the problematic question whether German Catholics, priests, and bishops have been true to their faith during the Third Reich, he writes: "Since their decisions were essentially personal ones, they cannot be ultimately criticized by science, and even less can they be offered scientifically." Even keeping in mind that the German word *Wissenschaft,* meaning "science" and "knowledge," is broader than the English "science," and with all respect for Huerten's sincerity, such a separation of the "personal" from the "scientific" is inadequate, insufficient.

❋ ❋ ❋

TO ignore the unavoidable personal—and participatory—element of human and historical knowledge is of course the great failure of objectivism. But there is another (and, in many of its instances, postmodern) danger, when the recognition of the shortcomings of historical objectivism results in Subjectivism. This is the case of (the once Marxist) E. H. Carr's *What Is History?* (1961). Carr's central argument is that "before you study the history, study the historian," and "before you study the historian, study his historical and social environment." This is a half-truth. The recognition that different persons see the past (and also the present) differently, and

13

that thus every historian is different, does not mean that because he is the product of his past he cannot do otherwise. How about the sons of rich parents who chose to become Marxist? Or—how about former Marxists who chose to become neoconservatives?[14] Carr's argument is nothing but a subjective form of determinism denying not only free will but hopelessly confusing motives and purposes.[15]

This kind of subjectivism is also inherent in the neoidealist R. G. Collingwood. Recognizing that a German historian who was born in 1900 would see the past differently from a French historian who was born in 1800, Collingwood concluded, "There is no point in asking which was the right point of view. Each was the only one possible for the man who adopted it." *The only one possible?* This is determinism—subjectivist determinism— again. That French historian in 1800 could have been a monarchist, or a republican, or a Bonapartist; that German historian could have been an imperialist or a liberal.[16] That would influence (influence, not determine) their perspectives of the past as well. (To carry this further: the French historian in 1800 could be a Germanophile or a Germanophobe; the German historian in 1900 a Francophobe or a Francophile. That could even affect the choice of their interests: it is at least imaginable that a German historian in 1900 could prefer to read and write about Louis XV and a French historian in 1800 about Frederick William I.)

It is here that the twentieth-century subjectivists, from the early Croce to Becker and Beard and many of the "postmoderns," slid into error. They could not liberate themselves from the scientific worldview, from Descartes' world divided into subjects and objects and from Newton's world where causes always and inevitably precede effects, and where the present is always the product of the past. They went wrong not because they were attacking the illusion of objectivity; they went wrong because, like the objectivists, they were thinking in terms of direct causes, of men as products. Thus subjectivism is also inherent in the neo-idealists Collingwood and Oakeshott, whose otherwise valuable recognitions of the errors of objectivism and materialism and positivism have moved them toward the morass of a merely philosophical—that is, abstract—idealism that is essentially subjectivist.[17]

However—my purpose here is not philosophical; it is, rather, a reminder for historians of some things that are real. Such recognitions of reality are inseparable from the knowledge of our own limitations, including the limitations of our profession, of our methods, of our craft. As in all human thought, in history these include the limitations of language. Historians must constantly keep in mind that the instruments of their craft (and of course of all their thinking) are words, because we think and teach and write with words. It is not only that memory is the womb of the human psyche, and that the Muses were the daughters of Memory: Mnemosyne. The sudden development of speech in children is indeed mysterious, because words are the fundamental signs and symbols of emerging consciousness. They are more than abstract symbols, or units of communication; they are symbols not of *things* but of *meanings*—not of something merely physical but essentially of something mental. Meaning always has an element of revelation in it (whence "literal" vs. "symbolic" meaning is a false distinction). And language exists, grows, and fades together with memory.[18]

Language is not perfect. It exists to communicate, but only what it can communicate. Some things it communicates badly. At the same time the language which can easily make the finest and most numerous distinctions of meaning is the best one. The great danger during our present passage from a verbal to visual "culture" is latent in the impoverishment of language. But language still contains an element of mystery within it: the mystery which is inherent in every human volition, in every human act, and which too is in essence a matter of quality.[19] And the quality of every human expression depends not only on one's choice of words but also on the intention of the expression and on its historical circumstances. This corresponds to the, alas, overdue recognition that ideas do not exist apart from the men and women who choose to represent and express them—and *when*.

❀ ❀ ❀

YES: historical circumstances—because the meaning of every human expression (and hence the meaning of every idea) is inseparable from not only how and where and to whom it is stated but *when:* conditions of historicity that are inseparable from and inherent in the speaker's or writer's intention. Here are two examples. "There are Communists who are murderers." Imagine a Pole or a Russian, say, in 1948, standing up and saying this in Warsaw or Minsk, at a public meeting ruled by Stalinist bureaucrats and chaired by a Communist government minister. Now imagine the same words shouted at a meeting of Young Republicans in, say, Chicago, 1952. Or: "A German Jew is at least as good as a Viennese Nazi." Imagine a German man or woman saying this loudly in a crowded Berlin trolleycar in 1942, as he sees a Jewish man pushed off the platform by an S.S. man bellowing with an Austrian accent. Now imagine the same words pronounced in New York before an audience of liberals and emigrés. The differences exist not only in the qualities of courage of the first speakers; and not only because they were directed to different people. I am inclined to think that in the given (that is, historical) circumstances somehow the first statements

15

were *truer* than the second ones: more precisely, they came *closer* to the truth, because they were more remarkable statements in the pursuit of truth, in the midst of the ugly presence and prevalence of accepted untruths. They rang with a higher quality of truth.

Justice is of a lower order than is truth, and untruth is lower than is injustice. The administration of justice, even with the best intentions of correcting injustice, may often have to ignore or overlook untruths during the judicial process. We live and are capable of living with many injustices, with many shortcomings of justice; but what is a deeper and moral short-coming is a self-willed choice to live with untruths. (All of the parables of Christ taught us to believe in truth, not in justice.) There is no need to expatiate upon this further, except that the difference between the propagation of justice and that of truth, resulting in the difference of the prevalence of injustice and of untruth, has perhaps never been as extensive (and startling) as it is now, at the end of the Modern Age, and in the midst of our democratic age. There may be less injustice—surely of institutionalized injustice—now than ever before. The governments of many states and all kinds of legal establishments profess to dedicate themselves to the elimination of injustice: slavery, exploitation, racial and economic and social discriminations. At least superficially these practices seem to have diminished throughout the world. At the same time there hangs over the world an enormous and spreading dark cloud cover of untruths—especially in this democratic age of mass and "electronic" communications (more often than not aimed at the lowest common denominator of their recipients). And amid this often suffocating discrepancy, which is replete with the gravest of potential dangers, few are aware that the indiscriminate pursuit of justice may turn to insane lengths—indeed, that it may lay the world to waste. (Consider but some of the inhuman techniques of modern war; or the puritanical character and fate of Captain Ahab in *Moby-Dick*.)

We have seen, earlier in this chapter, that there is a difference between historical and legal evidence. But: does the historian know what *is* truth? No, he does not; yet he ought to do better than Pontius Pilate (whom I, for one, could never contemplate without at least a modicum of sympathy). When Pilate asked: "What is truth?" he also implied: "What is untruth?" The historian ought to go one better than that. He ought to see untruth for what it is. His work, really, consists of the pursuit of truth (where Pilate had stopped), often through a jungle of untruths, bushes and weeds and thickets, small and large.

But it is not as simple as that. The pursuit of truth (and the often consequent belief, "Eureka! I found it!") is also historical—meaning that it changes through the ages. There was a time when an avowal of certain truths of faith amounted to a proof of one's belonging to a real community (or the reverse). This was followed by the so-called Age of Reason, when the assertion of a scientific truth became independent of any other belief (wrongly so). Yes: for God-believers Truth is God/God is Truth, which means: God is eternal. Truth is eternal. But we are not Gods but historical beings, and the fallible descendants of Adam. This has been beautifully expressed by the American Christian thinker Caryl Johnston: "There is, inescapably, an historical dimension in any truthtelling. . . . It is not that 'history' tells the truth (or disguises or determines the truth) as it is that we are ineluctably involved with history in any attempt to tell the truth." Note: *to tell the truth.*[20]

We cannot avoid the historicity of our thinking. As Owen Barfield wrote: "One way or another, what matters is our coming to realize that the way we habitually think and perceive is not the only possible way, not even a way that has been going on very long. It is the way we have *come* to think, the way we have *come* to perceive. Habit is the end product of repeated action in the past, of prolonged behavior in the past. This is as true of mental habit as of any other. And so, if men have at last become incapable of seeing what they once saw, it is because they have gone for so a long time not looking at it."[21]

But the historicity of our seeing and speaking does *not* amount to the relativity of truth. What history gives a mind, at best, is not a dose of relativism; it gives us certain standards, the power to contrast, and the right to estimate. The belief that truth is relative is no longer the assertion merely of cynics or skeptics but of postmodern philosophers, according to whom there were and are no truths, only modes of discourse, structures of thought and of text. Their relativization of truth is absolute. And yet: truths exist. Their existence, unlike the existence of ideas, is not a matter of our choice. But we are responsible for how, and where, and why, and when we try to express them.

"Facts"—inevitably dependent on their associations and, more important, on their statements—are not truths. Their statements or expressions can come close to truths—which is the best we can expect. A "fact" is never absolute. Nor is it given to us to fix, to nail down, to state unalterably an absolute truth. We may think that our *concept* (or *idea*) of truth is absolute; yet that, too, only hearkens toward the absolute. (Our very language reflects this. "This is true" is not quite the same as: "This is *the* truth.")

Pascal: "Truth is so subtle a point that our instruments are too blunt to touch it exactly. When they do reach it, they crush the point and bear down around it, more on the false than on the true." Kierkegaard: "The pure truth is for God alone. What is given to us is the pursuit of truth." This is not relativism. (If truth does not really exist, indeed, if it is wholly relative:

why pursue it at all?) And for believers, the sense that truths exist ought to be strengthened by the cognition (or consciousness) that the pure truth is for God alone—an existence that is independent of us and yet the potential sense of which is within us.

❀ ❀ ❀

A little more than a century ago the English historian Lord Acton claimed that historical science had reached a stage when a history of the Battle of Waterloo could be written that would not only be perfectly acceptable to French and British and Dutch and Prussian historians but would be unchanging, perennial, and fixed. Already Acton's great contemporary John Cardinal Newman said that Acton "seems to me to expect more from History than History can furnish." And a century later we have (or at least ought to have) a more chastened and realistic perspective. Acton believed that history (very much including the history of the Church) was a supremely important matter—yes—and that the purpose of history is the definite, and final, establishment of truth—no. Just as the purpose of medicine is not perfect health but the struggle against illness, just as the purpose of law is not perfect justice but the pursuit of it through vigilance against injustice, the purpose of the historian is not the establishment of perfect truth but the pursuit of truth through a reduction of ignorance, including untruths.

There are many historians who would not find such a statement sufficiently satisfactory. They are not to be blamed for this, nor are they to be blamed for a condition which is much larger than their own profession: the intellectual and mental and spiritual crisis at the end of the Modern Age, of which the bureaucratization of intellectual professions, including historianship, is but a consequence. But they ought to be blamed for their ignorance of (or lack of interest in) an amazing condition: the relatively recent development of a spreading appetite for history in the world, something that exists contrary to so many other superficial symptoms. For this happens at a time when many people know *less* history than their parents or grandparents had known; but when *more* people are interested in history than ever before. On the one hand, less history is being required and taught in schools than earlier in the twentieth century. On the other hand there exists an appetite for history throughout the world—and perhaps particularly in the United States—that has no precedents.[22] There are so many evidences of this that I can list only a few. There are history programs and history channels on television, historical films, historical "documentaries" and "docudramas," obviously responding to the interests of millions, dealing with topics that were hardly featured as late as two generations ago.

There exist popular historical magazines, with a widespread readership. There are three times as many local historical societies in the United States as there were sixty years ago: their membership includes many younger people, not only old ladies in tennis shoes whose interests are primarily genealogical.

Of course the historical appetite of people is served, and will continue to be served, with plenty of junk food. Of that professional historians may be aware. Yet the existence of this appetite for history is ignored by many of them—and, alas, by most administrators of educational institutions.

Perhaps the most startling evidence of this appetite—perhaps more precisely: of this recent evolution of consciousness—has been the (now at least fifty-year-old) change in the relationship between history and the novel. Within commercial publishing, popular histories have been outselling novels for at least fifty years. It is now accepted that serious biographies belong to history: biographies sell quite well, while the very methods of serious biographers have become historical. Interest in history and interest in the novel developed together about 250 years ago; they were part and parcel of the then-evolving historical consciousness. That was a new phenomenon, since the novel as such hardly existed before that. The novel was not really a new version of epic in prose. It described people and events who were not mythical but real, with whom people could identify themselves in one way or another.

Then arose the historical novel, in the nineteenth century, when writers recognized that they could create more interesting stories against a rich historical background. But during the twentieth century a reverse development occurred. More and more it was not the novel that absorbed history but it was history that began to absorb the novel. So far as readership goes, we have seen that the appetite for all kinds of readers for history and for biography has risen at the same time that their appetite and interest for novels has decreased. But—significantly—more and more writers began to sense this (even as they have not recognized its meaning), experimenting with new hybrid genres that are the opposites of the old historical novel, since in their confections history is not the background but the foreground. One manifestation of this is the new hybrid thing that has the silly name of "faction."[23]

"Our time is emerging as a golden age of American history and biography," writes the excellent historian of California, Kevin Starr. "As the American novel, in fact, has become more narrow, more internal and fragmented, more solipsistic in its inability to grasp and refract social dynamics in the manner of its [previous] masters ... American historians and biographers have come to the fore as the providers of imaginative as well as social scientific interpretation."[24] This may be especially true of biography. During the nineteenth century many professional historians, due to the largely German-inspired canons of their craft, eschewed biography. In this respect the English tradition was an exception, with enduring and widening results especially during the second half of the twentieth century (one of the few promising signs at a time of intellectual decay), to the extent that the appetite of the reading public for serious biographies is now larger than ever before, and that every serious biographer now follows the process of historical research.

Meanwhile two directions of the novel have become discernible: one tendency increasingly toward poetry, the other—more widespread and more important—toward history: and there is at least some reason to believe that sooner or later history may absorb the narrative novel almost entirely. New kinds of historical literature will of course appear—they are already appearing—including some very questionable ones. But Carlyle was probably right when he wrote, "In the right interpretation of History and Reality does genuine poetry lie." Or Maupassant (in his preface to *Pierre et Jean*): "The aim of the realistic novelist is not to tell a story; to amuse us or to appeal to our feelings, but to compel us to reflect, and to understand the darker and deeper meaning of events."[25] A historian could have written that.

More than one hundred years ago Thomas Hardy wrote:

> Conscientious fiction alone it is which can excite a reflecting and thoughtful and abiding interest in the minds of thoughtful readers of mature age, who are weary of puerile inventions and famishing for accuracy; who consider that in representations of the world, the passions ought to be proportioned as in the world itself. This is the interest which was excited in the minds of the Athenians by their immortal tragedies, and in the minds of Londoners at the first performances of the finer plays of three hundred years ago.[26]

I am convinced that *conscientious history* is now replacing that desideratum which Hardy stated as *conscientious fiction*. It is history which can excite a reflecting and abiding interest in the minds of thoughtful readers of mature age, who are weary (and how weary we are) of puerile inventions and famishing for accuracy (I should say: reality; truth).[27]

It should now appear that I have been writing about the historicity of our knowledge, rather than about the knowledgeability of all history; in other words, eschewing a philosophy of history but asserting the nature and evidences of a historical and monistic perspective of the world. A recognition of this, coming at the end of an age, is overdue.[28]

2

About Historical Factors, or the Hierarchy of Powers

(1968)

T he past; the remembered past; the recorded past. History is less than the first while it is something more than the last. But "the remembered past" harbors difficulties, too. For one thing, there is a difference between what we remember and what we think we ought to remember. We do not have much control over what we remember (though we have more control over it than what many modern psychologists imply); and we are often more conscious of what we want to know than of what we know. But what portions of the past are especially worth knowing? This depends, of course, on one's purposes: it is not the same for different people living in different times. Our historical interests are subject to change. There is, moreover, a difference between a "portion" and a "period" of history.[1] In any event, certain portions of it are better discernible and more intelligible than are others.

Why is this so? Why is a history of the United States in the nineteenth century a more intelligible and more meaningful "portion" than a history of North America? Or, in the twentieth century, a history of Philadelphia rather than that of Pennsylvania? Because the aggregates represented by the former of these pairs are more unique than are those of the latter. History is the history of human communities, and these communities must be, in more than one sense, particular and real. (Civilizations, Spengler declared and Toynbee preached, are the only more-or-less self-contained and intelligible units of history: yet what Spengler and Toynbee demonstrated, in their different ways, was that it was easier for them to write *about* this kind of history than to write it, to compare certain historical aspects of civilizations than to describe their histories.) This is why books and courses

From *Historical Consciousness; or, the Remembered Past* (New York: Harper and Row), 171–216.

in the history of the entire globe—World History—are still largely un-manageable. This is why a history of Eurasia (a real continent) would be, to a large extent, meaningless, while the history of Europe (a mere idea of a continent) is potentially meaningful—though only on certain levels, and perhaps only during the last few hundred years. For even Europe seems to be a community only when it is being regarded from the distance of an-other continent: for long centuries "Europe" existed only in the sense of a geographical area. Anyone attempting to write of recent European histori-cal developments in some depth even now will encounter inevitably the problem of the diversity of Europeans, of how the continued existence of different national cultures and of different national conditions makes it very difficult for the historian to generalize about Europe, to proceed from the particular to the general.

The proper study of history includes, principally, persons rather than social types, nations rather than classes, cultural rather than economic units. A history of science must be a history of scientists, a history of technology of the inventors, producers, and managers of technology: for the more the emphasis lies on the technical changes and the less on the human condi-tions and characteristics of their propagators, the less historical—and also the less interesting—the account. Of course everything is potentially in-teresting: it can be made interesting, possibly even the history of the alu-minum industry in western Ohio. A good economic history is better than a bad political history—that goes without saying. It is only that the good economic history is the one in which the human element is sufficiently emphasized and, therefore, real. For, generally speaking, the history of tech-nologies *is* less interesting than the history of nations, and the history of economics *is* less interesting than the history of wars. Less interesting, be-cause less real, and, consequently, boring; for, at least in one sense, the more boring something the less true it is.

This is not a facile statement. The reason behind it is the obvious con-dition of history being man's knowledge of man par excellence. Historical knowledge is inevitably anthropomorphic; consequently the more the or-ganism of the object of our historical research resembles human character-istics the greater its historicity, and the more interesting to us it is. We cannot really escape this condition. The histories of modern nation-states, for example, are not only among the relatively most intelligible "portions" of historical research: their histories are interesting because there exist con-siderable similarities, though not analogies, between the characteristics of certain communities such as modern nations and of the characteristics of human persons. "The life of nations," reads one of my favorite passages from Proust, "merely repeats, on a larger scale, the lives of their component cells: and he who is incapable of understanding the mystery, the reactions, the laws that determined the movements of the individual, can never hope to say anything worth listening to about the struggles of nations." We must, of course, be careful not to indulge in drawing biological parallels between nations and persons: we must not attribute "souls" to nations. Communities are not organisms, they are aggregations. But not only do national characteristics, such as "mercurial," "temperamental," "steady," "stolid," "imaginative," "unimaginative" exist; some of the functions of these characteristics do resemble certain functions of personal characteristics. A community, like a person, may be "humiliated," "downcast," "ashamed"—metaphors which cannot be applied to economies and rarely to civilizations. And this is a condition which reflects not only superficial appearances but deeper reactions, too: it may not be unreal, for example, to suggest that on certain occasions the military conquest of a nation by another may result in psychic conditions which, without being analogous, may resemble the results of a sexual conquest, since the sexual act does mean the imposition of the will of one participant on another, involving at least a partial acquiescence or even the collaboration of certain elements of the latter, and, as even Freud would say late in his career, the temporary creation of a community between two autonomous persons. It is from these recognitions that the ensuing speculations about the relative hierarchy of certain historical factors issue as a matter of course.

❈ ❈ ❈

WHAT follows are occasional, though not necessarily disjointed, observations concerning certain "aspects" or, as they are nowadays called, "fields" of history.

These observations must, by their nature, be existential rather than philosophical. It is true that any kind of comparison of the relative importance of, say, economic vs. political history will necessarily involve the metaphysical argument whether man is principally an economic or principally a political being. But this is not the place for such a discussion: for one thing, it is very difficult, if not altogether impossible, to convince people about such fundamental matters within the limits of a chapter or even of a book. On the other hand, the limitations of certain "fields" of research may be demonstrated on the historical, rather than on the philosophical, plane of argument—and this is what I am attempting to do.

Economic history, it is generally believed, is a very important "field"—or perhaps, "level"—of historical studies: it is the bedrock for the structure of general history. The present interest in economic history reflects an increase in the seriousness of historians, a concern to get beneath the surface, a deepening of our quest for understanding the past, an *approfondissement,* as the French say, *de l'état actuel de nos connaissances.* Yet the trouble with much of modern economic information is that it is abstract rather than solid, and superficial rather than profound. This is perhaps one of the reasons why most of our economists have been rather incapable of explaining much about the historical movement of events. I am not only referring to the present ways in which famed economists and public statesmen such as Professor Rostow dazzle the mind by devising historical periods such as The Economic Take-Off, which, according to them, are *the* decisive events in the histories of nations. Apart from the frequent follies of modern economists, there is ample evidence in modern and contemporary history to show that the so-called economic factors were less decisive than they may seem at first sight. The First World War; the Second World War; Mussolini, Hitler, Stalin; the Russian Revolution, the Hungarian Revolution; the Cold War, the end of the European empires—they are not explainable on an economic basis, by a principally economic interpretation of their origins. Obviously, economic conditions are historical factors. It is only that their operations are less direct, less profound, and, often, less powerful than what we have been accustomed to think.

I think that this will appear even in those instances of history where the economic interpretation of motives is generally recognized as principally valid. Most thoughtful people will dismiss the Marxist idiocy according to which Hitler was a tool in the hands of monopoly capitalism. Still, it is true that most German industrialists and capitalists supported Hitler in 1933, just as one of the principal, if not *the* principal, factor in the foreign policy of the Chamberlainites until 1939 was their fear of communism. But this preference of fascism over communism evinced by most German and by some English capitalists was something more than an economic preference; it was involved, on a deeper level, with their social, political, national convictions: they were afraid of the social consequences of communism rather than of the diminution of their personal profits. There are innumerable examples in the "pragmatic" and "materialist" English-speaking countries that illustrate that the most rabid and anxious opponents of communism are to be found among people who have very little capital of their own, and consequently very little stake in the economic order which they profess to preserve; on the other hand, some of the most influential advocates of pro-Soviet foreign, or pro-socialistic domestic, policies have come from among the principal capitalists of the British and American empires. Let me go so far as to say that there are no economic motives: there are only economic acts.

But my argument involves not only the impossibility of isolating eco-

nomic motives. It is addressed to the limitations of reconstructing economic acts from economic records. This is a more complex matter, since it
inevitably impinges upon economic thinking. A person may not act as a
capitalist, just as Stalin often acted in a very different manner from that of
a Marxian Communist: but as long as one person thinks that he is a capitalist, or that he is a Communist, this will have an important influence on his
actions. There may be no such thing as an economic motive, but there surely
are things such as economic ideas. Yet the latter are usually categories which,
by their very nature, are often systematic abstractions. For, unlike the material realities of this world, economics are human formulations. This is
perhaps the most important thing that we have learned—or rather, that we
ought to have learned—from the history of the last fifty years. A statement
such as the one made by the president of the British Board of Trade in
1914 (Walter Runciman, a Liberal M.P.; perhaps significantly a principal
Chamberlainite in 1938) that "no government action could overcome economic laws and any interference with those laws must end in disaster" is
inconceivable now not only because the ideal of Free Trade is dead but
because the idea of Economic Laws as if they were something like the Laws
of Nature is even more dead. This notion of economics as a mental construction, indeed, as a *fictio* in every sense of that word, may be hard for
many people to accept, but accept it they must if they want to think sensi-
bly about the functioning of economic factors.

For it is the functioning, rather than the measurability, of economic
factors that should be of interest to historians as well as to economists.
Whatever may be the merits of the new science of econometrics (not to
speak of "Cliometrics"—this obscene word having been recently proposed
in order to describe historical quantification), their practitioners would do
well to keep in mind how many economic data are the results of human
abstractions. I have written elsewhere about the illusion inherent in the
notion of Hard Facts: but let me now add that of all facts economic facts are
among the softest kind. (I cannot, for example, conceive of any economic
fact that is as solid as a demographic or an electoral datum, a birthrate
statistic or a percentage among voters.) And the reason for the softness
inherent in most economic data is that they are not only inseparable from
their interpretations but that they are the results of interpretations. They
are statistical answers not only to preexisting questions but to preconceived
definitions; and, moreover, to definitions which are far from being solid or
leak-proof, a good example of this being the now fashionable figure of the
Gross National Product, the very computation of which depends on questionable categories and variable definitions by econometricians. But then,
even the value of a stock, or of a currency, depends not so much on the

actual and computable assets and liabilities of a corporation or of a nation as on what the public thinks their value is. The principal factor in the development of such a *prima facie* "economic" event as the American depression beginning in 1929 was a loss of confidence, that is, a change in mentality (just as the American recovery beginning in 1933 was the result of the national recovery of confidence). What counts, often, is the popularity of an economic idea, rather than the "measurable" economic condition: indeed, changes in the first so often lead to changes in the latter that one is left to wonder whether the causalities of economics may not furnish *the* principal illustrations for arguments against materialist or determinist conceptions of the structure and sequence of events. But then, no economic idea is ever purely economic; it is inseparably interwoven with political and social preferences and tendencies. The history of the twentieth century is full of examples where all kinds of personal influences or psychological maneuvers resulted in actual economic changes (Roosevelt's first radio addresses, Hitler and the German money, de Gaulle's mathematically meaningless but psychologically most effective push of the decimal point two digits to the left, lopping off two zeroes from the franc).[2]

During the nineteenth century historians erred by generally neglecting the history of economic factors. We have become more sophisticated, not only in the sense that economic history made great advances and attracted a few master historians, but in the more important sense that our notion of history has become broadened so that in our times the general historian feels compelled—and, let me hasten to add, rightly so—to begin his description of a period or of a society by some of their economic conditions and developments. This is all to the good. Only, the historian must be very much aware of the limitations of economic data—and especially of certain data of recent times. All of our computers, all of our statistical information notwithstanding, there is reason to believe that the meaning of economic data decreases with their accumulation; that, historically speaking, many of these recent data are less meaningful than are certain data of the past. The information produced by Marc Bloch and his colleagues about medieval France, the household accounts presented by historians such as Eileen Power in her *Medieval People,* are wonderfully telling things.[3] A study such as J. Singer-Kerel's on the cost of living in Paris during the nineteenth century tells us very much, since the costs of living, *les coûts de la vie,* are inseparable from *les goûts de la vie,* the ways of living, from the prevalence of standards and tastes and aspirations. I read Boswell's detailed accounts of his expenditures in London of little more than two hundred years ago. They are marvelously illustrative. But let us suppose that an eager researcher gets hold of the tax returns and checking accounts of an American public figure in the 1950s. They will, I think, tell him much less about such a person's tastes and habits and problems, about his way of life, including perhaps his financial ups and downs, than what a cursory reading of Boswell's diaries tells about these things of two hundred years ago. The reason for this lies in the complexities of modern records of accounting, which may obscure even more than enlighten us about their underlying realities, just as the most detailed legal account of a corporation fight may tell us very little about the personal factors that are inevitably involved. The more the economic data—or rather, the more *demand* for economic data, by impersonal agencies such as governments, industries, accounting firms, all kinds of organizations[4]—the more complicated the accounting, which, after a while, becomes a closed system of its own, and consequently less and less meaningful, historically speaking. An example of this is a figure such as the "national debt," which in the twentieth century has become not much more than an abstract item within intra-national accounting.[5] Meanwhile certain international financial transactions have become abstract, too, in the sense that the movement of monies that they register are often transfers on the level of bookkeeping, not physical transfers from one country to another. This does not mean that they are meaningless: it means, however, that what happens during such transactions is something quite different from what we are told happens and that, consequently, some of their portents may be different, too, from what one would expect. As in much of contemporary political science, the old terms no longer fit the newer realities.

The development of the twentieth century has been marked by inflation, which has affected every nation to various extents. The historical meaning of this overall development may be summed up by saying that money has become more available while it has become less valuable—and, consequently, less important. What this means for economists is that a new science of economics is necessary for a new world: but this is, as yet, far from forthcoming. What this means for historians of the twentieth century is that they must be especially aware of the illusory nature of "purely" economic conditions and of the limitations inherent in many economic records, because they must recognize the increasingly papery characteristics of an increasing number of economic transactions, the new realities of which accord less and less with the traditional meaning of economic relationships. A modern and popular economics textbook, lying before me, defines *demand* as "desire backed up by ability to pay." Yes: but what is "desire" and what is "ability to pay"? In 1966 the meaning of these things—consider only the widespread existence of consumer credit—was something quite different from what it was in 1866. What do *ownership, property, possession* mean in a society such as ours, where most people are no longer employed in production but in administration, and where the principal purpose of the national economy is to produce employment rather than durable goods? In 1966 many more Americans owned their houses than at any time before in history: economic facts such as this are often employed proudly by public speakers in order to extol the merits of the American "people's capitalism." Yet what do these statistics of ownership mean when, at the same time, the average American family moves every three or four years, when no more than one out of twenty Americans expect to pay off their mortgage and fully own the house they occupy at the present, when not one in a hundred expects to be able to hand over his house eventually to his children? Surely in the second half of the twentieth century in the United States at least the very sense of the ownership of material goods has changed, together with the increasing impermanence of possessions: but then, even a century ago *ownership, property, possession* meant something very different in the Dakota Territory from what they meant in the Touraine.

❊ ❊ ❊

THIS is what I mean when I say that instead of studying history in terms of economic developments we must attempt to understand economics in terms of historical developments. This too is why no line separating economic from social history can be drawn. The movement of materials in and out of a man's life, the record of his possessions and of his management thereof is meaningful only because of his relationship with other human beings. The economic history of a man is an inseparable part of his social history. Let me illustrate this. X, the famous late-Victorian politician, switched his party allegiance in 187–, an event which led to all kinds of then unforeseen consequences in national politics. The records about this event having been fragmentary, X's motives have been debated by historians ever since. But now, nearly a century later, Alpha, a young historian, rummaging among private papers, discovers a set of letters and private memoranda, which furnish the Decisive Evidence. X was in debt to Y, to that great gray eminence of a banker who was beginning to press him; shortly thereafter he turned to become a National Liberal, and he came out in support of the Railways' Act from which the financial interests controlled by Y and his friends were to profit. Very well: let Alpha make his career. Still, after all is said, the attribution of the economic motive to X is not enough, not even in such a clear-cut case. X joined the National Liberals because he was in debt to Y; but is this "because" enough? Why was he in debt? Why was he in debt to Y? He *was* greedy: but why?[6] He wanted to cut a large figure in the world; he wanted to impress a certain woman; a set of people had snubbed him earlier; he wanted to identify himself with the *grand monde*, he wanted a townhouse, a carriage. And, still: why? Why did he want a certain kind of carriage and a certain kind of townhouse and a certain kind of club membership and a certain woman? We can never, of course, know the full answer to these questions: but we are, in a sense, back at the historiographical problem of motives vs. purposes. We do know something about the latter—from certain records of X's acts and words, from the surviving expressions of his ambitions and aspirations, which were personal as well as historical ones, since not only certain traits of his personality but even some of his intimate desires may not have been altogether inseparable from the habits, fashions, standards, and ideas of his times, that is, of a particular culture in a certain historical period.

In a sense, therefore, social history is the largest portion of cultural history. There are many problems with this field, however. The first is its relationship to sociology: history can never become sociology, even though it must become more and more sociographical[7]—meaning that the purpose of the conscientious historian as well as of the intelligent sociologist must be the description of societies rather than their categorization according to so-called laws, and that this description must be historical in the sense that it must focus on movement—that is, on the origins, developments, and changes of social habits and other social phenomena.

These phenomena include things such as classes that are for the social historian what states are for the political historian. It is here that the second problem, that of the terminology of social history, arises. This terminology must be historical, not sociological; it must depend, as much as is possible, on the vocabulary of everyday language. But it is not enough to say this. The social historian faces certain difficulties which are peculiar to his subject. Classes, for example, are more fluid and therefore more elusive realities than are states, which do have, after all, a concrete and geographical basis. And, as Professor Alfred Cobban wrote in a magisterial manner, historians have not been very accurate in writing about classes, since they have "borrowed their vocabulary, and therefore the presuppositions of their history, from the Marxian analysis, and continue to use the same terms even when their researches call for something different."[8] This does not mean that we should acquiesce in the defeatist thesis proposed by Professor Seignobos, that class terminology necessarily rests on a "mythological" vocabulary; it means, however, that we ought to reconsider the accuracy of the old categories and, with new materials at hand, we ought to be more precise about them. For example, the dominant "bourgeois" character of the Huguenots or of the Louis Philippe regime "deserve," in Cobban's words, "a little more investigation before we can take it for granted." Furthermore, we must keep in mind that the trouble with the old categories lies often not so much in their wanting accuracy as in their static character, for the very notion of class is dynamic rather than static. In the eighteenth century, for example, *manufacturer* in England meant industrial worker, whereas in France *ouvrier* meant what we now mean as manufacturer; as Cobban put it, thereafter "the English term has gone up in the world and the French one down." There is a difference between *bourgeois* and *middle class*: the former term is the more dynamic of the two. It refers to an entire sphere of functional and historical aspirations that are altogether missing from the more static and sociological term of *middle class*. These aspirations reflect tendencies which are different from the material conditions registered by economics: for, to a considerable extent, social history is not only the history of movements, it is the history of aspirations. Not only is what happens often inextricably involved with what people think happens; what people are is involved with what they want to be.

Typical of the Bourgeois Age was the powerful impulse of social ambitions. That Rastignac was a rake, Josiah Bounderby a pompous ass, Emma Bovary a fallen woman will be evident to readers a hundred years from now. What they may find difficult to comprehend is the exaggerated importance that certain characters of Balzac as well as of Flaubert, of Jane Austen as well as of Trollope, attached to social ambitions. At least for three centuries in the West such social aspirations were among the profoundest personal—and, consequently, historical—factors. It is because of their deep complexities that they have been described by master novelists rather than by historians. For, even if we recognize the powerful element of emotions and sentiments in politics, we can see that political ambitions are more or less rational ones, whereas this is less true of social ambitions, at the sources of which we find the gnarled roots of Vanity, luxuriating in cavernous recesses of the human spirit: and it is therefore that the penetrating eye of the novelist may furnish some guidance here to the cultural historian. For the social element is something more than environmental influence; it does not only surround, but through images and ideas it intrudes into the private spheres of thought and personal choice, including even the deep sphere of sexual choice. It is a mistake to categorize Madame Birotteau as having been the victim of her social, and Madame Bovary of her sexual, ambitions. There is a very close connection between these two things. They are involved with each other through personal aspirations generated by certain ideas through imagination. I shall have to return to this point later; let me only suggest here that, just as the Industrial Revolution was the consequence of certain ideas, the modern Sexual Revolution has been social rather than sexual. It is   especially in our democratic times—consider, for example, the marriage habits of young people in the

United States—that this primacy of the social over the merely sexual element so often prevails. It is only because of the peculiar intellectual confusion of our times that it has been seldom so recognized. But we ought to recognize that if the so-called Sexual Revolution in the twentieth century has been a revolution at all, it has been a social revolution, a leveling revolution; for sexual ambitions are almost often inseparable from social aspirations, just as sexual frustration is often social frustration, existential frustration, the sense of a personal failure within a society.

Meanwhile we face a new situation. The social historian of the second half of the twentieth century will have to consider the weakening of traditional social ambitions—at the very time when the impact of mass society on the individual is very strong, when social conformities of various kinds have become pervasive. We may face new phenomena of social history. Not only are "classes" difficult and, in retrospect, fragile historical categories: we may be moving into an era of a certain classnessness, at least in the traditional sense of the word. Surely many of the older class distinctions are dissolving, as we may be moving toward a neo-medieval society based on status rather than on contract, on recognized professional rank rather than on distinctions of birth or of wealth. Still, the momentum of accepted ideas is very strong, for people will think in terms of classes even when the realities of the latter may no longer function. (In any event, one of the most complex and most interesting factors within social phenomena is the discrepancy that almost always exists between two perspectives of one's position on the social scale: between the position in which a person sees himself and the different position to which others may assign him in their minds.) Moreover, with the gradual dissolution of class boundaries in many national societies, the desire for a kind of group self-identification has replaced the older personal propellant of social ambitions: we have a new type of person who wants to rise with his group, and almost never beyond it. This is altogether different from the bourgeois aspirations, this social phenomenon of the Organization Man, or Mass Man, or whatever we may call him; in any event, there are complex personal problems latent within his rootlessness, within the degeneration of his aspirations, and within the superficially manageable character of his ambitions. Some of the most telling observations of this structural change were made not by sociologists or by social historians but by the Italian-German theologian Romano Guardini. In a little book, characteristically titled *The End of the Modern World*, and again characteristically, written not during the desperations of the Hitler era but amid the flourishing prosperity of Adenauer's West Germany, Guardini said that the era of Mass Man is already succeeding that of the Modern Man, but that this mass "is not debased and decayed essentially as was the rabble of ancient Rome. The mass has assumed a genuine form of existence in human history." But with the "loss of personality comes the steady falling away of that sense of uniqueness with which man had once viewed his existence, which had been the source of all social intercourse. . . ."

Still, we cannot conclude that while political history was the history par excellence of the Modern Age with its bourgeois characteristics, social history is the history par excellence of the mass democratic age now developing. The description of societies, of their habits and of their ideas, has become more and more important—on the condition that such a description retains its historicity—as long as it remains "history" rather than "social."[9] The constant danger that social historians skirt is the tendency to gloss over what is unique and exceptional and resistant to the pattern of general developments. Of course we live in a world where we are more acquainted with the large than with the small: but "more" does not necessarily mean "better." The historian must remain introspective; he must avoid Comte's original error of trying, as Maxime Leroy put it, to explain "l'homme par l'humanité" and not "l'humanité par l'homme." There is no history to *every* categorized aggregate of individuals, so dear to the social scientist: there is not much history in the story of Tall Men or of Young Businessmen: there is history in the story of the Young Turks.[10]

❄ ❄ ❄

HISTORY is still principally the history of states and of governments. The now so respectable emphasis on economic and social developments obscures this fact. Yet the history of what used to be the governing classes no longer explains almost everything about domestic politics, just as the account of the relationships of states no longer explains all about foreign politics. The texture of history has changed, together with the structure of politics, in our democratic age. I shall not belabor this argument further, except to note that there is much more to be said about the problems of historiography and about the deteriorating authenticity of records in the democratic epoch in which we now live. Apart from these problems the practice of political history, especially in dealing with subjects after 1650 and before 1945, is relatively (but only relatively) in not too bad a shape. The main reason for this condition is that, all of their verbal respects to economics and to sociology notwithstanding, most historians are still interested principally in politics—indeed, it is probably because of their political interest in the past that they took their degree in history and not in economics or sociology.

There are, however, certain matters which may be worth mentioning at this point. There are many signs which suggest that the importance of local politics is decreasing: an alarming symptom for the future of traditional democracy. For one thing, the destruction, and not only the temporary defeat, of entire nations has now become possible because of atomic weapons, whereby foreign policy is literally a life-and-death matter for their governments. For another thing, the domestic life of peoples is influenced increasingly by administration rather than by legislation, permanent governmental agencies having become rather more important than even parliaments and other more traditional bodies. The most drastic curtailments of personal liberties and of traditional civic processes may be expedited by such agencies through their routine evolution—I need only to refer to such things as telephonic and electronic eavesdropping. Indeed, halfway to 1984, when this is written, the great danger in the West is no longer the possibility of the totalitarian and antidemocratic regime of a political Big Brother but rather the increasing regime of a totalitarian democracy, by which I mean the evolution of a society in which universal popular suffrage, including a minimum of party choice, exists, but where freedom of speech is hardly more than of theoretical value for the individual, whose life and ideas, whose rights to privacy, to family autonomy, and to durable possessions are regimented by government and rigidly limited by technology and mass communications. It will be difficult for a future historian to trace exactly the shapeless stages of these evolutions. In any event he will have to be exceptionally discerning in order to avoid becoming entangled in the thicket of antiquated adjectives—liberal, conservative, reactionary, progressive, rightist, leftist—which may obscure rather than enlighten his path.

This brings us to the problem of our political terminology. For not only is a "new science of politics necessary for a new world," but a now antiquated terminology may obscure our view of the historical developments of politics after 1914—indeed, perhaps during the last one hundred years. Since this is not a treatise in political theory I must sum up my argument as briefly as I can. We are still using the categories "Left" and "Right" even though they are often outdated and inapplicable. Here are a few examples. Has the United States been moving to the "Right" or to the "Left" during the last twenty years? Has the Soviet Union been moving to the "Right" or to the "Left" since Stalin died? Was Hitler more "rightist" than Mussolini, or less? These questions are unanswerable: the categories do not fit.[11] Of course they never fitted exactly, not even in the more remote past; still, Left and Right *were* relatively meaningful designations during the nineteenth century, whereas recently they have become meaningless in an increasing number of instances. And even less useful than "Left" and "Right" are the categories "conservative" and "liberal," especially as they are em-

ployed in the United States. I am not only referring to the evident transmutation of ideas whereby the liberals, the earlier champions of free enterprise, in the twentieth century became the champions of the welfare
state. I am referring to the condition that whereas the principal dialogues
in the nineteenth century occurred indeed between relative conservatives
and relative liberals, the principal relationship in the twentieth century
involves two elementary political tendencies of quite another order: they
are not liberalism and conservatism; they are nationalism and socialism.
They, and their relationship, are the principal political phenomena of this
century. For example, National Socialism has been the common denominator of the principal totalitarian regimes during the second quarter of this
century, a fact that has been deliberately obscured by the Communist,* and
regrettably, by the frequent liberal attribution of the adjective "fascist" to
all totalitarian regimes of the non-Communist variety. Yet, for once, the
German term National Socialism was a precise one. While it is nonsense to
call Hitler a Brown Communist or Stalin a Red Fascist, it makes a lot of
sense to recognize that, in one way or another, Hitler, Stalin, Mussolini
were all National Socialists. So were (and are), in their ways, Nasser, Tito,
Perón, Gomulka, Father Coughlin, Joseph McCarthy, Castro, Nehru,
Sukarno, Mao Tse-tung, Ho Chi Minh, and others: nationalist socialists or
social nationalists, all of them. Our political analysts and theorists have
consistently underrated the influence of the national factor upon socialism, even though this should have been evident as early as 1914, when the
nationalism of the masses, including the working classes, proved so much
stronger and enduring than the rational exhortations of the suddenly few
spokesmen of the international socialist ideology. After World War I, German National Socialism was but an extreme manifestation of this worldwide conjunction of nationalism and socialism, a phenomenon that, I repeat, is recognizable *not* only in its totalitarian varieties. I have often thought,
for example, that it is by these terms that the ideological mysteries and
complexities of the American two-party system may be explainable to
Europeans in the twentieth century, since it may be said that among our
two national welfare parties the Democrats have, by and large, emphasized
their socialist rather than their nationalist programs, while the Republicans have been, generally speaking, nationalists rather than socialists—even
though, of course, they would not admit this.

They would not admit this. The United States, as every other nation, has
been moving in the direction of a welfare state during the last sixty years at
least. This has involved legislation and administrative practices of the kind
which in other nations are called "socialist"; in the United States they
weren't. Americans have strenuously avoided this adjective; but, then, in

this evolution of an American socialism the role of American socialist parties was minimal. This should illustrate the importance of political terminology, and perhaps of rhetoric in general. Since the American people rejected (and they still reject) the word "socialist," and since what happens in the short run is inseparable from what people think happens, the legislation of the New Deal, for instance, was *not* socialist in the sense in which the legislation of British Labor or of Swedish Socialist governments *was* socialist. Of course this reluctance to call certain spades spades is a historical phenomenon involved with certain national traditions and national characteristics, including the reluctance of certain peoples to reconsider some of their ideas. As early as 1881 John Morley, referring to the English Factory Acts, wrote of "the rather amazing result that in the country where socialism has been less talked about than any other country in Europe, its principles have been most extensively applied." Two generations later, however, the word "socialist" (and not merely "Labor") has become more acceptable even in England. It is not inconceivable that, in the long run, future generations of Americans may recognize the socialistic transformation of American society, but this would involve a change in accepted ideas together with a change in the general political climate of the country. The course of the world, as Lord Percy of Newcastle wrote, is still "determined by what people believe," but it is also true that political terminology is not a mere matter of names, that, as René Rémond put it, "the changing fortune of certain political terms indicates corresponding changes in the fortune of certain political formations." Consider the recent fortunes of the political adjective "conservative" in the United States. As late as 1952, when the popular reaction against the liberal ideologies and policies of the previous Democratic administrations was in full swing, even Senator Taft shunned the word "conservative"; eight years later, however, "conservative" became acceptable, Nixon and even Eisenhower employing it approvingly on occasion, until by 1964, for the first time in American history, the presidential nominee of one of the two great national parties appeared as a "conservative"; by 1965 conservative third parties were forming, here and there, in the country. This antiliberal political reaction has had little to do with class consciousness (the mainstay of "conservative" strength in the United States is to be found generally among the lower middle class), just as throughout modern history in Europe there have been "rightist" and "leftist" peasants, "rightist" and "leftist" bourgeois.

In any event, the vocabulary of politics is dynamic not static, and its historical study amounts to more than antiquarian etymology. The growing acceptance or the increasing refusal of a term, the popularity of a new word, the change in the meaning of an old one, are reflections, symptoms, and sometimes even possible causes of political sentiments[12]—which, in turn, are almost always involved with some kind of a historical interpretation.

History, said the great English historian J. R. Seeley nearly a century ago, "is past politics and politics present history." This unilateral emphasis on the political factor in history marked Seeley's entire career as Regius Professor of Modern History at Cambridge; it was also fairly typical of the prevalent attitude among historians in the nineteenth century. (No chair for economic history existed, for example, in European or American universities before about 1895.) We know better now. The view prevalent among historians in the twentieth century tends to regard politics as if it were the superstructure—albeit a very important superstructure—of history, that is, largely a consequence of deeper economic and social developments. There is no doubt, of course, that a narrow preoccupation with political history may give us a relatively superficial version of events. But my point is that the necessary deepening of our professional historical concerns (which, let me repeat, is but a consequence of the deepening of the general historical consciousness) may come about not so much by a shift of interest from the field of political history to the fields of economic or social history but, rather, from a deepening of our interest and insight in every one of these fields. Instead of substituting the principally economic for the principally political interpretation of history we ought, rather, to search deeper into the structure of political events and social developments, as indeed we must probe into the essence of economic data. For it is through this deepening of historical interests, too, that the historian discovers the arbitrary nature of the division of fields of historical research; as the English economic historian Clapham said, "it is at the overlapping margins of disciplines and sciences that the most important discoveries are usually made." Even about Seeley, G. P. Gooch wrote that "though no historian of his time took a more limited view of the province of history . . . it was not because his own interests were few." To historians such as Seeley, history was the school of statesmanship (his contemporary Droysen said that "the statesman is the historian in practice"); and historians, beginning with Ranke, "regarded history as concerned mainly with the life and relations of states." To the best of the old-fashioned political historians such as Seeley domestic politics were always subordinate in importance to foreign relations. I believe that in this they were right. Their concerns were not as narrow as it may seem at first sight.[13] They recognized the tremendous importance and influence of a subject—perhaps *the* most important subject in modern history—to a cursory discussion of which I must now turn.

❀ ❀ ❀

"THERE is no nation on earth," said Ranke more than a century ago, "that has not had some contact with other nations. It is through this external relationship, which in turn depends on a nation's peculiar character, that the nation enters on the stage of world history, and universal history must therefore focus on it." This *Primat der Aussenpolitik* is even now incontestable. The foreign relations of states are still more instructive than are their domestic politics. There is no general history without them. Even today the history of Europe, and indeed of the world, no matter how ideologically divided, is still the history of states and of nations, the United Nations, NATO, Common Market, or the Soviet bloc notwithstanding. The implication of something external, secondary, foreign in the term "foreign policy" is misleading: it is a mistake to think that foreign relations, save on certain critical occasions, are something extraneous, different, and not directly relevant to the main, domestic, internal business of governments, states, nations. As this book is written, the relations of the United States and Soviet Union are more important than the relations of democracy and dictatorship, or of capitalism and communism. I am not writing here a theory of international relations but I am compelled to draw attention to certain, nowadays often obscured and confused and overlooked, factors in these relations. They are the geographical and the territorial factor in the relationships of states, and the cultural factor in the relationships of nations, the first two being a more or less traditional, the latter a more or less recent and democratic, phenomenon.

About the geographical factor we may as well observe that it has not been very much affected by the Space Age. History is not only anthropomorphic; it is geocentric.[14] "The policies of all the powers," said Napoleon, "are inherent in their geography." Events in Mexico concern the United States more than events in Tibet, just as events in Poland are of greater interest to the Russian government than are events in Brazil. The brave new worlds and their brave new words notwithstanding, the United States would not risk a war for Hungary in 1956, and the Soviet Union not for Cuba in 1962. It was, it is, and probably it will always be easier to bombard Florida from Cuba than from the moon; and if tomorrow we should learn that the Russians planted their flag on Mars but were compelled to haul it down in East Berlin there is no question that of these two events the latter one would be more important, not only for the history of Germany and Russia but of Europe and the world.

Geography circumscribes the limits, it governs the ambitions of states, it conditions the character of nations: it involves, however, not only the

effect of environment on human societies, it involves—increasingly[15]—
the effect, too, of human societies on their environment. The geographical
element in the relations of states, therefore, comprehends not merely proximity but possession. The term *real estate,* deriving from medieval usage,
admirably suggests this strong and unique reality of territory. It is even
now impossible to conceive of an autonomous community without some
kind of a territorial base. The territorial circumscriptions of communities
are clearer than are their social distinctions: a state frontier, an extraterri-
torial enclave, a capitulation, or even a modern air or naval base represent
"horizontal" divisions that are not only visible on maps but, in many ways,
more real than are the "vertical" divisions of society, things such as classes
or corporations.

But geography, while it conditions, does not determine the relations of
states and the interests of nations. There exist certain historically observable tendencies: the tendency for natural frontiers, for rounding off frontiers to seek alliances with one's "neighbor's neighbor," the dangers of sudden proximity (Russia and America bumping into each other in 1945, in
the middle of Europe, when Germany was eliminated as a power). Still, all
the appearances of *Geopolitik* notwithstanding, there is no such thing as a
Newtonian rule of gravitation among the powers of the world. When the
relations of states change, this happens because of their ideas of state and
of national interests. These ideas are neither mechanical nor progressive
matters. Not even technical progress determines (though it does, of course,
influence) the character of these relations. Americans, who have, after all,
many reasons to regard history as if it were the Story of Progress, regard
the progress of communications as if this technological development would
by itself have caused the increasing American involvement in wider and
wider affairs and areas of the world. American history textbooks have little
charts showing how the Atlantic has "shrunk": in 1620 it took six weeks to
cross that ocean, in 1820 three weeks, in 1920 six days, in 1960 six hours. ...
Of course today, in the age of the nuclear submarine, jet plane, transoce-
anic rocket, hydrogen bomb, America is more vulnerable than she was in
the past. Still, as we survey American history, we may see that American
involvements in the wars of Europe do not follow such a pattern of progressive increase. During the eighteenth century, indeed until 1815, America
was involved in virtually every European and world war. During the nineteenth century she was not. During the twentieth century she chose to be
involved again. Note that I said "chose": for geography, strategy, technology are important factors, yet ultimately it is not science or fate but human
choice that decides. Does the development of technology alter the relations of states and of nations? To some extent, yes; essentially, no. In 1914

the United States was safer from the danger of foreign invasions than one hundred years earlier, when a British force could occupy Washington and burn the White House. Does the diminution of distances mean the diminution of ignorance with which the peoples of the world regard each other? To some extent, yes; necessarily, no. By 1914 millions knew something about other nations, other millions had visited other nations as tourists, but did this great increase of communications correspondingly decrease misunderstandings among nations? As in the relations of persons, proximity may lead to understanding or to contempt, to friendship or to enmity. *Not the instruments but the tendency of the relationship counts; it is not the technical conditions of distance but the direction of ideas and sentiments* that determines the relations of human societies, and of their component human beings.

The sentiments and ideas of peoples remain the main motive force of nations. Even the totalitarian modern tyrannies are far from immune from their influences in the long run. It is these sentiments and ideas that are formulated into conceptions of national interest, which is not a fixed constant category adjusting itself automatically to ratios of geographical proximity and of military equipment. National interest, like self-interest, tends to produce its own rationalizations; but national interest, like self-interest, is produced by sentiments, inclinations, tendencies, ideas; national interest, again, is what people think it is, and there is more to it than meets the eye. It is certainly more than *Realpolitik* or *raison d'état*—especially in our democratic epoch, when the relations of states no longer preempt the wider and more complex influences in the relations of nations.

The modern term "international relations" is a misnomer; as I suggested earlier, it is almost always used for a study of supranational rather than of truly international history, since it deals with the relations of states rather than with those of nations. Both "nationalist" *Realpolitiker* and "internationalist" idealists often overlook the important historical condition that state and nation are not necessarily the same things. This is not the place to embark on the various historical origins of the two terms, except perhaps to suggest that if, as Figgis said, "the enduring work of the sixteenth century was the modern State," the enduring work of the nineteenth century was the modern nation. Now, it is true that during the nineteenth century state and nation became closer and closer; the old multinational empires were about to break up, while the modern national states were crystallizing, which is perhaps why Matthew Arnold would call the state "a nation in its collective and corporate capacity." During the last one hundred years, however, the relations of nations have become more important, since in this democratic age the historical development of nations, in the broadest cultural sense, underlies as well as supersedes the histories of states. The latter no longer preempt the general histories of nations, whose relations, in turn, have become something more than the foreign policies of their governments. With all of his emphasis on the foreign policies of governments, Ranke may have had an early insight into their truly international factor as he wrote that "we must understand the inner life rather than the abstract principle of the state."

I can only attempt to draw attention quickly, in passing as it were, to this enormous and important subject of the relations of entire nations, which by now encompasses all kinds of "foreign" relations, including literature, trade, translations, films, tourism, etc., all of them involved with the image that one nation has of another. This existence of national tendencies beneath state relations has not yet received the attention it deserves; and the preoccupation with political ideologies has only served to obscure its existence further. Obviously ideological sympathies may transcend patriotic loyalties. But this is not the end of the story. The allegiance of European and American Communist believers to Soviet Russia during the second quarter of this century was consequent to their sympathy for the Soviet state in its capacity as an ideological and political prototype. But, having focused their attentions and their hopes on that kind of thing, they failed to see from the beginning the existence of certain Russian national and historical characteristics that proved to be more real, enduring, and deeper than the ideological and political image of the First Communist State. The subsequent disillusionment of these Western believers was, therefore, to some extent predictable, even though few among them were brave or intelligent enough to admit this.

We tend to like or dislike persons rather than ideologies, whence the condition that the relationships of persons to certain nations may often be more significant than their relationships to certain ideologies, for national cultural traits may resemble personal traits more than do state political systems or ideologies. Since a nation is principally a cultural, while a state is principally a political, prototype, the tendencies of nations toward each other, the sympathies and the antipathies of certain nations, the rise and the decline of these sentiments, and the tendencies of certain people toward certain national cultures are on occasion powerful historical factors, very much worth our attention. It is possible that these factors functioned already during the religious struggles of the sixteenth century ("Calvinism," Burckhardt said, "was the Reformation of those peoples who did not like the Germans"). They are, in any event, more and more observable during the last one hundred years. Let me string out a number of examples. In the Russia of the nineteenth century Dostoyevsky's Germanophilia and Turgenev's Francophilia were not superficial or accidental matters: they reflected significant inclinations of the Slavophiles and of the Westernizers. After 1917, then, as the excellent Wladimir Weidlé remarked, "it was German socialism which triumphed at the expense of French socialism through the revolution conceived and executed by Lenin."[16] On the other hand, as John Plamenatz put it, had Germany and not Russia become Communist in 1918, the attractions of communism throughout Central and Eastern Europe would then have been much greater: because Russia and her culture enjoyed little respect among these nations at that time, while the prestige of German culture was much greater, and not only among Germany's allies. This German prestige was a very important factor in her fortunes and in the subsequent destinies of many European nations between 1870 and 1945. It may be even said that during these decades the lower middle classes in many parts of the world tended to be Germanophile, while the upper middle classes were Anglophile; this was evident among such different peoples and societies as Japan and Hungary, Rumania and Argentina, the United States and Turkey, Persia and Spain. Let me suggest, therefore, that while in a certain historical period there was such a thing as the "liberal" or the "authoritarian" type of personality, there was also such a thing as, say, a "Germanophile" or "Anglophile" personality, incarnating cultural rather than ideological preferences and inclinations. Even in the 1950s an American industrial worker would rather have his daughter marry a German than a Frenchman, if she was to marry a foreigner at all; for an American lawyer or banker, especially in the eastern United States, the converse may have been true. The so-called isolationism of many Americans in 1940–41, and the McCarthyism of others in the 1950s, often cloaked deeper, more hidden national and cultural preferences: relative Anglophobia and relative Germanophilia played their roles in these instances.[17] Among the American political elite the condition that, say, Walter Hines Page was an Anglophile and John Foster Dulles a Germanophile does not, of course, mean that they were disloyal Americans, British or German agents; it does not even mean that they were always conscious or even consistent supporters of these respective nations; it means, however, that on crucial occasions of their public offices their sympathies toward these nations were more significant than their recognized categories of having been progressives or Republicans or conservatives or isolationists or internationalists. (In a different vein the principal element, indeed the largest common denominator, in the French armistice party in June 1940 was not so much pro-fascism or right-wing conservatism but Anglophobia.)

One could multiply these illustrations endlessly. But let me conclude with an example that should show the powerful interactions of national inclinations and foreign policy. It concerns both the internal and the external relations of Austria between the two world wars. The history of Austria was then, in many ways, a paradigm of European political developments during the twenty years from 1918, when we can see in the dissolution of the Austrian empire the most important single consequence of World War I, to 1938, when Hitler's absorption of Austria marked the first of the great changes in the map of postwar Europe, leading to the outbreak of World War II in the following year. During the interwar period Austria was a weak state, torn by internal dissensions. Particularly in the early Thirties—the period that, in retrospect, appears to us as the hinge of fate not only in the interwar history of Austria but in the entire international history of the interwar years—the Austrian people were divided between three factions (whose origins go back to the 1880s), popularly known as "Blacks," "Reds," and "Browns": more precisely the Christian Socials (who after 1931 turned toward a partially clerical-fascist direction), the Socialists, and the National Socialists.[18] In February 1934 the Christian Social government crushed the Socialists; in July 1934 the Nazis prematurely rose; but in 1936 the government had to declare an uneasy coexistence with them; finally in 1938 Austria became a Nazi state. Now all of these events depended very much on the external relationships of Austria: more precisely, on her relations to her neighbor states. The principal weakness of the Socialists, who were the first to go under, lay in the condition that they had no strong patron states abroad; on occasion, they could count on sympathies from Czechoslovakia and France, but these states were relatively uncommitted and relatively unpopular among Austrians. The principal strength of the Christian Socials during the first crucial phase in 1933–34 lay in the condition that they were supported by Mussolini's Italy, which was, strange as this may seem in retrospect, a great power, perhaps the greatest in Europe, during those two years. It was, indeed, Mussolini who demanded that the Blacks crush the Reds in early 1934; and Mussolini's threat of military intervention during the July 1934 Brown Nazi *Putsch* contributed to the failure of that attempt. By 1936, however, Mussolini decided that Italy should align herself with Germany, and that Austria should not remain an obstacle to such an alignment; it was thereby that the fate of an independent Austria was about to be sealed; and in March 1938 Hitler occupied Austria without any opposition on Mussolini's part. It would seem, therefore, that the destiny of Austria in the Thirties was completely consequent to the relations of foreign states and of the ideological alignments of these great powers. Yet this is not quite the case. The strength of the Austrian Nazi cause was very much enhanced by the condition that while most Austrians disliked Italy (the protector of their regime), they had strong affinities for Germany. Most of these Austrians were pro-German rather than pro-Nazi; indeed, it is often difficult to distinguish convinced Nazis from convinced pan-Germans during that period. This was a condition that both Schuschnigg and Mussolini knew;[19] and it facilitated the surrender of Austria to Hitler in the dramatic days of March 1938.

❋ ❋ ❋

THE traditional ingredients of nationality are common language, common institutions, common culture, sameness of race, consciousness of history, consciousness of territorial limits, ancestral ties, permanence of residence. These are not categorical requirements: all of these eight ingredients need not always coexist: still, the majority of them must somehow coexist, in order to form nationality in the European sense. In the United States some of these ingredients do not exist, which is why being an American is still something different from being a Frenchman or a Pole. The American idea of nationality has been ideological rather than patriotic, populist rather than traditional, universal as well as distinctly particular in its portents, more superficial but also more generous than nationality in Europe. *Nomen est omen:* the United States of America, like the Union of Soviet Socialist Republics, is a general and open term; it suggests not a national society but rather something that is, at least implicity, universal: like "Soviet citizen," "American citizen" marks adherence to certain political principles rather than a certain nationality; there is theoretically no limit to what it may include.

The "nation," evolving from *patria* and *natio,* has been a particularly European phenomenon. In most Asian languages an equivalent for the word "nation" does not exist; for Arabs as well as for American Indians the same word serves for "folk" and "people" and "nation"; so does, in a way, the Russian *narod.* Most European languages, distinguish, however, between "nation" and "people." In most European countries, especially in Western Europe, including England, the sense of "nation" has been historical rather than racial, issuing from patriotic rather than folkish origins, with an emphasis on common land and common speech and common history rather than on common blood or common belief.

Patria carries the sense of a family, descent from a father; and *natio,* too, refers to relationship by birth. But early in European history this tribal sense was beginning to be replaced by something else: *patria* was becoming inseparable from a common place of settlement, which had not always been true of *natio.* No matter how atavistic the tribal bonds of the barbarian kingdoms after the fall of Rome may have been, they were not yet patriotic in this post-Roman and early-European sense; their laws as well as their territorial jurisdiction were fluid, resting not on soil but on blood. But when

Pepin drove the Moors out of Narbonne in 759 he allowed the Visigoths of that region to live according to their own laws, provided that they stayed there; and during the next thousand years in the history of Europe the relationship to land became more important than relationships of blood.

This is not the place to embark on the historical vicissitudes of these relationships: I have referred to the origins of *patria* and *natio* only because of my concern with the more modern phenomenon of the distinctions of patriotism and nationalism. While nationality, national ambitions, and national consciousness are discernible early in European history, nationalism, like the modern nation-state, is a more recent phenomenon, the result of the growing social homogenization of certain European peoples and the development of their historical consciousness—or, to put it perhaps in two other words in intellectual shorthand, democracy and romanticism. The history of the two modern terms reflects this condition: in England, for example, "patriotism" first appeared in print in 1738, "nationalism" more than a century later, in 1844. This may explain why Englishmen of the eighteenth century, for example Dr. Johnson, could not yet distinguish between patriotism and nationalism.[20] But to certain Englishmen of the twentieth century the distinction was more evident. "Nationalism," wrote George Orwell, "is not to be confused with patriotism. Both words are normally used in so vague a way that any definition is liable to be challenged, but one must draw a distinction between them, since two different and even opposing ideas are involved."

> By "patriotism" I mean devotion to a particular place and a particular way of life, which one ... has no wish to force upon other people. Patriotism is of its nature defensive, both militarily and culturally. Nationalism, on the other hand, is inseparable from the desire for power. The abiding purpose of every nationalist is to secure more power and prestige,[21] *not* for himself but for the nation or other unit in which he had chosen to sink his own individuality.

During the nineteenth century nationalism became an ideology: the older patriotic sentiments were often replaced by ideological nationalism. As Duff Cooper wrote, the jingo nationalist "is always the first to denounce his fellow countrymen as traitors"—a statement worthy of Dr. Johnson.[22] Adolf Hitler was to incarnate this tendency in the twentieth century. "By the time I was fifteen" (in 1904), he wrote in *Mein Kampf,* "I understood the difference between dynastic *patriotism* and folkish *nationalism,* even then I was interested only in the latter.... Germany could be safeguarded only by the destruction of Austria [Hitler's native country].... [T]he national sentiment is in no sense identical with dynasties or with patriotism."

What was startling and new in the twentieth century was the emergence of a certain antipatriotism in the name of nationalism. In 1809 the peasant Andreas Hofer led the patriotic resistance of Tyrolean Austrians against Napoleon's Frenchmen and their Bavarian allies; in 1938 a Tyrolean by the same name became Hitler's Gauleiter. Before and during World War II throughout Europe, "Nationalist" or "National Opposition" were often the names of those movements, blocs, and parties who worked against the legitimate governments of their countries, usually favoring an alignment of their country with Nazi Germany, and at times even the military occupation of their country by the latter. Of course there always have been all kinds of people, from traitors through ideological revolutionaries to persecuted minorities, who would welcome the occupation of their country by another power. But what is remarkable is the appearance of such tendencies in the form of a certain ideological nationalism, which was the result not only of modern nationalistic indoctrination but also of those conditions of modern society which make it possible for many people to be nationalists without being patriots.

Yet this may have been a transitional development, reminiscent of certain transitional developments during the sixteenth century, when, as Burckhardt put it, on occasion *Glaubensgenossen*, coreligionists, felt closer to each other than *Landsmänner*, compatriots. For ideological nationalism is a secular religion. And in Europe at least, the era of ideological nationalism may have come to an end: its attractions declined steeply after the last world war. Still, the factor of nationality, all superficial appearances to the contrary notwithstanding, continues to prevail, in Europe as well as all over the world. And this is the reason why I found it necessary to distinguish between patriotism and nationalism, or between the patriotic and the ideological varieties of nationalism. My argument is that nations are one thing and nationalism another. The former not only preceded but they survive the latter. Nations and national consciousness are enormously important historical factors even now, in the second half of the twentieth century, with its mass ideologies, in this age of superpowers, of the United Nations, of a rapidly spreading superficial internationalism on a global scale. History does not repeat itself: the Greeks had municipal *patriae* but no real nations in the modern sense. The Argive or Corcyran local quislings called in outside armies even when this meant the extinction of the particular characteristics of their communities. But this is not what happened even during World War II and after. Not even Quisling wanted to see Norwegian nationality and independence extinguished; not even Kádár wishes to witness the absorption of his nation by Soviet Russia. Indeed, the strongest evidence of the enduring importance of nationality emerges from the historical development of Communist states in Eastern Europe. I am not only referring to their conflicts of national interests, Rumania vs. Hungary or Bulgaria vs. Yugoslavia or China vs. Russia; I am referring to the personalities of their Communist leadership: from Trotsky through Stalin to Khrushchev, from Rosa Luxemburg through Bierut to Gomulka, from Kun through Rákosi to Kádár, from the 1920s through the 1940s to the 1960s the leadership in the Communist countries has become more and more typically national, reflecting a general historical development in a more national—though not always more nationalist—direction. For in Europe (as indeed in many other places in the world, including the United States) the meaning of nationality has become deeper, together with the development of some kind of a historical consciousness: it has entered the lives of many millions, penetrating their consciousness, transcending politics, through the democratization of societies and through the still powerful, only partially diluted, and occasionally emasculated national languages. On the one hand the world, in this age of television and air travel, is becoming more and more international (or rather, supranational). But on the other hand, the democratic societies of the world are also becoming not less but more national, in depth rather than in extent, through the now developing consciousness of nationality as a cultural, rather than a racial, phenomenon. Thus, nationality is still the most formative historical factor in our democratic times, despite powerful influences and technological institutions working against it. Even now, "French," "Dutch," "Polish" remain both more important and more meaningful historical realities than categories of classes such as "proletarian" or "bourgeois," or than political categories such as "liberal," "conservative," "Communist," many of which, as we have seen, have now become fuzzy and often increasingly meaningless.

In Europe the existing national states are now more homogeneous than ever before. They are settled down in their places; there are few outstanding frontier problems (this may have been one of the very few auspicious results of the last world war). The sovereign and independent national state may have had its day: but nationality continues to function, perhaps in a novel manner, corresponding to the change in the texture of history. Whether a truly united Europe will emerge before the end of the twentieth century is an open question; what is hardly questionable is that the era of wars among the national states of Europe is over. Wherever serious problems between nationalities exist in Europe—the conflict between Flemings and Walloons in Belgium, the South Tyrol controversy between Austrians and

Italians, Transylvanian and Macedonian problems in Eastern Europe—
these involve the rights of nationalities (and, moreover, cultural rather than
political problems) rather than questions about state frontiers: they are truly
inter-national, rather than "international" (meaning inter-state, or supranational) questions. We may be still far away from the development of a
strong decentralizing tendency, which would be a reaction against the
overcentralization in the present political structure of the world. This may
not come until some horrible experience, such as an atomic world war,
when the breakdown of the technological efficiency of overcentralized
power and authority will become obvious. But even now the reactions of
some of Europe's nations to the great intercontinental superpowers suggest that our nation-states may be acquiring certain of the characteristics
of the former city-states, that their historical function may reside increasingly in the uniqueness of their national cultures,[23] in their traditional customs, habits, and liberties, maintaining their national identities together
with the now unavoidable restrictions of their independent state sover-
eignties. The two countervailing tendencies now seem to be the increasing
dissolution of patriotic traditions, the weakening of national cultures through
the technological "Americanization" of the world on the one hand, and the
further cultural crystallization of nationality on the other. Our grandchildren should know which of the two tendencies will prove to be stronger.
Meanwhile we ought not overlook the existence of the second: for we cannot say really that Frenchmen have become less French, Finns less Finnish,
Poles less Polish—and Americans less American—no matter what has happened to their states and nations in the twentieth century.

And this leads me to the question of national characteristics. Intellectuals have found it to be fashionable to ignore them nowadays. But this is a
foolish thing to do: they'd be better off if they'd consider Henry Adams's
admonition, as he called national character "the most difficult and the most
important . . . of all historical problems."

The "historical problem" of national character consists of two comple-
mentary and reciprocal parts: national personality and personal nationality. There is such a thing as a national personality: a nation is not a person,
but it manifests certain personal traits, especially since it is a more organic
phenomenon than a state. Its character traits are nothing more and nothing
less than tendencies: but these tendencies underlie, and on occasion supersede, other tendencies, other historical conditions. They are manifest in
the history of politics: consider, for example, the differences between Russian and Polish and Yugoslav Communists. They are evident in the historical development of societies: consider, for example, the differences between
English and Italian industrial workers, or between French *bourgeois* and

Austrian *Bürger*. They are obvious in the historical unfolding of art: consider, for example, the differences between South German and South Italian baroque, or between German and Spanish "Victorian" architecture. They may be discernible even in the mechanical and standardized products of modern industrial mass manufacture. And the most meaningful reflections of these distinct tendencies of national character are to be found, of course, in the different national languages, the habits of which are veritable mirrors of national characteristics. Expression does have a nationality, even while thought may not always have one. And expression has a way of forming consciousness; it is therefore legitimate to speak of national mentalities, and of tendencies of national consciousness that are discernible on occasion.

National characteristics and a certain consciousness of nationality existed before the crystallization of most European national states. In the spreading of Protestantism, for example, national tendencies played important roles: certain people responded to Luther, others didn't. For, ultimately, the national characteristics of certain peoples are involved with certain religious and even spiritual inclinations (just as Weber and Sombart and Tawney attempted to demonstrate the connections between economic systems and religious ideas, we are in need of a historical investigation of the relationship between certain national characteristics and certain religious tendencies, of an inquiry into the inclinations of certain nationalities toward certain ideas).

For national character is inseparable from ideas: it is formed by geographical, social, racial, cultural, spiritual elements together. There is such a thing as a race, even though it is fashionable nowadays to deny this; however, race is a cultural even more than a biological factor, and this means that while we must recognize its existence we must understand, too, that the very function of its characteristics transcends deterministic causality (that, among other things, human beings may indeed acquire certain "racial" characteristics).[24] While this may be a complex development, its meaning is simple: national character is historical character: and this recognition is an intrinsic part of the evolution of our historical consciousness. Moreover, since history is a form of thought, national character is very much reflected in a nation's view of its own history, just as a person's autobiography—the expressions of his auto-historical thinking—his view of his own development and of his aspirations, affords us an insight into his character. On a more pragmatic level, then, just as the character traits of a person are best revealed in his dealings with other persons, the character of a nation is often best revealed by its actions and attitudes toward other nations[25]—whence the intrinsic significance of foreign policy.

Thus, it is not enough to say that we still live in an era of national states, and that the principal motive of their actions is still national interest. There is more to "national" than meets the eye: there is more to "interest," too. We may say of persons that the main motive factor of their actions is self-interest; but this is a truism. Take such different modern thinkers as Machiavelli, La Rochefoucauld, Bentham, Stendhal, Spencer, Tocqueville, Marx, Freud—yes, of course, this is what all of them say. But the better thinkers among them (Stendhal rather than Bentham, Tocqueville rather than Marx) do not leave it at that; they see deeper motives: fear and greed, guilt and ambition, all entangled; the best of them see vanity (a forgotten word nowadays) as the basic human motive. For what is self-interest, after all? Its formation comes from the concept of the self: an entangled thing, a complex thing, a tendency rather than a category, an aspiration rather than a constant.

The character of a person is formed as well as revealed by his own ideas of self-interest. These ideas change with time; they are often influenced by other persons; except in rare instances they cannot be accurately defined; they nonetheless exist. So it is with the interest of a nation: the character of a nation, too, is revealed by its own ideas of self-interest, by the nation's own image of itself, by its own concept of the place it would like to occupy, of the figure it would like to cut in the world.

Thus the geographical situation of a nation to a large extent defines its foreign policy, the conduct of which, however, is largely formed by the nation's character: thus, the history of a state is governed by its concepts of state interest, which reveal, in turn, certain important elements in the character of the nation. Britain's geographical situation is evident; but the conduct of British foreign policy has also reflected the willingness to mediate, to compromise, the tendency to pragmatism as well as the racial self-confidence that have been recognizable elements in the British character. Behind the Iron Curtain, did the Hungarian people rise in 1956 because of their economic conditions? No. Did they rise because they wanted to do away with the socialization of their industries, did they want to restore capitalism? No. Did they revolt because of their sense of deep injuries committed against their national interests? Yes. And were not their very ideas of their national interests, dissatisfied as they were with the initial Russian concessions, expressed in impulsive, occasionally heroic, and often unrealistic, demands? Yes; for these actions (and their very rhetoric) reflected typically Hungarian national characteristics. The Hungarian Revolution turned out to be the way it was not because it was post-Socialist, national-Communist, crypto-fascist or what not, but because it was a *Hungarian* Revolution—and, moreover, a Hungarian Revolution *in 1956*.

For these concepts of national interests are not always constant and not always consistent: national character may be tempered and conditioned by historical experience. (British self-confidence in 1960 may be something different from what it was in 1860; and in 1956 the otherwise impulsive, romantic, feckless Poles acted in a different way from their tragic revolutions in the past.)

National interest would be a constant factor, a geographically ascertain-able, strategically predictable category, if human beings were the same everywhere. And human beings *are* essentially the same: but their actions and reactions are different when their ideas and aspirations are different.[26] There is still much truth in what Charles Evans Hughes said in 1923:

> Foreign policies are not built upon abstractions. They are results of practical conceptions of national interest arising from some immediate exigency or standing out vividly in historical perspective. When long maintained, they express the hopes and fears, the aims of security and aggrandizement, which have become dominant in the national consciousness and thus transcend political divisions and make negligible such opposition as may come from particular groups. They inevitably control the machinery of international accord which works only within the narrow field not closed by divergent national ambitions. . . .

This somewhat narrow argument must, however, be tempered with the more profound considerations proposed by Johan Huizinga in 1936:

> States will continue to set their course of action predominantly by their interests or what they think to be their interests, and considerations of international morality will drive them only a fraction of an inch off their course. But this fraction represents the difference between honor and loyalty and the jungle, and as such reaches further than a thousand miles of ambition and violence.

Thirty years later we may observe that these "considerations of international morality" have, after all, grown in international esteem. As the world has become smaller and more interdependent, wars have become more dangerous in their consequences, and entire departments in the governments of states are now busying themselves with propagating benevolent and successful national images to the world. True, these considerations may be systematically obscured through all kinds of ephemeralities through publicity, their images may be falsified; nevertheless they exist. This may be but one manifestation of the continued importance of national characteristics, and of their apparent resemblance to personal characteristics: for, if few nations can nowadays afford the reputation of being arrogantly indifferent to other peoples' considerations of their morality, this is because these considerations are inescapably anthropomorphic in their nature.

And now let me turn rapidly from the characteristics of nations to the national characteristics of persons, which is a very complex thing. The legal criterion of citizenship, the geographical criterion of the birthplace, the cultural criterion of language, the racial criterion of parental and ancestral heredity: every one of these categories may leak. There are exceptions to every rule. In many instances—the Macedonian Alexander who wanted to be a great Greek, the Corsican Bonaparte the Frenchman, the Austrian Hitler the German, the Georgian Stalin the Russian—the exceptions count indeed. Earlier I suggested that in the conflict between Trotsky and Stalin the factor of their respective national differences was decisive. Trotsky had his Jewish characteristics, Stalin his Georgian ones; and in the struggle for political power in Russia this was to harm Trotsky more than it harmed Stalin. But this is not all. Trotsky did not want to be a Jew, and Stalin did not want to remain a Georgian. The former did not in the least identify himself with Judaism or with Zionism; the latter not with Georgian nationalism; they succeeded, indeed, in incarnating certain Russian traits. Consequently Trotsky was Jewish and non-Jewish, just as Stalin was Georgian and non-Georgian, Hitler Austrian and anti-Austrian, Napoleon Corsican and French, Disraeli Jewish and English at the same time.[27] Both of these characteristics existed within their lives: and, historically speaking, the second, the direction of their aspirations and ideas, was more important than the first, even though we must recognize the existence of the functions of the first. The decisive element is often not so much what a person "is" but what he wants to be. (Ortega y Gasset: "Life is a gerundive, not a participle: a *faciendum*, not a *factum*. Life is a task. . . ." Tocqueville: "a serious spiritual business.") And this is true of entire nations, too, whose character traits are formed but not caused: formed by their histories, and by their consciousness of their histories.

In the history of the consciousness of nationality in Europe speech has often been thicker than blood; and in certain instances patriotic and cultural affinities and aspirations superseded even speech. I am not only thinking of multilingual Switzerland, I am thinking of the German-speaking Alsatians, with their developing affinities for France, or of such relatively recent instances as when after World War I certain Slavic groups along the then new German-Polish frontier opted for Germany rather than for Poland: a clear case of cultural-national preferences. There are many examples in the histories of European nations that strongly suggest the non-Darwinian and supra-biological realities of historical life: that cultural-national aspirations may become historical, existential, personal, and, on occasion, even physical factors and that, consequently, acquired characteristics *may* be inherited.

A person is born with certain characteristics; he inherits certain tendencies; he acquires other inclinations through his life. Some of these are strong and enduring, others are ephemeral. Life consists of constant tensions: a person is formed, pulled, pushed by characteristics inherited from his father, by others inherited from his mother, as well as by his acquired personal desires, vanities, ambitions, obligations, loyalties, fears, which are often consequences of his ideas of his own situation in the world. So with the history of nations. Human, and historical, life is a succession of choices, which every conscious human being has to make every moment. At times these choices are decisive: and their very quality will often reveal that person's character and decide his fate. But that fate is by no means prescribed: for he may supersede his inclinations, inherited as well as acquired ones. The decision and the responsibility are his: for he is a free moral agent, responsible for his actions.

It is here that the semblance of analogy between the nature of persons and the nature of nations breaks down, in spite of the superficial resemblance of their characteristics. I said that a nation is a more organic phenomenon than a state; but the nation is not a person; and, apart from the persons and the communities that compose it, a nation has no life of its own. Thus, while a person is responsible for his actions, a nation is responsible only in part; for a nation has but a halfway sort of claim to immortality. Men die and disappear from this earth while nations do not die for a long, long time; but while the soul of a man is liable to divine judgment and is immortal, the soul of a nation is not.

❊ ❊ ❊

IT will be now evident that I have tried to suggest a certain hierarchy of historical factors according to their relative importance: a hierarchy the order of which goes considerably contrary to many recent assumptions. This hierarchy is far from being universally valid: but I believe it to be applicable, by and large, to the history of modern nations. Whether in the history of eighteenth-century England or nineteenth-century Germany or twentieth-century Russia, I believe that the changing structure of their economies was less decisive than the development of their societies, which, in turn, was less decisive than the history of their politics, including their revolutions, which were less decisive than the nation's relations to other nations through peace and through war; and these very relations, then, reflected national inclinations toward certain ideas that were, in turn, more universal than national, since they reflected certain concepts about human nature that were ultimately involved with certain cultural and spiritual concepts of more universal portents.

There is, thus, an order of ascendancy inherent in this thesis: the biological, racial, political, cultural, moral categories corresponding to the ascending order of social categories—mass, people, state, nation, religion—and perhaps even with certain cosmological categories: atom, elements, earth, man, universe. I believe that there is much truth in this, except that it is too much of a neat little shorthand sort of philosophy: for I believe, too, that historians ought to comprehend the pragmatic wisdom of the Latin proverb *primum vivere deinde philosophari,* that is, historical life is not only stronger than theory, it is, too, prior to philosophy. A merely categorical assertion of these hierarchies, or their definition, will not do. The categories, through the function of their component tendencies, overlap. We find microcosms at the two opposite extremes, within the atom as much as within the universe, just as in the life of a person his "lowest" material interests are often inseparable from his ideas and aspirations, while material forces often play roles within his "highest" intellectual experiences.

Still, I found it necessary to insist on the relative importance of certain historical factors: to put it in one sentence, that the motive factors in the history of the world even now ought not to be sought in economic developments as much as within nations and ultimately within the minds and hearts of persons in the midst of nations. The history of contemporary American-Russian relations is a good example of this relative hierarchy, since such a history, dealing as it must with enormous and complex matters, encompasses economics, sociology, ideology, politics, strategy, nationality, culture, religion: not only the relations of the United States and the Union of Soviet Socialist Republics but also those of communism and capitalism, Marxism and democracy, "East" and "West," the Russian and American empires, and nations. Economically, Russia and America have been growing more and more alike, as America was becoming a socialized welfare state, and Russia began to catch up with mass production. Yet in 1955, when these differences were smaller than what they had been in 1945, 1935, 1925, the hostility was greater than before. More important than the contest between communism and capitalism was the ideological struggle between Soviet Marxism and American democracy. Yet the difference between the two political ideologies was not the cause of the Cold War: were Russia a small country, like Yugoslavia, no matter how she may have been dedicated to revolutionary Marxism, the Cold War would not have developed as it did. Thus, the source of the Cold War must have been national interest: America and Russia, two great world empires, bumping at each other in the middle of Europe at the end of the last world war, suspicious of each other's strategies. We are getting closer to the more important factors in the origins of the Cold War: but this is not yet enough. This strategic view will explain many things but it will not explain many others: for, after all is said, American strategy during the entire Cold War has seldom been aimed at the Soviet Union proper (as distinct from her satellites and other areas), while in turn Russia interfered only occasionally, and hesitantly, with the immediate American strategic neighborhood in the western hemisphere. The animosities of these two states have not been wholly the results of their altered strategical situation: they have involved, increasingly, the images that the two nations have had of each other. Thus, in their competition for world leadership Russian suspicion and aggressiveness on the one hand, and the popularity of anticommunism in the United States on the other, were national tendencies that have played decisive roles in the relations of these two great nations; and, in turn, these ideas themselves have often reflected all kinds of cultural developments, including even religious ones.[28]

Let me repeat this then for the last time: Russian industrial statistics are less important than the condition that the masters of Russia are Communists, which, in turn, is less important than the fact that they are Russians, the masters of a long-standing empire and the children of a long-standing nation. The routine life of the Russian people depends on the development of their politics, but the national interests of the Russian empire are more important than its official ideology, and this pursuit of Russian national interests depends not only on geographical circumstances but on national characteristics that, in turn, are formed by cultural and historical and sometimes even religious tendencies. Thus, I seem to have narrowed the focus closer and closer, trying to penetrate deeper, peeling away the layers, getting down to what in the end may seem to be a very old-fashioned argument about national character, an approach that is not telescopic but microscopic in its direction. But the nature of human beings is such that close to the dark recesses of the human heart we find something universal again: for the human heart is a microcosm itself, reflecting the universe. "No man is an island"—these words of a poet, cited so often by superficial internationalists, have a meaning only because of the spiritual condition of man. The body of a man may be confined to a solitary island; but his heart and mind are not. A nation occupies a certain confined place in the world; but the origin and effect of the ideas that form its conduct are ultimately supernatural.

Let me now try to apply this argument to the history of history—say, to the history of the French Revolution. Many a historian found the analysis of the historiography of the French Revolution to be rather instructive: they investigated the politics of successive generations of French historians, the French Revolution For and Against. This *is* an instructive and intellectually enlightening endeavor: I believe, as does Professor Herbert Butterfield, that the historical study of the French Revolution may indeed be approached through the study of the historiography of the French Revolution. But now let me add my little bit as a nonspecialist and general historian. Instead of ranging the generations of radical and conservative, of pro- and anti-Jacobin, of republican and monarchist historians and evaluating them, let me take another approach in order to say that I believe that the exposition of the Revolution as a social movement (say, by Jaurès or by Mathiez) is less enlightening than its exposition in terms of politics and of political ideas (say, by Michelet or by Aulard), and that even more instructive is its exposition in terms of the persistent factor of foreign relations (say, by Albert Sorel), and that perhaps even more important is the consideration of the specifically French characteristics of the Revolution, together with its treatment as part and parcel of the greater and more universal ideas of the times (something that Tocqueville was about to try in the second, unfinished volume of the *Old Regime and the Revolution*). But now the important *caveat*. All of this does not mean that anyone who emphasizes the foreign relations of the Revolution is necessarily a better or more profound historian than someone else who concentrates on its social history. The hierarchy of importance of these relative factors is activated by the quality of the historian and his work: one may prefer Albert Sorel's approach to Jaurès's, or Tocqueville's to Mathiez's: still Jaurès and Mathiez are to be preferred over hundreds of second-rate writers who may have indeed placed the French Revolution within the great general historical movements of its times but whose vision and whose historianship are superficial.

There is a last point which I wish to make. I have tried to draw attention to the condition of the often inescapable involvement of what happens with what people think happens; and I have tried to illustrate that this is true of such things as economic events as well as of ideas of national interest. There are, however, different levels of our awareness of this condition—perhaps corresponding, conversely, to the relative hierarchy of levels I have suggested. By this I mean that while the axiom that what happens is involved with what we think happens is not immediately apparent in economic or in social matters, it is much easier to demonstrate it to people in instances referring to what they, with an unconsciously revealing phrase, often call the "higher things of the mind." When we speak of a telepathic event or what nowadays is called an "extrasensory" occurrence (when, for example, we are suddenly conscious of something happening to someone whom we cannot see or hear), when we speak of a religious experience (an inner vision or a sudden sense of a close understanding of a God), when we speak of art (the effects of a poetic phrase or of a painting), it is obvious that what we are speaking of deals with our thinking, that our consciousness is intimately involved, nay, inseparable from the experience itself. But as we move lower along this relative hierarchy of events, this involvement of consciousness becomes less and less obvious. While it is relatively easy to suggest how the factor of national characteristics involves not so much physical conditions as it does mentalities (that, for example, Dr. Johnson was a prototypically English while Voltaire was a prototypically French eighteenth-century thinker), this becomes more and more difficult to demonstrate in politics and in society and finally in economics, since we are accustomed to regard the latter as if it were involved with but the complexities of material circumstances. Thus, the economic historian is tempted to deal with what happened to people (a good harvest, or bad laws) or what they did to things (how they coined their monies, or how they invested them), without considering how the consciousness of people was modifying, and indeed on occasion creating, their very experiences. I am, on the other hand, tempted to think that some of the greatest contributions to historical thinking might be made in the future by historians of economics who would understand the historical, and therefore inevitably anthropomorphic, conditions of economic life, including the historical complexities of its causalities, and the essential and intrusive factor of human consciousness. I said "greatest," because such a radically new demonstration of the realities of economic life will be admittedly very difficult, if it is seriously pursued at all. I believe, however, that sooner or later more and more thinking people will have to recognize in every field this condition of the inevitable involvement of mind in matter, historically and not only philosophically speaking: the progress of this recognition in itself being part and parcel of the evolution of our consciousness, in the Western world at least.

3

History and Physics
(1968)

I have advanced the proposition that the outlines of the passing of a great phase of history are by now recognizable, and that people in all walks of life have begun to sense the collapse of hitherto generally accepted ideas—whence the extraordinary intellectual confusion of our times, the widespread feeling of mental seasickness, and the loss of appetite that many people have for life itself. And it might seem as if I have contributed to this confusion. My attacks on the scientific worldview and my admittedly "reactionary" emphasis on the historical view of the world may seem to some as if it were a burning of bridges, or else the erection of yet another wall in the already badly divided and rent house of the Western mind: a haughty and quixotic Immodest Proposal. For what I have argued was, mainly, that of the two great achievements of the modern European mind since the seventeenth century, of the scientific and of the historical form of thought, the latter is the more profound one; but, then, my argument was taken from the historical point of view; and I have merely suggested in passing, here and there, that certain scientists have themselves become skeptical of the scientific worldview, without explaining this in any way or detail.

My remaining task is, therefore, to explain, beyond humanistic assertions and generalizations, what the adjective *post-scientific* might really mean. And I cannot but reveal in advance one of the themes of this chapter, which is the hope that lies on the other side of despair. For I must begin by exclaiming a Good Tiding, which lies hidden in the increasing correspondences of certain recognitions: for, while the recognition of a disease does not amount to its cure, it does represent the potentiality of the cure. At the time when the still-popular concepts of mechanical science and the general ideas of progress have sprung leaks, the depth and the meaning of

From *Historical Consciousness* (New York: Harper and Row), 273–305.

these leaks have been recognized by certain great scientists, too; and this in itself is a testimony to the enduring vitality, to the honesty, to the *conscience* of Western thought.

The elements of a potential harmony between historical and scientific thought are already here. It is only because of the extraordinary intellectual confusion of our times that the existence of this harmony has gone either unrecognized or that it has been rather wilfully obscured by certain vested interests of the mind. And the recognition of this harmony, too, depends on the recognition of a certain development in the hierarchy of thought. As I am writing this a full one hundred years have passed since Bagehot wrote his *Physics and Politics:* but note that the title of this chapter is "History and Physics." This movement of the emphasis from the physics of historical force to the history of physics, marks, in itself, the developing historicity of our consciousness. Let me repeat that history cannot be explained scientifically, whereas science can, and indeed it must, be explained historically; and let me add that this is especially true of modern physics during our interregnum.

For this is not merely the audacious approach of a historian who professes his wide ignorance of the natural sciences. It is significant—and it suggests the present validity of the historical form of thought—that twentieth-century physics may be best understood through the history of its development. The most important books on the meaning of quantum physics, written by physicists themselves, have attempted to explain quantum theory through the intellectual history of its discoveries. And since the meaning of some of these discoveries (or perhaps we should say: of these new recognitions) is revolutionary, as they mark the collapse of the absoluteness of certain accepted categories of thoughts, I, an outsider, must also attempt to sketch the historical development, and the historical correspondences, of some of these recognitions. They at least suggest the direction in which Western thought may (though I cannot say it will) be beginning to move. They, in any event, suggest what we have already left behind.

Physics is the fundamental science of matter. (Indeed, it may be said that physics *is* natural science: that chemistry, for example, is but a subdivision of physics.) What, then, did the fundamental scientists of matter discover early in the twentieth century, at the apogee of the age of materialism? Around 1900 "science could well feel complacent." There are many testimonies to this complacency at a time when it seemed that the scientific explanation of the universe was becoming completed. In the words of Banesh Hoffmann, an American physicist, had not science, by 1900, "reduced the workings of the universe to precise mathematical law?"

Had it not shown that the universe must pursue its appointed course through all eternity, the motions of its parts strictly determined according to immutable patterns of exquisite mathematical elegance? Had it not shown that each individual particle of matter, every tiny ripple of radiation, and every tremor of ethereal tension must fulfill to the last jot and tittle the sublime law which man and his mathematics had at last made plain? Here indeed was reason to be proud. The mighty universe was controlled by known equations, its every motion theoretically predictable, its every action proceeding majestically by known laws from cause to effect.... The pioneering had been done and it was now only a matter of extending the details of what was already known. A few men with almost prophetic powers were able to discern the stealthy approach of distant storms, but their warnings did little to disturb.... Physics was essentially solved....[1]

It is symbolic that it was in 1900, at the opening of this century, at a time which in the history of the Western world is a kind of watershed (and not only because of the roundness of the figure), that the ideas of the great German physicist Planck had crystallized, as he himself told us. During a summer walk in the woods outside Berlin, Planck suddenly turned to his son and told him for the first time that he may have made a discovery comparable perhaps only to Newton's.

What was that discovery? What were its implications and its consequences? Since I am not a physicist I can but describe them in a necessarily imprecise manner.

Here is a rough sketch of their sequence. Since physics deals with all matter, sooner or later its systematic investigations will bounce against the most difficult and elusive of physical questions: what are the properties of light? Pythagoras solved this simply. He did not bother to define whether light consisted of waves or of particles. He stated that light flows out from luminous bodies in every possible direction (a statement which, incidentally, corresponds to some of the present rediscoveries of modern physics). Two thousand years later Newton defined light as formed by luminous particles. This theory began to be questioned during the nineteenth century until Maxwell's theories in the 1870s "established" that light consisted not of particles but of waves. In 1887 the experiments of Hertz found that Maxwell's electromagnetic waves had the same properties as waves of light.

But then, in 1900, Planck found that the pulsations of these waves did not flow regularly. They came in irregular jerks, representing bundles of energy. These he named *quanta*.

In 1905 Einstein found that, instead of being a wave, a quantum of energy was a particle—but that such a quantum of energy changes in time, and that thus matter and energy, in certain circumstances, are dependent on the dimension of time. This is the basis of his relativity theory (one of the implications of which, stated *vulgo,* is that two by two do not *always* make four).

By about 1920 confusion set in among physicists. Light was at once a wave and a particle: but, if so, how could one possibly imagine its size and shape? This was the central question. By 1923 de Broglie found that particles turn into waves as they move; he said that light was *both* particle and wave.

Between 1925 and 1927 Heisenberg confirmed that, indeed, *both* statements were true. The result was his principle of uncertainty or indeterminacy (amounting to the recognition, among other things, that we may never be able to see the atomic particle "as it is," since we cannot determine precisely either its position or its speed).

At this point the propositions of the German Heisenberg, of the French de Broglie, of the Danish Bohr, of the English Dirac, of the Swiss Pauli, of the Austrian Schrödinger, divergent and often opposed to each other but a few years before, converge: by 1928 the quantum mechanical revolution was accomplished and accepted among physicists.

Since that time certain physicists and philosophers of science were trying to draw the broader implications and the epistemological conclusions of these new principles of physics. These philosophical inquiries were retarded by the Second World War when the contacts between some of the most eminent physicists of the world were interrupted in more than one sense (and when many physicists were occupying themselves with the technological task of translating some of the discoveries of modern physics into atomic weapons). In 1955 Heisenberg proposed a wide-ranging philosophical synthesis in his Gifford Lectures at the University of St. Andrews; these were published in the United States in 1958 under the title *Physics and Philosophy.*

Twenty-five or thirty years, therefore, had passed from the first discoveries of the inadequacy of the Newtonian system of "classical" physics until the systematic realization of the meaning of these discoveries; and another twenty-five or thirty years passed until the broader philosophical meaning of these matters was to be presented. It is perhaps not wholly surprising that historians have devoted little attention to these matters during the time of Hitler, Stalin, the Second World War, the atom bomb, the Cold War. We shall see, moreover, how the deadening hand of time-lag in the movement of ideas lay heavy upon many physicists and, indeed, upon the minds of most of the contemporary scientists as they could not quite bring themselves to admit the radical philosophical implications of these new ideas. On the other hand *we* can no longer excuse our minds from this task. For we shall now see that many of the things that I have suggested about the structure of events have been confirmed, at first sight perhaps unexpectedly, from an entirely different prospect, coming from an entirely different direction. Save for isolated instances, a few pages in a posthumous Ortega article, in a few apocalyptic passages by Guardini, and in very scattered philosophical references by certain historians,[2] this has not yet been recognized or applied to the humanities, indeed not to most of our Western corpus of thought. Yet it has become, by and large, possible to say that "modern man has moved on beyond the classical, medieval and the modern world to a new physics and philosophy which combines consistently some of the basic causal and ontological assumptions of each," as F. S. C. Northrop put it in his attempt to introduce Heisenberg's Gifford Lectures to American readers in 1957. He added that this "coming together of this new philosophy of physics with the respective philosophies of the culture of mankind . . . is the major event in today's and tomorrow's world." He asked the question: "How is the philosophy of physics expounded by Heisenberg to be reconciled with moral, political and legal science and philosophy?" Let me attempt to answer: through historical consciousness; through historical thinking.

❄ ❄ ❄

LET me, therefore, insist that what follows is not the breathless attempt of an enthusiastic historian to hitch his wagon to Heisenberg's star, or to jump on Heisenberg's bandwagon, to use a more pedestrian metaphor. Rather, the contrary: my wagon is self-propelled, and a Heisenberg bandwagon does not exist (at least in the United States, among one hundred people who know the name of Einstein, not more than one may know of Heisenberg). It is the philosophical, rather than the experimental, part of Heisenberg's physics that I am qualified to discuss; my principal interest in this chapter springs from the condition that among the physicists of this century who have made excursions into philosophy I have found Heisenberg's philosophical exposition especially clear, meaningful, and relevant to my argument; and I have drawn upon some of his writings in this chapter because I want to present some of his courageous epistemological recognitions in a form which every English-speaking historian may read and understand easily. I have arranged these matters in order to sum them up in the form of ten propositions, the phrasing, the selection, and the organization of which is entirely my own: it is but their illustrations which come from the sphere of physics, described as some of them were by Heisenberg, mostly in his Gifford Lectures. They are illustrations in the literal sense: they are intended to illustrate, to illuminate new recognitions, certain truths, in the assertion of which this writer, as indeed any historian in the twentieth century, is no longer alone.

✿ *First: there is no scientific certitude.* Atomic physics found that the behavior of particles is considerably unpredictable: but, what is more important, this uncertainty is not "the outcome of defects in precision or measurement but a principle that could be demonstrated by experiment." Physicists have now found that while they can reasonably predict the average reactions of great numbers of electrons in an experiment, they cannot predict what a single electron will do, and not even when it will do it.[3] The implications of this are, of course, the limitations of measurement; of accuracy; of scientific predictability—all fundamental shortcomings of "classical," or Newtonian, physics—they suggest the collapse of absolute determinism even in the world of matter.

✿ *Second: the illusory nature of the ideal of objectivity.* In quantum mechanics the very act of observing alters the nature of the object, "especially when its quantum numbers are small." Quantum physics, Heisenberg says, "do not allow a completely objective description of nature."[4] "As it really happened," (or "as it is really happening") is an incomplete statement in the world of matter, too. We are ahead of Ranke. "In our century," Heisenberg wrote in *The Physicist's Conception of Nature*, "it has become clear that the desired objective reality of the elementary particle is too crude an oversimplification of what really happens. . . ." "We can no longer speak of the behavior of the particle independently of the process of observation. As a final consequence, the natural laws formulated mathematically in quantum theory no longer deal with the elementary particles themselves but with our knowledge of them." In *Physics and Philosophy* he explained this further:

> We cannot completely objectify the result of an observation, we cannot describe what "happens" between [one] observation and the next . . . any statement about what has "actually happened" is a statement in terms of the [Newtonian] classical concepts and—because of the thermodynamics and of the uncertainty relations—by its very nature incomplete with respect of the details of the atomic events involved. The demand "to describe what happens" in the quantum-theoretical process between two

successive observations is a contradiction *in adjecto,* since the word
"describe" refers to the use of classical concepts, while these
concepts cannot be applied in the space between the observations; they can only be applied at the points of observation.

❊ *Third: the illusory nature of definitions.* It seems that the minds of
most physicists during the present interregnum still clung to the old, "logical" order of things: they were always giving names to newly discovered
atomic particles, to such elements of the atomic kernel that did not "fit."
Yet the introduction of the name "wavicle" does preciously little to solve
the problem of whether light consists of waves or of particles; and it may be
that the continuing nominalistic habit of proposing new terms (sometimes
rather silly-sounding ones, such as "neutrino") suggests that illusion of the
modern mind which tends to substitute vocabulary for thought, tending to
believe that once we name or define something we've "got it." Sometimes
things may get darker through definitions, Dr. Johnson said; and Heisenberg
seems to confirm the limited value of definitions even in the world of matter:

> Any concepts or words which have been formed in the past
> through the interplay between the world and ourselves are not
> really sharply defined with respect to their meaning; that is to
> say, we do not know exactly how far they will help us in finding
> our way in the world. We often know that they can be applied to
> a wide range of inner or outer experience but we practically
> never know precisely the limits of their applicability. This is
> true even of the simplest and most general concepts like "exist-
> ence" and "space and time." . . . The words "position" and "ve-
> locity" of an electron, for instance, seemed perfectly well de-
> fined as to both their meaning and their possible connections,
> and in fact they were clearly defined concepts within the math-
> ematical framework of Newtonian mechanics. But actually they
> were not well defined, as is seen from the relations of uncer-
> tainty. One may say that regarding their position in Newtonian
> mechanics they were well defined, but in their relation to na-
> ture they were not.

The absoluteness of mathematical "truth" was disproven by Gödel's famous theorem in 1931;[6] but even before that, in the 1920s, physicists were
beginning to ask themselves this uneasy question; as Heisenberg put it:

Is it true that only such experimental situations can arise in nature as can be expressed in the mathematical formalism? The assumption that this was actually true led to limitations in the use of those concepts that had been the basis of physics since Newton. One could speak of the position and of the velocity of an electron as in Newtonian mechanics and one could observe and measure these quantities. But one could not fix both these quantities simultaneously with an arbitrarily high accuracy.... One had learned that the old concepts fit nature only inaccurately.[7]

Mathematical truth is neither complete nor infinite (the velocity of light added to the velocity of light may amount to the velocity of light; on the other end of the physical scale there can be no action smaller than the quantum of action; and under certain physical conditions two by two do not always amount to four). Quantum theory found, too, that certain mathematical statements depend on the time element: Heisenberg realized that p times q is not always the equivalent of q times p in physics (when, for example, p means momentum and q position). What this suggests is that certain basic mathematical operations are not independent of human concepts of time and perhaps not even of purpose. That certain quantities do not always obey arithmetical rules was suggested already in the 1830s by the Irish mathematical genius Hamilton;[8] and the Englishman Dirac, still to some extent influenced by nominalism, tried in the 1920s to solve this problem by asserting the necessity to deal with a set of so-called "Q numbers" which do not always respond to the rules of multiplication. But perhaps the "problem" may be stated more simply: the order in which certain mathematical (and physical) operations are performed affects their results.

❅ *Fourth: the illusory nature of the absolute truth of mathematics.* In biology, too, "it may be important for a complete understanding that the questions are asked by the species man which itself belongs to the genus of living organisms, in other words, that we already know what life is even before we have defined it scientifically."[5] The recognition of personal participation is inescapable.

❅ *Fifth: the illusory nature of "factual" truth.* Change is an essential component of all nature: this ancient principle reappears within quantum physics. We have seen that the physicist must reconcile himself to the condition that he cannot exactly determine both the position and the speed of the atomic particle. He must reconcile himself, too, to the consequent condition that in the static, or factual, sense a basic unit of matter does not exist. It is not measurable; it is not even ascertainable; it is, in a way, a less substantial concept than such "idealistic" concepts as "beauty" or "mind." We can never expect to see a static atom or electron, since they do not exist as "immutable facts"; at best, we may see the trace of their motions. Einstein's relativity theory stated that matter is transmutable, and that it is affected by time; but the full implications of this condition were not immediately recognized, since they mean, among other things, that the earlier water-tight distinctions between "organic" and "inorganic" substances no longer hold. "A sharp distinction between animate and inanimate matter," writes Heisenberg, "cannot be made." "There is only one kind of matter, but it can exist in different discrete stationary conditions." Heisenberg doubts "whether physics and chemistry will, together with the concept of evolution, some day offer a complete description of the living organism."

✵ *Sixth: the breakdown of the mechanical concept of causality.* We have seen how, for the historian, *causa* must be more than the *causa efficiens,* and that the necessarily narrow logic of mechanical causality led to deterministic systems that have harmed our understanding of history, since in reality, through life and in history this kind of causation almost always "leaks." But now not even in physics is this kind of causation universally applicable: it is inadequate, and moreover, "fundamentally and intrinsically undemonstrable."[9] There is simply no satisfactory way of picturing the fundamental atomic processes of nature in categories of space and time and causality. The multiplicity and the complexity of causes reappears in the world of physical relationships, in the world of matter.[10]

✵ *Seventh: the principal importance of potentialities and tendencies.* Quantum physics brought the concept of potentiality back into physical science—a rediscovery, springing from new evidence, of some of the earliest Greek physical and philosophical theories. Heraclitus was the first to emphasize this in the reality of the world: *panta rei,* his motto, "Everything moves," "imperishable change that renovates the world"; he did not, in the Cartesian and Newtonian manner, distinguish between being and becoming; to him fire was *both* matter and force. Modern quantum theory comes close to this when it describes energy, according to Heisenberg, as anything that moves: "it may be called the primary cause of all change, and energy can be transformed into matter or heat or light." To Aristotle, too, matter was not by itself a reality but a *potentia,* which existed by means of form: through the processes of nature the Aristotelian "essence" passed from mere possibility through form into actuality. When we speak of the temperature of the atom, says Heisenberg, we can only mean an expectation, "an objective tendency or possibility, a *potentia* in the sense of Aristotelian philosophy." An accurate description of the elementary particle is impossible: "the only thing which can be written down as description is a probability function"; the particle "exists" only as a possibility, "a possibility for being or a tendency for being." But this probability is not merely the addition of the element of "chance," and it is something quite different from mathematical formulas of probabilities:

> Probability in mathematics or in statistical mechanics [writes Heisenberg] means a statement about our degree of knowledge of the actual situation. In throwing dice we do not know the fine details of the motion of our hands which determine the fall of the dice and therefore we say the probability for throwing a special number is just one in six. The probability wave of Bohr, Kramers, Slater, however, meant more than that; it meant a tendency for something. It was a quantitative version of the old concept of *potentia* in Aristotelian philosophy.

We have already met Heisenberg's question: "What happens 'really' in an atomic event?" The mechanism of the results of the observation can always be stated in the terms of the Newtonian concepts: "but what one deduces from an observation is a probability function ... [which] does not itself represent a course of events in the course of time. It represents a tendency for events and our knowledge of events."

✵ *Eighth: not the essence of "factors" but their relationship counts.* Modern physics now admits, as we have seen, that important factors may not have clear definitions: but, on the other hand, these factors *may* be clearly defined, as Heisenberg puts it, "with regard to their connections." These relationships are of primary importance: just as no "fact" can stand alone, apart from its associations with other "facts" and other matters, modern physics now tends to divide its world not into "different groups of objects but into different groups of connections."[11] In the concepts of modern mathematics, too, it is being increasingly recognized how the functions of dynamic connections may be more important than the static definitions of "factors." Euclid had said that a point is something which has no parts and which occupies no space. At the height of positivism, around 1890, it was generally believed that an even more perfect statement would consist in exact definitions of "parts" and of "space." But certain mathematicians have since learned that this tinkering with definitions tends to degenerate into the useless nominalism of semantics, and consequently they do not bother with definitions of "points" or "lines" or "connection"; their interest is directed, instead, to the axiom that two points can be always connected by a line, to the relationships of lines and points and connections.

❄ *Ninth: the principles of "classical" logic are no longer unconditional: new concepts of truths are recognized.* "Men fail to imagine any relation between two opposing truths and so they assume that to state one is to deny the other," Pascal wrote. Three centuries later Heisenberg wrote about some of C. F. von Weizsaecker's propositions:

> It is especially one fundamental principle of classical logic which seems to require a modification. In classical logic it is assumed that, if a statement has any meaning at all, either the statement or the negation of the statement must be correct. Of "here is a table" or "here is not a table" either the first or the second statement must be correct. "Tertium non datur," a third possibility does not exist. It may be that we do not know whether the statement or its negation is correct; but in "reality" one of the two is correct.
>
> In quantum theory this law "tertium non datur" is to be modified. . . . Weizsaecker points out that one may distinguish various levels of language. . . . In order to cope with [certain quantum situations] Weizsaecker introduced the concept "degree of truth." . . . [By this] the term "not decided" is by no means equivalent to the term "not known." . . . There is still complete equivalence between the two levels of language with respect to the correctness of a statement, but not with respect to the incorrectness. . . .

Knowledge means not certainty, and a half-truth is not 50 percent truth; everyday language cannot be eliminated from any meaningful human statement of truth, including propositions dealing with matter; after all is said, logic is human logic, our own creation.

❄ *Tenth: at the end of the Modern Age the Cartesian partition falls away.* Descartes' framework, his partition of the world into objects and subjects, no longer holds:

> The mechanics of Newton [Heisenberg writes] and all the other parts of classical physics constructed after its model started out

from the assumption that one can describe the world without speaking about God or ourselves. This possibility seemed almost a necessary condition for natural science in general.

But at this point the situation changed to some extent through quantum theory. . . . [W]e cannot disregard the fact [I would say: the condition] that science is formed by men. Natural science does not simply describe and explain nature; it is a part of the interplay between nature and ourselves; it describes nature as exposed to our method of questioning. This was a possibility of which Descartes could not have thought of but it makes the sharp separation between the world and the I impossible.

If one follows the great difficulty which even eminent scientists like Einstein had in understanding and accepting the Copenhagen interpretation of quantum theory, one can trace the roots of this difficulty to the Cartesian partition. This partition has penetrated deeply into the human mind during the three centuries following Descartes and it will take a long time for it to be replaced by a really different attitude toward the problem of reality.

❀ ❀ ❀

WE cannot avoid the condition of our participation. Elsewhere I have tried to draw attention to the personal and moral and historical implications of this recognition, that instead of the cold and falsely aseptic remoteness of observation we need the warmth and the penetration of personal interest: but this is no longer the solitary longing of a humanist, a poetic exhortation. For "even in science," as Heisenberg says in *The Physicist's Conception of Nature*, "the object of research is no longer nature itself, but man's investigation of nature. Here, again, man confronts himself alone."[12] And the recognition of this marks the beginning of a revolution not only in physical and philosophical but also in biological (and, ultimately, medical) concepts, springing from the empirical realization that there is a closer connection between mind and matter than what we have been taught to believe. Still, because of our interregnum, decades and disasters may have to pass until this revolution will bring its widely recognizable results. Yet we may at least look back at what we have already begun to leave behind.

After three hundred years the principal tendency in our century is still to believe that life is a scientific proposition, and to demonstrate how all of our concepts are but the products of complex mechanical causes that may be ultimately determinable through scientific methods. Thus Science, in Heisenberg's words, produced "its own, inherently uncritical"—and, let me add, inherently unhistorical—philosophy.[13] But now "the scientific method of analysing, [defining] and classifying has become conscious"— though, let me add, far from sufficiently conscious—"of its limitations, which rise out of the [condition] that by its intervention science alters and re-fashions the object of investigation. In other words, methods and object can no longer be separated. *The scientific worldview has ceased to be a scientific view in the true sense of the word.*"

These are Heisenberg's italics. They correspond with the arguments of this book, in which I have tried to propose the historicity of reality as something which is prior to its mathematicability.[14] They represent a reversal of thinking after three hundred years: but, in any event, such recognitions involve not merely philosophical problems or problems of human perception but the entirety of human involvement in nature, a condition from which we, carriers of life in its highest complexity, cannot separate ourselves. The condition of this participation is the recognition of our limitations which is, as I wrote earlier, our gateway to knowledge. "There is no use in discussing," Heisenberg writes, "what could be done if we were other beings than what we are."[15] We must even keep in mind that the introduction of the "Cartesian" instruments such as telescopes and microscopes, which were first developed in the seventeenth century, do not, in spite of their many practical applications, bring us *always and necessarily* closer to reality—since they are interpositions, *our* interpositions, between our senses and the "object." We may even ask ourselves whether *our* task is still to "see" more rather than to see better, since not only does our internal deepening of human understanding now lag behind our accumulation of external information, but too, this external information is becoming increasingly abstract and unreal. Hence the increasing breakdown of internal communications: for, in order to see better, we must understand our own limitations better and also trust ourselves better. At the very moment of history when enormous governments are getting ready to shoot selected men hermetically encased in plastic bubbles out of the earth onto the moon, the importance of certain aspects of the "expanding universe" has begun to decline, and not only for humanitarian reasons alone; we are, again, in the center of the universe—inescapably as well as hopefully so.

Our problems—all of our problems—concern primarily human nature. The human factor is the basic factor. These are humanistic platitudes. But they have now gained added meaning, through the unexpected support from physics. It is thus that the recognitions of the human condition of science, and of the historicity of science—let me repeat that Heisenberg's approach is also historical[16]—may mark the way toward the next phase in the evolution of human consciousness, in the Western world at least.

❊ ❊ ❊

NEED I still insist that many of Heisenberg's propositions about physics—indeed, that sometimes the very language of his recognitions—correspond with many of my own propositions dealing with history? Of course these are correspondences, not analogies; they are not interchangeable; they do not form a system. Still, their portents go beyond the two fields of historical philosophy and philosophical physics. They suggest that in our times new ideas about the relationships of human life and of the universe, of mind and matter, may be emerging, often independently from each other, coming from the oddest sources, different places, through different routes. It would already be possible to string together a list of striking statements by certain scientists, historians, poets, writers, philosophers in the middle of the twentieth century, in order to illustrate certain profound convergences of the human spirit, indicating the evolution of what may be called postmodern thought in the Western world. Yet such a presentation, no matter how impressive, would be insufficient. It is almost always possible to find some people who tend to agree with you, no matter how unpopular or unrecognized your ideas may be; a mere listing of corresponding statements may give a disproportionate impression of their influence and importance or even of their significance. We must recognize the existence of certain correspondences: but it is through a historical approach that their significance may properly appear.

Once more I must insist how this eminent reasonableness of the historical approach has been recognized, in one way or another, by certain scientists. Nearly forty years ago E. A. Burtt wrote in *The Metaphysical Foundations of Modern Science* that "whatever may turn out to be the solution" of the modern problem of cosmology (and of physics) "an indispensable part of its foundation will be clear insight into the antecedents of our present thought-world."

> Possibly the world of external facts is much more fertile and plastic than we have ventured to suppose; it may be that all these cosmologies and many more analyses and classifications are genuine ways of arranging what nature offers to our understanding, and that the main condition determining our selection between them is something in us rather than something in the external world. *This possibility might be enormously clarified by historical studies* [my italics] aiming to ferret out the fundamental motives and other human factors involved in each of these characteristic analyses as it appeared and to make what headway

seemed feasible at evaluating them, discovering which are of
more enduring significance and why.

"To ferret out the *fundamental* motives" (again my italics) in the minds
of scientists long dead may be too much to ask; but when we use the historical approach we are on the right track, even though we must be more
modest. Our task is to sketch not the conditions of individual intellectual
creation but the historical correspondences of certain intellectual recognitions.

Some of these correspondences are relatively simple. Around the middle
of the seventeenth century, for example, as Ernest Mortimer observed in
his excellent study of Pascal, "only a few months separated . . . Galileo's
death, Newton's birth and the appearance of Descartes' *Principia Philosophica*
with its preface, the *Discours sur la méthode*." Darwin and Marx died within a
few months of each other, at the very time when Ortega was born. But
there is, of course, more to this historical problem of corresponding thinkers than correspondences in the life span of certain generations. In the
physical sciences, and particularly in their technical applications, there is
often an expectable convergence of certain achievements that are about to
be reached toward the end of certain phases of evolving research. Thus, for
example, the mutation theory in biology (something roughly corresponding to the form, but by no means to the essence, of the quantum theory in
physics, involving the discovery that genetic evolution may occur in
"jumps") was reached in 1902, at the same time by De Vries in Leyden,
Tschermak in Vienna, Correns in Berlin. This is the kind of achievement
which consists of the discovery of answers to questions that have been outstanding and precisely formulated for some time before: it involves the
"filling of gaps" whose existence and place has been recognized. (With all
the respect due to the before-mentioned eminent scientists these are, therefore, coincidences that are different in degree but perhaps not in kind from
the inventions of such things as electric light or the automobile engine: for
there are reasons to believe that, had Edison's experiments failed in 1879
or Benz's in 1885, someone else would have produced the first electric bulb
and the first automobile engine around the same time or, in any event, not
much later.)

Outside applied science the historical development of ideas is, of course,
less predictable—though, as I wrote before, in our democratic times much
of the earlier independence and unpredictability of the humanities also
has been eroding. Still, what happens when really significant correspondences occur? They involve not so much the "filling of gaps" as coinciding
recognitions of the inadequate level of "research," of the insufficient depths,

or heights, of the prevailing "dialogue" (Bernanos: "the worst, the most corrupting lies are problems poorly stated"); and this calls forth, of course, not so much new answers as new questions (or, perhaps, new recognitions of old questions) by solitary thinkers whose main fields of study may be quite different but who possess similar qualities of personal interest. It is thus that they are literally *dissatisfied* with the inadequacy of the prevailing categories of thought. It is thus that their different paths converge: for, let me repeat, the way to certain truths leads through a graveyard of untruths.

And this graveyard lives within the minds of living human beings. The graves, the tombstones, the thinning line of mourners, the grave-diggers, the lonely walkers through the nocturnal yard do not exist in the abstract. The history of science is the history of scientists, and the history of thought is the history of thinking men. This is why the historical conditions of new recognitions are so important; but at the same time the very conditions of our historical knowledge set limits to our pursuit of the historicity of their correspondences. These are the natural limitations of intellectual history, the inevitable circumscriptions of the otherwise so significant and meaningful pursuit of the pedigrees of certain ideas. I touched upon these limits earlier. In the deepest sense what we must keep in mind is the paradox that no human idea is entirely original and wholly independent—while, on the other hand, the personal perception and the expression of even the most obvious and most ephemeral platitude lends (*lends* rather than *gives*) the latter an inevitable minimum of originality.[17] In the narrower and more precise sense we must consider the inscrutable complexities of the distance from the "first" (the quotation marks are intentional) appearance of an idea within the consciousness of a person through its first rational formulation in his mind to its first public expression (which is really the farthest point back where the historian's tracing may start) and to the, in our times increasingly complicated, process of its dissemination among other people, its fertilization of their minds, its recognition by them. It is perhaps because of this necessity of a right "climate" that "dissemination" is a good word. On the other hand, the sprouting of seeds in men's minds is miraculous in its causal complexities; the physics of nature do not apply.[18]

Let me, therefore, attempt for the last time a quick survey of certain "climates of opinion": for this historical approach may explain something about the complex and confusing and difficult evolution of the Western mind toward the end of the Modern Age and during the present phase of an interregnum.

Much has been written about that climate of opinion of a little more than a century ago which helped to insure and, indeed, to create the conditions of receptivity for Darwin's propositions. Not only progressive scientists but Marx and Engels, too, hailed Darwin (the former said about the *Origin* that it was "a basis in natural science for the class struggle in history" and considered dedicating *Das Kapital* to Darwin; the latter that "just as Darwin discovered the law of evolution in organic nature, so Marx discovered the law of evolution in human history"). This does not, of course, mean that Darwin was a Marxist (though it does mean that Marx was a Darwinist). Darwin and Comte, the atheist Marx and Mendel the Moravian abbot, Buckle the liberal historian and Zola the dogmatic realist, Maxwell the physical and Spencer the social scientist, they were very different men. But there were broad correspondences in their principal ideas: as Gertrude Himmelfarb put it in retrospect about Darwin and Marx, "as their philosophical intent was similar, so was their practical effect": they all believed in the progress concept of history and in the mechanical-mathematical order of the universe, and this was to be typical of the thinking of an era. Of course these are imprecise generalizations. No period of history is of one piece. Anyone with more than a superficial knowledge of history can point out contrary currents of thought (and what is perhaps more important, of sentiment) within the so-called Victorian Age. But, no matter how deep, these contrary currents were of rivulet width, eventually washed under by the swelling stream of accepted ideas the power of which is still far from being spent, and the influence of which has spread far beyond Europe. In 1856, shortly before the *Origin* was completed (and a few months before Comte died) Buckle put down an archetypal statement of these ideas as he wrote: "In regard to nature, events apparently the most irregular and capricious have been explained, and have been shown to be in accordance with certain fixed and universal laws. This has been done because men of ability and, above all, men of patient, untiring thought, have studied natural events with the view of discovering their regularity: and if human events were subjected to a similar treatment, we have every right to expect similar results." These are the ideas that have become—thoughtlessly perhaps—accepted by large masses of people who for the first time received the benefits of modern education. Save for the sonorous Latinities of its prose, this 1856 statement is hardly different from what in 1966, 110 years later, a computer technologist at, say, General Electric's Space Center—or, indeed, an Official Advanced American Thinker such as Buckminster Fuller—was saying and, presumably, thinking. Darwin, who died in 1882, was justified in his optimistic assumption when he said that he would trust the definition of the human species to be settled by the opinion "of a majority of naturalists," as he knew that these were about to take their stand on his side. As Samuel Butler wrote around that time: "I attacked the foundation of morality in *Erewhon,* and nobody cared two straws. I tore open the wounds of my Redeemer as he hung upon the Cross in *The Fair Haven*, and people rather liked it. But when I attacked Mr. Darwin they were up in arms in a moment." Of course; for, as E. I. Watkin put it once in a pithy sentence, the liberal world at the end of the nineteenth century "went forward with triumphant assurance, confident in its own enlightenment in reason, freedom and progress, and failed to notice that its heart was a void."

Yet shortly before the twentieth century began, a European intellectual reaction against nineteenth-century categories of thought started to crystallize. Let me repeat that there had been many individual manifestations of such a reaction earlier, Nietzsche for example: but it was not until about 1894 that we may see a coagulation of recognitions. Around that time an antimaterialist reaction, particularly in the Latin nations of Europe, corresponds with the emergence of a new kind of philosophy, involving the phenomenology of consciousness, in Germany. Menéndez y Pelayo, Unamuno, Croce, Sighele, Pareto, Sorel, Bergson, Proust, Le Bon, Péguy, Dilthey, Rickert, Simmel, Einstein, Freud . . . but, again, a catalogue of names will tell us little. In the broader sense there is a kind of antimaterialist "vitalism" corresponding in the recognitions of such different workers in such different vineyards as, say, Bergson or Planck or Wilde, many of whom may have been entirely unaware of each other's existence. At any rate, between 1894 and 1905 Planck discovers a hole within the closed mechanical concept of the universe; various Latin European thinkers propose, independently of each other, the existence of principles of intuitive cognition; Bergson and Einstein and, in his way, Proust start to think and talk about the relativity in time in different ways. In the narrower, and more precise, sense, too, some of these correspondences are remarkable, since they are reflected by the very language of their different proponents. In 1899, for example, the German historian Alfred Dove wrote Rickert: "We do not enter into contact with the past through causality alone, but leap across the entire intervening causal space by the force of simple sympathy," a statement not only completely contrary to the assertion of the popular philosopher Haeckel, written in the same year, that "the great abstract law of mechanical causality now rules the entire universe, as it does the mind of man," but which corresponds amazingly with the terminology which was to be employed by Planck within a year.[19]

The second, and no less remarkable, wave of crystallizing correspondences occurred twenty-five years later, in the twenties, mostly in the intellectually supercharged atmosphere of Weimar Germany, at the time of the second great "jump" in the historical evolution of modern physics. Around 1926 the inadequacy of mechanical causality and of categorical objectivity, together with "indeterminacy," were recognized not only by the agitated physicists such as Heisenberg, Bohr, Pauli, Schrödinger, Bridgman, already in some contact with each other: corresponding statements were made at the same time by many different thinkers, including historians such as Huizinga and Meinecke. What is remarkable about the significance of these recognitions is that they go beyond the assertions of the 1894–1905 period, as they represent a striving for a higher kind of harmony. "Physics and history," Huizinga wrote in 1926, "are natural subjects for comparison.... [I]t appears that attempts of a new rapprochement are coming rather from the side of the natural sciences, whose theory of exactitude has not remained unmodified...." In an important essay, published in 1928, Meinecke proposed new and fundamental limitations of causality as he suggested the existence of "supra-causal" influences. Perhaps the most incisive expression of the themes then developing may be found in an essay by the philosopher Karl Joel, entitled "Superseding the Nineteenth Century in the Thinking of the Present"—an exquisite summation of a trend of thought that had been developing among the finest minds of Europe in the twenties. In what were once "exact sciences" this trend may have reached its culmination in 1930–31 with the Bruxelles-Solvay Congress of physicists (to which I shall briefly return) and in Gödel's revolutionary theorem about the inevitability of human preconceptions in mathematics.

Yet, for many reasons and, as we shall shortly see, perhaps principally because of political ones, these converging and crystallizing aspirations for a postmodern philosophical harmony were soon washed under. Within his above-cited essay Meinecke in 1928 wrote that "the aspiration toward harmony must continue as an impulse, and could only die out if our culture were completely to decay or to collapse"; yet he already warned not only against "ossified academicism" but also against "subjectivism running riot." He may have sensed something like the coming of Nazism, of a hurricane of an antibourgeois and antirationalist reaction against what seemed to have been the hypocrisies of bourgeois civilization; something ultimately destructive. And, of course, this is what happened through Nazism, whose antirational and often primitive and brutal intellectual practices drove many of the best Western minds back to the "Left"—a movement particularly evident in the English-speaking world. By the end of the thirties Heisenberg and some of his German physicist colleagues were suspected to have been working for Hitler; Unamuno, neglected by the masses and by the publicists of Left and Right alike, died tragically alone; Ortega was regarded as not much more than an unusually intelligent reactionary gadfly by those leading intellectuals of the West who, except for a few scattered conservative anti-Nazis on the Continent, pinned their remaining hopes and illusions again on the "Left."

At this point I must say something about the inevitable relationships of the history of ideas and of the history of world powers, though necessarily in a kind of intellectual shorthand. The history of ideas from 1875 to 1941, a period of world-historical importance, still remains to be written—precisely because the movement of ideas in this period amounts to much more than intellectual history. Let me sum it up with one generalization, surprising as this might seem at first sight. From about 1875 to 1941, all superficial impressions to the contrary notwithstanding, Europe moved toward the Right, not the Left. (The very categories of this generalization are, of course, not precise: the "Europe" in it does not apply to Russia; Britain is a partial exception, and "Right" and "Left" are not clear-cut categories nowadays. But for the sake of intellectual—or, rather, historical—shorthand this generalization must do.) From about 1875 to 1941 European thought was influenced increasingly by a reaction against, and in some cases by a transcendence of, the categories of the nineteenth century, by a reaction against liberalism as well as against positivism, against free-trade capitalism as well as against socialist internationalism, against democratic materialism as well as against the mechanical-scientific worldview. From about 1875 to 1941 in the political and social and cultural life of Europe's peoples the most powerful and dynamic factor was that of nationality: and the roots of this historical factor (speech, for instance) were fed from a deeper kind of consciousness than the political thought which had characterized the earlier nineteenth-century dialogue between liberals and conservatives about the proper compounds of liberty with equality. From about 1875 to 1941, contrary to the Marxist (and to the later Leninist and Wilsonian) predictions, it was not the struggle of classes, and not the struggle of liberal vs. Communist internationalists, but the struggle of nations that formed the principal and world-shaking events. From about 1875 to 1941 the history of the world was marked by the decline of multinationality, of the old Russian, Austrian, Turkish, Spanish empires and by the rise of new national powers such as Germany or Japan. From about 1875 to 1941 the principal development within Europe was the rise in the power and prestige (only briefly interrupted after 1918) of Germany. And after 1941 it was not only the defeat of German power but the bankruptcy of German-type nationalism which marked a turning point in the history of world politics as well as in the evolution of European ideas; for the very condition that Germany and Fascism represented some of the most extreme and primitive applications of this 1875–1941 reaction against the nineteenth-century worldview either alienated or disillusioned or literally drove underground some of the actual and potential intellectual advocates of this reaction.

Thus, while this antimaterialistic reaction of the European spirit—or, what may be more important, this *first* post-materialist and *first* postmodern movement in its history—did not have much to do with politics when it began to crystallize after 1875, it was destroyed by world political forces after 1941. In any event, it cannot be properly assayed without reference to the history of nations during the same period. It is true that, as Péguy said, the massive interference of politics and of its rhetoric leads to the degeneration of truth and of thought. But it is precisely because of this massive and pervasive interference of politics that the history of ideas cannot be treated in an isolated category. Not only were there correspondences between the late-nineteenth-century intellectual reactions against positivism and the political reactions against parliamentarism, or between the reactions against materialism and against capitalism, or later between philosophical neo-idealism and political Fascism. There exist, too, relationships between world political developments and the applications of the new ideas. There are some evident examples of these correspondences throughout the history of the new physics. Haven't we seen, for example, that 1900 marks the end of the indisputability of the Newtonian world order as well as of the confidence of the Bourgeois Age, that Planck's discovery of the hole in the mechanical-physical universe occurs at the very time when the cracks appear in what Mrs. Tuchman recently called *The Proud Tower?* The 1894–1905 period is, for example, not only an enormously important turning point in the history of ideas; it is an enormously important turning point in the political history of the world; it was then that the United States and Japan first arose as world powers, whereby the destinies of Britain and of Germany and of Russia changed radically (their statesmen took notice of this and altered the course of their respective ships of state, something that was to lead to the First World War). In the 1920s the indeterminacy revolution coincided with a defeat of the "Left" in Europe from which it has not yet recovered (the feebleness of the bourgeois parliamentary regimes and the depressing failure of capitalism led not to leftist revolutions but of rightist dictatorships enjoying widespread mass support).[20] And the "American" phase of the Second World War, after 1941, certainly corresponded with the construction of the first atomic bombs, by refugee scientists, in the United States. For it is history, not "science," that explains both how and why these atomic bombs were made. The "causes" of the atom bomb are historical (and, ultimately, personal); they are scientific and technical only on a secondary level of "causes." The principal causes of the making of the bomb include Hitler, the Second World War, and the persecution of the Jews in Germany. The bomb was made when it was made, in the way it was made, and for the purposes it was made, not merely because at a certain phase of scientific development a certain stage of technological know-how was reached but principally because in a certain phase of history in the consciousness of certain eminent scientists there had arisen the fear that other scientists might be building an atom bomb for Hitler. Technically speaking, the important stages in a history of the atom bomb are the splitting of the uranium nucleus by neutrons in 1938–39, the functioning of the first nuclear reactor in Chicago in December 1942, the exploding of the first bomb in New Mexico in July 1945, and the bombs finally cast on Japan in August 1945; but the technological character of these stages ought not obscure the principal motive factors in its creation which, as in every historical act, were formed by personal choices, through historical thinking and historical consciousness, and conditioned by the political, racial, national, religious, and ideological inclinations of responsible men.[21]

We may be too close to assay the meaning of the last twenty-five years with detachment. Yet certain things are hardly arguable about it. While the terrible record (and, what is more important, the defeat) of Hitler's Germany discredited, at least for a time, much of the cause of neo-idealism, the world triumph of the Soviet Union and especially of the United States after 1945 revitalized the cause, among intellectuals, of neo-positivism. I wrote "especially" of the United States, because the intellectual and the cultural influence of Soviet Russia proved to have been extraordinarily feeble after 1945, even in those countries which now belonged within her political sphere of influence. During the last twenty-five years we have witnessed the widespread and wholesale development of the cultural "Americanization" of much of the world. And yet it is quite possible that this phenomenon of Americanization may have been, by and large, more superficial than it seems at first sight. In most places of the world in the twentieth century "Americanization" simply means "modernization," or, in other words, the adaptation and application of American techniques of mass production and of mass distribution. Still, there are certain reasons to believe that the influences of American forms of thought have not penetrated deeply enough to affect the ways and the preferences of thinking (something that is quite different from the preferences of professional intellectuals) of the nations of Europe at least. I have dealt with this subject in *Decline and Rise of Europe;* let me only add here that one of the reasons for this continuing and, indeed, developing divergence between the United States and Europe is that while the predominant tendency of American thinking is still progressive, on certain levels of European thought after 1945 a predominant tendency has been "neoconservative."[22] "Marxism," said the physicist Max Born in 1957, "teaches that the communist economy is a historical necessity and derives its fanaticism from this belief. This idea comes from physical determinism, which itself arises from Newton's celestial mechanics. But, in fact, physics abandoned this theory about thirty years ago . . . in the light of which"—and, let me add, in the light, too, of historical experience—"the communist belief that Marxist predictions will necessarily be realized appears grotesque. American thought," Born continued, "for its part, is at the mercy of a superficial pragmatism which confuses truth and utility. I cannot adhere to it. . . . Europe is not bound to one or the other of these extreme and absurd doctrines. . . ." This is a prototypical expression of a European attitude seeking increasingly for its independence from accepted Soviet and American patterns of thought (it is perhaps symbolic how the date of the Born statement nearly coincides with de Gaulle's assumption of power in France in 1958). Born's condemnation of the United States is perhaps unduly summary and primitive in its phrasing; I shall have something to say about the increasingly elusive essence of "utility" a few pages later, as I shall attempt to demonstrate how the utility of much of present-day technology has become more and more questionable; and I must insist, too, that more and more Americans are beginning, for the first time, to nurture doubts about their once unquestioned idea of technological progress, while it is by no means sure that Europeans, at least in the near future, will reject the bondage of that "Americanization" of life (and, to some extent, of thought) which irritates men of the stamp of Born.

But this is a question of the future with which we are not here concerned. What concerns us here is the necessary recognition that the development of the really significant intellectual currents of our times, and of their correspondences, are, at least for the time being, disturbingly obstructed and severely circumscribed by the interregnal conditions of our culture at present. It is true, as Heisenberg said in his Gifford Lectures, that "the connections between the different branches of science have [recently] become much more obvious than they have at any previous time." Yet it is also true that the breakdown in internal communications, which is so characteristic of our interregnum, has led to the inability and the unwillingness of eminent scientists and intellectuals to act upon these connections, not to speak of their failure to recognize their inherent correspondences. Indeed, for the first time in many centuries, the basic assumptions of certain men of science and of certain professional intellectuals, otherwise members of the same culture and in some instances of the same country, are worlds apart. This general breakdown of communications has led, as we have seen earlier, to the condition that during our interregnum, ideas, all asseverations to the contrary, are moving with painful slowness indeed. And yet already in 1895 (again the date is significant) Gustave Le Bon could write that "the true historical upheavals are not those which astonish us by their grandeur and violence. The only important changes whence the renewal of civilizations results, affect ideas, conceptions, beliefs. The memorable events of history are the visible effects of the invisible changes of human thought. . . . The present epoch," he continued, "is one of these critical moments in which the thought of mankind is undergoing a process of transformation. . . . The ideas of the past, although half destroyed, being still very powerful, and the ideas which are to replace them being still in process of formation, [our] age represents a period of transition and anarchy. . . ." Indeed even now most people, including historians, and even including large numbers of applied scientists, have not recognized that the notion of scientific certitude was mortally wounded between 1895 and 1930. It was in 1941, for instance, that Jacques Barzun attempted to demonstrate to Americans, within the covers of one book, that the nineteenth-century idea of progress was full of holes, passé, even though Barzun recognized that the hold of old ideas was still very strong.[23] "To reverse such ingrained habits of thought and work," he wrote then, "cannot be done in an instant. It will take much work and a very different kind of thought in a fresh direction. But the difficulty of the task should only spur our efforts in the one realm which we have under some sort of immediate control: our minds. Failing this, the possibilities which Henry Adams foresaw seem likely to come true all at once: cynical pessimism among the leaders of mankind; a vast revival of semireligious superstition; a brutish dictatorship by capital or labor." Those, then, who read Barzun's *The House of Intellect,* published nearly a quarter of a century later, will recognize that this author has even deepened his own humanistic pessimism about the reign of cynical pessimism among the intellectual technocrats now clambering into positions of leadership in our Western societies.

For it is not among the common people that the slowness in the development of new ideas is most apparent. As Arthur Koestler wrote in *The Sleepwalkers* (1958), "The inertia of the human mind and its resistance to innovation are most clearly demonstrated not, as one might expect, by the ignorant mass—which is easily swayed once its imagination is caught— but by the professionals with a vested interest in the monopoly of learning. . . . Innovation is a twofold threat to academic mediocrities: it endangers their oracular authority, and it evokes the deeper fear that their whole, laboriously constructed intellectual edifice might collapse." And not only to academic mediocrities. Perhaps it is not even so much the hold of old ideas as of certain habits and tendencies of thought which is so deadening. "In our mind and speech the world is still Darwinian, Marxian, Wagnerian, but beneath the thick crust are the fires of new thoughts which must modify or destroy the old," Barzun wrote in 1941. *But the crust is very thick.* "It has taken more than a quarter of a century to get from the first idea of the existence of energy quanta to a real understanding of the quantum theoretical laws," Heisenberg wrote. "This indicates the great change that had to take place in the fundamental concepts concerning reality before we could understand the new situation." And despite the very great importance of these recognitions, "very little has been gained for the general situation of our age . . . very little of this development has reached the public so far . . . [even though] it looks very much as if this development [would] have repercussions in the sphere of philosophy." This was written more than ten years ago: yet nothing much has happened. The new ideas are difficult to accept, wrote the American mathematical physicist Banesh Hoffmann more than twenty years ago, "because we still instinctively strive to picture them in terms of the old-fashioned particle, despite Heisenberg's indeterminacy principle. We still shrink from visualizing an electron as something which having motion may have no position, and having position may have no such thing as motion or rest." For this difficulty of seeing involves more than difficulties of visualization that are caused by old and ingrained habits of an optical nature. It involves the deeper difficulty, consequent to the condition that we see with our minds and, indeed, with our hearts: that we are conditioned to see what we want to see. Perhaps this is why even Freud could not liberate himself from certain nineteenth-century concepts of science and of causality, and why Einstein stuck so blindly and obstinately to the contractual idea of the world, to the symmetrical and mathematical concept of order in an Old Testament manner ("God does not play dice," he said) as he would reject Heisenberg's recognitions. Like the majority of scientists, Einstein refused to think through some of the fundamental implications of the discoveries of the new physics, even though, in the long run, these implications might become more important than the discoveries themselves. And it is perhaps precisely because of their unwillingness to break with certain intellectual categories and mental circumscriptions, as well as because of certain historical and political conditions, that the reputations of Freud and Einstein,[24] especially among intellectuals in the English-speaking world, are still so high.

I said "intellectuals," because they are especially involved in the conditions of our interregnum. We have now entered a phase in history when the monopoly over learning and the publication of intelligence have fallen to professional intellectuals—an anomaly, especially in the history of the English-speaking peoples, going against the grain of the nonintellectual genius of their character, and against their traditions of nonspecialization and of common sense (the noun "intellectual," designating a specific kind of brain-person, became widespread in English only around 1890; like "intelligentsia," it was a term imported from socialist and Russian usage). This emergence of a meritocracy whereby distinctions of formal education re-place the older distinctions of wealth and of birth is, contrary to the once optimistic pipe dreams of nineteenth-century liberals and socialists, a poi-sonous development. It is, at any rate, typical of our interregnum.

❄ ❄ ❄

AND now I must end by returning to the theme with which I began: the growing disillusionment of people with whatever is called "modern," and their increasing doubts about "Progress." We have seen that at the begin-ning of the Modern Age the idea of progress and the historical conscious-ness arose together in the minds of men. I have tried to show what has happened—or, rather, what has been happening—to our historical con-sciousness: how important, and how widespread it has become now, toward the end of the Modern Age. And what has happened to Progress? Some-thing very serious has happened to Progress. Let me show this on a very basic and common-sense level, dealing with what, in everyday parlance, are called "the material facts of everyday life" in the Western world.

It is, simply, that we can no longer expect such radical improvements in our living standards as what had happened to our grandparents and to our great-grandparents in the half-century before the First World War. At any rate, the material conditions in *their* lives changed much more than have ours during the last fifty years. This may be surprising: and yet it is so. Let me illustrate this through a rapid retrospect, for which we are situated pro-pitiously, since the period from the Civil War to World War I and the pe-riod from World War I to the present are approximately of the same length. The following comparisons are, moreover, generally valid not only for the United States but for the industrially advanced countries of Western Eu-rope. Starting with the most fundamental phenomenon, the average ex-pectancy of life, for all classes, in this portion of the world was forty-two to forty-four years around 1865; by 1915 it jumped to fifty-eight, while by 1965 it climbed slowly to sixty-seven. The general average of infant mor-tality in Europe and North America was nearly 24 percent in the 1860s: this dropped to about 6 percent by 1915, reaching the present plateau of 3 percent two decades ago. Our ancestors were intimately acquainted with the terrors of pain: but by 1914, for the first time in the history of mankind, it was possible for a European or an American to live through long stretches of time, even decades, without ever experiencing acute pain in any form. It was not only the advance in anesthetics, it was the great general progress in medicine which had made giant strides during the fifty years before World War I, as indeed the above-mentioned figures indicate; it is true that medi-cal research and certain techniques have achieved astonishing things during the last fifty years dealing with relatively rare diseases and operations: but the overall portents of these cannot stand comparison with what had happened during the fifty years before World War I, and there is reason to believe, for example, that in 1914 the services of a good family doctor who had graduated from a reputable medical school were in many ways better than what the average family can avail itself of nowadays when general practitioners have become rare and when the once close contact between physician and family is almost nonexistent. In 1865 the great majority of the white race was still illiterate; by 1915, for the first time in history, in North America as well as in Europe the great majority of people knew how to read and write. Compulsory public education, in North America and in Western and Central Europe, by 1914 reached the average age of eleven, and after four or five years of schooling its recipients had acquired a minimum facility of expression, something that cannot be taken for granted today. So far as the standard comforts are concerned, very few of our ancestors enjoyed constant heat, running water, ample light one hundred years ago: but all of these amenities—house-wide heating, indoor plumbing, electricity, not to speak of hot water, fans, elevators—were invented during the nineteenth century and they were made available to something close to the majority of the people, at least in the United States, by 1914, the only post-1914 invention of this kind having been air conditioning. Let me repeat: living conditions, for large numbers of people, changed more radically during the fifty years before 1914 than at any time in recorded history before or after. The same thing is true about communications. Napoleon could progress from the Seine to the Tiber no faster, and no differently, than could Julius Caesar two thousand years before: yet a century later one could travel from Paris to Rome in less than twenty-four hours in a comfortable sleeping-car. The locomotive, the steamship, the motorcar, the submarine, the airplane; the radio, the telegraph, the telephone—they were all invented and put into practice before 1914, the only post-1914 invention of this kind having been television. Of course there is a difference between the supersonic jet plane and the Wright Brothers' contraption, but it is a difference in degree not in kind. Sixty-five years ago one could travel from New York to Philadelphia in one hour and forty minutes, on comfortable and well-appointed trains available at every hour of the day. Not only have comfortable and well-appointed trains, at least in the United States, nearly ceased to exist; but also, jet planes and superhighways and all the recent governmental double-talk about high-speed rail lines notwithstanding, I strongly doubt that we shall in our lifetime travel from city to city in such speed and comfort as could our ancestors more than fifty years ago.

It is, of course, true that much of the progress in the fifty years before 1914 affected only a small portion of mankind, certain nations and certain social classes; but then, this survey of progress is necessarily restricted to what we, with some imprecision, call "the Western world" (not to speak of the condition that the very idea of progress was a specifically Western idea). Moreover, in the United States at least, these radical improvements in the conditions of life already before 1914 had begun to affect the majority of people: they were no longer restricted for the use of a minority. My purpose, in any event, was not to paint the picture of a golden age before 1914: those Good Years were as maggot-ridden as any others in the history of mankind: all I wished to suggest is that those who keep talking about our Revolutionary Age of Dizzying Change and of Unprecedented Progress literally don't know what they are talking about.

What we have seen during the last fifty years are improvements and ever more widespread applications of earlier inventions as they have been made available to millions. Yet even in the routine spheres of life it may be arguable that the momentum of progress has slowed down to a mechanical crawl. With all the machines at our disposal, it is at least possible that many of the material standards of life for large numbers of people—especially in the most "advanced" nations of the Western world—may have declined as much as they have advanced. I do not only mean the upper classes; more is involved here than the servant problem or inflation, which are consequences rather than causes. These matters have little to do with per capita money income or with other economic statistics: they are involved, instead, with such things as the declining quality and the deteriorating durability of materials and, what is more important, with the declining sense of the permanence of personal possessions (very much including the increasing impermanence of residence)—all matters that reflect the general feeling of insecurity and of rootlessness which is characteristic of our times, and perhaps of every interregnum in history.

If we, then, turn to the motivating (that is, accepted and acceptable) ideas toward the end of the Modern Age we will find not only that, as I have been insisting often in this book, they move remarkably slowly, but also that they are painfully old. International organization, world government, disarmament, the population explosion, the administrative society, the welfare state, mass production, automation, progressive education, psychoanalysis, abstract art, Greenwich Village, tubular furniture, emancipated women—they were current, accepted, in evidence, *idées reçues* in . . . 1913. After everything is said, Kennedy's (and Dulles's, and Acheson's, and Hull's, and Hoover's) ideas were souped-up Wilsonian ideas, whereas Wilson's view of the world and of America's role in the world was very different from Lincoln's. . . . Our avant-garde have become a kind of rear guard. Consider the recent (1963) exhibition on the fiftieth anniversary of the famous 1913 Armory Show. The great jump was that from Ingres to Cézanne, not from Picasso to Picasso; from the *Salon des refusés* in 1863 to Utrillo, Pissarro, Vuillard in 1913 not from Armory Show (1913) to Armory Show (1963). From Tennyson to Yeats, from Brahms to Ravel, from Renan to Valéry, from realists to surrealists—jumps, all kinds of jumps; from Stravinsky to Stravinsky, from Kandinsky to Jackson Pollock, from the Dadaists to Genêt, from Blok to Yevtushenko, from Robinson Jeffers to Allen Ginsberg, from Frank Lloyd Wright to Buckminster Fuller a hobbled skip, and I am mentioning what are nowadays called "the exciting people," the "forward-looking minds" of our times.

I, for one, wish that President Kennedy had read something like the following passage from Georges Bernanos before he, in 1961, exhorted the people of the United States to "get moving ahead." "This world believes it is moving ahead," Bernanos wrote in 1946:

> [B]ecause it holds a most materialistic idea of moving ahead. A world in motion is a world that clambers up slopes, not one that tumbles down. No matter how fast you fall down a hill, all you are doing is falling down. Between those who think that civilization is a victory for man in the struggle against the determinism of things . . . and those who want to make of man a thing among things, there is no possible scheme of reconciliation. . . .[25]

I often think that in the Western world—and perhaps particularly in the United States—a new great division among men may have already begun to form. On the political and ideological level this is obscured by the continuing deadweight of old categories of ideas and of their antiquated terminology. As we have seen earlier, the adjectives "liberal," "conservative" and even the designations "Right" and "Left" make less and less sense now. Indeed, it was as early as a century ago, around 1870, that the importance and the meaning of the classical nineteenth-century antithesis of "liberals" vs. "conservatives" was beginning to fade. During the eighty-odd years that followed, liberalism and conservatism were giving way to the confrontation—and, eventually, to the compounding—of two rather more deep-seated and more elementary forces, nationalism and socialism. Is it not possible that the principal division in the political thinking of the future may crystallize on yet another, more profound level: between partisans of reason and partisans of progress, between those who *still* see no sense in resisting the increasing mechanization of the world and those who *no longer* share this outdated idea of Progress? I certainly find it to be significant that in the United States the opposition to superhighways and the moon rockets and computers and large-scale construction programs and supermodern gadgetry and gimmickry is crystallizing, perhaps for the first time, in the minds of the very people—"liberals" and "progressives"—who in the past used to be among the enthusiastic propagators of a materialist optimism; and, what is more important, among all kinds of people whom the old political and ideological categories no longer fit. Yet much time will have to pass until this opposition to the still-prevalent ideas of Progress becomes widespread enough to be effective: for this requires not only increasing efforts of propaganda but increasing consciousness in the minds of people of the reasons for their opposition—a difficult process, which, as we have seen, many decent people have not yet succeeded in thinking things through, in freeing their minds from many of the corroded shackles of ideas that were, after all, progenitors of certain monstrosities of which their minds have become only belatedly aware.

That epoch in the history of Western civilization that we call the Modern Age (it may be called, with more or less equal justice, the Political Age or the Atlantic Age or the Bourgeois Age, it matters hardly which), which opened about three or four hundred years ago, is now passing out of our lives, but, of course, not wholly: it is also changing into something new. As Ortega put it in 1914 (there is something symbolic in the coincidence that the printing of this first book of his, the *Meditations on Quixote*, was completed by a Madrid firm on July 21, 1914), each historical epoch is involved with a basic interpretation of man: but "the epoch does not bring the interpretation; it actually *is* such an interpretation." Consider, then, three stages in our view of human nature. The writers of the *Encyclopédie*, circa 1760: "Since all our direct knowledge comes by the senses, all our Ideas are consequently due to Sensations." Darwin, circa 1860: "I look upon all human feeling as traceable to some germ in the animals." Circa 1960, this no longer makes sense. On the occasion of the one-hundreth anniversary of Darwin's *Origin of Species* (1859), Joseph Wood Krutch, an American humanist and naturalist, surprised the readers of *The American Scholar* by setting up Darwin's view of human nature as against Dr. Johnson's radically different view of human nature and of human knowledge in *Rasselas* (1759), and expressing clearly his preference for Johnson. "Between the two centenaries," Krutch mused, "... there yawns a gulf that we may or may not someday cross again." I hope that we may: but then, this involves a mental bridge which we must cross before we get to it: we must recognize that the possibilities for crossings exist, though on a different level than heretofore. Or consider the prototypal "problem of modern man," as Aldous Huxley put it after the First World War. "God as truth, God as 2×2=4," that's not "so clearly all right," says Gumbril Jr. in *Antic Hay*. Is "there a chance of their being the same?" Are "there bridges to join the two worlds?" Well—has this 1922 problem retained its freshness? Doesn't it have a curiously musty, old-suit touch, like the theatricality of an old Bloomsbury cape? And I mean, even to people who may not be aware that the "gap" between "relative" moral and "absolute" scientific truths no longer exists, since, to start with, 2×2=4 ceased to be an Absolute Truth? "Scripture says that the sun moves and the earth is stationary, and science says that the earth moves and the sun is comparatively at rest," Newman wrote in 1845. "How can we determine which of these opposite statements is the very truth till we know what motion is? If our idea of motion is but an accidental result of our present senses, neither proposition is true and both are true; neither true philosophically; both true for certain practical purposes in the system in which they are respectively found." Fifty years later, in 1895, Andrew Dickson White[26] in his *History of the Warfare of Science with Theology in Christendom* attacked this statement with contempt. "A hopelessly skeptical utterance," White said, "For what were the youth of Oxford led into such bottomless depths of disbelief as to any real existence of truth or any real foundation for it? Simply to save an outworn system of interpretation into which the gifted preacher happened to be born." Yet at least in one important sense Newman's 1845 idea of the universe (or, rather, of our participation in the universe) has proved to be more enduring than White's 1895 positivism, just as some of us find Johnson's 1759 views of human nature more relevant to our lives than Darwin's 1859 propositions. In 1958 Professor Polykarp Kusch, an American physicist and Nobel prize winner, found it necessary to write in the *Columbia University Forum:* "I think that the modern scientific mind would be less outraged by Newman's statement than were his critics at the end of the nineteenth century; it would concede that Newman had some prevision of ideas that have become basic to much of contemporary scientific thought." (It is only that few "modern scientific minds" have either the convictions or the courage which would compel them to "concede" this as Professor Kusch has done.)

Between 1450 and 1690 there occurred a revolution in our concepts of the universe, at a time when most people in Western Christendom (the term "Europe" had only a geographical meaning in 1450) still believed in the divinity of Christ. By the end of this transition, great thinkers, such as Newton, practiced outwardly while they no longer believed.[27] After 1900 there began another revolution in our concepts of the universe, at a time when most people (including many churchgoers) do not believe in God, though a minority may—again or anew.[28] Certainly now, a century after

Pio Nono's Encyclical Letter and *Syllabus Errorum* (1864), which marked the maximum point of divergence between science and religion, the pendulum has swung back so that religion and science may be at hailing distance from each other. But this simile of a pendulum, with its circumscribed two-dimensional swinging back and forth, is not quite right. Our recognitions are historical: our historical consciousness has been evolving, that is, deepening; there is progress, here, after all, progress of a kind: the new recognitions develop on a higher level. (New religious recognitions, too, do not signify a return to earlier believing: they signify the results of non-unbelieving.) Descartes' mathematical conception of the world was not only insufficiently religious, it was unhistorical—which is why Pascal has at least as much to tell us as Descartes (and Tocqueville at least as much as Voltaire[29] and surely more than Marx).

As the Modern Age emerged, there emerged with it the modern concept of "Europe"—a political concept of a system of states which was replacing the earlier concept of Western "Christendom." This modern political concept crystallized during the second half of the seventeenth century, at the same time when the new idea of the universe and of the physical world had become accepted among savants, and when a number of important turning points occurred in the history of the Western world; among other things, it was then that the influence of Russia and of North America on the political history of Europe became discernible. Now, toward the end of the Modern Age, the *political* primacy of Europe is gone; yet it is now that the adjective "European" shows some signs of acquiring a *cultural* sense, beyond its geographical or political meaning. This development has, of course, little to do with economic associations and with international bureaucracies; but it may have something to do with the recent weakening of Russian and of American influences over Europe, influences which seemed to have been so dominant after 1945. It is by no means certain that we shall see an independent European confederation (note that I am not even speaking of a "United" Europe). Yet there is something symbolic in the condition that now, when "Western man" confronts himself alone, the notion of "Europe" may—but only may—assume a higher sense, too.[30]

Meanwhile ideas that had once come from Europe, the consequences of European genius, may destroy the world, a possibility which exists because of the fateful divergence between two forms of thought, between historical thinking and scientific method, these two supreme achievements of the passing Modern Age. I have tried to assert that scientific method is inseparable from scientific thinking, which is, really, historical thinking. This is now recognized by some of us, including certain scientists: but long perilous times may have to pass until these recognitions bear fruit.

On the one hand our interregnum is more dangerous and it might last longer than we think. "We live at a time," Tocqueville wrote 130 years ago, "that has witnessed the most rapid changes of opinion in the minds of men; nevertheless it may be that the leading opinions of society will before long be more settled than they have been for several centuries in our history; that time has not yet come, but it may perhaps be approaching." That time has certainly come. "It is believed by some that modern society will be always changing . . ." he went on. "For myself, I fear that it will ultimately be too invariably fixed in the same institutions, the same prejudices, the same manners, so that mankind will be stopped and circumscribed; that the mind will swing backwards and forwards forever without begetting fresh ideas; that man will waste his strength in bootless and solitary trifling, and, though in continual motion, that humanity will cease to advance." This kind of enormous intellectual stagnation marks already the age in which we now live. Circa 1960 the fine Italian poet Eugenio Montale wrote: "In the age of science and technology reason is towed along behind, and every effort is being made to pension it off."

On the other hand the striving toward harmony has not ceased: and some of us may glimpse, here and there, that kind of hope which is on the other side of despair. "Our civilization," Ortega wrote in one of his last essays, a decade or so ago,[31] "knows that its principles are bankrupt—dematerialized—and that is why it has doubts about itself. But it does not seem that there ever was a civilization that died, and a full death, from an attack of doubt. I seem, on the contrary, to recall that civilizations have perished for the opposite reason—from petrification or arteriosclerosis of their beliefs."

On the one hand, not only may the Modern Age or the European Age be over. Something much more important has happened. We have created monstrous institutions of scientific technology that are governed by puny men; and it is precisely because science is part and parcel of human history that, for the first time, *the end of the world is in sight.*

On the other hand, this now so suddenly closer Day of Doom can be adjourned, indeed it can be indefinitely postponed—by the sheer quality of our determination to live. And this quality—ultimately, and really, a quality of consciousness—has now become involved, irretrievably, with our historical way of thinking, with this new child which, out of the ancient marriage of realism and idealism, may yet become Europe's greatest gift to mankind.

4

Polite Letters and Clio's Fashions

(1998)

$\mathbf{M}$y title derives, in part, from my reading of the excellent bicentennial history of the Royal Irish Academy.[1] "Polite literature" was one of the sections of the Academy at its beginning. Indeed, its charter of incorporation defined the purpose of the Academy as "promoting the study of science, polite literature and antiquities."[2] The Chancellor of the University of Dublin, Professor W. B. Stanford, in his excellent chapter devoted to the history of that section, was elegantly apologetic about this. "Polite," he wrote, "obviously carried associations with a standard of elegance and refinement suitable for an Academy that was intended to be a 'select society of gentlemen.' But it would not be long before the era of dilettantism and amateurism in literary and linguistic scholarship would come into disrepute."[3] To which I now add that a similar, and perhaps analogous, development had occurred not only within literary, but also historical, scholarship. I further read that during the nineteenth century "historical topics became commoner" in the Transactions and Proceedings of the Academy; and then, in 1901, the Academy changed the title of the section from "Polite Literature and Antiquities" to "Archaeology, Linguistics and Literature." As Professor Stanford wrote, this showed a kind of demotion of "literature to a third place, but still, rather curiously, subsuming history under either Literature or Archaeology, despite the pleas of Bury and others that it was essentially a science."[4]

Now, the purpose of my discourse is to propose that there is no longer any reason to be apologetic about the phrase Polite Literature or, as I put it in my title, Polite Letters. I chose this title for my discourse not because of a *captatio benevolentiae* and not out of a wish to make some kind of a sly or arch reference to a phrase sodden with antiquated charm. To the contrary:

From Richard English and Joseph Morrison Skelly, eds., *Ideas Matter: Essays in Honor of Conor Cruise O'Brien* (Dublin: Poolbeg), 195–207.

my argument is that near the end of the twentieth century that phrase may be more timely than we are accustomed to think; that what is antiquated and corroded is the insistence of J. B. Bury and others (stated by Bury in the very first year of this century) that history is essentially a *science,* that when, at the end of the eighteenth century, the gentlemen of the Royal Irish Academy inclined to consider literature and history together they were not altogether wrong. What has happened, after two centuries, is that the relative hierarchy within their alliance has changed. It is not history that is a part of literature, but it is literature that shows signs of becoming a part of history, in a new and broader sense of that word, in the sense that history is more than a discipline: it is—or, more precisely, it has become—a form of thought.

Everything has its history, including history. A distinct historical consciousness—as distinct from historical existence, and then from historical thinking—may be said to have arisen only three or four hundred years ago in Western Europe and England. Consequently, during the eighteenth century the appetite of all kinds of readers for all kinds of history arose. So, during the last three centuries we may discern the following large developments. In the eighteenth century history was seen as literature. In the nineteenth century, largely (though not exclusively) because of the solid achievements of German scholarship, history was seen as a science—a development that reached England and Ireland more slowly and more hesitantly than elsewhere (which is why at the end of that century Bury's insistence that history was a science was already outdated). We must consider too that the word "science" in that century had a more spacious meaning than it has acquired since. It was somewhat akin to the German *Wissenschaft,* meaning both science and knowledge (the word "scientist," in English, appears only in the second half of the nineteenth century). Thus during two centuries history advanced from literature to science. And what about the twentieth century, near the end of which we now live, whereby we have the opportunity for a certain retrospect? About it we cannot make such a general statement. It seems, rather, that we are in the presence of two, essentially conflicting, different and divergent tendencies. One still-dominant tendency *is* to consider history as social science. The other is to consider history as a form of thought.

The consideration of history as a social science has sprung from several sources. The main one of these has been the general reluctance of academic historians to relinquish the prestige that the scientific notion of history brought to their profession—and thus to themselves. That was not only the result of the general acceptance, by 1914, of the PhD degree conferred upon historians throughout the world. It corresponded (and it still corresponds) to a general belief among the peoples of the world (a belief that had not existed a century earlier) to the effect that the historian is but another scientific specialist, that is, a professionally accredited scientific student of records. That such a narrow concept of the historian reduces him, in effect, to that of an archivist (as it reduces too the view of the past to merely that of the recorded, and not of the remembered, past) has not been recognized. (Nor has it been recognized that there is no difference between a source and a "historical" source, or between a document and a "historical" document.) Gradually during this century a slight, because inadequate, variant of the older nineteenth-century concept of history as a science gained acceptance: the notion that, well, if history is not quite like a science it is surely a social science of a certain kind. I say "inadequate" because most historians were fain to recognize the essential difference that men such as Dilthey had proposed as early as 1875, namely, the difference between *Naturwissenschaften* and *Geisteswissenschaften,* issuing from the comprehension that man's knowledge of man is essentially different from his knowledge of other, less complex organisms and matters. This is so not only because of the complexity of the human being, but because, perhaps especially in the case of history, the observer and the observed belong to the same species. As a consequence, not only the subjects of historical knowledge, but the very conditions, indeed, the nature of that knowledge itself, differ from the so-called natural sciences. Throughout the twentieth century we may observe evidences of a lamentable split-mindedness among many historians who will nod at criticisms of historical determinism as if those were truisms; and yet they go on writing and teaching history as if history *were* determined.

Another reason for the acceptance of history as a social science has been a more honorable one. One hundred years ago it was largely taken for granted what the English historian J. R. Seeley, the Regius Professor of Modern History at Cambridge, wrote: "history is past politics and politics present history." This was not very different from the standard nineteenth-century view as expressed, for example, by Droysen, who said that "the statesman is the historian in practice," or by Ranke, who saw history as concerned mainly with the life and the relations of states. Yet with the development of universal literacy and modern mass democracy it was already evident that a restriction of historical study to politics resulted in too narrow a scope; that history of governments and their relations, no matter how decisive and important, cannot but consider the history of the governed; that, in other words, the history of states must, on occasion, become both broadened and deepened by contemplating the history of peoples, including conditions of their everyday lives. With all due respect to the important achievements of the French *Annales* school, beginning shortly before the First World War, allow me to say that their recognition of this need was—or should have been—already a foregone conclusion at the time. What Oscar Wilde said about some men "who pursue the obvious with the enthusiasm of a short-sighted detective" must not be applied to those French social and intellectual historians of the *Annales* school such as Lucien Febvre or Marc Bloch, whose work, in retrospect, not only deserves our respect, but is worthy of emulation. But the pursuit of what seems to be intellectually fashionable and professionally profitable amounts to a temptation to which many scholars are, alas, not immune. The results are all around us, ranging from the huge confections of Monsieur Fernand Braudel, to the often unreadable and sometimes even ludicrous publications of specialists. On the one hand, we are faced with the boundless, and senseless, pretensions of someone like Braudel to the effect that what he had attempted, and achieved, is the *total* history of a place and of a period. On the other hand, we are faced with a disintegration of the discipline of history, through its implicit disregard of the political thread that, no matter how roughly, had once bound and still binds together the history of nations. This disintegration has created not only specialized "fields" such as social history and economic history and intellectual history, but such "fields" as black history and women's history pursued, alas, by ambitious men and women who seem to be rather less interested in the history of their people, and sometimes not even in that of their subjects, than in the prospect of their standing in the academy: that is, not in history, but historianship. The verminous fads of quantification and psychohistory are only extreme examples of the social-scientific attitude, with its wrongheaded practices of a thoughtless borrowing and adaptation not only of the methodology and the language of the natural sciences, but of the questionable terminology of Freudian psychoanalysis (about which another Viennese once wrote that it is the disease of which it pretends to be the cure). Thus *corruptio pessimi pessima*, but even for the *optimi* the acceptance of history as a social science has resulted in something that might appear as a more sophisticated and up-to-date way of dealing with history, whereas it is hardly more than a retrospective (and therefore hopelessly shortsighted) kind of sociology.

The alternative to this devolution, I propose, is the recognition of history as a form of thought—indeed, as a dominant form of thought in the twentieth century, consequent to the evolution of our historical consciousness during the last three hundred years; to a gradual evolution of our minds that in the very long run may be more profound than the discovery of the scientific method three hundred years ago. The phrase "history as a form of thought" is essentially epistemological. It suggests a historical philosophy that is the very opposite of a philosophy of history. It recognizes the futility of attempts to define universal laws or patterns for the knowledgeability of history. It issues from the recognition of the historicity of knowledge and—this is important—of language. Thus it may be said that implicit in the recognition of history as a form of thought lies the recognition that "facts" of history are merely so-called, since they are neither hard, nor distinctly isolable; that no fact exists by itself, but that its meaning depends on its association with other facts; that facts are not separable from the words in which they are expressed; that the statement of every fact depends on its purposes; that history is not only written, but spoken and taught and remembered in words and, moreover, in words that are not those of a scientific terminology, but words of the common and everyday language; indeed, that words themselves are not merely the symbols of *things,* but that they are symbols of *meanings*—meanings that in themselves have been formed by history.

Now, unlike the social-scientific school (if that is what it is), those who see history in this way do not coalesce into a school of thought. But they, often tucked away in the oddest places, have their great forerunners, historians such as Tocqueville, Burckhardt, Huizinga, in whose published works, lectures, and letters we find recognitions and elaborations of what I have tried to summarize above. Space does not allow for a detailed account of the pedigree of this alternative recognition of what history consists of. But I shall briefly turn to Jakob Burckhardt for two reasons. The first is the indisputable recognition that he was the founder of what we may call cultural history, something that is truer than are any pretensions to "total history," since what Burckhardt achieved was the historical representation of both the cultural forms and the modes of thinking of a certain place and time, often (though not always and not necessarily) expressed in its art. My second purpose in citing Burckhardt is to draw attention to the wisdom inherent in the humility of his purpose. "I never dreamed of training scholars and disciples in the narrower sense," he wrote in a letter:

> but only wanted to make every member of the audience feel and know that everyone may and must appropriate those aspects of the past that appeal to him personally, and that there can be happiness in so doing. . . . Furthermore, we must understand that when we try to immerse ourselves wholly in the reading of a classic, only *we alone* can find what is important *for us.* No reference work in the world, with its quotes, can replace that chemical bonding that mysteriously occurs when a phrase found by ourselves illuminates something in our mind,

crystallising itself into a real piece of spiritual property that is ours.... We are unscientific [*unwissenschaftlich*] and have no particular method, at least not the one professed by others.[5]

This conception, I once wrote, is something very different from amateurism as well as from subjectivism. With all of his stoic contemplation of the world, Burckhardt maintained his high faith in the potentiality of the human spirit:

> The spearhead of all culture is a miracle of mind, namely, speech, whose source, independently of the particular people and the particular language, is in the soul; otherwise, no deaf mute could be taught to speak and to understand speech. Such reaching is explicable only if there is in the soul an intimate and responsive urge to clothe thought in words.[6]

To which I should add: to *complete* thought in words; for speech is not only the clothing, but also the completion, of thought. Thus when speaking about cultural history we cannot avoid the relationship of history to language. And there are few places in the world where the consideration of that relationship is more appropriate than Ireland.

During a visit to Ireland several years ago, I found Professor F. S. L. Lyons's important and thoughtful book, *Culture and Anarchy in Ireland, 1890–1939*. Professor Lyons's thesis is that—contrary to what Matthew Arnold had set forth—culture might not be a unifying but a destructive force, leading to anarchy; that political problems may be the results of cultural problems; that in Ireland, surely since 1916, there was a failure "to find political solutions for problems which in reality are much more complex," because these problems are cultural, in the broadest sense of the word.[7]

Now allow this foreigner to essay his comments about this important thesis. What Professor Lyons said in this first chapter of his very valuable work is applicable not only to Ireland, but to most of the world. What he calls "culture" may be something that I might prefer to describe as "national characteristics" or "national tendencies," though I am aware that the two things are not quite the same. To put it in simpler and rougher terms: contrary to the lucubrations of Marxists and all kinds of social scientists, it is painfully evident that the main historical and political force in this world, even now, has little to do with economics. It is nationalism; and nationalism, a sense of nationality, national characteristics, national consciousness, are cultural, not material, factors.

Our problem lies with a definition of "culture." I think that Matthew

Arnold thought of culture and employed the term in a more narrow and aesthetic sense than we are wont to do. This is what T. S. Eliot implied when he found a certain "thinness" in Arnold's essay.[8] Lyons mentioned this in his crucial first chapter. But I think that Lyons was wrong when he wrote that there was "a prelapsarian innocence" in what Arnold wrote in the 1860s, because at that time (I quote Lyons) "the social sciences were still in their infancy. There were no social anthropologists or social psychologists to compel him to explain himself more intelligibly."[9] I think that Lyons, who was a first-class historian and not an academic votary of social science, gave here too much credit to the latter. In my opinion, the shortcoming of Arnold's old-fashioned essay consists in an unwitting philistinism of his own. He thought too much about art and aesthetics, and not enough about language and truth, almost like his American confrère, Emerson, who said that "the corruption of man is followed by the corruption of language," whereas it is arguable that the reverse sequence is true. To me, it seems that while one side—and a very important side—of Professor Lyons's thesis is correct, there is another side of which he was widely aware, but the importance of which he saw differently from this foreign observer: this is the tremendous asset of Ireland (and of Ireland's prestige in the world) that has been the result of the presence and of the effect of Irish genius on the literature of the English language.

Professor Lyons says somewhere that with the spreading of English and the shrinking of Gaelic during the nineteenth century "the marketplace" was bound to triumph over a remnant in the folk museum. Yet when Daniel O'Connell admitted that he did not mind the gradual disappearance of Gaelic—"I am sufficiently utilitarian not to regret its gradual passing"[10]—this was, I propose, a utilitarianism entirely different from the contemporary utilitarianism across the Irish Sea, that of poor Cobden, who wrote around the same time that he "advocated nothing but what is agreeable to the highest behests of Christianity—to buy in the cheapest market and to sell in the dearest." No: to my mind, Professor Lyons's "marketplace" was not the *mot juste*. The source and the driving force of that high mastery of the English language by Irish writers and thinkers and poets has not been utility, but attraction; not calculation, but affection, the affection that a master has not only for his tool, but for the scope and purpose of his work. To paraphrase Yeats: how can you separate the painting from the paint?

I should like briefly to refer to my native country, Hungary, because of the appositeness of a certain chapter of its history to that of Ireland at a particular time. Between 1867 and 1914 (it is uncanny how the limits of that period, from Butt to Redmond, correspond to the very same years of Hungarian history, from Deak to Tisza) many leading minds in Ireland (especially Griffith) saw in the home rule that had been secured by Hungary from Austria a reasonable and propitious model for Ireland. We also know, in retrospect, how this did not come about; and that many of its ideas proved to be illusory and outdated. Yet on a cultural—and not merely political—level (and, in terms of a *longue durée* much more meaningful than those enunciated by Braudel) some things happened that proved immensely beneficial in the long run. I am not only thinking of the sudden and extraordinary flourishing of literature and of the arts around the turn of the century, in Ireland as well as in Hungary, a flourishing that was not overcast by the pale neuroticism so evident in other cultural capitals of Europe at the time (as, for example, in Vienna and even in the London of the Yellow Book Nineties). I am thinking of a development that has been insufficiently recognized in Hungary even now. This was the extraordinary assimilation of German-speaking people in Hungary into Hungarian culture. Extraordinary indeed: because, with hardly any exceptions, this was the single such instance in Central and Eastern Europe at the time. For the German minorities before, say, 1865 their assimilation into what they saw as inferior and peasant-like peoples was unthinkable and—in more than one sense of the word—unspeakable. And yet in Hungary it happened: less because of political pressures than because of the Germans' recognition of the increasingly obvious qualities and merits of the native culture of the land where they lived. What I see here is a similarity—though not a parallel—between that Hungarian development and the identification of the Anglo-Irish with Ireland. And this would not have happened if, in the early twentieth century, the main demotic language of Ireland had not been English.

It is true, as Professor Lyons wrote, that the tragedy of the Anglo-Irish "was that, hesitating as they did between two worlds, they could never be fully accepted by either. To the English they came increasingly to seem an anachronism, to the Irish they remain an excrescence." I am not happy with that word "excrescence."[11] Or perhaps I am—not in the pejorative sense of it—because excrescence means an outgrowth; because excrescence is, after all, an organic function; and I happen to believe that much of Anglo-Irish, and also Irish-English, literature had a function more alive, and more enduring, than the sometimes bloodless appearances of Bloomsbury on the once robust tree of English letters. In this respect, I am thinking not only of worldwide celebrated writers of Irish origin such as Joyce or Shaw, but of representations such as *The Real Charlotte,* that small masterpiece which not only all lovers of English prose, but historians—and not merely historians of the Anglo-Irish—may ignore only to their loss. And I think I know that the mastery of the prose is inseparable from the deep-seated Irish loyalties of someone like Edith Somerville, who, born in the Ionian Islands, remained an Irish patriot through the most terrible and tragic years of the Troubles, probably aware of the condition of which Horace once wrote: "*patriae quis exsul se quoque fugit*"—an exile flees not only his country, but himself. Indeed, Professor Lyons himself wrote about "the man or woman in whom love of place transcended divisions based on origins, religion, or politics."[12]

"Love of place"—a phrase and reality that now makes me return to another, more recent, definition of culture: the celebrated—but senseless—one by C. P. Snow.[13] His thesis of the "Two Cultures" is alarmingly simple. There is a humanistic culture and a scientific one, and the solution is obvious: the humanists should know the Second Law of Thermodynamics and the scientists the *Areopagitica*. That such achievements may result in an aviary of stuffed owls should be obvious. The owl of Minerva, the Greeks told us, flies only at dusk; but *Snow's* owl will not fly. Less obvious, but more important, is the present condition: for, if there are two cultures in our world the division between them is not vertical, but horizontal. For the first time in the history of mankind there *is* a global, and therefore international, culture; a culture whose evident examples are airports that all over the world are alike; a culture whose most evident expression is a computerized and bureaucratic business language, a pseudo-scientific jargon artificially glued (not grafted) onto something that resembles Anglo-American. Yet next to—or, rather, beneath—this international language there are the national languages and cultures that are seldom translated and translatable, reflecting not only how people of different nations speak, but also how they live: not in their offices, not at their computers, not from nine to five, but after five, within their families and in their homes. In this respect, we may discern that, as this century proceeds, all *great* literature, prose as well as poetry, remains deeply national. There is no such thing as an international poem; and if there is such a thing as an international poet, he ought to be greeted—and kept—inside the waiting-lounges of airports, where he truly belongs.

But I wish to go beyond this evident recognition of the increasing presence of two cultures to propose that, in reality, there may be only one culture. The evolution of consciousness, perhaps especially in the Western world, is now such that every man and woman among us is a walking cultural historian. Or, in other terms: all of us are historians by nature, while we are scientists only by choice. We must admit that history is *not* a science and can never be one: because its very unpredictability issues from the complexity of human nature, whereby the mechanical causality on which all technology and Newtonian physics depend does not apply to the history of human beings. Thus history cannot be studied scientifically—while (and this is what I mean by history being a form of thought) science can be studied historically. While history is not part of science, it is science that is part of history: because first came nature, then came man, and only then came the science of nature. It is exhilarating, at least to me, to know that this commonsense truth has been confirmed by the recognitions of the greatest physicist of the twentieth century, Werner Heisenberg, who not only stated the fundamental condition of indeterminacy and uncertainty within the existence of the smallest particles of matter, but who also recognized the impossibility of separating the observer from the matter observed—whereby the epistemological recognition of man's own limitations ensues. The true scientific method can no longer assume that it deals with objects or subjects wholly apart from ourselves. To the contrary: it must take into account the process and the purpose of the observation itself—together with the inevitable limitations and suggestions of the human mind and of language. That this opens the way from the Cartesian dualism to a new, chastened, monistic view of the universe has been my conviction for a long time.

And so, nearing my conclusion, I now return to the relationship of polite letters and history. On the one hand, we are in the presence of a profound crisis in the study of history that is only partially due to the narrow-minded attraction of many of its practitioners toward something like a social science. Another element of the crisis is the inflation of materials, including records, with which the modern historian must deal. In the past, the historian was plagued by the fragmentary and insufficient survival of records. When dealing with the history of the last one hundred years (and sometimes not only with those) the problem of the historian has become the very opposite. An overwhelming mass of material threatens to suffocate him. The existence of this new condition calls (or should have called) for a drastic revision of the canons of historical research and scholarship (and perhaps of the training of future historians too). That this has not yet happened is a sorry reflection on the wanting vision and dedication of the professional historians guild. On the other hand, we are in the presence of a growing appetite for history on the part of many people and portions of societies who in the past were hardly interested in it—a fundamental and important phenomenon which few historians have, as yet, recognized. The evidences of this burgeoning interest in history are so protean that even a superficial sketching of them would require a substantial lecture on its own. Of course appetites can be badly fed; and an interest in history, indeed, the knowledge of history, can be damnably misused. We have had enough evidence of that during the last two hundred years. But that appetite is there: and its very existence proves, at least to me, the continuing evolution of historical consciousness.

Two centuries ago it was historical consciousness and interest in history that brought about the historical novel. But I think that we must go further than that—especially in this discourse dealing with the relationship of letters with history (or with history as a form of thought). My point is that every novel is a historical novel; and that the appearance of the novel, as a new literary form, was—like professional history—part and parcel of the same development. For a long time the novel was—and still is—seen as a new, prosaic form of the epic. Yet the novel and the epic, as Ortega y Gasset wrote in 1914:

> are precisely poles apart. The theme of the epic is the past as such: it speaks to us about a world which was and which is no longer, of a mythical age whose antiquity is not a past in the same sense as any remote historical time. . . .The epic past is not *our* past. Our past is thinkable as having been the present once, but the epic past eludes identification with any possible present. . . .[14]

It is not a remembered past (history is that), "but an *ideal* past."

Consider how, coming out of history, the novel grew with history. Consider, for example, not Walter Scott, but the preface with which his contemporary, Jane Austen, began *Northanger Abbey* in 1816:

> This little work was finished in 1803, and intended for immediate publication. It was disposed of to a bookseller, it was even advertised, and why the business proceeded no further, the author has never been able to learn. . . . But with this, neither the author nor the public have any other concern than as some observation upon parts of the work which thirteen years have made comparatively obsolete. The public are entreated to bear in mind that thirteen years have passed since it was finished, many more since it was begun, and that during that period, places, manners, books and opinions have undergone considerable changes.

It is unnecessary to press the point: Jane Austen's concern was decidedly, evidently historical. Now consider what Thomas Hardy wrote eighty years later:

> Conscientious fiction alone it is which can excite a reflecting and abiding interest in the minds of thoughtful readers of mature age, who are weary of puerile inventions and famishing for accuracy; who consider that in representations of the world, the passions

100

ought to be proportioned as in the world itself. This is the interest which was excited in the minds of the Athenians by their immortal tragedies, and in the minds of Londoners at the first performances of the finer plays three hundred years ago. . . .[15]

Another eighty years later it is my conviction that *conscientious history* has come to replace the desideratum which Hardy stated as *conscientious fiction*. It is history which can excite a reflecting and abiding interest in the minds of thoughtful readers of mature age, who are weary (and how weary we are!) of puerile inventions and famishing for truth.

I say "truth" because I shall venture to go further than Thomas Hardy. In the first place, I claim to detect the gradual absorption of the novel (indeed, of perhaps all polite letters) by history, not at all in the form of the historical novel, but through something else, indeed, by its opposite. In the second place, I venture to see in conscientious history, as well as in what Hardy called conscientious fiction, more than the far from ignoble attempts to present a mirror of real life; I see in their purpose something not very different from what had once impelled Thucydides to write his first history: the purpose of reducing untruth.

Someone once said that women are torn between the desire to be dressed and to be undressed. This is a half-truth. Culture is not nakedness, but it is not frippery either. Like all the other Muses, Clio is an inspiration of consciousness. To speak of Clio's subconscious exhibits a stupidity that borders on the obscene. A Clio stripped of her spiritual garments is no longer a Muse; and a Clio adorned with fashionable frippery is merely an antique frump. And this is worthy of our special attention now, when we must consider that the Muses, as Hesiod told us, were the daughters of Zeus and Mnemosyne, the incarnation of memory; and when Calliope and Melpomene, the personifications of epic and tragedy, may be witnessing their sister Clio's beneficent ascent in rank.

The reduction of untruth cannot be served by an inadequately retrospective and abstract sociologization, no matter how profitable that may be within the airless circles of professional historians straining to impress and write only for other professional historians. Allow me to paraphrase Yeats for the last time: Out of our colleges we have come; small minds, stuffy rooms; small hatreds, little art. That is one choice. The other is to recognize the truth inherent in Veronica Wedgwood's polite little formulation: "History is an art—like all the other sciences." For memory is an art, too: truly the mother of all arts.

5

American History:
The Terminological Problem

(1992)

During the nineteenth century the main events in the histories of Europe and the United States were different. In the history of the United States they were the westward movement, the Civil War, and mass immigration. In the history of Europe they were the revolutions of 1820, 1830, 1848, and then the—much more important—unifications of Italy and especially of Germany. These events were, of course, related to some extent, involving both continents, but not greatly so. When we come to the twentieth century the opposite is true. In the histories of both the United States and Europe, the main events for both were the two world wars. The rise of the United States as the greatest Atlantic power, the Russian Revolution, the Third Reich, the atom bomb, the end of the colonial empires, the establishment of Communist states, the division of Europe and of Germany, the emergence of the two world superpowers of the United States and the Soviet Union, the Cold War between them: all of these were the consequences of the two world wars, of those two enormous mountain ranges that towered over the historical landscape of the century, in the shadows of which we were living, until now.

The twentieth century was a short century. It lasted seventy-five years, from 1914 to 1989, its entire history dominated by the two world wars and their consequences. These consequences include, too, transformations of American society and transformations of American politics.

All of this should be obvious: but for many Americans it was not so obvious for a long time. For at least one American generation (and to many American historians) the most important event was the Depression and what followed it. That led not only to a change in the functions of Ameri-

From *American Scholar*, Winter: 17–32.

can government. It involved, in one way or another, the lives of more Americans than had the wars. Yet the Depression and its consequences were less important than the consequences of the two world wars. Whereas in Europe (and in England) World War I had already put an end to the limitations of massive government intervention into the economy, in the United States these limitations lasted until 1933, when government intervention was desired by the great majority of the American people. The Depression, and the reforms of the New Deal, brought no radical changes in American ideas and beliefs. (As a matter of fact, it often brought American families closer together, as both certain statistics and the reminiscences of certain thoughtful Americans reveal.) In sum, the transformations of American government and society consequent to the two world wars (and especially to World War II) were more decisive, in the long run more drastic, and—perhaps—less ineluctable than were the changes following the economic crisis of 1929–33.

The movement of American thoughts and beliefs toward a global involvement began to take form in the 1890s. This represented a profound, though gradual, change in the character of those beliefs. During the first one hundred years of American independence, most Americans believed that the destiny of the United States was to build a new world that was, and ought to be, different from the old world of Europe. During the next one hundred years, Americans came to believe that the United States was, and should be, the advanced model for the rest of the world. In many ways this happened: the Americanization of the world, ranging all the way from the adoption of American governmental practices to the adoption of American popular culture, made the twentieth century an American century. Add to this the remarkable fact (seldom seen thus by either American or European historians) that the American entry into the European war in 1917 was a more important—meaning: more consequential—event than the Russian Revolution in that year. So it was, both in the short and in the long run. In the short run, in 1917–18, Russia's withdrawal from the war did not decide its outcome, whereas America's entry did. In the long run Lenin's ideas about proletarian class-consciousness and the prospects of international revolution had a lesser effect on the world than had some of the ideas perpetrated by Wilson, that pale professor-president—including his propagation of national self-determination, instrumental in the destruction of entire countries more than seventy years ago, and continuing to be instrumental in our day. *Si monumentum requiris, circumspice.*

At any rate, when Tocqueville wrote *Democracy in America*, the United States was the only democratic country in the world; whereas in the twentieth century the democratization of many other societies should call for another work, a sort of Tocqueville in reverse: *American* democracy. Yes, there are elements in the democracy of the United States that make it different from, say, that of England or Germany or Spain or Japan, all democracies now. But: were the main political realities in American history still unique during the twentieth century, essentially different from those of Europe? Many Americans, including American historians, still think so. The purpose of this article is to demonstrate that they were not.

During the nineteenth century they *were* different. Yes, even during that century many of the nations of Europe were moving in the direction of democracy, albeit more slowly than the United States. Yes, the so-called Industrial Revolution (in reality, an evolution, not a revolution) affected countries in both continents. But during the nineteenth century the history of the United States was already the history of a people; whereas European history in the nineteenth century was still predominantly the history of states. (I am leaving aside the crucial term *nation,* to which I shall turn in a moment.)

The history of politics is the history of words. Tocqueville knew this when, 160 years ago, drawing the conclusion in part from his American experiences, he wrote that "a new science of politics is necessary for a new world." For 160 years this has not been really forthcoming, with the principal consequence that our political vocabulary has become antiquated and corroded, at times beyond usefulness, to the extent where not only confusion but corruption sets in.

It is at least remarkable that our present political terminology, in English, became current shortly before Tocqueville wrote *Democracy in America.* Of the three commonly used terms, the adjective *radical* is the only old English one. The political noun *liberal* (a positive and approbatory English adjective at that time, but only in a non-political sense) appeared in England in the 1820s; it was a political word borrowed from Spain. (For a few years the English used it in its Spanish form—that is, "*our Liberales.*") It was in the 1820s, too, that *conservative,* as a political term, was beginning to be employed in England; and it took another decade and a half before the Tory party began to call itself the Conservative one.

More remarkable is the fact that these terms—as well as those of "Right" and "Left"—rarely appeared in American political usage until well after the Civil War. The reason for this is simple. There was a fundamental difference between the United States and Europe, including England. All over Europe and England the debate and the struggle in most of the nineteenth century involved conservatives versus liberals. In the United States it did not. There was no conservative party in America. The very word *conservative* had a pejorative tinge in American usage when applied to politics (and even to other matters, on occasion). It may be argued that the Federalists were an American conservative party until their demise after 1816, or that the South was "conservative" when compared to the North (some of the southern political theorists and spokesmen began to employ the term in a positive sense, here and there, during the 1850s). In reality, they were not. Both the Federalists in the period 1810–20 and the Southerners in the 1850s were a peculiarly American mix of conservatives and radicals: both of them professed to believe in the sovereignty of the people—while in Europe no conservatives, and not even all liberals, had, as yet, accepted that. It was not until after the middle of the twentieth century—in 1954–55—that *conservative*, in the United States, began to acquire a positive meaning, and that a "conservative" political movement in the United States began to rise—one of the results of the decline of liberalism in America.

But in Europe the decline of liberalism had begun already around 1870. This has been remarked, and occasionally described, by some European (and especially British) historians. They saw the change from "classical"— that is, individualist—liberalism through the acceptance of universal suffrage, toward mass democracy, indeed toward the welfare state. What they often did not see was that after 1870 the entire antithesis of conservatism and liberalism (and, in some ways, that of Right and Left) was losing its meaning. Until about 1870 in England, and in much of Europe, the main debate and struggle was the one between conservatives and liberals. After 1870 this was less and less the case.

There were two factors in this transformation. One (and perhaps the less important) factor was that the advocacies of conservatives and liberals had begun to overlap. The British and European conservatives were becoming liberals, since they were now prone to accept (and were even willing to profit from) the functioning of mass democracy, including extensions of universal suffrage, the gradual disestablishment of state churches, the abolition of censorships of various kinds, and the predominance of industry over agriculture. The remaining old-fashioned liberals, on the other hand, had become conservatives, at least in the broad sense of that word. The liberal parties were still, by and large, the parties of reform, but less and less so; and their opposition to authority evoked fewer and fewer echoes in the minds of the masses. (There were exceptions to this, of course, old-fashioned liberals such as Gladstone or a newer type such as Lloyd George who was, in reality, a nationalist radical of sorts.) Something else had begun to appear, with plentiful echoes among the masses. This was the novel phenomenon of popular nationalism (misunderstood and ignored by Marx, who could not distinguish the *nation* from the *state*).

That was the second, and probably more important, factor of the piecemeal fading of the great conservative-liberal division. Unlike the Hegelian (or Marxian) scheme, the main result of the fading of the antithesis was not that of a new and transcendent synthesis. In reality, conservatism versus liberalism was being replaced by a new and near-universal antithesis—antithesis at first, conjunction afterward—resulting in nationalism and socialism. For about one hundred years, from 1770 to 1870, the main political realities were those of conservatism and liberalism, their struggles and their relationships. For the next hundred years after 1870 these were replaced by nationalism and socialism.

About socialism there is not much to say, since its development has been (or rather, should be) obvious. Democracy, as Tocqueville saw, involves the propagation and the extension of equality even more that that of liberty. The welfare state was in the making a generation before, say, Franklin Roosevelt or Léon Blum, by such diverse men as Bismarck or Theodore Roosevelt. Nothing is inevitable in history; but by the beginning of the twentieth century the inclinations of governments—whether freely elected or not—to provide for the welfare of the majority of their peoples was about as inevitable as anything. In 1894 Sir William Harcourt, an old and respected liberal leader in the House of Commons, uttered his celebrated and melancholy exclamation: "We are all Socialists now!" Only it was national, not international, socialism that was in the making. The first of these adjectives turned out to be more important than the second. "Socialism" was becoming a general phenomenon; but the word was avoided in certain countries and qualified in others. In England, the conscious and cautious policy of the early labor movement to eschew, at least for a while, the very word *socialist* attests to this. Another example was the emergence of "Christian" socialists in Central Europe. Despite their assertion of respect for the positive social teachings of the Catholic church (anti-Marxist as well as anti-capitalist), the new political adjective *Christian* was a nationalist term, negative and exclusive, meaning non-Jewish, nonliberal, non-Marxist, non-cosmopolitan, non-international. Where the socialists had a bad reputation this was not because they were dangerous radicals; they were dangerous because they were antinational.

Our problem with "nationalism," perhaps especially in English, is more complicated. The reason for this is its relatively late appearance in English (also in some other European languages)—an indication, in itself, that nationalism is a very modern, and not at all a reactionary phenomenon. *Nationalism,* in English, appeared first in 1844 (*O.E.D.*), by and large within the same quarter century when *conservative, liberal,* and *socialism* (as well as *capitalism:* 1854 [*O.E.D.*]) acquired their political meaning. Among all of these terms, the reality of nationalism is the least outdated, since it has proved to be the most enduring and powerful of all of them.

That *nationalism* differs—and often profoundly—from *patriotism* is a reality to which we should have paid more attention, especially in the United States where the two terms are still regrettably confused: when Americans speak of a super-patriot they really mean an extreme nationalist. When Dr. Johnson pronounced his celebrated phrase, "Patriotism is the last refuge of scoundrels," he meant nationalism, since the definition of the word in English did not yet exist. When Hitler, writing about his political philosophy in *Mein Kampf,* said that "I was a nationalist; but I was not a patriot," he knew exactly what he meant, and so ought we. Patriotism (as George Orwell noted in one of the few extant essays about its distinction from nationalism) is defensive, while nationalism is aggressive; patriotism is rooted to the land, to a particular country, while nationalism is connected to the myth of a people, indeed to a majority; patriotism is traditionalist, nationalism is populist. Patriotism is not a substitute for a religious faith, whereas nationalism often is; it may fill the emotional—at least superficially spiritual—needs of people. It may be combined with hatred. (As Chesterton wisely said, it is not love, which is personal and particular, but hatred that unites otherwise disparate men. "The ardent nationalist," said Duff Cooper, "is always the first to denounce his fellow countrymen as traitors.")

One hundred years ago it seemed that nationalism and socialism were antitheses, respectively on the far Right and the far Left of the political spectrum. The reason for this was not that of the difference between their economic, or even social, ideas. The reason was that socialists, at that time, were internationalists, anchored in the belief that class-consciousness was stronger than the sense of nationality. They were wrong. The Marxist idea failed—and how thoroughly!—not by 1989, at the end of the twentieth century, but in 1914, at its very beginning, when international socialism melted away in the heat of national enthusiasms like a pat of cold margarine in a hot skillet; when it appeared that a German (or a French or a British or an American) workingman had almost nothing in common with workingmen of another nation, whereas he had plenty in common with managers or even industrialists within his own nation. But already a few years before 1914, Mussolini, the young radical socialist and the brains of the Italian Socialist party, discovered that he was an Italian first and a socialist second—that is, a nationalist, and not an internationalist, socialist. All of this corresponded to another important change in the political vocabulary of the Western world. During the nineteenth (and late eighteenth) centuries, the words *people* and *popular* belonged only to the Left. Some time after 1890 these terms (in Germany, Austria, and also elsewhere) were beginning to be appropriated by the Right. In 1914, when he broke with the Italian Socialist party, Mussolini named his new nationalist newspaper *Popolo d'Italia.* This was five years before he would announce a new party, the Fascist one, and five years before Hitler joined a small National Socialist— *völkisch,* that is, populist—party in Munich. National socialism (and not only in Germany) was becoming a general phenomenon. The universal application of the adjective "fascist" to what people see as "the extreme Right" is wrong, and it confuses the issue. The worldwide phenomenon was not fascism; it was National Socialism. Neither Hitler nor Stalin were fascists; both of them were extreme nationalists, though the latter was careful not to admit this openly.

But this is not an article about the terminology of dictatorships. Hitler was only one of many who realized that nationality was more important than class, and that nationalism was more powerful than internationalism. Hitler was not the founder of National Socialism, not even in Germany; but he recognized the potential marriage of nationalism with socialism, and also the practical—and not merely rhetorical—primacy of nationalism within that marriage. He also knew that old-fashioned capitalism was gone: that belonged to the nineteenth century. (Before he had come to power someone asked him whether he would nationalize the German industries. "Why should I nationalize them?" he said. "I shall nationalize the people." Whether Krupp, in the 1930s, was nationalized under Hitler or not—and it wasn't—made as little difference as whether General Electric in the 1950s, whose main products under Eisenhower were no longer toasters but space rockets, was nationalized or not.) The economic structure that Hitler had in mind (and achieved) had few of the characteristics of either Marxian or state socialism; but it could not be called capitalist either.

Fifty years later nationalism still remains the most potent political force in the world. In this sense national socialism survived Hitler. Every state in the world has become a welfare state. Whether they call themselves socialist or not does not matter much. Of course the proportions of the compound of nationalism and socialism vary from country to country; but the compound is there, and even where Social Democratic parties rule, it is the national feeling of the people that really matters. What was defeated in 1945, together with Hitler, was his German National Socialism: a cruel and radical and hate-ridden version of nationalist socialism. Elsewhere nationalism and socialism were brought together, reconciled and compounded, without violence and hatred and war. International socialism remains a mirage. We are all national socialists now.

That in the history of the twentieth century the prevalence of this compound—and the primacy of nationalism within it—is as applicable to the United States as it is to Europe is the main argument of this article, to the explanation and illustration of which I must now turn.

The struggle between American nationalism and American socialism, their animosities and their combinations, are a—if not *the*—principal reality in American political history during the last hundred years.

Because of the American emphasis on equality, Tocqueville already foresaw that all of American "individualism" notwithstanding, democratic societies, including the United States, would eventually tend toward welfare states, administered by huge bureaucracies. Tocqueville (and in this he was not alone among foreign observers of the American scene at the time) noted, too, the extreme pride of Americans in their country and in its political system, including their often hyperbolic rhetoric. But Tocqueville did not yet distinguish between patriotism and nationalism (understandably, since the latter term did not appear until about the middle of the nineteenth century). Only recently did a thoughtful American historian (James McPherson) draw attention to the evolution of Lincoln's rhetoric during the Civil War, before and at the beginning of which Lincoln is speaking mostly of *Union*, while this usage gradually gives way to his evocation of the American *nation*.

This, of course, corresponds to the coalescing opinion among American historians to the effect that among all of the multifarious and confused causes of the Civil War the principal one was not slavery but secession; what Lincoln—and, indeed, the majority of his countrymen (as the electoral statistics of 1860, too, show)—would not tolerate was the breakup of the powerful nation into two separate states, whether peacefully or not. Notwithstanding all of the bitterness between South and North that continued after the Civil War, no Southerner, after 1865, would advocate secession again: but not only because of the shattering experience of the South's defeat in 1865. After the Civil War the South (partly because of its military traditions) became one of the most, if not the most, nationalistic portions of the United States; and so it remained. The war against Spain in 1898 had the enthusiastic support of the South. Most of the American pacifists and anti-imperialists came not from the South but from the North.

"Your Constitution," Macaulay wrote shortly before the Civil War, "is all sail and no anchor." This proved not to be the case in the long run, but it was true in the short run: the Constitution proved not to be strong enough to avoid the breakup of the Union in 1861. What, then, many Americans recognized after the Civil War was that many of the American freedoms inscribed in the Constitution were either inadequate or undefined or both; that the existential and physical welfare of many Americans was endangered either by corrupt interpretations or by a maleficent neglect of those freedoms; that, in sum, the American democracy had developed its particular social ailments and political problems. The result was what American historians, such as Richard Hofstadter, would describe later as the Age of Reform. The principal propagators—and, often, agents—of those reforms were the Socialists and the Progressives and the Populists. I am listing them not in the chronological order of their appearance, and not according to their political weight (or influence), but in the descending order of their endurance. One hundred years after their appearance the Socialists have, by and large, disappeared from the American political scene. The Progressives, too—recently, for the first time in three hundred years, many Americans have begun to question the very word *progress*, which has lost much of its earlier and universal shine. Yet American populism, albeit in somewhat changed forms, is still very much with us.

The American Socialist party did not get very far (by which I mean that while there was a moderate rise in its fortunes until 1912, the vast majority of the American working class refused to vote for it). This is at least remarkable because in few countries of the world were the unbridled ravages of capitalist greed as evident as in the United States at the time. But the main reason why socialism was unpopular in America was not because individualism or free enterprise or economic freedom were traditional American beliefs strongly embedded in the minds of the American working class. The Socialists were unpopular in America because they were (or at least they had the reputation of being) internationalist—that is, not sufficiently nationalist. American workingmen did not like American capitalists either. In that distrust, too, there was something deeper than an economic motive: they saw Wall Street and the Eastern financial establishment as dangerously cosmopolitan and un-American. (We are accustomed to attributing the origins of this peculiarly American usage of *un-Americanism* to the American right wing, especially after World War I; yet striking American workers would on occasion call their employers "un-American"—for example, as early as 1903, during the Cripple Creek crisis.)

Many American historians, including Hofstadter, thought and wrote that the governing ideology of the era of the robber barons, of untrammeled capitalism in America, was that of Social Darwinism. I am inclined to believe that they were wrong. The belief in and the propagation of "the survival of the fittest" was not a typically American (it was much more typically a German) idea. What Americans took from Darwinism (or, more precisely, a much older American belief that Darwinism seemed to confirm) was the great cloudy idea of Evolution, or call it Progress. The American Progressives, beginning to coalesce around 1880, exercised as they were by the corruptions of capitalism among the fittest of Americans, believed in Evolution wholeheartedly; it was inseparable from their belief in, and addiction to, Progress. They believed that when and where American democracy was imperfect, this was owing to insufficient education and to insufficient social and political planning. Consequently they were proponents of progressive improvement: not only of better but also of more government, of progressive education, of progressive law, in the end including international law. Thus, as time went on, the ideas and the propositions of the American Progressives differed less and less from—indeed, they often became identical with—those of American liberals and American socialists. Many of the Progressive intellectuals became left-wingers. Those were the main reasons for the Progressives' ultimate demise. They too were insufficiently nationalist.

The American party, or movement, that was unabashedly nationalist from beginning to end was Populist. The Populists believed that the trouble with American democracy was that it was not democratic enough, that the people must have more authority, that they must govern and rule. (The Progressives *seemed* to agree—but what they *really* believed was that there ought to be more authority for the educators of the people.) The social, the ethnic, the regional, the religious provenances of the Populists and the Progressives were very different, but for a while they were allied, or at least they were not in direct conflict with each other. From about 1896 to 1912 (with the partial exception of 1904) most Populists voted Democratic while most Progressives were Republicans, but during World War I these relative associations began to wash away. The break between Populists and Progressives came in 1917, when most Progressives (Republicans as well as Democrats) had become committed internationalists, championing the American intervention in the War to End All Wars, while among the minority of congressmen and senators who opposed the war, the majority were actual, or former, Populists. Like their subsequent hero Henry Ford, the Populists incarnated the peculiar American mixture of conservatism and radicalism.

Neither the Populists nor the Progressives knew much history. Henry Ford's famous "History is bunk" as well as the Populist state legislatures' radically nationalist censorship of history textbooks and of history teaching show this; but so does the dictum by Julius Klein, Herbert Hoover's Progressive Assistant Secretary of Commerce in 1928: "Tradition is the enemy of Progress." During their ridiculous confrontation at the Scopes Trial in 1925, William Jennings Bryan, the Populist protagonist, proclaimed his unhistorical belief in the Bible, while Clarence Darrow, the Progressive protagonist, proclaimed his, no less unhistorical, belief in Science. For a brief time—from 1932 until about 1935—American Progressivism and American Populism seemed to march together again, supporting Franklin Roosevelt and the New Deal. But that soon ceased to be. Roosevelt's most dangerous adversaries were not the candidates whom the Republican party fielded against him in the presidential elections of 1936, 1940, 1944; they were Huey Long and Father Charles Coughlin, incarnating the potential of mass movements: Populists both. The final, and irrevocable, break between American Populism and American Progressivism would then coincide with the great division among Americans as World War II approached, when the deepest of divisions were not between Republicans and Democrats, not between relative conservatives and relative liberals, not between Right and Left, but between so-called isolationists and so-called internationalists. The ideology of the former was strongly Populist, and of the latter mostly Progressive. The Progressives were mostly Democrats now, American international socialists of a sort. The Populists were American national socialists to a man (or woman).

Here I must emphasize again the concordances of European and American history. During that most decisive and dramatic quarter of our century, 1920 to 1945, the history of Europe *and* of the United States (and of many other parts of the globe, too) was marked by the struggle of three forces. There was Western parliamentary democracy, incarnated by the English-speaking nations and by some states in Western Europe. There was Communism, incarnated and represented by the Soviet Union alone. And there was a new force, radical nationalism, principally (though not solely) incarnated by National Socialist Germany. For a while the latter was the most powerful one; as World War II proved, neither the American-British empires nor the Soviet Union could defeat it; for its destruction the unusual alliance of democracts and Communists was needed. That, however, is not my main point here. The main point is that this triangular contest appeared *within* the politics—that is within the beliefs and tendencies and allegiances of people—of many nations, including the United States. Despite the crisis of the capitalist order, the American Communists remained a minuscule minority even in 1932 (though not minuscule among American intellectuals); and during the war they were allied with left-wing Democrats—that is, with some of the remnant Progressives. Their main enemies (and, as we have seen, Roosevelt's main enemies) were the nationalist Populists (whom Hitler once, in June 1940, correctly designated as American radical nationalists). Neither the sectarian quarrels among the conventicles of the American Left nor the inchoate character of the two large American political parties must obscure this issue. There were nationalist Populists in both parties, including Anglophobes among the Democrats, but Roosevelt's strongest opposition came not from the Left but from the nationalists of the Right—a new kind of Right. Only a few days before Pearl Harbor, Senator Robert A. Taft (who even after the war would claim that the war against Hitler's Germany was a mistake) emphatically said that he was standing for American Populism at its best.

The new world that came about with the defeat of Germany and Japan in 1945 may have meant the final defeat and disappearance of American isolationism; but isolationism itself was an imprecise term (most of those who had opposed intervention against Germany and National Socialism were soon enthusiastic advocates of an international crusade against Russia and communism). That was not really the issue. Hitler and his National Socialism were gone; but nationalism was not. Indeed, nationalism remained the principal political force in the world—and so it is still. Socialism, especially in the United States, ceased to be an issue. By 1948, at latest by 1952, the Republican party accepted all of the institutions of the welfare state that had been erected by the New Deal. Since that time, all superficial rhetoric and appearances notwithstanding, the deep differences between the two political parties have never been economic. In every presidential election since 1948, the majority voted for the—seemingly—more nationalist candidate. In 1948, despite the Democrats' increasing unpopularity, the memories of the New Deal were still close enough for Democratic working people to produce for Truman a narrow victory over Dewey (not to speak of the circumstance that Truman gave the impression of being at least as much, if not more, of a solid American than was his opponent). But in 1952 large masses of the same people for whom Roosevelt had provided during the Depression deserted the Democratic party; in 1952 almost *any* Republican could have defeated Stevenson or Truman. Anticommunism, that essential ingredient of populist nationalism, contributed to that, often and strongly, though not always decisively. Joe McCarthy was a radical nationalist and populist (he once proposed the nationalization of insurance), but people turned away from him after a few years; people voted for Kennedy in 1960, and they turned down Goldwater in 1964. These were exceptions that prove the rule. In the United States—as also in other countries—most people do *not* always vote for the party or for the candidate who is the most nationalist; but they will *not* vote for a party or for a candidate that does not seem to be sufficiently—or convincingly—nationalist.

This is not the place for an examination of the psychology of American nationalism. We must keep in mind, too—in addition to the earlier stated difference between nationalism and patriotism—that their sentiments often overlap and often within the same person. Nationalism is not always, and not necessarily, wrong. Historically, too, it may be argued that during the nineteenth century the comparison between the relative nationalism of the candidates was the principal issue in less than half of the presidential elections. Even in 1932, 1936, 1940, 1944, people did not vote for Roosevelt because he was (or seemed to be) the more nationalist candidate. Yet it is the—seemingly—insufficient nationalism (together with the increasingly unpopular liberalism) of the Democrats that explains the almost unbroken decline of their presidential fortunes during the last forty years.

Hence the necessary consideration of a more accurate political terminology, reflecting the historical realities of the last one hundred years. Our political commentators and political scientists still say that the American two-party system differs from that of the European democracies, and even from that of England. This may be true: but it is not true enough. Yes: even in England, unlike here, the ideologies and the political advocacies of the two great parties seldom overlap; there have also been great changes in the configurations of the two or three principal English parties during the last hundred years, whereas in the United States the configuration, since 1860, has remained the same: two huge parties, Republicans and Democrats. We do not have much of a socialist party, and we do not have a radical nationalist one. What we have are the American compounds of national socialism: *the Republicans who are more nationalist than socialist, and the Democrats who are more socialist than nationalist*—whence the rise of the former and the decline of the latter during the last forty-odd years.

Much of this corresponds with what may be the most significant development in American politics in the last hundred years. This is the emergence of a "conservative" movement and ideology in the 1950s. (*That* decade—and not the 1960s—was the turning point in the political history and in the character of the institutions of the United States during the second half of this century.) For two hundred years there was no conservative party in the United States. There is one now: the Republicans. The very word *conservative* was avoided by every American politician as late as 1950 (when even Taft said on one occasion that he was not a conservative but an "old-fashioned liberal"); but by the end of the 1950s, Eisenhower, that supreme opportunist, declared that he was a "conservative." That had ceased to be a pejorative, a controversial, or even a dubious term. By 1980 more Americans designated themselves as "conservatives" than as "liberals"—partly because of some of the evident mistakes and excesses of American liberals, partly because of the positive reputation that some American conservatives had acquired, slowly but surely. However, let me repeat: both *conservative* and *liberal* are long-outdated terms, well beyond the extent of their first compromising corruptions.

We have seen that, long before the conservatives' appearance, the nationalist populists had moved from the Democratic to the Republican party. The American "conservatives" (whose movement began as a radical McCarthyite movement) have been overwhelmingly nationalist, and populist too.

Thus their propaganda against "Big Government" has been inconsistent. (I am leaving aside the—increasingly significant—argument that our present "conservatives" are opposed to conservation—that is, to an attachment to land that is at least as patriotic as it is "environmental.") They may have argued against bureaucratic extensions of the welfare state—that is, against an American version of state socialism—but they have been enthusiastic advocates of extending the power and the purse of an imperial presidency— the size of the White House staff alone was six times larger under Reagan than under Roosevelt at the peak of World War II—of the FBI, the CIA, and, of course, of the American armed forces. The original core of the American conservatives consisted of the cadre who had opposed siding with the British against Hitler during World War II; but their isolationism disappeared soon, while their nationalism grew even stronger than it had been before. During the 1950s (as Section Nine of the Republican party platform in 1956 shows: it called for the extension of American air and naval bases "strategically dispersed around the world") the so-called "conservative" party had become the advocate of American intervention throughout the world, and then into space.

I need not draw further attention to the inaccuracy of the "conservative" usage. Yet it is indisputable that the popular nationalism avowed by the conservatives has often accorded with the preferences of the majority of Americans. That Americans' electoral preferences are the result of their economic motives, that they vote with their pocketbooks, has become less and less true (if it ever was true at all); and so is that other half-truth, that Americans are not really interested in foreign policy—that is, in their country's place in the world. In the midst of the Depression, in 1932, a poll showed that a majority of Americans wanted to increase the size of the armed forces, that they were willing to pay for "defense." As I write this my eye is caught by an article in the *New York Times* (July 14, 1991) stating that 62 percent of the people polled now favor Republicans and only 52 percent favor the Democrats; and while 51 percent say that Democrats, rather than Republicans (only 22 percent state that) are likely to improve the American health-care system, the greatest discrepancy favoring the Republicans is shown in the answers of people to the question: "Which party is more likely to make sure U.S. military defenses are strong?" Sixty-one percent say that it is the Republicans, and only 19 percent say the Democrats—and, as some of the comments of the people interviewed show, *that* is what really counts.

The history of American nationalism is still to be written. Whoever writes it ought to be aware of its varieties and mutations, including the differences between a traditionalist patriot and a radical nationalist, and including the differences (so often confused by historians of immigration) between nativism and nationalism, among other things. That historian must be aware, too, that at the very time when "nationalism" became a popular slogan in the United States, proposed as it was by Theodore Roosevelt, it meant something quite different from the nationalism current in our day. Despite Roosevelt's Big Stick reputation, his propagation of an American nationalism was not at all populist, and his employment of the term had nothing to do with foreign policy. By emphasizing an "American national-ism" Theodore Roosevelt was anxious to promote the cohesion of the na-tion, worried as he was (and, let me add, worried as we ought to be) about the changing ethnic composition of the American nation. That other, more recent, phenomenon, when American nationalism was equated with anti-communism, is largely over, too. The history of Reagan's foreign policy alone proves that; but the unabashedly sentimental and emotional nation-alism represented by Ronald Reagan is still widespread and strong (as the excessive popular reaction to the Gulf War shows). Indeed, it seems that nationalism, with its symbols and its functional rhetoric, may be the only religion that masses of otherwise inchoate Americans have in common.

The appeal of socialism is long gone, and nationalism is as strong as ever. Within their compound, nationalism proved to be the more enduring element. However, it behooves this historian to propose a last observation. Nationalism, though still strong, will not last forever—surely not in the forms in which it has appeared during most of the twentieth century. That century is now over. The thesis of this article was that while in the nine-teenth century the near-universal political phenomenon was the struggle between conservatism and liberalism, leading to their eventual overlap-ping, in the twentieth century it was that of the relationship of nationalism and socialism. That will not last forever, for two reasons. One is the near-final completion of the earlier socialist agenda: since the welfare state is a universal reality now, the conflicts and the compounds of nationalism and socialism have lost much of their meaning. The other is the gradual fading of the power of the state, by which I mean the authority of centralized government.

All over the world, especially in the Soviet Union and in Eastern Eu-rope, but within the regionalist movements in Western Europe, too, na-tionalism has been devolving into ethnic tribalism. Given the changing eth-nic composition of the American people, there is, alas, reason to fear that American nationalism, too, may devolve into tribal struggles of a pecu-liarly American kind. (Another factor may be the gradual growth of super-national bureaucratic authorities—the ultimate authority and efficiency of which, however, are still far away.) But this question about the primacy of the state appeared even earlier. It marked one of the few significant differences between the Fascist and National Socialist dictatorships. To Hitler, the populist, "the people" came before "the state," both hierarchically and historically as he once said ("In the beginning was the *Volk,* and only then came the *Reich*"). To Mussolini, Fascist nationalism meant the complete obedience of people to the state. Yet the centralized state was, after all, a product of the Modern Age, beginning four or five centuries ago. (Consider the title of Burckhardt's famous chapter in *The Civilization of the Renaissance in Italy*: "The State as a Work of Art." It surely is not much of a work of art now.) And now, when not only the twentieth century but much of the entire so-called Modern Age is passing, there are many signs suggesting that something else will replace the authority and the power of the centralized and sovereign national states of the world. We are all national socialists now; but not for long.

6

The Historiographical Problem of Belief and of Believers: Religious History in the Democratic Age

(1978)

There is a chapter in the second volume of Tocqueville's *Democracy in America* which, in spite of the lasting reputation of this great work, has not received the attention it deserves. What is particularly regrettable, it has been overlooked by the historical profession, in spite of the latter being its subject. This short chapter, entitled "Some Characteristics of Historians in Democratic Times," contains only forty-eight sentences; yet at times a single sentence written by Tocqueville contains a particular argument so condensed and so profound that it would be sufficient for an entire book, indeed for the kind of book that could establish the reputation of a twentieth-century thinker or scholar. What serves me for the starting point of this address is Tocqueville's argument that while the writing of history in the age of democracy may seem easier than in the past, this will be mainly so for mediocre historians or for idea-mongers. To the contrary, he says, this kind of task, if approached honestly, will not be easier but more difficult, because the causes of historical action "are infinitely more various, more concealed, more complex, less powerful, and consequently less easy to trace, in periods of equality than in ages of aristocracy when the task of the historian is simply to detach from the mass of general events the particular influence of one man or of a few men."

This is rather different from what most of the great historians of the nineteenth century said. Ranke, who established many of the canons of professional historiography, had a vision of universal history before his aging eyes; yet he was concerned with the inevitable extension of the horizon of

Presidential address delivered at the fifty-eighth annual meeting of the American Catholic Historical Association on December 29, 1977. From *Catholic Historical Review*, April: 153–67.

history, rather than with what Tocqueville was thinking about: evolving changes in the very structure of events, and with the necessary adjustment of our vision thereto. Acton, who believed (or, perhaps, who preferred to believe) that history was essentially the history of liberty, wrote to Newman that what was needed, especially in religious history, was "the encouragement of the true scientific spirit and disinterested love of truth." We may keep in mind that in 1861 Acton's usage of the word "science" was close to the German *Wissenschaft*, something considerably broader than the popular meaning of this term a century later; yet we cannot avoid the recognition that Acton, like Ranke, shared the nineteenth-century ideal of scientific history. On the other hand Burckhardt, in one of his majestic lectures delivered in the Museum of Basel in 1870 to the patrician bourgeoisie of his native city, said: "We have not yet experienced the full impact of the masses, of sheer numbers, on religion, but it may yet come." What would happen to religion in the democratic age? Like Tocqueville, Burckhardt did not expect it to disappear; but, like Tocqueville, he was aware that mutations were developing in the very structure of events—and, consequently, as Tocqueville saw it, also in the reconstruction of events—when more and more people would affect the history of states, of nations, and of churches.

Now, more than one hundred years later, we should be able to recognize some of the problems that this evolution of the democratic landscape presents to the historian, including the region which we—necessarily imprecisely—call religious history. Our task is to attempt—a very difficult task, this—a history of believers, a history of belief. The history of religion in the democratic age transcends church history on the one hand, and the history of ideas on the other. Enormous difficulties are latent in this task; yet the complexity and the magnitude of its problems ought not deter the serious historian.

And what are some of these difficulties? They involve, first of all, the description of large numbers of people. This, of course, does not mean that history has become, or that it ought to become, a kind of sociology. Sociology was the consequence of new numbers, not of new methods, of the development of democracy, rather than that of science. The historian, whose principal task is understanding, rather than certitude, finds it more and more necessary to practice a kind of sociography, rather than sociology: a description, rather than a scientific schematization of society. He must delineate the profile of certain societies, including those of churchgoers. We have seen but the beginnings, a few masterful examples of this kind of historical sociography applied to the religious behavior of peoples, sometimes by French historians, at times along regional and geographical lines; but large areas of this field remain uncharted, unexplored, perhaps because of the extensive difficulties of this kind of research. For here is the second difficulty: the increase in the quantity of materials confronting the historian. Whereas in the past the historian—and perhaps especially the historian of religion—was plagued by the relative scarcity of records, increasingly the historian of democratic times faces an overabundance of materials, very much including printed matter of all kinds. For the democratization of peoples involves their bureaucratization—a somewhat novel phenomenon, whereby the inflation of society grows apace with the inflation of money and with the inflation of paper and, consequently, with the inflation of "sources" with which the historian has to deal.

What this means for the historian is that he must find evidences about the behavior of churchgoing people on all kinds of levels; he must research matters reflecting on the growth or on the decline or on the mutation of beliefs in a previously nonexistent, and now rapidly burgeoning, variety of depositories, ranging from publications of all kinds (and not only religious ones) to certain statistics and perhaps even opinion polls—while, at the same time, he must not rest satisfied by demonstrating his ability in gathering such materials; he must maintain a healthy, and often unfashionable, skepticism of some of their essential limitations. This leads to yet another difficulty, to the degeneration of the quality of some of these materials, a matter that has developed apace with the increase of their quantity. By "degeneration" I mean nothing more or less than a decline of their authenticity. When it comes to state papers, say, a letter by a high public official, a president or a minister in the twentieth century, the old Rankean distinction of primary from secondary sources may no longer make much sense at a time when personal documents are often not written, not dictated, at times not seen and not even signed by the very men (or women) whose signatures are affixed to them, in some cases mechanically; and there are evidences that in an increasing number of instances the high public officials of churches, too, will avail themselves of these mechanical bureaucratic epistolary practices. This decline of authenticity exists on all possible levels: consider only the difference (it is an essential one) between a petition actually signed by, say, one thousand men and women, and an opinion poll taken of the same number of people. In the first event we see one thousand actual signatures, of all possible kinds and shapes, a mass document, to be sure, but with its marks of personal expression on the paper; in the second we face nothing which is personal, merely a mathematical result which may or may not be correct but which, even in the latter case, is nothing but an arithmetical computation of anonymous choices, formulated and predetermined by the alternatives made up by the pollsters themselves. I am leaving aside the all-too-evident problem posed to the historian by the advent of the telephone or of the radio or of the teletype whereby important matters are communicated without being recorded for posterity; I am inclined to think that whereas the end of the Middle Ages occurred together with a sudden development of communications, the end of the Modern Age may be marked by the breakdown of authentic communications, paradoxically because of their overwhelming and extensive nature.

Up to this point I have said little that is unique for the historian of religion in democratic times. He must, of course, realize, for better or worse, all of the above. But his principal task is yet another one. He must describe what large numbers of people believe. And who are these people? Do they form a community? Yes and no: this is one of the component difficulties of the problem.[1] We can, I think, at the risk of minor imprecision, speak of the English Catholic community, say, of one or two centuries ago—as John Bossy put it in his excellent *English Catholic Community, 1570–1850* (a work which in itself may be symptomatic of the evolving recognition of relatively novel tasks toward which certain historians must now direct their attention). But the situation of Catholics in England, say, in 1750 or even in 1850, was not only numerically different from the situation of Catholics in the United States in 1950 or even in 1850. I am comparing two communities not only of different size, and not only of different social structure; I am comparing two groupings of Catholics whose mental attitudes *about themselves* were quite different. As such different observers as George Santayana and Will Herberg put it, most American Catholics, certainly during the last one hundred years at least, have considered themselves to be Americans who happen to be Catholics, rather than Catholics who happen to be Americans—a distinction which was not necessarily true of Catholics in England two hundred years ago, before their legal emancipation and, what is more important, before the development of the democratic age. The history of Catholicism in America and the history of American Catholics overlap as a matter of course, but they are not identical.

It is difficult enough for the historian to ascertain and comprehend what people did; it is even more difficult for him to find out what people thought; and it is, I submit, very difficult for him to know what they believed. Statistics may help—a little. Quantification will not. Religion—including even the outward expressions thereof, the behavior of people—is a matter of quality, rather than that of quantity. And in this respect it behooves the modern historian to be both commonsense and humble. He may do well to ponder the words of Cardinal Feltin who spoke about the religious situation in France in 1955: "What is the religious situation in France? What is the situation of the Catholic Church in France? It is extremely difficult to give a true picture of the underlying state of religion in France. Nothing is more dangerous than to make a judgment from the outside; yet my survey must be from the outside, as I cannot pretend to penetrate the souls of my fellow countrymen. On the other hand, by their behaviour people to some extent reveal their disposition."[2] These words were said in the *Institut Français* in London, in the great city where Dr. Johnson had pronounced his thunderous commonsense dictum: "Intentions must be gathered from acts."

"I cannot pretend to penetrate the souls of my fellow countrymen." "Intentions must be gathered from acts." Two sentences that alone should be sufficient to disprove the pretensions of psychohistorians. Such recognitions of human limitations are neither antiquated verities, nor are they admissions of defeat. It is because of the accumulated evidence of all kinds of acts and of all kinds of words that the judicious historian should be able to approach his task—with all of the humility that such a task calls for, to be sure—his attempt to delineate something concerning the beliefs of certain people in a certain place, at a certain time: a quest of their *religio,* not a categorical and "scientific" analysis of their *psyche* or *pneuma.* It is an important task. And, in spite—rather than because—of statistics at his disposal, the historian is free to make certain statements. Here is a model of a statement that has taken into account the assistance of statistics as well as their limitations. Writing about religion in England during the Victorian age L. C. B. Seaman wrote:

> . . . [T]he combined effect of the Sunday school movement and the spread of compulsory education by the end of the century probably meant that working-class children knew their Bible better in 1901 than their predecessors in 1837. Unquestionably, a larger proportion of the population stayed away from church in 1901 than they had done so in 1837.[3] How far this reflected a decline in genuine religious feeling is impossible to judge, since religious feeling is not quantifiable.[4]

There is no dearth of serious works on the history of the Catholic Church in modern Germany; yet there is little that has been written about the Catholic population of the Germanies. Materials, as many of us know, are more than abundant for research into the painful and difficult years of the Third Reich. The German hierarchy has shown a new kind of largesse, opening their archives, a practice that can be only welcomed by historians. We have the correspondence of the princes of the Church; we have the Vatican collections of documents during World War II; we have the papers of the German Ministry of Religion and Education, all kinds of censuses and statistics, the confidential reports of *Gauleiter,* of *Regierungspräsidenten,* of *Bezirksleiter,* of various police organs, including their confidential opinion polls. Yet, after all is said—or, rather, read—it is surprising how limited is the historical information we have about the evolving attitudes of populations in the Catholic regions of Germany during this otherwise over-documented period. In the often valuable and impressively voluminous papers of the Bavarian hierarchy, for example, there is preciously little material that the sensitive historian can gather about the mutations of behavior among the largely Catholic population of the region—where, on the one hand, the Hitler movement had its beginning and its focus for many years, a movement whose leaders and spokesmen were, more than often, ex-Catholics, in the milieu of a traditionalist and Catholic city whose population could not be said to have been generally hostile to it at the time; and yet, on the other hand, this population, from all the evidence, was also the one in the Germanies which remained the relatively most impervious to the pressures and the propaganda of the Third Reich. Writing about an earlier era in German Catholic history, as Father James Hennessey put it in a recent review of the magisterial *Handbuch der Kirchengeschichte* (edited by Hubert Jedin, Volume VI: *Die Kirche in der Gegenwari, 11. Die Kirche zwischen Anpassung und Widerstand, 1878 bis 1914*), "Is it set in large enough a context? What is its definition of the Church?" It deals with the governors of the Church and with its relation to the rulers of the world—not with the lives and with the religion of the governed:

> There is a real need for the history of the Catholic Church, its people, its institutions, its theology, in the whole modern world, in the total social, political, intellectual, religious context in which it functions and has functioned. [This work] is not that. But it has, at the moment, no serious competitor. That is a tribute to the editor and contributors. It is also a challenge to the rest of us who claim to be modern religious historians.[5]

❈ ❈ ❈

SHOULD we, then, be surprised that the first serious study of certain painful matters involving German Catholics during the Third Reich came from the pen of an American Catholic sociologist, Professor Gordon Zahn, and, later, by certain polemicists, whose sensitivities ranged from those of Catholic Christians deeply vexed by the insensitiveness of their people regarding the recent past to those of certain non-Catholic historians who were not only wanting in their sympathy for the difficulties of German Catholics during the war but who were wanting, too, in their historical understanding?

In the superbly edited Vatican documents on World War II we may find a very large amount of significant information on the relationship of the Holy See to the government of the Third Reich; we may find much important material about the relationship of the German hierarchy to either; we may even find much that is interesting and intriguing about the relationship of certain German prelates to each other—and yet there is amazingly little about the attitudes, the currents of opinion, about the very behavior of German Catholics themselves. I say "amazingly," since every serious historian, weighing the evidence of the relationship of the papacy to the Third Reich during those burdensome years, will agree that the existence of German Catholics was *the* principal concern of the Pope at the time. On the other hand, perhaps this is not so amazing, after all. Fragile, friable, unreliable, and incomplete as they are, the surviving records reflect the principal concerns of people at a given time. After all, history *is* a reflection of what people actually did and thought. In a despairing letter, on January 23, 1943, the aristocratic bishop of Berlin, Konrad von Preysing, cited the recent words of the nuncio, Cesare Orsenigo: "Christian love, it is all very fine, but the most important duty is not to make difficulties for the Church."[6] Is it going far to suggest that the regrettable narrowness with which this unduly cautious prelate conceived the duties of the hierarchy of the Church during those tragic years corresponds, in one way or another, with the undue narrowness with which certain historians of the Church are wont to conceive their own tasks; and that, conversely, the broadening recognition of the wider challenge before historians may correspond to a recognition of the wider concerns of a truly catholic Church?

Three or four generations ago Catholics in the United States were often, and in many places, regarded as a distinct and particular community of people. Thereafter much—though, of course, not all—of this distinctness melted away. Even before the election of the first president who was a Catholic a phenomenon developed in this country which had no precedents: after 1945, or at the latest by 1950, the fact that the holder of, or the aspirant to, certain public or government positions was a Catholic was no longer a handicap; to the contrary, it was an advantage. This was not merely a transitory situation during a time when anticommunism was equated with Americanism. It also marked a stage in the increasing acculturation of the descendants of previously immigrant Catholics to wholly American standards of behavior, patterns of thought, ideals, including certain peculiarly ephemeral concepts of American patriotism. It is evident, for example, that during both the First and the Second World Wars the Catholic population of the United States was more inclined to isolationism than were many other groups; and my researches of the period from 1939 to 1945 indicate that a president such as Franklin Roosevelt was not only impressed with this condition but that it was this fact in domestic politics, even more than international considerations, which lay behind his unprecedented approach to the Vatican as early as October 1939, and which continued to be the underlying matter in his correspondence with the Pope thereafter. It is, of course, obvious that a principal factor in these political and ideological inclinations of certain American Catholics was due to their national origins rather than to their religion: the isolationists were predominantly Irish-Americans and German-Americans. But it is wrong to state this in a simple, and categorical, manner. The Anglophobia of Irish-Americans during World War II was noticeably less than during World War I; and there were significant and, on occasion, important differences in their attitudes according to different social and educational levels among them. In 1945 the American Catholic population reacted to the gradually developing (and, during that year, still generally hidden) national concern with the Soviet Union more swiftly than other segments of the population. Was this sudden transmutation from their recent isolationist preferences to interventionist attitudes merely a reflection of Catholic anticommunism? Were most of their political attitudes merely attributable to their religion?

Certain serious, and conscientious, Catholic historians have attempted to deal with some of these matters; but there remain certain phenomena that are, as yet, unexplored. There is, for example, the phenomenon of generations. Between 1945 and 1960, for example, there occurred a great change. The numbers and the power of American Catholics were rising fast. They seemed to have plenty of vitality at a time when the power and the influence of Protestantism in America were declining. Catholics produced more children; they were advancing in the political arena; they had become not only full-fledged Americans but first-class Americans, not only typical but prototypical Americans, the natural paragons of American virtues in many ways. I repeat: during this era of national anticommunism—unlike during its first wave, the so-called Red Scare that had followed World War I—for the first time in American history being a Catholic was an advantage, not a handicap. Anti-Catholicism continued to be "the anti-Semitism of intellectuals," in Peter Viereck's apt phrase (another phenomenon that was not true after World War I); but this made little difference in the politics of the time. Many of these developments culminated in the election of John F. Kennedy, the first Irish-American and Catholic president, in 1960. Thereafter this development lost much of its importance. By becoming indistinguishable from other Americans, American Catholics lost some of their identifiable characteristics; together with the weakening of their often particular convictions, their vitality may have been ebbing. Kennedy was a good example of this. His political career from 1946 to 1960 was also the story of his evolution from a Catholic nationalist to an internationalist; it corresponded to his rise from the world of his father (who was often vexed by the thought that in spite of his wealth he was not being regarded as a top-class American) to the glowing pinnacle of the Republic—but perhaps at the cost of his more authentic convictions. The brilliant observations of the Spanish philosopher, Julian Marías, in his *Generations: A Historical Method*, about the third-generation phenomenon, clearly applies to John Kennedy:

> The most representative figures nearly always are found here. But we must remember: what is representative is seldom what is most authentic. This is a generation of "heirs" who have begun to live within a tradition. Once established in this tradition, and with a wealth of beliefs that generally support it, the heirs begin to test new attitudes. The ease that has marked their life, their not having felt any need to innovate and struggle with their surroundings, allows them to begin seeing the limitations of this way of life. As a consequence, the basic beliefs ... begin to weaken gradually and to rupture in certain individuals.[7]

Another phenomenon—or perhaps we should call it a problem—is that of respectability. During the nineteenth century, "when respectability stalked unchecked," there were many early examples of a widespread as well as deep-running tendency, perhaps especially in the United States, that should have proved Marx wrong: the so-called working classes were, in many ways, the most conservative, instead of being the most revolutionary, elements in society, because of their desire for respectability which, in turn, undoubtedly influenced their churchgoing behavior. Historians of immigration often allowed their commendable sympathies for the masses of immigrants to lapse into an unhistorical kind of sentimentality, one characteristic whereof has been their sometimes uncritical acceptance of certain legends. I should hope that a historian, well versed in the social history of certain first-generation American Catholics, would arise one day to write the necessary counterpart—a counterpart, not a corrective—to the justly esteemed work, written in 1925 by Gerald Shaughnessy, *Has the Immigrant Kept the Faith?*, a book with the putative title: "The Immigrant Acquires the Faith," the subject matter of which would deal with the untold number of Poles, Italians, Hungarians, etc., who, some time after their arrival in the

United States, chose to take some comfort in their parish membership for the first time in their lives; who, in plain English, became regular church-goers not in their old countries but in the United States, with all of its agnostic traditions, with all of its vaunted separation of church and state.

These are phenomena which often do not fit into the accepted categories of ideas; they are more complex than they seem at first sight; and consequently their reconstruction calls for unusual sensitivity as well as for unusual independence of mind among historians. Certain oddities and mutations of sentiment within the ideological profile of Catholic Americanism may be glimpsed from the Catholic press, but the historian must be aware of the limitations of this kind of evidence. While, on the one hand, the press will reflect accepted opinions, on the other hand, it will seldom reflect deeper inclinations of thought and of preference; and it is especially the latter that will often escape the attention of pollsters and of other samplers, with their predetermined categories of public (meaning: already well-recognized) opinions. He must search for some of his telling sources elsewhere, looking for matters at times in the vast and uncharted realms of literature. Any historian worth his salt who wants to know something about north-midwestern American Catholic life around the middle of this century will ignore some of the novels of J. F. Powers or of Larry Woiwode at his intellectual peril.

Religious history, I submit, must be *inside* history. The historian ought to write about matters that he knows best. It must be microcosmic and sociographic, not sociological and generalizing. Of course there exists a wealth of material, ranging from yellowed parish papers to family reminiscences, in the parishes and the neighborhoods of the American people that remain to be explored by the affectionate and careful, imaginative and scrupulous hands of their descendants. This kind of historical sociography—which is something very different from sociological historicizing—of the Catholic peoples of the United States is, in my opinion, the principal task ahead of the young historians of our association, and of those future members thereof whom we hope to train.

A difficult task, but an inspiring one, the relative novelty of which ought not obscure the fact that there exists a very long and rich tradition to sustain it. Exhortations of presidents of historical associations at their annual luncheon or dinner meetings usually do not amount to much. Yet we, members of this small but honorable association, ought, I think, take a certain kind of pride in our record. Many of our members have, after all, addressed themselves, and cogently indeed, to the root of our very matter: What is history? I said before that to find out what people believed is very difficult; but it is not altogether impossible; and this re-search (note the hyphen) into the real *religio populorum* remains, after all is said, a far more common-sense attempt than the ludicrous and cramped endeavor of the psychoanalytic categorization of—more exactly, the application of an ephemeral and pretentious vocabulary to—people who died long ago. There are few things more wearisome in a fairly fatiguing life than the monotonous repetition of phrases which catch and hold the public or academic fancy by virtue of their total lack of significance. The current fad of psychohistory, as some of us know, was inaugurated in 1958 by the late Professor William L. Langer in his presidential address to the American Historical Association. How insubstantial were the speculations of this eminent scholar, compared to the manly and coruscating address delivered by the president of our association, Professor Eric Cochrane, in 1974, when he spoke about "What is Catholic Historiography?" Cochrane was attacking the ancient and all too evident shortcomings of ahistoricism as well as of rehistoricization in church history; but he said, too, that "a historian who is also a Catholic has several notable advantages over his secular colleagues."[8] Without enumerating or summing up the cogent arguments of my eminent predecessor, let me add that, in my opinion, one of these notable advantages is the one to which I alluded earlier, when I spoke of the particular tasks confronting the Catholic historian: it is the condition of his participation.

Historical knowledge, as distinct from the method (or rather, the desideratum) still universally accepted in the natural and even in the social sciences, is participant knowledge. Unlike in the Cartesian scheme of the world, the total and complete and antiseptic separation of the observer from the observed is not only impossible; it is not desirable. And it is in this respect that our task is a dual one: we must consider not only the democratization of religion, involving the very structure of certain events; we must also keep in mind the element of mental intrusion into the structure of events. The question is not only, as my cogent predecessor phrased it, "What is Catholic Historiography?" There is another question: "What is a Catholic?" "Who is a Catholic?"—a question now answerable with greater difficulty than at a time when Catholics were a distinct community of their own, and when the desire to believe and the capacity to believe were still equally strong. Now, whether their history is the history of a community or not, whether it is the history of a subculture or not, is it merely the subject that determines Catholic history alone? Is it not also that of the observer? Is it not also the spirit—spirit as well as method—of their participation, of their relationship?

As early as 1829 Carlyle wrote:

Of the Ecclesiastical Historian we can complain, as we did of his Political fellow-craftsman, that his inquiries turn rather on the outward mechanism, the mere hulls and superficial accidents of the object, than on the object itself: as if the Church lay in Bishops' Chapter-houses and Ecumenic Council-halls, and Cardinals' Conclaves, and not far more in the hearts of Believing Men; in whose walk and conversation, as influenced thereby, its chief manifestations were to be looked for, and its progress or decline ascertained. The History of the Church is a History of the Invisible as well as of the Visible Church; which latter, if disjointed from the former, is but a vacant edifice. . . .[9]

Exactly one hundred years later, in 1929, Lord David Cecil wrote in his life of Cowper:

Religious ideas are now confined to religion. His reason working on his usual assumptions about life no longer leads a man to search for a religious explanation of any phenomenon he does not understand. But it did in the eighteenth century. The visitation of God seemed to him the most probable explanation of an epidemic, as defective sanitation might seem the most probable explanation to us. A hundred and fifty years ago even those who rejected Christianity believed in a first cause. Voltaire himself would have been surprised at some of the views held by an orthodox clergyman of the Church of England in 1929. . . .[10]

Much of this is still true; but much of it is also outdated. Religious ideas are no longer confined to religion; and religious history is no longer confined to the history of the visible church. My purpose is not to define new frontiers for the categories of *Kirchengeschichte, Religionsgeschichte, Glaubensgeschichte,* let alone to engage in the mental fabrication of new ones. If we have been advancing at all, we have been advancing from ecclesiastical history to the historical sociography of certain people, of a more-or-less democratic sociography that in itself suggests the compatibility of democracy with religion, something that surprised Tocqueville in America, since it ran counter to so many accepted and even intelligent opinions one hundred and forty-five years ago.

The story of the Catholic Church is epic and history at the same time; but, as the young Ortega y Gasset said, history and epic are two different things:

The theme of the epic is the past as such: it speaks to us about a world which was and which is no longer, of a mythical age whose antiquity is not a past in the same sense as any remote historical time. . . . The epic past is not *our* past. Our past is thinkable as having been the present once, but the epic past eludes identification with any possible present. . . . No, it is not a remembered past but an ideal past.[11]

Or, as his principal exegete Marías put it:

We cannot understand the meaning of what a man says unless we know *when* he said it and *when* he lived. Until quite recently, one could read a book or contemplate a painting without knowing the exact period during which it was brought into being. Many such works were held up as "timeless" models beyond all chronological servitude. Today, however, all undated reality seems vague and invalid, having the insubstantial form of a ghost.[12]

The Catholic historian, as Eric Cochrane said, "will inevitably recognize that the history he writes is not necessarily the same as the history written by his non-Catholic colleagues"—to which I shall add that, at his best, the Catholic historian will take a kind of inner satisfaction from this condition, instead of being either complacent or uncomfortable about it. "He will," Cochrane went on, "insist that history not be just the pastime of an elite, but an essential category of human thought and action of great importance for mankind as a whole. He will, therefore, avoid isolating himself in wall-to-wall think-tanks, surrounded only by special students and PhD candidates. He will be solicitous for the teaching of history on all levels, from elementary to graduate schools, and for the diffusion of historical information and attitudes to the general public"—to which I shall add that, having acquired his union card, degree, or tenure, he will not regard it beneath his dignity to struggle against the deadening and dumbfounding practices of an ecclesiastical bureaucracy which has thoughtlessly permitted the elimination of not only church history but of much of history from the Catholic schools of this country, and which recently presented a sapless and ahistorical Catechetical Directory (a word that brings the telephone book to mind) to the American Catholic hierarchy for their approval. "Catholic historians," as my predecessor acutely said, "have an obligation to apply in their professional work a theological doctrine . . . of the sanctity of vocations. They must regard the work of historical inquiry not as a way of gaining social prestige, of building academic empires, or of making payments on suburban swimming pools."[13] To which I shall also add, in conclusion, that guardians of a tradition as we are, we are also its constant procreators. What we are fighting is not merely a rearguard fight; and we should be fully aware of its eventual dimensions. If history is philosophy teaching by example, we may add to Dionysius Halicarnassus that the historian ought to be a philosopher teaching by his own, existential, example. Or perhaps, to paraphrase Saki, the art of historianship consists to a great extent of knowing exactly where to stop and going a bit farther.

7

What *Is* History?

(2003)

W*hat Is History?* is the title of Edward Hallett Carr's 1961 Trevelyan Lectures, a book that, we are told, sold hundreds of thousands since that time. The authors of two of the books listed below consider *What Is History?* not only a milestone but a decisive turning point in the history of history itself. This is why I must begin this review-essay with a summary of my reservations about Carr's view of history.

I read *What Is History?* in 1961, when I was in the middle of writing my *Historical Consciousness* (published in 1968, with additions in 1985 and 1994), in the index of which I see at least eleven references to Carr, all of them critical or even dismissive. In my recent *At the End of an Age* (2002), there are only two short discussions of Carr, but I also wrote that "Carr's book was fairly well written (though poorly thought out)." Before writing the present essay, I thought I should reread Carr: I can now report that I found *What Is History?* better than when I first read it, fired as I had been with youthful energy and vanity, more than forty years ago. But my criticisms of his essential themes remain the same.

There was Carr's inclination to assert something like subjective determinism: "Before you study the history, study the historian." Yes: the understanding of history, as indeed all human knowledge, is participant. But this is not what Carr asserted. In his view the historian's background (especially his social background) virtually determines the history he will write. This is arguable, to say the least—consider but the sons of rich bourgeois who became Marxists, or the offspring of Jewish Marxists who chose to become neoconservatives. In the same book—and this is perhaps even more

From *Historically Speaking,* February: 9–12. Books considered in this essay include: Edward Hallett Carr, *What Is History?* (1961); David Cannadine, ed., *What Is History Now?* (2002); John Lewis Gaddis, *The Landscape of History: How Historians Map the Past* (2002); and Paul Veyne, *Writing History: Essay on Epistemology,* translated by Mina Moore-Rinvolucri (1984).

serious—the subjectivist Carr could not detach himself from the objective-subjective terminology: "It does not follow that, because a mountain appears to take on different angles of vision, it has objectively no shape at all or an infinity of shapes." But the more objective our concept of the shape of the mountain, the more abstract that mountain becomes. Moreover, the existence of the mountain was meaningless until men appeared and saw it, and eventually called it a mountain. (Much later they conceived it as an "objective fact.") There was the otherwise independent Carr's assertion of professionalism, insisting on a distinction between facts and historical facts. But is there a true difference between a source and a historical source, or indeed between a person and a historical person? There was Carr's insistence that no longer can historians eschew considering seriously a philosophy of history: "those historians who today pretend to dispense with a philosophy of history are merely trying, vainly and self-consciously, like members of a nudist colony, to recreate the Garden of Eden in their garden suburb." But, as Jakob Burckhardt said, a philosophy of history is a "contradiction in terms: for history coordinates, and hence is unphilosophical, while philosophy subordinates, and hence is unhistorical." Worse: to illustrate his thesis Carr cited approvingly A. L. Rowse, who had written that Churchill's history of World War I was "inferior" to Trotsky's history of the Russian Revolution, because Churchill's "had no philosophy of history behind it."

I must now, for the sake of this review-essay, attempt to place Carr's dicta within the evolving intellectual history of the West in the twentieth century. Some of his admonitions were proper and even overdue: that British historians ought to move beyond parochialism and direct their interests to hitherto largely untouched subjects and peoples. The most valuable pages of *What Is History?* were its very first ones, where Carr contrasted the historicist confidence of British historians around 1900 with the chastened view of other historians, including himself, sixty years later. He did this in a lucid and convincing manner; it was both proper and right (and, for the success of his book, immensely useful) that he began it with that very argument. But what perhaps most of his readers missed was that this recognition was not at all original. The Cartesian and objectivist and scientific conception of the world and of human knowledge was surely on the wane, reaching many historians during the twentieth century: Croce, Collingwood, Oakeshott, Becker, Beard, and others rejected objectivism well before Carr. And they were but a few examples of a deeper and much more powerful movement: a kind of subjectivist or idealist determinism (of which an extreme version was German National Socialism, among other things). Well before 1900 John Henry Newman already said that "Acton expected from History more than History can furnish," the Acton (not to speak of Bury, etc.) who believed and claimed that historical science had reached a stage where it could produce results that would be unchanging, perennial, fixed: that the purpose of history is the definite and final establishment of certain truths. No: the purpose of history is the reduction of untruths—which is not what Carr saw and wrote. Indeed, Carr still insisted that history is a scientific and not literary discipline.[1]

And so, as its title suggests, *What Is History Now?* is plainly and squarely dedicated to the fortieth anniversary of Carr's book. It is, by and large, a dreadfully boring volume for which its editor David Cannadine, an excellent historian, should not be blamed. He is but editor of a volume that reprints the lectures of a two-day symposium, held at the Institute of Historical Research in November 2001 in London, to mark the fortieth anniversary of *What Is History?*: "the classic we celebrate and commemorate in this volume," as one of its contributors (Linda Colley) says. Another contributor, Alice Kessler-Harris, begins her treatise: "My argument is predicated on a reading of Carr that is forty years old and originates in the United States. My generation of graduate students in the U.S. cut their teeth on E. H. Carr." (Much dental work badly needed, including orthodontics.) "For many of us who were in training in the 1960s, Carr offered a way out of the empirically based objectivism that had been the hallmark of historical studies till then, attacking full throttle its claims to truth." Borrowing Carr's epigraph, Kessler-Harris quotes Jane Austen's Catherine Morland who thought it odd that history "should be so dull, for a great deal of it must be invention." She concludes: "I would guess that Catherine Morland would not find gender history dull. . . ." *I* would guess she would.

Here are the chapters of *What Is History Now?* "Prologue: What Is History—Now?" (Richard Evans), "What Is Social History Now?" (Paul Cartledge), "What Is Political History Now?" (Susan Pedersen), "What Is Religious History Now?" (Olwen Hufton), "What Is Cultural History Now?" (Miri Rubin), "What Is Gender History Now?" (Alice Kessler-Harris), "What Is Intellectual History Now?" (Annabel Brett), "What Is Imperial History Now?" (Linda Colley), "Epilogue: What Is History Now?" (Felipe Fernández-Armesto). One trouble—besides the often poor writing—is that most of these writers' materials are taken from very recent articles and books. Many of these references suggest an obscurity that they may well deserve. I must mention something here that I, and presumably many others, have observed recently. This is the pervasive and frequent use of colons in the titles of historical monographs. (Two of the innumerable examples in this volume, culled at random: Anna Clark, *The Struggle for Breeches: Gender and the Making of the British Working Class*; or J. Tosh, *The Pursuit of*

History: Aims, Methods and Directions in the Study of Modern History, etc., etc.) A diagnosis of recent historiography suggests that, besides orthodontics, colonic irrigation is also needed.

Throughout these chapters, vocabulary often substitutes for thought. Phrases such as "female space," "valorisation," "consonance," and "critical heartlands" abound. (E.g., "a valorisation of this kind of material gained momentum, with the anthropological drift of history in the late 1970s.") The relatively—very relatively—most readable chapter is that by Richard Evans ("Prologue: What Is History—Now?"). But that, too, is full of questionable phrases. "The advent of the computer made it possible for historians to collect and analyse mass quantitative data" (well, yes) "on the past in a manner and on a scale previously undreamed of." (No: Evans ought to know the difference between a dream and a nightmare.) His conclusion: "within the limits of what the sources allow there is plenty of room for differing emphases and interpretations, and Carr's influence has allowed historians to make the maximum use of it." Too much allowance here. Besides, Evans's own account of history allowed him to make some amazing judgments: "Attempts to roll the tide of liberalism back in the 1970s, led by figures such as Heath and Nixon in the United States, had ended in ignominious failure." I cannot comprehend what Evans was writing about; but then this is the same Richard Evans who in December 1987 (!) wrote that German "reunification is simply not a realistic possibility, and to talk about it or to advance historical arguments in its favor is to indulge in political fantasizing."

However, Evans is right in saying that to Carr "history was, in essence, a scientific rather than a literary endeavor." And in the epilogue the intelligent Felipe Fernández-Armesto gives a fair summary of Carr's dualities. Carr proclaimed that history "includes all people" (Yes, it does, but what is so new in that?)—while at the same time Carr insisted that "history was a science[.] I do not think he appreciated, as we are beginning to do today, the degree to which historians have to be scientifically educated." But this merely repeats C. P. Snow's trumpeting of *Two Cultures*, again forty years ago.

I must now turn, alas, to *The Landscape of History* by John Lewis Gaddis. Alas, because it is an astonishingly bad book; alas too because it is more difficult to review a bad book than a good book, unless, of course, the reviewer contents himself with a mere dismissal. Gaddis is a prominent historian of the Cold War, the subject of every one of his six published books—a large topic, but possibly insufficient to furnish material for an ambitious work dealing with the epistemology of history. "Self-doubt must always precede self-confidence," thus Gaddis warns historians, an admonition that he himself should have kept in mind. The very title and subtitle of his book—"how historians map the past"—are questionable. "So what if we were to think of history as a kind of mapping?" So what? A mapmaker pinpoints and *defines* what is present; a historian *describes* some things and people from the past. Gaddis suggests that Carr is one of his masters, but his exegesis of Carr is more than often confused and confusing. When, for example, he cites, verbatim, Carr's objectivist assertion of a mountain, Gaddis adds: "What it suggests to me, though, is that Carr, without having a word for what he was describing, instinctively understood the concept of fractal geometry and saw its connection to history"—a statement that is as ridiculous as it is presumptuous. "Fractals," "consilience," "counterfactualism," occur throughout his writing—along with a breezy tendency to demonstrate a trendy worldliness: together with Carr, Bloch, Machiavelli, Thucydides, etc., there are plentiful references to Tom Stoppard, Edward O. Wilson (the "consilience" preacher), Harry Potter, dinosaurs, and movies such as *Zelig, Being John Malkovich,* and *Star Trek.* There is an embarrassing passage where Gaddis quotes himself as he compares the Soviet Union to a dinosaur ("a troubled triceratops") as well as a respectful reference to Virginia Woolf's "famous observation that 'on or about December, 1910, human character changed,'" which of course was, and remains, arrant nonsense.

The sad and sorry matter is that so many of Gaddis's examples and illustrations are entirely mistaken. An important example occurs in the beginning of the book. Gaddis juxtaposes the photos of two paintings, van Eyck's "The Marriage of Giovanni Arnolfini" (1434) and Picasso's "The Lovers" (1904) with the caption: "Two representations of the same subject, one from a particular time (van Eyck) and the other for all time (Picasso)." This is wholly wrong. The subjects are not the same. The famous van Eyck painting is that of an arranged betrothal, the two young people are distant, gelid, staring away, merely touching hands because so ordered. The Picasso is pornographic, a drawing of a naked copulation. But, as Gaddis writes— and alas, sees it: Picasso's "image, like van Eyck's, leaves little doubt as to the subject. But here everything has been stripped away . . . and we're down to the essence of the matter." The essence of the matter? Is it love? In the Arnolfini painting both spiritual and physical passion are entirely absent; the Picasso drawing shows a carnal act. And Gaddis goes on: "Switch now, if you can manage this leap, to Thucydides, in whom I find both the particularity of a van Eyck and the generality of a Picasso." Well—one finds what one is looking for. . . .

Another exegesis is that of Machiavelli. Gaddis cites him: "a prudent man should always . . . imitate those who have been most excellent, so that if his own virtue does not reach that far, it is at least in the odor of it." Gaddis: "This is as good a summary of the uses of historical consciousness as I have found." Machiavelli: "for a prince it is necessary to have the people friendly; otherwise he has no remedy in adversity." Gaddis: "This gets close to what historians do. . . ." No: this has nothing to do with historical consciousness, though it may have something to do with the consciousness of an assistant professor in search of tenure.

Gaddis, like Carr, will not and cannot abandon the dogma that history is a science. At times he expresses this in a plebeian manner: as in basketball, baseball, etc., "you have to know the rules of the game." But history has no such rules. "Individual historians . . . are of course bound by time and space . . . in ways they could never manage as normal people." "Historians have always been, in this sense, abstractionists: the literal representation of reality is not their task." Reading this I am—well, almost—speechless (like other normal people?). "The key to consensus, in science, is reproducibility. . . ." The key to consensus, in science, is professional ambition: agreement with other scientists. Gaddis about Henry Adams: "The connection Adams looked for between science and history now seems quite feasible, and in a way that does violence to the work of neither scientists nor historians." Absolute nonsense. Not to speak of the fact that Adams predicted—scientifically—the end of history around 1921. Finally, a sophomoric and trendy vulgarity: "'Physics envy' need not be a problem for historians because—metaphorically at least—we've been doing a kind of physics all along." That is exactly what "we" (a usage of the plural which is indeed singular) have not been, are not, and will not be doing.

An entirely different work is that of the French historian and philosopher Paul Veyne, *Writing History: Essay on Epistemology.* Title and subtitle ought to have been reversed, because this dense and profound work deals really with the knowledge, rather than with the writing, of history. Indeed, one criticism of Veyne's theses may be his insufficient emphasis on writing, even though he understands how words are inseparable from facts, as this classic example shows:

> When we utter the words "the Roman family" without further precision, the reader is led to think that this family was the eternal family—that is, our own—whereas with its slaves, its clients, its freemen, its minions, its concubines, the practice of abandoning some newborn children (especially girls), it was as different from our own as the Islamic or Chinese family. In a word, history is not written on a blank page; where we see nothing, we

suppose that there was eternal man. Historiography is an unceasing struggle against the tendency to anachronic misinter-
pretation.

This is the work of an author of immense erudition in the classics. His
voice is Gallic, clear, querulous; with a few caveats the translation seems
excellent. His conclusions are wholly different, nay, the opposites of those
in the previous two books. History is not a science; "it will never be scientific." Marxists and economists say that the infrastructure "determines the
superstructure. But, on the other hand, the infrastructure itself is human;
there are no forces of production in a pure state, only men who produce."
"History has no method (and that is why one can improvise oneself as a
historian)," but "the danger of history is that it looks easy, and it is not." No
method, "since it cannot formulate its experience in definitions, laws, and
rules." "The historical explanation thus consists of rediscovering in history
a mode of explaining that we have, in some way, 'always known'; that is why
it may be called comprehension, that is why history is familiar to us." "A
historical concept allows, for example, the designation of an event as a revolution; it does not follow that by using that concept, one knows what a
revolution is." The worst history books were written by Oswald Spengler
and Georg Lukacs; the best, *La société féodale* by Marc Bloch. "The only
possible progress of history is the widening of its vision." There—but only
there—Veyne and Carr seem to agree.

Veyne's clear and sharp aphorisms ought not mislead the reader. His
book is difficult to read. And Veyne's dicta, or at least his terminology, are
at times debatable. "There is no *historical* or *historians'* consciousness." "The
knowledge of the past is foreign to consciousness." I cannot accept this,
especially from a historian whose book deals primarily with knowledge
and consciousness. The problem *may* be in the different nuances of two
languages: *conscience* and *connaissance* in French mean both knowledge and
consciousness (example: to lose consciousness, *perdre connaissance,* in French
means losing knowledge).

I cannot tell. What I can tell is that there is not a single reference to
Carr in Veyne's erudite book, chock-full of notes and citations and references from all kinds of philosophers and historians. These include not a
few from Henri-Irénée Marrou's superb *De la connaissance historique* (1954),
evidently unknown by all of the previous mentioned authors, even though
an English translation of Marrou *(The Meaning of History)* appeared in 1966.
(The same is true of my *Historical Consciousness,* but I am used to that.) So
much for "the community of historians," "international scholarship," "sci-

entific consensus," "the blessings of the Internet," "the Information Revolution," etc., etc.—all of them shibboleths, serving ignorance and obscuring learning.

8

Historical Revisionism
(1999)

In the Compact Edition of the *Oxford English Dictionary* the word *revisionism* does not appear. *Revision,* says the *O.E.D.,* is "the action of revising or looking over again; esp. critical or careful examination or perusal with a view of correcting or improving." The related entries do not mention historians. *Revisionist*: "One who advocates or supports revision" appears, interestingly, in the 1860s; it refers to people wishing to revise texts of the Bible. (In 1888 the *Times* reported the meeting of a Revisionist Congress, mostly involving texts of the New Testament.) That historians have criticized certain versions of events is of course obvious. Perhaps the first, and most eminent, example of a writer whose main impulse was to correct then accepted versions of legends was Thucydides, as he stated in his introduction to the *History of the Peloponnesian War.* Yet there are few instances when the works of chroniclers were principally aimed at disproving other chroniclers' versions. Around 1700 in France there appeared a group of scholarly priests (especially Mabillon and Tillemont) who, for the first time, applied critical (or, as some people might say, "scientific") methods to their examination of medieval documents and other sources. These so-called Erudites or Antiquaries were perhaps the first modern academic historians; yet soon their influence faded. Instead, the professional study of history and the appearance of professional historianship arose in Germany about two hundred years ago, spreading thereafter across the world. Yet the notion of historical revisionism—that is, the necessary revision or criticism not of legends or of doubtful sources but of the accepted versions of events established by professional historians—was rare. Of course arguments and quarrels among academic historians were never absent. But somehow the nineteenth-century view, according to which the Cathedral of

From K. G. Robertson, ed., *War, Resistance and Intelligence: Essays in Honor of M. R. D. Foot* (Barnsley, U.K.: Leo Cooper/Pen and Sword Books), 71–82.

Historical Knowledge was being built brick by brick, by certified professional historians—leading, for example, to an account of the Battle of Waterloo not only acceptable to British and French and Dutch and Prussian historians but also one that would be *definite* and *final*—did not recognize, as we do, that *all* history is "revisionism" of one kind or another. Those French historians, for instance, who were divided among themselves about the virtues and the vices of the French Revolution or of Napoleon evidently belonged to opposite ideological and idealogical camps; but few of their works were seen as "revisionist" in the twentieth-century usage of that term. To what extent—or, rather, when and how—"revisionism" is justified or unjustified is, of course, a philosophical question, to which this essay is not addressed, except perhaps indirectly, and in a few sentences at its conclusion. Its scope is restricted: (1) to revisionism among historians; (2) among German, British, and American ones; (3) about the origins of the wars of the twentieth century.

The term *revisionism* is of German origin. It was first applied to those German socialists who, around 1875, chose to mitigate the doctrine of the inevitability of a proletarian revolution. This Marxist usage does not concern us. But the present use of historical "revisionism" has a German origin too. It arose after 1919, reacting to the punitive and condemnatory treaty imposed on Germany and on its First World War allies. The wish to revise these treaties, to change the then drawn frontiers of Europe, was a powerful impulse, potentially leading to Hitler and to another war. However, the aim of German historical revisionism was not directed at injustices of geography; it was directed at injustices of the record—that is, at the unjust condemnation of Germany as having been uniquely responsible for the war, stated in the Treaty of Versailles. The Germans had every reason to combat that. As early as 1919 the new republican German government began to publish documents to prove that the guilt for the outbreak of the war in 1914 was not Germany's alone. More extensive and scholarly documentation was published in a series of volumes a few years later. Germans felt so strongly about this that in 1923 a German amateur historian, Alfred von Wegerer, began issuing a scholarly journal, *Die Kriegsschuldfrage*—the War Guilt Question.

Seventy-five years after 1914 matters concerning the origins of the First World War are still occasionally debated by historians: but "revisionism" or "revisionist" are no longer applied to them. In any event, the origins of the First World War were more complicated than those of the Second World War. No Hitler, no Second World War—more precisely, no Second World War in 1939: this is hardly arguable. Yet argued it is, sometimes subtly, sometimes less subtly, by some German historians. In this essay, which is neither a research article nor a bibliographical essay, I cannot list most, let alone all of them: my purpose is to point out certain historiographical tendencies. I must also omit works of special pleading, as for instance those by survivors of the Third Reich's hierarchy (the memoirs of Ribbentrop's widow for one) or ideologically inspired defenders of Hitler (such as David Irving). However, during the last thirty years we may find works by serious German historians (examples: Dietrich Aigner, Oswald Hauser, Andreas Hillgruber, Ernst Nolte, Rainer Zitelmann) who, without explicitly defending Hitler, state that Polish intransigence and British hostility contributed, if not led, to the outbreak of the war in 1939. Their purpose accords with the purposes of those German historians whose writings led to the Historians' Quarrel in 1986–87: to qualify or to reduce the German responsibility for the horrors of the Second World War. That is an understandable and, in some instances, justifiable impulse; still the arguments of some of these "conservative" or "nationalist" historians have been, more than often, questionable. They include three, occasionally connected, theses. One is that the crimes of the Third Reich were not unique, when considering those of the Soviet Union—perhaps arguable, except when a respected German historian such as Klaus Hildebrand claims that there was no such thing as National Socialism, only Hitlerism. The other, connected argument, especially pursued by Ernst Nolte, is that Russian Bolshevism had not only preceded German National Socialism but that the latter was really a reaction to the former. The third, argued by the late Andreas Hillgruber but also by others, is that after 1939 Britain was as intent to destroy Germany as was Russia—an argument then leading to the more widespread and popular German two-war theory, according to which the war of the Third Reich against the Western Powers, especially against Britain and the United States, was perhaps avoidable and regrettable, while by fighting Soviet Russia Germany acted as a bulwark of European and Western civilization; and this Germany's Anglo-American enemies, blinded by their hatred as they were, regrettably failed to understand. In the 1990s then came another wave of revisionism—in this case involving not the origins of the war in 1939 but the German-Russian war in 1941. Depending on newly found Soviet documents whose provenance and value is often very questionable, some German and Austrian writers (Ernst Topitsch) argue that Hitler's attack on the Soviet Union in June 1941 was a preventive move, since Stalin had been making ready to invade Germany around that time or shortly thereafter—an interpretation which found a few scattered supporters even in the United States and also elsewhere, despite its lack of serious substance.

Few British historians concentrated on the origins of the First World

War (a recent exception is Niall Ferguson), many more on those of the Second. It is interesting that the slow but massive reversal of British opinion about Germany after 1920 had few consequences among historians. Some time in the early 1930s there developed what was at least a tacit consensus among the British people and many of their politicians that the Germans had been wrongly humiliated by the Versailles Treaty. This recognition contributed considerably to the so-called policy of Appeasement, the elements of which were complex, and the discussion of which does not belong in this essay. The willingness to give the New Germany some benefit of the doubt existed among historians too, but it was seldom expressed in their books. In any event the revolution of British public opinion and sentiment in March 1939 brought about a deep change. After that, an inclination to actually favor National Socialist Germany hardly existed at all, except perhaps in the case of Arthur Bryant who finally thought it politic to trim his sails, to say the least, in May 1940. Nor was there any substantial change in the consensus about the origins of the Second World War until decades later. There were British writers critical of the Nuremberg Trials, but they were not historians. The only considerable exception was General J. F. C. Fuller, who in his trenchant military history of the Second World War excoriated much of British strategy. (One must also consider that General Fuller had expressed his sympathies with the Third Reich as late as September 1939 and that he was at times close to the group around Sir Oswald Mosley.) In his *The Origins of the Second World War* (1961) A. J. P. Taylor, without wishing to rehabilitate Hitler, argued that Hitler was not very different from other ambitious German statesmen of the past; that, in sum, Hitler was more of a short-term opportunist and less of a long-range ideologue than it was assumed. On occasion Taylor presented his evidence on the sudden development of some of Hitler's decisions convincingly, at other times with considerable legerdemain. His principal error may have been his statement that "Only Danzig prevented co-operation between Germany and Poland"—entirely contrary to Hitler's own statements, according to which Poland had to accept a new status as becoming a junior ally of Germany, without an independent foreign policy of its own. A change then came about ten years ago—the first crack in the national consensus according to which Churchill in the summer of 1940 was "the savior of Britain" (as even A. J. P. Taylor put it in one of the biographical footnotes of his *English History 1914–1945*). None of this British "revisionism" related directly to the origins of the war in 1939, but rather to Churchill's policy in 1940–41, rejecting any possibility of an armistice with the Third Reich, with the ultimate result of the collapse of the British empire. Maurice Cowling wrote that "the belief that Churchill had understood Hitler . . . was not true"; others wrote that in 1940 Churchill was "Micawber," waiting for something to turn up. Such were the interpretations of 1940 by the Cambridge historians David Reynolds and Sheila Lawlor. John Charmley went much further, questioning not only Churchill's character but also his policy to fight Hitler at any cost, including the loss of empire, suggesting at least that not to acquiesce in Hitler's domination of Europe may have been a mistake. The main shortcoming of such arguments can be summed up by saying that with Hitler in 1940 or 1941 no Peace of Amiens (the short-lived arrangement between Britain and Bonaparte in 1802–03) would have been possible, and that the determination of the British people and of their politicians to maintain the empire had grown faint long before the Second World War broke out in 1939.

At the beginning of this essay I wrote that *revisionism* does not figure in the first four volumes of the Oxford English Dictionary; but it is included in the 1987 edition of its *Supplement*, where, rather significantly, it is stated prominently among other sub-entries: "mostly U.S., a movement to revise the accepted versions of American history, esp. those relating to foreign affairs since the war of 1939–45." This attribution or, rather, connection of "revisionism" to its American concept and usage is both significant and correct, since in no country other than the United States were the successive waves of revisionism so influential in molding public opinion and even national politics at large. The only exception to the *O.E.D.* statement to consider is its last clause: for revisionism, in the United States, meaning the very usage of the term, preceded 1945. Consequently, to a necessarily brief survey of the four waves of American revisionism, insofar as they relate to the origin of twentieth-century wars, I must now turn.

Of these four waves of revisionism the first was the longest and strongest. It began as an intellectual and academic (and sometimes also a political and ethnic) reaction against the extreme propagandistic condemnation of Germany in 1917–1919. It was a reaction by liberals and radicals against superpatriotism, not very different from (and often allied with) their opposition to American conformism to the postwar Red Scare, to the Ku Klux Klan, to the propaganda of the American Legion of the 1920s. As early as 1920, for example, the *Nation* attacked the dangers of French, not of German, militarism. In September 1921 this journal posed the question: "Who has contributed more to the myth of a guilty nation plotting the war against a peaceful Europe than the so-called historians who occupy distinguished chairs in our universities?" They were "willing tools" of "professional propaganda." The young and later distinguished Sidney Bradshaw Fay (not a typical revisionist, I must add) had already published three successive articles in the *American Historical Review* ("New Light on the Origins of the

World War"), a result of his reading of the then recently published German, Austrian, and Russian documents. Within five years this first wave of revisionism swelled into a tide. Revisionists now included respected members of the historical profession: the prominent Charles A. Beard, the University of Chicago historian Ferdinand Schevill, who wrote in 1926 that "there are today among reputable historians only revisionists." In the same year *The Genesis of the World War*, by the sociologist turned historian Harry Elmer Barnes, disdainful of France and Britain, while very favorable to Germany, was published by the reputable house of Knopf. The revisionist cause was supported by many amateur historians, also by celebrated literary figures such as Albert J. Nock and H. L. Mencken, and by the editors of some of the most prominent literary weeklies and monthly magazines of the United States.

By 1929–30 the revisionist tide was further swelled by the predictable confluence of another historical argument, about 1917 and not 1914. The time had come to revise not only the thesis of German war guilt but the story of the American involvement in the war. The first such substantial book was published in 1929 by C. Hartley Grattan, a onetime student of Barnes. By the early 1930s article after article, book after book, was attacking American intervention in the First World War. The most serious work was Walter Millis's *The Road to War*, published in 1935. The most determined book by a professional historian was Charles Callan Tansill's *America Goes to War* in 1938. By that time their arguments had filtered down from academia and from intellectual periodicals through the reading public to the broad lowlands of popular sentiment. *The Road to War* was a bestseller, with sixty thousand copies in print by 1936. A few months later Gallup reported that 70 percent of Americans thought it had been wrong to enter the First World War. Meanwhile Hitler, Mussolini, and the Japanese were rising in power.

In 1938 and 1939 another current in the revisionist tide came to the surface. Many revisionists were now worried about what they saw as an ominous change in Franklin Roosevelt's foreign policy. (In 1932 Roosevelt's foreign policy was generally isolationist, and as late as 1935 he went so far as to suggest his acceptance of certain revisionist theses.) In September 1939 Beard published a powerful small book against American intervention in Europe, *Giddy Minds and Foreign Quarrels*. Yet by 1940 the revisionist camp was badly split. Many of the liberals were coming around to support Britain against Hitler. Others were not. In 1940 Beard came out with another book, *A Foreign Policy for America*. Eleven years later Senator Robert A. Taft published a book with a virtually identical title; yet already in 1940 it was evident that the formerly radical and Jeffersonian Democrat Beard and the conservative Republican Taft were seeing eye to eye. But before the next year was out the news of Pearl Harbor roared over them both.

Revisionism was submerged but not sunk. After 1945 came the second wave of American revisionism, attacking Roosevelt for having maneuvered the United States into war; indeed, for having contributed surreptitiously and willfully to the catastrophe at Pearl Harbor. Many of the historians were the same ones as before, the two principal professionals among them Beard (*American Foreign Policy in the Making, 1932–1940* and *President Roosevelt and the Coming of the War*) and Tansill (*Back Door to War*). There were, and are still, many others, but this second wave of revisionism received relatively little attention, many of the revisionist books being now printed by minor publishers. Yet the effect of this kind of revisionism was wider than the publishing record might indicate. The majority of the so-called "conservative" movement that began to coalesce in the early 1950s was composed of former isolationists and revisionists. A principal element of the Republican surge after 1948 was a reaction against Roosevelt's foreign policy, including such different figures as Joseph R. McCarthy, John Foster Dulles, and the young William F. Buckley Jr. It was part of the emergence of the New Right in American politics. Still, Hitler and Tojo had few public defenders, and this second wave of revisionism failed to swell into an oceanic current.

The third, and much larger, wave of revisionism came not from the New Right but from the New Left. These were the historians who during the fretful 1960s attempted to rewrite the origins of the Cold War with Russia, arguing and claiming that American foreign policy and aggressiveness were at least as responsible, if not more, for the coming of the Cold War than was the Soviet Union. The principal ones (again, there were many others) of these New Left historians were D. F. Fleming (*The Cold War and Its Origins*), William Appleman Williams (*The Tragedy of American Diplomacy*), Gar Alperovitz (*Atomic Diplomacy*), David Horowitz (*The Free World Colossus*), Gabriel Kolko (*The Politics of War*), Diane Shaver Clemens (*Yalta*), and Lloyd C. Gardner (*Architects of Illusion*), all of these books issued between 1959 and 1970 by most reputable university presses and trade houses. Unlike the revisionists of the 1920s and 1940s these authors had little opposition from most of their historian colleagues: for such was the, generally Leftist, intellectual tendency of the American 1960s. These authors were praised and portions of their works were anthologized in college readers and textbooks. Whereas the revisionists of the 1920s and 1930s had their greatest effect among general readers, most of the consumers of this third wave of revisionist prose were college students. When Robert Maddox, in his precise and serious *The New Left and the Origins of the Cold War* (1973), pointed out many of the dishonesties of the documentation and the inadequacies of scholarship in these books, he was treated with tut-tutting and fence-sitting by most academic reviewers. However, as with so many fads and fashions of the 1960s, the tide of Cold War revisionism, though temporarily overwhelming, did not endure for very long.

By the 1990s we may detect the rise of the fourth wave of revisionism, coming again from the so-called Right rather than from the Left. We have now seen some of its evidences in Germany and in Britain. During the Reagan years in the United States there appeared a tendency to question not only the evident problems of the American welfare state but the establishment of its tenets by Roosevelt and the New Deal; and new indictments (and I fear not always well-warranted and judicious ones) of American foreign policy before and during the Second World War are also beginning to appear. In sum, there is reason to believe that this newest wave of revisionism, already apparent in Germany and Britain (and of course also in Russia), will spill over to the American side of the Atlantic too.

What revisionist historians claim, or at least emphatically suggest, is that their scholarship is better and their intellectual independence stronger than that of their opponents. Yet this has seldom been true. On the contrary, few of the revisionists have been immune to the ideological tendencies of their times. In 1917 Beard was an extreme interventionist. The United States "should help eliminate Prussianism from the earth." Germany represents "the black night of military barbarism . . . the most merciless military despotism the world has ever seen." By 1926 he was a Germanophile, influenced not only by the revelations in the German diplomatic documents but by German philosophies of history. Beard was not an opportunist, and even in the 1930s he insisted that he was not really an isolationist; rather, he was struggling with that seemingly concrete but, alas, often malleable concept of national interest. (In 1932 Beard received a twenty-five-thousand-dollar grant—a very large sum then—from the Social Science Research Council for the precise definition of "national interest." The result was one of his few unreadable books.) At that time he was a fervent supporter of Franklin Roosevelt, but soon he turned even more fervently against him.

The case of Barnes is even more telling. His first revisionist articles appeared in 1924, arguing for a division in the responsibilities for the outbreak of the First World War. By 1926 he was going further: France and Russia were responsible. Thereafter he became more and more extreme and violent. He was invited to lecture in Hitler's Germany, as was Tansill. In 1940 Barnes volunteered to promote the circulation of official German propaganda volumes. After the war he became an admirer of Hitler: "a man whose only fault was that he was too soft, generous and honourable." The Allies had inflicted worse brutalities on the Germans than "the alleged exterminations in the gas chambers." This, of course, was the extreme case of a once talented but embittered man, driven to such statements by what he called *The Historical Blackout,* one of his later pamphlets. Everything was grist to his mill, including the most dubious "sources" and "evidences." The same was true of Tansill, who in 1938 wrote in his introduction to *America Goes to War:* "Crusading zeal is hardly the proper spirit for an impartial historian." Yet Tansill was the prototype of a zealous crusader, in both of his big revisionist works about the two world wars. Eventually he became a member of the John Birch Society, an extremist group that even included President Eisenhower among unwitting helpers of an international Communist conspiracy.

Revisionists, especially in the United States and Germany, have often been obsessed with the idea of a conspiracy against them. During the German Historians' Quarrel the respected Hillgruber called his opponents "character assassins." Barnes called the anti-revisionists the "*Smearbund.*" He even thought that there was a conspiracy among booksellers not to reorder his *Genesis.* The famous American literary critic Mencken liked Barnes. In June 1940, when the German armies had marched forward into Holland, Belgium, and France, Mencken wrote to Barnes that "Roosevelt will be in the war in two weeks, and . . . his first act will be to forbid every form of free speech." Mencken, like Barnes and other revisionists, was bitterly against a war with Hitler's Reich, whilst after the war he thought that the United States should go to war against "the Russian barbarians." That inconsistency, if that was what it was, was typical of the inclinations of almost all the post–Second World War revisionists. The opposite was true of the Cold War revisionists of the 1960s, who accused the United States of having provoked the Cold War with Russia, while almost all of them approved the American involvement in the Second World War against Germany. They, too, did little else but project backward their then widespread and fashionable dislike of the Vietnam War to events that had happened twenty or more years earlier, manipulating that record for their own purposes. In the 1970s most of them turned to other topics, and at least one of them (Horowitz) became a neoconservative publicist.

There is, however, more involved here than a few historians adjusting their ideas to a prevalent climate of opinion. In some instances their writings affected national politics, through a momentum that was slowly gaining ground. In 1929 the writings of the revisionists had an influence on those members of Congress, mostly Western populists—George W. Norris, Gerald P. Nye, William E. Borah, for example—who had opposed the First

World War and the Versailles treaty. By 1934 the isolationist and revisionist tide ran so strong that a congressional committee, presided over by Nye,
found it politic to investigate the doings of bankers and munition makers
and other villainous promoters of the American entrance into the war seventeen years before. (One of the Nye Committee's five counsels was an
ambitious young lawyer, Alger Hiss.) In 1935 Congress passed the first
Neutrality Act, a definite reaction against the memories of the First World
War. It was extended in 1937. By that time Senator Homer Bone of Washington could report "a fact known even to school children in this country:
Everyone has come to recognize that the Great War was utter social insanity, and we had no business in it at all."

This illustrates a significant phenomenon to which few, if any, historians have yet devoted attention. It is the time lag in the movement of ideas,
the slowness of the momentum with which ideas move and then appear on
the surface at the wrong time, giving the lie to Victor Hugo's famous saw
about Ideas Whose Time Has Come. The high tide of revisionism (in the
United States; and in England of pro-German sentiments) occurred in the
mid-thirties when the German danger was rising anew—and not, say, in
1919 or 1929, when there had been cogent reasons to mitigate a mistreatment of Germany. The high tide of Second World War revisionism occurred in 1954 and 1955, when the reputations of Franklin Roosevelt and
of Yalta were at a low ebb. The high tide of the revisionism about the origins of the Cold War came around 1965, when American-Russian relations
were actually improving.

Of course it takes time for historians to complete their researches and
produce their books; but there is an agitated tone in many revisionist works
that stands in odd contrast with the slow momentum of their eventual effects. One reason for this is the often weak and tergiversating reaction of
the revisionists' historian opponents. In the beginning the seemingly radical performance of the former is often ignored, but then, gradually, the
revisionists' ideas may be adopted by respectable historians when it seems
politic for them to do so, or when they feel safely convinced by their ac-
ceptability. Thus, for example, Tansill's radical and Germanophile *America
Goes to War* was praised by some of the most prominent American literary
monthlies and by such eminent historians as Allan Nevins and Henry Steele
Commager. Tansill traced, "in magisterial style, the missteps which carried the United States along the road to war. It is an impressive performance, conducted with skill, learning, and wit, illuminating the present as
well as the past." This was written by Commager as late as 1938, the most
ominous and successful year in Hitler's career along the road to another
world war. The title of Beard's trenchant 1939 *Giddy Minds and Foreign Quar-*

rels is not really appropriate. So many of his colleagues' minds were not at all giddy; they were alarmingly slow. Even more disheartening was the reaction of many historians to the New Left revisionists of the 1960s, when the scholarship of those books was wanting. As Maddox wrote, "Reviewers who have been known to pounce with scarcely disguised glee on some poor wretch who incorrectly transcribed a middle initial or date of birth have shown a most extraordinary reluctance to expose even the most obvious New Left fictions," including false statements of fact to which tens of thousands of students were subsequently exposed in American colleges and universities. Finally, when it comes to the newest wave of revisionism, lamentably few historians have taken the trouble to track down and point out the selective methodology and occasionally sloppy scholarship in works such as Charmley's treatment of Churchill.

In science it is the rule that counts; in history, often the exceptions. And there have been exceptions to the shortcomings of scholars involved with revisionism. Millis, who, as we saw earlier, was the author of the most successful revisionist book in 1935, a few years later found himself appalled by the use people were making of his work, which, after all, had dealt with 1917, with the past and not with the then present. By 1938 Millis stood for resistance against Hitler and other dictators. "1939 is not 1914," he wrote in November 1939, when Roosevelt had to struggle against a senseless Neutrality Act. Maddox, whose study of the New Left revisionists was ignored or criticized by other historians, refused to make common cause with the New Right; he remained unimpressed by the selective argumentation of leftist and rightist, of Marxist and anticommunist, of neoliberal and neoconservative historians alike, because of his personal integrity, the essence of human integrity being its resistance to temptations, perhaps especially to intellectual ones.

Such temptations are the bane of historians, and not only of those who are in pursuit of attractive intellectual novelty. This does not mean a defence of "orthodox" history, because there is no such thing. Historians should be aware of the inevitably revisionist nature of their thinking and work. But the revision of history must not be an ephemeral monopoly of ideologues or opportunists who are ever ready to twist or even falsify evidences of the past in order to exemplify current ideas—and their own adjustments to them.

II.

HISTORIANS REVIEWED

*J*ohn Lukacs's judgments about the work of his fellow historians are informed as much by his convictions about the personal and participant nature of historical knowledge as they are by his sense of the bureaucratization of thought, which has infected the history profession as it has all scholarly disciplines. Writing history is, for Lukacs, an act and expression of character. He thus reserves his harshest criticism for those historians who not only succumb to the allure of ideology but who also expound upon "ideas whose time has come." Embracing intellectual fads and fashions, often in the interest of enhancing their professional reputation and status, these thinkers end by obscuring the truth, and worse, by adding to the sum of untruth. More propitious are those historians, whatever their shortcomings, who retain their independence and follow the interests of their own minds. After all, Lukacs notes, it is less important what ideas do to the minds of men than what men do with their ideas.

The essays in the following section, most of which were originally published as book reviews, explore many of the themes that dominate Lukacs's vast scholarship: the limitations of scientific history; the recognition of historical consciousness; the need to rethink the meaning of progress; the difficulties attendant on writing history in a democratic age; the origins and nature of the Second World War; the character of Adolf Hitler, the Third Reich, and German National Socialism; the relations between Hitler and Churchill and Hitler and Stalin; the transformation of American manners and morals that began in the 1950s; the failures of American foreign policy during the Cold War; and the historical writing of Winston Churchill. Like Alexis de Tocqueville, Jakob Burckhardt, and Johan Huizinga, Lukacs expresses complex ideas and offers astute observations within a brief compass. His characterization of George Kennan perhaps applies equally well to himself. Throughout his career, Lukacs's "principal ambition has been to share his private wisdom with the public—not so much to impress it with the powers of his mind as to help other people reach his convictions and conclusions," a worthy enterprise for a man who has spent most of his life as a writer and a teacher.

9

George Bancroft

(1961)

George Bancroft was the most successful of all American historians. Three generations ago, at a time when history was still considered literature, the volumes of his *History of the United States* stood on the shelves of thousands of American homes. During most of the nineteenth century it was a solid best-seller. Now his once so popular volumes are left untouched not only in the proverbial dusty attic but in teeming university libraries, too. His life, full of success, lasted long; his reputation did not.

In the history of American history George Bancroft was the central nineteenth-century figure. He lived at a time when historians still wrote for people rather than for other historians; and he got the best of the two now, alas, so separated worlds. Recognized as the dean of American historians during his lifetime, he also made some political history himself, and while he still receives textbook mention as an early founder of American historiography, his curious and manifold political career has scarcely been scrutinized at all. Yet he was not only historian but founder of the United States Naval Academy, American Envoy Extraordinary and Minister Plenipotentiary to London and Berlin, writer of presidential speeches, maker of presidential candidates, war-maker against Mexico. His political career runs through the rugged tapestry of nineteenth-century American democracy; his writing helped to establish its decorative historical pattern.

Bancroft was a central figure in several respects. His long life spanned most of the nineteenth century. The eighth child of a Massachusetts minister, he was born in 1800, within a year of Washington's death; he died in 1891, at a time when Eisenhower was already alive. He knew not many decisive setbacks during his life. He was among those fortunate beings who receive nearly all the fame they want during their lifetimes.

. . . .

From *American Heritage,* October: 65–68.

Steadily, throughout his days, George Bancroft burned with ambition; throughout most of the century he made himself known. As a youth he was serious and self-conscious, with a tendency toward priggishness (at fourteen he earnestly noted in his diary that he would rather closet himself with a "good moral book" than be amused, like his Harvard classmates, with athletics and fiction). The turning point of his life was the purse, quite a considerable forerunner of a Guggenheim or Fulbright, that sent him to Europe for four years; there he chose to be deeply influenced by Germany, the influence that is reflected throughout his *History* and also in his political career.

He sailed home to America, having acquired a few velveteen European clothes and some cosmopolitan mannerisms. He did not expect the disappointment he then saw reflected in the faces of his Puritan Harvard masters. Thereafter, instead of becoming a clergyman, as they anticipated, he started on a worldly career.

George Bancroft was a master of the art of timing. He founded a prep school when he sensed the excellent prospects for private schools in New England; twice he married well, socially and financially; and at the right time he perceived the advantages of entering Democratic party politics. He reckoned wisely. His years as American envoy abroad and his prominent political posts at home brought him the respectability he sought, if not in Boston, to which he never returned, then in New York and in Washington. There he settled after his last post in Berlin, to enjoy the fruits of his reputation. He had become a Washington eminence in more than one way. He kept a good table. He summered in Newport in his house, Roseclyffe. The Senate gave him the privilege of the floor. When he was eighty-seven, Browning sent a congratulatory verse:

> *Bancroft, the message-bearing wire*
> *Which flashes my "All Hail" today*
> *Moves slowlier than the heart's desire*
> *That, what hand pens, tongue's self might say.*

He died at what was virtually the height of his historical, political, and social reputation. President Harrison ordered the flags of official Washington to be flown at half-mast. No other American historian was ever so honored, either in life or in death.

But who reads him today? Among the now-myriad paper-bound reprints of early American historians you will not find his name. Adams, Prescott, Parkman, even Richard Hildreth, are reprinted, read, discussed, but not Bancroft. His figure is like those large iron statues of neglected governors that stand in the center squares of American state capitals, where now the traffic rushes around them but no one looks up. Our notion of his reputation is vague, romantic, incomplete, fragmentary. Nor is this a recent development. His reputation survived him by only a few years.

The reason is relatively simple. Bancroft died at the very time when a more objective, scientific, pragmatic, professionalized school of American historiography began to replace the earlier, more sentimental, rhetorical, nationalistic way of writing which he typified:

> The United States of America constitute an essential portion of a great political system, embracing all the civilized nations of the earth. At a period when the force of moral opinion is rapidly increasing, they have the precedence in the practice and the defence of the equal rights of men. The sovereignty of the people is here a conceded axiom, and the laws, established upon that basis, are cherished with faithful patriotism. While the nations of Europe aspire after change, our constitution engages the fond admiration of the people, by which it has been established. Prosperity follows the execution of even justice; invention is quickened by the freedom of competition; and labor rewarded with sure and unexampled returns.

These are the sentences with which Bancroft introduces his *History of the United States from the Discovery of the American Continent.* There follow another three pages describing an ideal, prosperous, and free national condition such as the world has never seen. "A favoring Providence, calling our institutions into being, has conducted the country to its present happiness and glory." Thus ends the introduction to the first volume, written and published in 1834, at the height of the Jacksonian era. The tone is unmistakable: it is indeed Jacksonian, optimistic, oratorical, somewhat loud, somewhat engaging. An eagle is proclaimed to soar, high above all, in what seems a cloudless blue sky, visible to the Children of Liberty, their vision yet untarnished by the battle smoke of the Civil War and by the factory smoke of the industrial expansion which followed it.

Bancroft left his introduction unchanged, though in 1882 he added:

> The foregoing words, written nearly a half-century ago, are suffered to remain, because the intervening years have justified their expression of confidence in the progress of our republic. The seed of disunion has perished; and universal freedom, reciprocal benefits, and cherished traditions bind its many states in the closest union.

—surely a somewhat incomplete description of the condition of the Republic under Chester A. Arthur.

The consistency and the complacency of Bancroft's historical optimism, of which his unchanged introduction is a fair example, suggest immediately why he was such a popular historian during his lifetime. They also suggest why he fell into neglect soon after his death, so that nowadays he is regarded as a lovable, simple, archaic nineteenth-century figure, a sort of bearded Founding Father of the historical profession whom, however, historians no longer read. But this is a superficial judgment; there are things in his *History* that deserve more than their present neglect.

Bancroft was essentially a one-book man. The book is a very long one, not only a *magnum opus* but an *opus vitae*. He began the *History of the United States* when he was thirty-two; he devoted much of his eighty-sixth year to a revision of the last edition. He wrote the first three volumes in his thirties, the next five volumes in his fifties: when he was seventy-five, he cut the ten volumes to six and brought out a so-called Centenary Edition; the old man and his wife then further corrected and cut out much, "slaughtering the adjectives" as she said, until ten years later "The Author's Last Revision" was issued. Altogether, from 1834 to 1890, almost thirty editions were published. Bancroft made a minor fortune out of them.

These thousands of pages, bound in somber pressed brown or dark blue, are heavy lumber, yet not quite as heavy as they seem at first sight. They are a curious mixture of splinter and gingerbread, of rough New England pine and brown mahogany varnish. They are the history of a Unique People, of a Unique Revolution, of the Providentially Chosen People of God. But there is more to them than the romantic naïveté of early nationalistic historiography. Though Bancroft still belonged to an age that looked upon history as a form of art, he also wished to consider himself a scientist. He refused to reconcile these two contradictory tendencies within himself, with the result that, at his worst, he sounds like a revivalist preacher on one page and a bored county clerk on the next.

Bancroft was a convinced believer in the social progress of democracy; yet there is astonishingly little social history in his long book. He wished to depict the large, dramatic panorama of American evolution; yet his last volume, describing the making of the Constitution, degenerates into dreary passages of long quotes; in the hundreds of pages dealing with 1786 there is but one paragraph about Shays' Rebellion. He exalts the American tradition of lawfulness and justice, yet he is eminently unfair about the Boston Massacre; he glowers about the acquittal of Captain Preston before a Boston court, a shining page of American justice that is unequaled in the history of the French or, indeed, of almost any other democratic revolution.

He believed in the advancement of morals; yet at times he could be priggish to the point of ludicrousness. He who first extolled the value of primary documents, the lesson he learned from Germany, did not make good enough use of his extraordinary access to European diplomatic archives.

His three years' tenure in London as American Minister to Britain (Polk's appointment after Bancroft's part in preparing the Mexican War message) had turned out to be profitable as well as enjoyable for him. Bancroft exploited his position by gaining access to many British and French state papers relating to the eighteenth century. Thus he could collect a mass of valuable material for the forthcoming volumes of his *History,* doing his "research" under conditions that past, present, and future historians might well envy.

Bancroft was perhaps the first American historian who did "collective research," since he had secretaries to make copies and to look things up for him; notwithstanding these advantages and the many revisions, factual errors abound in his *History.* He played tricks with his sources, misquoting them on occasion, stringing parts of texts together into fictitious speeches. Bancroft, who believed that history was an objective science, showing "the presence of law in the action of human beings," still treated his history as romantic literature. He looked at things not the way they were but the way they ought to have been; he was unwilling to admit the discrepancies between spirit and flesh, image and reality. "The warts on Franklin's face I wish omitted," wrote Bancroft in a curious note for the engraver who was to set Franklin's portrait on the frontispiece of Volume II of the *History.* (The engraver must have stood his ground: the warts on Franklin's face remain.)

At times Bancroft's narration is stately as well as lively—for example, when he writes about the silent bays of the continent as the colonists' little flotillas enter into their untouched waters: "The sea was enlivened by the shallops of fishermen." Many of his characterizations—especially of foreigners, curiously enough, rather than of Americans—are of enduring excellence, like his revised summation of Lord North:

> Yet Lord North was false only as he was weak and uncertain. He really wished to concede and conciliate, but he had not force enough to come to a clear understanding with himself. When he encountered the opposition in the House of Commons, he sustained his administration by speaking confidently for vigorous measures: when alone, his heart sank within him from dread of civil war.

His description of England in 1763, his characterization of Calvert, his contrast of Roger Williams with the Puritans, are better than good. It is a pity that they are not read nowadays. For, at best, a liverish New England nervousness and a thin stateliness harmonize in his prose, most of all in the more austere last editions.

The historian and his work are inseparable. Bancroft's person, like his *History*, was full of paradox. He was not very lovable, not altogether archaic, and far from simple. His prejudices are reflected throughout his *History*; they often form its worst, disproportionate faults. They are not merely nationalistic and democratic prejudices: they are Teutonic, Protestant, Populist, and Progressive. To Bancroft, the modern progress of Science and Virtue began with Luther, and the Chosen People were mainly those of the Germanic Race. To Bancroft the English civil war was a struggle between the simple, democratic, virtuous "Low Folk" Saxons and the "High Folk of Normandie"; the epic campaigns of Britain and France for the domination of the Atlantic world were but a war "between the Catholic and the Protestant Powers."

Bancroft, who at first rejected Darwin, was nonetheless an unconscious historical Darwinian. For him the Protestant democracy of America marked the inexorable march of progress. The victory of the Revolution "was the first decisive victory of the industrious middling class over the most powerful representative of the mediaeval aristocracy"—a peculiar description of British society in the 1770s. "The world is in a constant state of advancement"; things are getting better and better all the time. But this, then, is not really archaic at all. Indeed, it is the credo of American progressive historiography, stretching up to our present day. For even though the profession of history soon left Bancroft behind—abandoning social Darwinism and sentimental admiration for the Teuton race—the German-scientific tradition, of which Bancroft was the first central representative, still dominates American professional historical writing.

Bancroft was a successful man—so successful, indeed, that some of his friends reproached him for the very obvious eagerness with which he pursued wealth and prestige. His political ambitions were great, yet he was vexed and spurred by a sense of social inferiority throughout his life. He was a social climber rather than a self-confident aristocrat, and at least as much of an opportunist as a rebel. Though he was always extolling the Wisdom of the People and condemning the sins of aristocracies, he was evidently pleased by being invited to all sorts of high places in England and by the titles with which the Prussians flattered him.

As the American envoy to Germany, Bancroft spent the seven happiest years of his life, back in his beloved Berlin, surrounded by German professors, intelligently cultivated and inconspicuously patronized by his idol Bismarck, whose cause Bancroft ambitiously assisted with newspaper articles and undiplomatic speeches. (The French protested in vain against Bancroft's unneutral behavior.) The celebration of the great Prussian victory at Sedan in 1870 coincided almost to the day with the celebration of Bancroft's *Doctor-Jubilaeum*, the fiftieth anniversary of his doctorate at Göttingen. A stream of German academicians and high officials proceeded through Bancroft's Berlin house on that unforgettable day; the old Ranke hobbled up to him and planted a professorial kiss on Bancroft's beard.

Bancroft's judgment of nations and of persons was often lamentable. "It is still 'the scarlet woman of Babylon,'" he wrote about the papacy in 1870; "we have a president without brains," he said of Lincoln as late as 1860 (always privately, of course). He wrongly saw in 1848 the coming of the Universal Democratic Revolution in Europe; in 1870 he claimed to hear the sound of Freedom in the victorious bellowing of the Prussian guns at Sedan. It is not surprising that Ranke and Treitschke said that he was "one of us." Bancroft, in turn, called Bismarck "a lover of liberty," "a great republican," "a renovator of Europe"; he said that Moltke was a German Washington; on one occasion he even pledged, foolishly, the help of the United States Navy against France.

"Literary men indulge in humbug only at a price, and Bancroft abounded in humbug," wrote Van Wyck Brooks. "Did he believe what he was saying?" Anthony Trollope once asked. Emerson called him an opportunist, mercenary, a man with a tricky heart.

Much of what Bancroft had written was soon outdated and cast aside by the thousands of young American historians who followed him. In this respect even death came to him at a fortunate moment; near the time when Bancroft passed away, his idol Bismarck was sent into retirement and died soon afterward; within a few years American and German warships were glowering at each other in Manila Bay; soon Turner and Beard were at large, demolishing the edifice of American historical illusions that Bancroft had helped to build. The air was more electric; the mustiness was evaporating; the nation's vision of its own past was becoming clearer.

Bancroft was a lesser man, and a lesser historian, than he wished his contemporaries (and, of course, posterity) to believe; but in our times, when no one reads him, the balance ought to be redressed somewhat. His politics deserve a stricter scrutiny than they have received; his *History* deserves more consideration than the present neglect. It is another strange paradox that Bancroft stands condemned today for the wrong reason. He is neglected because of his romantic, effulgent qualities rather than because of his occasional insincerity and frequent cant. This is a pity, for his writing gains in contrast with the gray, cautious, dry, sociological, technical prose of mono-graphic historical writing that is so frequent nowadays. On the other hand, historians have slurred over the evidences of his astonishing political op-portunism. Ironically, they have fallen into Bancroft's own trap; they have treated him in the mode of professional and scientific historiography, as if the historian and the politician had been two different persons. This is never really possible—certainly not with Bancroft—though we may rea-sonably say that Bancroft the historian was better and at least more consis-tent than Bancroft the politician.

"Westward the star of empire takes its way"—this was the motto pressed on the cover boards of the first volume of Bancroft's *History*. It was pointed out to him that Bishop Berkeley's famous words spoke of the course, not star, of empire. Still he did not order his publishers to change it. He liked it better this way. On the covers of that early edition the Bancroftian version of the phrase remains.

10

Page Smith
(1965)

Among the now increasing number of books dealing with theories of history this book stands out as a shining example of thoughtful and brave convictions. Professor Smith, whose principal field of study is that of American history, is somewhat unique because of his deep interest in continental European, rather than Anglo-American, contemporary historical philosophies. It is symptomatic that his epigraph is taken from H.-I. Marrou, and that his book is dedicated to Eugen Rosenstock-Huessy, two European Christian historians. The first nine chapters of his book consist of a survey of general philosophies of history from the Hebrews and the Greeks to Spengler, Toynbee, and, somewhat surprisingly, Voegelin. The last five chapters represent a strong and honest attempt at demolishing many of the smug and unreasonable tendencies and categories of historical thinking and of social scientism which are now, regrettably enough, current within the historical profession itself. One of the chapters represents a "case example," a thoughtful, short, illustrative treatment of the history of the historiography of the American Revolution. This is a good book by a good man who is profoundly concerned with the widespread intellectual confusion of our times. It reflects a humanist and Christian view of history, without implications of the author's religious beliefs through rhetorical devices of his own.

It may be that the two parts of the book should have been made more distinct, for Dr. Smith does not make it quite clear whether he himself is aware of the difference between philosophies of history and historical thinking. This implicit contradiction appears, for example, in the very beginning, where the author says in his introduction that the final chapters represent an effort to state "some of the ways in which the study of history, and

Review of Page Smith, *The Historian and History* (1964). From *Catholic Historical Review*, April: 65–67.

perhaps, even more, *an awareness of the historic dimension of human experience* [his italics] may be of help to those who seek to chart a course through the turbulent waters of our time"; on the other hand, in chapter one he says that "briefly stated, history is a record of what has taken place in the past"— which contradicts the earlier statement with its strong and just sense that history is more than that: for history is not merely the *recorded;* it is the *remembered* past.

Generally speaking, this book is written in a somewhat pedestrian manner: but it is sure-footed rather than cautious, and it is enlivened by many important statements. Here are some of these. About the harm done by certain textbooks: "The ubiquitous textbook, which by the early decades of the twentieth century had come to dominate the teaching of history, can be taken as a symbol of the conviction on the part of historians that academic history could be reduced to simple declarative sentences and embalmed in the handsomely illustrated but blandly innocuous works that are, in one form or another, the constant companion of every American student from elementary school through college." Also: "The trouble with textbooks is not that they are illustrated in color, that they are 'written down,' that they are fuzzy and mealy mouthed and an insult to the intelligence of the teacher and the student. The inadequacy of the textbook goes much deeper. It is a reflection of the basic philosophy or nonphilosophy of the upper echelons of the profession—the scholars whose view, to a large degree, dominate our thinking about the central problems of historiography." About the inventions of national histories by some of the newly emerging independent states: "It is tempting to compare this process . . . with the therapy of the psychoanalyst, who, it may be suspected, is most successful when he invents, with the aid of his patient, a personal history which, however fictitious, reassures the patient and reinforces his ability to operate in the real world." About American intellectualism: "a basic intellectual conservatism, evident throughout American history, has made us content to import most seminal European ideas a generation or more after they have circulated on the other side of the Atlantic." The notion that history is scientific "is no longer believed but is still practiced as a consequence of intellectual sloth, inertia, and the strength of existing academic arrangements." "[T]o argue against the possibility of scientific history or to protest the phrase is, today, to beat a dead horse. Very few historians can be found who are willing at this hour to assert that the study of history is a science or can ever have the character of a science in any proper sense of that word. What is far more important is that many, if not most, historians think and write about the historical process as though it is very largely determined." "The historian must recognize that history is not a scientific enterprise but a moral one."

"My point," the author concludes, is not a pretentious one: it is "that many of the ills which maim and distort the modern psyche have their source in large part in a faulty sense of history or of the historic."

I have found very few errors in this book. The so-called "New Conservatives" know much less about Christianity and history than Smith suggests. A certain Viennese school (an English term) but not "Vienna" was the "stronghold of the logical positivists after World War I." Voegelin, at least in this reviewer's opinion, has as much obscured as he has "enormously enriched both the vocabulary and the scope of history." Smith's distinction between existential and symbolic history is somewhat wobbly. National histories are not yet "in any event, obsolete" (here Smith does not clarify the distinction between what is national and what is nationalistic). The difference between the historical ideologies of the French and the—largely unhistorical—ideologies of the Russian Revolution was much greater than what Smith implies. *Wie es eigentlich gewesen* was not so much "an unfortunate phrase" as a phrase that lent itself to unfortunate interpretations.

This book should be on the reading list of every undergraduate history major in the United States. It is useful, reasonable, readable, and on occasion, profound. Its very existence is an encouraging symptom.

11

Oswald Spengler
(1966)

By a remarkable coincidence the first volume of Oswald Spengler's *The Decline of the West* was published in Germany in the spring of 1918. The time was no longer the evening of an Augustan age. It was the cold dawn of a new Iron Age in which German forms of revolutionary thought would be prevalent in Europe; an atmosphere Spartan as well as Wagnerian. The Continent's center of gravity had already shifted east of the Rhine, notwithstanding the collapse of the Russian and of the German empires. In the new phase of world history the principal figures would be Lenin, Mussolini, Hitler, and Stalin.

Amid such conditions, Spengler's heavy, gloomy book set off a tremendous echo. Many philosophies of history had been published during the nineteenth century, and their writers were usually historical pessimists; but their influence was limited to a small audience of scholars and amateurs. Spengler's *magnum opus* was different. Not only did it appear at the right conjunction; its form and fate were different. And so was the categorical assertiveness of its title, the English version of which is but a pale and inaccurate translation that might properly have been "The Sinking" or "The Collapse" of the West.

For the next fifteen years Spengler was a prominent public figure. The occasional carpings of professional historians at some of his inaccuracies and questionable methods were drowned out by a solid chorus of approval, admiration, and assent from the highest ranks of German society and culture. Members of the German aristocracy, of the political hierarchy, the great roaring industrialists, the great renowned philosophers vied for his presence. He was lauded, respected, feared; he became rich, and he spurned the invitations of universities to professorial chairs of high repute. From

Review of Arthur Helps, ed., *Letters of Oswald Spengler: 1913–1936* (1966). From *New York Times Book Review*, March 6: 6.

Central Europe the influence of his genius traveled westward in curious waves—first to America, only then to England. His subsequent writings contributed heavily to an ideological atmosphere which the excellent Swiss historian Armin Mohler named "the conservative revolution" and which, in turn, created many (though not all) of the conditions for Hitler's assumption of power.

In the end, Spengler did not care for many of the things Hitler was to do; it seems, however, that Hitler cared even less for Spengler. In May 1936, Spengler suddenly died. Thereafter his reputation went through a phase of temporary eclipse. In Europe the terrible actuality of World War II and the consequent decline were far more dramatic and also considerably different from the great theories of Spengler; his cerebrations suddenly seemed oddly remote, more akin to Art Nouveau than to revolution. In England and especially in the United States the Spenglerian distinction between "culture" and "civilization" was distasteful to many philosophers and historians, who, perhaps too easily, claimed to see in this yet another symptom of German arrogance. In any event, the historian who after the war attracted worldwide attention with a large work devoted to the mysteries of the rise and fall of civilizations was the Englishman Arnold Toynbee, not Spengler.

In the early 1950s, Spengler's reputation revived again. References to him in American textbooks of cultural history now abound. In his short and thoughtful little biography of Spengler, the historian H. Stuart Hughes, continuing, perhaps unconsciously, the old New England tradition of intellectual fascination with German Giants of Thought, advanced the convincing thesis that Spengler, with all of his gloom, was a great thinker, an anti-Nazi conservative, and an intellectual aristocrat. In 1963, fragments of Spengler's correspondence were published by a Munich savant, A. M. Koktanek. Fragments of these fragments are now available in the present volume, translated and edited by Arthur Helps. This helps Spengler's reputation not at all.

The contents of the book are insubstantial. It is an editorial failure in many ways: a very poor translation, an incredible number of errors which ought to have caught any subeditor's eye, beginning with the very first sentence of the book in which the date of Spengler's death is given wrong. It seems that many of Spengler's letters were lost during the war, but Mr. Koktanek's introduction does not indicate whether there are more letters extant (this reviewer suspects there are). Nor does this American edition say anything about the number of letters by which the original German edition has been further diminished for American readers.

The result is fragmentary correspondence in which more than half of the letters are not written by Spengler but rather addressed to him by a variety of people. They include myriad party invitations and other momentous matters involving museum memberships, lecture fees, and free airplane rides. ("Among the hundreds of Spengler's correspondents," says the introduction, "are included important figures in the spheres of learning, industry and politics. Sometimes letters of thanks and invitations have been included in order to show the width of Spengler's circle of correspondents." This circle is composed of many squares.) The few interesting letters are those Spengler wrote to a friend while working on the first volume of *The Decline*. They run some fifty pages out of more than three hundred. Thereafter, the quality of the correspondence declines.

Does this collection of letters reveal anything? It reveals that Spengler was not a very admirable or attractive person. I say "reveal" because it was after the reading of these letters that this reviewer could no longer accept the now standard view of Spengler's personal and political character. The image of the military intellectual giant with his bronze cranium is now compromised by primary evidence suggesting that he was tetchy, petty, not devoid of opportunism, and in search of a kind of social approbation. ("One year," he writes in 1917, "without mental depression and with appropriate society, and I should have the whole gamut of my thoughts in ten small volumes ready for the public.") No aristocrat, Spengler was a bourgeois. It is only that instead of the bourgeois title of Herr Professor he preferred to be identified as The Thinker.

He was also humorless. Occasional flashes of enthusiasm appear in his descriptions of luxury hotels and the carcasses of roast pigs, of which he was extraordinarily fond. "In fact," says the introduction, "Spengler is not one of the masters of letter writing." This is a vast understatement.

He was also very shortsighted for a prophetic historian. In 1915 he writes that it is Russia "to which the succeeding millennium belongs, after we Germans have had the next few centuries for ourselves." His letters in 1932–35 make it clear that Spengler then emphatically preferred Hitler to the democratic parties of the German republic. (As late as January 1933, he commends a deranged abbot who had been censured by his superiors because of his pro-Hitler attitude.) A subsequent letter to Goebbels and the evidence of his interview with Hitler in 1933 suggest that Spengler was mildly itching to be taken up by the Nazi hierarchy, if this had been possible on his terms. But Hitler and Goebbels could do very well without him. Three years later, Spengler died of a broken heart.

Surely he found many things about Nazism distasteful and perhaps disastrous. Yet the hitherto accepted notion that his sudden death spared him from the fate of exile or execution (the translator's note suggests the concentration camp) at the hands of the Nazis now seems a vast exaggeration.

"The difference between Spengler and Toynbee," wrote a German archeologist a few years ago, "is that Spengler is a genius." The comparison is unfair. Both Spengler and Toynbee had much to say, but they said it in different ways and with different purposes in mind. At his best, Spengler is brilliant while Toynbee is only interesting. At his worst, however, Spengler writes a kind of bombastic and confusing mumbo jumbo while Toynbee is merely dull. The historian E. H. Carr has dismissed Toynbee as a "failure," which is not surprising from Carr; what is surprising is his statement that "Spengler is always clear."

The proper comparison is not between the German Spengler and the English Toynbee but between Spengler the would-be aristocrat and Jakob Burckhardt, the historical philosopher and German-Swiss patrician. If European civilization survives, it is a safe guess that the latter will be read by thoughtful historians a hundred years from now, when Spengler will be largely forgotten.

12

George Kennan

(1967)

George F. Kennan's *Memoirs* begin with his student years; he was far from having been an exceptional student in Princeton, but during his first years abroad his real aspirations, toward study and writing, crystallized. He was not yet twenty-five when, dissatisfied and depressed with the prospects of a career in diplomacy, he was about to resign from the Foreign Service in order to devote himself to the broad study of contemporary history and international relations. Fortunately it was then revealed to him that he could continue his studies, especially of modern Russia, in Berlin, under the then training program of the State Department. During the two exceptionally eventful and dramatic decades that followed, Kennan served his country in Tallinn, Riga, Prague, Lisbon, London, twice in Berlin, and twice in Moscow. Because of the sudden public receptivity to some of his opinions in 1946 he became well known; he was then called to Washington where he exercised an important influence during a fateful phase of American history. Again, but on a deeper level, he grew depressed with the general conduct of foreign policy in the American democracy. In 1950 he retired to the Institute for Advanced Study in Princeton. These memoirs end with this turning point in his life.

Those who are acquainted with Kennan's articles and books will not be surprised to find the quality of fine writing in his *Memoirs*. There are, however, certain surprising things in this book, all of them agreeable. Kennan was a compulsive writer from the beginning, though not necessarily with the purpose of publication. It now appears that he kept a detailed diary during most of his life. These *Memoirs* are interspersed with long passages from his diary and from other papers. Some of these passages consist of impressions of places and persons; others are political and historical in

Review of George Kennan, *Memoirs 1925–1950* (1967). From *New Republic*, October 28: 28–31.

character. Almost without exception they reveal not only their author's excellence of mind but an early and consistent addiction to good style:

> The windows of the apartment overlooking the *Giesebrechtstrasse* looked back into the pitlike courtyard, called the garden. There were a few trees there, and a bit of grass; also the garbage cans and an incredible number of tawny, dirty cats. On summer nights one heard the cats and occasionally the faint roar of the elevated trains on the *Stadtbahn*. On warm Sunday mornings, people would sit out on their high iron balconies, with coffee and the Sunday papers, and there would be a virulent chorus of radios, playing church music and Wagnerian opera mixed with strident … jazz.

This is Berlin, 1931. There are many such descriptions, of Riga in 1932, of Wisconsin towns in 1936, of Prague in March 1939, and of Moscow.

These memoirs reveal facets of this exceptional American which may have been unknown even to some of his admirers. Who would imagine that George Kennan, when in college, "went away and wept unmanly tears" as he read "the hauntingly beautiful epilogue" to *The Great Gatsby*? The fact that he couldn't resist, "weakly," as he says, marking a leftover recommendation from his own pen with the notation: "I find this a good idea, before the paper would disappear in the State Department files"? In Siberia, Kennan and a Russian host "visited a circus, watched a lady put her head in the lion's mouth, and after having a good second look at the lady agreed—to our great mutual satisfaction—that we were lost in admiration for the courage of the lion." Bravo.

This is not all, of course. For this book may well be not only a most excellent memoir but the single most valuable political book written by an American in the twentieth century, because of its instructiveness. It is in its political aspect that, for example, these personal memoirs surpass even Harold Macmillan's diplomatic work. There is a seriousness in Kennan which Kennan's otherwise excellent English counterpart approaches only on occasion. It is not only because of Kennan's familiarity with great events, famous persons, and because of his keen insight into them, that these memoirs are exceptional: it is because of his frequent exposition of a political philosophy, the range and the depth of which go far beyond the otherwise urbane and thoughtful attempts of his countrymen in understanding the reality of international affairs.

Kennan's political philosophy is, in an uncanny sense, profoundly conservative. I am using this now often misunderstood adjective in its original and traditional sense. History, tradition, the existence of national character, the variants of human nature, and the trueness of European civilization are part of Kennan's personal beliefs. Kennan thinks little of science, technology, planning, One World, mass democracy, economic determinism. Liberals and progressives will not like this book, and that not only because of Kennan's staunch refusal to entertain illusions about the Soviet system. ("Never—neither then nor at any later date," he declared about 1933, "did I consider the Soviet Union a fit ally or associate, actual or potential, for this country.") The sentimental idols of the liberal Left—the Causes of Czechoslovakia, League of Nations, Iberian League, Latin-American democracy—leave Kennan cold and skeptical. He admits his respect for the Catholic Church and the Habsburg empire; further, he recognizes that the Nazi regime, instead of having been reactionary, was something frighteningly modern. "If Germany had indeed set the clock back" as so many Americans had claimed, he writes in 1940, "we would be happier, for there is hardly anyone on the continent of Europe which does not speak of the superiority of the past. But what has happened has been no setting back of the clock." Only a few real fools appear in these pages (there are few, because Kennan often strains to be generous): people such as Joseph E. Davies, Edward Stettinius, the eager beavers of the wartime Treasury Department in Washington, and the conclaves of liberal professors at Berkeley. But then, Kennan has nothing in common with the unhistorical and ideological tendencies of that kind of radical nationalism which goes under the name of conservatism in the United States, and which became almost identical with a thoughtless and frenzied kind of anticommunism during the Cold War. And here we come to an important point.

The modest fame that became attached to Kennan's name originated in 1946–47, at the beginning of the Cold War. There have been a number of books lately about the origins of the Cold War. Their authors, for the first time, attempt to adduce evidence in order to blame American policies as much as Soviet ones for the beginning of that fatal conflict little more than twenty years ago. The more thoughtful among these writers sometimes suggest—and not without reason—that the years 1945 to 1947 mark the crystallization of the kind of American global interventionism which has now led, among other things, to our tragic predicament in Vietnam. Now George Kennan has been second to none in deploring the ravages of the American illusions of omnipotence and of omnipresence. But it is instructive to remember from these pages that during those fateful years Kennan's principal criticism of American foreign policy was the exact opposite of the recent cerebrations by young liberals. The trouble was not that Washington's opposition to Stalin's ambitions was exaggerated; the trouble was that it was inadequate; and that it did not develop early enough. In

Kennan's opinion, the moment "when, if ever, there should have been a full-fledged and realistic showdown with the Soviet leaders" was during the Warsaw uprising crisis, in the early autumn of 1944—a conclusion which this disdainful opponent of anticommunist ideology reached long years before Dulles and Taft and Eisenhower and MacArthur and McCarthy. Throughout the war years Kennan was impatient not only with the liberals but with the "disgraceful anti-British and pro-Soviet prejudices that certain of our military leaders had entertained"—in many instances the very same people who were to make ponderous preparations for the "inevitable" war with the Soviet Union a few years later.

Fox said about Burke that he was "a wise man; but he is wise too soon." The art of politics is the art of timing, but much more so in our times than in the age of Burke and Fox. It is a melancholy thought that the instruments which brought Kennan influence and fame in 1946 and 1947—the so-called "Long Telegram" and the "X" article—are among the more ideological and general, and among the least Kennanesque and specific, of his political papers. Suddenly: "My reputation was made. My voice now carried." And how did this happen? It is worth listening to what he says about this:

> Six months earlier this message would probably have been received in the Department of State with raised eyebrows and lips pursed in disapproval. Six months later, it would probably have sounded redundant, a sort of preaching to the convinced. This was true despite the fact that the realities which it described were ones that had existed, substantially unchanged, for about a decade, and would continue to exist for more than a half decade longer. All this only goes to show that more important than the observable nature of external reality when it comes to the determination of Washington's view of the world is the subjective state of readiness on the part of Washington officialdom to recognize this or that feature of it. This is certainly natural; perhaps it is unavoidable. But it does raise the question—and it is a question which was to plague me increasingly over the course of the ensuing years—whether a government so constituted should deceive itself into believing that it is capable of conducting a mature, consistent, and discriminating foreign policy. Increasingly . . . my answer would tend to be in the negative.

A biographer of George Frost Kennan may one day feel compelled to employ the epithet with which some scorned the philosophy of Dr. Johnson nearly two hundred years ago: "A Triumph of Character." While the perhaps deepest wish of Dr. Johnson was to apply the strength of his mind and of his dictum to the variegated problems of his personal existence—in other words, to verbally share his public wisdom with himself—Kennan's principal ambition has been to share his private wisdom with the public—not so much to impress it with the powers of his mind as to help other people to reach his convictions and conclusions. Kennan has been—and this is the consistent thread throughout his career—essentially a teacher and a writer. (Johnson abhorred teaching, and he did not like to write very much either.) But, then, the great Doctor, while eccentric, was not unclassifiable—while George Kennan, in twentieth-century America, has been unclassifiable without being eccentric. And it is within this characteristic that his personal triumph and, perhaps, also his tragedy—or, rather, the American tragedy—resides.

13

Guy Chapman and Alistair Horne

(1969)

Twenty-nine years ago the Germans conquered the French. This was a great event, without precedent in modern history. I write "conquered," because Germany had defeated France before but this time she conquered her just about entirely. I write "Germans" and "French," because this was a contest between entire nations, not only between states.

The German victory was planned and executed with a daring and a perfection virtually unprecedented in the history of modern warfare, certainly in the history of the twentieth century. The French had not won a single skirmish, let alone a battle. For a moment it seemed that Hitler's Germans had won the most astonishing war in the history of modern civilization. Eventually they would go under, though the French had little to do with their defeat.

The memory of 1940 lives deep in the consciousness of the most arrogant or even the youngest of Frenchmen. There are not many good French histories about it, perhaps with reason. When it comes to their own history the French simply disregard the contributions of historians of other nations. Sometimes they are right, since on occasion Frenchmen will write about the history of their own country in the way no one else can. With 1940, however, they have not yet come to terms.

They will ignore, too, the respectable contributions of these two English writers. We, on the other hand, ought to devote some interest to them. In view of their qualifications they could have done a little better.

Guy Chapman, a very fine historian and a sensitive writer, devoted many years to the study of the Third Republic of France; he also may have written the finest history of the Dreyfus Case in any language, which is no mean feat. Saddened and exercised by the collapse of bourgeois France in

Review of Guy Chapman, *Why France Fell* (1969), and Alistair Horne, *To Lose a Battle* (1969). From *Commonweal*, August 22: 520–21.

1940, he wrote *Why France Fell,* devoting himself to military history. The result is one of the most detailed accounts of the campaign of 1940 but little besides. There is the expectable, regimental and topographical, bog of details, all of it running one way. Throughout this serious volume one senses the sadness and the exasperation of this author with the French performance in 1940. He is extremely critical of de Gaulle and at times disillusioned with Churchill. One may wonder whether this kind of criticism would have occurred to the author had he written this book a decade earlier.

Alistair Horne's book is the last in a trilogy. I have admired the first two, on the Franco-Prussian War and on Verdun, and I am inclined to give *To Lose a Battle* a strong "B" but not more. After describing the decisive first fortnight of the campaign in more than 530 pages the author suddenly winds up his book, spending less than seventy on the crucial month that followed. Somehow one gets the impression that he got tired of his task. Unlike Chapman, he tries to paint an entire portrait of this decaying, overripe France, but he does not wholly succeed. He cannot help but admire the Germans' military qualities, but having said his bits about that, he seems a little woozy, not quite knowing what to say and think about them, as indeed are an increasing number of Englishmen who now write about the second World War. Horne, too, is critical of de Gaulle, in the opinion of this reviewer unduly so. De Gaulle was, after all, the only French general officer who in 1940 succeeded in actually pushing the Germans back for a few miles during a day or so. More than that he could not do, partly because of his own faults, but beggars can't be choosers, and in contemplating those brilliant and painful scenes of 1940 I believe that all civilized men, who have loved France, were and are beggars.

How we begged the French to fight! How we begged God to bless the French! How our minds begged for one sign, one small victory, one inspiring French act of courage, to suggest that Hitler's Germans were not invincible and that Western civilization would survive! In retrospect, our hopes were wholly devoid of reason. The French simply couldn't have stopped the Germans in 1940, not because of wanting armaments or wanting generalship but because of the way they then were and the way the Germans then were. Perhaps in those dazzling June days we all were beginning to sense this; and we hoped for one sign, one voice that would tell us, and the public world, that it wasn't so. There appeared one unknown French general who said that it wasn't so. And eventually it wasn't.

That weary and sad word, "eventually."

14

Jacques Barzun

(1975)

The history of history is probably the most significant path in the unending forest of the human mind. It marks, clearer than anything else, the evolution of our consciousness (which is probably the only kind of evolution there is). Let me, for the sake of my readers, most of whom are not professional historians—and also for the sake of many professional historians, alas, who know alarmingly little about this important matter—sum up the relatively recent history of history as briefly as I can. I must do this, in order to explain what Jacques Barzun has tried to do, and what he has not tried to do, in his recent book, *Clio and the Doctors*.

During the nineteenth century (for the first time in history) history became recognized as a science: the professional study of the recorded past. Toward the end of the century in Europe certain thinkers (many of them not professional historians) realized and said that the knowledge that men have of other men is subtly but fundamentally different from the knowledge that men have of anything else: of matter, of nature, of their environment, of other living beings. The roots of this argument had been stated before, by Vico, before Vico by Pascal, before Pascal by some of the great Greek thinkers: but there was a difference now. The antimaterialists of the late nineteenth century were not merely Platonists or anti-Cartesians. They were the first *post*-scientific—as distinct from *pre*-scientific—thinkers. They were reacting against the forcing of history into the Procrustean bed of the scientific method. Eventually some of the finest European historians and historical thinkers came forth, not only to restate forcefully but to argue with a kind of cogent common sense that history was both more and less than a science, that it was a form of thought.

Still, unlike the nineteenth century when the notion of history as a science became nearly universal, during the twentieth century the recogni-

Review of Jacques Barzun, *Clio and the Doctors* (1974). From *Salmagundi*, Summer: 93–106.

tion that history is something else than a science has not been universally accepted (or, rather, it has not been thought *through*). Another school of thought, to the effect that history was a social science, gained many influential adherents, especially in the United States, for a number of reasons. One was the continuing and unquestioned prestige of science among the peoples of the world. Another related reason was the continued belief of people to the effect that the historian is a scientifically trained researcher of records, a kind of archaeologist and archivist rolled into one, a professional specialist—all in all, an unquestioning belief which has accorded wonderfully with the needs (occupational, intellectual, social, psychic) of most professional historians. Yet another kind of related reasoning, particularly attractive to American Progressives, was that if history were treated as a superior kind of social science, its study could (indeed, that it ought to) produce utilitarian and pragmatic results.[1] Another cause (cause, rather than reason) for the prevalence of neo-materialism (a philosophy whereof social-scientism was but a variant) was the triumph of both the United States and the Soviet Union in 1945. The global victory of the two nations in whose intellectual institutions materialist categories were dominant, together with the defeat of the nation (Germany) and of the philosophy (fascism) which had incarnated some of the most extreme forms of antimaterialism, gave a powerful impetus to the revived respectability of materialistic philosophies throughout the world.[2] Unlike in the Soviet Union, in the United States certain historians nonetheless recognized the limitations of both Marxism and of social-scientism. Moreover, it would be wrong to think that a clear-cut struggle, or even division, existed between the non-scientific and social-scientific schools of thought. The vast majority of historians went ahead in their professions without wishing to give much or, indeed, any thought to the essential nature of their work (or of their thinking.) "Went ahead" is the *mot juste,* preoccupied as they have been with their professional advancement. In other words, during the twentieth century the teaching and the writing of history has been influenced principally *not* by changing ideas and modes of thought but by bureaucratic practices and professional ambitions—the argument to which I shall return.

From about 1945 to 1960 there was no essential difference between the concept of history as professionally practiced in the United States and in Western Europe. As a matter of fact, there was an increase of convergence, mostly because of the considerable progress in European, Medieval, and Ancient historical studies in the United States.[2] As late as around 1960 it seemed as if history remained largely unaffected by the degeneration of language and of thought that had affected the narrow professionalism of sociology, psychology, political science.[3] But this proved to be an illusion, for the simple reason that the vast majority of professional historians were not different from other professional intellectuals. Their judgments, their opinions, their political and intellectual preferences—including the very subjects and the very purposes of their research—were governed by the same kind of intellectual opportunism that has become near-universal in other fields of intellectual life, some of the manifestations of which were masterfully delineated by Jacques Barzun in *The House of Intellect,* about a dozen years ago. There have been three principal manifestations of these, essentially degenerate, tendencies in professional historianship during the last fifteen years or so. One of them has been the extreme persistence of the, regrettably American, tradition of historical presentism, that is, the preoccupation with "historical" subjects determined by the public "issues" of the present—whereby thousands of articles and books were written, millions of foundation dollars were spent, and hundreds of careers were made on histories of the Vietnam War or on Pacifism or of Blacks or of Women.[4] Another profitable endeavor was the pursuit of psychohistory. In 1958 the erstwhile diplomatic historian William L. Langer, a Pillar of the Establishment, announced in his presidential address to the American Historical Association that historians must henceforth consider the employment of psychoanalytic techniques. Shortly thereafter another fad emerged, that of quantification: the subjection of the study of the past to statistical methods, making it dependent on the computer (something dear to both the scientific and to the bureaucratic mind). By the early 1970s these two latter fads have become overwhelming within the profession. Jacques Barzun attacked them, first in an article, then in this book. His attack is cogent and lucid: but it does not go far enough.

❈ ❈ ❈

THERE are certain very good and profound things that Barzun says in *Clio and the Doctors.* Most of these involve the proper use and the misuse of imagination. The point of history, he says, is the imagining of past reality. About quanto-history, for example: "It would be interesting, if it were possible, to test the viewer of tables and graphs after his scrutiny and find out what images were formed and remained in *his* mind's eye. First, no doubt, some abstract shapes. . . . There is value for history in these perceptions. . . . But studies exclusively based on such modes seem better designed for reference than for comprehension." Of course: since the purpose of historical knowledge is understanding, even more than certainty. Again, Barzun about psychohistory *re* its so-called diagnosis of character: "An explanation by childhood determinants leaves no room for one of the most easily observed facts, the *development* of character. In other words, diagnosis is more likely to close and restrict the imagination than to open and enlarge it."[5] Barzun, moreover, knows enough literature and history to tell his readers who ought to know better that those who are making snide remarks against "uncritical" or "Victorian" practices of biography are merely setting up straw men. The practices of uncritical biography had been broken nearly a century ago: "It was Froude who in 1882 made the great break with Victorian ideas of biography by publishing the facts of Carlyle's domestic life—not, like Strachey thirty-five years later, in a spirit of snickering malice, but out of a finer notion of life and genius." Apart from the erudite reminder, "a spirit of snickering malice" in itself has a touch of genius, Barzun at his best.

But all of this does not go far enough. As we have seen, in 1958 the then president of the American Historical Association told the assembled historians under the title "The Next Assignment" that historians lacked "the speculative audacity of the natural scientists," that they tended to be "buried in their own conservatism." He admonished his fellow historians "to the urgently needed deepening of our historical understanding through exploitation of the concepts and findings of modern psychology." This description of historians "buried in their conservatism" leaves me speechless. Wasn't the overwhelming majority of American historians not a whit less liberal than the vast (and often oppressive) consensus of the majority of other American professional intellectuals? Wasn't it in America that historians have been taking up every possible social-scientific fad, at least fifty years before Langer's pronouncement?[26] More important: his extolling of the "speculative audacity of the natural scientists" makes me wonder in what kind of intellectual world this New England Sachem has been living, when the history of the last fifty years amply demonstrates the hidebound and bureaucratic nature of much of the speculation that goes on under the name of science, through the unwillingness and the incapacity of most scientists to liberate themselves from nineteenth-century concepts of causality.

In *The House of Intellect,* written more than a decade ago, and in *Darwin, Marx, Wagner,* written thirty-five years ago, Barzun had many telling things to say about the mental slowness and the stagnant conservatism of scientific thinkers. Why doesn't he return to this argument now, when he is aiming at essential errors at the very core of his own profession?[7] Perhaps there is one reason for this: Jacques Barzun is tired. In *Clio and the Doctors* his writing remains lucid, it is washed by his clear *bon sens,* there are flashes of insight, his wit flares on occasion—but one has the feeling of the kind of tiredness that overcomes even the best of teachers when he is unwilling to repeat himself: "I have been here before; I have said this so often before." He is, after all, up against a dense fog of stupidity closing in on him, within his own profession, up against idiots whose presence and publicity are depressingly ubiquitous. To wrestle down a weakling is easier than to struggle with a brute; but to argue with a bad mind is more difficult than to argue with a good mind: the latter effort is more pleasurable and somehow easier than the wearisome attempt to quarrel with someone who is not only ignorant of essentials but also largely devoid of common sense. There are passages in *Clio and the Doctors* when one senses that Barzun's mental image of his audience has become blurred, that he does not quite know whether he is talking at the history-doctors or to a crowd of artless and uninstructed students, when, for example, he feels compelled to explain to them the difference between Descartes' *esprit de la géometrie* and Pascal's *esprit de la finesse.* I understand, Père Jacques! I sympathize with you! *Clio and the Doctors* is essentially a sally, a spoiling attack against two fads—deadeningly, wearisomely recurrent attempts to make history into a science of sorts. But—and this is the main point of this review-essay—the issue is both deeper and broader than that.

❉ ❉ ❉

IN *Clio* at times it seems that Barzun attempts the assumption that interest in history has waned, that we are on the verge of a post-historical age. "Whether one looks at the numbers enrolled in history courses or the tendency of history departments to make sheep's eyes at bold quantifiers, or the declining popularity of history among general readers ... [t]he historical sense in modern populations is feeble or nonexistent, as Ortega pointed out. . . ."[8] But is this really true? Consider the popularity of all kinds of historical reconstructions, of amateur histories of many kinds, ranging from potboilers such as *The Day Lincoln Died* to the often solid researches of ex-actors or ex-journalists turned historians, such as John Toland or Cornelius Ryan or Bruce Catton or Barbara Tuchman (Barzun does mention her); consider the success of popular historical magazines, such as *American Heritage,* edited with a high level of competence, or the widespread popular appeal of early twentieth-century themes on television, or the existence of millions of World War II buffs. Very little, if any, of this kind of popular interest in history existed fifty years ago, or a century ago, certainly not in the United States.[9] There is an amazingly large appetite for history *in all kinds of forms*—and thus it is not only regrettable, it is criminal, that professional historians have been ignoring this, scurrying to adjust themselves to their professional and bureaucratic interests at the very time when broad evidences exist of a historical consciousness and of an appetite for the kind of *reality* that is offered by history. As I wrote in *Historical Consciousness,* more than a decade ago: "The historical form of reconstruction is one of the few things nowadays that can give people a vicarious mental connection with reality."

It seems (his sometimes unduly categorical distinction of biography from history suggests this) that Barzun cannot completely divorce himself from the essentially nineteenth-century notion of history being but the recorded past.[10] But history is more than that; it is a form of thought. About this Ortega was wrong and Huizinga was right. "Historical thinking," the latter wrote, "has entered our very blood." At times Barzun, too, recognizes this: "the public of today absorbs historical matter as part of its workaday life, almost without noticing that it is history." Yes: and it is precisely therefore that it is not enough to say that history is not a science. One must be bold enough to say that history is more than the recorded past; that just as there is no difference between a source and a historical source, there is no difference between a person and a historical person, or between an event and a historical event.

My purpose here, however, is not to argue that Jacques Barzun's view of history is insufficiently broad. I am principally interested in an intellectual phenomenon, the exploration of which has been insufficiently deep. *Why* the revived vogue of scientism in the 1960s, of all times?[11] Why have so many professional historians actually adopted idiocies? Because certain idiocies are intellectually profitable—though only in the short run. And this is a phenomenon of unusual enormity, involving the *Zeitgeist,* which I must now attempt to describe.

The enormity is this: the two fads of quanto-history and of psychohistory which have one thing in common—both are determinist (and, therefore, neo-materialist) in an extremely primitive way—flourish now, at the beginning of the last quarter of the twentieth century, nearly one hundred years after determinism and mechanical materialism had sprung their first leaks that were pointed out by the first post-scientific thinkers, and more than fifty years after determinism and materialism had been found wanting in physics, in the very study of matter itself. Ask any serious scientist and he will agree: twentieth-century mechanistic materialism is dead, it has been superseded in physics, chemistry, biology, etc., etc. Ask any serious historian and he will agree; the notion that history is determined, economically or materially, is long passé. And yet: there is a good chance that, having assented to this proposition, our colleague the scientist and our fellow-historian will go ahead with his professional work as if the world and nature and history *were* determined. This is our very problem, perhaps especially in the United States, and surely in the twentieth century:[12] not intellectual schizophrenia but something else: the reappearance of Byzantinism, with its characteristically split theological mind.

A little less than fifty years ago Johan Huizinga returned to Holland from a trip to the United States and wrote the following:

> ...American science in its dominant form appears to me to have a naïvely antimetaphysical focus.... The antimetaphysical attitude of mind automatically includes an antihistorical one.... In all these things, fashionable American thought gives us the sensation of an outdated or backward Europe.[13] Around 1890 there were some in Europe who attempted to impose on history the task of sociology and to compel it to be exact and general. It was not without difficulty that the sciences of the mind or culture resisted subjection to the norms and aims of natural science at that time. The most valuable gain won in that struggle was the realization that not every "science" strives always and exclusively for knowledge of the absolutely simple, for the extremes of analysis. Are men in America sufficiently aware of this methodological change? Or do they still hold the opinion that ... no term can be scientifically useful unless it is strictly exact?
>
> ... When one reads the writings of the radical representatives of the "new materialism," as its opponents call it, one detects in their facile explanations of psychological or social phenomena an appalling impoverishment of thought.... Something mechanical, something technological and schematic has entered their thinking. And there undoubtedly lies in this very abdication of reason an element in the large-scale process of mechanization of culture.... Strong feelings of social depersonalization must be at work.... [F]or these thinkers themselves the mechanization of society no longer means something to be feared.... [They say] that we must renounce the illusions of freedom and personality....[14]

Fifty years passed, and we are up against the same thing, resurrected and repeated over and over again.

But why this kind of intellectual stagnation? There is an answer: the great Tocqueville described it nearly one hundred and forty years ago. He denied what everyone, both partisans and critics of democracy, had believed at the time, that the coming age of democracy would spawn a dangerously revolutionary, rapidly changing movement of ideas. To the contrary: he believed that the movement of ideas would be slowing down. In a democracy an established opinion persists by itself and is maintained without effort, because no one attacks it. Those who at first rejected it as false ultimately receive it as the general impression, and those who still dispute it in their hearts conceal their dissent; they are careful not to engage in a dangerous and useless conflict. . . .

And he glimpsed something that would not come during the unfolding but later, during the decay of the democratic age:

> We live at a time that has witnessed the most rapid changes of opinions in the minds of men; nevertheless it may be that the leading opinions of society will before long be more settled than they have been for several centuries in our history; that time has not yet come, but it may perhaps be approaching. . . .
>
> . . . It is believed by some that modern society will be always changing its aspects; for myself, I fear that it will ultimately be too invariably fixed in the same institutions, the same preju-dices . . . so that mankind will be stopped and circumscribed; that the mind will swing backwards and forwards forever with-out begetting fresh ideas; . . . and, though in continual motion, that humanity will cease to advance.[15]

In other words, no matter what people say and think when they repeat that we live "in a revolutionary age," in reality we live in the midst of a monstrous kind of intellectual stagnation, typical of a decaying civiliza-tion, and of the end of an age. Certain institutionalized ideas, no matter how absurd, live on. Their essence may be dead but they are far from passé. There are enormous institutions, in enormous buildings, employing hun-dreds of thousands of people, with other millions as their indirect benefi-ciaries, incarnating and representing basic ideas in which hardly any of their employees and none of their beneficiaries really believe. (Two ex-amples of such institutions: the compulsory Education programs in the United States, the compulsory Marxism-Leninism courses in the Soviet Union.) No matter: they go on and on. So does social-scientism (to which both Marxism and Education belong). And this is the problem and the phe-nomenon—not the false *content* of certain ideas but their adoption and in-stitutionalization through a professional bureaucracy—to which Barzun does not now address himself.[16]

❀ ❀ ❀

AND now I have to take one more step: for I believe that here we are in the face of one essential issue that even the great Alexis, my admired mas-ter, has not clearly foreseen. This issue may be stated simply: it is quite possible that the age of aristocracy has been succeeded not by the age of democracy but by the age of bureaucracy. Bear with me, irritated reader: this is not a mere aphorism, just as bureaucracy is not a mere excrescence of the modern state, a passing phenomenon. Something akin to it existed in ancient Byzantium, and in old China, and in nineteenth-century Russia, where it was a phenomenon of relatively limited importance because the number of scribes and the extent of their influence then was strictly limited to certain administrative spheres of life. It is different now. The intellectualization of life has become enormous. What we are facing is the bureaucratization of intellectual life, and of the *entire* intellectual profession—a new phenomenon, this. We are faced with a new kind of man who thinks that the principal purpose of his mind is to represent or exemplify applications of ideas that have become public and current[17]—current among intellectuals and possibly becoming current in the mass media.[18]

To give an example: I find it quite possible that sooner or later the "scientific study" of occultism and/or astrology will be accepted as respected academic occupations. In that event it is merely a question of time that a respected (important qualifying adjective, this) historian will deliver a presidential paper: "Astro-History: The Next Assignment." And in this respect it really makes little or no difference whether astro-history precedes or succeeds quantohistory or psychohistory: for many, if not most of the same kind of professional historians who in the 1960s and 1970s chose to advance their career in making a "contribution" to quantohistory or psychohistory would embrace the cause of astro-history *when*—the operative word which, to them, is equivalent to *because*—it is opportune and respectable to do so. This is the main reason why in this essay-review I have not addressed myself to the dissecting of the very enormities of quanto-history and of psychohistory. I am not interested in the putrid body of the subject (which is evident) but in the diagnostic capacities of the physicians (which are not evident at all). I am dealing with medicine, not with biology. I repeat: on the one hand the constructions of quantohistory and of psychohistory are often so absurd that the task of dismantling them is enormous to the point of boredom. On the other hand the latter task is no longer of primary importance: for it is not so much the character of ideas as the character of the thinking of intellectuals which should be our main concern.

And in this respect Machiavelli, Hegel, Dostoyevsky, Freud, all may be outdated. The opportunism and the hypocrisy that Machiavelli ruefully described and suggested involved the necessarily self-conscious adjustment of one's acts and of one's words to the powers of the world—something quite different from the nearly automatic adoption of current opinions or ideas by people who believe that this is what their intellect is for. What

Hegel meant by the *Zeitgeist,* too, is quite different from the phenomenon we have to face: he concentrated on the category or the character of ideas, whereas our problem is that of the *process* whereby certain ideas are made to be current. There is a shortcoming in German categorical idealism which flows from the relatively primitive causality it attributes to the *Zeitgeist*—when, in reality, it is the person who is more important than *any* idea, since it is not the person who is part of the idea, but the idea which is (or rather, becomes) part of the person. Thus, historically speaking, it is even more interesting what people do with ideas than what ideas do to them. As H. C. Allen wrote in his *Sixteenth-Century Political Thought* (1928): "Men are constantly engaged in an, on the whole highly successful, effort to adjust their ideas to circumstances and also in an effort, very much less successful, to adjust circumstances to their ideas"—of which two processes the first has been, by and large, ignored by Dostoyevsky and by many modern intellectuals. Which leads me to Freud, an argument which I can sum up in one sentence: far more fascinating (and sometimes revolting) than speculations about the operations of the subconscious is what men, very much including intellectuals, do with their conscious minds.

Those of us who want to maintain the sanity of their minds must therefore recognize the time that has come in the evolution of consciousness: we must begin thinking, not about ideas, but about thinking itself.

15

Charles-Olivier Carbonell
(1977)

The French are a people who constantly think *for* themselves, while they do remarkably little thinking *about* themselves. This is surely true of their historians. There are few people whose knowledge is as saturated with historical memories as that of the French; at the same time they have been doing remarkably little thinking about the nature of historical knowledge itself. They take themselves very seriously; they take their past, which is the only thing they (or, for that matter, anyone else) know, very seriously; but while they think a great deal, they don't give much thought to how or why they are thinking. There are advantages in this condition: in the land of La Rochefoucauld a native psychoanalyst is a rare bird. There are disadvantages in this condition, one of them being that few French historians have concerned themselves with the problems of historiography, or with historical thinking. But then, the professional study of history—or, more accurately, of modern history—in France came into its own later than in Germany, only about one hundred years ago, during the somber and heavy bourgeois period. Or: this is what we have been told to believe. Until now.

Charles-Olivier Carbonell is a young historian, teaching in Toulouse. In the best French academic tradition he has written a number of small and succinct books on a variety of subjects. In this book he addresses himself to a very large topic. Between 1865 and 1885 the study of history in France became transformed. Certain people have claimed, not without convincing evidence, that during these twenty years the entire French intellectual attitude to the modern world was transformed. Carbonell examines these claims methodically,[1] and in a modest, often engaging manner, he suggests his conclusion: most of these claims are wrong.

Review of Charles-Olivier Carbonell, *Histoire et Historiens: Une Mutation Idéologique des Historiens Français 1865–1885* (1975). From *Salmagundi*, Spring: 155–60.

Early in the last century Augustin Thierry said that while the eigh-teenth century was the century of philosophy, the nineteenth century would be the century of history. Soon this idea became an accepted cliché, an *idée reçue*, repeated to this day. But was this true? In 1763, Carbonell shows, about one out of every ten books printed in France was a history; in 1873 the proportion remained the same. During the much-vaunted transforma-tion and expansion of historical studies, from 1870 to 1890, the proportion of historical works among other books printed in France actually declined a little. Another accepted idea has been that the nineteenth century, espe-cially after 1860, was that of *les bourgeois conquérants* (title of a famous work by Charles Morazé), and that this had profoundly affected the very struc-ture, and the sociology, of French intellectual life. Yet between 1866 and 1876 the author of every sixth historical book was a priest, and one out of every eight or nine was written by a titled nobleman. True, more than half of the books written by these men dealt with religious history, local his-tory, the history of the French nobility, etc. Still what these figures suggest is that as late as 1880 history writing in France was not the monopoly of the conquering bourgeois. Nor was there any significant change in the French historical perspective. The vast majority of classical and archeological stud-ies was concentrated on the Mediterranean. The perspective of world his-tory remained centered on Europe, on France. Henri and Charles Riancey, Catholic royalists, wrote a history of the world a little more than a century after Voltaire's attempt at universal history. During that century America and Russia had risen, the interiors of entire continents had opened up, Japan and China were no longer closed books. Yet the proportions of the Rianceys' book were almost identical to that of Voltaire's: more than one half of their history of the world deals with France, four-fifths of it deals with Europe.

The generally accepted idea is that the 1870s, at the latest, mark the beginning of scientific historiography in France. Yet even after 1870 the only truly scientific training school for historians was the Ecole des Chartres. Conservative in the twentieth as it had been in the nineteenth century, the Ecole des Chartres often produced superb archivists rather than historians. And here we come to an important question: perhaps history was too seri-ous a matter to be left to professional historians. Of all histories published in the 1870s only one-tenth were written by professional historians. Be-tween 1840 and 1880 there was hardly any variation in the subjects of doc-toral theses, the solid majority being devoted to the history of antiquity. Meanwhile journalists were writing a great deal of contemporary history, and their performance was not markedly worse than that of most of the professional historians. An astonishing number of lawyers were amateur historians, turning out all kinds of books in their spare time, addressing themselves to a remarkable variety of topics. Army officers, whose reputation, especially among intellectuals, was rather low after the Franco-Prussian war, produced many books, not all of them military histories. The great majority of professional historians did not wish to write about recent history, even indirectly. They skirted the topics of the Franco-Prussian War, there being a kind of tacit agreement among them about this, Carbonell writes. During the 1870s 205 books in France dealt with the Franco-Prussian War, of which only twenty-two were written by historians. Among 122 works dealing with the Paris Commune no more than seven were written by historians. What is more important, those few historians writing about these topics proved to have been "not more reliable as witnesses, and not more honest as chroniclers than other writers who had never studied or practiced the art of historiography." Carbonell shows this in a few tables of content analysis, dealing with the professional historians' language, in which the same phrases and adjectives appear and reappear in three, four, six, seven of the fourteen books by professional historians dealing with the period. The German soldiers are "barbarians," "butchers," "brigands," etc. Ernest Lavisse, the later-famous savant, in 1871 a recent product of the Ecole Normale Supérieure, described the Germans as "voracious," "animal-like," "filthy and sweaty," "their reek lingers on," etc. (Same thing in the seven books by historians on the Commune of 1871: "assassins," "bandits," "murderers," etc., etc.)

In the intellectual history of France the year 1863–64 is known as an important milestone, marking a breakthrough to modern historical thinking. In 1863 Renan first published his *Vie de Jésus,* Taine his *Histoire de la littérature anglaise,* in 1864 Fustel de Coulanges his *Cité antique.* Carbonell's conclusions are interesting. Contrary to what we have been told, none of the three had a real following within the academy. They were widely reputed, perhaps even widely read, but their influence was far less than what we have been accustomed to think. With all of his fineness and discriminating ability, Taine's method was less original than it then seemed. In spite of subtle changes in his later themes, he remained obsessed with the category of scientific naturalism. In 1870–71 came the catastrophe. The agnostic Renan said that the victory at Sedan was the victory of the Prussian schoolmaster. The Germans were better educated than the French. This was true of German soldiers as well as of German historians. The Catholic Fustel, a very different man than Renan, said much the same thing. In 1876 Gabriel Monod and his friends established the *Revue historique.* Their goal was a serious journal, a French equivalent of the *Historische Zeitschrift.* Ever since that time this event has been regarded as another milestone, marking the establishment of the objective-scientific tradition in French historiography. In reality the *Revue historique* reflected the views of a small clique of French Protestant, liberal, republican historians. They were later assailed bitterly by the nationalists of the *Action Française* stripe; but Carbonell shows that both the partisans and the attackers of the Monod group were far off the mark. Contrary to the general belief, Monod had no German ancestors (he did have interesting connections: the woman who finally consented to marry him after long years of unsuccessful courtship was Olga Herzen; and Nietzsche composed for them a piece for two pianos as his wedding gift); and he was a liberal and a democrat only in abstract terms ("Nine out of ten of the common people are idiots," this great republican said). He kept repeating over and over again that the *Revue historique* stands for values that are "strict and scientific," "scrupulously objective," "a compendium of positive science." He also reported over and over again that Catholicism is the religion of the dead, agreeing with Renan that it leads to the cretinization of the individual, because Catholic education arrests individual mental development, while Protestantism develops it.

In sum, the *Revue historique* served ideological purposes no less than the legitimist and conservative *Revue des questions historiques,* a historical journal which began to be published ten years earlier, in 1886, and which, as Carbonell writes, has been just about totally ignored by the few French historians who have written on the history of history in France. The common assumption is that the chasm between the two intellectual camps, with their profoundly different views of French history, opened up after 1900. But twenty years earlier the two camps, though with somewhat different compositions of members, already existed: practically no one who wrote for the *Revue historique* would write for the *Revue des questions historiques,* or vice versa. Fustel was a sporadic exception; so was Gustave Fagniez, who resigned from the *Revue historique* in 1881, disgusted as he was with the sectarian tendentiousness of the latter.

The attackers of the *Revue historique,* too, read things wrongly. Their accepted idea has been that the Monod circle propagated, and eventually established, the overwhelming influence of the German model for historians in France. Yet Carbonell suggests that the egocentric vegetation of the French intellect kept on flourishing green and thick after 1870 as much as before. During the entire decade that followed only one out of one hundred books published in France was a translation. Translations from English outnumbered those from the German. Between 1861 and 1885 there was hardly any change in the number of histories that had been translated from German. There was a slight—very slight—increase in book reviews of works of German historians. The indefatigable Carbonell made a quantitative study of bibliographical references and footnotes: the result shows the same condition, a minimal number of references to German scholarly works.

In 1966, Michel Foucault, instantly proclaimed as a Seminal Thinker of Our Times, published his famous *Les mots et-les choses,* "modestly subtitled as An Archaeology of the Human Sciences," as Carbonell puts it, in which pretentious book Foucault simply—or rather, complicatedly—restated the old thesis: the nineteenth century had become the century of progressive history because of the increasing interest and involvement of the bourgeoisie, with their inevitably progressive vision of history. Carbonell's answer: Not proven. And this is the result of solid research, not the product of a self-proclaimed revisionist or of an idea-monger. Even as it shows great erudition and considerable independence of spirit, Carbonell's work is not perfect. He is unduly apologetic about his method, many of his quotes are unduly extensive, and there is at least one piece of information that one would have liked to have: the number of copies printed (and eventually sold) of the various books and of the two principal historical journals he mentions. More important, Carbonell cannot entirely detach himself from the Cartesian division of the world. He sees through the often shabby pretensions of "objectivity" in history writing, but then he writes of "inevitable subjectivity," which is but the other side of the coin—the very error into which E. H. Carr had fallen when he pronounced that in order to study the history one must study the historian. On the other hand Carbonell does not slip into the determinism that Carr still accepted in *What Is History?* Carbonell understands something about the difference between the motives and the purposes of the historian.[2]

This is all to the good. But the French, as well as ourselves, have still a long way to go.

16

David Irving

(1977)

David Irving is a young English amateur historian of considerable industry, principally interested in the history of Germany during the Second World War. He has written useful, well-researched, and on the whole, fair books on the bombing of Dresden, on German atomic bomb research, on the *Luftwaffe*, and on the disaster that befell one particular Allied convoy sailing for Russia in 1942. But over a period of ten years, while he was producing these books, Irving was working on a biography of Hitler. He gathered an enormous mass of material, from which emerged this book of nearly a thousand pages dealing with less than six years of Hitler's life. A deafening silence has followed its publication. I have seen only one review, by Walter Laqueur in the *New York Times Book Review*, most of which consisted of an attack on Irving's earlier record as an author. This alone was sufficient to arouse my interest and predispose me in favor of this book, which I have now read and which, I must now say, is appalling.

Irving set a high goal for himself: to compose a blockbuster, a revisionist work not merely dramatic but of enduring importance; as he himself puts it in his introduction, with a strangely un-English lack of modesty, a *monumentum aeris*, a monument to an age. The pages of this book are marked by a kind of feverish nervousness, as if the author were spurring himself to something big: but this fretfulness is quite different from the pulsating impatience of genius, and his style is marred by it.

About his sources, too, Irving displays an amateurishness that is surprising, in view of his earlier books. He has pursued tirelessly the survivors of the Third Reich; the names of his interviewees listed in the introduction run to the hundreds. Yet he fails to consider that personal reminiscence is not necessarily a reliable source. *Hitler's War*, unlike Irving's earlier works, contains hundreds of errors: wrong names, wrong dates, and, what is worse,

Review of David Irving, *Hitler's War* (1977). From *National Review*, August 19: 946–50.

statements about events, including battles, that did not really take place. These errors, however, are not the result of inadequate research; they are not technical mistakes or oversights. They are the result of the dominant tendency of the author's mind.

Irving's main purpose in this book is to rehabilitate Hitler. He is convinced not only that Hitler was a very able man but that he was morally superior to his opponents. This latter conviction is not an easy one to sustain, to say the least; but then, all of his assiduous composition notwithstanding, Irving does not quite have the courage of his convictions. He refuses to say that Hitler was a great man (as in a certain sense he was, as were Stalin and Genghis Khan). Instead, he goes slyly about his self-appointed task, by denigrating all Hitler's opponents. He hints that just about everyone who opposed Hitler—Englishmen, certain Americans, German generals, it hardly matters who—where villains and dolts and cowards.

In this book Hitler appears as a very complex man, while Churchill seems a blundering simpleton; Hitler could be very careful in his speech, while Churchill was a fatal victim of his "very garrulousness"; Hitler was farsighted, while Churchill was "blinded by hatred"; Hitler was careful about details, while Churchill's rhetoric was marked by his "characteristic attention to accuracy." (Joke.) Speer, who "was planning less for Germany's defense than for his own," betrayed Hitler. So did the German General von Choltitz, who in 1944 had chosen not to destroy Paris: "an arrogant feckless military commander ... who had allowed the capital to decay into a rotten *Etappenstadt* of draft dodgers, malingerers, and army scroungers." The noble patriots who attempted to overthrow Hitler in 1944 were ambitious fools and villains, who lived in an atmosphere of "moral decay.... In a Germany bombblasted and rationed, these army plotters had lived the easy lives of grandgourmets. In Olbricht's cellars investigators found a thousand bottles of wine. A champagne orgy lasting far into the night had been their reaction to news of Hitler's 'death.'"

And how did Hitler compare to such miserable people? He, according to Irving, refused even to glance at the photos of their execution; he "irritably tossed the pictures aside." Indeed, this profoundly compassionate man arranged for "proper monthly subsistence payments to the next-of-kin of the hanged men." About the Jews, half of Hitler's ideas "were unconscious or the result of his own muddled beliefs, but half had been deliberately implanted by trusted advisors like Himmler and Goebbels"; Hitler also ordered that Jews should not be deported and liquidated, as in the case of Hungary in July 1944.

The evidence for all these assertions is inadequate; the references are either nonexistent or muddled; the names of Hungarian officers, among others, are hopelessly misspelled; errata in names and dates amount to hundreds, and unverifiable and unconvincing assertions to thousands. Here are a few random examples: in September 1939 the Polish army was "optimistically assembled at Posen for an attack on Berlin"; Hitler's invasion of Russia was a preventive measure, since "Stalin had obviously laid immense plans for an offensive into Europe"; in June 1941 "the Vatican also let it be known that it 'welcomed the war' with Russia"; one month before the collapse of the Third Reich, "the tough General Ferdinand Schoerner fought a grim twenty-day defensive battle for the industrial city of Moravian Ostrau (Ostrava) which ended on April 3 in a convincing victory for his Army Group Center"—all of which is complete (or rather incomplete) fantasy.

Yet a clue to Irving's method emerges from his use of language here. One of the rhetorical tricks of ideological advocates is their emphatic use of adjectives and adverbs, which they use not as qualifiers but to carry the main thrust of their sentences. They are rhetorical substitutes for evidence. (The Soviets do this all the time: they will speak of a "well-known fact" when the fact is not only far from being well known but not a fact at all.)

And so Hitler, in Irving's breathless prose, "*evidently* made some promise about the Jews" (there is no evidence); Schoerner fought a "*convincing* victory" (it was not a victory, and it convinced no one): the Polish army was "*optimistically* assembled at Posen" (a queer adverb for an English writer, but then the Polish army was not assembled at Posen, nor was it very optimistic); "Stalin had *obviously* laid immense plans for an offensive into Europe" (the very contrary was true: Stalin was so fearful of Hitler that he ordered the Soviet military not to proceed with defensive, let alone offensive measures, since these might have irritated the Germans). This last assertion, for example, appears on page 285 of *Hitler's War*. As in other instances, I looked up the reference to it. There are eighteen lines of footnotes relating to this page; they touch on all kinds of matters, and contain all kinds of codes and document numbers. But so far as evidence for the foregoing assertion goes, there is nothing: for Irving, obviously *obviously* will do. Another Irving (Washington) had warned his readers, in *Tales of a Traveler*: "I am always at a loss to know how much to believe of my own stories." This sense of loss, in David Irving's case, is not obviously apparent.

Why waste a long review on such a book? Because behind it lurks an issue which may be particularly relevant for the readership of *National Review*.

That readership will please note that the writer of this review has often been labeled a right-wing revisionist, and that his books, specifically those dealing with the Second World War, have been willfully ignored or, in one instance, treated with contumely by the New York liberal establishment.

In the introduction to *The Last European War,* I wrote that there has been regrettably little revisionist writing done about the Second World War. During the last fifteen years reams of profitable nonsense about the origins of the Cold War have been written, and published, by partisans of the fashionable Left, but there has been little serious reexamination of the clichés and accepted ideas about the Second World War—a vastly more consequential struggle of which the Cold War was but the almost inevitable consequence.

This situation is due partly to the liberals' near-monopoly on the intellectual and academic marketplace, including publishing; partly also to the fact that most of the few scattered revisionist books about the Second World War, published by small and relatively obscure right-wing houses, were single-minded, vitriolic, historically inaccurate, and devoted to a common theme sustained in the spirit of a pamphleteer: the war against Germany was a criminal mistake.

During the Vietnam War, now fortunately past, millions of decent Americans contrasted the melancholy condition of their divided people with their memories of unity of national purpose during the Second World War. Their memories were, however, inaccurate. There *was* a deep-seated division among the American people then—especially during the two years before Pearl Harbor—although it did not always show on the surface.

There were relatively few Americans who had an outright admiration for Hitler and the Third Reich. There were many Americans who had no sympathy for the American support given to Britain and France, let alone Russia, in the war against Hitler. The usual epithet of "isolationist" is imprecise, and it obscures the issue. There have been few consistent isolationists in the history of the United States; their preferences are usually determined by the particular war in question. Most of the so-called isolationists in the 1930s and 1940s did not wish England to win, which is the equivalent of saying that they did not wish Hitler's Germany to lose. Very soon after the war, they became the most vocal and extreme partisans of American intervention against Russia.[1]

Initially, the principal supporters of that remarkable and, on the whole, salutary phenomenon, the American conservative movement, were drawn from these people. They were the mainstay of the early *National Review.* When in the second year of its publication the magazine—for the simple reason that Nasser's Egypt seemed to be backed by the Soviet Union—supported the English-French-Israeli invasion of the Sinai and Suez, a large portion of its readers canceled their subscriptions. They were people who disliked the British and the French (and the Jews), with a distaste that lay deeper than their—often abstract—super-patriotic version of anticommunism: their memories and their preferences had been formed before and during the Second World War.

During the next twenty years the composition of the conservative camp, probably including the *National Review* readership, changed subtly but significantly. A new generation had grown up, with few or no memories of the Second World War; others had abandoned some of their earlier obsessions and dislikes. Conservatives earned a certain degree of respectability; their level of discourse rose; they became a recognized and recognizable and responsible and, I hope, increasingly influential element in the evolution of American political and historical thinking. The new generation is also interested in the Second World War, though from a viewpoint different from their fathers'; they find the phenomenon of Hitler fascinating, which indeed it is—whence this article, whose motto is simple: *Caveat lector.*

Should there be a place for isolationists in the conservative movement? I think that there should be, and that this place must include people who, whether young or old, think American involvement in the Second World War may have been a mistake. The caveat, however, is this: a person who supports Hitler's cause was not, is not, and never shall be a true conservative. And this issue is too important to be glossed over: let us leave special pleading and selective indignation to their master practitioners on the Left. An example of such special pleading from the Right is the lead article in the May 1977 *Alternative,* by John Chamberlain, entitled "An Innocent Ensnared: There Was Only One Lindbergh."

Lindbergh was not an innocent, and he was not ensnared. He believed that the war against Hitler's Germany was a mistake; and not only that American intervention in the war would be a mistake, but that American support of France and Britain against the Third Reich was a mistake, because France and Britain should not have opposed Hitler. The same point was forcefully argued by Truman Smith, a former American military attaché to Germany and a close friend of Lindbergh's and of Chamberlain's: Smith admired not only what Hitler's Germany had been able to achieve but much of what the Third Reich had stood for.

But Chamberlain fudges the issue, no less and no more than the liberal tergiversators. "When Churchill warned the British of Hitler's growing power, it was one thing. But when Lindbergh substantiated Churchill, it was quite another." What a travesty of the truth this is! Lindbergh opposed everything Churchill stood for. What Churchill said was that Hitler was arming, and the British had better get ready to fight. What Lindbergh said was that Hitler was so strong that there was no sense in fighting him at all.

Impelled by his own midwestern and Nordic conception of patriotism, Lindbergh went to Germany; he sought some kind of an understanding between the American democracy and the Third Reich, in which he saw the wave of the future. He was mistaken, but he was honest. Chamberlain writes that Lindbergh went to Germany on "patriotic, pro-democratic, and even pro-Jewish missions"—a statement which is not very honest. Later, Lindbergh "wanted to effect a reconciliation between the Germans and the British, in order to face the bigger menace from the Communist East. The idea was unrealistic, given Hitler's madness, but it was an idea held by such American worthies as Herbert Hoover, Harry Truman, and Bob Taft."

The idea was not unrealistic, it was Hitler's principal idea; Hitler was not mad; and there was an essential difference between these American worthies. When Hitler invaded Russia, Truman said: "If we see that Germany is winning we ought to help Russia and if Russia is winning we ought to help Germany . . . although I don't want to see Hitler victorious under any circumstances." Taft said on the same day: "The victory of Communism in the world would be far more dangerous to the United States than the victory of Fascism."

There is a profound difference between these two statements; and, at the risk of alienating my conservative friends, I must say that in this instance in 1941 (as also in others) Harry Truman was right and Bob Taft was wrong. Hitler's victory would have meant, at the very least, his domination of all of Europe, with incalculable consequences for the United States. Stalin's victory meant his domination of the eastern portion of Europe, an event with clearly calculable consequences, including the Cold War (which, as the excellent editor of the *Alternative* wrote elsewhere in the same issue, has not been a terribly gruesome struggle so far: "over the years our casualties have compared favorably with our highway death toll, and the cost was a bargain").

This writer, like Irving and Lindbergh and Chamberlain and Churchill and Taft and the best as well as the worst of the Germans, regretted and still regrets that the Second World War ended the way it did, in sordidness and tragedy rather than in decent triumph for the democracies. Unlike Irving, and perhaps others of his persuasion, I do not regret that the Third Reich lost the war. I believe that Hitler had it coming to him, and that his present admirers such as Irving have it coming to them still, whence this kick in the ass. *Caveat lector.*

17

William Appleman Williams
(1980)

The history of imperialism is the history of its rhetoric. From the beginning of their history the people of the United States and their leaders were often inclined to expansion, the justifications of which resided in patriotic and moralistic phrases that their public speakers kept repeating to the people in order to make them feel good. Certain historians in retrospect performed the often overdue duty of pointing out the mixed motives and unclear purposes of certain chapters of American territorial aggrandizement and of intervention abroad. Few of them were able to present a balanced picture when their vision was not sufficient to range beyond the concerns of their day. Many of the revisionists of the 1960s were primitive examples of this; at the cost of all kinds of falsifications and more often than not in the service of their own intellectual opportunism, they would simply project their then present opinions on the Vietnam War onto the past, applying them to the historical origins of the Cold War. In the early 1930s Walter Millis began his monumental *Road to War,* an eloquent and comprehensive account of Wilson's interventionism and of British propaganda during World War I. The book was published in 1937, at the height of the democratic and populist reaction against World War I, and became a best-seller. Yet Millis was disturbed by the protracted influence of his book, since less than two years after its publication he had come to believe that American intervention on the side of Britain against Hitler was a necessity. He, at least, was an honest man.

To write about national expansion is both easy and difficult. It is easy because the evidences are there for anyone to see, save for those who close their eyes because of their nationalistic piety or hypocrisy. It is difficult because, let us face it, every great nation became great because of its con-

Review of William Appleman Williams, *Empire as a Way of Life* (1980). From *New Republic,* October 11: 31–33.

quests, often at the expense of other peoples. This fact must be recognized, but it does not amount to an enduring trait of national character. Professional intellectuals will often chastise the character of their nation without recognizing that their profitable occupations have been made possible by the existing power and prosperity of their country. They are reminiscent of someone who publicly thanks God for his existence as a preacher of sexual abstinence, while forgetting how his father and mother produced him.

In one of his paradoxical essays Oscar Wilde suggested that "The Decay of Lying" is actually the result of the decay of truth: "everybody who is incapable of learning had taken to teaching—that is really what our enthusiasm for education has come to." In 1959 William Appleman Williams published an artless book, *The Tragedy of American Diplomacy,* which was wrong in many details but at least it was something out of the ordinary in 1959, when the fact—and it was a fact—of a new kind of American imperialism was not recognized even by American liberals and radicals, a condition of which this reviewer's own experiences amply attest. Now, more than 20 years later, comes Williams's *Empire as a Way of Life.* He has learned nothing, and forgotten everything. Truth has further decayed, and lying has become worse. Empire has become Williams's way of life, his profession, his capital, his bag. Because of my 1959 memories I approached this book with certain doubts in my mind but with no particular prejudice against its author. Now I am compelled to state that Williams is no American idealist but a vulgarian and a pedant.

The vulgarity of Williams's mind runs through this grandiloquent book, but it appears most clearly in his pop-confessional conclusion. He is compelled to tell us that he was born in 1921, that he was brought up to believe in The American Way of Life, and that once he stole a knife from a hardware store. His maternal grandmother, Maude Hammond Appleman, found him out and told him to return it to the store. After some painful hesitation the boy obeyed his grandmother (he calls her "Maude," which is peculiar enough, but let this pass), and took the knife back to the store where he was duly praised by the owner. What this has to do with American imperialism is difficult to gauge. (After all, the owner of that hardware store was not an Indian.) It seems that in the 1920s American kids were afraid of their grandmothers and American imperialism was popular. Now the grandmothers are afraid of the kids and anti-imperialism is popular. There must be a moral in this somewhere.

Now let us go from the very end to the very beginning. This William Appleman Williams (what a name! an American mouthful and suitable for an abbreviation like USA WAW) grew up to be an American professor, a pedant. It is all there in the first paragraph of the introduction:

> In order to think seriously about empire as a way of life, we
> must first choose a strategy of inquiry that is appropriate to the
> subject. Then we must define the basic terms involved, and out-
> line the process whereby the different elements of society are
> integrated into an overall outlook and culture. [The class goes
> to sleep.]

The pages that follow are reminiscent of Dickens's immortal Mr. Gradgrind,
who began his class by hectoring the students: "Define a Horse." Fortunately—or unfortunately—Williams's pedantry consists of short bursts; his
natural vulgarity will prevail, because it must. The title of his next chapter
reads: "A Psychologically Justifying and Economically Profitable Fairy Tale:
The Myth of Empty Continents Dotted Here and There with the Mud
Huts, the Lean-tos, and the Tepees of Unruly Children Playing at Culture." WAW. WOW.

He is not a simple pedant. If the history of imperialism—or at that, of
every idea—is the history of its rhetoric, then the mark of the hopeless
historian is his hopeless rhetoric. He will, on occasion, jargonize, using words
and terms such as "self-legitimatizing dynamism," "encapsulate," "reifi-
cation"—but, I repeat, his vulgarity (and what is worse, his *imprecise* vulgarity) will win out. The slogan of Manifest Destiny "was a mash that produced a 200-proof imperial snort." In the Navy in the 1920s "astute admi-
rals . . . leapfrogged into new electric power systems." In 1950 Herbert
Hoover "had no chance. He was in the position of a father of the 1960s,
trying to persuade his children that the jazz of the 1920s and 1930s was
worth a good listen and a good boogie."

There is worse to come. This eminent scholar, the president of the Organization of American Historians, the dean of revisionists, the recent James
Pinckney Harrison Distinguished Visiting Professor at the College of William and Mary, is not merely a shallow vulgarian and self-righteous pedant
and a single-minded idea-monger. He reveals a lack of knowledge of American history, of his very discipline, to an extent which in former times would
have debarred him from the lectern of any reputable institution of higher
learning. He battens on a quotation from Dwight Morrow, which he uses
repeatedly, whereafter he writes that Dwight Morrow "died soon after
speaking that wisdom. Hence no one will ever know how he would have
responded to the subsequent 1929 crisis of the American political economy."
For "no one" read the president of the Organization of American Historians. Some of us happen to know that Dwight Morrow died in October
1931, two years after the 1929 crisis, about which he had spoken and written plenty. Here are a few other examples:

> [In the sixteenth century] came the first Spanish and French, followed by the fleets of fishermen to the northern and the early colonies that failed to survive. The coughs, the sneezes, and the laying on of hands were like the bombs over Hiroshima and Nagasaki.

> The United States undertook to liberate North Korea by conquest and integrate it into the American Empire.

> The world looked relatively manageable in late summer 1949. The United States had won in Iran, the Soviets in Czechoslovakia.... Mao immediately asked to open serious discussions with the United States.

> While the Russians lost 20 million lives, for example, the United States created 17 million new jobs safe from bombs and bullets. These workers, including large numbers of women and teenagers—even some blacks and browns—sometimes had trouble finding places to live or other substantial ways to invest their money. As a result, the entertainment industry boomed. [A capsule summary of World War II.]

> [Around 1900 the American] policeman became ever more energetic in whacking the skulls of strikers and blacks at home, as well as thumping feisty natives abroad.

"Prior to the appearance of the Europeans there were probably between 10 and 12 million people living north of the Rio Grande River." Scholarly estimates are around one million, including Canada. In 1827 in Greece (yet another example of brute American interventionism) American "landing parties hunted pirates on the islands of Argenteire, Miconi, and Androsa." There are no islands by such names in Greece or indeed anywhere else. All of which tells us something of the Organization of American Historians, of the editors of the Oxford University Press (founded in 1478 and now at the sorry end of the Modern Age), and of the present state of professional historianship in the United States.

We are now coming to the essence of the matter. The ignorance of William Appleman Williams is very great. Some of it is, of course, the result of his single-mindedness. He will take any kind of evidence, from anywhere, and tape it together to illustrate his thesis, which is that Americans are obsessed with empire. To show support for his thesis he will cite, for example, a political commentator, a publisher's entrepreneur, an Australian rancher, and the Singapore minister for foreign affairs. This is a treatment of sources which in a genteel era cluck-clucking scholars used to dismiss as "cavalier," whereas it is, in reality, undiscriminating, ham-handed, sweaty, and breathless—and therefore, more than often, not only thematically but factually imprecise and wrong.

And what is the source of this kind of ignorance? Is it, simply and squarely, lack of knowledge, Williams not having done his homework? No, this kind of ignorance is not merely the result of insufficient brain-power. It suggests an insufficiency of self-knowledge. This statement is not the result of facile psychologizing. Its evidences are suggested by WAW himself, who makes—and not merely allows—his personality to intrude in his thesis-book again and again. At the end of his book he lists, and praises, famous Americans, men and women who at some time or other became anti-imperialists.

> It works, it happens, down the line. I live in a non-academic community. You have to earn your way in. My way is pool, I like the game and play it well. Professors playing pool with loggers and truck drivers and gippo fishermen properly go through an apprenticeship. You beat us at our game and we will try your game. Now my game at pool is to play the capitalist machine tables in such a way as most nearly to duplicate the real game of pool. No slop, no ball counts. You call your shots and bank the Eight Ball. The fascinating thing is that people like to be challenged to play the best they can in the most difficult circumstances. *They like the tough game.* [His italics.]

"And this is where we are in the relationship between empire and democracy . . ." (his words).

What does this have to do with empire and democracy? In any event, *le style c'est l'homme.* The earthy populist and the sensitive anti-imperialist, the professor among the truck drivers: his self-portrait is no more convincing than is his scholarship. It suggests that his "tough" game is only dirty pool.

18

Jakob Burckhardt

(1985)

Jakob Burckhardt was one of the profoundest of nineteenth-century historians, indeed perhaps of the entire modern age. His view of history was very different from that of his historian contemporaries, which is remarkable, for it was during Burckhardt's lifetime that modern professional historiography came into its own. The merit and enduring value of Burckhardt's work have been proved by the fact that during the last hundred years his achievement has been generally recognized and respected. There has been hardly any wavering in his reputation, even though his unique historical philosophy and method have had few emulators and though he has not been widely read. His vision remains as fruitful and timely as ever. In sum, Burckhardt, like all great writers and seers, transcends his time.

During his lifetime his reputation rose slowly; he did not seek the approbation of his fellow professionals and moved in their circles not at all. The German historian Friedrich Gundolf was the first who called him "the sage among historians" and the most imaginative among them. "My starting point is a vision," Burckhardt wrote, "otherwise I cannot do anything." This was very different from the nineteenth-century ideal of scientific and professional objectivity. In the introduction to *Reflections on History* Burckhardt writes:

> The word amateur owes its evil reputation to the arts. An artist
> must be a master or nothing. . . . In learning, on the other hand,
> a man can be a master in only one particular field, namely as a
> specialist, and in some field he *should* be a specialist. But if he is

From Jacques Barzun, ed., *European Writers: The Romantic Century*, vol. 6 (New York: Charles Scribner's Sons), 1225–44.

not to forfeit his capacity for taking general views or even his respect for general views, he should be an amateur at as many points as possible.... Otherwise he will remain ignorant in any field lying outside his own specialty and perhaps, as a man, a barbarian.

Burckhardt's main contribution to the writing of history was his creation of art history and cultural history. There his methods justify a recent comment by Gottfried Dietze: "Although a conservative, Burckhardt was nevertheless an innovator of the first rank." At least as important as this achievement are his philosophical reflections on history, delivered orally to small classes of university students and small audiences in his native city of Basel. Immediately after his death some of these texts were collected and published by his pupils, relatives, and friends, with the result that Burckhardt's reputation in his native world suffered no lapse. At least in the German language, most of his lectures (many of them equal to the contents of finished books) and most of his correspondence have become available during the twentieth century. His admiring students and successors have published the body of Burckhardt's work, in addition to a massive six-volume biography by Werner Kaegi, the foremost Burckhardt scholar of this century.

A principal reason for Burckhardt's renown is the excellence of his prose. Unlike many other German writers and historians, Burckhardt's sentences are short and direct; the character of the knowledge he wants to convey is such that he has no need of the many qualifying clauses on which most German writers depend. He is admirably clear, a master of the *mot juste* even in complex and recondite matters of philosophy or aesthetic judgment. Burckhardt's intellectual penchant for the Latin world, as well as his extraordinary comprehension of the classics, may have contributed to his literary gifts. His faultless knowledge of French and Italian, too, was the result not only of linguistic ability but also of the fortunate condition of his being Swiss, a son of a nation speaking the three principal languages of the Continent. Like the great Dutch historian Johan Huizinga, whose view of history was similar to Burckhardt's, he benefited from belonging to a small western European country closely acquainted with and deeply sensitive to the culture of the larger nations bordering its own. Still it was only gradually that the cosmopolitan—or more precisely the supranational—genius of Burckhardt emerged from his originally strong attachment to German thought.

❀ ❀ ❀

JAKOB Burckhardt was born in 1818 in the ancient town of Basel, in that historic triangle where three frontiers of Switzerland, France, and Germany meet. His ancestors were Baslers *(Bälois)*, many of them pastors and teachers; his father was a minister in the cathedral of Basel, founded in the eleventh century; his mother's family had settled in Basel in the fifteenth century. We must be careful not to draw an idealized picture from these conditions. As Burckhardt's biographer Kaegi writes, the society of Basel before Burckhardt's time was "hardly more human than the Athens of Socrates." The social standards and the intellectual climate were cramped and philistine, fearful of the new winds that wafted across Switzerland from revolutionary France. Even later, when Burckhardt's fame had been solidly established, there were patricians and bourgeois among the Basel families who muttered that this Burckhardt had a touch of the charlatan. However, the young Burckhardt was blessed with the spiritual and mental security offered by his bourgeois family, and especially by the serene integrity of his mother who, as Burckhardt states in one of his letters, "lived and died a saint." She died when Burckhardt was twelve years old. Several years before, she had begun a letter to Jakob's eldest sister, which was also meant for her son who, she feared, might one day grow skeptical of his father's simple and stern religious beliefs: "O, do not let yourself be cheated of your child-like faith; they will give you nothing, absolutely nothing, in return." Jakob Burckhardt was deeply moved by this admonition.

At first he was an indifferent student in the gymnasium. Then the romantic—or rather sentimental—*Sturm und Drang* idealism of the Young Germans took hold of his spirit. He depended on the close companionship of friends, to whom he wrote long letters:

> If only you could have gazed . . . into my storm swept mind, so much in need of affection! . . . I would exchange my life, at any moment, in favor of never having been born, and, were it possible, return to the womb—although I am not guilty of any crime and grew up in favored circumstances. . . . Poetry means more to me than ever, and I have never before felt its beneficent powers so active within me. But I have quite given up any idea of literary fame.

Thus he wrote at the age of twenty. He had just returned from his first journey to Italy. Violent and contradictory emotions surged within him. In Florence "the whole sky was deep blue; the Apennines were violet in the evening light; the Arno flowed at my feet, and I could have cried like a child." A few days later, still in Florence: "I felt utterly alone and realized how little the outer world counts if the inner world is not in harmony. That is the point where resignation is most painful: to do without the company of someone who loves us." And he quoted the German idealist poet Count August von Platen: "What heart is that which is untorn by pain?"

This was typical of the early, "Germanic" Burckhardt. He thought—with every reason—that the intellectual and political atmosphere of Switzerland was too cramped, insufficient for a healthy intellectual existence. He went to Germany to study in quest of a wider and clearer mental climate. From Frankfurt, at the age of twenty-one, he wrote his sister:

> I am like Saul, the son of Kis, who went out to look for lost asses, and found a king's crown. I often want to kneel down before the sacred soil of Germany and thank God that my mother-tongue is German! I have Germany to thank for everything! ... I shall always draw my best powers from this land. What a people! What wonderful young people! What a land—a paradise!

In another letter he wrote as if Germany were a holy land: "the debt I owe to Germany lies more heavily than ever on my soul." He was thinking of devoting himself to writing a history of the Counter-Reformation in Switzerland:

> But first and last I shall say to my countrymen: remember that you are Germans! Only a definite—though not political—union with Germany can save Switzerland. I am not disloyal, dear Louise, when I say this, for only someone who tries to further the interests of German culture can be of any use in Switzerland; there is only *one* remedy against the threatening decline of a people, and this is: to renew its links with the origins.... I will make it my life's purpose to show the Swiss that they are Germans.

Within a few weeks of his arrival in Berlin he wrote:

> My eyes were wide with astonishment at the first lectures I heard by Ranke, Droysen, and Böckh. I realized that the same thing had befallen me as befell the knight in *Don Quixote*. I had loved this science of mine on hearsay, and suddenly here it was appearing before me in gigantic proportions—and I had to lower my eyes. Now I really am firmly determined to devote my life to it, perhaps at the cost of a happy home life; from now on no

further hesitation shall disturb my resolve.... I have found my
main subject, *history.*

He was as good as his word. Yet the crystallization of his unique view of
history, something that soon would be very different from his professors',
had already begun. Within a few months he grew disillusioned with the
atmosphere of Berlin: "Berlin qua Berlin is a preposterous abode." His initial admiration for his instructors, especially for Leopold von Ranke, was
disappearing fast. Even before his recognition of the insufficiency of the
professional and academic and scientific method, he was aware that one
cannot separate history from the historian, that the ideal of scientific objectivity could be a self-serving professional illusion, and that—this was
his most important realization—history was more than an academic discipline: it was a form of thought. Burckhardt was not yet twenty-two when he
wrote to his friend Friedrich von Tschudi:

> My poetry, for which you prophesied fair weather, is in great
> danger of being sent packing now that I have found the height
> of poetry in history itself. There was a time when I looked upon
> the play of fantasy as the highest requirement of poetry; but
> since I must esteem the development of spiritual states, or quite
> simply, inner states as such, higher still, I now find my satisfac-
> tion in history itself, which exhibits this development in two
> distinct phases running parallel, crossing and intermingling, and
> indeed identical: I refer to the development of the individual
> and the development of the whole; add to that the brilliant *out-
> ward* events of history—the gorgeous motley dress of the world's
> progress, and I find myself back at the old and much misunder-
> stood saying that the Lord is the supreme poet. . . .

At twenty-four, Burckhardt's self-imposed task was clear to him. In June
1842 he wrote to another friend:

> Although you are a philosopher, you must allow me the truth of
> the following: A man like me, who is altogether incapable of
> speculation, and who does not apply himself to abstract thought
> for a single minute in the whole year ... my surrogate is *contem-
> plation*, daily clearer and directed more and more upon essen-
> tials. I cling by nature to the concrete, to visible nature, and to
> history. But as a result of drawing ceaseless analogies between
> *facta* (which comes naturally to me) I have succeeded in ab-

stracting much that is universal. Above this manifold universal there hovers, I know, a still higher universal, and perhaps I shall be able to mount that step too one day. You would not believe how, little by little, as a result of this possibly one-sided effort, the *facta* of history, works of art, the monuments of all ages gradually acquire significance as witnesses to a past stage in the development of the spirit. Believe me, when I see the present lying quite clearly in the past, I feel moved by a shudder of profound respect.... To me history is poetry on the grandest scale; don't misunderstand me, I do not regard it romantically or fantastically, all of which is quite worthless, but as a wonderful process of chrysalis-like transformations, of ever new disclosures and revelations of the spirit.

"Genius," José Ortega y Gasset wrote, "is the ability to invent one's own occupation." This apothegm clearly applies to the young Burckhardt.

His life in Berlin ("a sandy desert") was not difficult. He had many friends; he earned money as tutor in the house of a former ambassador from Holland. After less than three years in Berlin he returned to Basel. The town was in the midst of agitation: the political struggle between conservatives and liberals was rising in intensity during the 1840s. "I had the courage to be conservative and not to give in," Burckhardt writes. "The easiest thing of all is to be a liberal." But he was not interested in politics: "I am obliged to keep myself to myself, as I despise all parties: I know them all and belong to none." There was also a personal crisis about which even Kaegi's detailed biography tells us very little: Burckhardt offered marriage to a young woman; the offer was gently refused. In 1845 he took up the job of writing articles for the *Basler Zeitung*. Conditions in Switzerland, he writes to his friends, were disgusting and barbarous; they "have spoiled everything for me, and I shall expatriate myself as soon as I can.... God willing, in the summer of 1846." This expatriation led to results very different from what he had imagined.

In April 1846 Burckhardt indeed left for Italy: but his journey, which lasted five months, was soon aglow with an inspiration that he had not foreseen. If it was an escape, it was an escape forward; everything about the journey was exhilarating. There is a nervous, rapid quality of Burckhardt's letters of that time; the effusions of his *Sturm und Drang* period have evaporated. Art, and the history of art, have become the focus of his eye and mind. His political worries and disappointments about his native city and country lessen; and his enthusiasm for German civilization is being replaced subtly by something else; an enthusiasm for the reconstruction of the historic past of Europe: "We may all perish; but at least I want to discover the interest for which I am to perish, namely the old culture of Europe." He has now abandoned the idea of writing about the Counter-Reformation in Switzerland; newer plans—writing either about the declining centuries of the Roman empire or about the Italian Renaissance—replace it. Eventually he would do both of these. In September 1846 he goes again to Berlin via Basel, and after two months writes that his efforts are:

> now all concentrated on saving enough money to be able to go south once more; *then*, when once I am there, I shall not be got out so easily again. I hope to be able to get to the point of solemnly turning my back on the wretched and meretricious life here, its literature and politics. . . . In (present) Germany no man can develop harmoniously.

He writes two months later:

> My "fancy" is beauty, and it stirs me profoundly in all its forms more and more. I can do nothing about it. Italy opened my eyes, and since then my whole being is consumed by a great longing for the golden age, for the harmony of things, and the *soi-disant* "battles" of the present seem to me pretty comic.

Thus Burckhardt's short journey of 1846 to Italy was the turning point of his career. He had emerged from despair and saw the purpose of his life clearly. He returned to his native town, settling down to an outwardly dull but inwardly exciting existence as a writer and teacher, a pattern of life that, except for occasional travel, was not to be altered for the rest of his life, that is, for nearly fifty years. Burckhardt wrote three great books in less than eleven years: *Die Zeit Konstantins des Grossen* (*The Age of Constantine the Great*, 1853), the *Cicerone* (1855), and *Die Kultur der Renaissance in Italien* (*The Civilization of the Renaissance in Italy*, 1860). As a teacher Burckhardt devoted the rest of his life to his students. But what a teacher he was! Burckhardt, says Kaegi, was "not a specialist of the Renaissance but a historian of Europe"; to which we may properly add that he was *the* magisterial teacher of European civilization. He taught and wrote concurrently. He never missed a class in more than four decades of teaching. The purposes of his teaching and his writing were fused. The evidence is in Burckhardt's vast literary legacy, in the completeness of the texts and notes that he left behind. They could be and were published posthumously, some immediately after his death: *Errinerungen aus Rubens* (*Recollections of Rubens*, 1898), *Der Griechische Kulturgeschichte* (*History of Greek Culture*, 1898–1902), *Die Weltgeschichtliche Betrachtungen* (*Reflections on History*, 1905).

Burckhardt's conversion of 1846 reconciled him not only to returning to Basel but also to entering the teaching profession. The University of Basel, though ancient and respectable, was somnolent; when Burckhardt first went to Berlin, Basel had fewer than three dozen regular students. After receiving his doctorate (from Basel) Burckhardt taught for a time in a gymnasium, as Swiss university teachers were required to do; he earned money by contributing articles to the great German *Brockhaus* encyclopedia. In the mid-1850s he moved to Zurich for a few years to teach in the new polytechnic. In 1857 he returned to Basel, never to leave again. Already his close-cropped hair and moustache had turned entirely white. Ten years later Friedrich Nietzsche became first one of Burckhardt's students and then one of his younger colleagues. Their association and friendship lasted only a few years, but Nietzsche's respect for Burckhardt remained deep and strong: he said that every cultured citizen of Basel reflects the fact of having been born in the city of Jakob Burckhardt. Burckhardt's former student Albert Gessler writes that "for those who knew Burckhardt he was an 'educator,' a mentor [*ein Erzieher*], in the highest, most spiritual sense of that word."

By 1860, at forty-two, he had renounced, as he himself said, all scholarly ambition. He published nothing more during his lifetime. Invitations to German universities, including one in 1874 to occupy the chair of Ranke at Berlin, he rejected without hesitation. "In Basel I can teach what I like." In 1860 the old town of Basel leveled its remaining medieval walls; and Burckhardt wrote to a friend that "in the crisis of the declining nineteenth century things can only be changed by ascetics, men who are independent of the enormously expensive life of the great cities." He was himself such an ascetic in the original Greek meaning of the word, self-disciplined and austere, but he was neither a hermit nor a recluse. He liked food and wine; he loved music (he composed songs on occasion); he traveled to Italy again and again, and on occasion as far as London, Vienna, and Prague. He disliked professors, and was happy when he was not taken for one—except of course in Basel. There, he carried his large portfolio of photographs of art and architecture to class every day: the scene with "this old man with a portfolio" was captured in a charming photograph that survives. He prepared his lectures with the greatest care; but he did not bring notes to class.

The extraordinary range of his lecturing may be seen from this list for one semester in 1860 alone: the history of painting; tapestries; Calderón; Byron; La Rochefoucauld; Manzoni; Rabelais; Gothic monasteries; the

Corpus Christi festival in Vitter (1462); the beginnings of landscape painting; Greek sculpture in the British Museum.

Seven years later, after he had completed the section on architecture for his study of Italian Renaissance art, Burckhardt's interests moved toward the even larger sphere of the history of history and the relation of perennial forces to and within the history of civilizations. Between 1867 and 1872 he gave the series "Introduction to the Study of History" at the university and another series at the Museum of Basel for the Basel public. These lectures were not collected or published until many years after his death, when they appeared as *Reflections on History* and *Historische Fragmente* (*Judgments on History and Historians*, 1929). These two volumes have acquired a fame during the twentieth century equal to that of the works published in his lifetime. They expound Burckhardt's historical philosophy—something very different from a "philosophy of history." As Alexander Dru puts it, "In conformity with the requirements of a small university, he regarded his task as Professor of History as consisting less in the communication of special knowledge than in generally encouraging an historical outlook."

We do not know whether Burckhardt ever faced those hardly avoidable attacks of doubt that beset teachers when they face an audience of unimaginative students; what we know is that he enjoyed his teaching until the end of his life. He himself declares:

> In my experience, learned authorship is one of the most unhealthy, and mere teaching (however troublesome it may be, and however circumstantial the studies and preparations need to be) one of the healthiest *métiers* in the world. To be always standing, walking and talking, and to go for a good hike once a week, whatever the weather, now and then a bottle of the best, no overheated rooms in the winter, and an open collar, that is good for one.

He gave up his professorship of history in 1885 but kept his chair in the history of art until 1893, his seventy-fifth year. He enjoyed the company of students, who would visit him in the evening in his little rooms overlooking a river. His conversation was sparkling and light, like the northern Italian wines he preferred.

Burckhardt always found his trips to Italy invigorating. "I am in excellent health in spite of running to and fro," he writes from Rome in 1875; "among other things, I am enjoying not having to know ex officio who painted the reredos in the X-chapel of St. Thingumbob." When he visited London in 1879 he was full of excitement and wrote long letters to friends nearly every day. He muses: "Are the few drops of Italian blood that have come to me through several marriages since the sixteenth century still flowing in my veins?" The Italian people were good, their physical beauty had not declined, "although peasant coloring is becoming rarer. On the other hand, foreign tourists are much worse than they used to be, and the sight of the Piazza di Spagna, as it is now, makes me despair. I can stand the English, but a certain other nation somewhat less." He meant the Germans. He regarded "leisure as the mother of contemplation and of the inspiration that springs from it." This too was the very opposite of Ranke, who, upon being ennobled by the German emperor, chose the motto *Labor ipse voluptas* (Work itself is pleasure).

Leisure, compounded with the self-discipline of his tasks, remained the practical ideal of Burckhardt's life. He enjoyed his daily siesta, rereading the Greek tragedies as he lay on his sofa, as well as the conversations with his friends, and his correspondence. He was much more cheerful at sixty than at thirty. "One begins to feel as though one were going to evening service on a rainy Sunday," but the wisest thing is to be "as cheerful as possible, and not behave as though there were bad omens in the sky." He was witty and sociable till the end, a kind uncle and granduncle, a sage without being in the least oracular, cynical, or bitter. He was consistent in refusing to have his papers and lectures published, even though during his last years he agreed that his nephew Jacob Oeri might edit some for eventual publication. He often said of his lectures and notes that they would look "like carpets the wrong side up." They were, in reality, tapestries of unexpected magnificence of design.

❀ ❀ ❀

BURCKHARDT was not yet twenty-two when he wrote that "the history of art will always draw me like a magnet." Note that he wrote of the history of art, not of art alone. He was interested in the relation of art to life—more precisely, in its relation to historical life: that is, the ways in which the vision and work of artists reflect changing views of life itself. As early as *The Age of Constantine the Great*, his first published work and one that does not deal with the history of art, we find a passage that sums up Burckhardt's purpose:

> It is a fact that from approximately the middle of the second century the active production of works of art, which had hitherto flourished, ceases and degenerates to mere repetition, and that henceforward internal impoverishment and apparent overelaboration of forms go hand in hand. The deepest causes

of this phenomenon can probably never be plumbed or comprehended in words. If the developed Greek system of forms
could maintain itself for six centuries under all the vicissitudes
of history and always throw out new shoots, why should it lose
its power and its creative energy precisely from the age of the
Antonines downwards? Why could it not have lasted into the
fourth century? Perhaps an a priori answer may emerge from a
general philosophic consideration of the period, but it is more
prudent not to seek to determine the lifespan of a spiritual force
of such magnitude.

Three years later Burckhardt published the *Cicerone*. This extraordinary book, the first of Burckhardt's works translated into English, bears the
modest English subtitle: "An Art Guide to Painting in Italy for the Use of
Travellers and Students." The original German subtitle is even more telling: "An Introduction to the *Enjoyment* [italics are mine] of the Art Treasures of Italy." Of course the *Cicerone* is more than a guide. It describes all
of the valuable paintings in Italy, including those in the remotest corners
of abandoned churches, and it is equipped with a splendidly practical index of painters and places, from which the reader can instantly see where
this or that picture by, say, Bellini is to be found; or again, it tells us *what* is
worth seeing in, say, Bergamo. Yet the *Cicerone* is essentially historical.
Burckhardt begins with painting in the early Middle Ages and goes to the
middle of the seventeenth century. The work is encyclopedic in its scope;
yet unlike a guide, it can (and ought to) be read with profit from beginning
to end. It is not only a splendid walk with the best guide (*cicerone* means
"guide" in Italian) through the vast sunlit museum that is Italy, but also a
splendid walk through Italian history over a span of nearly 1,500 years.

Burckhardt does not hesitate to give summary judgments: "In emotional
scenes Mantegna is sometimes coarse and unbeautiful." Sandro Botticelli
"often painted with a great deal of haste." Burckhardt's best passages reveal
the relation between forms of art and forms of life and thought. In a mosaic

the artist no longer invents; he has only to reproduce.... The
repetition of something learned by heart is the essential characteristic of what we call the Byzantine style.... It is astonishing
to observe this complete dying out of individual character, which
is gradually supplanted by a uniform type, similar in every detail.... The expression of holiness always takes the shape of
moroseness, since art was not permitted to arouse the thought
of the supernatural by producing forms that were free as well as

grand. Even the Madonna becomes sulky, though the small lips
and thin nose seem to make a certain attempt at loveliness: in
male heads there is often a repulsive indignant expression.

Or consider this summary reflection upon the difference in spirit between the Italian Renaissance and the Flemish Renaissance, as exemplified
by a work of art:

> Another "Deposition" in the *Uffizi*, No. 795, ascribed to Roger
> van den Weyden, raises the question how it could be possible
> that the old Netherlanders should observe the details of reality
> with so sharp an eye, and copy it with such a sure and unwea-
> ried hand, and yet misconceive life and action as a whole.

The chapter on the Renaissance begins with a sublime introduction,
"The Character of the Renaissance":

> In the beginning of the fifteenth century a new spirit entered
> into the painting of the West. Though still employed in the ser-
> vice of the church, its principles were henceforward developed
> without reference to merely ecclesiastical purposes. A work of
> art now gives more than the church requires; over and above
> religious associations, it presents a copy of the real world; the
> artist is absorbed in the examination and the representation of
> the outward appearance of things, and by degrees learns to ex-
> press all the various manifestations of the human form as well as
> of its surroundings. Instead of general types of face, we have
> individuals; the traditional system of expression, of gestures and
> draperies, is replaced by the endless variety of real life, which
> has a special expression for each occasion. Simple beauty, which
> hitherto has been sought for and often found as the highest at-
> tribute of the saints, now gives place to the distinctness and
> fulness in detail which is the principal idea of modern art.

Burckhardt's introductory summaries about the great masters indicate
the breadth and sureness of his powers of description. Michelangelo was
an architect and sculptor

> but for the expression of that ideal world which he carried within
> himself, painting afforded materials so much more various that
> he could not do without it. . . . It was against his nature to enter

into any traditional feeling of devotion, any received ecclesiastical type, the tone of feeling of any other man, or to consider himself as bound thereby.... He creates man anew with grand physical power, which in itself appears Titanic, and produces out of these forms a fresh earthly and Olympian world. They move and have their being like a race apart from all earlier generations. What in painters of the fifteenth century is called characteristic finds no place here, because they come forth as a complete race—a people; but where personality is required, it is one ideally formed, a superhuman power.

Titian "either adopted, or himself created, or gave the original idea to the younger generation of all that Venice was capable of in painting. There is no intellectual element in the school that he does not somewhere exemplify in perfection; he certainly also represents its limitations." Burckhardt continues:

With Caravaggio and the Neapolitans drawing and modeling are altogether considerably inferior, and they think they may rely on quite other means for effect. Commonplace as their forms are ... in their vulgarity they are only too often vague as well.... From Luca Giordano downwards the drawing of the Neapolitan school falls into the most careless extemporization.

Burckhardt's *Recollections of Rubens* was not published until 1898, a year after his death. As early as 1842 Burckhardt said that Peter Paul Rubens had been "in general unreasonably criticized." The Rubens book is a perfect piece of work. Its synopsis, compiled and arranged by Burckhardt, is so detailed and comprehensive that we wonder not only at the scope of Burckhardt's knowledge and interests but also at his capacity to compress all of this in a relatively short space. Among his surviving manuscripts this was the easiest one to present to the printer because of its perfection. The book begins with a sublime consideration of Rubens's character:

It is an exhilarating task to evoke the life and personality of Rubens; good fortune and kindliness abound in him as in hardly any other great master, and he is well enough known for us to feel sure of our judgment of him. In the consciousness of his own noble nature and great powers he must have been one of the most privileged of mortals. No life is perfect, and trials came to him too, but the sum of his life so illuminates all its details that, looked at as a whole, it seems exemplary. It did not come to a premature end, like that of Masaccio, Giorgione, and Raphael, while on the other hand he was spared the weakness of age, and it was in his last years that he created some of his grandest work.

It was "extraordinarily fortunate for the Catholicism of the entire north to find so great, so willing, and so happy an interpreter, who was himself fired by enthusiasm for the life of all the great religious figures." Yet Burckhardt finds Rubens inadequate in his Madonnas, "not within the limits of the style we have once accepted as his, but in relation to the imaginative implications of the problem and to the rest of great art":

> At the risk of appearing most one-sided and unscholarly, and of judging a master by a standard that was not his, we must admit as witnesses against him not only Titian's "Transfigured Madonna" and Raphael's "Sistine Madonna" but even Guido Reni's Munich "Assunta" and his altarpieces of the "Holy Conception." And it is not the spirituality of the features in these pictures that we should have the right to feel the lack of in Rubens; it is the spirituality of the expression. . . . Her head shows that rich, matronly, unreligious modeling of Rubens's other Madonnas, and it is only in the Antwerp picture that she takes on a greater sweetness.

These passages indicate the extraordinary quality of Burckhardt's art criticism. There is in his writing a constant concern with the relation of art to history—not in the sense of chronological placing or even in the recognition of important correspondences of place and of time, but in the connection of a particular work of art with the culture of Europe in general. Burckhardt's description of Rubens's "Lesser Last Judgment" and of his "Fall of the Damned into Hell" (where Rubens's "mastery of space finds its ultimate expression") would alone qualify Burckhardt as one of the greatest analysts of art of all time ("the incredible spatiality is brought out by a powerful light falling from the sky onto every ghastly group"). But he wishes to remind us of something else, a corresponding verity on yet another level:

> If we survey the art and poetry of all times for a comparable imaginative power, we shall most probably recognize it in its exact opposite, namely, in a horrible description of nonspace. But the speaker is Mephistopheles in the second part of *Faust*, and he is giving Faust instructions for his journey to the "Moth-

ers." Thus by entirely different roads, men like Rubens and Goethe arrive at the same goal—the stirring within us of profoundest mythological feelings.

Burckhardt was not only one of the founding fathers of art history but also one of the original creators of cultural history. Yet his astonishing knowledge and insight were balanced by a modesty that was private rather than social, since it sprang from his demanding more effort and work from himself:

> There is nothing more precarious than the life of works dealing with art history. All things considered, I wish a better man than I had written a *Cicerone* (according to the plan I had before me)— but *what* was there excepting Murray, in 1853, by way of guide to art that made any attempt to take in the whole of Italy and all the forms of art?

We must not think that Burckhardt advanced from the history of art to the history of culture: many of the foregoing extracts reflect his inclination to see the history of an age in its syncretic wholeness. Remember what he wrote even in the *Sturm und Drang* phase of his youth: "I will at least seek out the interest for which I am to perish, namely the culture of Old Europe."

❊ ❊ ❊

JAKOB Burckhardt was the first master of cultural history—or of what may perhaps be more precisely called the history of a culture. This means that he visualized and attempted to describe the spirit and the forms of expression of a certain age, a certain people, a certain place. It does not mean that because of his fineness of perception Burckhardt regarded the high culture of a certain period as the most important element in its history. Although he was one of the first historians to lift his sights above the nineteenth-century notion that "history is past politics and politics current history," and although his concentration on the spirit of a certain age was very different from the Hegelian conception of zeitgeist, what moved Burckhardt were the richness and variety of significant evidence—significant where it reflected what people thought and believed at a certain time. This was something quite different from intellectual history or the history of ideas.

This resolve to describe the ideals and realities of an entire age— Burckhardt being aware of the fact that idealism and realism complement one another, the true antitheses being idealism and materialism—is evident in *The Age of Constantine the Great*. Dealing principally with the reigns of Diocletian and Constantine, the book begins somewhat slowly, but the author's purpose soon becomes apparent; then it develops with a verve peculiarly his own, especially in the later chapters, where Burckhardt moves further and further from matters of politics and imperial administration and closer to matters of culture and belief. Chapter 7, "Senescence of Ancient Life and Its Culture," is as masterly a chapter as Burckhardt would ever write; it is there that his conception of cultural history is set forth, in the superb wording previously cited. As Burckhardt says in a preface to the second edition of *Constantine* in 1880:

> When the material for this book was assembled, nearly three decades ago, and its writing was taken in hand, the objective in the mind of the author was not so much a complete historical account as an integrated description, from the viewpoint of cultural history, of the important period named in the title.

After *Constantine* Burckhardt wrote the *Cicerone*, and then began the most important, eventually the most famous, of his works, *The Civilization of the Renaissance in Italy*, published in 1860. Compared to *Constantine*, the *Renaissance* sold very poorly during his lifetime: during the first two years of its publication no more than 200 copies were sold. Then in the late 1870s Burckhardt's international reputation began to emerge; the first English translation of the *Renaissance* appeared in 1878.

That the *Renaissance* is cultural history rather than art history appears clearly from the order of its six major parts: the state as a work of art; the development of the individual; the revival of antiquity; the discovery of the world and of man; society and festivals; and morality and religion. This order—starting with politics and concluding with morality and religion—reflects Burckhardt's view of the hierarchy of historical factors, though he is never didactic about these levels of influence. Like a great painter who is not too conscious of his methods, Burckhardt is not concerned to explain his technique.

He begins this great work with a modest proposition: "This work bears the title of an essay in the strictest sense of the word." In this "essay" Burckhardt on occasion expresses the scope of his work as a matter of fact:

> Here, as in other things in Italy, culture—to which poetry belongs—precedes the visual arts and, in fact, gives them their chief impulse. More than a century elapsed before the spiritual

element in painting and sculpture attained a power of expression in any way analogous to that of the *Divine Comedy*. How far the same rule holds true for the artistic development of other nations, and of what importance the whole question may be, does not concern us here. For Italian civilization it is of decisive weight.

Here are examples of Burckhardt's questions:

> Why did the Italians of the Renaissance do nothing above the second rank in tragedy? That was the field in which to display human character, intellect, and passion, in the thousand forms of their growth, their strength, their struggles, and their decline. In other words: why did Italy produce no Shakespeare?

His ability to find the right kind of evidence for his kind of history is manifest throughout the book. In the chapter dealing with the revival of antiquity he directs our attention to an episode in 1485 when the rumor was current that the corpse of a beautiful young lady of ancient Rome, "Julia, daughter of Claudius," had been found, wonderfully preserved: "The touching point in the story is not the fact itself, but the firm belief that an ancient body, which was not thought to be at least really before men's eyes, must of necessity be far more beautiful than anything of modern date."

What was changing during the Renaissance was a state of mind, the way in which people were looking at things as well as at themselves. For example:

> Differences of birth were losing their significance in Italy. . . . Much of this was doubtless owing to the fact that men and mankind were here first thoroughly and profoundly understood. This one single result of the Renaissance is enough to fill us with everlasting thankfulness. The logical notion of humanity was old enough—but here the notion became a fact.

This is not a simple summation of Renaissance humanism. Burckhardt now draws our attention to the distinction between the desire for honor and the desire for fame:

> Let us begin by saying a few words about that moral force which was then the strongest bulwark against evil. The highly gifted man of the day thought to find in it the sentiment of honor. . . .

This sense of honor is compatible with much selfishness and
great vices, and may be the victim of astonishing illusions; yet
nevertheless, all the noble elements that are left in the wreck of
a character may gather around it, and from this fountain may
draw new strength. . . . It lies without the limits of our task to
show how the men of antiquity also experienced this feeling in
a peculiar form, and how, afterwards, in the Middle Ages, a special sense of honor became the mark of a particular class. . . . It is
certainly not always easy, in treating of the Italian of this period, to distinguish this sense of honor from the passion of fame,
into which, indeed, it easily passes. Yet the two sentiments are
essentially different.

At the same time Burckhardt warns us against categorical statements. In
his chapter on morality he says that these matters "may be investigated up
to a certain point, but can never be compared to one another with absolute
strictness and certainty. The more plainly our evidence seems to speak in
these matters, the more carefully we must refrain from unqualified assumptions and rash generalizations." Again, he states:

It is the most serious difficulty of the history of civilization that
a great intellectual process must be broken up into single, and
often into what seem arbitrary, categories in order to be in any
way intelligible. It was formerly our intention to fill up the gaps
in this book by a special work on the "Art of the Renaissance,"
an intention, however, which we have been able to fulfill only in
part.

Burckhardt's reference is to his *History of Architecture and Decoration of the
Italian Renaissance*, published in 1867. It is a continuation of the *Cicerone*
rather than a complement to the *Renaissance*. His *Notes on Renaissance Sculpture* were published posthumously. Of his intended *History of Renaissance
Painting* (a work distinct from the *Cicerone*) the three completed chapters
were published in 1898.

In cultural history Burckhardt's second great achievement was his *History of Greek Culture*, of which an abbreviated English edition exists. The
original edition in German was published in four volumes from 1898 to
1902 and republished twice after that time. This monumental work is composed of his lectures. When one of his friends urged him to publish it,
Burckhardt answered in a letter:

> No, my dear sir, such a poor outsider who does not belong to
> the guild should not attempt such a thing: I am a heretic and an
> ignoramus and my particular views will only arouse the anger
> of the Learned Savants. Yes, yes, believe me. I know these people.
> I need peace in my old days.

Nonetheless the *History of Greek Culture* is a complete, near-encyclopedic work. Again its contents tell us something about the character of Burckhardt's cultural history. From the Greek conception of state and nation he moves on to the fine arts, poetry, music, philosophy, science, and rhetoric. In his introduction he tells his students:

> What we are attempting is to make the history of Greek culture
> into the subject of a . . . course; but we admit in the beginning
> that this course is an experiment and will remain so; that the
> teacher is, and will remain, a colleague among his students; and
> he also wishes to remark that he is not a philologist.

Then Burckhardt warms to his task:

> The events are those that are easiest to learn from other books;
> we, on the other hand, must construct *perspectives* for the events.
> When we, during less than sixty hours, wish to communicate
> the really worthwhile things about Greek antiquity (indeed, also
> for nonphilologists) we can hardly proceed otherwise than
> through the history of culture.

> Our task, as we conceive it, is this: to give *the history of the Greek
> way of thought and of the Greek way of seeing* and to strive to grasp
> some understanding of the living forces, the constructive as well
> as the destructive ones, that were at work in Greek life. . . . It is
> *upon this*, upon the history of the Greek mind and spirit [Geist]
> that the study will concentrate.

In this introduction, written and delivered in 1867, Burckhardt says that although the study of history is undergoing a crisis throughout the West, the history of culture is less dependent on changing circumstances and standards of academic practice, for its sources are definite and obvious. The history of culture attempts to reconstruct, to recapture something of the inner life of past humanity; it tries to find out how people looked and

219

acted, what they wanted, what they thought, what they saw and attempted (*was er war, wollte, dachte, schaute und vermochte*). To his friend and correspondent Friedrich von Preen, Burckhardt confessed a few years later:

> To me, as a teacher of history, a very curious phenomenon has become clear: the sudden devaluation of all mere "events" in the past. From now on in my lectures I shall only emphasize cultural history, and retain nothing but the quite indispensable external scaffolding. Just think of all the defunct battles in the notebooks of all the Learned Savants in their professorial chairs!

❈ ❈ ❈

HAVING considered Burckhardt the historian of art and Burckhardt the historian of culture, we must now direct our attention to Burckhardt the historical philosopher. This was Burckhardt the unwilling philosopher and the unwitting prophet whose ideas struck a surprising variety of readers, especially in German-speaking Europe, with the shock of recognition. That shock occurred first thirty years and then again fifty years after his death. Burckhardt was indifferent to his reputation, although he thought that some of his most polished lectures (on Rubens, for example) might be published posthumously. But he would have been greatly surprised at his own posthumous fame. Eight years after his death, his nephew Jacob Oeri printed *Reflections on History*, but not until 1929 did *Judgments on History and Historians* appear, in the first edition of the *Collected Works*. During the deepening crisis of Weimar Germany in 1929–33 some of the best German thinkers and historians became aware of Burckhardt's prophetic historical views. After Adolf Hitler's assumption of power this feverish interest in Burckhardt died out, at least in public.

Again in 1947–49 Burckhardt's vision of history struck certain Germans as astonishingly relevant to the crisis of their nation and of European civilization after World War II. In those three years four separate editions of *Reflections on History* appeared in Germany. It was in 1948 that Friedrich Meinecke, the last great surviving German historian from the "classic" period, reflected on the differences between Ranke and Burckhardt in a lecture with that title, suggesting the temporal shortcomings of the former's and the enduring validity of the latter's view of history, and their respective relevance to German life. (See *The German Catastrophe*, Meinecke's last book, 1947.)

There were two reasons for these developments. One was Burckhardt's serene morality, which, unlike the avowed principles of many professional historians and philosophers of history, shone untarnished after the catastrophic experiences of dictatorships and two world wars; the other was his forewarning of the dangers of demagoguery in the rising age of the masses. Burckhardt was not only skeptical of the liberal and radical ideas of progress; his conservatism, too, differed profoundly from the nationalist conservatism that was to dominate German and central European historical thinking until at least 1945.

Reflections on History has three parts: the text of Burckhardt's university course "Introduction to the Study of History," given in 1868–69 and again in 1870–71; his three lectures titled "The Great Men in History," given at the Basel Museum in 1870; and the lecture "On Fortune and Misfortune in History," given at the museum in 1871. Burckhardt's *Judgments on History and Historians* was compiled by Emil Duerr from the lectures Burckhardt gave between 1865 and 1885. These are meditations on the history of the world; in other words, what the history of antiquity and modern Europe signified for Burckhardt about the relation of historical forces. The lectures differ radically from what is known as the philosophy of history and are as different from Oswald Spengler as they are from Arnold Toynbee. Burckhardt would have rejected the biological determinism of the former and the systematic categorizing of the latter. It might be argued that the *Reflections on History* is more philosophical and *Judgments on History and Historians* more historical: but such impressions arise only because the former is more general and the latter more chronological. The major part of *Reflections on History* deals with the relationships of state, religion, and culture, which to some extent indicates the evolution of Burckhardt's interests from art through culture to historical philosophy on the grand scale.

Just as Burckhardt the historian of art and of culture is unique, so is Burckhardt the historical philosopher. Instead of seeking a pattern for history, he was fascinated by the very opposite: by the historicity of our existence in all of its protean forms. "The philosophy of history," he writes, "is a centaur, a contradiction in terms, for history coordinates, and hence is unphilosophical, while philosophy subordinates, and hence is unhistorical." Instead of looking for a system that would eventually lead to the abstract knowability of all history, he was interested in the concrete historicity of knowledge, of consciousness, of thought. Nor was Burckhardt influenced by Darwinism or the consequent extension of historical studies to "prehistory." He told students that he wished to begin with the Greeks, and that he had relatively little to tell them about the Babylonians or Assyrians. For him, the "Hellenes embodied free will and hence have become the standard of excellence for ages to come."

Burckhardt also decries all kinds of prophecy: "To know the future is not more desirable in the life of mankind that in the life of the individual.

And our astrological impatience for such knowledge is sheer folly. . . . A future known in advance is an absurdity." Burckhardt did not believe in the cyclical theory or any other kind of determinism, whether biological, geographical, psychological, or Hegelian-idealist. If Burckhardt had a forerunner at all, it was Giambattista Vico, who also proceeded from the assumption that man's knowledge of man is not only more important but also prior to man's knowledge of nature. (But we have no evidence that Burckhardt had read Vico.)

History, says Burckhardt, differs from natural science; it is "the breach with nature caused by the awakening of consciousness":

> Every species in nature possesses complete what it needs for its life; if this were not so, the species could not go on living and reproducing itself. Every people is incomplete and strives for completion, and the higher it stands, the more it strives.

> In nature, individuals, particularly among the highest species of animals, mean nothing to other individuals except perhaps as stronger enemies or friends. The world of man is constantly acted upon by exceptional individuals.

> In nature, the species remains relatively constant: hybrids die or are sterile from the outset. Historical life teems with hybrids. It is as if they were an essential element of fecundation for great mental processes. The essence of history is change.

At times a single sentence in the *Reflections* illuminates a large subject: "During the great migrations we encounter first the remarkable attempt to elude a sharing of power with the priests by the adoption of Arianism." "Byzantinism developed analogously with Islam and frequently interacted with it." "The schools in the Catholic and Protestant countries oscillate between state and church control." In Athens "there was no exaggeration of music, for us the cloak that covers a multitude of incongruities; nor was there any false prudery concerning a mean and secret malevolence." "Originality must be *possessed*, not striven for." Such summations usually come either in the beginning or at the end of his remarkable short paragraphs. These summations were a stylistic habit of his. In *Constantine* we find the characteristic clarity of expression that strikes us with all the force of lightning: "A state is as able to survive nationality as a nationality a state."

Judgments on History and Historians is still more epigrammatic. "Aristocracies will abdicate but do not flee as princes do." Mohammed was "a trivial demagogue" and Islam "the triumph of triviality . . . but the great majority of people are trivial." "Mohammed is personally very fanatical; that is his basic strength. His fanaticism is that of a radical simplifier and to that extent is quite genuine. It is of the toughest variety, namely, doctrinaire passion, and his victory is one of the greatest victories of fanaticism and triviality." Cola di Rienzo (whom Richard Wagner and Hitler admired) was "no better than a poor deluded fool." Richard III of England "was no monster, but a terrorist. He did not commit a pointless crime; later he was fair to his victims. He acted in a spirit of 'expediency.'" "Calvinism . . . became the Reformation of those countries that did not like the Germans." Cardinal Richelieu "is the greatest accelerator of France's later political development, for good as well as for evil. Alone with his idea of the state, which he completely identified with his person, he confronts a world of selfishness." After the execution of Louis XVI "the spiritual survival of the monarchy is comparable to sensation in an amputated limb." Napoleon Bonaparte "had a sixth sense in all military matters and a seventh for everything relating to power. His deadly enemy, like that of all such people, was impatience; it brought his later career to disaster." "He believed that he had all the princes in his net, because they were afraid of the *democratic inclinations of their peoples* (which was the case in Austria); but he would not hear the peoples' despair and anger that were directed against *him* and that *must* in the end sweep along the princes, according to circumstance."

These epigrammatic passages give us a taste of Burckhardt's thought. What is important, too, is that the book is not disjointed, though *Judgments on History and Historians* is a series of lecture notes. True, its full savoring required some knowledge of the history of Western civilization. Whether even a century ago readers other than Burckhardt's best students possessed this kind of knowledge we cannot tell. What we can tell is that here as always Burckhardt is the historical thinker par excellence: a prophet of the past. And so we face what at first sight may seem a paradox: this prophet of the past was also a prophet of the future.

The quality and intensity of Burckhardt's vision was such that the light he poured on the past illuminated the then present and its sequel. He was telling people things about the darkened landscape that lay behind them, of what they and their ancestors had left behind; but the luminosity of his words would bathe, if only for moments, the mountainous route ahead. Indeed often the first thing that strikes people in reading Burckhardt is this vision of the future. The reason is Burckhardt's comprehension of the human condition, together with his comprehension of its historicity. He does not think that human nature essentially changes, although this does not mean that history ever repeats itself. Certain historical conditions may indeed recur; but the sources of this recurrence lie in human nature itself. Often one of Burckhardt's statements about a monarch, an institution, a crisis of many centuries ago strikes us with a sudden sense of its pertinence to the present. We are surprised because Burckhardt is seldom, if ever, didactic; his purpose is not to demonstrate historical parallels.

We have seen how Burckhardt, in his early maturity, turned away resolutely from speculations about the troubles of the present and its politics, devoting himself only to "Old Europe." Twenty years later the pessimism of that resolution had given way to a more stoical and less bitter concern with the present. Thus both *Reflections on History* and *Judgments on History and Historians* contain brief, but remarkably significant, statements about nineteenth-century Europe. He saw very clearly what the monstrous ascendancy of the modern state meant. He had no sympathy for G. W. F. Hegel, and especially not for Hegel's idealization of the state. Burckhardt respected Otto von Bismarck, but he also saw in the unification of the German states a great danger. He recognized the demonic element in Wagner. After a few years of friendship Burckhardt turned away from his admirer Nietzsche. (Their relationship had certain similarities with that of Alexis de Tocqueville and Joseph, comte de Gobineau).

Like Nietzsche, Burckhardt foresaw the degeneration of parliamentary democracy and the coming of the "terrible simplifiers," whom the emancipated and semieducated masses would naturally follow. But Burckhardt had no sympathy for Nietzsche's passionate attack on tradition as well as hypocrisy. Unlike Nietzsche, Burckhardt saw that the waning of the power of the churches was a complex and unpredictable phenomenon, not necessarily identical with the dying out of religious belief. Burckhardt abandoned many of his earlier prejudices against Catholicism; now he saw the weakening of liberal Protestantism and foresaw that the resistance to tyranny would, perhaps surprisingly, come from traditional beliefs and conservative churches. "In fact, we have not yet experienced the full impact of the masses, of numbers, on religion, but it may yet come." He had no respect for capitalists because of their often thoughtless materialism; but socialists too, he writes, are dangerous because of their ignorance, "their narrow optimism and their wide-open mouths." Capitalists as well as socialists will have little to do with a development he discusses in his letters to von Preen: "You may be surprised . . . but I fear that the military state will become industrialist." In the *Reflections* he says that by 1789 rulers had learned that

opinion makes and changes the world—as the traditional authorities had become too feeble to put obstacles in its way, and
as they themselves had begun trafficking with some of its features. . . . But today the success of the press lies more in the
general leveling of views than in its direct function. . . . [O]ften
the press shrieks so loud *because* people no longer listen.

Statements such as this may explain the relative neglect of Burckhardt
the philosophical historian (as distinct from Burckhardt the art historian) in
the English-speaking world. They stand in contrast to the Anglo-American
liberal and progressive intellectual tradition. Unlike Tocqueville, Burckhardt was indifferent to the United States and often sharply critical of modern democracy. Yet, latest of all his successes, after World War II Burckhardt
gained the recognition due him among historians and thinkers of the English-speaking world, in part because of his achievements in cultural history, in part because of the obvious truth of many of his views. The contemporary historian Hugh Trevor-Roper writes that while "the 'scientific,'
'factual' history of Ranke has now run nearly dry . . . the unscientific 'cultural' history of Burckhardt still excites us."

In 1871, at the end of his *Reflections on History*, Burckhardt had said that
the danger was now that everything has become possible, "mainly because
there are everywhere good, splendid, liberal people who do not quite know
the boundaries of right and wrong, and it is there that the duty of resistance and defense begins; it is *these* men who open the doors and level the
paths for the terrible masses everywhere." Still, Burckhardt would not take
refuge in an aristocratic kind of despair. Was the present tendency of Europe, he asked, "a rising or falling one? That can never be determined by
mere calculation. The peoples of Europe are still exhausted physically, and
in the intellectual and moral sphere one *must*, in order to think correctly,
reckon with *invisible forces, with miracles.*" As he wrote at the end of his subchapter on "Morality and Judgment" in the *Renaissance:*

What eye can pierce the depths in which the character and fate
of nations are determined?—in which that which is inborn and
that which has been experienced combine to form a new whole
and a fresh nature?—in which even those intellectual capacities
which at first sight we should take to be most original are in fact
evolved late and slowly? Who can tell if the Italian before the
thirteenth century possessed that flexible activity and certainty
in his whole being—that play of power in shaping whatever subject he dealt with in word or in form, which was peculiar to him

later? A tribunal there is for each one of us, whose voice is our conscience; but let us have done with these generalities about nations. For the people that seems to be most sick the cure may be at hand; and one that appears to be healthy may bear within it the ripening germs of death, which the hour of danger will bring forth from their hiding place.

❀ ❀ ❀

THIS essay is about Burckhardt the writer, rather than about Burckhardt the philosopher, inseparable though the two actually are. And the reason is clear: it is not only Burckhardt's practice in historiography but also Burckhardt's idea of the historian—of the duties and purposes of writing history—that is important to us. We have seen that Burckhardt's artistic inclinations were apparent from his formative years; even at the time when his interest in history had crystallized he was already dissatisfied with the established standards of "scientific" history. He was appalled by the pettiness, vanity, and opportunism of some of the most reputable professionals then at the pinnacle of their fame. "You can have no idea," he wrote a few months after he had arrived in Berlin, "of the envy and vanity of the greatest scholars here! Unfortunately, as everyone knows, Ranke, though very pleasant to meet, is lacking in character; you can see that in black and white in ... his writings." Burckhardt was shocked when he found that at a reception Ranke professed opinions and preferences that were the very opposite of what he had enunciated earlier that day. To his sister Burckhardt wrote: "If only all the professors were not archenemies! But what is the use of complaining when Ranke and Raumer always lecture at the same time (12 to 1) out of sheer spite?" Ranke

> learned a lot from the French, only he won't admit it. People are always talking about the art of writing history, and many of them think they have done enough when they replace [Schlözer's] labyrinthine sentences by the dry narration of facts. No, no my dear chap, what's needed is to sift the facts, to select what can interest man.

From this early emphasis on the necessity for an authentic human interest in history Burckhardt never departed.

At fifty-five Burckhardt summed up his philosophy of teaching in a letter to Nietzsche:

> I have done everything I possibly could to lead them on to acquire personal possession of the past—in whatever shape or form. ... I wanted them to be capable of picking the fruits for themselves; I never dreamed of training scholars and disciples in the narrower sense, but only wanted to make every member of the audience feel and know that everyone may and must appropriate those aspects of the past that appeal to him personally, and that there can be happiness in so doing. I know perfectly well that such an aim may be criticized as fostering amateurism, but that does not trouble me.

We must, however, go beyond Burckhardt's modest self-assertion, which might naturally lead to the conclusion that among the great historians of the nineteenth century Ranke was the prototype of the "professional" and Burckhardt of the "amateur." It would leave the impression that Burckhardt, for all his talents and the respect he inspires, belongs to a much earlier age, when history was regarded as a branch of literature. The opposite is true. Burckhardt was no amateur with a touch of genius, but an innovator whose view of a hierarchy of historical forces ran counter to the then professional concentration on the primacy of politics. His work also stands up against the dominant social-scientific tendency of twentieth-century intellectuality (including historiography) to seek (and then pretend to find) the motive power of human history in categories of material "factors." Burckhardt was convinced—and has convinced many of his readers—that the most important "force" is what people think, believe, and take for granted. At the end of his lectures on Greek civilization (as indeed at the beginning of the *Renaissance*) he repeats somewhat ironically his creed of "amateurism": "We are 'unscientific' (*unwissenschaftlich*) and have no particular method, at least not the one professed by others."

What was his actual method? It was very simple but at the same time complex. The student of history, Burckhardt says, "must *want* to seek and find; and *bisogna saper leggere*" (must know how to read). His interest in history must be authentic, not merely professional or bureaucratic; he must know how to read between the lines. This authentic interest must be personal. Burckhardt was profoundly aware of the inevitable relation between the observer and the observed. In this respect he was one of the earliest thinkers in the West who, without philosophizing about it, began to transcend the Cartesian division of the cosmos into "object" and "subject." For Burckhardt historical knowledge was neither objective nor subjective but participatory. He used to admonish his students so as to make them grasp the distinction between *Parteilichkeit*—partisanship—and *Vorliebe*—elective affection: the first the serious student of history must eschew; the second is his own privilege and possession. We find an elaboration of this point in his *History of Greek Culture.*

> Furthermore we must understand that when we try to immerse ourselves wholly in the reading of a classic, only we *alone* can find what is important *for* us. No reference work in the world with its quotes can replace that chemical bonding that mysteriously occurs when a phrase found by ourselves illuminates something in our mind, crystallizing itself into a real piece of spiritual property that is ours.

This conception is something very different from amateurism, as well as from subjectivism. Burckhardt wanted students and others to read certain works or passages several times, to find in them essences and ideas that might escape the mind on the first reading: "There are authors, such as Hesiod, whose each rereading opens new questions and new perspectives. Aeschylus' *Prometheus* reveals to us new characteristics upon every new perusal." The work of the historian, Burckhardt adds, is never finished. To him, of course, history was the constant rethinking of the past; the past ("not the reading of the newspapers") must be the source of our spirituality. Seeing the present with the eyes of the past and the past with the eyes of the present is a state of mind we must be constantly aware of: we may find in Thucydides something of the greatest present importance but "which may not be seen to be such until a hundred years from now."

Unlike many of the pessimist and fatalist thinkers of the twentieth century, Burckhardt, for all of his conservative inclinations and for all of his stoic comprehension of the world, maintained his high faith in the potentiality of the human spirit: "The spearhead of all culture is a miracle of mind—namely, speech, whose source, independently of the particular people and particular language, is in the soul; otherwise no deaf mute could be taught to speak and to understand speech. Such teaching is explicable only if there is in the soul an intimate and responsive urge to clothe thought in words." In keeping with this fundamental belief in the participant relation of people to the universe, Burckhardt was fond of quoting Goethe's great maxim "Unser Auge ist sonnenhaft, sonst sähe es die Sonne nicht" (Were our eye not like the sun, the sun it could not see).

Burckhardt distinguished between true and false skepticism: the latter was senseless and destructive, proceeding as it did from the false assumption that what human beings could not conceive could not exist. A historical skepticism, however, "has its indisputable place in a world where beginnings and end are all unknown, and the middle in constant flux . . . though the consolation offered by religion is here beyond our scope."

We live, Burckhardt said, not for ourselves alone but for the past and future as well. As James Hastings Nichols wrote, "He was thus more profoundly Christian than the good churchmen Hegel and Ranke." And he was no less a historian than the most accomplished of his fellow professionals.

For a long time Burckhardt was neglected. Upon the publication of the *History of Greek Culture* immediately after his death, the great classicist Uhlrich von Wilamowitz-Möllendorf attacked it. Two of Wilamowitz's students continued the denigration. After a time these attacks ceased; and the work came to be treated by the greatest German scholars with more than respect, indeed, with awe.

Like all works, even those of the greatest masters in art and letters, Burckhardt's were not without faults. In *Constantine* Burckhardt's chronological attribution of an important source has since been revised. In the *Cicerone* there are a few—in retrospect, astonishingly few—mistaken attributions of paintings. There is some evidence that in his *History of Greek Culture* Burckhardt may have been influenced by Fustel de Coulanges, whose *Cité antique* was published in 1864, though Burckhardt made no reference to Fustel. Burckhardt was certainly impressed (though not uncritically) by some of the writings of another contemporary, the Munich historian Ernst von Lasaulx. Burckhardt's intellectual relation to Tocqueville still awaits a monograph by a patient and perceptive historian. Burckhardt and Tocqueville differed greatly in background, personality, and character; but their historical philosophy had much in common and so had their historical interests. As Kaegi points out, Burckhardt began to write about the age of revolutions "almost in the same moment when Tocqueville had laid down his pen"—in 1859. Burckhardt wrote in his mature years:

> I like themes that straddle the frontier between the Middle Ages
> and modern times, because of their many different forms and
> vitality. And long before the dustmen have got their refuse carts
> moving and shout disagreeable things after us, we are already
> over the hills and far away.

Burckhardt lived what he preached. What he wrote about history being a participant's knowledge was integral to his own thinking self. Yet he was not thinking of himself when he wrote that "character is much more decisive for man than richness of intellect. . . . [P]ersonality is the highest thing there is," a statement applicable to him. Like Tocqueville, he was a great correspondent. A very important part of Burckhardt's legacy are his letters in nine volumes. They show his multifarious interests and the attractive facets of his versatile personality; they contain some of his deepest thoughts. Unlike Tocqueville, he was blessed with a devoted circle of students, some of whom were his relatives. It was they who after his death began the resurrection and the reconstruction of his immense legacy. In the hurried, troubled, at times catastrophic world of twentieth-century Europe, these modest scholars performed a feat comparable in kind, though not in extent, to the painstaking work of the monks copying and preserving the classics during the Dark Ages; they deserve our abiding thanks.

19

Harold Nicolson

(1985)

James Lees-Milne's two-volume *Harold Nicolson* is the biography of a biographer who did not believe that the art of biography had much of a future. Toward the end of *The Development of English Biography* (1928)—a brilliant history and analysis in less than a hundred-and-fifty duodecimo pages—Nicolson speculated about that future. Abandoning his earlier distinction between "pure" and "impure" biography, he wrote that there would be an increasing difference between "scientific" and "literary" works, and that the former would win the field. "The scientific interest in biography is hostile to, and will in the end prove destructive of, the literary interest," he wrote. "The former will insist not only on the facts, but on all the facts; the latter demands a partial or artificial representation of facts. The scientific interest, as it develops, will become insatiable; no synthetic power, no genius for representation, will be able to keep the pace." Harold Nicolson was often wrong about the future. (He was almost always right about the past.) In the appendix of his curious futuristic novel *Public Faces* (1932) he imagined with rueful amusement a biographical notice of himself written by his grandson in the early 1970s, in a communized Britain, where traditional English spelling would be replaced by something like a Shavian alphabet: "Harold Nikolson," all but forgotten, would have died in 1958. (Nicolson actually died in 1968.) What happened instead was a surge of interest in his life, stimulated by, among other things, *Portrait of a Marriage,* written by his son Nigel, which revealed the enduring love for each other of the homosexual Harold and his androgynous wife, Victoria (Vita) Sackville-West. I do not think that Nicolson, while perhaps rueful, would have been pleased by his son's book, no matter how intelligent, respectful, filial, and affectionate it is to the memory of his parents. I think that he would have been pleased by his biography as written by his friend James

Review of James Lees-Milne, *Harold Nicolson* (1980–84). From *New Yorker,* September 2: 82–86.

Lees-Milne, with its impeccable and often extraordinary research of the facts—pleased because of Mr. Lees-Milne's intimate comprehension of circumstances, because of his understanding of character, and because of the fortunate accord of its historical and aesthetic qualities, defying Nicolson's somber predictions of the future of biography nearly sixty years ago.

Mr. Lees-Milne's task was a difficult one for many reasons, among them the huge store of material that his subject left behind. Nicolson often referred to himself as indolent. There was indeed a moderate and epicurean facet of his character, reflected in his appearance: pink and plump, well dressed but a bit rumpled, with a slight touch of bohemianism, his collar points and hair curling away. At the same time, he was an indefatigable worker and writer, which at least suggests an astonishing kind of self-discipline. It was not only the quality but the quantity of work he imposed upon himself during his years in the Foreign Service which impressed his superiors. The corpus of Nicolson's written heritage is enormous. He wrote at least two dozen books; a monthly column and weekly reviews for about thirty years; reams of diplomatic memoranda and dispatches; a detailed diary for almost forty years; and more than ten thousand letters, often very intimate long ones, sometimes two or three a day. During his last years, when he was already senile and full of sleep, three volumes of his *Diaries and Letters* were published by his son Nigel. Their success was, as Mr. Lees-Milne writes, "phenomenal." Yet they contained only a fraction of his diaries and letters, and by no means the most interesting ones. (In one of his lucid moments, Nicolson told Nigel how odd it was to publish three books that he did not realize he had written.)

The amazing mass of his literary production hardly compromised its quality, except for his last two books (*The Age of Reason* and *Monarchy*). His mind was quick, and the facility of his style was extraordinary. He wrote many of his best books in a few months, some of them in a few weeks. Yet the prose of these was polished to perfection, while his speed of judicious reading made it possible for him to research in weeks a subject that would have taken years for other historians. This kind of virtuosity sometimes evoked the charge of dilettantism even in England, with its tradition of the amateur man of letters. His style was marked by a subdued but brilliant impressionism, which made some critics say he was unduly influenced by the French manner. Yet Mr. Lees-Milne records that as early as 1935 Michael Sadleir forecast that Nicolson would survive as one of the leading writers of his age. In 1960, John Betjeman at a Guildhall dinner pronounced Nicolson the greatest living master of English prose.

The subject of most of his books was biography and history. He wrote biographies of Verlaine, Swinburne, Tennyson, Byron, Sainte-Beuve, Benjamin Constant, Dwight Morrow, Lord Curzon, King George V—a list sufficient to illustrate the great range of his interests. He became famous with *Some People* (1927), which contains ironic and semi-fictitious portraits of people he knew. The best of his histories dealt with the Congress of Vienna and with the origins of the First World War. The latter, entitled *Lord Carnock: A Study in the Old Diplomacy* (1930), may be the most nearly perfect of his works. (He himself was inclined to think so.) It is also proof of the internal coherence of what might otherwise seem an excessively catholic and scattered oeuvre. Lord Carnock (Sir Arthur Nicolson, Bart.) was his father. During the first twenty-eight years of Harold Nicolson's life, his father was posted to Tehran, Budapest, Sofia, Constantinople, Morocco, advancing from consul-general to His Majesty's Ambassador to the court at St. Petersburg, and ultimately to the headship of the Foreign Office. *Lord Carnock*, as its subtitle tells us, is a history of the origins of the First World War; as the title tells us, it is also a history of Nicolson's father. This combination of history and biography, of the circle of a family together with the greater circle of events, was repeated in *Helen's Tower* (1937) and *The Desire to Please* (1943), in which Nicolson wrote about his uncle Lord Dufferin and his eighteenth-century ancestor Hamilton Rowan. They contradict his melancholy projection of the inevitable dichotomy between the "scientific" and the "literary" tendencies of biography. Their unity reflects the propitious complementarity of individual memory and professional history, of personal participation and detached intellection.

There was, on the other hand, an unusual difference between Nicolson's ability to judge the past and his ability to judge the present. As a historian, Nicolson was often unerring; as a politician, he was often wrong. During his political career, he made mistakes of judgment, of which the evidence is there in his diaries and letters, but few traces of such mistakes exist in his books. The division of Mr. Lees-Milne's two volumes corresponds to the turning point of Nicolson's professional life. He had a very promising diplomatic career. Yet he chose to abandon it in 1929, for a number of reasons. Even the prospect of ambassadorships meant nothing to his wife, who would not accompany him to his posts abroad, and who thought the routine life of an ambassadorial wife uninteresting and wearisome. He himself thought—wrongly—that his diplomatic duties would conflict inevitably with his writing career. His superiors, with few exceptions, respected (and after *Some People* some of them even feared) Nicolson's writing; many of them read his books with pleasure. What is true is that he did not have the toughness of character necessary for the successful ascent of a statesman. Mr. Lees-Milne properly includes a personal remark that Harold Macmillan made to him about Nicolson and another prominent Englishman with great intellectual powers. Yes, Balfour and Nicolson were highly civilized and cultivated, Macmillan said. "But although Balfour was extremely languid he was far from soft. He was lethargic but he was ruthless. Unlike Harold's, his spine was made of steel. He would sacrifice a friend of forty years without a murmur, without a moment's hesitation, if he decided that it was necessary to get rid of him. That was the difference. Besides Balfour did not care a damn what people said or thought about him. Harold did. He worried if he was criticised. He wanted to be liked. A fatal propensity."

Nicolson's life was not a triumph of character. Yet his work was a triumph of achievement. This is admirably set forth in this biography. Scholarly biographers—especially in these times, when there has been such a regrettable decline in the standards of documentation and in the management of evidence—would do well to emulate Mr. Lees-Milne's probity. He has read and used most of Nicolson's unpublished diaries and letters, always with the precise reference to their day, to their addressee, and sometimes to their circumstance. He went to the trouble (if that is the word) to read Nicolson's memoranda and dispatches in the British Foreign Office archives. Yet this biography is more interesting than the published diaries not only because of the biographer's opportunity to draw on a vast store of unpublished sources but also because he employs a style that, in this case, doubles the meaning of *le style, c'est l'homme. Il s'agit de deux hommes*: the biographer and the biographee. Mr. Lees-Milne has an exceptional empathy for Nicolson's style, which is not an easy one to emulate. He draws on some of Nicolson's inimitable images and weaves them into fine descriptive passages of his own:

> Conditions in Morocco at the turn of the century were archaic. There was no electric light in Tangier. There were no wheeled vehicles, not even a barrow. Rubbish was carried in panniers by donkeys. When asked out to dinner his father rode and his mother was carried in a sedan chair, preceded by a servant bearing a lantern. Harold too when a schoolboy would set out to a party on horseback, the flickering beams of the servant's lantern falling, now upon some iron-studded door in a blank wall, now upon a street fountain spluttering upon coloured tiles, and now upon a rat scuttling from an open sewer. His horse would pick its way cautiously through the mud and garbage. Suddenly a door would open in the silent street, disclosing a small courtyard, with a lamp hanging from a colonnade, its wick smoking angrily across the arches. The lamp was shaped like the lamps used at Pompeii. Years later Harold Nicolson, recalling these evening scenes in Tangier,

realised that it was not the glamour of the East which that smoking lamp suggested to him. It was the life of Rome and even Athens which he, as a boy, had been privileged to experience.

Such, too, are the descriptions of the icy St. Petersburg nights; of the
old, wizened Queen Victoria in her barouche, moving slowly through the
yard of Wellington College; of Harold and Pierre de Lacretelle "tacking
up and down the Bosphorus, dawdling on the sun-baked shores of the Black
Sea, dallying in a low-ceilinged room in Therapia, and all the while recit-
ing and talking about French poetry, while the water lapped against the
walls outside and steamers hooted in the distance." Or of Siena, where
Harold and his friends "strolled through the city gates and sat on the grass
and looked at the great cathedral growing out of the house tops, and at the
hills beyond, and caught lizards, and had tea and large cakes; and so back to
Harold's barrack-like room which already seemed to have assumed some
individuality. Every morning he walked across the Cathedral square, down
some steps, and knocked at a sinister little door of the house of his teacher.
Don Orlandi, a delightful old priest, lived in cool rooms smelling of violets
and incense, and adorned with one framed photograph of the Martyrs
Memorial in Oxford. He wore Balliol socks and did not approve of
d'Annunzio, which Harold found rather a relief. And every evening Harold
would pass through the red gates into the hush of the country outside."
After a visit to Keats's house in Rome, Harold and other friends "motored
down the Via Appia under a tomato-coloured sun. There was a little moon,
black silhouettes and the chirping of crickets."

Readers of Nicolson will recognize the style. Does this suggest that Mr.
Lees-Milne's portrait of Nicolson tends to emulation, adulation, the kind
of hagiography against which Nicolson had warned: an "impure" biography, in sum? No: this is, in many ways, an old-fashioned biography, with all
the virtues we may associate with that adjective, but without the vice of the
omission of unpleasant or difficult intimate details. (I can find only one
exception to this. Mr. Lees-Milne does not mention the Knebworth episode: Harold's acquisition of a venereal infection at a house-party, which
he then confessed to Vita, whose response was that of sympathetic forgiveness—possibly a psychic milestone in their then young married lives.) The
biography is candid about Nicolson's homosexuality and his wife's lesbi-
anism. Mr. Lees-Milne and his wife were close friends of the Nicolsons
during the last twenty years of their lives; he has included a few telling
passages from their private correspondence, tactfully and yet without being reticent. Harold's and Vita's love for each other grew out of a sense of
dependence, which was made easier by the condition that theirs was an

exceptional alliance rather than a marriage. "In fact it was because their marriage became totally divorced from the physical while based on the same cerebral interests that it endured so as to become one of the idyllic sagas of our century." Well, "idyllic saga" is perhaps too much: there was plenty in that relationship that was far from idyllic. But Mr. Lees-Milne understands matters that other recent commentators on this ménage have not. "Both of them had long been obsessed by the unorthodoxy of their marriage, and convinced that this unorthodoxy, coupled with the tolerance and understanding of both, was the main reason why their marriage had not only endured, but prospered." He also knows that Harold depended on his mother, because he "craved affection and protection. His love for his mother, which was deep and touching, suggests a certain vulnerability of character, an almost feminine dependence, in spite of his own strong will, upon psychical support in the harsh process of living. As he grew to manhood he realised that his gentle and unintellectual mother whom he never ceased to love and was in his turn to protect, was unable to provide the particular support he required. He had, like other sons before him, to seek it elsewhere." Mr. Lees-Milne reads Nicolson with a close intelligence, gathering evidence sufficient to eschew the attribution of subconscious motives. "What these words convey," he writes in quoting from one of Nicolson's letters to his wife, "is that Harold needed a strong prop against which to lean. . . . Vita was his prop. On the few occasions when he saw the prop threatened he panicked like the small boy he never ceased to be." And when, in one instance, Lord Curzon was cross with Nicolson, "this distressed Harold so much that he went downstairs at once and telegraphed to Vita, imploring her to come to him. It was a case of the little schoolboy, reprimanded by the headmaster, turning to his mother for consolation. Vita responded to his piteous appeal within a week." On another occasion, Harold wrote her, "I feel you are slipping away, you who are my anchor, my hope and all my peace." This to a woman who took selfish pride in being all sail and no anchor, surely no vessel in a domestic harbor of peace.

Nicolson was a complex man, who was well aware of his weaknesses and of his need to compensate for them. At seventeen, he wrote, "I am beginning to see that brain counts for little but that character counts for everything, and it is not a pleasant thought as my character is weak and easily influenced." Yet his entire life was marked by his preference for fineness of intellect. He was, in his biographer's words, "worldly-wise and yet childlike, sensitive and yet bluff, full of fun, with an irrepressible tendency to tease. Without being strictly handsome, he was cherubic, and very lively." He surely had the English upper-class male habit of excessive concern with his looks. He was obsessed with youth: at thirty-one, he referred to himself as "middle-aged"; on his fiftieth birthday, he was crazily unhappy. He also had the odd habit, which Mr. Lees-Milne does not mention, of posing in an emphatically masculine posture, with his legs wide apart and his hands on his hips. There is really no need to psychoanalyze this intelligent man, whose contradictory tendencies existed on the conscious level of his mind. When this class-conscious aristocrat and aesthete imagined that he was a socialist, his friend Christopher Sykes said that his Labour "proclivities were all talk and affectation." Critics have recently made much of his anti-Semitic remarks. Yet here was a man who early in his life proclaimed his support for Dreyfus, and who was among the first in England to stand up for German Jewish refugees.

John Sparrow, another friend, suggested (perhaps with a touch of exaggeration) at Nicolson's memorial service that his complicated character was that of a nineteenth-century Whig leading an eighteenth-century existence in the twentieth century. It is not the complications of Nicolson's character that ought to interest us. It is his writing; and his view of the world which is reflected in that writing. His cultivation and intelligence amaze us in retrospect; they belong to an age that is even further away than the Victorian and Edwardian circumstances in which he grew up. His biographer states, "Throughout his long life Harold never let a day pass without reading for half an hour some passage of Greek or Latin; he never went on a journey, even in the London tube, without carrying a Loeb edition of Euripides in his pocket." In 1944, Edmund Wilson wrote a critical essay about Nicolson for the *New Yorker* entitled "Through the Embassy Window," the gist of which was that, with a minor talent, Nicolson had an outdated and restricted view of the world, because of the class and the profession to which he belonged. In one sense, Wilson was right: if not Nicolson's style, his reticences in his biographies of Verlaine and Swinburne were almost Victorian. In the larger sense, Wilson was not. Nicolson's immense learning, his knowledge of the world, his understanding of diplomacy, his descriptions of character, his advocacy of certain enduring and humane principles were such that he, like every fine writer, transcends his background and his period. He is a writer whose descriptions of scenes in the late autumn afternoon of Western European civilization evoke not our melancholy but an almost sensual longing for the urbane elegance of those places. He thought that his writing would not survive. He also thought that in future biographies "psychological development will be traced in all its intricacy and in a manner comprehensible only to the experts," that a new kind of "impure" biography would prevail, identifying "an individual with some extraneous theory." It is pleasant to record that, by the hand of his friend James Lees-Milne, he escaped that fate.

20

Alexis de Tocqueville

(1988)

$\mathbf{B}$iographers of thinkers and of historians are a relatively modern literary practice. They began to accumulate less than a hundred years ago. It is at least arguable that interest in the life as well as the works of a thinker results from an evolution of consciousness which is not only a psychological phenomenon but a democratic one. Yet Alexis de Tocqueville, who has long been recognized as the greatest analyst of the democratic age, has not been the subject of an extensive and scholarly biography until the present decade; in 1984, André Jardin's biography was published in France, and now it is available in an English translation, by Lydia Davis and Robert Hemenway. *Tocqueville: A Biography* is a book of considerable importance, primarily because of its comprehensive treatment of both Tocqueville's public life and his private life—including many details necessarily absent from the two previous biographical essays, by Antoine Redier (1925) and J. P. Mayer (1939). There are reasons for the late arrival of such a biography. Tocqueville left an immense literary heritage, of which the major (and perhaps the most valuable) portion may be his thousands of letters, but not until 1951, ninety-two years after his death, did a commission in France begin to publish his complete works. Nineteen volumes have been issued, and eleven more are planned. M. Jardin, the editor of several of these volumes, has been an indefatigable Tocqueville researcher over the last thirty years; encouraged by the Comte Jean de Tocqueville, Alexis's great-grand-nephew and the present head of the family, he presumably decided that the materials for a serious biography were finally at hand.

Americans naturally associate Tocqueville with his classic *Democracy in America*, but *Democracy in America* is only a small part of Tocqueville's oeuvre. Besides his formidable correspondence, there is the innovative and pro-

Review of André Jardin, *Tocqueville: A Biography* (1988). From *New Yorker*, November 14: 136–40.

found history *The Old Regime and the French Revolution* (1856); its sequel, unfinished because of his last illness; his incomparable *Recollections* of the revolutionary year 1848, written during an earlier illness and also published posthumously; and many smaller works. The main theme of all these is, in various ways, the arrival of and the prospects for democracy in the modern world—a preoccupation that both preceded and followed *Democracy in America*. As Jardin observes, the surprisingly large success of its first volume, published in 1835, was not a result of fortunate timing. By then, French interest in the United States had actually abated, but intelligent readers knew that they were in the presence of a masterly philosophical and literary exposition of a democratic society. (One of the best reviews was written by the young Sainte-Beuve, at the very beginning of his literary career.)

Tocqueville, accompanied by his friend Gustave de Beaumont, had spent nine months in the United States, in 1831 and 1832. The pretext for their trip was a commission from the French government to make a study of the American penitentiary system. ("The penitentiary system was an excuse," Tocqueville wrote to another friend. "I used it as a passport that would allow me to go everywhere in the United States." But Tocqueville and Beaumont were not really precursors of modern grantsmen, since they paid for the trip themselves.) Tocqueville wrote the first volume of *Democracy in America* in less than a year. Then he began to write the second volume, which is very different from the first. Jardin exaggerates a bit when he says that in this volume Tocqueville's accounts of life in the United States are "no more than illustrations of a particular line of reasoning." Yet it is true that the second volume is about democracy rather than about America. At the same time, Tocqueville emphasized that the American experiment was not necessarily a model for democracy everywhere. Throughout both volumes he used the term "Anglo-Americans," mindful not only of the antecedents of the American people but of the specifically English origins of their freedoms. He worked on the second volume for at least four years. Although it had a mixed reception—critical, for the most part—to us, almost 150 years later, it seems even more penetrating than the first. Many of its chapters (shorter than those of the first volume; the very organization of the two books is different) are distillations of a wisdom that astonishes us, since they seem to be directly relevant to the democratic world of our times.

In the two volumes there is also a subtle difference in emphasis. What struck many readers in the first volume—and for a long time reduced Tocqueville's appeal to modern liberals—was his exposition of a new kind of danger, that of the tyranny of a majority. But in the second volume Tocqueville describes another kind of danger: the eventual growth of an all-provident and all-powerful government, which would rule more and more spheres of life, until its unwitting subjects became so accustomed to its powers that the independence of their thinking vanished—in sum, the devolution of democracy into a new kind of bureaucratic state. This idea corresponds to another important Tocqueville thesis, set forth in the chapter "Why Great Revolutions Will Become More Rare," in which he states that the exact opposite of the political conditions feared by opponents of democracy might develop. These opponents thought that an unbridled democratic society would necessarily tend to extremes. On the contrary, Tocqueville wrote; the incessant agitation on the surface of a democratic society merely obscures the slowing down of the true advancement of ideas, and a kind of agitated intellectual stagnation prevails.

Continuity was a principal perspective of Tocqueville's historical vision. His great and novel contribution in *The Old Regime and the French Revolution* was his observation that there had been more continuity between the practices of the monarchy and those of the revolutionary republic than people were accustomed to believe: the most harmful feature of the old regime—the centralization of governmental power—was unthinkingly extended by the new. Another significant element in Tocqueville's political philosophy—one generally overlooked by his commentators—is the recognition by this traditionalist aristocrat of the dangers to liberty from what we may call a radical Right. Just as his brilliant reminiscences of the revolutions of 1848 demonstrate insight and literary powers far superior to those of another contemporary observer, Karl Marx, Tocqueville had an understanding of the conservative inclinations of masses of people—their nationalism, for example, and their desire for respectability—which seems to have eluded Marx completely. In June of 1848, in Paris, Tocqueville supported the military suppression of what may have been the first socialist revolt in Europe (for this he was acidly and unfairly criticized by some radicals, including Alexander Herzen); yet very soon thereafter he recognized the danger latent in the appeal and the respectability of anticommunism. "The insane fear of socialism throws the bourgeois headlong into the arms of despotism," he wrote to a friend. "But now that the weakness of the Red party has been proved, people will regret the price at which their enemy has been put down." Concerning the widespread acceptance of Louis-Napoléon's dictatorship he wrote to his brother Edouard, "I am saddened and disturbed more than I ever have been before when I see in so many Catholics . . . this love of force, of the police, of the censor."

Tocqueville, as Jardin correctly states, was incapable of writing on a subject "that did not impassion him to the point of anguish." The evidence for this exists not only in his published works but in his letters and in his many notes. His friend Beaumont said of Tocqueville that "for one volume he published he wrote ten; and the notes he cast aside as intended only for himself would have served many writers as text for the printer." There was, however, a gap of twelve years between his completion of *Democracy in America* and the beginning of his archival researches for *The Old Regime*. The gap was due to his political career, to which this biography devotes nearly two hundred pages. The first full summary of that career, it is useful in many of its details, though perhaps of greater interest to French than to American readers. In 1837—after he began writing the second volume of *Democracy in America*—Tocqueville chose to stand for election to the Chamber of Deputies from his Normandy district. He lost, but two years later he was elected, and in the next ten years he won four such elections. He was not a parliamentary success. "His efforts to win over his colleagues ... seem to have been rather clumsy," Jardin writes. "He did not have the right hail-fellow-well-met parliamentary manner, and to others he appeared ambitious and proud." He himself wrote to his wife in 1842, "Yesterday once again I discovered that I absolutely lack the talent which, in this government, is everything—the talent for extemporizing." Yet his reputation was considerable enough (especially after a speech in January 1848, in which he predicted the coming revolution) that he was appointed to the commission drafting the Constitution of the Second Republic. In 1849, he was briefly the Foreign Minister of France, a task he fulfilled creditably (and of which a scholarly study remains to be written). He resigned after five months in office, unwilling to abide by the dictatorial tendencies of Louis-Napoléon.

More important than the detailed reconstruction of Tocqueville's political career is Jardin's accumulation of material about Tocqueville's personal life. For the first time, we have many details about the private Tocqueville. We have had different accounts of his temperament, and even of his physical traits. Some Frenchmen described him as cold and aloof; some Americans described him as nervous and excitable. Besides a few caricatures (one by Daumier), there is the beautiful portrait by the French romantic painter Théodore Chassériau. Tocqueville was not a vain man; Jardin tells us that Chassériau volunteered to paint his portrait out of gratitude for a favor that Tocqueville had done for the painter's brother. Jardin's verbal picture of Tocqueville corresponds well to the Chassériau portrait: he was "slight and thin," with a face "at once childish and rather sickly, framed by long silky black hair and brightened by large, sparkling black eyes." Tocqueville, who died at the age of fifty-four after a bout of bronchitis, suffered from recurrent gastric pains, a liver condition, and a serious pulmonary weakness. (His mother's health was also fragile, but Jardin is not convincing when he writes that Alexis inherited his inclination to moody anxiety from her.) Yet he was anything but a bookworm. He wrote in the mornings and took great pleasure in going out into the fields in the afternoons. He was a good rider. He was addicted to long walks, insisting on them even during his illnesses, save the last one.

Until this biography, even Tocqueville scholars knew very little about his relationships with women. Now we know that he had a love affair with a middle-class girl, Rosalie Malye, during his student years at Metz and wrote letters to her even after her marriage. More important, he rejected the custom of arranged marriages between aristocratic families. He was impressed by the American practice, in which marriage resulted from mutual affection, and also by the fidelity and assiduous domesticity of American wives. Jardin suggests that Tocqueville had a passionate temperament; in one instance, he implies (without citing his source) the existence of a few clandestine extramarital excursions. Many things about Tocqueville's marriage are still a mystery. Very much contrary to the habit of his time and of his family—and against his mother's wishes—Tocqueville, in 1835, married a not very attractive middle-class Englishwoman, Mary Mottley, who had been a governess in a French household. She was older than he was, and—at least temperamentally—his complete opposite. Opposites often attract, but in this case there were evident difficulties. On one occasion (also described by Jardin's predecessor Redier), Tocqueville is supposed to have thrown a plate at his wife, whose slowness at the dinner table he found insufferable. Yet she was an intelligent woman, and their ménage seems to have been more successful than not. Tocqueville's friend the essayist Jean-Jacques Ampère left a record of cozy days and good dinners at their château, of playing billiards with Mme. Tocqueville, of the couple reading aloud to each other on long afternoons and evenings. From Jardin we learn that Tocqueville loved Mozart's *Don Giovanni* and the music of Rossini.

A German visitor—one E. Gans—observing Tocqueville in a Paris salon, commented, "In his manner, there is a grace and a politeness to which the present generation of Frenchmen seems to attach less value than the preceding one." Yet some people accused this Comte de Tocqueville of being a traitor to his class, who made his peace with democracy too soon. Indeed, he carried himself with the minimum of pretension; among other things, he refused to use his title, and chose to take his place, whether in his parish church or in a line of voters, among the common people. It would be a great mistake, however, to consider him one of those aristocrats (and in the history of Europe there have been many) who sought popularity in a kind of reverse snobbism, or enjoyed rebelling against family tradition. Tocqueville was proud of his ancestry—for example, of his great-grandfather Malesherbes, who defended Louis XVI at the King's trial, and who was himself sent to the guillotine. He also took deep pleasure in his friendship with the Norman peasants, and in their loyalty to him. (Conversely, loyalty was one of Tocqueville's most admirable traits. He was sufficiently magnanimous not to nurse grievances. "My poor Hippolyte, what a sorry character, but what a heart of gold!" he wrote about one of his brothers, whose life and opinions could not have been more different from his, and who had often disappointed him.) His literary style was part of the heritage of the Tocqueville family, who read and discussed books constantly. During his early writing career, his father and his brothers "weighed every turn of phrase, down to individual words, and all three required the sort of exactness that gives Alexis's style, in places, a crystalline purity." His love and respect for his father, who was an amateur historian of sorts, were strong and enduring.

Tocqueville was one of those great thinkers who straddle their age by transcending it. His style was classical, yet his temperament was romantic. His reason carried many of the marks of the eighteenth century, yet the unwitting prophetic thrust of his thought carries us far into the twentieth. He was well connected—related not only to Malesherbes but to important writers, like Chateaubriand, and Prime Ministers, like Molé—yet independence of mind and character were the principal elements of his personality. This uncategorizable independence was doubtless the reason for the comparative obscurity of his reputation—an obscurity that persisted, especially in France, for many decades after his death. He transcended not only his times but also categories that are still prevalent. Was he a liberal or a conservative? Was he a social thinker or a historian? In the present sense of those words he was more the second of each pair than the first; but in a higher sense he incarnated the best and most enduring qualities of them all. There is, too, the question of Tocqueville's Catholicism. Few of his commentators have dealt with it adequately, most of them simply asserting that his faith was restricted to expressions of a belief in the necessary stability that religion brings to the social order. M. Jardin, recognizing the complexity of the issue, at the end of the book redeems his own speculations with an expression of modest wisdom: "In the case of a mind as active, as passionate, as secret as that of Alexis Tocqueville, we will not be so bold as to assume any certainty about his last thoughts. There are intimate reaches of the spirit that compel one to silence"—an honorable conclusion to this solid reconstruction of Tocqueville's agitated life.

21

Henry Adams

(1993)

"A weary Titan of Unity."[1] Thus Henry Adams referred to himself and to the work of his mind throughout his life in his *Education*. His commentators and biographers, very much in the American manner, have often attempted to give definitions of such a unity. Contrary to the ideas of some of his commentators—and of Adams himself—I see a division, as well as a split-mindedness, in Adams's life and in his thinking.

The division is that between Adams the historian and Adams the philosopher of history. Such a division is unusual. There is a connection, a well-nigh inevitable spilling over, in the works of those men who wrote histories and then tried to compose their philosophies of history. In Adams's case the distinction between his history writing and his philosophizing about history amounts to a real difference, to a definite division. I have a very high regard for Henry Adams the historian, but not for his philosophy of history. I am not only referring to the superb qualities of his nine volumes of the *History of the United States during the Administrations of Thomas Jefferson and James Madison*, but also to his fine biographies of Gallatin and Randolph and, perhaps especially, to his reviews and review-essays written in the 1870s, of books by historians such as Freeman, Maine, Green, Stubbs, Fustel de Coulanges, and many others. They are marked by a maturity that is not only rare but virtually nonexistent among historians writing in the fourth decade of their lives, whether in America or in Europe; and by a literary judgment and a quality of style probably without equal in the writings of American historians ever since.[2]

Then came a change: Adams turns away from history, to philosophy. I am not a Henry Adams scholar; and I cannot establish definitely when this

From David R. Contosta and Robert Muccigrosso, eds., *Henry Adams and His World* (Philadelphia: The American Philosophical Society), 322–24.

change occurred: in 1879, when he decided to leave Harvard? in 1885, consequent to the tragedy of the suicide of his wife? Is it possible that the generally unimaginative and insufficiently appreciative reception of his *History of the United States* contributed to it? In any event, by 1893 his turning away from history writing was complete. As Brooks Adams wrote about that year: "Henry thought that we would be crushed. And it was then, as Henry pointed out in his *Education,* that his great effort at thoughts began."[3] Yet his disappointment with the quality of his once fellow-academics (of which there is surprisingly little trace in the *Education*) began much earlier. In a pithy sentence he once wrote that "the teaching profession is, like the church and the bankers, a vested interest."[4] (One generation later Walter Rathenau said that there are no specialists, there are only vested interests.)

But besides and beyond this very evident and rather clear-cut division in Adams's life between its portion of history writing and the portion of philosophizing there is that other, more difficult, problem of Adams's split-mindedness. I must insist that by "split-mindedness" I do not mean what, in the twentieth century, is suggested by the term "schizophrenia." Split-mindedness, allow me to say, is a very American (and often Russian) phenomenon.[5] Contrary to the Freudian scheme, split-mindedness occurs when a mind is split vertically, not horizontally—that is on the conscious level, and not between the conscious and the so-called subconscious. It consists of the inclination and, even more, of the ability to maintain two different, and essentially contradictory, sets of ideas and beliefs in one's mind. Johan Huizinga pointed out that this had been typical of some of the Middle Ages, and especially of their late period.

An odd thing about Adams is that—rather unusually—he was to some extent aware of this duality, at least in some instances. It is suffused throughout his medievalism. It is discernible within the text of his famous passages about the Virgin and the Dynamo. He may have been ironic about himself when he wrote that "my idea of paradise is a perfect automobile going thirty miles an hour on a smooth road to a twelfth-century cathedral"[6] (a statement worthy of Dodsworth, or of Babbitt). Alas, one inevitable component of split-mindedness is self-deception. I am afraid that Adams was not ironic when around the same time he wrote to John Hay that in Normandy he found himself "among my respectable Norman ancestors. ... Caen, Bayeux, St. Lô, Coutances and Mont Saint-Michel are *clearly* [my italics] works that I helped to build. ..."[7]

One set of dualities that Henry Adams thought he had recognized and understood (and on which he often insisted) was his view of his own background and vision. He thought of himself as standing on one foot in the eighteenth century and on the other in the twentieth. Yet this was, strangely, a narrow-minded view. The Age of Reason, in late eighteenth-century Boston, was very different from the Age of Reason in Europe. Yes: "reason" at that time still had a spacious meaning, as had the German word *Wissenschaft*: science as well as knowledge. But the unfortunate and often undiscriminating New England adulation of "Science" was there from the very beginning, more often than not at the expense of true reason, even in the eighteenth century. The humane mentality, the humane reason of a Dr. Johnson, was entirely different from Henry Adams's idea of Reason. In the *Education* he wrote that during his youth he and his brothers had tastes far more "modern" than Dr. Johnson. Yet it is Henry Adams's scientism and not Dr. Johnson's humanism that strikes us as antiquated, corroded, hopelessly dated.

Of course much, if not all, of Henry Adams's scientism was his inheritance from Boston and from his Adams ancestors. Brooks, as was his wont, may have exaggerated his attributions of John Quincy Adams's thought,[8] but he hardly exaggerated when he wrote: "Granting that there is a benign and omnipotent Creator of the world, who watches over the fate of men, [John Quincy Adams's] sincere conviction was that such a Being thinks according to certain fixed laws, which we call scientific laws."[9] *That* was the naïve—but also narrow-minded and presumptuous—belief in scientism that Henry Adams had ingested and from which he never departed: "the principle that all history must be studied as a science," as he wrote in his *Letter to American Teachers of History* as late as 1910. In the *Education* he wrote: "Since Gibbon, the spectacle was almost a scandal. History has lost even the sense of shame. It was a hundred years behind the experimental sciences. . . . For all serious purposes, it was less instructive than Walter Scott and Alexandre Dumas."[10] Henry Adams failed to recognize not only that history cannot be studied "scientifically," that is, through the application of the methods borrowed or taken from the physical sciences; in a larger sense, he failed to see that "science" is a part of the history of mankind, not the other way around.

The scientism of Henry Adams was his undoing (as it may be the undoing of the United States). It is this scientism that makes his philosophy of history not merely an oddity, not only antiquated, but worthless. His acceptance of the dogmas of Buckle and Darwin was bereft of the elegant and worldly skepticism with which he looked at the confections of many of his contemporary historians. Perhaps his scientism was the natural reaction of a man who, with all of his honest respect of his ancestors, witnessed the fatal shriveling of the metaphysical illusions, of the rigid biblical beliefs and of the shallow spiritualism of New England. His melancholy recognition of Buckle and Darwin is marked by Adams's pessimism, a mood of near-despair. So he wrote in his *Education:* "The historian must not try to know what is truth, if he values his honesty; for, if he cares for his truths, he is certain to falsify his facts."[11] Facts! This is not an elegant paradox; it is a counsel of despair. Earlier, in the first number of the *American Historical Review,* he wrote: "On the average every history contains at least one assertion of fact to every line. A history like that of Macaulay contains much more than one hundred and fifty assertions or assumptions of fact. If the rule holds good, at least thirty thousand of these so-called facts must be more or less inexact."[12] Facts! Henry Adams, this literary artist and master was not able (or was perhaps unwilling) to understand that history is written (and spoken, and thought, and taught) in words; and, moreover, in words that are not made up by a scientific terminology but words of the common and everyday language; that "facts" cannot be separated from the words that express them; that no "fact" exists by itself but that its meaning depends on its association with other "facts"; that the statement of every "fact" depends on its purpose; that the purpose of historical knowledge is not scientific accuracy but human understanding; that man's knowledge of things and man's knowledge of man (which is what history potentially gives us) are not only two different matters, but that the second has a priority over the first, since they involve two different kinds of knowledge, that is, of thinking.

In 1899, almost a decade after he had finished his *History,* Adams wrote that the nine volumes were only "a fragment of history ... merely an introduction to our history during the Nineteenth Century.... [T]he real History that one would like to write was to be built on it, and its merits and demerits ... could be seen only when the structure, of which it was to be the foundation, was raised."[13] In reality, those nine volumes were (and still are) much more than that. What a history of the American nineteenth century he could have given us! Alas, he turned to his philosophy of history instead.[14]

Henry Adams had, as Ernest Samuels wrote, "scoffed at William James's talk of free will; he and Brooks had flatly asserted that the making of the human mind is mechanical."[15] His two communications to the American historical profession are chock-full with such assertions—dogmatically so:

> Any science assumes a necessary sequence of cause and effect, a
> force resulting in motion which cannot be other than what it is.
> Any science of history must be absolute, like other sciences, and
> must fix with mathematical certainty the path which human
> society has got to follow.[16]

> Those of us who read Buckle's first volume when it first
> appeared in 1857, and almost immediately afterwards, in 1859,

read *The Origin of Species* and felt the violent impulse which Darwin gave to the study of natural laws, never doubted that historians would follow until they had exhausted every possible hypothesis to create a science of history.[17]

How could [the historian] deny that social energy was a true form of energy.... For human history the essential was to convince itself that social energy, though a true energy, was governed by laws of its own.... [T]he only point requiring insistence is that sixty years of progress in science have only intensified the assertion that vital Energy obeys the laws of thermal energy.... [I]f Thought is capable of being classed with Electricity, or Will with chemical affinity, as a mode of motion, it seems necessarily to fall at once under the second law of thermodynamics as one of the energies which most easily degrades itself, and, if not carefully guarded, returns bodily to the cheaper form called Heat. Man, as a form of energy, is in most need of getting a firm footing on the law of thermodynamics.[18]

Anthony Trollope, having met George Bancroft, asked: "Did he believe what he was saying?"—a properly skeptical question, since Bancroft was not only a trumpeting bloviator; he was also much of a fraud. Did Adams believe what he was saying? Despite his fine aristocratic irony, despite his sophisticated pessimism, despite his paradoxical and humorous exaggerations in his intimate letters I think that—because of his split-mindedness— he did. Ernest Samuels wrote that "his attitude of desperate humor became the most persistent stance of his later life. One laughed for fear of being obliged to weep."[19] There is some truth in this statement; but not enough. Henry Adams's wit was different from a sense of humor that is not only skeptical but humble, since it issues from a self-deprecating understanding of the limits of human wisdom. In 1892, aboard the liner *Teutonic* (*nomen est omen*) he "was dismayed to notice the social decline in First Class. His two hundred fellow passengers seemed somehow all to be Jews. The ship, however, showed the first indubitable sign of mechanical progress."[20] What is remarkable in this kind of reminiscence is not Adams's snobbery or his developing prejudice against Jews: it is his unshakable prejudice for seeing evidences of "mechanical progress." Twenty years later he misread the symbolic meaning of the catastrophe of the *Titanic*. He wrote to Elizabeth Cameron that it may affect "the confidence in our mechanical success, but the foundering of the Republican Party destroys confidence in our political system."[21]

A knowledge of history, Henry Adams's near-contemporary Agnes Repplier once wrote, is the best fare for one's imagination. It leads to the understanding of people, to standards of judgment, to an ability to contrast and the right to estimate. Consequently, the political views of that modest literary essayist were almost always excellent, by which I mean that they have stood the test of time. The opposite was often true of Henry Adams, in spite of the strength of his mind, of his visionary power, of his historical learning. His contemporary political judgments were often very wrong. In 1893 he wrote to his brother: "I think we reached the end of the Republic here."[22] In 1895: "Once more we are under the whip of the bankers. Even on Cuba . . . we are beaten and hopeless."[23] This was less than three years before 1898. In 1891 he wrote to Lodge: "America has no future in the Pacific. . . . [W]e could Americanize Siberia, and this is the only possible work that I can see still open on a scale equal to American means."[24] "On a scale equal to American means" here is a matter of risible irony, since Adams wrote this at the very time when he was tape-measuring the breasts of Samoan girls. There *is* something wonderful in the innocent—yes, innocent—descriptions of his pleasures in Samoa, where he is American as well as aristocratic, where his fine, thin, Bostonian esthetic sense condemns the crude practices and ideas of low-church Protestant missionaries in Oceania. But there was that other side of his brain, with his tape-measuring that connects Adams's scientism to the silly primitivist ideas of Margaret Mead fifty years later—and perhaps even to the, alas, prototypically modern American stupidities of Drs. Masters and Johnson with their calibrations of genitalia.

And now to an important point: Adams's obsession with the acceleration of history. At times he had a Spenglerian vision of cyclical determinism, with its ever recurring symptoms of decline. In 1891 he wrote to Brooks that he saw "the age of Andrew Jackson and the cotton planters much as I see the age of Valois or Honorius—that is, with profound horror."[25] Writing from Sicily in 1899: "The extinction of Greece came with the extinction of the Greek coinage. When the mines are exhausted and population grows society will go to pieces."[26] (What would he have thought of the credit card?) He agreed with Brooks: the fall of Rome came "because of the silver denarius."[27] The Weary Titan of Unity wore down his mind with his wearisome, because senseless, efforts to arrive at a Mathematical Law that would explain everything. Through his split-mindedness, his philosophy of history amounted to an absurdity: to the search for the perfect and eternally valid marriage between (masculine) Mathematics and (feminine) Spirituality. "The ethereal phase," he wrote, will come "in 1921, when thought will reach the limit of its possibilities."[28] Some limit! Some possibilities! Adams should have heeded Tocqueville, who wrote in the 1830s that the extreme agitation of ideas in the age of democracy amounts to mere appearances on the surface of life, that the very opposite of what people fearful of democracy were predicting, would occur: the true movement of minds would slow down, and a long period of intellectual stagnation would prevail. What Adams saw as the acceleration of history—that is, of human thinking—was merely the mechanical acceleration of what we (perhaps wrongly) call "communications."

Sometime after 1875 Henry Adams began to lose touch with the most significant developments of European thought. This happened despite his wide learning, his knowledge of languages, his assiduous reading of English and German and French historians and scientists. The year 1875 is significant: Adams, who read the German philosophers of his time, was unaware of the distinction that Wilhelm Dilthey made in that year about the essential difference between *"Naturwissenschaften"* and *"Geisteswissenschaften,"* that is, between man's knowledge of nature and man's knowledge of man—a recognition in which Dilthey was not alone (consider but Nietzsche's essay *Über das Studium der Geschichte,* 1874). Through his somber acceptance of Buckle and Darwin, Adams remained ignorant of what I am wont to call the beginnings of post-scientific thinking—not only of Dilthey and Nietzsche but later of Valéry and Bergson, and surely of Jakob Burckhardt, the great historian and historical thinker and the philosophical and cultural historian of Adams's own lifetime (he died in 1897). It was not only Nietzsche who pronounced caustic aphorisms ("Building systems is childishness"). Burckhardt's profound vision denied the meaning of any attempt to erect a systematic philosophy of history. To the contrary: what Burckhardt attempted to write, and teach, was the historical way of seeing things, a historical philosophy, the very obverse of a philosophy of history. "A philosophy of history," Burckhardt wrote, "is a centaur, a contradiction in terms: for history coordinates, and hence is unphilosophical, while philosophy subordinates, and hence is unhistorical." Instead of cobbling together a system that would establish abstract "laws" governing the patterns of history, Burckhardt was interested in the concrete historicity of knowledge, of consciousness, of thought.

Henry Adams's despairing pessimism was not unlike that of other refined Americans of his times, if not of his exact generation. (Owen Wister or John Jay Chapman come to mind.) He died in the same year in which Oswald Spengler completed his *Untergang des Abendlandes.* We may regret that he had not read Burckhardt; but we must thank the Almighty that he was (and that we have been) spared of his reading of Spengler.

Henry Adams the historian deserves our respect—more: he deserves our gratitude. In his histories and in his reviews of other historians Henry Adams represented a maturity of learning and a style whereof the flowering of New England was once capable. Henry Adams the philosopher of history has nothing to teach or tell us. This is not only due to Adams's extreme scientism, which is (or obviously should be) antiquated and outdated by now. For the most dangerous and corruptible inclination of the American national mind and character is not really materialism. The speculations of Henry Adams should warn us against a deeper American danger: that of a split-mindedness, which includes the evils of a maddeningly abstract spiritualism running rampant.

22

Christopher Dawson

(1993)

To sum up the life of Christopher Dawson is not an easy task. Every man's life is inseparable from his ideas. But in Dawson's case his vision—by which I mean the coherence of his ideas—not only influenced but governed his entire life. And now, in *A Historian and His World*—of which "A Life of Christopher Dawson" is the subtitle—his daughter Christina Scott succeeds marvelously. Her own biographical text is not much more than two hundred pages. Yet this reviewer makes bold to say that it fulfills all of the requirements for a biography of her father. Surely someone, someday, will attempt an eight-hundred-page (or more) biography of this important historian and thinker. Surely such a work will not be a waste of effort, and it may include certain details hitherto unknown. Still, all of the essentials are here in this book, modestly and wonderfully crafted, full of affection and insight but also with a splendid kind of detachment, and excellently written.

All of this would be remarkable alone when considering the difficulties of a daughter writing about her father, with the need to eschew uncritical respect and admiration. It is more remarkable than that, because of Christina Scott's extraordinary knowledge of her father's work and ideas. I write "extraordinary" because, in many ways, we cannot expect the people closest to us—spouses and children—to have read everything, and critically indeed, of what we have written; that is, to expatiate on the meaning of a husband's or father's published work. The reason for this is—seemingly, but only seemingly—paradoxical. It is familiarity. What may be striking to others is commonplace within a family; they have heard those things and understood them long enough. Yet this book is not only fresh with insights. It is a first-class introduction to that enormous corpus of work within which

Review of Christina Scott, *A Historian and His World: A Life of Christopher Dawson* (1992). From *Intercollegiate Review*, Spring: 50–52.

we can discern Dawson's essential *idearium*. The great Jakob Burckhardt once wrote that the student of history must possess but one talent: *bisogna saper leggere*—he must know how to read. Christopher Dawson's daughter has passed this test with high honors.

Christopher Dawson was not a man of his time. Nor was he a period piece. Allow me to deal with the former statement first. Dawson was a late Victorian, by which I do not only mean that he was born in 1889. His childhood, his upbringing, his family, the surroundings, the climate, the atmosphere of his youth were all Victorian—in a now Arcadian and beautiful sense of that adjective. That, contra writers such as Lytton Strachey, was not a constraint but a tremendously vital asset in the lives of certain people, including the life of this otherwise unworldly man. The evidence is there in Dawson's own "Memories of a Victorian Childhood," a beautiful piece of writing first published in this volume. It is full of precise and evocative descriptions of the houses and the counties he knew when he was a child. They include Wales, Wessex, and the West Riding of Yorkshire. His knowledge and feel for these lands, of the essence of those countrysides, are amazing proofs of the rural affections of a man who led a bookish, in many ways closed, and sometimes even an ivory-tower-tinted life. Even in the beginning of this century the climate of Dawson's early youth was close not only to the world of *Kilvert's Diary* or to Trollope's Barchester but in some ways even to that of Jane Austen. And this, I repeat, was a very formative asset— because Dawson loved it and venerated it and sought no escape from it. There is a great difference between being a man for all seasons and being a man of one's own time. The latter, who fits in exactly with the customs and habits, including mental customs and habits, of his own time will amount to little; he has no enduring values. That Christopher Dawson was not. He carried with himself not only a proper nostalgia (in the sense of the original Greek term: *nostos* + *algos*, a longing for home) but a tremendous inherited capital of Victorian classical learning.

Nor was he a period piece. He belonged—or, more precisely, he contributed to—a period of Catholic intellectual revival in England, in the 1930s, together with people whose names are now, alas, unknown to an entire generation of American Catholic intellectuals: D'Arcy, Jerrold, Burns, Watkin, and others, at a time when the Chesterton and Belloc years were passing. Dawson's mind and vision ranged wider than those of many others. He was a great historian. The evidence is there in his books and articles. That evidence is so broad and so large that in any work, book, or article attempting to interpret Dawson's ideas the best and most apposite expositions of those ideas must be passages by Dawson himself. He once wrote, in a mildly critical article about that most pedestrian of living English modern historians Allan Bullock: "The academic historian is perfectly right in insisting on the importance of the techniques of historical criticism and research. But the mastery of these techniques will not produce great history, any more than a mastery of metrical technique will produce great poetry."

He was probably unaware that he was writing about himself. Yet he was very much aware that a largeness of vision is "the source of [the] creative power of any great historian."

Dawson's reputation was compromised by several handicaps, all of them severe ones. There was the fact of his conversion to Roman Catholicism, which, at least for the greater part of his life, rendered him suspect to many English and American historians of the time, when anti-Catholicism was the anti-Semitism of many academics and intellectuals. There was the fact of his amateur historianship—of course, amateur in the best sense of this often misused adjective—at a time when professional academic and amateur literate historianship began to separate more and more in England, and especially in America. Many historians, on both sides of the Atlantic, dismissed him as some kind of a more-or-less erudite Catholic publicist and apologist. Regrettably, there were (and still are) other historians who did not only refuse to read him but who were unaware of his existence. The very fact that his knowledge and writing spread to so many fields made many academic historians and public thinkers suspicious of Christopher Dawson, whereby they thought it best to ignore him. (It is lamentable how many American Catholic academics are unaware of Dawson now, merely two decades after his death, considering that one generation ago he was venerated more in America than in England). There was the fact that throughout his life he was more often than not shy; he was far from being a good public speaker, and he mumbled a lot—not in his writing, of course. His courtship and love for his wife were old-fashioned and exemplary; but while he was impractical, his wife was frequently restless; they moved often, which had sometimes adverse effects on the quietude and comfort necessary for his work.

He could be sharp and cutting on occasion—mostly privately or in letters to friends, with the not infrequent result of a few good aphorisms. But there was no evidence of a corroding bitterness in his writing, even when he could see—and how clearly!—the prospect of a New Dark Age unfolding. If his life was unmarked by triumphs of character, it was surely marked by a mind and a soul triumphant over adversity because of a deep knowledge of Christian hope, of providential goodness, and of a sense of meaning in human history.

23

Paul W. Schroeder

(1994)

This is a great—perhaps a very great—work by a historian who ought to be recognized as the leading American master of European diplomatic history. The scope and the quality of this volume surpass the achievement of the once classic American diplomatic history of modern Europe, William L. Langer's *European Alliances and Alignments*. Its quality is comparable to the diplomatic histories written by George F. Kennan, while its scope, because of its topic, is larger than those of Kennan. Much of this appears from the bibliography, which is not only compendious but excellent; and from the running references to works by historians of a startling variety, and in many languages.

Schroeder's book has a main thesis which should be apparent from its title: "The transformation of European politics 1763–1848." He states that a drastic change occurred in 1814–15, mostly through the Congress of Vienna. "This book attempts to . . . explain the process by which European statesmen, taught slowly and painfully by repeated defeats and disaster, finally and suddenly succeeded in learning how to conduct international politics differently and better." The eighteenth-century politics (and wars) were different. "Overall, the ratio of battlefield deaths to the total population of Europe was about seven times as great in the eighteenth as in the nineteenth century." This is debatable, but worth thinking about. Schroeder is in accord with the great French diplomatic historian Albert Sorel, and also with Burke: "The crime of the first Polish partition rose directly from the rules and needs of standard eighteenth-century politics."

Schroeder does not argue with Clausewitz: but, in a sense, his thesis is a contradiction of the latter. That war is a continuation of politics by other means was certainly true of the eighteenth century but less so after the

Review of Paul W. Schroeder, *The Transformation of European Politics, 1763–1848* (1994). From *Continuity*, Spring: 121–24.

Congress of Vienna, when the undisputed practice of balance-of-power was superseded, for the first time, by a tacit agreement for the upholding, or at least for some preservation, of an international order in Europe. A fine illustration not only of Schroeder's thesis but of his argumentative ability as a writer appears in this passage where he interprets Napoleon's and Metternich's famous failed meeting in Dresden in 1813: "At Dresden, it has been correctly observed, two different personalities with incompatible world-views faced each other. The confrontation was not, however, between a nineteenth-century romantic hero and an eighteenth-century *grand seigneur*, but between a sixteenth-century Italian *condottiere* and a nineteenth-century conservative European statesman representing a kind of politics the *condottiere* could not understand or even admit as possible. At this stage of their careers, Metternich was abreast of the times and Napoleon centuries behind." Then in 1814–15, "France here reaped the benefits of a new kind of European politics which it had not yet learned to practice itself." And after 1853 Europe reverted to balance-of-power politics; but somehow the achievements of the Congress of Vienna would be recognized later, much later.

Well, I have always been an admirer of the achievements (well, of some of the achievements) of the Congress of Vienna. A monograph ought to be written about the rise of the reputation of the Congress and of Metternich and Gentz and Castlereagh, etc., since 1945—and its sinking to the level of vulgarization (*basse*, not *haute vulgarisation*) by the Kissinger kind. But—not in spite of; because of, indeed, together with—my admiration for Schroeder, this is the place to argue with him … a little. Schroeder is an artist-historian; and sometimes he explains too much. A few examples: "Dynastic succession disputes ceased after 1815 to be a major international problem." Yes and no: there was Spain in the 1840s and again in 1870. Again about Spain in 1823, Schroeder says: "The statesmen of the Vieruna generation, to repeat, did not so much fear war because it would bring revolution as because they had learned from bitter experience that war was revolution." True, but perhaps not true enough. Schroeder argues that in creating the United Netherlands Vienna "was an astonishing success." Yes and no; or, rather, no and yes (in the long run). Schroeder's generalizations are sweeping at times. But that is not a vice: generalizations, like brooms, ought to sweep and not stand in the corner, stationary and dumb.

Here, in one sentence, Schroeder sweeps away the Accepted Big Thesis about the Era of Democratic Revolutions: "*pace* R. R. Palmer, Jacques Godechot, Franco Venturi, and other distinguished historians of this era, Europe in the 1780s was not heading inexorably toward revolution, but toward war, whether or not there was revolution. Revolution was contingent; war systemic and structural." Again: yes and no. Yes—because in the long run wars were more decisive than were revolutions; they changed the map of Europe. No: because Schroeder's last sentence may be true of "Europe" in the 1780s but not really of France. Perhaps this is the shortcoming in Schroeder's otherwise astonishingly brilliant (and also astonishingly well-documented) vision: his is a diplomatic history more than an international one; it deals with the history of states at a time when the internal movements of nations began to fill up (no matter how slowly, or gradually) the framework of states, where the "Primat der Aussenpolitik" was beginning to be affected. Schroeder knows this, and refers to it often, but perhaps not enough—especially in his last chapters, leading up to 1848 (the very consequences of which show that an age of wars would follow an age of revolutions).

Schroeder's vision of the world is conservative—in the best sense of that now so often obscenely inflated and perversely expropriated term. This goes beyond his respect for the Congress of Vienna. Here are a few of his throwaway remarks, all of them worth considering. "The statesmen of that era certainly did not believe in popular sovereignty, and wished to deal with governments rather than peoples (still a useful idea in international politics)," "the people (that dangerous abstraction)," and "the necessary, inescapable priority of the pursuit of order over justice in international affairs." Bravo.

His sureness of hand allows for exercises of wit, sometimes in the form of delicious footnotes, such as note three on page 522. Often his witty, and sometimes even elegant, formulation points to a serious need to reverse accepted ideas. He is justly critical of Canning: "Canning, long celebrated as the liberal opponent of the reactionary Holy Alliance, was really, in a literal sense, reactionary and restorationist, trying to restore the competitive international politics of the eighteenth century." "What happened in fact is that he summoned a threat to the New World into existence to redress his defeat [in Spain] in the old." In 1829–30 "Metternich, wanting to be Europe's coachman, resigned himself to the role of brakeman." Only once in the preface does Schroeder give way to modern social-scientific jargon ("the superiority of system-level explanations and structural analysis over unit-level explanations of international politics.") Elsewhere his pen writes swift and clear. For example, in 1813 "for Castlereagh and the British government, Russia was still Britain's natural ally; for the Russian government Britain was still a rival." Or, "It says volumes for the stability of British politics that in early 1809, at a critical stage of the war in Spain and with a new one brewing in Central Europe, Parliament could for two months be primarily engaged in investigating charges of corruption against the Duke of York and looking into his relations with his mistress. One can under-stand Napoleon's rage and frustration. With all his power, he not only could not bring the British down, he could not even gain their full attention." This is very good. Yes, Napoleon would not have understood Jane Austen—but then Chateaubriand would not, either. This is my formulation, not Schroeder's; but reading him I found myself in the presence of a masterful historian—as rare nowadays as finding a Jane Austen addict in a singles bar.

24

Brigitte Hamann
(1999)

T his is one of the most important books written about Hitler. Its scope is superbly crafted: it is a history as well as a biography. Its dual theme, Vienna and Hitler, reflects the chronological evolution of the work of Brigitte Hamann, who in her previous books demonstrated her more than considerable talents as a biographer and historian dealing with personalities of the last Habsburgs. Now, in her prime, she has turned to the topic of the young Hitler. The result is a masterpiece.

It is a masterpiece about Vienna. We have had a flood of books about Vienna around 1900, full of Freud, Mahler, Schnitzler, Klimt, etc. proclaiming Viennese "culture" and art as a fulcrum of modernity, with a fin de siècle more important and valuable than the Paris of, say, Debussy, Ravel, Monet, Pissarro, at worst suggesting noble rot, a fine dessert wine. I think that this is something of an exaggeration, but to analyze this is not within the province of this review. The other view, that of a Vienna which was backward rather than forward, is mostly found in less well-known political histories, suggesting that the collapse of the Habsburg monarchy was inevitable and that phenomena in Vienna had created the phenomenon of Hitler. That is an exaggeration, too, though not devoid of some truth. There was the old Irish biddy whom the neighboring women had asked whether the gossip about the young widow up the street was true or not. "It is not true,"she said, "but it is true enough." Well, a historian must proceed from the opposite end: he must recognize—and say—that certain things may be true, but they are not true enough. And this is one of Brigitte Hamann's virtues. Her portrait of Vienna circa 1910 is rich and balanced: indeed, it could amount to a fine little book even if all of the references and portions about Hitler were excised from it.

Review of Brigitte Hamann, *Hitler's Vienna: A Dictator's Apprenticeship* (1999). From *Spectator* (London), July 3: 31–32.

It is a masterpiece about Hitler (who, after all, is a more important topic in the history of the twentieth century than is Vienna). It stands out among the hundreds of biographies and studies of Hitler, many of them written by well-known professional historians, for at least two connected reasons. One is Mme. Hamann's assiduous research: she found and collected and collated facts and names and episodes and circumstances about Adolf Hitler's five years in Vienna that were either unknown or only fragmentarily worked up by most other historians. The other is that almost all of the latter have accepted, by and large, Hitler's own autobiographical account in *Mein Kampf,* to the effect that his mind, very much including his Judeophobia, was fully formed by his experiences, physical and intellectual, in Vienna.

For Brigitte Hamann that is not true enough. Yes, the dreadful vulgarity of the nationalist and anti-Semitic perorations and publications in Vienna— Hamann sums up and illustrates them so well—were there. Yes, what Hitler saw (and read) in Vienna had an important impact on him. But only partly so. His mind, his view of the world, and his vision of his own destiny and career crystallized not in Vienna but in Munich, almost a decade later. (I have written about this before, relying on evidence—but less evidence than Hamann now provides.) The young Hitler had Jewish acquaintances in Vienna, perhaps even a friend. He was an occasional guest in Jewish bourgeois houses. He admired a few Jewish artists, including Mahler. He made few (if any) categorical anti-Jewish statements before Munich, and in Vienna he certainly did not regard the Jewish "problem" as the key to history.

This leads—in my mind at least—to a question about Hitler that may still be open. Almost fifty years ago, Alan Bullock made the same statement that François Furet recently made about Hitler, that "history offers few examples of exploits so closely tailored to an ideological programme from start to finish." This is too simple. Hitler knew how to tailor his ideas to circumstances and certainly to his audiences. He was (or, rather, he became) a convinced, perhaps even obsessive anti-Semite by 1919. That was when he also recognized his great ability as a speaker. There was a connection between these two matters. In Vienna (as Hitler himself admitted) he was much more influenced by the success of the anti-Semitic rhetoric of the otherwise rather selectively anti-Semitic mayor Karl Lueger than by the fanatical pan-German and Judeophobe Georg von Schönerer. There is much other, later evidence that what Hitler said publicly, and to all kinds of people (not to speak of what he had dictated for *Mein Kampf*), did not entirely accord with his private opinions or convictions. What he said or wrote about what had happened to him in Vienna was not what he had thought then—and a demonstration of this is one of Brigitte Hamann's merits. In sum: did he believe what he was saying? While he was speaking, most certainly; but otherwise perhaps yes and no. And if he does not quite believe everything that he said, this does not reduce his responsibility— rather the contrary. But then this goes beyond the purview of Brigitte Hamann's book.

25

François Furet

(1999)

Until his recent and premature death, François Furet was a historian of France, with considerable talents. But in *The Passing of an Illusion* (originally published in France in 1997), he is writing not about French political history but about something else. "I have a biographical connection with my subject," he writes in his preface: "In my youth, I experienced the passing of an illusion as a Communist between 1949 and 1956." This is an honest admission but a qualification it is not. For one thing, it explains the chronological limits of his book; except for an epilogue, it virtually ends with 1956, which of course is not enough. For another, *The Passing of an Illusion* has all the marks of the skewed perspective of a convert. Now there is nothing very wrong with the zeal of converts for the future; but what is often very wrong with converts is their retrospective zeal—their inclination to exaggerate the universality of the evils from which they have escaped. In this instance, Furet vastly exaggerates the importance of the appeal that communism had for many intellectuals.

This book by an otherwise first-rate French historian contains all the symptoms of the myopia of French intellectuals, of people who (once known for the quickness of their minds) turned violently anticommunist in the 1970s—that is, pretty late. Furet's own writing has none of the once vaunted clarity of French intellect. It is both verbose and inaccurate. Here are a few examples: "Fascism fits completely into its own demise, whereas Communism retains some of the charm of its beginnings." (Some charm.) More about communism: "Now here was an intoxicating brew for moderns deprived of God. How could Hitler's brand of post-Darwinism or even the exaltation of nations hold a candle to it?" (Some mixed metaphor.) "Stalin sized Hitler up like a connoisseur." (Some connoisseur: In 1941, with nearly

Review of François Furet, *The Passing of an Illusion: The Idea of Communism in the Twentieth Century* (1999). From *Boston Sunday Globe,* July 4: F3.

two hundred German divisions pressing against his borders, ready to pounce, Stalin could not believe that Hitler would attack him.) About Hitler: "History offers few examples of exploits so closely tailored to an ideological program from start to finish." (Actually, history offers his pact with Stalin, among other things.) Fascism "had none of the symphonic beauty of Marxism." (Some symphony! Some beauty! Besides, has Furet ever heard Respighi's "Pines of Rome," written during the golden spring of Fascism, though not a celebration of it?)

Furet writes in his preface: "[T]his is not a history of Communism, even less a history of the Soviet Union; it is a history of the illusion of Communism during the time in which the USSR lent it constancy and vitality." But as this very sentence suggests, the history of communism and that of the Soviet Union cannot be simply separated; and throughout his more than five hundred pages and a wearisome sixty pages of closely typeset notes Furet himself cannot separate them. And by "constancy" and "vitality" Furet means little more than the image of the Soviet Union in the cerebrations of selected intellectuals. Ten pages about the "intrepid" Hannah Arendt—a fraudulent philosopher whose original manuscript of *The Origins of Totalitarianism* did not even include the Soviet Union, about which she appended two superficial chapters when the intellectual climate in New York had made that propitious. Another ten pages on Georg Lukacs, whom few people took seriously (or even read) in his native Hungary. More dozens of pages on the pro-Soviet idiocies of G. B. Shaw, H. G. Wells, the Webbs, Stephen Spender—people whose influence on the great events of this century was nil. It is like reconstructing the history of the New Deal from the writings of Upton Sinclair; or that of Reaganism from those of Ayn Rand.

Had Hitler captured Moscow and deflated Stalin in 1941, communism and Communists would have vanished from Europe—and, as Furet says, it is with Europe that his book is mainly concerned. As Proudhon (a deeper seer than Marx) wrote 150 years ago, people are not really moved by ideas about social contracts; they are moved by their perceptions of the realities of power.

There is worse to come. In addition to (or perhaps because of?) the fatal shortcomings of his perspective and scope, Furet's magnum opus contains an astonishing plentitude of mistakes, minor and major. The minor ones include dozens of erroneous dates and names. And the major ones? "After 1918," Furet writes, "the magic of the Soviet phenomenon would exercise a powerful force over the popular imagination, independent of the realities of the region." Well, after 1918, every nation bordering Russia rejected communism violently; and until 1945 there was not a single instance where Communists achieved power, whereas in dozens of countries fascists and National Socialists did.

Furet constantly confuses fascism and National Socialism. In the few instances when he attempts to separate them, he writes nonsense: "Unlike Fascism, Nazism was not basically nationalistic." In 1933 the Communist George Dimitrov "was acquitted, thanks, no doubt, to [Stalin's] secret deal with Hitler." ("No doubt"? No evidence, rather—not the slightest speck of it.) "For the British, the [potential] defeat of the pro-Franco forces in Spain signaled a step forward to Communism in Europe." (Despite the anticommunism of most Tories, "the British" thought that not at all.) "The Soviet Union had tenaciously supported and defended [Tito's] demands concerning Corinthia and Trieste." The very opposite is true: Stalin told Tito to lay off. He would not risk a war with the United States and Britain over Trieste, he said. The division of Europe was set: "What is ours is ours. What is theirs is theirs." Stalin's own words.

"The end of World War II was thus even more a political victory of the Communist idea than for the democratic idea." Where? In Eastern Europe Communist governments were installed by the presence of the Russian Army, not because of popular demand or revolution. Yes, in Western Europe there was a resurgence of Communist parties, but they did not get anywhere; it was liberal democracy that was resurrected in 1945 and thereafter, even in Western Germany. What a pity it is when an experienced historian fails not only to understand but even to know adequately the history of his own times.

26

Gabriel Gorodetsky
(1999)

The most consequential event of World War I was the American declaration of war against Germany. The most consequential event of World War II was the German invasion of Russia. Well before Pearl Harbor, Franklin Delano Roosevelt committed himself to oppose Hitler's Germany; indeed, the American navy was already fighting an undeclared war against German naval units in the Atlantic. Before June 22, 1941, however, Stalin's Soviet Union was not at all committed to opposing Hitler. Quite the contrary; Stalin refused to believe that Hitler would attack him, until the last moment—as a matter of fact, even for a few hours after the German armed forces had broken into Russia.

Stalin had tried everything to convince Hitler of his friendship. The Hitler-Stalin relationship between 1939 and 1941 is one of the strangest chapters—and perhaps the most interesting one—in the diplomatic, political, and personal history of this century. Some of it has been known to specialists for more than fifty years, mainly because of the Allied capture of German documents in 1945. Before the German invasion of Russia, for example, nearly two hundred German divisions were massing in Poland, pressing against the Soviet frontier. Hundreds of German planes were flying reconnaisance over the western Soviet Union. For all kinds of reasons Hitler did not conceal his plan of invading Russia. The evidence was overwhelming. Churchill tried to warn Stalin of what was coming, but in vain. Stalin made every effort to deflect Hitler's decision, in which he did not believe. Stalin thought that the German generals were preparing at worst something against Hitler's wishes.

Stalin's efforts were marked not only by delusion, but also by cowardice. They were manifold and abject, including gesture after gesture to Ber-

Review of Gabriel Gorodetsky, *Grand Delusion: Stalin and the German Invasion of Russia* (1999).
From *New Republic,* November 15: 47–50.

lin, signal after signal, with the purpose of demonstrating to Hitler his loyalty to their non-aggression pact. When the German declaration of war finally burst, Stalin's ambassador to Berlin asked Ribbentrop: "Isn't there a mistake?" And the foreign minister Vyacheslav Molotov said to Werner von Schulenburg, the German ambassador in Moscow: "Have we deserved this?" Von Schulenburg, an old Prussian nobleman who had tried his best to counsel Hitler against attacking Russia, but in vain, is the hero of this somber—and at times ludicrous—story. In 1944, he was executed by Himmler.

Gabriel Gorodetsky is a specialist in Soviet diplomatic history. His voluminous account essentially confirms the above summary of events. But there is more. His book, and its documentation, is exceptionally timely, because there has been, lately, a wave of revisionism about the record, mostly (though not exclusively) emanating from Germany and Austria. Of course, history is always revisionism of a kind. It must find room for the multiple jeopardy that the law eschews: historians must retry and retry again. But what matters is the purpose of the revisionists. And the purpose of the revisionists in this case is the—partial, at best—rehabilitation of Hitler's Third Reich: to argue (and, in some instances, to "prove") that Hitler's attack on Russia in 1941 was a preventive move, because Stalin, in 1941, was preparing to invade Germany.

It began in 1977, with David Irving's *Hitler's War* (a book that John Keegan recently, and very queerly, listed as one of the most important fifty books about World War II). Citing one or two pieces of utterly fragmentary and irrelevant "evidence," Irving stated that the Soviet Union in 1941 was about to attack Germany. Ten years later a spate of more reputable German historians turned to a more subtle attempt at the rehabilitation of Hitler, advancing two arguments: first, that Communism was as bad as Nazism, and so the Holocaust was in many ways a response to the Gulag; and second, that Stalin was about to attack Germany anyhow.

The latter argument was taken up by Gunther Gillessen, in the conservative *Frankfurter Allgemeine Zeitung,* and then by the Austrian Ernst Topitsch (who claimed that World War II "was essentially a Soviet attack on the Western democracies, in which Germany . . . served only as a military surrogate"), and the German military historian Joachim Hoffmann, and Werner Maser (one of Hitler's biographers), and even by an American, R. C. Raack. These writers got substantial support from Suvarov, a Soviet defector, from the very dubious former secret policeman Pavel Sudoplatov, and from the Russian historian V. A. Nevezhin. The purpose of this denigration of Stalin (and there is plenty to denigrate there) has been, alas, an ingenious mitigation of Hitler—again, that the latter's invasion of Russia was but a reaction to Stalin's plan to attack him.

The main merit of Gorodetsky's book is his documentation that such an attribution of Stalin's motives is thoroughly false. The evidence in this book fleshes out a picture of Stalin in which he is not merely deluded by others, but also suffers from an extraordinary measure of self-deceit. The wish is the father of the thought; and, in this instance, it was Stalin's wish to trust Hitler. The psychic dimension of the Hitler-Stalin relationship is a gruesomely fascinating story. They respected—if not admired—each other throughout the war.

On June 22, 1941, the German army has broken into Russia, and the Luftwaffe is destroying half the Russian air force, and Stalin is breathing heavily, he is helpless. "Hitler surely does not know it . . ." he mumbles: "If it were necessary to organize provocation, then the German generals would bomb their own cities." A few days before, when report after report showed that the German invasion was but a matter of days, if not hours, Generals Zhukov and Timoshenko asked Stalin's permission to make the most elemental defensive preparations. Stalin ordered Timoshenko not to fire at German planes flying across the frontier. He shouted at Zhukov in a rage: "Are you proposing to carry out mobilization, alert the troops now and move them to the western borders? This means war!" Stalin's slab-faced toady Molotov asked Zhukov: "Are you eager to fight the Germans?" On June 18, less than three days before the invasion, Stalin shouted at Zhukov again: "Have you come to scare us with war or do you want a war, as you are not sufficiently decorated, or your rank is not high enough?" He ended the meeting, "If you're going to provoke the Germans on the frontier by moving troops there without our permission, then heads will roll, mark my word!" Then he slammed the door.

No more military preparations. All the warnings—there were hundreds of them, ranging from German defectors to Churchill—were disregarded. Stalin preferred Hitler to Churchill. For almost ten days after June 22, Stalin was in a stupor; and then he gathered himself and spoke to his people for the first time. But that is another story. What belongs here is the evidence from another document that disproves, incidentally, the entire thesis of revisionists and conservatives and neoconservatives about Stalin, the International Revolutionary. Two months before the German invasion, Stalin told the Bulgarian Georgi Dimitrov, the president of the Comintern: "The International was created under Marx in the expectation of an approaching international revolution. The Comintern was created by Lenin in such a period too. Today, national tasks for each country have top priority. Do not hold on to what was yesterday. Take into account exactly the new conditions which have been created." The new conditions included the necessity for Soviet friendship with Hitler's Germany. A few days later, Stalin's henchman Andrei Zhdanov warned Dimitrov that what "Stalin regards as a 'fertile ground for spies and for agents of the enemy'" is "uncritical cosmopolitanism" (meaning mostly Jews—but that, too, is another story).

Gorodetsky found this in Dimitrov's diary, which is preserved in Bulgaria. But the bulk of his documentary evidence comes from Moscow. Its value is substantial, for more than one reason: the above-mentioned additional proofs of Stalin's cowardice, and of his nearly limitless trust in Hitler; and also the circumstances and the texts of Stalin's speech on May 5, 1941, at the military academy, when he did tell his listeners to be ready for war, if war must come—a speech that has not only been incorrectly cited but several times falsified by revisionists. There is also evidence that, contrary to the still-accepted general interpretation, Hitler's Balkan campaign in April 1941 did not really postpone or interfere with his timetable for the invasion of Russia.

Yet these Soviet documents have their limitations. Documents "make" history, but history also makes the documents: who is drafting them, and for whom, and for what purposes? Gorodetsky himself notes, on occasion, that many Soviet diplomats and agents abroad were opportunists, that they learned what Stalin wanted to hear. "By early May," Gorodetsky writes, "many intelligence reports were going all out to accommodate the Kremlin." This included the much-touted Ivan Maisky, the Soviet ambassador in London, who was afraid of Stalin: he contributed "to the self-deception which affected the Kremlin on the eve of the war." There is a good description of one of these Soviet diplomats, the Minister to Sofia, by his British colleague there: "a rather loutish creature, obviously terrified of committing himself." The Soviet ambassador to Berlin, one of Stalin's minions, began to "water down" his reports in May. Anyhow, "eventually fear of provocation drove Stalin greatly to decrease the intelligence work in Berlin."

There is trouble, too, with Gorodetsky's own account. Again this trouble comes from his reliance on Soviet documents. The names of dozens of important foreign diplomats of the period are hopelessly misspelled, and often unrecognizable, since Gorodetsky simply transliterated them from their Russian-Cyrillic sounds and letters into English. The most important among these figures was the excellent Swedish minister to Moscow, whose papers Gorodetsky seems to have consulted in Sweden, and yet Vilhelm Assarsson's name is misspelled throughout. Hitler's principal military adviser is written as "Alfried Jodl." Gorodetsky confuses Czar Alexander I with Czar Alexander II, and ambassadors with ministers. On at least two occasions he refers to significant diplomatic talks at the Quai d'Orsay or in Paris, when the French government existed not there but in Vichy. There are also considerable errors in both of the maps of the book.

Gorodetsky puts great emphasis on Soviet diplomatic maneuvers in the Balkans, but his account is often wrong about the Balkans, and includes many errors. On more than one occasion Gorodetsky contradicts himself. (On page twenty-nine, the Soviet move into two Rumanian provinces was "devoid of any motive for expansion"; but on page 179 we encounter "Stalin's dream of establishing a Soviet predominance in [the Balkans].") As in the case of many contradictions, neither of the two statements is correct.

One only hopes that his errors will not provide more ammunition to the revisionists. For they are not yet done. There remains their broad argument—proposed, among others, by Patrick Buchanan's recent book *A Republic, Not an Empire,* and by some British revisionists, such as John Charmley—to the effect that Churchill's resolution to fight Hitler was single-minded and obsessive; that the Western Powers should have let Hitler and Stalin fight it out in 1939 or in 1941, and thereby bleed themselves to death. Only a few weeks ago William F. Buckley observed in *National Review:* "Would things have been better if Hitler had conquered Moscow? They could hardly have been worse." These men do not ask the obvious question: And what if Hitler had won? He would have been unbeatable.

Regrettable, too, is Gorodetsky's interpretation of British policy. He obviously prefers Sir Stafford Cripps (who, with the best of intentions, was a most ineffective British ambassador to Russia) to Churchill (who was right about Russia in 1939–41 in most instances). Perhaps the most serious omission in Gorodetsky's work is his lack of any mention of Stalin's decisive replacement of Maxim Litvinov with Molotov in 1939, before the pact with Hitler. Gorodetsky regrets that "Churchill's voluminous history of the Second World War, with its persuasive and excessively self-centered interpretation of events, was regarded as authoritative and was frequently quoted by Soviet historians." Now read how Churchill summed up that most ominous event:

> The eminent Jew [Litvinov], the target of German antagonism, was flung aside for the time being like a broken tool, and, without being allowed a word of explanation, was bundled off the world stage to obscurity, a pittance, and police supervision. Molotov, little known outside Russia, became Commisar for Foreign Affairs, in the closest confederacy with Stalin.... There was in fact only one way in which he was now likely to move. He had always been favourable to an agreement with Hitler.

That is exactly how it was.

"One should not be distracted" Gorodetsky remarks, "by the simplistic presentation of war aims in [Churchill's] memoirs as the annihilation of Nazism. . . . This concealed his inherently imperialist outlook." Stalin's policy, by contrast, "remained essentially one of level-headed Realpolitik." In his conclusion, Gorodetsky admiringly cites this observation by Henry Kissinger: "Richelieu or Bismarck would have had no difficulty understanding [Stalin's] strategy."

There is some truth in this, but not much. Let us contemplate the scene on April 13, 1941, at the Moscow railroad station. Hitler had just overrun Yugoslavia in a matter of days. Earlier, Stalin had made a faint gesture to a Yugoslavian government trying to resist Hitler. But he regretted his gesture, and was worried plenty. There was one good thing that happened to him: the Japanese foreign minister was in Moscow, proposing a Soviet-Japanese pact, which Stalin gladly accepted. There was a long late lunch in the Kremlin, with much drinking. The Japanese delegation was about to leave; but the departure of the Trans-Siberian Express was delayed for an hour. Suddenly Stalin himself arrived at the station—a gesture without precedent. Molotov was stumbling along behind him, visibly drunk and shouting—another gesture without precedent. Stalin was looking for the German ambassador, but he could not find him. So he marched up to the German military attaché, embraced him, and said in a loud voice: "We will remain friends with you—in any event!" He repeated this twice, for everyone to hear. The Japanese ambassador was beside himself with excitement. Such honor! He jumped up and down, screaming in Russian: "Thanks! Thanks!" Later, the Japanese Foreign Minister addressed Stalin as "Your Highness."

No, this was not the world of Richelieu, and not the world of Bismarck.

27

Michael Burleigh
(2001)

T his is a very large book, nearly one thousand pages, and not
without some merits. But it is not really about the Third Reich, and it is not
a New History. There is the history of the Third Reich. There is the history of National Socialism. There is the history of Adolf Hitler. There is
the history of the Second World War. They overlap, but they are not the
same. Michael Burleigh's book is entitled *The Third Reich*, but, in an undisciplined way, its focus is directed to and its chapters deal with all four themes,
moving from one to another and back again. However, this is not the main
problem with the book. Its problem, besides its content, is its perspective.
Burleigh is right in detailing the brutalities and many of the horrors of the
Third Reich. Here and there he adds telling details generally unknown or
even unmentioned by others. But he writes that, because of its stupidities,
brutalities, fanaticism, and prejudices, the Third Reich was destined to be
destroyed. Unfortunately it was not.

By the Third Reich we should mean the great German state of 1933–45
that was a Germany different from its then recent past and of course from
its future. Despite the inevitable presence and continuation of the same
population and of many of its institutions, this was a new kind of state, with
a drastically new flag, designed by Hitler himself, the flag of his party having become the flag of the Reich. Symbols do matter, and this was more
than a symbol. There came a time when that swastika flag was hoisted and
flown across Europe, from the Pyrénées to the Caucasus, and from the
Aegean to the Arctic, carried by the armies of the Third Reich. For comparison, the French tricolor flew over a much smaller domain under Napoleon. The Second World War was a struggle of epic dimensions that the
Third Reich almost won.

Review of Michael Burleigh, *The Third Reich: A New History* (2001). From *National Interest*,
Winter 2000–01: 103–06.

Even before the Second World War began, the Third Reich had become the greatest power in Europe, far surpassing the extent and the
achievements of Bismarck's or William II's Second Reich. From a depressed
republic without allies, with many millions of unemployed, there arose a
new Reich within a few years, prosperous, arrogant, and powerful, incor-
porating Austria and Czechoslovakia without having to fire a single shot,
attracting powerful allies such as Mussolini's Italy and Imperial Japan, and
surrounded by smaller states unwilling to challenge almost anything that
the Third Reich desired.

By 1939 the Third Reich, in some ways, was the most *modern* country in
Europe. Then came a war that its leader deliberately chose to bring about.
Behind him his Third Reich produced armed forces and an organization
that stunned the world. In 1940 the Third Reich came close to winning the
Second World War. Had its leader not hesitated to invade England this
may have happened. In 1941 it again came close to winning the war by
knocking Russia out of it. Eventually the armies of the Reich were halted
before Moscow; but, obeying their leader, in the ensuing winter they stood
fast and deflected the fate that had befallen Napoleon's Grande Armée 130
years before. By that time the greatest powers of the world, with a combined population of at least four hundred million, were arrayed against the
eighty-odd million of the Third Reich, having formed a coalition of British, Americans, Russians, Capitalists and Communists, which held together
until the end. Even then, it took nearly four years before their overwhelming power was able to force the Third Reich to capitulate. The armies of
the Reich did not surrender even after most of their homeland was conquered by the Allies. Some of them fought on for another ten days after
their leader's death.

How was this possible? Burleigh's massive volume does not illuminate
this awful story. Yes, a catastrophe it was, including the deaths of many
millions, of even more innocent civilians than soldiers. Yes, the Third Reich
was a brutal machine—but an awesomely efficient one, alas. Doomed to
defeat it was not. And this had much to do with National Socialism. The
Third Reich was a National Socialist Reich.

The National Socialist character of the Third Reich is something that
Burleigh does not describe clearly and that he may not even understand
sufficiently. The power, the attraction, and the historical significance of
National Socialism was a phenomenon of worldwide import. Besides a very
long introduction, Burleigh devotes an unduly long chapter to the Weimar
Republic, to how Hitler came to power; but the emergence of national
socialism predated that. The classic categories of the political history of
the nineteenth century were conservatives and liberals, their dialogue and

debate (terms that are more and more outdated and yet employed even now). But, contrary to the Hegelian scheme, this Thesis-Antithesis did not lead to a Synthesis but to something else. After about 1870 two new forces appeared: nationalism and socialism. Their relationship, and their combination, rose above the conservative-liberal antithesis in almost every country of the world.[1]

Nationalist socialism has had different variants throughout the world. Its proper recognition has been confused by two imprecise terms that Burleigh uses throughout: fascism and totalitarianism. Fascism was an Italian phenomenon in practice (and for a while in essence), different from German National Socialism. The Leftist usage of applying the adjective "fascist" to any kind of dictatorship (or even non-dictatorship) of the so-called "Right" has been wrong (a misuse dictated by Stalin as early as 1932, since he wanted to deter the recognition that his own regime was turning in a *nationalist* "socialist" direction). What Hitler was able to do was to fuse nationalism and socialism into a particularly appealing and powerful ideology for Germans. This went farther and deeper than the imposition of party rule upon the state. Professors, lawyers, workers, generals, soldiers reacted to the ideology of National Socialism very positively indeed. Not every German was a National Socialist party member or believer; far from it. But that ideology was powerful enough to create new or reformed institutions and organizations, inspiriting the German armed forces that carried the swastika flag proudly across Europe and into the oceans of the world. It was because of National Socialism that the Third Reich fought until the very end. It had to be conquered in its entirety. To consider the National Socialist Third Reich as a crazed, reactionary episode, as so many—including Burleigh—do, is wrong. It was, alas, more than an episode. Even now, with communism having lost whatever appeal it may once have had, there are National Socialist believers and sympathizers, not only in Germany and Austria but across the world—people who are open or hidden admirers of the Third Reich and of its record, and who see it as a once healthy alternative to both international communism and to decadent international capitalism. We must not underestimate their potential— especially if the West slides into the final and sorry chapter of its decline.

The other term that Burleigh uses indiscriminately (he is not alone in this) is that of totalitarianism. That word, too, has a curious history. It was first used by Mussolini's Italy in the fascist version: what Mussolini meant was the total priority of the state over the individual (considering the Italian temperament, his particular problem). Hitler never cared much for the state: to him the National Socialist Reich was a Reich of the *Volk*. The state, as he said on occasion, was only an old-fashioned framework, cracking at its seams, a *Zwangsform.* (He also said that he was not a dictator: "every South American popinjay can be a dictator." He, instead, had a great people behind him—unfortunately so.) That stuttering polysyllabic word, "totalitarianism," became especially current in the United States after 1950, when some intellectuals (belatedly) were forced to recognize that Stalin's Soviet state was as much a police state as was the Third Reich (if not more so).

But a police state and totalitarianism are not the same things.[2] The best part of Burleigh's book is his long chapter, "The Demise of the Rule of Law," describing how easily and rapidly law and order were refashioned and corrupted in the Third Reich. Yet the awesome efficiency of the Third Reich and its awful brutalities were not always due to police rule: they were the outcomes of the popularity of its National Socialism. Besides, there was much more freedom—or rather, elbow room—in the Third Reich than in Soviet Russia: as long as people (those who were not victims of the state's racial policies, that is) did not act or speak openly against its leader and its institutions they were, relatively, free. "Totalitarianism" is a very imprecise term: no state, not even Stalin's Russia, can be entirely total.

Burleigh regards the Third Reich as but one example of "totalitarianism," which is both imprecise and unhistorical. The Third Reich was *sui generis.* In more than one way this book is about "totalitarianism," going well beyond the history of the Third Reich. This appears at its very beginning. On the second page of its long introduction, the second footnote (among the thousands of them) refers to a book about the 1999–2000 war in Chechnya. On page four there is a long (and well-known) quote from Tocqueville that has nothing to do with totalitarianism or with police rule (it was a prophetic description of majority rule and the coming welfare state). For an Englishman, Burleigh is curiously attracted to all kinds of unreliable and verbose philosophizers of the Hannah Arendt variety. There is a very long chapter on "Occupation and Collaboration in Occupied Europe 1939–1943" (why stop in 1943?), which, in the author's own words, is "a highly selective tour of occupied countries." Very well; but what has that to do with a history of the Third Reich? The political inclinations and the psychology of the various National Socialist collaborationists, from the Caucasus to the Atlantic, is an important but a different subject, and their activities could not even be subsumed by a work dealing with German police rule in the occupied countries, since there was more involved than that. The bibliography of Burleigh's book is also wanting.

The history of the Third Reich (and of German National Socialism) cannot be, of course, entirely separated from the history and character of Adolf Hitler. In this respect Burleigh's phraseology and his description are rhetorical at worst, and one-dimensional at best. Of Hitler he says that, in

1945, "A demented criminal converted himself into a martyred hero." This is way too simple. "Criminal" means defying the law. Hitler was worse, and more dangerous: like Genghis Khan or Ivan the Terrible, he *was* the law. "Demented"? He was a man who possessed many talents, well beyond his undoubted talent for demagoguery—talents that he consciously used for brutal and often evil purposes, which is exactly why he was responsible and should be regarded as such. Burleigh does not understand Hitler, which is one of the reasons his history is faulty. In the last pages of his book he misdates the day of Hitler's marriage, his dictation of his testament, and the day of his suicide. Perhaps such small details do not matter much. What matters, unfortunately, is that what Richard Sheridan said about a speech in the House of Commons more than two hundred years ago is apposite to *The Third Reich: A New History.* "There is much in it that is both new and true, but unfortunately what is true is not new and what is new is not true."

28

Lord Acton
(2001)

Lord Acton, who died ninety-nine years ago, may have been the greatest of English historians during the second half of the nineteenth century. He had dazzling connections and an impressive career. The Acton family was old English Catholic and cosmopolitan. They were intermarried with at least two of the most ancient noble families of the Holy Roman-German empire. Acton's grandfather, though English, was prime minister of the kingdom of Naples, for a while a close friend of Emma Hamilton and Lord Nelson. Acton's father was a cosmopolitan aristocrat, a period figure whose life and character may have been even beyond his contemporary Balzac's powers to limn. He died relatively young, at thirty-six, having caught pneumonia when he returned to his home in Paris after a night of gambling and drinking; his wife had him locked out. To his funeral came the ambassadors of all the great powers of Europe and a representative of the king of France. His widow married the future earl of Granville, eventually foreign secretary at the apogee of the Victorian Age. When his father died, John Acton (more precisely, Sir John Emerich Edward Dalberg Acton, Eighth Baronet, First Baron) was three years old.

His education was English and German. He read, spoke, and wrote perfectly at least five European languages, besides his sufficiency in Latin and Greek. His avocation was threefold: the causes of liberalism, Catholicism, and historicism. He lived at a time when publications of the largely German-inspired professional study of history multiplied rapidly. Astonishingly, most such books were noticed, collected, and read by a universal, multilingual historian such as Acton. He began writing studies and articles in his twenties. That was a time when journals and reviews were read by many influential people in England. He wooed and eventually married the young and beautiful Bavarian countess he loved. For a while he was a member of Par-

Review of Roland Hill, *Lord Acton* (2000). From *Los Angeles Times Book Review,* April 8: 1.

liament. Lord Tennyson and Cardinal Newman respected him; George Eliot admired him; the pope (Pius IX) feared him. He was one of perhaps the closest friends of Gladstone, one of whose daughters may have been a little in love with Acton. He had a private library of about seventy thousand volumes. Andrew Carnegie helped him out by buying that library, which, after Acton's death, went to Cambridge; Queen Victoria also helped him by making him her lord-in-waiting. Then she and the prime minister, Lord Rosebery, made him Regius Professor in Cambridge. He was one of the founders of the *English Historical Review,* and the appointed creator and director of the Cambridge Modern History series. When he was measured for the robes and the cap at his installation, his head was the largest on record.

He lived for another seven years and then died, surrounded by his family in their villa on the beautiful Bavarian lake of Tegernsee, in the sixty-ninth year of his life, 1902. During the century that followed, dozens of serious studies and books were written about him. The present one is the largest and fullest one-volume biography, superbly researched and well written by Roland Hill, whose interest in Acton and whose relations with some of his descendants had begun decades ago. It merits much praise because, in addition to the enormous amount of material relating to Acton's life and thought, that life and Acton's mind were not simple.

They were not simple for many reasons, the main one being Acton's struggle to reconcile his liberalism and his Catholicism. One of his obiter dicta became famous: "Power tends to corrupt, and absolute power tends to corrupt absolutely." (The "tends to" is often omitted, wrongly.) Acton's contempt and fear of absolute power formed his liberalism. He believed in intellectual freedom and in the protection of minorities; he was unalterably opposed to absolute power given to a state, a king, or a pope, including Pius IX's dogma of papal infallibility. He did not live to see the populist state dictatorships of the twentieth century. But his often trenchant and noble propositions of liberty inspired his various admirers during the century after his death. Politically too he was a committed and old-fashioned Gladstonian liberal. Hill is correct when he writes that "Acton meant the history of liberty to be a philosophy of history." Yet unlike Tocqueville (there is curiously little evidence that Acton read or considered Tocqueville extensively), Acton gave not much benefit of doubt to democracy. Despite his abhorrence of slavery, he favored the South in the American Civil War. Toward the end of his life, he recognized the rising forces of nationalism and socialism. Unlike Gladstone, with whom he agreed on so many things (including Home Rule for Ireland), Acton did not believe in "national self-determination." He, rightly, regarded nationalism as at least as dangerous and more ominous than socialism.

His Catholicism was more deep-seated than his liberalism. And more controversial too. His fear that Pope Pius IX strove for absolutism governed the most difficult and tortured period in Acton's life. He worked, assiduously and incessantly, against the proclamation of the dogma of papal infallibility before and during the First Vatican Council in 1869–70 in Rome, at times with the dedication of a political manager. He incurred many enemies, foremost among them the rigid Cardinal Manning of England. The greatest influence on Acton's mind was that of the extraordinary German Catholic Church historian and thinker Ignaz von Döllinger. As late as 1874, Acton feared that he would be excommunicated. Unlike Döllinger, he accepted the new dogma of infallibility and thought it necessary to state this privately and publicly.

The pope and the Infallibilists were probably wrong in exaggerating the dangers to the church and faith resulting from political and scientific liberalism, and especially from the loss of the temporal power of the papacy in 1870, when the Italians occupied Rome. But Acton was probably wrong too by exaggerating the consequences of the infallibility doctrine. In one of his notes there are the words of a friend, a priest: "Religion alone makes a good death," to which he added: "Religion alone cannot make a good life." His wife was often irritated with him. According to their daughter, his custom was to kneel next to the marital bed after lovemaking and pray that his act would lead to conception: We may assume that she was not amused. Yet his family and his neighbors loved him, and he died in his wife's arms in their Tegernsee villa. That villa is now a health spa, and Acton's grave in the local cemetery has been neglected: it is nearly impossible to find.

Acton never wrote a book. His aim was too high: to write the history of liberty. He wrote important and impressive articles, studies, and lectures, and an astounding amount of other papers and notes that, as the great English historian Herbert Butterfield once wrote, amounted to "a tremendous intellectual system, which has stimulated many commentators and interpreters in our time." Acton's fame is that of a historian, not of a liberal or a Catholic. Yet the three vocations of his mind and life were inseparable from one another. Through the science of history he wished to purify the record and the prestige of the church and especially of the papacy. He was liberal enough to dismiss all hero-worshipers such as Carlyle and to insist that the greatest names in history have been often coupled with the greatest of crimes. In an unquestioned and unquestionable acceptance of the universal infallibility of the papacy, he saw "a small-minded Catholic distrust and fear." He thought, as Hill puts it, that "Catholics everywhere were particularly suspicious of historical study, because, as the study of facts, it was less amenable to authority and less controllable by interest than philosophical speculation."

Yet Newman—with whom Acton's relationship was, alas, not close—was right when he said that Acton "seems to me to expect from History more than History can furnish." Till the end of his life, Acton believed, and claimed, that historical science had reached a stage when a story of the Battle of Waterloo could be written that would not only be perfectly acceptable to French and British and Dutch and Prussian historians, but that would be unchanging, perennial, and fixed. A century later we have (or at least ought to have) a more chastened and realistic view of historical objectivity, indeed, of truth. Acton believed that history, very much including the history of the church, was a supremely important matter—yes—and that the purpose of history is the definite, and final, establishment of truth—no. The purpose of history is the reduction of untruth.

29

Roy Jenkins

(2001)

At the very beginning of his book Roy Jenkins estimates the number of those who have written on and around Churchill as "somewhere between 50 and 100." A research librarian informs me that "in a broad sense, i.e. not just biographies but also works of history, fiction, juvenile literature, and works that may be about them but also about other individuals," books about Churchill in the U.S. amount to 283, in Canada 206, in Britain 652, in the Library of Congress 736. In every one of these statistics (including Britain) books about Hitler outnumber Churchill, often two to one; so do those about Roosevelt (except for Canada and Britain); except in the Library of Congress Stalin runs fourth, behind Churchill. There is an odd whiff of reality in these computerized and otherwise meaningless statistics. Had it not been for Hitler, in the history of Britain (not to speak of the world) Churchill would have been a perhaps interesting but assuredly secondary figure; and we may presume that Roy Jenkins would not have chosen him for the subject of a monumental biography, as he had done for Gladstone and Asquith.

Had it not been for Hitler . . . I think that here is, perhaps, the main reason for the continued interest in Churchill (and also for the relative eclipse of the reputation of those—incorrectly—defined "revisionists" of but a few years ago). For a long time most people were inclined to think that, of course, Churchill was brave and resolute in 1940, but after all, Hitler was bound to lose the war. That he was not bound to lose it, and that in 1940–41 he had come very near to winning it, has become more and more apparent and accepted by more people than a few specialist historians. Churchill knew that in the marrow of his bones—which explains much of his strategy, including his constant and fearful appreciation of the fighting

Review of Roy Jenkins, *Churchill: A Biography* (2001). From *Spectator* (London), October 13: 48–49.

abilities of the Germans. That much was simple. There has been a recent tendency to describe Churchill as complicated and "elusive." Complicated he was, but elusive? Not at all. Hitler, Roosevelt, Stalin were much more secretive than was Churchill, who spurted out many of his innermost thoughts and speculations to his staff, indeed to whoever was listening. As Jenkins puts it, "Churchill's life was singularly lacking in inhibition or concealment." That was, is, and certainly remains an asset for his biographers.

In his preface Roy Jenkins writes, "I can at least claim to be the only octogenarian who has ventured to write about Churchill." It does not show. His book may be too long (I shall come to this in a moment), but there is not much that is aged or creaky in his writing. Jenkins's ear shows none of the deficiencies of old age; he knows well who to listen to and then cite and when (example: Churchill's first love Pamela Plowden, later Lady Lytton: "The first time you meet Winston you see all his faults, and the rest of your life you spend in discovering his virtues"—remarkably acute, and true of many other people, including Jock Colville); and Jenkins has a few memorable phrases of his own (example: Churchill's decision to sink the French warships at Oran: "Nearly anyone else would have let sleeping ships lie, and hoped vaguely for the best").

To the above-cited prefatory sentence Jenkins adds, "I suppose I can also claim to have had the widest parliamentary and ministerial experience of his biographers." Yes, but there is some trouble with that. Early in his career Churchill, according to Jenkins, "showed slight signs of parliamentary incontinence." There are marks of literary incontinence in this book. Jenkins displays too much of his knowledge of parliamentary history; too many quotes from Gladstone and Asquith; too many comparisons of electoral arithmetic; there are long pages that deal not with Churchill but with the history of the Conservative party; there is too much about the Churchills' relationship with his erstwhile literary agent Reves (and Mrs. Reves). There is a surprising intrusion of recent Americanisms ("networking," "upwardly mobile," "window of opportunity"), and an often unnecessary sprinkling of French phrases, sometimes misspelled.

They do not matter. The book could have been cut by perhaps one-sixth but no more. Its main virtue is a comprehension of the complexity—no, not elusiveness!—of Churchill's character. There is a duality in every human being, but a balanced judgment of that is perhaps the best evidence of a biographer's talent. Jenkins understands this. Here is a prime example of his treatment of what was perhaps the duality in Churchill's character: the hedonist and the warrior. In December 1944 Churchill, weary and worn, decided to forgo the pleasure of a quiet Christmas with his family and flew off to a cold and dark scene in Greece. That was, to Jenkins:

[T]he triumph of duty over pleasure, and that, in spite of his self-indul-
gent tastes, was part of the pattern of his life. Whenever the two came
into head-on conflict, if the issue was big enough, he always came down
on the dutiful side. And this, like a lot of obvious explanations, contains a
large part of the truth, although not all of it. Duty always had a most
powerful ally in the shape of his desire to be at the centre of events, his
preference for danger over boredom, for risk over inertia.

This is very good. There were other dualities in Churchill: the conflict (if that was what it was) between his pro-Europeanism and pro-Americanism; between his anticommunism and his—at least occasional—liking of Stalin; between his irreligiousness and his strong belief in providence. Yet none of these dualities was essentially contradictory. There is a splendidly simple consistency in Churchill's view of the war in Europe, and of Hitler and Stalin, which—perhaps because of their geographical situation—English people may understand better than many Europeans. As early as 1940 (if not earlier) Churchill saw that the alternative was plain: either Hitler's Germany would rule all of Europe, or Stalin's Russia would rule much of Eastern Europe; and half of Europe was better than none. (He also knew, and said to de Gaulle and to Colville, that communism in Eastern Europe would not long prevail—an astonishingly prescient observation that seems to have escaped Jenkins's eyes). He must be commended for dealing with Eisenhower's and Dulles's inexcusably contemptuous mistreatment of Churchill, "who seemed in 1953–54 curiously unfazed by this display of insensitivity verging on brutality." This was so: for that was not only the time of a Churchill rapidly declining in health and in power, but of a chapter in American-British relations that no historian (including Jenkins) has, as yet, sufficiently explored. There is, finally, a splendid and moving proof of the capacity of Jenkins's ear, a quotation from Churchill's last speech in the House of Commons, 1955:

> . . . notable for at least one unforgettable phrase which illumi-
> nated the dreadful prospect like a sheet of lightning on a deso-
> late landscape: "Which way shall we turn to save our lives and
> the future of the world? It does not matter so much to old people;
> they are going soon anyway; but I find it poignant to look at
> youth in all its activity and ardour . . . *and wonder what would lie*
> *before them if God wearied of mankind?*"

The bourdon note of foreboding, as from the heart and mouth of an Old Testament prophet. The italics are Jenkins's. He is right.

30

Winston Churchill

(2002)

He was a writer. Was he a historian? There are many academics who are wont to deny that title to Winston Churchill: an amateur, no member of their guild; some of them (not merely professional but ideological critics) imputing that his methods of historianship were unscientific and insufficient (or, worse, self-serving and myth-making). That is one extreme. Entirely contrary to that is the commonsense assertion that every human being is a historian by nature while he is a scientist only by choice, historicity being the fourth dimension of man. However: not many men and women are conscious of that condition; few of them experience the need to write any kind of history; and even fewer make their writing of history not only "scientific" but works of art. Churchill did so: whence, in all probability, his award of the Nobel Prize for Literature (in 1953, and in a country where most professional historians were still inclined to regard history as a Science). But then he was in good company (although he did not travel to Stockholm for the ceremony): the only other historian who had received the Nobel Prize for Literature was the great German historian Theodor Mommsen in 1902.

In a stately (and plummy) essay J. H. Plumb writes that Churchill "was a rare and singular hybrid: a writer-statesman and a statesman-writer."[1] I would prefer: a historian-statesman and a statesman-historian. Churchill was a writer mainly because he was attracted to history, not a historian because he was attracted to writing. (Plumb, as we shall see, gives adequate and even moving tribute to Churchill's overwhelming sense of history, but is critical of Churchill's historianship.) To the best of my knowledge only one full-size volume exists about Churchill the historian, written by his once assistant Maurice Ashley; other assessments of Churchill's historianship

From *Churchill: Visionary. Statesman. Historian.* (New Haven, CT: Yale University Press), 101–28.

may be found in articles and addresses by Robert Blake, Victor Feske, John Ramsden, David Reynolds.[2] I think that (like "Churchill and Europe") a substantial book about "Churchill as Historian" is yet to be written.

One difficulty for such a work would be that the volume and the scope of Churchill's histories is enormous. But before I turn to a necessarily brief and certainly inadequate summary description and occasional analysis of his principal books, I think I must say something about his own perspective of his historianship. I think that this deserves interest, not only because it has been seldom analyzed by historians but also because (at least in my opinion) there is an element in that perspective which is not old-fashioned or traditional but perhaps surprisingly timely.

Churchill's perspective in many of his books is participatory. The purpose of writing is seldom separable from self-centeredness. There are many historians (perhaps especially those who categorize their craft as being a Science, not an Art)[3] who would prefer not to think of this condition—even though the very choice of their subjects of study is usually inseparable from their personal curiosity or interest. To admit self-centeredness is of course to admit that the ideal of scientific objectivity is wanting. Yet we, at least beyond the twentieth century and perhaps of the entire so-called Modern Age, ought to know that the ideal of Objectivity, meaning a complete, and antiseptic, separation of the observer from the matter observed, is impossible (and not only in the mental but also in the physical world); that the alternative to Objectivity is *not* Subjectivity (which is but another form of determinism); that all human knowledge is inevitably personal and participatory. Almost all of Churchill's written work illustrates this. Almost all of his books were inspired and researched and written because of his preoccupation with and his consequent interest in the history of people who were intimately related to him, and in historical events in which he was a participant. Thus his histories of the Indian and Sudan wars, thus the political biography of his father, thus the historical biography of his ancestor Marlborough, thus his histories of the First World War, of the Second World War, thus even his portraits of his contemporaries and, at least indirectly, of his history of the English-speaking peoples, the propagation of an idea whereof he was a principal proponent nearly throughout his life. (Exceptions could have been biographies of Garibaldi and of Napoleon that he once thought he might write.)

Personal and participatory: these adjectives sum up the historical philosophy inherent in Winston Churchill's writings. It is wrong to attribute this simply to the method of an amateur. Besides the argument that in history, unlike in many of the natural and applied sciences, *amateur* and *professional* are not and cannot be entirely separate and distinct categories,

Churchill was aware of the conditions and limitations of his historianship. At the beginning of his massive history of the First World War, *The World Crisis* (1923–27), he wrote: "I set myself at each stage to answer the questions: 'What happened, and why?' I seek to guide the reader to those points where the course of events is being decided, whether it be on a battlefield, in a conning tower, in Council, in Parliament, in a lobby, a laboratory or a workshop. *Such a method is no substitution for history, but it may be an aid both to the writing and to the study of history*" (my italics). Such an admission ought at least mitigate the bite of the witty remark made, I think, by Balfour, that Churchill had written a big book about himself and then called it *The World Crisis.* Churchill could be self-critical, at least on occasion. About *The World Crisis* he wrote: "Looking back with after-knowledge and increasing years, I seem to have been too ready to undertake tasks which were hazardous or even forlorn." In his first (and sometimes properly criticized) volume of *The Second World War* he wrote about the thirties: "I strove my utmost to galvanise the Government into vehemence and extraordinary preparation, even at the cost of world alarm. In these endeavours no doubt I painted the picture even darker than it was." In the preface to *The Second World War* he insisted again: "I do not describe it as history, for that belongs to another generation. But I claim with confidence that it is a contribution to history which will be of service to the future."

There are historians who may tend to dismiss that qualification "a contribution to history" as insincere or false modesty; but they will ignore his writing and his materials, "of service to the future," only at their peril. It should also be noted that while, for all kinds of reasons, Churchill omitted or toned down certain matters of controversy, including instances when he had been right and his opponents wrong, often he did not omit a record of his words and acts that at the time of publication would raise eyebrows, to say the least (as in the case of his descriptions of Stalin and of his dealings with him). In the prefaces of both of his world war histories he wrote that he followed, "as far as I am able, the method of Defoe's *Memoirs of a Cavalier,* in which the author hangs the chronicle and discussion of great military and political events upon the thread of the personal experiences of an individual." That method (or rather, structure and perspective) was then complemented, in almost all of his works, by copious, and sometimes too extensive, reproductions of letters and directives and other papers for the purposes of documentary illustration, suggesting at least an amateur historian's respect for the professional canon of dependence on "primary" sources.

Many of these documents inserted in his text, illustrating (but also occasionally interrupting) his narrative or his argumentation, are very valuable. They are also evidences of his assiduous attempts at research. Observe, however, that many of his books were long—often too long. His speeches were seldom long-winded. His writings—with some exceptions and of course with the exception of his journalism—often were. There was a tendency (as we saw before, in many of his important letters and messages) to expect much from his written record: Try to tell everything. And well!

His interest in—more: his appetite for—history matured very early. He was twenty-one years old and in India when he asked his mother to send him twelve volumes of Macaulay (eight of his histories, four of his collected essays). He wrote to her that he read fifty pages of Macaulay and twenty-five of Gibbon every day. "Macaulay is easier reading than Gibbon, and in quite a different style. Macaulay crisp and forcible, Gibbon stately and impressive. Both are fascinating and show what a fine language English is since it can be pleasing in styles so different."[4] They had an influence on his style. But he was already a writer (and a journalist: he was not yet twenty-two when he wrote and sold five articles to *The Daily Graphic*). And then came, soon, five volumes of Churchillian—that is, participatory and contemporary—history: *The Story of the Malakand Field Force* (1898), *The River War* (two volumes, 1899); *Savrola* (1900, his only novel and one written in a hurry); *London to Ladysmith* (1900); *Ian Hamilton's March* (1900). Five books written and published within three years, before he was twenty-six; and what eventful years those were, including his war in the Sudan, and then in South Africa, his capture by the Boers, and his escape. This is not the occasion to describe or analyze them in any detail. They were not long; many of them were rewritings of some of his journalist's dispatches. Eventually they became superseded by his incomparable memoir, *My Early Life: A Roving Commission* (1930), probably the most delightful book he wrote, summing up in a few short and sparkling chapters his own history of those years and adventures.

His talents for historical reconstruction are detectable in these early books (the first of them was already so recognized in a review in the *Athenaeum*: "a military classic"). Yet even more significant are those glimpses of his historical vision (and political thinking) that appear, here and there, in those early books. We have seen one visionary passage earlier, a vision perhaps comparable to the other, more famous dark vision of a contemporary, Kipling's poem "Recessional" in 1897. In his novel *Savrola* we may glimpse his conditional appreciation of a dictator, together with his melancholy perspective of mass democracy (or rather, populism). At the end of his first book he wrote this about his own people, the British: "a people of whom at least it may be said that they have added to the happiness, the learning and the liberties of mankind." These are the words of a patriot—though not of a nationalist. (Hitler said often, and wrote in *Mein Kampf,* that he was a nationalist: "but not a patriot.")

In 1902 Churchill turned to the writing of one of his most substantial works, the life of his father. *Lord Randolph Churchill,* "a political biography," consisted of two massive volumes, more than one thousand pages in toto. Such extensive political biographies were not unusual at that time, though this Victorian custom was beginning to fade. What was unusual was that most of these two volumes deal with but six agitated years of his father's career, 1880 to 1886. It is obvious that the son's inspiration and purpose was a vindication of his father. This is remarkable, perhaps especially because the son did not see his father often; their relationship was not a very close one; and the father died before his son reached twenty-one. There is also remarkably little about their family life (and, except for a few letters, very little about the relationship of Lord and Lady Randolph). And then, while Lord Randolph was certainly interesting, he was not altogether an attractive personality. He was a great speaker, he spoke easily (unlike his son, who had to prepare his speeches and even his pronunciation carefully), but he had many a prejudice[5] and strong inclinations to demagoguery[6] (which his son had not). Joseph Chamberlain and Randolph Churchill were principally responsible for destroying Gladstone's humane (and, at that time, perhaps workable) proposition of Home Rule for Ireland. He had a very quick mind, he was impatient (like his son); he was a maverick and at times a rebel within his own party—most of the Conservatives did not like him (again as the case of his son); he resigned from an important Cabinet post because of his unyielding principles (as asserted in the biography written by his son) but also in a huff (as asserted by his contemporary adversaries and critics). In 1888 certain newspapers would describe Randolph Churchill as "a boastful, rattling egotist with no principle and, apparently, with no conception of duty and honour." (Such very phrases and words were to be applied to his son often, at least during the first sixty-four years of his life.)

Yet: if a *grand plaidoyer,* as a vindication *Lord Randolph Churchill* does not succeed, as a great political history it does. There have been critics who declared it a masterpiece, some of them perhaps the finest book Winston Churchill had written. The circumstances of its composition are interesting enough. Churchill had some trouble to allow his father's literary executors to get access to all of his father's voluminous papers and correspondence. He especially needed the help of Lord Rosebery, which the latter gave, albeit a little reluctantly. Unlike his writing of his first rapidly composed and compiled books, Churchill worked four hard years on this one. (He did have some exceptional help: one of his cousins put him up at Blenheim while he was working there on his father's papers; another cousin let him work in a fine apartment in London.)[7] And the literary qualities of the book are often exceptional. It begins with a beautifully written and deeply evocative description of Blenheim. (Rosebery advised Churchill to omit this. Fortunately he didn't.) His critics have often deprecated Churchill for having been self-educated, an autodidact: but how rich are the evidences of his reading and learning in this political biography! The epigraph he chose for it is from Goethe (odd for a man accused of knowing little and caring little for Germany and its culture); other epigraphs of chapters and other superb quotations abound from Machiavelli, Horace, Burke, Disraeli, Crabbe, Dryden, the Book of Job. Scattered through the book's pages is a treasury of memorable phrases and descriptions. Perhaps more important: *Lord Randolph Churchill* is an extraordinarily valuable—and enduring—contribution to British political history during the mid-1800s, which in many ways was a turning point. About that let me cite the young Churchill's brilliant and grave description of that history at that time:

> There were important measures. There were earnest, ambitious men. But something more lay behind the unrest and uncertainties of the day. Not merely the decay of Government or the natural over-ripeness of a party produced the agitations of 1885 and 1886. The long dominion of the middle classes, which had begun in 1832, had come to its close and with it the almost equal reign of Liberalism. The great victories had been won. All sorts of lumbering tyrannies had been toppled over. Authority was everywhere broken. Slaves were free. Conscience was free. Trade was free. But hunger and squalor and cold were also free; and the people demanded something more than liberty. The old watchwords still rang true; but they were not enough. And how to fill the void was the riddle that split the Liberal party.

This is a summation by a great historian—evidence of his powers of grand and visionary summations in a work otherwise including often particular and excessive details. Passages such as this will—and should—live and inspire historians as long as English history is written.

They surely lived long in his mind.[8] And now I must leap ahead and break the chronological sequence and say something about his *Marlborough*, written thirty years later; because that, too, had the purpose of vindicating an ancestor.

Marlborough consists of four volumes. The first volume was published in October 1933, the last in September 1938. These dates are telling. For Churchill wrote these very large volumes at the very time when he was deeply engaged in more than mundane politics, when he was the self-appointed Cassandra of the prospect of a coming second world war. Also: during those years he wrote and dictated more newspaper articles than perhaps ever before or after. And while working on the last two volumes of *Marlborough* he was also beginning to dictate the first chapters of his *History of the English-Speaking Peoples* (which he interrupted in 1939, returning to it well after the Second World War). What extraordinary energy! True: he was now able to gather and employ a considerable staff of historian amanu-enses who brought documents to him, filled in gaps in his historical knowl-edge of a detail or even of a considerable period, the kind of assistance that other, less well-favored historians may justly envy: but the composition of the work, and its writing, were his own. We must compare Churchill's historianship not with that of professors (alas, there are such) whose re-search and other work is often the result of tasks they had farmed out to their graduate students. If there is any valid comparison at all, it must be with that of great artists such as Leonardo or Rubens or Rembrandt who, more than often, relied on groups of admiring painter-students to fill out details here and there, without compromising the genius of their master's grand design and of his craft. Maurice Ashley, who was one of Churchill's helpers in the work for *Marlborough,* wrote: "This gave me the opportunity to see Churchill at work as a historian, at a time when my heart was young, my mind malleable, and my memory good."[9]

Marlborough is Churchill's grandest, and strangest, work. Ashley thought that it was even better than *Lord Randolph Churchill,* which is debatable. More than any other of his works *Marlborough* could (and perhaps should) have been shortened. The four volumes (often published in two books, to which the following quotations refer) run more than two thousand pages.[10] The work is also—a word that I use with some reluctance—undisciplined. Its research was extraordinary. A great number of unpublished letters Churchill found in the muniment room of Blenheim (they are specially marked throughout the pages), but they are only a small part of all kinds of docu-ments culled from a very large variety of archives and papers and books in England and throughout Europe. Yes, many of these were dug out and brought to Churchill by his assistants, but then *he* chose which to employ and how to employ them (sometimes exceedingly), and at what point. The footnotes are daunting. At one point Churchill evidently found it proper and necessary to illustrate one sentence in his text with a small numerical table, the fluctuating prices of wheat in England from 1706 to 1714. But at another place, writing about John Churchill's proposed marriage to the beautiful but not rich Sarah Jennings, Churchill wastes a page and a half on composing fictitious letters by the grooms' parents ("We may imagine some of them") objecting to the troth. Yet there are other excursions that are masterly (for example, an entire chapter, "The Europe of Charles II," which could be a model for historians). Others are unduly instructional: about fortresses, drills, musketry, and so on. I think that Churchill was also attracted to the history of Marlborough, his wars, his period, because they involved what to Churchill was and remained the inevitable connection between the destiny of England and the fate of Europe, or at least of Western Europe—whereto Marlborough and an English army had returned after an insular absence of nearly three hundred years.

As in *Lord Randolph Churchill*, Churchill's magisterial depiction of the larger canvas, of the history of those times, succeeds better than his biographic vindication of his ancestor. Unlike *Lord Randolph Churchill*, we may wonder why he undertook this Herculean effort instead of a brief correction of the contemptuous rendering of Marlborough by Macaulay and other writers. We have seen that Churchill had a number of common traits with his father. With his ancestor John Churchill he had just about none. A great general Marlborough may have been. But he was also cold, calculating, frugal, secretive, avaricious—very much unlike his great descendant. (And, again unlike: "I do not like writing." One thing they had in common: their love for their wives.) By and large Churchill, with all of his justifiable emphasis on the character and conditions of those times, fails to convince us that his ancestral hero was not a shrewd and crafty calculator in his contacts with the exiled James II (his once great benefactor whom he abandoned in 1688) and with James's illegitimate son Berwick (whose mother, Arabella, true, was a former mistress of James, and Marlborough's sister). There was also a crudeness in Marlborough's character when he, for instance, wrote to Queen Anne in 1710, forcing her to choose between her confidante, the plain Mrs. Masham (who had been intriguing against Sarah), and him. When the queen wrote a letter dismissing him (on New Year's Eve, 1711), he threw that into the fire. His answer to her the next day was not one of his best.

A very obvious mistake of *Marlborough* is Churchill's excessive and vindictive campaign against Macaulay—a strange and unusual exception to Churchill's usual magnanimity and to his willingness to forget past wrongs. But then the entire purpose of his *Marlborough* he set forth at the very beginning: "A long succession of the most famous writers of the English language have exhausted their resources of reproach and insult upon his name. Swift, Pope, Thackeray, and Macaulay in their different styles have vied with each other in presenting an odious portrait to posterity. Macpherson and Dalrymple have fed them with misleading and mendacious facts." Churchill's campaign against Macaulay goes on and on and on. About John Churchill's affair with the older, very rich, and influential Barbara Villiers: "How disgusting to pretend, with Lord Macaulay, a filthy, sordid motive for actions prompted by those overpowering conclusions which lead flaming from the crucible of life itself!" Once in a while his research wonderfully succeeds: in a masterly footnote Churchill proves that in one instance Macaulay mistook William Penn for a minor writer by the name of Penne. In sum: "It is beyond our hopes to overtake Lord Macaulay. The grandeur and sweep of his story-telling style carries him swiftly along. . . . We can only hope that Truth will follow swiftly enough to fasten the label 'Liar' to his genteel coat-tails." Macaulay was not the only historian who aroused Churchill's ire: about the Austro-German Onno Klopp: "A whine and drone of baffled spite arises from these wearisome, laborious chronicles."

Perhaps the sharpest criticism of *Marlborough* was made in 1934, after the publication of the first volume, in a small book by the Jacobite historian Malcolm V. Hay, *Winston Churchill and James II of England.* "Can Mr. Winston Churchill be trusted?" "Mr. Churchill, sweeping out of his way everything likely to impede the progress of his argument, has followed the technique not of history, but of fiction." In his conclusion Hay cites Churchill's own preface: "We await with meekness every correction or contradiction which the multiplicate knowledge of students and critics will supply." "If Mr. Churchill is really so willing to accept correction, he will apologize in his next volume for his unfairness to James II. Fairness often requires an effort, and a watchful supervision of will; it is here that Mr. Winston Churchill has failed."[11] Yes, Churchill believed that "the Jacobite records preserved in the Scots College in Paris are one of the greatest frauds of history." Yet he could be marvelously fair to evidences and arguments contrary to his. "It is unfair to derive one's portrait of [Queen] Anne from the writings of the Duchess of Marlborough" (whom Churchill unreservedly admired). That he was not dogmatically anti-Catholic must appear from his exquisite portrait of Pope Innocent XI. And here is a fine example of balance, credit given to the pro-Jacobite *James II* of Hilaire Belloc: "A recent Catholic writer had portrayed the opposition to James as the resistance of the rich and powerful. This is true. It was successful because the rich and powerful championed the causes and prejudices which the masses espoused, but without superior leadership were unable to defend."

Finally, there are his splendid phrases and passages. Marlborough was supposed to have studied the Roman military writer Vegetius in detail. "It has often been suggested that by some occult dispensation our hero was able to extract various modern sunbeams from this ancient cucumber." About Harley's letters: "There is a personal awkwardness about them and a scent of lamp-oil, redolent after two hundred years." "Scotland chewed the thongs of union morosely through the misadventures of 1707." "An indifference to logic where it is likely to lead to serious trouble is one of the strongest English characteristics."

Yet another book that Churchill published in the 1930s was a collection of some of his pen portraits, with the title *Great Contemporaries.* In its way this is one of his three biographical works. Of course the craft of a biographer and that of a historian do not merely overlap, they are often the very same. And *Great Contemporaries* was much more than a collection of disparate pieces, and much much more than a potboiler. Many of Churchill's portraits of various personalities (not all of them British) are not only very well written but are marked with an understanding that ranges beneath and beyond the art of portraiture.[12]

I turn now to Churchill's histories of the First and Second World Wars. He wrote them in very different circumstances and during very different chapters of his life—*The World Crisis* in the 1920s, *The Second World War* between 1948 and 1953. He worked during ten years on the first, during five on the second. The first consists of five volumes, the second of six. He had far more help from historians and assistants for the second than for the first. Yet I am inclined to think that his Second World War history is the better of the two. The great military historian Sir Charles Oman was a severe critic of *The World Crisis;* there were also others.[13] Churchill devotes too many pages in it to justify some of his decisions, such as the Dardanelles—though not without an admission of self-criticism. Moreover, the quality of the successive volumes decreases. The last one, *The Eastern Front,* published in 1931 and the shortest one, was almost an afterthought. (He wrote it when he was already deeply involved in his writing of *Marlborough.*) Again, the Defoe-inspired compound of history and autobiography works better in *The Second World War* than in his voluminous history of the First: but then this is natural, for he was the Prime Minister and the chief antagonist of Hitler's Germany through most of the Second. The quality and the consistency and the rhythm of the six volumes of *The Second World War* is steadier, more even than that of *The World Crisis.*

But there are grounds for criticism there, too. The most substantial criticism is apposite to its first volume, *The Gathering Storm,* in which—to mention but one example—his description of Stanley Baldwin is unbalanced and unfair. There are other such examples, though perhaps less self-justificatory than in *The World Crisis.* In *The Second World War* Churchill's main purpose is less to justify himself than to justify his perspective: if only the

British and French governments had behaved better, this war could have been avoided. This is arguable. John Ramsden, not a customary critic of Churchill, in his valuable lecture cites Churchill who in *The Gathering Storm* insists that in 1936 Hitler could have been stopped, if only the French had mobilized: "There is no doubt that Hitler would have been compelled by his own General Staff to withdraw; and a check would have been given to his pretentions which might well have been fatal to his rule." "Note the way," Ramsden says, "in which that sentence slides imperceptibly from a confident 'there is no doubt' via two hopeful 'would have been[s]' to a suggestive 'might well have been.' It was on such a frail thread of syntax that hung Churchill's oft-repeated claim that (as he put it at Fulton), 'there never was a war in all history easier to prevent.'" This is very good.[14] On the other hand, there are many instances of Churchillian magnanimity in *The Second World War*—perhaps foremost among them his decision to omit entirely his struggle with Halifax, who wished to at least explore a potential negotiation with Hitler during five very critical days in May 1940. (Another example is the toning down of the record of his differences with the Americans in 1944–45.) Plumb, otherwise very critical of Churchill's historianship, admits: "Churchill the historian lies at the very heart of the historiography of World War II, and will always remain there."[15]

There is yet another difference between the two world war histories. There is a purpose of *The Second World War* that is also extant in *A History of the English-Speaking Peoples*.[16] Both of them are exhortatory. I think it was Samuel Johnson who said that we are here less to instruct people than to remind them. In both of these, otherwise very different, multivolume works Churchill's purpose is to remind the English-speaking peoples of the world of their inheritance, of what they had been capable of achieving, of their very virtues. This is evident from the "Moral" of *The Second World War:* "In War: Resolution. In Defeat: Defiance. In Victory: Magnanimity. In Peace: Good Will"—but also in his decision not to write anything about those dramatic days and nights in late May 1940 where he prevailed, and when he was right and Halifax wrong. Instead, he writes that in those very days "the War Cabinet were all of one mind." And: "There was a white glow, overpowering, sublime, which ran through our island from end to end."

"It must be admitted," Maurice Ashley says in the conclusion of his fine book *Churchill as Historian*, "that Churchill was wanting in that complete scientific application possible in university cloisters, though his powers of concentration and ability to master detail were terrific. . . . Churchill could be obstinate, as those who helped him write his books were aware, and though he might yield to persuasion, he was hard to persuade. This, I think it must be admitted, is Churchill's main weakness as a historical writer.

Clio is a tough mistress and requires a lot of service.... He never had either the time or the inclination to absorb himself in it completely or to revise his work in detail in the light of later knowledge: he preferred to make history than to write it."[17] This is largely true (except perhaps the question whether "complete scientific application" is what historical reconstruction consists of, and whether it is really and truly practiced in university cloisters). It rings truer, and fairer, than David Reynolds's conclusion in his paper of the 2001 Churchill conference: "In the 1950s, one might say, Churchill was a prisoner of history—his own history of the 1930s. It proved easier to make history than to unmake it."[18] Reynolds exaggerates when he states that the accepted notions of Baldwin, Chamberlain, Munich, appeasement had been largely Churchill's work. Yet Reynolds deserves credit for his research in the Churchill papers in the Churchill Archives, his reconstructing much about how *The Gathering Storm* was written. John Ramsden, more sympathetic to Churchill, points out other shortcomings of Churchill's research, one as late as in 1948, when he had failed to have some of Franklin Roosevelt's letters released by President Truman.

But let me look, now, at a larger and deeper issue, going beyond and beneath Churchill's method and purpose in writing his histories (even as we ought to realize that purpose is often inherent in method, as every "why" in every "how"). In 1933 A. L. Rowse in *The End of an Epoch* declared that Churchill, "unlike Trotsky[!], has no philosophy of history." This was cited and repeated in 1962 by E. H. Carr in his *What Is History?*[19] This is absolute nonsense. These famous British academic intellectuals fail to see that Churchill had something far more essential than a systematic philosophy of history. Churchill possessed something quite different: a historical philosophy. (Poor Trotsky! He *did* have a philosophy of history! It did him no good. I do not only mean his political career. His writings in exile show that his understanding of the historical realities of that time—the 1930s— were woefully wrong, the very opposite of Churchill's.) Thirty-five years and a Second World War later J. H. Plumb, in his essay about "The Historian," slips, slides (and falls) on another slippery slope, when he writes about Churchill's historianship: "There was, and is, in his work, a touch of the philistine." "He never mastered the giant intellectual figures of his youth and early middle age—Marx and Freud." (I am inclined to think that may have been to Churchill's advantage, not a handicap.) According to Plumb, omissions in *A History of the English-Speaking Peoples* are "indicative of Churchill's major fault both as a historian and as a statesman: he lacked a sense of the deeper motives that control society [economics, anyone?] and make it change, just as he lacked an interest in the deeper human motives [as, for example, in Hitler's?]."[20]

In 1962 E. H. Carr wrote: "Before you study the history, study the historian"; and "before you study the historian, study his historical and social environment." This half-truth[21] has been often applied to Churchill's historianship, wrongly. According to Plumb, again, "To understand Churchill the historian, one must look closer at his inheritance, particularly the historical assumptions of his class." This is much too simple. As one of his most recent biographers, Roy Jenkins, writes: Churchill's aristocratic background was not "the key to his whole career. Churchill was far too many-faceted, idiosyncratic and unpredictable a character to allow himself to be imprisoned by circumstances of his birth."[22] Such different historians as Plumb and Charmley have categorized Churchill as a prototypical aristocratic Whig, which is debatable from his historical judgments alone (examples of which are his treatments of the Whigs of the 1680s in *Marlborough* and those of two centuries later in *Lord Randolph Churchill*).

Yet Plumb, who asserts the insufficiency of Churchill's extensive research for *Marlborough,* writes: "Although open to criticism as history, it remains a splendid work of literary art." And about *A History of the English-Speaking Peoples*: "It contains his secular faith. As history, it fails, hopelessly fails; as a monument of a great Englishman's sense of the past, it is a brilliant success." But are those two matters entirely separable? If you have the right (and fine) sense of the past, can your history be entirely wrong? After all, Plumb also writes that "history was not, for Churchill, like painting, something one turned to for relaxation or merely to turn an honest guinea to meet his mountainous expenses. History was the heart of his faith; it permeated everything which he touched, and it was the mainspring of his politics and the secret of his immense mastery." "And I venture to think that only a statesman steeped in history could have roused and strengthened the nation in the way Churchill did during those years." As Maurice Ashley concludes about Churchill's historicism: "It is to his credit that he valued the verdicts of history and that he was conscious in all he did and said as Prime Minister that historians would one day examine and judge him."[23] These are proper tributes to Churchill the maker of history, to a statesman whose mind was steeped in history. Yet I think that another tribute may still be due: to Churchill the historical writer. There exist bad histories that are written tellingly or even well; but there can be no good history that is not told or written well. After all, whatever the research, there is no historical fact the meaning of which exists separately from its statement, from its very phrasing.

Churchill formed his own style. He was influenced by Gibbon and Macaulay but he did not emulate them. Stunning passages and phrases are abundant in every one of his books. I reproduce but a few of them, collected and jotted down on various scraps of paper in a near-lifetime of reading. In *Lord Randolph Churchill* about the Whigs: "The debate was heralded for several days by much parliamentary snarling." About some of the Tories: "the prosaic authoritarians who chafe the hearts of Celtic peoples." In *Marlborough* about Charles II: "Manouevre, fence, and palter as he might, he always submitted, and always meant to submit, with expedition to the deep growl of his subjects and to the authority of their inexpugnable institutions." About James II in 1686: "Nay, he would not reject even the dim, stubborn masses who had swarmed to Monmouth's standards in the West, or had awaited him elsewhere, whose faith was the very antithesis of his own, and whose fathers had cut off his father's head." In *The World Crisis* about 1914: Germany "clanked obstinately, recklessly, awkwardly towards the crater and dragged us all with her." And of July 28, 1914, the First Fleet leaving Portsmouth for Scapa Flow, through the English Channel: "scores of gigantic castles of steel wending their way across the misty, shining sea, like giants bowed in anxious thought." An immortal passage! Or about the German admiral, von Spee, cut off from refueling or repairing his ships: "He was a cut flower in a vase, fair to see, yet bound to die and die very soon if the water was not renewed." About a general who ordered the evacuation from Gallipoli: "He came, he saw, he capitulated." In *The Aftermath* about Russia after the Bolshevik Revolution: "Russia has been frozen in an indefinite winter of subhuman doctrine and superhuman tyranny." In *A History of the English-Speaking Peoples* about King Charles, sequestrated in Carisbrooke Castle, 1647: "Here, where a donkey treads an endless waterwheel, he dwelt for almost a year, defenceless, sacrosanct, a spiritual King, a coveted tool, an intriguing parcel, an ultimate sacrifice." (That solitary sad little donkey going round and round the waterwheel captured Churchill's imagination. He must have felt that he had to put it into his description. This was not the employment of a well-known historical cliché, not like the Capitoline geese or a kingdom for a horse: I know only of one history of Charles II or the English Civil War where that donkey has been recorded.)

Churchill's historical philosophy was evident. He did not only ponder history deeply, by which I mean its events and its course. What he wrote or said on occasion about the very nature of historical knowledge is worth citing, for many reasons, one of them being that they have stood the test of time. In *Lord Randolph Churchill*: "There is scarcely any more abundant source of error in history than the natural desire of writers—regardless of the overlapping and inter-play of memories, principles, prejudices and hopes, and the reaction of physical conditions—to discover or provide simple explanations for the actions of their characters." Or consider this passage about the Home Rule debates—echoing Burke, who said that one cannot and should not perceive men entirely separate from their historic circumstances: "A generation may arise in England who will question [their] policy ... as little as we question the propriety of Catholic Emancipation and who will study the records of the fierce disputes of 1886 with the superior manner of a modern professor examining the controversies of the early Church. But that will not prove the men of 1886 wrong or foolish in speech and action." (Well—some of them were. . . .) Or this great passage from his funeral oration for Chamberlain in November 1940: "It is not given to human beings, happily for them, to foresee or to predict to any large extent the unfolding course of events. . . . [But later] there is a new proportion, there is another scale of values. History with its flickering lamp stumbles along the trail of the past, trying to reconstruct its scenes, to revive its echoes, and kindle with pale gleams the passions of former days."

"The meanest historian owes something to truth."[24]

Churchill the Historian is a book yet to be written.[25]

31

Klaus Larres

(2003)

Winston Churchill's public career, which lasted from 1899 to 1955, was very long. The very large—and still accumulating—literature about him customarily concentrates on World War I and especially World War II, extraordinary and inspiring as his leadership during the latter was. Yet no less extraordinary (and debatable) were his efforts—and his vision—during the Cold War, both before and during his second premiership, from 1951 to 1955. Until recently, there has been surprisingly little scholarly study of Churchill and the Cold War.

There was, of course, his "Iron Curtain" speech in Fulton, Missouri, in March 1946, generally described and interpreted as one of the founding documents of the Cold War, together with George Kennan's Long Telegram and his "X" article in *Foreign Affairs,* as well as the Truman Doctrine and the Marshall Plan and so on. It was an early warning about Stalin and communism, just as he had warned early about Hitler and National Socialism: so Churchillian, so right. Such a reading of the great speech is not altogether wrong; but it is not subtle enough. It overlooks matters that suggest an essential difference between Churchill's and the Americans' (and also many other people's) view of the Cold War from the very beginning.

As late as March 1946, not only Harry Truman and Dean Acheson but also much of the American press, Right and Left alike, including many of the self-declared coldest (or hottest) warriors, still found it necessary to distance themselves from Churchill's stern Iron Curtain declaration; but that particular difference soon faded away. What would not fade away was a fundamental difference between Churchill's view of the conflict and Washington's view of it, a difference that devolved into a veritable chasm by the time Eisenhower and Dulles would steer the giant American ship of

Review of Klaus Larres, *Churchill's Cold War: Politics of Personal Diplomacy* (2002). From *New Republic,* January 13: 35–38.

state. Churchill's main subject and concern was the division of Europe. The main subject and concern of the American worldview, beginning in 1946 and lasting for four decades, was international communism. Churchill's principal preoccupation was the unnatural extension of a Russian military presence into the center of Europe, of which the establishment of Communist governments east of the Iron Curtain was merely a consequence, not a cause.

Churchill believed—as he said as early as September 1939—that the key to the Russian "enigma" (if an enigma it was) was "Russian national interest," something that had to be seriously considered. An undue extension of a Russian imperial domain was clearly dangerous for the West; but it was also a danger for Russia itself, and that had to be taken into account. Thus, unlike many of his latecoming American allies, Churchill still believed in an eventual renegotiation of Russia's newly acquired sphere of interest, rather than in a crusade against it. To correct the division of Europe: this was his principal ambition until the last day of his public life, nine years after his Iron Curtain warning. Yet the purpose of American policy, including NATO, was to maintain—indeed, to solidify—the division of Europe. This was a difference not of emphasis but of substance.

The disagreement came to a head during Churchill's second prime ministership. The Cold War, and the popular sentiments fueling it (including the McCarthy phenomenon), were then at their feverish heights. Yet significant events appeared to gather in a different direction, inspiring Churchill. Only six weeks after his wartime companion Eisenhower became the American president, Stalin suddenly died. The new and anxious Russian leadership showed many signs of unsureness. It announced reforms and—for the first time—the slogan of "coexistence" with the West. Revolts broke to the surface within its domains, including in East Germany in June 1953. There was a final armistice in Korea. The swollen Russian empire embarked on a policy of cautious retreat in Finland, Yugoslavia, Manchuria, and Austria; and in 1955, when Churchill finally retired, Moscow officially recognized the West German state without demanding that the Western powers recognize East Germany. Both publicly and privately, Eisenhower and Dulles declared these moves to be nothing but Communist trickery; on at least one occasion Eisenhower said to Churchill that Russia was a "whore" and would not change.

But Churchill did not think so. As early as 1950 he advocated attempts to renegotiate the conditions of the Cold War with Russia, foremost among them the rigid division of Europe. He said that "the central factor of Soviet policy was fear. . . . Moscow feared our friendship more than our enmity . . . the growing strength of the West would reverse this, so that they would fear our enmity more than our friendship and would be led thereby to seek our friendship." Thereafter he tried to impress the departing Truman and Acheson, and then the incoming Eisenhower and Dulles, to attempt a new kind of negotiations with Moscow at the summit.

On May 11, 1953, Churchill made one of his last great speeches in Parliament. In this historic speech, he questioned the Western tendency to accept the status quo and the division of Europe: "I do not believe that the immense problem of reconciling the security of Russia with the freedom and safety of Western Europe is insoluble." Eisenhower and Dulles rejected Churchill with contumely. Several times thereafter, in Washington and in Bermuda, Churchill tried to make them agree to a last Churchillian attempt to meet with the new Russian leaders (Malenkov and Molotov). He assured Eisenhower and Dulles that he was "not willing to appease the Soviet Union under all circumstances," but he insisted that they "ought to do justice to what is happening in Russia and to the many favorable events which have occurred." All of this was in vain. He wrote to Anthony Eden (then his foreign secretary) dejectedly: "it appeared as though the West was intent on maintaining and even stabilizing the partition of Europe . . . we cannot accept as justified or permanent the present division of Europe." He wanted to loosen that division, including some improvement of trade with the East: "friendly infiltration can do nothing but good." Eisenhower's retort was that the swords must be sharpened "for the struggle that cannot possibly be escaped."

There was, in sum, a period during the Cold War—more precisely, from Stalin's speech in March 1952 proposing a unification of Germany to the Geneva Summit in 1955, after Churchill's retirement—when a mitigation of the Cold War, including a renegotiation of some of its most troublesome tensions, was possible or even probable. It is regrettable that the horde of contemporary historians and politologues have almost entirely overlooked this, at least until recently. The first "revisionists" of the Cold War—a poor term, since all history is revisionist by its very nature—were opportunistic ideologues of the 1960s who simply projected their dislike of the Vietnam war onto the origins of the Cold War in the years between 1945 and 1948, arguing (often dishonestly) that the conflict mostly resulted from American provocations of the Soviet Union. Another kind of revisionism appeared after the collapse of the Soviet Union, when respected historians pursuing the obvious (or, rather, what seemed obvious) with the enthusiasm of short-sighted detectives, declared that "we now know" the historical truth: Communist Russia, and Russia alone, was the source and the origin of the Cold War, and of all the problems, including the division of Europe, during the Cold War.

Yet both "schools" entirely overlooked, or failed to see, the significance of the period between 1952 and 1955, and of Churchill's vision—until recently, when scholars, German scholars especially, have begun to masticate and to swallow and to digest the accumulating evidence, provided mostly by Russian sources. These prove that, at least in 1952 and 1953, a renegotiation of the division of Germany was seriously debated and pondered in Moscow, even during Stalin's last twelvemonth; that the Russians (possibly Stalin, but certainly his minion Lavrenti Beria, the head of the KGB) were even considering ditching the East German Communist state in exchange for a united and neutral Germany from which Russian and American troops would be withdrawn. (One of the more startling pieces of evidence is the brutal admonition of the Soviet high commissioner for Germany, Vladimir Semenov, to the shocked leaders of the East German state in Moscow, a week before the East Berlin workers' revolt in June 1953: reform and watch out, he said, because "in a few weeks you won't even have a state anymore.")

It is natural and expectable that a concerned reexamination of these past events should be of particular concern to German historians. Klaus Larres, a German-born scholar, is now a professor in Belfast. He does not read Russian, but he has read everything (well, almost everything) about this period; and the most interesting portion of his massive book deals with the Germanies in and around 1953. At times he admits what is still often unsayable among German *bien-pensant* historians: that Chancellor Konrad Adenauer thought that "reunification had to be sacrificed for the time being." Adenauer's distrust of Churchill throughout those years was evident; but Larres notes, too, that in contrast to his own Foreign Office, Churchill "doubted the desirability of the continued partition of Germany." His book is especially good and useful about the international origins and repercussions of the East German uprising in June 1953. Still, it is at least arguable that the revolt was principally "caused by the dire economic situation and rapidly deteriorating standard of living in [East Germany]." Churchill saw the situation more clearly: he said that the greatest crisis for a tyrannical regime occurs when it feels forced to reform—an effect that the great Tocqueville had noted as early as 1848. In any event, Larres's massive volume is a considerable contribution to scholarship. And massive it is, almost half of its contents consisting of long notes, set in small type, on 137 pages, and then a bibliography of nearly fifteen hundred items.

But there are problems. *Churchill's Cold War* is better about the Cold War than about Churchill. A book about Churchill and Germany, and another one about Churchill and "Europe," still remains to be written (the first primarily to revise the often-accepted notion, especially among German historians, that Churchill was a committed Germanophobe throughout his life). It was not necessary for Larres to begin his book with a long chapter on Churchill's "personal diplomacy" before 1914, involving the German and British naval programs: this is an undue extension. Another limitation is Larres's sometimes insufficient treatment of Churchill's relationships with Stalin and Roosevelt during World War II, from which of course much of the Cold War later resulted.

There are errors in this portion of the book. Larres writes that, when Churchill's confidential correspondence with Roosevelt began in 1939, he "believed too much in himself to worry about the fact that he was virtually ignoring the Foreign Office as well as the British and American ambassadors in his high-level diplomacy with Roosevelt." No: Churchill told and showed everything to Chamberlain and Halifax. In 1943 Stalin did not make a "decision to encourage intensive contacts with the German Embassy in Stockholm": the contacts were not intensive and they did not go through the embassy (more correctly, the legation). Roosevelt was not "strongly influenced by his Secretary of State," and he did not "avoid" meeting Churchill—they met in Cairo before the summit in Tehran. Larres's treatment of the very important Percentages' Agreement between Churchill and Stalin in October 1944 (when they made a rough sphere-of-interest division of the Balkans and Greece), and of the British decision to turn the concerns about Greece and Turkey over to the Americans in 1947, is perfunctory. "In late 1945 and early 1946," he writes, "it still appeared that Washington favored a policy of isolationism." Not so.

"The politics of personal diplomacy" is the subtitle of Larres's book. It is true that Churchill had a strong inclination to discuss and to settle things at the "summit" (he first employed this term in 1941), and that the Foreign Office, especially from 1951 to 1955, was critical of such an approach. But "personal diplomacy" is too much of a blanket term. Roosevelt, Stalin, and de Gaulle (not to mention Napoleon or Bismarck) all engaged in personal diplomacy, often successfully. Indeed, in the relations between states, high-level personal relationships are often more profitable than lower-level diplomatic relationships that are impersonal, legalistic, and technical.

Larres is unduly critical of Churchill. He berates him during World War II for his "grandiose and woolly rhetoric. . . .The United States had a much more lofty vision." Grandiose, perhaps; but woolly? And were not the Four Freedoms, or, say, the United Nations, also grandiose? On occasion, moreover, Larres contradicts himself, sometimes on the same page: he remarks upon "Churchill's vacillations about Europe," and a few lines later comments on Churchill's "own deeply held convictions regarding the shape of postwar Europe." Churchill "needed to avoid American domination of Europe after the war," but his main worry was that after the war the Americans would take their troops home from Europe. There are other contradictory statements in this otherwise valuable and serious tome.

I must now raise the only serious question about Larres's thesis, which is stated on page 123 and repeated again and again: "The key to a proper understanding of Churchill's summit diplomacy after the Second World War is his desire to maintain the power and influence of Britain." Well, during the war, yes. After the war, no. "After becoming Prime Minister once more," Larres asserts, "Churchill concentrated his energies almost exclusively to uphold Britain's great power status . . . by attempting to relax and perhaps even end the Cold War through an informal Anglo-American summit conference with the Soviet Union." But his emphasis was on the latter, not on the former. Ever since 1943—and Churchill admitted this at Tehran—he knew that Britain no longer had power even remotely equal to that of the United States and the Soviet Union.

Churchill wished to diminish the Cold War, and to avoid the deadly prospect of a nuclear war, by at least partly dismantling the Iron Curtain and thus mitigating the partition of Europe. On occasion Larres understands this: "Churchill's ultimate aim was the end of the Cold War and with it 'the unity and freedom of the whole of Europe.'" But elsewhere Larres states that Churchill was not interested in the eventual integration of Europe. Now, it is true that Churchill never proposed that Britain should join a united or federated or confederated Europe. Yet he certainly believed that the fate of Europe and the fate of Britain were inseparable; his statements about the primacy of Europe would fill a small book. This was, after all, the most significant difference between him and the appeasers during the 1930s: the latter were unwilling to contest Hitler's domination of Europe if the empire could remain intact, while Churchill was convinced that such a policy was not only immoral but impossible.

Consider also Churchill's memo to Eden on October 22, 1942, even before the military turning points of Stalingrad, El Alamein, or North Africa: "I must admit that my thoughts rest primarily in Europe—the revival of the glory of Europe, the parent continent of the modern nations and of civilization. It would be a measureless disaster if Russian barbarism overlaid the culture and independence of the ancient states of Europe." During the war Churchill remained unimpressed by Roosevelt's fanciful notions about world government; he argued that Europe ought to be Britain's "prime care." After the war he was the prime advocate of a closer union of Western Europe and a godfather of the Council of Europe, established by a congress at The Hague in 1948.

From 1951 to 1955, Churchill failed to make a dent in Eisenhower's and

Dulles's ideological convictions. This was at least partly his own fault. He had expected too much from his wartime comradeship with Eisenhower. There was a strong element of personal vanity in his belief that he could impress the new Russian leaders by talking to them directly, and thus end his historic career as an architect of the gradual cessation of the Cold War. He was also aging rapidly, and tired, and affected by a stroke, and wanting in self-discipline and stamina (often not doing his homework), and at times indifferent to the contrary advice of men of his own government. All this is true—and yet the historical record (and not only the revelations from the available Russian documents and sources) suggests that perhaps a great chance may have been missed fifty years ago, when Churchill, as so often during his life, was willing to act on his own vision and go against the tide, and when he was right and his opponents were wrong.

Here Larres misreads the evidence of public opinion and popular sentiment. It is not true that American politicians in 1953 were "worried of the popular appeal of the Soviet peace campaign." To the contrary: many of them quailed before McCarthy, and many more of them before the prospect of not seeming sufficiently anticommunist. "The great majority" of the populations in the United States and West Germany certainly did not welcome Churchill's 1953 initiative; nor was there "a radical change in American diplomacy after the uprising" in East Berlin.

Well before his resignation, Churchill predicted that West Germany would be admitted to NATO and that, more significantly, the Russians would agree to a mutual evacuation of Austria. There is, finally, a stunning piece of evidence about Churchill's vision that Larres has missed. On New Year's Day in 1953 (note that Stalin was still living then), Churchill told his secretary, Jock Colville, that if he lived his normal span Colville "should assuredly see Eastern Europe free from communism." Counting Colville's expectable threescore and ten, this would have been the 1980s—which was exactly what happened and when. Bismarck once said that the most a statesman could look ahead was about five years. Churchill did better than that. We must give him his due, as Klaus Larres also does; but less reluctantly.

32

Richard M. Gamble
(2004)

Consider the following statements:

"The greatest human power for good, the most efficient earthly tool for the uplifting of nations, is without question the United States."

The United States "must rise to the responsibilities of its position and put the commandments of God into action unilaterally, and then watch the effects on a startled world."

"The power of organized evil in this world could be only challenged by the organizing forces of righteousness."

"This country, strong and brave, generous and helpful, is called of God to be in its own way a messianic nation."

It is America's "divine destiny" to reaffirm the nation's special calling as a "city on the hill." America "is the hope of all mankind."

The last two statements are those of Ronald Reagan and the elder George Bush, respectively. Are the previous four those of the Christian Right, evangelical fundamentalists, conservatives, or Republicans? No, they belong to the Progressives, Democrats, intellectuals, and liberal Protestants before and during World War I. These include Gifford Pinchot, William Jennings Bryan, and Woodrow Wilson. "There is a mighty task before us, and it welds us together," Wilson said. "It is to make the United States a mighty Christian nation, and to Christianize the world." It is America's "duty and privilege . . . to show the paths of freedom to all the world. . . . [T]he American flag has vindicated its right to be honored by all the nations of the world and feared by none who do righteousness."

Such were the words of Wilson, whom Senator Carter Glass, a Virginia Democrat, called "the greatest Christian statesman of all time." Did he— did they—believe what they were saying? They did, alas; as did Reagan

Review of Richard M. Gamble, *The War for Righteousness* (2003). From *Los Angeles Times Book Review*, February 8: R9.

and Bush. (Was he "the greatest Christian statesman of all time"? There must be some who think so.) Many books have been written about the exaggerations of propaganda during World War I. Their authors, almost without exception, attributed those exaggerations to superpatriotism (not a good word) and/or to the influences of lobbies and profiteers. However, these are only half-truths, or more precisely, insufficient explanations. The Crusading Spirit of that time was inseparable from the dominant power of American liberal Protestantism, of prestigious churchmen who, very tellingly, adopted Darwinism and the religion of progress well before the war. These men included Lyman Abbott, Walter Rauschenbusch, Herbert Willett, and Harry Emerson Fosdick—public men whose influence lasted long after World War I.

"Their words," writes Richard M. Gamble in *The War for Righteousness*, "help open the interior world of the progressive clergy and reassemble the ideas they used to explain the war to themselves, to the American public, and to the world." Hence the great importance of this sober, convincing, and grave book.

Gamble's is not primarily an account of diplomacy and politics, although diplomats and politicians appear in these pages. In 1917–18, Protestant liberals pictured themselves living in a universe in which God's moral law reigned inviolable, in which the U.S. prospered as the nearest approximation yet to God's kingdom on Earth, and in which Germany struggled vainly as the last impediment to that kingdom, collapsing under its own repressive sins. The Federal Council of Churches declared that this war had "developed into a conflict between forces that make for the coming of the Kingdom of God and forces that oppose it." Willett, a theologian, said "the conception of God as a monarch, all-powerful, remote, transcendent, and autocratic, is no longer suited to the needs or the comprehension of the modern mind." Union Theological Seminary professor George Allen Coe proposed that the phrase "democracy of God" should replace "'Kingdom of God' as a more precise definition of Jesus' ideal."

And not only churchmen. There was the *New Republic*, launched in 1914, the flag-bearer of progressive liberalism, which in 1917 "proudly credited America's entry into the Great War to the political leadership of a new class, 'the intellectuals.'" They had done "effective and decisive work in behalf of war." Consider that in those times, not one American politician or public spokesman dared to call himself a conservative. Now, perhaps, many Americans call themselves that and "liberal" has become a curse word. That may be regrettable, but one must be honest enough to recognize how the wind (and the windbagging) we inherit was sown by liberals and progressives not so long ago. (George W. Bush in December 2001: "America must fight the enemies of progress.")

History is full of irony. Or rather, full of unintended consequences. Yes, we must see the fools of yesteryear for what they were and the consequences of their ideas and words. There is another, secondary question. The evidence in Gamble's book will serve those people who believe that the United States should not have entered either World War I or World War II. Yet, had we not entered the war in 1917, it is more than probable that Imperial Germany would have won. Would the world have been better off then? Would we? I cannot tell.

In any event, Gamble's is a well-written, thoroughly researched, impassioned, and yet detached book, a most important contribution not only to the history of World War I but also to the very intellectual history of the United States, as valuable as the earlier works of historians such as Henry F. May or Richard Hofstadter. Indeed, many of Gamble's insights are more telling than were theirs.

III.

DISSENTING OPINIONS

(OR: A FEW OTHER PROSAISTS)

*I*n a more genteel age when academic credentials and classifications mattered less, John Lukacs would doubtless have been hailed as a man of letters with catholic interests, tastes, and sensibilities. Although not formally a literary scholar and critic, Lukacs has written often about literature, especially in relation to the study of history. History once flourished as a branch of literature, and by the nineteenth century such writers as Austen, Balzac, Chekhov, Dickens, Dumas, Flaubert, Hardy, de Maupassant, and Zola enriched their work with all kinds of historical details in an effort to penetrate and understand the attitudes, opinions, manners, and morals of certain persons living in certain places at certain times. A sense of history infused much of the work of such twentieth-century writers as Faulkner, Fitzgerald, Giuseppe di Lampedusa, Mann, Pasternak, Proust, Solzhenitsyn, and Waugh. Either list could be extended indefinitely, almost to the point of meaninglessness. History has, in many ways, subsumed fiction. As Lukacs has observed, both novelists and historians must know not only what actually happened in the past, but they must also imagine what could have happened. Historicity makes the novel plausible and realistic.

The obsession with history, however, does not a good novel make. Lukacs argues in the essays on E. L. Doctorow and Tom Wolfe, for instance, that these writers fail not only because they put their own words in the mouths of historical figures, but also, and more importantly, because their imaginations are visual rather than verbal. Their works have more in common with film than with literature. Tolstoy presents other difficulties. Determined to write "scientific history," Tolstoy, Lukacs maintains, was an ideological rather than a historical writer. To a greater or lesser extent, the distortions of ideology, frequently though not always accompanied by opportunism, mar the thinking and writing of the "other prosaists" whose work Lukacs discusses: Hannah Arendt, Whittaker Chambers, Francis Fukuyama, Graham Fuller, and Arthur Koestler. Among the writers whom Lukacs considers in this section, only Simone Weil, humble, independent, brave, and pious, stands as an unsullied "witness for truth." Lukacs's reflections on Weil invite a comparison to those on Arendt and Chambers. Taken together, these three essays offer a brief but provocative commentary on the history of twentieth-century politics and thought since the Second World War.

33

E. L. Doctorow

(1975)

W hat do these books—some very bad, one of them very good (Dutourd)—have in common?

Their authors are obsessed with history. They are also attempts to break through to a new genre. Of this some of their authors are more aware than others.

The new genre is the converse of the historical novel. In *War and Peace* or in *Gone with the Wind* history is the background. In the books listed below (there are many others) history is the foreground. In the classic historical novel the great events of history are painted on a large canvas in order to lend depth to the story, to give an added dimension to the main characters. In the below-mentioned books the reverse: the main characters serve for the purpose of illuminating the history of certain events, of a certain time. In the historical novel the author's principal interest is *the novel*. In these books the author's principal interest is *history*—perhaps a new kind of history, but history nonetheless.

The historical novel (like scientific history) was essentially a nineteenth-century genre. The novelized history is essentially a twentieth-century genre. But—like so many matters in the twentieth century, which is a transitional century, at the end of the Modern Age—this genre has not yet crystallized. (Because the genre has not yet crystallized, "novelized history" is not a particularly good term, but for the time it will have to do.)

Still it represents a stage in the evolution of historical consciousness. Historical consciousness—a much more recent, and much more important

Review of *Ragtime* (1975). From *Salmagundi,* Fall 1975–Winter 1976: 285–95. Other books discussed in this essay include: Upton Sinclair, *Lanny Budd* (1950); Theodor Plievier, *Stalingrad* (1948); John Dos Passos, *1919* (1932); Aleksandr Solzhenitsyn, *August 1914* (1972); Truman Capote, *In Cold Blood* (1966); Jean Dutourd, *The Horrors of Love* (1967); and Norman Mailer, *The Armies of the Night* (1968).

development than we have been accustomed to think—led, among other things, to the novel in the second half of the eighteenth century; and a few decades later, to the historical novel. For the last two hundred years in the Western world an appetite for history has grown that has no precedents. By the twentieth century, as Huizinga wrote in 1934, "Historical thinking has entered our very blood." History has become a form of thought. Yet the vast majority of professional intellectuals, including historians, have remained unaware of this—because they could not free their minds from outdated categories of thought, and because of the bureaucratic character of their intellectual ambitions.

At the same time all kinds of writers—some of them not professional intellectuals—grappling with the elusive nature of truth, have become more and more absorbed with the historical dimension thereof. Most of them, too, have been incapable of freeing their minds from outdated ideas of politics, society, justice, reality. Few of them realized that at the end of the Modern, or Bourgeois, Age the novel, as a form of narrative, has been dissolving, tending in two directions: one toward poetry, the other toward history.

I am concerned with the latter, rather than with the former tendency, because of my conviction that here the future of prose literature may lie—unless all literature, as we have known it, is doomed to disappear: a possibility to which I must return at the end of this article.

In teaching history in the twentieth century some of us require our students to read certain novels, in addition to the histories and the biographies on our reading lists. We do not do this in order to acquaint them with the principal literary works of a certain period, or to give them a bit of extra culture (though God knows they are in need of that), hanging a literary tailpiece on the end of their historical readings. It is obvious that certain novels tell us certain things about a certain nation, a certain class of people, a certain time: how people behaved and, more important, what they thought and how they felt. Thus I, for one, do not assign to my history students the principal novels (and not even the principal historical novels) of a period but, rather, those that are particularly rich in this kind of sociography. Thus, for example, in a survey course dealing with nineteenth-century France it is Balzac rather than Stendhal, it is *Sentimental Education* rather than *Madame Bovary* that serves this purpose; dealing with mid-Victorian England it is Trollope rather than George Eliot; dealing with nineteenth-century Germany it is *Buddenbrooks*. In Russian history Gogol, some of Turgenev, and some of Chekhov will fulfill this purpose better than *Crime and Punishment* or *War and Peace*. I should not put the latter on a reading list dealing with Napoleon's wars.

This function of certain novels is even clearer in American history, because of its peculiar and, until recently, unique texture: a history of a people rather than the history of a state. The most obvious example: In the 1920s much of the history of the North American state, including that of its politics, was cramped and dull; but that was a decade of substantial, perhaps even profound, mutations in the behavior, in the manners, in the sensitivities of Americans. Thus for the history of the twenties a minor masterpiece such as *The Great Gatsby* serves a purpose. It suggests to American students more about those years than some of the standard histories. More things: more things worth knowing. This is obvious. What is less obvious, and more significant, is that *The Great Gatsby* serves such a purpose better than, say, Dos Passos's *1919,* in spite of the mass of journalistic, and contemporary, material in the latter. And, were I to give a course on the first decade of the American twentieth century, I would put *The House of Mirth* on the reading list but not Doctorow's *Ragtime,* in spite of the latter being not just a novel but novelized history, in spite of the large panopticon of historical stuff displayed in it.

E. L. Doctorow is a writer of great talent. A Sunday afternoon on the western New York side of Long Island Sound, circa 1906:

> ... Gulls wheeled overhead, crying like oboes, and behind him at the land end of the marsh, out of sight behind the tall grasses, the distant bell of the North Avenue streetcar tolled its warning.

More streetcar scenery:

> ... The moon was out, the temperature had dropped, and the trolley clipped along the broad reaches of this wide boulevard with only occasional stops. They passed grassy lots interspersed with blocks of row houses still under construction. Finally the lights disappeared entirely and the little girl realized they were traveling along the edges of a great hillside cemetery. The stones and vaults standing against the cold night sky suggested to her the fate of her mother.

Sentences such as these evoke in one's mind the sensation of instant, and far from superficial, recognition. Yes: that was the way it was. Yes: that's the way it must have been. I wish I had written these—both in my capacity as a writer and as a historian. Still I find *Ragtime* disappointing.

Doctorow performed the reverse trick, without sustaining it. Yes: history is in the foreground, it is the main theme. Yet Doctorow's figures are paper figures, almost wholly one-dimensional ones. He performs tricks with them, paper-silhouette tricks (as does his protagonist "Tateh"). Sometimes the figures are not much more than art nouveau caricatures resuscitated for contemporary interests: like fake-Tiffany objects, like the Beatles' Sergeant Pepper. One set of his main figures are "Father," "Mother," "Younger Brother." There is also a "Coalhouse Walker, Jr." They are not real. But this does not seem to bother Doctorow; we shall soon see why.

I see something here that is not a deficiency in literary skill but a deficiency in the author's thinking. Doctorow understands that Fact and Fiction are not entirely separate and watertight categories: but he cannot free his mind from thinking in terms of these categories—like a twentieth-century physicist or philosopher who knows that objectivity has been shown to be impossible but who nonetheless keeps on talking and thinking in Cartesian categories.[1] In *Ragtime* some of the figures are "fiction," the others are people who "really" lived: Houdini, Emma Goldman, J. P. Morgan, Henry Ford, etc. Like Houdini (who, Doctorow does not fail to remind us, was Jewish), he performs neat tricks, making Goldman, Morgan, Ford, Freud do things and say things they had not said "in fact" but which will make them more "real." But it doesn't. Now, if he had only written a parody. . . . But no—Doctorow wants to make them real, as in the movies. Yes: a novelist may invent a millionaire banker who is more interesting than J. P. Morgan, an automobile manufacturer who is more interesting than Henry Ford, a Jewish socialist mother-figure who is more interesting than Emma Goldman. But he cannot make *Emma Goldman* more interesting by making her do things and say things she never said because this will be not Emma Goldman, it will be someone else. What Henry Ford or J. P. Morgan really said is more interesting, it will always be more interesting (though perhaps less entertaining) than something we might invent and attribute to them, just as an authentic recording or newsreel of Churchill or Hitler speaking will always be more interesting (though perhaps less entertaining) than Churchill played by Charles Laughton or Hitler played by Alec Guinness. Fifty years before *Ragtime,* Thomas Beer, pleasantly intoxicated with literary ambitions, and slightly contemptuous of the bloodlessness of American academic historianship, attempted—with limitations, of course—a new kind of voluble history. Has Doctorow read *The Mauve Decade?*[2] With all of its foppishness and its verbal artifice, *The Mauve Decade* remains *both* interesting and entertaining, because of Beer's emphasis on the characters who are real: Beer was more interested in the persons than in the trivia of the historical procession, even as he put the latter to good use, because he knew a great deal of it.

The second limitation is ideological. In all probability it derives from the background of this author. E. L. Doctorow is a New York Jewish intellectual, grounded in a certain leftist worldview. "Grounded" is the *mot juste*. *Ragtime* is a much better book than Doctorow's *Book of Daniel*, the main theme of which is that the Rosenbergs were innocent. But in *Ragtime*, too, Doctorow's view of the United States in the early twentieth century is hardly distinguishable from a New York Marxist (or neo-Marxist; or neo-neo-Marxist) worldview current in the twenties (or in the thirties, or forties, or fifties, or sixties; it hardly matters when). He knows a world which is very limited. This, of course, leads to his weaknesses in characterization. In *The Book of Daniel* nearly all the characters were Jewish. In *Ragtime* Tateh and Mameh are at times near-real; "Father" and "Mother" and "Younger Brother" practically never. Unlike her counterpart Evelyn Nesbit, Emma Goldman is described with affection, she is sentimentalized; sometimes the reader can sense her real presence.

And there is more to this. Doctorow knows a certain Jewish environment intimately and deeply. He also knows many, many things about America. But what he does not know is that his knowledge of Jews in America is a different kind of knowledge from his knowledge of America. Doctorow may know *more* about America than, say, Philip Roth, another Jewish writer: but Doctorow does not know it *better*, all of Roth's coarseness and enormous lapses of taste notwithstanding. For in a book such as *Portnoy's Complaint* Roth's underlying theme is not Portnoy's problem with sex but Portnoy's problem with his Jewishness, the recurrent problem of his identity,[3] mostly among non-Jewish Americans. When Roth fails (he, too, knows Jews better than he knows Gentile Americans), he, unlike Doctorow, at least knows what he is trying to do. For Doctorow's interest in America, in the American past, is in *things* American—altogether on a different level from his knowledge of Jewish-American *thoughts*. And this brings us to the deeper limitation, to Doctorow's limited sense of history. Doctorow has a very large bin of knowledge. He has a real feel and talent for the accumulated contents of that bin—like a knowledgeable antiquarian, he knows the value of most bits of trivia. No, he is not on a nostalgia kick. Doctorow is a talented and enterprising man. He is right in battening on the years 1902–14—or, perhaps I should say, collecting stuff from those years, *the* years that gave form to the American century. It was not only Kafka who had a pallid nightmare about America circa 1910. When I came to the United States, an immigrant in 1946, I was struck by a comparable impression: looking up in the New York streets at the square and steely office-buildings and at the early skyscrapers, I thought how much they looked like the windrows of Theodore Roosevelt's teeth, how much this looked like America circa 1910. I came from a Europe devastated by war and yet, in New York, I had this feeling: how outdated much of it was, those iron buildings and streets with the terrible mechanical racket of their sounds. And now, reading Doctorow, a word swam into my mind, a name that I first encountered in New York in 1946 on juke-box machines, which carried a meaning—or rather, a sense—for me ever since. This name is Wurlitzer. New York circa 1910 (*Ragtime* takes place mainly in New York) was a Wurlitzer city rather than a ragtime town. Wurlitzer: the very shape and sound of the name being German and Jewish, not Anglo-Saxon or Negro, just as, with all respect to Scott Joplin, et al., there is some wurlitzery in the mechanical-tinny rhythm of ragtime, in the very musical origins of which there is a bit of Central-East European polka, besides the background of New Orleans and jazz coming up the Mississippi.[4] And it is the nickelodeon, this melodeon, this mechanical music that rings through Doctorow's short little sentences, through his stylistic trick, trying to write *Ragtime* in ragtime, one-two. But *Ragtime* is not really ragtime. It is Wurlitzer.

Still, Doctorow's visual talent, his interest in the American past—no matter how limited—represents an advance in historical consciousness. An advance not in novelized history but in the *participant* knowledge of a Jewish intellectual in America present and past. The Jewish participation in—quickly changing into contribution to—American culture in the twentieth century has been extraordinary. It had, in my opinion, three principal phases. First came the Jewish participation in American popular music—something that contributed to substantial changes in American sentimentality. Then came the Jewish participation in American literature—contributing to certain changes in the American language. And now comes this Jewish participant interest in the American past—contributing to certain changes in the interpretation of American history. Let me explain this further. As late as 1895 there were few Jewish composers, the Jewish contribution to American popular music hardly existed at all; twenty years later this Jewish participation was overwhelming. All of Stephen Foster, the talented Ives, the German-American melodic tradition, and the Negro element notwithstanding, this was not much of a musical country before 1900 because the vast majority of the native inhabitants were not a musical people. What is extraordinary is how the children of poor Russian and German-Jewish immigrants took to American music within one generation, and how they enriched American popular culture thereby. People such as Irving Berlin, Jerome Kern, and the most prototypical of all of them, George Gershwin, did not merely become assimilated Americans: their music became, within one generation, prototypically American. They produced a unique art form that flourished during the first half of this century, when American popular music became something entirely different, newer and more vital and more sophisticated than the popular music of European nations. This music enriched America; with its melancholy tones it even changed the tone of American sentimentality. It is futile to search for Jewish or even Negro elements in Gershwin's harmonies and tonalities. His harmonies and tonalities, the underlying texture of his music (which must be always considered apart from the often incredibly vulgar words written for his tunes by his brother Ira, George's business manager) suggests the love affair which this dark and ugly, talented Jewish boy had with America, his longing for the blonde *shiksa* that lay somewhere near the essence of the American dream—his American dream. Then came another generation, another phenomenon, though of course closely related to the first. As late as 1920 there were few Jewish novelists and Jewish poets in America. Since 1945 some of the principal—if not the principal—American writers, novelists, sometimes even poets, have been Jews. This, too, is a phenomenon of profound consequence and of enormous significance whose end may be approaching, though perhaps not yet. Philip Roth's appetite for the blonde *shiksa* has not been that different from Gershwin's, except that writers such as Roth (and Bellow) know something that Gershwin did not know: near the end of civilization, a great disappointment. And now, another generation later, to history. In 1945 there were very few Jewish professors of American history. The widespread Jewish presence in academia was already there, especially in psychology, sociology, cultural anthropology, and even in certain fields of European history: but not yet in American. Today this is no longer so. Many of the principal professional practitioners of American history are Jewish. And it is within this phase, which of course goes far beyond the restricted fields of professional history, to this participant interest in the American past, that Doctorow belongs.

But here, a fatal flaw. A generation earlier certain American Jewish patricians, a Lewis Einstein, a Thomas Beer, had a subtle feel for the history of this country that Doctorow does not possess. Their interest may be compared to that of amateur collectors of early American paintings, whereas Doctorow's historical interest is, as I said earlier, that of the manager of an antique emporium.[5] And this is revealed not only by his unduly narrow view of American historical realities but by the very style of his writing: unlike a Thomas Beer who knew American literature, all kinds of literature, Doctorow knows America less through history than through *the movies*.[6]

It is there in his style. *Ragtime* is very readable. But all of those short sentences, the prose clipping along, reflect the rapid images of cartoons, of comics, of *moving pictures*. The very opposite of a stream of consciousness, his sentences represent a sequence of short pictorial images—like the comics (another early twentieth-century American cultural phenomenon, of Central European origin), made for a people of *slow* readers. Doctorow's imagination is far more pictorial than literary. He writes with his eyes rather than with his ear. Let us look at the very first paragraph of the book, celebrated by reviewers: One paragraph running two full pages, sixty-four long lines without a break: and yet easily readable. It is a passage of essentially unconnected photographic images. But, as in the movies, the artifice is such that we do not see their disconnection. Here is a portion of it:

> (Father was a flag manufacturer.) . . . Patriotism was a reliable sentiment in the early 1900's. Teddy Roosevelt was President. The population customarily gathered in great numbers either out of doors for parades, public concerts, fish fries, political picnics, social outings, or indoors in meeting halls, vaudeville theatres, operas, ballrooms. There seemed to be no entertainment that did not involve great swarms of people. Trains and steamers and trolleys moved them from one place to another. That was the style, that was the way people lived. Women were stouter then. They visited the fleet carrying white parasols. Everyone wore white in summer. Tennis racquets were hefty and the racquet faces elliptical. There was a lot of sexual fainting. There were no Negroes. There were no immigrants. . . .

A sequence of pictures reminiscent of the best photographic pages of *American Heritage* magazine. Somewhere in the middle of the paragraph Doctorow's ideology intrudes: Wasp Americans did not know anything about immigrants, they did not even see them.

On page eleven "Father" is sailing out of New York on an expedition ship, the *Roosevelt*:

> A while later the *Roosevelt* passed an incoming transatlantic vessel packed to the railings with immigrants. Father watched the prow of the scaly broad-beamed vessel splash in the sea.

A marvelous sentence! But, then:

> Her decks were packed with people. Thousands of male heads in derbies. Thousands of female heads covered with shawls. It was a rag ship with a million dark eyes staring at him. Father, a normally resolute person, suddenly foundered in his soul. A weird despair seized him.

The picture of the immigrants and their encounter with the American patrician is idealized and ideologized until the old sepia photograph of the scene swims out of focus.

And, like that of most comedians of his generation, Doctorow's sense of humor is that of the absurd:

> (J. P. Morgan in Egypt.) He was placed on his camel and slowly led down from the pyramid. The sky was bright blue and the rock of the pyramid field was pink. As he passed the Great Sphinx and looked back he saw men swarming all over her, like vermin. They were festooned in the claws and sat in the holes of the face, they perched on the shoulders and they waved from the heights of the headdress. Morgan started. The desecrators were wearing baseball suits. Photographers on the ground stood by their tripods with their head poked under black cloth. What in God's name is going on, Morgan said. His guides had stopped and were calling back and forth to other Arabs and camel drivers. There was great excitement. An aide of Morgan's came back with the intelligence that this was the New York Giants baseball team that had won the pennant and was on a world exhibition tour. The pennant? Morgan said. The pennant? Running toward him was a squat ugly man in pinstriped knee pants and a ribbed undershirt. His hand was outstretched. An absurd beanie was on his head. A cigar butt was in his mouth. His cleated shoes rang on the ancient stones. The manager, Mr. McGraw, to pay his respects, Morgan's aide said. Without a word the old man kicked at the sides of his camel and, knocking over his Arab guide, fled to his boat.

This is sheer movie stuff, of the style circa 1970.

Ragtime doesn't come out of literature, but out of the movies—an originally American (and in many ways Jewish-American) art form in which everything is manufactured for effect and for entertainment, in which the complete illusion of reality is produced by a completely mechanical pictorialization. The turning point in the story of Doctorow's Jewish anti-heroic hero, of his protagonist Tateh, occurs when Tateh shows a rapidly flickable book of silhouettes in the store of the Franklin Novelty Company "to a man in a striped shirt with sleeve garters" (another period image: is it real?) who buys it, and future booklets, for twenty-five dollars. Like *Ragtime,* which is probably the great jump in Doctorow's career, this sale is the turning point for Tateh, who eventually becomes a movie magnate. "For purposes of the contract they were called movie books." And so is *Ragtime*, with all of its historical stuffing, a movie book.

This essay is about two matters: Doctorow's *Ragtime* and the novelized history. Granting all of Doctorow's considerable talents, *Ragtime* suggests that his interest in history is not sufficiently substantial. Yet I, for one, continue to believe that others may come to create a more perfect model of a genre that may be the genre of the near future, perhaps eventually dominating all forms of narrative literature.

And *Ragtime* suggests, too, the converse: a great danger. It is quite possible that the invention of photography may have put an end, not to pictorial decoration, but to the art of painting in the Western world. It is at least possible that the invention of movies may have put an end, not to the printed word, but to the art of literature in the West.

34

Isaiah Berlin and Leo Tolstoy
(1980)

Twenty-seven years ago, in 1953, at the height of the Cold War between the United States and the Soviet Union, a short essay by an Oxford don produced a swiftly swelling wave of praise among public thinkers and intellectuals, elevating its writer to a situation of unquestionable and unquestioned eminence undiminished to this day. By that time Isaiah Berlin had already achieved a reputation in Oxford and London circles as an erudite wit; but from that moment on his reputation rose even higher among American intellectuals than in England where, however, he was subsequently rewarded by a knighthood, a consideration to which the fortunes of his repute in the United States may well have contributed. Such success due to a little book of an essay is a rare event. *Habent sua fata libelli.* That book was, of course, *The Hedgehog and the Fox,* surely the most famous and most widespread and most popular—and also the most unchallenged—of all of the twentieth-century commentaries and analyses of Leo Tolstoy.

Berlin's main thesis is that "there exists a great chasm between those, on one side, who relate everything to a single central vision . . . and, on the other side, those who pursue many ends, often unrelated and even contradictory. . . . [T]hese last lead lives, perform acts, and entertain ideas that are centrifugal rather than centripetal." Building upon the metaphor by the Greek poet Archilochus, Berlin calls the first kind "hedgehogs," the other "foxes." "The fox knows many things, but the hedgehog knows one big thing." "Without insisting on a rigid classification," Berlin continues, "we may, without too much fear of contradiction, say that, in this sense, Dante belongs to the first category, Shakespeare to the second; Plato, Lucretius, Pascal, Hegel, Dostoyevsky, Nietzsche, Ibsen, Proust are, in varying degrees, hedgehogs; Herodotus, Aristotle, Montaigne, Erasmus, Molière, Goethe, Pushkin, Balzac, Joyce are foxes." I do not find this classification entirely

From *University Bookman,* Summer: 75–83.

satisfying—for example, it is easily arguable that there is more in common between Proust and Joyce than between Balzac and Joyce—but this is not my point.

"The hypothesis I wish to offer," Berlin writes, "is that Tolstoy was by nature a fox, but believed in being a hedgehog; that his gifts and achievement are one thing, and his beliefs, and consequently his interpretation of his own achievement, another."

This interpretation is—or rather, ought to be—open to challenge.

First, Berlin tends to treat the famous (or rather, infamous) philosophical treatise with which Tolstoy concludes *War and Peace* as if it were a separate intellectual creation of Tolstoy's genius. In reality, the philosophy of history that Tolstoy explains and expounds in those strange and often repulsive pages is woven into the text of the great novel itself, indeed is inseparable from the warp and the woof of it. Here are a few random quotations from the main text of *War and Peace*: "In searching for the laws of historical movements precisely the same things must be observed as in the laws of physics." We must study the motions of history just as we must study the motion of a locomotive. To discover what makes the engine move "I must entirely change my point of view, and study the laws that regulate steam, bells, and the wind." Until man "finds the ultimate cause of the motion of the locomotive in the steam compressed in the boiler, he will not have the right to pause in his search for cause."

Thus Tolstoy revealed himself a prisoner of the nineteenth-century, monistic view of mechanical causality, with its willful ignorance of purposes. With all of that folksy pretension of common sense, it did not occur to Tolstoy that the main "cause" of the motion of the locomotive might be its driver. "The only concept," Tolstoy wrote, "capable of explaining the motion of the locomotive is the concept of a force equivalent to the observed movement. The only concept capable of explaining the movement of nations is the concept of a force equal to the whole movement of nations." (Contrast this with a fragment from Tocqueville's unpublished notes: "The human spirit," he wrote, "cannot be treated along false and mechanical laws. In steam engines and hydraulic works the smaller wheels will turn smoother and faster, as power is directed to them from the larger wheels. But such mechanical rules do not apply to the human spirit.") "The farther back into history we carry the object of our investigation," Tolstoy remarked elsewhere, "the more doubtful appears the freedom of the men who brought events about, and the more evident grows the law of Necessity"—written with a capital N by Tolstoy himself.

Already in *Two Hussars* Tolstoy had written that "the best results always come involuntarily; the more one tries, the worse things turn out"; and in

War and Peace, XI, he asserted that "the assumption that the volitions of all men are expressed in the actions of any historical character are false *per se*" (the very opposite of Dr. Johnson's common-sense dictum that "intentions must be judged from acts" and not the reverse). "If the will of every man," Tolstoy wrote, "were free, that is, if every one could do what he pleased, then history would be a series of disconnected accidents." "In history," he wrote, "that which is known we call the laws of necessity, that which is unknown we call Free Will"—free will, for which Tolstoy had only contempt.

"If a single human action were free, there would be no historical laws, no conception of historical events." To Tolstoy, history and its "laws" are therefore inevitable: "Experience and reason have shown a man that in the same circumstances, with the same character, he will always act in the same way as before. . . ." The same causes will always and necessarily produce the same effects: a mechanical conception of human nature that is wrong, outdated, and hopeless.

To Tolstoy, the exceptional does not figure in history. Historical events appear wrongly as exceptions to the theory: "For History to regard the Free Will of men as a force able to exert influence on historical events, that is, as not subject to law, is the same thing as for astronomy to recognize freedom in the movement of heavenly forces." Freedom, for Tolstoy, was not a supreme potentiality of human nature; it was anarchy. "Whatever should be free could not also be limited," he wrote. "By admitting the Freedom of the Will, we arrive at an absurdity . . . it is essential to get rid of a freedom which does not exist." "Chance," declared Tolstoy, "brings the Prince d'Enghien into Napoleon's hands, and unexpectedly compels him to assassinate him." ("Napoleon," he opined, was a man of "no convictions, no habits, no traditions, not even a Frenchman.")

Unable as he is to separate consistently Tolstoy the philosopher from Tolstoy the novelist, Berlin will, at times, admit the inexorable overflow of the philosophical content of Tolstoy's appendix into the text of *War and Peace* itself. "The final apotheosis of Kutuzov," Berlin writes, "is totally unhistorical, for all Tolstoy's repeated professions of his undeviating devotion to the sacred cause of the truth. In *War and Peace* Tolstoy treats facts cavalierly when it suits him, because he is above all obsessed with his thesis—the contrast between the . . . delusive experience of free will, the feeling of responsibility, the values of private life generally, on the one hand; and on the other, the reality of inexorable historical determinism . . . known to be true on irrefutable theoretical grounds." Berlin is correct when he criticizes those who "politely ignored" Tolstoy's view of history; but he errs when he dismisses those who treated it as a characteristic aberration which they put down as a combination of the well-known Russian tendency to preach (and thereby ruin works of art) with the half-baked infatuation with general ideas characteristic of young intellectuals in countries remote from centres of civilization.

But whoever did so (George Orwell was among them) may have been right after all.

And here I arrive at my second point, the essential error in Berlin's interpretation of Tolstoy. To some extent like George Orwell (in the latter's terse and lucid essay on Tolstoy, Gandhi, and Shakespeare), Berlin claims that the trouble lies not with Tolstoy's obsession with science but with religion. "Tolstoy's purpose," Berlin writes, "is the discovery of truth, and therefore he must know what history consists of, and recreate only that. History is plainly not a science. . . ." In view of the frequent evidence of Tolstoy's writing, affirming his veneration for "Science" again and again, this is a curious thing to say; and Berlin himself notes Tolstoy's central faith in the great mechanical laws of the universe, that "Tolstoy blames everything on our ignorance of empirical causes." It is precisely therefore that Berlin's portrait of Tolstoy, the picture of a furious agrarian romantic, who distrusted and disliked all pragmatic and scientific knowledge, is unsatisfactory. When Tolstoy wrote that history is "one of the most backward of sciences," he obviously regretted this condition. It may well be that Tolstoy's obsession with Science was a schizophrenic obsession—but an obsession, while schizophrenic, is no less an obsession for that. And it is therefore, too, that we should not swallow uncritically Berlin's dictum that "there is a hard cutting edge of common sense about everything that Tolstoy wrote."

The bifurcation of the Berlin track assigned to the Tolstoy locomotive should appear from the following passage: "Tolstoy's notion of inexorable laws which work themselves out whatever man may think or wish is itself an oppressive myth," which is very true; but then Berlin concludes that "what is this but a wholly unhistorical and dogmatic ethical scepticism? Why should we accept it when empirical evidence points elsewhere?" It seems that one part of Berlin's mind keeps arguing that Tolstoy "slipped back," that he was not *sufficiently* scientific. This poorly constructed argument is contradicted by Berlin himself later, when he declares that "Tolstoy believed that only by patient empirical observation could any knowledge be obtained." It is, to say the least, difficult to accept Berlin's assertion that Tolstoy's view is "scrupulously empirical, rational, tough-minded and realistic."

In Berlin's opinion Tolstoy was an enlightened novelist, and even a potentially scientific historian, but unfortunately he stubbornly insisted on being a religious person. However, the cleavage may be elsewhere. An examination of Tolstoy's thought may reveal something else: the fundamental difference which has separated the Russian Orthodox from the Western Christian habits of thought, all of their liturgical, and sometimes even theological, closeness notwithstanding. This difference is what Isaiah Berlin, who manifests little interest in and little sympathy for the Western Christian tradition, fails to comprehend.

Berlin's argument stands or falls with his interpretation of Joseph de Maistre. Berlin says, in essence, not only that Tolstoy read de Maistre with considerable interest (which is true), and not only that this authoritarian and reactionary and ultramontane French Catholic thinker and writer had a great influence on Tolstoy, but that Maistre and Tolstoy stood for the same things. Berlin proposes what he calls a "deep" parallel:

> The Savoyard Count and the Russian are both reacting, and reacting violently, against liberal optimism concerning human goodness, human reason, and the value or inevitability of material progress.

But here the Berlin track, assigned to the Tolstoyan locomotive, really runs awry. There is no such parallel. Tolstoy's and Maistre's anti-intellectualism are as different as possible. Where Tolstoy is outspokenly anti-intellectual, his anti-intellectualism reveals his genuine hatred for the Western European idea of Reason—the very Reason that Maistre, whose habits of thought were formed by the eighteenth century, admired and which he believed were perverted by the revolutionary rationalists and ideologues. Tolstoy, on the other hand, throughout his life admired Rousseau ("the best book ever written on education"), whose ideas Maistre despised. All through Tolstoy's writings, including his portrait of Kutuzov, there lurks a Russian mythical and populist attraction to the idea of The Noble Savage; de Maistre found the idea of noble savages utterly contemptible and ridiculous. The essence of Maistre's religion rested on his belief in free will. There is not a trace of the kind of attraction to science, to the concept of mechanist causality that is so evident in Tolstoy. Berlin correctly points out the influence of the Russian Slavophiles on Tolstoy. But Maistre's anti-revolutionary ideas, his archconservatism is very different from those of the Russian Slavophiles, and Berlin is entirely wrong when he says that the Slavophile movement was similar to what he calls the "anti-industrial romanticism of the West." The Slavophiles' intellectual pedigree had nothing to do with Maistre or with Coleridge or with Chateaubriand. Slavophile origins were sentimental rather than romantic, and Germanic rather than French, or anti-industrial: Müller, Kleist, Herder, Vogelsang. Maistre was no Puritan; whereas there is an element of truth in Chesterton's aphorism about Tolstoy having been an amalgam of an "inhuman Puritan and a presumptuous savage." Curiously enough, the Marquis de Vogüé, the French discoverer of the Russian novel and another French conservative, described Tolstoy as "chemist and Buddhist"; and Custine, yet another French conservative, known for his lucid and profound description of Russia in the 1840s, of the generation that succeeded Maistre's and preceded Vogüé's, suggested that what passes for conservatism and religion in the minds of the Slavophiles has precious little in common with conservative and Catholic ideas and practices in Europe. Maistre defended the institution of marriage, while he refused to rationalize about it, while Tolstoy's fantastic attack on womanhood in *The Kreutzer Sonata* was a rationalization pushed to extremes by his personal fury. Berlin himself writes that Tolstoy "blames everything on our ignorance of empirical causes, and Maistre on the abandonment of Thomist logic or the theology of the Catholic Church." Where is the similarity? Maistre welcomed the admission of the Jesuits to Russia; Tolstoy hated them. Maistre was a post-Enlightenment thinker, whereas Tolstoy predated the Russian Enlightenment: a profound historical difference. Berlin calls de Maistre "an apostle of darkness" and quotes Maistre: "*C'est l'opinion qui perd les batailles, et c'est l'opinion qui les gagne.*" But this is pure Pascal.

"If it is admitted that human life can be directed by reason, then the possibility of life is annihilated," wrote Tolstoy within the main text of *War and Peace.* This goes against the grain of the Western tradition, including most of its most conservative or reactionary spokesmen. And it is in this respect that Tolstoy is inexorably bound to certain strains of Russian and populist orthodoxy, as is Dostoyevsky: something that among their contemporaries perhaps only Turgenev and Chekhov seem to have escaped. As the agnostic and bitterly anti-Catholic Edmund Wilson wrote: "it is impossible not to feel that Turgenev, the atheist, was a good deal more successful at practicing the Christian virtues than either the holy man of Yasnaya Polyana or the creator of Alyosha Karamazov." As Sir David Kelly put it, this combination of "fraternal evangelism and the most violent hate-inspired intolerance was peculiarly evident in the case of Tolstoy. The great attraction of his novels lies precisely in his lack of the sense of causality, his lack of orderly composition; they are like a cinema, with no perspective, all the scenes of equal importance." Curiously the young Proust noted this cinematic quality of Tolstoy's writing, in *Contre Sainte-Beuve:* "*dans cette création qui semble inépuisable, il semble que Tolstoi pourtant se suit répété, n'ait eu a sa disposition que peu de thèmes, déguisés et renouvelés, mais les mêmes toujours."* "The business of science," wrote Tolstoy, "is not to discover what happens but to teach men how they ought to live." This is all very different from Maistre; but it is not very different from Henry Ford, with his celebrated dictum: "History is bunk." And there is much in Tolstoy that is Fordian. Even his religious conversion, his being "newly born" at the age of fifty-five, has a curiously fundamentalist tinge, recognizable to Americans; while his sudden and vocal repentance of his sins, his turning away from the world in Yasnaya Polyana, repeats, in some ways, the pattern of Ivan the Terrible, who shortly before his death declared that he had become the monk Jonah, or that of the Czar Alexander I, who disappeared into a monastery and may have died mysteriously there.

Berlin, too, recognizes some of this: he writes that when it comes to brotherly love, "a state which [Tolstoy] could have known but seldom, an ideal before the vision of which all his descriptive skill deserts him and usually yields something inartistic, wooden, and naïve; painfully touching, painfully unconvincing, and conspicuously remote from his own experience." At the end of his now famous essay, Berlin rises to poetic heights:

> Tolstoy's sense of reality was until the end too devastating to be compatible with any moral ideal which he was able to construct out of the fragments into which his intellect shivered the world, and he dedicated all of his vast strength of mind and will to the life-long denial of this fact. At once insanely proud and filled with self-hatred, omniscient and doubting everything, cold and violently passionate, contemptuous and self-abasing, tormented and detached, surrounded by an adoring family, by devoted followers, by the admiration of the entire civilized world, and yet almost wholly isolated, he is the most tragic of the great writers, a desperate old man, beyond human aid, wandering self-blinded at Colonus.

This is one image of the great writer, and not entirely devoid of elements of truth. It is surely preferable to that of J. B. Priestley, who wrote that Tolstoy worked like "a happy god, with a whole world to play with." There exists another picture of Tolstoy late in his life. It is a photograph preserved in the archives of Remington Typewriters, Incorporated. It is a picture of an old man in a cable-stitch sweater, dictating away to an admiring girl in a middy, in a room where the typewriting equipment was furnished as a gift to the great writer and prophet by the Remington people.

327

The photograph was taken, with Tolstoy's consent, for the purposes of advertising. Half Christ-actor, half muzhik, the image is that of a popular genius, half fundamentalist, half scientist, for whom history is bunk.

"The actions of men are subject to invariable general laws expressed by statistics."

> The key for the study of the laws of history of society should not be sought in the brains of men, nor in the opinions and ideas of society, but in the mode of production practiced by society . . . the prime task of historical science is the study and discovery . . . of the laws of development of the productive forces . . . of society.

The first quotation is from Tolstoy, the second from the official *History of the Communist (Bolshevik) Party of the USSR*.

There are many things in common between the admiration of science and the sort of fideism often found among Slavophiles and Russian Orthodox thinkers and writers. Apart from the fact that fatalism and scientism are both deterministic, listen to the voice of the so-called reactionary and anti-conservative Dostoyevsky, from *The Diary of a Writer*: "In science, too, we [Russians] shall become masters and not followers of Europe." And one of the factors which binds Slavophilism, even in its admittedly religious manifestations, to the Bolsheviks, is the missing element of historical consciousness that both have in common and which compromised *both* the vision and the art of Tolstoy.

Now it is precisely this indifference to history, this unwillingness to consider history, which has deeply vexed such Russian writers as Pasternak and Solzhenitsyn; and it is my contention that, in this sense, the works of Pasternak and Solzhenitsyn represent, out of great suffering, an awakening of the Russian consciousness of history which is both remarkable and perhaps a promising portent for the present and the future of that vast and unhappy country.

Dr. Zhivago is not a historical drama like *War and Peace*. It is a poetic epic written in prose; it has no pretense of being history; and yet Pasternak's reconstruction of what has happened in Russia (and in certain Russian minds) between 1917 and 1924 is more precise and truthful than Tolstoy's rendition of history between 1805 and 1812. It is remarkable that Pasternak, like Tolstoy, found it necessary to conclude his novel with a curious and unexpected appendix, with an appendix which is something very different from a didactic exposition of a mechanical philosophy of history. It is a chain of religious poems, reflecting much of the *Western* Christian tradition.

Pasternak (who respected Tolstoy, and whose father was Tolstoy's friend and portrait-painter) has certain critical things to observe about Tolstoy in *Dr. Zhivago.* "Tolstoy says that the more a man devotes himself to beauty the further he moves away from goodness. . . ." "And suddenly I understood everything. I understood why this stuff is so deadly, so insufferably false, even in *Faust.*" The entire philosophy of *Zhivago* is far more suffused with history, and with a certain kind of historical existentialism, than anything written in Russia beforehand: "Direct causes," Pasternak writes, "operate only within certain limits; beyond them they produce the opposite effect." And, like Solzhenitsyn, his description of some of the Russian peasantry and soldiery and proletarians is light-years removed from the illusion of the Noble Savage that some of the Slavophiles, including Tolstoy, held as an article of faith.

We know about Tolstoy's contempt for Shakespeare and his attack on Shakespeare's art, surely one of the oddest outbursts from the pen of a great author. Pasternak not only admired and loved Shakespeare but his immersion into Shakespeare's language may have profoundly affected his entire philosophy of life, as Victor S. Frank adjudged in the *Dublin Review* (October 1958):

> The change over from purely personal lyricism to an epic me-
> dium, from the concentration on oneself to an intimate com-
> munion with others, may have been partly due to the many years
> of hard work which Pasternak spent in translating Shakespeare's
> plays. . . . Now one cannot live in daily contact with Shakespeare
> over a period of several years without being affected by his atti-
> tude to human affairs, without recognizing the inherent limita-
> tions of lyrical poetry pure and simple. It is in any case an at-
> tractive thought that the conversion of a great Russian poet to a
> Christian attitude may have been due to Shakespeare's influ-
> ence. . . .

Whatever the artistic merits of Aleksandr Solzhenitsyn, one thing is indisputable about his achievement. He is an unusual prophet, a prophet about the past, not about the future. He is obsessed with history, not with utopia or with apocalypse. And his obsession with history is remarkably un-Russian and remarkably novel. For historical consciousness—as differ-ent from unthinking traditionalism—is not a deep-rooted inclination of the Russian mind. Many critics have compared Solzhenitsyn to Tolstoy, especially in view of the former's *August 1914.* They are quite wrong. *War and Peace is* a historical novel—and yet with all of the limitations of what was essentially a nineteenth-century genre. The story is in the foreground, whereas history serves as an—admittedly gigantic—background. Now what Solzhenitsyn is trying to do is the very opposite. For him—and I am not merely referring to *August 1914* or *The Gulag Archipelago*—history is the foreground not the background; it is the main subject, not the secondary one; it is the matter most worth describing. It is not only that Solzhenitsyn's philosophy of history is the very opposite of Tolstoy's, who was an obsessed nineteenth-century determinist, whereas Solzhenitsyn is a believer and apostle of free will (as is *Zhivago*). It is also that Solzhenitsyn has been struggling with the problem of a new prose genre which is essentially historical. And this represents a tremendous step forward, an advance of Russian historical consciousness which is ahead not only of Tolstoy but also of such modern and partially Westernized minor Russian geniuses as Biely or Nabokov.

Even more than Tolstoy, Solzhenitsyn is a witness; and a witness with a desperate will to break through history. It was Mencken who said that the historian was a frustrated novelist. Tolstoy's example suggests the reverse, too: that the novelist may be a frustrated historian. In any event, what Solzhenitsyn may have recognized is that it is more difficult to write a great history than a great novel. The tremendous meaning inherent in his obsession with history may be obscured by some of the political as well as prophetic pronouncements by the public Solzhenitsyn. Yet it is inevitably connected to the condition that, all of the Slavophile excrescences of his thought notwithstanding, the historical consciousness of Solzhenitsyn represents—and not only because of his subject, which is the contemporary history of Russia—the living present, whereas both the form and the subject of Tolstoy's historical genre is part of a now receding and increasingly antiquated past, as must be also the philosophy of Berlin's *Hedgehog and the Fox*.

35

Hannah Arendt

(1990)

Hannah Arendt's *Origins of Totalitarianism* was published by Harcourt, Brace in 1951. It is composed of three parts, of which the first is a disquisition about anti-Semitism, the second about imperialism, and the third about totalitarianism. Evidently to its author's mind, these three "isms" are not only connected but inseparable from each other. The thesis (or rather, theses) of the book may be summed up as follows: Anti-Semitism is an inevitable ingredient of totalitarianism. "Race-thinking" (her term) is an inevitable ingredient of imperialism. Anti-Semitism and imperialism lead to totalitarianism in the age of the masses. Totalitarianism, which is dependent on mob rule ("a mixture of gullibility and cynicism had been an outstanding characteristic of mob mentality before it became an everyday phenomenon of the masses"), is bound to become more and more total as time goes on. ("The struggle for total domination of the total population of the earth, the elimination of every competing nontotalitarian reality, is inherent in the totalitarian regimes themselves. . . .")

The Origins of Totalitarianism is a long, difficult to read book of nearly 500 pages and nearly 300,000 words. Most of its materials, footnotes, and references are culled from German and other Central European sources with which American intellectuals are unacquainted. It contains very few references to the United States. These are not particularly perceptive ("America, the classical land of equality of condition and of general education with all its shortcomings, knows less of the modern psychology of masses than perhaps any other country in the world"). Yet the book received a very respectful recognition by the New York intelligentsia. A plausible reason for this was the book's timing. It was published at a time when— finally and much belatedly—most of that intelligentsia abandoned its illusions about the Soviet Union, and when evidences of Stalin's anti-Semitism

From *New Oxford Review*, April: 18–22.

had become publicized. In the last portion of her book Arendt equated Stalin with Hitler. This evoked expressions of approval, and perhaps also a psychological sense of relief, among that considerable number of American intellectuals who were ex-Stalinists or Trotskyists or Left-liberals, many of whom thereafter became the first cohorts of neoconservatism.

I read *Origins* at the time of its publication, and found it to be an extremely flawed book. I found many factual mistakes throughout its long and dense pages, and found much of Arendt's referential material, stuffed in long footnotes, to be selective, often presumptuous, and sometimes even ridiculous. This was material with which I, a European-born historian, was more familiar than were many American intellectuals. But at this point I must also refer to a personal element which, in this case, cannot be avoided. Besides the condition that I was a historian, whereas Hannah Arendt, an ideologue and political theorist, was not, there was another important element in my reaction to *Origins.* I had lived in Hungary, in the middle of Europe, during and immediately after the war, where I had experienced both pro-Nazi and pro-Communist tyranny during my most impressionable years. Very little of Arendt's speculations about totalitarian rule accorded with what I had seen and experienced. I write "speculations" because—as I learned later—she, unlike many other refugees in the U.S., had not really experienced totalitarian rule herself. She had left Germany but a few weeks after Hitler's assumption of the chancellorship and before his assumption of full power. She had never lived under communism of any kind. Her only experiences of internment consisted of a few weeks in a French camp in 1940. I am not a categorical believer in the eyewitness theory: An eyewitness is not necessarily right, and a distant observer of certain events is not necessarily wrong. Yet I thought in 1951 that Arendt's exposition of the origins and nature of totalitarianism was abstract and, despite (or perhaps because of) the dense mass of its material, insubstantial.

I also thought that events would soon disprove the validity of her thesis, which is indeed what happened. In *Origins* she had pronounced that it was in the nature of a totalitarian state to become ever more totalitarian. Yet less than two years later Stalin died, and Khrushchev not only relaxed many of his predecessor's police measures but proceeded to a long condemnation of Stalin's tyranny before a Communist party congress. She had declared that totalitarianism had the inevitable ingredient of "mob" (her favorite word) rule, and that therefore a revolution under totalitarian rule was both inconceivable and impossible. Yet less than five years after the publication of *Origins* came the Polish and Hungarian anti-totalitarian revolutions of 1956, with the active participation of the "mob." She had explained that "the struggle for total domination of the total population of the earth" was an inherent necessity of every totalitarian regime. Yet there is not one shred of evidence that Stalin, or even Hitler, had such a global plan. Stalin wanted to ensure domination of Eastern Europe and eastern Germany by all means possible, including brutal ones. Hitler wanted to make Germany the principal Eurasian power through his domination of Europe and Russia. Arendt had insisted that anti-Semitism and "race-thinking" are basic components of totalitarian rule. This is total nonsense. Mao Tse-Tung or Pol Pot, Ulbricht or Castro: Were (or are) they anti-Semites?

It is, as someone once wrote, a profound mistake to believe that Robespierre had slept with the *Contrat Social* under his pillow—even though there have been books whose political influence is indisputable. *Common Sense* had an impact in 1776, which even Washington acknowledged, though he soon came to the conclusion (rightly) that Tom Paine was an irresponsible radical and a fool. Referring to *Uncle Tom's Cabin,* Lincoln said to Harriet Beecher Stowe that here was the little woman who caused this great war (he was only half-serious, of course); Theodore Roosevelt *was* influenced by the naval history of Alfred C. Mahan. There is, of course, no reason to think that John Foster Dulles slept with Hannah Arendt's book under *his* pillow, or that any one of the American secretaries of state or presidents during the last thirty-nine years has ever opened *The Origins of Totalitarianism*. Yet that book has had an enduring influence on American intellectuals and academics for nearly forty years now—a condition which is even more lamentable than it is amazing.

Ten years after the publication of *Origins*—and well after most of her theses had proved to be nonsense—Alfred Kazin listed it among the Outstanding Books of the previous thirty years, in the Winter 1961 number of the reputable *American Scholar.* "Her thinking," Kazin declared, "has a moral grandeur suitable to the terror of her subject." In Norman Podhoretz's intellectual confessions, *Making It* (1967), he wrote of his "first invitation (at last!) to Hannah Arendt's annual New Year's Eve party." (The exclamation mark is interesting.) By that time, Podhoretz wrote, the newly found "hard anti-Communism" of New York intelligentsia

> rested on two major assumptions: (1) the Soviet Union was a totalitarian state of the same unqualifiedly evil character as Nazi Germany, and as such could not be expected to change except for the worse (this idea was given its most powerful theoretical support by Hannah Arendt in *The Origins of Totalitarianism*). . . . (2) the Soviet Union was incorrigibly committed to the cause of world revolution, to be furthered by military means when nec-

essary, and when possible by a strategy of internal subversion
directed from Moscow; only American power stood in the way
of this fanatical ambition to destroy freedom all over the world.
. . .

As late as 1985 Richard H. Pells wrote in *The Liberal Mind in a Conservative Age:* "I regard Hannah Arendt's *The Origins of Totalitarianism*" as one of
the few books "superior in quality to any comparable collection of works
produced in America during other periods of the twentieth century. Consequently, those of us who came afterward remain in [her] debt. . . ." And:

> Above all, Hannah Arendt, the Jewish refugee from Nazi Ger-
> many who spoke with greater authority than anyone else be-
> cause she knew more intimately [?] than anyone else exactly
> what there was to fear . . . by the late 1940s . . . was emerging as a
> towering figure among American writers because her preoccu-
> pations were increasingly theirs. . . . In most of the ways that
> count, Arendt's work remains the political masterpiece of the
> postwar era.

During the thirty-nine years after its publication, *Origins* was reprinted
several times. (Some of these editions carry new prefaces by Arendt, in
which she appears to revise some of the tenets of the original book; but
these explanations are as shortsighted as is most of the stuff in the original.)
It is still required reading in many courses in leading American universities and colleges. It is remarkable, too, how the unquestioned respect accorded its author has spread from the New York intelligentsia to liberals
and conservatives of almost all stripes.

Having read *The Origins of Totalitarianism* for the second time, I was
stunned to find that this book is even worse than when I had read it the first
time. I must now draw attention to certain essential faults of the book that
I had not known before and that I must state publicly now.

The Latin proverb *habent sua fata libelli* has a meaning that includes not
only the fate of a book after its publication but also the history of its making. And it is there that I found damning evidence not about the false and
outdated theses of *Origins* but, I am sorry to say, about the intellectual dishonesty of its making. Some of this evidence is, perhaps unwittingly, revealed by the admiring scholarly biography of Arendt by Elisabeth Young-
Bruehl; more of it is implicit within the text of *Origins* itself.

The greatest impact of *Origins* was due to its last part, where Arendt's
equation of Stalinist communism with Hitlerite Nazism made such a pro-

found impression on the American intelligentsia. This is curious enough when we consider that three-fourths of the book deals with Nazism. But what concerns me now is not how those intellectuals read the book but the making of the book itself. And about that there is plenty of evidence that Arendt's anti-Stalinist chapter was nothing—and I mean nothing—but a well-calculated afterthought.

From the Young-Bruehl biography it appears that Arendt had written almost all of her book in 1945 and early 1946—when Soviet Russia was still the principal ally of the U.S., and when among American intellectuals (except for a few fanatic Trotskyists) anti-Sovietism was unthinkable and unspeakable. At that time there was *no* reference to Soviet communism in her manuscript. But in 1947 the Cold War had begun. Her biographer tells us that "by the fall of 1947 she had changed her plan again." And: "The last part of *The Origins of Totalitarianism,* which expressed the conviction that the Nazi regime and Stalin's regime were essentially the same form of government, was written in 1948 and the spring of 1949"—that is, at the time of the Communist coup in Czechoslovakia, the Berlin Blockade, the Marshall Plan, and the formation of NATO, when the Cold War was in full swing.

A writer, like every human being, has the right and the reason to change his or her mind because of accumulated evidence. But the damning implications of Arendt's intellectual opportunism do not reside merely in the chronological coincidence of her intellectual adjustments (adjustments that, I must add, I find throughout the career of this writer revered for her intellectual integrity). They are there within the materials of those chapters. Whereas the previous three-fourths of her book are crammed with footnote references from a promiscuous variety of sources, the entire scholarly apparatus of the anti-Soviet part rests on multiple quotes from only two books, the memoirs of the then recent Soviet defector Kravchenko and the anti-Stalinist book of Boris Souvarine (published in Paris in 1935). Add to this the evidence of Arendt's careful adjustment of her ideology, not only to the then prevailing anticommunist thunder of American politics but to the currents among the New York intellectuals, aware as she must have been that most of them had been, or still were, Trotskyists. Consequently, in *Origins* Arendt praises Lenin and Trotsky, who, according to her, were not totalitarians—a very questionable thesis to which she in her later books would *not* return. "At the moment of Lenin's death the roads were still open." "Stalin won against Trotsky, who ... had a far greater mass appeal [in anti-Semitic Russia?]. ... Not Stalin, but Trotsky was the greatest organizational talent, the ablest bureaucrat of the Russian Revolution." "Stalin changed the Russian one-party dictatorship into a totalitarian regime." Etc.

"It seems clear that in . . . purely practical political matters Lenin followed his great instincts for statesmanship rather than his Marxist convictions." It seems clear that the very opposite is true, for this statement is applicable to Stalin, not Lenin.

And here I come to what, to me, is very telling evidence of the essential falseness of Arendt's writing. That falseness is unrelated to the shortcomings of her thick, inadequate, unwieldy Weimar-New York-intellectual prose. It is there within some of her—at first sight, strong and outspoken—statements that seem to be most revealing, *until* one suddenly realizes that they are not only historically wrong but completely *reversible.* If one reverses some of her statements—that is, if one reciprocally interchanges their subjects—their meaning (or rather, absence of meaning) remains exactly the same. Here are three examples:

(1) "The insane mass manufacture of corpses is preceded by the historically and politically intelligible preparation of living corpses." Now try: The historically and politically intelligible preparation of living corpses is preceded by the insane mass manufacture of corpses.

(2) In the camps "the basic experiences and the basic sufferings of our time take place in an atmosphere where innocence is beyond virtue and guilt is beyond crime." Or: where virtue is beyond innocence and crime is beyond guilt.

(3) "Tribal nationalism grew out of this atmosphere of rootlessness." Try: Rootlessness grew out of this atmosphere of tribal nationalism.

Both versions of each of these reversible statements are false.

One last observation: Few people know that *The Origins of Totalitarianism,* which she wrote in New York in her forties, was Arendt's *first* book (save for her 1929 German dissertation). The odd thing is that this dreadful book of hers is still a little more readable than her *On Revolution.* I read *On Revolution* in 1963, which was a memorable event in my intellectual life. I was confronted by an unreadable book. "Unreadable" is a metaphor, usually meaning something that is difficult to read. But large chunks of that book were not only difficult, they were virtually impossible to read. (Imagine a kind of dish, say, porridge, which is undercooked to a degree where it is not merely distasteful or indigestible but literally unswallowable because of the size of its lumps.) Having worked my way through *On Revolution* I came to the conclusion that *no one* had read this book through: not its editors, not its reviewers, not the scholars, many of whom subsequently found it propitious to include its title in their bibliographies, surely because of the intellectual reputation of its author. An eminent reviewer who had published a mildly favorable and respectful review of it in the daily *New York Times* admitted this to me: He couldn't *and* didn't read most of the book, he wrote. I still have his letter.

A quarter-century later the continued respect paid to *The Origins of Totalitarianism* is but another symptom of the cultural degeneration during which the frenzied agitation on the surface of intellectual commerce merely obscures a deadening stagnation in the movement of ideas. The recent events in the Soviet Union and Eastern Europe, meaning the abandonment not only of the theory but of many of the practices of communism, are only the most recent illustrations of the falsity of what Hannah Arendt composed some forty years ago. But then, most of this should have been evident at the very time of the publication of *The Origins of Totalitarianism*.

But the main purpose of this article is not the denigration of Arendt, no matter how much blackening her reputation deserves. My purpose has been to draw attention yet again to the self-willed—and therefore deep-seated—arteriosclerosis of American intellectual life.

36

Tom Wolfe

(1988)

$\mathbb{T}$om Wolfe's novel is a historical event. This statement requires explanation. A historical event is not necessarily an important event,
meaning something with an ascertainably lasting impact. There are historical events that are significant rather than important (like a small crack
on a large smooth surface). Tom Wolfe's novel may not be important; but it
is—more precisely: its writing, publication, and reception are—significant.
My purpose in this article is to draw attention to those significances on
four levels: the author's style of writing, his errors, his ideology, and, finally, his book's reception.

The Bonfire of the Vanities is 659 big pages long. Its plot describes the
pride, followed by the fall, of a young Old-American-Rich stockbroker,
undone by vicious and dishonest practices of criminal law and publicity in
New York in the 1980s. We cannot but be sympathetic to the protagonist,
who does not deserve the consequences of his comeuppance. These consequences are, in part, the accidental confections of a despicable English journalist (in the middle of the story), and, from the beginning to the end, the
result of the demagoguery of blacks and manipulation by Jews, who, in
Wolfe's view, run most of New York in the 1980s.

Tom Wolfe is a conservative nationalist and a stylistic modernist. There
is nothing wrong or even inconsistent in being a conservative nationalist
and an innovator, not even in being an innovator of style. There are ample
causes in this increasingly absurd world of ours for anti-progressive black
humor. Think of Pound or Céline. But a closer examination of Wolfe's style
will reveal an inconsistency—or, rather, the superficial quality of its seemingly radical modernity. Wolfe's device is that of the staccato sentence (*staccato* = broken), in this book punctuated by 2,343 exclamation points. Céline

Review of Tom Wolfe, *Bonfire of the Vanities* (1987). From *New Oxford Review*, September:
6–12.

wrote in much the same style; but while he could sustain it, Wolfe cannot. This is evident from the fact that in the most serious pages of Wolfe's "New" novel his "New Style" is entirely absent. There the author is still very voluble, but the staccato rhythm of his frantic-frenetic prose slows down. Exclamation points disappear. Of course every writer is free to change his style in mid-stream. But here one senses that not only the vitality but the very essence of Wolfe's imagination is wanting. The evidence of this is how in these more thoughtful portions of his book he falls back on repetition. "A sad, sad torpor set in." Five lines later: "It was all so sad and heavy, heavy, heavy." This kind of repetition would be, I think, red-penciled in any decent Freshman English Composition class.

Wolfe seems to need the staccato to cloak the feeble vitality of his imagination. The staccato, with its cascade of exclamation points, suggests vitality and energy: it is a stylistic device, geared to the fragmented attention span of the modern reader, whose eyes are used to the rapid flickering of images on screens, and also to the purpose of representing the quick, frantic, and fear-ridden reactions of modern people. We may or may not like a stylistic device, but if it is a representation of reality we must accept it as such. In Wolfe's writing, however, the stylistic device is specious, because it does not represent something telling and particular. It is applied randomly and interchangeably throughout Wolfe's prose.

Repetition, too, may be a stylistic device for emphasis. Yet the undue repetition of a word or phrase or a figure of speech indicates not only the poverty of a writer's vocabulary but also of his imagination. Wolfe describes the first fornication of his two protagonists: "King Priapus . . . now rose from the dead"; but this particular reference to this particular monarch recurs a few lines later, and again and again. Maria Ruskin has "loamy loins," and "loamy loins" return again and again and again. Again and again, too, Tom Wolfe, the self-proclaimed Anti-Trend Crusader, slips into trendy prose. He seems to like, for instance, the current but fairly senseless computer language word "mode": "The club facilities . . . were maintained, devoutly, in the Brahmin Ascetic or Boarding School scrubbed mode. . . ."

Wolfe's few negative critics have noted his obsessive habit of describing (and constantly returning to) the labels and prices of the suits and shoes of his characters. They attribute a kind of unnecessary superficiality to that Wolfe habit of writing. That habit is not only superficial, but absurd. Superficiality is not necessarily unreal, while absurdity is. Example: the protagonist's rage at a young Argentinian stockbroker in his office escalates because the Argie's trousers are held up by *red moiré* braces. Whereas Rawlie Thorpe, one of Wolfe's really good guys, "was a great wearer of button down shirts and Shep Miller suspenders." (What, pray tell, is a "great wearer"?)

In addition to clothes and shoes, one must describe other things about one's protagonist, including his physiognomy. There is, oddly, not much about that in the nearly seven hundred pages, despite Wolfe's obsession with physicality and its appearances. But there is one item, one phrase about Sherman McCoy, that recurs again and again, perhaps more than fifty times throughout the book. This is McCoy's *chin*. It is a strong chin (the obverse of that of Jews whose "wavy red beard . . . hide[s] a receding chin"). It is an "aristocratic chin." Wolfe employs that imprecise and silly phrase again and again. McCoy's father has an "aristocratic chin"; his son has a "budding aristocratic chin." But what is the main mark of that chin, according to Wolfe? It is the "Yale chin." That tag recurs over and over again, at least thirty times throughout the book. There is something wrong here. A person's bone structure may be the result of a particular heredity ("the party was given by someone of good blood and good bone"). But surely (unless that chin is the outcome of plastic surgery performed in the Yale University hospital) there is no such thing as a Yale chin. There may be such a thing as a Yale windbreaker or an Oxford accent or a Harvard book-bag or a Cambridge gait, but a Yale chin? There are further investments of this meaning (e.g., "his Yale Chin charm"). Elsewhere McCoy speaks "from the eminence of his chin." On yet another occasion, McCoy "lifted his Yale chin against the tide." Even a garage attendant is invested with Wolfe's mental mania (allow me this double entendre, "mentum" in Latin meaning "chin"): "You think I am your inferior, you Wall Street Wasp with the Yale chin, but I will show you." Oddly, Wolfe is here attempting to describe what a parking attendant thinks; yet the terms of thought are Wolfe's. (It is as if a chitty girl writing for *Vogue* were to describe a bag lady's thoughts: "You think I am your inferior, you woman in the Chanel suit and the Hermès scarf, but I will show you.") Wolfe does this sort of thing more than once.

Many years ago, in the beginning of his public career, Tom Wolfe declared that he was a new kind of journalist. Later, in 1973, he wrote that he had "grand ideas" about the New Journalism, that it would lead to a new kind of precise reportage that would replace the novel, that the techniques of the New Journalism would bring the writer "closer to the absolute in-volvement of the reader that Henry James and James Joyce dreamed of and never achieved." I think Wolfe was quite wrong about the dreams of James and Joyce, but that is not the point. The point is that Wolfe has repeatedly declared that the novel is either dying or dead, and that the task of a good and thoughtful writer now is to observe and record people and scenes with a new kind of journalistic precision, instead of inventing characters and plots. Well, this has been what such very different writers in New York as Norman Mailer and Truman Capote have tried to do (let me add, not very successfully). The writer as walking sociologist, as cultural anthropologist, as amateur psychologist—that is hardly different from what Balzac or Trollope or James did. There remains, however, one crucial desideratum. The writer must know what (and whom) he is writing about. Some time ago Wolfe announced that, yes, he was going to write a novel, *the* New York novel of our times. In one way—contrary to his earlier view against the need of inventing plots—he succeeded, because his plot is interesting; we are rooting for his hero till the end, which is why the book is a "good read" (an unattractive term, but let that go). But for a book with its aim (or rather, pretension) of giving us a social panorama, the plot alone will not suffice. Now, Wolfe suggests that he is a precise and detailed observer of certain people—of their behavior and speech and minds. But his detailed description of his protagonist is not only wanting because it is shallow (the chin syndrome; the repetitions of "aristocratic," etc.). It is especially wanting because of Wolfe's many errors in those very details about which, as he (and his critics) tells us, he is so accurate and knowledgeable.

The Bonfire of the Vanities pullulates with errors of fact—of facts upon which Wolfe's entire "panoramic knowledge" is supposed to rest. Here are some examples: Wolfe describes the palatial apartment houses on upper Park Avenue, where there are "German-Jewish financiers who have finally made it into the same buildings." "Finally" is all wrong; the New York German-Jewish upper class began to move into those Park Avenue buildings fifty or sixty years ago. (It was the rising descendants of Russian Jews who followed some of them a generation later.) On page 332 (in that "good bone and good blood" paragraph) Wolfe equates Park Avenue in New York with Beacon Hill in Boston and Rittenhouse Square in Philadelphia. But very few, if any, Philadelphia patricians have ever lived in an apartment house on Rittenhouse Square; and the fine townhouses in Rittenhouse Square were almost gone more than a quarter-century ago, the last proprietor of the last of them having died in 1986.

A Wasp lawyer says to McCoy: "The criminal lawyers aren't exactly the *bout en train*." That made me sit up and wonder, and I went to my large French dictionary which lists more than twenty usages of *bout*, but among them *bout en train* is not. Wolfe has a man saying that 1934 was "the greatest year there ever was for Armagnac"; but Armagnacs, like cognacs, are rated by their respective ages, not by their vintages. (The man also says he paid $1,200 for the bottle: but a fifty-year-old Armagnac can be bought for $120 in France, and at most for $180 in New York.) Wolfe makes reference to "an eighty-thousand dollar Duncan Phyfe piano"; there is no such thing. The McCoys' sumptuous apartment in New York: "It was the sort of [Wasp] apartment the mere thought of which ignited flames of greed and covetousness under people all over New York and, for that matter, all over the world." This is farfetched. Wolfe's notion that the men and women of the Wasp upper class in New York don't vote in local elections because then they cannot vote Republican is wrong, too. Sometimes he even can't get the spelling right: upper-class Wasp mothers and their children say "Mummy," *not* "Mommy."

Yes, this is nitpicking: and in a discussion of some other book by some other author such stickling would be unnecessary, and perhaps unwarranted. But in Wolfe's case we must keep in mind how, according to him and to just about every one of his reviewers, the accurate rendering of such details *is* his unique achievement, his forte.

And now to a more serious matter. Wolfe is a white Anglo-Saxon Protestant. Yet, after having lived in New York for thirty years and evidently being acquainted with some of the rich people there, Wolfe seems not to understand the kind of Wasp he picked as his protagonist. Here is a typical sentence (as Sherman McCoy walks his little daughter to the school bus): "As they crossed Park Avenue, he had a mental picture of what an ideal pair they made . . . himself, with his noble head, his Yale chin, his big frame, and his $1,800 British suit . . . he visualized the admiring stares, the envious stares, of the drivers, the pedestrians, of one and all." Is this how a "better-class" (or old-family) Wasp thinks? There is, God knows, plenty that is wrong with the way McCoy types think (or do not think). But this unceasing mental obsession with their exterior impact is not all that typical of them. To the contrary: a certain self-effacement, the avoidance of show, is a must of old-Wasp manners—sometimes to the extent of their unwillingness to think. I know of at least two Eastern American prep schools whose motto is the ancient Latin *Esse quam videri*, "to be more than to seem." That they, and their alumni, do not always live up to the motto is beside the point. The point is that, in Wolfe's mind, *everything* depends on how people seem. This appears, among other things, when Sherman McCoy is made to philosophize: "Your *self* . . . is *other* people, all the people you're tied to, and it's only a thread." So this is the Wolfe motto: *Videri quam esse*: to seem, to seem, to seem.

These, then, are examples from the work of a man who insists on the accuracy of his observations. That insistence is represented by yet another—unattractive—stylistic device. There are hundreds of instances where Wolfe chooses to mimic the accents of certain people—especially Jewish accents, sometimes picking out not a phrase but the pronunciation of a single word (e.g., "kehpehsity" for "capacity"). We know that the shifting of prose to dialect seldom works well, because it slows down reading: the eye must stop as one attempts to re-mouth the words, trying to echo them in one's ears. But in this instance it is not only Wolfe's stylistic device that is troubling. It is more disturbing to contemplate his apparent purpose in presenting these vulgar and ugly mispronunciations of American English.

Anyone who is seriously exercised by the behavior of certain races or classes—in Wolfe's case by his evident view of the savagery of blacks and the arrogance of Jews in New York—has the right to express his concerns by writing about such matters: at considerable risk, of course, to his reception and reputation. But the seriousness of Wolfe's concerns is compromised not only by the relentless effort at funniness in his writing; it is corrupted by his apparent malice. And yet it would be a mistake to label *The Bonfire of the Vanities* a racist novel. Wolfe's view of the world is not so much racial or social as it is ideological. *The Bonfire of the Vanities* is an ideological novel. This, despite its author's assertions, makes it entirely different from (and stylistically inferior to) novels of society like, say, Balzac's portraiture of Paris or Thackeray's of London; but it is different, too, from political novels such as, say, Solzhenitsyn's, where that writer's somber condemnation of a tyrannical regime is meant to underline the main story, which consists of the conditions of human life and thought in a prison. In Tom Wolfe's portrait of New York in the 1980s the reverse is true. The main story is an illustration of this author's coherent ideology.

Coherent: but not consistent. Tom Wolfe sets himself up as an Old American and a Defender of Old Values. That would amount to a philosophy: but his inconsistency and his shallowness reveal that his philosophy (as also Ronald Reagan's) does not amount to more than an ideology. The ideology of Tom Wolfe is his American nationalism. A distinction is in order here, the distinction which separates the flag-waving radical from the true conservative, the nationalist from the patriot, and which separates Wolfe from most other American writers of Southern origin. He comes from Virginia, but there is nothing identifiably Virginian or Southern in his ideology or his style. He has been living in New York for many years now.

In his many articles and books he has exposed the fraudulent hypocrisies and pretenses of radical chic, of leftist slogans and ideas, of fads in clothing and behavior, and of "modern" art together with the thoughtless acceptance and corrupt commercialization of it. Conversely, in *The Right Stuff* he extolled the courage and manliness of American fighter pilots. In *The Bonfire of the Vanities* he laments—sort of—the decline in influence of an old American class to which he suggests that he, too, belongs. Yet there is something wanting in his defense of old values (as happens, too, with many of our "conservatives" nowadays).

In all of Wolfe's writing there is not the slightest trace of any interest in or respect for religion, with all his anti-trendiness and antimodernism he shows no interest in any tradition. His heroes in his only "positive" book, *The Right Stuff,* are not merely fighter pilots but sexual athletes whose successful adulteries and carnal conquests he approves; in *The Bonfire of the Vanities,* too, he has no respect for—indeed, he is sarcastically contemptuous of—marital fidelity. He satirizes certain immoralities: but his standards and values are wholly amoral.

Wolfe's Americanist xenophobia appears throughout *The Bonfire of the Vanities,* too, where, next to blacks and Jews, the third despicable category is Europeans. When McCoy is looking for a criminal lawyer and hears the name of the firm Dershkin, Bellavita, Fischbein and Schlosse, "the torrent of syllables was like a bad smell." He is derisive and contemptuous of McCoy's wife, describing her in very different terms from his mistress (the one with the "loamy loins"), who wears a blouse and shoes whose "price alone would have paid for the clothes on the backs of any twenty women on the floor." Wolfe briefly describes Mrs. McCoy's family. Her father was a professor in Wisconsin "in his rotting tweeds, whose one claim to fame was a rather mealy-mouthed attack . . . on his fellow Wisconsinite, Senator Joseph McCarthy . . . in 1955." Wolfe the ideologue is showing through.

Several years ago in writing about the American ideological *stasis,* I noted that liberals had become senile, while conservatives were immature. (In normal times the reverse would be true.) There is an unappealing juvenility throughout Tom Wolfe's work: in his writing style, his ideology, his obsession with externals, and his inability to distinguish character from appearance, and manners from fashions. At the end of *The Bonfire of the Vanities* Wolfe's brutal immaturity comes to a peak at the dénouement, when the erstwhile hesitant and confused McCoy, trapped in the execrably corrupt labyrinth of the criminal justice system in New York, on his way out of the courtroom, suddenly strikes out and knocks down a screaming black. "Into the Solar Plexus" is the title of Wolfe's last chapter, the climax of Wolfe's novel, and the epitome of Wolfe's standard of justice and norm for the proper behavior of a virile American male. The Marines Have Landed. Or (in the terminology of *Star Wars,* beloved and repeated by Ronald Reagan): The Force Is with Us.

So this is supposed to be a great book about New York, the latest in a long tradition of, say, Edith Wharton and Henry James. The jacket of *The Bonfire of the Vanities* reads: "It is a big, panoramic story of the metropolis— the kind of fiction strangely absent from our literature in the second half of this century—that reinforces Tom Wolfe's reputation as the foremost chronicler of the way we live in America." It is, of course, possible that a great novel about New York can no longer be written, because fact has become stranger than fiction.

That our conservatives—so called—would cheer Wolfe on was, alas, predictable. No matter what they assert about being defenders of tradition (and of religion; and of Western civilization), most of our conservatives— a motley crowd nowadays—are united only by their hate for their opponents. (This is no laughing matter since, as Chesterton once said, it is hate that unites people—or at least brings them together—not love, the latter being, by its very nature, individual.) I was not in the least surprised that Christopher Buckley praised *The Bonfire of the Vanities* to high heaven in the *Wall Street Journal*, though I was rather surprised that George Will wrote of the novel as "Victorian, even Dickensian . . . in its capacity to convey and provoke indignation"—which suggests that when it comes to literature mere Will will not do. That the *American Spectator* would exalt Wolfe as the greatest of American writers was expectable. So was the lead review in *National Review* by Richard Vigilante, called "The Truth about Tom Wolfe." Wolfe, wrote Vigilante (whose name may be telling), is "*saving American literature*." "No one has portrayed New York society this accurately and devastatingly since Edith Wharton. . . ." Vigilante's summation reads: "Wolfe is the most contagious force the good guys have. Things are looking up."

I think that for the Konservatives this is so. They, and Wolfe, will continue to command attention; they will continue filling the vacuum of American thought that the bankruptcy of American ideological liberalism has brought about. That collapse is an ugly sight, because it involves the collapse not merely of ideas, but of character, as the vacuum is being filled by the poisonous exhalations of opportunism and fear.

To New York the new Dark Ages have come, with the decline of urban civilization and the rise of all kinds of epidemics, physical and spiritual; with the collapsing standards of security, permanence, and discourse. A *new* Dark Ages: because this time the barbarians are not approaching the ramparts, they are inside the city. The conservative defenders of "order" are inside, too; but, in a sense, worse than the barbarians, because they ought to know better. There is a certain similarity to what befell Europe half a century ago. Nazism was, among other things, a reaction against communism; the Nazis fought against communism; they defended countries against communism. But the Nazis were not really defenders of old traditions and standards and religion. If the defense of the West against communism meant going along with Hitler, then there was not much hope for the West, and if the defense of Old America means going along with the Wolfe pack (or even with some of the Buckley crowd), then there is not much left of it that is now worth defending.

There is not a single black man or woman or child in this book who is not a loathsome criminal or a cheat or a fraud. (It would be interesting to read a review of *The Bonfire of the Vanities* written by a black; I have not seen one.) It is interesting that Wolfe's apparent malice seems to be directed at Jews even more than at blacks. While he has at least one black speak in polished English phrases and accents, not one Jew does. There is not one Jewish man or woman in this book who is not vulgar and ugly. This phenomenon of ugliness is of great importance here, because of Wolfe's extraordinary emphasis on physicality, on physical appearance. This is even true of Judge Kovitsky, who (at the very end of the novel) turns out to be the only one of dozens of Jewish characters who is not altogether loathsome; but vulgar and ugly Kovitsky is too (he first appears in a scene when he spits a yellow-oyster gob of slime at the grating of a police van of yelling prisoners). I find it at least possible that Wolfe brought in this single redeeming New York Jew—ugly and vulgar, but at least not despicable—because of his opportunism: but I will not attribute motives to a writer. Rather, I am concerned with acts, in this case acts of expression, acts of writing, which constitute evidence that may indicate something about intentions. I have very seldom read such injurious descriptions of Jews as those in Tom Wolfe's Big American Novel. And here I am comparing *The Bonfire of the Vanities* to the often vicious publications of the Nazis in Germany and of their sympathizers in other European countries, including the rabid anti-Jewish prose and rhetoric of *Der Stürmer,* directed by Julius Streicher—a man and a publication that even some of the leading Nazis in Hitler's court shunned, as Streicher himself was shunned by the other defendants at Nuremberg—and who was hanged from the gallows simply and squarely because of the record of his anti-Semitic publications. Whether a fanatical anti-Semitic writer or editor *is* a "war criminal" is a moot point, and whether Tom Wolfe is an anti-Semite is another one. That is not for me to decide, and I am inclined to think that, given the complicated nature of anti-Semitism, he may not even be one, certainly not in the Nazi sense. My point is simply this: a writer should be responsible for what and how he writes.

The striking thing, in Wolfe's case, is the favorable and respectful treatment his book has been receiving from much of the liberal press. When a book such as this one receives serious, extensive, and, I repeat, respectful attention from the chief liberal newspapers and journals in New York, there is something ominous going on. That *The Bonfire of the Vanities,* with its odious descriptions of New York Jews, should receive such a positive reception in New York (where the slightest suggestion of anti-Semitism will not only compromise a writer's reputation but may even affect the publishability of his works) is significant. There can be only two plausible explanations for this. One is opportunism; the other is fear. The opportunism, in this case, is yet another manifestation of Conservative Chic—the phenomenon which, for example, accounts for the now standard critical celebration of Bill Buckley's spy novels. There may be an element of irony in the circumstance that Tom Wolfe, who coined the phrase Radical Chic,[1] has become such an eminent and successful beneficiary of Conservative Chic twenty years later. That is: to dismiss Tom Wolfe means not to Be With It. That kind of literary or cultural opportunism is, of course, nothing new.

But there is, I believe, another—ideologically suffused—element involved here. Fear and opportunism are two inclinations that are often connected, since opportunism is often prompted by fear. In 1910 the great and lonely French Catholic poet and visionary, Charles Péguy, wrote in *Notre Patrie* about modern Paris: "It will never be known what acts of cowardice have been motivated by the fear of not looking sufficiently progressive." In "postmodern" New York it will never be known what acts of cowardice have been motivated by the fear of not looking sufficiently ... well, at least neoconservative.

In the daily *New York Times* Christopher Lehmann-Haupt, its standard reviewer and an erstwhile liberal, praised *The Bonfire of the Vanities* unstintingly. The lead review in the Sunday *New York Times Book Review* was very respectful; in the Christmas number, Wolfe's novel was one of the Editors' Choices, one of the eight "Best Books of the Year." But two "mixed reviews," in the *New Yorker* and in the *New York Review of Books,* are telling, too. In the first, Terence Rafferty, feeling compelled to balance a negative judgment with repeated noddings of respect, made this erroneous distinction: while Wolfe's insights may be superficial, "Wolfe's precision is impressive," each character "a perfectly matched composite." Rafferty went on: this novel is "composed entirely of meticulous observation and perfectly worked-out illustrations of theories of the relationships among classes. ... It has everything that intelligent research [and] precision tooling ... can give a narrative ... a sensational display of craftsmanship." What Rafferty *did* get right is that the novel's reception has been "so euphoric." The review in the *New York Review of Books* was short; the reviewer, a pale academic, argued mostly with George Will, saying that, no, Wolfe's novel is not really Dickensian. Even Levine's caricature on the same page was not really successful.

Yes, liberals (and some Jews) are afraid of Wolfe, who, whatever the power of his intellect, has enough good animal instinct to smell that fear. He knew he could get away with this book, and he did. His book's objects of attack are barbarism and vulgarity; what he—and, alas, so many other people—did not and do not know is how the publication and reception of this book represent a small but significant triumph of that same barbarism and vulgarity. It is not only that the barbarians and the vulgarians are here, within the gates. It is that their allegiance is coveted and their approval is sought. This is not only applicable, as Wolfe puts it, to black demagogues in Harlem. With regard to the respectful reviewers sweating cold, it is also applicable to Tom Wolfe and his cheering "conservative" partisans.

37

Whittaker Chambers

(1989)

About forty years ago, at the time of the Hiss Trial, Alistair Cooke wrote a book with the title *A Generation on Trial.* I have not read the book, whereby I cannot say anything about the validity of its contents, but even then I sensed that the title was very appropriate. Indeed, in 1948 I had an instinctive feeling that Alger Hiss was guilty. I felt this not because of my then so strong and impatient anticommunism; I thought that I recognized that Quaker inclination to the far Left; I thought I recognized his type. More important: Hiss was not an untypical example of a certain American bureaucrat who made his career in the Roosevelt administration and who was attracted by the idea of international communism—and, even more than by that idea, by the prospect of his being, or becoming, an important member of a future ruling elite. Later I found that the truest insight into such inclinations came not from historians or political scientists but from certain American writers. The inclination of certain liberal Protestants to the extreme Left was described by Santayana in *The Last Puritan,* and the ambitions of that bureaucratic would-be elite by Edmund Wilson in *I Thought of Daisy.*

Everything I read about Hiss since that trial, including his own memoirs and the (unwittingly) damaging revelations about his character by his son, confirm this view. To this I will add that—in some ways not unlike the "revolutionaries" of the 1960s—there was a fatal superficiality in the inclinations of this man. The former were, in reality, merely playing at revolution; Alger Hiss was, to me, playing at spying. When I read those State Department documents that Hiss gave to his blustering Soviet agent in 1938, I found that they contained information and secrets of minimal value. I am also inclined to think—but, of course, for this I have no evidence—that by 1945 Hiss, who had risen high in the government bureaucracy, may

From *New Oxford Review,* November: 5–8.

have ceased actively working for the Soviets, and that, had he not been caught, he may have gone on as a high and respected member of the American foreign policy establishment, perhaps returning to government service in the 1960s, shedding not only his earlier Communist connections but all of his old notions about communism and the Soviet Union. (He might even have become a neoconservative—who knows?)

I had, and still have, nothing but sympathy for Whittaker Chambers, who struck me as an unhappy and serious man, far more profound than Alger Hiss, and by this I do not only mean his conversion from communism. I read his *Witness* with respect. Unlike some of his critics, I did not and do not hold it against him that in this searing personal confession he did not mention the homosexual relationship that, among other things, had bound him to Hiss in the 1930s. But: one's sympathy for a tortured and decent man does not necessarily mean a trust in his view of the world.

As for Hiss, my irritation also arose because the revelation of his former Communist activities led to an extreme preoccupation with domestic communism, because it was the Hiss case that led to the rise of Richard Nixon, and because the Hiss phenomenon led to a political atmosphere in which ideological anticommunism became an even greater obstacle to the conduct of an intelligent foreign policy than the influence of procommunism in 1945 had been. In the case of Chambers I saw no dishonesty—but rather the, perhaps not easily avoidable or surpassable, inclination of a man to attribute most, if not all, of the evils and problems of the world to the wrong from which he had, after great inner troubles, escaped.

The influence of Hiss and others, Chambers wrote, promoted the triumph of Communism in China, and it

> decisively changed the history of Asia, of the United States, and therefore, of the world. If mankind is about to suffer one of its decisive transformations, if it is about to close its 2000-year-old experience of Christian civilization, and enter upon another wholly new and diametrically different, then that group may claim a part in history such as it is seldom given any men to play. . . .

Had Hiss, in 1948, succeeded in destroying Chambers (or rather, had Chambers not succeeded through their confrontation), "the fight against Communism would have suffered such a reverse that no second man would have dared for a long time to stand up against the secret Communist party whose entrenched power would have been more untouchable than before." So Chambers had to "help save what was left of human freedom, and specifically, that nation on which the fate of all else hinged." Writing this at the height of the McCarthy era, he would even write: "It is not the Communists, but the ex-Communists who have cooperated with the Government, who have chiefly suffered."

Toward the end of his book Chambers attacked American liberalism and, indirectly, the Roosevelt era:

> The simple fact is that when I took up my little sling and aimed at Communism, I also hit something else. What I hit was the forces of that great socialist revolution, which, in the name of liberalism, spasmodically, incompletely, somewhat formlessly, but always in the same direction, has been inching its ice cap over the nation for two decades. . . . And with that we come to the heart of the Hiss Case and all its strange manifestations. No one could have been more dismayed than I at what I had hit, for though I knew it existed, I still had no adequate idea of its extent, the depth of its penetration or the fierce vindictiveness of its revolutionary temper, which is a reflex of its struggle to keep and advance its political power.

And more:

> It was the forces of this revolution that had smothered the Hiss Case (and much else) for a decade, and fought to smother it in 1948. These were the forces that made the phenomenon of Alger Hiss possible; had made it possible for him to rise steadily in Government and to reach the highest post *after* he was already under suspicion as a Communist in many quarters. . . . Alger Hiss is only one name that stands for the whole Communist penetration of Government. He could not be exposed without raising the question of the real political temper and purposes of those who had protected and advanced him, and with whom he was so closely identified that they could not tell his breed from their own.

It is thus that Chambers's conspiratorial memories and experiences made him believe in a conspiratorial view of the world. There are, alas, many such passages in *Witness:* some of them, as some of those above, nonsense. They were nonsense then; they are, more evidently, nonsense now. I hope I need not detail this in 1989, when there are hardly any Communists left in the United States, when communism is failing throughout Europe (and also in many other parts of the world), when the very ideas and practices of Communist rule are crumbling within the Soviet Union itself, and when various Communist governments have become ridiculous imitators of the U.S., enamored as they are with fast-food outlets, Coca-Cola, credit cards, "people's capitalism," and much else besides. The road from the Hiss-Chambers case to a popular American president's advocacy of the idea of the Evil Empire and of Star Wars has been straight, though slow. And the fact that Ronald Reagan was forced to announce on Red Square that the Evil Empire was no longer evil in the very same week of 1988 when he and his friends succeeded in passing the bill that made Chambers's Maryland farm (where Chambers had hid those films in his pumpkins) a National Monument confirms that the movement of ideas in our so-called fast-paced and revolutionary times is not only slow but ludicrous. It also confirms how the equation of anticommunism with American patriotism—indeed, with Western civilization itself—has not only been senseless and wrong but how it could corrupt the minds of some of the best—in this case, of Whittaker Chambers. *Corruptio optimi pessima.*

38

Francis Fukuyama and Graham Fuller
(1992)

I had heard about, but not read, "The End of History?" Francis Fukuyama's starburst essay published in 1989; but I felt a twinge of sympathy for him as his critics chortled and pointed at history rumbling anew: people dancing atop the Berlin Wall, the Soviet Union falling to pieces, an American Army flying into Arabia. The end of history? I thought that perhaps that was not really what Fukuyama meant, that what he was espying was a new structure for history after the idea of democracy—of popular sovereignty—had been instituted everywhere in the world. But after reading Fukuyama's ideas in full elaboration, I regret to say that I was wrong; and I am appalled to find that Fukuyama is a fool. I do not use the epithet lightly. Fukuyama is "a former deputy director of the U.S. State Department's Policy Planning Staff." To paraphrase Henry Adams, the evolution of American foreign policy planning from George Kennan to Francis Fukuyama is sufficient evidence to disprove all the theories of Darwin.

Fukuyama thinks that liberal democracy has conquered the world. Totalitarianism is gone forever. Nationalism is something that he does not, or cannot, consider. The globe is becoming one vast international network. Freedom and the market economy (whatever *that* is) have become, or are about to become, nearly universal. He is concerned with a world bereft of useful and useless strife. Yet that, according to Fukuyama, may become a moral problem. History will not only become unintelligible, but will cease to exist. This may or may not be regrettable, but "The Worldwide Liberal Revolution"—the title of his central chapter—has seen that it will happen.

The world as seen by Fukuyama consists almost entirely of "Liberal Nations," with Bosnia or Georgia or Cambodia or Zambia awash with people

Review of Francis Fukuyama, *The End of History and the Last Man* (1992), and Graham Fuller, *The Democracy Trap: Pitfalls of the Post–Cold War World* (1991). From *Chronicles,* December: 39–40.

incarnating the ideas of John Locke, William Gladstone, Benjamin Constant, and Felix Frankfurter. But of course the very opposite is true. Intellectuals not only excel at not seeing forests for trees; they often cannot see a hog from a log. Liberalism is dying throughout the world, including in the United States, where its decay and the rise of the "conservative" movement began at the precise moment—1955—when another intellectual, the Harvard professor Louis Hartz, published his prizewinning book *The Liberal Tradition in America*, pronouncing the liberal tradition as the *only* political reality in America. Hartz, though an academic plodder, was by comparison with Fukuyama a sage.

Fukuyama's mind is philosophical, whence his troubles arise. Like his mentor Leo Strauss he knows (or thinks he knows) plenty of philosophy, while his ignorance of history is lamentable and abysmal. Among other things, Fukuyama is enamored of a Greek term favored by the Straussians: *thymos*, meaning (to him) the essence of the human condition. (Another of his key chapters bears this title: "The Rise and Fall of *Thymos*.") This word he stuffs promiscuously into his fruitcake, while coining other words such as "hypothymia" and "megalothymia," etc. According to my Greek dictionary *thymos* means thyme, a pleasant spice. Unfortunately Fukuyama's *thymos* has nothing to do with spices.

Owing to lack of space, but also because history (and human nature) do not follow the laws of physics—meaning that while it is easier to wrestle with a weak body than with a strong one, it is more difficult to wrestle with a weak mind than with a strong one—in this review I must let Fukuyama speak for himself. Fukuyama has given his chapters such titles as "The Weakness of Strong States II, or, Eating Pineapples on the Moon," and "The Victory of the VCR." In his introduction, he writes: "In lieu of conventional thanks to a typist for helping to prepare the manuscript, I should perhaps acknowledge the work of the designers of the Intel 80386 microprocessor." He should. It shows.

Early in his book Fukuyama says that what he meant by the end of history was not history, but History (his capitalization): "history understood as a single, coherent, evolutionary process, when taking into account the experience of all peoples in all times." *Whew*. Fukuyama says that he gets this concept of History from Hegel, but he later adds that his philosophy is really a compound of Hegel and of the latter's modern exegete, Kojève. Thereafter he refers sometimes to "Hegel-Kojève," which to me evokes something like "Häagen-Dazs." "Our deepest thinkers," he writes, "have concluded that there is no such thing as history—that is, a meaningful order to the broad sweep of human events." "Deepest thinkers" is good. "Virtually everyone professionally engaged in the study of politics and foreign policy believed in the permanence of communism; its worldwide collapse in the late 1980s was therefore almost totally unanticipated." Not by this reviewer, but that is not the point. The point is Fukuyama's uncontrollable affection for such words as *virtually* and *totally.* "For many Americans the family, now no longer extended or nuclear, is virtually the only form of associational life or community they know." Tell that to the Marines. (Or to the Mafia.) "People in the Soviet Union and PRC turned out not to be the atomized, dependent, authority-craving children that earlier Western theories projected them to be. They proved instead to be adults who could tell truth from falsehood, right from wrong, and who sought, like other adults in the old age of mankind [what was *that?*] recognition of their own adulthood and autonomy." (I saw one of these young Chinese adults in Tiananmen Square, beaming at an American television reporter, speaking into the camera: "I like American girls, American girls can see me now!")

To continue: "It is possible for a country to be liberal without being particularly democratic, as was eighteenth-century Britain." (The political term "liberal" did not then exist, but no matter.) "Not everyone can be a concert pianist or a center for the Lakers, nor do they have, as Madison noted, equal facilities for acquiring property." "Ken Kesey's 1962 novel, *One Flew over the Cuckoo's Nest,* provides an illustration of the totalitarian aspiration." "People today resemble Woody Allen's character Mickey Sachs." Then Dr. Fukuyama climbs Mount Fujiyama, looks around, and ponders: "What is man?"

Clap and Trap. The other grand contemporary work dealing with the condition of mankind and with its principalities and powers is Graham Fuller's *Democracy Trap.* (The proof copy says that the introduction is by Francis Fukuyama, but I was relieved not to find that in my copy.) Fuller is more realistic and pessimistic than Fukuyama, but for the wrong reason. Someone once said (it is not a very clever saying) that a pessimist is an optimist with experience. Yet quality of experience (including bureaucratic experience) depends entirely on quality of thought. Fuller has plenty of thoughts, but of what quality? He writes of the "Cold War Century," whose "struggle began in 1917 with the challenge to the capitalist world posed by the Bolshevik revolution." I would have thought that the world struggle started in 1914, with a horrible world war of which the revolution in Russia was but a consequence; but who am I to argue with a master policy thinker such as Fuller? "The invention of the teenager, in fact, is probably one of the most far-reaching acts of American social creativity," he adds.

A fact is a fact, no doubt. Compared to Fukuyama's jappy calligraphy Fuller writes like a red-faced ham-handed American, vulgar to the core: "Whatever value the Cold War had in helping to keep the West's ideological socks up in Europe and at home. . . ." Oh, for the Order of the Garter! In the end, Fuller on Fuller: "As a senior-level Intelligence Officer responsible for long-range National Estimates at the Central Intelligence Agency (essentially crystal-balling the future of strategic issues for policymakers at the White House and the State and Defense Departments), I had been regularly required to think about global issues and trends as the heart of my daily work for the Director of Central Intelligence."

This is a laughing matter no longer. For anyone honestly concerned with the destiny of the republic, it is a matter for rage, bitterness, and tears.

39

Ian Buruma

(1999)

*A*nglomania is a book about a truly remarkable—and now historic—phenomenon, which lasted for two hundred years or more, and which
was a deep-seated element in international relations. The accepted use of
the term "international relations" is, alas, false: for it deals with the relations of states, rather than of nations. Yet the relations of nations have often
become even more important than the relations of states. They are surely
deep-seated because they involve the images—including the attractions
and the enmities, the sympathies and the antipathies—that nations and
peoples have for each other.

The historical study of such relations is relatively recent. And the greatest
of such topics is Anglophilia: the extraordinary affection for England, for
Englishmen (rather than for Englishwomen), for Englishness and English
things—all of this adding up to England's prestige that survived many of
its retreats and mistakes and shortcomings—a grand inclination appearing
across the globe, illusory as it often was, and having elements of an unrequited love, and yet manifest among diverse peoples and all kinds of classes
(especially the upper-middle.) I am very loath to quote myself, but at least
in two of my books, some of them written decades ago, there appear sentences such as "[t]he history of Anglomania is yet to be written." I meant
Anglomania in general, not in particular (there exist a few worthy studies
about Anglomania in France in the eighteenth century, which was the first
overall appearance of that phenomenon). And now here is *Anglomania*, a
book not by a historian but by a fine writer whose understanding and erudition, meaning his knowledge of literature and of people and of a fair
amount of history, are first-class.

Yet it is only an hors d'oeuvre, a kind of tasty introduction to a vast and
profound topic. And the title given by its American publishers is deceiving.

Review of *Anglomania* (1999). From *Los Angeles Times Book Review,* June 6: 2.

Ian Buruma's book is a series of portraits, sometimes brilliant ones. That is why the proper title of his work should have been *Anglophiles*. (The bibliographical information on the back of the title page indicates that the original, and probably English, title of the book was *Anglophilia*. Even that would have been good enough; but Random House evidently chose to hype it.) This is not quibbling: In his first chapter, Buruma explains that he is writing about Anglophiles (and occasional Anglophobes) but not of Anglomania. And he does this very well, moving from Voltaire and Goethe and Schlegel and the Shakespeare cult in Germany to all kinds of paragons of Anglophilia, some of them unexpected. There is also Kaiser William II, who was a sorry mix of a love-hate relationship for England and the English, the only Anglophobe principal in the book. Much of the book, perhaps as many as four or five of its fifteen chapters, is devoted to the nineteenth- and twentieth-century affection that Jews in Europe had for England (in America the Anglophilia of, say, Ralph Lauren or of the *New York Review of Books* are later, more superficial phenomena), including portraits of entirely—well, almost—anglicized Jewish refugees or émigrés in England.

All of this is very telling, and even illuminating. But a history or even a summary sketch of Anglophilia it is not. Of course that is a very large topic, ranging from the Orleanists in France to Argentine polo clubs, from the anglicized Huguenots in England to the Spanish intellectual "Generation of '98," from the Hungarian Count Szechenyi who undertook to reform and rebuild an entire nation about 170 years ago by adopting English institutions and practices to foreign masters of the English language such as Joseph Conrad and admirers of British standards such as the Indian writer Nirad Chaudhuri—and the adoption (too often mistaken) of a mass of English words and phrases into every European language. (One example: the Russian word for railroad—vokzal—was simply taken from Vauxhall Station in London in the 1840s.) Such examples are endless.

But on many an occasion, Anglophilia had powerful and even dramatic consequences in the very movements of states—for the benefit of England and, yes, for the cause of liberty in the history of the world. During World War II, for example, Anglophilia (and Germanophobia) transcended Right and Left (it motivated millions, and often their governments) across the globe and inspired people during their darkest hours. (Conversely, in France, after its worst defeat, the common thread that tied all of Marshall Petain's supporters together was not fascism or Germanophilia but Anglophobia.)

In any event, Anglophilia was not merely a political or ideological but a cultural preference. As Buruma understands, it was well-nigh inseparable from the ideal of the gentleman. Yes: More than two hundred years ago the ideal of the gentleman began to replace the ideal of the nobleman. (Not so long ago I read the memoirs of an old-fashioned conservative diplomat, writing about the Emperor Franz Joseph, whom he had once met, enumerating the qualities of this monarch of the oldest imperial and royal family in Europe, and the best thing he could say about Franz Joseph was that he was a "gentleman.")

And what will replace the gentleman? And what will be the relation of England to Europe? Buruma does not know. Neither do I.

40

Arthur Koestler

(2000)

Arthur Koestler had an interesting life. He was born in Hungary in 1904 but lived for most of twenty years in Austria and Germany and then for more than forty years in England. There were many interruptions: years in Palestine, another year in Russia, yet another year in Spain, four in France and then long residences in the United States, in Austria, and again in France. He was a twentieth-century Central European émigré intellectual, not atypical of a group of people now largely, though not entirely, extinct. Twentieth century: because his migrations, both physical and mental, were largely the consequences of the two world wars. Central European: because the cast of his intellectual inclinations was largely Austrian and German, while his character had a few Hungarian (more precisely Budapestian) traits—but then that was typical of many intellectuals in the Weimar-German period. Émigré: because, in midlife, he found refuge in England, which gave him both security and comfort during the second half of his life. Like other Central European émigré intellectuals, such as Marx and Freud, he died in London, where his ashes remain.

Unlike Marx and Freud, he was agile and restless. He needed many friends around him. He was prone to travel, at little notice and often. He had an instant appeal to women, many of whom he treated crudely, on many occasions which are related by his present biographer, David Cesarani. He had three wives, each of them quite different. Racked by illness (though not yet in the throes of unendurable suffering and not yet facing imminent death), he chose to kill himself by poisoning in 1983, having convinced (or, as some people say, suborned) his younger wife, Cynthia Jefferies, to die with him.

He left a legacy of more than forty books, the last thirty of them written

Review of David Cesarani, *Arthur Koestler: The Homeless Mind* (1999). From *Los Angeles Times Book Review*, January 9: 9.

in English. Widely read and noticed, he had unusual successes in his literary career. The themes of his books are very different, which is why it is not easy to sum them up within a review. Many of them are period pieces—but then so was their author. Most of them deal with "isms": communism, Zionism, behaviorism, Darwinism, materialism. Koestler was Zionist and then anti-Zionist; materialist and then antimaterialist; Communist and then anticommunist; liberal and then antiliberal. His conversions were sincere. The flyleaf of *Arthur Koestler: The Homeless Mind* designates him as "this intellectual titan of the 20th century." That he was not. He was a brilliant journalist and, like many brilliant journalists, a not inconsiderable thinker.

His novels will not endure. The most famous of these (originally written in German), *Darkness at Noon,* has proved thoroughly false since its publication in 1940. In this book, Rubashov, an idealistic Communist condemned to death, confesses to nonexistent crimes in order to remain loyal to the party and to the cause of communism. It had a great impact, especially in the English-speaking world, where novels dealing with political ideas have been either rare or nonexistent. What we now know about the Moscow purge trials of the 1930s is that their hapless defendants, almost without exception, were forced into cowering submissions and confessions, including Mikhail Bukharin (after whom, to a large extent, Rubashov was modeled), without a trace of the Koestlerian fable. Cesarani writes: "The final rout of the Soviet imperium in 1989–90 began with the publication of *Darkness at Noon* (fifty years earlier)." This is complete nonsense. (It began with Khrushchev and Gorbachev, whose recognitions of the grave shortcomings of the Soviet system were the results of experience, of a reality that had nothing in common with the intellectual self-torturings of Rubashov.) "Koestler led the intellectual counter-attack," Cesarani writes, "that culminated in the fall of the Berlin Wall." That is a vast misreading of history. Koestler was but one among an estimable group of ex-Communists who had explained their break with communism convincingly.

Better than Koestler's novels are his biographies—though they too are journalistic rather than historically accurate. Perhaps his most valuable and enduring book is *The Sleepwalkers: A History of Man's Changing Vision of the Universe,* a well-researched and rather profound exegesis of the life and work of Johannes Kepler. This appeared in 1959, at the beginning of a period when Koestler devoted himself, more and more, to a questioning of the materialism of "natural" science. (In this case too he had brought within himself to England valuable intellectual baggage that was essentially Central European, indeed mostly German, in origin.) His related writings (and lectures) were more than excursions of an ever restless mind. What Koestler recognized was the presence (in his view, a presence rather than the increasing intrusion) of mind into matter. In this respect he was even more of an estimable pioneer than in his anticommunism: His understanding of the uneven "progress" of "science" well antedates Thomas Kuhn's much celebrated but essentially flat-footed academic thesis *The Structure of Scientific Revolutions* in 1962. But here too Koestler's potentially great contribution was marred by some of his characteristic shortcomings. His scope and the range of his reading were broad; but they would not extend to people beyond his ideological ken. When it came to the primacy (chronological as well as perceptual) of mind over matter, Koestler seems to have entirely ignored the important books of his contemporary Owen Barfield in England (just as he largely ignored such contemporary English "right-wingers" as T. S. Eliot and C. S. Lewis). And sometimes he went too far, first into psychology and then into parapsychology. His biographer cites Koestler's statement (in *Arrow in the Blue*, 1952): "[A]ll evidence tends to show that the political libido is basically as irrational as the sexual drive, and patterned, like the latter, by early, partly unconscious, experiences." All evidence? Political libido? Basically? Patterned? "The heart has reasons that reason knows not": Pascal's great maxim is shorter, better, wiser, deeper.

Cesarani's book is a most detailed and, in many ways, useful account of Koestler's life. There are only a few factual errors in it. In 1944, the British refused to enter into negotiations with Adolf Eichmann for obvious reasons and not because they "feared" that too many Hungarian Jews "would want to enter Palestine." Henry and Clare Luce were not "pillars of the American liberal establishment." Cesarani readily accepts Koestler's own story about having urinated into the radiator when his car boiled over (Koestler was five feet, seven inches tall). He overstates Koestler's talents as a writer: "A world without Koestler would have been noticeably different; but there would have been little difference to a world without [Cyril] Connolly. [Koestler] was the better writer." More successful, or more recognized, yes. But "better?" That is not within Cesarani's province to state.

Yet the trouble is not with Cesarani's details. It is with his argument, declared in the subtitle of this biography, *The Homeless Mind*: "His homelessness." "He condemned himself to homelessness." "He stigmatized the longing for home." Not at all. Yes, Koestler wanted to belong: to this or to that cause, and eventually to England. But the desire to have a home and the desire to belong are not the same. You can belong and not have a home—like a nomad, or an American hippie; conversely, you can have a home and not belong—like an émigré. And this brings me to the central, and fundamental, thesis of Cesarani (who is professor of modern Jewish history at Southampton University), stated throughout as well as in the beginning and at the end of this massive volume: "Koestler was a Jew who exemplified the *Jewish* [Cesarani's italics] experience in Europe during the 20th century." "It is clear that previous commentators and biographers have missed perhaps the most fundamental element of his story: that Koestler was a Jew." He was Jewish, Hungarian, Austrian, German, English, in succession. (Koestler felt little or no allegiance to Hungary, and he just about never wrote in Hungarian, or for Hungarians.) Besides his speaking ability (never quite perfect) in these languages (he did not speak Yiddish or Hebrew), his association, his assimilation, and his adaptation to these nations and to their customs was very impressive—though not exceptional. Perhaps it may be said that he was more non-English than English and more Jewish than non-Jewish, but these are only matters of proportion. To argue that his Jewishness was the most fundamental and essential fact of his person and of his work (in other words: that race predetermines mind) is a vast exaggeration, amounting to special pleading at best and to racism at its worst.

41

Stephen E. Ambrose, Steve Neal,
James C. Humes
(2002)

People with adult memories of the 1950s are by now a minority in this country. They have been defined for us as "The Greatest Generation" (title, or subtitle, of Tom Brokaw's three recent best-sellers), a phrase denoting those Americans who fought the Second World War, during which there was less division—at least on the surface—among the American people than during any other war, before or after. Yet something is missing from this description, even at the start. What the Greatest Generation books describe were, in reality, "The Best Years of Their Lives" (title, almost, of a famous sentimental movie circa 1946). It was in the fifties that the Greatest Generation came into the prime of their manhood (and womanhood), but the history, not to say the lives, of a generation encompass more than nine or ten years. What came next? *Were those* the best years of their lives?

Apart from the evidence of a few personal memoirs, we do not know. Nonetheless, an American legend has been constructed around the fifties. This legend has become a national monument, marvelously preserved, like a giant aircraft carrier polished and scoured, free of rust and barnacles, a tourist attraction worth visiting and contemplating. It bears the name The Eisenhower Era. The contractors of this monument of national memory have been, and continue to be, historians and journalists (more precisely: historians writing like journalists and journalists attempting to be historians). Foremost among these are Stephen E. Ambrose, the first historian in the history of history who has transformed his writing and speaking busi-

From *Harper's,* January: 64–70. Books discussed in this essay include: Stephen E. Ambrose, *Ike's Spies: Eisenhower and the Espionage Establishment* (1999); Steve Neal, *Harry and Ike* (2001); and James C. Humes, *Eisenhower and Churchill* (2001).

nesses into a corporation, and his satellite, Douglas Brinkley, director of the Eisenhower Center for American Studies at the University of New Orleans (founded by Ambrose).

Among Ambrose's innumerable books and other publications dealing with Eisenhower, the recent edition of *Ike's Spies* (introduced by Douglas Brinkley) gives us a sense of his prose. "Both the grin and the bald pate seemed as wise, broad, and sunny as the Kansas prairie," Ambrose writes, describing Eisenhower the general. Somewhat later: "As President he intended to fight the Communists just as he had fought the Nazis, on every battlefront, with every available weapon. His arsenal was a mighty one, capped by the atomic bomb." Besides the vastness of this inaccuracy (did Eisenhower fight the Nazis, or indeed the Communists, on *every* battlefront?) consider Douglas Brinkley's Ike, who "did mention the horrors of World War II, such as the bodies he had seen at Auschwitz" (where he had never been).

It is regrettable that these often self-contradictory dithyrambs are seldom picked out by historians. Geoffrey Perret, in a recent adulatory biography of Eisenhower, writes, "Eisenhower explicitly ruled out preventive war, but not a preemptive strike"—a distinction without much of a difference (or what an Englishwoman in her cups once called an odorous comparison). Perret also writes that "Like Kennan, [Eisenhower] believed that over time the Soviet Union would mellow." This was the Eisenhower who agreed with Dulles to sack Kennan from the Foreign Service in 1953, and the same Eisenhower who kept repeating to Churchill throughout the fifties that the Soviet Union would never "mellow."

The past year has seen the appearance of Steve Neal's *Harry and Ike,* a somewhat tenuous examination of Eisenhower's relationship with Harry Truman, and James C. Humes's *Eisenhower and Churchill.* Neither of these books adds much to our understanding of Eisenhower other than to testify to a continued interest in him and an idea of him as in some sense the epitome of fifties-era decency and solidity—the father figure of the Greatest Generation. There is now a long shelf of books dealing with Eisenhower, longer even than the one of books about the fifties. Among the latter, David Halberstam's *The Fifties* is best known. An attempt at a social and cultural history, the book is, in reality, not much more than a garland of a journalist's memories of some public happenings and personalities of that decade. Again, its shortcomings may be gleaned from Halberstam's summary judgment of Eisenhower—another contribution to the national monument, as superficial as it is wrong: "Eisenhower was cautious, pragmatic, modest, and given to understatement; Dulles, bombastic, arrogant, and self-important." The contrast will not stand. Self-important both of them were, and with all of his faults (there were many) Dulles was less bombastic than preachy, while

Eisenhower was hardly given to understatement. Indeed, the history of the fifties, and of Eisenhower (from the long-awaited announcement of his candidacy in early 1952 to his retirement from the presidency in 1961), remains to be written.

In more ways than one the fifties were a good time for the great majority of Americans. Most of them had lived through the Depression of the 1930s, but by 1950 it had become evident that the fears (and the economists' predictions) of a postwar depression or recession were unwarranted. There came, instead, an almost uninterrupted rise of incomes and wages, with widespread consequences, among them the easy availability and tremendous growth in ownership of new houses and (of course) new automobiles. The number of marriages did not quite reach the astonishing postwar peaks of 1946–47, but then neither did the number of divorces; throughout the fifties the divorce rate did not vary much. And the American birthrate, for both whites and nonwhites, reached a startling high in 1956 and 1957, a figure not surpassed since. All in all, the fifties were a decade of security (rather than of stability, since people were moving all the time); of "togetherness" and, of course, no war. By 1952 the Korean War was essentially over; the Cuban Missile Crisis and the Vietnam War were yet to come. There were plenty of reasons for optimism (perhaps optimism rather than contentment). And, looking back, there has been the contrast with the raucous and divisive sixties; it is because of this contrast that the fifties shine so cleanly in retrospect.

But the roots of the troubles of the 1960s—indeed, of our very troubles fifty years later—were all there: the decline of American industry, of American manufacturing, of saving habits (gross personal savings in 1960 were actually less than in 1951); we had become a credit-card society (they all began then—Visa, MasterCard, and the rest—their startling effects were there by the late fifties). Before 1960 the United States produced more automobiles than all other countries together; after that, no longer. Both in quantity and in quality the competitive advantages of American products began to wane. Very few people, including historians, have noted how short the industrial age was, compared with the previous agricultural and the succeeding postindustrial ages: a few decades, not more. In 1955 and '56, for the first time in American history, the majority of working people were no longer engaged in production (either agricultural or industrial) but were instead working in "administration" and "services," a change that led to a posturban and bureaucratic society. It was during the 1950s that the greatest American cities began to deteriorate and to decrease in population, a devolution that has not stopped since. I once wrote about the "American bourgeois interlude," that in the 1950s "the relatively short efflorescence of an urban and bourgeois culture in the history of American civilization came to its end."

In the fifties the cult of "growth" became an unquestioned shibboleth, without any thought given to the affinity of growth and inflation. In this respect, as in many others, the mid-fifties were a turning point. 1955 was the last year when the consumer price index actually *dropped* by a fraction of a percentage. During the mild recession of 1957–58, prices still kept rising. At the end of World War II the United States was the greatest holder of gold in the world. For ten more years gold continued to flow into American vaults. But in 1956, for the first time in decades, gold began to flow out of the United States. Fourteen years later, half of the nation's gold stock was gone—until in 1971 Nixon prohibited the outflow of gold altogether.

The superficiality, indeed the fatuity, of the nation's confidence in American "exceptionalism" in the fifties appears startlingly in some of the declarations made by "conservative" eminences of that time. In 1955, Herbert Hoover wrote, "With only about six percent of the world's population we have almost as many youth in our institutions of higher learning as the rest of the world put together. We could probably enumerate more libraries and more printed serious works than the other 94 percent of the people of the earth." In 1957, Edward Teller, "Father of the Hydrogen Bomb," stated that American teenagers would soon be "as enthusiastic about science as they are about baseball." These pronouncements were enunciated at a time when many American public schools had already devolved into custodial institutions. By the end of the fifties the disorder in the schools had spilled out into the streets: in cities such as Chicago and Philadelphia the police had to be advised of early dismissals. Consider too that in "first reader" books for six-year-old children the average number of words fell from 645 in the 1920s to 330 in 1950 to 150 in 1962. Meanwhile the number of pictures in the primers doubled; that was, of course, part and parcel of the devolution from a verbal to a pictorial culture, which was probably not what Herbert Hoover had in mind (friend of Louis B. Mayer though he had been). In 1954 a panel of experts gathered by the National Association of Manufacturers declared, "Guided by electronics, powered by atomic energy . . . the magic carpet of our free economy heads for distant and undreamed horizons." David Sarnoff, the chairman of RCA, predicted "5,000-mile-an-hour rocket planes, controlled weather, and push-button homes by 1976." In 1955, Admiral Lewis Strauss, chairman of the Atomic Energy Commission, predicted that nuclear energy would be so cheap that by 1970 electricity would no longer have to be metered.

Looking at the 1950s in retrospect, the accepted view seems to be of a decade marked not only by a benevolent, smiling president but by now old-fashioned American scenes, as painted by Norman Rockwell (whose reputation—rightly—has lately begun to rise). Yet read what Rockwell wrote himself in the *Saturday Evening Post,* in 1960, about the governing idea of one of his most famous paintings: "In 1951, for the Thanksgiving issue of the *Post,* I painted a cover showing an old woman and a small boy saying grace in a shabby railroad restaurant. The people around them were staring, some surprised, some puzzled, some remembering their own childhood; but all were respectful. If you actually saw such a scene, some of the staring people would have been different, some insulting and rude, and perhaps a few of them would have been angry." I don't think so. And how could Rockwell be so sure of that? Here is another sad revelation of how the public optimism of certain Americans in the 1950s was the result not of naïveté but of a corroding pessimism.

The 1950s were a boom time for religion in America. It was the era of Fulton Sheen, of Cardinal Spellman, a decade when, for the first time, American Catholics could justifiably feel that they were not only first-class but the best, the most reliably patriotic of Americans, because of their near-doctrinal anticommunism. When, in 1956, the American Institute of Management pronounced that its survey of the Roman Catholic Church reported A-1 in Management and 90-plus in Efficiency, this imbecility was welcomed in many American Catholic publications with self-congratulatory satisfaction. In 1953 five of the six nonfiction bestsellers had a religious theme. In 1958 the cost of new church construction amounted to more than twice the funds allotted for the building of public hospitals. President Eisenhower, who had not found it necessary to attend church before, found it politic and useful to be seen in church before his election. Soon thereafter he announced, "Our government makes no sense unless it is founded in a deeply felt religious faith—and I don't care what it is." Is this what the neoconservative Paul Johnson meant when he wrote in his *History of the American People* that "Eisenhower presided benignly over what was termed 'Piety on the Potomac,' a generalized form of the Christian religion very much in the American tradition . . ."?

It is a great error to believe that the sixties amounted to a radical break with the fifties. There is plenty of evidence that the puerility of the 1960s (for that was what it was) existed already in the 1950s: the increasing influence of the pictorial imagination, for instance—especially as embodied in television—or what happened to popular music. American popular music from about 1915 to 1950, whether we call it jazz or not, was a great, wondrous contribution to the world. It was democratic, but it was also elegant and sophisticated, mainly because of its complex harmonic structures, which elevated even simple melodies to the level of a beautiful art. In the early

1950s this dried up, finally vanishing almost entirely, notwithstanding occasional attempts at revival. What followed was rock and roll, which spread like wildfire beginning in about 1957, after a faint, Eisenhowerish transition marked by Doris Day, Lawrence Welk, and, at best, Bing Crosby. From the South it was not Flannery O'Connor but Elvis Presley who would eventually be invited to the White House (and to whom Bill Buckley, leader of the American "conservative" movement, only recently devoted an admiring novel). The sexual "revolution" of the sixties, too, was there in the fifties, and not only below the surface. In 1956 the median age of first marriages for women fell to an astonishing low: more than half of American women who married in that year were younger than twenty years of age. In 1957, *By Love Possessed*, a dreadful novel by James Gould Cozzens, described copulation in mechanical detail and introduced the word "fuck" into print, for which it was hailed on the cover of *Time* and in *Ladies' Home Journal*.

But the most lasting—and damaging—consequences of the American fifties involved the Cold War; and, after half a century, there is ample reason (and evidence) for this historian to attempt a summation of what happened then and there.

The Cold War was not the consequence of International Communism (this was what the government and most of the people of the United States believed at the time) but of the Second World War. About the Second World War we know something now that we did not know then: that Hitler's Germany had been much more powerful than it seemed in 1945, and that Hitler had indeed come very close to winning the war in 1940–41. About the Cold War the opposite is true: we know now (and not only because of the collapse of the Soviet Union a decade ago) that Soviet Russia was much weaker than what the American government told its people in the 1950s. It was, indeed, retreating rather than advancing in the 1950s, and so was International Communism, especially in America and Europe. That the so-called Missile Gap, favoring the Russians, much touted in 1957 and after, was a myth, we now know; but we ought also to know that this kind of military-industrial propaganda was trumpeted by men in the government who not only should have known but indeed did know better. I shall come to the military-industrial transformation of the country in a moment, but before that let us establish a few things about the world situation during the fifties, when the Soviet empire was retreating, and when its leaders were seriously contemplating a radical improvement of their relations with the United States.

In March 1953, merely six weeks after Eisenhower's inauguration, Stalin died. Instantly there was accumulating evidence of the reality that Churchill had glimpsed as early as 1944 about Eastern Europe, when he said to General de Gaulle that although Russia was indeed then a big hungry wolf in the midst of sheep, "after the meal comes the digestion period." Russia, he believed, would not be able to digest its swollen intake. When Eisenhower became president, Churchill was again prime minister, and Churchill hoped that much would come from their wartime comradeship. But he was to be bitterly disappointed. Eisenhower and Dulles treated him with contumely and disdain. (One of Churchill's respectable English biographers, Roy Jenkins, recently described this treatment as "insensitivity verging on brutality"; another, Geoffrey Best, has written of "the bellicosity and intransigence epitomised by John Foster Dulles"; James C. Humes chooses, as have many other writers, not to deal with evidence contrary to the notion of Eisenhower and Churchill as affectionate "partners." There is, for example, the diary entry made by Churchill's private secretary in 1953, which states that Churchill was "[v]ery disappointed in Eisenhower whom he thinks both weak and stupid.")

Three times, in 1953 and 1954, Churchill came over, attempting to convince Eisenhower that the time had come to try some kind of settlement with the new Russian rulers, perhaps to correct, at least partly, the conditions of the division of Europe. Prodded by Dulles, Eisenhower dismissed Churchill. He said to some of his supporters that Churchill had become senile, that he had sentimental illusions about who and what the Russians were. (This was the same Eisenhower who eight years before had ignored Churchill while approaching Stalin directly, and who at that time—early 1945—saw Churchill as dangerously imperialist and anti-Russian.) It is at least possible that had Eisenhower at least listened to Churchill in 1953, the Cold War would have wound down thirty years sooner.

That we cannot know for sure. What we know (and what Washington then dismissed as of little or no importance) are the Russian retreats: that in 1955 the Russians agreed to remove themselves from Austria; that they accepted the political independence of Tito's Yugoslavia; that they withdrew from their naval base in Finland; that they gave up the bases and concessions in China and Manchuria awarded them at Yalta; that they officially recognized the West German government without demanding that the Western Powers recognize the East German one; and (this is now confirmed by papers in the Russian archives) that on many occasions they advised Polish and Hungarian and East German Communist leaders to go slowly, and perhaps to experiment with less rigid forms of government.

All of these moves were publicly declared by Eisenhower to be meaningless trickery. In 1956 came the explosive Polish and Hungarian revolutions. These put to the test Dulles's famous propaganda of Rolling Back Communism behind the Iron Curtain. In reality, Eisenhower and Dulles did nothing. In his memoirs, Eisenhower wrote that the Hungarian Revolution of October 1956 caught him by surprise. He was lying: Washington was very well informed of what was happening there. Eisenhower was anxious that nothing should be attempted to change the accepted division of Europe. He and Dulles profited from the spectacle of the brutality of Russian suppression of the revolution; it amounted to wonderful propaganda, which contributed to Eisenhower's landslide victory over Adlai Stevenson in November, during the very days in which the Russians reinstated their domination of Hungary. The Russians, in turn, now knew that they needed not fear the Americans, who had no intention of renegotiating the division of Europe. In 1959, after repeated and pathetic requests, Khrushchev got himself invited to Washington, where he was received by a sour-faced Eisenhower without a single gesture of goodwill or generosity; among other restrictions, Khrushchev was forbidden to travel, as he had wished, across America (this included prohibition of his desired visit to Disneyland in California). Meanwhile American spy planes were crisscrossing and photographing the Soviet Union week after week. There were no such Russian incursions into American skies. Finally one of these American planes was shot down in May 1960, during a summit meeting in Paris, when Eisenhower (perhaps justifiably, in this case) had to lie again, claiming that the plane had been on a weather mission.

Eisenhower's head of the CIA, Allen Dulles, was already preparing an invasion of Castro's Cuba at the Bay of Pigs when Eisenhower retired.

Readers will note that I have not written about the excrescences of the Second Red Scare that had developed within the United States, reaching its peak in the early fifties, 1950–55 marking the rocketing rise and subsequent fall of the political career of Joseph McCarthy. True, there had been undue Communist influence and even conspiracy within the United States for many years, and the evidence shows that people like Alger Hiss were amateur traitors. It must also be said in favor of the American rule of law (however bent by politics on occasion) that, unlike in Russia, few opponents of the government were executed or cruelly imprisoned or exiled. Yet all of this pales before the oceanic tide of American popular sentiment and public opinion, which reached its height in the fifties and then went on, reappearing again during Ronald Reagan's Evil Empire years: the identification, indeed, the substitution of anticommunism for American patriotism. To detail the myriad, often absurd and shocking examples of this is not within the province of this article. What belongs here is the myopia of American political thinking, apparent within the political terminology and the rhetoric of those, in retrospect, halcyon—but in reality, often fraudulent—years. One startling example (hitherto, alas, overlooked by most historians, "liberals" and "conservatives" alike) is that in 1956 the foreign-policy platform, Section Nine, of the Republican party, called for "*the establishment of American air and naval bases all around the world.*" (These italics are mine.) This was the party still called "isolationist" by some of its critics. What is relevant is that by the end of the 1950s there were American air and naval and military bases in nearly sixty countries. There is every reason to think that neither the president nor anyone else in Washington was able to list and identify most of them. Nor can they now.

What kind of a man was "Ike"? The general and accepted impression is that of a benevolent, often smiling, moderate man of judgment behind whose outwardly simple demeanor lay the considerable hidden wisdom of a great soldier and statesman. Douglas Brinkley has recently described him as a representative of "frugal, old-fashioned, Main Street values." This portrait is largely incorrect. Even when Eisenhower was the supreme commander of the Allied forces in Europe, many of his strategic judgments were outright mistakes. At the same time, his performance as the chief executive of a coalition was commendable, and it was because of his politic ability to compromise that General Marshall had proposed him for that supreme task in 1942. As a politician and president, Eisenhower was an opportunist. One of his most lamentable acts was his open endorsement of Joseph McCarthy in 1952, after McCarthy had brutally denounced Eisenhower's benefactor General Marshall as a traitor. Eventually, more than two years later, Eisenhower turned against McCarthy (or more precisely, allowed him to be destroyed by others), but not before he had calculated that this was no longer politically dangerous (Steve Neal does an adequate job of documenting this betrayal in *Harry and Ike*, though he is perhaps too eager to smooth over—on his way to a happy ending—the serious rift it caused between Truman and Eisenhower). We have seen how, prodded by Dulles, Eisenhower had turned his back on Churchill in a contemptible way. Indeed, during the fifties the course of the giant American ship of state was set by the two Dulles brothers, even as Eisenhower sat on the captain's seat.

Several of Eisenhower's biographers have described him admiringly as a man of principle, shrewd, a master at "hidden-hand leadership." In reality, Eisenhower was devious rather than straightforward, ideology-ridden rather than pragmatic, governed by calculations rather than by convictions. He was well aware of the prime importance of publicity. He was the first television president, cosmeticized and bureaucratized. In 1948, Harry Truman appeared on television for a short three-minute appearance, urging the citizenry to vote. In 1952, Eisenhower hired the actor Robert Montgomery to help with his television grooming and appearance; in 1956 another actor, George Murphy, did the same with assiduity. (Eventually

Murphy became a senator in California—a forerunner of the Hollywood-ization of American politics that led to Ronald Reagan.)

If Truman was the last old-fashioned president in the White House, Eisenhower was the first bureaucrat. He campaigned on a Republican platform against Big Government, but the bureaucracy under his administration grew and grew: by 1960 his full-time staff in the White House was nearly three times that of FDR and nearly twice that of Harry Truman. His speechwriters numbered in the dozens. Paul Johnson proclaimed that "[t]ranscripts of his secret conferences show the lucidity and power of his thoughts. They reveal an excellent command of English which he could exercise when he chose." But in fact the very opposite was true: his speeches furnished ample material for superb parodies that have often been reprinted since. Perhaps the most famous of these was Oliver Jensen's "Gettysburg Address in Eisenwese," the brilliance of which makes worth quoting at length:

> I haven't checked these figures, but 87 years ago, I think it was, a number of individuals organized a governmental set-up here in this country, I believe it covered certain Eastern areas, with this idea they were following up based on a sort of national independence arrangement and the program that every individual is just as good as every other individual. Well, now, of course, we are dealing with this big difference of opinion, civil disturbance you might say, although I don't like to appear to take sides or name any individuals. . . .

In "Eisenhower the Dove," an article that appeared in the September 2001 issue of *American Heritage* magazine, Douglas Brinkley compared Eisenhower's farewell address with that of George Washington, writing of "the depth of thought in their enduring appeals to humanity's better nature." Ike's farewell address was "a call for prudence and compassion." Yet in the same farewell address Ike declared, "We face a hostile ideology, global in scope, atheistic in character, ruthless in purpose, and insidious in method." Eisenhower the Dove?

There are many, and serious, reasons to assert the opposite. It is true that Eisenhower signed the armistice in Korea in 1953, but this was two years after the warfare in Korea had ceased and a virtual armistice had come into existence along the Thirty-Eighth Parallel (the line still in effect today). It is also true that in 1954 Eisenhower chose not to intervene with American forces in the French-Vietnamese war in Indochina, but that would have been catastrophic nonsense at that time, not to speak of the fact that the gradual American military infiltration into South Vietnam, eventually leading to the Vietnam War in the sixties, began during his last years in office. In 1958, Eisenhower sent Marines into Lebanon: a ludicrous excursion, for no purpose, with the Marines withdrawn soon afterward, having achieved not much more than being photographed with Lebanese beauties on the beaches. Eisenhower ringed American cities with Nike missile bases, waiting for Soviet bombers. Earlier I wrote that there are reasons at least to consider whether, had it not been for Eisenhower and Dulles, the Cold War may have wound down in the fifties (without, of course, disappearing entirely). That is a hypothesis. But what is not a hypothesis is the meaning—and the authenticity—of Eisenhower's farewell address about the dangers of a military-industrial complex, language that has since that time grown into a legend, now emphasized by Brinkley. That speech was largely drafted by Malcolm Moos, one of Eisenhower's speechwriters, a man without a significant influence in the White House either before the celebrated speech or after.

Let us give Eisenhower the benefit of the doubt. He did want to give a farewell address; and some of the phrases in Moos's draft appealed to him. Warning against the dangers of an inextricably conjoined military-industrial economy and chain of command, he obviously meant what he said. But did he know what he was warning against? Did he know what he himself had created? It was in the 1950s, during his presidency, that the military-industrial concubinage, and the imperial expansion of the United States, had grown to monstrous proportions. In 1960, military spending was three times that of 1950, the year of the Korean War. Military expenditures for scientific research and development had risen from an annual average of $245 million during World War II to $15 billion in 1956 (and that was before the Russians' success with their orbital Sputnik accelerated these American expenditures, funding missiles many times over). That year Eisenhower decided to fund and construct the Interstate Highway System for military and industrial purposes, leading to the disastrous deterioration of America's railroads.

There was another great landslide in the fifties around which a handful of historians have been paddling lately, without really considering the importance of its extent. In 1950 "conservative" was a word to be avoided; that year even Senator Robert A. Taft, on the right wing of the Republican party, declared that he was "an old-fashioned liberal." Yet the decline and the erosion of liberalism, now reaching its last phase, had in reality started in the fifties. As late as 1955, Louis Hartz, a mediocre Harvard history professor, published *The Liberal Tradition in America,* stating that liberalism was not only the American political tradition but the only American political reality. Poor booby! That was the very year when William F. Buckley Jr. started his *National Review,* when the American "conservative" movement rose, growing so rapidly that the cautious Eisenhower noticed it: in 1960 (lo and behold!) he said that he was "a conservative." By the 1980s the "conservative" movement helped to propel Ronald Reagan into the White House; indeed, by the 1980s more Americans identified themselves as conservatives than as liberals. This was, and remains, a mutation of enormous proportions and consequences. That our "conservatives" (my quotation marks are intentional) have become the loudest and most effusive proponents of the military-industrial state, of Star Wars, of missile shields, of massive promotions and fundings of "defense," of maintaining, if not extending, the American military presence all over the globe (indeed, into space) while being indifferent, if not hostile, to the conservation of America's land and its resources—that is another story. And all of that started in the fifties.

42

Simone Weil

(1990)

I am not a Simone Weil scholar—by which I mean, among other things, that I have *not* read all of her available works. But she has inspired—not merely inspired, and not merely interested—me for many years. Our philosophical inclinations—and our view of the modern world— have much in common. Also—although she was considerably older, very much wiser, and more experienced than I—our most searing experiences accumulated during the Second World War, which she did not survive but of which she remains a truly extraordinary witness (and, moreover, "witness" in the ancient religious sense of that word). What connects these two matters is the fact—and it is a fact of an unusual character, *a fact of quality*—that one of the great principles that Simone Weil incarnated was that of *resistance*. By this I do not only mean the quality of her patriotism that ranks her among the heroes and the heroines of Charles de Gaulle's Free French resistance movement. What I mean, too, is her unusual, brave mental and spiritual resistance to so many of the accepted ideas and intellectual categories of the modern world. I do not flinch from saying that— completely contrary to the tendencies of our present "conservatives"— Simone Weil was a radical reactionary, in the proper sense of that so often misused word: an argument that I shall not belabor further through semantic definitions, except to remind you that this noble word *resistance* is a reactionary, rather than a progressive one.

Simone Weil only lived thirty-four years—of which her most shattering experiences accumulated during the last seven, a period from which the relatively best-known of her writings survive. That this period was not marked by a sudden maturation of her thought, or by a conversion, but that the principal direction of her convictions, the luminosity of her thinking,

First delivered as a lecture at Skidmore College in October 1988. From *Salmagundi*, Winter-Spring: 106–18.

her resistance against the accepted false ideas of the twentieth century had matured much earlier is now evident in many of her *Formative Writings*, beginning in 1929, when she was only twenty years old. She was born in 1909 in Paris of a respectable Jewish family, long resident in France, of Alsatian provenance. This is important to consider, because it is a mistake (as some of her American commentators had done) to connect some of her ideas to her reaction to French anti-Semitism. The year 1909 came ten years after the peak of the Dreyfus agitation; and in no European city with a considerable Jewish population was the assimilation of Jews as secure as in Paris during her youth. She loved her parents and admired her older brother, a mathematician.

She was an Ugly Duckling. Unlike most ugly ducklings, she seems to have been wholly devoid of self-pity. She was attracted to the poor, as are all the saints. She was a little girl when she gave away her superbly comfortable winter coat to someone during the last freezing winter of the First World War. She was an excellent student. She had a deep-rooted, that is *radical*, in the original and literal meaning of that word, inclination to struggle against social injustice—indeed, to be a participant, an active witness, a sufferer of such struggles. She went off to be a lowly worker in a factory in Paris. She went off to Spain to engage in the Republican ranks during the Spanish Civil War. All of this suggests her place among the idealist—so-called—leftists of the period, many of whom had been ugly ducklings and who then began flapping the oily water from their wings, trying to fly. But in her case—as in the case of George Orwell with whom she had this very profound recognition in common—she found that the struggle against social injustice was not enough; indeed, that such a struggle could, at times, serve evil purposes. There is something in this world that is more important than the pursuit of justice. It is the pursuit of truth. We, in this world—and perhaps especially in the twentieth century, when the air of our cities is polluted by a viscous film of empty words—are menaced less by the prevalence of injustice than by the prevalence of untruths. It was Georges Bernanos (whom she discovered, and wrote to, during her Spanish experience) who later wrote that the pursuit of justice can lay the world to waste—which, when you think of it, is a particularly American predicament.

Like George Orwell (on the Left) and Georges Bernanos (on the Right) Simone Weil was appalled by the governing lies and cruelties of the Spanish Civil War. Bernanos was a reactionary Catholic, who once had written a fiery admiring biography of the French social prophet and anti-Semite Edouard Drumont, but who also saw the monstrous dishonesties and cruelties committed by the followers of General Franco, and wrote the stunning book, *Les grande cimetiéres sous la lune*, the exact counterpart (on the

Right) of Orwell's *Homage to Catalonia*. Simone Weil (who had suffered a serious burn in Barcelona and came back to France) read it. She wrote Bernanos. From that time on we can see her engagement in something that is deeper and more important than the struggle against injustice, even as she was a prime victim of the vile injustices imposed upon Jews during the Second World War. Simone Weil was a votary, a witness for truth. A humble witness, because she had so chosen. A new phenomenon, rare in the twentieth century, a witness who is also a martyr, but without the slightest inclination to make her martyrdom public. (As Bernanos wrote in *The Diary of a Country Priest:* "Chosen humility can be truly regal, but vanity run to seed is not a pretty sight.")

Like Bernanos, she was a patriot. She tried to volunteer when Hitler started the war, in 1939. Then came the collapse of France and the persecution of the Jews. She lost her modest teaching job. She then chose to work in the fields, first in the garden of a Catholic writer and philosopher and then on a truck farm. She also had to take a hand in guiding the destinies of her endangered family in Marseille: for Simone Weil—like most humble saints and unlike most intellectuals—was a practical person. In 1942 they escaped from the dragnet that was closing over Jews all across Europe, to New York, through French Morocco and Casablanca (that Casablanca route about which in that year one of the most famous but also one of the stupidest American movies was made by a group of fortunate screenwriters sunning themselves in Hollywood). Unlike for most European refugees, New York was not to be a safe harbor for Simone Weil, only a stepping stone from which to make her way somehow across the war-infested Atlantic to London, for the purpose of enrolling herself in the ranks of General de Gaulle's resistance army, Free France. She made it to London. She was not chosen to be parachuted into France. She worked on, and she chose to adapt her physical condition to those of starving people in France. She was sick. She ate very little. She died.

Such is my brief, and certainly inadequate, summary of her brief, and more than adequate, life. Did she starve herself to death? We do not know. Only God knows that. For the purpose of this essay, it does not matter. All I wish now is to draw attention to some of her recognitions of certain truths, resisting the accepted ideas of our times. That resistance was more than political or ideological. It was philosophical, personal, and participant.

The main thread binding (and not merely running through) Simone Weil's thought is her resistance to, and rejection of, materialism. But that rejection is much deeper, and much fuller, than either that of a philosophical idealist or that of a converted anti-Marxist. She rejected Marxism and capitalism; not only positivism but determinism in every form. She rejected

Marx *and* Comte *and* Darwin *and* Freud *and* Einstein. She was aware of the shortcomings of any modern philosophy which fails to admit that all philosophy must be epistemological now (this is my formulation, not hers). At any rate she was entirely aware of the deadening and false formulations and categories of verbal logic, that is, of a mathematicization of language. In 1942 she wrote in Marseille: "It is true that quantum mechanics finally delivered philosophy from the fashionable scientism of the nineteenth century; but with a little intelligence philosophers could have delivered themselves without the help of quanta."

This is a statement of astonishing insight. It precedes the philosophical recognitions of the greatest physicist of the century, Werner Heisenberg, the discoverer of the principles of Uncertainty and Indeterminacy, the philosophical meaning of which he expressed in his Gifford Lectures in 1955. I thought until recently that a statement such as the above one was an example of the final crystallization of Simone Weil's philosophy, of the phase that reached its Pascalian heights in 1940–42. Now it appears that the essence of her epistemology was clear in her mind as early as 1930, when she was only twenty-one years old, as expressed in her extraordinary study of "Science and Perception in Descartes." In this long and difficult dissertation she does not reject Descartes (although her resistance to the Cartesian duality of the world is already there). Instead she approaches Descartes and recognizes an essential element in his perception in a thoroughly new and unorthodox way: "although from a distance Descartes seemed to offer a coherent system befitting the founder of modern science, on looking into it more closely we no longer find anything but contradictions. . . . How could the man who had thus adopted the Socratic motto 'know thyself' devote his life to the kind of research into physics that Socrates scoffed at?" She does not *reject* Descartes (although it is rather evident that she is a Pascalian and a Platonist); but in recognizing Descartes' contradictions she is already moving from a categorical philosophy to an existential epistemology. In this essay, which is largely devoid of intellectual self-indulgence, the most important recognitions are expressions of her concern—concern, even more than self-centered interest—with the conditions of her own consciousness:

> . . . nothing that transpires in my consciousness has any reality other than the consciousness I have of it; the only knowledge I can have is to be conscious of what I am conscious of. To know a dream is to dream it; to know a pain is to suffer it; to know a pleasure is to enjoy it.

Again:

> I used to believe, with regard to any problem whatever, that to
> know was to solve the problem; now I realize that it means to
> know how the problem concerns me.
>   The world weighs on my free will in such a way as to make
> me, if I do not resist, the plaything of my impulses; in return,
> the exercise of my free judgment cannot leave the world un-
> touched.

This is an early statement of her resistance to the determinist idea of
human passivity, of the restriction of human consciousness to sense reactions. The later, much more pronounced, religious essence of her conviction of a monistic universe is already there, in 1930, within this passage:

> . . . simple ideas are created by God, since the role of God in
> relation to me is to warrant, in some manner, the union of the
> soul and the body. The great correlations that form the core of
> the doctrine become apparent; there is no longer any contra-
> diction between freedom and necessity, idealism and realism.

It is not idealism and realism that are opposites; to the contrary, they
encompass corresponding verities. The antithesis of idealism is materialism, including its quantitative formulations, especially when they are wholly
dependent on the abstractions of mathematics:

> . . . in applying analysis to physics there is a risk that what legiti-
> mates it may be forgotten; it is only in geometry and mechanics
> that algebra has significance.

Again:

> If mathematical ideas give me a feeling of clarity and obvious-
> ness that sensations do not provide, it does not follow that this
> feeling exists independently of my consciousness of it.

It should appear from these passages that while Simone Weil rejects the
universality of the—man-made—"logic" of mathematics, her recognition
of the limits of a cold and abstract rationalism includes not a single word
suggesting a tendency to seek refuge in the recognition of irrationality, of
the subconscious—a tendency so typical of many twentieth-century think-

ers. To the contrary: Simone Weil's attention is directed to the workings of the conscious mind. She is *thinking about thinking.*

Ten years later, in her *pensées* collected by Gustave Thibon in *Gravity and Grace,* her recognitions are the results of the same resistance to determinism, to every kind of determinism—startling and pithy formulations that issue from her understanding of how the recognition of the limitations of our intelligence enriches that intelligence: "We know by means of our intelligence that what the intelligence does not comprehend is more real than what it does comprehend." Then her recognitions soar to great heights: "Faith is experience that intelligence is enlightened by love." In the intellectual order, the virtue of humility is nothing more nor less than the power of attention.

To this allow me to add: What does attention have to do with the subconscious? *Nothing.* And Simone Weil is one of those—few—important people who in the twentieth century recognizes that many—very many—of our problems are the results not of a bewildering complexity of imagination but of an—often fatal—want of attention.

Simone Weil's understanding of the conditions of our knowledge was matched by an equally astonishing insight into the history of the twentieth century. This it is possible to show even with a handful of randomly chosen illustrations. In a few rapidly written articles ("The Situation in Germany") composed in the winter of 1932–33, before Hitler's assumption of power, she demonstrated an understanding of the mental condition of the German masses—and a comprehension of the fatal and corrupting weakness of the German Left—in a way that was unequalled at the time and which, except for a few minor errors, is as valid now as when it was written by this then barely twenty-three-year old and unworldly French girl-philosopher. She was already aware of the truth latent within her aphorism put down ten years later: "It is not religion but revolution which is the opium of the people."

As early as in October 1936, she wrote from Spain (the title of her article, "Reflections That No One Is Going to Like," is telling): Spain may be undergoing "an experience that so many workers and peasants in Spain are paying for in blood."

> Europe has already undergone one experience of this sort, also paid for with a great deal of blood: the Russian experience. In Russia, Lenin publicly demanded a state in which there would be neither army, nor police, nor a bureaucracy distinct from the population. Once in power, he and his associates set about constructing, through a long and grievous civil war, the heaviest

bureaucratic, military, and police machine that has ever burdened an unfortunate people.

In May 1938 ("A European War over Czechoslovakia?") she recognized
many things that virtually no one, whether Right or Left, recognized at
that time (and that many people have not recognized even now, including
historians, such as A. J. P. Taylor). "A kind of protectorate would suit Hitler's
general policy much better than annexation of Czech territory," she wrote.
"To Hitler the main thing is that Czechoslovakia, regardless of whether or
not it is dismembered, become a satellite state of Germany."

A patriot is *not* a nationalist, but someone who is deeply troubled by the
faults and the self-deceptions of his own country. In the same essay Simone
Weil wrote about France and its foreign policy in the twentieth century:
"France tried to use the small nations to compensate for her own inferiority. At the same time she gives herself a sort of halo of idealism—entirely
undeserved, for what atrocious woes did the carving up of Central Europe
twenty years ago not create!"

After the war came in September 1939 she wrote:

> . . . we need first of all to have a clear conscience. Let us not
> think that because we are less brutal, less violent, less inhuman
> than our opponents we will carry the day. Brutality, violence,
> and inhumanity have an immense prestige that schoolbooks hide
> from children, that grown men do not admit, but that everyone
> bows before. For the opposite virtues to have as much prestige,
> they must be actively and constantly put into practice. Anyone
> who is merely incapable of being as brutal, as violent, and as
> inhuman as someone else, but who does not practice the oppo-
> site virtues, is inferior to that person in both inner strength and
> prestige, and he will not hold out in such a confrontation.

This was exactly what happened in 1940; and in a fragment written
after the great French collapse in June of that year, she foresaw what resistance meant—almost as if she had been a philosopher sitting next to Charles
de Gaulle in the night:

> We must . . . keep from falling into inertia, believing that the
> liberation will be carried out by others. Each of us must know
> that one day it will be his duty to take part in it, and hold him-
> self in readiness. . . .
> . . . We must think of the precious things we allowed to be

lost because we did not know how to appreciate them, things that we have to regain and that we will have to preserve, things whose value we now know. . . .

In 1942 she wrote, in a then unpublished essay, a searing and profoundly realistic dismissal of what is still, laughably but also lamentably, called "the science" of economics. It was included in a short and extraordinarily profound analysis of Hitler—in my opinion, without equal among the thousands of descriptions of that man.

"If Hitler despises economy," she wrote

> . . . it is probably not simply because he understands nothing about it. It is because he *knows* (it is one of the notions of simple common sense that he clearly possesses and that can be called inspired, since such ideas are so little understood) that economy is not an independent reality and as a result does not really have laws, since in economy as in all other spheres human affairs are ruled by force. . . . It seems to me difficult to deny that Hitler conceives, and conceives clearly, a kind of physics of human matter . . . laws that he has not invented but that before him were presented so forcibly and distinctly only by men of genius. He possesses an exact notion of the range of the power of force . . . [and] Hitler would be inconceivable without modern technique and the existence of millions of *uprooted men.*

She sacrificed her earthly life in the struggle against Hitler. Yet she refused the technological determinism that threatened the world, represented in the ruling philosophies of the two merging Superpowers, Russia and America. She saw not only through the failures of Marxism but saw the fatal shallowness of the Marxist view of human nature, that such a view was not only intellectually false but a spiritual evil, because it rested on a lie. But she saw, too, what Bernanos would pronounce in 1945, that the atom bomb was a triumph of technique over reason. Three years before 1945 Simone Weil wrote, "It is inevitable that evil predominate everywhere where technology is either completely, or almost completely, sovereign."

I think that it is especially apposite for us to contemplate the abyss that separates the spirit and the mind of this deeply traditionalist and Christ-attached woman (I shall have to say a few words about the mystery of her Christianity at the end of this essay) from the so-called Christian conservatives and traditionalists of our befuddled country now. Only think of the difference that separates Simone Weil's recognition of the evils of technology from Mrs. Phyllis Schlafly's statement: "God gave America the atom bomb." How incomprehensible her rejection of a technological materialism would be to our public conservatives and neoconservatives, especially now when humility and a knowledge of sinfulness—these essential essences of a Christian belief—have become entirely absent in the pronouncements, and presumably in the minds, of American "conservatives." On a mundane level this has a special meaning now, when there exists some similarity between the political forces of 1940 and today. For then, as now, the Left and the Marxists were an outdated defeated force. The struggle was that between two forces of the Right. On the one side stood Hitler, and those conservatives, nationalists, who were willing to go along with him. On the other side stood Churchill and de Gaulle, and those conservative and reactionary and traditionalist patriots who saw Hitler as an incarnation of a very *modern* evil, and who were inspired by the task of resistance to that evil.

"Between those who think that a civilization is a victory of man in the struggle against the determinism of things . . . and those who want to make man a thing among things, there is no possible scheme of reconciliation," Bernanos wrote in 1946. Here too Simone Weil was a forerunner, not only of this Bernanosian statement, but of the destruction that determinism, quantification, computerization and its inhuman consequences over life will mean—a new kind of evil abstractness where reality is being discarded not only in the communications but from the very minds of men. She wrote that as "the relation of the sign to the thing being signified is being destroyed, the game of exchanges between signs is being multiplied of itself for itself. And the increasing complication demands that there should be signs for signs. . . . As collective thought cannot exist as thought, it passes into things—signs, machines. . . . Hence the paradox: it is the thing which thinks, and the man who is reduced to the state of a thing."

To speak of Simone Weil without offering a full summary of her philosophy or a thorough account of her writing is perhaps to emphasize too much the prophetic quality of her thought. I am fully aware of the fact that Simone Weil would have found it utterly distasteful to be seen and described as a prophetess. But no matter: a true prophetess speaks prophecy despite herself, and clearly many of the things Simone Weil said a half-century or more ago have already gained an especial timeliness for our present—and for our immediate future.

And she was very humble. That unselfish quality makes her figure especially attractive in retrospect. Now it is a mysterious condition of humility that it becomes inseparable (and not at all for merely "psychological" reasons) from an attachment to a loving, and forgiving, God. But this is not the place to speak about Simone Weil's religion, and her steady movement in the direction of Catholicity. We know about a revelation of the beauty of a humble saintliness that came to her when she visited Assisi in 1937; of her deep impression of the days and nights she spent a year later in the French Benedictine Abbey of Solesmes; of the impact of the poem "Love" by the seventeenth-century English mystical poet George Herbert; and of many other mental and spiritual impulses that led her, wide-eyed, during the pilgrimage of her life, especially in its last humble phase. Only God knows whether she had come into His Church in the last days of her earthly life. We know that she wished to become a Catholic; and that her intellectual honesty and scrupulosity had kept her from an emotionally satisfying conversion. But she was buried in a Catholic cemetery in England; a priest said prayers over her grave; and flowers tied with a thin ribbon of the French tricolor were thrown into that grave. This much we know.

Kierkegaard once said that the truth is not given to us. That is for God alone. What *is* given to us is the pursuit of truth. The pursuit of truth—of truth, even more than of justice—became Simone Weil's self-imposed task. It guided her through the pilgrimage of her life. And there is more to that than a rare and inspiring achievement at which we should glance with respect, from a great and ever growing distance. It is a very worldly duty, too, in the best sense of that word. As she herself wrote: "The object of our search should not be the supernatural, but the world. The supernatural is light itself; if we make an object of it we lower it."

IV.

PLACES AND TIMES

*H*erodotus, the "Father of History," traveled widely throughout the eastern Mediterranean and Asia Minor, collecting information about the lands he visited and the peoples he encountered. He recorded many of the curious legends, strange tales, and extraordinary accomplishments of which he learned in order "to prevent the traces of human events from being erased by time." Since antiquity, the longing to wander and the writing of history have been intimately connected in the West. Philosophers may suffer no irreparable harm from remaining at home, but historians enjoy incalculable benefits from seeing the world.

Lukacs's writings about place are infused with the sights, sounds, and aromas of the past. The novelist would envy his ability to evoke both the external appearance and the interior life of a place in relation to its past—a past alive in bed linens, breakfast dishes, old-fashioned evening dress, cuisine, tables, chairs, and buildings. Nowhere in his large body of work does Lukacs call the past to life more vividly than when he writes about the streets and cafes of fin-de-siècle Budapest, the comfortable parlors of bourgeois Philadelphia, or a somber evening performance at the Dresden opera. A sojourn in the countryside and villages of ancient Transylvania; a holiday in the Gasteinertal; a journey through the battlefields and military cemeteries of northern France; a trip to London to attend Churchill's funeral; and a visit to Hitler's birthplace herein occasion poignant and often melancholy reflections on the past, present, and future of the West.

43

Budapest 1900: Colors, Words, Sounds
(1988)

On the night of the first of May in 1900 Mihály Munkácsy, the Hungarian painter, died in a private sanatorium in Germany. He was buried in Budapest nine days later. His funeral—like that of Victor Hugo in Paris fifteen years before, on another day in May—"was not to be the obsequies of a dead man. It was to be the celebration of an immortal. The nineteenth century was to enter into history with the man who had echoed its enthusiasms and its passions."

The catafalque rose on Heroes' Square in Budapest (Victor Hugo's body had lain in state under the Arc de Triomphe), before the six Corinthian columns and the neoclassical peristyle of the Hall of Arts. The sarcophagus of Munkácsy rested on top of a catafalque, forty-five feet high. The sarcophagus was designed, and completed in haste, by a well-known Hungarian sculptor, assisted by his students; the catafalque by a famous Hungarian architect, an apostle of Magyar modernism. This was odd because, except for a large bas-relief of a prancing stag in front, there was nothing either very Magyar or very modern in these designs. The sarcophagus was white, the catafalque velvet-black. Two enormous masts, draped with black flags, were crowned by white-painted laurel wreaths. There was a double row of topiary standards, with their black-green leaves. Amid these cascades of blackness another large white bas-relief in the lower center of the bier stood out, with Munkácsy's profile in a gilded frame. Four bronze torches flamed and smoked around the catafalque. It was a cool, windy day in May.

There was one element of an asymmetrical and Hungarian panache above this monumental funereal *mise-en-scène*: a huge black veil, draped on one side from the attic peak of the Hall of Arts, sweeping down in a half-circle. It suggested something like a great national actress in the act of mourning.

From *Budapest 1900* (New York: Weidenfeld and Nicolson), 3–28.

There was the national government and the municipality of Budapest: ministers, the mayor, black-coated, top-hatted. There were bishops, hussars, four heralds in costumes copied from one of Dürer's funeral paintings, three riders holding tall silver staves with black lanterns affixed to them. Incense and myrrh wafted away in the breeze. At half past three the funeral procession began to move: the hearse (decorated, too, in medieval style, by Hungarian painters) drawn by six black-blanketed, silver-caparisoned horses, and eight carriages packed high with wreaths.

The noise of the city died down. On the Pest side of the Danube the trolley cars had stopped. Black flags flew. The procession wended westward, on to the broad expanse of Andrássy Avenue. At that moment the sounds of the loud clip-clopping of the horses were softened, because Andrássy Avenue was paved with hardwood blocks. The Minister of Culture and Religion had ordered the schools closed for the day; the students were commanded to line the streets along the funeral route. The great procession flowed down that avenue, the pride of Pest, past the villas and the wrought-iron railings of the new rich, the consulates of the Great Powers, the May greenery and the young horse chestnuts.

At Octagon Square, a mile down Andrássy Avenue, a trumpeter halted the march, to direct the procession to turn leftward to the Ring. The bishops and the ministers stepped into their carriages. In front of the terraces of the coffeehouses gypsy bands played Munkácsy's favorite Hungarian songs. Stiff in black stood the Carpenters' and the Housepainters' Guild, and the choral society of a factory sent the bass of their threnody up the afternoon sky. There was a moment of disturbance: the chorus of the School of Blind Children was told to step forward to sing, but the mounted policeman in front had not been alerted, he rode into their frightened ranks to push them back. But there was no other commotion, save for the fear of some people that the narrow ornamental balconies of the newly built monumental apartment houses might crumble under the weight of the assembled spectators. On the second-story balcony of No. 44 Elizabeth Ring stood a small white-bearded figure, the grand old man of Hungarian literature, Mór Jókai. He lifted his hat as the procession passed under him. Women curtsied; there were women who knelt. A mile down the Ring, then another turn, on to Rákóczi Avenue, toward the city cemetery. By that time the crowd was dispersing in the violet twilight.

The lights were coming on along the boulevards of Budapest. In their shadows the vinous nocturnal energy of the city sprang to life, with its raucous, vinegary sounds filling the gaps of the night air. There was the sense of an odd holiday just past, of a mourning after. Again there was a curious parallel with that day in Paris fifteen years before, when the British

Ambassador wrote to Queen Victoria that "there was nothing striking, splendid or appropriate either in the monstrous catafalque erected under the Arc de Triomphe, or in the trappings of the funeral. There was nothing mournful or solemn in the demeanour of the people...."

This was the second time in six years that such a giant funeral took place in Budapest. In March 1894 the body of the great exile, the national leader Lajos Kossuth, had been brought home. Kossuth and Munkácsy had been the two most famous Hungarians known abroad. Hungarians knew that. It was one of the reasons, perhaps the main reason, for Munkácsy's apotheosis: the honor Hungary gained through his reputation in the world.

His path was the path of a comet. He was born in 1844, of German-Hungarian parents, in a dusty, backward town in northeastern Hungary: Munkács. Like many other people in his time, he would Magyarize his name—in his case, with an aristocratic flourish, appending the nobilitarian *y* at the end—from Lieb to Munkácsy. His early life was sad. His parents died. The orphan became a carpenter's apprentice in the home of a relative. He was a poor, thin wisp of a boy, racked by illnesses. During his adolescence he showed a talent for drawing. A sympathetic painter took him as a companion to the provincial town of Arad. From there he went up to Pest, and then to Vienna (where he failed to enroll in the Academy of Fine Arts—whether because of lack of tuition money or want of accomplishment we do not know) and back to Pest and then to Munich and Düsseldorf, where he made some kind of living from sketching but failed to make an impression either on his Hungarian painter companions or on his occasional German teachers. Then came the turning point. In 1868 he painted a large canvas, *Siralomház* ("The Last Night of a Condemned Prisoner"). It is a dark and exotic painting, exotic in its theme rather than in its execution: a Hungarian brigand, in peasant dress, sits and leans against a table, surrounded by shadowy figures in anxious grief. The background is dark, the brushstrokes strong, naturalistic, showing considerable talent in composition and in the art of contrast; the style is reminiscent of Courbet. It was an instant success. One of the earliest American private collectors, the Philadelphia merchant William P. Wilstach, bought it for two thousand gold thalers. Munkácsy was not yet twenty-six years old.

In 1870 this painting was shown in the Paris Salon. It earned the Gold Medal and celebrity for its painter. Munkácsy moved to Paris. He married the widow of a baron. Mme. Munkácsy had social ambitions. They had a palace built on the Avenue Villiers. Cabinet ministers, artists, ambassadors, Russian dukes, and the King of Sweden attended their dinners. Munkácsy was handsome. He had dark eyes, a beautifully kept beard, there was a suggestion of an elegant bohemian in the lavallière cravat that he habitually wore. *"Dieu, qu'il est beau,"* a Parisian woman said. He chose a mistress, the wife of a Parisian painter. A powerful art dealer from Munich, Sedlmayer, became his agent—more, his factotum. He kept telling Munkácsy what to paint. Munkácsy's paintings were sold for very large sums, more than sixty of them to rich Americans who had begun to collect art. They included Cornelius and William Vanderbilt, Jay Gould, William Astor, August Belmont, the financial genius Edward T. Stotesbury of Philadelphia, General Russell Alger the Governor of Michigan, Joseph Pulitzer the newspaper magnate (who was born in Hungary), Delmonico the New York restaurateur. His most successful enterprise was the large painting "Christ before Pilate," a subject that Sedlmayer had suggested. It was bought by the "Merchant Prince," the rising department store magnate John Wanamaker from Philadelphia, for $150,000, the equivalent of nearly $2 million one hundred years later. It is still exhibited every Easter in Wanamaker's department store.[1] Before it was shipped to Philadelphia Sedlmayer showed "Christ before Pilate" on a European tour, for three years. At the time (1881–84) there were people, including critics, who wrote that Munkácsy was the greatest living artist, the creator of the greatest modern work of art in the world, the peer of Michelangelo and Rembrandt. We know this from a folio volume that Sedlmayer had printed and that included reviews of Munkácsy, who had become so famous that a letter by an American admirer, addressed to "Munkácsy, Europe," was delivered to him in Paris. In 1886 Sedlmayer arranged for a triumphal tour in the United States. More of Munkácsy's paintings were sold (including a sequel to "Christ before Pilate" to Wanamaker). President Cleveland received Munkácsy in the White House, the Secretary of the Navy gave a dinner in Washington and Delmonico a festive banquet in New York. A "Hungarian" gypsy band played a "Munkácsy March" on the New York pier when he boarded the liner *La Champagne* for France.[2]

His success reverberated in his native country, to which he remained loyal throughout his life. He funded a modest purse for young Hungarian painters for their study in Paris. When "Christ before Pilate" was shown in Pest there were eighty thousand paying visitors; the chairman of the committee was Bishop Arnold Ipolyi, the most learned Hungarian prince of the church at the time. Around 1890 the Hungarian government commissioned Munkácsy to paint a monumental canvas for the new Parliament building, *Honfoglalás* ("The Conquest of Hungary"). Árpád, the founder, prime prince of the Hungarian tribes, sits erect on his white stallion, receiving the homage of the inhabitants of the Hungarian hills and plain. It is well beneath the standards of Munkácsy's best work. But he was already a sick man. A disease, latent from his youth, probably syphilis, had affected his body and his brain. Few people in Hungary knew that. He was a national hero; a national treasure; the most famous son of Hungary in the world.

A comet: or rather, a meteor. People speak of a meteoric rise when, in reality, a meteor is marked by its fall. That was the case with poor Munkácsy. He was a self-made painter, an artist of remarkable gifts, with a considerable talent for depth and contrast; but perhaps his best paintings are those surviving ones that are the least known—a few summer landscapes and a few portraits. There was a duality in his talent and, perhaps, in his entire personality. He could be profound, yet he was habitually superficial. He was obsessed with technique, yet he worked very fast. His masters, besides Rembrandt, were the late-Renaissance painters; yet he seldom visited Italy, and never traveled beyond Florence. He was a Francophile who never learned to speak or write French well. We may now see that his canvases—their subjects as well as their execution—are period pieces. At his best he could approximate the standards of Courbet, perhaps of Millet. But the Munkácsy meteor lit up the Parisian sky only briefly, and at the very time—in the 1870s—when the new generation of the Impressionists left the Salon well behind. Munkácsy execrated them. Before his death he wrote his wife that what he would really like was to start an academy "to do away with the exaggerations of the Impressionists." Long before that the French critics turned away from Munkácsy. Dumas *fils*, who liked him personally, said to his Hungarian friend Zsigmond Justh: "Munkácsy is an inflated reputation who has both profited from his wife and been damaged by her."[3] Huysmans looked at "Christ before Pilate" and wrote that Munkácsy had a taste for nothing but décor: "*le rastaquouère de la peinture*," a dubious adventurer. Others called his house a "*palais de poncif*," a palace of a hack. Two years before Munkácsy's death the contents of the house on the Avenue Villiers were auctioned off: the Gobelins, china, Persian rugs, antique guns, and some of his paintings went for almost nothing. A later generation was to find that the very material of his paintings was deteriorating. Munkácsy habitually used a black bitumen ground for his large canvases. This tended to fade his colors with the passing of time.

The pomp and the circumstance of Munkácsy's state funeral obscured all of this;[4] and in the grandiloquence of the Budapest newspapers in May 1900 there was no trace of a reflective tone. But it must not be thought that the recognition of Munkácsy's limitations was the particular reaction of Parisian critics, of a culture five hundred miles to the west and many years ahead of Budapest. As so often in the history of Magyar intellect and art, worldwide fame was one thing, true merit another; and the two would rarely correspond. At the very time, 1873, when the Munkácsy comet reached its apogee in the salons of Paris, a Magyar painter, Pál Szinyei-Merse, painted a canvas, "May Picnic" *(Majális),* that eventually came to be regarded as the finest Hungarian painting of the nineteenth century. I write "eventually," because its initial reception in Budapest was so inadequate that Szinyei-Merse turned away from painting for many years to come. Yet it is significant that both the composition and execution of "May Picnic" corresponds exactly with the time and the emergence of the vision of the great French Impressionists, the early Monet or Renoir. In Paris Munkácsy had a young Hungarian friend, László Paál, who died tragically young, but whose canvases, as we now know, represent superb individual variants of the Barbizon school. (Millet regarded him as the most promising of the younger painters.) In the Budapest of 1900, of every thousand people to whom Munkácsy's name was a household word, perhaps one knew the name of Paál. Yet years before Munkácsy passed away painters in Hungary had already rejected the pictorial tradition that he represented. That tradition—despite Munkácsy's Francophilia and his Paris residence and his Paris success—was essentially a German, a Munich one; but by the 1890s the best Hungarian painters had broken away from that. They withdrew, not into bohemian conventicles, but to serious workshops in the country, in Nagybánya, Gödöllo, Szolnok, to open their windows, to go ahead with a Hungarian school of plein-air painting, built up with colors that would not fade. The first exhibition of the Nagybánya painters took place in 1897; and by 1900 modern painting in Hungary had not only begun, it was in full development.

These painters were criticized, indeed, excoriated by some of the conservatives whose bastion was that Hall of Arts from where Munkácsy's body was sent forth on his last journey, but no matter: these painters knew not only what they were doing but also where they stood—and sat. In 1900 in Budapest the painters', sculptors', and architects' habitual coffeehouse was the Japan on Andrássy Avenue, with its tables that sometimes bore their penciled drawings on their raspberry-color marble surfaces (on one occasion a respectful art collector cajoled the owner of the coffeehouse into selling him one of these tables, which he then had carted home). The Japan was only a few steps away from the grandiose apartment houses of the Ring. That Elizabeth Ring—not only its buildings but its atmosphere, colors, sounds, and the language along its pavements—was typical of Budapest in 1900; but so, too, were the minds and the talk of the people in the Japan.

"This city," wrote Gyula Krúdy about Budapest, "smells of violets in the spring, as do mesdames along the promenade above the river on the Pest side. In the fall, it is Buda that suggests the tone: the odd thud of chestnuts dropping on the Castle walk; fragments of the music of the military band from the kiosk on the other side wafting over in the forlorn silence. Autumn and Buda were born of the same mother." In Budapest the contrast of the seasons, and of their colors, is sharper than in Vienna. It was surely sharper in 1900, before the age of the omnipresent automobile exhausts and diesel fumes. Violet in Budapest was, as Krúdy wrote, a spring color; it was the custom to present tiny bouquets of the first violets to women as early as March. They came from the market gardens south and west of the city, sold along the Corso and in the streets by peasant women. In March, too, came the sound and the smell of the rising river. The Danube runs swifter and higher in Budapest than in Vienna. It would often flood the lower quays, and the sound and sight of that swirling mass of water would be awesome. By the end of April a pearly haze would bathe the bend of the river and the bridges and quays, rising to Castle Hill. That light would endure through the long summer mornings, lasting until the mature clarities of late September.

At night the shadows retreated, and a new, dark-green atmosphere grew over the city like a canopy of promise. This was not the acid green springtime of Western Europe: May and June in Hungary, even in Budapest, have something near-Mediterranean about them. The smoke from the myriads of chimneys retreated with the shadows (except, of course, the high blown smoke of the mills and factories in the outer districts). The chairs and tables were put out before the cafés and in the open-air restaurants. It was then that the nocturnal life of Budapest blossomed, a life with singular habits and flavors that began early in the evening and lasted into the dawn, in which so many people partook. There were avenues in Budapest which were more crowded at ten at night than at ten in the morning, but not because they were concentrations of nightlife, such as Montmartre or Piccadilly. The freshness of the dustless air, especially after the May showers, brought the presence of the Hungarian countryside into the city. Somewhat like parts of London in the eighteenth century (or Philadelphia in the nineteenth), this smoky, swollen, crowded, and metropolitan Budapest was still a city with a country heart, with a sense that a provincial Arcadia was but an arm's length away. By May the violets were gone but there was a mixture of acacias and lilacs and of the apricots, the best ones of which in Hungary were grown within the municipal confines of Budapest. There was the sense of erotic promises, earthy and tangible as well as transcendent. It penetrated the hearts of the people, and not only of the young; and it was not only a matter of espying the sinuous movements of women, movements more visible now under their light summery frocks. It was a matter of aspirations.

Summer was hot, hotter than in Vienna, sultry at times, broken by tre-

mendous thunderstorms, but almost never damp. When the dark thunder-
heads convened high over the dry, dusty streets, they carried the promise
of relief and the return of the long pleasant summer evenings, for the evenings were almost always cool. There is not much difference between a
May and an August night in Budapest, except of course in the vegetation.
Even on the hottest of days the trees were green, never sere. Summer was
the recurrent feeling, the promise of pleasure in *le bel, le frais, le vivace
aujourd'hui*; and a Budapest bourgeoise or a young gentry wife threw open
the double-leaved windows and leaned over her geraniums with the same
movement—and perhaps, too, with the same movement of the heart—as a
Frenchwoman on the Côte d'Azur at summertime circa 1900, a little out of
season but *fraîche, belle, vivace,* nonetheless. Surrounded by the yellow, pow-
dery Hungarian countryside, Budapest then spread along the banks of the
Danube like a green bower; or, perhaps (for those who prefer vegetables to
flowers), rather like a super-large green cabbage whose outer leaves were
edged, here and there, with the black rime of smoke from the factory chimneys. The crowded town, packed with people and rows of apartment houses,
gave the impression—and the feeling—of a summer resort, perhaps even
that of a spa. Few people complained of the summer in Budapest, except
for those who employed it as the pretext to proclaim their departure to
vacation places well known. A profusion of fruit, greenery, and fish spilled
out from the markets to the sidewalks. Young people stayed up late, into
the dawn. Older people, daydreaming on hot afternoons, turned their
thoughts to the winter season to come, thinking of new circumstances, new
quarrels, new flirtations.

Autumn can be a short season in Budapest; in any event, its beauties are
unpredictable, like those of rapidly maturing women—or, perhaps, unpredictable like the melancholy of Hungarian men. It is not only that the owl
of Minerva flies at dusk; it is also that the best writers of Hungary, living in
Budapest around 1900, had autumn in their hearts. The instruments of
their internal music were not springtime violins, or the summery bravura
of the gypsy bands whose music in the summer mixed with the crunch of
the gravel and with the clanging of the dishes in the open-air taverns and
restaurants. The deepest, the truest sound of Magyar prose is not that of a
canting and chanting violin; it is that of a cello.

March, not April, is the cruelest month in Budapest; and November the
saddest. A century ago it was the only month when that great bell of clear
air over the Hungarian plains became striated with damp fog. That fog
swirled around the broad pillars of the Danube bridges, it rose to cloud the
high hills of Buda. On All Souls' Day thousands of people streamed toward
the cemeteries of Budapest, with flowers in their hands, on that holy day

which is perhaps taken more seriously in Hungary than elsewhere because of the national temperament. *Temetni tudunk*—a terse Magyar phrase whose translation requires as many as ten English words to give its proper (and even then, not wholly exact) sense: "How to bury people—that is one thing we know." The greatest tragedies in the history of modern Hungary—the hanging of twelve martyred Hungarian generals after the collapse of the War of Independence in 1849, the collapse of the ancient monarchy in the defeat of the First World War in 1918, the collapse of the deeply torn and divided effort to free Hungary from its deadly alliance with Hitler's Reich in 1944, the collapse of the great national rising in 1956, centered in Budapest—all happened in October or early November. For Budapest in 1900 the last three of these great tragedies were still unknown.

And then, one morning—it would come as early as in the third week of November, and surely before the middle of December—one of two new things was happening. A clear sky had risen over Budapest again, with the paler gold of a winter sun refracted by the crystalline cold. Or the sky was gray but rich, great flakes of snow were coming down all over Budapest: a celestial filling, like the goose down in the comforters of its bedrooms. In 1900 in Budapest winters came earlier than they come now. They were colder and snowier. There were still years (though not in the calendar year 1900) when the entire stretch of the Danube was frozen, and adventurous men could walk across the ridges of ice from Pest to Buda. There was a sense of feasting and of innocence in the air. Unlike in the snow-laden country, winter in Budapest was something else than a season of long rest and sleep; it was another season full of promise and excitement. The streets of the Inner City were filled before noon, with women and girls parading in their winter finery, and with promenading gentlemen in their fur-collared great-coats. Girls without furs were equipped at least with a furry muff. They were stepping in and out of the confectioneries and the flower shops and the glove-makers with tiny packages wrapped in rosy, crinkly papers, hanging daintily from the tips of their little fingers. Among the horse-drawn carriages on the avenues in 1900 there still slid in and out a few sleighs—black-lacquered, drawn by black horses, and with silvered tackle, with the laps of their passengers wrapped in ancient fur-lined blankets. What the city offered was this agreeable and satisfying contrast of exterior ice and interior fire: of the diamantine, light blue, crackling cold climate of the streets only a few steps away from the inner atmosphere of the houses with the cozy warmth of their cosseted bourgeois interiors, with deep-red carpets underfoot and perhaps with crimson tongues of fire not only in the grates of the tile stoves but in many hearts. Even in the dark, grimy streets, with their forbidding doorways and freezing entrances, the white snow thick around provided not only a contrast in color but in atmosphere: gazing inside to sense the hot interior fug, or looking outside from their cramped interiors into the snowy streets was equally good. The crunch of the snow, its odd chemical smell, the roofs and the windowsills and the shop signs and the monuments of Budapest picked out in white gave the city a compound of secure feeling. Behind those windowsills the housewives patted the long square insulating bolsters between the double windows into place; and the few walkers along the quays or up along the deserted streets and parapet walks on Castle Hill must surely have been lovers.

It was the season of long dinners, of heavily laden tables with the roasts, sausages, bacons, fowl, and game sent up to the families from the country; of the smells of wet wool and leather and pastry cream and perfume in the shops of the Inner City; of the anticipations of Christmas, of dancing assemblies and balls; and for the young, the chance of meeting on the skating rink of the Budapest Skating Club, on the frozen lake in City Park, under electric lights on weekday evenings. When the little blue flag of the club was up at Octagon Square it meant that the ice was sufficiently hard for the skaters—and for their flirtations, while the girls' chaperones would gossip behind the windows of the clubhouse that was warm as an oven, aglow in the dark like the redness behind the isinglass of a stove, reeking of oiled leather, coal-smoke, and the melted ice on the rough floors of that waiting room. It was a city of distinct anticipation and of distinct seasons, more distinct than now.

The year 1900 was the noon hour of Budapest, even in winter. Summer was galloping in its skies and in its heart. Foreign visitors arriving in that unknown portion of Europe, east of Vienna, were astounded to find a modern city with first-class hotels, plateglass windows, electric tramcars, elegant men and women, the largest Parliament building in the world about to be completed. Yet the city was not wholly cosmopolitan. There was the presence of the Hungarian provinces within its streets and within its people, so many of whom had come to Budapest from the provinces where they were born. In another sense, too, it was less cosmopolitan than the backward, unkempt town of a century before, whose inhabitants had been a mixture of Magyars, Germans, Swabians, Greeks, and Serbs. Now everyone, including the considerable number of Jews, spoke and sang, ate and drank, thought and dreamed in Hungarian. This was a very class-conscious society: there was as great a difference between the National Casino of the feudal aristocracy and the Café New-York of the writers, artists, and artistes as there was between the elegant clubhouse and the plebeian grandstand at the racetrack. These worlds were separate, yet they were not entirely unbridgeable. Certain aristocrats respected the writers and painters; in turn, most of the writers and painters admired the aristocrats, especially when these were to the manner born. They read the same papers, sometimes the same books, saw the same plays, knew the same purveyors. They dined in different places, their tables were set differently; but their national dishes, their favorite musicians, their physicians, and their actresses were often the same. In Budapest there was no particular *vie de bohème* restricted to writers and artists; indeed, the city did not have an artists' quarter—no Bloomsbury or Soho, no Montmartre or Montparnasse, no Munich Schwabing.

It was a grand place for literature. The ancient Magyar language, the vocabulary of which was reconstructed and enriched with great care, sometimes haltingly, by the patriot writers and classicists of the early nineteenth century, had become rich, muscular, flexible and declarative, lyrical and telling. But the Magyar language is an orphan among the languages of Europe. It does not belong to the great Latin, Germanic, or Slavic language families. Mostly because of this, Hungarian literature had no echoes, no reverberations, no reputation beyond Hungary. During the entire nineteenth century only one Hungarian writer, Mór Jókai, was frequently translated abroad; and by 1900 Jókai—as well as the style and scope of his novels— had grown very old. But in 1900 Budapest rang with the reverberations of literature. Every Hungarian writer knew that. During the literary, cultural, and political revival of the nation in the nineteenth century none of the great poets and writers had been born in Budapest. In 1900 this was still largely true, but they all had gravitated there. They lived in Budapest not only because of the evident advantages of living close to the newspapers and publishers who would purchase their words. They needed the atmosphere of the city. This was true even of such fine writers as Géza Gárdonyi or Kálmán Mikszáth,[5] who were truly provincial in the best sense of that adjective: country writers, saturated with the colors, odors, and music of the countryside and with the speech of its people. But for the first time in the history of Hungarian literature, in 1900 there were writers who chose not only to write in, but *of* Budapest. They were not necessarily the greatest writers of that period, though some of them were. In 1900 Budapest and Hungarian literature had become inescapably intertwined.

So I am compelled to describe three writers who wrote about Budapest in 1900—in the ascending order of their talents. They were Tamás Kóbor, Ferenc Körmendi, and Gyula Krúdy. The very title of Kóbor's book and the very date of its publication fit our theme exactly. The title of his novel was, simply and squarely, *Budapest,* written in the year 1900 and published in 1901. Portions of it actually appeared, seriatim, in 1900 in the literary periodical *A Hét,* which was the principal literary periodical at the time; Kóbor was one of its principal contributors. He was the very first Hungarian novelist who was actually born in Budapest.[6] Kóbor's *Budapest* is a period piece, largely forgotten now, but not without some merit, and of considerable interest for our purposes. What Kóbor attempted in *Budapest* was a Budapest version of Arthur Schnitzler's *La Ronde*, the famous book published in Vienna as *Reigen* four years before.[7] It is surely possible, and almost probable, that Kóbor was influenced by Schnitzler. The theme of both books is a chain (in *Budapest* a sequence rather than a circular chain) of sexual liaisons, of love affairs. There is, however, a great difference between the two books. Schnitzler was a very talented craftsman; Kóbor's writing is more uneven, cruder. Schnitzler's main interest was sexuality; Kóbor's the social portrait of a city. Schnitzler is a sometimes brilliant journalist, an exponent of that bourgeois neurosis within a culture that agitated and inspired the theories of Freud; but his portraiture of a place is definitely secondary to his main theme. Kóbor's book is deeply pessimistic, whereas Schnitzler's pessimism is implied: in almost all of Schnitzler's writing one senses a cynical smile on his lips, whereas there is no smile on Kóbor's face at all. In Kóbor's *Budapest* the conditions of the sexual lives of kept girls and married women and their husbands are meant to illustrate his main concern, which is the immorality—immorality, rather than neurosis—of a city where misery and riches, servility and haughtiness, abjectness and power, the still-strong presence of a feudal class-consciousness and the ever stronger, ever increasing influence of money live side by side. And it is the abjectness of moneylessness, the poverty-ridden lives of women and their daughters in the dark warrens of apartment houses with which Kóbor was so familiar, which shocks and moves us in his book. His description of the lives and the conditions of the upper class is much less successful. It is a book of miseries rather than of grandeurs, a somber book full of harsh smoke and strong, unrefined flavors. As Kóbor wrote in his introduction in 1901: "I directed my light to the depths above which Budapest is being built." He did not quite succeed, in part because its depth does not a building make. Yet Kóbor's *Budapest,* with its dark wintry scenes, remains a significant corrective to that no less real climate of summer that in 1900 galloped in the skies of Budapest and in its heart.

Another book that illuminates that place and time, in a very different way, is the monumental novel of a writer who is largely forgotten, even in his native country, despite the fact that his *A boldog emberölto* (*The Happy Generation*) had indifferent and abbreviated translations in Paris and New York. Ferenc Körmendi's writing career in Hungary was very short, a mere seven years in the 1930s, after which he left Hungary for England and then the United States, where he wrote little. Significant of *The Happy Generation* is, again, its chronological condition—in this case, the linchpin of Körmendi's entire theme. It is the story of a man who is born in Budapest on January 1, 1900, on the first day of the new century. It is a great Budapest *haut-bourgeois* novel, even though, I repeat, it is not (perhaps not yet) so recognized. Körmendi was as much influenced by Thomas Mann as Kóbor had been by Schnitzler's *La Ronde.*[8] But there is an essential difference between Mann's *Buddenbrooks* and *The Happy Generation. Buddenbrooks* is the story of the rise and tragic decline of three generations of a family; *The Happy Generation* is the story of a half-generation, the life and family of a single thirty-year-old man, a descent from a sunlit plateau of prosperity and security to the tragic collapse of his own desire for more life. It is entitled *The Happy Generation* because in 1900, when its protagonist is born on Andrássy Avenue, everything is suffused with the optimism of security, respectability, cultivation, and progress; indeed, on one occasion his father says so. "The generation," he tells his two sons, "in which you will grow up will be fortunate[9] . . . there seems to be no reason why it should not be so."

Of course this novel, unlike Kóbor's *Budapest,* was written and inspired by retrospect, by the painful and melancholy retrospect of the 1930s (it was published in 1934, the year after Hitler had assumed power), when the world of 1900 seemed so blessed, so far away, so irretrievably lost. In this, *The Happy Generation* precedes Stefan Zweig's *World of Yesterday* by nearly a decade, a work that is a novel, not a wistful memoir; but the respect for the secure standards and values of the world of 1900 is as strong in Körmendi's novel as in Zweig's nobly pathetic reminiscences written in his Brazilian exile. For our purposes, *The Happy Generation* is important because it shows the sunny atmosphere of the Andrássy Avenue bourgeoisie at and after the turn of the century: not only the sureties and the securities but also the presence of the solid bourgeois virtues of personal and civilizational probity, perhaps concentrated in the admirable doctor and father, the head of the Hegedüs family. Their spacious apartment may be full of bibelots, their curtains may be heavy, but the sunshine of that summery Budapest of 1900 filters through. It is a world of protective affinities: of a few old family portraits, many comfortable armchairs, and the noonday scent of the forever first course of the Sunday family dinner. With all of this, *The Happy Generation* is not really tainted with nostalgia, while it is a nearly perfect rendition not only of the atmosphere but of the mental aspirations of a class of people, of a place, of a time. It is the greatest work of Körmendi (surely in size: 850 pages), who was not a *very* great writer; yet *The Happy Generation* deserves recognition not only in the annals of literature but also by historians who wish to know much about that place and time.

And now we come to the greatest writer of Magyar prose in the twenti-

eth century, perhaps to the greatest prose writer in all Hungarian literature, and surely one of the great writers of Europe—even though he is
seldom translated and remains largely unknown outside Hungary. This is
Gyula Krúdy, who arrived in Budapest in 1896, when he was not yet eighteen, and whose first contributions had been printed by provincial newspapers when he was thirteen. He was one of those writers in the Hungarian
provinces for whom Budapest had become a magnet. His father wanted
him to be a lawyer. "I shall be a poet in Budapest," the son said. (He never
wrote a single poem there.) The father, a member of the old, impoverished
gentry of his province and country, disinherited him, for more than one
reason. It was a break not only between two generations but between two
centuries. Again there is a chronological coincidence. The father died on
December 30, 1900, the exact last moment of the old century. By that time
his son was a published writer in modern Budapest. The first volume of his
stories was printed in 1899, when he was twenty years old. His first long
novel appeared in 1901.

Except for short absences, he remained in Budapest for the rest of his
life. But for many years he did not write about Budapest. He wrote about
melancholy provinces on the great Hungarian plains, about little towns in
the shadows of the Carpathian mountains. It was not until later, about 1912,
that he began to turn the magical searchlight of his memories on Budapest.
Thereafter he would write often about the city, and about the city around
1900, in his own lyrical style, with a depth and with an evocative music, in
ways in which no one has written about it either before or since, and perhaps—no, most probably—no one ever will.

I must translate a few of his passages about Budapest at some length.
This is inevitable, since he is the writer of colors, odors, and sounds. His
descriptions of Budapest were scattered in hundreds of places in his novels, sketches, and feuilletons. Here and there some of them have been put
together in small volumes, published decades after his death. In this fantastic profusion of his passages and writings about Budapest there is a duality
or, rather, an evolution. Krúdy, who with all of his liberality of spirit and
startlingly modern prose style was a very historically minded writer, a reactionary in the best sense of that much abused word, would flail, on occasion, the loud, commercial, shamelessly eager metropolis of 1900—con-
trasting its spirit with its slower, calmer, respectable, near-provincial past.
At times he wrote that the city lost its virtue around the time—perhaps in
1896, the year of the great Millennium Fair—when cannons boomed and
the city glowed, celebrating the greatness of Hungary, the very year when
he had arrived in Budapest. He wrote once about Franz Josef's visit to
Budapest in 1896, to this once town of "smaller houses and modest citizens,

of young, rosy, patriotic girls waving their handkerchiefs, of a quiet and unrebellious antiquity." But now "Pest had thrown off its mask of modesty; each year she put on more and more jewelry; the unassuming had become loud, the thrifty had turned to gambling, the virgins brought up in severe convents had begun to take pride in the fulness of their breasts. . . . Pest had become unfaithful. . . ."

> This *raffinée* courtesan of a city had forgotten the triumphs of the young monarch at whose bosom she had once thrown herself, in the time of her fresh innocence. . . . Her shoulders no longer breathed the odor of holy water. Pest lifted her once downcast eyes; she was no longer satisfied with little presents of honey and gilded walnuts. She had become conscious of her developing charms; she discovered her new side that was both *gamine* and cosmopolitan; this once little wallflower had begun to appreciate herself; and the thrifty old gentleman was disturbed to find that the demanding cocotte that Pest had become no longer loved him. The naïve virgin, who in the 1860s so happily imitated the crown-like hairdo of the thin-waisted Queen Elizabeth whom she had seen at the Merchants' and Artisans' Ball— she had become a wide-hipped, eager, unbridled female. The gentlemen, who at the time of the Coronation had begun to train their sideburns with the help of the Kishid Street barbers, had become fewer and fewer; and now only old janitors, veteran soldiers and ancient civil servants wore the Franz Josef beard. . . .

The mythical hero of an unfinished Krúdy novel

> saw that in the forest of the town the white-waisted, sentimental, virginal birches trembling in the wind had become fewer and fewer; he saw that those embroideries and needlepoints and laces that had been stitched by busy, light, feminine fingers were disappearing from the drawing rooms in the houses of the old citizenry; that the coiffures and the countenances of women no longer resembled the antique Madonnas in the churches of the Inner City or of Buda, but that the fashions were now dictated by infamous transient female personages, dancers and cocottes. . . . The tone of talk is ever more frivolous, the pursuit of pleasure ever more shameless as it whispers its selected phrases bending over the uncovered shoulders of the women in the theaters, or on the streets bending at the sides of their veiled hats, or even

in the apartments of families where one can still smell the scent
of the wax candles from a Christmas Eve hardly past. . . .

He saw, too:

> . . . the blue-white towers and the endlessly rising roofs; the white
> ships multiplying on the river and the rainbow-hued Danube
> bridges . . . the coming and going of wrinkles on the faces of
> those ladies whom one could find out of their houses every time,
> and who keep a spirit from the *Thousand and One Nights* in their
> homes (in the form of a scrubby little maid who does all the
> work, who sews the torn clothes of the children and cooks the
> midday meal for the husband). He saw the proud gentlemen
> forced into higher and higher collars to hide the premature folds
> of their necks and the premature trembling of their heads; he
> saw those heart-rending days in spring when the new frocks
> bedeck the pavements like flowers in the meadows; and the lilt-
> ing, snowy days in winter when the sun comes out at noon on
> Andrássy Avenue to encourage the poor office girls to step out
> with the gait of duchesses. . . .

Sometime during the darkening years of the First World War Krúdy's
flagellation of Budapest began to give way to a quieter, lyrical kind of nostalgia, a remembering of what was lovely and good in Budapest at its once
noontime. And by 1920 and 1921, when Budapest—surely the spirit of
Budapest—was under attack by a nationalist wave of sentiment and by the
nationalist regime, "They are reviling Budapest in the Parliament," Krúdy
began.

> Well, Pest has never been an agreeable town. But desirable, yes:
> like a racy, full-blooded young married woman about whose flir-
> tations everyone knows and yet gentlemen are glad to bend down
> and kiss her hand. . . . No matter how we country people may
> have been irritated, it was in Budapest that Hungarian culture,
> about which so many of the old, blessed Magyar people had
> dreamed, received its hallmark. Here the dancing in the the-
> aters is the best, here everyone in a crowd may think that he is a
> gentleman even if he had left jail the day before; the physicians'
> cures are wonderful, the lawyers are world-famous, even the
> renter of the smallest rooms has his bath, the shopkeepers are
> inventive, the policeman guards the public peace, the gentlefolk

are agreeable, the streetlights burn till the morning, the janitor will not allow a single ghost inside, the tramcars will carry you to the farthest places within an hour, the city clerks look down on the state employees, the women are well-read from their theater magazines, the porters greet you humbly on the street corners, the innkeeper inquires of your appetite with his hat in hand, the coach drivers wait for you solemnly during an entire day, the salesgirls swear that your wife is the most beautiful of women, other girls in the nightclubs and orpheums hear out your political opinions politely, you find yourself praised in the morning newspaper after you had witnessed an accident, well-known men use the spittoons in the café gardens, you are being helped into your overcoat, and the undertaker shows his thirty-two gold teeth when you take your leave from this city forever.

Yes, in those times:

How much is there to say about those blessed, peacetime years! Of the air of Budapest which, true, was often dust-laden in the wind blowing from the Rákos fields; but that air became that much sweeter in spring when the wind had turned and began to breathe from the direction of the Buda hills; dependable old gentlemen insist that one could then smell the violets from Mount Gellért within the city.... And listen again to the talk of these respectable men, because you will learn that in those times it was not at all shocking to wear houndstooth trousers in the spring, and a tiny bouquet in one's lapel, to wait on a certain street corner as if one were the swain of the Swabian flower seller and not of the lady in the blue veil who would approach from Váci Street....

Váci Street—the main shopping street of the Inner City:

The little squares of the Inner City were like confectionery boxes. There the breeze from the Danube was pirouetting with the rays of the sun, there gleamed the hired carriages at their stations from which countesses with their delicate feet had just descended; old pensioners sat on benches in their spotless clothes; the grocer with his wicker baskets and the baker smelling of his fresh kaiser rolls kissed the hands of the chambermaids in their black bombazine when these had rung the bell;

405

the serpentine waists of the vendeuses, the white blouses of the millinery girls . . . and the silvery heads of the booksellers gave the tone to this district. Whoever settles in the Inner City will remain a distinguished person for the rest of his life. It was easy to dress well from its shopwindows, easy to learn how to be fashionable, and every purchaser could have credit. The famous shops that sold the best goods from London, suits, hats, gloves, were memorable like a grand foxhunt in autumn. The merchandise from Paris arrived directly, scented like women before a grand soirée. . . . The waiter in the coffeehouse put the recent *Le Figaro* in your hands. The barber had learned his trade in Paris; virgins embroidered initials on linens; the spiceshop had the odors of a great freighter just arrived from Bombay. Around the hotels shone the footwear of wealthy foreigners, the carriage curtains would seldom veil the adventurous demi-mondaines, the jewels blinded with their shine and the bank tellers paid out brand-new bills. Blessed Inner City years! Like youth—will they ever return?

And in other streets, too:

Women smelled like oranges in Japan. Rákóczi Avenue was full of women of doubtful repute; yet they were pretty and young enough to be princesses in Berlin. Around the Emke coffeehouse stiff lieutenants and fake country gentlemen kept reviewing them. . . . The youngest girls wore silk stockings, and whitehaired women found their own brand of connoisseurs. The city was blessed with its cult of women. The eyes of men trembled, the women were so beautiful: black-haired ones, as if they had come from Seville, and in the tresses of the blond ones tales from an Eastern sun were playing hide-and-seek, like fireflies in the summer meadows.

The tone of the cello was deepest when Krúdy saw the duality of Budapest:

They kept on building every day, palaces topped by towers rising toward the sun; and at night it was as if there were endless burials—an everlasting row of tumbrils hauled the old broken matter out of the town, the cadavers of old people and of old houses, of old streets and old customs.

Perhaps from these translated excerpts English-speaking readers may be able to recognize, or at least sense, the particular tone not only of Krúdy's language but of the Magyar literary language—and of the Magyar spirit—which is that extraordinary combination, the constant presence of a minor key within the basic key of a major.

So beneath the noisy boom of Budapest there was that presence of a wistful and melancholy tone; and there was more to it than the echo of nostalgic memories, heard only in solitude and silence in the deep of the night, when the city noise had died down. But that blending of major and minor, of optimism and pessimism, of light and darkness is, after all, the inevitable human condition, and also the condition of any culture that is worthwhile. It is only that some people—and this is true about Hungarians—are more conscious of it than are others. As Pascal said, men are both beasts and angels. Hungarians know that—which is the reason why the fanatic insistence of a Dostoyevsky about that duality and about its coexistence in the human soul leaves them, by and large, unmoved: that unkempt Russian tells them nothing that they do not know.

In 1900 not only the colors and tastes and sounds but also the psychic tones of Budapest and Vienna were very different from each other. Budapest was still full of self-confidence. Its building fever, its financial prosperity were the consequences of that condition. This had much to do with the Magyar temperament, in which a deep-rooted (and nonreligious) pessimism is often broken by sudden bursts of appetite for life, of a physical appetite stronger but perhaps less finely woven than what the French phrase *joie de vivre* suggests. The results of this were visible, and palpable, in 1900. Vienna may have been neurotic; Budapest was not. There were plenty of troubles, dissatisfactions, shadows, darknesses in the life of the city; but there was, as yet, no definite desire to break with the past and no self-conscious doubts about the future. Within Magyar pessimism there is the sad music of the futility of human endeavors, but none of that Germanic *Angst:* the tone is often melancholy, but the appetite for life—including the material pleasures of words, sounds, colors, tastes, and touches—abounds. The Hungarian mind inclines to psychosis rather than to neurosis; but the German idea of the subconscious (as distinct from the unconscious), the idea that something is truer because it is "deeper," has had no appeal to the Hungarian mind, especially when it is expressed in intellectual categories whose very language is removed from the everyday realities of life. The Hungarian mind is very observant and sensitive to every psychic nuance, but it tends to recognize these from expressions of the conscious mind. Long after 1900, Freud's influence in Budapest was slight. One of the reasons for this is the declarative character of the Hungarian language and of

Hungarian habits of speech. There is this odd contradiction of the Hungarian temperament: a deep masculine reserve, but without the inclination to hide one's prejudices, loves, and hates. There were Hungarian disciples of Freud (Sándor Ferenczi), and there were Hungarian writers of great talent, Mihály Babits and Géza Csáth, who wrote profoundly about schizophrenia; but the great Magyar writers, knowers and alchemists of the human soul such as Krúdy, obsessed as they were with dreams and with the reality of dreams, never felt any need to expatiate upon the "subconscious"; and what they did not know about the strange inclinations of the male and the female, of the child and the mature spirit and mind, may not have been worth knowing.

Much of this is fairly evident from the literature of the relations of the sexes at the time, when the erotic life, too, of Budapest was less neurotic than that of Vienna. It was largely untainted by the late nineteenth-century despair of the Romantic Agony. At worst, erotic life was crude and male-dominated. At best, it was late-aristocratic rather than late-bourgeois, in the sense that the desire to please had a definite priority over the wish to be loved. Perhaps this is why foreigners found Hungarian men even more attractive than they found Hungarian women, whose beauty did have a definite renown at the time; for instance, many Viennese women married Hungarian men in 1900, while the reverse of such alliances was rarer. Romantic love, the desire to please, is the main theme of writers such as Krúdy, who otherwise was startlingly and at times even shockingly knowledgeable of the frailties of the sexes. The very different, but thoroughly Budapestian writer Erno Szép, in one of his best novels: "I was telling myself: I am in love, I love. To enjoy this woman physically: ah! there's an animal. I *am* an animal, too, but what I feel is not only that but its very opposite.... And, as a man, what I want from a woman I'll take in a way that is a hundred times sweeter for her than it is for me. She will be happy with me between her faintings and tears. Her fever will come, her tremblings will come, and her mouth will smother in the pillow a burning scream that cannot be heard beyond the wallpaper. . . ." And the serious Catholic Mihály Babits in his otherwise dark novel, *Halálfiai*: "That was the age of love in Hungary, of the love learned from the oldest Magyar novelist, a love that had turned to a phraseology: for what else could have been interesting in life?" A great poem by Babits is entitled *Two Sisters*. The two sisters are Desire and Sorrow. The poem is a deep, pessimistic tour de force of parallel and paradox (Sorrow becomes Desire, and Desire becomes Sorrow), but there is nothing neurotic or decadent in it. In the Budapest of 1900 desire and sorrow may have been sisters, but desire surely dominated that family scene; and, for once, Desire was the older sister and Sorrow the younger one.

This Hungarian comprehension of human nature (a comprehension that, however, is almost always individual, never collective), together with the reluctance of the Magyar mind at abstractness—may have been a factor not only in the quality of modern Hungarian literature but also in the worldly success of so many Hungarians after 1900. I wrote "after 1900" because this, too, is something that we can recognize only in retrospect: the extraordinary and varied success of a generation of 1900 coming out of Budapest. For it was around that time that from the gymnasiums and the universities, from the bourgeois homes of Budapest and the gentry families of this then fairly obscure and relatively small nation an extraordinary generation of scholars, scientists, writers, thinkers, inventors, philosophers, financiers, *faiseurs,* painters, composers, musicians—a generation of Nobel Prize winners and mountebanks (in some cases, perhaps the same persons were both)—came into the outside world that knows the names of many of them even now, while it knows the names of some of the best of them not at all. In the succeeding tragedies and vicissitudes of Hungary many of them left to seek their fortune and acquire their fame elsewhere. And some of the seeds of those tragedies and vicissitudes were already there in 1900.

Three generations and nearly ninety years later the Budapest of 1900 looks better than it was. In 1920 the Budapestian culture of 1900 was excoriated by many Hungarians, and very definitely by the official public philosophy of the nationalist and counterrevolutionary regime. Fifty or sixty years later, the officially Communist and Marxist government of Hungary has found it proper not only to permit but also to promote the commemoration and the celebration of monuments and of people, and the publication of the arts and letters of that bourgeois era, through historical reconstructions that are suffused with respect and often even with admiration. But then, much of the same has happened with the reputation of Vienna in 1900 (or with the urbane and bourgeois civilization of much of the Western world at that time). Who, in 1920 or even in 1950, would have thought that "Vienna 1900" would be the subject of the most successful and fashionable exhibitions in New York and Paris; that it would become the subject of a spate of books by non-Austrians; and that the cult of Franz Josef and of the Habsburgs would become sacrosanct in Vienna, with public homage paid to it by socialist governments in Austria? Yes, Budapest 1900, too, attracts us; but we must watch for the symptoms of an uncritical and, therefore, unhistorical nostalgia.

Still, 1900 was both a milestone and a turning point in the history of Budapest. It has a meaning that is more than chronological. It provides a contrast with Vienna 1900 and Paris 1900—two capital cities of capital importance for the culture of the Western world—about which so many books have been written. The *belle époque* is a pleasant nostalgic phrase, but the crisis of an older France and the breaking away from the ideas, ideals, and standards of the nineteenth century had begun in Paris fifteen or even twenty-five years before 1900. In Vienna, too, 1900 was the end of the Austrian *fin-de-siècle*, with many of its interesting artistic and intellectual symptoms and alarming manifestations. In Budapest, *le mal* (if it was a *mal de siècle*) was only about to begin. Yes: in that sense, perhaps, Budapest was behind Vienna. But what is "behind" and what is "ahead"? Yes: the crisis of the old Liberalism, the breakdown of the old political and capitalist order and of the urbane social and financial equilibrium had come in Vienna seven or ten or twelve years before Budapest. It is, of course, not arguable that what happened in Vienna (and what was happening in some Viennese minds, too) would influence the twin capital, that junior one, the Budapest about which many Viennese in 1900 were supercilious. They (as had Freud, for example) looked down on Budapest and on its Hungarians, that semibarbaric country and place. But what the Viennese did not know— and how could they?—was that in 1900 in Budapest the breaking away from the nineteenth-century habits of thought, vision, manners, and even speech was occurring even faster than in Vienna, and in different ways. At the very moment when Budapest became the indisputable focus of Hungarian culture, a new generation of Hungarian painters, writers, and composers sought and gained their inspiration from the Magyar countryside. The new Hungarian painters Ferenczi, Hollósy, Rippl-Rónai, and Csontváry had learned nothing from Klimt, Schiele, and Kokoschka; the writers Krúdy, Kosztolányi, Ady, and Babits were very different from Musil, Trakl, Hoffmansthal; Bartók and Kodály had little in common with Schönberg and Webern. Only in the architecture of Budapest can we still see a definite Austro-German influence.

For Budapest 1900 was the noon hour. The zenith of its prosperity in that year coincided with the zenith of its cultural life; and a few years later— rather precisely, again, in 1905–06—the breakdown of its parliamentary and political order coincided with many of the first appearances of new forms, shapes, manners, expressions. A new generation of men and women were coming into their own. Some of the colors, sounds, and words—the atmosphere, language,[10] and music of Budapest—would eventually change. "*Les parfums, les couleurs, et les sons se répondent*"[11]—there are few times and places in the world that illustrate that famous line from Baudelaire's *Correspondances* better than Budapest in 1900.

44

Philadelphia 1950

(1981)

$\mathcal{R}$epublican rule in Philadelphia ended in 1951, after sixty-seven years. In the 1940s the mayor was Bernard Samuel, an amiable non-entity, a figurehead among the Republican politicians. There was something typically Philadelphian in the placid indifference with which these politicians padded along on their self-appointed rounds through the corridors of City Hall, even when they heard the snapping noises of investigators gathering behind their tracks. The Republicans took some comfort from the standard figures of the voters' registration: as late as 1950, there were more than two Republicans for every registered Democrat in Philadelphia, 718,000 to 308,000. They also took some comfort from the national political temper that was running anti-Democratic and anti-liberal at the time.[1] Yet in Philadelphia things had begun to change. In 1947 Samuel had defeated Richardson Dilworth in the contest for the mayoralty; but in 1949 Dilworth and Joseph Sill Clark won the offices of city treasurer and controller. Grand juries were investigating various and long-standing practices of corruption in City Hall. Independent Republicans decided to support Clark, even though he was the local leader of Americans for Democratic Action. A new city charter was adopted. The *Philadelphia Inquirer,* daily trumpet for Republicanism, endorsed Clark for mayor. In November 1951 Clark won the race for mayor, and Dilworth the race for district attorney. The Democratic victory was complete.

It was reminiscent of the New Deal; this long-overdue but eventually overwhelming surge of the popular vote for reform (the symbol of the Clark-Dilworth party was a broom), this return of attractive patricians to head a popular government. If the Philadelphia New Deal was twenty years behind the national pattern,[2] so were the Philadelphia Republicans. In 1950

From *Philadelphia: Patricians and Philistines 1900–1950* (New York: Farrar, Straus and Giroux), 310–44.

their politics were still a kind of Business-Biblical Americanism of the Old Protectionist Dispensation; their candidates, real-estate men and Masons, brownish men with owlish faces, were politicians out of the twenties. The Republican national committeeman who ran state politics bore the name of G. Mason Owlett: *Nomen est omen,* again. He was the fugleman of Joseph P. Grundy, the latter in his eighties, still sprightly and hale, the boss of the still-powerful Pennsylvania Manufacturers' Association: a Taft Republican, he led the fight in the primary against the more liberal Duff. The Republican candidate for mayor of Philadelphia in 1951 was a clergyman, the Reverend Daniel Poling, known for his pursuit of profitable publicity and for the commercial pieties with which he larded his speeches from the pulpit. He lost.

All of this was reminiscent of something else, too: of the reform movements of the early 1880s, before the Republicans established their long hold on the city. Then, too, the reformers were supported by some of the older civic leaders, many of them independent Republicans. Then, too, a new city charter was written, against the low growlings of the ward politicians. Then, too, the final electoral triumph of the reform party came after years of determined work by the mugwumps. So in 1948 the distinguished old Edward Hopkinson Jr. was raised to the chairmanship of the City Planning Commission; his executive director was Edmund N. Bacon, Dilworth's ally, a sharp-featured modernist city planner (whose favorite of all painters was, as he once told this incredulous writer, Klee). In December 1948 a Greater Philadelphia Movement was founded, studded with patricians and independent Republicans: the chairmen were C. Jared Ingersoll, Robert T. McCracken, and W. Fulton Kurtz; the executive committee chairman was Lewis M. Stevens, a Wilsonian Progressive and lay Presbyterian leader; the executive director was Robert K. Sawyer, a liberal Quaker. The composition of the City Charter Commission, established in 1949, was similar. These were honest people, exercised by the sight of corruption and by the indifference to it of self-satisfied politicians. "In a democracy," Evelyn Waugh wrote in *The Ordeal of Gilbert Pinfold,* "men do not seek authority so that they may impose a policy. They seek a policy so that they may achieve authority." This was not true of these worthies. Their concern with the government and with mismanagement was authentic and sincere.

Most of them were lawyers. Nineteen-fifty was the Last Rally of the legal aristocracy of Philadelphia, their last assumption of civic leadership. Very few people were aware of this at the time; yet it was evident that, together with the composition of the city, the structure of its politics was changing—just as the composition of its bar association had changed, together with the very practice of the law.

Until about 1890 the education of a lawyer in Philadelphia took place in law offices rather than in law schools. The fundamentals were pleading, equity, trusts, and estates. There were, of course, lawyers on all kinds of levels (what the English called "accident-tout" had become the American "ambulance chaser" well before 1900); but the specialization of corporation lawyers, estate lawyers, divorce lawyers, criminal lawyers had not yet taken place, and the tax lawyer was just about nonexistent. Consequently, large firms were few. Most of the law offices (offices, rather than firms) bore the single name of the distinguished lawyer who headed them. Philadelphia lawyers were not necessarily hardened veterans of litigation, as the cliché suggested, nor were they experts in loopholes of accounting. They were advocates of civic law and civic order. Their offices were small and somber,[3] smaller than the increasingly luxurious and impressive offices of the burgeoning firms in New York; they were bereft of Persian rugs and chandeliers, replete with uncomfortable furniture and books. They had a family touch, which would in time include their clerks and their secretaries, women who were monuments of reliability and rectitude, devoting their lives to their employers. George Wharton Pepper recalled that, in 1939, fifty years after he had bid the Biddle office goodbye.

> I paid a courtesy call on Mr. J. Rodman Paul who, as a partner in the old firm, had fed me my first ration of Blackstone and had conducted many of the office quizzes. There he sat in the modern suite into which in recent years the firm had moved. Around him were the furnishings of half a century before, including a familiar framed facsimile of Magna Carta. "What ever happened to Morris?" I asked, referring to Mr. Biddle's clerk who in student days had seemed to us already an old man. "Nothing has happened to him," was the reply, "you will find him in an adjoining room." I gasped. "There were three stenographers in those days," I said, "Miss Shubert, Miss McGarry, and Miss McNutt. Whatever became of them?" "They are still with us," he said—and so they were.[4]

Of George W. Biddle (who had been trained by Binney and who, fifty years later, trained Pepper) his grandson Francis Biddle wrote: "He was the last of the old school of Philadelphia lawyers, trained in the classics, a little austere, courteous, artless, with his professional and personal standards."[5] The Lawyers Club of Philadelphia adopted a resolution that spoke of "his mastery of his cause, and his graceful oratory and delightful presence, whilst his spotless integrity and devotion to Christian principles evidenced the purity of his character." Reminiscing about her *fin-de-siècle* Philadelphia, Elizabeth Robins Pennell wrote before the First World War: "The recommendation to Philadelphia of its lawyers was not the high esteem they were held throughout the country, but their social standing at home—family gave distinction to the law, not the law to family."

Her next sentence destroys this truthful impression: "Approved Philadelphia names adorned the signs at almost every office door and not for some years was the evil day to dawn when the well-known Philadelphia families who inherited the right of the law would be forced to fight for it with the alien and the Jew."[6] Whatever "the right of the law" might mean, they did not fight for it. In 1952 the bar association for the first time elected as its chancellor a Jewish lawyer, Bernard Siegel—incidentally, not a descendant of an old Jewish family in Philadelphia—without a murmur.

The devolution that took place between 1899 and 1952, between the era of the Bispham and of the Siegel chancellorships, was of another nature. Throughout the United States the practice of law changed; and Philadelphia moved along with it. It was a devolution of legal practices rather than the result of the transformed ethnic composition of the bar—a rare instance when the changing character of a practice led to change in the character of the practitioners, rather than the reverse. The increasingly technical training of the law schools, the emphasis put on the case method, the geometrical growth of legislation and of regulation on all levels of government, the spreading intricacies of taxation, the crowding of the courts; in sum, the bureaucratization of the law amounted to an American devolution during the first half of this century, the consequences of which abide with us and the end of which is not yet. It developed apace with the bureaucratization of business and industry. As late as the 1920s, the main institutions of industry and banking in Philadelphia were still governed by men of old and known families. Corporate managers were to succeed them. As Edwin Wolf wrote, before 1929:

> Horace P. Liversidge was Philadelphia Electric; his successors were merely presidents of the company. Effingham B. Morris was Girard Trust and Joseph Wayne, Jr., Philadelphia National; those who followed them were but successful and competent employees. Nowhere was the change more clearly seen than in the legal profession, long the pride of Philadelphia and the reservoir whence many of its leaders came. Whereas George Wharton Pepper was recognized as the dean of the bar, Morris Wolf as the force behind the fastest growing office, and Robert T. McCracken as the most influential lawyer in town, it was firms

made up of galaxies of specialists which emerged as important. By 1940 no Morgan, Lewis, or Bockius was known as an individual but the firm was the biggest, richest, and most active in the city.[7]

This was, I repeat, a national phenomenon, not a Philadelphia one; but what happened in Philadelphia was a gradual (and, at times astonishing) disinterest in the law among the Philadelphia Quirites. In many instances disinterest in the law succeeded disinterest in politics within two generations. During the nineteenth century there were few prominent men who abandoned their legal practice after they had been admitted to the bar. During the twentieth century disillusionment with the law became more and more apparent.

This disillusionment took different turns. We have seen how in the lives of eminent men, such as Johnson and Ingersoll and Price, interest in art had grown apace with their waning interest in the law. This was not merely the consequence of a broadening view of the world that they acquired through the individual development of their minds. It corresponded with the change of legal practice in the United States; and also with the change—slower and less visible on the surface—in Philadelphia proper. What people would sometimes call "the Web," a close, interlocking relationship of families and boards and directorships, in Philadelphia still existed; but its influence became more restricted, and it was weakening. In 1900 one could detect two governments of Philadelphia side by side, a political and a social one, neatly separated but tolerant—perhaps too tolerant—of each other. It was the legal aristocracy which provided both the inevitable contacts and the relatively trouble-free functions of both. After the Civil War—in Philadelphia a little later than elsewhere—The Best Men No Longer Went into Politics (this was what Lord Bryce, after Tocqueville the most important foreign observer of the American scene, wrote at the head of a famous chapter in his *American Commonwealth*). After the First World War the best men were less and less interested in the law. This was a gradual development. They did not abandon it altogether; after all, men such as Johnson and Ingersoll and Price went on practicing some kind of law till the end of their active lives, and a career at law was still the expected and preferred occupation for the sons of the Philadelphia patricians until 1950 at least. Moreover, for every Johnson and Ingersoll and Price, there existed a Pepper, a Drinker, a McCracken, a Gates, Proper Philadelphians for whom the practice of the law was eminently satisfactory and who continued to occupy eminent positions in the civic order. Some of them combined their vocations with their avocations, like Henry Drinker, an amateur musician of a high order and an accomplished musicologist. Yet they represented a Philadelphia tradition which, though long-standing, was narrow. They were Republicans, embittered by the New Deal. At least on one occasion Justice Holmes thought that the Philadelphia lawyers were oddly circumscribed: they did not argue well before the Supreme Court. During the first half of the twentieth century, the law school of the University of Pennsylvania was probably the best in the country; yet Philadelphia and Pennsylvania ceased to be the legal Athens and Attica of the United States. During the 1880s John G. Johnson was offered a place on the Supreme Court of the United States on two occasions, but he declined: he'd rather be a lawyer in Philadelphia. In 1912 George Wharton Pepper would have accepted such an august appointment; but it was not tendered him. During the entire twentieth century, Philadelphia had but one Justice on the Supreme Court, Owen J. Roberts, a liberal Republican. His career on the Court was undistinguished, his main note of fame being his chairmanship of the investigation which absolved Roosevelt from responsibility for the disaster at Pearl Harbor.

The days of a legal aristocracy were passing. What Tocqueville had written in the 1830s: "The lawyers form the political upper class and the most intellectual section of society," a century later was no longer true. He was "aware of the inherent defects of the legal mind"; nevertheless, he doubted whether democracy could prevail for long "without the mixture of legal and democratic minds, and I hardly believe that nowadays a republic can hope to survive unless the lawyers' influence over its affairs grows in proportion to the power of the people."[8] The lawyers' profession was no longer a counterweight to a democracy, and the liberal lawyer was replacing the conservative one. Instead of the principal task of preserving traditional and private liberties, throughout the Republic the most successful and most renowned lawyers were trying to extend liberties to more and more areas of public life. "Judges," Blackstone had written, "are not delegated to pronounce a new law but to maintain and expound the old law"— and during the nineteenth century, generations of Philadelphia lawyers were brought up on Blackstone. During the twentieth century, that "certain scorn for the judgment of the crowd," which Tocqueville noted, was no longer true among American lawyers, including the most conservative Philadelphia ones. Among the younger ones the bureaucratization of the law resulted in existential frustrations, involving personal tragedies on occasion. There were a few instances in the 1940s when brilliant Philadelphia lawyers, full of promise, turned to the practice of criminal law, a choice previously unheard of—not, as some of their cluck-clucking colleagues thought, for monetary reasons, but because they found the standard practice in their large offices hopelessly dull: the combat in the courts was more interesting, and personally more satisfying. In other instances, the existential frustrations of young lawyers led to premature resignation, depression, alcoholism, even suicide. In an increasing number of instances, Philadelphia lawyers were no longer able to transmit the taste for the law to their sons, and many of the long ancestral chains of tradition were broken.

Still, in 1950, after nearly a century, the Best Men had returned to politics again. A coalition of patrician lawyers, including Republicans who turned Democrats, of eager young men, of civic reformers, would sweep the tired and corrupt Republican government out of City Hall. They elected Clark, who left the practice of law to enter politics, together with Dilworth, who eventually succeeded Clark as mayor. Many of their reforms, political or architectural, were long overdue. Yet the people who congratulated themselves on this failed to notice that it was but a belated adjustment to a national pattern—and precisely because of this, no longer particularly Philadelphian.

In any event, the result was a civic renaissance, in more than one way. The physiognomy of the city, long neglected, was refurbished. During and after World War I, the first plans had been made for a grand transformation, for a wide prospect to be cut diagonally athwart the petrified brownstone jungle northwest of City Hall. The Benjamin Franklin Parkway was to be rather magnificent (and, thus, quite un-Philadelphian), with splendid neo-classical buildings flanked by broad green parterres as it swept toward the first damp hillocks rising in Fairmount Park to the north. There was a French inspiration to it; its draftsmen were Paul Cret and Jacques Gréber, two eminent French architects, together with two Francophile architects of great talent, Horace Trumbauer and C. Clark Zantzinger. Their plans matured during World War I, and construction began soon afterward. Along this Champs-Elysées of Philadelphia Logan Circle was the Rond-Point;[9] like the Champs-Elysées, the parkway would slowly and majestically rise to its western culmination, the Philadelphia Museum of Art. Beyond it toward Fairmount Park, Philadelphia's Bois de Boulogne, a few modern apartment houses would rise, not unlike smart buildings in Passy or Auteuil.[10] Toward the end of the 1920s, however, building along the parkway ran out of steam (parts of the parkway remain barren and unfinished even now). Eventually its very name became vulgarized through its slangy abbreviation: it is—officially—the "Ben Franklin Parkway" now.

Around 1950, synchronized with the movement for civic reform, came two great surgical improvements on the face of Philadelphia. The demolition of the so-called Chinese Wall was about to begin. This was a large brick barrier, interrupted only by viscous, dark roadway tunnels forever dripping with black water, built originally to carry the Pennsylvania trains into Broad Street Station in the center of town.[11] The Chinese Wall was hideous—and, more important, unprofitable—so that even the lethargic Republican administration decided in 1946 that it had to go; but nothing much was done until the Philadelphia New Deal occupied City Hall, after which the demolition began to proceed. The eventual results were not altogether the best: within a decade Penn Center (an unimaginative name, to start with) consisted of a row of stiff and unimaginative square boxes of skyscrapers, indistinguishable from New York office buildings in the late 1930s, including a parochial imitation of Rockefeller Center, complete with an ice-skating rink and the pathetic possibility of an outdoor café. The café soon closed, the skating rink is sparsely used; it is overshadowed rather than washed by sunlight, the surface of the ice is soiled and gray.[12] When Philadelphia tries to go modern, she merely follows New York: and when she follows New York, the results are usually, and expectably, indifferent.

Still, Penn Center was an improvement over the Chinese Wall. The other great change involved Society Hill. That name, unlike Penn Center, had a snobbish (though, again, somewhat provincial) ring to it, perfect for the appeal of a new urban neighborhood whereto smart young couples would move. The revival of the name included a touch of publicity legerdemain: few people knew, even after 1950, that "society" in Society Hill had nothing to do with Society, that it was named after a Quaker neighborhood in colonial Philadelphia. In 1949 Harold R. Kynett, an eccentric old Philadelphian,[13] composed a little book, privately printed, with the title *For Better or Worse? Rambles on Progress and Otherwise,* in which he wrote:

> Once, in the flush of newly acquired information I made the statement that the region of Second and Pine Streets was a hill, known as Society Hill and on it, a Friends Meeting House commonly called the Hill Meeting. Polite incredulity greeted the statement and even quotations from the antiquaries could not quite erase the suspicion that I was a monumental liar.
>
> Today's visitor to Second and Pine would find never a trace of hill nor meeting, although traversing the streets in a car might leave the impression of crossing the Alps. Pine Street, between Front and Second, is a disconsolate clutter of wholesale establishments, interlarded with morose dwellings whose entire atmosphere is one of near-collapse. To say the neighborhood breathes a dispirited air is to put it mildly. At Second Street, the tattered remnants of Old Second Street Market, with shuttered windows and abandoned stalls, enhance the feeling of a deserted city.

But after 1950 this would rapidly change. The Philadelphia Redevelopment Authority set to work. Within a decade Society Hill would be in existence. A strict set of architectural regulations forbade the demolition or the transformation of buildings that had been erected before 1840.[14] Gradually this portion of the city emerged from dirt and neglect and obscurity. It became a reconstructed portion of Old America, restored and inhabited by a younger and more transient generation, together with a few Old Philadelphians who moved into small town houses. By 1970 Society Hill had become a tourist attraction.

There were arguments in the 1920s about the site and the shape of the Philadelphia Museum of Art. (Some of its opponents called it a Greek garage.) It dominated the skyline from across the Schuylkill River, the first impressive monument to be glimpsed by people coming by train from New York: the Acropolis of Philadelphia. Nineteen-fifty was its Golden Age. It was the focus of what was best in Philadelphia, or at least that was what some Philadelphians thought. Membership in the Museum had a social cachet to it. At the Museum parties the social and cultural aristocracy of Philadelphia would gather—often the same people, by and large, who were the leaders of political and civic reform. They took a great deal of pride in this institution. There was a sparkle to this civic renaissance of 1950, at those Museum parties where the handsome men and the attractive women of the older families would mingle, perhaps for the first time in the social history of this city, with the newer patrons and providers of art. A classical-music FM station began to broadcast in Philadelphia, without interruption by commercials. Six theaters were open regularly. The University of Pennsylvania was revitalized. For the first time in thirty-five years the Phillies won the National League pennant.[15] Nineteen-fifty: Philadelphia's New Deal.

This civic renaissance in Philadelphia was, as we have seen, similar in many ways (though unsimilar in others) to the reform movements of earlier times. Like the short-lived provincial reform efforts of the nineteenth century, it did not last. For underneath it all coursed a deeper development that was essentially unbroken: the decline of the power of the erstwhile patricians. In 1950 they still had considerable power—in part because of their material assets; more important, because of their authority. Eventually their authority would erode as fast as their power.

In 1950 this was, as yet, hardly visible at all—save, perhaps, from the odd perspective of an outsider, as this writer then was, and in so many ways still is.

Nineteen-fifty was a milestone in the history of Philadelphia; but it was not a turning point. Around the turn of the century John Jay Chapman (a close friend of Owen Wister) wrote: "We have escaped an age of tyrants, because the eyes of the bosses and their masters were fixed on money. They were not ambitious. . . . Mere financial dishonesty is of very little importance in the history of civilization. . . . The real evil that follows in the wake of a commercial dishonesty so general as ours is the intellectual dishonesty it generates. . . . The literary man is concerned for what 'will go,' like the reformer who is half politician. The attention of everyone in the United States is on someone else's opinion, not on truth."[16] This was as true in 1950 as it was in 1900. There was much in that civic renaissance in Philadelphia that was necessary, useful, perhaps even inspiring. There were attractive men and women who—at times admirably—spent their time, energy, money on causes involved with the improvement of the city and with the patronage of its art collections. Yet a certain cast of conformism went on to prevail everlastingly among most of them. The categories of the conformism had changed, but it was conformism nonetheless. *De rigueur* at those Museum parties (or at the Redevelopment Authority meetings) was the possession of the proper kind of opinions. These opinions in 1950, unlike twenty or thirty years earlier, were politically liberal and artistically avant-garde; but what difference did that make? In November 1950 the Diamond Jubilee of the Museum was celebrated by a glittering party. Fiske Kimball had brought together the One Hundred Greatest Paintings and One Hundred Greatest Drawings in America. It was the moment of his highest glory,[17] though he was already a sick man. He had lately succeeded in persuading some of the richest collectors in the United States to give their possessions to the Museum; he had the Golden Touch, half-Midas, half-Hollywood (his greatest triumph at the time consisted in getting the modernist-abstract collections of Arensberg and of Edward G. Robinson, the ex-Bessarabian movie actor, both from Beverly Hills). When the Museum went up, in the 1920s, the philistines of Philadelphia would make self-consciously complacent jokes about it as they drove past the construction. In 1950 many of these philistines were inside, parading past the abstract paintings, no less self-conscious, but also no less complacent. What Saki wrote circa 1910 was true of 1950 as well: the sure way of knowing nothing about life is to try to make oneself socially useful.

They surely knew little of the Philadelphia outside their confines. During the 1930s and the 1940s, certain Philadelphia painters painted scenes and vistas of the hilly neighborhood of Manayunk. Often their patronesses failed to recognize the scene, even though Manayunk is less than two miles from Chestnut Hill and clearly visible from across the Schuylkill. Some of them thought that it was an Italian hill town, a kind of Umbria impressionized or ashcanized.[18] As an addition to the Art Museum crowd the University Museum had become a social enclave, with its prehistoric stuffing and archaeological expeditions, replete with Old Philadelphians and their matrons going on the "digs," so very Philadelphian in its Franklinesque mix of Society and Science.[19] So was the American Philosophical Society (rich beyond the dreams of avarice), where a kind of somnolent philistinism reigned supreme, with measured pinches of incense bowl offered to the cold statuary of the scientific Franklin spirit, the society governed by the safest of professors, usually from the upper reaches of the University of Pennsylvania, descendants of Lancaster County Pennsylvania Dutchmen, thoroughly Philadelphianized, Anglophile, and Republican, having achieved their academic fortunes through passionate subjects such as histories of American medicine.

By 1950 some of the older Philadelphia traits had faded. One of them was the Philadelphia accent. In 1894 Owen Wister, out West, was often taken for an Englishman. As late as the 1940s there survived something like a Philadelphia accent, including a High Episcopalian *a*, its timbre different from the upper class *a* of New York or Boston or their suburbs.[20] More significantly, the Southern touch was fading, too. As late as the early 1940s, few of the girls who graduated from the best Philadelphia private schools would go on to college (they were the "brains," when compared with the debutantes); in this respect Philadelphia was still closer to Baltimore, Richmond, Charleston than to Boston or New York. Ten years later this was no longer true. And while the Southern touch was fading, the Maine attraction was stronger than ever; it survived the disastrous fire that destroyed most of Bar Harbor in 1947; indeed, around 1950 in Northeast Harbor ("Philadelphia on the Rocks"), much of Philadelphia society could be more often "at home" than at home. During the 1950s a painter who attained great national fame was Andrew Wyeth, from a family of talented illustrators. His careful craftsmanship was, however, inspired not so much by the rich Chester County land where he lived as by the climate of Maine; unlike the great traditional Philadelphia painters, Eakins, Cassatt, etc., his themes were, and remained, essentially cold. A painter of stubbled March fields and of stony textures, his landscapes and barns (and often even his models) differed from the old warm Philadelphia tradition; he was, in spite of his provenance, a Maine painter rather than a Philadelphia one.

In 1900 there was in Philadelphia, as we have seen, an appreciable, and often sharply nuanced, distinction between the older patrician families and the—relatively—new rich. This distinction did not exactly correspond to the difference of what sociologists would call the upper and upper-middle classes, even though it had certain similarities to it. In 1950 many of the erstwhile new rich of two generations before were, more or less securely, lodged within society; the old patrician families still existed, while the new

new rich were no longer predominantly Anglo-Saxon: a more or less normal and expectable development of social acceptance in which the catalyst was no longer intermarriage or business or church or club membership but rather, the patronage—public and social—of certain arts. This was the Philadelphian pattern of a national devolution, whereby Society had more and more to do with Celebrity. In Philadelphia the two were still far from being equivalent, or even related: but the first was—already—aware of the second. After all, celebrity means to be publicly known; the bridge between Society and Celebrity consists of publicity; and publicity will have its inevitable effect on people whose particular and discriminating manners are not matched by particular and discriminating mental interests of their own. The charmed privateness of the Philadelphia patriciandom had begun to erode. Evidence of this was there, among other things, in the social columns of the Philadelphia newspapers. In 1900 the social pages of the Philadelphia newspapers were filled with reports of all kinds of receptions, dinners, social events, no matter how inconsequential, item by item, column by column; the newspapers would print the items that had been brought to them, massive lists representative of the inclination of democracy for publicity, for people who believed what was printed in newspapers—while many of the events in the social calendars of the older patrician families went unreported. In 1950 much of this distinction between what, on the one hand, was old and private and secure and what, on the other, was self-conscious in its aspiration for publicity had disappeared. The social columns of the Philadelphia newspapers around 1950 were silly beyond caricature. The plainness and the innocence of the endless lists was gone; a kind of adolescent snobbery that is both bristling and unrefined had taken its place. The social columns were now something like gossip columns, but gossip columns that were extremely parochial. Unlike the then national gossip columns composed for people hopelessly distant from Society and Celebrity, and therefore prone to take a vicarious interest in the brilliant social lives of legendary men and women, the Philadelphia newspapers' social columns were now catering obviously to the needs of people who thought that the meaning of their membership in society might be further enhanced when that fact was publicly shown.

For one thing, the space given to these columns was enormous. In one newspaper alone there were *five* social columns each Sunday, running to as much as ten pages. "The Main Liner," "Jane Wister," "Philadelphia Pepper Pot by 'Frank and Phoebe,'" "Judy Jennings' Notebook," "Deborah Debbie" (the last the most insipid, composed for the younger set). Examples:

After church this morning we all went over to Uncle Robert's and Aunt Helen's for lunch. The conversation centered on their forthcoming trip to Palm Beach. Aunt Helen was busy debating over the clothes she would take while Uncle Robert and Daddy sorted fishing gear. They plan to stay until March, so perhaps I may go down for awhile. 'T would be divine! ("Deborah Debbie," February 5, 1950)

"Susie" La Baw and "Sonny" Knode seen at a party on the Main Line recently.... "Connie" Lavino riding in Chestnut Hill every day.... "Noodles" Knode still raving about the party "Eddie" Adams gave recently.... "B. J." Furley among the debs of the coming season as are "Zara" Bentley and "Ellie" Drinker.... ("The Main Liner," *ibid.*)

A couple we know got a record of the background music of *Lost Weekend.* They put it on the automatic phonograph and it played all night while they slept. Next day the husband joined Alcoholics Anonymous. The same thing happened to them last week—this time with the zither music from the *The Third Man.* Both have applied for permanent reservations at a well-known institution for mental disturbances. ("Philadelphia Pepper Pot," by "Frank and Phoebe," April 21, 1950—the lead story)

Sorted out my last year's summer clothes this morning to see what was still wearable.

Tonight Steve and I went to see *Battleground* which was one of the best movies I've ever seen. ("Deborah Debbie," April 21, 1950)

In the same number of the *Philadelphia Inquirer* the lead editorial bore the title: "For Vast Truth Drive against Red Lies." The lead editorial a week later: "Cold War a Task for All Nations."[21]

In 1950 the *Philadelphia Inquirer,* owned and directed by an unscrupulous newspaper magnate, was probably one of the worst morning papers of any great city in the world; it had all the features of cheapness and sensationalism, while preserving the format of a respectable morning newspaper, preaching an Americanism alternately sentimental and strident.[22] Few Philadelphians grumbled about this; they took the *Inquirer* for granted, for their reliable morning paper. It supported, as we have seen, the reform mugwumps on the local level—conforming to what seemed to be an irreversible popular movement—but beyond that, its nationalism was indiscriminate, vulgar, harmful. For in 1950 the hitherto last great wave of American extreme nationalism was rising fast: in January Alger Hiss[23] was properly convicted; in February Joe McCarthy fired the first star shell of his improper crusade, with his speech in Wheeling, West Virginia; in June the Korean War burst forth. The editorials, the headlines, the chortling columnists of the *Inquirer* scratched and screeched with the brummagem ideology of the day, elevating the banner and the slogans of anticommunism as if the latter were simply and squarely identical with American patriotism.

This was not the first time that something like this would occur in Philadelphia; but there was an underlying difference now. There was, for the first time since the 1840s, a swelling undercurrent of distrust between certain classes of people in Philadelphia—or more precisely, between people of different provenance and background. In 1950 the social leadership in Philadelphia was still predominantly Anglo-Saxon; but numerically the Anglo-Saxon element was a small minority. Many of its members were, as we have seen, active participants in the Philadelphia New Deal; their political convictions were, generally speaking, more liberal than that of the majority of the population. And just as the Cold War had developed out of the Second World War, the second Red Scare in the history of the United States coagulated, in many ways, out of the uncomfortable and undigested memories of the Second World War. In 1950 there were many Americans who saw in the national alert to the Soviet danger a belated vindication of their uneasiness with Roosevelt's foreign policy, with America's alliance with the British and Russians earlier in the decade. This was especially true of many Americans of German, Italian, Slovak, Ukrainian[24] and even Irish[25] origin. This—and not some kind of superficial "conservative" political philosophy—was the source, as well as the appeal, of McCarthy's (he was half-Irish, half-German) Wisconsin rhetoric; his anticommunist crusade was a stick with which to cow American liberals and to humiliate Anglo-Saxons of the Eastern establishment. In Philadelphia Communists were few and far between; but the sentiment of considerable sections of the population followed this transnational pattern.[26] A new kind of American nationalism, anticommunist and ideological, had risen, in which a genuine concern about the Soviets was commingled with fears of treason, with suspicion, and with envy. I recall how, in 1949, a local post of the American Legion publicly accused the Philadelphia chapter of the World Federalists of anti-Americanism, demanding that the latter be investigated and dissolved. The names of the World Federalists—an innocuous group, with their bland program in pursuit of the illusionary ideal of world government under international law—were, without exception, English, Welsh, or Scottish, some of them bearing the names of the oldest Quaker and patrician families; the names of the people who accused them of anti-Americanism were, without exception, Italian, Ukrainian, and Slovak.[27]

In 1950 the ethnic composition—and more important, the relative strength—of the groups of people living in Philadelphia had changed. The enormous influx of blacks and Puerto Ricans was only beginning; there was, in 1950, still relatively little change in the traditional, and sometimes almost hermetic, national composition of different neighborhoods; but the Americanization of the sons and daughters of earlier immigrations was now nearly complete. The results were not always propitious. It was not only that the "Americanism" with which certain people (often second-generation Americans) identified themselves was both strident and shallow; they were also wont to lose particular features of their popular culture—features which had, after all, enriched the American stew in the melting pot. Among the Catholic working people in the picturesque streets of Manayunk in 1950 the Irish and the Polish and the Italian parishes were still as separate as before, but the monies and the ambitions of their parishioners had been accumulating; and when, in the 1950s, the people of St. Josaphat's decided to build a new church, it was made of steel and concrete and pre-cut stone blocks, modern and oil-heated, indistinguishable from other churches built across the country during the bland and affluent Eisenhower years. The old St. Josaphat's, with its wooden balconies and hand-painted statuaries, a unique piece of nineteenth-century Poland wedged into the streets of an American mill town, was pulled down in no time at all; a few years later something similar happened to St. Rita's, the old gray Italian church around the corner on Green Lane.

Around 1950 the Irish were rising fast; and the Italians would soon follow. The peculiar Philadelphia atmosphere of restricted social ambition had affected the Irish in this city: despite their increasing numbers, there were no Irish mayors of Philadelphia, and even the oldest and most distinguished Irish families kept aloof from the social and cultural elite. But by the 1950s the new nationalist tendency, part and parcel of the anticommunist crusade in accord with which, for the first time in the history of the United States, being a Catholic was no longer a handicap but an advantage, began to be sensed in Philadelphia too: the makers and the managers of the Philadelphia New Deal found that they were very much dependent on certain Irish politicians.[28] The social elite, too, were interested on occasion in such Irish families as the Kellys, whose charming and engagingly modest daughter Grace had risen to cinematic fame and in the 1950s became the reigning Princess of Monaco; yet this kind of interest was not reciprocated by the Irish families themselves.[29]

In South Philadelphia the second and third generation of Italian-

Americans, too, became more assertive than they had been before. Their own particular peculiar contribution to American popular culture was beginning. As late as in the 1920s, Christopher Morley recorded the somewhat patronizing but also charmed reaction of certain Philadelphians to the more or less colorful Italian neighborhoods that existed in the otherwise drab industrial climate of the city, including the popular operatic tradition of their people, when organ grinders in the streets and Victrolas through the windows and on the back tables of the few and unpretentious Italian restaurants rang with the arias of Verdi, Donizetti, Leoncavallo. The musical ability of the Italian population was indeed such that by the 1940s some of their talented sons and daughters had risen to respectable positions in the Curtis Institute or in the Philadelphia Orchestra and, on occasion, even on the national operatic scene; but soon after 1950 there arose another element. The high schools of South Philadelphia became the breeding grounds of American popular music of a new kind: for 1950 was a milestone not only in the history of Philadelphia but in that of American popular song. The unique half century during which American songwriters, from Berlin and Gershwin to Porter, had made American popular music known and loved and played throughout the civilized world was over. Jazz was being replaced by rock, the lilting tunes and sophisticated harmonies of the former by the crude mechanical tones and adolescent beat of the latter. Many of the performers of this new kind of popular music came from the public high schools of South Philadelphia: "Fabian," Frankie Avalon,[30] Bobby Rydell (Ridelli), James Darrin, Buddy Greco, from the Italian-American population of the city.

As almost always, politics would follow. In 1950 an Italian mayor in Philadelphia was still difficult to imagine. The first Irish mayor was elected in 1963, the first Italian mayor in 1971, long after New York; but while James Tate differed from other Irish mayors of American cities perhaps only in his blandness, Frank Rizzo was utterly different, not only from Fiorello La Guardia, but also from Vincent Impellitteri, the first "purely" Italian mayor of New York in 1950. Rizzo was not a liberal (and not really a conservative, either) but an Italian-American of a new and assertive breed. His enemies would call him a fascist, which surely he was not; but there was enough of the bully in the character of this uneducated man for us to say that, compared to him, Mussolini was a philosopher and a humanist.

But we are running beyond the confines of our story, which ends, as it must, in 1950. There was something else happening in and around Philadelphia in and around 1950 which was significant. The great estates had closed their gates; they were sold to institutions. We have seen how, around 1900, the then new rich had built their estates on the outskirts of Philadelphia, palatial mansions with turrets and Norman roofs and parterred parks, erected on foundations twenty feet deep and two feet thick, impressive monuments to the founders of family fortunes, to the glory of themselves and to that of their wives and children. Yet their glory lasted nary beyond a generation, and sometimes not even that.[31] By 1950 more than two dozen of these estates, including the magnificent houses of Wideners, Elkins, et al., were empty; they could no longer be kept up. The reasons for this were taxes and the dearth of servants. Their owners could no longer afford them— this is what they said; it seemed reasonable enough then, it seems even more reasonable now. Yet there *was* another reason, on a deeper, more personal level: for when people say that they cannot afford something, this usually means that they don't really want to afford it. Unlike some of the owners of old houses in England who stick it out, if need be in a wing, these owners were unwilling to stay on, at the cost of more expenses or of some cutting back, or of some discomfort. But then they, and their fathers, had not had these houses for long.

I saw some of the houses in 1950 and again twenty years later. Most of them were sold to institutions, often to Catholic religious orders. There was something sadly telling in the aspect of these estates, but there was also something in their prospect that was very American and perhaps even inspiring. Here were these palatial houses, these merchants' castles, erected at a time when Protestant financiers and men of business had gathered much wealth and began to live as if they were the Borgias and Medicis of the rising twentieth century, the richest and most powerful representatives of American civilization in the world. Well, it did not happen. After thirty or forty years of opulent (and often uneasy) living, they sold their houses to the grandchildren (and sometimes to the children) of their Irish gardeners and handymen and chauffeurs. And so, around 1950, their estates became the novitiates and the scholasticates and the convents, the training schools of nuns, brothers, priests, of the children of the common Catholic people of America, full of vitality. In occupying these houses the latter would sometimes change things around with a kind of thoughtless vulgarity; still, they brought a new kind of life into these abandoned premises, tending their gardens where elegant thin-stemmed flowers had leaned against the walls, growing thick-stemmed vegetables for their own plastic-sheeted tables, keeping the rose beds, and pointing out to their visitors the rich mullioned windows, the carved moldings, the Renaissance mantels over the fireplaces, with respect and with pride. There was, after all, a strange kind of historical justice in the fact that some of these objects of the old European civilization now reverted to the possession of a new, American, and Catholic people; that the mantel carved by a French *ébéniste* four hundred years before, that the old stained-glass window set by an Irish glazier sixty years before, that the stucco swirls and crenellations on a ceiling kneaded into place by an Italian immigrant plasterer fifty years before now looked down on a crowd of some of *their* descendants, who came to occupy these buildings after the cold men and women who had ordered them to be built had left them for good. The smell of hot dogs, of sweet popcorn, and the sound of television now wafted across these baronial halls—and also the occasional scent of incense, the communal murmurs of the rosary, plainchant, and lusty caroling.

It did not last. Twenty years later many of these houses were abandoned again by their occupants.[32] There is a story, a story with a grave moral, latent in the histories of these houses; it will probably never be written. In any event, it does not belong here: for this story of the estates and the mansions of the new rich, replete with the last transitional chapter, was repeated, *mutatis mutandis,* across the Republic, on the edges of its cities; it was not especially Philadelphian.

The Philadelphia (and Pennsylvania) renaissance of 1950—by now a tenet accepted by historians—is contradicted by certain prosaic figures. During the prosperous wartime decade of the 1940s, the population of the United States grew faster than during any other decade in its history, a fact that is especially remarkable when we consider that almost all this growth was natural increase, since there was very little immigration at the time. Yet Pennsylvania and Philadelphia were declining, dropping behind the national averages. Between 1940 and 1950 the American population increased by 14.5 percent; but the population of Pennsylvania grew by only 6 percent, and that of Philadelphia by 6.9 percent. (The neighboring state of New Jersey had increased its population 16.2 percent during the same decade.) Between 1930 and 1940 Philadelphia had actually lost population. In 1950, for the first time, Pennsylvania slipped from second to third among the most populous states of the Union; shortly afterward Philadelphia followed suit, she was now fourth-ranked among the largest cities; Chicago had passed her before 1900; now it was Los Angeles's turn.

One of the things that was now happening to Philadelphia was mass suburbanization. The increase of "Greater Philadelphia," meaning the city plus the three suburban counties adjoining it, was 14.1 percent between 1940 and 1950, only slightly below the national average; the population of Montgomery County increased by nearly 22 percent, of Delaware County by nearly 33 percent. But here we run into a geographical problem, since the boundaries of "Greater Philadelphia" defy rational (that is, non-municipal) definition. Not only in 1950, but even now, after more than thirty years of unceasing suburban sprawl, large areas of the surrounding counties have remained rural—meaning that they, unlike the suburbs of New York, for example, have almost nothing to do with Philadelphia: their residents neither live nor work there, and perhaps the majority of them almost never visit the city. Closer to Philadelphia, unsightly suburban developments began to spring up after 1945. (The first large development on the edge of the city was built on the abandoned Stotesbury estate.) Philadelphia differed from other American cities during the last portion of the nineteenth century: in Philadelphia it was rich people, not the middle-class, who moved out of the city, while within the city rents remained relatively low and the house-owning population remained extraordinarily stable. Shortly after the end of the Second World War, the building boom began: for the first time in the history of Philadelphia, large numbers of middle-class and lower-class families moved out to the suburbs, a movement that is still going on, and the consequences of which on the composition and the character of the city were, and remain to this day, incalculable. In 1950 none of this was yet a response to neighborhood pressures by blacks or Puerto Ricans. Nor was it a result of inflation: the prices of houses in Philadelphia had risen but little, apartments and condominiums were almost nonexistent, real-estate taxes were among the lowest in the great cities of the nation.[34] It was, rather, the result of increasing conformity, propagated by the pictures on television and in the shiny national picture magazines, with their advertisements showing a suburban paradise of togetherness, where happy American families, enviable and respected, would live in their modern houses and spick-and-span gardens in suburban neatery. The massive movement to the suburbs was not yet a flight, not a response to certain economic or social conditions; it was a movement toward the image of a better, more modern kind of life, as well as toward a novel kind of respectability. The result was increasing indistinctiveness, increasing blandness: much that was unique about life in Philadelphia was being washed away; except here and there, conformity to the national pattern became overwhelming.[34] And just as the architecture of the dwellings and the grassy plots of the people of the suburbs conformed to the national pattern, so did the architecture of their minds.

After 1950 much that used to be distinctly Philadelphian—both bad and good—was beginning to crack, melt away, disappear. Cracks appeared everywhere across that proverbially flat, dun, provincial-Sunday dullness. The Blue Laws about which so many comedians made jokes, and which had been imposed on Philadelphia by a coalition of politicians and low-Protestant ministers after the Civil War, began to be eased in the 1920s, though as late as in 1950 some of their curious features prevailed.[35] But ten years later there were restaurants and apartment houses athwart Philadelphia by the dozen, and all vestiges of the Sunday ban on liquor were gone. This was all to the good, except that this abolition was accomplished not so much on its own merits, resting on arguments of common sense, as by the city representatives' insistence on the potential blessings of mass tourism, on the necessity of making Philadelphia conform to whatever was going on in other cities of the nation.

This urge for conformity brought other changes, not all to the good. It was after 1950 that the automobile began to devour the city in earnest. "Suburbanites are traitors to the city," Agnes Repplier wrote with her precise ire around 1920; yet for a long time the abandonment of the city for its countrified suburbs remained, by and large, the privilege of the upper classes, at a time when public transportation within Philadelphia was more ample than in many other cities of the nation. As late as 1950, the parking of cars within the city was easy even during business hours, and even in the center of the city. Soon thereafter the construction of the Schuylkill Expressway began at enormous cost, disfiguring, among other things, the entire western bank of the Schuylkill within the city, with the foreseeable result— not, of course, foreseeable to its planners—of creating a traffic problem instead of solving one, of attracting masses of automobiles instead of distributing their movement, of clogging the approach to the city through a hideous coagulation, a crawling flow of colored steel. The decline of public transportation and the swelling of the suburbs would inevitably follow; to go downtown became even more difficult; what was more important, it made less and less sense.

It was because of some of their particular qualities, including their financial practices, their investment policies, and first of all, because of the characters of their leading figures, that many traditional Philadelphia institutions and Philadelphia banks weathered the financial crises of 1873 and 1907, and even that of 1929–33, considerably better than had many comparable institutions elsewhere in the nation.[36] Soon after 1950, however, the management of these institutions became indistinguishable from the national corporate pattern. They would abandon many of their traditional and particular procedures, adapting themselves to techniques that were standardized, transnational, and popular at the time. Many of them would select outsiders, men reputed for their management wizardry, to direct and preside over these operations; they would convince themselves of the advantages of merger with large corporations, their former competitors; in some instances they would move their headquarters to New York. There they would dwindle ignominiously and, in some instances, collapse and disappear entirely. This was the destiny—self-chosen destiny, rather than inevitable fate—of such monumental Philadelphia institutions as the

Pennsylvania Railroad,[37] the Curtis Publishing Company, Lippincott's (the principal Philadelphia publishing house), Eden Hall (Agnes Repplier's erstwhile forcing school of the madams of the Sacred Heart). Except in the case of the last, these decisions were made by the men of the city, its financial leaders at mid-century. The dénouement of these events occurred in the 1960s, otherwise a time of national expansion and of—increasingly dubious—prosperity. But they had ripened around 1950, because of the decline of certain convictions and of the belief in the viability of certain traditions in the hearts and minds of men.

Such were some of the results of this inclination to conform to the national pattern of progress. And thus many things in Philadelphia changed; but not everything. Much of the coziness, the slowness, the warmth, the privacy of the Philadelphia spirit continued to prevail. They were not always palpable to visitors: for a visitor in a hotel, bereft of friends or acquaintances in Philadelphia, a weekend in this city remained as dreary as ever. There were, however, things remnant in the Philadelphia nooks and crannies—snowy afternoons in Germantown before Christmas, with yellow lights shining serenely out of the gray-stone Quaker houses, with all of the promises of decency and of the sentimental warmth of an American small town; the coruscating lights through the fog settling on Rittenhouse Square, muffled and elegant, reminiscent of a vanished London; Reading Terminal Market, with a thin coating of sawdust on its floors and its stalls heavy with mountains of produce, sides of meat, shimmering hills of fish equal to the best in the market halls of Europe; the inimitable and irreproducible scent of old Chester County farmhouses inhabited by Philadelphians, a potpourri redolent of furniture polish, mustiness, and freshly dusted carpets; the stores in Chestnut Hill, managed by the descendants of their owners and founders, crisp and straight in their tweeds, knowing everyone, though not all; the flowers in ironstone bowls and vases, everywhere. There was something Philadelphian in the smell of the sea in the remaining oyster houses as well as in the well-lit dining room of the Barclay Hotel, so very different from the rich hotel restaurants of New York even in the 1950s, with its own kind of a smart provinciality, with a dependable majority of recognizable faces all around, something akin to the placid climate of county in England, but in a more comfortable and easygoing American version. If Philadelphia was twenty years behind New York, so be it; and for this writer, coming from Europe and the Second World War, there was something else, too: the utter charm of an American city behind the times, the odd survivals of an earlier and better century as late as 1950; and by these survivals he did not mean artifacts or pieces of overdone Victorian furniture for which he did not care, even when these had become fashionable again, but certain civilities of the heart for which he cared very much indeed. What George Orwell wrote about England during the welter of the last world war applied to Philadelphia perhaps more than to any other city in America: no matter how things would change, it would not lose all its peculiar flavor: the gentleness, the hypocrisy, the thoughtlessness, the respect for law would remain; like England after 1941, Philadelphia during the last half of the American century would still be Philadelphia, "an ever-lasting animal stretching into the future and the past and, like all living things, having the power to change out of recognition and yet remain the same."[38]

And so Philadelphia did not change beyond recognition; in the private habits of its people it probably has changed less than New York or Boston or Washington, even now. Were Penrose or Miss Repplier or Bok or Bullitt or Pepper or Wister or Barnes to reappear today, they would be surprised by some of the changes and downcast by others; but their city would be as recognizable as ever, and so would many things in the private lives and preferences of the descendants of some of the people they had known. Perhaps Bok would be the only one among them who would be shocked beyond belief by the disappearance of the empire he had built in Philadelphia; but then, Bok was unlike the others, not only because of his non-Philadelphia provenance, but because of his publicitarian Americanism, which, in spite of the Franklin touch, was not very Philadelphian after all.

One more thing remains to be said about such people and about the spirit of the city where they lived and which they reflected in so many different ways. In 1950 most of them were gone; Agnes Repplier, whose life lasted close to a century, died during that year. What did they have in common? In spite of certain similarities of breeding and education, not much. There was, however, one significant thing. Their mothers, without exception, were stronger than their fathers. These mothers lived during the nineteenth century, when Victorian women are thought to have been subservient, when families were paternalistic, when masculinity was unchallenged and dominant, when not only the orderly hierarchies of domestic and social life but the very appearances and countenances of men were meant to reflect the virile hegemony of the male. Yet, all these appearances and all the accepted clichés about the age notwithstanding, the feminine gender, in these cases, as in many others, was the stronger one. Owen Wister was one of the few people who noticed this. In his unpublished *Monopolis* he wrote about the women of Philadelphia before 1900: "In a few generations they surpassed the men." He was right; but then he was wrong again. "The simplicity of their crystal faith and their unworldliness made them into something spiritually so gentle and serene, that America has seen nothing lovelier in the shape of womankind. When the breath of the cock-tail [sic] and the cigarette blew them away, Monopolis was not a gainer of this change of wind."[39] No: all the latter did not make that much difference, not in Philadelphia. This kind of feminine strength was not dependent on a pristine and Quaker unworldliness; its substance was not that of the more modern version of the sentimentalized (and in reality, often blue hair-tinted) American grandmother baking the turkey or saying the blessing on the covers of the *Saturday Evening Post*. Nor was it the proverbial strength of the Puritan woman, or of her West-going descendant, a woman with a sunburned face under her bonnet, peering sternly ahead. The best qualities of American women, as represented in Philadelphia, have always included a fine compound of reticence and understanding: reticence about matters of belief, understanding of matters of the world. They were strong, but they were not assertive. Their strength had much to do with their sense of family and of tribe; and this sense would manifest itself not in an unworldly kind of gentility but in a profoundly female comprehension of the requirements for a decent life. It was not the result of suppressed instincts but of an understanding that was more thorough than mere intellect. I saw, on certain unforgettable occasions, the gently reserved and yet wise and worldly smile of grandmothers among the *grandes dames* of Philadelphia reappear on the faces of old Irish nuns and on those of the two middle-aged Jewish spinsters sewing in a loft where I once ventured in quest of two lampshades of a particular shape and color. The faces were different, but the substance of the smile was the same.

The women were stronger, they were more deeply civilized, than the men. They, not the men, were the true conservatives. So often their domesticity fulfilled the prescription of Dorothy Wordsworth: "It calls home the heart to quietness." There may have been a historical substance to this, relating to the destiny of this country: they were not the Last Best Hope of Mankind (a maudlin phrase, when you think of it); they were, toward the end of the Modern Age, guardians of what remained, and of what still remains, of civilization.

45

In Darkest Transylvania

(1982)

When I tell my American friends that I traveled in Transylvania, their response is predictable, automatic, universal: "Dracula!" with a grin. I am irritated by this example of the dismal influence of movies on entire categories of American knowledge—or, rather, anti-knowledge. "Dracula" was a Wallachian tribal chief who had little to do with Transylvania. His "castle" was outside Transylvania. For fourteen years he was imprisoned by King Mathias of Hungary, who was the real ruler of Transylvania then. In that gilded prison, "Dracula" (this means Little Devil in Rumanian; his real name was Vlad Tepes, the Impaler) allegedly gave up his Byzantine Orthodox religion to become a Roman Catholic in exchange for his freedom. This was the worst of the sins that the Russian historian Kuritsyn (one of the first chroniclers of Dracula's cruelties) held against him; but then, Kuritsyn was the favorite chronicler of the immediate predecessors of Ivan the Terrible. Some humanists, these Muscovites! The Russians did not like the Rumanians then and do not like them now, and the mistrust is mutual.

The real trouble in Transylvania, however, is not between the Russians and Rumanians but between Rumanians and Hungarians, as we shall see.

Transylvania is a beautiful region, a beautiful part of Europe. I write "part of Europe," because this is essential, the key to its history, to the very configuration of its landscape and of its shapes, of its colors and scents, and of the taxonomy of its flora and fauna, including the human fauna. Transylvania had its high Middle Ages, cathedrals, Cistercians, a whiff of the Renaissance, its Reformation, its Counter-Reformation, its Baroque, its Enlightenment— the historical ages that made Europe, entire historical ages that did not exist in Russia or in Rumania, Moldavia, Oltenia, Wallachia, Bessarabia, Bulgaria, Serbia, Macedonia, Albania, Thrace, Greece, the Ukraine.

From *New Republic,* February 3: 15–21.

Before Vienna the Alps peter out. But there are other mountains in the old Austro-Hungarian empire, the largest among them the Carpathians. They form three-quarters of a ring around old Hungary, fir-laden dark mountains, not as young as the Alps but not very old either, black-green with sunlit clearings, mysterious rather than ominous, sparsely populated even now. On the map they resemble a tightly coiled wreath of the hair of an Eastern European peasant girl, girding the Danube basin as the girl's hair engirds her head. Eleven hundred years ago the Magyars (a name that I prefer to Hungarians) came into that basin. Its eastern portion was the land of the forests, Transylvania, Erdély, Ardeal.

To sum up the history of Transylvania in a page, or even a dozen pages, is nearly impossible: it is one long series of exceptions. The Magyars were, and are, exceptions, in a sense that they do not belong to any of the principal European ethnic families they have lived among—Germans and Slavs and Latins; and the Székely, the main Magyar tribal people in Transylvania, were exceptions among the exceptions. The Rumanians, too, are exceptional people: they claim to be descended from the near-mythical Dacians and from Trajan's Roman legions, which is near-nonsense. What is not nonsense is that their language is clearly neo-Latin, though for long centuries the Rumanian script was Old Slavonic, and until nearly two hundred years ago the few Rumanian books were printed in Cyrillic. The Turks conquered almost all of the Balkans, including Wallachia and Moldavia (there was no "Rumania" then) during the fifteenth century. They conquered half of Hungary during the sixteenth. They did not penetrate into Transylvania; the Magyars fended them off. On two or three occasions the hot rake of war ran up several Transylvanian valleys, and Turks and Tatars ravaged scores of villages, but for nearly two centuries Transylvania was something of an independent state, governed for most of that time by Magyar princes. Transylvania existed between East and West. Its then status had remarkable similarities to that of Finland since World War II. The rest of Europe noticed this, exercised by a recurrent fear of the Turks. As in the case of modern Finland, the civilization of Transylvania was remarkable: there was religious toleration, decreed in 1560, and for most of the time Catholics and Protestants lived peaceably together. (William Penn knew this: impressed by the extant example of religious toleration, his original idea was to name his American Quaker colony "Transylvania.")

At the end of the seventeenth century the Turks left Hungary and the western fringe of Transylvania (though not Wallachia and Moldavia—that is, present Rumania). Transylvania reverted to a province of Hungary, which, in turn, was a semi-independent province of the Habsburg empire. The Rumanian population grew: Rumanians came through the mountain passes, getting away from the Turks, coming into that (often empty and open) land of the forests. In 1918, Transylvania, for the first time in its history, was given to Rumania—the gift of Wilson, Lloyd George, and Clemenceau, those pettiest and most hapless of middle-class statesmen in the twentieth century.

There are now about 2.1 million Magyars in Transylvania, amounting to perhaps one-third of the population. The Magyars have not been a very prolific people. They are badly suppressed by the Rumanians. Before 1918 the Magyar treatment of the Rumanians was hardly exemplary either, but the present kind of suppression is different. There are relatively few political prisoners in Rumania now, but the secret police is ubiquitous, more ubiquitous than in any Eastern European country excluding the Soviet Union—and, as Rumanians themselves will tell you, the Soviet Union is not really a European country. The number of Magyar schools is systematically diminished by the government. The largest university, until recently bilingual, is now entirely Rumanianized. The Magyar faculties are gone, though here and there Magyar professors linger on. This is in Cluj-Napoca, the largest city in Transylvania, which was originally Kolozsvár in Magyar (Klausenburg in German), then it became Cluj in Rumanian, and lately it has been renamed Cluj-Napoca, a resurrection of a Roman place-name from the time of the Emperor Trajan. Official Rumanian propaganda and official Rumanian historiography claim that the Rumanians are direct descendants of Trajan's legions, which is as if Ronald Reagan were to declare his descent from Pocahontas. Yet many Rumanians have something mock-Latin about them; they are curiously reminiscent of the mock-European quality of Argentinians (and there is something Indian in Ronald Reagan's face).

The broadcast and television slots allotted to the Magyar language on the Rumanian state network are distressingly brief, and hardly more than official Rumanian propaganda. The speakers and the interviewed and the musicians must identify themselves as "we Rumanians." In the predominantly, and sometimes purely, Magyar villages and towns, all of the inscriptions are in Rumanian—bilingual signs and directions are not allowed at all. Those Magyars who succeed in struggling up through the bureaucracy to acquire diplomas or qualifying degrees are given jobs in Wallachia, Moldavia, Oltenia, and Bucharest. There have been cases when patients in state hospitals in Magyar towns and with a Magyar staff were forbidden to talk to their doctors in Magyar.

On the Rumanian side of the frontier with Hungary, the wait is three hours. There are not more than seven or eight cars in line, but the hoods and the trunks have to be opened, the seats are pried apart, the luggage taken out and deposited on concrete slabs of benches. It is not my American passport that entitles me to a bit more courtesy from the Rumanian customs men, but the fact that I have only one piece of luggage; the other cars are crammed with people, children, and packages of food that they bring into Rumania. The Rumanian police are looking for foreign books, including books from Hungary, which are confiscated. I was warned about that in Budapest and left my books behind, but on top of my clothes there is an offprint of an article by a Magyar medievalist, printed in a German scholarly journal, about the commercial and diplomatic relations of the Caucasian principalities with the city-state of Genoa during the fifteenth century. The Rumanian customs people pore over this for twenty minutes, they take it into their booth, they study it. They return it to me, and one of them asks: "Where is this Georgia?" "A republic of the Soviet Union," I say. He is reluctant to believe me, but then he returns my passport and waves me on.

This is the frontier between two Communist states, two Eastern European states, two member states of the Warsaw Pact. The difference between them is enormous. Passing back into Hungary—and this is southeastern Hungary, a relatively poor portion of the country—I am instantly back in the West. The difference between Rumania and Hungary is much greater than that between "Communist" Hungary and "Western" Austria. This is not merely the difference between two states, but between two nations and two cultures—indeed, the deepest boundary is not on the map. It is unmarked and yet immediately palpable, there between peoples: the boundary between Roman Catholic Europe and Byzantine Europe, between Western Christianity and Eastern Orthodoxy. (The fact that many of the Magyars in Transylvania are Calvinist shows that in Transylvania the exception is the rule.)

I could regale my American friends and readers with stories about Rumanian corruption: the official who exchanges currency, but who wants a tip; the "luxury" hotel which has (finally) a bath, but which will not furnish a stopper for the tub except for extra consideration; the fundamental difference between the cleanliness of the places populated by Magyars and those populated by Rumanians. I won't continue, because my readers will already be saying that, of course, this writer is a Hungarian and that explains everything. I cannot help this. I am a Magyar but I am an American too, and I am writing for Americans. The most important thing in Transylvania, as perhaps everywhere else in the world, is this existence of deep national differences, something that is obscured not only by ideologues (including those of anticommunism) and by their appalling ignorance of geography and of history, but by the dominant social-scientific pattern of academic and bureaucratic thinking that dismisses national character as a reactionary nineteenth-century myth.

What is happening in Transylvania (and what is happening to many other places in Eastern Europe) has little to do with communism or anti-communism. What is even more significant, it has almost nothing to do with the Russians. As a matter of fact, during the Russian occupation of Transylvania, the Magyar population was treated a little better; the Russian rulers wanted no trouble in that regard. As the Russian flood receded from Rumania the atavistic inclinations rose again, and the crude suppression of the Magyar population reappeared. The principal, and sometimes courageous, spokesmen for the Magyar people are members of the Rumanian Communist party, who on occasion are persecuted and dismissed from their jobs. Whether or not you are a Communist makes little difference in Transylvania. What counts is whether you are Rumanian or Magyar; or, to be more precise, whether you are anti-Magyar or pro-Magyar, regardless of your party membership, regardless even of your native language.

In many of the Magyar apartments and houses the radio is tuned to Budapest. The news from Radio Budapest does its little bit for pro-Soviet obeisances and propaganda, but for the Transylvania Magyars this hardly matters at all; it is so much more objective than the Rumanian radio. "Sometimes we listen to Budapest, sometimes to Radio Free Europe," they say. "It hardly makes any difference."

Rumania used to be the richest agricultural country in Europe. The American fliers who were shot down over Ploesti in 1943 and then parachuted in were amazed at how well they were fed. (They were the only prisoners in World War II who gained ten to twenty pounds in one year of captivity.) The Communist regime depleted the land. The oil wells, the largest deposits in Europe west of Russia, are running dry. The fields are speckled by children in blue smocks; classes in the fall are ordered out to gather potatoes. The state of the economy is as bad as Poland's. As in Poland, the shops are empty; unlike in Poland people often do not bother to stand in line. In most restaurants there are no menus. The waiter will tell you what there is to eat, and the food is foul.

The regime, however, is fairly solid and strong, and not only because of the secret police. In Rumania, not unlike the Soviet Union, the government is seen by the masses as a necessary evil, an unquestionable force of nature. The Rumanian government caters to mass sentiment by feeding it nationalism, suppressing the Magyars, and on occasion making sly references about the Russians. Thus the most rigid Communist regime in Eastern Europe is also the least pro-Russian one. The dictator of Rumania is Nicolae Ceausescu, a former cobbler, whose wife and whose numerous relatives occupy dozens of the highest posts in the government. His private train has twelve cars. He had himself photographed with a jeweled scepter in hand, as well as standing over the carcasses of wild boars and bears which he shoots as they are driven before his august presence. He was also photographed dancing the Rumanian *hora* with Richard Nixon: the grinning, dark, and jowly faces of the Californian and Wallachian presidents, both chief executives from the edges of civilization, oddly resembled each other.

The Eastern European landscape is now that of a valley where the flood and the fog are receding, and the ancient towers and turrets, broken and begrimed but nonetheless recognizable and standing, slowly emerge from under the fog. This devolution is promising and should not surprise anyone except for ideologues and theorists of international relations. Yet it is not as simple as that. In Russia, too, the towers and the turrets of Old Russia reappeared when much of the red chaotic fog of the Lenin-Trotsky years was wafting away. Yet in the streets of that Russian scene appeared not the New Soviet Man (that invention of intellectuals), but a people reminiscent of something old and dark, as was their leader, a new reincarnation of Ivan the Terrible. In Rumania, too, Ceausescu is reminiscent of something old and rooted in the dark recesses of Balkan history, of those Wallachian and Moldavian *voivods* who knew the Byzantines and the Turks and how to get along with them or against them, depending on circumstances, people whose calculations of power are in their blood, and compared to whose life stories Machiavelli's *Prince* was but an elegant theory spun out by a rationalist skeptic.

But Dracula was not a Transylvanian, and Transylvania is different. There is the Saxon minority, for example. As early as in the thirteenth century, the kings of Hungary invited Germans to settle in Transylvania. The latter called themselves the Saxons. They were an early variant of the bourgeoisie; they built admirable and industrious lives in their towns. They lived a tight little existence, disliking the Magyars and despising the Rumanians. With the Reformation they discovered their German nationalism in an instant and became the grimmest Lutherans in all Christendom. Four hundred years later they were proudest followers of the Führer. As I drive through a village, a young boy in lederhosen, seeing my Viennese license plate, gives the Hitler salute.

All over Eastern Europe after World War II, the Germans were deported to Germany. The Rumanians did not deport them (though many of the Saxons left for West Germany through the years). An intelligent Rumanian told me several years ago: "Who knows? The Germans may become a great power again." There is that Hollywoodian witticism about the Hungarian who enters behind you in a revolving door and comes out ahead. Nothing could be further from the truth. Hungarians, with all of their talents, are the least able politicians. The political history of Hungary is marked by a series of disasters. It is the Rumanians who are masters at politics.

Here are a few examples from our contemporary history. To a certain extent, the modern Rumanian state had been a creation of France, but when France fell in 1940 the Rumanians turned pro-German more quickly, and more shamelessly, than any other state and people in Europe. Well before the Third Reich demanded compliance with the "Final Solution," the Rumanian Iron Guard hanged elderly Jews on butcher-hooks in the side streets of Bucharest. They murdered, among others, Professor Iorga, the nationalist historian, whose only sin was his Francophilia. (Before killing him they tore out his beard, hair by hair.) Now, forty years later, Iorga is respected anew; and some of the former Iron Guardist historians occupy chairs in the Rumanian universities. Marshal Antonescu, a Rumanian patriot of considerable character and stature, succeeded in crushing the Iron Guard with Hitler's tacit approval; as a matter of fact, Hitler respected Antonescu even during their last interview in August 1944, when Antonescu suggested to Hitler that Rumania must now follow her own interests. As early as 1943 the Antonescu government made all kinds of secret arrangements with American Jewish organizations. The awful pogroms, perpetrated by Rumanians themselves in 1940 and 1941, were forgotten; the time had come to curry favor with the winning side. In August 1944 the Rumanians executed the most successful *coup d'état* during World War II. With an entire German army in their midst, they turned around within twenty-four hours and proclaimed their alliance with the Soviet Union, Britain, and the United States. (Again the comparison with Italy is instructive: compared to this acrobatic feat, the descendants of Machiavelli were mere bunglers.) A few months later the Rumanians installed a pro-Soviet government in full compliance with Stalin's wishes. Stalin gave them their reward: all of Transylvania was put back under Rumanian administration, the way it had been under the kings and the Francophile capitalists of Rumania. And just as two, three, or six centuries ago the behavior of certain Wallachian chieftains was the surest indication whether Ottoman power in the Balkans was waxing or waning, Ceausescu's gestures of independence from Russia, the first of which were made seventeen years ago, indicated that the Russian influence in Eastern Europe was becoming less ubiquitous and fearsome.

It is because of this Rumanian political genius that the political future of my native people in Transylvania is largely hopeless. There may be an occasional member of Congress with Hungarian-American constituents who will insert an occasional item in the *Congressional Record*; there may be an article or two in *Le Monde* (for the first time in more than one hundred years, informed opinion in France is no longer one-sidedly pro-Rumanian); but a change in the Rumanian sovereignty over Transylvania, or that noble dream, an independent and autonomous Transylvania, is so remote that it doesn't even qualify as a possibility. The Magyar sovereignty is gone for good, and even some of its stones and turrets are destroyed.

I drove off on a side road to look at Bonchida, the baroque country house of the Bánffys, of the Transylvanian Magyar nobility (which was, with few exceptions, the most liberal and cosmopolitan of perhaps all Central and Eastern European aristocracies). They left in 1944. The Rumanians had gypsies settle in the house. I lived through the war in the middle of Europe, but destruction such as this I had never seen. Untouched by artillery or by bombs, the interior of the house has been scoured down to the bare brick, the very plaster scraped from the walls, and the Italian putti from the parapets smashed to pieces, lying in the rank grass. Unlike Dracula's "castle" (which the Rumanians have now built to attract American tourists—there is a "Dracula Tour," a Rumanian variety of Disneyland), places like Bonchida can never be restored.

Yet history is unpredictable, which means that the texture of history changes. The obvious alternatives disappear, and new conditions arise, on another level. Culture is no longer a luxury, the possession of a minority; on certain levels of life it is replacing politics, and it becomes the precious possession of many, not only of a few. Life goes on among the Magyars of Transylvania, who are a bitterly serious people. They write their books (published in Bucharest, but published nonetheless) and they teach and they crowd their churches. Their presence, including their intellectual and spiritual presence, has not been eradicated. In the midst of this wretched Communist state the houses in the Magyar towns are restored and repainted; small municipal museums grow out of near nothing, tended and arranged with infinite care. When the long Transylvanian autumn and winter set in, a kind of decent nineteenth-century existence is palpably at hand, with stoves and larders, the Magyar teachers' houses with their books overflowing from room to room, and two big healthy pigs scratching in the yard. It is a nineteenth-century existence because of the interior quality of this kind of life. Outside, Transylvania is dark. It is dangerous to drive after dusk, since the occasional ox carts and horse carts have no reflectors on their backboards; in the cities the streets are badly lit, because the electric current is poor and weak. The lights are pale, hardly flickering in the squares, reminiscent of a Central Europe sixty or more years ago. But in the sunny autumn mornings the plane trees are drenched with gold and the cities are real cities, with people milling in the old streets, visibly propelled by the difficulties and by the purposefulness of everyday life. And thus certain things in these cities still breathe the life of decades ago, when Magyar (and sometimes Magyar-Jewish) geniuses took wings to fly to the greater world of Budapest and Paris. It was then, in the coffeehouses of Kolozsvár and Nagyvárad, that the Baudelaireans and the folklorists argued and drank into the night, a Transylvanian night in which the coffeehouse smoke instantly wafted away in the clean dark air in the narrow streets, between the uneven rows of the yellow-stuccoed, one-story provincial houses with their earthy odors and sometimes erotic promises and the lone swaying electric tram car lighting up the cobblestones at the far end.

The cityscapes have changed in many ways, yet the landscape remains almost untouched. By September the grass is down, the large, unpeopled, and untended hills resemble the nineteenth-century deer park of a great Anglophile lord. There are lakes in the mountains, agate-pure, secretive, and calm in bowls of pine forests, without a single inn or a house or even a tourist tent nearby. And beyond the mountain ridges lie Moldavia and the snow, a different world of bearded priests and gypsies and Levantine merchants in their cordovan boots. Ancient roads and mountain passes, which were used by Transylvanian craftsmen to haul their boots and finished goods and furs to the markets, are still traversed now and then by bullock-carts, a truck passing them every five minutes or so. On the other side of Moldavia, a mere one hundred miles further to the east, almost all of the roads peter out, disappearing before the Russian frontier where the few crossing points are hundreds of miles apart. It is as if Russia were thousands of miles away; as if the Russians had never been there.

So this is the beautiful and the bitter end of Europe, poor beyond its deserts, rich with its past, and where the past is present not only in the remaining houses with their high-ceilinged rooms and tile stoves, but in the minds and the hearts of the people. In George Orwell's *Nineteen Eighty-Four*, Winston Smith, on one occasion, secretly and daringly offered a toast "to the past." In darkest Transylvania, as 1984 approaches, such a toast would be as out of place as a toast to Dracula. There the past is real; it illuminates the everyday necessities of life; it is the living hope not only of the oppressed Magyars but of those younger Rumanian writers and thinkers who, perhaps for the first time since the Turks, have something in common with the Magyars. They, too, despise the police state, the mechanical surveillance, and the senseless acres of chemical factories in the valleys of Transylvania, spewing sulphurous yellow and scarlet fumes into the air. The Russian flood is retreating, one day the Communist state will be gone, and when that miasmatic fog has lifted perhaps the multifarious people in the streets and squares of Transylvania will not be condemned to repeat the past, precisely because they, unlike the Russians, have learned to know it. There will be no place for petty Draculas in Transylvania. They will take their vampirish flight to Hollywood, to those Californian castles where they belong.

46

Gasteinertal
(1990)

The valley of Gastein—Gasteinertal—is a long crevasse between two stretches of high mountains in Austria, coming to an end at a still higher wall of mountains, snow-capped all year round, blocking it from the south. This is one of the two Austrian Alpine regions which are not yet crossed by stunning automobile highways poised on ferroconcrete gooselegs one thousand feet in the air; but an indeed spectacular rail line does bore through it, a triumph of engineering achieved during the last years of the Austrian empire, the time which intellectual fashion demands that it be defined as "inevitable" dissolution and decay.

But then the history of the Gasteinertal has had its share of exceptions. Thousands of years after the Celtic peoples had settled in the far western islands and headlands of Europe some of them came to the Alpine valleys of the continent and left their marks of habitation during what is called the Austrian Late Bronze Age. As in other parts of Germany, the Christian missionaries came from the far west, not from the south: not from Italy and the Mediterranean but from the rainswept islands of Ireland and England. Eight centuries later Lutheranism took root among the gnarled, headstrong peasantry of the Gasteinertal, together with a tribal kind of prosperity: gold and silver were hacked out of the mountains through the enterprise of a few determined families. They had risen from the peasantry; in less than two centuries they would descend to the peasantry again.

At that time the Gastein valley was the southernmost portion of the archepiscopal state of Salzburg. We are accustomed to regard the Germanies before Bismarck as divided, and the Habsburg monarchy of Austria as united; indeed, the Germanies consisted of as many as seventeen hundred states during the seventeenth and eighteenth centuries (of which even thirty-nine remained after the Congress of Vienna), while Austria was governed

From *Four Quarters*, Spring: 9–15.

centrally from the grand capital of Vienna. Yet the Salzburg archbishopric was a separate state until as late as 1816. Its destinies differed from those of the surrounding lands. During the Thirty Years' War a diplomatic archbishop of Salzburg, Paris Lodron, a kind of Alpine Richelieu, succeeded in keeping the horrific armies of that war away from his domains. But one hundred years later, when the fires of religious wars had burned out elsewhere in Europe, another archbishop, Firmian, chose to force the Protestants of the archbishopric, including those of the Gasteinertal, to emigrate. By that time the gold and silver mines were closed down. A great silence fell upon the valley. The shadows of mountains made it remote again.

Another one hundred years later the name "Gastein" became familiar all over the Habsburg lands and the Germanies. The thermal waters of Gastein were known for a long time but few people availed themselves thereof. The waters were known for their healing properties to the extent that around 1800 there was a thermal pool for horses, not people. During the nineteenth century spas and watering places became famous. A commonsense explanation of this is the swollen girth of the Bourgeois Age, including the swollen stomachs and livers of its beneficiaries. But there was more than that. The central belt of the European continent teems with thermal resources—potential spas—yet not all of them grew to fame during the nineteenth century. Gastein had an additional attraction: its mountains. This attraction was the result of Romanticism. As the great English thinker Owen Barfield once wrote in a memorable sentence: "A hundred and fifty years ago when mountains were still 'horrid,' the foundations of the present economic structure of Switzerland were being quietly laid by the dreams of a few lake poets and their brother romantics." Mountains had become beautiful. Consequently physicians discovered the healing essences of the mountain air, and of the mountain waters. The mountain spas came into existence. The Emperor Franz I visited Hofgastein. The water of Badgastein, four miles away and one thousand feet higher, was channeled down in wooden pipes. Except for the water, thereafter everything went uphill, from Hofgastein to Badgastein.

One generation after Kaiser Franz's visit, Gastein was in the league with the most famous European watering-places: Baden-Baden, Bad Ems, Homburg, Vichy, Evian, Aix-les-Bains, far surpassing the reputation of the original Spa (in Belgium). General von Moltke visited Badgastein in 1859 and told his ruler about it. William I of Prussia (later the Emperor of Germany) came to Gastein twenty times during the next twenty-five years. In 1863 Franz Joseph and William met in Gastein for the first time. Its reputation now earned it a place in the diplomatic history of Europe. Bismarck (who suffered from gastric trouble throughout most of his life) maneuvered his Austrian counterpart in 1865 to the short war between Prussia and Austria. Thirteen years later it was in the Hotel Straubinger (it still exists) where Bismarck and the Austro-Hungarian Foreign Minister Andrássy signed the Dual Alliance between the two empires. The Kings of Greece, of Rumania, of Saxony were Gastein visitors; so was the Emperor of Brazil in 1876 (he must have been a forerunner of the jetsetters; he had visited the Philadelphia Centennial Exhibition in the same year). In July 1886 the last great meeting of the imperial families took place at Gastein, the *Kaiserbegegnung*. Franz Joseph, the Empress Elizabeth, the ninety-year-old William I, and his grandson (soon to become William II) met there. During the next four years the melancholy Empress Elizabeth came to Badgastein every summer. She walked far into the mountains.

By the turn of the century Gastein had become more bourgeois than aristocratic. The Central European bourgeoisie, Lutheran, Catholic, and Jewish, as well as occasional English visitors, were layered among the dozens of Kurhotels, cheaper hotels (especially for the frugal North German clientele), guest-houses, and *pensions*. The North Germans particularly preferred Gastein with its mountain atmosphere, the pert waitresses with their easy manners, the green velvet aprons of the mountains and of the women, the Austrian *Gemütlichkeit* of domesticity, prettiness, and comfort. As the pretext of coming for the waters receded, the pace of the social life increased. Then, in 1909, the railway was completed and the Gastein boom went on.

There is a 1909 atmosphere in Gastein even now. The hotels of the turn of the century are still there, embedded in the mountainside. The great Gastein waterfall thunders day and night; at night the hidden arc lamps bathe its precipice at the bottom, and the spray of the crashing foam rises in a wondrous swirling cloud, as romantic and mysterious as anything in the paintings of Johann Caspar Friedrich. Principal walks still bear the names of the Kaiserin Elizabeth and of Kaiser Wilhelm. In the evening the promenades are deserted but the windows of the elegant shops with their expensive silks and scarves and the fine leathers glisten, a jeweled setting surrounded by the darker glassy shapes of more modern hotels, situated further down. If—all of the industrious nostalgia of the Austrians notwithstanding—the scene is reminiscent of Franz Joseph and of Elizabeth only on occasion, it is at least reminiscent of Stefan Zweig. (The bookstore carries all of his books in paperback.)

That was the first period of opulent prosperity in the Gasteinertal. Then came the catastrophe of 1914. In the vestibule of the parish church of Hofgastein there is a marble memorial tablet, and next to it, under glass, the faded photographs of the men of that community who died in the First World War, faded grey and yellow photographs of sad, serious, wide-eyed peasant faces under their Austrian chakos. "Gefallen" or "Verschwunden": fallen or disappeared. But another decade later Gastein revived. It had survived the dissolution of the Habsburg empire, as indeed had Austrian culture during its last high period. Tourism, that great industry of the twentieth century, reappeared again. Between 1926 and 1936 the prosperity of Gastein returned, together with many of the prewar guests. There was a difference now. There were, for the first time, many Englishmen and Englishwomen, even Americans. At dinnertime the pianists and the trios played Lehár, Kálmán, Strauss, Millöcker, as of yore; but they also played the music of the Berlin jazzy operettas and tunes by Gershwin and Kern. The Austrian government allowed the opening of a casino.

There were now two seasons in Gastein, not only the summer one from May to September, but also a winter one. For every guest who came to take the waters there were now five or more skiers. Yet the scene and its comforts remained the main attraction: the hotels furnished with brown plush *Stilmöbel* as well as the handcrafted wrought iron gates and lamps and dirndl costumes, that discovery of the charms of Austrian peasant baroque which became fashionable in places as far east as the villas of Budapest and as far west as Curzon Street in London. It was a meeting place for two generations: that of my grandparents, both born in 1872 who came to Gastein several times with their serious bourgeois clothes and modest hats; that of my mother, born in 1902, hatless, with her shimmering short dresses and long pearl necklaces, who was in Gastein after and before her marriage, when she was still chaperoned by my grandmother, and who was asked to tea-dance several times by an English duke (or was he a viscount? or an earl?), a story which I heard more than once, which no doubt contributed to my beautiful mother's Anglomania, a consequence of which was her insistence that her son be taught English from the age of five and sent to English schools, one of the things for which he remains forever grateful.

But underneath this hotel civilization—and literally thus, for they lived in the basements of the great hotels—was the world of the waiters and waitresses and porters and mechanics, the sons and daughters of the Gastein valley peasantry riven by the national identity crisis of the Austrian people. Some of them were to be impressed with the fantastic success of their countryman Hitler across the Alps, whose fatherland was Austria but who identified himself with his great tragic mother Germania who took him for her husband. And on a cold March Saturday in 1938 Hitler made the union of Austria with Germany. Soon came the Second World War, in which another one hundred of Gasteiners lost their lives. There is no memorial commemorating them; and the histories of Gastein skim over those tragic years in a few sentences.

447

In the last week of the war, in the brilliant late spring of May 1945, the American Army arrived and occupied the hotels and the *pensions* of Badgastein and Hofgastein for a year or so. And thereby hangs the thread of this short essay, which is the Americanization—and the non-Americanization—of the Europe of Gastein, something that is intertwined with the existence and with the memories of this writer, whose mother is Europe and whose wife is America, whereto he came in the year when the Americans were in Gastein.

The Americanization of the world, of which the Americanization of Gastein is of course just a part, is probably the main story of the twentieth century, but it is a story of such enormous proportions, so worldwide and so protean in its manifestations and evidence, that no historian will ever tackle it. It is a development which is cultural and social even more than political and military. Its main element is the emulation of the social order (and at times, of disorder) that made the United States famous and rich. Its economic and social substance may be summed up in a single phrase: giving credit to the masses. This, even more than the outpouring of American dollars, or the Marshall Plan, led to the democratic prosperity of Western Europe soon after the war. As in the United States, consumer credit became an everyday matter. *On ne prête qu'aux riches*—only the rich are able to borrow—was typical of European capitalism before the Second World War; this rings hollow now, a *bon mot* from a sunken time.

The third, and largest, wave of prosperity for places such as the Gastein Valley began around 1950 and has continued without abating until this day. (One example: the peak in the number of visitors occurred in 1974, the very year when the oil crisis hit Europe.) Every two or three years another soaring ski-lift is completed, wafting people to hitherto unreachable Alpine peaks. There are ever more hotels. The building regulations are very strict; there are but a few buildings, here and there (and usually down in the valleys), whose artless surrealist appearance disfigures the scene.

There are all kinds of results of this Americanization, good and bad, in Gastein. There is a Convention Center in Badgastein wedged in between the hotels, a great concrete turtle, as ugly as anything conceived by a graduate of the Yale School of Architecture; its bookstore contains the German editions of *Playboy* and *Penthouse* which are now, I think, the only American magazines published worldwide. Even in the Grand Hotel of Hofgastein, where the manager's beautiful wife appears at the weekly reception for the guests in a velvet-panelled long-skirted dirndl, the salad table features Thousand Island dressing. The mimeographed program listing the daily events and the menus of the hotel ends with a Joke of the Day, as if the Grand Hotel were a Holiday Inn in California. But all of this does not matter against the long run: without the American contribution to the defeat of Hitler, without the American presence in Europe thereafter this kind of sunny, late-afternoon prosperity could not have happened. Material prosperity is often destructive as well as constructive: but here its destructiveness has not carried the day, the Americanization of the Gasteinertal left plenty of opportunity for restoration as well as for leveling, and this includes the Promenade Kaiserin Elizabeth and the continued presence of the human music of the past.

And now it seems, at least to this writer, that this Americanization is slowly, gradually, coming to its end. This change is beginning to appear on different levels of life.

There are two cultures in the life of the world now, not at all the Two Cultures about which the fatuous Lord Snow trumpeted forth his theory, which was the existence of two separate parallel cultures, the humanistic and the scientific-technological, whose representatives knew little or nothing about each other's "field." No: the two cultures are neither separate nor parallel. They overlap, and they exist on different levels. One is the international; the other is national. One is represented by the international language of the network of business, of technology, of conference centers, of sociological jargon, of computers, of telex, of airline and airport lingo; the other by the language of domestic life. The first language is Americanized and in many instances outright American: the phenomenon known as *franglais* in France has its equivalents everywhere in Europe, including Gastein. The second, in vocabulary as well as in tone, is as Austrian as ever; and there is no reason to believe that it will gradually disappear. Outward appearances, too, reflect this: blue jeans and fringed cowboy jackets come and go, while the local dress of women and men stays as prevalent as it was fifty years ago.

The American physical presence, too, is less than it was twenty or thirty years ago. For every American visitor or tourist in the Gastein valley there are one hundred, perhaps two hundred Germans. And when we drive on the Autobahn in Germany the occasional signs indicating an American military enclave or command post already give the faint impression of anachronism, a leftover impression from the era of the German-American symbiosis, when the principal political reality in West Germany was the American military presence stretching ahead to the Iron Curtain.

For nearly one hundred years, from the middle of the last century to the middle of this one, Austrians had an identity crisis: if they could not keep their position as the ruling nation of the Habsburg empire they might as well join their German-speaking brethren across the Alps. It was because of this identity crisis that the inspiration of the Nazi movement was often South German and that the presence of the former Austrians in the SS was more than considerable. But now another identity, another role has come into being: Austria as another Switzerland, a neutral Alpine republic, a bridge connecting not Berlin and Rome but West and East, prosperous between the two power blocs, America and Russia.

Democratic and partially Americanized as she is, with a Communist party that is one of the least significant of Europe, Austria is moving slowly, imperceptibly toward the East. Vienna has already regained her former position as the great cosmopolitan Danubian central capital city, a meeting place of Western and Eastern Europe, in many ways and on many levels. To demonstrate this could be the subject of a long article, perhaps even a book: suffice it to say that the historical rhythm of Central Europe has begun to draw Austrians (and Germans) closer to the European East than to the American West; but communism has nothing to do with this.

This is a relatively new development, the consequences of which are unpredictable, but I do not think that we ought to be unduly worried about it. The European East has been moving westward, too, for more than twenty years now. The Austrians know that the Soviet empire (and the Russian danger) is not what it used to be; but, then *mutatis mutandis,* that is true of the American empire too.

The darkest writer and the darkest seer of this century, the Frenchman Louis-Ferdinand Céline, thought that the defeat of the German army at Stalingrad meant the death knell of European civilization; later, toward the end of his life, he thought that the Americanism and the democratization of Europe meant nothing; sooner or later the Chinese will be at the English Channel, *les Chinois à Brest.* Well, the Chinese now imitate America even more thoughtlessly than the Europeans ever had; they are not in Brest, and the Russians are not in Gastein. However, the latter may arrive one day: a new Russian tourist class, emerging from the transformations of Russian society. I cannot see the Chinese in Brittany, or even the green tunics of Russian soldiers in the Gastein valley; but I can imagine the Russian and Prussian tourists, in their heavy tweeds, eventually promenading on the Elizabeth and the Kaiser-Wilhelm alleys, sometime in the twenty-first century.

The fields are spangled with dandelions, the meadows with wildflowers, the Mercedes swish on the highways, the golden and wheat-colored baroque sconces and swirls are freshly painted around the window-frames, the bright red geraniums glow in the dark green windowboxes, the pastryshops are chock-full with young people and choc-full tortes, the lodencoated visitors walk in the thin rain with their sensible shoes. In America the age of democracy is in its third century. Here the age of democracy has only recently begun. It was in the Gasteinertal, not in the United States, that one hundred years ago history began to accelerate. The imperial phase was followed by the bourgeois phase, after which came the short and painful Third Reich chapter, after which came the American phase, and that, too, will pass. In any event, the mountains, the skiing, and its Americanization notwithstanding, the Gastein valley is not at all like Colorado, and while Austrian-style chalets and German investors may crowd into Aspen and Vail, the lives of Hofgastein and Badgastein are less and less like those of Aspen and Vail every year.

All of this has something to do with the spiritualization of matter—a difficult phrase by which I mean simply that in the history of mankind the relationship of mind and matter is not constant, because the intrusion of mind into matter increases, something which, Darwin and Marx and even Freud notwithstanding, is the only meaningful evolution there is. For two thousand years the material existence of people in the Gastein valley depended on agriculture. They lived from the soil and the trees. Then came a century or so of hollow poverty. Then, five hundred years ago, they dug into the mountains for gold and silver. They could not eat silver: they lived from what they were paid for their industry. When the mines ceased to be worked there came another trough of poverty. Then came the prosperity due to the thermal water. That water was material; but what attracted the paying crowds was not altogether material. The people of the Gastein valley now lived off what they were paid for their services to visitors.

There are still the people who come to Gastein to soothe their bodies; but their numbers do not compare to the numbers of those who come for that kind of well-being which modern humanity wants, of which the beautiful landscape is as much an ingredient as is the comfort of hotels, and the peaceful rhythm of the day as is the mountain air: they seek the agreeable healing of their minds as much, if not more, than the agreeable pleasures of their bodies. Thus the people of the Gasteinertal now prosper from the very perception of the atmosphere of their valley. From agriculture through industry to service and maintenance—from the chancellors of the archbishops through the Vienna financiers and the bourgeois and then to Americanization—and what is next to come? I do not know.

But I know one thing: mountains will never become "horrid" again. That is inconceivable: because it is unimaginable. Romanticism was not merely the reaction to rationalism, a swing of the pendulum. We are—for better or worse—all Romantics now.

451

47

A Night at the Dresden Opera
(1986)

At the curve of the highway, there appears, some five miles below us in the valley, the famous city of Dresden. More thoroughly than any other city, Dresden was destroyed during the last world war. Now it glimmers and breathes in the sunlight. There is a whitish flatness about it: no architectural landmarks, and none of the giant smokestacks that herald the other cities of East Germany from afar. And from that distance we can see none of the famous ruins. As our car moves into the city, we begin to comprehend why this is so. Most of Dresden has been razed. We stop at a parking lot on one side of the Pragerstrasse, an enormous pedestrian mall. We cannot drive farther. Our hotel looms, fifteen stories high, on the other side of the mall, which is a half mile long—a flat, paved expanse between large concrete buildings of different heights: hotels, department stores, government offices. This mall has an Eastern, Soviet look rather than a midwestern American one, but with an Aztec (or perhaps Mongol) element here and there: concrete piles of buildings without eyebrows but with outcropping cheekbones. The Russians have been here for forty years, of course. Our hotel is the Hotel Newa, and its address is the Leningraderstrasse.

So this is the new Dresden, a modern city got together on top of the rubble and situated within the imperial sphere of the Soviet Union—this once princely rococo Saxon city, which, with its music conservatories and cream cakes, was much favored by Americans before the First World War (and also by Russians of the czarist era). It is still very German. As so often happened during the Second World War, the bombers missed one essential target. The old railroad station is still there, beyond the mall. It was built in the 1890s, a massive, solid building with a roof of glass and steel; its profile suggests that of a First World War German battleship. Something of an older Germany is more visible and palpable here in East Germany than in

From *New Yorker*, March 17: 95–100.

the prosperous West. The government of the German Democratic Republic knows this. It has gone beyond earlier pathetic and servile efforts to establish its presence, and has reached a stage of self-consciousness wherein it proclaims the G.D.R. to be the legitimate successor of the old, the historic, Germany. Its banners, draped on the fronts of buildings, announce, "DIE D.D.R. IST UNSER VATERLAND!" In West Germany, the railroad and the postal service are identified as those of a federal republic: Deutsche Bundesbahn, Bundespost. Here the names are harsh and assertive: Deutsche Reichsbahn, Deutsche Post—the railroad, the post office of the German Reich. Meanwhile, some of the streets carry the names of international Communists of the 1930s; the hotel chain is Interhotel, and the airline is Interflug. This much remains of the erstwhile Communist International, nothing more.

This *Vaterland* is not prosperous. Along the mall, at two in the afternoon, we can buy lunch only in the bowels of an office building; beyond the plate-glass door, one finds oneself immediately in the midst of the sad grimness of a German communal restaurant during the war. We are in need of a road map of the G.D.R. There are none to be found, even in the large bookstores, which are crowded with people. The young women at the hotel desk allow us to borrow, for an hour or two, one that was printed in England many years ago.

They cannot procure tickets to the state opera for us. It is now five o'clock. We have come back to the hotel, tired after a long walk, having crossed the concrete desert of the mall twice. We went to look at the Altstadt—the old city—at the north end of the mall. It was not difficult to find. An hour later, we go back; there is nothing else to do. Beyond the Sovietish mall, beyond the new Dresden, the first ruins appear: a great semicircle of them, perhaps a square mile in extent, stretching from the mall to the flat banks of the Elbe. They are the largest reminder of the Second World War in Europe— perhaps in the world. In Hiroshima and in Berlin, a few buildings were left in ruins as a reminder; the rebuilt city flows around them. But this is different. In Dresden, the old city is a monument of ruins. In the West—in London or Nuremberg, say—the ruins were cleared away; ten years after the war little or nothing of them remained. In the East, in Budapest and Warsaw (the latter destroyed by the Germans in two installments), the old districts have been rebuilt almost completely—an outlet for patriotism and traditional pride, and an activity for which their unpopular governments got some credit. Here it almost seems as if the ruins were meant to be preserved, instead of cleared or reconstructed—as if the destroyed Altstadt were meant to be a piece of propaganda to show people what the war was like and what the Western enemies of Germany wrought. Restoration has been going on only desultorily, here and there.

For someone who lived through the war in Europe, these ruined acres are an instant reminder of forty years ago. Some things about the ruins, however, are different. Forty years have aged the walls. They are no longer stone-colored or burned black. Four decades of grime and smoke and rain have made them dark brown, so that they look even more startling than the ruins among which one trudged in 1945. They are somber and macabre enough, but there is an element of beauty in their midst. Trees have grown up within these walls, among these toothless giant buildings. Trees, not weeds—we are in the northern half of Europe, where vegetation is not riotous. There is something melancholy and peaceful in these young and middle-aged trees filling with green light the courtyards of death. In the park of the palace of the Saxon kings, German and Russian soldiers amble about. One of the palace buildings is half restored. Band music is playing over loudspeakers. We walk down to the Elbe. Old-fashioned paddle steamers (bearing such names as Friedrich Engels and Karl Liebknecht) are tied up along the quay. With their paddle boxes, they are white and broad-hipped, like Saxon women of the past. Here, at least, Dresden looks as it must have looked in the past, the river surely reminiscent of the scene Bellotto painted two hundred years ago. (Warsaw, Dresden—the famous riverscapes. He must have appreciated that green-and-blue flatness, like the Venetian lagoons.) Yes, the afternoon sky over the Elbe at Dresden is pale-blue, fine, unbroken porcelain—a Bellotto sky.

In the Theaterplatz, the equestrian statue of Johann I, King of Saxony during the *Reichsgründung,* has been erected again, midway between the array of burned ruins and the opera house, which has been rebuilt. This is the Semper Opera, named after its architect, Gottfried Semper. It is an oval neo-Renaissance building, with a curious history. The first Semper Opera, built in 1841, burned down in 1869 and was rebuilt less than a decade later; in 1945, the bombs all but destroyed it, and it has been completely reconstructed—an achievement begun in 1977, finished in 1983, and commemorated by a tablet at the main entrance. *Fidelis Semper!* Around a side entrance, its doors painted a shiny dark brown, men and women are gathering. It is half past six. The performance tonight is a "Klassischer Ballett-Abend"—an evening of classical ballet—beginning at eight. People are standing in line for the remaining tickets. I do not like standing in line for anything—surely not at the end of the day. But I give in. There is nothing else—absolutely, completely nothing else—to do in Dresden at night.

There are three public entrances to the Semper Opera. The main entrance is for those who possess tickets or special passes. Another is for those who have reserved tickets. The entrance in front of which we are waiting is for people who hope for standing room, or for seats if any are left. The gathering now becomes a small crowd. People come in groups, and some congregate in front of the main door, too. Precisely at seven o'clock—I look at my watch, because there is no sound of bells from the dead, burned towers of the churches around us—something happens: the Semper Opera bursts into light. Hundreds of electric candles glow and glitter from their chandeliers through the great, palatial Renaissance windows. It is still light outside; all this grand illumination is interior. The Semper Opera is a brilliant jewel box ablaze.

At once the main door is opened; men and women press in. More and more people are coming out of the evening, across the broad, cobblestoned square surrounded by the silent, unmoving, darkening ruins. The scene is semicircular, and probably unrecordable even by the widest-lensed of cameras. It is unforgettable, a scene beyond the means of the most imperious of theatre directors, a true piece of *Welttheater:* this nineteenth-century jewel box drawing the stunned, the desperate, the determined, the fortunate, the hopeful to its lights, and three hundred feet away the gigantic backdrop of the ruins. They are black now, and the green, living trees inside them have turned black, too—indistinguishable from those ominous towers in the moonless falling night. A backdrop is always a reminder of sorts. (For once, a German word is more telling than the English one: "*Mahnung*" combines the meanings of reminder and warning, its tone intensely somber.)

Between the ruins and the theatre, the square is largely empty, except for the statue of Johann I and the groups of people arriving. Most of the people come on foot. On one side of the square is a paved roadway, where cars may pull up to drop off their passengers. Every few minutes, a Volvo or a black Russian-made limousine appears, carrying what are rather obviously members of the governing class of the German Democratic Republic—content, smiling men and women of the bureaucracy, who make their way with ease through the crowd and enter the golden light of the Semper's foyer to be led to their boxes and seats. From one of the limousines emerges a group of North Koreans in European clothes. They wear red badges bearing the enamelled portrait of their dictator, Kim Il Sung; they are smiling rigidly, their features, I am sorry to say, proletarian and cruel. Later, two or three tour buses pull up. One of them is from West Germany. Its license plate indicates that, but so do its passengers—middle-aged men and women who are much better dressed than their East German compatriots. But perhaps "compatriot" is not the right word; they inhabit a different world from the people of Dresden—different economically, politically, and ideologically, as well as in dress. They belong to another age of history, these pros-

perous envoys from the West, on a prepaid package visit to their impoverished relatives.

The opera-loving people of Dresden seem the older Germans, and not
only because in the Eastern part of Europe life is harder and people age
faster. The shapes, the clothes, the faces of so many of these men milling
before the opera, waiting for their wives, are reminiscent of the Germans
of Germany before the war, sometimes to the point of caricature. They are
heavy, thick-necked, odd-lipped, with hard creases around their mouths,
and heavy jowls. They have George Grosz countenances, though without
the uniforms and high collars, and without the arrogance that that vengeful
German artist attributed to them circa 1923. In the Weimar period, a German photographer, apparently full of hatred for his own people, brought
out an album of monstrous portraits of the stiff and distorted faces and
figures of ordinary German citizens; I saw it a few years ago, in an edition
that was published in New York. Some of these men remind me suddenly
of the faces in that album. But, I repeat, they are devoid of arrogance. Their
wives have brought them along to the music and the splendor. I must bow
my head before these wives of Dresden. Here they are, heavier than their
coevals in the West, serious and patient. It is they who have a sense of
occasion. Many of them wear long skirts, which, for fashionable evenings,
are going out of style in West Germany; but these women don't know that,
and it's not important. They come to pay homage to a culture they hope is
still theirs, to the high-bourgeois nineteenth-century virtues represented
by an evening at the state opera. They come for the ballet and the music,
but, beyond that, for the occasion: to spend three hours once more in their
opera house, which—unlike the Zwinger, that eighteenth-century rococo
palace, which lies a hundred yards away—has been redone with all the
opulence of a century that for them is irrevocably past and yet not unfa-
miliar.

We are told that most people arrive at seven, an hour before the performance, because the buffets of the opera house open early, offering sand-
wiches and Russian champagne that is very cheap. It is now ten minutes
before eight, and still not everyone is inside. The shiny brown doors are
opened from time to time by an official, who admits eight or ten people at
once. At one minute before eight, we are let in. We are among the last, and
get tickets to the highest gallery, for a few cents—standing room only. So
we enter the Semper Opera. It is the 1870s, to the last jot and tittle. Crimson carpets, crystal forests of chandeliers, monumental black marbleized
columns with creamy capitals, enormous mirrors—all in the eclectic neo-
Renaissance style of the nineteenth century but somehow all of a piece.
Only the colors of the many frescoes on the ceiling are a bit too new, too

sharp. (Gottfried Semper, that neoclassicist, was a great advocate of poly-chrome.) The opera house is stuffed to the gills, but there is little of the loud, titillating hum that reverberates in theatres before the curtain rises. The air is not still, however; it is full of the subdued sounds of a silent respect.

The performance is very good: excerpts from *Swan Lake, Sleeping Beauty, La Bayadère.* In contrast to the florid richness of the interior, the spectacle is reduced to simplicity. The ballets are performed on an empty stage, on a black slate floor. The dancers of the Dresden State Opera Ballet are like white butterflies, flying and gliding above the dark slate. More surprising than the lack of stage décor is the fact that the orchestra is not visible; but perhaps an array of serious German musicians in frock coats and white ties—yet another image from the past—would have been too much.

The respectfulness carries over to the end, with no thunderous applause, no pompous bourgeois shouting of "Bravo!" There is something like a hushed thankfulness instead.

During the long wait outside I had seen an old, quiet German woman in the crowd at the door. Her grey hair was pulled back in a bun, and she wore a long grey evening dress. She waited patiently, holding her program and leaning with one elbow on a crutch. Sometimes she rested her thin frame against the rusticated stone wall. She must have had some difficulty hob-bling up to the fourth tier of the opera house. There she stood, not far from us, wearing a little smile and leaning forward on her crutch. There was no need to speculate about her: this was clearly something very important in her life. After the intermission, fortunately, she found a seat. I had the urge to say something to her in my halting German. I did not do so; and perhaps she would have been embarrassed if I had. It was then that the meaning of the evening crystallized in my mind.

This must have been how the people of the Middle Ages entered the vast, magical spaces of their cathedrals for high Mass, the only splendor in their lives. There was, however, a difference. That experience in the Middle Ages came to people with no consciousness of history. For the people of Dresden today, the Semper Opera was the tangible presence of a better past—a past that some of them still remembered. They thought that they were being faithful to what was best in themselves. Did they shut out from their minds the dreariness of their present, of their everyday lives? Perhaps not. When the evening was over and they left that building burning with the fullness of beautiful things, these people, still stunned forty years after their defeat, found the black monumental ruins staring at them. Whether they stared back or not, I could not see.

48

Letter from Normandy
(1995)

The town of Bayeux—five miles inland from "Gold" Beach, at Arromanches—was taken by the British on the first day of their landing in 1944. It was one of the few towns in Normandy hardly damaged by the fighting and the bombing, unlike its neighbor Caen, which was largely destroyed, since the Germans had held on to it for weeks. Bayeux is a pleasant little town with a moderately impressive cathedral, many flowerbeds arranged in the courtyards of its municipal buildings with their classic buttery stone façades, and brilliant colors in the clear autumn air. An old waterwheel flanks a placid rivulet next to a museum where the Bayeux Tapestry is housed.

It is from here, and from these very beaches nearby, that William had set out to conquer England in 1066, nine hundred and twenty-nine years ago this October. And conquer he did, with the greatest consequences for the history of England. Men flushed with victory do not always have a proportionate sense of occasion. William must have had some of that. He had a tapestry made soon after his victory at Hastings, to commemorate his great enterprise. For a long time people—and the local tradition—attributed the embroidery to William's wife; but it is almost certain that the work was done by English embroiderers, ordered by William's half-brother Odo, the bishop of Bayeux, and was to be eventually placed in his cathedral (which had not yet been built in 1066).

The Tapestry is not only a venerable relic but also an astonishing work of art. It is 231 feet long and twenty inches wide. The needlework is in worsteds of eight colors. It depicts a long story, including the preparations and the intrigues preceding the Normans' invasion and then the crossing, the landing, and the battle. The sequence of the scenes is nearly complete: only the end of the strip, the post-Hastings portion, has been lost. (Perhaps

From *American Scholar*, Summer: 359–70.

this is for the better: would there have been some excessive adulation of the conqueror and victor?) Along the margins of the strip runs a continuous narrow fringe of heraldic animals, and above the scenes a running Latin commentary in what, for the eleventh century, is amazingly classic and clear lettering. Most startling is the fineness of the design. The angularity of the figures is not at all primitive—there is a near-perfect suggestion of their movements throughout. When we think of a tapestry, we think of a great wall hanging, a *Gobelin;* but the Bayeux Tapestry is a strip, a veritable cartoon, an art form perhaps especially familiar to twentieth-century Americans; and (to paraphrase Henry Adams) the evolution of cartoon figures from those of this eleventh-century masterpiece to those of, say, Saul Steinberg is sufficient to refute all the theories of Darwin.

However, it is the meaning of the Bayeux Tapestry that grips me as I move slowly past its glass case with the crowd, as I contemplate it, as my mind wanders. Napoleon knew that meaning. In 1803 he had this strip of cloth removed from Bayeux; he ordered it to be exhibited in Paris. That was when he laid his plans for *his* invasion of England. He had a sense of history; 737 years after William, he wanted to remind the people of Paris of that first invasion, just as he wanted them to remember Charlemagne when, in December 1804, he brought the pope to Paris to crown him emperor, the first emperor of France receiving his crown from a pope after almost exactly one thousand years. However, by that time he had given up his plans for an invasion of England; and the precious band of linen was brought back to Bayeux.

It is 1995 now, and I am thinking of Hitler. Had he invaded England, would there have been another episode in the history of the Bayeux Tapestry? Perhaps not: the German occupants left it where it was during World War II. (During the Franco-Prussian War of 1870–71 the people of Bayeux rolled it up and hid it from their potential German occupants.) But had Hitler invaded England, he would have been its first conqueror in nine hundred years, with incalculable consequences, greater than those of William's invasion in 1066. William had conquered England and added it to his dukedom in Normandy. Had Hitler conquered England, he would have added it to his already acquired European empire. William won his war against a king of England; Hitler would have won his world war.

He came close to that. So many people are inclined to think of him as a madman—and of the entire, rapid, and dramatic history of his rise and fall as a crazy episode in the history of the twentieth century, as if the collapse of that horrible episode had been inevitable, foreordained from the beginning. It wasn't so; and two things come to my mind here, in Bayeux.

One is that—like William, and unlike Napoleon—the Germans could have made a successful landing in England in the summer of 1940. The British army, reeling back in defeat from Dunkirk, was unready. The British navy—which in 1803 could have blown the ships and barges of the approaching French into smithereens—in 1940, in the air age, could not have destroyed the invading forces of the Germans. (Against parachute landings it would have been useless. Besides, the British, including Churchill, were loath to risk their entire fleet for one desperate battle in the Channel. They—again including Churchill, who said that much to Roosevelt—knew that if the Germans were to conquer Britain, the only card in the hands of a future British government, seeking some kind of peace with the Germans, would be the existence of the fleet.) There are at least two British military writers who, during the past fifty years, wrote books speculating about a German invasion of Britain; both think that it could have succeeded.

And—this is now roiling in my mind—what would have happened then? We know something about that, here and there, from Hitler's own words. He had always wished for an alliance with the British empire. Now he would have that—on his own terms. He would have taken few colonies— perhaps none—from the English. His steely fingers would have clamped down on England—but clothed in a velvet glove. England was not Poland; he did not want a new province for the German empire. He wanted a British government that would make peace with him, that would administer Britain but in accord with his wishes; he wanted a British government that would accept his domination of Europe, a government and a people that would accommodate themselves to being a minor partner of the continental Great German Reich, discarding their hopes across the Atlantic, for a partnership with the United States. And what would Roosevelt have done— what could he have done—then? "Fortress America," well and good; but the isolationists and the America Firsters would have been proved right: it was futile and wrong to tie the destiny of the United States to the cause of Britain, to a combat against Germany in a war that the Germans had already won.

More was involved here than the power of German arms; and more than what had happened nine hundred years earlier—that is, the conquest of one kingdom by another. What Hitler represented in 1940 was a new elemental force in the history of the world, the force of an idea, a wave of the future (which was the title of a book that summer, published and widely read in the United States, written by the thoughtful and intelligent Anne Spencer Morrow Lindbergh). And Churchill understood that—even better than his colleague in defeat, the premier of France, Paul Reynaud. A few days before the collapse of France, Reynaud made his last broadcast. If Hitler wins this war, he said, "it would be the Middle Ages again, but not illuminated by the mercy of Christ." Fine words: words symptomatic of a Frenchman of the Age of Reason, fearful of a return to the Middle Ages. But Churchill's vision was nearer to the truth. On June 18, 1940, in one of his most famous speeches, he evoked the prospect, not of a return to the Middle Ages, but of an enormous lurch into a New Dark Age. If Hitler wins and we fall, he said, "then the whole world, including the United States, including all that we have known and cared for, will sink into the abyss of a New Dark Age made more sinister, and perhaps more protracted, by the lights of perverted science." Note the word *protracted*. He knew that Hitler represented a new revolutionary force in the world, with a new revolutionary appeal to many people—especially in the event of his victory. Had he won, his Reich might have lasted—perhaps not for a thousand years, as he had once said, but for a long time. So Churchill's words were more apposite than Reynaud's.

But now I am thinking of 1944, not of 1940. I am no longer thinking of what could have happened in 1940 across the Channel but of what happened in 1944 here in Normandy. After all is said, Hitler did not attempt to land in England. But four years later Americans and British landed in Normandy. There may be something symbolic in their crossing the Channel along the route of William the Conqueror, but in reverse. (Hitler had expected them to land near Calais and Boulogne, reversing Napoleon's planned route.)

Now I leave Bayeux. We are driving to the coast. Fifty years have passed, and there are no sights of destruction left from the war. There are, of course, the thick spiky hedges of Normandy, the fields where the Normandy cattle graze, the clean and prosperous villages; and the American, British, and Canadian flags on many of the tourist houses and restaurants and inns, and a few signs: "Welcome to Our Liberators." (What would William the Conqueror—or William II the Kaiser—have thought of that?) Now we are in Arromanches, where there *is* a reminder of 1944, out in the water: the remnants of "Mulberry," the artificial harbor thought up by Churchill. It is a lovely day and Arromanches is as bright as a button, a few tourist buses along its main street, a warm early-September breeze bringing the salt smell of the sea softly coiling around us as we eat a nice lunch on a terrace. Then I walk into the D-Day Museum and I cannot hold back my tears.

But why? There is no one in my American family who died or fought here. I have no American or British friend who died here. I am not a veteran. Now, three months after the anniversary of D-Day, there are a few veterans wending their way through the museum. They are genuinely interested, but they do not seem to be particularly moved. I talk to a Welshman who had been here fifty years ago in the 53rd Infantry Division, whose

461

regimental badges we eventually find on one of the wall displays. He had landed here seven days after D-Day. Later he was captured by the Germans. (They treated their British and American prisoners fairly well, he says.) He was *there.* He knows much more about it than I can ever know. But I know something that he did not and does not know: that he was there because of me, a European. Hitler did not want to war against the British empire, and he did not want to go to war against the United States. What he wanted was the domination of Europe. But Churchill and Roosevelt and, with them, the British and the American people did not accept that. And their young men came here, to fight and die, for the liberation of Europe and of Europeans, including myself.

My thoughts run on and on. The conquest of 1066 was the last—and the only—conquest of England from the Continent. But 1944 was probably the last time that the armies of English-speaking peoples would come from across the sea to help decide a war in Europe. No matter what happens in Europe, this will not happen again. Besides, D-Day was a turning point—more than a milestone—in the history of England. Well before D-Day there was no way for the British to win a war against the tremendous might of the Third Reich without the Americans and the Russians. But until June 1944 there were more British than Americans in actual combat against the Germans. After June 1944 all that would change. Not only was an American general the Supreme Commander; but the mass of American soldiers would carry the war forward on the western front. The diminution of British power set in. Churchill's prestige worldwide was still great, equal to that of Roosevelt and Stalin, because of 1940. But his power was diminishing. Still, if the price for the liberation of Europe meant the transfer of most of the wealth and many of the possessions of the empire to the Americans, so be it. That was the policy of the half-American Churchill ("a half-breed," some of his enemies in London called him in May 1940). He had a larger vision, a vision that accompanied him throughout his life, a vision again partly owing to his American ancestry. That vision was an ever closer union of the English-speaking peoples. And there he failed—for many reasons, but first of all because America was becoming less and less English.

Turning now west, along the Route Nationale 13, we see here and there some of the other beaches and German bunkers and gun emplacements. They do not seem terribly formidable, but then they are kept up only as mementos of what happened here fifty years ago. And now another thought swims up to the surface of my mind. Suppose the invasion had failed: What would have happened then? A great wave of shock would have run across the world—and across the minds of the American people. It would have shaken FDR's position more than Churchill's—the British had been accustomed to terrible setbacks throughout the war. But remember, too: six days after June 6 the first German rockets began to fall on London. Would there have been another invasion attempt? And where? And when? And what would Stalin have done, the Stalin who for three years had been gravely suspicious of his allies for not trying for a second front, for not relieving the Russians who were carrying the brunt of the struggle against the Germans? He would have responded to an offer of a separate peace from Hitler—whose entire strategy since late 1941 was to split the coalition of his opponents. Had the invasion failed—what would have happened with the liberation of Europe then?

But it did not fail.

We have now skirted Omaha Beach (bloody Omaha, where for an hour or two the winning of the bridgehead *almost* failed), the Pointe du Hoc (where the Rangers made a daring climb up the cliff only to find that the great German guns on the top were dummies—the real ones had been pulled back another half a mile or so); Utah Beach (where almost everything went well). At St. Laurent-Colleville is the American Cemetery. More than nine thousand graves are there, a white field of crosses. I know what I feel; but I do not know what to say. "Those farm boys from Iowa . . . those young Americans from the small mining towns of Pennsylvania . . ." I know that but I feel something perhaps too precious for words. Not so long ago I read what a Dutch woman at Arnhem had said: "They came to help us to be free again, and I feel very grateful. But 'grateful' is too small a word. There are feelings you cannot really put into words properly."

There is a small tablet on one of the walls of the cathedral of Bayeux about the First World War. "In memory of the more than one million young men of the British empire most of whom fell and are buried in France." The Americans who fell here in both world wars were fewer than that, thanks be to God. When those ten thousand fell here in 1944, the American empire was rising to its zenith, to the zenith of the American century in 1945. But they did not die for the American empire. They were sent here to fight and die for the survival of a civilization—a civilization that is in great danger today, fifty years after that bloody summer month. That thought burns in my head now as I am approaching Tocqueville.

The hamlet of Tocqueville is a dozen miles off the N 13, which is also the main route along which the First American Army had pushed northwest to liberate Cherbourg. It consists of a few gray stone houses grouped around a small church that is surrounded by a narrow oval of grass containing a few graves, among them that of Alexis de Tocqueville and his wife, the inscription of which has already grayed, most of the letters of which are now washed away. Two miles away is the Tocqueville chateau. A

Tocqueville ancestor received his estate and patent of nobility from William in 1054—that is, a dozen years before the latter set out for England. It has remained in the family ever since—but now, for the first time in more than nine hundred years, there are no male Tocquevilles left. The last Comte de Tocqueville (a lateral descendant of Alexis, who had no children) had two daughters.

Alexis de Tocqueville (the two hundredth anniversary of his birth will come ten years from now) was the greatest, and most prophetic, seer and thinker of democratic civilization, the Plato-cum-Aristotle of the democratic age that had begun to rise during his lifetime. His great book about America was only one of his accomplishments, though an extraordinary one: the greatest book about a country written by a foreigner; astonishingly, much of it remains valid 160 years after its composition, though the country and nation are vastly different. The title of this famous book is precise and telling. *De la Démocratie en Amérique—Democracy in America—*suggesting, at least, that it is about democracy even more than it is about America.

Tocqueville had a vision of history that transcends the divisions Ancient-Medieval-Modern. There were the aristocratic ages, ruled by hereditary minorities; and now, in his very lifetime, the democratic age, the age of majorities, had begun. And that was irreversible, no matter what his conservative friends may have hoped or thought. But the democratic age would have its own dangers. The tyranny of the majority, enthralled by a popular leader, was one of them. Still: "I cannot believe," he wrote, "that God has for several centuries been pushing two or three hundred million men toward equality just to make them wind up under a Tiberian or Claudian despotism. Verily, that wouldn't be worth the trouble. Why God is drawing us toward democracy, I do not know; but embarked on a vessel that I did not build, I am at least trying to use it to gain the nearest port." The tyranny of the majority—Tocqueville was able to see the prospect of a Hitler—was but one of the dangers. The other was the treatment of the majority as a dumb and selfish and inchoate mass, when an incessant agitation of ephemeral novelties on the surface only cloaks an ever deepening spiritual apathy and intellectual stagnation. The question, he wrote, was no longer whether democracy would prevail or not; the question was: what kind of democracy? Would it be a mediocre order, with no great spiritual advancement, but where common decency and prosperity would exist for a majority of people who, for the first time in history, would have risen from poverty with the help of bureaucratic government—a society held together by its respect for law and religion? Or would it be a decaying democracy—its bonds of public morality and law and order loosening—

tending toward anarchy (from which a popular tyranny may be the only way out)?

For the United States this question was still open fifty years ago. Is it still open now?

Fifty years ago here in Normandy the armies of democracy liberated Western European civilization from the barbarism Hitler and his Reich had incarnated. That was a barbarism of a new populist nature, obeyed by a great people accustomed to discipline, obedience, and a military tradition. But Hitler had not only husbanded the energies of an entire people; he had married the two principal movements of the twentieth century, nationalism and socialism. There was a triangle of forces in the world then. There was liberal parliamentary democracy, represented mostly by the English-speaking and Western European peoples. There was communism, represented by Soviet Russia alone. And there was National Socialism, risen to power among a variety of peoples, but principally incarnated by Hitler's Germany, which was so powerful that it took the combined forces of democracy and communism to conquer it.

Fifty years later this triangle no longer exists. Hitler was defeated; and less than fifty years later, communism, even in Russia, has disappeared. Yes, Nazi and fascist sympathizers exist here and there, but do not worry about that; history does not repeat itself. But there is plenty of reason to worry about something else—the democratic decay that Tocqueville had feared might come, "the abyss of a New Dark Age made more sinister, and perhaps more protracted, by the lights of perverted science," as Churchill had put it in June 1940, though he was speaking of Hitler then. But his words remain as apposite now, half a century later, when, within and without the great conurbations of the Western world, many of the signs and symptoms of a New Dark Age are rising. "The democracies have been decomposing, too," another great seer, the Frenchman Bernanos, wrote after the war, "but some decompose more quickly than others. They are decomposing into bureaucracies, suffering from it as a diabetic does from sugar, at the expense of his own substance." Bureaucracies that are less and less able to protect personal safety and dignity from the internal rise of barbarism and savagery, a rise inspired and spawned by the promotion of the sovereignty of a popular "culture" at the expense of the preservation of civilization.

Its signs are all around us. Hitler's propagandist Joseph Goebbels wrote in 1939: "National Socialism has understood how to take the soulless framework of technology and fill it with the rhythm and hot impulses of our time." National Socialism did not quite do this; but the New Barbarians, of whom the Nazis were one variant of forerunners, did. Rhythm and hot impulses! Fifty-one years ago, in 1944, American popular music was the wonder of the world. That meant more than a subchapter in the History of Jazz. Over the Channel flew not only the big American Liberator bombers but the liberating—yes, liberating—sounds of the swinging music of the American big bands. In 1944—there are historic evidences of this—all over Europe (including Germany) those who loved American music despised the barbarism of the Nazis. In 1994 the New Barbarians (including Nazi skinheads) are the most fervent addicts of rock.

In 1944 there was a vast American working class that, with all of the narrow-mindedness of its conformism, was wondrously patriotic and conservative, upholding and representing conservative values in a country where the class struggle hardly existed at all, where the lower classes were not an underclass, where they kept rising and rising to middle-class status, where credit was given to the masses in multifarious ways, so that the national prosperity of the United States was a wonder, soon to be emulated by much of the world. In 1994 there is less and less of a working class in the United States, while there is a vast and growing underclass; where credit cards are given to the masses while they are credited with little else—because of a pervasive and corrosive cynicism that goes against the very traditions of a democracy whose institutions and public policies as late as fifty years ago rested on a (perhaps arguable, but nonetheless generous) overestimation of the intelligence of people—until now, when education, information, and entertainment in America are governed by their cynical underestimation. That is no longer an intellectual argument. Its material consequences have come. I know that I will return to a country where not only are people less safe but, for the first time in two hundred years, they are poorer than are people in Western Europe. And even Tocqueville had not foreseen that.

Fifty years from now—will there be many visitors to the American Cemetery at Colleville? That will be 2045, and I can imagine that the United States will have gone through a long period of decline and that the dollar is worth ten German pfennigs. There may still be a director of the cemetery living in his white house near the entrance, who tells a group of visiting Americans (among them, perhaps, American exiles living in France) that, for the time being, the Gettysburg National Theme Park and this last of the American cemeteries in Europe were saved by a Southern senator from the budget cuts declared by the National Bottom Line Internet. "My job is still here," he might say, "but I may be the last director here, and the cemetery may have to be kept up by volunteers and the French."

That may happen. Or it may not. In any event, Churchill and Roosevelt, whatever their faults, helped to save Europe and Western civilization from barbarism fifty years ago. Save—and restore. Churchill was not a progressive, Roosevelt thought that he was one, but never mind; they were savers and restorers. At best, civilization may survive and exist, in part because of what these young soldiers fought and died for in Normandy fifty years ago. At worst, Churchill and Roosevelt gave us—especially those of us who are no longer young but who were young then—fifty years. Fifty years before the rise of a new kind of barbarism, not incarnated by the armed might of Germans or Russians, before the clouds of the New Dark Ages darken the lives of our children and grandchildren. They gave us fifty years. Perhaps that was enough.

49

Three Days in London:
Churchill's Funeral
(1979)

January 29, 1965, Friday
It is a very quiet London, a humdrum day. No sense of crowds, no excitement, no feeling of something big and ceremonial. Even at the airport there are not many people; it is a winter arrival day; the kings and the prime ministers are driven away quickly, silently, there is little of that raincoated and gumsoled rushing around them of slovenly photographers with their hanging ogling equipment. The English are, of course, very good at this quick and efficient whisking of important people out of sight. Still it is very different from the June atmosphere of coronations, and even of royal funerals.

That grey airport bus, through the western suburbs of the great city. It is a long and humdrum approach through what were not so long ago solidly respectable rows of houses but which bear some of the outward marks of social decay. There is not much traffic in this snow and driving sleet. Past the huge dumb-impassive square aluminum buildings set up by construction companies, indistinguishable from American ones. And then, rather suddenly, near the end of the new concrete highroad, rows of brown brick buildings, a Victorian English sea of houses after the grey wintry continental cloudiness of the motorway. The lights burn yellow through the mist now, at eleven in the morning. And everywhere what, for a writer, must be one of the most evocative things of all: the inscriptions of London. The street signs and the shop fascia, the bus stops and the public lettering, most of it in that already traditional and very English modern sans-serif which Eric Gill had created in 1928, I think, for the London transport system and which was, indeed, one of the few fine achievements of the En-

From *American Spectator,* August: 7–14.

glish creative spirit between the wars. Of all countries that I know England has the finest public lettering.

At first this is curious that this should be so, for an unrhetorical and unintellectual people. At second thought it is perhaps not so surprising at all. This people, with all of its Old Testament traditions, is not really a pharisaic people: with their respect for The Law there is mixed a deep strain of their love for The Word. That is just why Perfidious Albion is, really, a mistaken phrase; that is why this is the Shakespearean nation; that is why they understood Churchill when he had to be understood, in that dramatic moment of their long existence.

But there are very few signs of the funeral now, less than twenty-four hours before it will begin.

❊ The flags are at half-mast, of course. But there are not so many of them.

Noon. We walk out from the hotel, not quite sure where we shall presently head to.

It is still sleeting and grey. Hyde Park stretches out, green, wet, and empty. The traffic on the great street has dropped down to a Sunday-afternoon level; many empty cabs and only the red busses lumbering past without rumbling, much like English middle-class spinsters who had grown to maturity in the King Edward age, with a Queen Alexandra bearing, and now often their conductors are young black women and men.

We walk somewhat hesitantly eastward, into the wind. Then one notices the many different national flags, at half-mast, flying from the buildings. This row, fifty years ago the townhouses and the flats of a rich upper-middle class, during the short peachy-creamy period of Peter Pan Kensington, houses many consulates now; the banners of many unknown new African countries, and Tito's red star flapping in the wind. (He, too, owes much to Churchill.)

There is something else, too. Something that towers, kindly, over the white Kensington houses with their now tattered fluorescent and bureaucratic insides. This thing stands above the intrusive, the uncomfortable thoughts of what the James Barries and the inevitable reaction to them— Bloomsbury, further down—had done to the spirit of England. The building that now houses the Dutch Consulate. It is a large red apartment building, built in the Queen Anne style, I presume, around 1910; its white curved roof-gables have a Dutch impression, though this is surely coincidental. Set back from the pavement behind a low wall and a small gravelly courtyard this house stands like a large solid ship, anchored forever. Its brick walls have a tinge of vermilion; like all colors, this impression is inseparable from the association which goes with it, and this is that of quiet, reddish, small square rooms inside, with dark comfortable furniture and brass fenders. Above the doorway, with its crest with the Royal Netherlands seal, flies the bourgeois red-white-blue horizontal flag of Holland, half-mast, in mourning.

It stands but a few hundred feet from Hyde Park Gate, from another, even more English, red-brick house where Winston Churchill died. And now, for the first time, I am gripped by the kind of emotion that is compounded by historical memory and personal association. This London house, and the Holland Legation, and Churchill—they are, all three, a monument of decency, commingled now in my mind and before my eyes. Large, tolerant, solid, and decent—this is what they stood for. Houses like this have buttressed the now so ramshackle edifice of a thousand years of European civilization, during its last great Protestant and Northwestern and bourgeois phase. Holland and England. Marlborough and Churchill; Holland the first England; England the second Holland; brown warm rooms and Edwardian Queen Anne; nations of families, presided over by royal families, by decent and unpretentious ones. The Dutch mourn Churchill, they understand how he tried to save a certain kind of civilization.

From the house of the Holland Legation we now drive to Westminster Hall.

✻ The cab rolls by an endless queue. We come upon it suddenly, on Millbank, as it stretches out of the New Palace Yard and from Westminster Hall; its thousands of people stand straight and somber, huddling from the wind, scuffling slowly, close against the iron railings, way down Millbank; and then the queue is turned inward, through the small flat garden between the street and the eastern end of Westminster and the river embankment; and then it turns back again, a little sparser but long, very long. It goes all the way to the Lambeth Bridge. This will take hours. My eight-year-old son is wearing cotton socks. Still, we'll see. With a cold empty feeling in my stomach I pay off the cab on the Lambeth Bridge and there we are, in the queue.

It is a good queue because it is moving. The wind is awfully cold, blowing from the grey sheet of the Thames, but there is not that sense of hopeless democratic impatience as when one has to stand and wait and stand and wait for what seem to be endless minutes without explanation. I am surprised how far we have progressed in fifteen minutes, how long already the queue is behind us. And it is a good queue because it is an English queue, disciplined and good-natured, without jostling. After fifteen minutes I know that we'll go through with it. Behind us a group of schoolgirls,

470

with impossibly long scarves, are joking and occasionally snickering, but somehow this does not seem out of place here: a grim, self-conscious solemnity would be. We are standing and walking and standing and walking, surrounded by a variety of people, most of them working-class, charwomen perhaps. They must know that we are not English. Paul wants to tell them that we have flown over from Toulouse for the funeral but I dissuade him. We are not English. I came because of my conviction of respect and my sentiment of gratitude: to suggest their appreciation of us would compromise the conviction and the sentiment.

The papers wrote later that in the crowd lived the spirit of '40, that there was a great democratic upsurge of Englishmen, with men in bowler hats and elegant women standing in line with the cockneys and the stevedores. Perhaps. I don't know about that. It might have been that way, in the cold evenings and at night, in the pubs and the teashops behind Westminster where the frozen fragments of the crowd went to restore themselves with a warm cup of something. The way I see this queue is that of pale knots of different people, a long quilted afghan made out of patches of multifarious humanity: schoolgirls, working people, businessmen, and the cheap-furred, straight-backed women of the conservative middle class, a few foreigners here and there, including a few dark faces, smiling Pakistanis or Malayans or whatever they are. For a moment I feel a slight irritation: what do *they* have to do here? mere curiosity-seekers, that is, wanting to be present at the ceremonies of the Great Imperial Guru? But I dismiss the thought in a moment: because it is ungenerous and unreasonable: in *this* cold wind, through *this* frozen garden, for such hours, it is wrong, absolutely wrong, to question motives.

✾ The working people. We have now made the first turn in the queue and people are talking. The charwomen. (But are they charwomen?) In their greenish old tweed coats, the brown wool scarves, the little glasses resting on the bumps of their pale faces, their bad teeth, their thin mouths. "I was here in '40." "There was St. Paul's with all the City blazing around it, you know." But these are standard memories which have been repeated over and over again, presumably in the papers all through this week. How much of the memories are real? How much a mixture of associations? It doesn't matter. What matters is that they came, in this cold, which is no ceremony and no coronation, a hundred thousand of the working people of England, with their good nature and their knobby faces, out of a still living feeling rather than of memory—to the bier of a man who led them not to a great victory but who saved them from the worst of possible defeats, from the collapse of English self-respect.

Now their houses are warm and their television is going and they live better than ever before. . . . Better: well, in a way. And they sense, too, the transitory malleability of this comfort, the old working people of old England, the tired members of the island race even in this airplane age: still members not fragments: selfish but self-respecting: unimaginative but fair. *Fair.* One day when the last portions of the green fairness of England will be gone or meticulously fenced in by planners and antiquarians that old green fairness will still exist, I think: it is the green copper bottom of the hearts of the working people of England.

❊ But the middle class is here, too. And my heart goes out for them.

I mean the middle class, and not the more elegant members of the upper-middle class. I mean men in their thin towncoats, women with their bony cheeks and blue eyes who have already lived longer than they shall live, erect and tired; I do not mean the children of Saki, the men and women of the once world of Evelyn Waugh and of the boring world of Anthony Powell. I need not describe them. I mean the people who were once the backbone of England.

It is a strange thing: but they, the upholders of the Conservative Party and of the once Imperial Spirit and of the Country Right Or Wrong were not those to whom Churchill meant the most. Like all of the really grands seigneurs, Churchill was closer to the aristocracy and also to the lower classes of the people. To the lower classes not because he had much of the vulgar demagogue in him (earthy he could be but rarely vulgar) but because the lower classes sometimes instinctively understood him even on his terms, on his own level. (In a news film I once saw a flick of a Churchill gesture that I cannot forget. He is coming through the ruins of an East London street after one of the bombardments. There are people, including a woman, with blowing hair, like the spirit of a proletarian Boadicea, running up to him from the ruins, gathering around him as he marches through the rubble in his tall hat and coat and cane, smoking with his incomparable chewing smile. As one of them runs up, he pats her on the back with his left arm, with an All Right! All Right! gesture. It is an amiable, patronizing, and nonchalant everyday gesture. For a moment one senses that feeling of utter trust and confidence which only certain grandfathers can give.)

It was at that time—October 1940?—that the grey ice on the faces of the middle class melted enough to reveal a racial facet of their true selves. He infused some kind of a sense into their long decline, from Kensington to Kensington. They were not the lot of hard-faced men who had made out well from the first war: but they were, let's face it, the people of Baldwin and of Chamberlain, stiff and unimaginative, with a tight kind of patriotism that was no longer enough. It was not merely a clique of narrow Germanophile politicians who distrusted Churchill in the Thirties, it was the once large middle class of England who instinctively distrusted him: they were the people who had a natural trust in the Chamberlains: Churchill's pugnacity, his rhetoric, his brilliance, his Francophilia and his Americanisms, these were things they shunned, uneasily, stiffly, shyly. Then, in 1940, all of this flashed away. Even then they did not quite understand him: but in this country of common sense this was irrelevant then, and it is irrelevant still. For, after the war, it was this thinning and threadbare and sorely tried middle class that continued to believe in some of the older patriotic virtues no matter how out of date these seemed to have become. Slowly, instinctively, through their bones—their bones warmed by this feeling through the chilly austerity years of British decline—their minds received Churchill, with his prose and through the memories of the war.

Oh, this shy race of men and women, how very different they are from other middle classes of other nations, from the bourgeois of the continent! They are shy because they are kind. Kindness is not yet generosity, just as fairness isn't all honesty. But it is still from among their children that there may come forward one day an angry and generous Englishman, at another great dark hour of civilization, an avenging angel remembering Churchill.

Now, in his death, the pomp means less to them than to the others; it is not the might and the parade, the flags and the bands that impress them, but they, perhaps for the first time, have an inner comprehension of the magnanimity of this man now dead. Now, in his death, he belongs to them perhaps even more than to anyone else in England.

❊ 1940 is close now: the volunteer vans. We have turned away from the Thames; we are in the line moving slowly toward Millbank. There are three old blue vans of a volunteer service parked on the grass, and old small women address us with paper cups, offering blackish tea and Bovril. Two of the vans bear these inscriptions in small white paint: "London 1940–44. Coventry 1940. Bristol 1941." 1940 is close now; and the soft little rumble of the long queue seems to have dropped.

It is perhaps an appropriate thing that the American delegation to this Churchill funeral, because of some kind of Washington complexity and confusion, is unimpressive and second-rate. It is appropriate because 1940 has no great meaning for Americans. 1940 is a high year, a historic date, a sharp and poignant association for Britain and for Europe, not for America. There was, of course, Churchill's romantic Americanism, the very, very necessary help that Roosevelt chose to give him at that time, the sympathy, the interest, the willingness that millions of Americans had for Britain's struggle late that summer. But 1940 was still the peak of the European War, before America, Russia, Japan entered the scene; it was the gripping great crisis of the civilization of Europe rather than that of the "West" (a word hurriedly resuscitated and put into currency only after 1945) or, at that, of the United Nations. The lines were clear in 1940. Hitler, Mussolini, Stalin, the Japanese, the opportunists as well as the Jew-haters, the Anglophobes of the lower-middle classes, greasy Spanish functionaries as well as the dark peasant masses of Russia, they all had their mean little enjoyments in witnessing the humiliations of Britannia. The other side was incarnated by Churchill, simply and clearly. It was good to know that summer—and not only for the British—that the struggle was ineluctable; that even in this century where everything is blurred by the viscous wash of public relations, there were still two camps as close to Good Versus Evil as ever in the terrestrial struggles of nations.

All of this touched the United States but indirectly. This is even true of the great English speeches of Churchill that year. Despite the evocative power of the same—or, rather, of almost the same—language, his great June and July resolution meant something much more to certain Europeans than to Americans then. I say "certain Europeans" because at that time many of them were only small minorities, those who knew they lived in the dark, who had lived to see Hitler triumphant, who had experienced the quick sinking of a new kind of iron night on their once civilized evenings. They were the ones who needed the most that spirit of defiance and of inspiration and of British self-confidence which Churchill alone gave.

❧ Westminster Hall. First there is the sense of relief from the cold, the sleet and wind dropping behind one in an instant; it is mingled with that other sense of relief that the long cold progress is over. Here, for the first time, the gestures of the policemen are quicker. The crowd surges forward for a moment, many abreast, on the steps—and there we are, formed into two lines, in a hall. We are already moving to the left. It is very simple. In that enormous hall, under its English Gothic beams, a very tall catafalque, like a great memorial stone cut in dull black, and his coffin under a large generous British flag. The rest is what one would expect: the four Royal Marines standing like statues, and the tall candles burning.

So there we go, rather quickly now; and as we come closer I sense that the catafalque is perhaps purposely higher than usual, the flag larger than usual, which is why it is so fitting. There lies an old corpulent man whose flesh had begun to dissolve some time ago. He loved life very much; and he made life possible for many of us because he had a very old, and very strong, belief in the possibilities of human decency and of human greatness. History is not a record of life but life itself: because we are neither human animals nor perpetual slaves. In the long and slow and sad music of humanity he once sounded an English and noble note which some of us were blessed to receive and to remember.

Now up the stairs and before us we see the open door where the crowds file through and immediately dissolve, taken up by the stream of everyday London. But: instinctively, at the top of the stairs, everyone of us turns around, for a moment. I wrote "us" because, for the first and only time, I felt that I can write this honestly: not an Englishman, my grief was different from theirs, but at this moment—this very individual moment, since there is, curiously, not a speck of crowd psychic reaction in this turning around—we are all one. Again the tall catafalque and the candles blowing and the four ceremonial guards and the flag covering the coffin, all palely shining through the thin light which comes in through the large window, with its small and reconstituted unimpressive stained-glass panels. It is not perhaps the scene that is unforgettable: it is the occasion. Farewell Churchill. Farewell, father of a foreign family. Farewell British empire. I loved you once. I love you still.

❄❄❄

JANUARY 30, SATURDAY

The thirtieth of January. Dawn thoughts. On this day Franklin Roosevelt was born in 1882, and Adolf Hitler came to power in Germany thirty-two years ago.

Roosevelt and Hitler died within the same month, in April 1945. Churchill survived them by twenty years. His relationship with Roosevelt was a complex one: a mixture of genuine affection (on Churchill's part, that was), a strong recognition of obligations, a sense of loyalty together with what was a very Churchillian unwillingness to fight for certain things. It is difficult to say what were the deeper sources of his unusual deference to Roosevelt during the last two years of the war: his absolute conviction of the necessity of American benevolence for Britain, together with a certain weariness, played a role in that. Roosevelt, in turn, was the smaller person of the two—not because of his breezy American seignorialism shining at times on his face (that Churchill liked) but because of a certain uneasiness toward Churchill (and toward Britain, Europe, history)—a compound of sentiments of inferiority and of superiority, the by-products of a Rooseveltian intellectual attitude that professed to see the twentieth century as The Century of America and Of The Common Man: in these terms Churchill was a brave roast-beef Tory, an almost Dickensian figure. This was the same kind of American myopia which made Oliver Wendell Holmes consider Harold Laski to have been the greatest brain in England. Still, in 1940 at least, Roosevelt's heart was in the right place. Hence Churchill's enduring gratitude, too.

Much has been written about Hitler's love-hate relationship to England. In reality, this theme is overdone. This evil genius, capable of great instinctive flashes of comprehension when dealing with some of the motive forces of various national characteristics, never understood the English, and least of all did he understand Churchill. He did not understand that behind This Far And No Further there was something more than a stubborn dumb pragmatism; he could not understand the romantic springs of English sentiment; he mistook Churchill's bravery for mere panache; Churchill's peculiar compound of resolution and nonchalance was one of the few things that remained far beyond the reach of Hitler's wild and powerful mind.

Churchill and Hitler were, at any rate, the two protagonists of the dramatic phase of the last war, even though Roosevelt and Stalin played the decisive roles in its epic phase, in the end.

A young man was supposed to have said yesterday: "Let's hope that Hitler can see this now."

❊ But the crowds are not big. Four, five deep at the most. And how silent they are. We had risen early, in a black dawn; dressed and walked down to the Gloucester Road. The streets had a quiet Sunday feeling. A few polite posters telling motorists that some of the Thames bridges will be closed for the funeral. But the Underground is running—the Underground, with its sultana-cake plush seats, with its peculiar coal-and-cocoa smell. At Westminster Station we rose to the surface, into the jaws of the large long crowd—and great, great quiet, well an hour before the great procession was to move out of the New Palace Yard.

I read later, and heard it discussed on the plane back to Paris by a famous American reporter, that what had impressed him was the pride of the crowd, that this was a day of great inner pride, that the people of England had pulled themselves up this week and showed a proud face to the world in their mourning. This is not what I saw. Perhaps certain foreigners, television reporters, Americans felt this, because of some of their preconceived ideas: but foreigners, and especially Americans (this is strange) are prone to mistake the English aloofness for some kind of haughtiness instead of seeing what it is: the essential shyness of this people. I saw less pride than a kind of disciplined resignation, and a respectful sadness: a sadness full of the remembrance of the past for those who had memories of 1940; and, for the young, full of a strange, vague, almost medieval respect for a distant and legendary figure, someone removed even from their parents' generation, someone with real authority, someone they could respect. . . . That was strange: the papers remarked it, too: the large number of young people in the crowds, long-haired, sad-faced young barbarians, in search for something, with their strange, watery eyes.

For the others self-respect rather than pride, and a self-respect tinted with the sense of passing time. There was in this a thin thread of resigned realization that for *this* England, in her present situation, the Churchillian generation was too old: that he was the right man at the right time but not for the grey, the difficult, the technical present. I do not think that there are very many Englishmen, including Conservatives, who regard the election of July 1945 that turned Churchill out of power as some kind of a national disaster. They have an instinctive feeling that he was right for the war rather than for the postwar time. (And this is true in a way: with all of his great gifts, with his great understanding of world history, with his great insights into movements, connections, correspondences, tendencies, Churchill was not a good diplomatist—especially not when it came to dealing with Americans. . . .)

A Churchillian generation: there was, really, no such thing. Eden, Beaverbrook, Macmillan, Duff Cooper . . . Of all of them the latter was closest to Churchill in spirit: but he never had more than a minor position. The shock that grips all of England at this moment is the sight of Macmillan, Eden, Attlee, among the honorary pallbearers. How infinitely old they look! Attlee is bent over twice. He has to sit down in the cold wind, in a big black overcoat, protected carefully by a tall guards' officer. Then, for a moment, Eden—infinitely old, infinitely weary, too—bends over Attlee with a kind of great solicitude. It shows how far away we are now from the Churchillian Days, from the time of the Low cartoon of May 1940, "We're all behind you, Winston!"—Attlee, Bevin, Morrison, Eden, all of them rolling up their sleeves and marching in a broad file behind Churchill. Low drew them (how well I remember that cartoon) in a somewhat unimaginative outfit, like English shop stewards in their Sunday best they looked. But they were, at that moment, the good, the reliable, the last best hope, the shop stewards of European civilization.

❊ The RAF pilots escorting the coffin. "Never in the field of human conflict was so much owed by so many to so few." That was, to some extent, a Churchillian exaggeration. (His 1940 rhetoric was not always exaggerated, the "We shall fight in the streets" passage, for example: there are witnesses to whom he had said in May that if the Germans were to land and push into London he would go with a rifle to the sentry box at the end of Downing Street and keep firing at them 'til the end.) Would the Battle of

Britain have been won without American support? I do not mean the material support, which was not decisive at that time; I mean the knowledge, by Churchill and by the people of England and by the world, that America was moving away from neutrality, toward their side. And the legendary figures announced in '40 *were* exaggerated. "You can always take one of them with you": the RAF pilots *did* take more than one of them but not five or six. The score was a little less than two to one. Still, it was an appropriate thing to have the officers of the 1940 fighter squadrons form the first escort. They are grandfathers now, most of them; slightly corpulent training officers in pacific command posts; it is not difficult to imagine their suburban homes, their habits, their families. They have nothing of Valhalla heroes' marks on their faces. They, in 1940, they only did their duty, they would say. Now, too.

✳ The Polish officer. He is in the crowd, with his Slavic, creased face, in an angular black suit, wearing the ribbons of his medals. So this man came to pay his respects, too. For a long time the exiled Poles were bitter about Churchill. They had reason to be. From the very beginning he had found it necessary to compromise with Stalin. He wanted to let the Russians have the eastern portion of Poland up to the Curzon (or, rather, Lloyd George) Line, in exchange for a Russian agreement for a Russophile but free Polish government. In this he failed: in the end Stalin got both the frontier and the government he wanted, a big Soviet Ukraine and a subservient Communist regime in Warsaw. At Yalta, too, Churchill fought for the cause of Poland and lost (he won for France instead). Having lost, he put up a good front and went far in defending Yalta in the House of Commons. How bitter it must have been for the brave Polish exiles, with their large wounded army, these months in the ruined 1945 landscape of London! They had fought and bled in three continents, for six years, and they were abandoned in the end: large Russian armies installed forever in the terrible landscape of their ravaged country, and with the acquiescence of Churchill. (The Yugoslav exiles fared worse: Churchill had put his chips on the bandit Tito well before the end of the war.)

A German Christian-Democrat newspaper in Bonn, paying homage to Churchill, wrote among other things that he was nevertheless responsible for the division of Europe, having let Stalin come too far into the heart of the continent. And yet that is all wrong. Churchill tried to save what he could. At least his basic idea was right, as it was indeed in 1915, in the Dardanelles business, even though he could not carry it out—in 1915 because of the British government, in 1943–45 because of the distrust of the American government. Churchill knew that a price had to be paid in Eastern Europe for the Russian contribution to Germany's defeat; also, he knew the Russians better than did Roosevelt, knowing that this price ought to be fixed in advance, since with the Russians no postponing of unpleasant things and no vague declarations of universal goodwill would do. He was more concerned with the tragic destinies of Poland than Roosevelt, who was, at worst, concerned with his Polish-American voters, and Hull, who pleaded moral indignation in refusing to enter into Territorial Deals. And when in October 1944 Churchill, exasperated with American procrastination, sat down with Stalin and divided with him on a sheet of paper the rest of Eastern Europe, only a simple-witted person or some kind of a special pleader may see in that the evidence of Traditional and Perfidious Machiavellian Diplomacy: for at that time, as indeed on other occasions, what Churchill did was to try to save what was possible. And he did. He made sure that the Russians won't interfere in Greece, which he then saved from a Communist revolution. His support of Tito, too, paid off in a way: it contributed to Tito's sense of his independence: surely this made the latter less dependent on Stalin: it helped to make his future break from Moscow possible. Even Poland remained a nation, after all, far from being independent but, still, a nation and a state at a time when Stalin could have done anything he wanted in that part of Europe: he did not incorporate Poland into Russia, after all.

In that way, too, Churchill was a great European. But how bitter and lonely must have been those exile years to men and women such as this angular, wooden Pole, alone for more than two decades now in this grey and unemotional London! And yet he is here, on this icy street, silent and stolid. What must be the thoughts and the memories that burn slowly in that creased, war-worn skull! Churchill and he *were* fighting comrades in a great European War, after all. And when I read in the paper, next day, that Poland (Communist Poland, that is) was the only East European nation that was represented by a cabinet minister, and that he sat in St. Paul's among the official guests, and so did the old spare leaders of the Polish national army, Anders and Bór-Komorowski, I thought that this was only fitting and just, and that in issuing the invitations to the latter the British had, instinctively, done the right (and not merely the proper) thing again.

❁ The monarchs of Northwestern Europe. Olav of Norway (rubicund); Frederick of Denmark (genial); Baudouin of Belgium (still like a student); Jean of Luxembourg (looking surprisingly like Otto of Habsburg); Queen Juliana (surprisingly heavy). It is right that they should be here. Churchill saved their countries twenty-five years ago.

And, so, this is a sad family occasion. They have an instinctive tie of memory with Elizabeth, who, like some of them, was very young at that time. They know what they owe to this great commoner now dead. That there is this great array of royalty paying their respects at the bier of a statesman is not the important thing. The important thing, again, is the memory of 1940: those dazzling, feverish evenings of the brilliant and deadly May and June of that year. Four times in six weeks King George and his queen had driven in the evening to Victoria Station to greet the fleeing monarchs and presidents of Europe with dignity, sympathy, and solicitude. The sky was enormously blue in London, the German air attacks had not yet begun, unlike those black clouds that had risen from the fires of Bergen, Rotterdam, Antwerp. In the white rooms of London hotels these royal persons of Europe were surrounded by gentleness and courtesy, by the fading flowers of a civilization. They had come to be thus received in its then last island house.

They are respectable men and women, these constitutional monarchs of the small democratic nations of Northwestern Europe. For a moment, as they stand, some of them uneasily, on the steps of St. Paul's, they are a family unto themselves. They represent those lands of the world where there are still many living monuments to an older kind of humaneness. On the surface map of the world they represent the central cluster of decency, these bourgeois monarchs of Northwestern Europe. Churchill knew that: for he was a monarchist not merely out of sentiment but because of his deep historical reason. In a fatherless world they are sources of a certain strength and of a certain inspiration. May they live and reign for long! May their presidency over the Sunday afternoons of Western Europe be prolonged!

❀ Above them towers now de Gaulle. "The Constable of France": thus Churchill saw him in June 1940. The constable of a new Europe, now? There is something to this. His presence is regal: naturally, without the slightest pomp. There he stands in his ill-fitting French army greatcoat, blinking occasionally, putting on his glasses, leaning down to Prince Jean of Luxembourg, saying something with a bearing that reflects a familiarity and solicitude. Many, many people in this great royal assembly look at him often. Later the London papers describe him in terms of unstinted admiration and respect. Very little of that uneasy suppressed dislike with which some Americans regard de Gaulle. But, of course, their quarrels and the phrase of the heavy burden of the Cross of Lorraine notwithstanding, Churchill understood and respected de Gaulle; so far as their conceptions of history (and of human nature, too) went, Churchill and de Gaulle, two national leaders of the Right, had more in common than Churchill and

Roosevelt. This is what most intellectuals failed to understand: that in 1940 the truest opponents of Hitlerism were men of the Right, not of the Left: Churchill and de Gaulle, each representing a certain superb kind of patriotism, not internationalism.

❀ A ragged group of Frenchmen. They, as well as groups from Denmark and from elsewhere, flew over here representing their Resistance. Their silken tricolors wave smartly as the coffin moves by. These colors, together with the few red-and-white-crossed Danish flags, enlighten for a moment the somber tints of the procession, beneath the cold blackened imperial buildings of Whitehall. They are a ragged group of men and women, marching disordered as in any French civic parade, many of them paunchy, with their rimless glasses: small *fonctionnaires* and *propriétaires* (one old Frenchman with an angelic white beard shuffles on, pink-faced, waving an enormous flag).

The French owe much to Churchill. Unfortunately not many of them recognize this. (De Gaulle does: despite the struggles and the quarrels and the high-hatted arguments in his *Memoirs* he did write down a crucial sentence that without Churchill he and Free France would have been nothing, nothing. "Shipwrecked from desolation," he wrote, "on the shores of England, what could I have done without his help?") It is a curious thing that while elsewhere on the continent the national traitors and the fascist politicians were the Germanophiles, in France the party of surrender, the nationalist party, consisted of Anglophobes. Anglophobia, not Germanophilia, was the key to the behavior and to the attitudes of Pétain, Laval, Darlan. They had had reasons for distrusting Chamberlain: unfortunately they distrusted Churchill even more. That tremendous, ill-considered but genuine Churchillian offer for an Anglo-French Union, uttered on the sixteenth of June in 1940, was one of the gravest pronouncements in modern history and in the history of Great Britain. How different would the United Europe look today had the French accepted it at that time! Throughout his life Churchill was a genuine Francophile. This shines through not only in his great generous gestures of 1940 (that inimitable broadcast to the French in October: *Dieu protège la France!*) but in the way he fought for France and for de Gaulle five years later, at Yalta, and six years before '40 as he spoke in the House of Commons: "Thank God for the French Army!" he said. (He also noted the utter annoyance and disbelief on the faces of the Members.) This was more than a political choice for Churchill. He belonged to a generation of aristocratic and patrician Englishmen who, coming to maturity in the Edwardian Age, were, among all British generations, the most conversant with the political history of the continent and the most deeply attuned to the delights and civilities of French culture. Churchill was never prone to take a philistine view of Europe, not even when the continent was ruined, when the governments of the ancient states of Western Europe had been reduced to the role of tattered suppliants, when it seemed that America and Britain and Russia would rule the world. His distaste for the Birmingham municipal radicalism of the Chamberlains was part and parcel of his distaste for the Germanic inclinations and sympathies of that kind of British middle class. (His artistic inclinations reflected these tendencies, too: his disinterest in music, his painting in the manner of the French impressionists.) Unlike those of some of his Edwardian contemporaries, Churchill's Francophilia was more than an acquired taste for certain pleasant and civilized delights. He enormously admired Joan of Arc and Napoleon, two of the greatest opponents of England. He understood something of what D. H. Lawrence once noted, that the Rhine was a peculiar frontier of the European spirit. He believed in the alliance, in the necessary alliance, of St. George and St. Denis; and he represented that short-lived Anglo-French conflation of spirit which, with its elegance and nonchalance, marked some of the highest levels of European civilization early in this century.

❉ The Churchill family. Despite his aristocratic inclinations (among them his thoroughbred characteristic of impatience: the most aristocratic and least helpful of his characteristics), Churchill had a deep understanding of the patient virtues of patrician family life, of that fragment of bourgeois civilization. One must know something of the English aristocracy to recognize how unusual that was. Thus the beauty and the dignity with which his family walks behind his coffin is a living apotheosis to his personal ideals. Not a trace of that self-conscious pride which would make them a center of attention. Suicide, divorce, degradation, they have all fallen away. There are no signs of the ravages of life, only the tragic quiet of discipline on Sarah Churchill's pale jewelled face. (She is fifty years old now!) Her father would have been solicitous of her on this day.

❉ On this day of Sabbath the British people mourn a great David-like figure who is buried with the pomp and reward of a great Old Testament Patriarch. It being Sabbath, the president of Israel couldn't ride in a car; he had to walk to St. Paul's.

That, too, is fitting for the occasion. The heads of the state of Israel walking, small and solemn, to Churchill's funeral. Enormous are the debts that the people of Israel owed, and still owe, to Churchill. I am not thinking of his support for the Jewish state, which goes back a long time. It is all a one-way debt. Unlike Roosevelt, he owed little to Jewish political support.

Churchill had few vested interests in supporting Israel; he was a new King Cyrus without an Esther. He saw the evil incarnated in Hitler instantly, immediately. Then he rose like a hero, highest in those months in 1940 when the future of human decency was at stake, and when Jewry and Christianity were on the same side, which was the side incarnated by him, which was his side. It is therefore that no Jewish intellectual should ever call Churchill "a splendid anachronism"; it is therefore that every conscientious Catholic should pay respects to this Englishman who, in a supreme moment, saw Evil even clearer than had the pope.

❊ The procession has reached the Thames.

We are told that this is the end of the state funeral, and that from now on the private progress of mourning belongs to the Churchill family. In reality there is no frontier between the two portions of the procession. But the progress is thinning out. The crowds are lighter; on the bridges, closed to traffic, there are not more than three deep, and some of them will scurry across the width of the bridge to follow the watery wake of the launches.

And it is because of the royal procession melting away in the city that, somehow, the funeral becomes sadder and more poignant. There is the wail of the bagpipes, keening across the cold river: but their impression is only aleatory now. There is something very sad in the aspect of this river, and in the small neat launch that will carry Churchill's coffin upstream. It is said that he himself, in instructions he had left for his funeral, wanted his coffin to be carried up the Thames, as was Nelson's. But how different is the Thames now from Nelson's, or even Wellington's time! Two hundred years ago Canaletto himself painted it and wondered at it, when it was a great green river, ample and rich like the empire, with gardens and rich terraces on its borders. Now it is a grey and narrowing flow, with but faint memories of the ocean sea whose scummy tides race inland on dark evenings; the once rich shipping of the Port of London is sparse and far downstream. No longer could a warship, even a destroyer, come upstream for Churchill. The *Havengore* is a launch used for hydrographic tasks by the Port of London Authority.

Swiftly she sails up the cold narrowing river, bordered by warehouses, barges, and cranes. And as she is small, the coffin, covered and now protected by that large and lovely flag, is visible to all.

❊ The train. In a black automobile, simply, the coffin is now driven to the train. The crowds are very sparse now: but still that enormous silence, all over London.

Up to now everything connected with the arrangement of the funeral was stately and appropriate; now it has become appropriate in a familiar sense. The midday silence of the great iron railway hall, for example. Waterloo Station. That peculiarly English, steady, stutterless hissing of the steam locomotive. Far on the other side of the station other trains are standing and people moving, the regular Saturday traffic of the British Railways. The train is appropriate: it brings to life the Edwardian memories, the comfortable English patrician tastes of Churchill's age: those butter-and-chocolate British Pullman cars, including the van in which the Irish Guards will place the coffin, painted cream and maroon, including the momentary sight of the tables laid in white napery with their little yellow fringed lamps in a dining-car for the family, including the portly engine. In the procession there is now the sense of the few small hitches of a family occasion: the Pullman waiter, standing respectfully but somewhat uneasily in his white spencer jacket, the nervousness of the stationmaster who looks at his watch too often, because, for the first time, this perfectly managed timetable is a minute or two late.

Then—and how appropriate this is!—the locomotive blows twice. The sound of the whistle is melancholy and raucous at the same time. The steady hissing of the steam valves remains the same; there is no dramatic huffing and puffing as the train gathers speed and glides out of the iron station into the pale sunlight of the Western Saturday afternoon.

In a minute its rumble dies away; the end of the last coach vanishes; now, for the first time, we are face to face with the emptiness of the afternoon.

❋ That afternoon and evening I walked in the streets and across the squares of this great city.

Everything resumed now its course, the theatres and the cinemas and the shops were open, the football matches were played and there was racing in the wet parks, the crowds filled the streets but the sense of silence remained. I felt nothing of that inner, quiet glow of relief that so often follows funerals and other ceremonial occasions. I am sure that there were few gatherings in great houses this day; that, instead, at the same time, the inner silence was something oppressive.

There was now, in London, some of that yellow fog that, in the cold, reminds one of what one knows of the nineteenth century; of imperial London with its large Roman paving-blocks, and the black processions of thousands of cabs, and the great throngs of people in the cold shadows of the stony classical buildings built by an imperial race. This dark-bright evening of London was closer to, say, 1875 than to 1935. Now the city was full, fuller than a century ago, and yet there was a sense of emptiness or, rather, an emptiness of sense: something had gone out of the spirit of these imperial buildings: Trafalgar Square was brilliantly lit but it was not Nelson's Column and the lions that were strange: it was Admiralty Arch, that well-proportioned Edwardian building with its proud Latin inscription chiseled large and deep over the seething roadways; it seemed ancient and emptied out now.

It was because of Churchill that Macaulay's awful prediction still had not come true, that tourists from New Zealand standing on London Bridge may contemplate a large living metropolis and not merely a few broken buildings. London had risen from her partial ruins, and her imperial monuments, lit by floodlights and by the eerie sideglows of her cinemas, still stand. But it was a purposeless crowd who swirled among them on this silent evening.

Meanwhile I had a sandwich in a place called a Wimpy. The waitress in a wimpy maroon uniform was very English, with her bun-like face and her shyness and adolescent incompetence. I thought of the fat-faced Advertising Managers and the horde of public relations men who decide on names such as Wimpy, who spread the cheeseburger all over Britain, and the end result of their American publicity bang being a weak British wimpy.

There came in a man, a fortyish man with glasses and a mouse-colored moustache, and a turned-down mouth between a woolen scarf and his grey tired face. He may have been a teacher in a poor school in the Midlands. He looked at the plastic menu for a while. Then he said to the waitress: "A Wimpy, please." As he said that there passed a shadow of embarrassment, a flicker of resigned disturbance across his face. I thought that I could detect something of the same on the otherwise nearly vacuous, pale face of the little waitress too. *That* embarrassment they shared in common. Surrounded by Wimpies and the cheap metallic filth of plastic dishes and the sex magazines, in the midst of this vast process of thin liquefaction that flicker of embarrassment was a faint sign of the atavistic resistance of the race: a faint sign but a sign nonetheless: a weak glow but still a glow of the once fire, of some kind of a fire below the ashes.

✻ ✻ ✻

JANUARY 31, SUNDAY

The Sunday papers. In the quiet of the morning, the Sunday papers. (All of the weariness in the civilization of the great English-speaking cities in the twentieth century lies latent in these two words and in their associations: Sunday papers.)

The long accounts of yesterday's funeral and the excellent photographs are there but, somewhat surprisingly, the articles are not very good. There are slips even in the evocative details—one of the young leader writers saying, for example, that as the launch moved off Tower Bridge Pier, "a band crashed out with the tune that was a last Churchillian brag: 'Rule Britannia'": how wrong it is, the crash instead of the muffled keening across the long dampness, and the Last Churchillian Brag, as if it had not been something infinitely different and melancholy. There are also such things as the article by the Fellow and Director of English Studies (in reality a New York intellectual eager beaver) at Churchill College (in reality a Lord Snow institution), ending with a real Madison Avenue phrase: "Given the tools, Churchill College can do its part of the exciting job."

All through the week the writers of articles did capture many of the fragments and some of the atmosphere of the occasion: but now the reminiscences have a curious kind of nervous tiredness about them. The more intelligent among the commentators, thus, write that this funeral was indeed a proud and ceremonial occasion but the last occasion for something that is irrevocably past, the last time when London was the capital of the world: for after this last solemn homage to the glories of a British imperial past the worn weekdays of a compressed modest England begin anew. This may be true: but it does not quite explain that slight awkwardness of the eulogies by some of the more perceptive younger writers. I think I know the sources of that awkwardness of sentiment: it is the knowledge, especially of those who had grown up in the postwar years, that the Churchill victory of the Second World War was, after all, not much of a victory indeed.

That, too, may be true. But this intellectual recognition, lurking uneasily beneath the immediate impressions of the occasion, does not really conflict, for once, with the sentiments of the people: the sense of gratitude by this unemotional people of England that is now untainted either by nostalgia or by self-pity: because it has little to do with the glory of victory. It is the sense that *Churchill had saved them from defeat* rather than the knowledge that he had led Britain to victory. This is, I think, what accounts for the absence of any amount of nostalgic jingoism among the people—who, even more than the journalists and the statesmen and, of course, than the intellectuals, may feel in their bones how close England was to disaster in 1940.

Now this seems to be rather obvious: but few people, I think, comprehended its historical portents.

To most people, in England as well as abroad, the Thirties are, in retrospect, something like a rather incredible episode, an era of philistine stupidity. The older generation who lived through it are not prone to analyze it in any detail, partly because of the fortunate British mental habit of letting bygones be bygones, partly because of the less fortunate British unwillingness to face certain unpleasant truths. To the younger generation it is yet another example of the myopia of the then governing classes. The consequence of these beliefs is, then, that Churchill came forth, at a time of great distress, to attune the spirit of England to its standard condition.

But was this really so? As one contemplates the devolution of Britain during the last half-century one gets the impression that it was the lassitude which was the standard condition, in the Twenties and the Thirties and the Fifties and the Sixties. The Bonar Laws as well as the Lansburys, the donkey generals of 1917 and the asses of the 1935 Peace Ballot, the Chamberlains as well as the Ramsay Macdonalds, the spirit of Harold Laski as well as the Great Ideas of Lord Snow: what did they, what do they, have in common with Churchill? In one of the few fortunate phrases in the post-mortems Dame Rebecca West wrote that she remembers Churchill in the Twenties shining with vitality as if it had been sluiced over him with a pail. This at a time when the spirit of England had begun to smell like weak cocoa.

This does not mean that Churchill was completely isolated, absolutely alone: he was out of spirit with the *Times*, he was out of spirit with "the times" (whatever that is), but there was something else: he knew that he could bring an entire people with him, in 1940. This was one of the great differences between Churchill and de Gaulle at that time. But even this does not mean that 1940 represented England in her standard conditions. And the people know this better than the intellectuals. Hence their deep emotional regret. They know how there loomed in 1940 the possibility of something that is still unspeakable and perhaps unthinkable: that England, despite her island situation, despite the riches of her then empire, despite the aid from the United States, could have indeed collapsed before the strong and purposeful Germany, because England already then was at the tail end of a long period of lassitude and abdication, because in the spirit of England, then as now, the vitality of aspirations shimmered very low.

To the present generation it seems unthinkable that Hitler could have ever won the war at all. To the intellectuals Hitlerism represents a strange and perhaps fascinating, barbaric and reactionary episode of a temporary madness going against the broad stream of the twentieth century, against the long and broad history of mechanical progress. England, together with the United States and the Soviet Union and the Progressive Forces of the world, was bound to defeat fascism: foolish and stupid statesmen and vested interests had led her close to great painful disasters, whereupon Churchill, who only did in great style what had to be done anyhow, restored the balance of reason and democratic virtue with Shakespearean words and gestures; that was his role; that was all. But that wasn't it at all. People still do not know how close Hitler and his cohorts came to winning the war in '40. Certain men and women who are attuned better to the listening to the movements and the sentiments of large masses of people in Europe know this better than do the intellectuals, including certain professional historians; and the common people of England who had lived through the war sense it better, too.

They could have been conquered. Their island history would have come to an end. Their self-respect would have gone for good. Churchill saved them from this fate: and he had appealed to them as he did so. It is a mark of the decency and of the common sense of the people of England that they were not, and are not now, puffed up with pride in remembering those days, and that the stillness reigning over Churchill's funeral reflects their now profound sentiment of still gratitude to him for having done so.

Several of the men now writing about Churchill's life say that he was at his best, at his most courageous, when he was alone in the Thirties, the lonely political Cassandra, the warning trumpet, the voice in the wilderness. This is an arguable proposition. Churchill, though of a small minority, was not entirely alone in the Thirties; he had certain newspaper columns at his disposal; and there is, at any rate, a difference between speaking out when one has no official position at all and between leading a half-armed nation, urged by instinct, on a proud course of defiance in face of the strong possibility of disaster. And: is it really true that Hitler could have been stopped easily in '38 or in '36, at the time of Munich or at the time of the Rhineland? I am not so sure about that. Of course Churchill was right. But who would have followed him in '36? Not Baldwin. Not Chamberlain. Not the Liberals. Not the Laborites. Not the Trade Unions. Not the Fabianists. Not the Socialists. Not the Pacifists. Not the Popular Front. Not the Commonwealth. Not the Americans. Not Roosevelt. And why?

Why? Why did they—an enormous, a heterogeneous *they*—distrust him so much? with an emotional as well as an intellectual distrust whose echoes lived strong in England until the gunfire drowned them out in the high summer of '40, and which was to flare up again, across the ocean, later in the war. *They* all distrusted him because he was uncategorizable. He was the kind of person whom mediocrities instinctively fear. "He was not steady" said conservative respectability. "He is a reactionary" said progressive intellectuality. But at the bottom the sources of their distrust were much the same. Neville Chamberlain and Eleanor Roosevelt, Harold Laski and Edward Stettinius distrusted Churchill out of the same human motives. He did not have the kind of intellect that has a natural appeal to Overseers of Harvard University and to deans of womens' colleges in New England. At the time when Churchill began to sputter against the Hitler German danger he was dismissed not only by the stolid dumbness of the Baldwins and the Chamberlains; it was at that time that Harold Laski wrote that Hitler was not much more than a tool in the hands of German capitalism, it was the time when Alger Hiss was the chief advisor of the Nye Committee, investigating the misdeeds of British militarism left over from the First World War; ten years later the same Hiss was to sit on Roosevelt's right at the Yalta table, with his long ambitious Quaker face, that intellectual mug, calculating, self-conscious, and smug.

A man by the name of Henry Fairlie wrote in the *Sunday Telegraph*: "Mr A. J. P. Taylor said last week that historians of the future would ignore at their peril the spiritual contact which one man found in 1940 with the rest of his fellow-countrymen. . . . If Mr. Taylor is not afraid to talk of a 'spiritual contact,' I see no reason why one should be afraid to talk of a vision. . . ." "Afraid" is good. For God's sake, why should one be *afraid* to admit the existence of something that was a matter of spirit, something that was not a matter of "production" or, at that, of "opinion" statistics? This is no longer the outcome of racial shyness; it is a kind of perverted crampedness of mind. It is this belated triumph of Josiah Bounderby that had laid the spirit of England so low that Churchill had to come to lift it up at its greatest danger: this Bounderby philosophy which, bruited now in the name of Freud and of Marx (how curious it is that both of them are buried here in London) is again abroad in this land.

What remains then, for England, on this Sunday? The nervous tic on the face of the man when he ordered a Wimpy. The essential, the ineradicable reticence graven into the hearts of the girls and women of England even as they leaf through the latest sex book or magazine. This Sunday stillness.

At midday we went to Mass in a Roman Catholic church on High Street in Kensington. It was not a very attractive church, set back between the brown brick houses. It was full of people: a few Poles and in the pew ahead of us the earnest and solicitous heads of Central European converted Jews: but the majority of the congregation was English, infinitely serious English men and women with their children. Living through the last phase of the Protestant episode, of the long unhappy chapter of Roman Catholicism in England, with the old suspicions and the mistrust melting away, with reconciliation setting in, these English Catholics, perhaps better than any other Catholics in the Western world, know what it means to be Christians in a post-Christian land.

In a superficially post-Christian land, that is. In England, the existence of something like Christian morality may have survived the decay of religion. And yet is it "Christian morality," this thing which is dissolving and changing into the pale fluid of a vague universal humanitarianism? Yes: and no.

In this people who ushered in the modern age there is still a mystical, a near-medieval strain, a strain that has been part and parcel of their Protestantism, their Puritanism, their Industrial Revolution, their English socialism. It is there in this living strain of English Catholicism, which, in the twentieth century—curious paradox in the spiritual history of England—has become one of the strongest subterranean streams of a peculiar Englishness. To be hounded by heaven was one way to put it—but it was not only the Gerard Manley Hopkinses who sensed this. Even Aleister Crowley. Or Malcolm Muggeridge. Hounded by the sense of Satan or of God in a new-old, postmodern way, preoccupied, unlike many other people in the Western civilization, with the living reality of the question of whence we have come and where we are to go. Even now.

Then to midday dinner in an English home; we sat in friendliness for a little while; after that the cold wind whipping the torn papers in the doorways; through the brown Sunday afternoon and the wide streets to the steel tower of the airways terminal, with its inscriptions in many tongues. In a foreign airplane we rose into the winter evening sky.

In the hot droning airplane the Sunday papers again. *His name. Churchill.* How the very sound and the shape of his name fitted him. Pouting, aristocratic, flecked by sunlight. The round and juicy sound of the first syllable, formed by lips curling to speak just as his, the air filling up the cheeks of a seventeenth-century boy with a young and churchy sound. The pout makes it human and humorous rather than churched (but, then, the sound of the English *church* is so much more attractive, rounder, than the high guttural Gothic of *Kirche,* than the cold Roman-law *église,* than the hard angular Celtic *kell*). The pout merges, in a genial way, into the second syllable. There is nothing chilly about that final syllable, it is short, shiny, even brilliant, that springy sound of a rill. The sound of the full name is serious and humorous: it has a male charm about it: it is like the baroque fountains of Blenheim. (English rather than British; an English name whose bearer is now buried in English earth; English earth with its Roman and Saxon and Norman layers; an English man who had a romantic and exaggerated, an expansive notion of Britishness perhaps precisely because he was neither Scottish nor Welsh.) The shape of the name, too: like the shape of his body: compact, slightly corpulent, with the glimmer of a single jewel, jaunty. The fluted cylindrical second portion giving clear form to the roundness of the first. Wearing his black 1940 hat, he looked like that dome of St. Paul's on occasion. Churchill. Churchill.

50

Hitler's Birthplace
(1994)

In March 1989 I went to Hitler's birthplace.

The town of Braunau, where Adolf Hitler was born one hundred years ago, is off the tourist-beaten track—that is, distant from the Munich-Salzburg-Linz-Vienna superhighway. It is in the Innviertel, a region of the province of Upper Austria, which, even before the Autobahn, had few tourist attractions comparable to the pretty shining lakes farther to the south, on the shores of which innkeeping had become a source of income for Austrians during the nineteenth century. About forty miles north of Salzburg and seventy miles east of Munich, Braunau is a good two-hour drive from both, on two-lane roads. There are few local trains between Munich and Simbach, the German frontier town across the Inn River. The train no longer comes to Braunau.

Partly because of this relative remoteness Braunau has been undamaged by the tempestuous ravages of the Second World War and by the less tempestuous but more endemic ravages of modern architecture. In 1874, three years after Hitler's father had come to take up his post as a customs official there, many of the wooden buildings of Braunau were destroyed by fire. But most of the houses of Braunau, built of stone, still stand in tight rows along the main city square, which serves as an open-air market once a week. They jut out more irregularly in some of the side streets. Many of them are buildings of the seventeenth and eighteenth centuries, and some even older. There are two particularly handsome prospects in Braunau. One is the remnant of the city wall (Braunau was a fortified town for centuries), with a few ramshackle gardens and houses set atop the grey stone ramparts in the cracks of which clumps of greenery have pushed their way through. The other is the view east from the large market square whose eastern edge is unobstructed by buildings and slopes slightly downward.

From *Destinations Past* (Columbia, MO: University of Missouri Press), 158–72.

The prospect is of a range of green-brown mountains under an unusually wide expanse of sky. But that bright lightness opens up away from Braunau, many of whose narrow streets, including the small square around its high-spired church, are seldom washed by sunlight. What is perhaps unusual is this combination: Braunau is both handsome and somber.

The somber quality resides in the darkness of some of its old houses, with their heavy buttresses. Their appearance is but a representation of the history of this town and of the complicated story of the loyalties of its inhabitants. The Inn River is the boundary between Austria and Germany; but that was not always so. For centuries Braunau was a Bavarian frontier town facing Austria. In 1706 it was a center of a peasant rebellion against the Habsburgs. It passed back and forth from Bavarian Wittelsbach to Austrian Imperial Habsburg rule. It was in Braunau that in 1810 Napoleon's new bride, the Archduchess Marie Louise, was festively transferred from her Austrian to her French entourage. During his campaigns against Austria in 1805 and again in 1809 Napoleon spent the night in this frontier town—in the same House Schüdl (and presumably in the same second-story rooms) where seventy years later Hitler's father came to live. It is a well-proportioned building on the south side of the large market square.

The house where Adolf Hitler was born stands a hundred yards farther down on the main street. In 1889 it was the Gasthaus zum Pommer, one of the two main inns of Braunau, an old hostelry once owned by a brewery—that is, a "Brauhaus." Hitler's father moved often, at least until he could buy his own house during the last years of his life; before that he had often preferred to live in inns. The Gasthaus zum Pommer is partially occupied now; it houses a hostel for handicapped children. Earlier it was a kind of public library. After Hitler had annexed Austria, Martin Bormann bought it for the purpose of ceremonial preservation. At that time, and also during the war, it was a place of pilgrimage for many people, most of them coming from Germany to contemplate the Führer's birthplace in awe. The house has something of a dual aspect now, almost as if it were divided against itself. The ground-floor façade is heavy and Germanic; the top two stories have the pale wash of yellow Austrian stucco. The back of this L-shaped house, with its arched corridors of the upper stories, seems abandoned and in poor repair. During my visit to Braunau the building was closed. I could not ascertain the location of the room where Adolf Hitler was born.

People in Braunau do not seem to be divided against themselves. They are a fairly homogeneous people, which is somewhat unusual, since during the 1940s (near the end of the war and for several years afterward) millions of the German-speaking peoples of Central Europe had moved from north to south and from east to west, leaving their great bombed cities, fleeing before the avenging Russian armies, expelled from their once homelands among other Eastern European peoples, eventually establishing themselves in postwar West Germany and Austria. (By 1950, for example, most of the inhabitants of Munich were no longer its natives.) But this great inchoate migration of peoples touched the Innviertel only marginally. Its people are stubby, gnarled, muscular, with some of the marks of inbreeding. (Hitler's father and mother, too, were second cousins.)

I came to Braunau in early March. A friend had reserved a room for me in the main hostelry of the town, Hotel zur Post, an old inn with gloomy rooms and a good sturdy cuisine. I ate my dinner alone, behind a table occupied by locals, including the owner, a man of a long line of Braunau innkeepers. I knew that they knew why I had come to their town; I was obviously a forerunner of the many journalists who had booked the Post solid for the nineteenth and twentieth of April. Their conviviality eventually spilled over the low back of the bench separating my table from theirs. As the dining room of the inn was emptying, one of them, a wiry little man, a bit in his cups, stepped over to sit with me. I told him that I was not a professional journalist but a historian, something that impressed him not at all. What seemed to impress him—and, I fear, not altogether agreeably—was that I knew something about the history of his town. I asked him where the Gasthaus zum Pommer was. We went out in the pelting rain. We looked at it. Then he invited me to go on drinking in another tavern. "My father was a Nazi," he said. "I don't know about myself." Then he added: "I am an engineer." At breakfast next morning the owner came over to sit with me. He started the conversation by telling me that "der Hitler" had lived but the first three years of his life in Braunau. (Actually he lived there even less than that.) Then he went on to say that, yes, there were people around here who had been Nazi sympathizers in the 1930s, but this had been a depressed region then, and people were influenced by the prosperity and the high level of employment of factories in German Simbach, a few hundred yards away across the Inn.

That was typical of the few conversations I had with people in Braunau—which is why I write that people in Braunau do not seem to be divided among themselves. There is, at the same time, a division, a kind of split-mindedness, within their minds. When it comes to memories of the Hitler years, they are defensive but not remorseful. When it comes to foreigners, the attitude reflects what, to them, is a commonsense skepticism; foreigners cannot, and will not, understand those things. But this is not an attitude of the people of the Innviertel in particular; it is an attitude still widespread among the people of Austria at large. What is particular about the people of Braunau and the Innviertel is their insistence that Adolf Hitler was not a typical son of their city and their land, that he was not really one of them. And in this they are, at least to some extent, correct.

There are three things in Hitler's early years about which he misled people: about Braunau, about his father, and about his years in Vienna.

He dictated—dictated rather than wrote—*Mein Kampf* in the winter and spring of 1924–25. *Mein Kampf* consists of (and originally was to be printed in) two volumes, of which the first is autobiographical. Hitler declared this in his preface: from his own history "more can be learned than from any purely doctrinary treatise" about the development of himself and of the movement. Now he had "the opportunity to describe my own development, as far as this is necessary for the understanding of the first as well as the second volume, and which may serve to destroy the evil legends created about my person by the Jewish press."

Mein Kampf begins with a paean to Braunau. "Today I consider it my good fortune that fate designated Braunau on the Inn as the place of my birth." Again: "this little town on the border appears to me the symbol of a great task." And again: "this little town on the River Inn, gilded by the light of German martyrdom." Yet it is not only that the Hitler family moved away from Braunau in the third year of Adolf Hitler's life. All of his repeated emphasis on his native roots notwithstanding, he did not return to Braunau until his forty-ninth year.[1]

He came back to Braunau on the twelfth of March in 1938, on a Saturday, the day of the week when he was born. That Saturday in 1889 had been grey. Now Braunau was washed by the sun. The resistance of the Austrian government had collapsed the day before. That night people poured into the streets; there was a triumphant torchlight parade. A large swastika banner was draped over the stone carving of the Habsburg Imperial double-headed eagle at the top of the arch of the old city gate. From the early morning of the twelfth, German army units were coming over the bridge, passing through Braunau, cheered on by the crowd. A little before four in the afternoon there was a hush. In a big open Mercedes touring car Hitler came slowly across the bridge. He received a large bouquet of flowers. His face was unsmiling. The automobile halted before the house where he was born. He did not descend; he did not wish to enter. Braunau did not mean much to him. He never saw it again. After March 1938 party officials and other enthusiasts designed embellishments and commemorative erections in Braunau. Hitler was not interested.

That afternoon he drove on, in the direction of Linz. His triumphant progress followed, by and large, the route of his family during his childhood and early youth. The year after his birth his father was posted from Braunau to three different places in Upper Austria, eventually settling in

Leonding, a suburb of Linz. On the thirteenth of March in 1938, more than one hundred thousand people crowded into Linz to cheer Hitler. Their frenetic jubilation made him change his original plans; he proclaimed the union of Germany with Austria then and there. Till the end he had a soft place for Linz in his heart. A few days before killing himself in the Führerbunker in Berlin, he looked dreamily at a plan of a future Linz that he had wished to make into a great cultural center (and to which in his personal will he had donated most of his paintings). Leonding is on the way from Braunau to Linz; yet it was Linz first and Leonding second. From Linz Hitler drove to pay a short visit to his parents' grave, in the parish churchyard of Leonding. I saw that grey gravestone, with his father's photograph set in it under glass. In May 1945, after American troops had set them free from the concentration camp in nearby Mauthausen, a schoolmate of mine and a friend had their memorable first picnic lunch sitting on the wall of that churchyard. They saw an enormous wreath left on the grave of Alois and Klara Hitler, with a wide ribbon: the homage of the party of the district. In March 1989 there were two small pots of flowers on the grave.

Across the street from the churchyard stands an ochre-stuccoed one-story house where the Hitler family lived for eight years. Not far from the other side of the church stands another ochre-colored building, the tavern where Hitler's father was sitting when he was struck dead by a stroke. Adolf Hitler was thirteen years old then.

Hitler wished to obscure certain things in his youth. Unquestionable is the evidence of his love for his mother, a sad-eyed, oval-faced woman, the third wife of his father. This was a filial love about which Dr. Bloch (Klara Hitler's Jewish physician in Linz) said that he had seen nothing like it in his career. What remains contradictory (and these contradictions exist within Hitler's own statements) is his relationship to his father. Alois Schicklgruber was the first of his line to rise in the world. He was better situated and better off than his son would later admit. Without anything more than a lower-school education he rose to be a customs official in Braunau. He was a sanguine, willful, respectable civil servant: his photographs exhale the picture of an official of the Habsburg empire, self-confident almost to the point of caricature. He was an illegitimate son (something that was neither rare nor particularly demeaning among Austrian peasant families then) and changed his name from Schicklgruber to Hitler thirteen years before his son Adolf was born. For this alone Adolf should have been grateful. (The reminiscences of his schoolmate Kubizek sound convincing: Hitler said that "Schicklgruber impressed him as too rough, too peasantlike; besides, too long and impractical.") He inherited other things from his father, too: the latter's restlessness (Alois's frequent moves), perhaps also some of his attractiveness to women; his handwriting and his signature resembled his father's for a long time. Yet he was vexed, perhaps painfully, about his father throughout his life. In *Mein Kampf* he wrote about his father with glowing respect, in phrases of superficial sentimentality that are otherwise absent in that book. "I honored my father and loved my mother," he wrote. But during a long nocturnal conversation, replete with memories, with the Austrian general Edmund von Glaise-Horstenau (who was also born in Braunau) in April 1939 Hitler said something different: "I feared my father, but I loved him not at all."

He wished to distance himself from his family as soon as he could. As he told Glaise-Horstenau that night, he wanted to break away, "with the definite aim to become something really great." In this, as also in many other things, Hitler was very different from Napoleon, whose ties to his family had bound him (often burdensomely) throughout his life. Yes, Hitler was an Austrian who wished to be a great German, just as Napoleon the Corsican wanted to become a great Frenchman, or Stalin the Georgian a great Russian, or Alexander of Macedon the greatest Greek. Yet Hitler was perhaps less influenced by Austria than Napoleon had been influenced by Corsica, or Stalin by Caucasian Georgia.

He wrote at length in *Mein Kampf* about his progress from Braunau through Linz to Vienna, insisting that it was in Vienna that his entire ideology had crystallized. Most of his biographers and commentators have, by and large, accepted his explanation, emphasizing his Austrian background and his experiences in Vienna. There is some truth in these explanations, but not enough. Yes: his five years in Vienna influenced him in many ways. The life of a great city opened his eyes, in more ways than one. He read all kinds of political and ideological publications and he was, at least to some extent, impressed with their contents. But there is evidence that even before coming to Vienna he thought of the Austrian state as corrupt and ramshackle, while he admired the power of Germany. When he was twenty-three he left Vienna forever. The painstaking researches of certain German historians have since established that the picture he drew of himself of a poverty-stricken young man in Vienna was not correct. His small inheritance provided him with more money than he would assert later. It is questionable, too, whether his encounter with Jewish people in Vienna (where 90 percent of the Jews of Austria lived at that time—he had known no Jews in Braunau or Leonding and very few in Linz) was as decisive as he declared in *Mein Kampf,* since we have virtually no evidence of his essential anti-Semitism before 1919. It seems that the sudden crystallization of his worldview came relatively late, in his thirtieth year, in early 1919 in Munich.

It was then and there that the critical mass of Hitler's ideology congealed, out of his feelings about the defeat of his beloved Germany but even more out of what he saw as hateful and ugly in the few agitated months of the short-lived Munich "Soviet Republic." The other matter that this formerly shy and reticent young man had discovered within himself was this: he was a gifted public speaker, a *Redner.*

He was not a typical son of the land he had been born in; not in his elective affinities, not in his temperament or even in his appearance. In that part of Upper Austria there is a sun-bleached toughness in the faces of the people: a subalpine race, taciturn, suspicious of authority, conservative in their traditionalism, combative but not revolutionary. But Hitler was very far from being a traditionalist or a conservative. He was that frighteningly modern phenomenon, the revolutionary nationalist. "I was a nationalist; but I was not a patriot," he wrote. That distinction, that difference between nationalism and patriotism, is often obscured in our modern usage. The two terms are often used interchangeably. Yet "patriotism" is an old English word, while "nationalism" is a relatively new one, appearing first in the 1840s. The difference between patriots and nationalists has marked some of the deepest rifts in the history of the twentieth century. Patriotism is traditionalist, deeply rooted, introverted, and defensive; nationalism is populist, extroverted, aggressive, and ideological. Adolf Hitler chose to uproot himself from his family and his homeland. He wanted to identify himself with Germany, and he did.

Consequently Hitler did not have an identity problem. But an increasing number of Austrians did. The political manifestation of Austrian nationalism was born in the same decade in which he was born—among other things, in the form of Georg von Schönerer's Pan-German party, which strove for the union of Austria with Germany and, implicitly, for the dissolution of the traditional Habsburg monarchical state. Thereafter a paradoxical linguistic usage came into being. *Ein Nationaler,* a nationalist, in Austria was someone who wished to see the abrogation of an independent Austria and of a distinct Austrian nationality, in favor of their absorption into a German *Volk* and state. When in 1918 the Habsburg monarchy ceased to exist and Austria remained a truncated state, many Austrians thought that such a small country was not viable. Not every Austrian who thought so was a Nazi; conversely there were Nazis who wanted to maintain some kind of separate Austrian identity. Especially after Hitler had risen to power in Germany, a difference emerged among the Austrian people, between patriots who struggled to maintain the independence of Austria, and nationalists who fought for its union with the Third Reich. Added to this division between themselves there was a split-mindedness within themselves. The last Austrian chancellor who tried to maintain the independence of Austria from the Third Reich felt compelled to say that he stood for a "German and Catholic" Austria. After Hitler had marched into Austria, he chose to sanctify the union of Germany and Austria with a plebiscite. On April 10, 1938, only five people out of nearly thirty-six hundred voted against Hitler in Braunau.

That was the year of his greatest and most convincing political triumphs. He was the greatest revolutionary of the twentieth century, whose entire political career was a refutation of Marx. In that year Simone Weil wrote this refutation of Marx: "It is not religion, it is revolution that is the opium of the people"—words fitting Hitler all too well.

Twenty miles to the south, in the small village of St. Radegund, only one man voted against Hitler. This was Franz Jägerstätter, a Catholic peasant, the father of a young family. More than fifty years later few people in Braunau wish to remember Hitler. Few among them know anything about Jägerstätter. But the number of those who know about him seems to grow every year. Earlier I said that Hitler may have been the greatest revolutionary of the twentieth century. But Jägerstätter was a revolutionary too—in the prophetic sense in which the great French Catholic poet and visionary Charles Péguy wrote, even before the First World War: "The true revolutionaries of the twentieth century will be the fathers of Christian families." In this sense the true revolutionary was Jägerstätter, not Hitler.

❀ ❀ ❀

THE village of St. Radegund is on the ledge of a low hill, away from the road running from Braunau to Salzburg. I drove there on a cold spring day. When the clouds tore away from the sun, the fields glistened in the cool green colors of a northern spring. Except for a small tractor here and there and the distant shapes of modern factories toward the horizon, the scene was reminiscent of a Europe fifty or more years ago. I saw a few women working in the fields, some of them (this is very rare in Europe now) in their traditional peasant clothes. Because of an enforced detour at Ostermiething where a crew was laying pipes, St. Radegund was not easy to find. Half an hour later I felt the errant motorist's customary sensation of relief as I saw the road sign for St. Radegund, below which I was pleased to see another marker: GRAB JÄGERSTÄTTER—Jägerstätter's grave.

St. Radegund was empty. There was silence everywhere. From somewhere I heard the lowing of an energetic cow. After a few hapless minutes, across the road I espied a man who showed me the way to the little church in a hollow, against the wall of which lies Jägerstätter's grave. He was guillotined in Brandenburg Prison on August 9, 1943.

He had refused to serve in the German army; not because he was a pacifist, not because he was an Austrian patriot, but because of his Catholic convictions. This war, Hitler, and National Socialism were causes of evil; he said as much to the military court, and in what he wrote both before and during his imprisonment. That was the last station in the pilgrimage of his otherwise unremarkable life. Franz Jägerstätter was the son of a servant girl who could not marry his father. Both were too poor for that—the unwritten law among the Upper Austrian peasantry at that time. His grandmother cared for the boy. Two years later a better situated peasant married his mother. He adopted Franz, giving him his name, Jägerstätter. That was near the end of the First World War. Franz Jägerstätter's formative years followed in a poverty-stricken land. He was a hard worker, respected in the village where he was the first to acquire a motorcycle, a handsome young peasant, rambunctious and tough, with a taste for merrymaking. At the age of twenty-six he sired an illegitimate daughter. Three years later he married another young woman. They had three daughters. It was a happy marriage. But trouble came between them in the spring of 1938 when he said that he would not vote for the Anschluss. Afraid of the consequences, his wife turned against him. He was deeply hurt. In time she learned not to question his convictions again.

The faith and goodness of his grandmother had left an impression on him; but he had not been very religious in his early youth. Sometime between 1933 and 1936 his religion had deepened. After his twenty-sixth year the meaning of his faith became a growing concern in his mind. The evidence is in some of his letters to his godson and in some of his own notes from his reading of the Gospels, recently published by his biographer. They are extraordinary because of their simplicity, purity, and insight. They are untouched by the neo-baroque language and the otherworldly spirituality of much of the Austrian religious literature of his time. They concern the responsibilities of a believing Catholic in this world. For Franz Jägerstätter these responsibilities included his recognition of the dangers of National Socialism, and the consequent duty to oppose it.

This was not easy for him. In an important sense he was alone among his people. In 1931 the Nazi votes in Braunau had doubled. In 1933 an entry in the parish chronicle of Ostermiething reads: "Our people are devoured [*ganz durchfressen*] by their enthusiasm for National Socialism, their inspiration for Austria about zero." In 1935 Braunau declared Adolf Hitler its honorary citizen, which was then countermanded by the government of Austria. Political parties had been outlawed but there were many illegal Nazi party members (though not in St. Radegund, where Jägerstätter was offered the post of mayor in March 1938, which he refused).

His loneliness weighed upon him in another important way. The guidance that he received from his Church was often neither clear nor strong. He could draw sustenance from certain allocutions: until 1938 the Austrian hierarchy supported the Catholic Dollfuss and Schuschnigg governments against the Nazis; there was Pope Pius XI's encyclical *Mit brennender Sorge* in 1937 condemning Nazi racism, which Jägerstätter would often re-read and cite; and the bishop of his diocese, Gföllner of Linz, was an old traditionalist who said that a Catholic cannot be a Nazi and that was that. But on March 27, 1938, a pastoral letter issued by the entire Austrian hierarchy and read at every Mass welcomed the union with Germany, praised National Socialism, and told the Catholic people of Austria that it was their duty to vote for Hitler. There were Austrian bishops (not Gföllner) who had been sympathetic to the nationalist-folkish persuasion; many others were unwilling to stand in the way of enthusiastic popular sentiment; and perhaps especially significant, in retrospect, are those passages of that pastoral letter which declared the bishops' trust in the compatibility of Catholicism and National Socialism: "We joyfully recognize what the National Socialist movement has achieved ... [and] that through the National Socialist movement the danger of destructive and godless Bolshevism is being defeated." Jägerstätter came back to this pastoral often. "The Church in Austria allowed itself to become a prisoner," he wrote. Nor could he have gained sustenance from the allocutions of the bishops of Germany. In 1939 Cardinal Bertram of Breslau said: "Heil Hitler: that is valid for this world. Praised be Jesus Christ: that is the tie between earth and heaven." No neater formula could be imagined. In April 1940 Hitler answered the congratulations tendered him by the German Bishops' Conference on his fifty-first birthday: "I am especially pleased by your expression of your conviction that the efforts of the Catholic Church to maintain the Christian character of the German people are not opposed to the program of the National Socialist party."

Jägerstätter was not completely alone. In St. Radegund the priest, Father Karobath, was Jägerstätter's close friend. He was arrested briefly in 1940. Several of the priests of the Ostermiething parish were taken away by the Gestapo. In the Innviertel, indeed in Upper Austria, more priests were imprisoned or executed during the war than in any of the other provinces of Austria. In 1939 a Gestapo official told the pastor of the Braunau cathedral church: "In the Braunau district [to which St. Radegund belonged] we're getting nowhere." There was only one convinced Nazi sympathizer among the clergy, Father Weeser-Krell, a native of Germany, who tried everything to become the pastor of that church in Hitler's birthplace; but Bishop Gföllner refused to appoint him. In 1941 the resident pastor, Father

Ludwig (in 1989 he was still alive, in his late eighties), was arrested by the police. When Germany invaded Russia, Hitler and his government expected Catholics to support his "crusade" against atheistic Bolshevism. No matter how wrong the ideas and practices of communism, Jägerstätter said, this was but another invasion wrought upon innocent people. There was nothing in the practices and doctrines of National Socialism that was preferable to those of communism.

He wrote down his thoughts in copybooks at home, and spoke about them when the occasion arose, among his family and friends. It is to the credit of the St. Radegunders that he was never denounced to the police. Yet many of his neighbors were of two minds about him. The village men were doing their duty to the fatherland, serving in the army; Jägerstätter was not and said that he would not do so. His wife no longer questioned his convictions and his choice. His mother did, and was bitter against her daughter-in-law for failing to support her. His parish priest told him that he was not wrong when following his convictions. The two of them asked for an audience with the new bishop of Linz, Fliesser (Gföllner had died in 1941). He tried to dissuade Jägerstätter: it would be better for everyone concerned if he obeyed the order to serve in the army, he said.

In March 1943 Jägerstätter was called up. He went to the provincial military center and stated his refusal to serve. He knew where this would lead in the end. But in the prison in Linz doubts beset him. There was his responsibility to his family, to his wife—even though she did not ask him not to follow his conscience. There was the temptation to convince himself that what he was doing amounted to a choice of suicide, a mortal sin for a Catholic. By the time he was moved to a military prison in Berlin these tormenting thoughts had left him. His faith, his serenity, his concern for those other prisoners with whom he had some contact, impressed them. He wrote many letters to his wife, who was allowed to visit him once. He kept writing notes to himself. Among other things he wrote: "It is not given to the powers of this world to suppress the conscience of a single human being." And: "Whoever is ashamed of his faith shows that he knows not Jesus Christ." Jägerstätter was far from being a religious fanatic. It is natural for a true believer, and especially for a man condemned to death, to direct his thoughts to the world to come. Jägerstätter believed, and hoped, in the world to come; but even more he believed in a Christian's duties in this world. Many of his statements remind me of another of Hitler's martyrs, the Protestant pastor Dietrich Bonhoeffer, who wrote, also in prison and before his execution: "The way of Christ goes not from this world to God but from God to this world." Or of Simone Weil: "The object of our concern should not be the supernatural but the world. The supernatural is light itself: if we make an object of it we lower it." (She died in the same month Jägerstätter died.) Jägerstätter was beheaded on the ninth of August. That night the prison chaplain told two Austrian nuns that they must be proud of their countryman. "For the only time in my life I had met a saint," he said.

One year after the war Franziska Jägerstätter brought her husband's ashes back to St. Radegund. Father Karobath had returned to his pastorate. Some of the villagers did not know what to make of Jägerstätter's story. Many of their husbands and sons had fallen in faraway Russia; many of them returned wounded or maimed. Centuries of tradition and custom had made them obey the call of their country's rulers. Why was Jägerstätter a special case? For some time the Austrian government rejected Franziska Jägerstätter's application for the standard pension of war widows: some bureaucrat declared that her husband had not been a soldier. For many years the widow and the priest were criticized by veterans and their relatives for honoring a man who had "abandoned" his fellow Austrians. Some of them said that Jägerstätter had "betrayed" his people. Sometime in the 1960s there came a gradual change. It had much to do with the growing up of a younger generation of people to whom the memories of comradeship in the war meant nothing, but also with the respect of the St. Radegunders for the widow who brought up her three orphaned daughters and managed their family farm in an exemplary way.

An important part in the recognition of Jägerstätter was taken upon himself by an American. I first read about Jägerstätter more than thirty years ago, in an article by Gordon Zahn, who was a conscientious objector during the Second World War, a committed pacifist and adherent of Dorothy Day's Catholic Worker movement. He had read something about Jägerstätter and chose to follow it up. The result was a fine book, *In Solitary Witness,* published in 1966—for a long time the only book about Jägerstätter. Many more documents and details have come to light since then; yet Zahn's book has stood the test of time well—as Jägerstätter's biographer, Dr. Erna Putz, told me. I found her in Ostermiething, in the parish house (where she is the pastor's helper, busy with, among other things, bringing up two small Vietnamese children of the boat people), an hour or so after my solitary visit to St. Radegund.

The little white church of St. Radegund is lovely, perhaps remarkably so even in this part of Austria where onion-domed parish churches abound. I walked down to it on an alley of cobblestones. The church (founded in 1422) was open but empty. As in many other places of the world, in Austria there are now not enough priests to go around; the Mass is said and the other sacraments administered by the pastor who comes over from

Ostermiething. Against the white wall of the church lies Franz Jägerstätter's grave. It has no marker except for the crucifix above it. But there is a single bronze tablet set in the church wall to the left of it. I translate its words from the German:

> THANKS BE TO GOD FOR JÄGERSTÄTTER!
> HE KNEW THAT ALL OF US ARE BROTHERS
> AND THAT CHRIST'S COMMAND IS MEANT
> FOR ALL OF US. HE DID NOT DIE IN VAIN!
> MAY THE GREAT LOVE OF GOD
> AND THAT OF HIS SON JESUS CHRIST
> FILL THE HEARTS OF ALL PEOPLE!
> MAY THIS GREAT LOVE MOVE THROUGH
> THE WORLD, SO THAT THE PEACE OF GOD
> ENTER INTO THE HEARTS OF ALL MEN. AMEN.
>> A BROTHER IN CHRIST
>> Missoula, Montana, U.S.A.
>> 9 August 1968

I felt a sense of pride being an American.

I went back into the church. There was a guestbook of sorts, open near the entrance. It was filled with the handwriting of people from far away: Irish, English, Poles, Hungarians, Rumanians and many, many Germans. I copied only one of the entries. "I was a German soldier. I know now that Franz Jägerstätter was the one who did his duty to our people." That afternoon in Ostermiething Erna Putz told me that all kinds of people came to St. Radegund every ninth of August, the anniversary of the martyrdom. On that day there is a pilgrimage walk from St. Radegund to the church in Ostermiething. This has become, she said, a local tradition now—one hundred years after Adolf Hitler was born. I thought of those few flowers on Hitler's parents' grave in Leonding and of the somber fact that, alone among the historical figures of this century, Hitler had no grave. On that cold March day in St. Radegund, Franz Jägerstätter's grave was covered with fresh flowers.

V.

SOME TWENTIETH-CENTURY

QUESTIONS

In writing the history of the twentieth century John Lukacs has illustrated his own theory that historical knowledge is personal and participant. His lifetime coincides with much of the period to which he has devoted years of study. Born in 1924, as a young man in Budapest near the end of World War II Lukacs "saw the fiery retreat of the last German troops and the cautious advance of the first Russian soldiers on a dark, frozen morning." He thus surveys the twentieth century as both a historian and a contemporary.

Historians do not mark the passage of time according to the calendar. For Lukacs, the twentieth century was a short century. It lasted only seventy-five years, from the outbreak of the First World War in 1914 to the collapse of the Soviet empire in Eastern Europe in 1989. The two world wars, he argues— rather than, for instance, the Bolshevik Revolution or the Great Depression— were the principal events of the twentieth century, the enormous "mountain ranges" that dominated its landscape. The events and conditions that defined the century, including the Bolshevik Revolution, the Cold War, and the division of Germany and of Europe into American and Soviet spheres of influence, were the consequences of the First and Second World Wars. When those circumstances changed, the twentieth century came to an end.

Most of the essays in this section examine the conditions of twentieth-century history and the individuals responsible for creating them. In several essays, Lukacs also investigates the tumultuous ideological currents that surged and broke between 1914 and 1989: the growing threat of "totalitarian democracy" and majoritarian tyranny; the inherent defects of communism; the self-serving delusions of anticommunism in the United States; the enduring strength of nationalism and National Socialism; the senility of American liberalism and the immaturity of American conservatism; and the degradation of American political and social life that has been effected through the cynical machinery of public relations and manufactured popularity. In "The Bourgeois Interior," however, Lukacs extols the opposite of publicity and celebrity: the "inner security" and "inner freedom" of the Bourgeois Age, "the most precious heritage of the Western civilization of the last five hundred years."

51

Questions about Pius XII

(1964)

he Deputy is less of a play than it is a historical document. It is a historical document in two ways. In the first place, most of it rests on what may be called historical evidence (the most valuable part is "Historical Sidelights," the more than twenty-five-thousand-word appendix to the printed edition of the play). In the second place, Rolf Hochhuth has been preoccupied with what is essentially a historical-moral, rather than a religious-moral, problem. In this respect The Deputy reflects a certain deepening of historical consciousness which is, indeed, one of the salutary developments of the European mind since the last war; Hochhuth may not know it, but his approach is historical-existential rather than historical-theological; and it is in this respect, too, that The Deputy is not a historical drama in the traditional sense (just as Dr. Zhivago is not a historical novel in the sense of War and Peace).

But while the play cannot, of course, be considered apart from history, the reverse is true, also: the author's attitude in the writing of his play casts a reflection upon his understanding of the history. Thus the faults in Hochhuth's play and in Hochhuth's history are inseparable. The principal fault is obvious. It is the exaggerated, and somewhat juvenile, description of Pius XII. Hochhuth's Pius is a mixture of passive villain and intellectual Tartuffe. A more perceptive writer would have portrayed Pius rather in the form of a bespectacled Hamlet. This has been remarked by so many critics that I need not go into it in detail. The second and lesser fault is a matter of emphasis. The historical clue to the problem of The Deputy involves not so much Pius's relationship to the Jews as his relationship to the Germans; and that, in turn, involves the national situation and the national condition of the German Catholics themselves. Hochhuth is aware of this: but he does not deal with the problem sufficiently.[1] This, however, is the

· ·

From *Continuum*, Summer: 183–92.

problem which I propose to deal with here.

The Germans, more than any other people in Europe, were deeply aware of what they used to call "the Jewish problem." This does not mean that the Germans were, even during the Hitler era, the most anti-Semitic people in Europe: they were (and are) less anti-Semitic than Ukrainians, Lithuanians, Russians, Bessarabians (and on occasion, even less than French or Poles), but it means that they were anti-Semitic in a different way, just as most German Catholics were Catholic in a different way. The reasons for this are complex and numerous: the two principal ones are the relatively late flowering of nationalism in southern, Catholic Germany, and the peculiarly German form of rhetoric which (contrary to Freud's and Joyce's views of the functions of rhetoric) were not merely expressions of feelings and of thoughts but formative influences on feelings and on thoughts. At the very time, after 1870, when German nationalism was becoming more and more an ideological and less and less a patriotic phenomenon, German Judeophobia became transformed into anti-Semitism: what had been a religious and social consideration became a cultural and racial attitude. These developments came to a head after the First World War. It was not a coincidence that the cradle of Nazism was not Prussian Berlin but Bavarian Munich, not the industrial metropolis of the Protestant north but the capital of the Catholic south of Germany, a *Kulturstadt*. The long-range cause of this was the nationalism of German (and Austrian and Sudeten) Catholics and ex-Catholics (of whom Hitler was one); the principal, and short-range cause was the ridiculous but painful episode of the Bavarian Soviet Republic in 1919, whose leadership had been largely Jewish—as indeed was the case of the Béla Kun regime in Hungary, and of the Bolshevik regime in Russia during its early period. We must understand, first, that, to a great extent because of these experiences, the success of Nazism and of Fascism was due to anticommunist sentiments; and second, that in the twenties continental Europe entered into an anti-Marxist (and in some respects, a post-Marxist) phase of its history. We must understand that after the First World War anticommunism and anti-Semitism were closely allied, indeed, that they were hardly separable in the minds of many people. Americans may find this difficult to comprehend now, in the era of Goldwater; but it was nonetheless a historical factor then. It was especially prevalent in Weimar Germany (but also in Austria, Hungary, etc.), where even those who were able to distinguish between Communists and Jews felt that great national ideals and religious realities were directly threatened or indirectly undermined not only by international communism but also by the cultural, social, financial influences freely exercised by international (or rather, non-national) Jews.

Though this diagnosis was superficial, the sufferings of Germany after the First World War were real. They had a great, and enduring, effect on Pius XII when he was papal nuncio (and a very popular nuncio) in Germany after the war. Eugenio Pacelli was a Germanophile.[2] There is not the slightest evidence that he had any sympathies for Hitlerism; he had, however, sympathies for national conservatism in Germany, and for the anticommunism which was later represented by politicians such as Papen or Monsignor Kaas, who, perhaps for the first time since the Reformation, were not only nationalist Catholics but principal political figures on the national scene with an all-German reputation. Pius XI was not a Germanophile: but the Lateran Treaty concluded with Mussolini in 1929 and the Concordat concluded with the Third Reich in 1933 at least contributed to a climate of Catholic opinion which was not altogether unfavorable to a nationalist Germany. During the last two years of his reign the old Pius XI made his concern with Hitlerism manifest; but even then there were many members of the Curia who regarded Hitlerism as a far lesser evil than communism. There was, after all, no full-scale persecution of Catholics in Germany comparable to what was happening in Russia, Mexico, or Spain; there was a Concordat functioning with great difficulties but functioning nevertheless. There were, in the first six years of the Hitler regime, fewer manifestations of barbarism than was reflected in the horror stories seeping out of Russia; and until the outbreak of the Second World War the principal policy of the Hitler government was not the extermination of the Jews of Europe but the expulsion of all Jews from Germany.

This is the way things were in early 1939; and it is rather senseless to criticize these attitudes in retrospect. But at that time a new factor entered: the election of Eugenio Pacelli to the Throne of St. Peter in early March 1939. It was one of the swiftest and most clearly unanimous papal elections in modern history. It also coincided with the zenith of Hitler's prestige, coming but a few months after his diplomatic triumph at Munich, in a period of lull, at the time of Franco's decisive final anticommunist victory in Spain. In lieu of documentation the historian should not impute motives: nevertheless there are many weighty reasons to believe that, besides his excellent record as papal secretary of state, Eugenio Pacelli's pro-German reputation was an important, and perhaps decisive, factor in his swift elevation to the papacy. And there is evidence to sustain the argument that the Germanophilia of Pope Pius XII remained one of the principal characteristics of his political attitude during the whole nineteen years of his rule. There is, I repeat, no evidence at all that he may have sympathized with Hitler (as, for example, did certain Croatian, Ukranian, Slovak, and Spanish Catholics). There is the evidence of his allocutions, his warnings against racialism, cruelties, terror; there are the many instances when the Vatican, as indeed many members of the Catholic hierarchies and Catholic institutions and individual Catholics throughout Europe, made inspiring and brave attempts to help the persecuted, including many thousands of Jews. On the other hand Pius XII wanted to maintain a Vatican relationship with the German government; he was deeply sympathetic to the German people throughout the war and after; and there is every reason to believe that he unquestioningly preferred Hitler to Stalin.

As his principal confidant and later apologete, Father Leiber, wrote in regard to Hochhuth's play: "of the two systems, National Socialism and Bolshevism, Pius XII, with his gaze on the future and on the greater whole, held Bolshevism to be the more dangerous." At first sight this does justice to the long-range wisdom of the Vatican, and to the historical perspective of Pius XII: it is because of this perspective that, for example, Pius XII comes out rather well from his wartime correspondence with President Roosevelt. A closer view, however, may reveal that this was the kind of Catholic anticommunism with which we in the United States are all too familiar: an anticommunism of a rather superficial nature. It is not only that the end does not justify the means—that Pius's preoccupation with the long-range perils of communism should not have obscured his mind to the present and clear danger of Nazi terrorism. It is that most of the Catholic (and the non-Catholic) populations of Central Europe (as already the Munich example of 1919 had showed) were rather immune to Communist ideology, while they were by no means impervious to radical nationalist ideas. How much more profound (and at the same time traditional) were the concerns of the nuncio Roncalli, who in October 1942 (at the very time of Stalingrad!) wrote in his diary: "the two great evils which now intoxicate the world are secularism and nationalism."[3] Even though it seemed to be confirmed by events, Pius XII's preoccupation with communism was, to some extent, shortsighted. A family father who neglects sickness in his own house because of his fear of robbers in the neighborhood is not necessarily justified because, at the end of the story, the robbers really appear. Furthermore, in this case it was the robbers who were attacked by the bully of the household in June 1941. It is true that the Vatican was careful not to lend substance to the Nazi propaganda of a German-European Crusade against Bolshevism; but there were many Catholics who saw it that way. There is ample evidence that Pius XII, as indeed perhaps the majority of Catholics of his time, still shared the anticommunist attitudes of the continental nationalist conservatives of the Papen or Pétain type. Somewhat like Hilaire Belloc who, after a lifetime of valiant struggles against the evils of shallow Marxist and liberal thinking, proved that he did not understand

Hitler at all, Pius XII may not have altogether understood Hitler very well. In any event, his subordination of the dangers of Hitlerism to the dangers of communism was, if not superficial, then somewhat abstract.[4] This appears, for example, from the war memoirs of Winston Churchill, as he records his meeting with the Pope after the liberation of Rome by the Allies. Among all of the Allied statesmen it was Churchill who at that time was most deeply concerned with the prospects of Russia's advance into Europe; he was involved in bitter arguments with the Americans who either did not understand or did not sympathize with his political strategy, which wished to set definite limits to the Russian conquests. He did not get much help from the Pope: there is a faint sense of irritation in his record of their conversation:[5] what Churchill seems to have felt was that *this* kind of abstract anticommunism wouldn't get them anywhere.

So far about the pro-German, and anticommunist, attitudes of the late Pius XII. I deal with them at some length because they are, in my opinion, inseparable from the principal problem. The reasons which made him maintain relations with Hitler's Germany to the end were not altogether different from the reasons which kept him from condemning the slaughter of Jews with greater energy and fervor. But that slaughter *was* the greatest crime in modern history—and *not* because its victims were Jews. It was the greatest crime in its extent, in its quantity, this organized and scientific extermination of five million human beings within two-and-a-half years.

Hochhuth's primary mistake is his primitive portraiture of the Pope. His secondary mistake is his somewhat inadequate understanding of the historical situation. He, at least by inference, imputes certain base motives to the Pope[6] which have no substance at all—instead of concentrating on Pius's hesitations, on the extraordinarily involved, circumlocutional characteristics of his rhetoric, on his genuine inability to understand the historical evils which were inherent in the problem of German behavior. Nor does Hochhuth altogether understand the Vatican's circumstances. For example, it is true that the Pope's condemnation of the events in October 1943, which led to the deportation and the eventual slaughter of more than nine hundred Jews of Rome, was extraordinarily weak. But it is also true that the compromising subtleties of the Vatican's policy at that time paid off from the viewpoint of sheer numbers, since more than seven thousand Roman Jews could go into hiding, supported by the Vatican, and survive until the liberation of Rome. Had the Pope made a strong and energetic stand against the Germans at that time, Hitler may have reacted by insisting on full-scale *razzias* in Rome, on the hunting down of most of the seven thousand Jews of whose survival and hiding places German intelligence was, of course, aware. Thus the very story of the Jews in Rome, which is the central episode of Hochhuth's play, confirms, in a way, what Albrecht von Kessel, a German diplomat stationed in Rome at that time, wrote in what is still the most intelligent, and moving, defense of the Pope's position.[7] In 1943, Kessel wrote, a fiery protest by the Pope "would not have saved a single Jewish life." I am inclined to agree with von Kessel on this point: *in the short run*, probably nothing that Pius XII might have said against Hitler and for the sake of the Jews would have saved Jewish lives during the war.

I say "probably"—because now, two decades after these terrible events, I, as a historian, am beginning to have certain second thoughts on that subject. In 1943 Hitler had all of the characteristics, as von Kessel writes, of a "hunted fanatic": but he, not to speak of other members of his government, was not *altogether* devoid of certain elements of political realism. "There are bad people," La Rochefoucauld wrote three hundred years ago, "who would be less dangerous if they had no good in them." There are political fanatics who would be less dangerous if they had no political realism in them. There are evidences that while Hitler, having painted his European Lebensraum with blood, was painting himself into a corner, he was occasionally scanning the four walls and the doors and the windows. His relations with the Vatican were a two-way affair. He kept up the diplomatic relationship with the Vatican because it was in the interests of Germany to do so. During the last two years of the war he was thinking more and more in terms of a split among the Allies who were closing in on him. He had tacitly permitted certain tentative feelers to the Russians, and after September 1944 to the Americans. From April 1944 onward, for example, the Germans were willing to suspend the Final Solution altogether, to trade instead the lives of the remaining millions of Jews for American money or trucks.[8] The Germans had already permitted the emigration of some Jews to neutral countries, in exchange for certain financial considerations. They did not mistreat Jewish prisoners-of-war, including Jews who had been recently German citizens and who were now members of the American armed forces. Finally, in November 1944 they ended the gassings. Many of these arrangements were, of course, ordered not by Hitler but by Himmler, and some of them even behind Hitler's back: but it is at least probable that many of them were undertaken at least with his tacit consent. They fit into an erratic, but not senseless, pattern, at the end of which stands the often overlooked fact of Hitler appointing Admiral Doenitz as his successor—not a Nazi official but someone who could be considered a "Westerner," an anti-communist and a conservative, a kind of naval Papen. In brief, perhaps the Pope was not such a subtle diplomat at all. In brief, it is not certain that a more active policy of the Pope might not have led to the suspension of the mass killings at least in 1944, involving the largest number of the victims.

These are speculations. We do not know what would have happened *if.* ... What is not a speculation is the very important factor which dominated Pius XII's thinking at that time: the spiritual condition of German Catholics. The control of the Nazi state over German Catholicism was not absolute. Mass was being said, the sacraments were available, the churches were open, the religious orders were functioning, the training of priests went on, the armed forces had their Catholic field chaplains, the members of the hierarchy were not imprisoned, even a few Catholic newspapers were allowed to exist. At least one-third of the German population, and at least three out of eight German soldiers, were Catholics. A fiery condemnation of Hitler (something which, in any case, was utterly alien to the temperament of Pius XII) may have meant a radical rupture between Germany and the Vatican, swift suppression of the remaining religious privileges which German Catholics still enjoyed, and perhaps even a profound spiritual crisis for most German Catholics. The Pope had to weigh the prospect that his condemnation of the crimes against the Jews, besides being futile, would endanger the spiritual welfare of millions of Catholic Germans.

There remain, however, these considerations: If the Catholic Church is the *catholic* church, and if the pope *is* the Vicar of Christ, should his concern for the spiritual privileges of Catholics have a necessarily categorical preference over his moral concern for the life and death of non-Catholics? Moreover—was it not possible that the spiritual welfare of German Catholics may have become undermined in a subtle way, by the very fact that their Church and their Pope did not clearly and unequivocally condemn what was wrong?

At the beginning of this essay I suggested that Hochhuth's play is a historical document in the sense, too, that it reflects the author's interpretation of history at a particular time of his own historical thinking. By this I mean that his play or, rather, the thinking that his play manifests, represents an attitude toward the Catholic Church which is curiously recent, curiously contemporary. It is an attitude of high expectations. I do not hesitate to say that in this respect Hochhuth's play could be called pro-Catholic. It also reflects the great rise in papal prestige after 1945, which is one of the most remarkable developments in the postwar history of the world. Amidst the godlessness, the plasticity, the materialism, the communism, and the neo-Marxist twaddle and patter of intellectuals about a "post-Christian" world the prestige of the papacy during the last decade of Pius XII's reign was higher than at any time since the Middle Ages. Why this should be so is an extremely complex matter which I shall not attempt to discuss at this point. In any event, it is a historical phenomenon as well as a spiritual one. Hochhuth is a sometimes immature writer who does not always have a

sense of proportion: his very expectations flow from his belief that the prestige and the power of the papacy was the same twenty years ago as it is now.
Also, he, a Protestant, misunderstands the central authority of the pope:
He expects too much from it *in practice*: he does not understand the actual,
the existential limitations of the functioning of that authority on the everyday lives of Catholics. And yet we cannot simply dismiss the issue by
pointing out Hochhuth's disproportionate expectations—whose very existence, I repeat, are a curiously encouraging spiritual phenomenon for all
of us.

About the question of papal prestige during the war we may as well
admit that it was high. After all, the proof of the pudding is in the eating.
Qui mange du pape en meurt: Napoleon had taken a bite; Hitler did not. Napoleon did not have any scruples about arresting a pope; one hundred and
thirty years later the infinitely more diabolical Hitler would not touch the
Vicar of Christ. During the First World War the Italian government insisted that the Vatican be excluded from the peace conference, and President Wilson coolly dissociated himself from Benedict XV; during the Second World War President Roosevelt found it politic to inaugurate a correspondence with Pius XII, and on dire occasions the people of Rome acclaimed the pope as if he were the true sovereign of Italy. It was not the
dull Stalin but the spirited Napoleon who first said, very long ago, "Bah!
how many divisions has the pope?"—whereas in the spring of 1943, Hitler
told Weizsaecker that there were three powers in Rome, the King, the Duce,
and the Pope, and of the three the last was the strongest. Thus, while
Hochhuth was wrong in attributing in 1960 a kind of prestige to the Pope
which the latter in 1943 may not have possessed, it may well be that in 1943
Pius XII underestimated his already accumulating spiritual capital, the
power at his disposal.

About the second question concerning the authority of the Pope, I shall
say this: only those who regard the Roman Catholic Church as *the* catholic
church of mankind have the right to criticize Pius XII in regard to the Jews.
If the Catholic Church is only one church among the many churches and
religions and sects of this world, then its recent record is certainly not
worse, and probably even better, than the record of other churches, other
religions, other sects. After all, if the Catholic Church was relatively indifferent to the persecution of Jews in Eastern Europe during the war, most
Jews and Jewish spokesmen in the West were even more indifferent to the
persecution of Catholics in Eastern Europe after the war.[9] This is a very
weak argument, one may say. Of course, I know that it is a weak argument:
but *why* is it a weak argument? It is weak only because Catholics believe
that the Catholic Church *is* the true church, that the Pope *is* the Vicar of

Christ, that Catholics are unique not because they are uniquely blessed but because their burdens and their responsibilities are unique, because more is expected from them than from others. I must say that I welcome Hochhuth into the company of those who are, no matter how inadequately, aware of this condition. It is, after all, this condition, and not a brainwave of Pope John XXIII, that created the present ecumenical movement. And there are subtle and deep reasons for believing that this movement of rising spiritual expectations, this movement recognizing the increasing catholicity of the Catholic Church and of its concerns, was already hidden in the hearts of millions of Christians, of pre-Christians[10] and post-Christians, that it was already here twenty years ago during the Second World War.

There is one last thing that I wish to say. The principal faults of certain German Catholics during the war issued not from the fact that they were too Catholic but from the fact that they were too German. Aspects of the problem of German Catholicism during the Hitler era have been treated recently in valuable works by Gordon Zahn, Guenter Lewy, Böckenförde, and Carl Amery: I need not discuss this further. But I must conclude this article with a glance at the national condition of Catholics in Germany, since this has a disturbing relevance to the present. What Pius XII did or did not do during the war was to a great extent determined by the attitudes of the German Catholic hierarchy. There are reasons to believe that, had the German bishops protested energetically against Hitler's crimes and had they been consequently persecuted, the Vatican would have spoken out strongly in their favor—but then, the very attitudes of the German Catholic bishops were to a great extent determined by the attitudes of the German Catholic population (it is for that reason, for example, that only the German hierarchy's protests against Hitler's euthanasia program were effective: the bishops spoke out because they knew that the population was behind them). During the nineteenth century, before and during the First Vatican Council, the argument of liberal Catholics was that the authority of the Pope ought to be lessened, in order to bring the Church closer to "the people." During the recent discussions of *aggiornamento,* during the Second Vatican Council liberal Catholics have unanimously hailed the papal decision to grant greater authority to the national hierarchies, and the—in my opinion, regrettable—substitution of national languages for Latin in large portions of the Mass. In view of our experiences of the Second World War, in view of what we know about the problem of German Catholics, I have a few questions. Wasn't it precisely the national conditioning of German Catholics, the dependence of the German hierarchy on popular sentiment, their *völkisch* populism, the *aggiornamento* of *deutsches Christentum* ever since Görres[11] and Bismarck, that was the principal cause of their eventual failures? Had there been more responsibility vested in the German national hierarchy, had the Mass been safe in German for a generation, wouldn't the record of German Catholicism during the war have been even more pitiful? Was the problem of the German Catholics that they were hopelessly outdated, out of line with the modern national development of Germany? Was it not, rather, that their rhetoric and their political beliefs fitted in very well with that development? Who was a sturdier opponent of Hitler, the old traditionalist Pius XI or his in many respects more modern and up-to-date successor? Wasn't the problem precisely that the authority of the Holy Father was not sufficiently paternal, not sufficiently authoritative, not sufficiently universal? Isn't it true that what the world needed then, and what many of us (including Hochhuth) expect now is something quite different from an august spiritual chairman of the board of an international organization of national companies, that the world is looking for someone whose singular authority should have spoken to us in a strong and clear voice: the Representative, the Vicar of Christ, the Sovereign standing on the rock of Peter?

52

Halfway to 1984

(1966)

We are now halfway to 1984. George Orwell, the author of *1984*, finished his book in 1948. That was fifteen years ago, and it is not more than another eighteen years before that ominous date rolls around.

It is *ominous*, in every sense of that antique adjective. There is reason to believe that eighteen years from now thousands of people will experience a feeling of uneasiness, perhaps a light little shudder of trepidation, as they first encounter that new year's numerals in print. In the English-speaking world, at least, "1984" has become a household term, suggesting some kind of inhuman totalitarian nightmare. And since millions who have not read the book now recognize the term, it is reasonable to assume that both the theme and the title of the book have corresponded to an emerging consciousness among many people in the otherwise progressive-minded English-speaking democracies, to the effect that things are *not* getting better all the time—no, not at all.

The plot of *1984* is well known but it may be useful to sum it up briefly. By 1984 most of the world has been divided by three superstates—Oceania, Eurasia, and Eastasia. They are perpetually at war with one other, but no one of them is completely able to subdue the others. This state of war enables the rulers of these states (the ruler of Oceania being Big Brother) to keep their peoples both ignorant and submissive. This is achieved by totalitarian and technical methods, by the absoluteness of one-party rule, and by a kind of censorship that controls not only the behavior but even the thinking process of individuals. The hero of *1984*, Winston Smith, born in 1945 (both the date and the first name are significant), is a simple party member and a functionary of the Ministry of Truth in London, which is the chief city of Airstrip One, for that is what Britain became after she had been absorbed by the United States to form Oceania. (Continental Europe,

From *New York Times Magazine,* January 2: 8 ff.

having been absorbed by the Soviet Union, had become Eurasia.)

Winston is a weak and forlorn intellectual who, however, is sickened not only by the dreary living conditions in 1984 but by the prevalence of official lying and the almost complete absence of personal privacy. One day he stumbles into a love affair, which in itself is a dangerous thing since the party punishes illicit relationships severely. Winston experiences happiness and a sense of personal fulfillment, especially as Julia shares his hatred of the existing system.

There is a high official in the Ministry of Truth, O'Brien, whom Winston instinctively trusts. He and Julia confide in O'Brien. They are deceived. All along, O'Brien has set a trap for them: they are arrested in their secret little room. They are tortured. Winston, despite his strong residue of convictions, not only confesses to everything imaginable, but in the end, faced by an especially horrible torture, he even betrays Julia. He is finally released; he is a completely broken man; he has even come to believe in the almightiness and goodness of Big Brother.

But it is not this plot, it is rather Orwell's description of everyday life in 1984 that is the principal matter of the novel and, one may suppose, the principal matter of interest to its readers. Life in 1984 is a mixture of horror and dreariness. What is horrible is not so much war as the shriveling of personal freedoms and privacy, with the planners of the superstate controlling vast portions of once independent lives. What is dreary is that within these totalitarian conditions the living standards of masses of people in what were once civilized and prosperous countries are reduced: food and drink are little better than standardized slop; mass entertainments are primitive and vulgar; personal property has virtually disappeared.

One of the profound differences between *1984* and Aldous Huxley's *Brave New World* (published in 1932, the latter still had many of the marks of the light-headed twenties: Its philosophy compared with that of *1984* is a rather irresponsible *jeu d'esprit*) lies in Orwell's view of the past rather than of the future. Looking back from 1984, conditions in the early, capitalistic portion of the twentieth century seem romantic and almost idyllic to Winston Smith, so much so that on a solemn occasion he offers a toast "to the past." Unemployment, revolutions, fascism, and, to some extent, even Nazism and Communism are lesser evils than what is going on in Oceania in 1984, since by that time the rulers of the state have perfected brainwashing and thought control to the point that the memories of entire generations, and hence their opinions about the past, have been eliminated.

This, of course, does not happen overnight: It is a brutal but gradual development. In *1984,* Orwell set the decisive turning point in the middle sixties, "the period of the great purges in which the original leaders of the

Revolution were wiped out once and for all. By 1970 none of them was left, except Big Brother himself."

Let us keep in mind that *1984* is the work of a novelist and not of a prophet; Orwell ought not be criticized simply because some of his visions have not been borne out. On the other hand, Orwell was concerned in the late forties with certain tendencies of evil portent; and *1984* was a publishing success because around 1950, for great numbers of people, the picture of a society such as he described was not merely fantastic but to some extent plausible.

It is still plausible today, but not quite in the way in which Orwell envisaged the future eighteen years ago. Halfway to 1984 we can say, fortunately, that most of Orwell's visions have proved wrong. It is true that the United States, the Soviet Union, and China correspond to some extent to the superpowers Oceania, Eurasia, and Eastasia. But the United States has not annexed Britain, the Soviet Union has fallen far short of conquering all of Europe, and even China does not extend much beyond her traditional boundaries.

What is more important, the superpowers are not at war with one another. It is true that during the so-called Cold War between the United States and the Soviet Union many of the practices of traditional and civilized diplomacy were abandoned; but the Cold War has given place to something like a cold peace between these two superpowers. Even the dreadful and ominous war in Asia is marked by the reluctance of the United States and China directly to attack each other.

Orwell proved correct in saying that "war . . . is no longer the desperate, annihilating struggle that it was in the early decades of the twentieth century. It is a warfare of limited aims between combatants who are unable to destroy one another. . . ." Yet Orwell was interested principally not in international but in internal developments. For example, in *1984* the peoples of Oceania are isolated; travel is forbidden except for a small minority of the elite; and the press is controlled to the extent that no meaningful information from the outside world is available to the public.

But now, halfway to 1984, the opposite has been happening. It is not warfare but torrents of automobiles and mass tourism that threaten to destroy entire landscapes and cityscapes; great amounts of information are available to us about an undigestible variety of matters; and at times it seems that the cultural traditions of great Western nations are endangered less by the persistence of isolationism than by a phony internationalism drummed up by a kind of pervasive publicity that drowns out the once truer music of the arts.

Also, in the world of *1984* most people are ill-fed, badly clothed, run-down. But this, too, has not happened. Now, halfway to 1984, almost everywhere in the world, living standards have risen, and the danger is not, as Orwell envisaged it, that entire generations of once prosperous countries will no longer know such things as wine, oranges, lemons, and chocolate; it is, rather, that our traditional tastes and table habits may be washed away by a flood of frozen and synthetic foods of every possible kind, available to us every hour of the day.

The reasons why Orwell's visions of 1984 have been wrong seem to be bound up with the time and the circumstances of the book's conception. About the circumstances Orwell himself was supposed to have said that *1984* "wouldn't have been so gloomy if I had not been so ill." He wrote most of the book in self-imposed isolation on a rain-shrouded Scottish island, finishing it in an English country hospital in late 1948. Shortly thereafter, he was moved to a hospital in London, where in January 1950 he died. As for the time of writing, in the late 1940s Orwell's imagination succumbed, at least in part, to the temptation of conceiving the future as an increasingly acute continuation of what seems to be going on at the present. (In one of his earlier essays, Orwell had criticized the American writer James Burnham for this very fault.) Around 1949, when most intellectuals had come around to recognizing that Stalin's tyranny was hardly better than Hitler's, many of them concluded that it is in the nature of totalitarianism to become more and more tyrannical as time goes on. Indeed, some of them established their reputations by the ponderous books they produced on this theme. (Hannah Arendt's *Origins of Totalitarianism* is an example.) Yet only a few years later, events in Eastern Europe and in Russia showed that history is unpredictable and that the projections of intellectuals are often oversimplified. But this Orwell did not live to see.

He foresaw the horrible features of 1984 as the consequences of totalitarianism, of political tyranny, of the despotism of a dictator. But halfway to 1984 we can see, for example, that the era of totalitarian dictatorship is sliding away, into the past. Even the Soviet Union seems to be moving in the direction of what one may call "post-totalitarian"; all over Eastern Europe (though not yet in Asia) we can perceive regimes that, though dictatorial, are no longer totalitarian. The danger for us is, rather, the obverse: the possibility of totalitarian democracy.

Totalitarian democracy? The words seem paradoxical; our eyes and ears are unaccustomed to the sight and the sound of them in combination. Yet I believe that we ought to accustom our imaginations to the possibility of a democratic society in which universal popular suffrage exists while freedom of speech, press, and assembly are hardly more than theoretical possibilities for the individual, whose life and ideas, whose rights to privacy, to family autonomy, and to durable possessions are regimented by government and rigidly molded by mass production and by mass communications.

Let me, at this point, fall back on a personal illustration. For a long time the term *1984* evoked, to me, the image of a police state of the Eastern European type. But when I think of 1984 now, the image that swims into my mind is that of a gigantic shopping center and industrial complex—something like the one which has been erected a few miles from where I live in eastern Pennsylvania.

The undulating rural landscape around Valley Forge, with its bright dots of houses and its crossroads, has been transformed. There is now the eerie vastness of the General Electric Space Center, whose square edifices spread across hundreds of acres. Beyond it stand other flat windowless blocks of buildings—the King of Prussia shopping center, around the trembling edges of which bulldozers roar from morning to night, boring their brutal tracks into the clayey soil which they must churn before it can be covered by concrete. The predominant material is concrete, horizontal and vertical concrete. Twice a day, thousands of people pour into and out of this compound, in a tremendous metallic flow. But no one lives there. At night and on Sundays, these hundreds of acres resemble a deserted airport, with a few automobiles clustering here and there, or slowly cruising on one of the airstrips, occasionally peered at by uniformed guards. Why fly to the moon? Stand on a cold January night in the middle of a parking lot in a large shopping center in the American North. It is a man-made moonscape. This is how the moon will look after our Herculean efforts, after we reach it, colonize it, pour concrete over it.

This is how 1984 looks to me, in the middle sixties, but I know and feel that this view is neither solitary nor unusual. There are millions of Americans who, passing a similar space-age complex of buildings, will say *1984,* covering up their resignation with a thin coat of defensive humor. What strikes us is not just the ugliness of the buildings but something else, something that is not so much the reaction of middle-aged earthmen against brave new worlds as it is the expression of a feeling which is, alas, close to the Orwellian nightmare vision; a sense of impersonality together with a sense of powerlessness.

The impersonality is there, in the hugeness of the organization and in the anonymous myriads of the interchangeable human beings who make up most of their personnel. The powerlessness is the feeling which I share with so many of my neighbors—that we cannot stop what in America is called the March of Progress, the cement trucks coming toward us any day from across the hill; the knowledge that our voices, our votes, our appeals, our petitions amount to near-nothing at a time when people have become accustomed to accepting the decisions of planners, experts, and faraway powerful agencies. It is a sickening inward feeling that the essence of self-government is becoming more and more meaningless at the very time when the outward and legal forms of democracy are still kept up.

Let us not fool ourselves: Now, halfway to 1984, with all of the recent advances of civil rights, with all of the recent juridical extensions of constitutional freedoms, we are facing the erosion of privacy, of property, and—yes—even of liberty. This has nothing to do with the Communist Conspiracy or with Ambitious Government Bureaucrats—that is where our New Conservatives go wrong. It has nothing to do with Creeping Socialism. It has very much to do with Booming Technology. The dangers that our modern societies in the West, and particularly the United States, face now, halfway to 1984, are often new kinds of dangers, growing out of newly developing conditions. What ought to concern us is the rootlessness of a modern, technological, impersonal society, with interchangeable jobs and interchangeable people, on all levels of education.

We ought to dwell less on the possibility of unemployment arising out of automation, in a society which, after all, feels obligated to produce full employment; rather, we ought to consider the growing purposelessness of occupations in a society where by now more people are employed in administration than in production. And in such a society we ought to prattle less about the need for more "creative leisure" when the problem is that work becomes less and less creative. We ought to worry not about the insufficient availability of products but about the increasing impermanence of possessions. We ought to think deeply not so much about the growth of the public sectors of the public economy at the expense of private enterprise (which, at any rate, is no longer very "private"), but rather, about the cancerous growth of the public sectors of our existence at the expense of the private autonomy of our personal lives.

We ought to concern ourselves less with the depreciation of money and more with the depreciation of language; with the breakdown of interior, even more than with the state of exterior, communications—or in other words, with the increasing practices of Orwell's doubletalk and doublethink, and with their growing promotion not so much by political tyrannies as by all kinds of techniques, in the name of Progress.

I cannot—and perhaps I need not—explain or illustrate these concerns in greater detail. They are, in any event, 1966 concerns about the future, not 1948 ones. Still, while many of the phantoms that haunted Orwell's readers eighteen years ago have not materialized, the public currency of the term 1984 has lost none of its poignancy. The tone of our literature, indeed of our entire cultural atmosphere, is far more pessimistic than it was eighteen years ago. "Alienation" and "hopelessness" are no longer Central European words; they are very American. This broad, and often near-nihilistic, cultural apathy and despair is relatively new on the American (and also on the British) scene. Its existence suggests that, despite the errors of Orwell's visions, the nightmare quality of *1984* continues to obsess our imagination, and not merely as the sickly titillation of a horror story. It haunts millions who fear that life may become an Orwellian nightmare even without the political tyranny that Orwell had predicted.

"It is by his political writings," Bertrand Russell once wrote, "that Orwell will be remembered." If this is so—and at this moment, halfway to 1984, it still seems so—he will be remembered for the wrong reasons, and one can only hope that the slow corrective tides of public opinion in the long run will redress the balance.

Orwell was not so much concerned with the degeneration of justice as with the degeneration of truth. For Orwell, both in the beginning and in the end was The Word. This is true of *1984*, too, which had three levels. On the top level there is the "plot," the love affair of Winston and Julia, which is really flat and inconsequential. On the second level there is the political vision which, as we have seen, sometimes holds up, sometimes not. It is the third level, of what is happening to words and to print, to speech and to truth in 1984, that agitated Orwell the most. Indeed, this spare and economical writer chose to end the novel *1984* by adding an appendix on "The Principles of Newspeak." Orwell was frightened less by the prospects of censorship than by the potential falsification of history, and by the mechanization of speech.

The first of these protracted practices would mean that the only possible basis for a comparison with conditions other than the present would disappear; the second, that the degeneration of traditional language would lead to a new kind of mechanical talk and print which would destroy the meaning of private communications between persons. This prospect haunted Orwell throughout the last twelve years of his life. Some of his best essays dealt with this theme of falsifications of truth—even more than totalitarianism, this was his main concern. As long as people can talk to one another meaningfully, as long as they have private beliefs, as long as people retain some of the qualities of Winston Smith's mother (she had not been an "unusual woman, still less an intelligent one; and yet she had possessed a kind of nobility, a kind of purity, simply because the standards she obeyed were private ones. Her feelings were her own, and could not be altered from the outside. . . ."), tyranny was vulnerable; it could not become total.

Orwell was wrong in believing that the development of science was incompatible with totalitarianism (by 1984, "science, in the old sense, has almost ceased to exist. In Newspeak there is no word for science"). As we have seen, he foresaw a decay of technology ("the fields are cultivated by horse-ploughs while books are written by machinery"). This is not what has happened; now, halfway to 1984, the fields are cultivated by bulldozers while books are written by machine-men. But Orwell was right in drawing attention to doublethink, "the power of holding two contradictory beliefs in one's mind simultaneously, and accepting both of them," and to the desperate prospects of doubletalk, of the degeneration of standards of language through varieties of supermodern jargon, practiced by political pitchmen as well as by professional intellectuals. There is reason to believe that, were he alive today, Orwell would have modified his views on the nature of the totalitarian menace; and that, at the same time, he would be appalled by many of the present standards and practices in mass communications, literature, and publishing, even in the West, and perhaps especially in the United States.

In short, the 1984 that we ought to fear is now, in 1966, different from the 1943 version. Politically speaking, Tocqueville saw further in the 1830s than Orwell in the 1940s. The despotism which democratic nations had to fear, Tocqueville wrote, would be different from tyranny: "It would be more extensive and more mild; it would degrade men without tormenting them. . . . The same principle of equality which facilitates despotism tempers its rigor." In an eloquent passage Tocqueville described some of the features of such a society; above the milling crowds "stands an immense and tutelary power, which takes upon itself alone to secure their gratifications and to watch over their fate. That power is absolute, minute, regular, provident and mild. . . ." But when such a government, no matter how provident and mild, becomes omnipotent, "what remains but to spare [people] all the care of thinking and all the trouble of living?"

Orwell's writing is as timely as Tocqueville's not when he is concerned with forms of polity but when he is concerned with evil communication. In this regard the motives of this English socialist were not at all different from the noble exhortation with which Tocqueville closed one of his chapters in *Democracy in America*: "Let us, then, look forward to the future with that salutary fear which makes men keep watch and ward for freedom, not with that faint and idle terror which depresses and enervates the heart." Present and future readers of *1984* may well keep this distinction in mind.

53

Questions about Roosevelt and the Second World War
(1990)

T he two world wars are the two mountain ranges that dominate the historical landscape of this century. The main features of that landscape were set forty-five years ago, and there was no essential change until last year. The two superpowers of the world in this period were the United States and the Soviet Union; their potential conflicts; the end of the Western European colonial empires; the division of Europe and of Germany and of Berlin—all of these were the results of the Second World War. Some of the characteristics of the present constellation have begun to change recently. Yet what happens is—at least for a while—inseparable from what people think happens. To many, if not most, people it still seems as if the two competing forces of the twentieth century were capitalism and communism, incarnated, among other things, by the United States and Soviet Russia. This view of the world is wrong. The main force in the history of this century has been, and still is, nationalism (within the United States and within the Soviet Union, too). Also, the conflicts between "capitalism" and "communism," indeed, between America and Russia, had nothing to do with the two world wars, during which—and especially during the second—they were effectively allied. Their enemy was the brutally aggressive nationalism incarnated by Germany (and also, to some extent, by its allies): a historical force which was so powerful that it took the, admittedly difficult and in some ways unnatural, alliance between the Anglo-Saxon de-

From *Virginia Quarterly Review*, Summer: 547–64. Books discussed in this essay include: Waldo Heinrichs, *Threshold of War: Franklin D. Roosevelt and American Entry into World War II* (1988); Frederick W. Marks III, *Wind over Sand: The Diplomacy of Franklin D. Roosevelt* (1988); Robert Nisbet, *Roosevelt and Stalin: The Failed Courtship* (1988); and Robert James Maddox, *From War to Cold War: The Education of Harry S Truman* (1988).

mocracies and Stalin's Russia to defeat it: neither side could have accomplished that victory alone. That was the source of the division of Europe and of Germany and of the entire Cold War, and of many other things besides.

Because of the extraordinarily dramatic texture of many of the events of World War II (and of its horrors) the history of World War II remains of abiding interest to many people around the world. At the same time (unlike what happened after World War I) there has been a perhaps vague but general consensus among the majority of academic historians about the ins and the outs, about the immediate origins and the consequences, of World War II. (I am leaving aside the short-lived, and insubstantial, faddish neo-Marxist interpretations of the 1960s.) This consensus has recently begun to break up, in many places. In the Soviet Union the Stalinist and other more-or-less official versions are being revised. In much of Eastern Europe these changes have advanced further. In England the monumental respect for Churchill has begun to be chipped away not only by fanatical enemies of Churchill such as David Irving but by the Cambridge historian Maurice Cowling. In Germany the so-called *Historikerstreit,* unlike other *Gelehrtenstreite* in the past, involves not methods but neonationalist interpretations of German destiny at the beginning and near the end of World War II, revealing inclinations that were largely suppressed in professional German historiography until lately. These changes differ from country to country, but at this time they do have something in common. The dominant tendency is no longer the so-called "revisionism" of the Left. Most of this revisionism, in nearly every country, is nationalist—more precisely, nationalist and/or neoconservative.

Some of this revisionism has been warranted and overdue; some of it has not. "Revisionism" is (and will always be) a mixed bag. Indeed, the very term of historical revisionism has two different meanings. Contrary to current memories, the ephemeral meaning of the term originated not with the new-Left "revisionist" historians of the Cold War in the 1960s but with those historians who in the 1920s worked to revise the notion of the principal German responsibility for World War I. In the late 1940s and early 1950s the term was again applied, and applicable to those, mostly American, historians and political writers (a small minority then) who condemned Roosevelt's foreign policy and his participation in the war. These different waves of revisionism represented historical arguments consequent to the political and ideological inclinations of their writers—which is what was wrong with most of them. Yet in a larger and higher sense all history is, because it must be, revisionism of a kind, because all history consists of the rethinking of the past. Thus the revision of history ought not be an ephemeral monopoly of opportunists who are ever ready to twist or turn or even falsify the records of the past in order to exemplify their current ideas.

It was Tocqueville who first remarked (not that this remark has had much recognition among historians) that the history of a democracy may be more difficult to write properly than the history of an aristocracy—despite the accumulation of all kinds of evidences and records, including open archives. An example of this is the foreign relations of the American people; and examples of that example are the immediate origins and the immediate consequences of American participation in World War II—complex events about which a general consensus prevailed among American historians for at least fifteen years after 1945, and which prevails among the most respected practitioners of that history even now. Yet, on more than one level, this consensus has begun to weaken. Here, then, are two books, exemplifying revisionism in the aforementioned narrow (and bad) sense of that word, one exemplifying it in the large (and good) sense of that word, and one representing it not at all. The principal theme of two of these books is how Franklin Roosevelt led the United States into the war; the other two deal with the consequences of Roosevelt's policies at the end of the war.

❊ ❊ ❊

3. Morris to SecState, 2, 6, 7 Aug. 1941, 740.0011 EW/13626, 13745, 13781, RG 59, radioed to president, 4, 7, 8 Aug. 1941 as ibid./13649A, D, E; Joint Intelligence Sub-Committee, "German Intentions up to the End of 1941," minutes of War Cabinet meeting, 8 Aug. 1941, FO 371/26523, C9529/19/18, PRO. The American Berlin Embassy's report of 6 Aug. was conveyed to the British, but probably not in time for the 8 Aug. paper (British delegation in Washington to Admiralty, 8 Aug. 1941, FO 371/29489, N4456/78/38, PRO).

This is an impressive footnote. It suggests the precision and thoroughness of its author's research. A historian is often judged by his peers for the extent of this kind of "scholarly equipment." Unfortunately, few of them take the trouble that one of the authors of the books here reviewed (Maddox) had done years ago, in a crucial instance, to which I will return—that is, checking the quotations and footnotes against the text they are supposed to illustrate. In *Threshold of War* Professor Heinrichs (who is not a revisionist) does not—unlike others—misconnect or falsify his illustrations. What he does is to reconstruct the sequence of great events as if these had been hidden in third-hand references: so-called "primary" materials that are not really "sources." The paragraph which the above-reproduced footnote is supposed to prove (147–48; the footnote is on 248) deals with the Russian front in early August 1941. The sequence and the meaning of those events are cobbled (or rather, Scotch-taped) together with snippets of information sent to Washington from the then severely restricted American embassy in Berlin, at a time when the staff of that embassy hardly knew more about the Russian front than what an intelligent reader of newspapers elsewhere could gather. There *were* instances when American diplomats in Berlin gathered confidential information about important matters: but this was not one of them.

I took this, not really scandalous, example because it illustrates the shortcomings of much that goes under the name of academic historianship. For if *le style c'est l'homme,* then *la méthode c'est l'historien.* Still, history is not chemistry; and when the historian's method is wanting, his experiment, unlike a chemist's, may still result in a definite concoction. That concoction, then, may be palatable—palatable, rather than useful—to other academics; but beyond their circles it is useless. That is a fateful limitation and to a great extent responsible for the crisis of historianship in our times. That limitation appears, too, from the limits of Heinrichs's reading—in contrast to the industry of his archival researches as was shown above.

At the threshold of war, the most decisive event—a fortnight before Pearl Harbor—was Roosevelt's (and Hull's) decision to cancel the so-called "modus vivendi," an American proposal that might have been a negotiable response to the last-minute proposal of the Japanese. There are details about that matter which are still obscure. What is hardly arguable is that on that night of November 25–26 Roosevelt stepped across the threshold. Yet Heinrichs hardly deals with that momentous decision at all. Nor does he mention Stimson's crucial words: "The question was how we should maneuver them into the position of firing the first shot. . . ."[1] Here the fatal limitations of an academic historian appear again. A most detailed treatment of the modus vivendi business may be found in John Costello's *Pacific War 1941–1945;* and much of the intelligence background before Pearl Harbor in Ronald Lewin's *American Magic.* Neither of these works is listed in Heinrichs's bibliography, suggesting at least that Professor Heinrichs had found them unworthy of inclusion or presumably that he had not read them at all. But, of course, Costello and Lewin are not academic historians.

In history, method and style are not separate matters. When a story is poorly told, this means that there is something wrong with the storyteller. The trouble is not only that Heinrichs's prose is wooden. The shortcomings of his very research are not only implicit but evident in the shortcomings of his style. When he writes, for example, that "On May 14, Pétain was reported to have stated on the radio. . . ." Well, had Pétain stated it or not? "Shortwave broadcasts from Boston and Philadelphia heard across the Atlantic claimed that the Germans were already in Dakar"—such a statement is unworthy of a historian: were they in Dakar or not? (They weren't.) "On December 1, word arrived that the Soviets had retaken Rostov, saving the Caucasus." The Russians had retaken Rostov on November 28, whether word arrived or not (and Rostov is four hundred miles from the Caucasus). "So far as diplomacy was concerned, Japanese-American relations were a wasteland in 1941." What does that mean? This super-industrious researcher's prose is full of breezy and imprecise journalistic phrases ("key generals," "the high-rolling foreign minister," "this heartening naval clasp," "a hard-bitten, make-do fighting organization," "at what point in time was this national effort aiming," "war pounced on the United States on December 7, 1941"). Often an entire sequence of events is a patch of successive headlines from the *Washington Post*. This is not only a criticism of style. Since "facts" do not exist apart from their associations and from words in which they are expressed, the employment of the proper word or phrase amounts to more than stylistic precision: it is a reflection of judgment. Heinrichs (who *is* a Roosevelt partisan) describes FDR as "this most elusive and dissembling of presidents." More elusive than Eisenhower or Wilson? More dissembling than Nixon or Johnson or Coolidge? This is not a shortcoming of vocabulary; it is a shortcoming of judgment.

In the end, shortcomings of judgment inevitably involve errors of accuracy. Thus *Threshold of War* is full of errors of facts, of dates, of misspellings. Generally speaking, its author's knowledge of the European war in 1941 is inadequate, despite his flat statement that "world politics was not compartmentalized . . . the configuration of world power was moving from one of interconnected regional crises toward a unitary global balance of forces." (Vocabulary triumphs over thought.) But then, Heinrichs's understanding of the history of his own country and of his protagonist is wanting, too, as when he writes that in 1937–39 Roosevelt's domestic programs "failed, leaving him a weakened, presumably lameduck president." This is nonsense— alas, not atypical of this book dealing with one of the most crucial months in the history of the United States, carrying the "advance acclaim" of some of our most reputed historians (specialists in Heinrichs's field) on its jacket: "Brilliant, thoughtful, meaningful, illuminating" (Frank Freidel); "deeply researched and splendidly written" (Robert Dallek); "likely to remain the most authoritative account" (Akira Iriye).

No—there remains plenty of room (and need) for revisionism, in the large sense of that word. Roosevelt's approach to the American threshold of war must still be rethought and retold, by truly first-rate historians. But *Wind over Sand* is something else. It is a blast of hot air—as, ironically and unwittingly, its very title suggests. But with what a compilation of "scholarly equipment"! This book contains no less than 112 pages of closely printed footnotes, including some that may be among the longest footnotes in the history of history: note forty-one on page 397 running to three and a half pages, a total of 154 lines; note thirty-nine to more than three pages, or 128 lines. The notes section is followed by a forty-one-page bibliography.

Again there is a direct connection between the quality of this referential equipment and the shortcomings of this author-scholar. He is a monomaniac, which is especially grievous when it comes to the reconstruction of a history, since monomania inevitably involves monocausality: and there is no single event in history that is the result of a single cause. Marks believes, and writes, that Franklin Roosevelt's character and his foreign policy and his view of the world were woefully wrong, always; that Roosevelt could not do anything right. There *are* ample reasons to criticize Roosevelt's foreign policy, as there are other, related, reasons to question his perspective of the evolving history of the world. But since this review-essay is not an ideological argument (though at least in the case of two of the authors I am compelled to deal with ideologues) I must again limit myself to an exposition of how a historian's method may contain evidences of his honesty or lack thereof. I write "lack of honesty" because, unlike in Heinrichs's book, where most (though not all) of the shortcomings are intellectual, in Marks's case the problem is essentially moral. Whereas in *Threshold of War* the bibliographical and reference notes are often inadequate illustrations of the text, in *Wind over Sand* these notes often do not relate to the text at all. Marks's practice is to end a paragraph with a strong (and often astonishing) statement; but when one looks for the proof in the relevant (and often very long) footnote there is none; indeed, the jumbled mass of references within the footnote refers to other things. On page twenty-one Marks describes Roosevelt's denial of his connection with Bullitt; the relevant footnote consists of fifty-five lines, of which fifty-two do not mention Bullitt at all. On page seventeen Marks writes that when Hitler, in 1933, made "an unexpectedly mild-mannered address to the Reichstag, Roosevelt leapt to the conclusion that he had averted a German attack on her neighbors." The footnote consists of nine items in eleven lines, devoid of proof. The statement on page twenty-eight, that in 1933 "Roosevelt yielded gratis the very thing the Soviet Union desired most: diplomatic recognition" is incorrect: but its "evidences" in the footnote include letters written by Roosevelt's mother in 1927 and 1932 and 1937. On page ninety a strange statement about British trade in the Yangtze valley in 1940 refers to a footnote which mentions neither British trade nor the Yangtze but states the presence of certain American army officers in London. A clipping from the *Los Angeles Times* and the title of a book by one of Mussolini's most extreme apologists furnish most of the footnote justifying (in Marks's view) Italy's attack on Abyssinia in 1935. In footnote eighteen on page 283 he cites a book of mine, among other things. It is pleasant for a historian to find a reference to a book that he had written more than thirty-seven years ago: but, alas, there is not the slightest relationship between what I had written on the page cited by Marks and his text.

As in *Threshold of War,* a main shortcoming of *Wind over Sand* is its author's insufficient knowledge and understanding of European history of the period, despite (or perhaps because of) his obviously long *séjour* in the French and British archives. Many mistakes of facts and dates pullulate throughout this book, without enlivening it. When and where Marks's prose heats up, it is when it comes to depictions of Roosevelt. "Clowning antics, a sarcastic tongue, mimicry, and a magnificent smile were all part of the act, and the act was the man." Roosevelt was "repeatedly fumbling the ball"; he "displayed a bland insensitivity to foreign culture"; he revealed "multiple cases of bumptious insularity"; according to Marks, not only Churchill but Stalin knew more of the world than the patrician American president. Roosevelt, to Marks, cannot do right: at times Roosevelt is unduly anti-Russian and anti-Semitic; but then he is even more unduly pro-Russian. And, as the book proceeds, the increasingly recognizable ideological thesis begins to hover over the monomania. Roosevelt delivered half of the world to Stalin. "The smiles, jests, and territorial concession which he felt would be disarming served merely to whet Russia's appetite for more." Roosevelt was responsible for communism in Latin America, too—both because he encouraged it *and* also because he acted as an American imperialist. Because of Franklin Roosevelt "America's reputation fell into semi-eclipse," Marks writes. "The ideas upon which he rested his case from 1933 to 1945 proved to be a veritable bed of sand. The rain fell, the floods came, the winds blew and beat against that house, and it fell."

That house? *What* house? In 1945 America was the skyscraper—the only skyscraper—of the world. The United States was the only great power whose territory had been untouched by the war, the only power that fought a war across two oceans simultaneously and won it, the only rich power, the master of much of the globe.

What remains true is that in 1945 the United States, led by Roosevelt (whose lead was followed by Truman) divided the spoils of that victory with the Soviet Union. In Europe he had to; in the Far East he chose to. This division, in Europe, could have been effected in ways, and along geographical lines, that would have been less advantageous for Stalin, and that could have preserved a larger portion of Europe from its then brutal Sovietization: and Roosevelt's unwillingness to face, or perhaps even to recognize, these prospects contributed to that tragedy and to the consequent crystallization of the Cold War. But he was by no means alone in this; and, as I wrote earlier, *some* kind of a division of Europe, and *some* kind of an agreement with Stalin could not have been avoided. This is willfully ignored by Frederick W. Marks but also by Robert Nisbet. *Roosevelt and Stalin: The Failed Courtship* represents this social thinker's interest in history, which is (and should be) unquestionable; but this book deserves questioning and criticism because it represents something else, too: as in the case of much of Marks's book, Nisbet's is an application of a neoconservative ideology to the history of the Second World War, and a very faulty application at that.

Nisbet's argument is that Roosevelt allowed—more, that he preferred—himself to be duped by Stalin; that Roosevelt should have listened to Churchill, instead of distancing himself from the latter as the war went on; and that much of this was the result of Roosevelt's immature and uncritical adoption of a Wilsonian view of the world. There are elements of truth within such an argument; but Nisbet's presentation of it is wildly disproportionate, and his arrangement for its proofs are wholly insufficient. The strongest evidences against this author, too, are there in his method and his style. This book, too, contains dozens of factual errors—which, in most cases, are the results of an author's impulse to make extreme statements for which there is little or no evidence. Thus, for example, on page eight Nisbet attributes words to Churchill that the latter had not then spoken; a few pages later he cites an astonishing statement by Roosevelt ("I think that something entered into [Stalin's] nature of the way in which a Christian gentleman should behave") for which Nisbet gives no reference. "Stalin's Russia was by religio-ideology sworn to destroy capitalism in any shape, form, or fashion . . . this is the message such wise and experienced minds as Harriman and Kennan tried so hard to convey to Roosevelt, and then to Truman": but that was not their message at all, there was nothing about "capitalism" in any of their dispatches. And again the faults of the method are inseparable from the faults of the style: for here the prose of this otherwise eloquent and often judicious sociologist hardly rises above vituperation. Roosevelt "played the credulous ape," "this embarrassing schmooze," Roosevelt's relationship to Stalin was "the puerile courtship of a despot." Nisbet's word-pictures of the latter are so unreal that they do not even amount to caricature: "Behind his stony exterior, Stalin must have been a veritable geyser of geopolitical joys." Tehran was "a cornucopia of delights for Stalin"; the Far Eastern concessions at Yalta "a handsome smorgasbord of territorial delights"—samples of a feverish, agitated sloppiness which is not typical of Nisbet's erstwhile prose.

In writing about Roosevelt and Stalin Nisbet takes satisfaction (if not pride) in trying to be brutally honest; but in this book (as also in Marks's) there is plenty of brutality and very little honesty. There are, alas, many people in this world who take more pleasure (and profit) in brutality than in honesty. This is especially true of ideologues—and, more than often, of ideologues of nationalism. For a historian brutal honesty is a doubtful purpose, for the simple reason that hatred and truth are seldom, if ever, reconcilable. And when they are reconciled, the result is, more often than not, selective indignation. Thus Berlin was Roosevelt's "final war gift to Stalin"; but Eisenhower who, far more than Roosevelt, was responsible for opposing Churchill and stopping the American advance toward Berlin, is exonerated by Nisbet. Nisbet attributes all of Roosevelt's faults to his Wilsonianism, forgetting that Herbert Hoover was even more of a "faithful apostle" of Wilson than was Roosevelt. Or perhaps, not forgetting it at all. For the argument of this book is not only marked by selective indignation. It rests, alas—more explicitly than in Marks's case—on an ideological thesis, a thesis dear to certain Republicans and so-called "conservatives": not only was Roosevelt's alliance with Stalin a mistake; it was but one result of an ongoing conspiracy. At the end of *Roosevelt and Stalin* Nisbet concludes his argument with a diatribe against the New Deal and the welfare state. Roosevelt's idea "that the Soviet Union is basically a forward-looking, progressive state seeking a prosperous, democratic, and classless society not unlike that struggled for by William Jennings Bryan, Woodrow Wilson, and Franklin D. Roosevelt—has by no means disappeared. There is still today a substantial sector of the American intelligentsia, one with considerable influence upon some of our otherwise excellent newspapers and broadcast news agencies, that comes very close at times to holding precisely that view."

In sustaining this ideological theme, Nisbet of course cites and praises James Burnham, Jeane Kirkpatrick, Robert A. Taft. He should have cited Mrs. Phyllis Schlafly, too, who wrote a few years ago that "God gave America the atom bomb": for, according to Nisbet, only the American atom bomb "forced Stalin to drop any ideas he had about sending the Red Army into devastated Western Europe in late 1945." Whatever ideas Stalin may have had at the time, that was not among them.

From 1945 to 1947 there occurred a revolution in the course of the American ship of state and in the direction of American public opinion which had few precedents in the history of the Republic. At the time of Roosevelt's sudden death (and for some time afterward) the government, and most of public opinion, preferred to see the Soviet Union as the principal ally of the United States. Less than two years later the government and public opinion concluded that the Soviet Union was the principal adversary of the United States. This radical transition has been the subject of many works during the last decades. Most of their authors make a sharp distinction between the Roosevelt and Truman eras. Few of them describe the gradual and complex character of that transition and the continuity between the last months of the Roosevelt and the first months of the Truman administration as cogently as Robert James Maddox in *From War to Cold War*. Harry Truman, who had a mind of his own, who knew an estimable amount of history, and who had a view of the world considerably—though not entirely—different from Franklin Roosevelt's, began to change his views of the American relationship to the Soviet Union only gradually: in most cases not because of his own inclinations but because of his crystallizing recognition of where and when Stalin's actions and intentions were irreconcilable with American approval or acquiescence. But this recognition was a complex development. Among other things, there are two significant details to which Maddox draws attention. Defenders of Roosevelt's foreign policy have made much of the—in reality, few and fragmentary—evidences, according to which during the last twelve days of his life this president was beginning to consider, or even implement, a tough policy toward Stalin. Maddox examines these evidences which, in any event, come to an end with Roosevelt's sudden death. More important is his analysis of Truman's meeting with Molotov, a mere ten days after Roosevelt's death, in which many historians have seen a drastic reversal, because of Truman's unusually strong language. Some of them describe it as the threshold of the Cold War. Maddox shows that it was not; that Truman himself, in retrospect, gave an exaggerated version of his statements. That Truman's coming to the White House meant a sudden and drastic reversal of Roosevelt's Soviet policy is a "myth . . . that, in various guises, persists. . . . Contemporary journalists and political commentators had reason to believe this version of events. . . . Perpetuation of the reversal myth in works written by scholars having access to the documents is harder to explain." Yet *From War to Cold War* is not an argumentative work. It is a perceptive summation of a period, where matters such as Truman at the Potsdam Conference, the issue of Japan, Truman's relationship to Byrnes, and American policy—or rather, the absence of a definite policy—in regard to Eastern Europe are treated with the quiet and unassuming authority of a knowledgeable scholar.

From War to Cold War is not orthodox history: but neither is it revisionism of the narrow-minded and ephemeral kind. That kind of revisionism is merely the result of projecting one's political and ideological preferences of the present into the past—which is what happened with the Cold War revisionists, then coming from the Left, beginning about 1964, with the Vietnam War. In 1972 Maddox wrote *The New Left and the Origins of the Cold*

War, in which he demolished their works—not through ideological argumentation, but by pointing out the dishonesties of their quotesmanship and the inadequacies of their most basic methods of scholarly proof. For this he was not only savaged by the Left but treated with a cowardly skittishness and fence-sitting by other liberal reviewers, so many secular vicars of Bray. Lesser men than Maddox would thereafter have made common cause with the anticommunist ideologues, the Roosevelt-haters, etc. But Maddox remained unimpressed by the selective argumentations of leftist and rightist, of Marxist, neo-Marxist, anticommunist, neoconservative historians alike. Thus the modest mastery of *From War to Cold War* reflects a quality of personal integrity—the essence of human integrity being its resistance to temptations, perhaps especially to intellectual ones. Besides its scholarly achievement, *From War to Cold War* is a triumph of character.

Few people are aware (and more should be aware) that the present American "conservative" movement began as a reaction against America's participation in World War II. That was its common denominator. Such different men as Senator Taft, Joe McCarthy, Bill Buckley, John Kennedy (the latter a secret contributor to America First in 1940–41) were isolationists. There *is* something to be said for the arguments of isolationists before World War II—except that consistent isolationists were few and far between. The "isolationism" of most of the "conservatives" was deeply compromised because of their selective indignation. Most of those who had been critical of the American intervention on the side of Britain (and of Russia) against Germany very soon became the most vocal advocates of ideological and political and military intervention against Russia. They believed that the most grievous result of World War II, the defeat of Germany at the cost of the rise of communism and Russia, was the result of leftist conspiracies and, at best, of Rooseveltian naïveté.[2]

There are three important matters about Roosevelt's moving in or out of war. One is Roosevelt's perception and management of Stalin, which had many shortcomings, including the regrettable tardiness of some of Roosevelt's reactions. This was the result of his habit of procrastination, which grew worse during the last year of his life. Yet to argue and believe, as Marks and Nisbet do, that during the war Roosevelt should not have treated Stalin as any kind of an ally is nonsense: for without that, admittedly unorthodox, American-British-Russian alliance Hitler would have been unbeatable. There is also, as Maddox states, some evidence to suggest that, had he lived, Roosevelt may not have been unwilling to contradict Stalin as the war came to its end.

The second matter is a more complex one with which no historians have yet dealt adequately. It is that it takes two to make a war. It involves not the endless picking over of the cryptoanalytic and other intelligence puzzles before Pearl Harbor, and not even the aforementioned enigma of how and why Roosevelt cancelled the modus vivendi, but the *approach* to that threshold of war with Japan: a period of about three months when it seems that Roosevelt (and Churchill) had not really made up their minds whether to back into a war with Japan or not.

There was, in 1941, a similarity between the Stalin-Hitler and the Hitler-Roosevelt relationships. For more than two months before Hitler's invasion of Russia, Stalin cravenly refused to respond to any of the Germans' provocations, including flights over his country. Eventually this did not save him; Hitler (who continued to respect him personally) attacked the Soviet Union on June 22, 1941, without the slightest pretext. The day before (a very important decision that Heinrichs misdates on one occasion) the same Hitler (who hated Roosevelt) forbade German submarines or warships to respond to American attacks on them. Hitler knew how far Roosevelt had moved from neutrality, that Roosevelt wished to provoke an incident in the Atlantic: he, Hitler, would not do that favor for Roosevelt. There *were* a few naval incidents (the *Greer,* the *Reuben James,* etc.) but not enough for Roosevelt to go before Congress for a declaration of war against Germany. He knew that the American people were not sufficiently united for that. In August 1941, during their first summit in Argentina Bay, Roosevelt and Churchill began to think that perhaps the best way to get America into the war was through the back door, through war with Japan. By that time American relations with Japan had gone downhill for more than a year, with faults on both sides. Yet during the next three months everything, including their often contradictory private statements, indicate that Roosevelt's and Churchill's minds were still not made up about this. The British, of course, would have preferred the American war effort in the Atlantic, instead of a division between the Atlantic and the Pacific theaters: but if there was no other way? Roosevelt—who should have accepted in September the conservative Japanese Prime Minister's (Prince Konoye) proposal for a personal meeting—also seems to have been divided, hoping (rather than wishing) to avoid war with Japan, and yet thinking of its eventual inevitability, if not desirability. He finally made up his mind on November 25–26, after which his dilemma was reduced to the problem of having the Japanese fire the first shot.

But all of this pales before the importance of his earlier decision, in 1940, to support Churchill and engage the United States in the effort to overthrow Hitler's empire. *That* was the crucial decision. Had the United States had an isolationist president then, suspicious of Britain (as, for example, were Hoover or Taft, idols of the present "conservatives" and neoconservatives), Hitler would have won the war. Was there, in 1940, an American alternative other than the acceptance of Hitler's rule over most of Europe, with the acquiescence of a defeated Britain? There was not. Yet that was what most isolationists thought in 1940, and that is what some of the "conservatives" think even now, satisfied as their minds are with the vision of the world dominated by the struggle of "capitalism" and "communism." With them our now increasingly numerous and vocal neoconservatives are now allied—an alliance at least as strange as that of Roosevelt and Stalin during the war.

54

Revising Joseph Goebbels
(1988)

The diaries of Joseph Goebbels are an extraordinary find, for many reasons, including their size and their history. Goebbels was a truly compulsive writer as well as speaker—an unusual combination. He began to write a regular diary in July 1924 (there are indications of an irregular diary even earlier) at the age of twenty-six. The last entry is probably that of April 9, 1945, three weeks before his suicide along with his wife and children, and the complete collapse of the Third Reich. The total of the retrieved hand- and typewritten material may amount to more than sixty thousand pages. When completed, their publication will comprise ten large volumes, of which the first four have now been published by the Institut für Zeitgeschichte in cooperation with the West German Federal Archives. These four volumes of Goebbels's diaries from July 1924 to July 1941 are a unit by themselves. Goebbels wrote them by hand, often every day, even when he was at his frenzied work as the minister of propaganda and culture in the Third Reich.

He turned to dictating them to a first-rate stenographer in July 1941. A few months earlier he had the written diaries transported to an underground safe and commissioned the same man to begin transcribing them on a typewriter. Thus there are portions of these diaries of which two or even more transcripts exist. This is one guarantee of their authenticity, about which there should be no question. The extensive introductions of Elke Fröhlich, their compiler and editor, describe the extreme care and precision of their analysis and transcription. (Goebbels's handwriting became increasingly difficult; besides, many of the retrieved pages were damaged by moisture.) In reading these nearly three thousand large printed pages I found only a few, very minor, errors in the annotations.

Review of *Die Tagebücher von Joseph Goebbels: Sämtliche Fragmente*, vols. 1–4, 1924–1941. From *New York Review of Books*, July 21: 14–17.

The story of the recovery and the detection of these manuscripts is long and complicated. Elke Fröhlich has given an account within her 103-page introduction in volume one (and in an article in the October 1987 number of the *Vierteljahrshefte für Zeitgeschichte*). Some of the material was found by a German woman who had been ordered by the Russians to clean up the *Führerbunker* soon after the fall of Berlin; another portion was found within a mass of paper sold by a junk dealer a year later; much of the material, in large aluminum boxes, was carted away by the Russians; more boxes were found by the East Germans in the late 1960s. The Russians eventually turned over microfilm rolls to the East German authorities, who, after some of the material was leaked to a West German publisher, agreed to their publication. One odd detail is Goebbels's request to a German phototechnician in November 1944 to begin the photographic reduction of these thousands of pages ("I may lose everything, but these personal papers of mine must be preserved for posterity"): the technician was the man who either invented or at least was a pioneer of what much later became known as microfiche to librarians and archivists around the world. By a strange coincidence this man, who is still alive, bears the name of Dr. Joseph Goebel.[1]

What is remarkable, significant, and new in this enormous mass of papers? The answer to the first question is obvious: their bulk. I know of no comparable example of such extensive continuous diaries by any political leader of any country at any time. (There *are* a few important gaps, in 1938 and 1939.) But obviously, too, quantity and quality are different matters. There are not many truly startling revelations in these pages. Most of the interesting revelations involve Goebbels himself. But apart from what these diaries may tell about this frantic and compulsive diarist there are at least two elements—elements, rather than specific individual items—of these diaries that should make historians rethink some matters.

One of these concerns the political history of the German people before, not after, the Depression. The accepted view is that the sudden rise in Nazi votes (the tremendous, ninefold increase in September 1930 from 12 to 108 Nazi seats in the Reichstag) was a result of the economic crisis that befell Germany soon after the New York stock market crash in October 1929. Most historians have attributed most of the Nazi successes to the Depression in Germany. Yet in 1929—which was a prosperous time in the history of the Weimar Republic—the appeal of the Nazis had already begun to grow. In the communal elections of Saxony, Apolda, Coburg, Mecklenburg, and Berlin Nazi votes doubled and trebled. Goebbels of course records these minor (though significant) electoral events. But what is astonishing is the absolute confidence—and, alas, the foresight—that

Goebbels and Hitler possessed and that they demonstrated about their prospects, even before the economic and political crisis of the Weimar Republic: that is, before the late summer of 1930, at a time when the Nazi party was only an extremist faction, holding fewer than 3 percent of the seats in the Reichstag. Once the people speak up, we'll be in power—this was Goebbels's conviction as early as 1929.

Later, a year before Hitler's astounding rise to the chancellorship, Goebbels writes (February 4, 1932): "It is wonderful to observe how sure and unhesitating the Führer looks at the coming assumption of power. He does not doubt that for a second, not even in his private thoughts. He speaks and acts and thinks as if we were in power already." He goes on: "Gröner [the anti-Nazi minister of war] must fall. Then Brüning. Then Schleicher"— the exact sequence of what happened. On April 14, 1932, "we are discussing questions of personnel, as if we were already in power." Alas, these were not the daydreams of fanatics. Goebbels and Hitler understood the tides of German popular sentiment. This suggests the need not only to revise (and drastically diminish) the economic interpretation of the crisis of German democracy in the years between 1930 and 1933 but to recognize the political savvy of Hitler and of his cohorts—and also to recognize that National Socialist propaganda well before 1932 and 1933 had struck deep chords in the consciousness of increasing numbers of Germans, involving sentiments and inclinations that were more powerful and older and deeper than the novel responses to economic need.

Another potential revision suggested by these diaries involves Hitler's relationship to Goebbels. (The converse, that is, Goebbels's relationship to Hitler, is a different matter, to which I shall return.) The accepted opinion is that Goebbels was one of Hitler's closest advisers, and surely his intellectual adviser. But from the evidence of these diaries there can be no question that Goebbels was subordinate to Hitler in every way: not only administratively or psychologically but also intellectually—a condition that Goebbels admits throughout his career, again and again. More important: it appears from the mass of evidence of these diaries that, Hitler's need for Goebbels's propaganda activities notwithstanding, Goebbels's influence on Hitler's decisions—decisions and choices on all levels—was minimal.

Perhaps even more important is the evidence accumulated here that confirms something that few people (one exception was General Jodl) remarked: despite his more than occasional volubility, Hitler was a very secretive man. His frequent, and often cunningly planned, monologues and haranguings were not always the result of self-indulgence. He used them to influence, inspire, overwhelm, and, at times, intimidate others. Yet some of his most important political and military decisions he kept entirely to himself. It was Jodl who said in 1946 (and a few fragments of evidence since then support this view) that, contrary to the accepted view, Hitler knew before almost anyone in his circle that he would lose the war: but how could one expect that he would admit this to his staff, let alone to the German people at large? Goebbels's diaries confirm Hitler's secretiveness, well before the war. Yes, he was close to Hitler; but for Hitler to tell him what he, Hitler, was about to do (except for his sometimes dreamy speculations and long-range designs) happened very seldom.

One example is Hitler's decision to attack Russia. Hitler ordered the planning for the invasion to begin nearly eleven months before it took place, and he gave the definite directive for it six months later; but Goebbels was not privy to these plans except shortly before the actual attack. In this respect the meeting of the two men on June 16, 1941, as recorded in these diaries, is significant. It may be the longest of these thousands of diary entries. It contains yet another revelation of Hitler's brutal and amoral convictions of what war was supposed to accomplish ("Right or wrong does not matter. We must conquer [*siegen*]"); but it is another confirmation, too, of the fact that Hitler was less certain about the prospects of a rapid collapse of Russia than were Goebbels and his generals—which may explain why, for once, he was compelled to harangue Goebbels and others about this.

And now: what about Goebbels himself? Again there is reason, supplied by these diaries, to correct the accepted view that this master of propaganda was something of a genius, and "the most interesting of the men around Hitler." This was the view of Alan Bullock, Hitler's first serious biographer, whose views about Hitler have not quite stood the test of time. That this is still the accepted view should appear from the fact that, next to Hitler, none of the Nazi leaders has been the subject of as many biographies as Goebbels (of these Helmut Heiber's is the best);[2] and during the last forty years at least four portions of Goebbels's diaries—fragmentary, incomplete, and, at least on one occasion, pirated editions—have been published by American and English commercial houses. Was Goebbels really the most interesting man among the Nazis? There was an extraordinary consistency in the vision of this man, the very shape and sound of whose name suggests, like a small rubber ball, the bounce of compressed energy. Yet these diaries show how his mind was more limited in its scope and more shallow than one has been inclined to think.

Goebbels was addicted to the diary form. His two books (the novel *Michael*,[3] written in 1923 and published in 1929, and his account of Hitler's achievement of power, *Vom Kaiserhof zur Reichskanzlei*, published in 1934) were also written in the form of diaries—it is significant how the text of the latter corresponds largely to his diaries of the same period. For many years he scribbled these long diary entries at night, often ending them with sentimental exclamations, and calling his diary "My father confessor!" He appears early as a prototypical example of an unhappy German neo-idealist, a radical revolutionary youth with a Spenglerian cast of mind, an extreme nationalist with sympathies for a nationalist bolshevism. Tearing himself away from his lower-middle-class Catholic family, critical of his father, a factory foreman who rose to be a clerk, filling his mind with a hatred for anything that is middle-class bourgeois, he is extremely moody, too; and his moods, very frequently, involve women.

Large portions of his diaries during the twenties are devoted to his love affairs. Here, again, a minor revision is in order. Goebbels has had the reputation of an obsessed womanizer, a physically unattractive man who would use his powerful position and prestige to bed women, including young movie actresses. This is not altogether untrue; yet everything indicates that this partially maimed man (it is odd how much Goebbels looked like Joel Grey in *Cabaret*: a swarthy, energetic little man, with a diabolical grin and large, popping eyes) attracted all kinds of women early in life, probably because of his immediately apparent dynamic personality. He needed women (the platitude "women are the motor of life" he repeated often). Yet it was the women who flocked to him, including his future wife, Magda Quandt, the second great love of his life (the first, Anka Stahlherm, kept returning to him after her marriage). Until now it had seemed that the beautiful Frau Quandt, who was something of an upper-middle-class woman, was courted by Goebbels and served as his means of rising in society. It now appears that it was she who seduced Goebbels, not the reverse. (With all of the importance of his erotic drive the only entry in these diaries in which a physical consummation is even suggested occurs when Magda appears at his apartment on the night of February 15, 1931: "And she stays very late.") But—and this is more important—his sexual ambitions were wholly subordinated to his political ones. On June 17, 1931, he wrote: "First comes the Party, then Magda. Love does not restrict me; it drives me on." Around that time he made "a solemn agreement" with Magda that they will not marry "until we have conquered the Reich." (Actually their marriage took place before this.)

But by that time the style and the very purpose of his diary had changed. He wrote less and less about his private life, more and more about his public life. He was much happier than before. Like Hitler, he discovered his talent for public speaking. His references to his speeches are full of self-praise. The fairly vulgar word *Bombenerfolg* (whose English translation, "an explosive success," is but a pale version) recurs, over and over again. He now saw himself as the great chronicler of the party; and, after that, of the Third Reich. He said that his diaries will provide his children a substantial inheritance (in 1934 he received a very large advance for their eventual publishing rights); he became more obsessed with his self-appointed task as chronicler of the Reich. The result is a gradual decrease of interesting material.[4] There are two reasons for this. One is his increasing habit of beginning each diary entry with a summary of the military and political events of the previous day. (By this time he was writing his diary every morning, and not at night.) This is especially evident in the later portions, after 1941. Yet these summaries tell us relatively little that is new.[5] The other reason is the already mentioned secretiveness of Hitler.

At this point we must say something about Goebbels's adulation of Hitler. In one of the earliest entries in his diary, on July 4, 1924, Goebbels wrote (it is not certain whether he had met Hitler by that time): "Germany is longing for the One, the Man, as the earth in summer is longing for rain. . . . Could a miracle still save us? Lord, show the German people a miracle! A miracle!! A man!!!!" The miracle was coming. It was Hitler. (On July 19: "The people's movement needs an ideal, a great Führer personality. Yes, we are looking for the born Führer.") Then he met Hitler. On October 14, 1925, having finished reading *Mein Kampf:* "Who is this man? Half plebeian, half god! Is he in fact The Christ, or only the John [the Baptist]?"

Yes, there are a few—very few—instances in which the diaries record disappointment with Hitler's tactics. They do not last. From the very beginning Goebbels is wholly under Hitler's sway. The adulatory passages are copious. But they do not only refer to Hitler's ideas. They refer to his private personality. (November 6, 1925: "Hitler now jumps up, he stands before us. He grasps my hand. Like an old friend. And those great, blue eyes. Like stars. He is glad to see me. I am very happy. . . . This man has everything to be a king. The born tribune of a people. The coming dictator." April 13, 1926: "At the end Hitler embraces me. Tears in his eyes. I am so happy. . . . He is our host. And how great he is in that too!" July 31, 1928: "Hitler is a universal human being. He is a glorious storyteller.") Much later, when Hitler chooses to telephone him on New Year's Eve, Goebbels is in tears. It appears that Hitler knew very well how to deal with him. Goebbels was only eight years younger than Hitler but "he is like my father." (June 22, 1929: "His fatherliness is touching. I love him very much. Of all men I love him most, because he is so good. He has a great heart." Nine years later, August 16, 1938: "The Führer is like a father to me. I am so thankful to him for that.") Goebbels was not a particularly loyal character, but his loyalty to Hitler remained unbroken until the end. Some time after 1929 his references to Hitler begin to change. He no longer refers to him as "der Chef." Now he writes "der Führer." It was not only National Socialist fanaticism but Goebbels's adulation of Hitler that made him (contrary to Hitler's request that Goebbels abandon the *Führerbunker*) accompany Hitler beyond the end, into death. In their twenty years together there are a few times when Goebbels is disconcerted with Hitler's hesitations. The brutalities of Hitler, his vulgarities, do not trouble Goebbels for a moment. He admires Hitler for them. Hitler is the stronger character and—it is Goebbels who says this—the greater mind.

This tells us something not only about Goebbels's character but about his mind. Was he altogether a good judge of people? It does not seem so. He was very vain. His reactions varied extremely according to how he was seen and treated by others. There was a time when he despised Göring and liked Ribbentrop; later he would reverse himself. His assessments of foreign statesmen were very poor. He knew little of the world beyond Germany. In *Michael* he wrote about the German people: "We are the most intelligent but, alas, also the stupidest nation in the world." If by "intelligent" we mean the original meaning of that word, the ability to read between the lines, then Goebbels does not come out very well. He had a quick mind, and his self-discipline was often amazing. (In 1931 he could write—besides his diary—three hundred typewritten pages in fourteen days.) But his mind was both fanatical and superficial. He wrote his diaries in a feverish haste, with a minimum of contemplation. He had read much in his youth, but after 1929 his main intellectual pleasure and interest were directed to films. (He was an admirer of American movies, especially of *Gone with the Wind*: "a great achievement of the Americans," which he showed several times in his private movie-room, including the agitated night before the invasion of Russia.)

If there was a glimmer of genius in his insights it was in his ideas about propaganda. (February 8, 1932: "The intellectuals think that the more often a theme is repeated the less its effect on the public. This is not true. It depends how one treats that theme. If one has the ability to repeat the same theme over and over again but in different ways, from different sides, with ever increasing drastic arguments, then its [acceptance] by the public will never fade; to the contrary, it will become stronger.")

Goebbels was not a simple person. There were dualities in his character. There was his obsessive erotic drive; yet his relationship to the many women in his life seems fairly normal. He broke away from his Catholic parents early; yet he remained a good son, often to the point of sentimentality. He was a cynic about people (September 25, 1924: "90 percent of people are the gutter, 10 percent halfway decent"); yet his admiration for and faith in German soldiers and workers were excessively strong. Much of the prose of his diaries is sentimental and petty, with many expressions of kitsch; often it seems almost a caricature of German middle-class sentimentalities. Yet the most consistent element in his ideology was his hatred of the sentiments of the bourgeoisie, of the middle-class mentality (which is why both in the beginning and near the end of his public career he favored an alliance with Russia and Communists). Even at the end of the war (which he never opposed, and into which he had thrown himself with enthusiasm), looking at the destruction of German cities, he took some comfort by saying that at least the bourgeois world of Europe had been destroyed forever. He was, fortunately, wrong.

It is a curious coincidence that Goebbels ended his antibourgeois novel *Michael* with "that catastrophic day, January 30" when his hero Michael died. Ten years later, in 1933, January 30 was to become the culmination, the greatest triumph, in Goebbels's life, the day Hitler became the chancellor of Germany. From the consequences of that catastrophic thirtieth of January we have not yet recovered—leading as it did to the world war in the shadows of which we still live.

55

Hitler: The Historical Problem

(1997)

On October 14, 1944, the Dutch historian Pieter Geyl concluded the preface of a book, the subject of which had preoccupied him for
more than four years. Those were dramatic years indeed in his life. In May
1940 his country was suddenly and brutally invaded and conquered by
Hitler's Germany. Geyl had written an essay about Napoleon, which in
September 1940 he used for some lectures at the Rotterdam School of Economics. A month later he was arrested and sent to Germany, where he had
occasion to repeat those lectures "in very different surroundings and for a
very different public, namely in the Buchenwald concentration camp for
my fellow hostages." The subject was Napoleon; but it was "the parallel
[between Napoleon and Hitler] that roused the keenest interest and amusement." A few months later, Geyl was returned from Buchenwald to Holland, where he spent another three years of internment. In February 1944,
he was freed on medical grounds, and then he began to write his book on
Napoleon.[1] It was completed eight months later in a small room, in the
cold and the darkness of a still-subjugated Holland, under the shadow of
the Gestapo. Seven months still had to pass until Holland was liberated.
The book—*Napoleon: For and Against*—was published in 1947, the first English and American editions in 1949.

As the title shows, the subject of this fine and most readable work by
probably the second-greatest historian of Dutch origin in this century (the
other being Johan Huizinga) was Napoleon, not Hitler. As a matter of fact,
Hitler's name does not appear in the text at all, except for a tiny footnote
on page 278. But it appears throughout the preface. After all, as Geyl admitted at the very beginning of the preface: "This book is a by-product of
our recent experiences." But this was not to be a book of Parallel Lives.[2]
Listen closely to what Geyl wrote in that preface: "Let me state, in fairness

From *The Hitler of History* (New York: Alfred A. Knopf), 240–68.

to my own word, that I found a good deal more than the parallel to attract me. Napoleon had his own fascination, and French historiography a charm of its own. Not even the article of 1940 had been in the first instance suggested to me by the problem of the resemblance or contrast between Napoleon and Hitler, *but by the historiographical problem, the problem of the endless variety of interpretations of Napoleon, his career, his aims, and his achievements.* [The italics are mine.] Yet—how could it be otherwise? I had been struck by the parallel no less than had my readers or hearers, and in this book, too, it has undeniably remained an element, even though I have alluded to it only very occasionally and have nowhere worked it out."

The rest of Geyl's preface, then, *does* compare Napoleon with Hitler; I will return to some of his trenchant statements in a moment. But there is a paragraph in this otherwise brief preface that struck me when I first read Geyl's book, almost a half century ago. Geyl wrote that he did not wish to give the impression "that it was written for the parallel and owed to the parallel, in my opinion, its principal interest." But: "There [is] a point to which it is difficult not to fear that the parallel may extend—it is only a later generation that will know for certain."

> When one sees the French licking the hand that had chastised them; when one notices how the errors and crimes of the Hero, the trials of the people, the disasters and losses of the State, were forgotten in the glamour of military achievement, of power, unsound and transitory though it was; when one notices the explanations and constructions, ingenious, imaginative, grandiose, that were put up as much as a century later by historians—and such excellent historians!—then one seems already to discern among later generations of Germans[3] the apologists and admirers of the man who was our oppressor and who led them to their ruin.

Pieter Geyl wrote this in October 1944—exactly fifty years (to the month) before I began to plan and write the present book. I would not name it *Hitler: For and Against.* Yet readers who have followed my book until now will know that a pro-Hitler literature by "apologists and admirers" does exist, and will continue to exist, and not only among "a later generation of Germans." There *are*, as we have seen, admirers and rehabilitators of Hitler, hidden and open. Their influence is limited, and perhaps their significance, too. But the future is still ahead of us.

In any event, the subject of this book is both like and unlike Pieter Geyl's. It is not the history of a man but the history of his history; but then its chapters are not divided among his historian opponents and his historian admirers. And this last chapter is—inevitably—historical rather than historiographical (though of course history and historiography overlap): a putative answer to the question of where and how Hitler's place may be, in the history of the twentieth century, at least. And that question does involve a comparison with Napoleon.

The parallels, or more precisely, the similarities—between Napoleon's and Hitler's careers (their careers, rather than their lives) should be apparent even to general readers who do not possess detailed historical knowledge. We may sum them up in the briefest possible manner. Both rose—unexpectedly—as national leaders. They incarnated—even more than they represented—a new element in the politics and history of their countries. Their popularity was—for a long time—extreme and indubitable. Their conquests abroad were astonishing. They wished to rule—and for a time did rule—most of Europe. The main obstacle to the acceptance of their conquests was England, which they were not able to invade. Having convinced themselves that England's last continental hope was Russia—after having first made a surprising treaty with Russia—they decided to invade Russia, where they met with disaster, whereafter they could no longer conquer and were defeated utterly. All of this is well known, and some of the coincidences are spectacular: for example, the very beginning of their invasions of Russia, Napoleon's starting on June 24, almost on the same day (June 22) as Hitler's.

But the differences are even more substantial than the similarities.[4] I can hardly improve on what Geyl wrote in his preface in October 1944—which I feel now compelled to cite in detail:

> "I always hate to compare Hitler with Napoleon," so, listening to the BBC the other day, I heard that Winston Churchill had been telling the House of Commons, only to continue with a "but" and to enter upon the comparison all the same. So it is with all of us, and so it is with me. It is simply impossible not to do so. The resemblances are too striking. No doubt—and I want to state this with unmistakable emphasis—the differences, the contrasts, are such that, even when as in my case one had hated the dictator in Napoleon long before the evil presence of Hitler began darkening our lives, one almost feels as if one should ask the pardon of his shade for mentioning his name in one breath with that of the other. . . . I do not want to say that French civilization was made of so much finer stuff than German: the difference is that under Napoleon French civilization, albeit stifled

and narrowed by him, still accompanied the conquest, while the character of the conquest that it has been the lot of our civilization to undergo is not compatible with any civilization at all. Lastly, the personality of Napoleon—indeed, when I think of elaborating the comparison on that score, I suddenly feel a surge of revolt against [his] "detractors" with whom generally (as will be seen) I am on quite friendly terms.

There follows now a paragraph summing up Napoleon's tyranny and his atrocities. And yet:

> Methods of compulsion and atrocities? The worst that our generation had to witness . . . had no parallel in Napoleon's system. Indeed that system remained true, from first to last, to conceptions of civil equality and human rights with which the oppression or extermination of a group, not on account of acts or even of opinions, but of birth and blood, would have been utterly incompatible. And yet methods of compulsion and atrocities are inseparable from the character of the dictator and conqueror, and we shall see that Napoleon incurred bitter reproaches, at home and abroad, for some of his acts. Nevertheless this is one of the points where the comparison is bound to do good for his reputation. What is the proscription of "the general staff of the Jacobins" beside the annihilation of all opposition parties in jails or concentration camps such as has taken place in the Third Reich? What is the murder of the Duke of Enghien beside those of Dollfuss, of General Schleicher and his wife, and of so many others on June 30th 1934? What are the executions of Palm, of Hofer, what are even the severities with which so many villages and towns in Germany and Spain were visited, beside what in our time all occupied territories have had to suffer from Hitler's armies? The French police were hated and feared in the occupied and annexed territories, but when one reads about their conduct with a mind full of present experiences, one cannot help feeling astonished at the restraints and resistances they still met within the stubborn notions of law and in the mild manners of a humane age.

Written in October 1944, this still rings true. But now allow me to continue this comparison a little further. It may be of some interest to note that throughout his life, Hitler made very few references to Napoleon.[5] In June

1940, during his fast and almost furtive visit to Paris at dawn, he spent a few moments contemplating Napoleon's tomb in the Invalides; and in December 1940 he ordered that the coffin of Napoleon's son be brought from Vienna to a wintry Paris, to be deposited next to that of his father—a gesture that evoked little reaction among the French people. To this we may add that a contemptuous dislike for France and the French marked Hitler's thinking from his earliest years.[6]

There were grave differences between Napoleon's and Hitler's personalities and temperaments. Unscrupulous cruelty—of a calculating Machiavellian and Mediterranean kind—marked what was probably the worst element in the mental habits of the former; hatred—and the cultivation of unbridled hatreds—was perhaps the worst element in the latter. It is at least arguable that Napoleon, that supreme egoist, was more confident—and often more optimistic—than was Hitler.[7] Another difference between the two lies in their attitudes toward the past. In that sense Napoleon was much less revolutionary than was Hitler. One attractive—and surprisingly human—facet of Napoleon's personality was his hereditary and family feeling, his 1810 inclination to settle down with a family, for his affection for Marie Louise and his love for his son amounted to more than the calculated purpose of consolidating his power through a grand dynastic marriage. There was a bourgeois (in the best sense of that often maligned word) side of Napoleon that was missing in Hitler. At his most grandiose, Napoleon saw himself as a new Charlemagne at his coronation in 1804; he chose Roman emperors as models; Hitler had none (except perhaps Frederick the Great, at the end).[8] There is, too, the contrast between Napoleon, who said that his marshals were bloodhounds straining at the leash, so that he had to hold them back, whereas Hitler said that it was he who had to incite and drive his generals forward.

More significantly, Napoleon saw his place in history as that of a third force between Revolution and Reaction. He said, before his downfall: "After me, the Revolution—or rather, the ideas which formed it—will resume its course. It will be like a book from which the marker is removed, and one starts again at the page where one left off."[9] Hitler's vision was entirely different. After his disappearance there would be no return, only darkness; and then, perhaps after fifty or a hundred years, a revival of his own revolutionary ideas.

Again, I must insist (for the last time) that I am not writing a biography of Hitler; but I am preoccupied with the problem of his place in history. And it is in this respect that a comparison with the ups and downs of Napoleon's historical interpretation may be proper. Most of the substantial biographies and histories of Napoleon were written and published forty or fifty years after his death, whereas we have seen that substantial scholarly biographies of Hitler began to appear within a decade of his death. During his lifetime, many of the great artists and thinkers of Europe admired or respected Napoleon (Beethoven and Goethe, for instance, if only for a time); this does not apply to Hitler (though cases such as Knut Hamsun or Ezra Pound ought not to be ignored). There were prominent Englishmen who respected Napoleon; with Hitler the only substantial exception was Lloyd George (who thought Hitler the greatest figure in Europe since Napoleon). There were great French writers and poets (Stendhal, Béranger) whose unstinting admiration for Napoleon remained constant;[10] about Hitler we find no German writers of comparable caliber. Last but not least—and especially for the purposes of this book—the biographers and historians of Napoleon may be divided into For and Against categories (which Geyl has so impressively done); but—at least during the first fifty years after his death—such an equal or near-equal balance among Hitler's biographers and historians does not exist. There are, as we have seen—besides a few outright but questionable admirers—more cautious and circumspect historians who are inclined to revise the commonly accepted portrait of Hitler, but, unlike some of Napoleon's French biographers, they are not his outright defenders.[11]

In any event, Hitler, unlike Napoleon, was not loved or revered across Europe.[12] Among his own people, yes; but even there we must consider that the phenomena of the "public" and of the "people" were different one hundred and thirty years before Hitler. But while history does not repeat itself, there exist a few startling similarities: the sunny prosperity of the Third Reich in the 1930s and what many French historians have called "the golden spring of the Consulate"; Napoleon's and Hitler's Concordats (and such things as the pro-Consulate and pro-imperial inclinations of the subsequent papal nuncio to France, Cardinal Caprera; and those of the nuncio to Berlin under Hitler, the accommodating Monsignor Orsenigo).[13] There was Napoleon's explanation to Caulaincourt that his Eastern and Russian policy was not due to his excessive ambitions but to his aim to deprive England of hope and compel her to make peace—we have seen that this was Hitler's explanation too. There remains, in the history of both, the obvious evidence of the profound limitations of the importance of "economics." After all, it was the Marxist Georges Lefebvre who proved that in 1801 and 1802 bread was even more expensive in France than it had been in the crucial year of 1789, and yet it was in 1801 and 1802 that Napoleon's popularity was at its highest, in the "Golden Spring of the Consulate." (But Tocqueville had noted that, too, in his unfinished second book about the Revolution, about Bonaparte's taxes.)[14]

Last but not least, there is one profound difference between the two men. It involves the secret practices of statesmanship. Like Hitler ("It is the Führer's wish"), Napoleon intentionally left no written instructions of some of his most brutal orders. But, unlike Hitler, Napoleon made it clear that he wanted to be dissociated from them.[15] Hitler's most brutal instructions may have been secret or oral or even too general to pin down; but he never disavowed them or their results; nor did he attribute them to others, in order to exempt himself for the sake of the historical record—another example of the difference between his and Napoleon's sense of history.[16]

In 1901, the French positivist historian Alphonse Aulard wrote his *Histoire politique de la revolution française*: his aim was to study and appraise in an objective, scientific way, "historically and not politically." Eighty years later German historians expressed the desideratum of Hitler's "historicization" [*Historisierung*] in similar terms. Yet "objective" and "scientific"[17] are outdated Cartesian categories (as are their symmetrical antonyms: "subjective" and "artistic"). Like all human knowledge, historical knowledge is both personal and participant[18] (and, its expressions are less motive-bound than purpose-oriented). Or, to repeat: Perspective is an inevitable component of reality—to which I must now add that no perspective is ever devoid of the element of retrospect. And it is in the retrospective perspective of a century that we must consider Hitler's place in it. If the two world wars were the two mountain ranges dominating the historical landscape of the twentieth century, in the shadows of which we were living until 1989, in Europe and America and Germany and Russia alike, wherefore World War II was the culmination of these world wars, and with results lasting longer than those of World War I, then it follows that the peak figure of the century was Hitler[19]—which brings us to the unscientific question of historical greatness.

The question of historical "greatness" is hardly more than semantic. (Of nearly ten thousand words under the entry "great" in the *Oxford English Dictionary*, among its twenty-two definitions, historical greatness, as such, does not figure.)[20] The history of mankind is the history of the evolution of its consciousness, which includes—indeed, it is inseparable from—the history of words. And there has been such an evolution lately. The last three monarchs to whom the epithet "Great" was applied were all of the eighteenth century: Peter, Frederick, and Catherine (when it had something to do not only with quality but with magnitude). This attribution has declined, if not altogether vanished, since. It is perhaps significant that Napoleon has not acquired the epithet "Great," except for the indirect and sarcastic suggestion that his nephew Napoleon III should be called "Napoleon the Little."

And so, for the last time, a comparison of Napoleon with Hitler. Many things that Napoleon had made or brought about have proved enduring, many of his institutions, laws, reforms, buildings, including an architectural and decorative style (that, to be precise, actually began during the late years of Louis XVI and then continued to develop during the Directory, but still . . .), and some of his sayings, crisp expressions of an extraordinary mind. Hitler, who had an occasional sense of the comic but not much wit and hardly any sense of humor, left few sayings worth remembering (except for a few trenchant observations). What remained and ought to be remembered are his automobile highways and a mostly destroyed array of neoclassical buildings, most of whose designs are attributable to his architects, whose designs he may have approved but whose style was not entirely in accord with his own.[21]

Konrad Heiden, Hitler's first serious biographer, chose a passage from Goethe for the motto of his book, about the "daemonic" quality of certain people—not necessarily statesmen: "All moral powers are helpless against them; in vain are enlightened minds [*der hellere Teil der Menschen*] against . . . the mass will be attracted to them." I wrote before about Hitler's extraordinary talent for adjusting circumstances to his ideas—to which I also added that as the war proceeded he was forced to adjust some of his ideas to circumstances over which he had no control—and that the guilt (or rather, the want of civic responsibility) of most Germans was that they found it easy to adjust their ideas to circumstances—as indeed many people are inclined to do.

The old Germanomaniac and Wagnerite Houston Stewart Chamberlain praised Hitler in 1923: "the great simplifier of all problems." But sixty years before that, Jakob Burckhardt had written: The time of "the terrible simplifiers" will come. In 1981 Vappu Tallgren, a Finnish historian, made a significant contribution in his study of Hitler's "creed of heroism." Through the "cult of heroism in National Socialist Germany, Hitler wanted to prepare a new religion." The creed of heroism, for Hitler, was "a principle, not a rhetoric—which is why he believed that with that he expressed the most essential element of his ideology."[22] That may be largely true. Yet, as I tried to state earlier, Hitler's mind and willpower may have been extraordinary, but mind and willpower alone do not a hero make. Nor does hero worship. The cult of heroism and being a hero are not the same thing.[23]

There was no nobility in Hitler's makeup—or in his actions. But an easy dismissal of Hitler by ridiculing him is arrant nonsense.[24] The list of people—thinkers, writers, artists—who said and wrote that Hitler was a genius is long. They include such otherwise unexceptionable antitotalitarians as Jules Romains in 1934 and André Gide in 1940. An unpleasant but symptomatic case is that of the English writer and thinker Wyndham Lewis, an anti-Left modernist and radical who—and this was true of many others—despised the tawdry commercialism and decadent intellectualism of the 1920s (he also abhorred Chaplin). In 1931, he wrote an admiring book entitled *Hitler*—about whom he changed his mind in 1939, writing *The Hitler Cult*. But then another fifteen years later, in his novel *Self-Condemned*, the hero is an English historian who loses his position and is forced to live in exile in a frozen Canada in part because of his unorthodox opinions of what Hitler represents in the modern history of Europe.[25]

Still, it is with this question of "greatness" that many of Hitler's biographers have been struggling.[26] Haffner, for example: "Of course one hesitates, and justly so, to call him 'a great man.'"[27] "Those who are only vigorous destroyers are not great at all," says Jakob Burckhardt, and Hitler certainly proved himself a vigorous wrecker. But beyond any doubt he also proved himself a star achiever of high caliber, and not only in wrecking. Admittedly, without his decidedly exceptional vigor the disaster which he accomplished would have turned out less enormous, but one should not lose sight of the fact that his road to the abyss led across high peaks."[28] Fest wrestles with the semantic question: "All known history shows no phenomenon such as he; should one then call him 'great'?" He says yes and no; "still one is reluctant to call him 'great.'" But then he cites Burckhardt in the opposite sense from Haffner, since Burckhardt "spoke about a remarkable dispensation of the common laws of morality" when it came to the consciousness of "great" individuals.[29] Perhaps the question of "greatness" is best managed by Schramm. "In terms of sheer magnitude of what he wrought during his twelve years and three months in power he was one of the 'great' men in history. But his perverse greatness was informed less by creative energy than by some malevolent genius, so that even his most positive intentions and deeds acquired a dubious and ultimately sinister character."[30]

"By virtue of his personality, his ideas, and the fact that he misled millions, Hitler poses an historical problem of the first magnitude."[31] This is well put. Great and profound is the problem of Hitler's place in history—not whether he deserves or not the sentimental, imprecise, and perhaps antiquated adjective "great."

In November 1936 (after his long discussion with Cardinal Faulhaber), Hitler sat with Speer at the large window of the Berghof, looking out at the mountain twilight. After a long silence he said, "For me there are two possibilities: to succeed with my plans entirely, or to fail. If I succeed, I will be one of the greatest men in history—if I fail, I will be condemned, rejected, and damned."[32] When, on May 1, 1945, his great opponent heard the news of his death on the radio, Churchill said at the dinner table: "Well, I must say I think he was perfectly right to die like that."[33]

He left the name at which the world grew pale
To point a moral or adorn a tale.[34]

The first line is applicable to Hitler; the second is not.

"There is no argument,"George Orwell once wrote, "by which one can defend a poem. It defends itself by surviving, or it is indefensible."[35] So we judge achievements by their consequences. And what were the consequences of Hitler?

His war (and World War II was *his* war) ended with the greatest catastrophe for the German and also for the Central and Eastern European peoples—for the latter, because the Russian occupation and the subsequent Communist rule in that part of Europe was the consequence of that war. A consequence of the war was the division of Germany, which lasted for more than forty years, with mass expulsions from the east and protracted sufferings for the German people in the so-called "German Democratic Republic." A more enduring consequence was the drastic reduction of Germany in the east: the entire loss of East Prussia, together with other substantial portions of the former Prussia, Silesia, Saxony to Poland (and, in the case of the Königsberg enclave, to Russia). Even more enduring: the almost complete elimination of the presence of ethnic Germans from countries in Eastern Europe where some of their ancestors had lived for eight hundred years.

The year 1945 marked, too, the end of the predominance—political, cultural, intellectual—of Europe in the world, the end of the European age, and the end of the European state system.[36] There was something else, too: the end of the predominance of German intellectual influence in the world. For what had happened, for about seventy years after 1870, was not only that the practices and standards of German education and learning had influenced and were adopted in many places of Europe and of the world, including nations that were opponents of Germany in the two world wars. Something had begun after the French Revolution: a romantic (and often sentimental and categorical) idealism, reacting against the materialism (and often against the rationalism) of the Enlightenment. This most important and potentially fruitful intellectual achievement—a great chapter in the history of the European mind—was mostly represented and exemplified by Germans; and then it was carried by some of them to extremes, to a deterministic idealism that proved to be more inhumane than the deterministic materialism that had preceded and (lamentably) survived it—at least for a while.[37] And an incarnation of an unstinting belief in a determinist idealism was Adolf Hitler.[38]

The English historian of religion Owen Chadwick wrote: "The Reformation would have happened without Luther. But without Luther it would not have happened in the way it happened."[39] Four centuries later the same condition—*mutatis mutandis*—applies to nationalist socialism and Hitler. He was the greatest revolutionary of the twentieth century. That is not an approbatory adjective. "Great" may be applied to criminals or terrorists, too. (Also, one need not be a reactionary to sense, especially at the end of the twentieth century, that to designate someone as a Great Conservative may be even more approbatory—at least in the Western world—than the epithet of a Great Revolutionary.) In any event, what followed Hitler was our still-present era of no great wars and no great revolutions—something that he had not foreseen, though Tocqueville had.

What he had seen—and, more or less, accurately—was the formidable attraction of populist nationalism in the age of the masses. That nationalism proved to be the principal political reality in the twentieth century. He was its most extreme representative. He sensed that sometime after 1870 nationalism and socialism came to supersede the older nineteenth-century categories of conservatism and liberalism, indeed perhaps even of Right and Left; and that, of the two, nationalism was more influential than socialism. The categories of socialism and capitalism themselves began to be outdated, because strength was more powerful than wealth, because nationality was more powerful than class, because nationalism was more powerful than internationalism. When there was national unity, the formerly rigid categories of socialist and capitalist, public and private ownership began to leak; what mattered was not ownership but management; and ownership and management and labor would be ultimately obedient to the dictates of nationalism.

Hitler was not the founder of National Socialism, not even in Germany. Among the principal figures of the century, Mussolini was the first National Socialist who recognized, around 1911, that he was an Italian first and a socialist second—this eight years before his creation of "fascism." There were differences, not only in the practices but in the ideas, of Hitler's National Socialism and Mussolini's fascism. But that becomes inconsequential when we look at the reciprocal influences of the main dictators in the 1930s and 1940s: Mussolini, Stalin, and Hitler. That comparison of reciprocal influences—more precisely, of their development—ought to tell us something. Mussolini was not (and did not become) a Communist; Stalin was not (and did not become) a fascist; but both of them became influenced and impressed by Hitler's ideas and achievements to an extent that makes it both proper and precise to say that they became more and more nationalist socialists as time went on. That development (including their increasing inclination to anti-Semitism) ended with their deaths. So much for the war and the short run. But we must recognize that in the long run, too, in one sense Hitler's vision survived him. During the twentieth century the compound of nationalism with socialism has become the nearly universal practice for all states in the world. International socialism is a mirage. At the same time every state in the world has become a welfare state of sorts. Whether they call themselves socialist or not does not matter much. Hitler knew that. The economic structure of Germany that he had in mind had few of the characteristics of either Marxian or state socialism, but it could not be called capitalist, either. Fifty years later it cannot be denied that nationalism remains the most potent force in the world. We are all national socialists now. Of course, the proportions of the compound of nationalism and socialism vary from country to country; but the compound is there, and even where social democracy prevails it is the national feeling of people that matters. What was defeated in 1945, together with Hitler, was German National Socialism: a cruel and extreme version of nationalist socialism. Elsewhere nationalism and socialism were brought together, reconciled and then compounded, without remotely comparable violence, hatred, or war. But Hitler's nationalism was profoundly different from traditional patriotism, just as his socialism had few of the marks of the traditional philanthropy of the earlier socialists.[40]

To this the objection may be raised: After all, has not the appeal of communism long survived that of Hitler's National Socialism? Despite all the superficial evidence—examples: the surviving appeal of "Communist" parties in Russia and Eastern Europe, Chinese "communism," Castro in Cuba—the answer is no, for three reasons at least. The first is that the surge of communism that enveloped much of Eastern Europe after 1945 was not the result of popular revolutions but was simply the result of the presence of Russian armed forces in that part of Europe. The second is that the sporadic rise of Communist regimes in the oddest places of the so-called Third World—Cuba, Ethiopia, Angola, among others—was the obvious result of anticolonialism (and in Castro's case, of anti-Americanism) rather than of the appeal of communism as such or the example of the Soviet Union. The third reason, connected with the second, is that the present—and probably transitory—reappearance of Communist or pro-Stalinist parties, especially in Russia, is not only inseparable from but fundamentally bound to a resurgent and populist nationalism. If international socialism is a mirage, international communism does not even qualify as an optical illusion.

As Karl-Dietrich Bracher put it: "The kernel of the phenomenon of Hitler was a fundamental underestimation of [the attraction of] National Socialism"—that is, not only of Hitler but of the idea he seemed to represent.[41] And in this respect it behooves us to consider the corresponding, and perhaps ominous, statement by another German historian, Hagen Schulze, buried in the debates of the Historians' Controversy, about that important experience "in our history: that the constitutionalists of the first German republic had nothing effective to counter the enormous emotional appeal of the nationalists. Certainly the experience of the Third Reich has considerably dampened the German inclination to nationalistic extremes," but it is questionable "whether this kind of dampening will last more than one or two generations, despite all of the political pedagogy about the efficacy of which one should have no illusions."[42] Neither should we have illusions about the permanent constitutional validity of laws according to which in Germany the public display of the swastika and of pictures of Hitler remains forbidden forever. What we must hope for and trust is that when the time for the removal of such proscriptions comes, such a legal decision will reflect a climate in which the symbols of Hitler's era will attract nothing more than historical curiosity.[43]

That time is not yet; and now when the German state has become united, when the entire postwar period marked by fifty years of the so-called Cold War has unraveled, when the entire century is ending, let us conclude with an attempt to identify—identify, rather than define—Hitler's place in the history of it.

The twentieth century—historically speaking—was a short century. Whereas the historical eighteenth century lasted 126 years (from 1688 to 1815), marked by the world wars principally between England and France; and the nineteenth century lasted ninety-nine years (from 1815 to 1914), marked by the absence of world wars; the twentieth century lasted seventy-five years (from 1914 to 1989), marked by the two world wars and by their consequence—the so-called Cold War between America and Russia. It ended in 1989, with the withdrawal of Russia from Eastern Europe and the reunification of Germany. The crucial period of this—transitional—century (marking the passage from the so-called Modern Age into something else) was its early one-third (1920 to 1945) in which, of course, the career of Hitler belongs.[44] During this period—again contrary to the popular and mistaken impression about the importance of the Russian Revolution in 1917—the history of the world (and not only of Germany or of Europe) was marked by the existence and the competition of a triangle of forces. There was parliamentary democracy, incarnated principally by the English-speaking nations, by the states of Western Europe, and Scandinavia. There was communism, represented only by Soviet Russia, incapable of assuming power elsewhere. And there was National Socialism (and also other, to some extent similar but by no means identical, nationalist movements) in Germany, after 1933 incarnated by Hitler and the Third Reich, which proved to be so powerful that it took the unnatural and temporary alliance of liberal democracy and Russian communism, of the English-speaking and the Russian empires, to defeat and conquer it. Neither side could do it alone.

That by itself identifies Hitler's place within the history of the twentieth century. But there was even more to it. This triangle, represented by liberal-conservative-democratic people, and by Communists and radical nationalists, repeated itself in every country in Europe, and in almost every country of the world—including the United States, South America, China, and Japan. (In 1945, the radical nationalists were silenced or subdued—temporarily. Later their successors reappeared again.) Not all of the radical nationalists were followers or admirers of Hitler, though many of them were.[45] Schramm wrote that we cannot ignore the fact that Hitler represents a key phenomenon in the history of Germany in the twentieth century, but not only in the history of Germany.[46]

The German term *Ortsbestimmung* is defined as "position-finding" in a dictionary sense; but it is a word often used by German historians, meaning the definition of a place in history, and suggesting that while historical judgments of an event or person may vary, the *place* of the events or persons within the sequence of history is—eventually—ascertainable. In this respect Schreiber's relatively recent conclusion is still valid: "The place of the National Socialist period in history [*die historische Ortsbestimmung*] still remains a desideratum of further research."[47] But is the problem still that of "research"? Perhaps—even though there is reason to believe that no more important, or even significant, documents by or about Hitler will come to light. But then history does not only consist of documents.

Allow me now, at the risk of presumption, to sum up three long-range considerations: (a) about a necessary Christian view of Adolf Hitler; (b) about his place in the culture-civilization antithesis; and (c) about his place at the end of the so-called Modern Age.

On June 2, 1945, hardly a month after Hitler's suicide, Pope Pius XII spoke before the College of Cardinals about "the satanic apparition [*Gespenst:* ghost, apparition] of National Socialism." With all respect due to this much, and sometimes unjustly, criticized Pope, I am inclined to agree with Friedrich Heer: "Again this is being metaphysical, removing something from history and from the responsibility for history, acquitting Catholics of their responsibilities. For a 'satanic apparition' no one is responsible—at best, an exorcist. ... The Pope overlooks entirely that this 'satanic apparition' was a very concrete human incarnation who, before all in the Munich so loved by the Pope but also elsewhere, was promoted and helped into power by very responsible and notable men. ..."[48] In the first chapter of this book I wrote that Hitler represented many half-truths; and that a half-truth is not only more dangerous but worse than a lie, because human acts and expressions are not frozen into mathematical categories: hence a half-truth is not a 50 percent truth but something else. To this let me add La Rochefoucauld's great maxim: "There are evil men in this world who would be less dangerous if they had not something good about them."[49] Let me repeat: Does this mean that Hitler was "only" "50 percent bad"? No. It was not only that he had great talents given to him by God which he used for evil purposes, whence his responsibility; it is also that his evil characteristics were spiritual. In this day and age it is unfashionable to cite great Fathers of the Church; but it was St. Thomas who wrote about a half-truth being worse than a lie; and allow me now to bring up St. Augustine, who wrote that "whatsoever things are, are good," while evil is spiritual, because it is part of the human condition. What this means is not only that the sins of the spirit are worse than those of the flesh but that the two are inseparable; that there are no sins of the flesh without their—preceding as well as simultaneous—sins of the spirit.[50]

Another consideration—because, but only partly because, of Hitler—may be the originally German, but by now worldwide, accepted notion of the superior nature of Culture over Civilization. Civilization is essentially material and bourgeois; culture is spiritual and creative. Civilization, at best, is marked by a security and a solid social order, at worst, it is hypocritical and philistine. The origins of this idea go back to the nineteenth century, but it was something that appealed to Germans and then to a class of people, intellectuals, worldwide, and then it was loudly asserted and categorically hammered down by Oswald Spengler. For intellectuals, culture follows or, rather, rises beyond civilization: from Babbitt's Zenith, U.S.A., to places like Greenwich Village, or from Belgravia to Bloomsbury. For Spengler the direction is the reverse, from a youthful culture to an ossified civilization.[51] It was something Hitler believed in. Germans and Aryans, to him and his followers, were more than the supreme custodians of culture. "True art is and remains eternal," he said on one occasion. "It does not follow the law of fashion; its effect is that of a revelation arising from the depths of the essential character of a people."[52] Besides his, here again expressed, belief in populism (rather than in refinement) we cannot deny that Hitler was both a proponent and promoter of art and of "Kultur"; but was he a champion of civilization? Not at all. As a matter of fact, he was its enemy. This is not the place to discuss the origins and development of the two terms, except to note that the Greeks had no word for culture, whereas they and the Romans were the founders of our still-extant urbane notions of a civilization; and—more important—that "civilization," as *we* know it, is a concept and a product of the last four hundred years. In English, "civilization" first appeared in 1601 and was defined as the antithesis of "barbarism."

I hope that my readers will allow this brief summary disquisition, if for no other reason than the existence of a recognizable condition: at the time of this writing, fifty or more years after Hitler took his own life, we in the Western world are threatened not by an endangerment of "culture" but by grave dangers to civilization.[53] Let me repeat: The kind of civilization that we still know was the product of the so-called Modern Age. The term "Modern" is both unhistorical and imprecise, suggesting that this "modern" age would last forever.[54] It would be more accurate to name the last five hundred years the Bourgeois Age, characterized as it was by the coexistence of aristocracies and bourgeois, and with the gradual and uneasy rise of the latter. That Hitler was the enemy of almost everything that was "bourgeois" needs no further explanation.[55] He belongs to the end of an age, and he was defeated, and—for a while—bourgeois civilization has been restored, at least in Western Europe and West Germany. But if Western civilization melts away, threatening to collapse, two dangers lie in the future. During a rising flood of barbarism his reputation may rise in the eyes of orderly people, who may regard him as a kind of Diocletian, a tough last architect of an imperial order. At the same time he might be revered by at least some of the New Barbarians. But this book is the work of a historian, not of a prophet.

56

The Poverty of Anticommunism
(1999)

The basic statement of American anticommunism, as well as the basic conception of the Cold War, is the one expressed by William Buckley Jr., who got it from James Burnham. I quote: "In 1917 history changed gears." Apart from the weirdness of such a mechanical metaphor— as if history were an automobile—the meaning of it is that the Russian Communist Revolution was *the* principal and decisive event of this century, which thereafter was marked by the struggle between International Communism and the Free World (whatever *that* is). There are few statements about the history of the world of which one may say that they are complete nonsense. This is one of them.

The principal event of the twentieth century—which was a short century, lasting seventy-five years, from 1914 to 1989—was the outbreak of the First World War in 1914. I need not expatiate what this catastrophe meant for Western civilization. The First World War led to the Second World War, and the Second World War to the Cold War. The two world wars were the two enormous mountain ranges in the shadows of which we lived until 1989.

The Russian Communist Revolution in 1917 occurred during the First World War. This alone ought to reduce its historical importance. Unlike the French Revolution, which had spread across Western Europe, and which then led to a quarter century of great wars, the Russian Revolution was one consequence of a war then current, not the cause of it. Again, unlike the French and American Revolutions, the Russian one did not spread anywhere. Indeed, until 1945 the Soviet Union was the *only* Communist state in the world. Also, communism in Russia could survive only at the price of the very retreat and diminution of Russia itself. From 1917 to 1920 five new states—Finland, Estonia, Latvia, Lithuania, Poland—broke off from

From *National Interest,* Spring: 75–82.

Russia. They were determinedly anticommunist ones—again, the very opposite of what had happened after the French Revolution.

Lenin thought and said that the location of the first Communist revolution in Russia was an accident, that further revolutions would very soon occur across Europe, and especially in Germany (he is waiting still in his unquiet grave). Lenin was a revolutionary, and a statesman not at all (Stalin turned out to be the opposite). Had the first communist regime been established in Germany, its influence would have been immeasurably greater: because of German discipline, German energy, German organization, and German reputation. The fact that communism was incarnated in backward and semi-barbaric Russia was fatal to its reputation—except for conventicles of intellectuals and wannabe "revolutionaries" elsewhere in the world.

During the quarter century after 1920, there were three great forces in the world. They were not only apparent on the political map but repeated within almost every nation of the globe, even in Asia and in the Americas, where each of the three ideologies had its partisans and its opponents. There was Western parliamentary democracy, incarnated by the English-speaking peoples and in Scandinavia and Western Europe. There was communism, incarnated, I repeat, solely in Soviet Russia. And there was a new force, anticommunist and nationalist socialism, incarnated in many places in the world but most forcefully in the Third Reich of Germany. Of these three forces, communism, in spite of its assertion of being international, was the weakest, while national socialism was the strongest. Eventually this became evident in the Second World War. To defeat the German Third Reich, the in many ways unnatural coalition of Communists and capitalists, of Russia and the English-speaking democracies, was needed. Neither of them could do it without the other. The Russians could not have conquered Germany without the Anglo-Americans, and the Anglo-Americans—in spite of their tremendous superiority in manpower and material resources—would not have been able to conquer Germany by themselves. That alone should give us pause to think; but, then, this is not the main argument of this essay.

I move on now to the history of the Cold War (the coming of which Hitler had predicted but which came, fortunately, too late for him). If there is a key document for the evolution of the Cold War it is not Stalin's speech in February 1946, nor Churchill's Fulton speech about the Iron Curtain a month later, nor Yalta or Potsdam or Tehran. It is Churchill's statement to de Gaulle in November 1944 (recounted, incidentally, not in the former's but in the latter's war memoirs). After the liberation of Paris, Churchill had come to visit de Gaulle. The Frenchman tried to wean him away from the special Anglo-American alliance, but in vain. Among other things, de Gaulle said: Look at the Americans. They are inexperienced. They are letting half of Europe go to the Russians, without thinking much about it. Churchill responded, "Yes, Russia is now a hungry wolf amidst a flock of sheep. But after the meal comes the digestion period." As early as 1940 Churchill saw that in that war there were only two alternatives: either Germany would dominate all of Europe or Russia would dominate—temporarily—the eastern part of it; and one-half of Europe (especially the western half) was better than none. After the war would come the digestion period; and the Russians would not be able to digest their East European conquests.

And so it was to be. And how soon these digestion problems appeared! In 1948 Tito's Yugoslavia broke off from Stalin's empire. In 1949 Stalin thought it best to put an end to his—partial—blockade of West Berlin. In 1950 his prudence and caution dictated that he give no support to the North Koreans, requesting the Chinese do that instead. The result was this; before 1950 North Korea had been largely a Russian satellite; by 1952 it had become a Chinese one. In 1952 Stalin (and his successors through 1953) was seriously considering the ditching of the East German Communist state, in exchange for an establishment of a "neutral"—that is, not American-allied—united German state. In 1954 the Russians agreed to retreat from Austria, and they gave up their privileges and ports and bases in eastern China. In 1955 they abandoned their naval base in Finland. In 1956 came the Hungarian and Polish revolutions. In 1958 their quarrel with China became public. In 1959 Khrushchev came to the United States, hoping among other things to get American support in his developing conflict with Communist China—in vain. In 1961 the drain of people fleeing from Communist East Germany had become so dangerous that its regime was forced to close up East from West Berlin by a wall.

In 1962 came the Cuban Missile Crisis, from the beginning to the end of which it was (or rather, should have been) evident that the Russians would not risk anything like a war for the sake of Cuba (just as in 1956, all anti-communist rhetoric notwithstanding, the United States did not for a moment consider a war for the sake of Hungary). Indeed, the foreign policy of the United States was not only content with the existing division of Europe and of Germany and of Berlin, but would do nothing to risk upsetting it. As for the Vietnam War, Russian policy was similar to their Korean one: do little or nothing, don't risk anything.

Now the interesting—and, at least in some ways, lamentable—thing to notice is that the highest tide of American anticommunism (which many people at the time equated with American patriotism), the highest peaks of American military and nuclear preparations, the greatest burgeoning of an American military-industrial state, occurred precisely in those periods when the Soviet Union was in retreat: in the 1950s in the Eisenhower years, and again in the 1980s during the Reagan era, propelled by the ideology of anticommunism. In the latter period the Russians gave up communism and their East European empire and their presence in Germany and Berlin; and not because Reagan forced the Soviet Union into bankruptcy but because no one believed in communism any longer—something that, with all of its fabulous intelligence apparatus, even the CIA was unable to foresee, as indeed was admitted when it came to the demolition of the Berlin Wall.

But then this article is not meant to be a one-sided or potted summary of the Cold War. Its purpose is to argue the yawning failures of the ideology of anticommunism. So let me close this portion of it with what I think is a trenchant observation. In 1945 *many thousands* of Germans committed suicide. Many of those who killed themselves were not National Socialist party leaders, some of them not even party members, but all of them believers. But I know not of a single instance, in or around 1989, when a believing Communist committed suicide because of the collapse of communism, in Russia or elsewhere.[1] Dogmatic believers in communism had ceased to exist long before, even as dogmatic anticommunists continued to flourish.

One argument that may be raised against the historical overview I have sketched is that, in the United States at least, Communists were more influential in the interwar period than were American pro-fascists or pro-Nazis. This, too, may be arguable: for it can be said that in the 1930s Franklin Roosevelt's most dangerous popular challengers came from the Right, not from the Left: from Huey Long and Father Coughlin, for example. Still, the influence and the intellectual appeal of communism in America *was* considerable, an influence that spread well beyond the limited number of American Communists. Again there is one statement that sums up the matter succinctly and precisely—a sentence in the first volume of George Kennan's *Memoirs*:

> The penetration of the American governmental services by members or agents (conscious or otherwise) of the American Communist Party in the 1930s was not a figment of the imagination. It really existed: and it assumed proportions which, while never overwhelming, were also not trivial.

There is no need to rehearse the history of the CPUSA during the crucial second quarter of the twentieth century. There exists a sufficiency of serious studies about the topic, including the sociology—more precisely, the sociography—of immigrant and native American Communists. But, again, there is a written passage (ignored by the authors of the aforementioned studies) that I find especially telling. It is germane to the history of the 1930s, when some American Communists and Communist sympathizers succeeded in advancing themselves to certain governmental and bureaucratic positions in which they were no longer mere members of a revolutionary and largely uninfluential fringe group. The author of this passage is Edmund Wilson, who, like many other American intellectuals, had not been at all intelligent, or even perceptive, about what communism meant. (In 1935, after a journey to Russia in the midst of Stalin's purges, he wrote that while there he had been "at the moral top of the world.") But in 1953, in his new foreword to the paperback edition of his 1929 novel, *I Thought of Daisy*, he wrote:

> Some time in the late thirties, at the time when . . . [the Soviets were] coming to seem respectable and Communism a passport to power in an impending international bureaucracy, I thought of doing a brief sequel to *Daisy*, in which some Washington official would be giving himself a sense of importance and enjoying a good deal of excitement through an underground connection with the Communists. . . . [Their] set would go on drinking, playing bridge and making passes at one another's girls with the conviction that these activities had been given a new dignity by being used to cover up operations which would eventually prove world-shaking and land them somehow at the top of the heap.

I consider this passage to be the best, and most perceptive, description of a certain kind of American Communist agent—to wit, the Alger Hiss type. In certain positions, and in certain circumstances, their influences, as Kennan put it, were "never overwhelming" but "also not trivial." They were able to do harm. Still, marked by their fateful immaturity, most of these people were playing at spying—not unlike most of the "revolutionaries" of the 1960s, who were only playing at being revolutionaries.

This should also reduce—or at least qualify—the importance of the recent "revelatory" documents from Moscow. In the first place, an agent must make work for himself, to prove that he is doing his job well. This was particularly true of members of the Soviet secret services when they reported that they had succeeded in recruiting X or Y, and when they listed others as "agents"—which, in many cases, was a vast exaggeration. (In the same way, many of the victims of the internal Soviet purges in the 1930s were the victims of overzealous secret policemen.) In the second place, at least in the 1930s, the materials their American collaborators provided to their Soviet contacts were not always valuable, for example the few pieces that Alger Hiss seems to have typed and given to his Soviet "drop" in 1938. I never doubted that Hiss was one of these sorry birds; but looking at some of these "documents" with the eye of a diplomatic historian, I found them of little or no value whatsoever. But then consider what every experienced historian knows (or at least ought to know), which is that documents do not make history, but rather it is history that makes documents: who wrote them and when and why and how? intended for what and for whom?

However, as I have said, a fair amount of harm *was* done: perhaps less by the passing of American state or nuclear secrets to the Soviets than by the protracted influence of Communist sympathizers in American publishing, as well as other academic and opinion-forming activities in the 1940s. While on the one hand we have the new revelations of Moscow documents (sometimes of questionable value), we also have the special pleading of nostalgic reminiscences about American Communists under siege in the climate around 1950—as for example in Philip Roth's recent novel, *I Married a Communist,* or the protracted attempts at a rehabilitation of the Rosenbergs. I have no sympathy for such views and arguments, for the simple reason that, at the latest by 1945, those American Communists and their sympathizers ought to have known better. By that time there was enough evidence about the brutalities of Stalin and of Communists, not only in Russia but in many other places of the world. Factual accounts of such conditions, acts, and events were available in a great variety of books and articles, there for anyone who could read. Yet many thousands of Communists and their sympathizers refused to give them a thought. And here we meet with what seems to be the most essential weakness of the human mind, leading straight to a corruption of character, something that has nothing to do with Intelligence Quotients or with functions of the brain: for it involves not an inability to think about certain matters, but an unwillingness to do so.

In June 1848, less than a year after Marx had written his *Communist Manifesto,* Alexis de Tocqueville walked across a Paris in the throes of the first "Red" revolution in history. Here and there he talked with the troops of General Cavaignac, gathering before the barricades. The Russian émigré Alexander Herzen (hero of many liberals ever since, including Isaiah Berlin) wrote that he despised Tocqueville for that. Yet it was the same Tocqueville who soon saw that the new danger for France and freedom was the popularity of anticommunism, leading to the dictatorship of Louis Napoleon. "The insane fear of socialism," Tocqueville wrote in 1852, "throws the bourgeois headlong into the arms of despotism. . . . But now that the weakness of the Red party has been proved, people will regret the price at which their enemy has been put down."

"In this sense," I wrote in 1959, "I do not hesitate to say that Tocqueville was an anti-anticommunist."[2] And so am I. Allow me to sum this up as briefly as I can. There are variations of anti-anticommunism. There are those anti-anticommunists who convince themselves that all enemies of freedom are to be found on their Right and not on the Left: their colors are, plainly, pink. And there is another kind of anti-anticommunist who has no sympathy for communism but who is appalled by the errors and dishonesties of anticommunist ideology and of its propagation. (Such a posture does not necessarily imply moderation; "moderation in everything, including moderation.") Mathematically thinking, of course, an anti-anticommunist is a procommunist. But we neither speak nor think mathematically. "Numbers," said Kierkegaard, "are a negation of truth."

There are variations of anticommunism too. Again, as with many documents, they depend on the *when* and the *where* and the *how*. I have nothing but admiration for the slightest evidences of courageous anticommunist acts or words in Stalinist Russia; or under whatever Communist regime; or even within Communist parties or procommunist conventicles anywhere in the world. But I have hardly more than contempt for those who think it best to adopt anticommunism as an ideology when that is not only safe, but popular and even profitable for themselves.

Of course, this tendency is apparent not merely among intellectuals but among statesmen. Churchill and Hitler were both anticommunists, even as both of them recognized that the dominant impulse of the century was nationalism, not communism. Both knew that Stalin was much more of a Russian nationalist than an international Communist. But Churchill would, on occasion, publicly say so, while Hitler never would. What Hitler recognized was the popular respectability of anticommunism—among "conservatives" but also among the working classes. (The wish for respectability among the masses was one of the many things that Marx had completely failed to recognize.) It was the respectability of Hitler's anticommunism— not the respectability of his anti-Semitism—that brought him to power in Germany. In November 1932 he said to President Hindenburg, "The Bolshevization of the masses proceeds rapidly." He knew that this was not true; but he also knew that this kind of argument would impress Hindenburg and the German conservatives. Less than three months later they installed him in power.

Another eight months on he said, "The Red revolt could have spread across Germany like wildfire. . . . We have been waging a heroic struggle against the communist threat." This at a time when the Communists in Germany had been annihilated, with their leaders in prison or in exile. To Germany's Catholic bishops he said, "The defense of Europe against Bolshevism is our task for the next two or three hundred years." That was the argument that inclined many (though not all) European, British, and American conservatives not to oppose Hitler. In 1941 Archbishop (later Cardinal) von Galen spoke out openly from the pulpit of his church against the Nazi policy of euthanasia, a rare and perhaps unique public statement of opposition during the entire history of Hitler's Reich. Hitler thought it best not to move against or to restrain Galen, for in the same speech Galen had welcomed the German invasion of Russia, that crusade against atheistic Bolshevism. (And he did not say a word about the German persecution and murdering of Jews.) There, in a nutshell, we may find the essence of the Germans' tragedy.

In the history of the United States, too, the ideology of anticommunism long predates the Second World War, not to speak of the Cold War. As early as 1854, George Fitzhugh, an intellectual defender of the South, wrote that the enemies of the Southern order were "communists." The history of the first Red Scare in 1919–21 is well known. Less well known are the statements of members of Coolidge's cabinet, including the otherwise moderate Secretary of State Frank B. Kellogg, to the effect that the troubles in Mexico in the 1920s, and in Nicaragua, were due to "Bolsheviks." In December 1941, three days before Pearl Harbor, Senator Robert A. Taft (a hero of many of today's conservatives) proclaimed that while "fascism" only appealed to a few, communism was a much greater danger because it appealed to many. (This when Hitler's armies stood fifteen miles from Moscow.)

Between 1947 and 1955 the Second Red Scare—admittedly, with more justification than the first—swelled into an oceanic tide, leading to the entire identification of anticommunism with American patriotism. We need not list its many excesses here, except to note two matters. One is that the ideological vision of international communism obscured and compromised the very perceptions, and the conduct, of American foreign policy. The other is the then contemporaneous emergence of an American conservative movement, the composition and ideology of which was as anticommunist as it was anti-liberal. Men and women who had been isolationists but a few years before now became extreme internationalists, arguing not only for the containment but for the conquest of the Soviet Union.

The consequences of this mutation of the political and ideological climate were considerable. They included the opportunism of President Eisenhower, who in 1945 had chosen to reject Churchill when it came to Anglo-American political and military strategy in Central Europe, preferring to approach Stalin directly instead. Less than eight years later, the same Eisenhower refused Churchill again (privately referring to him as

senile and naïve) when the English leader proposed an attempt to negoti-
ate a revision of the division of Europe with the Soviet leadership, after
Stalin's death. Or there was Henry Luce's *Life* magazine, which in 1942
printed a full-page photograph of Lenin with the caption: "This was perhaps the greatest man of the century." Nine years later it editorialized that
while communism was a Mortal Sin, McCarthyism was but a Venial one.
The ultimate beneficiary of this ideological revolution was of course Ronald
Reagan in the 1980s—when, for the first time in American history, more
Americans identified themselves as "conservatives" than as "liberals."

And, as so often, intellectuals were quick in climbing onto the bandwagon. There was Hannah Arendt, in her *Origins of Totalitarianism* (1951), a
flawed and fraudulent book from beginning to end. Flawed, because her
analysis of "totalitarianism" was nonsense; fraudulent, because, after her
manuscript had been rejected by publisher after publisher, she quickly added
two chapters about Stalin at the end.

Whittaker Chambers, who deserves our sympathy, was not fraudulent;
but he certainly was wrong in attributing to international communism the
ability to engineer "mankind's decisive transformation . . . about to close its
2,000-year experience of Christian civilization." Of course, these were the
inclinations of an honest man to attribute all of the evils of the world to the
wrong from which he had, after great inner troubles, escaped. Still, both
Chambers' sense of proportion *and* his perspective of history were flawed.

Some of the shrillest prophets of anticommunism in the "conservative"
camp (Chambers did not identify himself as "conservative") were former
Communists or Trotskyites. Then in the late 1960s, the wave of neoconservatism arose—composed mostly of men and women for whom it had
taken fifty years to discover that the Russians were anti-Semitic. Since then,
all of the dishonest and imbecile Revisionists and Revolutionaries of the
1960s notwithstanding, and all of the lamentable presence of Political Correctness in American universities notwithstanding, the influence of these
so-called neoconservatives has become more and more evident, and in certain areas of public discourse even prominent. Are they more honest, or
better, than the pinkish Lib-Lab intellectuals of the twenties and the thirties? In some instances, perhaps yes; generally, alas, no.

"Totalitarianism," as understood by Hannah Arendt, had certain recognizable general characteristics. First, all totalitarians tended to be anti-
Semitic. Second, totalitarians aimed at the conquest of the entire globe.
Third, totalitarian rule was bound to become not only broader but stricter
and stricter as time went on. A mere few years after her magnum opus
appeared, events proved that all of this was nonsense. Was Castro, or Pol
Pot, or Ho Chi Minh anti-Semitic? Was Khrushchev an even greater tyrant

than Stalin? All of this in no way harmed her reputation, but that is not the point. "Totalitarianism," not only to Hannah Arendt, but to libertarians and to all kinds of conservatives, means the overall power of the state. But look at Russia now, when the danger is the exact opposite: the weakness, not the power, of the state.

We have experienced a phenomenon unparalleled in history, and there are not many things unparalleled in history: a great empire giving up its possessions—without external pressure, and without a bloody revolution in its midst. By the 1980s the only people who believed in the existence of international communism—though there were, alas, still many of them— were the conservatives and neoconservatives and their plethora of time-servers in Reagan's administrations. Compared to them the number of believers in communism in Russia, or in the Communist states of Eastern Europe, were a minuscule remnant. And now we have the promoters of wild capitalism in Russia, Harvard savants such as Jeffrey Sachs—a successor of another Harvard illusionist eighty years ago, the then celebrated John Reed. It is at least possible that the consequences of the Ten Days That Shook The World may have been nothing compared to the consequences of the Ten Years That Are Now Shaking Russia.

I fled my native country in 1946, fifty-three years ago, when I knew that sooner rather than later it would fall under Communist rule. But I did so not because communism was strong, nor because communism was the ideology taken up by masses of my people. On the contrary: communism was unappealing; it was antiquated; it was unpopular, except with a few. The reality was the presence of Russian armed forces, not communism; and that, I believed, would stay in my part of Europe for a long time, perhaps fifty years. (I was ten years off, thank God.) This distinction between Russian armed power and the ideology of communism was something that many Americans did not comprehend—or perhaps did not wish to comprehend—or, perhaps more precisely, were made not to comprehend by politicians, ideologues, and propagandists of all kinds.[3] To illustrate this would take an entire volume, and not a small one. Alas, the history—including the psychology—of anticommunism is yet to be written.

57

The Problem of American Conservatism
(1984)

$\mathcal{O}$f the three political adjectives, "conservative," "liberal," "radical," only the last is ancient and English. The political usage of "conservative" and "liberal" derives from France and from Spain. They were not applied to politics in the English-speaking nations before about 1825— that is, fifty years after the American Revolution. Of course there were conservatively inclined people within the new nation, including not only Loyalists but men among the founding fathers; but while we must recognize their existence, it would be wrong to invest them with the categorical label of "conservative." After all, even Burke was a Whig, not a Tory; and there were enough radical elements in John Adams's vision of the world to keep us from designating him as a conservative, *pur et simple.* But it remained for Tocqueville to recognize, and explain, that many of the institutions and the character of society and public opinion in the American democracy were neither radical nor revolutionary—which was what conservatives and even certain liberals in Europe at the time had feared.

This does not mean that American institutions or the American national temper is altogether conservative. It means that conservative tendencies of American democracy existed from its very beginning. It also means that American conservatism differed even more from European conservatism than American radicalism differed from European radicalism, something that went back to the very psychic origins of American consciousness.[1] Scratch the American conservative and you'll often find a radical of sorts. That the South was more conservative than was the North is fairly obvious; but the conservatism of its few political theorists had a radical tinge. (Fifteen years before the publication of the first volume of *Das Kapital* in 1867, George Fitzhugh, one of the few southern political theo-

From *Outgrowing Democracy: A History of the United States in the Twentieth Century* (Garden City, NY: Doubleday), 327–41.

rists, wrote that slavery was "the only political alternative to worldwide communism.") The radical strain was there within the Federalists, who around 1800 ranted and raved in favor of "real Americanism" (by which, of course, they meant federalism). That component of radicalism was there within the conservatism of the otherwise humble Abraham Lincoln, who spoke in Cincinnati shortly before his election in 1860: "The good old maxims of the Bible are applicable, and truly applicable, to human affairs, and in this, as in other things, we may say here that he who is not for us is against us; he who gathereth not with us scattereth"—an argument identical with that employed by Joseph McCarthy a century later, arrogating to himself the power and the glory of Christ. Still, Richard Weaver, an early intellectual apostle of the American conservative movement in the mid-twentieth century, called Lincoln "a Conservative in the legitimate sense of the word. It is no accident that Lincoln became the founder of the greatest American conservative party, even if that party was debauched soon after his career ended. He did so because his method was that of the conservative." Yet the Republicans began as a radical party, "an assemblage of Whigs, Abolitionists, Know-Nothings, Sore-heads and fag-ends."[2] The English conservative historian Lord Acton called the New England Republicans, and particularly their chief, William Henry Seward, dangerous radicals. Wendell Phillips, the prophet of Republican abolitionism, said in 1871 that "there is no hope for France but in the Reds," since the Communards were "the foremost, purest, and the noblest patriots of France." Yet during the presidency of Benjamin Harrison the American ambassador to France joined the British ambassador in disassociating himself from the one-hundredth-anniversary celebrations of the French Revolution, in 1889. There was a conservative strain within the Republicans' populist opponents too: a man such as William Jennings Bryan may have been radical in his domestic politics while he was a religious conservative. A parochial conservatism and a populist radicalism coexisted in Henry Ford's mind. The Populist Ignatius Donnelly in *The Golden Bottle* foretold the coming of universal peace through the establishment of literacy in Russia and through world government—a forerunner of Woodrow Wilson's beliefs.

My purpose in this scatteration of paradoxical examples was to illustrate the frequent coexistence of conservatism with radicalism in the same minds. Yet thirty years ago Professor Louis B. Hartz of Harvard, in *The Liberal Tradition in America* (1955), argued that the liberal tradition *was* the American tradition. This was one of those bland Harvardian works which, to paraphrase Wilde, pursue the obvious with the enthusiasm of a short-sighted detective: but in one important sense Hartz was right. Even though the political meaning of "liberal" came in the 1820s, the liberal vision of the world came from the eighteenth century. That vision was *the* dominant vision of the modern age: the vision that society was perfectible, that there was no such thing as original sin, that it was within the power of man (and especially of the New Man) to transform the world: a vision which, with all of its then merits and with its optimistic progressivism, was essentially antihistorical, or at least ahistorical. Against it arose the recognition of history by a thinker such as Burke, who was not behind but ahead of Paine, just as fifty years later Tocqueville was not behind but ahead of Marx. For Burke was not merely a defender of tradition: he recognized and expressed the inevitability of the historical dimension of human nature, something that not many Americans were willing to accept. In a broad sense, the liberal vision was the dominant American vision, propounded by Jefferson as well as by Paine. Until now—because the most important event in the recent history of the American people is that the liberal dogma of linear and evolutionary progress is no longer shared by many Americans.

It is noteworthy that Hartz's book was published at the very time when the American conservative movement had begun to crystallize. Hartz composed his book during the McCarthy era, when a powerful wave of antiliberalism seemed to overwhelm, at least temporarily, American popular sentiment. Yet as late as 1955 few Americans would accept the designation "conservative," while twenty-three years later opinion polls (whatever their limitations) showed that more Americans preferred to designate themselves as conservatives than as liberals. But perhaps even more important than these semantic preferences is the condition that most of the principal figures of that American conservative movement, which from 1955 to 1980 had grown to the extent that it helped to propel Ronald Reagan into the White House, have not only shared but espoused the originally Jeffersonian and Painean ideas of progress and modernism and American exceptionalism—at the expense of the kind of historical understanding that had been enunciated by Burke.

In any event, it is historical development, rather than abstract ideological analysis, that tells us something of the character of a political movement, as indeed of the character of a man.

The antithesis between liberalism and conservatism was typical not of America but of Europe; and it was typical not of the twentieth century but of the century before 1870. Thereafter this antithesis was superseded by the newer, and more universal, relationship of nationalism and socialism. I write "more universal" because during the twentieth century these realities have applied to American politics too, the difference between Republicans and Democrats being that Republicans, by and large, have been more nationalistic than socialistic, whereas Democrats have been, by and large, more socialistic than nationalistic—a difference which is also applicable to the modern American "conservative" and to the American twentieth-century "liberal." Because of the general acceptance of the practice of the welfare state during the twentieth century (in this the differences between Republicans and Democrats, and between "conservatives" and "liberals," were differences of degree, not of kind), the development of various nationalisms have been generally more interesting and significant than the development of various socialisms—a worldwide phenomenon from which the United States was not exempt.

In the United States during the first half of this century a division, at times amounting to a chasm, came into visible existence, a division which temporarily corresponded to that between conservatives and liberals. This was the division between American isolationists (who could be more accurately called American nationalists) and American internationalists. The differences between them went deeper than disagreements about domestic politics, deeper even than arguments about foreign policies. They involved different ideas and different sentiments about the destiny and the character of American nationhood and of American civilization.

There was, in this division, a great and perhaps even profound similarity between Americans and Russians. The American division between internationalists and isolationists corresponded to the Russian division between their "Westernizers" and "Slavophiles." The Russian Westernizers were those who believed that Russia had to come closer to Europe, that she had to become more progressive, more cosmopolitan, more liberal, less Asian, and more European. The Russian Slavophiles were orthodox nationalists, often isolationist and expansionist, conservative and messianic at the same time: Europe was decadent, while Russia had her unique destiny; she was the greatest and most Christlike nation in the world. Thus the difference between Westernizers and Slavophiles involved more than advocacies of different domestic and even foreign policies; it was ideological and cultural. Among Americans, too, the division was less political than it was geographical and ideological and cultural, with religious undertones. It was a division between two different geographical and historical views of American destiny, between those who believed that the advance of American civilization should bring the New and the Old World closer together, and those who believed that American civilization was meant to represent the opposite of that of the Old World. The national rhetoric of American exceptionalism produced plenty of believers who were suspicious of Europe: the United States had little to gain from a closer contact with Europe, and not much to learn from it.

The existence of a duality in the emotional relationships of Americans with the Old World was evident from the beginning, but we ought not indulge here in its psychoanalysis. Our interest must be directed to the pedigree of ideas. Most of the ideas that led to the first conscious appearance of a "conservative" political movement after 1950 were inseparable from the development of American isolationism—that is, from a peculiarly American form of nationalism—during the first half of this century.

American isolationism was a powerful factor during all of the Twenties and most of the Thirties, at the very time when in many ways—physically, financially, culturally—America and Europe were closer than they had been before. This division had existed for some time among American writers and artists too: between those who believed in American exceptionalism, moving away from and ahead of Europe, and those who believed that Americans should and finally could not avoid the realization that they shared the traditions of Europe, essentially the same problems and conundrums of human nature—the difference, say, between Mark Twain and Henry James. Somewhat later this division was dubbed, fairly successfully, as one between Redskins and Palefaces. That the formulator of these labels was an American intellectual of Russian birth (Philip Rahv) was perhaps not an accident.

Isolationists, nationalists, Redskins; internationalists, cosmopolitans, Palefaces: these categories are simple and often telling; but, as always in historical life, the human realities were more complex. Consistent isolationists and consistent internationalists were few. Many, if not most, of the isolationists were so only in regard to Europe; when it came to foreign policy they were often Asia-Firsters. The adoption and the advocacy of isolationism or of internationalism depended on the particular object, on the particular foreign nation. Many of the isolationists who were opposed to the American commitment to Britain and to the liberation of Western Europe from Hitler's Germany very soon became advocates of military commitments against Russia and of the liberation of Eastern Europe from communism. The reverse was also true: many liberal internationalists and enthusiastic advocates of the wartime American alliances after 1945 were opponents of American commitments restraining communism and Russia. Most American isolationists who believed in America for Americans also believed that what was good for America was good for the world: but wasn't that, in reality, a broad American version of internationalism? Most American internationalists believed that it was America's destiny to Make the World Safe for Democracy: but wasn't that, in reality, Americanism broadly applied unto the world? Scratch the American nationalist and you may find an American internationalist: scratch the American internationalist and you may find an American isolationist underneath—but then, as we have seen, much of the same thing applies, too, to American conservatives and American radicals.[3]

In sum, these terms of isolationist and internationalist are telling only inasmuch as they refer not to constant categories but to tendencies of American minds. A statement of human paradox may be entertaining: but, after all is said, human paradox is the result of the often inevitable primacy of life over theory. Here lie the roots of yet another similarity in Russian and American developments. In 1917 in Russia the triumph of the Westernizers over the Slavophiles seemed complete. Orthodoxy and Tsarism had collapsed; and the inheritors of the collapse were the Bolsheviks, who claimed to represent that most radical of Western ideas, Marxist communism. Yet within a few years it became apparent—apparent, that is, except to Western intellectuals—that Stalin and his Soviet Union incarnated in many ways the inclinations of Slavophilism, which were then institutionalized in a police state that was reminiscent not of Marx or Engels but of Ivan the Terrible. In 1945 in the United States the triumph of internationalism over isolationism seemed complete. Some of the most influential isolationists in Congress announced their adoption of internationalism, which, to them, had become inevitable. American internationalism—the externalization of a liberal and progressive ideology—was now in full development. Yet less than a generation later the appeals of liberalism and of progressivism were melting away. As late as 1970 the principal proponents of an American internationalism, of an Americanized world order, were the conservatives, descendants of isolationists, representing an antiliberalism that corresponded to the sentiments of many Americans, as indeed Stalin's neo-Slavophilism had corresponded with the sentiments of many Russians.

In this respect there was yet another similarity of Russian and American nationalism, and perhaps especially of Russian Slavophiles and American conservatives of a certain kind. Their inclinations, and their propaganda, were conservative at home and revolutionary abroad. During the second half of the nineteenth century the Russian Slavophiles propagated revolutions and Russian intervention in the Balkans against the Turkish and, on occasion, the Austro-Hungarian empire. During the second half of the twentieth century American conservatives propagated American interventions everywhere in the world against the vague monster of international communism—unaware of John Adams's warning in 1821 that the United States will and should not go "abroad in search of monsters to destroy."

In tracing the pedigree of the ideology of the American conservative movement we must note that from, say, 1935 to 1955 (more precisely from the rise of Father Coughlin to the demise of Joseph McCarthy) the emergence of a powerful radical Right in America was a possibility. This, too, followed a development in Europe, though with the usual time lag. In the history of Europe the twenty-five years from 1920 to 1945 were a quarter century during which radicalism was no longer the monopoly of the Left, when neither communism nor capitalism but what is—inadequately and imprecisely—called "fascism" was the rising and dynamic political phenomenon, eventually leading to the Second World War, when such men as Hitler and Mussolini proved to be the dynamic world leaders after Wilson and Lenin were gone. In the United States, too, the Depression was followed by the rise of the popular appeal of radical nationalists. There was a mass potential for a radical Right in the United States even after the death of Huey Long and the episcopal (and partial) silencing of Father Coughlin. This was evident in 1940–41 and again after 1950. Anne Morrow Lindbergh described this potential, having witnessed it at the Madison Square Garden rally of the America First Committee in May 1941. Her description is especially telling not only because of her sensitive intelligence but because she was the wife and supporter of Charles Lindbergh, the popular hero of that movement. There, she wrote, she felt "the animal quality of the crowd," and she sensed "for the first time in my life—the rumbles of revolution. Would it break now? Or was this only one of those instants when a grain of the future has by accident fallen in among the grains of the present? But one knows in a flash of insight: of such will the future be."[4] In some ways this was so. When in 1941 Senator Taft said that the danger to America was not Hitlerism but communism—"for fascism appeals but to a few, and communism to the many"—his diagnosis was entirely wrong; yet less than a decade later the majority of Americans would agree with him, having convinced themselves that communism—outside as well as within the United States—was a far greater danger than fascism had ever been.

It was then, shortly after 1950, that the American conservative movement made its appearance; and the great majority of its early proponents and supporters shared these sentiments. During the late 1940s the designation "conservative" was still shunned by every American politician, as if it had pejorative and unpopular connotations. Yet by 1950 the opposition to liberalism and to the Democratic Party and even to the philosophy of the New Deal was not restricted to wealthy Republicans; it had broad popular support, including masses of people who had been the beneficiaries of the reforms of the New Deal. The development of the Cold War with the Soviet Union and the successive revelations about domestic Communists seemed to have vindicated Franklin Roosevelt's nationalist opponents in the minds of many people. The consequent opinion that the American alliance with Britain and Russia against Germany had not only been wrongly

handled but that it may have been a mistake altogether was held by a minority within that majority, mostly by German-Americans and midwestern
Populists; but the realignment of American politics that took shape twenty-
five years later was already in the making. Still, in the 1950s the radical
Right—the potential mass movement behind Joseph McCarthy notwithstanding—did not carry the day, for many reasons: Joe McCarthy, despite
all of his demagogic instincts, did not have the political savvy of a Hitler
(or even of a Perón); Eisenhower, in spite of all of his procrastinating opportunism, was not really a Hindenburg; and all of the several similarities
between modern Americans and Germans notwithstanding, the United
States was not really like Germany.

The first national magazine of the conscious conservative movement,
William F. Buckley's *National Review,* appeared in 1955, a few months after
McCarthy's meteoric fall from political grace had begun. Many of its subscribers were isolationists, resentful of the American participation in the
Second World War. When in November 1956 *National Review* approved the
Israeli-British-French attack on Suez/Egypt (only because Egypt seemed
to have had the support of the Soviet Union) the magazine lost thousands
of, presumably anti-Jewish, subscribers. But thereafter a dual development
was taking place. On the one hand most of the isolationism, a fair amount
of the Anglophobe nationalism, and a considerable portion of the religious
conservatism among Irish-Americans and many other American Catholics
melted away.[5] On the other hand the American conservative movement
was widening. Its ranks were no longer composed mainly of the isolationist
remnant but of all kinds of people: disillusioned old radicals,[6] ex-liberals,
individualist libertarians, and ideological anticommunists—the latter being the common denominator of the conservative movement till this day.

As late as 1950 the isolationist Robert A. Taft—Eisenhower's opponent
within the Republican Party—refused the label "conservative." By 1960
Eisenhower, the broad-smiling democratic soldier handpicked by Roosevelt
for the command of the crusade against "fascism," said that he was a conservative. In 1941 Charles A. Lindbergh, the leading figure of American
isolationism, said that his principal opponents were "intellectuals, Anglophiles, and Jews."[7] Less than thirty-five years later a fair number of American intellectuals and American Jews opted for neoconservatism.[8] This revolution in American intellectual history still awaits its judicious historian.

One of the main elements in this revolution was the changed image of
Soviet Russia. In the 1950s the American conservative movement came into
existence at the time when anticommunism was being equated with American patriotism. That equation was as wrong as it was shallow. In the minds
of many people it was but another manifestation of their belief in Ameri-

can sinlessness. God had given America a monopoly of virtue, and communism a monopoly of sin. Communism represented the exact opposite of what America stood for; conversely there were few evils in the world that were not the creation of Communists and their sympathizers. Apparently as late as 1983 this was still the essence of President Ronald Reagan's beliefs. In 1982 Mrs. Phyllis Schlafly, the heroine of many American conservatives, said that "God gave America the atom bomb." No: the atom bomb was made in America by Central European refugee scientists whose ideas of morality could not have been more different from those espoused by Mrs. Schlafly. Yet concerning the Soviet Union the ideas of the conservatives and of the ex-liberal neoconservatives had now become largely the same, while many Americans (and not only liberals) had grown uneasy with the nuclear prospects of an American global strategy of anticommunism.

The other element was the decay of liberalism. During the 1950s American liberals became fearful of democracy itself. Persons accused of Communist associations were not only hiding behind the antique constitutional barrier of the Fifth Amendment; in almost every instance they preferred to avoid their trial by jury, since they were afraid of the American people. The liberal interpreters of the McCarthy phenomenon were the prisoners of their own outdated intellectual categories. In 1954 Edward R. Murrow said that Joseph McCarthy was "to the Right of Louis the Fourteenth"; in 1955 Bernard De Voto called the Reece Committee of the House of Representatives "reactionary: they hate and defy the twentieth century."[9] These images defied reason. (Imagine Joe McCarthy at Versailles, or Carroll Reece from Tennessee in the company of Metternich.) In 1953 McCarthy was investigating a former Broadway Communist. This former disciple of Lenin and Stalin now invoked Tacitus and Suetonius. "On his part," the *New York Times* reported, "Senator McCarthy quoted former President Woodrow Wilson as writing that 'the informing function of Congress should be preferred to its legislative functions.'"[10] In 1958 a gang in Harlem called themselves "Conservatives." (They would no more call themselves "The Liberals" than would children play at being pacifists rather than soldiers.)[11] Meanwhile the number of adherents to the conservative movement grew. The civil rights movement, its legislation, the extension of welfare, the reaction to the Vietnam War did show that the generous impulse of the American character was not yet spent. What was bankrupt were the institutionalized ideas of liberalism, very much including the modern liberal view of human nature. The realization that the liberals had contributed to—indeed, that they had vested interests in the maintenance of—the bureaucracies and the institutionalized legalism that were choking free choice, obstructing freedom, and creating disorder in so many American places was swimming up to the surface of consciousness in many minds.

The conservatives contributed to this recognition. By 1970 the constituency of the conservative movement had changed. It was no longer overwhelmingly Irish, German, Catholic, western Republican—indeed, it had become internationalist. The number of conservative journals and the intellectual quality of their contents increased. Even in the universities and colleges the presence of conservative professors began to make itself felt. The Republican Party now openly avowed its conservatism.[12] Republicans and conservatives together survived the shattering defeat of Barry Goldwater (the first avowedly "conservative" candidate) in 1964 as well as the shameful resignations of their erstwhile heroes Agnew and Nixon ten years later. In 1980 the landslide triumph of Ronald Reagan coincided with the twenty-fifth anniversary of the founding of Buckley's *National Review*. A glittering celebration took place in the Plaza Hotel in New York; and the very names of those present showed that in the realms of intellectual as well as political celebrity the monopoly of the once liberal establishment was gone.

Less than two years after that auspicious celebration it was evident that the conservatives had not fulfilled their own expectations. Here was a peculiarly American paradox: *the liberals had become senile, while the conservatives were immature.* Their intellectual—and moral—substance was not sufficient to fill the postliberal vacuum. The reason for this was not the cultural inferiority of American conservatives when compared to American liberals: that was a condition that the conservative intellectual movement had, by and large, outgrown. The reason for this was the conservatives' split-mindedness—suggesting that split-mindedness, too, was not a monopoly of American liberals. The conservatives argued against big government: yet they favored the most monstrous of government projects, laser warfare, biological warfare, nuclear superbombs. They were against the police state: yet they were eager to extend the powers of the FBI and the CIA.[13] They were against government regulations of "free" enterprise: yet they supported at times the government shoring up or bailing out large corporations. They stood for the conservation of America's heritage: yet they were indifferent to the conservation of the American land. They proclaimed themselves to be the prime defenders of Western civilization: yet many of them had a narrowly nationalist, and broadly Californian, view of the world—narrow enough to be ignorant, broad enough to be flat. "I was a nationalist," Hitler wrote in *Mein Kampf* about his youth, "but I was not a patriot." So were, unfortunately, most American conservatives, unaware of the crucial difference (George Orwell described it in one of his prime essays) between the ideological nationalist and the true patriot: the former is moved by the desire to extend the power of his nation, the latter is moved by the love of his country. They were nationalist rather than patriotic: they put their nationalism above their religion, their nationalism *was* their religion. Thus American conservatives welcomed (at worst) or were indifferent (at best) to the dangers of excessive American commitments to all kinds of foreign governments or—what was more important—to the flooding of the United States by countless immigrants from the south who would provide cheap labor but whose increasing presence could only exacerbate deep national problems. There were many Catholics among the conservatives; but their publications would criticize popes and bishops when the allocutions of the latter did not coincide with the desiderata of their ideological nationalism. The true patriot and the true conservative is suspicious of ideology, of any ideology: yet the American conservatives were, more than often, ideologues, disregarding John Adams's pithy statement that *ideology* amounted to *idiocy*. Their view of the world and their consequent advocacies of foreign policies were lamentable, since their view of the Soviet Union as the focus of a gigantic atheistic conspiracy and the source of every possible evil in the world was as unrealistic, unhistorical, ideological, and illusionary as the pro-Soviet illusions of the former liberals and progressives had been. Even though intellectuals of the American conservative movement were often more generous and less narrow-minded than were liberal intellectuals, they seldom hesitated to ally themselves with, and to seek the support of, some of the most uncouth and slovenly minded people and politicians. That was just the trouble. As Jonathan Swift said, certain people "have just enough religion to hate but not enough to love." Many American conservatives, alas, gave ample evidence that they were just conservative enough to hate liberals but not enough to love liberty.

As a matter of fact, they were not really conservative. Their insubstantial heroes were Coolidge, Hoover, Taft. Their very advocacy of a materialist capitalism was merely a negative reaction to socialism—they overlooked, among other things, that capitalism and industrialism were the great anticonservative and antitraditional forces of the nineteenth century and after.[14] The wanting appreciation of tradition among American conservatives was evident not only among some of their politicians but also among their star intellectuals. Bill Buckley was an unquestioning admirer of Secret Agents, of computerism and nuclear technology; Tom Wolfe of fast-flying and fast-living pilots; the two twentieth-century heroes of Hugh Kenner were Ezra Pound and Buckminster Fuller. Jeffrey Hart, senior editor of *National Review*, wrote in 1982 that American conservatism amounted to American modernism: that the progress of technology, the breaking away of modern literature and modern art from all traditional forms, and the new loosening of the family and sexual mores were matters that American conservatives should welcome, indeed, that they should espouse. In another article in *National Review* in 1983 Hart advocated not only the public listing of those Russian cities that American nuclear missiles would pulverize in the event of an atomic war but that this novel kind of diplomacy (he called it a "new conceptualization of atomic strategy") "has numerous connections elsewhere. In one area after another, we appear to be entering an epoch in which reality will be defined increasingly in terms of abstract analysis.... [A]bstract analysis becomes the only knowable reality.... [W]e now appear to be entering a distinctively new phase, in which abstract thought will again become [as in the Middle Ages] a decisive part of our sense of the real." For at least two hundred years, beginning with Burke and Dr. Johnson, the commonsense argument against abstract reasoning has been the strongest and the best intellectual weapon of conservative thinkers against the celebration of modernism. Yet the admiration of the mechanical and the abstract, in the age of computerization and of nuclear international relations, seems to have had a strange and particular appeal to many American conservatives.

Not to all of them, of course: but then the conservatives have not been really united. The marriage—more properly, the cohabitation—of conservatives and neoconservatives has been uneasy. There has not been much compatibility in an alliance of nationalist Redskins with worried intellectuals who thought that their neoconservatism completed their acculturation in America. One need not be a prophet to see that in the event of a dangerous crisis the nationalists would prevail. Their radical and populist strain was there from the beginning of the conservative movement, within the ideas of the otherwise thoughtful Richard Weaver, who said that Tom Paine, "philosopher of a starker principle," was preferable to Burke, or within those of Willmoore Kendall, who advocated a populist majoritarianism that was a half-mad expostulation of what Tocqueville had called the tyranny of the majority into a virtue.

Fifty years ago the greatest conservative thinker of the twentieth century, the Spaniard José Ortega y Gasset, wrote in *The Revolt of the Masses,* "Liberalism—it is well to recall this today—is the supreme form of generosity; it is the right which the majority concedes to minorities and hence it is the noblest. ... It announces the determination to share existence with the enemy; more than that, with an enemy which is weak. It was incredible that the human species should have arrived at so noble an attitude, so paradoxical, so refined, so acrobatic, so antinatural. Hence, it is not to be wondered at that this same humanity should soon appear anxious to get rid of it. It is a discipline too difficult and complex to take firm root on earth." He was right. Forty years ago the English Christopher Hollis, representative of the Burkean and Chestertonian tradition, wrote that "the phrase 'conservative mind' is today almost a tautology. There are no minds but 'conservative minds.'" He was right. By 1980 these concordant—meaning, only superficially contradictory—statements became applicable to the United States. They reflected a certain kind of American reality. American life was still multiform and protean. On the one hand, the dissolution of religion, the loosening of families, the deterioration of older beliefs and customs and manners went on, together with the growth of the political appeal of conservatism: by 1980 millions of *Playboy* readers voted for Reagan.[15] On the other hand, for the first time in their history large numbers of Americans had become conscious of their essential conservatism—a movement of ideas in which the conservatives played but the role of a minor catalyst. For the first time the unquestioned belief in progress, in the beneficial results of man's increasing management of nature, was no longer held as an article of faith by many Americans. Their growing opposition to the pollution of nature or to genetic engineering or to atomic plants or to nuclear weapons could not be simply attributed to liberalism, the impulses of which were still alive, but the attraction of whose ideas was fairly gone. In sum, conservatism and neoconservatism have been but a partial phenomenon of the larger, postliberal and postprogressive, development of the American mind.

One indication of this maturation existed among the young. For almost a century before 1970 one could take it for granted that most of the brightest American students would be more liberal than were their fellow students. After 1970 this was no longer so: often its opposite was true. On the stock exchange of American words, too, the adjective "conservative" has risen. Perhaps even more significant are the increasing approbation and respect granted to adjectives such as "old-fashioned" and "traditional" at the time when the connotations of "modern" or "progressive" are no longer very approbatory. We must at least essay the supposition that these are marks of a profound sea change, of an ebbing away not only of the rhetoric of a superficial public optimism but of the erstwhile dogmatic American belief in the inevitable benefits of Progress. Such postprogressive realizations, opening around the end of the second American century, may have meant the painful but evident maturation of the American mind, rising toward its acceptance and comprehension of the tragic sense of life, and perhaps even toward a new synthesis.

That was one possibility. The other was the floundering of the majority of the American people between two hard (and, on occasion, increasingly vicious) minorities: the so-called conservatives, enthusiastic advocates of technological "progress," indifferent to the poisoning of the land, propagating the American (and nuclear) domination of the world; and the so-called liberals, opposed to nuclear technology while tolerant of the poisons of pornography, propagating the public and legalized abolition of personal moral restraints in every possible form, indifferent to the killing of millions unborn by abortions. This was the danger: that without a more mature conservatism the American political alternatives would be dominated by the thoughtless proponents of atomic war or by those of the suicide of the race.

58

The Elective Monarchy

(1984)

During the twentieth century, the president of the United States became the prince of the world. Much of this was due to American prosperity and power; even more of it was due to mass communications. Abraham Lincoln was probably unknown to the vast majority of mankind during his lifetime. People in the British Isles may have recognized his name; most of the people on the continent of Europe probably did not. Forty years and one generation later the name of Theodore Roosevelt was far more widely known than that of Abraham Lincoln. During those forty years the greatest extension of popular literacy, of newspaper reading and printing, had occurred throughout the world. Another twenty years later Woodrow Wilson appeared as a new world apostle: when he landed in England and France in 1918 little girls in white dresses threw rose petals at his feet; in unpronounceable and unspellable new republics such as Czechoslovakia, hotels, boulevards, and railroad stations were given the name of Wilson. The veneration of this particular president was transitory; the worldwide interest in the American presidency was not. In 1940, another twenty years later, during the most dramatic phase of the Second World War, the United States was not yet a belligerent: but the American presidential election, for the first time in the history of the world, played an important part in the calculations of the rulers of the greatest powers. When Hitler's invitation to receive Molotov in Berlin finally arrived in Moscow, Stalin chose to set the date of that long-desired meeting in Berlin after the American election. (In November 1940 Hitler, too, wrote Mussolini that Italy's attack on Greece ought to have been postponed at least until after the American presidential election.) Another twenty years later, a President such as John Kennedy could have been elected as first President of the World, including

From *Outgrowing Democracy: A History of the United States in the Twentieth Century* (Garden City, NY: Doubleday), 256–88.

President of Europe, had elections throughout the world been popularity contests. To hundreds of millions everywhere Kennedy and his family represented the image of the successful New World: youthful, powerful, suntanned, and rich. This marked something that went beyond the nineteenth-century image of America: it marked the Californization of the dreams of people everywhere. During the second half of the twentieth century the peoples of the world followed the American presidential elections with an interest that, on occasion, would surpass their interest in elections of their own. The most celebrated journalists and television people of many nations crowded into Washington and New York to signal the early omens and to report the results (for the first time in 1948). There remained now two elective monarchs in the world: the president of the United States of America and the pope of the Holy Roman Catholic Apostolic Church. The occasional elections of the second may have been, in the long run, more consequential than the regular quadrennial elections of the first; however, few people thought that way, and the interest in the first far exceeded the interest in the second among all kinds of people, including the Catholic population and clergy in the United States.

This is an interpretation of the history of the United States, not a history of the world and not even a history of the American image before the world, topics that are so huge and so amorphous that no decent historian ought to attempt to write them. Yet there is a correspondence between this development and the developing problems of American historiography. The tremendous increase in the projection and reception of the image of American presidents in the twentieth century corresponded with the enormous increase in the quantity of records that Americans amassed about their presidents and that the latter amassed about themselves. The canons of scientific and professional historiography, laid down in the nineteenth century, required that the historical reconstruction of the life of a person, of a certain place, of a certain period exhaust all of the written and printed sources related to the topic. Yet by 1900 at the latest this requirement became impossible to fulfill. Theodore Roosevelt may have been the first president about whom so much was written and published that even the most assiduous biographer or team of biographers could not read or even find most of the "material." This did not mean that a first-rate biography of Roosevelt, or a history of the Roosevelt years, could not be written. It meant that a change in the historian's perennial problem had occurred. The problem was no longer the insufficient quantity, it was the overwhelming quantity of "materials"—an increase that involved a decrease in quality, that is, a decrease in the authenticity of presidential "documents."

The increase in the number of documents was involved with the enor-

mous increase of the executive bureaucracy. The consequences of this bureaucratic growth around the presidency were increasingly strange, and at
times ludicrous. Herbert Hoover was the first president to establish a library bearing his name. Every president since that time followed with this
practice, depositing the papers of his presidency in a presidential library
building somewhere in the United States. The largest and the most opulent of these is the Lyndon B. Johnson Library in Austin, Texas, housing
the papers of a president who almost never wrote letters on his own, and
whose principal means of communication was that of multiple telephon-
ing, including his occasional reliance on a telephone set installed within
easy reach of his toilet seat. But then, this development corresponded with
the general development during the passing of the Modern Age: the increase in the holdings of libraries developing apace with the decrease in
the habit of reading.

The list of presidents of the United States during the second century of
the Republic does not compare favorably with those who led the nation
during the first century of its existence. Of course there was a devolution
from the generation of the founding fathers (this term was, oddly enough,
coined by Harding) to such mediocrities as Pierce or Buchanan or Arthur—
a decline about which Henry Adams said that the evolution of the presidency from Washington to Grant was alone sufficient to disprove the theory
of Darwin. Adams's acidulous witticism in the 1870s may have been premature. One hundred years later the comparison of Grant, Hayes, Garfield
with Nixon, Ford, Carter suggests a difference not of degree but almost of
kind—not to speak of the devolution from the literacy of a president such
as Ulysses S. Grant, whose own memoirs, composed and handwritten during his painful illness, are an American classic, to the movie and television
personality of Ronald Reagan, who preferred to be briefed by film clips.
During the last one hundred years the names of the two Roosevelts stand
out; perhaps Cleveland, perhaps Truman. The development of the reputation of the latter is significant. Truman was not an especially popular president; had he chosen to run against Eisenhower in 1952 he surely would
have been defeated. Yet there is hardly any relationship between the temporary popularity of a president and his eventual reputation; as a matter of
fact, the relationship is often obverse. (The most popular president during
the twentieth century was Calvin Coolidge.) Truman's reputation began to
rise several years after he left the White House. During the 1960s and the
1970s it reached nearly unprecedented and sentimental heights. The reason for this was not so much (or perhaps not at all) a retrospective judgment of his achievements: it was a retrospective judgment of his character.
It was the national appreciation for a man of the older American type: out-

spoken, courageous, loyal to his friends, solidly rooted in his mid-American past, and *real*—a self-crafted piece of solid wood, not a molded plastic piece. In his private notes Truman once wrote, "I wonder how far Moses would have gone if he'd taken a poll of Egypt? What would Jesus Christ have preached if he'd taken a poll in Israel? . . . It isn't polls or public opinion of the moment that counts. It is right and wrong."[1] Less than a decade after Truman had quit the presidency there was an appreciable rise of national nostalgia for this kind of old-fashioned president, an authentic relic of Americana compared to his successors.[2]

Perhaps this was not only a matter of retrospect. In 1948 the American people, surprisingly and contrary to the projections of all of their pollsters, voted for Truman against Dewey, surely for all kinds of reasons, but perhaps because they sensed that the character of the former was stronger, that he was more of a traditional political person than the latter. In any event, during the last hundred years the majority of American voters seldom chose wrongly on the first Tuesday of every fourth November. This, of course, is a personal estimate—but it may be shared by responsible historians. There was only one presidential election during the last one hundred years whose outcome was surely deleterious for the nation and for the world in the long run. This was the election in 1912, when Woodrow Wilson was chosen instead of Theodore Roosevelt. But then, it was not really the American people who denied Roosevelt the presidency. Had he been nominated he would have won over Wilson. His nomination was denied him by the Republican politicians.

During the twentieth century the voters were, generally speaking, wrong less often than were their self-styled political representatives. What went wrong were not elections but the procedures of nomination. From 1840 to 1900 in every presidential election more than two thirds of the eligible voters voted. Since then there has not been a single presidential election when more than two thirds of the eligible voters voted. From 1840 to 1900 there was only one election (in 1852) when less than 70 percent of those entitled to vote did so, whereas twice in the twentieth century less than half of those entitled voted. After 1960 the trend became definite: 62.8 percent in 1960; 61.9 in 1964; 60.9 in 1968; 55.5 in 1972; 54.4 in 1976; 52.3 in 1980. Perhaps this meant a decrease of civic responsibility among the American people. But other factors contributed to the decrease of voting, ranging from the increasing complexities of voter registration, through the broadening of the electorate, to the decrease of the nineteenth-century custom of politics as grand entertainment. Still, this decrease happened during the century when voting rights, the education of voters, the length, extent, and cost of the campaigns were increased, the latter astronomically so.[3] Since

World War II, in the democracies of Europe 80 to 95 percent of those eligible voted in national elections, in the United States barely half. After 1970 federal laws provided for the public financing of the campaigns of presidential candidates and lowered the requirements of voting age to eighteen. Yet the portion of actual voters dropped significantly and steadily.

All of this happened as the transformation of the Republic to a mass democracy was completed—and when the measurement and the production of popularity had become a scientific practice and an accepted fundament of the electoral process. Those chastened observers and conservative critics who attributed this to popular irresponsibility and to the inevitable shortcomings of egalitarian populism may have been right on occasion, but I believe that we must go beyond their ideas. During the twentieth century American politics in general, and the politics of the presidency in particular, passed beyond the stage where democracy devolved into a popularity contest. Note the title of this chapter: the elective monarchy of the United States has come to mean the degeneration of popular democracy to a contest of *publicity*, which is not identical with *popularity*—a difference that their connections must not obscure.

❀ ❀ ❀

MORE than two hundred years ago Americans became a republican people. "Republic," in the eighteenth century, did not mean quite what it would later. The word was not necessarily connected with democracy. During the eighteenth century most of the few existing republics in Europe, such as Venice, were aristocratic republics, not democratic ones. In England, too, a considerable segment of the Whig party was composed of noblemen whose inclinations were aristocratic and antimonarchical. In the Declaration of Independence and in the Constitution the word "democracy" did not figure once. When Jefferson established his political party, he gave it the name "Democratic-Republican," of which two adjectives the first was the qualifying and the indicative one, emphasizing what kind of a republic he and his friends wished to see. The other party was the Federalists, the more conservative of the two (relatively and imprecisely speaking: the adjective "conservative" was not yet applied to politics then). At any rate, the Federalists went out of business after 1816, and during the next fifteen years the ideological transition of the United States from a republic to a democracy was completed. The political transition to democracy was completed by the time of the election of Andrew Jackson, who defeated the patrician John Quincy Adams in 1828; there was that famous scene the day of Jackson's inauguration, with his partisans, many of them rough people and farmers from the then West, crowding into the White House with their muddy boots. What followed Jackson's election was even more important: the first convention of political parties nominating a president—in his case in 1832. By 1836 the Whigs, the party opposing the Democrats (who had by then dropped the adjective "Republican" from their name) resorted to the same kind of electoral practices as had their opponents.

It was then that American campaigns, including the election of the president, became full-fledged popularity contests. This development was regarded bitterly and skeptically by the few remaining conservatives in this country, and by some of the liberals in England (Macaulay, who said, "Your constitution is all sail and no anchor"). Their criticism was often judicious, yet it mattered little. In one important sense most critics of popular democracy missed an essential point.[4] What loomed ahead was not the rule of the mob; it was the manipulation of the masses by the politicians. A brilliant description of what happened may be found in three obscure papers (one an honors' thesis at Harvard) written by the young Boies Penrose in the 1880s. Penrose wrote that with the election of Jackson the sovereign people had "asserted their power. But in reality Jackson, the man of the people, was but a puppet in the hands of the politicians. In reality, the majesty of the politicians, not of the people, was asserted. . . ." It was Martin Van Buren, not Jackson, who "marks the transition in American politics from statesmen like Adams and Webster to the great political bosses and managers of today. . . . Adams was the last statesman of the old school who was to occupy the White House, Van Buren was the first politician president . . . the first of that class of statesmen who owe their success not so much to their opinions or characters, as to their skill in managing the machinery of party. . . ." And this was "the inevitable outcome of the development of the country. . . . In the rivalries of parties the mechanical arts of electioneering were soon reduced to a system. . . . Political opinions, in fact, were a secondary consideration. All the statesmanship that the times required was the artful adaptation of general propositions to the existing temper . . . of the masses."[5] The mechanization of politics, in other words, developed apace with the cult of the people. Penrose's career exemplified his vision: after a few years of a dull life as a young lawyer, this Philadelphia patrician abandoned his early support of reform and chose the low life of politics, not for financial reasons, but because of his disabused and stoical recognition of what American politics was all about. Even more trenchant than Penrose's analysis of the transformation of American politics in the 1830s was his criticism of the reformers of his time.[6] He had a contempt for them. They were "watery-eyed," "pious fools," hypocrites from the so-called better classes, priding themselves on having opinions higher than those of the common man.

Yet Penrose's public career, from 1885 to 1920, coincided with the American Age of Reform. The proponents and the movers of reform were the Progressives and the Populists. They were different in their backgrounds and in their social and political aims. The one thing they had in common was their belief that democracy ought to be improved through its extension—through education and by increasing political participation—since political corruption meant that the just desires of the people were being thwarted. They did not understand that "the people" were (as indeed they are) an abstraction. For who are the people? A statement by a king is a statement by a king; a statement by a group of nobles is a statement by a group of nobles; a statement by Napoleon is a statement by Napoleon. Yet a statement by the people is a statement by one remove, it is a statement made *in the name of the people*. That such a statement may, on occasion, be in accord with the sentiments of the majority of the people may be true; yet its potential truthfulness does not alter its indirect nature. This is, too, why the historian of democratic times faces problems different from those of the past: "the people wanted," "the people thought," "the people resisted" are vague phrases. They may not be entirely untrue. Yet the historian of democratic times must be very careful, aware, as he ought to be, of the difficulties inherent in his task of reconstructing who the people really were,[7] and what they thought and believed at a certain time—problems which are less statistical than they are structural.

One of these problems is the difference between public opinion and popular sentiment. Like "the people," "public opinion" has a history of its own. Its classic age was the nineteenth century. The first generation of American statesmen was still keenly aware of the difference between "public" and "popular." "Popularity" for John Adams was not an approbatory term. "The form of popular government," *Federalist* 10 stated, "enables it to sacrifice to its ruling passion or interest both the public good and the rights of other citizens." In the United States before the 1830s, in England before the 1880s, public opinion meant the opinion of the more-or-less educated classes,[8] while popular sentiment belonged to the masses. With the extension of democracy and public education the two categories began to overlap. "The public" was no longer synonymous with an educated class; it was less and less separable from "the people." More and more people were entitled to vote; more and more people read newspapers; more and more people had opinions on more and more subjects. Whether these opinions were ready-made or not mattered little. What mattered was the preoccupation with popularity, to which the entire electoral process was being subordinated.

"Public opinion is strong," Samuel Butler wrote toward the end of the nineteenth century, "while it is in its prime. In its childhood and old age it is as weak as any other organism." In Europe, too, the great historian Jakob Burckhardt saw as early as 1870 that the prime of public opinion was passing.[9] Earlier it was still taken for granted that the public was the more articulate portion of the population; that it was almost always a minority;[10] that public opinion was, simply, opinion made public; that it was articulate, active, actual, while popular sentiment was potential rather than actual, its expressions often dependent on the ideas presented to it by public opinion. By the end of the century suffrage and literacy were being exploited by manufacturers and distributors of publicity. They were making a living out of what people still called public opinion, but which they tried to transform into something that was inseparable and, on occasion, indistinguishable from popular sentiment.

In the 1830s John C. Spencer, an American lawyer, impressed Tocqueville when he said that certain "leaders" of public opinion in the United States should be reproached not so much because they flatter the people but because they "do not struggle with enough courage against an opinion believed to be shared by the people." "You can't be a leader," said Governor Meyner of New Jersey in 1957, "unless you know where the people want to go." That this was something different from the tyranny of the majority had been noticed by James Fenimore Cooper as early as 1838: "In a democracy, as a matter of course, every effort is made to seize upon and create publick opinion, which is, substantially, securing power," he wrote in *The American Democrat*. "One of the commonest arts practiced, in connection with this means of effecting objects, is *to simulate* the existence of a general feeling in favor, or against, any particular man, or measure; so great being the deference paid to publick opinion, in a country like this, that men actually yield their own sentiments to that which *they believe to be* the sentiment of the majority." The italics are mine. Note that this thoughtful American writer was concerned less with the tyranny of the majority or with the deference paid to public opinion than with its simulation.

During the nineteenth century, and for some time thereafter, the main instrument of the mechanization of politics, with its subsequent creation of electoral majorities, was the political party. Party loyalties were near-sacred, unbreakable, they often ran in families through generations; party affiliation, among Americans, was often not altogether different from religious affiliation. In this respect there was something medieval in the American process of nominating and electing presidents, especially in the unanimity with which the temporarily and bitterly divided nominating convention closed.[11] "The shout is the test": whereafter, as during the Middle

Ages, the unanimity was taken for granted, it could not be broken. In the Middle Ages as well as in the United States people would deny the existence of divided opinions for a long time,[12] in political parties as well as in small-town life. Yet it was a mistake to attribute the occasional wrongheadedness of majorities to mere partisanship, as it was attributed by the progressive reformers. An editorial in the first issue of the *New Republic*, the then quintessential intellectual voice of modern progressivism, in 1914 bewailed that the new practice—recently established by a constitutional amendment—of the direct election of senators made little or no change to the better. A "severe blow to non-partisan progressivism" had occurred, said the editorial. Machine politicians with unsavory records were elected, even though they were opposed by the progressive elements in their parties. "Yet they were all nominated and elected by popular vote, and no adherent of popular government can question their title to their offices. The meaning of the lesson is unmistakeable. Direct primaries and the direct popular election of Senators will not contribute much to the triumph of genuine political and social democracy as long as partisan allegiance remains the dominant fact in the voter's mind. . . ." But the problem was no longer the domination of partisan allegiance. It was the domination of publicity.[13] For by 1914 the second transformation of the American political system, that from a contest in popularity to a contest in publicity, had begun.

❊ ❊ ❊

THE word "publicity," in its present sense, "the business of making goods or persons publicly known," appeared as late as 1904, the *Oxford English Dictionary* tells us. This was different from the first English usage of the word (1791): "The quality of being public; the condition or fact of being open to public observation or knowledge." "Publicity agent," "public relations," "public relations expert," "the public relations industry" (or "business") are Americanisms of the twentieth century. Some of these words were coined by Edward L. Bernays, an American publicity magnate, in 1919. Forty years later the abbreviation "PR" had entered the American popular vocabulary; it was recognized by everyone.

The American respect and attention paid to publicity was older than that.[14] Benjamin Franklin was an early public relations man. His famous asseveration that all that an American had to do was to build a better mousetrap was nonsense. What he had to do was to *advert* people—often at the cost of frequent and incessant repetition—of the existence of this or that mousetrap, the prerequisite of people's acquaintance with the quality (and even with the price) of aforesaid mousetrap. During the nineteenth cen-

tury the effort to direct the minds of people to the availability of something or somebody began to merge with the effort of adverting them of the
particular quality of the thing or person—especially when the effort was
directed at large numbers of people. This was happening, too, with advertisements in the press. The press was beginning to depend more and more
on advertising; but, unlike in the earlier newspapers, the language, and later
the pictorial content, of the advertisements changed. The earliest newspapers, during the eighteenth century, merely published notices about the
availability of certain goods. During the nineteenth century the emphasis
shifted to their qualities and prices. This corresponded to the entire history of newspapers during the centuries of the Modern Age. In the beginning they printed snippets of news among their advertisements, which indeed had been their principal profit-making function. Later their dependence on advertisements became predominant again.

During the nineteenth century the space occupied by advertisements
in American newspapers and on American streets, walls, and roads was
growing very large. In this field American practices were well ahead of
those of Europe. The pictorial appearance of advertisements became more
perfected and more startling. Their language was, at times, strikingly modern, having acquired early the often surrealistic tone of twentieth-century
advertising, with the purpose of attracting attention rather than of emphasizing the unique (and specific) qualities of a product or store—in other
words, with the purpose of creating a general image rather than concentrating on a particular reality.

The electoral campaigns adopted these developments. At the time of
their first transformation, in the 1830s, the change of the verb was telling: it
was then that candidates began to "run," and no longer "stand," for office.
But there was more to it than that. In the crude presidential campaigns of
1836 and 1840, which disheartened James Fenimore Cooper and other
Americans of the older political persuasions, the Whigs had unearthed the
old General Harrison because of his potential popular appeal: the slogans
of "Old Tip," and then "Tippecanoe and Tyler too," the exaggeration of
the contrast between the rough-and-ready frontier hero and "silver-spoon"
Van Buren was manufactured by the Whig politicians. It is significant, and
telling, that the Whigs were, relatively (but only relatively), the more conservative party of the two.

Yet publicity, as a business, was still in its infancy. Except here and there,
the politicians were the publicity agents. Besides the newspapermen it was
the politicians themselves who labored mightily in the creation of popular
men and popular slogans. During the first decades of the twentieth century
came a subtle change. This involved the transition from verbal to pictorial

images; the invention and production of photography, movies, and pictorial reproduction in the newspapers greatly contributed to it. Warren Harding was the first presidential candidate in whose selection his solid good-looking appearance played an important part.[15] It is senseless to speculate whether Abraham Lincoln—who, no matter how impressive, was an ugly man—could have been nominated in the age of the pictorial newspaper or in the age of television. It is not senseless to argue that, had television existed in 1932, Franklin Roosevelt's crippled condition would have been a serious, and perhaps insurmountable, obstacle to his nomination. However, he was the president who made the best use of the radio, where the tone of his voice was inspiring, even as the content of his speeches reads somewhat less inspiring in retrospect.

During the first decades of the twentieth century the effectiveness of verbal politics was weakening. This was noticed by Van Wyck Brooks in 1915; "The most striking American spectacle today is a fumbling about after new issues which no one as yet has been able to throw into relief. We have seen one president advocating a 'New Nationalism,' another president advocating a 'New Freedom' . . . phrases that illustrate just this vague fumbling, this acute consciousness of the inadequacy of habitual issues, this total inability to divine and formulate new issues that really are issues. With us the recognized way of pinning down something that is felt to be in the air is to adopt some cast-off phrase and tack the word 'New' before it."[16] When Theodore Roosevelt said that the presidency is "a bully pulpit," he was only restating forcefully what had become obvious in his lifetime (the presidency had not been a bully pulpit one or two generations earlier). Yet it was the pale professorial Wilson, not the sanguine and impatient Roosevelt, who instituted new practices in the presidency. Wilson was the first president to hold "news conferences" (about which wags were wont to say that they contained no news and were not conferences). In 1917 he created the Creel Committee on Public Information. That this committee perpetrated many a fraud in the service of wartime propaganda is not our concern here; what is significant is the president's creation of the first official American government agency dedicated to large-scale national opinion-making. Wilson was also the first president to encourage the investigative function of congressional committees. These functions tended to become publicity stunts. Like so many other progressive "reforms," their functions often developed at the cost of American civil liberties. Harding, who was chosen because of his image, was a limited man; he sought popularity in his artless ways while he kept private some of his beliefs, not to speak of habits.

An interesting case was the complex character of Calvin Coolidge. The accepted image of Coolidge was, and still is, that of a tight-lipped New

Englander, a kind of Last Puritan in the presidency, a taciturn Yankee with certain private convictions. In reality Coolidge was an unsure man, rarely at ease; and when "Coolidge was at ease and not on public display, he was the most garrulous occupant that the White House has ever had."[17] He was constantly concerned with his public image, which he cultivated endlessly. He delivered more speeches in four years than any other president before or after him; he also held more press conferences than any American president before him. His press secretary, C. Bascom Slemp (a name which would have been dear to Anthony Trollope or to Artemus Ward), was very much aware of the importance of the Coolidge image, including the pictorial representations thereof—whence the famous photographs of Coolidge wearing Indian headdresses and the one of Coolidge in a New England farmer's overalls (over gleaming city shoes), from which picture the photographers failed to crop out in the upper corner the presidential Pierce-Arrow limousine and the presidential chauffeur, cap in hand, respectfully waiting for the august subject of this kind of iconography.[18]

I am again referring to pictorialization, since the Twenties was the last decade of the Golden Age of the Press. By the 1930s their monopoly on the "news," on informing the people, had been cracked by radio, newsreels, newsmagazines. During the interlude between the Golden Age of the Newspaper and the Silver Age of Television much of public opinion was made, and reflected, in the newsmagazines. In the newsmagazines such as *Time* many of the proper distinctions between information and opinion were washed away. The newspapers were still influential, but the character of their influence was changing. Apart from the important condition that they were now increasingly dependent on advertising, in most of the newspapers, too, the previous attempts of at least a half-decent separation of information from opinion, of reporting from editorial content, were progressively obliterated. "This era," Douglas Cater wrote, in an article in the *Reporter* magazine in 1959,

> illustrates the degree to which the reporting of events can itself be a major political event. Publicity is a force that has become uniquely essential to the American system of government. . . . Within the Executive branch itself, grown large and infinitely compartmentalized, the publicity competition often takes on the character of a life-or-death struggle. . . .[19] This tendency for the development of news to influence reactively the development of events is a force that cannot be precisely charted.[20] The interaction can be a result of pure chance. It can, as modern practitioners of the art of public relations appreciate, be made the

object of manipulation. It can even be a product of conscious cooperation, or lack of it, between the politician and the press.

Twenty years later this analysis is still valid, but with two exceptions. The influence of the press became limited to the few remaining national newspapers, to the *Washington Post* perhaps even more than to the *New York Times*. Meanwhile the influence of the newsmagazines decreased, while the influence of television grew.

About ten years before the advent of television another phenomenon appeared: that of the pollsters. (Again, the development of the language is telling. Before about 1940 the word "poll" was associated with elections; after that, with public-opinion research.) Sporadic attempts to "measure" public opinion were made earlier, here and there; but it was during the Thirties that public-opinion research institutes came into being, the most celebrated among them that of Dr. Gallup in Princeton. Soon political figures and organizations became interested in their findings. This included Franklin Roosevelt, who, all of his patrician self-assurance notwithstanding, was fairly well aware of the existence of certain undercurrents of popular sentiment. Twice, in 1936 and in 1948, the pollsters' predictions of presidential elections were wrong. Yet the public interest in their findings continued, and their techniques of sampling improved, until in the 1950s the sampling of popularity, on every conceivable issue, became an accepted practice for most politicians and especially for presidential candidates and presidents.

This seemed as if it were the ultimate extension of popular democracy.[21] Yet the pollsters' pretensions were essentially fraudulent. They pretended to be in the business of "researching," that is, of ascertaining, public opinion. In reality they were making soundings of popular sentiment—by means of primitive and crude questions about precooked alternatives, and by cooking the results into percentages. Whatever the difference between public opinion and popular sentiment, they have this in common: neither opinion nor sentiment can be enumerated, quantified, and therefore measured, since they involve broadly and profoundly varying elements of quality, of intensity, and authenticity. It is therefore that almost any numerical representation of "opinion" is, by necessity and by definition, false.

How, then, have the pollsters and their rapidly growing research organizations become accepted, necessary, successful? That their influence grew was not surprising: modern democracy has a dumb kind of respect—even though not unmixed with resentment—for all kinds of experts. Despite the frequent failures of their performances, it seems as if modern democracy cannot do without them. But the pollsters have gone one better than most other experts. After a decade or so of trial and not infrequent error they improved their technique of samplings to the extent that their predictions of elections became less inaccurate. Their margin of error was diminishing, even though as late as in 1980 their predictions of the popular vote were fairly wide of the mark. This happened because their work had little to do with opinion or with sentiment. They were dealing with choosing, not with thinking. Now choosing and thinking are different things—especially when the choosing involves predetermined and unalterable alternatives, whether in presidential elections or in market research. Which box of soap powder a tired housewife will choose from the shelves of a supermarket depends, of course, on many things: on her memory (ranging from definite consciousness to subliminal reactions) of the incessant, or at least frequent, repetitions of the name or image of the product in all kinds of advertisements; on the color and shape of its packaging; on its positioning on the shelves; and, of course, on its quality and price—but the last two matters are not always the determinant factors. This kind of choice, involving usually a low-level kind of consciousness and a low level of personal and private commitment, is fairly predictable, especially when it comes to large numbers of people. When it comes to electoral choice, the level of commitment is to some extent different (after all, voting requires some kind of personal effort, including that of registering); but the difference is often that of degree, not of kind; and the prediction of the pollster is made easier by the fact that the choice involves only two predetermined alternatives.[22] Hence the approximate accuracy of the pollsters' predictions when it comes to electoral choices—a rather low level of achievement at that. (This is probably why the pollsters, with all of their extensive efforts and sophisticated equipment, were seldom able to predict the total number of voters—or, conversely, the number of voters who did not bother to vote.)

There was worse to come. We have seen that the choice, or at times even the voice, of the people has often been an abstraction, one remove away from reality. We have seen that more than 140 years ago James Fenimore Cooper was exercised not so much by the prevalence of political popularity-seeking as by the simulation of popularity. In the twentieth century this meant that popularity could be manufactured by publicity—amounting to a distortion of the political process to which the pollsters then contributed. This was the political and social phenomenon corresponding to the so-called Heisenberg principle (which in the world of matter was a discovery more fundamental than the relativity theory of Einstein): that the observation of a certain matter may influence and change the matter itself. By repeating and repeating that someone is popular he may become popular. (This, too, may have been one of the reasons for the im-

mense increase of the national interest in athletic achievement, which, after all, *is* measurable and real. By repeating that this or that artist or record
is popular, he or she or it may become popular; but by repeating that this
tennis player or that sprinter is the best is not enough; he has to beat all his
opponents or run faster than anyone else.)

During the 1950s the Department of State got involved in the manufacture of popularity, in assisting politicians allegedly friendly to the United
States in all parts of the world. In Washington arrangements were made to
the effect that the motorcades of foreign dignitaries arriving in Washington should move through Constitution Avenue around 12:30 "just as Government buildings will be discharging lunch-bound workers. This will give
the visitor the impression of a spontaneous demonstration in his honor."
(From a government pamphlet of the Dulles period.) In New York, worried
lest some of the distinguished foreign visitors receive an unduly small share
of ticker tape descending on their motorcade, the agents of the Department of State got together with those of the New York City Department of
Sanitation and with the president of the New York Stock Exchange. They
agreed that the Exchange would save ticker tape for a week or ten days
before the arrival of prominent visitors from abroad, after which assiduous
preservation the leftover tape would be gathered and delivered to the Department of Sanitation, whose workers then would ascend to the lofty offices of stockbroking firms and help to toss down the mounds of tape which
thereafter they would sweep up from the street again.

By the middle of the century all principal political candidates had their
own pollsters, whose multiple tasks included not only the selection of popular programs or issues or phrases but the public pronouncement (often "a
news release") that their candidate or client was doing well in the polls,
that he had become a popular choice. (A consequence of this was the increasing practice of announcing that a candidate was "ahead"—ahead, that
is, days, weeks, months before people were actually to enter the voting
booths to register their choice.) In this way the functions of the pollster and
the publicity agent overlapped, often to the extent of their inseparability.
The same thing happened to the lobbyists for special interests, who in the
past had attempted to influence legislators by emphasizing the material
interests of the latter, tempting them with financial advantages. After 1950
this kind of corruption became less material, more intellectual, and therefore more insidious. The job of the lobbyist, and of the jobber, was to simulate and to produce expressions and "evidences" of popularity.

This corresponded with certain mutations in the American political
process. The old-fashioned ward-leader, whose principal task and purpose
was to bring out the vote, gave way to the newer kind of publicity expert,

whose principal concern was the public image of his candidate. At the same time partisanship and party membership among the voting public at large declined until it became a secondary, at times even a nugatory, factor. By the 1970s the traditional Democratic and the traditional Republican voter were disappearing from many a political scene. Certain thoughtful conservative observers of the American scene said that what happened in the 1830s was a transition on the part of the elected legislator from delegation to representation. One hundred and twenty years later there was another transition, from representation to "presentation." This was what "public opinion" was all about: publicness, rather than opinion. Through publicity an enormous overhead to American industry and business had been created, allowing them to spend huge amounts on advertisements that could be deducted through Byzantine tax laws, as if they were production expenses, eventually at the cost of the efficiency of production itself. It was through publicity, too, that the function of what had gone under "society" in older America was transformed: old society in America was rather private, the newer society determinedly, anxiously public. To be well known— or, more accurately, to be widely known—was what counted, in political as well as in social, business, and intellectual life.[23]

❊ ❊ ❊

DURING the twentieth century the American president became an elective monarch. In the history of Western civilization the hereditary (as well as the so-called absolute) monarchy was more typical of the early Modern Age than of the Middle Ages. In many instances and in some ways the medieval king was an elective monarch, dependent on the nobles. The principle of elective monarchy had been, of course, established in the constitution of the Republic from the beginning. In accord with their preferences for the English concept of "balanced government," the founders of the American state invested the president with certain monarchical prerogatives, yet dependent on the other two, relatively aristocratic and relatively democratic, branches of the government, as well as on the electoral process. During the nineteenth century the presidential powers were not especially strong. Tocqueville thought that with the further extension of democracy the president would be more and more dependent on Congress. About 1900 the congressional domination began to weaken. Because of the complexities of an industrialized country, executive orders were needed in an increasing variety of instances in order to regulate matters that could not be left to the slow and cumbrous and often inadequate process of congressional or state legislation. Even more important was the growth of the publicity machinery. "The people" wanted a leader, a father, a husband.

This was a worldwide phenomenon. The revolutions of the eighteenth century, whether in France or in America, were antimonarchical. The mass movements of the first half of the twentieth century were not. I am using the word "monarchy" in its original Aristotelian sense of one-man rule, and not in the sense of hereditary, that is, aristocratic, royalty. The examples of Mussolini, Hitler, Perón, or of many others, showed that democracy and monarchy were even more compatible than aristocracy and monarchy had been.

During the twentieth century, and especially after 1920, popular participation in presidential voting fluctuated and actually decreased. Yet popular interest in the person of the president did not. With the advent of mass publicity, an increasing amount of information (mostly tawdry) about successive presidents was produced, much of which was false. Because of publicity the distance between image and reality was widening. There have been few revelations about presidents of the nineteenth century that contrast sharply with their contemporary image, or that are really surprising in retrospect. In the twentieth century this began to change for the worse. Conscious as he was of the effects of publicity and the press, Theodore Roosevelt was too much of a piece, whence there is no sharp contrast between his real (and historic) personality and that of his contemporary public image. The same thing may be true, *mutatis mutandis,* of his successor, Taft. But when it came to Wilson the contrast between the public and the private president was indeed very large, in some instances strikingly so. Without going into a character analysis of that most complex of presidents, let us note only an indubitable fact: that the physical and mental condition of Wilson, incapacitated as he was after his stroke in September 1919, was kept from the American people for more than a year, in spite—or perhaps, because—of the enormous influence of the press and of the publicity machinery at large. There was the startling contrast between the public image of the tight-lipped and determined Coolidge and the garrulous and insecure private Coolidge. Millions knew all kinds of details about Franklin Roosevelt's private life—the name of his dog, the fact that he served hot dogs to the king and queen of England when they visited him in 1939. Often the very same millions were unaware that this president was crippled and dependent on a wheelchair. They were unaware, too, that during the last year of his life he had weakened drastically, indeed, that he was a dying man. During Franklin Roosevelt's presidency the hereditary impulse began to influence the elective monarchy of the American presidency. Roosevelt was elected four times in a row; perhaps he could have been elected again, had he so wished and had providence allowed. Theodore Roosevelt was the first president in whose family life the American people took excessive interest; Franklin Roosevelt's wife was an important public figure, perhaps for the first time in the history of the presidency. Yet the Roosevelts, patrician Americans as they were, still guarded their private lives from undue publicity (with more than one reason). Eventually this kind of separation of public from private lives was further eroded by the machinery of publicity.

For a while the hereditary tendency ran strong. Had John Kennedy not been assassinated there is reason to believe that he would have been re-elected triumphantly and that four years later his brother Robert would have been elected, had he not been killed in turn by a deranged Arab. The public image of John Kennedy, that of the prototype of the ideal young American husband, gloriously and happily married, seems to have been very different from the realities of his private life; but very few people knew that at the time. Americans now took more and more interest in presidential wives. That President Nixon's daughter married President Eisenhower's grandson was not surprising; their alliance was reminiscent of the hereditary inclination as well as of the intermingling of the new bureaucratic and state aristocracies, as happens frequently within leading families in the Soviet Union. The kind of American populism that during the nineteenth century had been often suspicious and hostile to rich people in high political offices was vanishing. Before 1920 the name of Rockefeller or Vanderbilt would have been a decided obstacle, if not anathema, to candidacies to public office, though that of a Ford would not. A generation later Rockefellers were elected to governorships of states. One of them went on to become a presidential candidate and vice president, without appreciable popular hostility. What counted in his favor was not his philanthropic record but his political celebrity, the public recognition of his name. An unknown brother or relative of a president did not stand a chance; a well-known brother did. Celebrity in the 1950s and 1960s made movie actors into senators and governors, until eventually one of them became president.

Let me insist again that the increasing influence of publicity did not mean the increasing democratization of American politics. Critics of populism or of democracy, whether in the nineteenth century or in the twentieth, have feared or castigated "the common man," believing that the further democratization and popularization of any process, of any institution, would necessarily lead to anarchy and/or extremism. In many ways the opposite has been happening. The American people, overwhelmed by the oceanic tides of daily (and nightly) publicity, have been surprisingly docile. Many of them may not have liked this or that president; yet their fear of not having a president was very great—this in spite of the fact that, beginning with Eisenhower, presidents have often absented themselves from the White House for unconscionably long periods of time. An evidence of this has been the enormous sense of national relief in the swift and smooth resumption of the presidency after a president in office had been suddenly eliminated by death (or, in Nixon's case, by abdication). During the nineteenth century, presidents died in office, other presidents were murdered, but there seemed to have been none of the fretful anxiety to have their successor sworn in within hours, if not minutes. As late as in 1901 the news of McKinley's death reached Theodore Roosevelt in the more-or-less normal way, when he was vacationing in the Adirondacks. (It is true that when Roosevelt arrived in Buffalo to take his presidential oath he made sure that plenty of newspapermen were present.) The first dramatic innovation in this instance involved Calvin Coolidge, a man whom most people still regard as a nineteenth-century survival in the America of the Twenties, whereas he was, in more than one way, a prototypical man of his times, excessively aware of the advantages of publicity. When Harding died on a hot August night his vice president, Coolidge, was in Vermont. A congressman friend (Porter H. Dale) rushed up to him. "The United States has no President!" he shouted. "Mr. Coolidge, the country should never be without a President!" (All of this happened before the age of cold wars and intercontinental rockets.) So Coolidge, known to the nation as a businesslike president who went to bed early and slept soundly, stayed up in the night and was sworn in by his father, a local official, at 2:47 a.m., after which his swearing-in was restaged for the photographers.[24] When President Kennedy was assassinated, his successor was sworn in even before the presidential plane took off for Washington. When President Nixon resigned, his successor was sworn in in a matter of minutes; when President Reagan was wounded by an assassin's attempt, his secretary of state rushed to the White House to announce to the nation with trembling lips that according to the Constitution he was in charge. (He was wrong.) In each of these instances there was an immediate feeling of national relief; the senators, public figures, newspapermen, and television commentators gave vent to their immense satisfaction that the Constitution "worked," there *was* a president, after all. . . . But in the Middle Ages, too, people could not *imagine* not having a king.

"The emergence of the physical and symbolic defining characteristics of the modern presidency is evident in the several city blocks surrounding 1600 Pennsylvania Avenue," Professor Fred Greenstein wrote:

> William Hopkins, who began working as the White House stenographer under Hoover in 1931, went on to become executive

clerk, and held his White House position until his retirement in the Nixon years, remembers that he had shaken hands with President Hoover the year before going to work in the White House. Hoover still found it possible to carry on the leisurely nineteenth-century New Year's Day tradition of personally greeting any person who cared to join the reception line leading into the White House.

In Hoover's time, the presidency had not become so central a symbol for public emotions and perceptions about the state of the nation that elaborate procedures for protecting the White House from potentially dangerous intruders were deemed necessary. The White House of our time is surrounded by a high, electronically sensitized fence; its gates are locked and carefully guarded; and the fence extends across West Executive Avenue to the ornate Old Executive Office Building, creating a two-block "presidential compound." In Hoover's time, the lower, unelectrified fence surrounded only the White House grounds and had open gates. Anyone walking east of the White House from what then was not a presidential office building, but rather the site of the State, Navy and War Departments, customarily did so by strolling across the White House grounds.[25]

The 1950s represent another turning point, including a mutation in presidential character. General Eisenhower, who was elected by a large majority in 1952 and again in 1956, was not a mere creation of publicity. Nor was he the first example of a presidential candidate who was chosen by the politicians because of his reputation as a victorious general. Yet already in 1942 General Marshall and President Roosevelt had chosen Eisenhower as the commander of the Allied forces in the European theater partly because he was the kind of American general—democratic, agreeable, accommodating, and well equipped with a photogenic smile—who would be acclaimed by the press and who, in the difficult position of having to command all kinds of allies, would be a good chairman of the board. Eisenhower's favorable publicity potential as well as his bureaucratic capacities decided in his favor. These qualities propelled this general after the war to the presidency of Columbia University, to the command of NATO, and eventually to the White House. He was well aware of the importance of publicity. If Truman was the last old-fashioned president in the White House, Eisenhower was the first bureaucratic one. Eisenhower campaigned on a Republican platform against Big Government and Big Bureaucracy, but the bureaucracy of the White House during the Eisenhower years grew very fast. By 1960 the full-time staff was nearly three times as large as that of the Roosevelt period and nearly twice as large as that of the Truman years. Eisenhower delegated all kinds of authority to his staff. The most important task of this staff was to choose who could see and talk to the president, a dubious practice that restricted his reception to information, people, policies, and ideas of which certain influential men on his staff approved. He wrote none of his speeches. In the 1950s the number of speechwriters in the White House began to abound; eventually dozens of them would snip and paste and assemble the text of a presidential speech.

Eisenhower was not the first president who found his task onerous. From John Adams to Truman, presidents had complained about the presidency being a kind of gilded prison. Still Eisenhower was the first president who regarded his occupation as that of a chairman of the board, on a nine-to-five schedule, absenting himself from the White House on golfing vacations as often as he deemed possible. He was also the first television president. In 1948 Truman appeared on television only for a short, three-minute appearance, urging the citizenry to vote; in 1952 Eisenhower hired the actor Robert Montgomery to prepare his television grooming and appearances; this actor remained on the staff of the White House for some time. In 1956 another actor, George Murphy (eventually to become a senator from California) took his place. Eisenhower's countenance was photogenic and reassuring, more impressive than his voice. The shift to the pictorialization of the American imagination as well as the bureaucratization of American life was now amply represented by the very functioning of the American presidency—that elective monarchy which in more than one way contained elements of neo-medievalization. The great historian Huizinga had described how imagination and life in the late Middle Ages were excessively public and pictorial. Like the medieval monarch, the American president now depended on a court of advisors who planned his public appearance and who presented not only the various options but the very selection and the formulation of those problems which, in their opinion, and always with an eye on immediate publicity, the elective monarch had to address.

In the 1950s another transformation of the American procedure of presidential elections was developing fast. This was the increasing influence of presidential primaries. It was yet another example of the shortcomings of the populist and progressive ideas propagated half a century earlier. (The first presidential primary took place in 1905, in the prototypically populist-progressive state of Wisconsin, the same state whose voters supported the demagogue Joseph R. McCarthy with enormous majorities in the 1950s; in

1952 he received 72 percent of the vote in the Republican primary.) At first sight the introduction of primaries seemed to be a further extension of the democratization of the American political process—another move in the direction of making the election the equivalent of a popularity contest. A closer look ought to reveal that, instead of an extension of popularity, the hullabaloo of the presidential primaries resulted in the achievement of popularity through publicity. In 1954 the state of Oregon enacted a primary law, according to which "the names of those persons who the Secretary of State of Oregon determines in his sole discretion to be 'generally advocated or recognized in national news media throughout the United States' as presidential candidates are placed on the ballot." In other words, the nominators were the "national news media," not the people.

In 1960 the first televised "debate" of presidential candidates took place. As with all subsequent ones, this was a debate only in the broadest (and flattest) possible meaning of the word. It consisted of a few selected and alternating statements by the two candidates, who had not only been prompted and trained for these decisive sixty minutes, but who had also been combed, primped, dressed, and face-smoothed for many hours and after interminable consultations with advertisers, movie people, hairdressers, and other assorted beauticians. Since in 1960 John Kennedy won the election by a narrow margin, there is at least reason to believe that his attractive appearance on the screen was an important contribution to his victory over the less attractive Nixon. These television "debates" subsequently became prime events in the presidential contests. Their most absurd example occurred in 1976. The scene was a theater in Philadelphia, chosen by the respective staffs of the two candidates after months of assiduous consultation, carefully apportioning the audience, who served as theatrical props, mechanically applauding now one candidate and then the other. An electrical failure cut off the sound toward the end of the "debate." The president of the United States, Gerald Ford, and his eventual successor, Jimmy Carter, stood for fifteen minutes numb and dumb, facing the nation (and the world) without saying a word, not daring to turn toward or to talk to each other, standing uneasily behind their lecterns, with their eyes downcast. Consumed by fear and embarrassment, they looked as if they were unable to move because their trousers had fallen down.

Their predecessor, Richard Nixon, was the only president in the history of the Republic who had to resign, threatened as he was with the prospect of impeachment. Nixon was an extremely complex character, not devoid of certain talents and even of vision, yet in many ways deeply unsure of himself. He was not especially successful with the publicity media. Thus, it would not be accurate to say that Nixon, like other presidents and presi-

607

dential candidates of his era, was the creature of publicity. There was also an appreciable difference between the public and the private Nixon; as a matter of fact, the frequent, and unconsciously revealing, occasionally startling, expressions of the private Nixon greatly contributed to the dislike, ranging from disdain to outright hatred, that many people felt for him. Yet this unusual man was as much, if not more, obsessed with publicity than were any of his immediate predecessors or successors. In this respect Nixon, too, was an example—and perhaps an extreme example—of the *homo americanus* of a new breed, in regarding and treating his image as if it were not a reflection of reality but reality itself. His first successful election campaign in 1968 was criticized in a best-selling book as *The Selling of the President*, even though this campaign differed from others of that period by degree, not in kind. What was incontestable was that by the 1960s many of the principal agents and aides of presidential candidates were publicity men, whose main experience and achievement was not in the field of industry or business but in public relations. They, too, were a new breed: neither political partisans nor even ideologues, for the most part. Such people, for the first time in the history of the presidency, became the most trusted aides of Richard Nixon. Since Nixon was the first elected president in the history of the United States who openly avowed that he was a "conservative," supporters as well as opponents of Nixon thought that he would depend on people with such an ideological persuasion. Yet the principal liegemen and barons of his staff were California public relations men such as Haldeman and Ehrlichman, uninterested in ideological persuasions, which is perhaps the reason they felt surprisingly at ease with the police bureaucrats whom they met in Moscow or Peking. Their principal preoccupation was to shield the president from people and influences opposed to their own vocation, which was the maintenance of their president's power through every conceivable kind of publicity and practice justifiable in the name of "national security." In this, mostly because of their own shortsightedness, they failed. Still, the president himself attributed the rising wave of his popular opposition to the power of the public "media," obsessed as he was with his image.[26]

The superficial good looks of both Spiro Agnew and Gerald Ford were the main elements in Nixon's choosing them for his vice presidents. He was also confident that these men of mediocre talents would not overshadow him in his office, which was indeed the case. The public relations men and the pollsters had become the important people in the White House. By 1970 the very selection of a presidential press secretary (previously a former journalist giving handouts to reporters) had become an event that was analyzed with more assiduity than the selection of a cabinet member. In 1976 the main element in the election of Jimmy Carter was a wave of national empathy for the picture of an unassuming person emerging from the rural America of the South. In reality the character of this self-styled simple and frugal person was as complex as that of Nixon or Wilson. It may be at least arguable that Carter was the first American president whose purpose in becoming president consisted entirely of his wish to win the presidential race, and who gave little, if any, thought to what he would do once that race was won. Having won the governorship of Georgia once, he decided to try for the big one, somewhat like a TV contestant trusting his luck (and the sympathy of the producers) in a quiz show. He depended on pollsters and public relations experts even more than had his predecessors. The insubstantiality of his character defeated him in the long run. (Napoleon once said that he who fears his reputation is sure to lose it; Maurice Baring wrote, "Nothing in the world is more insuperable than the obstinacy of the weak.") Finally, in 1980—in part due to the disillusionment with the utter incompetence of Carter's administration, in part because of a conservative surge— the American people, for the first time in the history of their Republic and in the history of modern Western civilization, chose a former movie actor for president.

Of course Ronald Reagan was not only a movie actor; he had been governor of California. Still, his emergence as a public statesman was due in part to the pictorialization of the American imagination. When in 1956 the U.S. Air Force Academy came into existence, Eisenhower's secretary of the Air Force announced that the uniforms of the Air Force cadets were being designed by the movie producer Cecil B. De Mille and his associates. In 1971 President Nixon had the entire White House guard dressed up in movie-parade uniforms. (This was not a success: eventually the costumes were sold off piecemeal, some of them going to high school bands in the West, some to Bolivia.) In the 1970s, the movie actor John Wayne became an American kind of national hero because he represented in his films—in contrast to most other films of the period—traditional American virtues (traditional, that is, since the movies and *The Virginian*) that seemed to be incarnate in the western cowboy or sheriff. In 1979, when the United States was humiliated by a Persian mob in Tehran, students of San Jose University in California marched around the streets holding up pictures of John Wayne. What counted even more than the stereotyped roles that Wayne played was his well-publicized personal image, whereby in the minds of millions the political opinions and the social preferences of this virile actor corresponded exactly with his roles on the screen. His death was mourned by a congressional proclamation; in California airports and high schools were named after him. About Ronald Reagan we may say, even at this time of writing (1983), that few of his predecessors depended on pollsters and public relations "experts" as much as he has. His cabinet and his advisers included certain "neoconservatives" or even "conservatives": but power in the White House was exercised by three of his advisers, every one of them involved in public relations previous to their appointment, one of them the previous owner of a public relations firm in California. "In the middle of this enterprise," reported an article about the Reagan administration in the *New York Times Magazine*, "stands David Gergen, whose official title is Assistant to the President for Communications.... Gergen now serves as the chief White House spokesman, oversees the operations of the press and communications offices and plays a highly influential role in setting strategy and policy."[27] In other words, the packaging, presentation, and advertising of the "product"—that is, the deliberations of the highest statecraft—not only influenced the product but were part and parcel of its creation.

Ronald Reagan's election was not the result of a publicity hoax. He was, and for some time remained, a popular president, popular with the American people at large. Yet it was evident from the beginning that most of the decisions and statements of this amiable and benevolent president were made with the immediate impact of publicity in mind; a disturbing and potentially disastrous practice, especially when it comes to foreign policy. When, for example, a few months after the election, the pollsters in the White House began to worry about the popularity of the president slipping because of proposed policies involving El Salvador, Richard S. Beal, one of the president's speechwriters and publicity analysts, admitted to the reporter, "What was wrong with El Salvador was the packaging of the activity, in terms of policy and presentation to the public. It wasn't well staged or sequenced." (His very language was telling; "sequencing"—the timing and order of a series of actions—"voter cohort targets," "resistance ratios," "opportunity windows," "and the need to be 'proactive' rather than reactive.") At the time of this interview this pollster was engaged in writing the president's State of the Union speech. Of his work he told the reporter, "We lay out the scenarios of winning and losing. Our work concerns the identification of issues, goals and principles at the macro level. . . ." "By analyzing polling results," the reporter added, "[Beal] believes he can tell what public views on what question are likely to prevail at a given time.... This helps the president [or rather, the president's men] decide how to proceed."[28] That this was something very different from presidential leadership in the past—or perhaps from any kind of leadership in the traditional sense—should be obvious. The transformation of the political process from a popularity contest to a publicity contest did not begin in 1980, but it was now nearly complete. The very word "popular" was fading in political usage, while "image" and "publicity" became more frequent.[29]

One of the main themes of Ronald Reagan's presidential campaign was the reduction of governmental bureaucracy. Yet with all of the reductions ordered in government, the staffing of the White House diminished not at all. When the New Deal came in in 1933 the White House staff numbered less than fifty. Fifty years later it consisted of 600 or more—and this includes only full-time White House employees.[30]

> Something more than Parkinson's law has been at work in the growth of the White House staff. . . . The shift from exclusive use by Roosevelt of behind-the-scenes advisors to use of a staff authorized by statute is recorded in the *United States Government Manual* released in October 1939. Listed immediately following the page identifying the President of the United States is what continues to be the umbrella heading under which presidential agencies are grouped—the Executive Office of the President (EOP). The White House Office (WHO) is listed next. (In October 1939 only three WHO aides had been selected. In the 1970–1971 *Manual,* about the peak year for size of WHO staff, over fifty were listed.)[31]

That the transformation of the American presidency to a publicity enterprise is inseparable from the existence of such a vast "executive" bureaucracy should now be obvious. In the Middle Ages, indeed, until about the seventeenth century, kings had no cabinets; they depended on councils of advisers. In the second half of the twentieth century the elective monarchy of the American presidency assumed more and more of the characteristics of medieval kingship, with the liege lords having the power of determining access to the monarch, to the extent that even cabinet officers could no longer see the president on their own, that is, without the consent of the aforementioned liege lords who determined not only what and whom the president should see but also what he should hear—and perhaps, subsequently, think. That such a near-absolute preoccupation with publicity involves an underestimation of the character (and, implicitly, of the necessary intelligence) of the elected president—as well as of the American people—should be obvious too.

For a long time American democracy has been criticized by many a skeptical conservative for proceeding on the basis of overestimating the intelligence of the democratic masses, of the people at large. This may have been true on occasion. Yet, after everything is said, idealism is preferable to cynicism, and even gullibility to distrust. The habitual overestimation of popular or public, private or personal intelligence, too, is infinitely preferable to its habitual underestimation. The traditional, and often thoughtless, strain of generosity in the American character prevailed, by and large, through two centuries: this was what F. Scott Fitzgerald, in a memorable sentimental phrase, called the American "willingness of the heart." But underneath its superficial symptoms grew a dark countercurrent: the unwillingness of the managerial mind. Thus the paradox: the very people who professed their faith in the reality of "public opinion" now depended on a cynical estimate of it.

In American education, too, the fatal decline of its institutions and purposes in the twentieth century was the result of a corroding kind of cynicism within a vast educational bureaucracy, increasingly dependent on their assumption that of American youth not much should be, because not much could be, demanded. As with the presidency, the material costs and the administrations of the schools grew monstrously expensive; yet the duties and the learning and the very imagination of the youth declined. There was more than a parallel, there was a connection between these devolutions. With the pictorialization of instruction and imagination, to which television contributed, the American cult of youth extended the period of confused adolescence rather than that of youthfulness. An increasing number of public figures gave the impression of immature men. A kind of puerilism marked many American attitudes—an unnaturally extended puerilism that tended to transmute itself into senility alarmingly and swiftly. As Johan Huizinga wrote, "Puerilism we shall call the attitude of a community whose behavior is more immature than the state of its intellectual and critical faculties would warrant, which instead of making the boy into the man adapts the conduct to that of the adolescent age. The term has nothing to do with that of infantilism in psychoanalysis." In 1851 Tocqueville wrote about the first democratically elected national assembly in France in 1848, "I am sure that nine hundred English or American peasants chosen at random would have had much more the look of a great political body." A century later this was no longer true.

Yet this condition can no longer be blamed exclusively on the people themselves, true though the old adage—every people has the government it deserves—remains. By the 1970s the dangers of the Revolt of the Masses, of the Mass Man, of the Tyranny of the Majority faded; they had an unreal sound. The danger of the tyranny of the majority belonged to that phase of American and democratic history when politics and presidential elections *were* popularity contests. Now the wishes of the people and the inclinations even of majorities could be submerged, while the influence and the very existence of certain minorities could (and would) be exaggerated by publicity, beyond proportion and reason.

During and after the two world wars of the twentieth century the power and prestige of the American presidency became enormous. Some of this prestige was the result of American power; much of it was due to the flooding of the world with "communications," that is, with publicity.[32] But this kind of democratic Caesarism was different from the past, and even different from what Tocqueville had feared. (He had seen it come to pass during his lifetime, in 1849, when the first democratic presidential election in France brought Louis Napoleon to power, clear evidence that the progress of Liberty and Equality were not the same, or not even necessarily parallel.) Yet some time during the twentieth century it began to appear that the danger to democracy was no longer the tyranny of the majority but that of certain insistent, influential, and powerful minorities. Their pursuit of popularity through the commercialization of politics, entertainment, education, and art obscured this. The taste of the public may have become debased, but it was not vicious by nature. It was not the people who decided what was being shown on television; it was not the students who decided what was being taught and required in their colleges; it was not the choice of the public that governed the reputation of artists—it was the television producers, the faculty committees, the art critics, and the foundation executives. And so we cannot really speak of the Tyranny of the Majority, except in an indirect sense: for the majority has been often silent, passive, acquiescent, and in certain instances long-suffering.

This relationship of "hard" minorities and "soft" majorities has not only compromised the democratic process of legislation and government, including the knowledge of what really happens. It has also compromised the chances of the reconstruction of what happened: the task of the historian who—unless he is equipped with a great deal of independent probity and insight—will be easily misled in his "research" of majority opinion and sentiment that may have been simulated by minorities but that, in reality, represented the true state of opinions and sentiments current among the people hardly or not at all.

The great historian Burckhardt wrote that during the Renaissance, in the beginning of the Modern Age, an important mutation occurred in the Italian attitude toward leadership:

> The highly gifted man of that day thought to find it in the sentiment of honor. This is that enigmatic mixture of conscience and egotism which often survives in the modern man after he has lost, whether by his own fault or not, faith, love, hope. This sense of honor is compatible with much selfishness and great vices, and may be the victim of astonishing illusions; yet, never-

theless, all the noble elements that are left in the wreck of a character may gather around it, and from this fountain may draw new strength.... It is certainly not easy, in treating of the Italian of this period, to distinguish this sense of honor from the passion for fame, into which, indeed, it may easily pass. Yet the two sentiments are essentially different.[33]

In our times, toward the end of the Modern Age, the difference—indeed, the discrepancy—between fame and honor has become so great that in the character of presidents, and in those of public figures in all kinds of endeavor, the passion for fame has well-nigh obliterated the now remote and ancient sense of honor.

There remained, too, a discrepancy between those who still believed in original sin and those who believed in secular progress, a discrepancy between two articles of belief: according to orthodox Christian doctrine the prince of this world is Satan; according to the kind of American doctrine that became a kind of American orthodoxy in the twentieth century, the prince of this world is the president of the United States.

59

The Bourgeois Interior
(1970)

The Modern Age, or Modern History, are now misnomers. They were farsighted misnomers centuries ago, when they were coined and put into intellectual currency by our ancestors who were overoptimistic in this regard; they took the growing and sprouting landscape of new trees for a perennial forest opening up around them. They are shortsighted misnomers now. Sometime in the future the now closing period of history will receive another name. This giving of names is the kind of intellectual exercise that ought not preoccupy us at this time. Yet I must say something about a principal characteristic of this so-called Modern Age that is still with us, because of its protean manifestations, many of which will, I am sure, survive into the New Dark Ages or whatever comes next.

I am thinking of the bourgeois spirit. In writing about this I must break through an amorphous intellectual obstacle. "Bourgeois" and "bourgeoisie" are not English words. (From my experience with examination papers I suspect that probably the majority of the three hundred million people whose native language is English cannot spell them without one mistake or two.) The reason for this is that the phenomenon of a bourgeoisie was largely peculiar to the continent of Europe. In England and in the United States large middle classes have existed: and the term "bourgeois" has been considered as if it were their French equivalent. But this virtual equation of bourgeois and middle class has been wrong. They were not, and are not, the same things. Every society has a class that is situated in the middle, between the upper and the lower classes. Not every society had, or has, a bourgeoisie. The existence of a middle class is a universal, a sociological phenomenon. The existence of the bourgeois, on the other hand, has been a particular phenomenon, a historical reality.

From *The Passing of the Modern Age* (New York: Harper and Row), 191–207.

The difficulties of the word "bourgeois" have been compounded by its reputation. For more than a century now it has been a bad word: it suggested not only "middle-class" but also "unimaginative," "pedestrian," "philistine." There was a romantic and an aesthetic element in this attribution of vileness to the bourgeois. The self-professed artist, sometime after 1820, especially in France, claimed to be an aristocrat of the spirit, and even the brummagem aristocracy of the bohemians professed to be the very antipole of the bourgeoisie. Ridiculed by aristocrats as well as by radicals, during the nineteenth century the bourgeois were hated by the extreme Right and Left alike.

This nineteenth-century, sometimes snobbish, and later Marxist, usage of the term was, in reality, narrow and inaccurate. Marx equated, in effect, the bourgeois with the capitalist spirit. He was wrong. Anti-Marxists, such as the German social thinker Werner Sombart in his monumental *Der Bourgeois* (1911), made the same mistake, from a different angle. They did not consider sufficiently that one could be a bourgeois without being a capitalist, which was true of many people in the rising professions; or that, conversely, one could be a capitalist without being a bourgeois; that in many instances rich people were excluded from the ranks of the bourgeois for all kinds of reasons. In America, Charles A. Beard wrote that the United States has only one large class, "the petty bourgeoisie—despite proletarian and plutocratic elements which cannot come under that classification . . . the American ideal most widely expressed is the *embourgeoisement* of the whole society—a universality of comfort, convenience, security, leisure, standard possessions of food, clothing, and shelter." Standard possessions of food, clothing, and shelter? These are middle-class aspirations, not bourgeois ones. The philosopher Berdyaev, in *The Bourgeois Mind* (1934), again equated the middle class with the bourgeois: the bourgeois mind, he wrote, is both materialist and smug, "self-satisfaction is one of his characteristic traits." This is nearly nonsense. The principal criticisms one might level against the bourgeois mind are its caution, its calculation, its cowardice, its seeking refuge in conformism: the kind of thoughtless self-satisfaction of which Berdyaev writes was more characteristic of the European aristocracies than of the bourgeoisie.

After the Second World War certain discriminating writers, especially in France, recognized that the meaning of "bourgeois" was not so simple, after all. Pierre Gaxotte suggested, in passing, that it meant something more than a social class.[1] In one of his aphoristic essays Jean Dutourd had some rather intelligent things to say about the term "bourgeois": "It is one of those ambiguous and inconstant terms that change at every turn of history. In spite of Molière's mockeries that anticipate Flaubert's, the word means something different at the time of the Fronde and under Louis XV, during the reign of Robespierre and of Napoleon III, for the Communards of 1871 and for the surrealists under the reign of André Breton...." "Flaubert himself, so violently antibourgeois, heartily approved the suppression of the Commune, regretting only that too few of the workers had been executed. ...." "In our days the bourgeois have abdicated. In fact the bourgeois democracies of the second half of the twentieth century are socialists. To apply their old discredited name to them is nothing but hypocritical propaganda."[2] In a thoughtful book, *Métamorphose du bourgeois,* Professor Jacques Ellul has tried to come to terms with this fluidity of meaning. "The bourgeois is Proteus himself," he writes. "A grotesque weakling and a man of iron, an imbecile and a powerful executive, a cold-hearted egotist and a founder of philanthropies, a Milquetoast and an adventurer, a lecher and a family man.... [W]ho is the bourgeois?"[3] The question evokes the most extreme and contradictory answers. "Was there ever an enterprise greater than the Industrial Revolution?... Strangely enough, we admire that revolution and we despise the bourgeois who invented it and put it into effect."[4] He goes to a fashionable contemporary dictionary where he finds that "bourgeois," "thinking bourgeois," "seeming bourgeois" is defined as "vulgar." This dictionary (the *Robert*) uses certain selective citations to buttress its point. Flaubert: "I call a bourgeois anyone who thinks low" ("*quiconque pense bassement.*") Gide: "... there are bourgeois workers and bourgeois nobles. I recognize the bourgeois not by his habits and not by his social level but by the level of his thinking. The bourgeois... hates everything that he cannot understand." This is not much help.

Professor Ellul is quite right when he criticizes some of these "definitions." He, too, insists that the institution of private property is not necessarily characteristic of the bourgeoisie. Yet his book, too, is unsatisfactory on an important point. Obsessed as he is with the protean and changing forms of the "bourgeois," Ellul in effect equates him throughout with "modern man."

Bourgeois: modern. Let me now try to sort out what I have in mind.

Instead of the Modern Age we *could* speak of the Bourgeois Age. Those who talk of the age of aristocracy before the First World War, or before the War of American Independence, do not know what they are talking about. The aristocracies may have kept their social, and in certain countries their political leadership, but by the eighteenth century in most of Europe the prevailing ways of thought were bourgeois. A sociography of the principal thinkers, writers, artists, poets, inventors of the last three hundred years would show that their vast majority came from a bourgeois background— no matter how many of them may have attacked the bourgeoisie.

The mathematicability of reality, the cult of reason, free trade, liberalism, the abolition of slavery, of censorship, the contractual idea of the state, constitutionalism, individualism, socialism, nationalism, internationalism—these were not aristocratic ideas. For bourgeois means something more than a social class: it means certain rights and privileges, certain aspirations, certain ways of thinking even more than of living. Note that I write "ways of thinking" rather than "frames of mind": for the bourgeois standards and habits of thought were constantly changing; and what was characteristic of them was not their fixity *but the way in which they have been changing*. (Had the aristocracies had their way there would have been little change.) The bourgeois spirit—and this is its least admirable characteristic—has been too conformist, not sufficiently independent. The bourgeoisie tried to conform to the powers that prevailed. With a few inspiring exceptions the European aristocracies during the entire Modern Age have done the same: they, perhaps even more than the aspiring bourgeoisie, knew how to adapt themselves to new rulers, new powers, new times; they did this a trifle more gracefully than most of the bourgeois: that was all.

There was a difference nonetheless. The aristocracies would conform indifferently. The bourgeois would conform with a kind of nervous energy. The behavior of the former conformed more than had their minds. The minds of the latter conformed as much as had their behavior. (The idea-mongering philosophers and writers of the nineteenth century, including Dostoevsky, missed this; obsessed with their ideological discovery of what ideas can do to men they overlooked the more complex problem of what men can do to ideas.)

The Middle Ages were marked by the domination of aristocracies: but during the Modern Age democracy was not yet dominant. True, the ideas of popular government became more current and finally respectable: but democratic standards were not wholly translated into practice, not even in the English-speaking nations, until literally our very times. Typical of the bourgeois era was the coexistence of democratic ideas with aristocratic standards. The half-thousand years from about 1450 to 1950 were no longer an age of aristocracy and not yet that of democracy: in many places of the Western world it would not be altogether wrong to designate them as the Bourgeois Age.

Free citizens: this was the original aspiration of a bourgeoisie whose emergence, in Europe, long preceded that of capitalism. "The first mention of the word [bourgeois] occurs in France in 1007" (Henri Pirenne). It had nothing to do with capital: it had very much to do with the city. "Bourgeois," "Bürger," "burgher," "borghese" meant city dweller. For the European city as it grew during the Middle Ages was different from the Greek *polis* and the Roman *urbs* as well as from the modern American city. It had walls which provided for security. They made for a sharp physical separation of the city from the surrounding countryside. This lasted for hundreds of years. There was a definite distinction of citizen from countryman. It was a privilege to belong to the community of the city. "*Stadtluft macht frei,*" some Germans were wont to say: the city air makes you free. This was true at least in a metaphorical sense. Citizenship meant a real community, not an artificial one. The otherwise rich Russian language, for example, has no word that is the equivalent of bourgeois: the nearest word means "city dweller," devoid of the implications of civic and political rights, of an urban community, of permanence of residence. But Russian cities, with few exceptions, had no walls separating them from the surrounding land. The walled portion of the city, as the Kremlin in Moscow, was there to keep the rulers apart from the rest of the people, as in China.

In England, too, with few exceptions (and, of course, in America) cities had no walls. In the English-speaking countries the rights acquired by the gentry, by the yeomanry, by the merchants, by these developing classes in the middle of the social structure were not predominantly urban. On the other hand the controlled confluence of democracy and aristocracy was the special strength of English civilization: the social attraction of certain aristocratic standards marked the prevalence of an English kind of civility which, except perhaps for a brief period, could not be properly called bourgeois, while it was certainly patrician.

The great achievements of European civilization during the last half-thousand years were predominantly patrician in their inspiration, urbane in their manners, urban in their spirit. This kind of urban civilization, with its liberties, had little in common with those of ancient Athens or Rome and not much in common with the liberties that had been extracted by the nobility from their weak kings during the Middle Ages. This kind of "urbanization" was different, too, from the external spreading of cities with the subsequent disappearance of all distinctions between city and country, from that enormous suburbanization of everything that has set in during the twentieth century and that people who should, but don't, know better mistakenly call the "urbanization" of the world. The monstrous conglomerations of a Tokyo or a Los Angeles are not at all urban in the traditional sense. They have much to do with the enormous swelling of a middle class: they have little to do with the bourgeois spirit. In a country such as Japan we can speak of a swelling middle class, we can even speak of the swelling of capitalism, but not of a bourgeoisie in the older European sense, just as the "Westernization" of Japan (as also of many other countries) means, simply, Americanization.

The transition from an aristocratic to a democratic era, or the increasing admixture of aristocracy with democracy, explains the bourgeois spirit only in part. The Greeks and the Romans experienced the former without ever being bourgeois. Their thinking was different from that of our closer ancestors. Their consciousness was different, as their aspirations were different. The bourgeois kind of "urbanization" was a later phase in the evolution of human consciousness, it marked the beginning of the "internalization" of the human condition.

Free, and also secure: these were marks of the bourgeois spirit. Not for nothing did satirical draftsmen and writers depict the bourgeois wearing a nightcap, tucking himself under a large comforter on a rainy or wintry night. When we think of a bourgeois scene, we seldom think of nature outdoors; we usually think of something that is human, comfortable, cozy. We seldom think of a bright glittering morning; we think of an afternoon or evening. Is it thus true that the bourgeois epoch was the long autumn afternoon of Western civilization, following, say, the glorious dawn of Antiquity and the glorious noon of the Renaissance? This is what thinkers such as Spengler tell us, insisting even that there were bourgeois colors such as brown. But there is something else that Spengler did not understand: that the increasing "interiority" of the bourgeois era was involved with the increasing "internalization" of the human condition in the West.

All of its spiritual aspirations notwithstanding, the medieval civilization was strongly external, "all things in life were of a proud or cruel publicity" (Huizinga). The bourgeois era of European civilization, on the contrary, was marked by the internal deepening of human consciousness of which Erasmus, Montaigne, and even disillusioned aristocrats such as La Rochefoucauld were early prime examples. As the exploration of the external world accelerated, at the same time our ancestors became more and more aware of the interior landscape of their minds.

Words such as *self-love, self-confidence, self-command, self-esteem, self-knowledge, self-pity;* other words such as *disposition, character, ego, egoism, conscience, melancholy, apathy, agitation, embarrassment, sensible, sentimental,* appeared in English or French in their modern sense only two or three hundred years ago. And as their appearance marked the emergence of something new in the minds of peoples, something new appeared, too, in their daily lives. As the self-consciousness of medieval people was spare, the interiors of their houses were bare, including the halls of nobles and of kings. The interior furniture of houses appeared together with the interior furniture of minds.

There are many potential illustrations of this. One may suffice, from the extraordinary book of our contemporary French historian Philippe Ariès, translated into English under the title *Centuries of Childhood*. He reminds us that in paintings before the end of the fifteenth century interior scenes are extremely rare.

> But from that century on, they become increasingly common. The gospel-writer, hitherto placed in a timeless setting, becomes a scribe at his desk, with a quill and an erasing-knife in his hand. At first he is placed in front of an ordinary ornamental curtain, but finally he is shown in a room where there are shelves lined with books: we have come from the gospel-writer to the author in his room, to Froissart writing a dedication in a book. In the illustrations to the text of Terence in the Palace of the Doges, there are women working and spinning in their rooms with their maidservants, or lying in bed, not always by themselves. We are shown kitchens and inn rooms. Love scenes and conversations are henceforth set in the enclosed space of a room.
>
> The theme of child-birth makes its appearance, the birth of the Virgin providing the pretext. Maidservants, old women and midwives are shown bustling round St. Ann's bed. The theme of death appears too: death in the bedchamber, with the dying man fighting for his life.
>
> The growing practice of depicting rooms corresponds to a new emotional tendency henceforth directed towards the intimacy of private life. Exterior scenes do not disappear—they develop into the landscape—but interior scenes become more common and more original, and they typify genre painting during the whole of its existence. Private life, thrust into the background in the Middle Ages, invades iconography in the sixteenth and above all in the seventeenth century: Dutch and Flemish painting and French engraving show the extraordinary strength of this hitherto inconsistent or neglected concept.[5]

Even in the richest and noblest houses before the seventeenth century there were hardly any rooms which served for specific purposes since the notion of privacy scarcely existed. Much of the furniture, including even beds and tables, were collapsible and, therefore, portable. "In the same rooms where they ate, people slept, danced, worked and received visitors."[6] In the seventeenth century this was beginning to change. The collapsible beds, for example, became permanent pieces of furniture, even though for a while the bedroom remained a public room, but the beds were now curtained off. (Later the bedroom becomes *the* private room: the only room in the house that will be called not *salle* but *chambre, camera*.)

What is involved here is far more important than the history of furniture: it involves the history of the family and of the home. Domesticity, privacy, comfort, the concept of the home and of the family: these are, literally, principal achievements of the Bourgeois Age. How wrong it is to believe, for example, that the German insistence on the patriarchal family, surviving into the twentieth century, was medieval in inspiration! The idea of the family in the Middle Ages was much weaker than we are accustomed to think. In any event, it was much different from ours.[7] In the Middle Ages the lives of children were separated from those of their parents; this practice endured for a long time, especially among the aristocracy and among the poor. The idea that children were full-fledged human beings, that they were entitled to a kind of protected equality within the family, this, too, was the result of the bourgeois spirit. By the seventeenth century it ceased to be customary to entrust children to strangers. As Ariès puts it: "This return of the children to the home was a great event; it gave the seventeenth-century family its principal characteristic, which distinguished it from the medieval family. The child became an indispensable element of everyday life, and his parents worried about his education, his career, his future. He was not yet the pivot of the whole system, but he had become a much more important character."

It was only then that, through the bourgeois insistence on privacy, the family became the most important unit of society. Not in the admittedly Christian Middle Ages, when the idea of the house or home was still weak. "The concept of the home is another aspect of the concept of the family." Between the eighteenth century and 1950 "the concept of the family hardly changed at all." It grew: it extended further and further through society. As late as a century and a half ago medieval habits of family life, including the absence of the children from the home, still prevailed among the poor of many a nation. But finally family life "embraced nearly the whole of society, to such an extent that people have forgotten its [largely bourgeois] origins."[8]

The family: the home. If we, in our situation, have any kind of nostalgia at all, it is for this: for the security, and for the freedom, of the Bourgeois Age, for its *inner* security, and for its *inner* freedom, for a kind of life that some of us have once known and that others among us can still imagine. … The very word *nostalgia* in Greek meant, literally, homesickness, a painful longing for a place like home, for something that we have once known. Thus we ought to abandon our superficial and sentimental (and, therefore, false) nostalgia for the chivalry of the Middle Ages, because that is a nostalgia for a world that we have not known: it represents an interest in a past that is ideal, not real—unlike our occasional longing for some of the verities of the Bourgeois Age, still so familiar to us.

How curious this is! At the end of the Modern Age millions of people become attracted to bourgeois things. Certain bourgeois scenes have now become idyllic to our minds. This would have surprised the Romantics: they would have revolted against the very notion of it. And yet it was they, the Romantics who, having made a breakthrough in the direction of consciousness, provided for the development of this rich and still interiority, all of their aristocratic and neomedieval pretensions notwithstanding. The bourgeois were once the deadly enemies of the Romantics. Or, rather, they only seemed to be. Now we know that the Romantics were bourgeois, and that the bourgeois were Romantics, to a considerable extent, far more than we (and, of course, than they themselves) were accustomed to think. These are not abstract or literary speculations: we can understand them historically. The zenith of Romanticism was the period around 1820. That was the beginning of the bourgeois zenith, of the Modern Age, too, before the enormous smoky swelling of cities, before the revolutions of 1848, before even in Eastern America Jacksonian democracy set in. Characteristic of the architecture and of the furniture before the 1830s was a kind of patrician, rather than aristocratic, elegance, something that evokes in us a real nostalgia: for we could live in those rooms ourselves, unlike in the glittering, coldly magnificent rooms of the eighteenth century. Not only the rooms and the houses, the landscapes of the period around 1820 breathe a kind of comfort to which we instantly respond because, to some extent, they are still familiar and comprehensible for us. The idyllic component is real, not merely Arcadian. Perhaps this interior stillness reflected a momentary state of high equilibrium, the peak achievement of an age. The spirit, even more than the style, of bourgeois interiority suffused the landscape, and it penetrated the minds of millions even in countries and places where a bourgeois class hardly existed at all.

Here is an example: *Stille Nacht,* "Silent Night," the song that is probably known by more people in the world than any other. It was composed by a village priest in 1818, in the Austrian Tyrol. At that time the Tyrol was one of the more backward mountain provinces of the still largely feudal Habsburg empire. The common ways of life in the Tyrol of 1818 were close to the seventeenth century. The Tyroleans wore the clothes of the past, their towns were isolated, apart; they would not encounter many bourgeois even in the somnolent provincial capital of Innsbruck where the *Bürger* were few, mostly artisans, members of guilds, a few teachers, a few bureaucrats. Even now the childlike simplicity of *Stille Nacht* suggests to us a pastoral (if not *the* pastoral) scene: the village church in a mountain valley, the snow, the silent night. Even people who know little history associate it with a faraway, feudal and pastoral, premodern past.

And yet the success, indeed, the spirit of *Stille Nacht* was not feudal, it was bourgeois. For our cult of Christmas is a bourgeois phenomenon, more recent than we are inclined to think. During the Middle Ages, and for centuries afterward, the principal holy event of the year was Easter, not Christmas, in accord with the Christian theology of the supremacy of the Resurrection, Christ becoming God being an event even greater than His coming to earth. This habit lasted for a long time in Russia, Spain, Ireland, nations that have been touched but little by bourgeois humanism. In Puritan New England, too, and in many places in Scotland Christmas Day was an ordinary workday as late as a century and a half ago. But during the nineteenth century the cult of Christmas began to spread. Eventually Christmas became associated with commercialism and with publicity, much of which reflected the prevailing need of most people for the kind of sentimentalism that Oscar Wilde, wittily and quite correctly, designated as the Bank Holiday of cynicism.

And yet there is more to this. Christmas has an element of interiority that Easter does not have. Beyond the growth of middle-class sentimentality, beyond the transitory revival of the respectability of religion that occurred during the first quarter of the nineteenth century, this evolution of the cult of Christmas in the lives of people reflected the evolution of "internalization." The growing cult of Christmas was involved with the rise in the cult of the child, indeed, with that of the family whose origins, as we have seen, were less feudal than they were bourgeois. The central figure of the child, God coming to Earth, the giving of gifts, the element of peace and warmth in the middle of winter—this modern cult of Christmas responded to some of the deepest aspirations of the bourgeois spirit. So did "Silent Night." Its appearance marks the zenith of the Bourgeois Age, in some ways like the words of Goethe's *Wanderers Nachtlied*, expressing the sense of a sublime equilibrium, a sublime stillness. Of all Christmas songs *Stille Nacht* is the simplest and the most childlike; it is not a song for a great choir, it has little of the baroque in it that marks most of our carols even now. Perhaps this was why it had such an attraction for the bourgeois of the world, this *Biedermeyer* melody (for it is far more *Biedermeyer* than folkish) to which the *Bürger* of Vienna, including Protestants and Jews, responded instantly. It traveled thereafter across frontiers and oceans. In the 1950s the Eastern European Communist governments gave up their struggle against the cult of Christmas. In Tokyo "Krismasu" became the greatest feature in the annual program of department stores. I believe that "Silent Night" will be sung one hundred years from now. And thus this final paradox: the most massive survival of a religious cult has been the product of the bourgeois spirit.

We have seen that it is wrong to confuse bourgeois with middle-class, for the latter term is sociological, not historical. It is also static, not dynamic. The Bourgeois Age was marked by aspirations, by social ambitions. During the Middle Ages ambition flourished only within the aristocracy; but the Bourgeois Ages did not only introduce social mobility, it made a virtue out of it: nobody should rest satisfied with his lot, he should always think of bettering it. For a while "this eagerness to rise in the world" was mixed with the spirit of the Renaissance; it pretended to fulfill something of a heroic ideal: but after the seventeenth century it became involved with the propagation of education. In any event, even after the somewhat compromised heroic ideal was passing, the desire to rise in the world remained strong. The ambitious men and women and adolescents within the new middle classes emulate successful people within their own group. The aspiring bourgeois emulated the classes which still stood above them.

In one sense this led to a social selfishness which was the worst characteristic of the bourgeoisie. In the Middle Ages "people lived in a state of contrast; high birth or great wealth rubbed shoulders with poverty, vice with virtue, scandal with devotion. Despite its shrill contrasts, this medley of colours caused no surprise." But "there came a time when the [bourgeois] could no longer bear the pressure of the multitude or the contact of the lower class." Instead, they cultivated, selfishly, their "homes designed for privacy, in new districts kept free from all lower-class contamination."[9] This kind of narrow selfishness revolted sensitive people; it still repels us. There gleams a kind of naked selfishness in some of the faces of handsome and successful people, surviving in photographs of an Edwardian ascot or of the Avenue des Acacias around 1910, that is unappealing, as it reflects a kind of superficial rigidity that may mask something that is either decomposing or already hollow. Certain satirists would capture this better than social thinkers or political philosophers. Saki would record "a garden party in full swing, with smart frocks and smart conversation, fashionable refreshments and fashionable music, and a fevered undercurrent of social strivings and snubbings." The large-spirited and amused Wilde would write of the late-Victorian English bourgeoisie, with "their strange mixture of romance and finance." It is true, of course, that our very sensitivity to such faults of human nature has been the result of our own evolution: we have become more self-conscious of such things, more introspective and, therefore, more critical.

But in another sense the bourgeois aspirations sprang often from a conscious emulation not merely of aristocratic habits but of the classic virtues. These virtues included not only moderation and prudence and a kind of humanism that was cautious in its demophilia; they included the cult of justice, of temperance, and of reason. Such patrician standards of culture and of responsibility were the sources of some of the finest achievements in the civilization of the Bourgeois Age. This is why we should no longer abide by the narrow and distorted Marxist usage of the word "bourgeois": we should recall, instead, its more spacious sense, including its precapitalist suggestion of a free urban citizenry. Beyond this, we should extend its reputation. During the last one hundred years this word has penetrated the vocabularies and the conscious minds of the English-speaking peoples of the world: and it is high time to grant it not only citizenship but to nominate it to a respectable office in the building of the English language which, besides being a means of communication, is a historical building, a living structure of a people's past that has much to say to the present.

But then, our languages are beginning to reflect this. In the United States, for example, the reputation of "bourgeois" has lately started to rise, at least among cultivated people. Thus the stock of words rises and falls through the years. Their histories are our histories, they both reflect and create the prevailing tendencies of consciousness which are the deepest matters in the histories of peoples. In this stock exchange within our minds "modern" has been falling, "bourgeois" has been rising: a small trend, probably not without some significance.

If I could select but one painting by a master of the past five hundred years, for the purpose of illustrating its historical aura, I would probably choose a Dutch or a French master, of the seventeenth or of the late nineteenth centuries, near the beginning or near the close of the age: a Vermeer or a Rembrandt, a Monet or a Sisley—very different painters who, nevertheless, have one thing in common. Their works exemplify the rich interior lives of our ancestors. By this I do not merely mean their subjects, the rooms painted by Vermeer: this rich interiority shimmers through the trees of Monet. What unites them is their preoccupation with illumination, the attempt of their genius to paint not so much what exists around us as what is visible to us, their understanding of this deepening human recognition that the sense of reality exists within. Their enlightenment is of an interior, not of an exterior nature. Their masterworks embody a human condition to which the word "modern" is too vague and too thin to be properly applicable at all.

This interiority that we are attempting to cultivate and to preserve (for it is a living thing, which cannot be preserved unless it is cultivated) is our bourgeois heritage. It is not merely a cherished image out of the past, a rich knick-knack, an heirloom. It is the most precious heritage of the Western civilization of the last five hundred years.

60

Mechanic

(2002)

In 1654, when Oliver Cromwell was Lord Protector of England, some of the followers of the exiled Charles II issued "a proclamation in the King's name offering five hundred pounds, knighthood, and a colonel's commission, to anyone who succeeded in killing 'a certain mechanic fellow' called Oliver Cromwell, 'by pistol, sword, or poison.'" The Pretender did not entirely discourage them, insisting only that such a killing should be part of a general royalist rising and "not an isolated act."

What I find interesting is not the Pretender's hesitation but the peculiarly English and pejorative sense of the word *mechanic*—according to the *Oxford English Dictionary*: "Belonging to or characteristic of the 'lower order'; vulgar, low, base. Obs.," meaning "now obsolete." Yet it was not *obs.* for a long time. It was preceded by *mechanical*, "which in its early uses is somewhat closer to the sense of the Latin word"—again according to the *OED*—and also close or almost identical to what was then its meaning and appearance in many other Western European languages. In English, *machinist*, too, seems never to have had a pejorative association; in any event, it is more precise than in French, where both *machiniste* and *mecanicien* may refer to a driver of engines, besides the charming and probably now obsolete use of *mecanicienne*: a girl using a sewing machine. But the history of the English *mechanic*, both as an adjective and as a noun, is different.

In the broadest sense it meant having a manual occupation (though not in agriculture), or even working at a trade; in the somewhat narrower but common sense it was clearly disparaging—a connotation that seems to have emerged in the sixteenth century. Shakespeare used the word on occasion. In *Coriolanus*: "Do not bid me to dismiss my soldiers or capitulate again, with Rome's mechanics." Or in *Henry IV, Part II*: "mechanical and dirty hand," "of mean mechanical parentage." Among Shakespeare's contemporaries

From *American Scholar*, Winter: 107–10.

there was Hakluyt, 1589: ". . . mechanical men of base condition, [who] dare to censure the doings of them, of whose acts they be not worthy to talk." Another Elizabethan, John Marston, cited in the *OED*, 1599: "each mechanic slave. Each dunghill peasant . . ."

In one instance, Swift described an apocathary as "a base mechanic." Someone else in the eighteenth century abjured both "Mechanick Theists and Atomic Atheists." As late as 1842, Lord Tennyson: "Lest . . . his nice eyes should see the raw mechanic's bloody thumbs / Sweat on his blazon'd chairs." In *Daniel Deronda*, George Eliot wrote of "four mechanic wings that would not fly." There is mention as late as 1880 of "mechanical orders," meaning the working class. Earlier, John Vanbrugh, the Restoration playwright and wit, wrote in *The Confederacy*, "A woman must indeed be of the mechanic mould, who is either troubled or pleased by anything her husband can do for her." Evidently *mechanic* in this sense meant automatic or thoughtless.

But it was Edmund Burke whose criticism of *mechanical* was something new. It signified his reaction to the inorganic and cold rationalism of the French Enlightenment. In his *Reflections on the Revolution in France*, 1790, he wrote: "On the principles of this mechanick philosophy our institutions can never be embodied." This is no longer a dismissal of occupation or class. It is, instead, an assertion of the primacy of what is historical and organic over the mechanical and the abstract. In *Coningsby*, Disraeli in 1844 extolled that primacy: "The supreme control obtained by man over mechanic power." That "supreme control"—its assertion as a human ideal as well as its translation into practice—may be our main problem in the twenty-first century.

It is interesting to note that during the nineteenth century, about the same time when in England the reference to mechanics as a social class began to disappear, in the United States that sense of the word was current and strong; indeed, it became an assertion of working-class pride, infused with nativism and the ideal of popular sovereignty. In 1827, the first American party of urban workers, or trade union, was founded in Philadelphia, bearing the name "The Mechanics Union of Trade Association." In the 1830s and 1840s, many new American hamlets or villages took names such as Mechanicsburg or Mechanicsville (it was in Mechanicsville, Virginia, that Robert E. Lee received his command in June 1862); in my state, Pennsylvania, there is also a Mechanics Grove, and in Maine, a Mechanics Falls. In the late 1840s and 1850s, the official name of the nativist and populist Know-Nothing Party was "the United Party of White American Mechanics." (One hundred and twenty years later there was at least a resonance of such inclinations among the hard-hat unionists who were encouraged by

President Nixon's supporters to demonstrate against anti–Vietnam War protesters in downtown New York City in 1970.) There is no entry for *mechanic* or *mechanics* in H. L. Mencken's supplement to *The American Language*, but recently I read that among American gamblers in the 1930s, *mechanics* was a dismissive word: it referred to professional cardsharps.

❊ ❊ ❊

MY interest in *mechanic* is not philosophical or epistemological but historical. The earlier—but also *surprisingly* long-lived—identification of *mechanics* with *working-class* has been obsolete. But how about the association—indeed, the identification—of *mechanical* with *industrial?* In its earlier English usage, a mechanic was an industrial worker but not a peasant. Yet what is happening now, when the structure of entire societies, with their occupations and professions, has changed drastically? We have already entered a postindustrial age. (The Industrial Age was much shorter than we have been accustomed to think. It was in 1874 that, for the first time in history, there was a nation, England, where more people were involved in industrial than in agricultural production; and in 1956, for the first time, the United States had more people employed in services and in administration than in agricultural and industrial production *together*.) One consequence is that the terms *working class* and *middle class* now convey a meaningless distinction. Both categories have been stripped of their original, or even sensible, meaning; and, as far as possessions or income are concerned, the two former "classes" have become almost indistinct.

And yet: we live in a mechanical age. Much of our agricultural production has become mechanical. This postindustrial age, wrongly called the Information Age, depends on computers that are wholly mechanical; and not only are the instruments and the transmission mechanical, but so is the digital composition of images and sounds. Well before these technical transformations, a mechanical thinking (and seeing) had entered the American language. At the beginning of the Industrial Revolution, people called the first railway locomotives "iron horses." A century later, in America, an energetic businessman was approvingly described as "the spark plug of the organization," suggesting that at least as many people were acquainted with spark plugs as with horses. Well, there was a loss here; for while the first locomotives looked, at least a little, like iron horses, what man (or woman) looks like a spark plug? And, sooner or later, a smart whizzer will be called The Chip, or The Modem, and we will be yet one more step away from reality. Meanwhile, the very term *Information Age* is inaccurate; for what is really happening involves not information but the mechanical transmission and representation of preprogrammed data, numbers, sounds, and texts.

❀ ❀ ❀

IN sum, the mechanical age is postindustrial. One paradox of this condition is that now, when more and more of our work and everyday living is mechanical, there are fewer and fewer mechanics—meaning experts and repairers of machines. Another paradox is more meaningful, at least to this writer. All of our machines, and indeed the entire mechanical world, depend on mechanical causality, the prime conditions of which are: (1) the same causes must produce the same effects; (2) there must be an equivalence of causes and effects; and (3) the cause must always precede the effect. Yet in the twentieth century we learned—or at least ought to have learned—that mechanical causality (which was but one of the three or four causalities described by Aristotle) is insufficient. It is insufficient when it comes to the relations of human beings to other human beings (the most important and decisive of all relationships, because they involve not only religious or moral factors but also the interactions of the universe's most complex organisms). Mechanical causality is insufficient because of the intrusion of mind into the structure of events—in plain English, because what happens, while not identical, is not separable from what people think happens. But mechanical causality is insufficient, too, because of the collapse of Cartesian determinism within the physical study of the smallest components of matter. Whether we call it Indeterminacy or Uncertainty, Werner Heisenberg and Niels Bohr have not only asserted but proved the insufficiency of the above-mentioned desiderata of mechanical causality (which is why the very phrase "quantum mechanics" is, at least in one sense, an oxymoron).

Two centuries ago it was the romantic reaction against the rationalism of the Enlightenment that first formulated the difference—indeed, the contrast—between what is mechanical and what is organic. Out of this came the exaggerated German distinction between the categories of *Zivilisation* and *Kultur*. Oswald Spengler inflated that into a world-historical system. I happen to believe that this distinction has become at least as *obs.* as the equivalence of *industrial = mechanic* (just as the absolute categorical distinction of *organic/inorganic* is now *obs.* when it comes to the smallest particles of matter). There can be no culture without civilization; they are inseparable. Indeed, because of many conditions, including the relentless mechanization of life, it is civilization, even more than culture, that is now endangered. Two centuries after Edmund Burke, the American farmer, writer, and thinker Wendell Berry wrote: "It is easy for me to imagine that the next great division of the world will be between people who wish to live as creatures and people who wish to live as machines."

VI.

READING, WRITING,
AND TEACHING HISTORY

*J*ohn Lukacs has spent most of his professional life as a writer and a teacher, so it is fitting that this volume concludes with his reflections on the nature, purpose, and significance of writing and teaching, and with his mature advice to students on how to approach and understand the study of history. It is also appropriate that the final section of this book includes a loving portrait of Agnes Repplier, a Philadelphia writer with whom Lukacs shares much in common. Like the intelligent, urbane, witty, and cosmopolitan Miss Repplier, Lukacs has an "interest in all kinds of details of social and of everyday life: the petits faits dear to . . . some of the best historians of the twentieth century." He agrees with her that the ignorance of history "impairs our judgment by impairing our understanding, by depriving us of standards, or the power of contrast, and the right to estimate." "History," Lukacs writes, "is the best fare for one's imagination." To students of history, he repeats the counsel of Jakob Burckhardt: "Bisogna sapper leggere" ("You must know how to read"). With G. M. Young, Lukacs urges students to "go on reading till you hear the people speaking," while always and faithfully bearing witness to the truth.

61

Teaching
(1990)

Had someone told me before the age of twenty-one that I would become a teacher I would have laughed. In the Gymnasium and even at the university our professors were our enemies. This had much to do with the strict and stiff Germanic and bureaucratic organization and requirements of Hungarian schools and universities that, otherwise, were on a very high academic level: the standards of the Gymnasium graduation examination, at seventeen, were well beyond what is required of a graduate of a top American college or university now. It took me a long time to recognize that I had profited from this kind of schooling, after all: from six years of compulsory Latin, for example. However, our requirements were rigid and terrifying, not only because of their demands but also because of their arbitrariness. An unlucky theme, or the whim of a teacher, could decide one's grade. In order to get by, most of us tried to cheat as much as was possible, resorting often to the most inventive stratagems. As in Germany, this kind of education may have done much for one's brain but not much for one's character. The results are obvious in retrospect. When I look back at my Gymnasium and university classmates, I find no relationship between their achievements in school and their achievements in life: as many of the top students turned out to be bad eggs as did mediocre ones. (I was not a top student.) At the same time most of the poorest students did come from poor families, living in bookless homes, sometimes in rough conditions. So even then I knew what I know now: what mattered in Hungary, as in the United States, was not what one acquired in school but what one received, often indirectly, from one's family, at home. And it was therefore, too, that the few teachers and professors we respected were men of probity: gentlemen in the broad sense of that word, old-fashioned in their manners, steeped in their learning rather than in

From *Confessions of an Original Sinner* (New York: Ticknor and Fields), 198–221.

their occupational situation, serious but fair with their students. Most were older men. There was something timelessly clean in their very appearance: they did not exhale that airless smell out of the cramped circumstances in which many of the Gymnasium professors lived. At the risk of being pompous, let me say that even then we sensed—without really knowing it—the essential, the unavoidable connection (or rather, interdependence) of integrity and knowledge.

Then, in 1945, there came a change—a small transitory episode in my life then, but something whose significance rises before me in retrospect. I was still a university student, but I had all kinds of secondary occupations during that awful year at the end of the war and the Russian conquest. I had a connection with the Hungarian Institute for Foreign Affairs, whose temporary office was in one of the relatively undamaged but unheated rooms of the Parliament Building. There someone suggested that I give a course in the English language, for a minimal tuition, for whoever wished to come. There came a gray, desolate, hopeless rainy day in late September. The room was crowded to the walls with people whose faces were full of hope. They were, for the most part, people of the defeated Hungarian gentile middle classes, who at that time put all their hopes—and I mean *all* their hopes—in the English-speaking Powers that might as yet liberate Hungary from the Russians. The course ran for three or four months—I cannot now remember how and when my teaching there came to an end. What I remember is the unexpected satisfaction that my teaching there gave me. The sources of this satisfaction existed on different levels. There was the pleasure of purpose, at that confused, sad, downcast phase of my young life; I was, at least for a few hours each week, doing something useful. There was an element of intellectual pleasure: the sudden realization that by explaining things, my own knowledge was becoming clarified and reasonable—and not, as in a conversation, with the purpose of drawing attention to my person. (It was years later that, in reading St. Augustine, I found what this meant: that by giving out something we are not impoverished by it. Rather, the contrary; that the "laws" of the natural world do not apply to those of the human spirit and mind; that expressing something may lighten one's mind and even enrich it.) Finally there was the element of vanity. I was still a student, yet now it was I who stood in front of a table, writing on a board, my words sometimes avidly followed by this crowd of impoverished and hopeful men and women, sitting bundled up in their shabby overcoats, whose very presence in that once richly decorated but now suddenly antediluvian room invested me with a kind of authority that I never had before—in sum, the pleasures of vanity. I have now sorted out these unexpected satisfactions in descending order; but I do not for a moment doubt that the last and the lowest one of these, that of vanity, was the most important one, surely at that time.

In late 1946 I arrived in New York with few connections but with a few letters addressed to university people.[1] Almost immediately I had a part-time job at Columbia because of the large wave of students flooding American universities and colleges in 1947, veterans turning the G.I. Bill of Rights to good account (and I mean to good account: they were, by and large, admirably serious students, as all teachers of that period will remember). I taught a course in nineteenth-century European history twice a week. My reaction and experiences in those superheated classrooms in New York accorded exactly with those in that unheated antediluvian room in Budapest, one calendar year and one light-year away. I was sure now: I wanted an American college appointment; I could teach and have time to write. (What it was that I wanted to write I did not yet know.) I had all kinds of part-time jobs in New York to sustain me;[2] my part-time salary from Columbia paid me, of course, very little, but it contributed to my opportunity to secure a full-time appointment at Chestnut Hill College.

I am—sometimes—a bit of a gambler, wherefore I was not disheartened by the task of teaching, in English, including one or two courses about the contents of which I was not very sure. Lecturing, after all, has had for me much in common with another habit of mine, that gambling spirit of impertinence—impertinence, rather than daring—when it comes to speaking in a foreign language of whose grammar I might be uncertain and of whose vocabulary my knowledge is incomplete. There is a spirit of enjoyment when after a long time I attempt to speak Italian or Spanish; it is like walking a high-spirited dog on a thin leash. Like every beginning teacher, I began by preparing copious notes. Alarmingly soon I came to think that I did not much need these and threw them away. I was a voluble young man, to be sure.

One thing still worried me in the beginning. Chestnut Hill is a girls' college. There I stood, day after day, in front of an audience of young rosy girls, some of them not more than two years younger than I. I write rosy because I found these American girls, en masse, very pretty. I thought that sooner or later there would be trouble; I would get interested in one of them and this, in a strict Catholic institution! I thought that I mustn't. Then I found that this kind of self-discipline was even easier done than said, since I evinced no temptations, not even on those rare—and they were very rare—occasions when a girl sitting in front of me showed a remarkable extent of leg and thigh. This was not a matter of the weakness of flesh but of spirit, because our chronological and biological proximity of age meant nothing: these girl-students were so much younger than I. With all their American goodwill and eagerness we had very little in common. All my life I had little interest in females with whom I could not much talk; until about the age of twenty-six I never had a love affair with a girl who was younger than I. In forty-one years of teaching I can remember only one girl in the classroom who appealed to me as a woman. I made a point of talking to her after class. She was a very intelligent girl: I suggested that she go on to graduate school. I am sure that my purposes were mixed: I wanted to keep in contact with her, and on one occasion I inveigled her to attend a history lecture or forum at a nearby university. This was shortly before her graduation; and a day or so later I found an odd, sad letter from her on my desk. No, she would not go on with her history studies, she wrote. This was a different country; what I was trying to do was a fine thing, but not really applicable to her world and at this time. It was too idealistic, too impractical.

By this time—it was around 1949—I began to realize something that kept bothering me for a long time: the oh-so-limited aspirations of many Americans, and the extraordinary docility of the young ones among them. Their lightheartedness, their optimism, their explosions of energy: yes, I knew all of that American dynamism, I saw its expressions every day. Yet so few of them aimed at anything beyond the brief radius of their immediate circle. It was not only that they knew so little of life outside that circle. They were not interested in looking, let alone going, beyond it; and those among them who really wanted to rise in the world wanted to rise only within the group of their friends and acquaintances. They were afraid to think beyond their class—so much more afraid than many young people in the restricted society of half-feudal Hungary had been. Of course there were shortcomings in their intellectual education that made them so incurious. But there was more to it than that. I thought then, and I think even now, when social conformism among young Americans is perhaps (but only perhaps) less than it was thirty or forty years ago. They were not self-confident enough to aspire to anything that, to them, was unusual. To these young, often undisciplined and, on occasion, wild and strident girls, success in life meant safety and respectability, with the emphasis on the latter: respectability among people they knew and were to know. And as the range of their imaginations and their ambitions was limited, so was its time span. They all wanted to get married, the sooner the better; and beyond the wondrous prospect of becoming engaged and the dazzling white-and-gold glory of the wedding day their contemplation of their future was so very vague.

Teaching was not always pleasurable; but teaching was easy. My fear (the fear, I believe, of every beginning teacher) that I might not have enough "material" to fill this or that fifty minutes evaporated very soon. The problem turned out to be the opposite: I had (or I thought I had) too much to say, wherefore I kept running out of time. I needed money, and I taught a lot—on Saturday mornings, in the summer, part-time at another college, a schedule that I kept up for about fifteen years. Professors in higher institutions of learning were appalled when they heard that I was teaching that much, sometimes eighteen hours a week. It contributed to their suspicion that this kind of person cannot be taken seriously, he could not be a good teacher. I think that they were wrong. They were right, however, in their suspicions in one important sense: I cared little about an academic career. I wanted to be a writer. I wanted to make my money and my reputation as a historian whose works are read by more than an academic readership, at the same time maintaining—and possibly even elevating—the standards of professional historianship. It took me more than thirty years to realize that this was not going to work; but the story of that belongs to the next chapter, about my writing. What belongs here is my confession of my hopes that accompanied me for at least fifteen years of my teaching career. I hoped that, by the age of fifty at the latest, my main income would come from my writing, subsequent to which I might reduce some of my teaching. This did not happen. But something else was happening, something that developed slowly, something that was positive not negative, something different from a compromise, from an accommodation of one's life and career to the necessity of one's circumstances. I began to realize—gradually and slowly— that I *am* a teacher as much as a writer. In the beginning the principal purpose of my job as a teacher was that it enabled me to write. Thirty years later this relationship of means to ends was no longer so simple. I found that teaching was not only relatively easy but, on occasion, inspired by occasional impulses of intellectual pleasure. At the end of this chapter I shall say more about how my teaching helped my writing. Here I will only state the recurrent—and fortunately still sometimes alive—pleasure of fresh mornings, driving alone on country roads, smoking my matutinal cigar, mentally planning the contents of my coming lecture whose sequence and organization are falling wonderfully into place, crystallizing in sparks of sunlight. I think that every writer worth his salt will know that this kind of pleasure does not exist when one is in front of one's typewriter. One may be driven to write; but the pleasures of writing (whatever those are) are something quite different, if indeed they exist at all; they consist in having written something, not in writing it.

One of the pleasures of teaching—it is, I hasten to say, a pleasure on a fairly low level—is that of having a captive audience. Vanity and irresponsibility are inherent in that pleasure. Vanity: because of the often serious, and sometimes even shining, faces of one's students; because of the sense of one's intellectual, institutional, and almost tangible authority; because here are people who are actually listening to you, something that has become a rarity at this time of the twentieth century. During the twentieth century the capacity and the practice of listening have deteriorated. In all walks of life, in all kinds of circumstances, the capacity of attention has become disrupted and curtailed because of the incredible—literally incredible— amount of noise and sounds and music and words and slogans whirling around people's heads and ears. This condition is, in itself, a matter worthy of the attention of a historian. It is the condition that the very consciousness of people changes through the ages: not only their ideas or the subjects of their thoughts but the functioning of their senses and their minds as well. We have reason to believe, and evidence to prove it, that six hundred years ago, before the Renaissance rediscovery of perspective, people's eyes moved differently from the way they move now. We also know that, say, three hundred years ago not only did people hear different sounds but they used their ears and, therefore, their minds differently. Consider only the duration of sermons in the seventeenth century when otherwise there was so much for the simple people to do, at a time when their lives were indeed poor, nasty, brutish, and *short*: we know, for example, that during the English Civil War the fact that the Puritan preachers' sermons were longer and better than those of the Anglicans mightily contributed to the popularity of the Cromwellian army. The converse of that mental habit, the inability to concentrate, has, of course, woefully affected our people, and perhaps especially the young, in the second half of the twentieth century. Millions have lost the ability to concentrate on anything, and especially to listen—the automatic responses of a secretary being but one last step ahead of the ultimate insult, the answering machine, that diabolical instrument which responds but does not listen to you. By insulting a person, you do, at least, pay attention to his existence; but by refusing to listen to him, you have refused to acknowledge his existence at all. Plainly, it is easier to talk than to listen—not to speak of what Goethe said: "To communicate our thoughts to others is nature; to assimilate what is communicated to us, with understanding, is culture." "In the intellectual order," Simone Weil once wrote, "the virtue of humility is nothing more or less than the power of attention"—to which allow me to add that attention has nothing to do with the subconscious: *nothing*.

Having a captive audience was a luxury. Here, for fifty minutes at a time, I could tell students about interesting things and they were actually listening to me. After nearly forty years of experience as a writer, having written thirteen books, I do not think that I have ever seen a person who was actually engaged in reading one of them. Do people really listen to a famous man who is on the radio or television? Yes and no. But in those classrooms, because of my authority as a teacher, they had to listen—and I could tell them, at my own choice and pleasure, many things.

I must say something here about the authority of an American college teacher. It is, plainly, enormous—in most cases unwarrantedly so. It is abused by many professors who otherwise cultivate a phony camaraderie with their students, a camaraderie that may include an entire range of execrable practices, from calling each other by their first names to a professor fornicating with a selected student. At first sight nothing could be so dissimilar as the authority of a German university professor and an American college one. Since teaching is a two-way relationship, that comparison is deceiving. What American students may lack in discipline they make up in docility. An old-fashioned German professor is often so remote from his students that he is a semi-divinity, an archbishop of learning, sexless. A modern American professor is a father figure, a male figure, and not sexless at all.[3] (Nor is an American priest, but that is another story.) I am not a Germanic type, but that American camaraderie, so often artificial, so often phonily democratic, had no attraction for me, not even at the beginning of my teaching career. I have never called my students by their first names.[4] I would have liked, I would still like, my American students to ask me more questions, but this has not happened because of their docility and shyness. This was a loss but not a great one, since that celebrated American desideratum of a dialogue between students and teachers is often false. The lack of curiosity among students is, of course, to be regretted. Yet their unwillingness to say something or to ask questions is not always attributable to a dull shyness; they know that their knowledge is less than yours, and that's it. American students, indeed, American youth, admire and, yes, even love authority, perhaps even more than their German counterparts, though in different ways. During forty-one years as a teacher my students occasionally saw me, or heard about me, driving a truck, going to the races, dancing at a ball, playing squash or jazz piano.[5] They seemed to be fascinated with such tidbits of individual life: probably less out of curiosity than out of a want of imagination.

Want of imagination, indeed! A few years after I began teaching I grew conscious of something that I did not know before, that my teaching American students at this time of our decaying civilization has a dual purpose—a recognition that took some time to coagulate in my mind. The dual endeavor was this: I was teaching them history, but I also wanted—more: I felt compelled—to teach them a historical, that is, a human way of thinking: about the past, about human nature, about themselves. It took some time before the summation—that history is a form of thought—crystallized in my own mind. Before that I had recognized the obvious: that teaching involved unteaching. Yes, I was aware—and often appalled—by their dreadful ignorance of history. But I also began to understand that this involved something else than a mere lack of knowledge, that it involved a mode of thinking—not merely the subjects of their minds but the very functioning of those minds. I learned that teaching was more than the dissemination of information because we must remind people as much, if not more, than to instruct them.[6] What I have tried to remind them of was a commonsense historical way of thinking, a form of thinking that has not always existed, and the emergence of which may have been even more important (though seldom so recognized) than the emergence of the scientific method three or four hundred years ago—that historical thinking was, plainly, past-thinking, including the conscious knowledge of their own past; that they knew more about that past than they thought they knew; and that they knew more about history than science, which was natural, since it is science that is part of history and not the other way around. In sum, I have been teaching my students history *and* a historical philosophy—something that is the very reverse of a "philosophy of history," the latter often little more than a compound of gassy theories systematized by speculative historians.

I liked my classrooms. I taught in the same one for thirty years. It was in that classroom that important news came to me: the telephone message that my wife was in labor with our first child, the same kind of message with my second child, the news that John Kennedy had been shot, and, during one examination as I read my mail, the news in a sad letter from my aunt that my mother would soon die—moments not easily forgotten. I am now teaching in a less attractive and comfortable classroom, but that doesn't matter. What matters is that it was in these classrooms that I realized the melancholy truth, stated by George Orwell, to the effect that in the twentieth century we have sunk so deep that it is our duty to restate the obvious; and another, perhaps more exhilarating truth, stated by Jean Dutourd, to the effect that in this dreary century a little bit of common sense is enough to give the impression that one is a first-rate philosopher. At any rate, when I hear from a student or a former student that he or she remembers my teaching because of my "philosophy" (the inverted commas may be proper) I think that I prefer this to their telling me that they were particularly taken by my knowledgeable lectures in nineteenth-century German intellectual or twentieth-century American diplomatic history. This does not mean that I am more of a philosopher than a historian. The reverse is true, especially now when all that remains meaningful in philosophy is, by necessity, epistemology, and, moreover, an epistemology that is inevitably historical; for it is philosophy that is part of the history of mankind and not the other way around. First was nature, then came man, and then the science of nature (a moment's contemplation of which sequence should be enough to refute all the pretensions of the Darwinists); I am, therefore I think, therefore I am: a supersession, more than a mere reversal, of Descartes.

In any event, a student's grateful memory is pleasing to one's vanity, though perhaps not on the lowest levels of that fundamental human weakness. And there is another weakness attendant on having a captive audience: the temptation to irresponsibility in the classroom, which I often failed to avoid. I must confess that I often enjoyed it. Irresponsibility: because a professor, perhaps especially in America, can, and indeed will, say some things in the classroom that he might not say elsewhere—a scathing remark about a contemporary politician, for example. This temptation, in my case, was stimulated by my classes at La Salle College, where I was teaching boys, not girls: young men, not young women. My mother, extricated from Hungary, arrived in Vienna in 1949, cared for by her unmarried older sister; she was very ill. I had to support her out of my meager salary, I looked for an additional part-time teaching job, and the president of Chestnut Hill allowed me to do so. There began an altogether pleasant association with La Salle for thirty-four years, until the history department (some of them former students of mine) preferred to end it. I enjoyed the often solicitous friendship of the Christian Brothers who ran the school, their increasingly useful library with its excellent librarian, those early-summer faculty picnics rich with food and drink, so much more generous and easygoing than the stiff affairs of faculty clubs at prestigious schools; and I particularly enjoyed the students, sometimes rough-mannered and poorly prepared young men, the best of whom, however, were better than my best students at Chestnut Hill because, unlike the girls, they were avid for more learning. They were instantly, if perhaps unfortunately, receptive to the occasional crudities and vulgarities with which I felt free to pepper my language on sudden impulse, perhaps not for effect but for the sake of striking a direct point in a kind of rhetorical shorthand—a kind of language that I would employ before an audience of young men but not in a class of young girls. This was perhaps a minor weakness and not more than an occasional one. As time went on, I abandoned this practice, while I did not altogether abandon my occasional habit of exaggeration (a habit in my conversation, and not only in my lectures), again for the purpose of shocking my students into the instant awareness of something that otherwise would take too long to explain.

There is still another weakness of my teaching that I must confess. I am a lazy teacher—perhaps no more but no less than most college teachers,

who are a lazy crowd indeed. I have always put most, if not all, of my energies into my lectures. I am punctual and precise about the requirements of
my classes, their examinations, my reading lists and their administrative
details; but there is an array of instruments at the disposal of a teacher that
I have willfully neglected through the years. For one thing, in spite of my
knowledge of their awfully poor writing habits, I require few term papers
from my students because a conscientious reading of such papers would
take an unconscionably long time. I know that, to do any good, I would
have to correct every sentence and perhaps every third or fourth word, and
I have not enough time for that. As it is, I, who am so convinced that history
is a seamless web, who stress in my lectures the evident connectedness of
art and customs and fashions and politics in history—that, for example, in
the seventeenth century the French obsession with the mathematical nature of things was there not only in Descartes but also in the organization
of their government and in their military engineering and in the topiary
shapes of their gardens; or that there was such a thing as a First Empire
style of painting and even of a Third Reich style of architecture—well, I
do nothing beyond telling them that, without showing them pictures or
films or whatnot. I know that "total history" is impossible, and that M.
Fernand Braudel is a *faux bonhomme,* but I also know its webbed nature. Last
but not least, I know how the lamentably weakened imagination of this
generation is pictorial rather than verbal. Yet I do not find time to illustrate
my lectures with pictures, filmstrips, movies, music—a kind of laziness, I
think. But perhaps I really do not have time: I have too much to tell to that
captive audience; and on the handful of occasions when I chose to darken
the classroom and show a film I found myself sitting suddenly mute in the
dark, in the position of a numb, and surely dumb, fool; a supernumerary, a
superfluous teacher and man.

My admittedly reactionary view of history and of human nature includes the belief that continuity is as important as change. I find this to be
true as I contemplate the ever-succeeding student generations during more
than forty years of teaching. Yes, I know: there have been changes, and even
important ones, among them. The students' clothing is different, something that is perhaps especially apparent in a Catholic girls' college. Yet
their behavior in the classroom has hardly changed at all: their, at best,
attentive and, at worst, rigid faces; their sometimes respectful, sometimes
unthinking acceptance of authority. Some of their ideas may have changed,
but the workings of their minds have not. Yes, they are ignorant about the
world at large and about the history of their entire culture, meaning the
provenance of just about everything to which they are physically and mentally accustomed: but they are not stupid. They are probably more igno-

rant and less stupid than were students thirty or forty years ago because they are aware, sometimes woefully, of their own ignorance, unlike thirty or more years ago when so many young Americans took an odd kind of social pride in the fact that they were not "brains."[7] Television and the dreadful decline of high school requirements have affected them profoundly. The world of books is unknown to many of them, whereby I reached the conclusion many years ago that what the American college must do is really something very simple (the goal is simple while its accomplishment is not): we must teach these young people how to read and write. Their very imaginations have become pictorial, not verbal—a subterranean slide away from the traditions of the last five hundred years that were irretrievably connected with books. Yet their respect for books may have increased, not decreased: I remember how, around 1950, people looked oddly at a young woman who in a Philadelphia trolley car was actually reading a book. This would not happen today, while at the same time my students' ability to read and their capacity to absorb what they are reading have decreased, together with their very appetite for reading. Yes, therefore I had to make adjustments in my teaching. I have had to take less and less for granted—alas, in a Catholic college, the very knowledge of the essentials of their religion, including the Gospels and the very episodes in the life of Christ, is often sadly wanting—and I have had to reduce my requirements. (Soon after the start of my teaching career in America I found that one of my tasks was to introduce these students to good books. I put a strong emphasis on my required reading lists, but while thirty years ago I could require my undergraduates to read seven or eight books per semester, I have reduced this to five or six.) Yet I do not believe that my students are worse—by which I mean, worse human beings—than those whom I taught thirty or more years ago. I am inclined to believe the opposite; and not because I have become more resigned, or even more mellow, with age. Even now, twenty years after their "sexual" and "social" liberation, American college students are less cynical and less worldly than their European counterparts.

These are generalizations. Generalizations, like brooms, ought not to stand in a corner closet forever; they ought to sweep as a matter of course. There may be a particular reason they are excusable here. This is the uniformity of student vintages across the vast United States. Ask any sensible professor, from any kind of institution: which were the good years? 1946–52, 1958–65, etc., etc. This in a nation and in a society where the characters, the backgrounds, the provenance, the social training, the fashions, etc., of young contemporaries could not be more different: where a girl, say, from Bryn Mawr College would prefer the company of a male student from Zambia than that of her coeval from, say, Villanova University, less than two miles away—whom she would not meet and would not want to meet. During more than forty years in the teaching profession I have been amazed, again and again, by how my estimation of my students at Chestnut Hill, in this small, isolated, Catholic (and for a long time predominantly Irish-Catholic) middle-class college corresponded exactly, uncannily, with what other professors at very different institutions found among their students at the same time.

I have served as visiting professor at a number of universities during my teaching career. Some of these stints were agreeable, and not only because of the added income: I could go into some detail in subjects that interested me, since these visiting professorships involved graduate classes. Yet I found less of a difference between my graduate students and the undergraduates at Chestnut Hill than I had expected originally.[8] One of my visiting professorships was at the Fletcher School of Law and Diplomacy in Medford, Massachusetts, in 1971 and 1972. The acting head of that institution was attracted by one of my books and was about to offer me a chair, with the consent of his professors of course. This chair would have meant twice the income for half the teaching I was doing at Chestnut Hill, but I was not tempted by it. I offered a compromise: I would fly up to Boston once a week and teach for two days, without having to diminish my teaching in Philadelphia significantly, and see what happened after a year. Whatever temptation I may have had evaporated during the first day. The professors whom I met at the reception tendered me were a sour bunch. Medford, Massachusetts, was plainly awful—plain *and* awful. I began to dread these weekly expeditions—and I do not necessarily mean the necessity of having to rise before six, not even the heartrendingly ugly drive to the Philadelphia airport, perhaps not even the dirty yellow ice coating the Medford streets. I hated the poisonous warm fug and clattering din of the Tufts cafeteria, where I had to take my breakfast, a period place and scene of masses of unkempt, unwashed, and sleepy-eyed students shuffling along in their Russian-style padded jackets in clouds of malodorous steam; the padlocks and chains on doors, entrances, gates everywhere, evidences of a universal distrust of humanity; the atmosphere of Cambridge, where I would go in the evenings in search of a place to dine; the darkness of Harvard Square, interrupted only by cold vapor lights; a kind of Nordic tropics, or Soviet America, or an American version of what was worst in the surrealist atmosphere of Weimar Berlin, much of it fake to the core, like the Baltic-Latvian compound name of Häagen-Dazs, the rich ice cream that my eyes met first up there in Boston. One night I dined at the Harvard Faculty Club—the only faculty club in America whose atmosphere produced a bit of wistful longing, as I imagined bins of claret kept there by a few old and well-heeled professors. But this impression, too, evaporated soon. My hosts excused themselves for the relative limitations of the menu, since it was the day of the week of the ethnic smorgasbord: Scandinavian that week, Italian next week, and Soul Food the previous week, they said. My plate was more than adequately filled by the stumpy New England ladies standing like sturdy little trees in white uniforms, with their marcelled gray hair, behind the steam tables, relentlessly smiling. I could imagine them with that smile during Soul Food day the week before, with perhaps an extra smile for the black professor of sociology, in his serious three-piece suit, who may or may not have preferred roast beef, but who must have thought that Soul Food was one of those things from which he had sprung with a determination of no return.

I came to the United States at a time when almost all American intellectuals and most American professors were liberals, to the "left" of American politics, supposedly full of a naïve and humane idealism. Their pride in belonging to a class of opinion was there; but it was a fairly low kind of pride. As Dr. Johnson's Imlac said in *Rasselas,* pride "is seldom delicate, it will please itself with very mean advantages; and envy feels not its own happiness, but when it may be compared with the misery of others." Yet what Johnson's Rasselas saw among intellectuals did not apply. Rasselas "went often to an assembly of learned men, who met at stated times to unbend their minds, and compare their opinions. Their manners were somewhat coarse, but their conversation was instructive, and their disputations acute, though sometimes too violent, and often continued till neither controvertist remembered upon what question they began. Some faults were almost general among them: every one was desirous to dictate to the rest, and every one was pleased to hear the genius or knowledge of another depreciated." This was truer of Hungarian and European intellectuals than of American ones, who did not really meet to unbend their minds or to compare their opinions; whose conversation was seldom instructive and almost never violent; who seldom, if ever, were desirous of dictating to the rest; and those who were pleased to hear the knowledge of another depreciated took ample care to camouflage their pleasure with rhetorical practices suitable to the subtleties of a Chinese court, even though their manners were not good enough to keep their jealousy in abeyance.

For a long time I thought that most American academics were hampered by their naïveté. They were more isolated from the world, they knew less of the world than their colleagues in other countries—a curious condition in a democratic country such as the United States, but so it was. It was not only that intellectuals were writing for other intellectuals, with sometimes deplorable consequences for their rhetoric, language, and style. Their social life was restricted to the narrow circle of other intellectuals with consequences that were deplorable, too. It took me some time to recognize that this naïveté, with its attendant abstract optimism of the world—say, their early belief in the United Nations or in World Government or in the Progressive Left—was complicated rather than simpleminded. Mixed within it was a dose of corroding pessimism, the kind of despair that, at best, is a pathfinder out of a cemetery of dead untruths and, at worst, a pathfinder of cynicism—something not entirely different from what Joseph Conrad wrote about Russians in *Under Western Eyes:* "a terrible corroding simplicity in which mystic phrases clothe a naïve and hopeless cynicism."[9] The intellectuals' fear and loathing of nonliberal—or, indeed, any academically unacceptable—opinion was the intolerance of the tolerationists. This kind of airless isolation was already there a century ago in the progress—or, rather, devolution—of Emerson, who in 1837 had issued his famous proclamation of democratic learning in "The American Scholar," while thirty years later in his Phi Beta Kappa address at Harvard, "The Progress of Culture," he said that that progress depended on small "minorities," on the "few superior and attractive men," forming "a knighthood" of learning and virtue. (That this "progress" from the Open Workshop to the Ivory Tower was not much of a progress toward refinement should be obvious to those of us who recognize that life in an ivory tower may be as unsanitary as it is stifling.) For a long time this uneasy compound of optimism and pessimism, of naïveté and despair, did little harm to America, precisely because what was taught in the colleges did not matter much: what mattered was the college "experience." But by the 1960s the dependence of institutions and even of the government on intellectuals—consider only those presidents who had to have foreign-born academics from the very dubious "discipline" of International Relations, such as Professors Kissinger or Brzezinski, to twirl the globe and explain the world to them—became a fact. And it was then that the lack of responsibility among the professorate, amounting to a shameful abdication in the 1960s, became disastrous. It was they—more than the students, and even more than the bureaucratic administrators of their colleges and universities—who allowed, in most cases thoughtlessly, the elimination of history, literature, the classics, etc., from the requirements of colleges and high schools, about the latter of which they were ignorant as well as indifferent. Their ambitions, aspirations, intellectual energies were concentrated on their own bureaucratic situations and advancement, in committees, conferences, foundation grants, publicity within the academy. The habit of flitting from conference to conference hardly widened their knowledge; while it may have sharpened their ambitions, it narrowed their discourse. One of my most disillusioning experiences was a week-long conference in 1966, arranged by the followers of Michael Polanyi, an "anti-reductionist," funded by the Ford Foundation (about which Dwight Macdonald once wrote that it "is a large body of money completely surrounded by people who want some"). Soon after my arrival in the United States I decided to avoid conferences, finding them uninstructive and, more often than not, depressing. But here, I thought, was something worth going to. I would meet a group of people, from different disciplines, who were engaged in the same task as I (I had just finished ten years of work on my *Historical Consciousness*): in breaking through to a new recognition of our situation in the universe, in a rethinking of the conditions of thinking itself. I was sadly disappointed. Instead of a happy band of a moral minority, instead of a group of men and women who were interested in the same thing, I found that most of these people were uninterested in anything beyond gathering additional security for their self-esteem.[10] This kind of self-esteem was a puny one, wholly restricted within the radius of academic respectability; and that academic respectability was further constrained by ambitions that were less intellectual than they were bureaucratic. Most professional intellectuals are now hardly interested in anything beyond their "fields"; but even within their "fields" they profess to ignore what is truly exceptional and unpredictable. There is a sentence in one of Evelyn Waugh's last books that applies to intellectuals as much as it applies to politicians. "In a democracy," he wrote, "men do not seek authority so that they may impose a policy. They seek a policy so that they may achieve authority." This is why intellectual life, the very production of books and the circulation of ideas and styles, has become drearily predictable in our times, presented by men and women who are engaged in the incarnation and the representation and the projection of ideas that are (or rather, that seem to be) already current, since they think that this is what their minds are for, this is what intellectual creativity is all about.

Well before that conference I had met scholars whose private opinions about teaching were either cynical or despairing or both. I also met professors, and well-known ones at that, who had an impressive office, the walls padded with all kinds of interesting volumes, including recondite and expensive ones that I longed to borrow and look at, while in their neat suburban houses there were alarmingly few books lying around. In one instance I counted them: there were less than fifty. (Perhaps he had a few more in his bedroom, though I doubt it.) Was this man really interested in history? I thought, driving home. Well he was, but what really interested him was his historianship. But perhaps I am too harsh. Was this man cynical? I do not really think so. What limited him were his aspirations: a cause, perhaps even more than a consequence, of the limitations of his imagination. Conversely, my best friends among intellectuals, the lovable men and women I know, are people whose aspirations may be limited but whose imaginations and attentiveness—a rare combination nowadays—are not. They enlighten my life, because in their company I am lighthearted and happy. What saddens me sometimes is the unhappiness among teachers: their unhappiness in a profession where, after all, one is doing what one can do best, one does what one wants to do, and where the work, if not the living, is easy.

Well I know that I have been making a virtue of necessity: an explication, if not altogether an apology, of my teaching in a little-known college for more than forty years. Yet "virtue" is not really the right word; choice would be a better one. I had my moments, and even periods, of unhappiness—at worst, recurrent moments, rather than lasting periods, because of my fortunately volatile temperament. I have taught much; and I have learned a few things, not unimportant ones. That teachers learn from their students is a bromide, though not a euphemism; at any rate, learning is to a great extent osmotic, and in the case of learning from students probably as much as the other way around. In any event, I have learned less about them than about myself: for example, where my teaching was without much effect, where it went wrong. I had, and have, my disappointments with the students: with their wanting imagination and curiosity, with their alarmingly feeble sense of humor, with their inexperience with books, with their execrable and habitual errors in writing—the latter flowing from their crampedly self-conscious inclination to the effect that in their writing they must employ a different language from speaking: different words, and phrases, sentences, and tenses (especially the dreary and dreadful passive tense) that they never use when they speak. Yes, there is a difference between the written and the spoken word, but on a higher and subtler level than what appears in students' papers: if they only wrote the way they speak! And I knew, very soon after my first book, that my profession as a writer has nothing to do with my profession as a teacher, because my books in most instances have not been really applicable to my courses and to my reading lists, and not because of excessive modesty on my part. One of the purposes of my reading lists has been to introduce my students to good historical books, perhaps even more than to acquaint them with the principal histories relevant to this or that course. And even when, at the risk of being immodest, I know that this or that book of mine was fairly well written, I think that they ought to read something else. All through my years of teaching I have seldom felt any compunction about taking short excursions from my scheduled lecture topics when the spirit, rightly or wrongly, so moves me, taking the opportunity of a captive audience to discourse on a subtle matter that sputters or sparkles in my mind at a given moment. Yet I have very seldom directed them to something I have written. I think I know why; and yet somehow I don't.

All of this shows a definite divorce between my two careers of teacher and writer. Perhaps things would have been better if, say, I had been a professor of graduate students at Harvard, but I am inclined to think not very much. I am sure that I would be as loath to foist my published writings on them as I am at Chestnut Hill, and I am not sure whether I would like to discuss my actual work with them, or read them portions of my manuscripts in progress—a dreadfully boring seminar practice, I think. There has been, however, one tremendously profitable result of my teaching these young girls: a veritable golden bridge between my twin crafts of teaching and writing. It took me years to recognize its existence: I may exaggerate its importance, but I honestly don't think so. This golden bridge consists of the fact—and, for once, it is a fact—that my writing has profited from my teaching. Whatever clarity and economy my writing possesses has often been the result of my teaching uninstructed undergraduates. I am not referring to the condition that a college teacher's life, with his many free hours and vacations, enables him to write. I am referring to the necessity— a gradually more and more self-imposed necessity—of speaking about large and complex topics briefly and clearly, and yet without superficiality. This necessity of a verbal economy helped my mind and my practice of writing so much that perhaps in this instance virtue *has* grown out of necessity—if virtue it still is (something that readers of this book may indeed question). I am not alone in this, for I received sustenance, an electric spark of recognition, only a few weeks ago when, picking up a book in the college library, I ran across these splendidly unassuming words in the gracefully short acknowledgments of a very fine scholar, in Professor David Buisseret's *Henry IV,* a splendid (and short) book about that great and complex monarch, the *Vert Galant*: "Much of this work was written while I was teaching at the University of the West Indies, where my students forced me to explain myself carefully about a period and place so foreign to most of them."

62

Writing

(1990)

The relationship between the spoken and the written word is not simple. Speech, contrary to Freud's doctrine (and perhaps also to Joyce's idea), is not the transcription of thought; it is the realization of it. Hitler realized that the spoken word counted with the masses: *Mein Kampf,* which he had dictated, was a book to be spoken, he said. Churchill, who, contrary to the accepted notion, was a better writer than speaker, wrote about Balfour in *Great Contemporaries:* "This most easy, sure, fluent of speakers was the most timid, laborious of writers. . . . The spoken word, uttered from the summit of power, gone beyond recall, had no terrors for him; but he entered the tabernacles of literature under a double dose of humility and awe which are proper. He was sure of the movement of his thought; he was shy in the movement of his pen. The history of every country abounds with brilliant and ready writers who have quailed and faltered when called upon to compose in public, or who have shrunk altogether from the ordeal. Balfour was the reverse example, and in this lies a considerable revelation of his character." I am the reverse of Balfour, wherein lies a considerable revelation, if not of my character, then of my mind.

I can hardly remember a time in my life when I did not want to write, surely not after the age of five when I had learned to read. The relationship between reading and writing is even more complicated than that between the spoken and written word. The mental connections and disconnections between them are odd. There are millions of readers who do not like to write. A devoted reader would like to talk about what he or she had read: but that is different from the desire to write. As any writer knows, reading often serves as an escape from the duty of writing. Yet there have been writers, sometimes very good ones, who read very little. Reading is easier than writing: but the impulse to write is deeper than the impulse to read.

From *Confessions of an Original Sinner* (New York: Ticknor and Fields), 222–75.

Somerset Maugham said that when a young author "discovers that he has a creative urge to write ... [this] is a mystery as impenetrable as the origin of sex." I do not believe this is so. Writing, after all, is yet another form of self-expression. The motive to write is the desire to vanquish a mental preoccupation by expressing it consciously and clearly. The purposes of writing almost always contain at least a minimum of self-love, that is, of vanity.

All my life I have felt and recognized the presence of history within descriptive prose. This happened long before I began to realize that the novel, unlike the epic, has been part and parcel of the evolution of our historical consciousness; and long before I concluded and dared to say that in the near future history may absorb all narrative prose—a process that is well on its way. But this is not the place to repeat or even to sum up matters, however important, about which I have written elsewhere. Earlier I wrote that I was a devoted reader of novels at an early age. Even now I often get more pleasure—and instruction—from reading a fine novel or a biography than from a mediocre history. I do not mean historical novels: I find *War and Peace* interminable, false, and boring. I think that *Madame Bovary* and *Sentimental Education* are more historical than Tolstoy. What attracts and inspires my mind are the details and the poignant impressions of how people and things seemed, how they behaved, how they spoke, thought, and presumably even felt in a certain place and at a certain time. By the end of the second decade of my life an impulse was beginning to form in my mind. At some time, in some place and in some ways I would attempt a new kind of history.

This impulse has been plaguing me ever since. For a long time, even during my career as a professional historian, it led to the occasional temptation of trying my hand not at a new kind of history but at a new kind of novel. I have a few fragments, usually not more than a few pages, of such attempts somewhere in my files. It took me many years to recognize what should have been obvious. Such attempts were not going to succeed, for a simple reason. This is that while I can be fairly good at describing characters and places, I cannot invent a plot. There is this plain shortcoming in the very functions of my mind. Strings and knots hopelessly discombobulate my brain and my hands. I am very poor at checkers, let alone chess; I can play poker, but I am incompetent at bridge. Probably consequent to this I find descriptions of complicated characters and scenes and places and developing conditions infinitely more interesting than the development of plots. When I read a detective story I am instantly lost. In following the thread my mind is all thumbs. The other element is my acute interest in what really happened, rather than even the most imaginative plot (not to speak of science fiction, which immediately puts me to sleep). I love Dickens and I could speak (or write) at length about his characters and even about his philosophy, but ask me to reconstruct the plot of, say, *Great Expectations*: I can tell only the roughest sum of it. I have a great admiration for what Chesterton and C. S. Lewis wrote, for the philosophical cast and strength of their minds; but I find the Father Brown stories distasteful, and the "Narnia" kind of book painfully difficult to read.

The research and the description of what really happened—*wie es eigentlich gewesen*—this separation of "fact" from "fiction" is, of course, the central statement of purpose and the standard desideratum of professional history, with its canons established by Leopold von Ranke and mostly German historians during the nineteenth century, with many solid and enduring results. Ranke's famous phrase, *wie es eigentlich gewesen*, has been dissected, interpreted, and misinterpreted often since his time. But more important than the most precise translation and exact rendering of that phrase, apposite and proper for his time, must be our later realization that history is not a science. (Again the context is important: the German word *Wissenschaft*, especially a century ago, included the more spacious meaning of science *and* knowledge.) What "really happened," to my mind, inevitably includes not only what happened but also what could have happened: actuality mixed up with potentiality. This is why history differs from the Newtonian or Cartesian categories of science. More obviously, history is less than a science but also more than a science, because everything has its history, including science. It took me more than a decade of professional historianship to recognize this and put it in something like this way. Long before that I felt, and thought, that history was closer to art than to science, that indeed history-writing *was* an art. But I outgrew that, too. Around 1958 the final crystallization formed in my mind, to the effect that the entire objective/subjective, science/art (and even fact/fiction) antitheses were inadequate and outdated; that we have outgrown them; that knowledge, very much including historical knowledge, is neither objective nor subjective but personal and participant; that history is not only "an art, like all the other sciences" (Veronica Wedgwood's fine formulation) but a way of thinking, a now inescapable form of thought; and that the awareness and description of this may be my most important task.

Before that, I knew something more directly related to my writing. This was that the historian, like the novelist, is plagued by the elusive nature of truth. Very early in life I learned in Hungary that it is possible to write a history in which every "fact" may be precise and yet the general impression of which may be—often deliberately—false. This happens because a "fact" does not exist in our minds except through its associations; because it has no meaning except through its statement; and because the statement of every fact depends on its purpose. History consists of words, not of "facts"—or, more precisely, of "facts" that are inseparable from (and even unimaginable without) words. Therefore, too, the purpose of writing a piece of history could not be really the final, fixed, finite establishment of "factual truth" or "solution of a problem" (i.e., "The *definitive* history of the origins of the Civil War"), but—as Thucydides, the first critical historical writer, intimated—the reduction of untruth. And what is the purpose of that purpose itself, of the reduction of untruth? It is not only that of enlightenment or correction or even instruction; it is one of *reminder*. We have to remind people of some things that they, in one way or another, already know.

This brings me to an avowal of a democratic impulse that may surprise some of my readers. I am reactionary enough to admit my thoughts about the dangers of democracy. These exist because of the democratic tendency to interpret equality and freedom in ephemeral, superficial, and abstract ways, and of institutionalizing them in deadening and impersonal forms; in sum, because of the deadly inclination of democracy to inflation and to bureaucracy. I am, moreover, aware that the writing and teaching of history have their special dangers in democratic times, something that Tocqueville summed up in forty-eight sentences, in a short chapter entitled "Some Characteristics of Historians in Democratic Times," in the second volume of *Democracy in America.* It may even be argued that writing fine history is an aristocratic art. There are many reasons why it is easier to write a mediocre history than a mediocre novel, and why it is more difficult to write a great history than a great novel—foremost among them the inevitable restrictions of the historian, who cannot invent people who did not exist, statements that were not made, things that were not about to happen and that did not happen. These conditions are true enough. But even their importance pales before the overall commonsense and democratic truism, which is that history does not have a language of its own. It is thought, imagined, taught, spoken, and written in our everyday languages (which is, too, why history is a form of thought). This is why there is no difference between a document and a historical document, between a source and a historical source, between a person and a historical person, between an event and a historical event. Any attempt, especially in the twentieth century, to insist on (or even to proceed from) such differences is self-serving, false, and, at least potentially, corrupt; and it only helps to diminish further the sense of our connection to the past.

History is not only the study of the recorded past; it is also that of the remembered past.[1] I was twenty when I chose to work for a history degree; but even then I was aware of two matters from which I have not departed since and never will. One is that there is no categorical division between professional and nonprofessional history-writing. Yes, there is a difference in some of the training (and in the aspirations) of a PhD in History and in that of an amateur historian. But—unlike, say, in the cases of a professional surgeon and a paramedic—there is no difference in the instruments of their craft, which is everyday language. Nor is there any difference in the character of their knowledge, that is, in the process whereby the reconstruction of history occurs in their minds. There ought not be any difference in the extent of their research and reading. But amateur historians sometimes write better prose than professional historians. The reason for this is simple, even though its consequences are complicated. Many professional historians are writing principally for other professional historians. That limitation of purpose may reduce their range of vision, including their very understanding of human nature. Of course that happens during the bureaucratization of every intellectual profession. The greatest historians (for example, Burckhardt) were aware of this.

There are countless examples of this amateur-professional problem, if problem it is. One example is that of Churchill. I have thought for many years that he was a great historian (for once the Nobel people were right when they awarded him the prize in literature because of his history writing). Yet I have been amazed how professional historians have paid little or no attention to his histories.[2] I am not uncritical of Churchill's historianship, not even about his monumental volumes of the history of the Second World War, which have their share of errors; still, more than forty years after he wrote those volumes, they have stood the test of time extraordinarily well. They withstood the inevitable changes of our perspectives, and also the inevitable revelations in the immense mass of publications and documents that have accumulated through four decades. I am particularly impressed by a passage in Churchill's first volume of that work (*The Gathering Storm*). This is Churchill's brief description of the young Hitler; three long paragraphs. I do not recall that this made an especial impact on me when I first read it more than forty years ago. Since that time I must have read one hundred books, a dozen biographies, tens of thousands of pages about Hitler, whose character and mind still interest me and about whom I believe I have made a few serious contributions. But when I recently reread these passages my heart beat faster, for I found that Churchill was absolutely right. What he must have dictated circa 1948, pacing up and down in Chartwell, in perhaps less than twenty minutes, sums up just about everything that scholars have learned to know (and one important thing that they have not yet learned to know) not only about Hitler's early life but about the crystallization of his political mind.[3] What I am saying is not only that Churchill was a great writer-artist, capable of summing up, in his own kind of masterful prose, something that would take another historian at least a chapter. What this involved is not only manner but matter, not only style but substance. What these paragraphs reveal is that Churchill possessed the rare insight that is the fruit of genius. His portrait of the young Hitler is a high achievement of genius whose essence is an understanding of human nature that is profoundly and unavoidably historical. He knew because he understood; and he could employ his understanding to the best of his knowledge—all of it on the acutely conscious level of his mind.

This issue of the flexible boundary between professional and nonprofessional history has affected the purpose of my writing for more than forty years. My perennial desire to write a new kind of history sprang not from the desire for novelty but from the impulse to demonstrate how history— perhaps especially now, in the democratic age—must include what and how many people thought and acted and hoped for in their everyday lives: in short, the design, the limning, and the coloring of the sensitivities of a certain place and period. I shall presently sum up the history of my books, the very structures and the materials of which ought to—necessarily inadequately—illustrate this; but I must insist on something else at this point. This is that this recurrent, and perhaps chronic, aspiration of mine has been involved with my interest in the inevitable overlapping of "fact" and "fiction" (in the sense, too, of the original Latin meaning of the word *fictio*, that is, mental construction), in a kind of prose that may be found in the best of histories and in the best of novels. It will thus be evident that my own attempts toward this kind of history have had certain similarities in scope—but none at all in method, approach, or perspective—with the kind of "total" history that people such as the celebrated Fernand Braudel have been composing in our times. Yes: we have come to the unavoidable (and by no means very brilliant or profound) recognition that the lives and the minds of great numbers of people do matter, and that in describing a place and a time and a people we must attempt to reconstruct and to understand many things, including the material conditions of their lives and the formative influences of their minds. But this must be achieved through the *esprit de finesse* rather than through that of *géometrie*; through a sympathetic and evocative attempt of comprehension and not through a kind of retrospective sociology, cobbled together with fragmentary (and sometimes even fraudulent) statistics—and through the recognition of the intrusion of mind in the structure of events, indeed, of matter itself.

If I had any great masters before my eyes they were Burckhardt, Tocqueville, Huizinga. *If* I had any Great Masters . . . I have been blessed (and sometimes cursed) with a fairly independent mind. But I also know that my mind is not really very original. I am only good (and sometimes original) in seeing (and perhaps describing) kinds of connections.[4]

There is something more important. It involves that particular kind of imagination which is historical. I must leave aside the important argument that *all* imagination is, to a great extent, historical; as C. S. Lewis wrote, no one can imagine a wholly new color or a wholly new monster or a third sex, only a new combination of colors or monsters or of the two sexes that we already know. I must also leave aside the fascinating possibility—and some of its evidences—that in some cases human perception actually *precedes* sensation. In any event, imagination, like perspective, is not only a consequence but an inevitable component of the act of seeing. But here I am writing not about imagination itself but about certain odd elements that stimulate or vitalize or even inspire the imagination of a writer such as myself.

Names, for example. When Peter Quennell in his autobiography writes about "the fashionable dandy Napier Alington," this, to me, is instantly evocative of a place and of a period. I find a slip of paper among my notes: "A British officer, Vivian Usborne, a wonderful 1918 name." In *Heart of Darkness* Conrad wrote of "all the ships whose names are jewels flashing in the night of time." In March 1940 Churchill, visiting Scapa Flow, remembered Kipling's

> *Mines reported in the fairway, warn all traffic and detain. Send up* Unity, Claribel, Assyrian, Stormcock *and* Golden Gain.

There is a sublime music in such things,[5] as there is a mysterious connection of the very sound and the shape of certain names with the character of their bearers: Bismarck: the strong mark of a fist; Mussolini: the Italian muscleman; Goebbels: the bouncing, compressed energy of a small rubber ball; Stalin; Nixon.

Another example: the evocative power of certain dates. I remember when, before coming to America, I saw a picture of a railroad station in Montana in 1915. It showed a great powerful Great Northern steam locomotive, with white-rimmed driving wheels and a plume of smoke rising from its flat, modern funnel; two or three tall Americans in uniform, standing on the narrow wooden-slatted platform of the station; and behind them mountains, dark and un-Alpine because there was no sign of any kind of habitation on them. I kept gazing at that picture for a long time. What excited my interest was the combination of that place and the year: the year, more than the place. I had had mental pictures of *1915*: of Flanders fields, of the Western front, of the Eastern front, of the Dardanelles, of wartime London or Berlin and the cobblestoned main streets of Budapest and perhaps even of a teeming New York in 1915; but that picture evoked the mysterious vastness and the momentous modern power of America in a certain year, *at a certain historical time,* instantly filling my mind with an avid, palpable curiosity whereof the only crude approximation would be a new dish on a buffet table of delicacies whose very sight incites one's appetite. Another occasion: I remember that when I read that Greta Garbo had begun her acting career in Stockholm in 1916, an entire slew of associations and images flew into my mind. Stockholm *in 1916*: how must it have been in that neutral hyperborean city then, with its dark three-storied houses, white islands, pearly sky, a foggy bath of pale electric lights, high-wheeled boxlike Adler automobiles crunching forward in the snowy streets, Germanophile patricians in their high-crowned felt hats and fur-collared coats; how did those Swedish people live then, what did they think?

Summering in Spain in 1962 I was reading a history of that country in the early twentieth century, including a footnote about an agricultural strike in the Spanish Levant in 1917. And then, walking through the dusty botanical gardens of Valencia I was suddenly overwhelmed by an acute wave of curiosity, by the wish to know more about that sunbaked, semi-African scene, litigious, thin, black-clothed men and women behind and outside of a Europe at war and yet at the same time: Valencia *in 1917.*

Not so long ago I spent two weeks on the French Caribbean island of St.-Barthélemy (mostly to please my wife, since I am not attracted to the tropics; I have, instead, *la nostalgie du Nord*). Walking down to the harbor one day I passed a monument engraved with the names of those French islanders who had served in the 1939–45 war. I recognized the names of the prominent families of that island. I also knew that in 1940 the French Antilles had opted for Pétain, that they were governed by a Vichyite admiral, and that it was not until 1943 that these sun-scorched, somnolent islands joined the Allied ranks and the Allied cause. But how did St. Barts look *in 1940*? Now, in 1982, it was full of sails and yachts and cruise boats. Then it must have been empty, perhaps with a gray-painted American destroyer standing offshore on certain days, watching lest a German submarine come to a short rest in its territorial waters. But what must have been more interesting were the lives and the thoughts of the French families. What did they think and feel when France fell in June 1940? How were they divided, between pétainistes and gaullistes, gradually adjusting their minds in the gathering course of the war and to the gathering presence of American power? How interesting it would be, I thought, to spend a year here and in Paris among the archives of the *département* or perusing the files of the local newspaper; but I also knew that many of the scenes and the evidences of the kind of historical truth I would pursue were not to be found in those archives that would be, at best, their reflections.

A few months earlier I had traveled in Transylvania, spending a few days in those towns that had been inhabited by Lutheran Saxons for centuries, in houses that still had their German look. The Rumanians executed a very successful coup d'état in August 1944, passing instantly from the German to the anti-German camp; but I knew that it took a few weeks, until in the wake of the retreating Germans, the Russian and Rumanian armies arrived in that portion of Transylvania. And what happened during that tense time in these towns when the Russians were approaching, where but a few weeks or even days before a persecuted and cowed community of Jews and an arrogant and stolid community of Nazified Germans lived side by side? Some of the Germans were packing up and leaving, but most of them stayed. How did they behave? Did they and the Jews talk to each other? Would a Saxon lawyer lift his hat when passing a former Jewish colleague in the street? *In late August, in 1944.*

I wished, and still wish, to know more about such matters, a wish that has all the attributes of appetite. Like appetite, this kind of mental interest is neither aseptical nor objective. Yet this kind of interest (and its mental absorption) goes counter to the "laws" of the physical world. When we are truly interested in something we want to know more and more about it; and the more we know about something, the more easily we include more knowledge about it in our minds. Yet here is, I think, a difference between the functions of my mental appetite when reading a novel and when reading or researching history. In the former my imagination is principally vitalized by the atmosphere. In the latter case my principal curiosity is directed to events, facts, details—adding to a plot the main course of which I already know. I often cannot remember the subplots (and sometimes not even the main plot) of some of my favorite novels; but I remember not only the plot but also the subplot of the histories I read. This is partly because of the earlier-mentioned weakness of my mind in following plots; but it is also because the concreteness of history in our minds solidly attaches our imagination and memory to certain unique places and times.

I must now sum up the story of my thirteen books: not their contents but their histories; their conceptions and their purposes. My first book, *The Great Powers and Eastern Europe,* was an ambitious attempt at contemporary or near-contemporary history, mostly because of the unusual availability at that time of diplomatic and other international documents of a recent past. The largest mass of German diplomatic documents had been captured by the Allies in 1945 and was beginning to be published. Other governments had published particular volumes during or before the war. Yet other governments (the British, the Italians, the Americans, the Swedish) were publishing other documentary collections about those years. Without this new mass of materials I would surely not have undertaken that book. But the impulse to write it may have been deeper than that. I was very much interested in many of the obscure episodes and still-unresolved questions of the last war, through which I had lived during my formative years. I was not ashamed of this interest in so contemporary a history; I thought (after all, so had Thucydides) that my book would perform a service in correcting or reducing untruths still current. This work took me about five years with the usual ups and downs. Among the ups, the wintry evenings in the old Furness Library of the University of Pennsylvania stand out in my memory. The downs were my troubles with my first American publisher. The American Book Company was a textbook house that had chosen to go into the "trade" field shortly before my manuscript had come to their attention by way of their chief history reader. He was a saturnine, strong-minded, well-prejudiced, and extremely intelligent scholar, Professor Gaudens Megaro, who became one of my close friends, until his strange disappearance and sudden death a few years later. The trouble came because sometime before the completion of my book the managers of the American Book Company had changed their minds about going into the trade field. Consequently, they regretted their contractual commitment to such a large work—not a textbook—such as mine, which they now could not let go. In short, they had something like a muskrat—not a tiger but nevertheless a sizable and difficult animal—by the tail. The book sank without a trace; but not only because of the, by then, drastically reduced marketing budget of its publisher. The ideological climate of the American professorate was still governed by the orthodox liberal ideology of the 1940s and before.

Before I finished my work on *The Great Powers and Eastern Europe* my mind had begun to wander to different fields. My interests, at that time, were even more undisciplined than ever before or since; they were perhaps especially inchoate. Intellectually speaking this was an unhappy phase of my life—while at the same time that life was lightened and merrified by my engagement and marriage. The page proofs arrived at my apartment on the day of our wedding. I had to do the index during our honeymoon. I was, of course, unhappy with the lack of recognition of this first book of mine, something that I immediately attributed—perhaps exaggeratedly—to the ideological (and also methodological) narrow-mindedness of so many intellectuals, including, alas, historians. Meanwhile I went on reading indiscriminately and voraciously, including the works of some of the great historians of the nineteenth and early twentieth centuries, filling in large gaps left over from my Hungarian university education. I have written elsewhere of the condition, unknown to Americans, whereby the blessings of America made it possible for refugees from Europe to travel and discover a Europe that they might otherwise not have known. Here I must record my indebtedness to another blessing of this country whereby a refugee from Europe might learn here more about European history or literature or art than almost anywhere else in the world, because of the freedom and richness of the large American libraries and because of the relative leisure of the life of an American college teacher. In 1955 I began to write the first portions of what eventually became *Historical Consciousness,* my most important book.

This was not completed for many years, and was published more than thirteen years after I had begun it. I had to interrupt its writing several times, often because of my doubts about its form. On more fortunate occasions I stopped because of commitments to other, smaller books. One of my articles in *Commonweal* was read by Dwight Macdonald, who praised it in a letter to their editors that they then sent to me. I was pleased because I liked Macdonald's writing; I called on him in New York, and soon we became the closest of friends. He mentioned me to Jason Epstein and Nathan Glazer, who were then in charge of what was becoming the paperback revolution, having convinced Doubleday of the existence of a large tappable reservoir of potential buyers of quality books in paperback reprints, especially in colleges and universities but also among intellectuals of all kinds, somewhat similar to the Penguin series in England. Epstein published one of the subchapters of what was to become *Historical Consciousness* in his *Anchor Review.* Was there anything I'd care to write for them? he asked. Well, there was, I said. There existed parts of Tocqueville's second, unfinished book on the French Revolution and his correspondence with Gobineau, too, that had not been published in English. I would translate them and write an introduction. We agreed.

This work took me about a year—1956, the year when my son was born. Translating long texts is something that does not really accord with my temperament; and I remember a few beastly summer days when I was forced to descend to the cool damp cavern of the cellar of our rebuilt old house, with drops of dirty water plopping periodically onto the pages of the Tocqueville *Oeuvres Complètes* at my right hand. Yet I was fairly enthusiastic about this work because of my tremendous respect for Tocqueville. *Monsieur le Comte, mon semblable, sinon mon frère.* Alexis de Tocqueville died in the year when the oldest of my grandparents, my paternal grandfather, was born. Is he a Great Contemporary of mine? Yes he is: because he is the

Aristotle (and perhaps the Plato, too) of the democratic age, the greatest of its political and social thinkers and writers and one of the greatest of its historians. He will be our Great Contemporary for many generations to come, until the age of political democracy (and the bureaucratic morass into which it now devolves) will disappear and a new kind of society will form. Like other European intellectuals in America, I had found *Democracy in America* the most profound and the most telling book ever written about the United States. From there I went on to realize that its second volume is even more important than the first, since it is more about democracy than about America in the 1830s. Then I began to read everything that Tocqueville wrote about the history of France, and also about himself: the incomparable *Souvenirs,* his history of the Old Regime, his unfinished book about the French Revolution and the extant collections of his letters, some of which contain the most startling illustrations of his extraordinary vision and mind. I was also critical of and impatient with the standard liberal American commentaries of Tocqueville. In the introduction to my translation I tried to suggest the main Tocqueville questions. Was he a liberal or a conservative? Was he a sociologist or a historian? Was he an aristocratic agnostic or a believing Catholic?—indicating that, even as he transcended customary categories, the second halves of these pairs were truer than the first.

In 1959, when my *Tocqueville: The European Revolution and Correspondence with Gobineau* was published, Tocqueville had become a subindustry in academia. Thereby, rather expectably, my work and my interpretation were either studiously ignored or dismissed as "special pleading" (the words of one commentator). Because of an odd compound of sloth and pride (as Christopher Sykes once wrote, "Scruples and sloth make happy bedfellows") but for other reasons, too, among them the undisciplined ranging of my interests, I often have been inclined to abandon my scholarly efforts in fields where they are treated as unwelcome intrusions by most scholars. This was surely true about my Tocqueville work. I knew, however, that there was evidence somewhere about Tocqueville's religion in the last phase of his life, something that I could prove beyond (or perhaps, beneath) "special pleading." Well, if they wanted documents, I will find documents. (Research: we find what we are looking for—at least most of the time). And indeed, in August 1962, on a long day trip from Paris to the very modest convent of the Sisters of the Notre-Dame de Secours in Troyes, I found three overlapping, separate, and contemporary manuscript accounts by the nuns who had cared for Tocqueville in 1859. The superior of the house allowed me to take these handwritten documents to America—a rare generosity, especially in France. I returned them a few months later. I published these accounts, in a long article, in the July 1964 issue of the *Catholic*

Historical Review. They made no difference: none of the Tocqueville scholars in America has referred to them ever since (though the leading French Tocqueville scholars have).

Directly upon completing my Tocqueville manuscript in 1957, I returned to my book about historical thinking. I took advantage of my first sabbatical and of a small but very useful grant from RELM Foundation, a conservative institution whose director was brought into contact with me by Russell Kirk. The history of my writing of *Historical Consciousness*, 1955 to 1968, is summed up briefly in its appendix, wherefore I am loath to recount this story again. Instead, I am compelled to say something about its gestation and structure because these matters relate to the history of my writing. *Historical Consciousness* is not a philosophy of history but its opposite: a multifaceted statement and exposition of a historical philosophy. Its purpose is not the demonstration of a systematic knowledgeability of history; to the contrary, it wishes to demonstrate the profound, yet considerably unsystematic, historicity of our knowledge. It deals with many things: with the evolution of our consciousness of history since the seventeenth century; with the emergence of the now widespread historical form of thought; with the necessary rethinking of the essential problem of causes, and of more mundane matters such as public opinion and popular sentiment; with what "fact" and "fiction" really mean; with a reasonable hierarchy of historical forces in our times, ascending from what is least significant (economics) to what is most significant (thinking); with the difference between categories and tendencies, leading to the question of human characteristics and including the persistence of national characteristics; with the relationship of imagination and memory, indeed, with that of "evolution" and history; with the necessity to recognize the inevitable involvement of the historian and his subject, that is, of the "observer" with what is "observed," leading, in the end, to the correspondences between this view of historical knowledge and the proven recognitions of quantum physics, whereby near the end of the so-called Modern Age the Cartesian and Newtonian views of man and of the universe must be rethought. It is a great mistake to write about more than one thing. The best parts of one's book become invariably lost. It befuddles a few readers and most reviewers. It is a great mistake, too, as Stendhal once wrote, to be more than one or two steps ahead of the public mind: if an idea is "five or six degrees ahead, it gives them an intolerable headache." A century and a half later even two steps are bad enough. What Stendhal wrote about the public mind is true of the professorate only in the sense of a metaphor, since professional intellectuals are good at avoiding headaches. It is the author whom they will treat as intolerable, whereby his ideas and his books won't count.

In 1958 I had no publisher for this book. This did not matter; the manuscript was far from complete. What mattered that year was the great event of my discovery and reading and comprehension (in that order) of Werner Heisenberg's 1955 Gifford Lectures. I knew that some of my views about the nature and the limits of our historical knowledge corresponded with what certain contemporary or near-contemporary writers and philosophers—say, Ortega and Unamuno; Bernanos and Péguy; Pieper and Wittgenstein; Guardini and Frankl; Camus and Simone Weil; William James and Santayana, and, of course, Tocqueville and Burckhardt—had at least suggested in some of their writings. I suspected that there might be a few correspondences between the discoveries of modern physics and my own convictions of the indeterminacy of historical—that is, human—thinking. Yet I had not imagined that so many of these correspondences would appear, in startling and concrete ways, until I read those Heisenberg lectures (after which came my reading of his other writings). I can recall those sunny mornings in the sea-grape arbored booth of a restaurant in Siasconset, where I had to work after the college girl waitresses—as was their habit, disdainfully—had cleared the breakfast dishes and cutlery away. (With my wife and baby we were poor relations on the already then trendy and expensive Nantucket Island; our room was small and cramped, which was why I would work best in that restaurant after an ample breakfast, scribbling furiously while my wife and child were on their way to the beach.) It was then that I found how not only the philosophical recognitions but sometimes the very phrases of that great German physicist corresponded uncannily, and at times literally, with what I had written about the structure of events, about how things happen and how their "happening" is inevitably involved with our own "observation"—that is, with our own participation, *and* with our knowledge of its limits—in the very world of matter. I worked up a large two-page chart of these correspondences for my book. (Eventually I left that chart out of it; it is still somewhere among my leftover papers.) I knew then what this meant. It meant a new, anthropocentric recognition of the universe: the end of the Cartesian division and separation of "object" from "subject," of observer from the observed, of matter from mind. It would lead to a new anthropocentrism that is complex and not primitive, chastened and not arrogant, issuing from our recognitions of the inevitable limitations of human knowledge, of every kind. Later that year—it was a beautiful Friday in September—my wife and I were driving out to dine with another couple. On our way I told my wife that I may have arrived at an intellectual discovery of great magnitude.

She did not understand this at the time. She was a very intelligent and deeply honest woman; we had many intellectual interests and preferences in common, and the kind of mutual respect that is the foundation and the refuge of every enduring marriage. She was, however, influenced by her earlier reading of the first drafts of the putative chapters of my developing book, which she had found verbose, opaque, and sometimes difficult to follow—rightly so. That natural and pragmatic experience carried over to her reaction to my excited declaration on that melancholy evening. She would understand the essence of my historical philosophy later. It was, after all, a commonsense one, she would say—and she was, I daresay, right. But her first reaction depressed me because of my isolation. I needed her to talk about this matter and, at least for a while, I couldn't. Less disheartening—because they were more expectable—were my subsequent experiences with physicists. I had been, after all, interpreting paragraphs and passages from the texts of a physicist whose *meaning* I thought I wholly understood; but was I correct in my understanding of *what* he was writing about? My knowledge of standard physics was, after all, close to being nonexistent. During the next two or three years I wrote, and attempted to talk, to a number of physics professors, local as well as eminent ones. I got nowhere. With one exception (Henry Margenau, of Yale) their answers to my written or spoken queries were a compound of tut-tutting and disinterest. Yes, they knew all about Heisenberg; yes, the indeterminacy principle was obviously proved; yet what it meant, and even what it encompassed, interested them not at all. About that *meaning*—well, Heisenberg might be right, he might be wrong. Their answers and their lack of interest suggested that the matter was not much worth thinking about. In sum, their reactions (or rather, the lack of their reactions) reminded me of so many of our professional historians who, in the second half of the twentieth century, would admit that, yes, historical determinism is outdated, and then go on teaching and writing as if history *were* determined. However, I got over this through the simple expedient of writing and then calling on Heisenberg himself, in 1962 and 1968. I was relieved to hear and read (in some of his letters to me) that I had not been mistaken in attributing certain observations or ideas to him. He wholly agreed with what I had written in my "History and Physics" chapter, which was all that I wanted to know.

But I am running too far ahead. In 1959 none of my book was in near-finished form. During that fall I suffered a letdown. There was the recurrent illness of my wife. Among other matters, I was disheartened, too, by the enduring and dangerous unwillingness of American public figures (and of many intellectuals) to understand the conditions of the American relationship to the world and to Soviet Russia. Khrushchev had come to the United States that September. There was something pathetic in this Russian peasant czar's hardly suppressed admiration for everything American at the same time that his hosts, including President Eisenhower, walked beside Khrushchev with their noses in the air and with suspicion and distrust written all over their faces. More important: I was getting a bit tired of writing my historical philosophy book. There I have been exhorting historians to write history rather than write about history. But wasn't this exactly what I was doing now? What was the use of all these theses and theories and arguments? As Santayana said, "In the great ages of art nobody talked of aesthetics." Wouldn't it be a more reasonable thing to take a piece of recent history and write it—and demonstrate there the validity of my arguments about the hierarchy of certain historical forces? On a yellow legal pad (another small American blessing) I wrote out a table of contents for two books. One of these potential histories would deal with the history of the world conflict of the United States and Russia. I sent it to the new editor of Doubleday Anchor. A few days before Christmas late in the evening the telephone rang. This editor offered me a contract. Directly next morning my writing of *A History of the Cold War* began.

There followed the happiest six months of writing in my life. Immediately I went out to buy typing paper, a new ribbon, a box of good cigars, and a case of Bass Ale. I wrote this book—a not insubstantial one, either in size or in its composition—during fourteen or fifteen weekends, a draft of each chapter (thirteen overall) each weekend, closeted in my little fruitwood-paneled library, enveloped in a cloud of tobacco. The entire book had been wonderfully clear in my mind. Except for the penultimate chapter, I hardly stopped at all. I set a very wide left margin on my typewriter and wrote the entire book in one full sweep, in one draft, making my corrections and emendations on that wide, pristine, snow-white expanse on the left side of the paper. I especially remember a Saturday in late March 1960 when I had finally wrestled down the first draft of that long, difficult, and fairly verbose penultimate chapter. Having worked without stopping from eight in the morning to six in the afternoon, I took a deliciously hot bath, dressed and drove with my wife a mere half-mile away to a dinner party of my favorite friends, the Drakes, where, to Larry's dismay, as I later found out, I was sufficiently ebullient to consume half a bottle of brandy after dinner. On the way back from dropping off the babysitter I drove our car into the side of a telephone pole. My wife was already safe at home. I didn't care. I was happy.

The next Christmas was dark. My wife was in the local hospital, very ill with an undiagnosed high fever. Yet the year 1961 opened as *annus mirabilis,* for many reasons in my private life. A few days after the New Year my wife's condition turned around; she was recovering beautifully, coming home on the Sunday morning when *A History of the Cold War* had a splendid congratulatory review by Cyrus Sulzberger in the *New York Times Book Review*. I also received a much cherished long letter from George Kennan, who wrote that, among other things, my book was "a really great work of philosophical-historical analysis . . . the deepest and most important effort of this sort that has been made anywhere to date. It abounds with things which to my mind need saying; many of them things that I have tried to say myself, but never so comprehensively; others—ones that I have dimly realized but never pushed to the point of formulation; still others—insights that had never occurred to me, but the validity of which I instantly recognize." How I have been pleased with that. A paperback and German and French editions were to follow. Jason Epstein, who had left Doubleday for Random House, took notice. He offered me a contract for *Historical Thinking*. So I was on my way—or so I thought. I had enough money to send my wife to Florida for the coming winter, for her to escape her recurrent pulmonary illnesses in the cold months. (In the end that cost me little money, since she took it upon herself to work at two jobs and came home in April shining, tanned, and with an unexpected saving of $1,500.) We traveled in Europe next summer. On my return I found that Epstein had sent my manuscript back, with such editorial suggestions that I could not in conscience consider, let alone follow. I returned my contract and put *Historical Thinking* away. I wrote *Decline and Rise of Europe* (a long historical essay) for Doubleday in 1963–64. I went off to teach in France for a year. I added two chapters to the paperback Cold War history in 1966. Then I met (in the same house where I had drunk that unconscionable amount of brandy six years before) Cass Canfield Jr., who gave me a contract for *Historical Thinking*. I rewrote the entire manuscript, boiling some of it away, making it a better book. Two months before its publication another department of Harper & Row, unbeknownst to Cass, published a textbook with that very title. Then and there I had to change my title to *Historical Consciousness*. I did not really mind. After thirteen years my book was in print. It sank without much of a trace, faster than any other book of mine. That did not surprise me—I was inured to it, it had happened before. I now had a double contract. One was for *The Passing of the Modern Age*—the title echoing Huizinga's *The Waning of the Middle Ages*, but otherwise a very different book, a historical essay, not much more than a summation of the devolution of institutions and standards at the end of our age. It was published on the day my wife died, November 15, 1970.

The other book was to be *The Last European War, 1939–1941*, which I consider my second most important work. I had lived through the Second World War in my youth. I kept up an interest in it. It was not only a great, searing, and at times mentally inspiring experience. I sensed then, as I knew later, that this world war was not only enormous in its extent but also more complex than its predecessor, because it involved much more than the movements of armies and of states; it involved the movable sentiments of entire peoples. In many ways the mental earthquake of that war was bigger than the physical one. And this was especially true of its first part, of the twenty-seven months in 1939–41, before Pearl Harbor. After December 1941 Hitler could no longer win his war because the British and the Russians had held out against him until finally the Americans joined them with full force. But before Pearl Harbor he could have won it. At times he came close to winning it, which is what so many people either forgot or did not wish to think about. So my book would include the movements not only of the armies and of governments, but of public opinion and of popular sentiments and perhaps even beliefs during those years. The reactions of peoples to the stupendous German triumphs were one thing. Others were the beginnings of the end of bourgeois politics, of the British empire, the beginnings of the Americanization of Europe and of the extermination of masses of Jews. I wanted to write a large and profound book about those years, a newly designed and crafted vessel whose structure would naturally incarnate my own ideas about how history ought to be seen and therefore written, a representation of some of the governing ideas of *Historical Consciousness.* I divided *The Last European War* into two parts: a "narrative" and an "analytical" portion ("The Main Events" and "The Main Movements")— in other words, a description of *what* happened, followed by a description of *how* and *why* events, tendencies, and developments came about. In the second, longer part I moved from the lives of the peoples to the march of the armies to the movements of politics to the relations of states to the sentiments of nations to the convergences of thought and of belief, in that order (these were the titles of successive chapters), in accord with the hierarchy already suggested in *Historical Consciousness,* along an ascending order. I had done this earlier, in *A History of the Cold War,* and would do this later, too, in my *Outgrowing Democracy: A History of the United States in the Twentieth Century.* I knew that the first portion—as important and in many of its details as new as the second—would be overlooked, even by sympathetic reviewers. But because this book was much more than a historical essay, because it filled many gaps in our knowledge, because it was the only near-encyclopedic work on the years 1939–41, because its materials had come from my research and reading of many thousands of books and articles and documents in many languages, I hoped that the very structure and the method of the book would be noticed and perhaps discussed by other professionals. It wasn't. The very writing and the publishing of the book went through years of vicissitudes. I began it in 1967 but interrupted it twice, once for the writing of *The Passing of the Modern Age* and again during the tragic year of my wife's fatal illness and death. I finished it in 1973, but it was not published until March 1976. In one instance, the book was delayed when the secretary who was supposed to retype the manuscript (the ephemeral paramour of the chief editor) forgot it in the broom closet of her summer rental apartment on Fire Island. Another torpedo befell it around the time of the book's launching: the excellent and sympathetic editor newly assigned to it was fired. But never mind: the book was published, and I am pleased with it still. Before it sank out of sight it had received a few respectful salvos of star shells; and a few foreign lifeboats hauled around to salvage it, whence its German, French, British, and Brazilian editions. Thus, unlike many other books of mine, it did not quite sink without a trace. There were a few bubbles on the surface, including, alas, the ugly oily slick exuding from one of its reviewers, who suggested that my treatment of the Jewish tragedy could be exploited by anti-Semites. This, of course, was not only wrong but the very opposite of what I had intended and written; but it surely accelerated the disappearance of this, I believe, well-wrought vessel, to the extent that its remains on the bottom are unmarked in many of the maritime charts of its region. Enough of this figure of speech: what I mean is that *The Last European War, 1939–1941* is often omitted from the very bibliographies of works dealing with its subject.

Often during the last phase of writing a book I grow tired of it—less tired of the work itself than of the place it preoccupies in my mind. Then I begin to think what I should write next; and, to use Jean Dutourd's fine phrase, the *petite musique* of certain ideas and phrases is beginning to form in my mind. The idea of a book about Philadelphia was already crystallizing when I finished *The Last European War*. However, I had no other publisher than Doubleday at that time; and I loathed the effort of addressing unsolicited letters to publishers and editors who presumably knew nothing of me. Thus Doubleday and I agreed on my writing a short book about the year 1945. *1945: Year Zero* was smaller and different from the structure of my other books; its writing took me a year and a half. It was a good little book, a destroyer compared to the aircraft carrier of *The Last European War*. Long before its proof stage I returned to my Philadelphia project, which was perhaps the second of my most delightful book-writing experiences. I was longing to get away from large canvases, from portraying great wars and civilizations. I wanted to try my hand at a miniature. But the crucial inspiration was, of course, not the size of the canvas but the scene. I had an amateur and secondary interest in the history of my adopted city (I live nearly forty miles west of it, but in Philadelphia it is not geography that matters) for many years. In 1958 *Encounter* had printed my short and impressionistic article about Philadelphia and Philadelphians, which led to the agreeable result of its inclusion in the University of Chicago's manual, *Selected Writings in English,* among samples of fine English writing. In my private library alone there were hundreds of the oddest books about Philadelphia. So I began this book in 1976, leading to its eventual title, *Philadelphia: Patricians and Philistines, 1900–1950.* The first chapter was a detailed description of the city in 1900, the last in 1950; the rest were biographical portraits of seven famous or not so famous Philadelphians, *qui floreabant* during the first half of this century, with odd dualities in their character.

There were particular pleasures attendant to the writing of this book. One of them was the search and the finding of material (including photographs) in various Philadelphia libraries, where my discovery of material oddities was enhanced by the atmosphere; and at the end of the darkening afternoons stood the prospect of a short walk in the cold wintry air and a good dinner downtown with one of my friends.[6] Another pleasure was talking about this book and its characters with my second wife on warm summer evenings over dinner on our screened porch in the country, high above the bushes but secluded under trees, with the sounds of bullfrogs and cicadas lightening the heavy green stillness from the dark pond and the creek. I had plenty of trouble getting a publisher for this Philadelphia book. Eventually, through a rare stroke of fortune, the manuscript landed on the desk of Robert Giroux who, *rara avis,* actually *read* those hundreds of pages of an unfinished manuscript by an unknown writer. I was delighted to meet him, this last old-fashioned gentleman in what once had been an occupation for gentlemen. He convinced me to add a chapter on Albert C. Barnes, the collector of art, something that my wife, too, had urged and that previously I had refused to do. This took another summer's work, but it was worth it. My Philadelphia book was published in March 1981; Farrar, Straus & Giroux printed a physically very attractive book. It may be one of my best written ones. It was a book whose publication was followed by a series of agreeable events. By this I do not only mean that it had a few very respectful reviews but that I had the occasion, too, to do a few lighthearted causeries (relating, among other things, a fair number of anecdotes that I left out of the book) in two or three of the small Philadelphia clubs, to audiences consisting of many men and women whom I knew, in pleasant little clubhouses built in the twenties, including the ineffable Philadelphian climate of civility, that urbane atmosphere further enhanced by the great trees swaying outside the windows and the yellow lights bathing the small alleys and squares of the city in the windy autumn evenings.

It will now be seen that the topics of my books have been different ones;

and that I have been moving from European to American history through the years. And why not? I have lived in this country for a long time. Whether I was becoming a part of it I cannot say; what I can say is that it was becoming a part of me. In 1981 I began an attempt to write a history of the United States of the last one hundred years, along a structure again in accord with those of some of my previous works and *Historical Consciousness*. I was assisted and inspired by a great and good friend, Nick Rizopoulos (then of the Lehrman Institute), whom I gained during this work. *Outgrowing Democracy: A History of the United States in the Twentieth Century* was published by Doubleday in March 1984. A year later a new, enlarged edition (by two important chapters) of *Historical Consciousness* was published by Schocken Books.

That year William Shawn, the editor of the *New Yorker*, took notice of my writing. During the next eighteen months I was a grateful beneficiary of his sympathetic appreciation of my work. He printed six articles of mine in the *New Yorker*, carefully wrought pieces on very different topics,[7] encouraged by his interest and polished with the aid of the unusual and old-fashioned editorial scrupulousness of his magazine. When Shawn left the *New Yorker* in January 1987, I was saddened. I also thought how odd the tides of American development have been. When the *New Yorker* had started out in 1925, at the high tide of modern American urbane sophistication, someone said, or wrote, that the *New Yorker* was not meant for "the old lady in Dubuque." Sixty years later many of the readers of the *New Yorker* were old ladies in Dubuque and other traditional readers of literature tucked away in the oddest of places.

So my interests were not only moving in the direction of American history, but simultaneously in the opposite direction as well. In 1985 I began to think about a book dealing with the cultural history of my native country; more precisely, about life in its capital city around 1900. So many books had been recently addressed to intellectual life in Vienna around 1900; I thought that the time had come to direct English-speaking readers to the, in many ways, no less interesting culture of Budapest, the other capital city of the Dual Monarchy, in 1900, which was unknown to them. Materials about that subject had become available, and were accumulating; and the libraries in Budapest were now open for research.

Looking back at my books I can see certain similarities that I had not recognized before. I have written thirteen books in four decades, so the average time for my writing a book has been about three years. This is the case of my last three books, so perhaps I am only now hitting my stride, though I doubt this. Another curious coincidence that I found only lately is that most of my books, including this one, consist of nine chapters—something that has never been a conscious decision at the time of their planning. All my books have been published by trade publishers. This has been my definite preference, for two reasons. One is my conviction that historians should not write only for other historians—even though there are important occasions when they must, and should. The other is money. Well, these preferences have not really worked. When a professor succeeds in having a book printed by a reputable commercial publisher some of his colleagues will profess a kind of pristine disdain that often cloaks their less pristine sentiment of envy. They are wrong to be envious. There is little money in this kind of writing. (There is more in the grants and appointments that may be accumulated because of one's academic publications, affiliations, and connections.) They are wrong, too, in being disdainful. To write for more people than academics does not necessarily connote superficiality. Often the very contrary is true. I may have been a prolific writer; but I have not been superficial.[8] I have, I think, profited from the self-imposed condition of living apart from the sometimes airless circles of academics. This explains, too, why among my many articles I sent relatively few to academic journals. The exceptions to this are my scholarly book reviews. While my books and essays often contain—sometimes inordinately—more than a single topic and a single argument, my book reviews do not, for then a single topic is given: a single book. The intellectual commerce of our times has led to the habit of book reviews that serve as instruments for displaying the reviewer's opinions and prejudices, and his scholarship at its feeble best. My practice of reviewing is the old-fashioned one: telling what the book contains and trying to include a mention or at least a summary of anything that I find new or significant in its details.

I have been a prolific writer, for all kinds of reasons. I think I can express certain thoughts and matters better in writing than in speaking. My impulse is to the expression and not really to its reverberation (as Eliot said of literature: it is "the impulse to transcribe one's thoughts correctly")—which is not the case with speaking, nor that of writers whose aspirations are celebrity and money. I am not indifferent to these things, and only imperfectly immune to their temptations. (Gibbon in 1763: "I do not wish that the writer make the Gentleman wholly disappear.") Yet I also feel that we have fallen to a level of intellectual commerce where the instant academic and/or commercial success of a book of mine may mean that there must be something wrong with it. (It would give me great pleasure to have to revise this sentence.)

In any event, there are in this vast country a few hundred men and women, mostly unknown to me, who will read anything I write—if and when they become aware of its availability. Still I have failed in my self-designed task. I have not been able to create that new genre, that new kind of history whereof I have been the occasional John the Baptist, at best. Yes, I have, here and there, attempted the great task for a historian, the tale of some subjects of the last one hundred years, not a retelling of the Decline of the West, surely not a Spenglerian speculative systematization of it, but the *conscious* historical recognition of the opening of a new phase in the evolution of our consciousness. Or, in other terms: the great, the profound difference between evolution and history.

But how I desired to paint some of this in a microcosm! I would paint a clear and beautiful slice of the sad music of humanity, on the surface canvas of which people, their characters and their episodes, their words and thoughts and actions and reactions, would reflect the conditions and the tendencies of a certain historical time—and suggest, at the same time, the potentialities of what lay before them. For example, the rise and fall of Anglomania in Europe, 1815–1955, and not only from its political and literary evidences. Or the fading of the Anglo-Saxon Eastern patriciandom in the United States: the fading of their strength and of their presence; of their convictions rather than of their optimism, out of evidences that are implicit rather than explicit, describing their reactions and their actions, of what they came to understand rather than what they knew, their sometime despair of life rather than their fear of death, the stiff bravery of their race still in their brittle bones but with the sense that the instinct of their courage had become solitary, it would no longer be national or communal. Edith Wharton once wrote about the society of Old New York more than a century ago that it was a bottle now empty but at the bottom of it there still remained a fine kind of lees, an essence of rarefied, and often unspoken, sentiments. I should not only describe the lees but its components and, of course, its devolution: the evaporation of the wine, a description in which, again, the *why* would be implicit in the *how*. Yes, somewhere I could write about a party, say, in one of the Philadelphia suburbs, of young handsome couples recognizable to me and therefore describable: people thinking, without much feeling, that they and their country were at the top of the world, drinking and dancing under the roofs of large trees, to the music that their kind liked, tunes such as "Dancing on the Ceiling" or "What's New?" without knowing that while their ears were attuned to the rhythm of that music, its essential harmonies were melancholy—this around the time, say, 1947, when Washington had become The Capital of the World and when someone like Dean Acheson thought that he was Present at the Creation. For there had been a connection between these things—and well before what was going on in the sixties in the lives of decent middle-aged people, when their sons and daughters chose to go barefoot and filled the inadequacy of their resistless freedom with drugs and an unceasing, battering, primitive music—and also of many other things besides. Here and there in some of my books I related and connected such materials, fragments of evidence and life whose connections were clear, at least to me, no matter how unusual and perhaps even startling their correlations were. But not enough for a book: a few coherent vignettes do not amount to a creation. History is a seamless web and not a collage. And a description of any portion of that web is neither the business of an arachnologist (*vide* a social scientist or a quantificationist historian), nor of a modernist painter (*vide* a "nonfiction" novelist) who cannot see, and therefore cannot paint, beyond a collage of colorful shapes. It requires a new, a stunning conjunction of an old-fashioned master draftsman and a visionary master painter.

I have now written about painting with words. Yet I am a writer, not a painter. I think that my travails in writing a book have more in common with the work of a sculptor than with that of a painter, the first draft especially corresponding to the heavy labor of someone striking and hammering and beating and carving something recognizable out of a large lump of stone, before the chiseling can begin: recognizable, that is, only to him at that stage. (My first drafts are not only crude; they are undecipherable for anyone except myself.) But because I chose to be a writer, not content with being not much more than a competent researcher and archivist, I must say something about the awesome handicap of having to write in English, which is not my native language.

This has been a handicap, not a dilemma, because this was my choice. In 1946 I left Hungary behind when Hungary was left behind the Iron Curtain. Whether I would leave now I doubt; but had I lived in my native country till now, I would surely be a different man. Since this book is written in English, for English-speaking readers, I will not say much about my relationship to my native language, except to state that I speak it accurately—at times with a few old-fashioned mannerisms and words that people on occasion notice when I visit my native country: when they remark that, this gives me pleasure. While I still *feel* Hungarian (an inadequate shorthand statement for something complex and important), during the last forty years I have come to think in English. Almost always I dream and count in English. (Counting in a language is significant. I was once told by a French police officer that when they are not sure about the nationality of a suspect, experienced detectives will attempt to listen to him when he is counting.) Because of my lack of practice I sometimes find it more difficult to write Magyar than English, and I am unwilling to speak Magyar in public without a prepared text. In 1983 the Historical Institute in Budapest invited me for a talk. I wrote my lecture with care, polishing it with greater concentration than if I had been asked to speak anywhere else in the world. Afterward the chairman said: "We haven't heard such language in this room for a long time." This compliment touched the depths of my soul.[9]

I wrote about my lifelong love affair with the English language earlier. I have been married to it now, and there can be no question of divorce, or even of a long separation. When I am away from an English-speaking country I begin to worry about the dangers of absence, of the unfaithfulness of the dear thing in my mind. It is a dear thing, like my wife—also, as Cyril Connolly once wrote, "Our language is a sulky and inconstant beauty and at any moment it is important to know what liberties she will permit" (again, like my present wife). But my marriage to English is a prosaic marriage, meaning that it involves mostly prose, not verse—especially not free verse.[10] Yes, good prose, like a good prosaic marriage, may *contain* told and untold depths of poetry within it; but it does not *consist* of poetry. While I enjoy and, I think, comprehend modern and classical English and American prose as well as I enjoy and comprehend the prose of my native country, this is not true of poetry. I comprehend poetry, good and bad, in Magyar better than in English. I think that the reason for this is simple. It includes not only my education in Hungary but the fact that all genuine poetry is tribal, like a family joke.[11]

Such reflections have led me to wonder what would have become of me as a Magyar writer. I was overwhelmed by such sentiments in 1981 when I read Jean Dutourd's breathtakingly scintillant, witty, proud, and supremely elegant speech as he took his chair at the Académie Française. I envy Jean for many things. How fortunate he is to write in his native language! As I read his prose in a language that, at best, is my third or fourth one, I knew how my fortune and my abilities were hopelessly (and I mean hopelessly) remote from his. He was able to summon his highest talent and produce a masterpiece of a traditional address in his living, shining native language, one of the finest addresses that must have been delivered in three hundred years under that cavernous dome on the banks of the Seine. I wrote him about this; and he answered with his usual brevity, generosity, and wit. He soothed me with a phrase by Rivarol: "My country is the language in which I write." Yes, or rather, of course: my country is America now; but in Rivarol's French "my country" is "*ma patrie*"; and in spite of my American loyalties and my marriage to English my fatherland remains Hungary, after all is said.

Every careful writer possesses certain cherished examples of prose that stimulate his imagination: in my case, a historical rather than a literary imagination. I have a folder in which I occasionally stuff small slips of paper copied out after I have run across a passage that I find very good. That folder (it is, alas, not a thick one; it is disorderly, and desultorily kept), marked Fine Writing, contains a bunch of such slips. I read through them as I was preparing this chapter on my writing. Now I think I ought to reproduce some of them, for the sake of illustrating myself.

Here is a description that has the material smell of historical truths and is, at the same time, a wonderfully economical summary of complicated facts:

> The royal household was a gigantic nest of costly jobbery and purposeless profusion. It retained all "the cumbrous charges of a Gothic establishment," though all its usage and accommodation had "shrunk into the polished littleness of modern elegance." The outlay was enormous. The expenditure on the court tables only was a thing unfathomable. Waste was the rule in every branch of it. There was an office for the Great Wardrobe, another office of the Robes, a third of the Groom of the Stole. For these three useless offices there were three useless treasurers. (John Morley, *Burke*)

Here is a very different sample of prose, which is autobiographical. It is a rich evocation of a vanished decade—masterly, with its mixture of scherzo and adagio, because its author's style, probably unconsciously, breathes the atmosphere of an impressionism that was not merely a retrospectively regnant style but that is so suited to depictions of the 1890s:

> Then came a summer term at Scoones, distracted and dislocated by many amusements. I went to the Derby that year and backed Persimmon; to the first performance of Mrs. Campbell's *Magda* the same night; I saw Duse at Drury Lane and Sarah Bernhardt at Daly's; I went to Ascot; I went to balls; I stayed at Panshanger; and at Wrest, at the end of the summer, where a constellation of beauty moved in muslin and straw hats and yellow roses on the lawns of gardens designed by Lenôtre, delicious with ripe peaches on old brick walls, with the smell of verbena and sweet geranium; and stately with large avenues, artificial lakes and white temples; and we bicycled in the warm night past ghostly cornfields by the light of a large full moon. (Maurice Baring, *The Puppet Show of Memory*)

Here is Joseph Conrad, a foreigner who never learned to speak English faultlessly but who was not only a great master of English prose: these lines, to me, amount to a historical and pictorial—not epic or poetic—written apotheosis of an England, evoking, to me, England circa 1888 (though this passage comes from *The Nigger of the Narcissus,* published in 1898):

> A week afterwards the *Narcissus* entered the chops of the Channel. . . . Under white wings she skimmed low over the blue sea like a great tired bird speeding to its nest. The clouds raced with her mastheads; they rose astern enormous and white, soared to the zenith, flew past, and falling down the wide curve of the sky, seemed to dash headlong into the sea—the clouds swifter than the ship, more free, but without a home. The coast, to welcome her, stepped out of space into the sunshine. The lofty headlands trod masterfully into the sea; the wide bays smiled in the light; the shadows of homeless clouds ran along the sunny plains, leaped over valleys, without a check darted up the hills, rolled down the slopes; and the sunshine pursued them with patches of running brightness. On the brows of dark cliffs white lighthouses shone in pillars of light. The Channel glittered like a blue mantle shot with gold and starred by the silver of the capping seas. The *Narcissus* rushed past the headlands and the bays. Outward-bound vessels crossed her track, lying over, and with their masts stripped for a slogging fight with the hard sou'wester. And, inshore, a string of smoking steamboats waddled, hugging the coast, like migrating and amphibious monsters, distrustful of the restless waves. . . .
>
> At night the headlands retreated, the bays advanced into one unbroken line of gloom. The lights of the earth mingled with the lights of heaven; and above the tossing lanterns of a trawling fleet a great lighthouse shone steadily, like an enormous riding light burning above a vessel of fabulous dimensions. Below its steady glow, the coast, stretching away straight and black, resembled the high side of an indestructible craft riding motionless upon the immortal and unresting sea. The dark land lay alone in the midst of waters, like a mighty ship bestarred with vigilant lights—a ship carrying the burden of millions of lives—a ship freighted with dross and with jewels, with gold and with steel. She towered up immense and strong, guarding priceless traditions and untold suffering, sheltering glorious memories and base forgetfulness, ignoble virtues and splendid transgressions. A great ship! For ages had the ocean battered in vain her enduring sides; she was there when the world was vaster and darker, when the sea was great and mysterious,

and ready to surrender the prize of fame to audacious men. A ship mother of fleets and nations! The great flagship of the race; stronger than the storms! and anchored in the open sea.

Here now the same period, though a different place, recalled with the spare romanticism hidden underneath the narrow shoulders of an austere (though not unambitious) Scotsman:

> There was the bridge with the river starred with strange lights, the lit shipping at the Broomielaw, and odours which even at their worst spoke of the sea. (John Buchan about Glasgow, circa 1890, in *Pilgrim's Way*)

Jan Morris is not a historian; but her sense of a place and of a time, flowing from a historical imagination dependent on solid knowledge, suffuses her prose at times with images whose appearance is not only evocative but tangible:

> Victoria returned to her palace in the evening, exhausted but marvelously pleased, through the blackened buildings of her ancient capital, whose smoke swirled and hovered over the grey river, and whose gas-lamps flickered into tribute with the dusk. (About the Diamond Jubilee, 1897)

One more sophisticated appreciation of that decade:

> To appreciate the gulf between that period and now, one may recall that when the brilliant man-about-town Harry Cust, editing the *Pall Mall Gazette* in the '90s, wrote a leader on the downfall of the Casimir-Perier cabinet he gaily headlined it: "Perier Joué." (D. B. Wyndham Lewis, *English Wits*)

There is nothing fancy, or even artistic, in this description. But I can think of no better summary of the Dual Monarchy before 1914:

> Only those who knew what life was like in old Austria-Hungary can judge the country fairly. To sit in the Mirabell Gardens and look up at the castle of Salzburg, to saunter down the Stradone in Ragusa, to see the Goldmacherhäusl, the alchemist's cottage, gleaming on the Hradschin in Prague, to hear the tolling of the bells of the Stefansdom in Vienna, to admire the frowning castle

in Budapest, the mosque in Mostar, the Mickiewicz memorial in Cracow, and the Dante memorial in Trient—is to realize that tradition and selfishness, geographical necessity and the play of chance, had collaborated here to build a structure supremely individual, of which three men so different in outlook as Palacky, Bismarck, and Disraeli remarked that if it did not exist, for the sake of European peace it would have had to be invented. (G. Reiners, *The Lamps Went Out over Europe*)

Again 1914. From the diary of an ordinary Englishman. I do not think that even Sir Edward Grey's famous phrase of that night ("The lamps are going out all over Europe") strikes a note comparable to this singular, deep tone:

> *Rake. Night of 4 August, 1914.* Out in the garden of my house at 11 P.M., listening to what I imagined to be a War signal: a gun fired at Portsmouth, very faint in the distance, this whole thing a climax to my various private troubles.... [Train ride to London]. Wind, hot sun and coal dust, and over all the great shadow of the War. (*The Ordeal of Alfred M. Hale*, Paul Fussell, ed.)

Here is the frozen Petrograd of 1920, described by someone more sensitive (and perhaps even more knowledgeable) than political historians of that period:

> *(1920. Petrograd.)* That was the time to see the Palmyra of the North in the majestic misery that endowed it with a new beauty: its suddenly yawning squares, its distances subtly merging into haze; its main streets all silent after the noisy tumults of war and insurrection, forgetful of the familiar sounds of the time gone by when the city was still alive; its stations now without trains, its port without ships, the palaces along the quays all staring blindly; the Stock Exchange, on the other side of the river, again a temple, and there was the Smolny convent, all whirls and spirals, entablatures and rock work, Rastrelli's astonishing currant-and-cream cake, royally served on a vast platter of snow, which in the days of October had been the revolutionary headquarters. During the yellow thaw, at the end of 1920, there were few people to be met in the center of the city; these walked in the middle of the street, the houses on either side being riddled with bullets, revealing their nudity through crumbling plaster

and the planks that served as a dressing for their wounded windows and plate glass. People passed under the triumphal arch and then seemed to lose themselves, adrift in the great square; at the far side of it the Winter Palace, in that livid light in which the city slept, seemed merely its own shadow, haunted by the ghosts of those who had once dwelled in it. But far into the night, and into the fate there was no escaping, the city preserved her own spectral beauty, looking fairer than ever in the washed air of spring, untarnished by smoke from the now silent factories, her porticos and colonnades displaying once again the graces no longer enjoyed, no longer of this world. (Wladimir Weidlé, *Russia: Absent and Present*)

(1920. Kolchak's Siberian army.) Men with axes were busy freeing the trains of their colleagues which, as always after a prolonged halt, were anchored to the permanent way by great stalactites of discoloured ice depending from lavatories and kitchens. The half-battalion of Japanese infantry who had arrived on Skipetrow's heels were enigmatically ensconced in a siding; it was given out that they had come to supervise the evacuation of their nationals. (Peter Fleming, *Kolchak*. The question arises whether the second sentence is unintentionally funny.)

The evocative power of certain place-names: because such names are not only inseparable from their places but from a certain time:

(1923.) My mother's favourite sister had married a rich man. Aunt Mab was very beautiful but she also had special smells, smells of furs and Edwardian lure. Uncle Walter gave me a steam train and a watch for Christmas. Wherever we went with Aunt Mab there were presents and large houses and the appeal her wealth made for an imaginative child was irresistible. Bishopscourt, Loughananna, Rochestown, Marlay, the names of her houses (for she moved every six months) held a poetry for me. ... (Cyril Connolly)

And to me Compton Wynyates sounds and spells more elegant than Choisy-le-Roi. ...

I have included these samples of prose for two reasons. They will illustrate some of my own inspirations and aspirations: if *le style, c'est l'homme,* so

679

is *le goût*. More important is my conviction that these excerpts are deeply historical. They are "material" that I like to use and that historians ought to use. By "use" I do not necessarily mean their inclusion or precise citation. What I mean is that they are wondrous instruments for a deeper and more satisfying comprehension of certain places and certain periods, which is exactly what historians must achieve. History is a descriptive business, not a defining one. This business of description versus definition is the essence of the difference between history and "science"; between words and numbers; between Pascal and Descartes; between two views of the world. Without description history cannot live in our minds because history, I repeat, is not only expressed but *thought* in words.

These samples, picked at random, are not necessarily samples of the best kind of historical-atmosphere descriptions that I know exist. I have not included anything from my favorite writer, the Magyar Krúdy. Nor are there American writers in the previous sample, even though I have many slips from them in that Fine Writing folder of mine. That file, as I said, is a desultorily kept and disorderly one. Yet I must still add some things from it, in order to illustrate the inspiration that certain kinds of writing give me. "Silence. The subdued hum of London was like the bourdon note of a distant organ." (William Gerhardie. The music of a period.) Somerville and Ross describe (in *The Real Charlotte*) the landing of the Irish Mail at Kingston: "The paddles dropped their blades more and more languidly into the water, then they ceased, and the vessel slid silently alongside the jetty, with the sentient ease of a living thing"—well, I have not seen a paddleboat coming in from the sea, but I have seen the Irish Sea when it was flat and calm and that is how it must have been. When Charlotte "had the unusual gift of thinking out in advance her line of conversation in an interview, and, which is even less usual, she had the power of keeping to it"—useful to keep in mind for describing an able diplomat.

So are some of the philosophical aphorisms tacked up above my desk. And so are the very histories of words—how, for example, *spiritual* in the Middle Ages meant the opposite of what it means now; how *melancholy* meant a bodily function four hundred years ago; how the word *anachronism* three hundred years ago did not exist; how *old-fashioned* was a pejorative adjective two centuries ago in England and less than a century ago in America, and how its reputation is now rising, while that of *modern* declines. When new words appear and endure, when old words disappear or change their meaning, this means that the thinking of a certain people at a certain time changed, which is what history is mostly about—for words are not the symbols of things; they are symbols of meanings.

Does this then mean that history is art, after all, *impur et complex*? No, there is a difference between an art and a form of thought. Yes, every novel is a historical novel; yes, "fact" and "fiction" overlap. But an evolution has occurred. Exactly a century ago Thomas Hardy wrote that "conscientious fiction alone it is which can excite a reflecting and abiding interest in the minds of thoughtful readers of mature age, who are weary of puerile inventions and famishing for accuracy; who consider that in representations of the world, the passions ought to be proportioned as in the world itself. This is the interest which was excited in the minds of the Athenians by their immortal tragedies, and in the minds of Londoners at the first performances of the finer plays of three hundred years ago." I am convinced that *conscientious history* is now replacing that desideratum which Hardy stated as "conscientious fiction." It is history "which can excite a reflecting and abiding interest in the minds of thoughtful readers of mature age" who are "weary" (and how weary we are) of "puerile inventions" while they are "famishing for accuracy"—and for reality and truth in representations of a world.

Jean Dutourd wrote in his *jeu d'esprit, Mary Watson: "écrire une histoire, c'est transformer un morceau de temps en un morceau d'éternité."* "To transform a fragment of time into a fragment of eternity"—easier said than done. But one must go a bit beyond art. "*En art, comme ailleurs, il faut vivre au-dessus du ses moyens*"—"In art, as elsewhere, one must live beyond one's means." Or Saki: "The art of public life consists to a great extent of knowing exactly where to stop and going a bit farther." Are these aphorisms applicable to history-writing? I know that in my writing and in my life I have had the old Magyar habit of living beyond my means. This includes my fondling of that dear and sulky and inconstant beauty, the English language. (There is a funny repartee in one of Waugh's books: "He probably speaks perfectly good English." "Oh yes . . . but we must not encourage him.")

I chose to write and teach, in that order, even though these priorities became eventually, and not necessarily disagreeably, confused. But chronologically my writing outlasts my teaching. I began to write before I became a teacher; I can foresee the time when I will have to give up my teaching; I can hardly imagine a time when I would no longer write. What I could not foresee, until lately, is the prospect of something somber. This is the end of the Age of the Book. I have known for a long time that the Modern Age, the great chapter of Western civilization that began about five hundred years ago, is passing. The invention of printing was one of its early features. It developed together with the rebirth of learning (which was a term long used in England for the Renaissance. More people in Western Europe knew how to read Greek and Latin in 1520 than in 1320). But it is only during the last twenty years or so that I have begun to see how the now rapidly declining habit of book reading is not a transitory or a super-ficial phenomenon. Living in the United States I have been well situated to observe this. I am now living among a people, teaching its young, whose imagination is no longer verbal but pictorial. Television and the movies have, of course, contributed to this. Yet this development preceded televi-sion. Its evidences are all around us. They involve more than habits. They involve the very functioning of people's minds. Yes: there are fewer book readers. But contrary to accepted ideas—that is, illusions—there were not many American book readers or French book readers (and book buyers) fifty or one hundred years ago, either. Their influence, however, could be considerable on occasion; it is not now. There is another difference. We are now in the increasing presence of people who don't read because they don't want to. They don't want to because they are unused to reading. There are fewer bookstores. Most of these are not really bookstores: they do not store books. They will not stock (or even order) books that are not currently mass produced. Many American libraries are emptying, too, not yet of books but of people. I am afraid that sooner or later a diminishing number of their visitors will be followed by their diminishing acquisitions of books. Oddly—or perhaps not so oddly—this is happening when "education" has become truly universal, when four out of ten American high school stu-dents go on to college, that is, spending at least twenty years of their lives in schools; and at a time when the number of new books published is still increasing.

Again we face a phenomenon when numbers do not matter; or, rather, they matter in an inverse way. The inflation of education and the inflation of printed matter are part and parcel of the general phenomenon of infla-tion in the age of democracy, especially in the twentieth century. Whether it is money or books or degrees or sex, when there is more and more of something it is worth less and less. The Hungarian poet János Pilinszky wrote: "Just as masses of automobiles paralyze traffic, publishing masses of books impedes reading. When you are getting published, while no one reads you, this is not really publishing. I feel that we are moving back toward a kind of anonymity, somewhat like artisans in the Middle Ages who were great creative artists, having found their own spheres of art within their lives."

This somber perspective is not devoid of a silver lining. I believe that the necessarily small minority of men and women who take pleasure in books will find each other and draw closer together. There are already signs of such a development across the isolated (isolated from books and culture, that is) suburban wastelands of this great country. I also find it probable that the otherwise catastrophic technology that led to the deadly flood of external and impersonal "communications" at the expense of authentic and personal ones may have some interesting consequences. This may include the possibility that in the future writers might not only write but type, print, bind, pack, and send out—that is, "publish"—their own books, depending on an existing network of their potential readers and buyers (and on the mails). This would mean a return to the early modern centuries when the printer and the publisher and the bookseller were the same person. It would lead to the breaking of the increasingly cumbrous and entangled chain of middlemen whereby writers and their readers are supposedly brought together but, in reality, more often kept apart. (It would also mean that writers, not publishers, would get most of the profits.) But I am a historian, not a prophet.

Like many contemporary authors I have a string of horror stories about publishers. I shall not dwell on them unduly. Because of the frantic pace of the publishing business, the editors assigned to five or six of my books left their firms between the delivery date of the manuscript and its publication. Another of my books was already printed and bound when its title had to be changed in a frenzy: the same firm had just published a textbook reader with my title, a fact of which my chief editor and his entire department were unaware. Six months after the publication of yet another book of mine the computer of the publishing house twinkled the information to bookstores that no such book existed on their lists. I mentioned earlier how an entire manuscript of mine was lost by the girlfriend of the editor. Despite insistent requests from publishers to submit my corrections for a second printing, sometimes the result was that these corrections were left out of that printing, for "technical reasons." One day my telephone rang early in the morning: Tokyo was calling, inviting me to come to Japan, offering a substantial honorarium and the luxury of first-class airfare halfway across the globe. Not until I landed in Tokyo did I learn the reason for this invitation. One of my books had been translated and published in Japan four years before. I had had no information from its New York publishers about this. Such ludicrous happenings (in many cases leading not only to my financial loss but to that of the publishers) are, of course, not particular to the publishing industry. They are typical of the impersonality, of the standardization and of the consequent inefficiency, of large corporations, with their computer-thinking (or lack of thinking) in our days. They are not very different from the troubles one might have with his credit-card account or with the Internal Revenue Service. They are the results of impersonality: of inattention, not of ill will.

In our times the fate of books—together with much else in the world of merchandise—is largely, though not entirely, predetermined, even before they are published. This is relatively new. The critic Richard Schickel recently wrote a telling passage about this: "Art," he wrote, "was a classically free market until recently. It was, indeed, one of the last such in our corporate economy. Now, however, with the intervention of marketing . . . it becomes a market organized as a series of self-fulfilling prophecies. . . . [Y]our work is either a hit or a flop; there is no viable middle ground. And that status is decided beforehand in the marketing meetings, which may well precede production, and assuredly do precede distribution. The chance of the market reacting unpredictably, resisting the massive interventions of promotion and publicity, of consumers revolting against the prophecy that is really a fix, is minimal." This surely applies to the publishing of books. In the past the decision to publish a book was made by the editors; the sales manager was called in afterward. Now the sales manager is a principal in the decision whether to publish a book or not. Of course there are practical reasons for this. One is the large increase in the actual cost of matter: the paper. Another factor is the passing of an urban civilization in the age of suburbs: what matters is what books can be placed on the shelves of the book-supermarkets there. The size of the first printing and the promotion budget are what matter, since because of the decline of book readership and the passing of an urban civilization the reputation of a book can hardly expect to prosper by word of mouth. When Franklin and Emerson said that in this country all someone has to do is to build a better mousetrap they were mouthing nonsense. What he has to do is to *advert* people (often at the cost of frequent and incessant repetition) of the existence of his mousetrap. This is probably even more so in the book business. A manufacturer of an unusually good mousetrap may, after all, acquire a modest reputation among his neighbors in want of dead mice. The writer of an unusually good book does not have such a chance.

However, I have my consolations. The first of these is that I cannot do otherwise. Writing and teaching are my métiers. My writings are being published. They may disappear rapidly; they do not earn much money; but I do not think that the conditions of a writing career are in every way worse than they were in the past. They are surely different; but what Walter Scott wrote more than a hundred and fifty years ago is still apposite, at least to me: "Literature," he said, "is a good staff but a bad crutch." I am fortunate in not having to depend entirely on my writing income. My son, without the slightest pressure from his father, but inspired by his own great intelligence and talent, chose a similar career of teaching and writing. I am fortunate because my writing brought me exceptional friendships. Through my writing I have gained the correspondence and the confidence, and sometimes the close friendship, of great contemporaries: very different men and women, such as Dwight Macdonald, George Kennan, Jacques Barzun, Malcolm Muggeridge, Jean Dutourd, Owen Barfield, Dervla Murphy. To this random and incomplete list of great and honorable men and women I add the existence of people who will read what I write with the kind of acute and abiding interest that fills me with gratitude and does me honor. At times, in a wildly optimistic mood, I hope that I may gain the reputation of someone who is the opposite of a celebrity. A celebrity is famous for being well known. I prefer honor to fame; but I won't mind being famous for not being well known.

We would have more book readers and book buyers if the publishing and book-distributing people did a better job. At the same time they *would* do a better job if more people were interested in books. This reciprocal relationship between the providers of goods and their consumers does not prevail in the world of scholarship. There are more and more people attending schools at the same time when the standards of teaching have fallen. The deterioration of teaching in an age of democracy is, of course, especially deplorable; but this is a relatively new phenomenon, for the estimation of which we have, as yet, little historical perspective, since mass education is hardly more than a century old. The world of scholarship is a different matter. It is of less importance than people and, of course, many scholars believe. In the great ages of culture universities often did not count. Oxford and Cambridge mattered little during the Elizabethan Age; during the Golden Century of Spanish art and literature the universities of Spain were wretched, abysmal places; during the entire French Enlightenment the universities of France hardly figured at all. Of course there were many private scholars and artists and scientists in those times, a tradition that has now almost entirely disappeared. Now there is practically no scholarship left outside universities and research institutes. One hundred years ago in England scholars smiled at the idea that a historian ought to have a doctorate. We may yet see a world where every "serious" poet would be required to have a PhD. In the long run this would not matter much either. The life and the culture of peoples would go on, more or less independent of their universities. Certified academics would keep on writing for other academics. Consequently their knowledge of the world, and the value of their productions, would be limited. That, too, is nothing new. It is not the unworldliness but the petty worldliness of scholars that such different men as Juvenal and Abelard and Rabelais and Montaigne and Samuel Johnson and Randall Jarrell have described, in different ages, laughing about it rather than deploring it.

What is new is the contemporary inflation of scholarship. There are fewer publishing houses and fewer bookstores than fifty years ago. There are many more professors with the highest professional degrees. In the past scholars knew of each other, but this is no longer so. Four hundred and seventy years ago, at the beginning of the Modern Age, Erasmus's books were read eagerly by the kings of England and France, by the Pope and by many other people of various ranks, including a customs' collector on the Rhine at Basel who was delighted to meet that author. Unlike Erasmus, Giambattista Vico two centuries later was an unknown scholar, and not at all a peripatetic one; yet soon after his first book appeared he received long letters and comments from scholars in France and Germany. In our times many scholars flit around the world from conference to conference; they and their books cross the ocean in a few hours; yet professional scholars specializing in the same "field" are often ignorant of the existence of colleagues living but a few miles away. Fifteen years ago, introducing my bibliographical remarks in *The Last European War,* I wrote: "Five hundred years ago the Modern Age began with the sudden increase of all kinds of communications, including printing. This age is now ending with a breakdown of communications, because of their inflation. There are public idiots who proclaim this flood of communications as the 'knowledge explosion.'" I think I must clarify this statement further. What is still advancing is the technology—the mass and the speed—of communications. What we must understand is the difference between mechanical transmissions and authentic human communications; between the speed of communications and the slowness of the movement of ideas; between the availability of communications from a distance (i.e., *tele*communications) and the deteriorating receptivity of minds. The existence of this kind of ignorance is undeniable, though its sources are complex. They include the devolution of liberal democracies into bureaucracies. In a democracy more and more people speak. In a bureaucratic society fewer and fewer people listen. The result is the increasing institutionalization of ignorance, with fateful consequences well beyond the world of learning. As Christopher Dawson once wrote, "The more ignorant men are, the more inevitable their fate."

The insistence, within the academies, on publication, the syndrome of "publish or perish," hardly affects this condition. The reason for this is seldom acknowledged, though it is obvious. Scholars no longer read much, not even each other's books. They will read *some* books; more often, articles; even more often, reviews; and the latter only in certain publications. That reading reviews rather than reading books is an intellectual shortcut is obvious; also, so much is being printed in so many places that only a few assiduous readers can keep up with it. Yet the sources of this practice (or malpractice) are more complicated than that. We are in the presence of a situation that has had few precedents in the past, surely not in the history of the West. This is that not only have common people lost the time and the inclination for reading; so have many academics. That people who don't read don't write is natural. What is unnatural is that we have now entire slews of professional experts who read little while they write much, for the sake of firming up their professional status. In this respect, too, we may see the devolution of democracy into bureaucracy; or from a largely contractual to an increasingly status-dominated society. It is the affiliation, not the quality of the work, of an academic that matters. It is thus that the estimation of scholarship tends to degenerate into something like a cultural anthropology.

I cannot comprehend why successful, recognized, and celebrated writers have been downcast by a single example of adverse criticism. Harold Nicolson was deeply and lengthily depressed by Edmund Wilson's superficial criticism of his writings in the *New Yorker*. A poor review of one of their books would send such different authors as Virginia Woolf and Ernest Hemingway to their particular slough of despond, where they would wallow and thrash for some time. I cannot understand this. I admit that when, during an hour or so between my classes, I repair to the college library and look at some of the recent scholarly periodicals, I am sometimes overcome with furious rage when I see shoddy or dishonest stuff printed—and also, alas, when I find that my own work has been ignored by scholars who ought not have done that. I am compelled to admit such things in what is, after all, a kind of intellectual autobiography. Yet if my story is a story of failure, much of the reason for this has been myself. I chose my profession to be intellectual, which is not identical with the choice to be a professional intellectual. This was a mistake, because the world of professional intellectuals does not wish to know that. I am not slow-witted, but it took me perhaps thirty years to recognize—to recognize, and not merely to sense—that this distinction was fatal to the reputation of my works. The results have been obvious. I did not stoop. But I did not conquer. Many of my books remain and will remain unread by those to whom they have been directed: scholars and students and amateur readers of history. This includes academics who are supposed to be specialists in our "fields." Walter Rathenau was supposed to have said that there are no specialists, there are only vested interests.

I am compelled to illustrate this with what is perhaps the most abysmal experience in my scholarly life. *Historical Consciousness* is, I repeat, my most important work. During the thirteen years of its gestation and writing, interest in historical philosophy grew among American and English academics. One of the results of this was the publication of a new scholarly journal, with the somewhat ungainly title *History and Theory*, dedicated to the detailed discussion of philosophical problems of history. This journal failed to print a review of *Historical Consciousness.* I was not surprised by this, nor was I particularly distressed. But when, a few years after my book's publication, I was browsing in the college library and I ran across the latest issue of *History and Theory,* I was overwhelmed by a black cloud of rage. *History and Theory* had published an entire thick issue, a *Beibeft,* consisting of an extensive bibliography without equal. It listed *everything* that had been published in every retrievable language, relating to topics, themes, and problems of historical philosophy, during the four years 1965 to 1969, when my book, too, had been published. This list of more than one hundred pages included hundreds of works not only in English but, on occasion, in Bulgarian. Its entries listed not only books but articles; not only articles but also reviews; not only reviews but even reviews of reviews. It did not list the book *Historical Consciousness.* I sent a short angry letter to the editors, "to assure you," I wrote, "that by having tried to render my work into an Unbook you have not succeeded in making me an Unperson."

I am asking my readers to stop for a moment to consider what this means. For once, I believe, this has little to do with vanity. When a book is omitted from a bibliography, and from possibly the most complete bibliography of a limited subject, this means that future students of this subject will be, naturally and excusably, unaware of its very existence. Such practices exist in the Soviet Union, for political reasons. But this kind of thing happened, and is happening, in the United States. I have been thinking about this for some time. The omission from a bibliography, in that case, was not the result of malevolence or of conspiracy. I am not important enough for that. But my book (like some of my other ones) was probably uncategorizable. It did not fit. And thereby lies an ominous lesson for the future. My purpose in detailing this episode is not to draw attention to my misfortunes, which, like all human misfortunes, are at least partially the result of my own making. It is to draw attention to what can happen, indeed, of what is already happening, to books during The Knowledge Explosion. Let me insist that I am interested in the pursuit of truth, not in that of justice. And the instruments and the instrumentators of the pollution of untruths that lie like a cloud cover over our world, a mental pollution whereof the physical pollution of the world is but a consequence (as indeed those candy wrappers and beer cans lie on the roadside because some people had thrown them there), include, alas, many Experts with Degrees from Institutes and Ministries of Truth. They are processing words, answering machines, and computing very selective data. The year 1984 is now well behind us. Our world is not, as Orwell wrote it might have become, one of political totalitarianism. Nor is it reactionary (in *1984* Orwell wrote that science and technology would decay under totalitarianism: "science, in the old sense has almost ceased to exist.... [T]he fields are cultivated by horse-ploughs..."). Just the opposite: Newspeak and doublethink and untruth are "scientific" and "progressive." They are instruments of a new bureaucratic kind of tyranny that Tocqueville had envisaged though Orwell did not. Their main instrument is the computer, which is not a robot, since it is "programmed" by men. Whatever does not fit in it will remain unrecorded for posterity. It reduces life to a system. A system, by its very definition, is exclusionary. Whatever is not part of it must be discarded, forgotten, destroyed. It was not a historian but a computer scientist, J. Weizenbaum, who wrote (in *Computer Power and Human Reason,* 1976) that the computer "has begun to be an instrument for the destruction of history. For when society legitimates only those 'data' that are in one 'standard format' and that 'can easily be told to the machine,' then history, memory itself is annihilated. The *New York Times* has already begun to build a 'data bank' of current events... how long will it be before what counts as fact is determined by the system, before all knowledge, all memory, is simply declared illegitimate? Soon a supersystem will be built, based on the *New York Times*'s data bank (or one very like it), from which the 'historians' will make inferences about what 'really happened,' about who is connected to whom, and about the 'real' logic of events. There are many people who see nothing wrong in this."[12]

The measuring and ordering of time is a human invention. But, as St. Augustine said, it is impossible for us to imagine what happened before God created time. In any event, there is another time than clock time—which may be a consolation even for those who do not believe that there is another world than this. Thus every one of us—a father, a mother, a lover, a scholar, an artist, a writer—may take some comfort from hoping, and knowing, that his efforts might be recognized and perhaps even appreciated after he will be gone. This is a thin diet for the minds of most of us, and not much sustenance for our daily lives, but there it is. For a writer, an artist, a scholar it takes strength to find consolation in this kind of lonely and faraway prospect.[13] Because of what is happening in our world some of us may now be deprived of that, too. Yet this ultimate deprivation—ultimate, that is, for some people—does not overwhelm me. I think much about the future of those whom I love and whom I shall leave behind, and I am, perhaps deeply, concerned with the prospect of the human world: *avant moi le déluge?* I believe in the existence of another world than this. I believe in the immortality of the human soul. I am even inclined to believe in the immortality of human memory, in some form or another. Yet I am indifferent to the immortality of my writing. Perhaps I am not such a serious writer, after all.

63

What Is Happening to History?
(1977)

In 1979 millions of Americans will have spent twenty-three to twenty-six years (about one-third of their expectable lifespan) in schools without having had a single history course. During the late sixties the majority of colleges and universities abandoned all history requirements; in a minority of higher institutions the latter survive in drastically diluted or diminished forms. For every four or five undergraduates who chose a history major fifteen years ago there are now one or two. The decline in the number of graduate students in history has been even more precipitous. In the past fifteen years, among the more than two thousand colleges and universities in the United States—employing nearly half a million teachers—there have been but a few hundred new teaching jobs open to holders of advanced degrees in history, most of these appointments of temporary nature.

About twenty years ago books were appearing on the intellectual scene with titles like *Post-Historic Man*. A little later Marshall McLuhan came forward to propose his argument, with an unusually complex vocabulary, the essence of which was that pictures were replacing books, and that the epoch of the image was about to replace the epoch of the word. These developments seem to be but confirmations of these generalizations.

At the same time consider the following:

In 1979 there are in the United States more than three thousand historical societies, most of them in small towns, nearly twice as many as twenty-five years ago.

During the past twenty years, when the circulation of most periodicals declined, the only popular periodical that has earned its way without advertising has been *American Heritage* magazine.

From *University Bookman*, Spring, 51–58.

Since about 1945, in "hardback" commercial publishing, popular histories have regularly outsold popular fiction.

Historical bestsellers now exist on all kinds of levels. Many of them have sold in the millions. The trend may have begun with Toynbee's abridged *Study of History* in 1947, which tens of thousands bought but few read, through books such as Tuchman's *The Guns of August*, Lasch's *Eleanor and Franklin*, Bishop's *The Day Lincoln Was Shot*, Ryan's *The Longest Day*, etc., books which millions have bought *and* read.

Since about 1960, we have a new kind of best-selling phenomenon: varieties of books, the substance of which is some kind of reconstruction of a certain historical past. *Ragtime* and *Roots* come to mind, huge publishing successes during the last three years. Many things suggest that this new kind of hybrid historical genre is not only growing in popularity, but that it may eventually overwhelm the genre of the novel.[1]

Another example of this burgeoning of the historical genre is that of instant-replay histories, such as Theodore H. White's *The Making of the President*, a heavy quadrennial bestseller of a kind that occurred to no publisher and, presumably, to no author, fifty or a hundred years ago.

Television and the movies are conforming to the same popular tendency. Example: the increasing frequency of cinematic "documentaries," to the success of social-historical soap operas like *Upstairs, Downstairs*.

In 1976 a survey of the Harvard class of 1968 showed that more than 60 percent of them were engaged in restoring old houses.

Upon reading this survey I asked my students: How many would choose to live in an old house, how many in a new house, all other things (comforts, neighborhood, price, etc.) being equal? Without exception they chose old houses. I found this interesting, to say the least: when in 1955 students learned that my wife and I, newly married, were living in a restored old house, they thought that this was very eccentric.

I am a member, and former chairman, of the Planning Commission of Schuylkill Township, Chester County, Pennsylvania, where old houses were demolished for the sake of highways, office buildings, industrial plants, and suburban-type modern developments twenty years ago without any opposition from the people. During the past dozen years, the preservation of older houses has become a popular issue among my fellow citizens, no matter what their neighborhood or their social or economic status. (A minor but significant point: more people are interested in "conservation" and "restoration" than in "ecology," a word which, to them, has acquired a faddish and abstract-scientific touch.)

The word "modern" has hardly any appeal for the younger generation, who for many years now have been flaunting the outdated character of their clothes, gear, posters, and accumulated junk. One of the most derogatory words in their limited vocabulary is "plastic": a shiny and modern word in the 1920s, indeed, as late as 1945.

In 1933 George Orwell wrote in *A Clergyman's Daughter* about lower-class children in London: "History was the hardest thing to teach them.... A boy of the middle classes, no matter how poorly educated, has at least a mental picture of a Roman senator, of an Elizabethan Englishman, of a French courtier.... But for these children these words were incomprehensible, they could not imagine them at all." This condition no longer prevails (perhaps, in part, because of television).

The 1876 Philadelphia Centennial exhibition was dedicated to machinery, not to history. The buildings housed exhibits of industry and of manufacture. Americans took enormous pride in the mechanized achievements of their present; their interest in history was almost nonexistent, as shown by the nature of the exhibits, and by the character of the perorations. The Bicentennial, in 1976, was entirely consumed by history. (By history on all kinds of levels, to be sure, overwhelmed by tasteless junk and souvenirs, but by history nonetheless; and there are reasons to believe that it was precisely the commercialization and the tawdry publicization of the Bicentennial that left large numbers of people dissatisfied with it.) What pleased and excited the imagination of Americans in the Bicentennial year was a parade of old-fashioned sailing ships.

"It is the nature and the duty of an American to rise above the station of his parents in the society," wrote an ornament of the New York Bar in 1868. As late as thirty years ago many Americans, especially the children of first-generation immigrants, were ashamed of their parents; they sought, therefore, refuge in the ephemeral and standardized conformities of American life. Most Americans knew nothing about their great-grandparents; as late as twenty-five years ago more than half of them could not name all four of their grandparents. This is no longer so. What is more important, most Americans are no longer ashamed of their ancestry; the opposite is true.

On an autumn Sunday evening in 1977, I am in the house of friends in a Philadelphia suburb, for a buffet supper. The house was built around the turn of the century. My friends have a penchant for Victorian furniture—not altogether my taste, but this is not what matters: what matters is what springs to my mind as I stand in a corner and contemplate this evening scene.

I see high ceilings, large mahogany pieces of furniture, massive sideboards, a piano, a harvest bouquet for a centerpiece, ironstone plates, large-size cutlery, thick curtains with large folds suggesting a certain kind of femininity, and carpets darkly florid; the electric light from the unwieldy chandelier shines like old light; it is all, comfortable, slightly stiff, heavy with cushioning, pale, brown, and warm.

What occurs to me is this: If my great-grandfather would reappear here, in 1977, coming from 1877, much of this scene would be easily comprehensible to him: he would find a few things to be strange and curious but he would find much of it essentially familiar.

And if *his* great-grandfather had appeared in 1877, after a century of absence? Nothing of the kind. There were very few people, certainly not in the United States, who lived in a 1777 house in 1877. How many rooms, in Europe or in America, were filled in 1877 with the furniture of 1777? Not one in fifty thousand, I think.

There are many rooms and many houses like this one now. But there is more to this. It is not a matter of things alone. I look at the people. Many of the women wear long skirts and long-sleeved blouses; the drapery conforms to them. Many of them wear their hair long; many of the men wear beards. They are lawyers, teachers, architects, representatives of a professional class. They stand in clusters, they talk in moderate tones. Some of them are talking about old things, from the history of this city a century ago, about odd details of which many of them—and they are not professional historians—are quite knowledgeable and aware. In sum, they are—physically and mentally—much closer to the world of 1877 than their ancestors in 1877 were to the world that was then one hundred years ago.

And this is something new.

The Acceleration of History? Henry and Brooks Adams were quite wrong about this. The Virgin and the Dynamo? These people have no interest in the Virgin; but, then, they have no interest in the dynamo, either. They are attracted by the reality of the past. The great Dutch historian Huizinga knew, better than Adams, what was going on in the twentieth century. Few people were as aware as was Huizinga of the corrupt superficialities of this century. Yet he wrote in 1934: "Historical thinking has entered our very blood."

There exists now in the United States a widespread, and deep-seated, appetite for history—more exactly, for physical and mental reminders of the past—which, in the entire history of this country, has had no precedent.

This appetite developed at the very time when much of the teaching of history was thoughtlessly and shamefully abandoned by those responsible for it.

The reasons for this massive thoughtlessness may be summed up as follows:

In the first place—in order, and perhaps also of importance—the vast majority of professional historians have not the slightest interest in what happens to teaching in the secondary schools. I know of no country where the worlds of the college professor and that of the high school teacher are as separate as they are in the United States; they have less in common than the nineteenth-century worlds of the bourgeois and of the beggar.

At the same time when the college and university professorate were riding high in power and prestige (circa 1960–65), the enormous educational bureaucracy ruling American high schools eliminated the traditional European and American history courses, with the admitted purpose of making high schools more relevant to the modern world (of the realities of which this bureaucracy remained of course entirely ignorant). All of this happened in the name of stagnant and wholly outdated social scientism which swallowed up courses of history like a marsh that swallows up the courses of creeks.

The professorate, blissfully preoccupied with the delightful intrigues consequent to its bureaucratization, paid not the least attention to such mundane matters. Indeed, in accord with its own simian inclinations for demonstrating the capacity of its members to sit on boughs and saw them off simultaneously, it contributed to the abandonment of traditional history teaching within its own institutions. It put up but a weak and disorganized and unconvincing opposition to the elimination of history requirements within its own colleges. It went along with the confection of all kinds of nonhistory history courses, with fashionable subjects such as Feminism, Africanism, Sexuality (courses enthusiastically proposed by younger department members, accompanied by the occasional clucking of their older colleagues whose smiles shone with all of the gleam of a silver plate on a coffin). It took a certain pleasure in talking up the two novel fads of Psychohistory and Quantification, the recondite characteristics of which would further contribute to the image of the Historian as a Social Scientist of a premier kind, a practitioner of skills and a possessor of arcane knowledge to which the artless and uninstructed public could not hope to aspire.

Projecting the continuation of whatever seems to be going on (the occupational disease of most intellectuals and bureaucrats), the professorate, during the corrupt and inflated 1960s, kept on turning out more and more graduate students *ad maiorem professori pecuniam*, until it suddenly came face to face with the condition that teaching jobs for history graduates in the United States had become as rare as berries for birds in the winter.

It is both symptomatic and telling of the mental state of professional historians that during their belated self-searching and occupational analysis, among all of the above reasons they have been concentrating exclusively on this last one—in itself an effect as much as a cause. The greater issue—the increasing divergence in interest for academic and popular history—occurred, or occurs, to the majority of professional historians not at all.

What we should recognize, therefore, is not the ebb and flow of academic and intellectual fads, but the bureaucratization of American life. What this means is that professional historians will have less and less to do with the living history of the American people.

To give but one example, relating directly to the subject of this article: the unprecedented appetite for history which has developed among the American people in recent decades not only had no consequences in their schools, but the public recognition of this very fact—and it is a fact—has been entirely nonexistent.

This is one of the tragic ironies of history in our otherwise "open" and vastly documented democratic age: what happens on the surface often has no connection with the real currents of thoughts and inclinations among large numbers of people, with the deeper and more enduring currents of events.

It is true that, at the time of this writing, certain universities and colleges have been restoring history requirements, here and there: but this reversal has been too modest and, as yet, too short-lived to constitute a general trend.

And, since history—surely in the short run, and sometimes even in the long run—consists not so much in what happens but in what people think happens, when people are told that they live in a post-historic age, they may think and act and choose accordingly.[2] We have to face the possibility: when publishers and television producers convince themselves (in no matter how ephemeral a fashion) that history does not "pay," many of the earlier listed evidences of a public appetite for history might disappear, at least for a long time.

The silly term "self-fulfilling prophecy" does not explain this phenomenon, which is, rather, the result of that stagnation in the movement of ideas about which Tocqueville wrote in *Democracy in America*.

And, just as the massive bureaucratization of life has come out of democratization, the near-abolition of history (and also of other kinds of learning) from our schools may have been the end-result of universal education. Few people realize that universal education and the teaching of history in schools developed at the same time, less than one hundred and fifty years ago; that history was not taught anywhere during the "historic centuries," just as during the great centuries of Western art no one knew anything about aesthetics.

In sum, popular interest in history preceded the teaching of history in schools; and there are many reasons to believe that it will survive it too.

❋ ❋ ❋

IN the small college where I have been teaching for more than thirty years we are making a modest attempt toward some kind of a restoration of learning. We are now offering a so-called "History School" program (the designation may be somewhat grandiloquent, but, having racked my brains, I could not find a more appropriate term for it). It simply means an option for certain students during their undergraduate studies. Its purpose is to broaden as well as to deepen the background of certain majors. The student who chooses the "History School" option within a major will, upon completion of four years, have an understanding of the major subject through a more-or-less thorough acquaintance with the historical development of it.

It is not a "minor" in history. Students electing the "History School" option will have to take a minimum of six historically grounded courses among the offerings in their majors. Historically grounded courses in English, for example, include courses such as "Shakespeare" or "Poetry of the English Renaissance"; in political science, they include courses such as "Ancient and Medieval Political Theories" or "Socialism and the New Left." Conversely, they do not include courses such as "Journalism" or "The Short Story in English"; or "Methods of Political Analysis in Political Science," for example.

The historically grounded courses are marked by an asterisk in the college catalogue. At this time this option is available for majors in five fields; we hope to be able to extend this option to at least six more departments thereafter.

Because of present conditions, whereby most students arrive in colleges knowing hardly anything about the historical substance—I write "substance," not merely "background"—of their projected fields of study, such an option may be eminently desirable. Yet the foundations to which I have written have shown no interest in this program. We have now started it with the aid of a modest, so-called "pilot," grant from the National Endowment for the Humanities.

Were it not for the fortunate condition that the bureaucratic practices of academic life are limited in a small Catholic college such as Chestnut Hill, my original proposal for such a program would not have had a ghost of a chance. Even here we have certain problems with incomprehension among some of the faculty members who received their professional training in the sixties. But when I read of the public soul-searching going on in our most powerful and rich and prestigious institutions of higher learning, I often feel that I must thank God for having placed me thirty years ago where I am; when I look at the "new" curriculum offered by Harvard I see but another litter of academic mice scurrying forth from the tremulous caves of what passes for a mountain; and I am saddened, to the point of despair, as I contemplate yet another example of the overwhelming failure of life in America, which is that of waste—the endless waste not so much of the environmental but of the *human* resources of the country.

I do not for a moment claim that this is a daring or revolutionary or even important program, though I do wish to attract some attention to it. It is a unique program in the United States at this time: but there is no reason for taking pride in this uniqueness. It does not even deserve the usual encomium attributed to the one-eyed monarch in the country of the blind. It is, at best, an example of what the profound French writer Jean Dutourd recently remarked: when a massive imbecility reigns, it is the easiest thing to appear wise: a minimum of common sense will do.

64

Selections from *A Thread of Years*: 1901, 1945, 1968

(1998)

A *Thread of Years* does not have a story. But it has a theme. That theme is the decline of a particular civilization, and the decline of the ideal of the gentleman; two inseparable matters. In 1901 the British and the American empires were the greatest powers in the world. On the map of the globe the British empire was greatest; but the center of gravity had already shifted across the Atlantic, and was moving westward. The threat to the Atlantic predominance was represented by Germany, with the result of two world wars. All of this is well known. Less well known are the inevitable, and often intangible, relations of power and prestige. The power of the Anglo-American world in 1901 was inseparable from the worldwide prestige of the originally English ideal of the gentleman. That ideal, transformed and qualified by specifically American conditions and ideas, existed in the United States, too, incarnated and represented by a minority of people whose influence still exceeded their numbers. For many reasons: because of some of the inadequacies latent within the ideal itself; because of the shortcomings of many of those who thought, or pretended, to represent it; and finally because of their waning self-confidence—the ideal faded. That this belongs within the history of this century may be the theme of this book.

History has now entered the democratic age, which simply means (the meaning is simple, but its reconstruction is complicated) that the historian must deal with all kinds of people, and with all kinds of events. Every event is a historical event; every source is a historical source; every person is a

From *A Thread of Years* (New Haven, CT: Yale University Press), 1–9, 13–22.

historical person. This book does not deal with the Roosevelts, Churchill, Stalin, and so on. They do not figure in it—when they are mentioned at all, it is only in passing, here or there. Its "1917" does not deal with the American declaration of war on Germany—at least not directly. None of its scenes has drumfire in it. They do not consist of great dramatic events. They are period pictures: vignettes. But the underlying theme exists, alluded to here and there: the *petite musique of grande histoire*, the decline of a civilization (civilization, not culture).

In this book I am writing about everyday people whose plausibility exists only because of the historical reality of their places and times. This book may be an attempt at a new genre. Do not take this too seriously. My attempt is imperfect, and I have no interest in inventing new and startling forms. At the end of this century (and indeed of the so-called Modern Age) I am dubious about anything and about anyone who claims to be avant-garde; and as for an Idea Whose Time Has Come (Victor Hugo's hoary nineteenth-century phrase), well, it is almost certain not to be any good. Meanwhile, historical writing still has a long way to go. Max Beerbohm said about the 1880s, "to give an accurate and exhaustive account of that period would need a far less brilliant pen than mine." That was funny and even telling, but in the long run Beerbohm was wrong. History has not yet had its Dante or its Shakespeare. That will come one day, and this book is not that. For, if it is not a novel, it is not history either. In this book I invent people (though not places and times)—yes, I hope plausible and telling types, but who did not actually exist. That is not history. But my purpose is not literary and not political; it is historical. The pictures, the vignettes, of this book are meant to attract the reader's interest to certain people in certain places and in certain times: *couleurs locales* that ought to be good enough to linger in the mind.

If there is beauty in some of these scenes, it is meant to evoke an iridescent mix of sadness and pleasantness in the minds of readers. Yes, *A Thread of Years* is about the sad decline of a civilization, but the colors are not heavy bitumen colors, and the music is not Mahler, while there are a few remnant memories of beautiful things and of decency and goodness. (My original title for this book was *Remnants.*) But the purpose of each vignette is also sentimental (and historical) education, because inherent in each of these vignettes, *petites histoires*, are reflections of the larger tides of history. And this connection, or meaning, is *debatable*, in the literal sense of that word—hence the ensuing dialogue, a conversation and sometimes a debate with my alter ego, which is meant to explain or, more precisely, justify the vignette.

The question thus arises (as one of my potential publishers posed it):

why not restrict this book to the vignettes? My answer is, again, simple: I am a historian, not a novelist. I am more interested in the historicity than in a literary portraiture of a place or of a person, even of my pseudoprotagonist. And it is the suggestion of that historicity that is a subject of debate and that I wish to point out further, together with other related matters, sometimes light, sometimes more profound, through a breezy conversation with myself. For in these discussions, in the second part of each annualized chapterette, I challenge myself. *Myself*: because my interlocutor is my alter ego. He is not an imaginary person; he is not a composite or a confection of someone else. He is more commonsensical, more pragmatic, more direct, more down-to-earth than is the narrator of the vignette, and we argue, add, subtract, agree, disagree.

When the idea (or, rather, the plan) of such a construction first occurred to me I cannot tell. It may be that while the author of my vignettes and their occasional defendant is my European self, my challenger and debater is my American one. "It may be"; perhaps not. But it is no use to discuss this further. This book is not about me, and I am not writing about myself.

Allow me to end by expressing what is obvious: that everything that is human is history, including history and, in this case, including this book. Its original title was *Remnants*, not *A Thread of Years*; instead of going from 1901 to 1991, I chose to end it with 1969; and I changed its original introduction also. That, too, I wrote in the form of a dialogue. I discarded that version, for more than one practical reason; but I am keeping its end, which read as follows:

"Good luck. Are you on to something that seems to have intrigued you through most of your life? An attempt at a new genre. That's not easy. God only knows why you're doing it. There are so many other books that you can, or ought to do. Well, I guess that whatever I say, you will do it—because, as Bernanos once said, 'le bonheur, c'est un risque.'"

Yes, happiness is a risk (and happiness is a task).

"Well, if you succeed, you will have *done* it."

And if I don't succeed, it will be just another of my books.

"Now you sound like your old friend Owen Barfield, who wrote about one of his friends that he writes, not for a living, not for reputation, but because he can't help it."

Not quite—but I can't help writing *this*.

1901

TWO men sit at the large windows of the Philadelphia Club on a Friday evening. The windows are open, it is early September, warm enough for that. The noise of Walnut Street has died down, because Philadelphia is not a crowded city with iron clangor. The men are second cousins, around forty, resembling each other not very much, one taller and leaner, less rubicund than the other, who has just returned from California. The latter has made an important decision. He will move to Pasadena. He is explaining his reasons. They include more than the legendary California weather. He and his wife—as much as himself, he insists, if not more—have sized up the civilities and people in Pasadena: urbane people, most of them Easterners, many of them Bostonians. (That is always a recommendation among proper Philadelphians, who have a sense of respect, because of a sense of intellectual inferiority, for the proper people of Boston.) He talks about some of those men and women, including a few recognizable family names; he speaks of the schools, the club, the theater, and the house they are about to have built, the gardening, the California flowers, the salubrious omnipresence of outdoor life year-round. Of course Pasadena is not Philadelphia, but that "not" carries at least a prospect of "not yet." Already civilization is developing there that will encompass and typify what is best in America. It amounts to more than a floriferous setting and a healthy climate; it is also a good place for the children to grow up, who will of course go on to their boarding schools and then colleges back in the East, no more than five days away from their parents by train. Yes, California is the West, with all of its pluses and with fewer and fewer of its minuses: civilization there is overcoming the pioneer roughness every day, sometimes incredibly fast, and the evidences of that evolution are all around.

It is a big move for a Philadelphian to leave and go to live in California, from a place where people move less than in any comparable city in the United States, where the web of family connections is as comforting as it is constricting, where respectability is the primary ideal, and not only in public. Queen Victoria has died in January 1901, but Philadelphia is sill quite Victorian (all right: Victorian-American). It is not fin de siècle, not belle époque, and will not ever be Edwardian—because in Philadelphia the cult of respectability is inseparable from the cult of safety. That is, at least in part, the Quaker inheritance: the desire for safety, sometimes so rigid as to be uncomfortable. It is thus that his cousin and friend is not going to try to dissuade him, or even to ask more questions than are needed to stitch their conversation along. One of the reasons for this is the Philadelphian custom of refraining from discussing (and, more than often, from thinking about) unpleasant things. That is a habit that sometimes leads to regrettable consequences, when the excessive wish to keep safe is oddly, or perhaps not so oddly, allied to the reluctance to exercise more than customary foresight. But within this habit there resides, too, a modicum of the ingrained respect for privacy; and one of the reasons for his reticence comes from that. He is aware of a certain restiveness in his cousin's temperament, evident in his cousin's few known escapades, usually short-lived to the extent of harmlessness. He, unlike his cousin, is hardly given to enthusiasms—partly out of character, partly out of temperament. His cousin is a Progressive, of sorts; he is not. He has just returned from his summer place in Maine, from Northeast Harbor (Philadelphia on the Rocks, in the epithet to come in the late twenties), that Philadelphian appendage in the cool, rockbound, pale-blue-eyed North (call it Down East, if you wish), with its large and often ungainly gray cedar-shingled houses, where the sharp tinge of the outdoors is complemented by the knowledge of comfort indoors, large brick fireplaces puffing woodsmoke through big chimneys in midsummer, reminiscent of the smell wafting above the gardens of Philadelphia suburbs in the autumn: a comforting sense, as is the knowledge that Philadelphia is but one night away on the Bar Harbor Special of the Pennsylvania Railroad. Yes, for him there is something neither quite safe nor respectable about living in California; and his cousin's phrases about the blossoming of civilization in Pasadena do not greatly impress him. He is American enough to believe not only that change must be tempered by continuity but that change is a kind of continuity in itself—which is why both of them are unable to question the theory of Evolution that they somehow equate with Progress.

There is, however, a difference in their beliefs. One of them is inclined to think (an inclination to think may not be tantamount to a belief, even though it is sometimes more important than a belief) that America is growing ever more able to represent what is best of the civilization of the white race, of England, and of much of Western Europe—and that thus Philadelphia is somewhere in the middle between England and California, and that is how it has been, is, and should be. His cousin believes that the course not only of empire but of all civilization is inevitably westward and without cease; that what is still good in the American East is spreading to the West; and that because of the richness of this country he can partake in that movement with no loss, indeed, with physical and mental profit to himself and to his family. He believes that the future of America may be California, and sooner rather than later. His cousin believes that as America goes so will the world, even though that may not yet be around the corner.

What they talk about are doctors, lawyers, banks, insurance, schools, relatives, railroads, in the Philadelphian manner, restricting the scope of their conversation to what is practical since, again in the Philadelphian manner, what is practical is not only real but safe. They do not know that they are talking about more than that. About the future of America. Of the century. Of the world.

The twentieth century has begun. They espy no trouble in that. Both of them see a world in which the most important portion is being governed by the Anglo-Saxon, the seafaring, the Teutonic, the industrial and industrious races. That seems certain. Like Progress.

I'd like to imagine that their conversation occurs on Friday, September 6, 1901, on the afternoon of the day when President McKinley was shot in Buffalo. The news has not reached the Philadelphia Club. They do not know it yet. Nor do they know that a week later (on Friday the thirteenth) McKinley will be dead, and Theodore Roosevelt will be the president of the United States.

❊ ❊ ❊

NOW you must know I will return to one of these people—to the California-bound one, in, say, 1912 or 1913.

"When you will, I presume, describe what is happening to his Arcadian illusions out there."

Not Arcadian but Progressive; and ideas even more than illusions.

"All right, except that the idealization of the American West was both Arcadian and Progressive."

And few people, if any, saw the inherent contradiction between these two things. This includes Teddy Roosevelt, who once said to Charles Fletcher Lummis: "I owe everything to the West! It made me! I found it there!" And in 1911 or 1912 he spoke to Lummis again: "California has come mighty close to my governmental ideals." This Lummis, who had been at Harvard at the time of Roosevelt, was a big promoter of Pasadena, a big booster of California, a patron of the arts and crafts, a Health and Culture enthusiast, an interminable spokesman for Arcadian Progressivism. He also said that "the ignorant, hopelessly un-American type of foreigner which infests and largely controls Eastern cities is almost unknown here." "Here" was Los Angeles. He was a pompous, insufferable fool, which Roosevelt was not, but both of them were wrong about what would become of California.

"You're telegraphing your punch. What will become of California, what will become of Philadelphia, what will become of America, what will become of civilization. Your Big Questions. But I don't know whether it is sufficiently telling to hang the *Auftakt* of this theme on these two buttoned-up Philadelphia gents, even though they are your friend's relatives, and even though one of them seems to be ready, if not altogether itching, to loosen his high collar. Besides, you have done a little cheating here, using the device of this conversation between two men in the Philadelphia Club. There *was* such a conversation, right there, a small turning point in the history of American literature, and I think you know what I mean."

You mean Owen Wister talking to Walter Furness in September or October 1891 at the Philadelphia Club. The record is there, in Wister's own words. He had just returned from the West. Let me find it. Here it is. Wister: "Why wasn't some Kipling saving the sage-brush for American literature, before the sage-brush and all that it signified went the way of the California forty-niner, went the way of the Mississippi steam-boat, went the way of everything? Roosevelt had seen the sage-brush true, had felt its poetry; and also Remington, who illustrated his articles so well. But what was fiction doing, the only thing that has always outlived the fact? Must it be perpetual tea-cups? The claret had been excellent. 'Walter, I'm going to try it myself! I'm going to start this minute.'" He stood up, bid good night to Furness, and wrote his first Western story, "Hank's Woman" in the library of the Philadelphia Club that night. Then out of "Hank's Woman" came *The Virginian*, the legend of the West for a century to come.

"Which is just about unreadable now."

Which is why it was a milestone less in the history of American literature than in the history of American popular imagination. In any event, Wister was a most peculiar person. His illusions turned into the blackest kind of despair. A few years later Wister wrote a better book than *The Virginian*, a novel about Charleston and the South, *Lady Baltimore*; in 1912 he began a book about Philadelphia, *Monopolis*, which he abandoned; in 1934 he wrote the centennial history of the Philadelphia Club, after insisting that the book written by another member (already printed) be withdrawn and destroyed; and the last thing he was writing before he died in 1938 was to be a book on French wines.

"So he began his writing inspired by the club claret, and his last inspiration returned to the claret."

Spare me these paradoxes, though there is something to them. A true and startling biography of Wister is yet to be written, since the revolution of his ideas is more interesting than the man himself. There is an American tragedy of that mind, the tragedy of the insubstantial virility of his American illusions. It is not like Dreiser or even Fitzgerald, since the American tragedy is not about people who want to rise, rather impatiently, in American society. The history of those who attempted to write about the tragedy of American patricians is yet to be done, starting with Fenimore Cooper and perhaps ending with John O'Hara, *alas*.

"Stop right there. You're going on too long."

I know I am, and besides, my California-bound Philadelphian is not at all a Wisterian or Rooseveltian believer in muscular Christianity. He is something of an American hedonist. Like many people, including the former Bostonians who are moving to Pasadena, he and those westering Americans are not moved by a bravado nurtured by Kipling or the Bible.

"I presume that our man's wife is charmed by the tinkling of teacups among the ladies formerly of Boston, sitting in the gardens of Pasadena. But, good God, what are they and their husbands talking about, except congratulating themselves frequently for how smart they have been in moving there?"

Well, you may be right about the scope of their conversations and even about their tone. But let's not be too tough on those men and women in Pasadena in 1901. They are still full of an American vitality, and they are not so much hedonists as idealists, which makes almost all their illusions not only understandable but defensible. Let's be honest: it could have been quite pleasant to live in Pasadena in 1901. But there was one thing that few people have noticed, including historians. This is that while California was ahead of Eastern America, and while of course the United States was ahead of Europe, ahead in many things and practices, and I mean not only machines or industry but popular democracy, public education, the secret ballot—at the same time, and in a very important way, America was *behind* Europe, because most of the prevalent American ideas, especially those of the Progressives, were already antiquated and unreal.

"You mean the sempiternal American addiction to Progressive Evolution, including the belief that, through science and education and political and social reform, society and mankind can be made perfect, or at least near perfect. But not far beneath this progressive optimism about the improvability of society lay a deep and hidden but at times sorrily apparent distrust about the improvability of human beings."

That is not my argument here. It is that the moving vision within all those illusions, all that movement toward the West, the advance toward a healthier, open life untrammeled by brittle conventions and by hypocrisy— a vision eagerly taken up by Englishmen and many continental Europeans, too—was the vision of the American West as a *return* to a simpler ideal of manhood, a rebirth of a once lost and legendary but now actually achievable way of life, against the ever paler ideas of the Age of Reason ("the stinking brain" was one of Wister's uglier phrases), which the ever smokier clouds over the cities and the factories of the Old World (and of the American East) had stifled and obscured. Evolution, indeed; but together with Return. In 1895 Wister wrote an article for *Harper's*, "The Evolution of the Cow-Puncher." The West, he wrote, gave the Anglo-Saxon race another chance. "The race was once again subjected to battles and darkness, rain and shine, to the fierceness and the generosity of the desert. Destiny tried her last experiment upon the Saxon, and pluck[ed] him from the library, the haystack and the gutter, . . . [whereupon] his modern guise fell away and showed again the medieval man." This hankering after the Middle Ages was one example of something that not many people recognize: the medieval facet of the American heart. Wister was thinking and writing this around the time when Henry Adams was turning toward Mont-Saint-Michel and Chartres.

"But he wrote this stuff sitting in the Philadelphia Club—after having asserted several times that he did not like to live in Philadelphia, but then he could not shake the Philadelphia dust from his feet, he was to return to it, wearily, and earlier than he had imagined."

Yes, and good-bye to Owen Wister. I repeat: our California-bound Philadelphian is not at all like Wister. What he envisages are pleasantries in the life of an American capitalist in California. Wister would have scorned him. Our man is no amateur cowboy, not at all. Not for a moment does he see himself as the Last Cavalier, except perhaps at some New Year's Eve costume party in Pasadena. For Wister the Last Cavalier was the Anglo-Saxon cowboy that was the drawing with which Frederic Remington illustrated "The Evolution of the Cow-Puncher" for *Harper's*, showing a cowboy, tall and lanky, with a bronzed Anglo-Saxon face, including a drooping mustache, in front of a misty tableau of assembled ancient halberdiers, Templars, Crusaders, Knights of the Roses, and a seventeenth-century cavalier looking wistfully at this American horseman. "There ought to be music for the Last Cavalier," Wister wrote Remington. "The Last Cavalier will haunt me forever. He inhabits a Past into which I withdraw and mourn." But our Pasadena Philadelphian sees nothing of the Past in the West. His vision (if that is what it is) is a blossoming, garlanded near future, here and there braced with a necessary scaffolding of stainless steel, and warmed everywhere by perennial sunshine. He is probably less split-minded than was Wister, who mourned for the past and cheered on the spirit of the future at the same time, to be incarnated by the new American, the Western man. "It won't be a century before the West is simply the true America, with thought, type and life of its own kind" he also wrote. He believed that, too—at least for a while.

"That may be very interesting, but you're not writing a historical thesis.

One of the things I miss: you must clarify that scene of those two men sitting at the windows of the Philadelphia Club. Your readers may think that they are those large windows on the ground floor of a majestic club, with Morganatic bankers puffing at their cigars, as drawn by numberless cartoonists of the old *New Yorker*. The dining room and those windows of the Philadelphia Club were, and are, on the second floor, well above the street. More description, please."

All right. The Philadelphia Club is a red brick building, with marble steps and white window ledges and frames. It is handsome rather than elegant, not at all majestic but solid, and noticeable only to those who know what it houses, that is, the most selective of the clubs of that city, its membership made up mostly, though not entirely, of men of the older Philadelphia families. In 1901 it was more exclusive than the Rittenhouse Club with its Beaux Arts building and of course much more exclusive than the Union League (a monumental brown-front). That had been erected during the Civil War by Republican nouveaux riches. Well, now, on this Friday evening in September 1901 the rooms of the Philadelphia Club are rather empty, with few diners at the long table, since many of the members live in the leafy suburbs, and the weekending habit is already widespread, even though nearly all of them keep small townhouses for the winter. Agnes Repplier's later acid apothegm ("Suburbanites are traitors to the city") apply to many of them, too. On other Friday nights there are many more diners, with their wives; but in early September the theater season has not yet begun, and in 1901 the Philadelphia Orchestra does not exist. (Philadelphia is habitually about thirty years behind New York: the Philadelphia Orchestra and the art museum came about thirty, even forty, years after the Metropolitan Museum of Art, the Metropolitan Opera, Carnegie Hall, and the New York Philharmonic.) I will now add that before their serious talk the two cousins had an excellent and typical dinner at the club: turtle soup or terrapin, or oysters perhaps (September being an *R* month), veal-and-kidney pie, et cetera—no, no Madeiras, though the family bins of the Philadelphia Club still had plenty of those. After that the two men translated themselves to the windows. Some of the parquet flooring and the fine wainscoting were still washed in the evening light, while the gas lamps on Walnut Street below them were being lit.

1945

IN 1945 the wind carries centuries in its mane.

In April 1945 the European war—the last European world war—is near its end. On Saturday the twenty-first, American troops are deep in the middle of Germany. Now they are entering the city of Leipzig. There are small clouds of smoke and the crump and the rattle and the sizzle of battle, but unlike in Berlin to the north, here it is intermittent and not constant, with long minutes of an unearthly quiet. The April weather is unseasonably cold, but the sky is bright and the linden trees in the streets have begun to green and bud and the telephone still functions and so does most of the electricity.

At eleven in the morning Herr A., the city treasurer (*Schatzmeister*), lifts the receiver on his desk. He listens to the dial tone buzzing for a long moment. Then he puts it down. He sits straight in his office chair. Then he puts two pills in his mouth, bites down on one of them, and in less than a minute he is dead.

It is a clean and orderly desk. Perhaps the leather-bordered pad on the top will be slightly stained by the dead *Schatzmeister*'s saliva, but it is still a clean desk, not cleared for a last stand but typical of this city treasurer, unencumbered except for the telephone, an inkstand, a small reading lamp, that large pad with its green blotting paper, and three or four thick reference volumes standing stiff at its far left end: an orderly desktop of an orderly man, this large bald German. This is how the American army photographers will find him, three hours later. They will be startled. It is a frozen scene, a still life of death, because across from that desk, a few feet away, two women, his wife and his daughter, are dead, too. Their skirts are properly pulled down, their eyes closed (did their husband and father close them?), their faces not distorted, though the daughter has slid halfway down from the sofa to the floor.

The treasurer was a party member, but he does not have the small round enamel party badge in the buttonhole of his stiff dark suit now. He is no last-ditch Nazi but a German civil servant who drew the consequences. His world, his German world, had collapsed. Beyond that he would not think or wish to live. He took his family with him. Had his wife and daughter ever talked to him, did they question his resolution? I doubt it. What was going on in their inner selves he of course did not know, and neither do I. I am inclined to think that *I* wish I knew, but he did not.

That Saturday afternoon, on April 21, 1945, in a hospital in Los Angeles, B., a German émigré musician, kills himself. He is a sick man with a cancerous bladder. His illness is not yet terminal; his pain grows and fades, it is endurable, perhaps particularly this afternoon. But he hopes for nothing, and he is in the depths of despair. He has no appetite for life left—or, rather, that is what he thinks, and for him thinking amounts to knowledge. He does not understand that some feelings are best ignored, which is what courage amounts to. But then courage also amounts to the numbing of fear, and his last act of courage is to reach for the strychnine pills. They are in one of the recesses of his wallet in the drawer of the night table. He swallows them, and in a few minutes he suffers a horrible death.

Now please consider that what I want to write about is not death but despair. What I am interested in are not motives but purposes. All modern psychology and even the present-day use of the language confuse the meanings of motives and purposes, more than often illegitimately so. But there is a profound difference between mechanical and human causality. Life amounts to the wish for more life, and when that wish flickers out and dies, we die. Every human action or thought is more than a reaction, because we are not merely pushed by the past but pulled by the future, by our own vision of the future. And when that wish for the future—any future—is extinct ... Pirandello had a nice phrase: The dead are "les retraités de la mémoire." They have retired from memory, they are the pensioners of memory. True, but not true enough. Yes, everything—every human thought—depends on memory. But what made A. and B. kill themselves on a cruel April day? Was it some unbearable memory? No, not in their cases. It was their despair of the future, of their future.

There were many Germans who chose suicide at the end of the Third Reich. (This in itself was a significant phenomenon: few Communists chose to kill themselves when their rule collapsed.) It is at least interesting that many of these suicides were not committed Nazis, most of whom were or had become cynics and survivors with a sense of cruel humor. (I find it difficult to imagine a resolution to suicide coexisting with any spark of humor.) Our city treasurer was a humorless German—unfortunately not untypical of his generation. His very countenance reflected that: a big bald head and thick neck, small eyes, small nose, the thinnest of lips, a rigid mask that moved up into the officious rigidity of his eyes when looking at papers, people, the world. He was a nationalist, a Lutheran, a veteran of the First World War, *Deutschnational* in the twenties, and not a National Socialist but a believer in duty and in German greatness; in 1933 came Hitler, who was not entirely his favorite, but what a national leader Hitler turned out to be, and what a Reich he built and achieved! So he joined the party, at least partly because of conviction and not merely because of opportunism; his position in the city government was secure. And he followed all the orders and the regulations with utmost strictness. He was responsible, per-haps a bit old-fashioned; as the local Nazi *Gauleiter* remarked about him, "verantwortlich durch und durch." This was the fatal tragedy of Germany, then: the unquestioning and unquestionable obedience of such people as this superbureaucrat to the state, to the *Vaterland*—and now, as Hitler pro-nounced, to the *Volk*. And now the end of the Reich was at his doorstep.

He should have at least considered that the Americans were coming, not the Russians. He didn't: they were enemies of the Reich. He should have considered that his party membership did not condemn him to be executed: yes, at worst imprisoned for a while, but weren't there untold millions of party members in Germany? No: he could not imagine any life, and least of all a respectable life, in a city and a Reich occupied by the enemies of Germany. He could not, because he did not want to. The future for him and for his wife and for his daughter was not merely bleak: it did not exist. When he first spoke of the suicide plan to his family, he repeated a famous German saw: "Better an end with horror than horror without end." That sounds good, but it is very German. It seems to make sense, but really it doesn't.

There were not many Americans—certainly no refugees among them—who chose to kill themselves around the time of V-E Day. B., this refugee from Europe, did. Yes, he was ill with cancer. Yes, for him too, "better an end with horror" and so on. He thought that he had nothing to look for-ward to but pain, shame, and loneliness. He was fifty years old. His man-hood was gone. If he was to live, the doctors said, there were chances but not the best ones, and he would have to live with a colostomy bag attached to him, day and night. He had no family here, and his last woman had left him. But above and beneath all this there coursed an intellectual feeling now hardened into a conviction, an acrid and black conviction that, his life aside, his world had arrived at its end. This, I believe, even more than the bladder cancer, made him decide on the strychnine pills. Perhaps I should describe this man in a little more detail. He had been a cellist in the Leipzig Philharmonic. He was gaunt, dark-haired, large-eyed and large-eared, large-lipped but talkative not at all, devoted not only to Bach and Haydn but to Rembrandt and Rilke, to Biedermeier cabinetry and the drawings of ships, to fish dishes and Sobranie cigarettes. He was a lonely man, an only child; his parents died young, he hardly recalled them at all. He was one of the Good Germans. One of those who chose to leave the Germany of Hitler, even though his existence was not threatened there, either for racial or for political reasons. He went at first to Switzerland, then to France; he was an excellent cellist, but refugee musicians were a dime a dozen. He played here and there in provincial orchestras and survived in his great loneliness.

In 1940 he got his American visa—late, even though his name had been inscribed on the quota lists years before, but others pressed and elbowed their way before him. He arrived in New York, where he did not have the right connections, and then to Los Angeles and Hollywood, where he had a few jobs, though eventually he had to accept a fixed post in a movie orchestra.

There was a large refugee colony around Los Angeles then, its members ranging from Thomas Mann to Bertolt Brecht: writers, artists, musicians, movie people, scriptwriters, intellectuals of every kind. There was even a salon of sorts in Beverly Hills where they regularly gathered, with plenty of Central European argle-bargle, most of it in German, some in English. He felt out of place there. The relentless sunshine of southern California blinded him and darkened his inner eye. In 1942 he met a Czechoslovakian girl who left him in 1944. (But then women never played the most important roles in his life.) He was lonelier in California than in that wretched pension in Zurich with its soupy smells, than in the dank provincial hotels in Nancy or Dijon with their horrid wallpapers, than in the furnished room on West Ninety-Sixth Street in New York. He had no friends, only acquaintances. He knew a few Americans and liked some of them; most of his fellow Central Europeans he did not like. They were bombinating in the sunshine, resounding with ideas of and about the world. The war was ending in Europe. Good things had come to them in America, and now they were ready to tell the Germans what they deserved. He thought about the devastation of Germany. In his notebook were the addresses of his remnant relatives and a few remnant friends. Would he now write them, would he now contact them, would he return to them? He turned his mind away from that. Then he became ill. He read Stefan Zweig's *World of Yesterday*— *Die Welt von Gestern*—written shortly before Zweig's suicide in Brazil in January 1942. He kept thinking and thinking about that. Zweig also could not face the world of tomorrow; Zweig, who had been healthy and safe and respected in Brazil, chose to die. He, B., is very ill and about to die. So . . . ?

In the city treasurer's room in Leipzig, an ugly clock in its dark oak Wilhelminian cabinet on the wall goes on ticking; it is ticking at two o'clock when the American army photographers come through the door. I doubt the *Schatmeister* took a last glance at the clock, for, if he had, he might have walked across the room (stepping over the legs of his daughter?) in order to stop it. On the white and shiny walls of the hospital in Los Angeles, an electric clock is relentlessly moving and humming. Our man looked at it before the last minutes of his life. There it was, the American world of Today adding up to Tomorrow, the New World forever, with enormous and growing hospitals and airports, all electrically humming. Immutable Progress.

❈ ❈ ❈

"I know what you're after: Hollywood was as bad as the Third Reich in 1945. That won't get you very far, and it will be misunderstood by many people. There is no equivalence there, and hardly any connection. Besides, your two men are very different."

Of course. And of course I have more sympathy for B. than for A. I am sorry for B., and perhaps sorry for Frau A. and for Fräulein A., but I think that A. was a very stupid man. Stupidity, of course, is not a sin, except when it is willful, and in this German civil servant it *was* willful. All I can say is, God have mercy on their souls—on all of them. But there is one more thing I want to say.

"You have already said enough—or rather, too little."

Yes, you are right—though this is not a short story or a novel. But what I want to say is that both of them were foolish, and so was Stefan Zweig in 1942. Well, foolishness is not a sin, but suicide is. And because it is a sin, it is not really practical.

"Sin is not practical?"

It is often practical but only in the short run. Pleasurable, yes. Practical, no. Consider old Zweig. A little less despair and he would have survived, comfortably in Brazil. He would have survived not only the war but The World of Yesterday. Soon after the end of the war he would have been welcomed in Austria and Germany, been greeted with flowers offered by some who had betrayed him and by many others who had denied him, but what does that matter? In 1945 and thereafter there was a good deal of appetite for The World of Yesterday and for people who claimed it and belonged to it—many would have been ready to receive and adorn the famous exile writer, returning without much remorse. In sum, he spared himself a good lot of old-age happiness.

"Would Zweig have been at home in that ruined Vienna after the war?"

Perhaps not in Vienna but in Salzburg. He would have complained that things and people were not what they had been, but then this was true of everyone else, too. But let us not talk about Zweig. That stupid A.! All right, he would have lost his job, a city position, and would have had to go through a difficult year or two of de-Nazification, but nothing much else would have happened to him. Four or five years after the war he would live in a small modern apartment somewhere in Württemberg or Baden, perhaps even with a federal government pension, his daughter married to an American captain with whom he in the evenings could discuss the evil threat of communism.

"And B. could have met a warm-hearted American nurse, Miss Tender

Loving Care, and eventually gotten rid of the colostomy bag and perhaps even played cello again, if not in a great orchestra then in a well-paying television one."

You are not a cynic, and you ought not talk this way. I do not know what would have happened to him, and I doubt whether he would have lived long with that cancer of his. What I am certain of is that he would have had moments, perhaps long moments, of comfort and maybe even of happiness. Not only is our existence God's greatest gift to us, but His other gift to us is that life is unpredictable. I am not saying that death is not a change of state; what I am saying is that life is a long chapter of consciousness that is not for us to terminate.

"What you say is what French telephone operators kept saying to callers before France-Telecom became fully automated."

What was that?

"'Ne quittez pas.' And you, too—go ahead. But watch out. You are always taken by coincidences. I suppose you chose the end of April 1945 because it was then that the Reich was cut in two, when the first Americans coming from the West were to meet the first Russians coming from the East."

Yes, that was really the end of an age and the beginning of a new one, even though it happened five days before Hitler killed himself and almost a fortnight before the Germans laid down their arms—the end of an age even more than the end of a war. Year Zero, 1945. What has stuck in my mind for a long time is the surrealism of 1945—the surrealism, for example, of the fantastic contrast between, say, life in Berlin and life in Hollywood, 1945. People dying and crawling in the ruins of Berlin, people sunning themselves in California. There was this connection: Goebbels admired Hollywood, and not only the technology but some of the scriptwriters' creations, which he wanted to emulate—even as in Hollywood a goodly number of the scriptwriters and composers in 1945 were refugees from Berlin.

"Well, wasn't there a difference between life at the court of Versailles and life at the court of Peking, say, in 1789 or 1689?"

Yes, but there was no connection there then. Now let me go out on a limb: there is something surrealistic in these very figures, *1945*, which pull in different directions. The *19* marks the twentieth century, of course; the *4* is a German number, a marching number; and now it is followed by the jaunty bow-legged American *5*, a colt number, an American figure, a cowboy cipher, a Far Western year. And not far from California, under a brazed and burnished sky, in the American West—yes, that was a Far Western year—men put together a new kind of fire, as the Indians had once done in the unrecorded and unhistoric past, in the desert. They constructed a bomb from the electric particles of matter. Most of the scientists had also come from Germany; they grew up in gray *Mietkasernen,* dark Wilhelminian apartment houses in the gloomy streets of Central European cities. And now they were in the western American desert, in baggy suits pinned with badges marking their persons, chattering and excited under the complicated eyes of their American military masters, alternately wringing and clapping their hands as the hour of the sorcerer's apprentice drew near. And in 1945 there were fluorescences on the shining pages of *Life:* photographers with odd names like Ivan Dmitri or Gjon Mili, strange names that foreshadowed the names of the shadowless, dead-white, poisonous coral isles of the atomic age: Rongelap, Etorofu, Eniwetok . . .

"You stopped short of Bikini."

That was in 1946.

"You began this with a sentence: 'In 1945 the wind carries centuries in its mane.' Good, it is all right for a historian to employ poetry—once in a great while—but is it your job to bag the wind?"

1968

A man stands on a small island in an estuary, hesitant whether to wave once more to his friends. Their boats have moved off the landing, in different directions; one has already turned away in the middle of the bay and the light is fading fast. This is the central portion of the Maine coast, Muscongus Bay, and there is more than a touch of autumn in the air, since it is almost mid-September, the Saturday after Labor Day. This has been the last party of the season; tomorrow there will be nothing but packing, and either that afternoon or Monday morning these people will start the long haul of their driving southward, to the suburbs of New York and Boston and Philadelphia and Baltimore and Pittsburgh. Here in the bay (or "in the river," as some of them say, a habit taken from the Maine mainlanders) they have their island properties, acquired many years ago or inherited from their parents or grandparents in the early years of the century, when these ancestors had elected to advance from the humid torpors of the mid-Atlantic summers to the coastal cools of Maine, establishing their modest summer seats in the rustic austerities of these islands, each with a white wooden or gray shingled house of its own. A little below, both geographically and socially, of the enclave of Northeast Harbor, perhaps even as comfort goes, since these houses are not mansion-like, and some of their owners even now pride themselves on not having electricity; but they are well built, comfortable enough, with bottled gas and plenty of fireplaces drawing well. These owners do not have yachts or large sailboats, but their outboard motorboats (at least two are a must for each island house) are broad-beamed and substantial. Each year they arrive in June and leave after Labor Day, their arrivals less synchronized than their departures, which occur, habitually, on the same weekend or two. They are either retired or well-off enough to spend three months of the year away from their suburban or country homes and offices and occupations, save for the occasional necessities of quick midweek forays south via Portland, by air. Some of them take regular winter vacations or even own houses in the Caribbean. An agreeable annual rhythm of life for these American couples in or just beyond middle-age, as agreeable as the rhythm of their daily life up here in Maine, which includes frequent parties on one island or another, the hosts signaling across the water with a rigged-up flag at one house or with the bang of a small brass cannon cemented down on the front lawn of another but more usually going out on their boats, sailing in a circle, and shouting across: "Drinks at five!" And now, I repeat, this is the last party of the year, a little later than usual, which is due not to the weather or to the calendar in 1968 but to the consideration that their friends feel they owe to their host and his wife: for these two will not be leaving now, they will stay on, during the entire fall and perhaps even the whole winter, here and later upriver in the village of Bremen, Maine.

There is always a touch of melancholy about these last parties, partly because of the ever swifter coming of the darkness in the evening. But, while *partir, c'est mourir un peu,* the melancholy is not unpleasant; it is washed away by plenty of drinks ("did you think we're leaving all those bottles of gin for the scavengers?") and by the anticipations of their houses and families at home. But this evening is somewhat different. Now their host turns back from the small dock and walks up on his lawn, getting smaller and smaller when seen from this distance; he wears white shoes, white duck pants, and a white sweater, but soon he diminishes into a white wisp and then disappears. I must not overdo the melancholy because that would be incorrect. He and his wife chose to discount it some time ago. They had talked long enough about their decision to stay here. Self-discipline, including a stiff reluctance to gnaw over anxieties, has long been bred into their bones. Now that they have cleared up the glasses and the plates and brought the dishes into the kitchen, there is a very determined blaze in the fireplace and the prospect of an easy supper with the many leftovers. Their

talk is all about practical matters, about the new man in charge of the winter storage of one of the boats, about letting the mainland chandler know
that they will need another two bottles of cooking and heating gas, about
the house in Bremen, about their daughter's wedding reception. There is
even a touch of adventure knowing that they have now cast off from New
York, facing the chances and the conditions of the coming tide of autumn
and of winter by themselves, here, alone.

Then he sleeps badly. At dawn it is as if the cold Maine morning has
been invading the house, as if its gray light hangs over all the furniture like
a cobweb, coming relentlessly closer, depriving him of further rest. This is
rare for him, for he usually sleeps well; he is in good physical shape, trim,
still athletic in the sixty-sixth year of his life, little to worry about when it
comes to his health or to the tasks he has set ahead of him, for he is a good
amateur carpenter and handyman and sailor. But a new chapter of his life
has now opened, which is like stepping over a threshold and entering a new
room, closing the door behind. Yes, there is a sense of adventure in this, in
the plans ahead of him, some features of which he indeed anticipates; but
he knows, too (and so does his wife, even more acutely), that the purpose of
leaving their life in New York for Maine was the seeking of a refuge there,
and when either of them says, "We've escaped from New York," they say so
because in people's minds escape and adventure are often the same things,
whereas refuge is not.

He is now sixty-five. His great-grandfather had moved from Massachusetts to Ohio, his grandfather from Ohio to New York, his father from New
York to Montclair, New Jersey, where he was born, and now he is back in
New England again. His grandfather made welding equipment, and after
he had become a successful manufacturer, he died young, in a tuberculosis
sanatorium in the Adirondacks. His son went to the best schools money
could buy, became a stockbroker, entered the middle-upper-class ranks of
New York, and settled in Montclair, which became an upper-class suburb
around 1900. The present son's schooling and occupation resembled his
father's, but their personalities were different: the father was a secret drinker,
he an open one, sometimes slipping over into the no-man's-land of alcoholism. But he got cured of that around sixty, indeed to the extent that now,
a few years later, he allows himself to drink again moderately and keeps to
that without difficulty. He is a very disciplined man, insistent and precise
in his business, used to taking tiny draughts of pride in his old-fashioned
standards with his clients and with his firm. But the composition of his firm
has changed, and their practices have changed, and life with his wife in
New York has changed. It was different from the way he had envisaged it,
and he decided one day this spring that he had to leave New York, a deci-

sion that—perhaps surprisingly—met with no opposition either from his wife or from his children, though no doubt for reasons of their own; in his wife's case, her agreement was in exchange for his promise to spend their money and the two worst of Maine months, February and March, in a rented villa known to them in the British Antilles. Their son lives in California, their late-born daughter (this is 1968) is a college dropout, has caused many a worry for her father, and lives with the son of another retiree (an artist) in Maine; he is a lobsterman in the summer and a sign painter in the winter. At this moment they are upriver, in Bremen, in the small house that her father bought some years ago, one of those thousands of gaunt and New England Gothic square wooden buildings whose windows have a cold stare of their own, but in this case they have enough modern heating and plumbing and good pieces of furniture to be livable.

The imperfect sleep did not discombobulate her father. It is a squally morning now, and his mind and hands are full with plenty to do. But when in the afternoon he takes his first drink, he knows only too well that this is now the middle of the autumn of his life, as it is autumn in Maine, and winter will come soon, with its beauties and difficulties arriving together. Outside everything is flat and gray, with the green tufts of the islands getting pale in the melting fog. In a few days he will be alone. His wife will be going down to Boston for two weeks, after which he will close and nail and pad and shut the house down, and they will go to Bremen, where their daughter will be married on a late October day marred by sheets of rain, though the reception at the inn will be bright and smart, arranged to a tee by his still mahogany-tanned, rich-voiced, alcoholic wife; in one of her three new dresses, she will be a beacon of elegance in that plain little church, as if it were a wedding in Montclair or Chestnut Hill. He will be there, with his trimmed white moustache, with his blue-eyed smile, and with God knows what anxious sentiments swelling in his breast. There will be quarrels and then loneliness. The price of refuge, but he hopes to have his hands full. There is work to be done on both houses, he says to people, to her, and to himself.

But there will be coziness in the yellow lights of the little houses of the village of Bremen, and the evening will have swallowed up the afternoon, and the fog the rain. As they walk into their house, now vacated by the bride and groom, who are on their way to Quebec in her parents' station wagon, his wife says to him, "Well, that's what she wanted. We always gave her what she wanted. I only hope that it works for her." What she doesn't say is "This is what you wanted, and I only hope that it works for you." But that is what she thinks, even as she knows that "for you" does not quite mean "for us."

❋ ❋ ❋

"I fear that your crucial word is wrong. This couple does not seek *refuge*, they *retreat* from New York."

Perhaps the wife, but not the man with whom I am concerned. Retreat suggests the possibility and the potential desirability of returning, which is not what he wants. He does not want to return to New York.

"Well, he does retreat into the wilderness, which is a very American thing to do—"

You know very well that this is not the case. He may—I am not sure of that—be aware that he belongs to the last generation of family that has risen in the world (occupationally, financially, socially) and that this is no longer happening or even possible for what remains of his family. What he wants to do is to save what he still can, and I don't mean money: his remaining chance for a few reasonably safe—and healthy—years.

"The American dream turning into a nightmare in New York. You suggest this, but too faintly. What has happened to him in New York? There was this *bon mot* (I'd call it a *mot mauvais*) surfacing around 1968, that a conservative (of course meaning a neoconservative) is a liberal mugged by reality. Your man is not a liberal and not an intellectual, he is a not untypical though creditable Wasp (forgive this silly term), and was he ever mugged?"

No, he was not mugged, though he witnessed something like a mugging. It happened in broad daylight, at a shining noon hour in midtown Manhattan, on Forty-Fifth Street, between Madison and Park. A black deliveryman and a white deliveryman were fighting on the pavement while shouting obscenities. People watched. Another black climbed down from a truck. Together they kicked and pummeled the white one; in the end they pushed him down to the pavement, laughed and spat at him, and then jumped into the truck and drove away. No one stopped them. He wanted to stop them (he had been in the Navy), but his wife screamed and held him back. What upset him was not the brutality and the ugliness of the scene. He suddenly realized that whites were now afraid of blacks. That hit him in the craw—

"That this was racism in the reverse, because in the past blacks used to be afraid of whites?"

This was something new. Blacks are a minority, just as Jews were a minority in Germany, but were there any Nazis afraid of Jews? And there was this in his mind too: that somehow these white people in New York were hopeless because they were responsible for what was happening, though not only because of the former mistreatment of blacks by white Americans. They were responsible because of their own acceptance of the cult of brutality and of ugliness. The law of the jungle had broken to the surface here, in midtown Manhattan, and the people there were not up to it.

"One street scene in New York, and he is off to Maine. You're going too far again."

No, there was more to it. Don't forget that it was you who asked whether he had been mugged or saw a mugging. It came together with other things: for instance, he was not an Old New Yorker, meaning that he was more keenly aware of what he saw as the decay of the city than some of the Old New Yorkers who thought (thought, rather than felt) that New York has always meant change and that they must stay reconciled to that. He saw, more keenly than others, the quick decay of all those monumental buildings only a few decades after their and his youth, when they had been the wonders of the world, not only because of their majestic presence but because of the opulence of their decorations, which had been made possible because of the abundance of an American civilization. His office was on Park Avenue South, and he saw the signs of that devolution every day. The crenellations and the machicolations of the bastions of American prosperity were crumbling. Not only did he see the stucco replaced by plastic inside those buildings, but he was dismayed by what was going on within his firm. The coming of new people and their doings, cutting corners, and I do not of course mean the physical rearrangement of the office but the novel practices of people that were distasteful to him. So he was ready to retire, in more than one way. He knew that he was more and more out of place and that these people knew that. And of course there was his place in Maine.

"But isn't that retreat—or, all right, refuge—in Maine an illusion, too?"

I hope not. But about New England . . . well, somewhere in my files there is a poem from the April 1945 *Atlantic,* "Indian Summer," by someone whose name is unknown to me, a Constance Carrier:

> *New England is a savage still at heart,*
> *hiding in every empty cellar-hole,*
> *in ambush at the edge of every field,*
> *lurking behind each granite-ridden knoll.*
>
> *The gaudy violence of an autumn day*
> *prevails against white house and whiter steeple:*
> *the scarlet leaves, like feathered arrows flying*
> *blow in the wind above an alien people.*

This is a land unconquered and aloof,
secret and harsh and ribbed with stubborn stone.
As watchful as an Indian warrior waiting,
it keeps an ancient silence of its own.

"All right, though not a great poem. And I don't know how pertinent it is for 1968. Let me remind you that I was in Brunswick, Maine, in 1968 and found that there were at least five barbershops on the main street. The land unconquered and aloof had been conquered by the tourist industry."

Conquered, or merely overrun? Well, at least partly so. But I am anxious not so much about this man's illusions of Maine, where he knows things and most of the people well enough. I am anxious about his old age, which, despite his excellent physical and existential condition, will now be coming fast. Yes, old age *may* bring some wisdom—but it brings more tiredness than wisdom. And that tiredness (whether it includes wisdom or not) is the soft deepening feeling and recognition of what one is, leaving behind the feeling and the recognition of what one wants to be. That may include wisdom—but not necessarily so.

65

The Great Gatsby?
Yes, a Historical Novel
(2001)

According to F. Scott Fitzgerald's principal exegete, Matthew J. Bruccoli, "*The Great Gatsby* has become an international source for American social history and is read as a record of American life at an actual time and place." (It is at least possible that such an international appreciation of *The Great Gatsby* may have been due to the movie rather than to the novel.) In any event, this international association of *The Great Gatsby* with the social life of rich Americans is relatively recent. (*The Great Gatsby* was not a publishing success when it first appeared, in 1925; its qualities were discovered or rediscovered only after World War II. I recently read a fairly serious book about society and social life in Sicily of the 1980s, peppered with adjectives about "Gatsbian" or "Gatsby-like" parties, meaning less parties that were "American" but parties that were excessively sumptuous. *Sic transit gloria Gatsby*).

It is probably because of the peculiar American, and democratic, structure of history that certain novels tell us more about a certain time and about certain people than even the best of histories. When I taught American history, particularly in my 1890 to 1945 undergraduate course, I put *The Great Gatsby* on my reading list, I think at the expense of requiring my students to read about the politics of the 1920s or otherwise good biographies of, say, Harding or Coolidge or Hoover. I had put some novels on my reading lists of other times, though not for the 1910s or 1930s. For what had happened in the twenties was that the development and changes in society, including the modes of everyday life in America, were both more interesting and important (meaning: more consequential) than the history of its

From Mark C. Carnes, ed., *Novel History: Historians and Novelists Confront America's Past (and Each Other)* (New York: Simon and Schuster), 235–44.

politics and of its government. (In spite of the suffrage given to women, there was, for the first time in many decades, a definite drop in the percentage of voters after 1920.) So between the Progressive Age (including World War I) and the progressive decade of the New Deal, there was this Jazz Age—the twenties, a phrase that is recognizable even now. (As a matter of fact, "The Jazz Age" is a phrase that was coined and thrown into circulation by F. Scott Fitzgerald himself, in 1920.)

It will not fade soon, or easily. Our associations of the Jazz Age are essentially the same as they were decades ago. In this respect, Bruccoli is wrong. In the preface of "the authorized text," Bruccoli wrote, "*The Great Gatsby* was published in 1925; therefore many of its details now seem as remote as those in the world of Charles Dickens's fiction." Not so. Automobiles, short skirts, movies, gramophones, lots of liquor, adulteries, the cult of celebrities, suburban life, airplanes, the increasing fusion of middle class with upper class and of working class with middle class were all there in the 1920s as they are here now. (Only television and the computer and air-conditioning are—perhaps—missing.) After all, it may be said that the twenties (and not only in America) were the *only* "modern" decade. For what else were the sixties, with their miniskirts and cult of youth and sexual freedom, etc., but an exaggerated repetition of the twenties? I am looking at the original jacket cover of the first edition of *The Great Gatsby*. Its designer was a Spanish artist in Hollywood by the name of Francis Cugat, who also worked for Douglas Fairbanks. Fitzgerald's publisher, Charles Scribner III, wrote that this cover "is the most celebrated—and widely disseminated—jacket art in twentieth-century American literature." Fitzgerald's editor, Maxwell Perkins, "believed that the jacket was a masterpiece." I do not think that it was (or is) a masterpiece, but that is not the point. The point is that the midnight eroticism of Daisy's eyes and luscious mouth hovering above a bright yellow explosion of electric glitter and sequins and background neons could easily serve as a modern (or postmodern) jacket for a sexy book published in AD 2000.

The protracted influence of, or respect for, *The Great Gatsby* alone suggests that *The Great Gatsby* is more than a period piece—except in the sense that all works of art are, to some extent, period pieces, including even such immortals as Mozart or Vermeer. Whether *The Great Gatsby* is immortal is arguable; what is not arguable is that it is representative of a period, not only because of its contents but also because of its style. And that there is nothing wrong with a period piece—and that there is also more to *The Great Gatsby* than a period piece—may appear from a comparison of *The Great Gatsby* with *An American Tragedy,* Theodore Dreiser's large novel, also published in 1925. The story of Clyde Griffiths, the tragedy, his aspirations, and his comeuppance could fit into the decades before or during or even after the twenties. This is not true of *The Great Gatsby*, which is suffused with the atmosphere and with some of the actual evidences and effects of the early 1920s—which is one, but only one, reason why it is such interesting and even informative and valuable reading. And now consider that *The Great Gatsby* (which was not Fitzgerald's original or preferred title) could be easily entitled "An American Tragedy." As with all fine creations of art and letters, *The Great Gatsby*—its meaning and its style—also transcends its period (which *An American Tragedy*, at first sight more of a historical novel than *The Great Gatsby*, does not).

The protagonist Gatsby, a successful and attractive man of dubious origins, is in love with Daisy Buchanan, a young woman of the American upper classes. His social ambitions are not simple. Yes, he wants to impress people, but even more important is his romantic quest for Daisy—which suddenly ends in tragedy (because of an accident involving Daisy, though not because of her wish to end their affair); Gatsby is killed (again, by an erratic coincidence); and no one, virtually no one, comes to his funeral. (In *An American Tragedy*, Griffiths kills his plain girl because of his social ambitions: he is about to be involved with a richer, more glittering girl. He is a villain, from beginning to end.) In the eyes of Nick Carraway, the narrator, Gatsby, with all of his faults, is not only not worse but better than the horde of rich people who had profited from his hospitality (and business), including Daisy. That *is* an American Tragedy—perhaps even more than that: *The* American Tragedy—the hollowness (rather than the failure) of social aspirations.

There are few such sad funerals in the history of literature: perhaps Emma Bovary's is one. And Jay Gatsby is a male American Emma Bovary at least in one sense—even as, unlike Emma Bovary, he dies suddenly when he is still healthy and rich. He is a romantic. Bruccoli is wrong when he writes that Gatsby "does not understand how money works in society. He innocently expects that he can buy anything—especially Daisy. She is for sale: but he doesn't have the right currency." No: Gatsby does not want to buy Daisy with money. Money is very important, but he wants to win her through love. He is innocent—in the way he idealizes Daisy, who, in the end, is hardly worth it—but that, too, is not the main point of the novel. He still has some of his midwestern innocence. His easterners have none. It is the people of West Egg and East Egg of Long Island, and their guests and visitors and spongers and hangers-on, mostly from New York, who are worthless—whether they have money or not. The tragedy that F. Scott Fitzgerald describes is not really that of American materialism; it is that of a—peculiar—American idealism. It is a gem, a historical cameo not of

American thinking but of American feeling; not of calculations but of aspirations.

And that was an idealism that F. Scott Fitzgerald himself had imbibed and shared. Describing the automobile ride into New York from Long Island: "The city seen from the Queensboro Bridge is always the city seen for the first time, in its wild promise of all the mystery and beauty of the world." That was how a few people, including intelligent foreigners, saw New York in the 1920s; or how sensitive immigrants saw it within the city. It was F. Scott Fitzgerald, not Woody Allen, who comprehended the kind of Manhattan oddly resonant in George Gershwin's melancholy chords. But then that is, too, why the last famous lines of *The Great Gatsby* are so often misunderstood or at least imperfectly understood. Yes, Gatsby was drawn to the green light at Daisy's dock, now so close. And Daisy did come, easily, from across the water. Besides that green light—which has become a veritable literary-cultural cliché, employed by critics over and over again—there is on that last page that other, so often cited, famous Fitzgeraldian passage of the narrator, alone after Gatsby's death and looking across: "[I] became aware of the old island here that flowered once for Dutch sailors' eyes—a fresh, green breast of the new world." Well, there is something wrong here: for what the narrator sees is not the view of "the fresh, green breast of the new world" from the Atlantic but the brummagem Connecticut shore across from Long Island Sound, which is not what the Dutch sailors had first glimpsed. Yet it is F. Scott Fitzgerald's historical romanticism which suffuses *The Great Gatsby,* and not only on that famous last page: a soft, almost subterranean music that makes it transcend a period piece—something that is expressed, too, in another famous Fitzgeraldian phrase, that of America being the willingness of the heart. It is the willingness of Gatsby's heart, not his aspiration for more and more money, that characterizes him, while it is the unwillingness of the heart that characterizes most of the book's minor characters, perhaps especially Tom Buchanan, Daisy's muscular and brutal husband, a veritable villain who is somewhat overdrawn: a heartless, rather than mindless, American, a rich Yalie.

There exists a rather thoughtful book, *Another Part of the Twenties* (1973), by the historian Paul A. Carter: "My father was attending an Eastern men's liberal arts college when *This Side of Paradise,* F. Scott Fitzgerald's archetypal novel by, for and about the college student, was first published. . . . Although an avid reader all his life, my father never read it. When he was in college he could not have afforded a raccoon coat, but years later in the bottom of the Depression he bought one in a second-hand store. My mother went to a coeducational church-related college in the Midwest. Snapshots and a portrait of her from the twenties show a strikingly attractive, high-spirited woman, but she was hardly a flapper as that term is ordinarily employed. Her idea of fun was a church social, and for vacations she and my father inexpensively went camping." From further queries and research, Carter "got the impression that my parents in their day were not alone in having missed a good deal of what we ordinarily characterize as 'The Roaring Twenties'...." "In fact... gazing away from Manhattan's Great White Way any night during the decade following 1920, one could have seen wide, dark stretches of the continent where the roar of the Twenties was muted indeed; where life was lived in a rhythm in which there was not the faintest echo of jazz." This is very true: but, then, this was (and still is) a big country. And *The Great Gatsby* is still a near-perfect period piece—and more: a description of a small segment of American society but also something beyond that: a concern with the insubstantial essence of what so many Americans thought (and still think) reality is.

There are—and this is a minor point in this essay—many interesting details (and phrases) that tell us something about Fitzgerald's people and places and times, in retrospect. Here are some of them: a mistress is called "a sweetie"; another, that already in the early 1920s, Celebrity was beginning to replace, or at least merge into, what was still called Society (though Fitzgerald's term was somewhat different: "celebrated people"). Another, perhaps interesting, detail: James Gatz changes his name to Jay Gatsby, for the sake of elegance; a few decades later it is arguable that "James" may be at least as classy as, if not even classier than, "Jay." And sometimes Fitzgerald's ambition of social perceptions carries his prose too far: "my second glass of corky but rather impressive claret." About some of the partying girls: "I have forgotten their names—Jaqueline [sic], I think, or else, Consuela or Gloria or Judy or June, and their last names were either the melodious names of flowers and months or the sterner ones of the great American capitalists whose cousins, if pressed, they would confess themselves to be." And: "'He's a bootlegger' said the young ladies, moving somewhere between his cocktails and flowers. 'One time he killed a man who had found out that he was a nephew to von Hindenburg and second cousin to the devil.' 'Reach me a rose, honey, and pour me a last drop into that there crystal glass.'" This is too much. But then there are near-immortal perceptions, or summary phrases: for example, how Americans move "with the formless grace of our nervous, sporadic games." And the true mark of a fine writer, which is the splendid choice of some of his verbs, rather than the easier choice of his adjectives: in Gatsby's tragic swimming pool "there was a faint, barely perceptive movement of the water, as the fresh flow from one end urged its way towards the drain on the other." And then much (if not all) of the Jazz Age (and the American Dream?) is summed up in this exquisite paragraph:

For Daisy was young and her artificial world was redolent of
orchids and pleasant, cheerful snobbery and orchestras which
set the rhythm of the year, summing up the sadness and suggestiveness of life in new tunes. All the night the saxophones wailed
the hopeless comment of the 'Beale Street Blues' while a hundred pairs of golden and silver slippers shuffled the shining dust.
At the grey tea hour there were always rooms that throbbed
incessantly with this low sweet fever, while fresh faces drifted
here and there like rose petals blown by the sad horns around
the floor.

Theodore Dreiser was not capable of writing such sentences. Nor was
Henry James or Hemingway. It is impressionistic, elegant, and romantic: a
rare American combination. But then this is an essay not about literature
but about history. Fitzgerald's lyricism is not only stylistically extraordinary but also historically telling. Yes: "*le style c'est l'homme*"; but *le style c'est
aussi l'histoire.*

66

Agnes Repplier, Writer and Essayist
(1981)

Among the surviving photographs of Agnes Repplier there is one in which she sits, not very comfortably, fidgeting with her cup, with the looks of a retired schoolmarm, dowdy, thick-ankled, her humorless countenance topped by a black pot of a hat, or one resembling a caricature thereof. The picture is a period piece. It shows a library of a late-Victorian or an early-Edwardian kind: an entire wall constructed of ornate shelves and books, the latter mostly Collected Editions in fine bindings, a heavily sumptuous collection. Tightly framed by the shelves, a portrait of Samuel Johnson hovers over the assembly. A. Edward Newton, the host and noted book collector, is holding Miss Repplier's recently published volume (a collection of essays in praise of tea) in his left hand and a cup of tea in his other hand; he is sporting a large checked tweed suit and the expression of a large and benevolent retriever. His wife and another gentleman complete the human components of the picture. Between them stands a delicate galleried tea table, top-heavy with a very elaborate silver tea set, the entire assembly resting on a correspondingly ornate, rich Oriental carpet. By contemplating the atmosphere I can *smell* the fine dust of that carpet. And when was this picture taken? My friends look at the furnishings, the clothes, the library; they say, without much hesitation: "Nineteen-twelve." "Nineteen-oh-nine." "Nineteen-nineteen."

They are wrong. The picture was taken in November 1932. It is a period piece of a certain kind—which tells us something about Philadelphia, but not about the then celebrated author for whom this depressingly genteel tea party was given. Photographs, like phonographs, can blatantly lie. Agnes Repplier did not teach school, she was not retired, she had a great sense of humor, she was extremely witty, she was tall and long-legged. What is more

From *Philadelphia: Patricians and Philistines 1900–1950* (New York: Farrar, Straus and Giroux), 85–146.

important, she was not a period piece. The few literati (very few) who remember her name may think so. They are wrong.

She came into this world in the year of the Charge of the Light Brigade, and she left it the year after the hydrogen bomb; she preceded Theodore Roosevelt by four years and she survived Franklin Roosevelt by another five. When she was a child steel pens were beginning to replace quill pens, and she lived to see (if that is the word) television beginning to replace what was left of reading; the last of the Brontë sisters died the year she was born, and she outlasted James Joyce by nearly ten years. Her life was solitary, vexatious, and long.

For ninety-five years she lived in Philadelphia, this woman whose tastes and whose learning were as cosmopolitan as anything. She was utterly honest, and assertive without pretense, a rare combination. There were only three instances when she chose to alter her record. In the supreme court of her feminine conscience she decided that she was born a few years after her arrival in this world. That was her own dread decision: she liked the years 1857 and 1858 so much that they occasionally became the years of her birth. She loved France so much that France eventually became the land of her ancestry.[1] Since she was not merely a Francophile but her mind was in ways thoroughly Gallicized, was this not what counted, after all? She was not *une française malgré soi*; she was that vastly preferable kind of person, *une française à cause de soi*. In the third place (in order, though probably first in importance), she spun a veil over her unhappy childhood. She wrote about it as if it had been sufficiently sunny and reasonably secure: it wasn't so.

Her father was handsome and weak; her mother was plain, strong, and intelligent. Her own qualities were compromised fatally by the fact that Mrs. Repplier, born Agnes Mathias in 1832, was a Thoroughly Modern Woman in more than one way. She hated domestic duties, and she disapproved of children, including her own. Such inclinations, widely current a century later, were luxuries then. The Reppliers were not rich. Rich parents could afford to be uninterested in their children, since they could deputize nannies and governesses and tutors and domestic servants of all kinds for the discharge of those domestic and educational responsibilities for which they themselves had no particular taste. Other children would be permanently maimed by the deliberate withholding of parental affection. Agnes was not.

She got a Spartan taste of life from the start. "My mother," Agnes told her niece many decades later, "was perfectly just, but her justice was untempered by mercy. No one loved or tried to understand me, and I think I was an interesting child, if anyone had cared enough to find out."[2] Her mother tried to force her to read, for a long time in vain. Agnes taught herself how to read at the age of ten. Before her opened a world of unexpected delights. Her reading capacity was extraordinary; it was wedded auspiciously to an astonishing memory. Well before she knew how to read she could recite alarmingly lengthy poems by heart.[3] Throughout her life she could draw on her astonishing memory with astonishing ease. She seemed to have read everything, and forgotten nothing. She would instinctively react to the resonance of words—an unusual inclination, since she was otherwise tone deaf, and her interest in music nonexistent.

When she was twelve her mother enrolled her in Eden Hall, the Convent of the Sacred Heart, in Torresdale. Liquidated exactly one hundred years later because of the temporary insanity of worldliness that infected the nuns in charge, Eden Hall was then a singular institution: a Catholic school in America attempting to maintain the traditions of the Sacré Coeur of the Old World. From Eden Hall—a pile of a building in the middle of what was then a country estate—issued generations of unusual American women, not all of them Catholics.[4] Eden Hall was *très Sacré-Coeur:* strictly pious and hierarchical, aristocratic in aspirations and slightly brushed with snobbery, French with touches of the Second Empire, sentimental and disciplinarian, Victorian as well as classical, the regimentation of its days and the corridors of its building decorated by a statuary that was marble-cold. Wealthy parents drove out in their carriages to visit their daughters. "Energetic parents made the trip by street car and train. Mrs. Repplier, who was neither wealthy nor energetic, stayed home."[5]

Agnes Repplier, often called "Minnie" (she despised the name), occasionally "April Fool" (she was born on April 1), was not a popular child. She was a self-conscious little girl, independent, and occasionally rebellious. At the end of her second year her parents were told not to bring her back.[6] Her convent days were over. *In Our Convent Days* is the title of the memoir of those two years that she wrote more than thirty years later, dedicated to her closest friend from Eden Hall, the difficult Elizabeth Robins Pennell. It is a small hand-wrought piece, one of the finest of her writings, shot through with silver threads of delicacy and proportion: light and serious, shimmering and somber, a recollection of pieties and impieties, of young girlhood and enduring childishness, this *bonbonnière* of a book is more than a precious trinket of period recollections; it is a minor masterpiece that ought to rank with that other *fin de siècle* book of a similar milieu, Valéry Larbaud's *Fermina Marquez.* Agnes Repplier had at least as much, if not more, cause for bitterness about her school as the well-known English writers of the succeeding generation; she had a healthy talent for irony, and a reserve capacity of sarcasm; moreover, she had been expelled from school, an achievement of which Maugham, Greene, Orwell, Waugh, et al., could not boast. Nonetheless, she elected to spin the tale of her convent days into a fine lacy book, unweighted by sentimentality and not at all genteel. She simply chose to come to the best possible terms with her memories. She decided that her childhood had not been unhappy; and that was that.

Perhaps she knew that it is more difficult to be happy than to be unhappy, and she must have realized the silliness of Tolstoy's famous first sentence in *Anna Karenina*: "Happy families are all alike; every unhappy family is unhappy in its own way." (She never liked Tolstoy very much.) She would have, I am certain, agreed rather with La Rochefoucauld, whom she admired: "We are seldom as happy or as unhappy as we imagine."

In that year, 1869, Miss Agnes Irwin took over the school of Miss Tazewell, victim of a properly Philadelphian nautical tragedy. (She had drowned on a boating excursion off Mount Desert Island in Maine.) Mrs. Repplier and Miss Irwin were friends. In the latter's West Penn Square Seminary for Young Ladies, Agnes Repplier was now enrolled. There, too, she was not a success. Most of the girls, less interesting than her friends in Eden Hall, snubbed her.[7] Miss Irwin appreciated her intellectual talents.[8] She also considered the consequences of Agnes's rebellious nature, concluding that they were considerable. One afternoon, Agnes, confronted with the task of reading a disagreeable book, looked straight at Miss Irwin and threw the book on the floor. That evening she met Miss Irwin on the steps of their house. She had come to visit her friend Mrs. Repplier, a not unusual occurrence. Nothing was said. Agnes retired in peace. As she put on her coat and scarf and cap next morning, her mother stopped her. Where was she going, she asked, with an asymmetrical smile on her dark face. To school, Agnes answered—wide-eyed, serious, a little frightened perhaps. Her mother told her that she was not going to school that morning, or ever again.

There and then began the most difficult years of her life, stunted and scarred and poor. Her mother would scratch her own bitterness with diamond-hard lines on the interior window-pane of her daughter's eye. "Your daughter has strong opinions," said a guest to Mrs. Repplier. "Yes, indeed," replied the mother, "in spite of their being worthless." "One morning at the breakfast table, when Agnes was about fifteen, her mother regarded her critically and observed, 'You look like a leper who has had small-pox.' Agnes burst into tears. Her mother went on to say that it was silly to behave this way because one had a bad complexion. 'Mirabeau was ugly and pockmarked, yet he grew up to become one of the great writers of France.'"[9] This was not the voice of the Modern Woman. It was the voice of a hard Victorian eccentric who knew talent wherever she saw it, including in her children. She turned Agnes to a career of writing, while she nearly crushed her spirit. Mrs. Repplier was not strong enough to avoid the temptations of self-pity, an indulgence the results of which can be more disastrous to those close to us than to ourselves. When she was "beaten down by life and knew she was dying, she asked Agnes' forgiveness for bringing her into so undesirable a world."[10]

It was an undesirable world. Agnes's adversities were oppressive. Her gentle and taciturn father lost most of his money in his business: added to the social handicaps of being German and Catholic, the Reppliers were now impecunious as well. Agnes had to live through that saddest of young experiences, moving away from a house in which many things were close and familiar. From Twentieth and Chestnut, a mildly fashionable and genteel portion of the swelling city, the Reppliers moved to Fortieth and Locust in West Philadelphia.[11] She was no longer a child, but she was deeply affected by the move to this somber portion of the city, with its dusty trees, hardwood porches, Methodist respectabilities, and the waiting in the rain for the horsecars, ramshackle and crowded, nearly an hour away from the lights of central Philadelphia, with its theaters, stores, and badly lit library. What kind of life was this, composed of tiresome duties of the day, the dullness and dampness of the house, even when the sun was shining, when the depressing heat lay on West Philadelphia like a beached and breathless whale; with the vulgar decorativeness of the hydrangeas, with the dark green weediness of it all.

When the financial catastrophe overcame John George Repplier, his wife, quite reasonably, decided that her daughters would contribute to keeping the Repplier household afloat.[12] She was an intelligent woman, after all. The younger daughter (Mary) would teach. Mrs. Repplier dismissed the idea, bruited about the family earlier, that Agnes should enter a convent. Agnes should write. Agnes was barely past sixteen, but "from that very moment she was fired with both desire and need, the best of all possible goads for the artist."[13] The best of all possible goads, perhaps; but the worst of all possible circumstances. The chances for an untutored and ungainly girl, plunked down in the dullest portion of dullest Philadelphia, to earn a respectable living by becoming a writer were not minimal; they were virtually nonexistent. Compared to such circumstances, the lives of Agnes's English contemporaries, of Gissing's writers in New Grub Street, struggling at the feet of the moloch of Commerce, were melodrama. Here is this gawky girl, this early caricature of a bluestocking, scratching away with her pen on the second floor of a West Philadelphia house, weighed down by the dreariest conditions of enforced domesticity, without friends, without a swain, without any knowledge of the world. During the most formative years of her life, her imagination is not nourished by any kind of experience. It is no less powerful for that. It is nourished by books, by the best of books.

The American newspaper, then even more than now, had some of the characteristics of a magazine. It needed "fillers": sketches, odd pieces of information, stories of all kinds. Thousands of now forgotten scribblers, housewives and clerks, filled these gaps for a few dollars. Few of them aspired to much more. Agnes did. As her niece wrote eighty years afterward: "She had abandoned many early hopes, only to cling with increasing tenacity to one dominant ambition—to become a writer of distinction."[14] In 1937, when she was more than eighty years old, she wrote about herself in this autobiographical fragment:

> *1877.* I am twenty years old, and I have begun to write. It is the only thing in the world that I can do, and the urge is strong. Naturally I have nothing to say, but I have spent ten years in learning to say that nothing tolerably well. Every sentence is a matter of supreme importance to me. I need hardly confess that I am writing stories—stories for children, stories for adults. They get themselves published somewhere, somehow, and bring in a little money. Otherwise they would have no excuse for being; a depressing circumstance of which I am well aware.[15]

For seven years more she wrote and wrote, for seven years that were as lean as any. Her mother died. She had to take care of her old and sick father and her paralytic brother. She struggled on in the night. She was getting closer and closer to the summit of her talent, though she did not know this. In July 1884 a very important thing happened. She met Father Isaac Hecker, a German-American priest of some renown, a compassionate and cultured man who was the founder of the Paulist order and of the *Catholic World* magazine. He had been publishing some of Agnes Repplier's stories.

> Father Hecker told me that my stories were mechanical, and gave no indication of being transcripts from life. "I fancy," he said, "that you know more about books than you do about life, that you are more a reader than an observer. What author do you read the most?"
>
> I told him "Ruskin," an answer which nine out of ten studious girls would have given at that date.
>
> "Then," said he, "write me something about Ruskin, and make it brief."

That essay turned my feet into the path which I have trod-
den laboriously ever since.[16]

This was that rare thing of perfect advice perfectly accepted and carried out. Less than two years later Agnes Repplier reached the summit of
her ambitions. The *Atlantic Monthly* would publish her essay.[17] Its editor,
Thomas Bailey Aldrich, saw that he was in the presence of a writer of talent. She was invited to Boston to meet the Aereopagus of American intellect, the circle of Lowell, Holmes, et al. Against all odds (and what odds!)
Agnes Repplier achieved what she wanted. Her talent was now public. The
pattern of her future was set.

She was thirty-one years old, tall, with a serious mien, no longer very
young. How acutely, how permanently, she was aware of that! In 1937, when
she was eighty-two, she recounted her crucial conversation with Father
Hecker, an account every word of which rings true. There is, however, one
white lie. She wrote that this meeting had taken place in 1877. It occurred
in 1884. Add to this the two years that she customarily deducted from her
age, as in this account in *Eight Decades,* when she writes about herself as "a
girl of twenty" in 1877. The crucial interview with this good Father Hecker
happened not when she was twenty but when she was rising thirty, past the
twenty-ninth birthday of her life. Even at the age of eighty-two she wanted
to direct minds away from the stunting sadness of those struggling solitary
years. She wanted to give the impression of a young girl, succeeding in
literature not merely through her gifts but with the help of great good luck.
She dreaded giving the impression that her eventual success was the result
of her perseverance: the world might think that she was married to books
because no man had wanted her when she was marriageable and young.

She had been in love with her half-brother, and perhaps also with a
cousin.[18] She liked the company of men, she knew how to flirt, she was
sensitive to male flattery; while she was not beautiful, she was not in the
least unattractive; but the pattern was set; she would remain a maiden woman
for the rest of her long life.

The pattern was set: her first publication in the *Atlantic* brought her a
kind of renown that would not cease for the next fifty years. Every man and
woman of letters in the English-speaking world learned her name. Within
four years of her first publication in the *Atlantic,* Gosse and Saintsbury wrote
her complimentary letters. Awards, medals, honorary doctorates came to
her in succession. She was the dean of American essayists.[19] Even in her
own "dull, tepid" Philadelphia she was discovered. She became a cherished
friend and the pride of some of the best patrician houses. She was eighty-
one when Ellery Sedgwick, then editor of the *Atlantic,* wrote:

733

> For two full generations Miss Agnes Repplier has not ceased to
> be a bright and finished ornament of American letters. Who
> matches her in craftsmanship? Who excels her in discipline, in
> the honest withholding of praise, or in its just bestowal? She is
> the inheritor of a more ancient excellence than ours, and among
> Americans she has become a sort of contemporary ancestor, a
> summation of the best that has gone before....[20]

Few American writers received, or deserved, this kind of encomium.

The pattern was set, by her talent and by her sense of duty. She was
compelled to live with her older sister and with her half-paralyzed brother,
in modest circumstances, without domestic help.[21] They took their meals
in a small residential hotel in the neighborhood, including breakfast: perhaps the most depressing of their meals, as the three of them sat hardly
saying a word. Wilde, whose work she admired, said that he put all his art
into his life. Agnes Repplier, whose wit and learning and whose appreciation for the finer things in life were comparable to Wilde's, subordinated
her life to her art. Returning from those silent breakfasts through the dreary
emptiness of city streets (the streets of American cities do not shine in the
morning), she would hasten toward her room. When she was younger she
took refuge in books. Now she would escape to her work. Her cat would
perch on the chair, or on the far edge of her writing table. She would take
up her pen; and in her large, curious, stilted handwriting the words were
beginning to form.[22]

She kept up her work for sixty-five years: more than two dozen books,
perhaps as many as four hundred essays. The books are now difficult to
find, not very attractive in their looks: dun little Quakerish books in gray
covers.[23] (A handsome exception is *Eight Decades,* printed in 1937, her own
selection of her best, and probably the best introduction to her prose.)

She was a superb craftsman. "Every misused word," she wrote, "revenges
itself forever upon a writer's reputation."[24] She knew the value of words:
"For every sentence that may be penned or spoken the right words exist."[25]
She rose above the not inconsiderable accomplishments of a linguistic pre-
cisionist; she was sufficiently strong-minded to improve upon Shelley. ("For
the mind in creation is as a fading coal, which some invisible influence, like
an inconstant wind, awakens to transitory brightness.") Agnes Repplier: "The
substitution of the word 'glow' for 'brightness' would, I think, make this
sentence extremely beautiful."[26]

Words are not mere instruments of precision. They ought to convey
delight. "'The race of delight is short, and pleasures have mutable faces.'
Such sentences, woven with curious skill from the rich fabric of seven-

teenth-century English, defy the wreckage of time."[27] The history of mankind is the history of mind; and the history of mind is the history of speech: "How is it that, while Dr. Johnson's sledge-hammer repartees sound like the sonorous echoes of a past age, Voltaire's remarks always appear to have been spoken the day before yesterday?"[28] She was one of those writers who have a special affinity for the mysterious evocative power of names: "It took a great genius to enliven the hideous picture of Dotheboys Hall with the appropriate and immortal Fanny, whom we could never have borne to lose. It took a great genius to evolve from nothingness the name 'Morleena Kenwigs.' So perfect a result, achieved from a mere combination of letters, confers distinction on the English alphabet."[29]

Her own descriptions were no mere combinations of adjectives. Besides her *mots justes* there was, often unexpected, evidence of her own preferences. She was Catholic; she loved Spain; but she was no Hispanomaniac. Here is a great phrase: "The Escorial," she writes, "is Philip, it is stamped with his somber, repellent, kingly personality."[30] Three perfect words: compressed and jeweled expressions of a lifetime of historical thinking.

She read everything; indeed, what she reread would be sufficient unto a department of English in our colleges now.[31] One of the most attractive features of her writing is its unpredictability: neither frivolous nor impulsive, it sprang from the independence of her spacious mind. Of the fifty years in English letters that preceded the death of Byron she knew just about everything that is worth knowing. She sometimes regretted that she had not lived during that "happy half-century"[32] of "sunlit mediocrity"; yet writing about it, she remained as clear-eyed as ever: she took great pleasure in pointing a descriptive, a definite finger on the inane writings and opinions of that period—indeed, of any period.[33] Accepted opinions! *Idées reçues!* They got what they deserved: an impatient but precise sweep of her verbal broom, leaving an elegant pattern on the museum floor, with an upward swirl in accord with the very tone of English speech. In a private letter about Alma-Tadema, whom she met in London: "a kind, self-satisfied man, who told venerable stories all wrong."[34] When in Boston James Russell Lowell descended from upstairs to take her coat, the ladies oohed and aahed. She did not. Why, oh why, Lowell asked her, did people in Philadelphia call Whitman the good gray poet. "I dare say," the great Boston panjandrum growled, "nobody calls me the good, gray poet, though I am as gray as Whitman and quite as good—perhaps a trifle better." "He paused," Agnes adds to a friend, "and I was on the point of saying, 'Then there is only the poet to consider,' but I forbore."[35] Yet she was not an indiscriminate admirer of Whitman: "The medium employed by Walt Whitman, at times rhythmic and cadenced, at times ungirt and sagging loosely, enabled him to write passages of sustained beauty, passages grandly conceived and felicitously rendered. It also permitted him a riotous and somewhat monotonous excess."[36] A bearded sage whom she profoundly disliked was Tolstoy, who, perhaps "with the noblest intentions, made many a light step heavy, and many a gay heart sad." She greatly preferred Wilde, at a time when such preference was not fashionable, especially in America. About Lytton Strachey's principal shortcoming she was unerring: "the amazing and unconcerned inaccuracies of the modern biographer" (and perhaps about Virginia Woolf, too: "thin" and "self-conscious").[37]

She was Catholic: in England she found Canterbury Cathedral "an empty shell inside. The shrine of the Saint has vanished, and his very bones were burned by that brute, Henry VIII. A chattering verger leads scores of scattering tourists over the level marble floor, once the holiest spot in England."[38] Yet she had none of the sentimentalities of the Chesterbelloc type: when she spent a Holy Week in Rome, "the processions were scrubby little affairs."[39]

She saw it her duty to point out the shortcomings of popular idols as well as of popular ideas. "The fact that Miss [Helen] Keller has overcome the heavy disabilities which nature placed in her path, lends interest to her person, but no weight to her opinions, which give evidence of having been adopted wholesale, and of having never filtered through any reasoning process of her own."[40] She saw through the superficialities of Victorian as well as of post-Victorian sentimentalities. "When we permit ourselves to sneer at Victorian hypocrisies," she wrote, "we allude, as a rule, to the superficial observance of religious practices, and to the artificial reticence concerning illicit sexual relations. The former affected life more than it did literature; the latter affected literature more than it did life."[41] She admired Thackeray: "The world is not nearly so simple a place as the sexualists seem to consider it. To the author of *Vanity Fair* it was not simple at all." Yet her ire rose when "Trollope unhesitatingly and proudly claimed for himself the quality of harmlessness. 'I do believe,' he said, 'that no girl has risen from the reading of my pages less modest than she was before, and that some girls may have learned from that that modesty is a charm worth possessing.'"

"This," Agnes adds, "is one of the admirable sentiments which should have been left unspoken. It is a true word as far as it goes, but more suggestive of *Little Women*, or *A Summer in Leslie Goldthwaite's Life*, than of those virile, varied, and animated novels which make no appeal to immaturity."[42] She had a great admiration for male virtues, including martial ones; she took a romantic delight in beholding certain warriors. She quoted Ruskin: "All healthy men like fighting and like the sense of danger; all brave women like to hear of their fighting and of their facing danger": *but* then she flew at

Ruskin, "who has taken upon himself the defense of war in his own irresist-ibly unconvincing manner."[43] She spared not Carlyle, "whose misdeeds, like those of Browning, are matters of pure volition," and who is "pleased, for our sharper discipline, to write 'like a comet inscribing with his tail.' No man uses words more admirably, or abuses them more shamefully, than Carlyle."[44] Like Carlyle, Meredith could be tiresome. When "he is pleased to tell us that one of his characters 'neighed a laugh,' that another 'tolled her naughty head,' that a third 'stamped: her aspect spat,' and that a fourth was discovered 'pluming a smile upon his succulent mouth,' we cannot smother a dawning suspicion that he is diverting himself at our expense, and plum-ing a smile of his own, more sapless than succulent, over the naïve simplic-ity of the public."[45] Her admirations were never undiscriminating: Sir Walter Scott "always shook hands with his young couples on their wedding-day, and left them to pull through as best they could. Their courtships and their marriages interested him less than other things he wanted to write about—sieges and tournaments, criminal trials, and sour Scottish saints."

The sour Scottish saints of Scott!

"When we read, for instance, of Lady Cathcart being kept a close pris-oner by her husband for over twenty years, we look with some compla-cency on the roving wives of the nineteenth century. When we reflect on the dismal fate of Uriel Freudenberger, condemned by the Canton of Uri to be burnt alive in 1760, for rashly proclaiming his disbelief in the legend of William Tell's apple, we realize the inconveniences attendant on a too early development of the critical faculty." This kind of wit, taken from the first paragraph of her first book, was her hallmark: polished and dry, it has none of the upstaging one-liner characteristics of much of American hu-mor. How many pearly sentences rolled off her pen, to vanish unremarked! They were too fine for many of her readers, as was often the wittiness of her conversation. In Philadelphia, perhaps especially among her fellow Catholics, she suffered often from the reputation of being a "cynic," from the age-old habit of people finding themselves ill at ease in the presence of unaccustomed opinions, dubbing them "cynical" even when, in reality, the speaker is far more of an idealist than are her unwitting listeners. "We can with tranquility forgive in ourselves the sins of which no one accuses us," she once wrote.[46] This is emphatically not the voice of a cynic—rather the contrary.

"Wit," she said, "is the salt of conversation, not the food, and few things in the world are more wearying than a sarcastic attitude towards life."[47] A man should live within his wits as well as within his income: she liked this Chesterfieldian maxim. Her wit was never forced. Since it came to her naturally, it had none of the marks of effect-writing, none of the absurd, surrealistic, oxymoronic verbal juxtapositions so typical of present-day American humor. Her wit was all intertwined with her learning. Madame de Montolieu was a, now justly forgotten, French sentimentalist novel writer, the author of *Caroline de Litchfield*. Her equally witless English admirer, a Miss Seward, wrote that "the merits of graces" of Madame de Montolieu's volumes were due to their author's "transition from incompetence to the comforts of wealth; from the unprotected dependence of waning virginity to the social pleasures of wedded friendship." "In plain words," Agnes Repplier adds:

> we are given to understand that a rich and elderly German wid-
> ower read the book, sought an acquaintance with the writer,
> and married her. "Hymen," exclaims Miss Seward, "passed by
> the fane of Cytherea and the shrine of Plutus, to light his torch
> at the altar of genius"—which beautiful burst of eloquence makes
> it painful to add the chilling truth, and say that *Caroline de
> Litchfield* was written six years after its author's marriage with
> M. de Montolieu, who was a Swiss, and her second husband.
> She espoused the first, M. de Crousaz, when she was eighteen,
> and still comfortably remote from the terrors of waning virgin-
> ity. Accurate information was not, however, a distinguishing char-
> acteristic of the day. Sir Walter Scott, writing some years later
> of Madame de Montolieu, ignores both marriages altogether,
> and calls her Mademoiselle.[48]

She carried her learning as lightly as her wit. "Erudition," she said, "like a bloodhound, is a charming thing when held firmly in leash, but it is not so attractive when turned loose upon a defenseless and unerudite public."[49] What she (like Wilde) held principally against the Victorians was their dead-ening seriousness. She asked herself, in 1890, "whether the dismal serious-ness of the present day was going to last forever."[50] "Humor would at all times have been the poorest excuse to offer to Miss Brontë for any form of moral dereliction, for it was the one quality she lacked herself, and failed to tolerate in others."[51] She could not stomach the Brownings. "It is hard to tell what people really prize. Heine begged for a button from George Sand's trousers, and who shall say whether enthusiasm or malice prompted the request."[52] She admired the essentially aristocratic virtue of gaiety: "Cheer-fulness and melancholy can be, and usually are, equally odious; but a sad heart and a gay temper hold us in thrall."[53] She could achieve a felicitous alliance of common sense with wit: "Poetry weds King Cophetua to a beg-gar maid, and smilingly retires from any further contemplation of the catastrophe."[54] She once "saw a small black-and-white kitten playing with a judge who, not unnaturally, conceived that he was playing with the kitten."[55]

Humor is a mark of maturity: it "is seldom, to the childish mind, a desirable element of poetry."[56] In national life it "illuminates those crowded corners which history leaves obscure."[57] This view of humor accorded entirely with her *persona,* and with her style of expression. She was a prose writer, steeped in the French tradition of letters, and thoroughly urban.

She was urban, urbane, cosmopolitan in the literal sense of these words. Philadelphia was not much like Dr. Johnson's London; but, like Dr. Johnson—and probably even more like all true Parisians of her own time—she found little of life that was worth living outside a city. In one of her acutest essays, "Town and Suburb," written during the 1920s, she saw clearly what the abandonment of the city meant: the abandonment of civilizational, even more than civic, responsibilities by the very class of citizens upon whose support, and cultivation, urbane life in America had to depend. "Suburbanites are traitors to the city." As in many of her essays, sixty years of distance has not dimmed the acuity of her insights, often prophetic ones. "The present quarrel is not even between Nature and man, between the town and the country. It is between the town and the suburb, that midway habitation which fringes every American city, and which is imposing or squalid according to the incomes of the suburbanites."[58] Much of this was the result of the adolescent national mania for automobiles, and of their sanctimonious spokesman, Henry Ford, for example, whom she could never stand and who has "added the trying role of prophet to his other avocations." Her preferences for city life were not merely those of practical convenience, and she had little time for the pious preachings of nature lovers: "... it is hardly worth while to speak of city life as entailing 'spiritual loss,' because it is out of touch with Nature.[59] It is in touch with humanity, and humanity is Nature's heaviest asset."[60] She cited Santayana, her favorite American philosopher, who also prized "civilization, being bred in towns, and liking to hear and see what new things people are up to."[61]

Her independence of mind, her love of conversation, were as French as they were English. ("It is not what we learn in conversation that enriches us. It is the elation that comes of swift contact with tingling currents of thought. It is the opening of our mental pores, and the stimulus of marshaling our ideas in words, of setting them forth as gallantly and as graciously as we can.")[62] Yet the often endless volubility of Parisian talk was not for her; her love for the English temper of speech defined her prosody as well as her rhetoric: "If everybody floated with the tide of talk, placidity would soon end in stagnation. It is the strong backward stroke which stirs the ripples, and gives animation and variety."[63] She minded not a certain kind of restraint: "a habit of sparing speech, not the muffled stillness of genuine and hopeless incapacity."[64] When Henry James came to Philadelphia in 1904, Agnes Repplier was asked to introduce him. The lecture was a muffled disaster, James mumbling for an hour and shuffling his papers. The introduction was a small triumph: perfectly minted, witty, engaging, modest, and short.[65]

Delighted as she was with the music of words, immense as was her mnemonic genius for verse, she was essentially a prose writer. Her one collection of verse, including her introduction to it,[66] belongs to that very small minority of her writings that has a musty and dated touch, and which is rather late-Victorian in its limitations. Her inclination for the fine-turned phrase was at least as French as it was English; she liked paradox, and expression that was elegant and sharp, rather than blunt or muted by suggestiveness. "When Voltaire sighed, 'Nothing is so disagreeable as to be obscurely hanged,' he gave utterance to a national sentiment, which is not in the least witty, but profoundly humorous, revealing with charming distinctness a Frenchman's innate aversion to all dull and commonplace surroundings."[67] "It is bad enough to be bad, but to be bad in bad taste is unpardonable."[68] She preferred the qualities of French lyric expression: "The delicacy of the sentiment is unmatched in English song. The Saxon can be profoundly sad, and he can—or at least he could—be ringingly and recklessly gay; but the mood which is neither sad nor gay, which is fed by refined emotions, and tranquilized by time's subduing touch, has been expressed oftener and better in France."[69]

She was a *moraliste* in the French tradition—something different from what "moralist" in English means. She liked Sainte-Beuve ("I always tremble when I see a philosophical idea attached to a novel"); and Sainte-Beuve "was spared by the kindly hand of death from the sight of countless novels attached to philosophical ideas."[70] Philosophical ideas were one thing, the need for discrimination quite another. "There is no measure to the credulity of the average semi-educated man when confronted by a printed page (print carries such authority in his eyes), and with rows of figures, all showing conclusively that two and two make three, and that with economy and good management they can be reduced to one and a half. He has never mastered, and apparently will never master, the exact shade of difference between a statement and a fact."[71] Sentimentalist nonsense, whether in literature or in education, made her angry. "The assumption that children should never be coerced into self-control, and never confronted with difficulties, makes for failure of nerve. . . . The assumption that young people should never be burdened with responsibilities, and never, under any stress of circumstances, be deprived of the pleasures which are no longer a privilege, but their sacred and inalienable right, makes for failure of nerve. The assumption that married women are justified in abandoning their domestic duties, because they cannot stand the strain of home life and housekeeping, makes for failure of nerve. . . . The assumption that religion should content itself with persuasiveness, and that morality should be sparing in its demands, makes for failure of nerve."[72]

She was intellectual; but she knew the limitations of the intellect. "The clear-sighted do not rule the world, but they sustain and console it. It is not in human nature to be led by intelligence. An intelligent world would not be what it is today: it would never have been what it has been in every epoch of which we have any knowledge."[73] She—a rarity among women writers, this—had a very strong, a deep knowledge of history. Her *Philadelphia: The Place and the People* (which she wrote in 1898 upon a publisher's suggestion) remains to this day the most readable history of her native city. Her often superbly detached and witty style of writing; her strong, and instinctively intelligent, judgments are complemented by her talented evocation of atmosphere, and by her interest in all kinds of details of social and of everyday life: the *petits faits* dear to Taine and to some of the best historians of the twentieth century. (In this respect, too, Agnes Repplier proved herself to be a "threshold" writer: standing firm on what was best in the standards of the nineteenth as well as of the twentieth century.) The book suffers from a certain lack of proportion: three-fourths of it deals with the eighteenth century, and hardly more than one-eighth of it with the nineteenth; she may have become somewhat bored with her task, even though the writing of the last chapters surely matches that of the earlier ones.[74] Agnes Repplier belonged to the tradition that considered history to be the narrated past, a form of high literature, and her histories are none the worse for it, to say the least; but she understood history well enough to know in her bones that history was more than that, too: not only a form of literature, but also a form of thought.

> The mediæval chroniclers listened rapturously to the clamor of battle, and found all else but war too trivial for their pens. The modern scholar produces that pitiless array of facts known as constitutional history; and labors under the strange delusion that acts of Parliament, or acts of Congress, reform bills, and political pamphlets represent his country's life. If this sordid devotion to the concrete suffers no abatement, the intelligent reader of the future will be compelled to reconstruct the nineteenth century from the pages of *Punch* and *Life*, from faded playbills,

the records of the race-track, and the inextinguishable echo of
dead laughter.[75]

She wrote this in 1893. Eighty-seven years later this historian, after a
lifetime of studying the character of modern history and the requisites of
modern history writing, can but lift his imaginary plumed hat and shout:
"Brava!"

"The neglect of history," she wrote more than sixty years ago, "prac-
tised by educators who would escape its authority, stands responsible for
much mental confusion." "I used to think that ignorance of history meant
only a lack of cultivation and a loss of pleasure. Now I am sure that such
ignorance impairs our judgment by impairing our understanding, by depriving us of standards, or the power to contrast, and the right to estimate."[76]
"In the remote years of my childhood," she wrote, "the current events, that
most interesting and valuable form of tuition which, nevertheless, is unintelligible without some knowledge of the past, was left out of our limited
curriculum. We seldom read the newspapers (which I remember as of an
appalling dullness), and we knew little of what was happening in our day.
But we did study history, and we knew something of what had happened in
other days than ours; we knew and deeply cared."[77]

History is the best fare for one's imagination; it also provides for a
thoughtful conservatism whose absence, especially in America, she regretted.[78] "Political conservatism may be a lost cause in modern democracy;
but temperamental conservatism dates from the birth of man's reasoning
powers, and will survive the clamour and chaos of revolutions."[79] For "in-
novations to which we are not committed are illuminating things."[80] "The
reformer whose heart is in the right place, but whose head is elsewhere,
represents a waste of force...."[81] "It is well that the past yields some solace
to the temperamental conservative, for the present is his only on terms he
cannot easily fulfill. His reasonable doubts and his unreasonable prejudices block the path of contentment. He is powerless to believe a thing
because it is an eminently desirable thing to believe. He is powerless to
deny the existence of facts he does not like. He is powerless to credit new
systems with finality. The sanguine assurance that men and nations can be
legislated into goodness, that pressure from without is equivalent to a moral
change within, needs a strong backing of inexperience. 'The will,' says
Francis Thompson, 'is the lynch-pin of the faculties.' We stand or fall by its
strength or its infirmity."[82]

To cheat ourselves intellectually that we may save ourselves
spiritually is unworthy of the creature that man is meant to be.

And to what end! Things are as they are, and no amount of self-deception makes them otherwise. The friend who is incapable of depression depresses us as surely as the friend who is incapable of boredom bores us. Somewhere in our hearts is a strong, though dimly understood, desire to face realities, and to measure consequences, to have done with the fatigue of pretending. It is not optimism to enjoy the view when one is treed by a bull; it is philosophy. The optimist would say that being treed was a valuable experience. The disciple of gladness would say that it was a pleasurable sensation. The Christian Scientist would say there was no bull, though remaining—if he were wise—on the treetop. The philosopher would make the best of a bad job, and seek what compensation he could find. He is of a class apart.[83]

"Human experience," she wrote during the First World War, "is very, very old. It is our sure monitor, our safest guide. To ignore it crudely is the error of those ardent but uninstructed missionaries who have lightly undertaken the re-building of the social world."[84] She belonged to the rare company of realistic idealists, whose knowledge of history and whose self-knowledge go hand in hand—which provided her with the necessary balance in perceiving, and describing, people and places and scenes to which she would be otherwise sentimentally inclined. "Touraine," she once wrote, "is full of beauty, and steeped to the lips in historic crimes."[85] This kind of demanding realism was part of her religion: "It was Cardinal Newman who first entered a protest against 'minced' saints, against the pious and popular custom of chopping up human records into lessons for the devout. He took exception to the hagiological license which assigns lofty motives to trivial actions."[86]

She was a *moraliste*, not a Puritan. She believed in the virtues of cultivating human self-discipline; but also in the virtue of cultivating human pleasure. In 1890 she wrote: "Why should the word 'pleasure,' when used in connection with literature, send a cold chill down our strenuous nineteenth century spines? It is a good and charming word, caressing in sound and softly exhilarating in sense."[87] Also: "Joy is a delightful, flashing little word, as brief as is the emotion it conveys."[88] And about an emotion: ". . . when a happy moment, complete and rounded as a pearl, falls into the tossing ocean of life, it is never wholly lost."[89] Her taste for pleasure was as fine as it was strong. In her essay on Horace, she wrote, about his retreat in the country, that it was "what was then called the simple life; but, as compared with the crude and elemental thing which goes by that name in this our land today, it is recognizable as the austere luxury of a very cultivated poet."[90] She generally despised preaching, especially Puritan preaching. "'Christ died for a select company that was known to Him, by name, from eternity,' wrote the Reverend Samuel Willard, pastor of the South Church, Boston, and author of that famous theological folio, *A Compleat Body of Divinity*. 'The bulk of mankind is reserved for burning,' said Jonathan Edwards genially; and his Northampton congregation took his word for it. That these gentlemen knew not more about Hell and its inmates than did Dante is a circumstance which does not seem to have occurred to anyone. A preacher has some advantage over a poet."[91] And here is a prize:

> Agnes Edwards, in an engaging little volume on Cape Cod, quotes a clause from the will of John Bacon of Barnstable, who bequeathed to his wife for her lifetime the "use and improvement" of a slavewoman, Dinah. "If, at the death of my wife, Dinah be still living, I desire my executors to sell her, and to use and improve the money for which she is sold in the purchase of Bibles, and distribute them equally among my said wife's and my grandchildren."
>
> There are fashions in goodness and badness as in all things else; but the selling of worn-out women for Bibles goes a step beyond Mrs. Stowe's most vivid imaginings.[92]

She did not like Mrs. Stowe.[93] She cared little for Bostonians, including Emerson:[94] "Unlike Emerson, we are glad to be amused, only the task of amusing us grows harder day by day."[95] Her "amusing" was a rapier word with double edges: "It is amusing to hear Bishop Copleston, writing for that young and vivacious generation who knew not the seriousness of life, remind them pointedly that 'the task of pleasing is at all times easier than that of instructing.' It is delightful to think that there ever was a period when people preferred to be pleased rather than instructed."[96]

"Any book which serves to lower the sum of human gaiety is a moral delinquent" (proof that she could be flippant when she wanted to be).[97] She could be as impatient with the cant of the modern critic as with that of the ancient Puritan preacher:

> It is the most significant token of our ever-increasing "sense of moral responsibility in literature" that we should be always trying to graft our own conscientious purposes upon those authors who, happily for themselves, lived and died before virtue, colliding desperately with cakes and ale, had imposed such de-

pressing obligations.

"*Don Quixote*," says Mr. Shorthouse with unctuous gravity, "will come in time to be recognized as one of the saddest books ever written"; and if the critics keep on expounding it much longer, I truly fear it will.[98]

She herself counted the "obnoxious word 'ethics' six times repeated in the opening paragraph of one review, and have felt too deeply disheartened by such an outset to penetrate any further."[99] Her strong heart as well as her appetite found the vague and bland white sauce of ethical culture repellent. "There is," she wrote, "nothing new about the Seven Deadly Sins. They are as old as humanity. There is nothing mysterious about them. They are easier to understand than the Cardinal Virtues."[100]

She had a compound attitude toward Quakers. She had a genuine feeling for their humaneness. Unlike most people—unlike, alas, many Philadelphians—she much preferred the melancholy Penn over the ambitious Franklin.[101] She had a good deal of respect for "that old-time Quakerism, gentle, silent, tenacious, inflexible, which is now little more than a tradition in the land, yet which has left its impress forever upon the city it founded and sustained."[102] Yet the unimaginative tightness of the Quaker mind grated on her nerves. She admired Elizabeth Drinker for her singularly detailed and disciplined diary of Philadelphia during the Revolution; but she was exasperated with her self-imposed limitations, with that whalebone corseting of a soul. "The most striking characteristic of our Quaker diarist is precisely this clear, cold, unbiased judgment, this sanity of a well-ordered mind. What she lacks, what the journal lacks from beginning to end, is some touch of human and ill-repressed emotion, some word of pleasant folly, some weakness left undisguised and unrepented. The attitude maintained throughout is too judicial, the repose of heart and soul too absolute to be endearing. . . ."[103] Because Agnes Repplier could not stomach Puritans, she stood for tolerance; because she was not a Quaker, tolerance could also leave her cold. "The languid indifference . . . which we dignify by the name of tolerance, has curtailed our interest in life."[104] (She would have agreed with her contemporary compatriot and potential confrère, the Philadelphia literary gentleman Logan Pearsall Smith, who fled to England from the bosom of Quakerdom: "Only among people who think no evil can Evil monstrously flourish.") "There are always men and women," she wrote, "who prefer the triumph of evil, which is a thing they can forget, to prolonged resistance, which shatters their nerves. But the desire to escape an obligation, while very human, is not generally thought to be humanity's noblest lesson."[105] She was not an abstract moralist; she had, as we have seen, a stern sense of duty. She was impatient with stupidity—and impatience has not been a Quaker or Philadelphia habit. "Sonorous phrases like 'reconstruction of the world's psychology,' and 'creation of a new world atmosphere,' are mental sedatives, drug words, calculated to put to sleep any uneasy apprehensions. They may mean anything, and they do mean nothing, so that it is safe to go on repeating them."[106] "The combination of a sad heart and a gay temper, which is the most charming and the most lovable thing the world has got to show"; this was emphatically not a Quaker combination.[107]

Her mind, in many ways, represented the best of combinations: she was a realistic idealist and a tough-minded romantic. I wrote before that she *chose* to regard her childhood as not particularly unhappy: a choice which was conscious, not a subconscious one, for which all Freudian terms such as "sublimation" or "repression" would be woefully insufficient. She, who had no children, thought and knew a good deal about the trials and tribulations of childhood, and she wrote some of her finest essays about children's minds. She detested people who wrote books such as the one "with the somewhat ominous title *Children's Rights*."[108] She understood, because she loved, the imagination of children (". . . no child can successfully 'make believe,' when he is encumbered on every side by mechanical toys so odiously complete that they leave nothing for the imagination to supply").[109] Because she was not a sentimentalist, she understood how very complex the minds of children (not at all little adults, as Americans are wont to believe, and to treat them) are:

> The merriment of children, of little girls especially, is often unreal and affected. They will toss their heads and stimulate one another to peals of laughter which are a pure make-believe. When they are really absorbed in their play, and astir with delicious excitation, they do not laugh; they give vent to piercing shrieks which sound as if they were being cut in little pieces. These shrieks are the spontaneous expressions of delight; but their sense of absurdity, which implies a sense of humor, is hard to capture before it has become tainted with pretense.[110]

A passage worth an entire library confected by child psychologists.

It was a kind of participant knowledge: neither objective, nor subjective, but personal. So was her understanding of the psychology of nations. "National traits," she wrote, "are, as a matter of fact, as enduring as the mountaintops. They survive all change of policies, all shifting of boundary lines, all expansion and contraction of dominion."[111] She understood how the struggles of nations are more important and decisive matters than are the struggles of classes; that the sympathies and the antipathies which the images of certain nations inspire are deep-seated and weighty matters, more profound than the superficial and current categories of "international relations." She understood that Anglophilia and Francophilia and Germanophilia were not merely the results of ethnic or ancestral memories; that they were more than political preferences. They were cultural preferences, representing certain inclinations of spirit and mind. On the highest level of her own cultural preferences Agnes Repplier aspired to those peaks of sensitivity which were unique for that Anglo-French civilization that, around 1900, may have marked the pinnacle of the Bourgeois Age.

The *entente cordiale* between these two great Western European nations existed in her mind decades before their alliance became a reality on the battlefield, and well before it had become a reality in the form of a treaty. This was no coincidence. She, who was not particularly interested in politics, sensed that Germany represented a danger, not only to the British and the French, but to the kind of civilization she cherished. This is why her impatient and, on occasion, insistent, admonitory writings during the First World War should not be considered as if they were odd political excursions during her literary career, which is what some of her critics took them to be. She was convinced that a victory of Germany over France and Britain would be a disaster to the entirety of Western civilization, and she was bitterly impatient with the majority of her countrymen who were unwilling to face this condition, comforting themselves instead with pious sentiments.

How she loved England! "I, without one drop of English, Scotch, Welsh, or Irish blood in my veins, have come into the matchless inheritance of the English tongue and of English letters, which have made the happiness of my life."[112] She had no sympathy with the frequently narrow Anglophobia of Irish Catholics in the United States;[113] she had even less sympathy with the kind of redskin American nationalism which, wishing to fill the Indian land, preferred to turn its broad back on the English heritage. But she met with the same cold and shrouded obstacles with which so many lovers of England had had their chilly encounters: the English were diffident, with gray ice over their faces.[114] She wrote a beautiful essay about the relationship of England and America, "The Estranging Sea." She, who understood the English so well, felt their unwillingness to respond, to the marrow of her bones. It was an unrequited love.

She was sixty years old when, in 1915, she asked her friend Dr. White to take her to France to serve in the American Ambulance Hospital.[115] (He, wisely enough, refused.) She hated the sanctimonious William Jennings

Bryan ("a past master of infelicitous argument, and very ugly to boot"). She did not like Germans, and she would have agreed with the wag who said that Wagner's music was better than it sounds; she did not like their heaviness;[116] she did not like Schopenhauer, "the great apostle of pessimism" who made "so much headway in reducing sadness to a science." She could be critical of the faults of the French, and especially of their talent for egocentricity: "When Voltaire sneered at the *Inferno*, and thought *Hamlet* the work of a drunken savage, he at least made a bid for the approbation of his countrymen, who, as Schlegel wittily observes, were in the habit of speaking as though Louis XIV had put an end to cannibalism in Europe."[117] Her initial sympathies were monarchical and aristocratic and romantic: when she first visited Paris she kissed the tattered cassock of Archbishop Darboy (murdered during the Commune in 1871) "when no one was looking. Republican France held no place in her heart."[118] She changed her mind about this; she rallied to the cause of the French Republic before, during, and after the First World War.[119]

During the war she would write scathingly about suffragettes and pacifists.[120] "The Honourable Bertrand Russell," she wrote, "whose annoyance at England's going to war deepened into resentment at her winning it (a consummation which, to speak the truth, he did his best to avert). . . ."[121] She read in the newspapers about a high-flown American project: a "World Conference for Promoting Concord between All Divisions of Mankind," "a title," she added, "that leaves nothing, save grammar, to be desired."[122] After the war she went to a Philadelphia dinner party with her friends the Pennells. Joseph Pennell was unkempt and boisterous, wishing to shake the Philadelphia bourgeois.[123] "Mark my words!" he roared across the table. "You'll all live to see the day when the German Army and the British Army march arm in arm down Chestnut Street!"

> An impressive silence followed this astounding declaration. Then, leaning forward ever so slightly in her place, Agnes Repplier spoke up in a voice that was deadly calm. "Oh, dear Mr. Pennell," she said slowly and distinctly, "do have them come down Pine Street. Nothing ever happens on Pine Street."[124]

She believed in the uniqueness of Western civilization. She was neither an American isolationist nor a Pan-Americanist: "friendship and alliance with those European states whose aspirations and ideals respond to our own aspirations and ideals, are as consistent with Americanism as are friendship and alliance with the states of South America, which we are now engaged in loving. It is not from Bolivia, or Chile, or Venezuela, or the Argentine that we have drawn our best traditions, our law, language, literature, and art."[125] "You cannot make the word 'freedom' sound in untutored ears as it sounds in the ears of men who have counted the cost by which it has been preserved through the centuries."[126] She was the finest of Americans. Her mind was cosmopolitan in its scope, she was a devoted Anglophile and Francophile; yet she had nothing in common with her contemporary American exiles, whether of the rarefied or of the merely spoiled kind. She knew more about France and the French than a whole slew of American expatriates; yet she would not have retired to a salon-equipped château even if she had all the money in the world. She was more like Willa Cather than she was like Edith Wharton, even as she was unlike any of her contemporaries. She saw in the United States the potentiality for what was best in the world: not the last best hope of mankind, not the seat of world government, but something somberer and greater: the representative and the repository of the heritage of Western civilization.

Therefore, with all the refined qualities of her mind, she detested and feared American vulgarity less than she detested and feared American sentimentalism (she would have agreed with Wilde, who said that sentimentality was the Bank Holiday of cynicism), beneath the superficialities of which she would instantly detect the deeper element of a corruption of purpose:

> We are rising dizzily and fearlessly on the crest of a great wave of sentiment. When the wave breaks, we may find ourselves submerged, and in danger of drowning; but for the present we are full of hope and high resolve. Forty years ago we stood in shallow water, and mocked at the mid-Victorian sentiment, then ebbing slowly with the tide. We have nothing now in common with that fine, thin, tenacious conception of life and its responsibilities. . . . A vague humanity is our theme. . . .[127]

So she wrote in 1915. "Americans returning from war-stricken Europe in the autumn of 1914 spoke unctuously of their country as 'God's own land,' by which they meant a land where their luggage was unmolested."[128] She, who habitually kept her ironic talent in restraint, let out the reins when it came to evidence of American self-satisfaction. An American critic, a Mr. Haweis, "guided by that dangerous instinct which drives us to unwarranted comparisons,"

> does not hesitate to link the fame of Knickerbocker's *New York* with the fame of *Gulliver's Travels*, greatly to the disadvantage of

the latter. "Irving," he gravely declares, "has all the satire of Swift, without his sour coarseness." It would be as reasonable to say, "Apollinaris has all the vivacity of brandy, without its corrosive insalubrity."[129]

"That failure in good sense which comes from too warm a self-satisfaction" raised her ire even at the age of eighty-one, when she recalled the national temper around 1900:

> Those were good days in which to live. Our skirmish with Spain was over, and we talked about it and wrote about it in terms that would have befitted Marathon. Mr. Hennessy is as enthusiastic about our "histing the flag over the Ph'lippeens" as if he had not just found out that they were islands, and not, as he had previously supposed, canned goods. A sense of well-being permeates Mr. Dooley's pages. The White House cat is named "Gold Bonds"; mortgages spell security; the price of whisky, "fifteen cents a slug," remains immovable in days of peace and war; the "almighty dollar" has the superb impregnability that once attached itself to Roman citizenship; and devout men breathe a prayer that Providence may remain under the protection of the American flag.[130]

She read a letter from Walter Hines Page, printed after the First World War: "In all the humanities, we are a thousand years ahead of any people here. . . . God has as yet made nothing or nobody equal to the American people; and I don't think He ever will or can." "Which is a trifle fettering to omnipotence," she would add.[131]

She was over seventy when she wrote that "like the little girl who was so good that she knew how good she was, we are too well-informed not to be aware of our preeminence in this field." In the spring of 1925 the American Ambassador to the Court of St. James's delivered himself of a speech before the Pilgrims' Dinner in London. "In it he defined with great precision the attitude of the United States toward her former allies. His remarks, as reported, read like a sermon preached in a reformatory."[132] Her fine indignation carried over into the twenties, and beyond. Her preferences became slightly more conservative;[133] she was concerned with the ultimate effects of admitting an unlimited number and variety of immigrants to the United States, and wrote sharply about this. Yet she kept her irascibility at the American trait of self-congratulation burning with a glow. "It is a bearable misfortune to be called un-American, because the phrase still waits analy-

sis," she wrote in 1924.[134] In 1927 she spoke about "Success and Ideals."
"Every message, every address, every editorial, every sermon had faithfully echoed this chant of triumph over the unparalleled prosperity of 1926
and the magnificent prospects of 1927. We are the super-state and we have
been assiduously taught that, to be good and happy and prosperous, is to
fulfill the designs of a singularly partial Providence."[135] "It is not efficiency
but a well-balanced emotional life which creates an enjoyable world." And
the American "lacked the moral and intellectual humility, which would
bring him an understanding of tragedies in which he has no share and su-
premacies in which he sees no significance."[136] Here is Agnes Repplier, the
so-called conservative period piece, writing in the twenties. Walter
Lippmann and the American liberal and intellectual consensus would agree
to all the above. She would, however, lash out at silliness from every quarter, no matter how intellectually fashionable or timely. In 1931, the *New
Republic* "says that the United States is a belligerent country. Assuredly not!
Bullying, perhaps, but not belligerent."[137] One source of her best qualities
was her instant contempt for any kind of intellectual opportunism. "The
man who never tells an unpalatable truth 'at the wrong time' (the right
time has yet to be discovered) is the man whose success in life is fairly well
assured,"[138] Agnes Repplier wrote in 1924 a sentence that alone is worth
the contents of an, as yet unwritten, volume on the vice of the twentieth
century, which is intellectual opportunism.

"Stupidity," she wrote wisely, "is not the prerogative of any one class or
creed."[139] She knew that most stupidity is not the result of neuro-cerebral
incompetence but that it is self-induced and willful.[140] "What the world
asks now are state reforms and social reforms—in other words, the reformation of our neighbors. What the Gospel asks, and has always asked, is
the reformation of ourselves—a harassing and importunate demand."[141]
Democracy "is not the final word of progress.... Democracy is rational but
not luminous."[142]

She preferred Theodore Roosevelt to Wilson:

> Nothing is easier than to make the world safe for democracy.
> Democracy is playing her own hand in the game. She has every
> intention and every opportunity to make the world safe for her-
> self. But democracy may be divorced from freedom, and free-
> dom is the breath of man's nostrils, the strength of his sinews,
> the sanction of his soul. It is as painful to be tyrannized over by
> a proletariat as by a tsar or by a corporation, and it is in a mea-
> sure more disconcerting, because of the greater incohesion of the
> process. It is as revolting to be robbed by a reformer as by a trust.[143]

She loved her country, and knew all its faults: "a mad welter of lawless-ness, idleness, and greed; and, on the other hand, official extravagance, ad-ministrative weakness . . . and shameless profiteering. Our equilibrium is lost, and with it our sense of proportion. We are Lilliput and Brobdingnag jumbled together, which is worse than anything Gulliver ever encoun-tered."[144] Certain American assertions drove her to despair. "Mr. Rockefeller is responsible for the suggestion that Saint Paul, were he living today, would be a captain of industry. Here again a denial is as valueless as an asser-tion."[145] Yet she saw, and wished to encourage with every nerve of her be-ing, the finer potentialities of the American mind:

> When we leave the open field of exaggeration, that broad area which is our chosen territory, and seek for subtler qualities in American humour, we find here and there a witticism which, while admittedly our own, has in it an Old-World quality. The epigrammatic remark of a Boston woman that men get and for-get, and women give and forgive, shows the fine, sharp finish of Sydney Smith or Sheridan. A Philadelphia woman's conversa-tion, that she knew there could be no marriages in Heaven, be-cause—"Well, women were there no doubt in plenty, and some men; but not a man whom any woman would have,"—is strik-ingly French. The word of a New York broker, when Mr. Roosevelt sailed for Africa, "Wall Street expects every lion to do its duty!" equals in brevity and malice the keen-edged satire of Italy.[146]

And of American speech:

> If some Americans can speak superlatively well, why cannot more Americans speak pleasingly? Nature is not altogether to blame for our deficiencies. The fault is at least partly our own. The good American voice is very good indeed. Subtle and sweet inheritances linger in its shaded vowels. Propriety and a sense of distinction control its cadences. It has more animation than the English voice, and a richer emotional range. The American is less embarrassed by his emotions than is the Englishman; and when he feels strongly the truth, or the shame, or the sorrow his words convey, his voice grows vibrant and appealing. He senses his mastery over a diction, "nobly robust and tenderly vulner-able." The former and finished utterances of an older civiliza-tion entrance his attentive ear.[147]

She would not care for that quintessentially modern American-intellectual type, the social scientist;[148] but she would care even less for the unctuous foreigner who bilks and misleads Americans by offering credit to their worst intellectual vices:

> That astute Oriental, Sir Rabindranath Tagore, manifested a wisdom beyond all praise, in his recognition of American audiences. As the hour for his departure drew nigh, he was asked to write, and did write, a "Parting Wish for the Women of America," giving graceful expressions to the sentiments he knew he was expected to feel. The skill with which he modified and popularized an alien point of view revealed the seasoned lecturer. He told his readers that "God has sent woman to love the world," and to build up a "spiritual civilization." He condoled with them because they were "passing through great sufferings in this callous age." His heart bled for them, seeing that their hearts "are broken every day, and victims are snatched from their arms, to be thrown under the car of material progress." The Occidental sentiment which regards man as simply an offspring, and a fatherless offspring at that (no woman, says Olive Schreiner, could look upon a battle-field without thinking, "So many mothers' sons!") came as naturally to Sir Rabindranath as if he had been to the manner born. He was content to see the passion and pain, the sorrow and heroism of men, as reflections mirrored in woman's soul. The ingenious gentlemen who dramatize Biblical narratives for the American stage, and who are hampered at every step by the obtrusive masculinity of the East, might find a sympathetic supporter in this accomplished and accommodating Hindu.[149]

Miss Repplier was a solitary person. She would have agreed with the French maxim "*On trouve rarement le bonheur en soi, jamais ailleurs*"—one finds happiness rarely in oneself, never elsewhere—but her *bonheur* was seldom, if ever, separable from the conscious activity of her mind. Her adult work was all of a piece. Her adult life was all of a piece. Only they existed on different planes. People who did not know Agnes Repplier may have thought (indeed, they often did) that she was an eccentric dowager, an aristocrat of sorts, all dove-gray silk, instructing the world, keeping her impatience and brilliance, like a pair of greyhounds, on display and on the leash. Agnes Repplier was a *grande dame* of letters all right, but her character was not that of an aristocrat; she was a bourgeoise, which did not bother her much.[150]

She had, as I wrote before, few pretensions. Or, to be exact, she had a hundred strong convictions for each of her pretensions—an attractive ratio.

She was not happy, because her life was not easy. She had little money.[151] She earned almost all her income by writing—writing erudite essays, and hardly ever compromising her high standards—a truly extraordinary achievement. Around the age of thirty-two, as we have seen, she reached a high plateau, and from there on, her essays flowed from her pen during those solitary mornings and she had no trouble publishing anything. Her main outlet was the *Atlantic,* but for more than twenty-five years she also wrote for *Life,* the *Yale Review, Century Magazine, Forum, Harper's,* and so on. The recognition of her work brought her other benefits. She could travel to Europe. She first crossed the Atlantic in 1890 with her sister on the steamer *Normania.* During the next ten years she was able to visit Europe three more times, for ever longer periods, as the chaperone of two accommodating young girls, the Boone sisters from Eden Hall (who were the wards of Cardinal Gibbons of Baltimore). Between the thirty-sixth and seventy-fifth years of her life she visited Europe half a dozen times, usually in the company of friends, the last time as a member of the official American delegation to the Ibero-American World Exhibition in Seville in 1929, a trip which she enjoyed at least as much as (perhaps even more than) her first, and of which she wrote a short and witty account. Knowledgeable, expectant, perceptive, thoroughly aware of her surroundings and of the people, yet always ready for new impressions and experiences, she was an excellent traveler,[152] and an excellent companion, so far as we can tell. She crisscrossed the United States on innumerable occasions, mostly on lecturing engagements. Her public life corresponded to the age of the public lecture, a peculiarly American form of instructional entertainment. She did not like to lecture; she was far less confident at the lectern than at her desk; but lecturing produced an income that she could not afford to relinquish.[153] After most of these trips she returned to Philadelphia bone-tired. Her finances required that she accept lecturing invitations even after she had reached seventy.

She was not a domestic woman. She was thoroughly urban, fond of good food and wines, smoking innumerable cigarettes (and, on occasion, small black cigars). She did not know how to cook. Her domestic life was not comfortable. After ten years of successful writing, she, her sister, and her brother were able to move from West Philadelphia to downtown Philadelphia, renting apartments successively on Spruce, Chestnut, and Pine Streets.[154] In 1921 they moved to 920 Clinton Street, the house which eventually became her trademark; one of those old Philadelphia streets with red brick houses of good proportions and solidity.[155] For the first time in her life she found a house that suited her character, her image, her personality. Yet the perfection of the milieu was external rather than internal. The interior was dusky, Victorian, not particularly distinguished, full of old bibelots.[156] Her surroundings stood still even when her mind did not.

She would receive single visitors in Clinton Street from time to time; she would never entertain there. (Later she would invite friends for lunch at the Acorn Club.)[157] Yet her friends meant the world to her—literally, not merely figuratively speaking. She relished the friendship and the intellectual companionship of men. She was thoroughly at home with them; they, in turn, relished the masculine strength and directness of her mind. She was not a professional intellectual; she belonged to that select minority of strong minds who disdain being considered "intellectual," as if mental refinement were some kind of skill. Yet she came into her own at a time when there was a perceptible tendency among men and women who were attracted to the intellectual life to seek some comfort and warmth in each other's company in what was otherwise a very indifferent world. During winter evenings in the late eighties and nineties Agnes Repplier was part of a small Philadelphia circle of such people, of whose limitations she was amiably, rather than condescendingly, aware.[158] Around 1890 she met four patrician gentlemen, each of whom had a great influence in her life. Harrison Morris, later editor of *Lippincott's Magazine,* became her lifelong friend and literary adviser; Horace Howard Furness, the Shakespeare scholar, cherished her friendship and treated her as an ornament at the gatherings in his suburban house "Lindenshade."[159] S. Weir Mitchell, the talented patrician physician and writer, received her at his more formal entertainments with a kind of avuncular deference; J. William White actually became her occasional collaborator. Like Mitchell, White was part of the Philadelphia medical tradition, at the peak of its reputation around the turn of the century. He was an attractive man and an excellent surgeon. He probably saved her life. He diagnosed cancer in her left breast. He removed it in a masterly operation.[160] She was then forty-three years of age. They were close friends for the next two decades, very close during the First World War. Both were thoroughly convinced Francophiles and Anglophiles. They collaborated on political pamphlets. White went off to France in 1915.[161] He died in Philadelphia a year later. Agnes Repplier wrote his short memorial biography.

Her friendships with women were long-lasting and profound. Elizabeth Robins was her oldest friend, from their convent days. She was a complicated woman, consumed by social ambition, a Quakeress with aristocratic aspirations, tending to subordinate her undoubted intelligence to certain pretensions. After she married Pennell, Elizabeth and Agnes drifted a little apart. The former may have resented the fact that the girl who once was Minnie now outshone her in the literary world. Agnes Irwin, who, as we have seen, thought it best to disembarrass herself of little Agnes in her school, recognized her talents nevertheless at an early age; her solid support and affection for the young girl blossomed into the best kind of friendship, with reciprocal affection resting on the solid foundation of mutual respect and esteem. "Miss Agnes" Irwin died suddenly in 1914; her school remains her monument even now; another monument is the fine short biography that Agnes Repplier wrote after her death. Cornelia Frothingham was a New England woman, an in-law of the Brinley family in Philadelphia; in spite of her sometimes tiresome insistence on civic virtues and self-improvement, this neurotic woman[162] and Agnes Repplier became close friends, traveling often to Europe, Nova Scotia, and Maine together. Mrs. Schuyler Warren was the mistress of a sort of literary salon in New York circa 1905; well-read, exceptionally handsome, and rich. Agnes Repplier took great pleasure in her company. Two close Philadelphia friends were Caroline Sinkler and Cecilia Beaux, the painter. During the last quarter of her life Miss Repplier often appeared in public together with Miss Frances Wister, a formidable Philadelphia patroness of the arts; their friendship was extraordinary perhaps only because of Miss Wister's enthusiasm for music, to which Miss Repplier was, perhaps by nature, indifferent.[163]

There were people who believed that this bluestocking, this lifelong spinster, had, like her contemporary Willa Cather, a secret longing for people of her own sex. I do not believe this to be true. The evidence of a handful of letters to her friends, perhaps especially to Mrs. Warren and to Miss Frothingham, is insufficient, save for those who are hopelessly inclined to the attribution of sexual motives to every expression of human sentiment.[164] The contrary evidences are more impressive. We have seen how thoroughly she enjoyed masculine company and its attentions. Her occasional references about sexual attraction in her writings are sane and healthy compounds of the commonsensical and the Gallic. They are devoid of sentimentality; with a touch of the *femme moyenne sensuelle* they are much closer to Jane Austen than to the Brontës, and much closer to Colette than to George Sand. When President Eliot of Harvard pronounced Becky Sharp a despicable creature, she corrected him impatiently:[165] to the contrary, she said, the heroine of *Vanity Fair* had many admirable qualities. In some of her writing, passages exist that suggest her healthy sensuality, or at least her natural appetite for it. She wrote of a pampered cat, who grew so tired of his dull orderly life that "he ran away with a vagabond acquaintance for one long delicious day of liberty, at the close of which, jaded, spent, starved, and broken, he crept meekly back to bondage and his evening cutlet."[166] At the same time she had a very clear understanding of the virtues of restraint—especially in art:

In French fiction, as Mr. Lang points out, "love comes after marriage punctually enough, but it is always love for another." The inevitableness of the issue startles and dismays an English reader, accustomed to yawn gently over the innocent prenuptial dallyings of Saxon man and maid. The French storywriter cannot and does not ignore his social code which urbanely limits courtship. When he describes a girl's dawning sentiment, he does so often with exquisite grace and delicacy; but he reserves his portrayal of the master passion until maturity gives it strength, and circumstances render it unlawful. His conception of his art imposes no scruple which can impede analysis. If an English novelist ventures to treat of illicit love, the impression he gives is of a blind, almost mechanical force, operating against rather than in unison with natural laws; those normal but most repellent aspects of the case which the Frenchman ignores or rejects. His theory of civilization is built up largely—and wisely—on suppression.[167]

She regretted that she never married; and she learned not to make an issue of it.[168] She was a spinster, and she learned not to mind it. She was appalled at the crudity with which American humorists treated spinsters, and wrote a sensible little essay about spinsterhood. "It is not an easy thing to be happy. It takes all the brains, all the soul, and all the goodness we possess. We may fail of our happiness, strive we ever so bravely; but we are less likely to fail if we measure with judgment our chances and our capabilities. To glorify spinsterhood is as ridiculous as to decry it. Intelligent women marry or remain single, because in married or in single life they see their way more clearly to content. They do not, in either case, quarrel with fate which has modelled them for, and fitted them into, one groove rather than another; but follow, consciously or unconsciously, the noble maxim of Marcus Aurelius: 'Love that only which the gods send thee, and which is spun with the thread of thy destiny.'"[169] She admired that stoic Roman ruler. Horace, she wrote on another occasion, was like Marcus Aurelius, "able to be alone; but he was far too wise to make of himself that lopsided thing called a recluse."[170] So was she.

She was impatient with the self-conscious respect and the superficial sentimentalism with which American men treated their women. There were many things wrong with ancient Rome, but "she was far from being a matriarchy like the United States. She was not a nation of husbands, but a nation of men."[171] "The superlative complacency of American women is due largely to the oratorical adulation of American men—an adulation that has no more substance than has the foam on beer."[172] She was an intelligent feminist, who took a long-range view of things. "Since Adam delved and Eve span, life for all of us has been full of labour; but as the sons of Adam no longer exclusively delve, so the daughters of Eve no longer exclusively spin. In fact, delving and spinning, though admirable occupations, do not represent the sum total of earthly needs. There are so many, many other useful things to do, and women's eager finger-tips burn to essay them all."[173] "Perhaps the time may even come when women, mixing freely in political life, will abandon that injured and aggressive air which distinguishes the present advocate of female suffrage," she wrote in 1894.[174] The Michigan magistrate who in 1918 "gave orders that a stalwart male angel presiding over the gateway of a cemetery should be recast in feminine mould may have been an erring theologian and doubtful art-critic; but that he was a stout-hearted American no one can deny."[175]

She knew the follies of the exclusively male, as well as the exclusively female, viewpoint. "'Never,' said Edmond de Goncourt, 'has a virgin, young or old, produced a work of art.' One makes allowance for the Latin point of view. And it is possible that M. de Goncourt never read *Emma*.'"[176] But "the pitfall of the feminist is the belief that the interests of men and women can ever be severed; that what brings sufferings to the one can leave the other unscathed."[177] "In Mr. St. John Ervine's depressing little drama, *Mixed Marriage,* which the Dublin actors played in New York some years ago, an old woman, presumed to be witty and wise, said to her son's betrothed: 'Sure, I believe the Lord made Eve when he saw Adam could not take care of himself'; and the remark reflected painfully upon the absence of that humorous sense which we used to think was the birthright of Irishmen. The too obvious retort, which nobody uttered, but which must have occurred to everybody's mind, was that if Eve had been designed as a caretaker, she had made a shining failure of her job."[178] "The too obvious retort" of a fine conversationalist. "Whenever Adam's remarks expand too obviously into a sermon, Eve, in the most discreet and wife-like manner, steps softly away, and refreshes herself with slumber. Indeed, when we come to think of it, conversation between these two must have been difficult at times, because they had nobody to talk about."[179] She had a finely tuned appetite for malicious humor in conversation, including the eternal topic of how and why certain people are attracted to each other, in which she, rightly, saw the essence of sex. She did not take Freud seriously, which was a good thing. In her essay on "Three Famous Old Maids," the Misses Austen, Edgeworth, and Mitford, she described their "serene, cheerful, and successful lives . . . all rounded and completed without that element we are taught to believe is the mainspring and prime motor of existence."[180]

Her fierce independence of mind,[181] as we have seen, rested on the understanding that freedom is not merely the absence of restraints but that, to the contrary, it springs from the restraints one imposes on oneself. Her independence was sustained, rather than compromised, by her religion. She was a Roman Catholic with a very independent mind, a rarity in her country in her times, but no less a Catholic for that. Weaker or more self-indulgent women than Agnes Repplier could find it comforting to turn against the memories of an unhappy childhood that culminated in cold convent days and expulsion, to explain to themselves and to the world that they could sustain no inner nourishment from those rigid pieties whose hypocritical and superstitious nature they claimed to know only too well. At the same time, the majority of Catholics during Agnes Repplier's life, "when respectability stalked unchecked," chose not to think much, if at all, about the deep differences between what they believed and what they professed to believe. Some of the middle-class Catholics in Philadelphia did not like her, and pronounced some of her writings scandalous. She, on her part, disliked many of the German and Irish Catholics, a petulant kind of dislike that flared especially high during the First World War. The vulgarized Americanisms of some of the clergy haunted her throughout her entire life.[182] Yet even during her lifetime the Church was a house of many mansions. Not all American Catholics were parochial.[183] Cardinal Gibbons, many of the bishops, the heads and the nun-teachers of the small Catholic academies and colleges welcomed her with eagerness and affection. Catholic universities awarded their highest honors to her. The Catholic community of Philadelphia, indeed of the United States—it was more of a community then than it is now—eventually took pride in the achievement of this solitary woman, who was, after all, one of their own. She patronized and befriended the handsome and civilized priest Henry Drumgoole, choosing him for her escort to many a gathering. The Monsignori Drumgoole,[184] Sigourney Fay, Edward Hawks were priests after her heart (the last two converts from Anglicanism), representing a higher and more elegant and broad-minded Catholicism that was definitely not isolationist; a minority among the clergy, they supported the British and French cause during the entire First World War.

The character of Agnes Repplier was compendious enough to encompass a taste for the baroque as well as for the classical, even though she had a profound distaste for easy enthusiasms. Her philosophy of life was reflected in "The Chill of Enthusiasm," one of her favorite essays. "If we had no spiritual asbestos to protect our souls, we should be consumed to no purpose by every wanton flame," she wrote.

> If our sincere and restful indifference to things which concern
> us not were shaken by every blast, we should have no available
> force for things which concern us deeply. If eloquence did not
> sometimes make us yawn, we should be besotted by oratory.
> And if we did not approach new acquaintances, new authors,
> and new points of view with life-saving reluctance, we should
> never feel that vital regard which, being strong enough to break
> down our barriers, is strong enough to hold us for life.[185]

Yet, with all her self-restraint, reserve, and irony, she was not a rational-ist. "If knowledge alone could save us from sin, the salvation of the world would be easy work."[186] She had a respect for emotions, and the New En-glanders' dichotomy of Reason vs. Emotion made no sense to her.[187] Her understanding of life—and not only of letters—was spacious enough for her to comprehend the reasons of the heart.

Like Dr. Johnson's, her life was in many ways a triumph of character. Her accomplishment may be summed up in one short sentence: She was the Jane Austen of the essay. That she is not so recognized is a great—and one hopes, temporary—loss. Her essays are always lucid, often profound, and worth rereading. Few of them show the marks of her age. In spite of her quickly faded reputation, there is little of her writing that is a period piece.

We must, however, recognize the essence of a certain kind of truth within that epithet, even though we must qualify it. From her first essay, published in the *Atlantic* in 1886, to the last, published there fifty-four years later (in 1940), there is hardly any difference in the style or in the quality of her writing. Agnes Repplier did not grow. She reached a high and exceptional level of expression when she, against extraordinary odds, first earned her national reputation. She kept up this high level, with few exceptions, until the end of her industrious life. To sustain this was achievement enough; and there may have been an internal relationship between the scope of her art and that of her life. She took pleasure in her own writings (during the last years of her life she would, on occasion, request that her nurse read some of them to her aloud, only to ask that the volume be quickly put back on the shelves when the bell rang, announcing a visitor), but she never let herself be carried away by a wave of unwonted self-confidence; she never overestimated her talents.[188] She did not try her hand at a novel, or a play, or even at a compendious work of literary criticism. The small essay re-mained her genre; she was satisfied with it, just as her social ambitions never bloomed beyond the particular comforts she found in the often dull but always cozy quietude and familiarity of Philadelphia. "My niche may be small, but I made it myself," she would say. Much of the wit and the wisdom in her essays was not grasped even by her closest friends. She knew this. Yet she did not long for wider intellectual or literary companionship. She was content with the genuineness of the affection from her friends whose intellectual sensitivities may have been wanting, here and there, but whose personal sensitivities were not. In this respect—and in this respect only—she was like Edith Wharton, who once said about the society of Old New York that it was a bottle now empty but at the bottom of which there still remained a fine kind of lees, an essence of rarefied and unspoken sentiments.

There is another, related, element to consider. Her first books of essays were composed and published when she had passed the age of thirty. From her solitary reading she brought forth an immense accumulation of intellectual capital, upon which, assisted by her prodigious memory, she could draw for the next fifty years, replenishing it with ease. This capital was large enough not to be exhausted. Thus she was unaffected by the disease that affects American native talent: the brilliant early accomplishment unequaled in later years, never again blossoming in maturity. It was not her genius which was precocious; it was her maturity. Perhaps it was because of this precocious maturity—a rare accomplishment, to the point of being an oxymoron—that she remained unaffected by senility even in her eighties.

Because of this maturity she knew the limitations of public recognition. In this Philadelphia was, as usual, wanting—or, rather, slow.[189] (After she made her reputation in Boston, through the *Atlantic*, a certain lady in Philadelphia would occasionally ask her friends whether they knew a "Miss A. Riplear.") Unlike many other Philadelphia artists, she took this without much agitation. There is a passage in her fine little history of Philadelphia which applies very well to herself. "Philadelphia, like Marjorie Fleming's stoical turkey, is 'more than usual calm,' when her sons and daughters win distinction in any field. She takes the matter quietly, as she takes most other matters, preserving with ease her mental balance, and listening unmoved to the plaudits of the outside world. This attitude is not wholly wise nor commendable, inasmuch as cities, like men, are often received at their own valuation, and some degree of self-assertion converts many a wavering mind. If the mistaking of geese for swans produces sad confusion, and a lamentable lack of perspective, the mistaking of swans for geese may also be a dangerous error. The birds languish, or fly away to keener air, and something which cannot be replaced is lost. Yet anything is better than having two standards of merit, one for use at home and one for use abroad; *and the sharp discipline of quiet neglect is healthier for a worker than that loud local praise which wakes no echo from the wider world.*"[190] The italics are mine.

Gradually, slowly, the neglect disappeared. After 1900 she was well recognized, well respected, on occasion celebrated.[191] She often said that she enjoyed her years between forty and sixty the most. But after the First World War, which, as we saw, was a searing experience for her mind, she complained more and more often of being tired, especially from her lecturing.[192] Yet her writing remained lively and sharp.[193] She found a certain satisfaction in her Clinton Street house. In her seventy-fifth year she embarked on her official trip to Spain, where she outwalked and outtalked many of the younger members of the American delegation. She was seventy-seven when she saw the Gershwin musical *Of Thee I Sing,* which she enjoyed thoroughly; she was pleased with the fact that her compatriots delighted in seeing "the inglorious nature of their absurdities."[194] As she gave up lecturing, she depended only on her writing. It was then, in the last decade of her writing career, that she turned out a number of books in which we can detect, here and there, a certain decline of verve. Between the seventy-fourth and seventy-seventh years of her life she wrote three biographies, as well as a book on cats and a book on tea.[195] They were followed by a book on laughter, which she wrote and had published after her eightieth birthday. The motto under the title read: "*Un gros rire vaut mieux qu'une petite larme.*" A big laugh is worth more than a small tear. This is not the motto of a Genteel Lady of Letters.

In Pursuit of Laughter showed some of the marks of tiredness. Miss Repplier was becoming a bit predictable, and on occasion even repetitious. If *In Pursuit of Laughter* was not a potboiler, well, it was a *pot-au-feu:* a *pot-au-feu* put together by someone thoroughly at home with Gallic and American cooking, with the inherent qualities of all kinds of condiments and meat. "Our passionate loyalty to our humourists, our tolerance of the 'comic' in newspapers and cinemas," she wrote of her fellow Americans, "proves our need of laughter; but we are not gay. The appalling grin with which men and women are photographed for the press is as remote from gaiety as from reason."[196]

On her eightieth birthday the Cosmopolitan Club, of which in 1886 she had been a founding member, gave her a dinner (she was, in reality, eighty-two). The book collector A. Edward Newton was the toastmaster; there were many speeches in her honor. That year (1937) Houghton Mifflin published her own selection of her best essays, entitled *Eight Decades.* We encountered it before; there she did a sleight-of-hand about her age. *Eight Decades* begins with a forty-page autobiography. It is sprightly and colorful, amusing and witty, spangled with small particles of glitter that would be characteristic of the ornament of a woman half her years. Yet it tells very little about herself and her life. She was profoundly aware of the limitations of autobiographies, and she would not abandon the kind of rectitudinous reticence that accompanied her through her life.[197] During the following year she was found to be suffering from acute anemia. She also feared that her memory was fading, which worried her far more than anemia. She now retired to her bed. For the first time in her life she would not go to Mass on Sunday. "No, I won't. God is a good deal more understanding than relatives." "I am light-headed and heavy-footed." "All my time is now wasted. It has no meaning. Work is over."[198] This was an exaggeration. Her last essay, on the Housmans, was published in the *Atlantic* in January 1940. That year she was complimented and charmed by a young Philadelphia scholar, George Stokes, who had begun writing a biographical study of her. She received him in Clinton Street, sometimes staying in bed, puffing on innumerable cigarettes. The scene should remind us for the last time: she, the contemporary of literary women such as Mrs. Humphrey Ward and Julia Ward Howe, had nothing in common with them; she had many things in common with her younger contemporary Colette.

She lived to see her beloved France conquered and humiliated anew by a Germany much more brutal than that of the Kaiser or the heavy-footed tourists; she lived to see England alone against the wall, in its finest hour. But the fires of her anger now had died down; the awful scenes and issues of the Second World War flowed on the surface of her mind. Like the aged Hilaire Belloc, the erstwhile fiery Francophile and Germanophobe, everything she had proclaimed about the danger of the Western nations from Germany came true; but she could no longer rouse herself to an indignant passion comparable to hers during the First World War. Unlike Belloc, she was not senile. She was eighty-eight years old when a bequest brought her an increase in comfort. She moved to an apartment in Overbrook. Meals, including breakfast, were brought to her. She had fallen in her bedroom and moved very little. Yet her mind was amazingly sharp. Reporters from the Philadelphia newspapers came to interview her on her birthdays; she waved them away with a kind of petulant charm. She had the pleasure of the company of her intellectual niece; and she lived to see the publication of a biographical study of her by Professor Stokes. She lived to be ninety-five. "Her face was a picture of distinguished intellect, reticence, sensitiveness, and tolerance, yet she never seemed old. She did not regret or complain, for a lifetime of stoicism was not easily discarded. She still possessed ardor and contemplation, and when death came to her, he came softly, imperceptibly, hardly distinguishable from his half-brother, sleep."[199]

67

A Student's Guide to
the Study of History
(2000)

AN INTRODUCTION—TO YOURSELF

What is history?

No definition will do. Earlier in this century, two German historians tried to give such definitions. They were ludicrous, running to sixty words or even more. They remind us of Dr. Johnson's great saying: "Definitions are tricks for pedants." Ha! I just wrote: *remind*. And that *re-minds* me, instantly, of another great Johnsonian saying: that we (teachers or, indeed, everyone) are here less to instruct people than to remind them. Re-mind: to think, and to become conscious, of something that we already know—even though we have not been thinking about *that* in *this* way.

A good description—a description, not a definition[1]—is this: "History is the memory of mankind." Now, memory—every kind of memory—is enormous, just as the past is enormous. (The past is getting bigger every hour, every day.) But it is not limitless. There is the entire past. There is that portion of it (a varying portion, but let that go for a moment): the remembered past. And there is a yet smaller portion of that: the recorded past. For a long time—and for many professional historians even now—history has been only the recorded past. No, it is more than that: it is the remembered past. It *does* depend on records; but it is not merely a matter of records.

But this is true of every human being. You have your own history, because you have your own past—ever growing and ever changing;[2] out of this past surges your memory of your past; and here and there exist some tangible records of your past. I am coming to your records in a moment, but, first, a few matters about memory.

. . . .

Published as *A Student's Guide to the Study of History* (Wilmington, DE: ISI Books).

All human thinking—conscious *and* unconscious—depends on memory. There is no function of the human brain that is not connected with memory. For a long time neurologists thought that memory was a very important part of the brain, but only a part; their present tendency is to recognize its central function. (Even our dreams are inseparable from memory: it may be said that when we dream we do not think differently; we only remember differently.) If our memory ceased we could not go on living; we would, for example, walk through a window instead of through a door, not knowing— more precisely, not recalling—that *this* is a window and *that* is a door. As the great Christian thinker Søren Kierkegaard said: "We live forward, but we can only think backward."

One more thing about the past. The past is the only thing we know. The present is no more than an illusion, a moment that is already past in an instant (or, rather, a moment in which past and future slosh into each other). And what we know about the future is nothing else than the projection of our past-knowledge into it. We know that it will get dark at night, because it has always been so. Notice, too, that even in "Science Fiction" the author puts himself at a point from which he relates the fabulous events he de- scribes *backward*—that is, he writes in the past tense. The reason for this is that the human mind cannot for long sustain attention to a narrative that is composed in the future tense. In sum: our sense of the past is profoundly inherent in the functioning of our minds.

Socrates said that all knowledge must come from human knowledge and from knowledge of the self: *Gnothi se auton*—Know Thyself. (Shake- speare: "To thine own self be true.") What this also means—and what it has come to mean (about this condition, see later)—is that knowing yourself means knowing *your* own history, your own past. This knowledge of the past is the very opposite of a burden—a good example of how the function of the human mind differs from the functions of matter. By *knowing* some- thing our mind may or may not be enriched; but it may be *eased*.[3] Of course memory may be inaccurate and even fallible. But human memory is inevi- tably historic, to some extent. Your grandfather tells some of his experi- ences during World War II; their content is historical at least in some ways and to some extent. In sum: it is not only the history of mankind that is the remembered past; so is everybody's, including your own.

But then you may ask: My grandfather keeps telling us this fabulous story about the war. And he always talks so much. How much of *that* is true? But one day he brings out a newspaper clipping from *Stars and Stripes*, re- porting the exciting capture of that German armored train by Battalion C, Company A, of the 28th Division—his division. That printed record seems to *confirm* the Grandfather Story. (That this newspaper story may be sensationalist or inaccurate is another matter—that, too, we must leave for a moment, except that your eye may be caught by something slightly disturbing therein: your grandfather's name is misspelled in it, and his hometown is wrong.) And here I get to the matter of *records*. Aren't they what history *is*? Yes or, rather, no: because history is something more than mere records. But—and that is *the* important point—your own records are historical, too. Yes, you don't have many of them. There is your high school yearbook; a few ticket stubs; some photographs; in your mother's cupboard, a few old postcards; and, lo, there is a letter from your great-grandmother describing her honeymoon trip to Havana in, say, 1924. Well, *all* of these are historical records, not only because their very shape or form or color or scent vitalizes one's memory and imagination. In that letter of your great-grandmother's the handwriting is old-fashioned, spiky; the paper has yellowed, and the ink has faded; they bear marks of the past, of *a* past: but there is more to that. That plain old letter is *as much of a historical record* as, say, a typescript record of a cabinet meeting of the Eisenhower presidency. As a matter of fact, *more* of a historical record. Why? Because the record of that cabinet meeting was probably drafted and typed by a secretary, without President Eisenhower's seeing it, and perhaps even without his signing it.[4] But your great-grandmother's letter was handwritten, by herself. Even if it contains a few routine phrases such as "wish you were here," it is genuine and authentic. And it is the authenticity, the genuineness, of every human document—of every human expression—that counts.

In sum: your great-grandmother was as much of a historical person as was President Dwight David Eisenhower; and her remnant "records" are but one proof of that. In sum: there is no difference between a historical source and a "nonhistorical" source, because there is no difference between a "historic person" and a "nonhistoric person." (Shakespeare, in *Henry V:* "There is a history in all men's lives.") Let me reformulate this: All men's lives are historic. It is not only that there is *some* history in their lives. They are components of the history of their times.

Now, this is a relatively recent recognition. Let us see how we got there.

The History of History

Everything has its history, including history. And in the history of mankind we can see a certain evolution: from historical being to historical thinking and then to historical consciousness.

Let us begin by asserting what is unquestionable: only human beings are historical beings. All other living beings have their own evolution and life spans. But we are the only living beings who *know* that we live while we live—who know, and not only instinctively feel, that we were born and that we are going to die. Animals and other living beings have an often extraordinary and accurate sense of time. But we have a sense of our history, which amounts to something else.

This sense of history—in other words, the knowledge that we are historical beings—is detectable in some of the oldest human records and achievements left to us from the most ancient of cultures. It is there in the Bible, in the Old Testament. There, unlike in other mythological scriptures, is a mass of material that is not only spiritual or exhortative but historical: accounts of men and women and places and events that have since been proved by archaeology and by other evidence. Yet the Old Testament often combines history and legend;[5] that is, material or genealogical information on the one hand, and symbolic descriptions of people and events on the other. The New Testament—that is, the life of Jesus Christ—is *more* historical. Consider the very words of the Gospel of St. Luke, chapter 2:

> And it came to pass, that in those days there went out a decree from Caesar Augustus, that the whole world should be enrolled./ This enrolling was first made by Cyrinus, the governor of Syria./ And all went to be enrolled, every one into his own city./ And Joseph also went up from Galilee, out of the city of Nazareth into Judea, to the city of David, which is called Bethlehem: because he was of the house and family of David. To be enrolled with Mary his espoused wife, who was with child./ And it came to pass, that when they were there, her days were accomplished, that she should be delivered./ And she brought forth her firstborn son, and wrapped him in swaddling clothes, and laid him in a manger; because there was no room for them in the inn. . . .

This description—or account—is exactly and thoroughly *historical*. There is nothing even remotely comparable to that in the accounts of the coming of other gods or founders of religions, whether Greek or Roman or Oriental. Unlike other founders of religions *before* him, Jesus Christ was a historical person. For believing Christians he was not *only* a historical person of course, but that is not our argument here. The historicity of Jesus Christ (which we may regard as God's great gift to mankind) is incontestable: there exist Jewish and Roman and other sources about the fact of his existence, though not of course of all his deeds and sayings (or of their meaning). The very writing of St. Luke is marked by the evidence of something new at that time: of *historical thinking*.

However—in this sense St. Luke had his forerunners. They were the Greeks. As in so many other instances, the Greeks were the creators of many of the fundaments of our entire culture and civilization. Among them we find the first examples of historical thinking (and, therefore, of historical writing)—indeed, the very word "history," which in ancient Greek meant something like "re-search." The three greatest classical Greek historians were Herodotus, Thucydides, and Xenophon. It is interesting to note that all of them wrote something like contemporary, or nearly contemporary, history about events and people that they knew and that they had witnessed. (Xenophon had marched with ten thousand Greek soldiers across Anatolia—today's Turkey—to the sea and described that in his book *Anabasis*, that then became near-immortal.) Herodotus was sometimes called the Father of History: he was a man of the world, and perhaps his most lasting achievement was the ease and the clarity of his style.[6] But for our purposes here, running through the history of history, perhaps the most telling achievement is that of Thucydides. In the introduction to his *History of the Peloponnesian War* he asserts his purpose. This war is not yet over, he writes: but there are already so many false stories of this event or that, of this man or another, that he is compelled to tell what really happened. This search for the truth—which most often consists of the reduction of untruths—is the essence of historical research: a fabulous achievement of the Greek mind. There is also Thucydides' conviction of the permanent value of history. He hoped, he wrote, that his *History* would be read "by those who desire an exact knowledge of the past as a key to the future, which in all probability will repeat or resemble the past.[7] This work is meant to be a permanent possession, not the rhetorical triumph of an hour."

And now we must note that for the next two thousand years (Xenophon, Thucydides, Herodotus all lived in the fifth century, BC), there was no profound change in the nature of *historical thinking.* Important and readable historians existed during the Roman empire, the Dark Ages, and the Middle Ages; but their achievements, though often considerable, were not very different from those of the Greeks. At least the names of Tacitus or Livy or even Julius Caesar (who "made" history as well as wrote it) must be known to you. There were many others—Polybius, Plutarch, Procopius, Symmachus (necessarily an incomplete list)—Roman and Byzantine and Christian historians, writers in the Middle Ages. Let us pause, if only for a minute, at Plutarch, who is eminently readable.[8] He was a biographer. (That word did not exist in his time; it is only relatively recently that we have come to consider biography as history.) His portraits of famous and infamous Greeks and Romans are most readable and inspiring even now. But there is one great difference that separates Plutarch from every modern biographer. When Plutarch describes, for example, the Emperor Tiberius, he describes him in the way he was, including certain acts during his reign; but he writes nothing about how Tiberius had come to be that way; he writes almost nothing about his childhood and his adolescence—in sum, about his *becoming*. In this sense it is not psychoanalysis but our *historical consciousness* that has taken another step forward—in the sense of being profoundly aware of *becoming* and not only of *being*.

This kind of historical consciousness was only dormant during the Middle Ages. There *were* important historians then, too, but many of them were *chroniclers* rather than historians. They and their masters found it important to record what happened and when[9]—but were seldom inspired by a finely developed critical sense. And then came the Renaissance, with a sudden flourishing of interest in history, inspired by an admiration of all that was grand and fine in Greece and Rome. (Consider that more people in Europe spoke and read Latin in 1500 than in AD 1000—a fact unknown to those who think that Latin has been a "dead" language for ages.)[10] But, in an important way, the Renaissance respect and admiration for men and things past were still inadequate. They *idealized* the Greeks and the Romans, with a kind of idealization that was often insufficiently historical—though not without grand results of their own.[11]

Here are a few examples of the difference between our consciousness and that of the greatest thinkers, writers, and masters of art four hundred years ago. Shakespeare's attraction to and interest in history was already amazing. Consider his many plays about kings of England. Yet in his famous Globe Theater the most ancient of kings or Romans were dressed in his contemporary, that is Elizabethan, robes and costumes. Or: when Titian or Raphael painted Biblical scenes, their immortal paintings show figures dressed in sixteenth-century Italian clothes, and in the background there are villas and carriages typical of sixteenth-century Italy. But then, less than two hundred years later, even the most amateurish theatricals would drape Caesar or Marc Antony in some kind of a toga; and the classical landscapes of a Rembrandt or a Poussin represented Joseph or Mary or Herod in biblical costumes.[12]

That is a mark of our then developing *historical consciousness*, which is a sudden evolution of the Western mind as important (and as profound) as the evolution of the scientific method in the sixteenth and seventeenth centuries. The latter resulted in an entirely new view of the Earth's (and of man's) place in the universe. The former resulted in recognizing a new dimension of human consciousness. One example (or, rather, symptom) of this new kind of consciousness was the appearance of the word "primitive" in English, French, and other Western European languages about four hundred years ago. It marked a new concept of evolution (or even of education)—indeed, of "progress." To the Greeks, for example, "barbarian" meant people who lived outside Greece, beyond Greek civilization. It was a designation of certain people in a certain place, rather than at a certain time. But the word "primitive" obviously designates people who are *behind* us in time, rather than beyond us in space. And then, in the seventeenth century, especially in France, England, and Holland, this new sense of progress and of historical evolution multiplies. It is there in the appearance of a spate of new words, for example, "century," "age," "modern"—words that either did not exist before or that had then acquired an entirely new meaning. ("Century," for example, before about 1650 had meant only a military unit of one hundred men.) And it was only toward the end of the seventeenth century that some people began to look back and call the Middle Ages "the Middle Ages."

There are two matters to consider about this. First, in the Middle Ages people did *not* know that they lived during, or even near the end of, the Middle Ages—whereas we know that we are living at the end of the Modern Age.[13] Second, the notion of the "Modern" (meaning: today's) Age reflected a certain kind of enlightened optimism, meaning that this "Modern" Age would last and progress forever; that, even through many difficulties, things (and probably human nature, too) were bound to get better and better all the time. We have (or ought to have) a more chastened view about that; but it is more and more obvious that the so-called Modern Age itself is a recognizable historical period, one approximately from AD 1500 to 2000 (hence, its very designation, "Modern," may eventually change in the language of our descendants).

This growing consciousness of history went apace with a growing interest in history. That, in the eighteenth century, led to more and more fine books about history, to the extent that we may generalize about history having become in that century a branch of literature. Probably the greatest example of this development was Edward Gibbon, who, suddenly inspired in Rome by his view of the sunken monuments of the Roman Forum, decided to re-search and write a monumental book. The result, *The Decline and Fall of the Roman Empire,* remains to this day not only one of the greatest histories ever written but, even more, an enduring monument of English prose literature. Besides that tremendous achievement it must be noted that while Gibbon was not a professional historian (he lived just before the beginning of professional historianship), he was historian enough to rely on original Latin sources, which he would amply cite in his footnotes. There are many things in the Gibbonian interpretations that we have come to see differently; but there can be no question that two hundred or more years ago he exemplified a new sense of history, when a wide spreading of historical interest and of historical consciousness was in the air. Symptoms and examples of this were so numerous that there is no space here to detail them or even to sum them up.[14]

One (but only one) example of this burgeoning interest in history was the birth of professional historianship in Germany, which resulted in the first academic degree in history established by the University of Göttingen around 1777: the first PhD in history, a university doctorate. One hundred years later this concept and practice of professional historianship had spread around the world. By 1900 there were very few nations where universities did not grant a PhD in history. In sum, whereas in the eighteenth century history was regarded as literature, in the nineteenth century it had become a Science. This was mostly (though not exclusively) the achievement of German historians. The results were enormous. The position—and the recognition—of the professional historian was born. The methods of professional historianship became established: the insistence on "primary" sources, the requirements of seminars and of doctoral dissertations, monographs, bibliographies, footnotes, professional journals. Great historians, in every country, produced astonishingly learned and detailed works, shedding light into some of the remotest recesses of history. All of this went together with the general interest in history in a century when, among other things, the historical novel was born, and when architecture tended to emulate many historic styles. By the end of the century there was hardly anyone who would question the famous phrase of the German historian Leopold von Ranke, that the historian's task was to reconstruct a past event "wie es eigentlich gewesen," "as it really was." Indeed, most people accepted the professional historians' claim to Objective History; as the great English historian Lord Acton said, civilization was now able to produce, say, a history of the Battle of Waterloo that would not only be acceptable to present and future English and French and Prussian historians but that would be complete and definite and perfect—because of its objectivity, and because of the rigor of the scientific method of its research.

One hundred years later thinking historians do not share such an optimistic belief. We must recognize that history, by its very nature, is "revisionist." To put it in other terms, history, unlike law, tries its subjects through multiple jeopardy. History is the frequent, and constant, rethinking of the past. There may be one thousand biographies of Abraham Lincoln, but there is no reason to doubt (indeed, it is almost certain) that sooner or later there will be a 1,001st one, with something new in its contents, and not necessarily because of new materials that its author has found, but because of his new viewpoint.[15] In any case, the general cultural and civilizational crisis of the twentieth century has also reached the historical profession.

While in the eighteenth century history was seen as a branch of literature, and in the nineteenth as a branch of science, for the twentieth century we cannot make such a summary statement. One general tendency, which most historians accept or at least share, is the view of history as a form of social science. This does not merely mean the application of such "disciplines" as sociology, economics, geography, and psychology to history, but the recognition that history cannot be exclusively, or perhaps not even primarily, the history of politics and of wars and of rulers (as the English historian Sir John Seely said around 1880, "History is past politics, and politics is present history"); it must deal with the lives and records of large masses of people. Another tendency is to recognize history as a predominant form of thought—as, for example, the American philosopher William James put it: "You can give humanistic value to almost anything by teaching it historically. Geology, economics, mechanics are humanities when taught with reference to the successive achievements of the geniuses to which these sciences owe their being. Not taught thus, literature remains grammar, art a catalogue, history a list of dates, and natural science a sheet of formulas and weights and measures." In other words, "Science" did not and does not exist without scientists; and the history of science is the history of scientists and of their achievements. Thus Science is a part of history, rather than the reverse: for in the history of the world, Nature came first, and then came Man, and only then the Science of Nature.[16]

PROFESSIONAL HISTORY

We have now seen that the appearance and the recognition of the professional historian—of a man or a woman with a PhD in history—is a relatively recent phenomenon. Among the great nations of the world, England was the only one whose universities in 1900 did not grant such degrees (because of the then uniquely British high degree of the MA), but soon after 1900 they adopted this practice too. This qualifying of professionals has had of course many positive results. Since this essay is written not for graduate but undergraduate students, I must sum them up briefly.

In our American system the vast majority of students who, either by obligation or by choice, take a history course in college do not go on to study history further in graduate schools. This is also true of students who major in history. The training of professional historians begins in various graduate schools. There, at most after a year or so, they must decide in what "fields" or "periods" they wish to specialize: American? European? Ancient? Renaissance? Modern? etc. They must take certain methodological courses and seminars. In the latter, they work under the guidance of one of their professors, a specialist in his "field." This kind of apprenticeship must, in the end, lead to their selection (with their professor's approval) of a limited topic that has not been researched or treated before in detail. They must research and write a monographic dissertation of it. This must be accepted by their professor and later "defended" before a faculty committee (defending a thesis is at times not more than a formality), after which they will be granted their PhD. This kind of graduate period may last as few as three and as many as ten years, depending on many circumstances. After obtaining this degree, our new professional historians are qualified to apply for college or university teaching positions, or for other occupations that nowadays require an advanced professional historian's degree (government, museums, publishing, public or private archives, etc.).

The origin of all of these procedures was German, including that of the apprenticeship. Like all university institutions, including apprenticeships, they are of course all too liable to vagaries, fashions, academic politics, ideologies, and personal intrigues among the faculty. The historical profession, no more and no less than other professions, is not immune to the intrusion of ideological fads such as Psychohistory or Feminist History or Multiculturalism. There are many sorry examples of these, especially in our times. Yet, by and large, this originally nineteenth-century and German-designed training cannot be abandoned—that is, not until a radically new system of education and of higher learning, involving a new need for new kinds of certified teachers, comes about, something that is not likely in the immediate future.

There is, however, one overwhelming argument against a thoughtless acceptance of the professionalization (and of the consequent bureaucratization) of history. It is that there is *no essential difference* between the "professional" and the "amateur" historian (just as there is no difference between a person and a historical person, or between a source and a historical source). No one would prefer to undergo brain surgery at the hands of someone who is not qualified as a professional brain surgeon. But many of the greatest historians, not only before but also since the nineteenth century, were men and women who did not possess the PhD. To say that you cannot be a historian unless you have a PhD in history is not quite as absurd as to say that you cannot be a poet unless you have a PhD in poetry—but there is at least a touch of absurdity in it. We are all historians by nature, while we are scientists only by choice; and history is not a Science. (Or, as the English historian Veronica Wedgwood said in her aphorism: "History is an art—like all the other sciences.") The writing of a first-class history (or biography) is open to anyone who has thoroughly read everything he could find about his topic; who has an ability to express himself clearly; and who is mature enough to understand some things about human nature itself—three general requirements that, then, depend on the very authenticity and quality of his interest. His main interest must be history, rather than the positioning of his historianship.

The Methods of History

One of the greatest of professional historians, the German Theodor Mommsen, wrote more than one hundred years ago: "The elements of the historical discipline cannot be learned, for every man is endowed with them." The (probably even greater) Swiss historian Jakob Burckhardt said to his students that there is no such thing as a historical method. "*Bisogna saper leggere*," he said (in Italian): "You must know how to read." And by this of course he did not mean speed-reading or other devices, but that you must acquire the practice and particular quality of your reading.

Yes, strictly speaking history has no method. (Some academic historians will not like to hear that, since that may seem to reduce the achievement of their degree and of their expertise. Ignore them.) A main reason for this is that history has no technical jargon, it has no language of its own: history is written, spoken, and taught in our everyday languages. (It is also thus that you cannot be a good historian if you are not a capable writer.) You must know how to read; but also how to express what you know. That expression is not merely the packaging of your knowledge; it is the content itself. (Every human expression is not just the packaging of a thought, but its completion.)

There are, however, some limitations. History is the knowledge that human beings have of other human beings; and every human life is unique. Theodore Roosevelt was not merely the twenty-sixth president of the United States, or a President Type A. He was Theodore Roosevelt, born in 1858, died in 1919. As unique as your great-grandmother, the jolly and rotund Mrs. Myrtle Brown, 1902–87.

There are a few small methods, or "tricks," to historical study and writing, as there are to any human endeavor, such as cleaning or cooking. They can hardly be avoided. As with cooking, you must know where to begin: you must know what you want—indeed, what you'd like—to cook. After that, go to a cookbook. You must know what subject or theme or period or person interests you. After that, there are bibliographies (general and specific ones, and others at the ends of books already written about your topic), guides, encyclopedias, etc., leading you to more reading material. Nowadays this is made easier through various programs on the Internet; but none of that will spare you from the—we hope, interesting—task of reading, which is, really, what most of "re-search" may mean. There are also historical journals (often quarterlies), with articles and book reviews and bibliographies in every "field."[17]

After a while you will have gathered an amount of material. That will usually fall into three categories. Some of this you will not use (it is a great mistake to use *everything*). Some of this you will use. Some of the latter will be extraneous to your text, belonging in a footnote. Roughly speaking there are only two kinds of footnotes: one that *must* give the *exact* reference of where your quotation or material comes from; the other, an illustration or explanation of something that may be interesting or significant as an "aside," worth mentioning, though not within the particular paragraph of your main text.

About these methods—including much more than a description of "methods"—see the superb book entitled *The Modern Researcher,* by Jacques Barzun and Henry A. Graff, now in its umpteenth edition. (Better: buy it. You will be able to use it for the rest of your life, whether you become a historian or not.) Now note that the title of this superb handbook is not *The Modern History-Writer* but *The Modern Researcher*. The reason is that this book is a guide not only for history students but for *anyone* writing a paper in *any* discipline. Yes, you will find footnotes and bibliographies not only in history books and articles, but in such various places as *The Journal of Oph- thalmology* or *Musical Instruments of Turkey* or *The Physiology of the African Gnu*—because this practice of footnotes and bibliography (which some people call "a scientific apparatus") was adopted by *all* other disciplines in the nineteenth century, emulating the then developed methods of profes- sional historiography.[18] In this respect—at least in the method of authenti- cation—all scientific literature follows the historical method now.

There is, finally, one important rule that the nineteenth-century Ger- man historians established: their distinction between "primary" and "sec- ondary" sources, the first being "original," the second not. Example: a per- sonal letter by Theodore Roosevelt telling Mrs. Roosevelt that she ought to hire a new maid is a primary source; a relation of this event in a book or article entitled *The Roosevelts' Household in the White House* is a secondary one. This distinction is important and ought to be observed (for example, almost all PhD dissertations in history require research in at least some "primary" sources).[19] Yet it is no longer as ironbound as it once seemed— because communications in the twentieth century (letters signed but not written by important people; telephonic and other communications) tend to wash away the once rigid line between "primary" and "secondary" sources.

What matters, first and foremost, is the genuineness of your interest in history—almost no matter what history. And this is as true of undergradu- ates as it is of graduate students. This leads to the relatively new advan- tages of history majors. A history major who does not go on to graduate school has lately become prized by intelligent employers, since they know that a history major is not some kind of apprentice archivist, but someone who knows how to read and write relatively well—and whose knowledge of some history gives him at least a modicum of understanding of the variety of human beings. History is, as I wrote earlier, the knowledge that human beings have of other human beings, a kind of knowledge more valuable and, yes, even more practical, than the knowledge human beings have of more primitive organisms and of things.

THE INTEREST IN HISTORY

At the end of this century—indeed, for some decades now—we are witnessing a dual development. Many people know *less* history than their parents or grandparents had known; but *more* people are interested in history than probably ever before. On the one hand, less history is being required and taught in our schools than earlier in this century.[20] At the same time there exists an appetite for history throughout the world—particularly in the United States—that has no precedents.[21] There are so many evidences of this that I can list only a few. For example, while few history courses are required in high schools and colleges, in *all* colleges history courses are among the first elective—that is non-required—courses chosen by students. There are history programs and the History Channel on television, historical films, historical "documentaries" and "docudramas," obviously responding to the interests of millions, dealing with topics that were hardly featured as late as two generations ago. Within commercial publishing, popular histories are outselling novels for the first time in two hundred years. It is now accepted that serious biographies belong to history; biographies sell very well, while the very methods of serious biographers have become entirely historical. There exist popular historical magazines, even about specialized periods, that have a readership more solid and widespread than that of most other magazines. There are three times as many local historical societies as there were sixty years ago; their membership includes many young people, not predominantly old ladies in tennis shoes whose interest is primarily genealogical. The historical appetite of Americans has become unprecedented and large. Of course it is served, and will continue to be served, with plenty of junk food. Of that professional historians may be aware. (Yet the existence of this appetite for history is unknown to many of them.) Around 1980 the extraordinary English thinker Owen Barfield wrote: "The Western outlook emphasizes the importance of *history* and pays an ever increasing attention to it ... there is a new concept of *history* in the air, a new feeling for its true significance. We have witnessed the dim dawning of a sense that history is to be grasped as something substantial to the being of man, as an 'existential encounter.'"

And now, moving from the recognition of this universal and national growth of interest in history, I must say something about *your* interest. Someone who does not know how to cook must depend on a cookbook; but before opening the cookbook he must have an appetite. That interest— that appetite—must be recognized, nurtured, and cultivated. It comes not from the outside, but from the inside—as all human appetites and interests do. When you are interested in something—whether it is the taste of a good glass of wine, the sound of a certain kind of music, or a certain book— you must not only recognize it but literally *keep it in your mind* and follow it up, making the effort to find another kind of that particular wine, or another record of that particular composer, or another book by the same author, or yet another dealing with the same topic or a similar one. That effort will be worth all the trouble (if trouble it is), because that is how the human mind works—different from the laws of natural science. The more you know about something (and about something that really interests you), the easier it will be for you to absorb more knowledge about it. When a sack or a box is full, it becomes more and more difficult to force more stuff into it. But when we really know something (and especially when we are interested in something), it is easier not only to absorb but to know and understand and remember more and more things about it. In sum, the *quality* of your interest will not only enrich your mind; it will govern the very *quantity* of your knowledge. And that is true of historical knowledge, the knowledge of the past—which, in a way, is the fundament of just about all of the human knowledge we have.[22]

The Greatness of Historical Literature

To direct you now to, or even to list, the greatest of histories is almost impossible, for one simple reason: in one way or another *all* literature is, to a great extent, historical. It is quite possible—and there is nothing wrong with this—that your interest in history may have been stimulated by a movie or by a television play or by a novel. The varieties of historical literature are enormous.[23] One word about the novel may be in order here. The novel is a relatively new form of literature. It appeared in the eighteenth century, together with the evolution of our historical consciousness, and around the same time that professional history was born. (I am not referring to "historical novels"—a later phenomenon and one now rather past.) Novels such as Jane Austen's *Pride and Prejudice,* or William Makepeace Thackeray's *Vanity Fair,* or Arnold Bennett's *Old Wives' Tale,* or Honoré de Balzac's *Old Goriot,* or Thomas Mann's *Buddenbrooks,* or F. Scott Fitzgerald's *Great Gatsby* do not tell us only a story; they do not only remind us of many everlasting truths about human beings and about their inclinations;[24] they tell us, plausibly, how *certain* men and women, in a *certain* place, and *at a certain time* (!) lived and talked and thought and desired and believed. So does a good biography, of course.

But this is *A Student's Guide to the Study of History.* So here is a very incomplete and random list of some of the greatest historians whose writings you may find and should eventually read. Many of them should be available in paperbound editions; all of them are available in any decent library. But from time to time you should buy some of them for yourself, and not only for purposes of a history course or a research paper or essay. You must begin to enrich your own library, a personal library that is not merely a collection of once acquired books—that is, remnants—but of books that you will read—and perhaps reread again.

SOME OF THE GREATEST HISTORIANS

This is *not* a bibliography or a bibliographical essay. There are at least three reasons for this. The first is that the mass of writings about history is so enormous that, except for very limited periods or areas or fields of study, not even a selective bibliography will do. The second is that many of the greatest books about a particular people or place or period were not written by historians, and this list contains only the names and main works of historians. The third is that this is a *guide* to the study of history, and not to history *in toto.* (Consider here the difference between a guide to the study of literature—difficult but manageable—and a bibliographical guide to all literature: nonsense—a guide to everything that has ever been written by men and women?)

Ancients

Herodotus (c. 484–425 BC) was—somewhat exaggeratedly, but not without substance—sometimes called "the Father of History." He was born under Persian rule, but was thoroughly Greek in every respect; in a sense he was to history (a word that he brought into wide circulation) what Homer had been to the epic. He read widely and traveled; he wrote very well and was perhaps the first writer to demonstrate the critical qualification of a historian. This kind of style and substance is there in his *Persian Wars.* That critical sense—allied with an impatience for legends and untruths, together with not only great learning but a wise experience of human nature—was next exemplified by **Thucydides** (ca. 471–399 BC) in his *History of the Peloponnesian War,* of which he was a contemporary and participant (for a short time he served as a general). His style and his analysis of human nature are exceptional and at the time very new. A generation later, the great speaker Demosthenes was supposed to have said that he learned everything from Thucydides. **Xenophon** (c. 430–355 BC) was a conservative Athenian, a participant in a great military campaign across Asia Minor, whence his nearly immortal *Anabasis* (and the rarely known but also splendid *The Hellenica*), a thrilling history of his times. His style was plain and direct, like that of Julius Caesar, whom he influenced.

The bridge between the Greek and Roman historians is **Polybius** (c. 204–122 BC),[25] a Greek who lived under Roman rule and who wrote and traveled much (as a matter of fact he accompanied Scipio to the siege of Carthage). He wrote thirty-nine books, of which five survive. They deal with Roman history, including the Romans' conquest of Greece and then of Carthage. He was a tireless researcher and somewhat verbose; but he influenced the Roman historians directly, even though all of the latter were but individual successors to the Greek "founders of history."

These great Roman historians lived and wrote mostly during the dramatic age when Rome changed from republic to empire. **Livy** (Titus Livius, 59 BC–AD 17) wrote his long—but very readable—*History of Rome* from the very beginnings of the city to the then present. He was a Roman aristocrat who often insisted that the purpose of history is to teach us something by contemplating examples of morality.[26] Only about one-third of his writings survive, but he had written very much and continues to be an invaluable source for the early history of Rome. **Julius Caesar's** (100–44 BC) *Commentaries,* including *The Gallic War,* are classics: easily readable accounts by a statesman and general who was also an excellent writer and historian of his own times (two thousand years later his equivalent is Winston Churchill, about whom below). **Pliny the Elder** (c. AD 23–79) wrote many books, but he is not comparable to his nephew **Pliny the Younger** (AD 61–113), whose superbly—and easily—readable books include his description of the catastrophic eruption of Vesuvius and the destruction of Pompeii in 79 BC, during which his uncle perished. By that time we may observe a shift of emphasis of Roman historians toward biography (even though that word did not yet exist), particularly of the lives of successive emperors. This biographical talent is evident in the—again, very readable—*Parallel Lives* of **Plutarch** (AD 46–120), another Greek who was a Roman subject, comparing the lives of great Greek and Roman personages and rulers. His contemporary was **Tacitus** (c. AD 55–117), whose *Twelve Annals* deals mostly with imperial Rome during the first century AD, but who is best known for his *Germania,* an excellent description of the Germanic tribes, their habits and lives, and contemporary histories north of the Alps. The *Twelve Caesars* of **Suetonius** (c. AD 75–160) are often amusing as well as shocking, containing scandalous and racy stories about the lives of successive, and sometimes very different, emperors of Rome.

These excellent men were followed by hundreds of Roman historians during the last four centuries of the Roman empire and by many thousands of others who have written about Greece and Rome during the last two thousand years. But now comes a change: we must, by necessity, limit this short essay to the names of those who were no longer contemporaries of the times of which they wrote, but whose books illuminate the past in incomparable and novel ways. Their works are the result of the new phase of *historical consciousness*—a step beyond historical thinking, about which evolution I wrote earlier. A classic example is **Edward Gibbon** (1737–94), whose *Decline and Fall of the Roman Empire* is unique because of its imaginative qualities, the splendor of its English style, and Gibbon's thorough reliance on the ancient writers and sources.

The Middle Ages

When it comes to the Middle Ages, the best introduction to them may be found not in the surviving works of medieval chroniclers, but in the works of twentieth-century historians, such as the Belgian **Henri Pirenne** (1862–1935), a great modern historian of the Dark and Middle Ages, perhaps especially his *Mohammed and Charlemagne* and his short and brilliant *Medieval Cities*. **Eileen Power** (1889–1940) gave us superb portraits of half a dozen men and women in *Medieval People,* describing their everyday lives. **Johan Huizinga** (1872–1945), perhaps the finest historian who lived in the twentieth century, wrote *The Waning of the Middle Ages,* an extraordinary book encompassing a very new approach of historical description, including his reconstruction of the mental inclinations of people at a certain time.

The Nineteenth Century

We have seen that professional history had come into its own in the nineteenth century: its results were protean and wide-ranging. Yet let me mention two men who lived in that century who did *not* wholly share the scientific concept of history but who, in retrospect, emerge as very great writers. One is **Alexis de Tocqueville** (1805–59), who is mostly known for his classic *Democracy in America* (which is not a history); but his *The Old Regime and the French Revolution* again amounts to a new, and increasingly appreciated, kind of history, penetrating beneath the surface of political events. The Swiss **Jakob Burckhardt** (1818–97) was perhaps the greatest of historians in the last two hundred years, immensely wise and wide-ranging, the founder of modern cultural and art history. His *History of Greek Culture, The Civilization of the Renaissance in Italy, The Age of Constantine the Great,* and his *Judgments on History and Historians* (the latter from recorded notes of his lectures) will still be read centuries from now.

The three classic American historians of the nineteenth century include, first, **Henry Adams** (1838–1918). The last "great" of the Adams family, a direct descendant of two presidents, is mostly known for his *Education of Henry Adams,* which may remain less enduring than his many brilliant histories, especially *The History of the United States during the Administrations of Jefferson and Madison* (of which abbreviated versions are available). **Francis Parkman** (1823–93) is the incomparable historian of the French and British empires in North America during the eighteenth century, but also of *The Oregon Trail.* **William H. Prescott** (1796–1859) was the classic historian of the Spanish conquest of the Americas, especially in his *Conquest of Mexico* and *History of the Conquest of Peru.*

The Twentieth Century

When we arrive at histories of the twentieth century written by historians living in the twentieth century, they are innumerable, including the best of them—in many, many languages. But let me single out one great amateur: **Winston Churchill** (1874–1965). All of his books are worth reading, including his six-volume *History of the Second World War.* He loved and revered history. His style is exceptional, and so are his insights. Among other works he wrote a four-volume *History of the English-Speaking Peoples.* (And note in this instance the original meaning of the word "amateur," which was not the opposite of a "pro," but someone who loves his subjects and his work.)

One more brief note—about *the philosophy of history.* Many historians (and also other thinkers) have been preoccupied with trying to find a system in history, meaning the coincidence of certain conditions and tendencies recurring at somewhat comparable stages in the histories of different civilizations. The three great twentieth-century names in this regard are the German **Oswald Spengler** (1880–1936), whose *Decline of the West* is a stunning, though erratic, work, reflecting German pessimism about the fate of our civilization after World War I; the Briton **Arnold Toynbee** (1889–1975), who in his multi-volume *Study of History* attempted to find parallels and similarities in the development of many civilizations; and the English Catholic **Christopher Dawson** (1889–1970), an "amateur" historian of great erudition, who found religion to be the deepest and most enduring element in different civilizations. His assertion of the Christian nature of Europe may be found in many of his scattered volumes, perhaps especially in *The Making of Europe* and *Religion and the Rise of Western Culture.* However, two warnings may be in order here. Reading such philosophies of history may give the reader startling and illuminating generalizations about history in general; but history necessarily consists of particular events, peoples, places, problems, periods. Thus the reading of philosophies of history ought to come *after*, and not *before*, a reader has developed his own interest and preference in reading about particular matters of his own civilization. Also (as Jakob Burckhardt has said), history is not a system, and your own development of a *historical philosophy*—that is, a historical way of looking at and thinking about people, nations, events—ought to precede, and supersede, your interest in *philosophies* of history.

And now a last *however*. There are *no* rules about this, *no* rules about reading, *no* rules about what should—or will—interest you. What you must do is follow and feed your own interests—through which practice (and pleasure) you will acquire what Burckhardt named as the *only* historical method: *You must know how to read.*

Let me end with two great statements about what happens if you do *not* have an interest in history. One, ancient, is from Cicero: "To be ignorant of what happened before you were born is to remain a child always." The other, modern, is from the fine American essayist Agnes Repplier: "I used to think that ignorance of history meant only a lack of cultivation and a loss of pleasure. Now I am sure that such ignorance impairs our judgment by impairing our understanding, by depriving us of standards or the power of contrast, and the right to estimate." And, "We can know nothing of any nation unless we know its history."

782

BIBLIOGRAPHY OF THE
PUBLISHED WRITINGS OF
JOHN LUKACS

1947–2003

*T*his is a bibliography of the published writings of Professor John Lukacs, my grandfather, from 1947 through 2003. The structure, the conditions, and the limitations of this bibliography are the following:

It is divided into four parts: books; articles (including essays and pre- and post-publication excerpts from books); reviews (including review-essays); and a fourth section including articles in encyclopedias, verbatim texts of interviews, letters to editors, contributions to symposia and roundtables, obituaries, and other miscellaneous items.

This bibliography consists only of his writings that were actually published. It does not contain unpublished articles or reviews or other writings (for example, manuscripts or notes of certain lectures.)

The basis of the bibliography is Professor Lukacs's collection of his published writings, arranged in sequential boxes in his private library. To the best of his knowledge, this bibliography is 95 percent to 98 percent complete. However, especially for foreign publications but sometimes for domestic ones as well, it was occasionally difficult if not impossible to provide information regarding page numbers.

Obviously, there is also a chronological limitation. The items listed do not go beyond December 31, 2003. Moreover, John Lukacs published a few writings in his youth (in Hungarian, approximately 1943–46) before he came to the United States in October 1946. These are not included, since most of them are unavailable. The reader might notice that, starting around 1990, items in Hungarian begin to accumulate. This is due not to his occasional visits to Hungary but to the unexpectedly large interest in his books and interviews there. (Unless otherwise noted, all Hungarian items listed were printed in Budapest.) In the fourth section of this bibliography, under "Interviews," only those in which his statements were quoted verbatim are included.

It must be kept in mind that editors formulated some of the titles of his articles, often without consulting the author. On occasion, other articles have been changed, abridged, or even mangled by editors. Whenever possible, I noted this in these bibliographical entries.

Almost all of the original texts of his books, articles, reviews, and other of his manuscripts are extant in either his personal library or in the Rare Book/Department of Special Collections of the University of Pennsylvania's Van Pelt Library. This library is to be the eventual inheritor of his papers, including his professional correspondence.

This bibliography does not contain audio or videotapes, recordings of Professor Lukacs's interviews, or taped lectures in this country or abroad.

❉ Helen Lukacs
December 2003

Part I: Books

1953

1. *The Great Powers and Eastern Europe.* New York: American Book Company. Bibliography and index.
    a. Reprinted: Chicago: Regnery, 1953.

1959

1. Tocqueville, Alexis de. *"The European Revolution" and Correspondence with Gobineau.* Introduced, edited, and translated by John Lukacs. Garden City, NY: Doubleday. Index.
    a. Reprinted: Gloucester, MA: Peter Smith, 1968.
    b. Reprinted: Westport, CT: Greenwood Press, 1974.

1961

1. *A History of the Cold War.* Garden City, NY: Doubleday. Index.
    a. Paperbound edition: Garden City, NY: Anchor Books, 1962.
    b. German edition: *Geschichte des Kalten Krieges.* Gütersloh: Sigbert Mohn Verlag, 1962.
    c. French edition: *Guerre Froide.* Paris: Gallimard, 1962.
    d. Spanish edition: *Historia de la Guerra Fria.* Mexico City: Herrero, 1962.

1965

1. *Decline and Rise of Europe: A Study in Recent History, with Particular Emphasis on the Development of a European Consciousness.* Garden City, NY: Doubleday. Bibliography and index.
    a. Reprinted: Westport, CT: Greenwood Press, 1976.

1966

1. *A New History of the Cold War.* Extended edition of *A History of the Cold War,* 1961. Garden City, NY: Doubleday Anchor. Index.

a. German edition: *Konflikte der Weltpolitik nach 1945*. Lausanne: Editions Rencontre, 1970.

b. German paperbound edition: DTV-Weltgeschichte des 20. Jahrhunderts, Band 12. Munich, 1970.

1968

1. *Historical Consciousness; or, the Remembered Past*. New York: Harper and Row. Idearium and index of names.
    a. Reprinted: New York: Schocken Books, 1985. New and extended edition, with a new introduction and new conclusion.
    b. Reprinted: New Brunswick, NJ: Transaction Publishers, 1994. Includes a new introduction by the author and a foreword by Russell Kirk.
    c. Hungarian edition: *A t rt nelmi tudat: avagy a m lt eml kezete*. Budapest: Európa Könyvkiadó.

1970

1. *The Passing of the Modern Age*. New York: Harper and Row. Index.
    a. Paperbound edition: New York: Harper and Row, 1972.
    b. Spanish edition: *El fin de la edad moderna*. Mexico City: Editorial Novaro, S. A., 1975.
    c. Japanese edition: *Dai katoki no gendai*. Tokyo: Perikansha, 1978.

1975

1. *A Sketch of the History of Chestnut Hill College, 1924–1974*. Chestnut Hill, PA: Chestnut Hill College. Appendices.

1976

1. *The Last European War: September 1939–December 1941*. Garden City, NY: Anchor Press. Bibliographical remarks, abbreviations, and index.
    a. Reprinted: London: Routledge and Kegan Paul, 1977.
    b. Paperbound edition: New Haven, CT: Yale University Press, 2001.
    c. German edition: *Die Entmachtung Europas. Der letzte europäische Krieg, 1939–1941*. Stuttgart: Klett-Cotta, 1978. (Somewhat abbreviated edition.)
    d. Hungarian edition: *Az európai világháború, 1939–1941*. Budapest: Európa Könyvkiadó, 1995.
    e. Portuguese edition: *Á ultima guerra européia, Septembro 1939–Dezembro 1941*. Rio de Janeiro: Editora Nova Fronteira, 1980.
    f. French edition: *La dernière guerre européenne, Septembre 1939–Décembre 1941*. Paris: Fayard, 1977.

1978

1. *1945: Year Zero.* Garden City, NY: Doubleday. Index.
   a. Hungarian edition: *1945, a nulla év.* Budapest: Európa Könyvkiadó, 1996. Includes a special appendix for this edition.

1981

1. *Philadelphia: Patricians and Philistines, 1900–1950.* New York: Farrar, Straus and Giroux, 1981. Bibliography and index.
   a. Paperbound edition: Philadelphia: Institute for the Study of Human Issues, 1982.

1984

1. *Outgrowing Democracy: A History of the United States in the Twentieth Century.* Garden City, NY: Doubleday. Index.
   a. Paperbound edition: Lanham, MD: University Press of America, 1986.
   b. Hungarian edition: *Az Egyesült Államok 20. századi története.* Budapest: Gondolat, 1988. Also: Budapest: Európa Könyvkiadó, 2002. Includes a new appendix.

1986

1. *Immigration and Migration: A Historical Perspective.* AICF Monograph Series, paper no. 5. Monterey, VA: American Immigration Control Foundation.

1988

1. *Budapest 1900: A Historical Portrait of a City and Its Culture.* New York: Weidenfeld and Nicolson. Bibliography and index.
   a. Paperbound edition: New York: Grove Press, 1990.
   b. Japanese edition: *Budapesuto no seikimatsu: toshi to bunka no rekishiteki shozo.* Tokyo: Hakusuisha, 1991.
   c. French edition: *Budapest 1900: portrait historique d'une ville et de sa culture.* Paris: Quai Voltaire, 1990.
   d. German edition: *Ungarn in Europa: Budapest um die Jahrhundertwende.* Berlin: Siedler, 1990. Includes "Vorwort zur deutschen Ausgabe," a special foreword for this edition.
   e. Hungarian edition: *Budapest 1900: A város és kultúrája.* Budapest: Európa Könyvkiadó, 1991. Also bilingual edition: Budapest: Európa Könyvkiadó, 2003.

1990

1. *Confessions of an Original Sinner.* New York: Ticknor and Fields.
   a. Reprinted: South Bend, IN: St. Augustine's Press, 2000.
   b. Hungarian edition: *Egy eredendö bûnös vallomásai.* Budapest: Európa Könyvkiadó, 2001.

1991

1. *The Duel: 10 May–31 July 1940: The Eighty-Day Struggle between Churchill and Hitler.* New York: Ticknor and Fields. References, abbreviations, bibliographical essay, and index.
   a. British edition: *The Duel: Hitler vs. Churchill: 10 May–31 July 1940.* Oxford: Oxford University Press, 1992.
   b. Paperbound editions: New York: Ticknor and Fields, 1991. Also: Oxford: Oxford University Press, 1992. Also: New Haven, CT: Yale University Press, 2001.
   c. Danish edition: *Duellen.* Copenhagen: Fremad, 1991.
   d. German edition: *Churchill und Hitler: Der Zweikampf: 10. Mai–31. Juli 1940.* Stuttgart: Deutsche Verlags-Anstalt, 1992.
   e. French edition: *Le Duel Churchill/Hitler.* Paris: Laffont, 1992.
   f. Dutch edition: *De Krachtmeting 10 Mei–31 Juli.* Amsterdam: Uitgeverij Contact, 1992.
   g. Italian edition: *Il Duello.* Milan: Longanesi, 1991. Also: *Il Duello 10 maggio–31 luglio 1940: ottanta giorni decisivi della storia del nostro secolo.* Milan: TEA/Longanesi, 1995.
   h. Hungarian edition: *A párviadal.* Budapest: Európa Könyvkiadó, 1993. Includes a special appendix for this edition.
   i. Swedish edition: *Duellen: Kempen mellan Churchill och Hitler 10 Maj–31 Juli 1940.* Stockholm: Tidens Förlag, 1994.
   j. Hebrew edition: *ha-Du-kerav: shemonim yeme hitmodedut ben Ts'erts'il le-Hitler, 10 be-Mai-31 be-Yuli 1940.* Tel Aviv: Misrad ha-bitahon, 1994.
   k. Japanese edition: *Hitora tai chachiru: hachijunichikan no gekito.* Tokoyo: Kyodo Tsushinsha, 1995.
   l. British paperbound edition: *The Duel: Hitler vs. Churchill, 10 May–31 July 1940.* London: Phoenix Press, 2000.
   m. Swedish paperbound edition: *Duellen: Kempen mellan Churchill och Hitler 10 Maj–31 Juli 1940.* Stockholm: Raben Prisma, 2002.
   n. Portuguese edition: *O Duelo.* Rio de Janeiro: Jorge Zahar, 2002.

1993

1. *The End of the Twentieth Century and the End of the Modern Age.* New York: Ticknor and Fields.

a. Dutch edition: *Het ende van de moderne tijd.* Amsterdam and Antwerp: Uitgverij, 1993.

b. Turkish edition: *Yirminci yüzyilin ve modern çagin sonu.* Istanbul: Sabah Kitaplari, 1993.

c. Hungarian edition: *A XX. század és az újkor vége.* Budapest: Európa Könyvkiadó, 1994, 436. Also: Budapest: Európa Könyvkiadó, 2000. 2nd ed.

d. Bulgarian edition: Sofia: Obsidian, 1994.

e. German edition: *Die Geschichte geht weiter: Das Ende des 20. Jahrhunderts und die Wiederkehr des Nationalismus.* Munich: List, 1994.

f. Portuguese edition: *O Fim do Século 20 e o fim da era moderna.* Sao Paulo: Editora Nova Cultura, 1995.

g. Swedish edition: *Slutet på det tjugonde århundradet och den moderna tidens slut.* Stockholm: Raben Prisma, 1998.

1994

1. *Destinations Past: Traveling through History with John Lukacs.* Columbia, MO: University of Missouri Press.

    a. Hungarian edition: *Visszafelé... Utazások 1954–1996.* Budapest: Európa Könyvkiadó, 2001.

1997

1. *The Hitler of History.* New York: Alfred A. Knopf. Bibliography, abbreviations, and index.

    a. German edition: *Hitler: Geschichte und Geschichtsschreibung.* Munich: Luchterhand, 1997.

    b. Paperbound edition: New York: Vintage, 1998.

    c. Italian edition: *Dossier Hitler.* Milan: Longanesi, 1998.

    d. Portuguese edition: *O Hitler da história.* Rio de Janeiro: Jorge Zahar, 1998.

    e. Hungarian edition: *A történelmi Hitler.* Budapest: Európa Könyvkiadó, 1998.

    f. Swedish edition: *Hitler i historien.* Stockholm: Prisma, 1999.

    g. Dutch edition: *Hitler en de geschiedenis. Hitler's plaats in de 20ste eeuw.* Antwerp/Amsterdam: Carus/Anthos, 1999.

    h. German paperbound edition: *Hitler: Geschichte und Geschichtsschreibung.* Berlin: Ullstein-Propyläen Taschenbuch, 1999.

    i. Italian paperbound edition: *Dossier Hitler.* Milan: TEA/Longanesi, 2000.

    j. British edition: *The Hitler of History: Hitler's Biographers on Trial.* London: Weidenfeld and Nicolson, 2000.

2. *George F. Kennan and the Origins of Containment, 1944–1946: The Kennan-Lukacs Correspondence.* Introduction by John Lukacs. Columbia, MO: University of Missouri Press. Bibliography and index.

a. Paperbound edition: Columbia, MO: University of Missouri Press, 1992.

1998

1. *A Thread of Years*. New Haven, CT: Yale University Press.
   a. Paperbound edition. New Haven, CT: Yale University Press, 1998.
   b. Hungarian edition: *Évek*. Budapest: Európa Könyvkiadó, 1999.

1999

1. *Five Days in London, May 1940*. New Haven, CT: Yale University Press. Bibliography and index.
   a. Hungarian edition: *Öt nap Londonban: 1940 május*. Budapest: Európa Könyvkiadó, 2000.
   b. German edition: *Fünf Tage in London: England und Deutschland in May 1940*. Berlin: Siedler, 2000.
   c. Swedish edition: *Churchills Ödesstund: Fem Dagar I London, maj 1940*. Stockholm: Prisma, 2001.
   d. Portuguese edition: *Cinco Dias em Londres: negociações que mudaram o rumo da II Guerra.*. Rio de Janeiro: Jorge Zahar, 2001.
   e. Italian edition: *Cinque Giorno a Londra, Maggio 1940*. London: Carbaccio, 2001.
   f. Korean edition: Seoul: Jungsim Publishing, 2001.
   g. Paperbound edition: New Haven, CT: Yale University Press, 2001.
   h. Australian edition: *Five Days in London, May 1940*. Carlton, VIC: Scribe Publications, 2001.
   i. French edition: *Churchill: Londres, Mai 1940*. Paris: Odile Jacob, 2002.
   j. Spanish edition: *Cinco dias in Londres: Mayo de 1940*. Madrid: Turner, 2001.

2000

1. *A Student's Guide to the Study of History*. Wilmington, DE: Intercollegiate Studies Institute.

2002

1. *At the End of an Age*. New Haven, CT: Yale University Press.
2. *Churchill: Visionary. Statesman. Historian*. New Haven, CT: Yale University Press.
   a. Portuguese edition: *Churchill: Visionario, Estadista, Historiador*. Rio de Janiero: Jorge Zahar, 2003.
   b. Hebrew edition: Tel Aviv, 2003. Translated by Arie Hashavia.

Part II: Articles

1947

1. "Communist Tactics in Balkan Government." *Thought,* June: 219–44.

1949

1. "Political Expediency and Soviet Russian Military Operations." *Journal of Central European Affairs* (January): 390–411.
2. "A Hungarian Traveler in Pennsylvania, 1831." *Pennsylvania Magazine of History and Biography,* January: 64–75.

1950

1. "The Inter-Service Dispute Viewed with European Eyes." *U.S. Naval Institute Proceedings* (November): 1237–47.

1951

1. "The Resurgent Fascists." *Current History* (April): 213–18.
2. "The Story behind Hitler's Greatest Blunder." *New York Times Magazine,* June 17: 10ff.

1952

1. "The Policy of Containment" (Part 1). *Commonweal,* August 29: 503–6.
2. "Diplomacy in a Vacuum: The Policy of Containment" (Part 2). *Commonweal,* September 5: 530–32.
3. "Foreign Policy: The Confusion of Ideology." *Catholic World,* December: 195–201.
4. "The Last Days of the Ritz." *Commonweal,* December 5: 219–22.
5. "The Winning Side." *Freeman,* December 29: 242.

1953

1. "On Literary Correspondence." *Commonweal,* February 20: 500–504.

1954

2. "The Totalitarian Temptation." *Commonweal,* January 22: 394–99.
    a. Reprinted (abridged) in *Commonweal Confronts the Century,* edited by Patrick Jordan and Paul Baumann, 56–62. New York: Simon & Schuster, 1999.
3. "The Return of A. Pruett Ripperger." *Commonweal,* May 28: 202–3.
4. "The Crusaders." *Commonweal* (under the pseudonym "Tacitulus"), June 18: 263–66.
5. "Russian Armies in Western Europe: 1799, 1814, 1917." *American Slavic and East European Review* (October): 319–37.

1955

1. "The Meaning of Naval Prestige." *U.S Naval Institute Proceedings* (December): 1351–60.

1956

1. "New India and 'Age-Old Christianity.'" *Medical Missionary,* May/June: 67–70.

1957

1. "On Public and Popular Opinion." *Anchor Review.* 221–40.
2. "Lessons of the Hungarian Revolution." *Commentary,* September: 223–30.
    a. Pursuant correspondence: December: 188.

1958

1. "Intellectuals, Catholics and the Intellectual Life." *Modern Age* (Winter 1957–1958): 40–53.
2. "The World's Cities—Philadelphia." *Encounter,* February: 34–41.
    a. Reprinted in *English: Selected Readings,* vol. 1. The University of Chicago, Syllabus Division, University of Chicago Press, September: 257–70.
3. "Was Fascism an Episode?" *Commonweal,* March 14: 606–9.
4. "Dwight Macdonald: Another Orwell?" *America* (under the pseudonym "Orville Williams"), May 17: 224–27.
5. "Conversation in Vienna." *Commonweal,* August 8: 466–67.
6. "The Death of Hard News." *Encounter,* September: 72–73.

1959

1. "De Tocqueville Centenary." *French Historical Studies* 1: 250–51.
2. "The American Imperial Disease." *American Scholar* (Spring): 141–50.

   a. Pursuant correspondence: *American Scholar* (Summer): 402–8; (Autumn): 540–41.

   b. Reprinted in *Executive* (Harvard University Graduate School of Business Administration) (May): 16, 21.

   c. Reprinted in *The Challenge of Politics: Ideas and Issues,* edited by Alvin Z. Rubinstein and Garold W. Thumm, 392–97. Englewood Cliffs, NJ: Prentice-Hall, 1965.

3. "Letter to England: A Second Holland Is Not Enough." *Encounter,* May: 59–62.

4. "Ten Misconceptions of Anti-Communism." *United States Naval Institute Proceedings* (May): 64–69.

   a. Summary and excerpts in *Commonweal,* May 29: 227.

   b. Reprinted in *An American Foreign Policy Reader,* edited by Harry Howe Ransom, 635–42. New York: Thomas Y. Crowell, 1965.

5. "De Tocqueville's Message for America." *American Heritage,* June: 99–102.

1960

1. "Intellectual Class or Intellectual Profession?" In *Intellectuals,* edited by George B. de Huszar, 517–23. Glencoe, IL: Free Press.

2. "The Grand Mountain Hotel." *Harper's Bazaar,* May: 210.

1961

1. "What 'Moonlighting' Reveals: Certain Problems of American College Teachers." *University Bookman* (Summer): 86–90.

2. "Bancroft: The Historian as Celebrity." *American Heritage,* October: 65–68.

   a. Reprinted in *A Sense of History: The Best Writing from the Pages of* American Heritage, with an introduction by Byron Dobell, 410–17. New York: American Heritage Press, 1985.

1962

1. "Poland's Place in the European State System." *Polish Review,* vol. 7, no. 1:47–58.

2. "The Sense of the Past." In *Chester County Day.* Annual newspaper of the Chester County Day Committee of the Women's Auxiliary to the Chester County Hospital (Chester County, PA), October: 6.

3. "Les origines de la guerre froide: le problème historiographique." *Comprendre* (Société Européenne de Culture, Venice) vol. 25: 17–24.

1963

1. "Poker and the American Character." *Horizon,* November: 56–62.

   a. Reprinted in *Philadelphia Inquirer,* March 1, 1964, Today's World section, 6.

b. Reprinted in *Horizon Bedside Reader*, edited by Charles L. Mee Jr., 252–67. New York: American Heritage Press, 1970.

1964

1. "The Last Days of Alexis de Tocqueville." *Catholic Historical Review* (July): 155–70.
    a. Translated into Hungarian as "Alexis de Tocqueville utolsó napjai." *Vigilia* (Budapest) no. 10 (2002): 739–47.
2. "The Roots of the Dilemma." *Continuum* (Summer): 183–92.

1965

1. "Internationalism and the Nations of Europe." *Worldview*, March: 5–8.
2. "De l'idée d'Europe—son evolution historique." *Revue des sciences politiques* (Toulouse) (June): 349–60.
    a. Excerpted in *Current*, May: 26–37.
3. "The Battle that Began a 100-Year Peace." *New York Times Magazine*, June 13: 10–13.
    a. Excerpted in *New York Times International Edition*, June 18.
4. "Magyar Wedding, Irish Funeral." *Esquire*, August: 34-39.
5. "A magyar nemzet és az európai öntudat." *Irodalmi Ujság*, October 1.

1966

1. "It's Halfway to 1984." *New York Times Magazine*, January 2: 8ff.
    a. Reprinted in *A Complete Course in Freshman English*, edited by Harry Shaw, 761–68. New York: Harper & Row, 1967.
    b. Reprinted in *The Odyssey Reader: Ideas and Style*, edited by Newman P. Birk and Genevieve B. Birk, 59–68. New York: Odyssey Publishing Co., 1968.
    c. Reprinted in *The Lively Rhetoric*, edited by Alexander Scharbach and Ralph H. Singleton, 159–68. New York: Holt, Rinehart and Winston, 1968.
    d. Reprinted in *Perspectives on Our Time*, edited by Francis X. Davy and Robert E. Burkhart, 177–85. New York: Houghton Mifflin, 1970.
    e. Reprinted in *The Experience of Writing*, edited by William D. Baker and T. Benson Strandness, 189–92. Englewood Cliffs, NJ: Prentice Hall, 1970.
    f. Reprinted in *Insight: A Rhetoric Reader*, edited by Emil Burtik, 61–70. New York: Lippincott, 1970.
2. "The Changing Face of Progress." *Texas Quarterly* (Winter): 7–14.

1967

1. Excerpt from *A History of the Cold War*. In *Great Issues in Western Civilization*, vol. 2., edited by Brian Tierney, Donald Kagan, and L. Pearce Williams, 669–78. New York: Random House.
2. "Magyar széljegyzetek." *Irodalmi Ujság*, August 1: 3.
3. "A Dissenting View of the Day that Shook the World." *New York Times Magazine*, October 22: 32ff.
    a. Pursuant correspondence: January 7, 1968: 112–13.

1968

1. "How Ideas Move: Notes for a Future Historian of 'Revisionism.'" *Worldview*, July/August: 6–9. (Mangled by editors.)
2. "Speaking of Books: Historians and Novelists." *New York Times Magazine*, February 25: 2ff.
3. "The Changing Campus." *Grackle*, Spring: 16–18.
4. "Elkerülhetö volt—e Magyarország orosz megszállása 1944 ben?" *Irodalmi Ujság*, April 1: 1–16.
5. "Magyar széljegyzetek." *Irodalmi Ujság*, August 1: 5.
6. "America's Malady Is Not Violence, but Savagery." *Commonweal*, November 15: 241–45.
    a. Reprinted in *Violence in America: A Historical and Contemporary Reader*, edited by Thomas Rose, 349–58. New York: Vintage Books.

1969

1. "American Expansion" and "The Great Historical Movements of Our Times." Excerpts from *A History of the Cold War* in *Aspects de la civilization américaine*, edited by Jean Guiget, 271–77. Paris: Libraire Armand Colin, 1969.
2. "The Night Stalin and Churchill Divided Europe." *New York Times Magazine*, October 5: 36–50.
    a. Reprinted in *Richmond Times-Dispatch*, October 5.1970

1970

1. "The Paradox of Prosperity." Excerpt from *The Passing of the Modern Age*. *Commentary*, February: 64–69.
    a. Translated into Italian as "Il paradosso della prosperità." *Mercurio* (Rome), November: 7–11.
2. "The Heritage of Yalta." *ACEN News*, July/August: 6–9.
3. "Emancipation or Degradation?" Excerpt from *The Passing of the Modern Age*. *National Review*, August 11: 833–35.
4. "The Bourgeois Interior." Excerpt from *The Passing of the Modern Age*. *American Scholar* (Autumn): 616–40.
    a. Reprinted in *Dialogue*, no. 1: 89–96.

5. "The Transmission of Life: Certain Generalizations about the Demography of Europe's Nations in 1939–1941." *Comparative Studies in Society and History,* October: 442–51.

1971

1. "America May Be in the Last Phase of Its Adolescence." *New York Times Magazine,* December 5: 58–60.

1972

1. "Pornography and the Death Wish." *Triumph,* January: 11–14. Reprinted in *The Spirit of* Triumph, *1966–1976,* by the Society for the Christian Commonwealth, 45–47.
2. "The End of the Cold War (and Other Clichés)." *Worldview,* February: 5–8.
3. "Rêveuse Bourgeoisie: The Vitality of the European Bourgeoisie during the Decisive Phase of World War II." *Societas: A Review of Social History* (Autumn): 291–306.

1973

1. "The Origins of the Cold War." Excerpts from *A New History of the Cold War,* in *From Metternich to the Beatles: Readings in Modern European History,* edited by Richard C. Lukas, 196–205. New York: New American Library.
2. "'Right and Left,' in America, That Is." *Art International,* January: 81–84.
3. "Bare Ruined Choirs." *Triumph,* April: 22–24.

1974

1. "Wilson Is Overtaking Lenin." *National Review,* February 15: 199–203.
2. "A German Inheritance." *Triumph,* June: 32–34.

1975

1. "The Kirovogard Mystery." *National Review,* January 31: 106–8.
2. "So What Else Is New?" *New York Times Magazine,* February 9: 38ff.
   a. Pursuant correspondence: March 9: 4.
3. "Thirty Years since World War II." *Louisville Courier-Journal and Times,* March 23: 8–13.
4. "The College Is Now a Grandma." *Philadelphia Sunday Bulletin,* June 22, Discovery section, 4–5.
5. "What Solzhenitsyn Means." *Commonweal,* August 1: 296–301.
   a. Pursuant correspondence: October 10: 475–79.
6. "The Postwar World." *New Republic,* August 29: 18–21.
7. "Doctorowurlitzer, or History in Ragtime." *Salmagundi* (Fall 1975–Winter 1976): 285–95.

1976

1. "FDR: The American as Idealistic Pragmatist." Excerpt from *Year Zero. Four Quarters* (Summer): 31–46.

1977

1. "Sans Caviare." *National Review,* April 15: 450–52.

1978

1. "What If? Had Hitler Won the Second World War." In *The People's Almanac # 2,* edited by David Wallechinsky and Irving Wallace, 394–97. New York: Bantam Books.
2. "The Historiographical Problem of Belief and Believers: Religious History in the Democratic Age." Presidential address of the American Catholic Historical Association, 1977. *Catholic Historical Review* (April): 153–67.
3. "Slouching toward Byzantium." *National Review,* April 28: 539–41.
4. "Power and the Twentieth Century." *American Spectator,* June/July: 13–15.
5. "Big Grizzly." (Version of Boies Penrose chapter in *Philadelphia: Patricians and Philistines: 1900–1950.*) *American Heritage,* October/November: 72–81.
6. "A nemzeti becsület védöje: Lukács János történész visszaemlékezére Auer Pálra." *Magyar Hiradó* (Vienna), October 1.

1979

1. "The Continental Express." *National Review,* March 2: 311–13.
2. "What Is Happening to History?" *University Bookman* (Spring): 51–58.
3. "Three Days in London." *American Spectator,* August: 7–14.
4. "The Light from the East" *National Review,* October 26: 1352–60.
   a. Reprinted (abridged) in *The Joys of National Review, 1955–1980,* edited by Priscilla Buckley, 228–30. New York: National Review Books.
5. "The Monstrosity of Government." Excerpt from *The Passing of the Modern Age.* In *The Politicization of Society,* edited by Kenneth S. Templeton Jr., 391–408. Indianapolis: Liberty Press.

1980

1. "The Tolstoy Locomotive on the Berlin Track." *University Bookman* (Summer): 75–83.
2. "Old World to New," *Salmagundi* (Fall 1980–Winter 1981):105–14. See also Lukacs's remarks in panel discussion, 116–17, 136–37.
3. "American History? American History," *Salmagundi* (Fall 1980–Winter 1981): 172–80. See also Lukacs's remarks in panel discussion, 185–86, 189–92.
4. "The Light in the East." *New Republic,* September 20: 17–19.

a. Reprinted in *Criticón* (Bonn), November/December.
b. Reprinted in *La Prensa* (Buenos Aires), March 1, 1981.
c. Reprinted in *Western Civilization*, vol. 2, edited by William Hughes, 189–93. Guilford, CT: Duskin Publishing Group, 1983.
5. "Obsolete Historians." *Harper's*, November: 80–84.
6. "Polish Omens." *New Republic*, November 29: 14–17.

1981

1. "From Camelot to Abilene." *American Heritage*, February/March: 52–57
2. "Poland: A Lesson of Eastern Europe for the Soviets: Symptomatic of Coming Decline, Hungarian-Born Historian Says." *Pittsburgh Post-Gazette*, March 11: 1–6. Also see insert: "A Very Quotable Historian."
3. "Kovács Imre 1913–1980. Kivételes férfi." *Uj Látóhatá* (Munich), March 30: 425–27.

    a. Translated into Spanish as "El Triunfol de Evelyn Waugh." Suplemento cultural de *La Nueva Provincia* (Bahia Blanca, Argentina), April: 1–6.

4. "Easter in Warsaw." *National Review*, June 12: 658–65.
5. "Agnes Repplier," Part I. *New American Review* (Fall): 13–21.
6. "L'Urss, una pianeta senza più satelliti." *Il Giorno* (Milan), October 6: 7
7. "Uno storico di origini magiare rivisita l'Ungheria. Tremi il potente Cremlino: E rinato l'amor di patria." *Il Sabato* (Milan), October 24–30: 21–22.
8. "Bracing Praise." Excerpt from *Philadelphia 1900–1950. National Review*, December 11: 1450.

1982

1. "In Darkest Transylvania." *New Republic*, February 3: 15–21.

    a. Translated into Hungarian as "Erdély. Európa legszebb és legsötétebb része."*Délamerikai Magyar Hirlap* (Buenos Aires), May.

2. "Open Your Eyes, for God's Sake!" *National Review*, March 5: 223–30.
3. "Alexis de Tocqueville: A Historical Appreciation." *Literature of Liberty* (Spring): 7–34.
4. "Agnes Repplier," Part II. *New American Review* (Spring/Summer): 30–36.
5. "Hitler Becomes a Man." *American Scholar* (Summer): 391–95.
6. "Schuylkill Retains Its Rural Character." *Evening Phoenix* (Phoenixville, PA), October 4, sec. A.
7. "Progress, Our Least Important Product." *Philadelphia Inquirer Magazine*, October 24, Today section, 18ff.

1983

1. "When Hitler Came. Fifty Years Ago." *American Spectator*, May: 11–13.
2. "Happy Birthday, Benito." *American Spectator*, August: 13–17.

3. "A Foreigner in Philadelphia." Excerpt from *Confessions of an Original Sinner. Philadelphia,* November: 91–103.

1984

1. "The American Conservatives." *Harper's,* January: 44–49.
    a. Excerpts translated into Hungarian in *Külföldi folyòiratokból,* 116–18.
2. "Two-Faced Germany." *American Spectator,* July: 21–23.

1985

1. "Alexis de Tocqueville" and "Jacob Burckhardt." In *European Writers: The Romantic Century,* vol. 6, edited by Jacques Barzun, 893–912, 1225–44. New York: Charles Scribner's Sons.
2. "American Pacifism—A Historical Perspective." In *Die Kampagne gegen den NATO–Doppellbeschluss,* edited by Gunther Wagenlehner, 70–83. Koblenz: Bernard and Graefe.
3. "Történetirás és regényirás: a mult étvágya és ize." *Történelmi Szemle,* no. 2: 280–88.
    a. Reprinted in *Korunk* (Cluj), January 1999: 44–55.
4. "Remembering Yalta: What Happened and What Did Not." *Harper's,* March: 75–76.
    a. Translations published in many periodicals, including: *V.I.P. Weekly* (Madras), June 17; *Srinitgar Bulletin,* June 18; *Ourvi-Zilly* (Buesti), June 4; *Srinagar,* June 9; *El Heraldo de Mexico,* May 13; *La Estrella de Panama,* May 27; *Swatantra-Gbharat,* May 14; *Gaumi-Hamdard,* May 15; *Kausar,* April 30; *El Diario* (La Paz), May 5.
5. "The Gotthard Walk." *New Yorker,* December 23: 57–77.

1986

1. "A Night at the Dresden Opera." *New Yorker,* March 17: 95–100.
2. "The Lampedusa Mystery." *New York Times,* May 7: sec. A, 31.
3. Excerpts from *Philadelphia: Patricians and Philistines, 1900–1950.* In The Scene, by Clark DeLeon. *Philadelphia Inquirer,* 31 August: sec. B, 2.
4. "The Soviet State at Age 65." *Foreign Affairs* (Fall): 21–36.
    a. Excerpt in *World Peace Report,* December: 2–3.
5. "The Dangerous Summer of 1940." *American Heritage,* October/November: 22–31.
    a. Reprinted in *World History,* vol. 2., by David McComb, 146–50. Guilford, CT: Dushkin Publishing Group, 1990.
6. "The Displaced Persons." *World and I,* November: 675–82.
7. "Après Ski." *National Review,* November 7: 57–59.
8. "The Sound of a Cello." *New Yorker,* December 1: 43–60.

a. Excerpt translated into Hungarian as "Egy cselló hangja." *Valóság*, no. 5, 1987: 124–25.

b. Excerpt translated into Hungarian as "A gordonka hangja." *Mozgó Világ*, no. 7, 1987: 674–75.

c. Excerpt in *In Quest of the Miracle Stag: The Poetry of Hungary*, edited by Ádám Makkai. Chicago: Atlantis-Centaur, 1996.

1987

1. "Heisenberg's Recognitions: The End of the Scientific World View." Excerpt from *Historical Consciousness*. In *Science and Culture in the Western Tradition*, edited by John G. Burke, 257–61. Scottsdale, AZ: Gorsuch Scarisbrick Publishers.
2. "America in the 1980s: Under the Sway of 'Conservative' Constantinism." *New Oxford Review*, April: 7–11.
3. "Unexpected Philadelphia." *American Heritage*, May/June: 72–81.
4. "The Constitution: Could It Be Written Today?" *Philadelphia Inquirer Magazine*, July 5: 101–15.
5. "The Evolving Relationship of History and Sociology." *International Journal of Politics, Culture, and Society* (Fall): 70–88.
    a. Abstracted in *Sociological Abstracts*, October 1988: 1261.
6. "Philadelphia." *TWA Ambassador*, August: 18ff.
7. "Im Schatten von gestern." *Frankfurter Allgemeine Zeitung*, August 29.
8. "Soviets Aren't the Point of Conflict: While We Curse the Old Foe, Threats from the Third World Grow." *Los Angeles Times*, October 2: 7.
9. "Casablanca Revisited." *Four Quarters* (Winter): 35–38.
10. "The Alps." *TWA Ambassador*, November: 32–41.

1988

1. "U.S. Policy towards Eastern Europe: Past, Present and Future." In *The Uncertain Future: Gorbachev's Eastern Bloc*, edited by Nicholas N. Kittrie and Iván Völgyes, 203–14. New York: Paragon House.
2. "The Riviera in Winter: Menton Then and Now." *Gourmet*, January: 58–61.
    a. Reprinted in *Provence: An Inspired Anthology and Travel Resource*, edited by Barrie Kerper, 262–68. New York: Random House, 2001.
3. "Afghanistan Was Misread by Both Sides." *Los Angeles Times*, February 15: 7.
4. "Budapest 1900: Colors, Words, Sounds." Excerpt from *Budapest 1900*. *American Scholar* (Spring): 253–61.
5. "Budapest in 1900: City and People." Excerpt from *Budapest 1900*. *Hungarian Studies* (April 1): 65–92.
6. "The Reagan Administration—Bitter Afterthoughts." *World and I*, April: 581–87.
7. "A Muscle-Bound America Truly Has Few Options to Chase Bad Guys Away." *Los Angeles Times*, 15 April: 7. (Titles of articles such as these are seldom the choice of the author.)
8. "Nationalism, Not Communism, Is Today's Threat." *Los Angeles Times*, July 4: 6.

9. "Tom Wolfe's Novel and Its Reception as a Significant Historical Event." *New Oxford Review,* September: 6–12.
10. "Corrupt and Diminished, the Communist Party Has Finally Met Its Match." *Los Angeles Times,* October 18: 7.
11. "American Manners." *Chronicles,* November: 9–15.
12. "Budapest in Love and War." Excerpt from *Confessions of an Original Sinner. Harper's,* November: 72ff.

1989

1. "America's True Power." *American Heritage,* March: 74–79.
2. "The Rhine." *TWA Ambassador,* July: 38ff.
3. "The Coming of the Second World War." *Foreign Affairs* (Autumn): 165–74.
    a. Reprinted (abridged) in *World History,* vol. 2, edited by David McComb, 146–50. Guilford, CT: Dushkin Publishing, 1993.
4. "The Conspiratorial World View of Whittaker Chambers." *New Oxford Review,* November: 5–8.
5. "Let History Be Our Guide." *Los Angeles Times,* November 18.
6. "Hungary in 1938." *New Hungarian Quarterly* (Winter): 46–51.
7. Excerpt from *Budapest 1900. Világosság,* December: 910–21.

1990

1. "Resistance: Simone Weil." *Salmagundi* (Winter/Spring): 106–18.
2. "Hannah Arendt's Intellectual Opportunism." *New Oxford Review,* April: 18–22.
    a. Translated into Hungarian as "Totalitarizmus és érelmeszedés." *Magyar Nemzet,* September 7, 1996.
3. "A Valley's Voyage through Time." *Four Quarters* (Spring): 9–15.
4. "Eastern Europe." Excerpt from *Confessions of an Original Sinner. Wilson Quarterly* (Spring): 37–47.
5. "Born Again Budapest." *Condé Nast Traveler,* April: 140–49.
6. "Der achtzigtägige Zweikampf." *Frankfurter Allgemeine Zeitgung,* May 5.
7. "Scared by Reds, Mugged by Thugs." *Los Angeles Times,* May 21, sec. B, 7.
8. "The Stirrings of History." *Harper's,* August: 41–48.
9. "Letters and Physics, or the Race to the Swiftest." *Salmagundi* (Winter/Spring): 195–96.
10. "Fifty Years Ago: The Eighty-Day Duel." Excerpt from *The Duel. New Hungarian Quarterly* (Autumn): 7ff.
11. "A Professor among Politicians." *Philadelphia,* September: 59–67.
12. "A burzsoá enteriör." Hungarian translation of "The Bourgeois Interior." *Világosság,* October: 739–47.
13. "Connecting with Eastern Europe." *American Heritage,* November: 47–58.
14. "Die Schweiz als Vorbild. Europasymbol und Europagedanke." *Frankfurter Allgemeine Zeitung,* December 15.

1991

1. "Polite Letters and Clio's Fashions." Address at the Irish Conference of Historians, Trinity College, Dublin (1989). In *Ideology and the Historians*, edited by Ciaran Brady, 199–210. Dublin: Lilliput Press.

    a. Corrected version in *Ideas Matter: Essays in Honour of Conor Cruise O'Brien*, edited by Richard English and Joseph Morrison Skelly, 195–210. Dublin: Poolbeg.

2. "'Fictio,' or the Purposes of Historical Statements." Excerpt from *Historical Consciousness*. In *From Texts to Text*, edited by George H. Jensen, 417–21. New York: HarperCollins.

3. "A New World Is Opening Up." *New Hampshire International Seminar*, Center for International Perspectives, University of New Hampshire, Durham, New Hampshire, 1–22.

4. "Response." In *The Opening of the Second World War: Proceedings of the Second International Conference on International Relations, Held at the American University of Paris, September 26–30, 1989*, edited by David W. Pike, part 1, 56–58. New York: Peter Lang. See also, "Excerpts from the Debate," part 1, 61–62, and "Excerpts from the Debate," part 5, 242–245.

5. "The Greatest Danger Ahead: Soviet Breakup." *Arizona Republic,* January 20: sec. C, 2.

6. "The Ultimate Urban Village." *Mid-Atlantic,* February: 36ff.

7. "The Short Century—It's Over." *New York Times,* February 17: sec. E, 13.

    a. Reprinted in *Readings in Global History*, vol. 2, edited by Anthony Snyder and Sherri West, 322–24. Dubuque, IA: Kendall/Hunt, 1992.

8. "Berlin Letter." *Harper's,* March: 66–70.

9. "Churchill és Magyarország." *Élet és Irodalom,* April 5: 5.

    a. Reprinted as appendix to *A párviadal* (Hungarian edition of *The Duel*). Budapest: Európa Könyvkiadó, 1993.

10. "The 'Other Europe' at Century's End." *Wilson Quarterly* (Autumn): 116–22.

11. "The Church in Hungary Today." *America,* October 5: 219–21.

12. "Concept and Symbol of Europe." *New Hungarian Quarterly* (Winter): 3–7.

13. "About the Psychology of the Émigré." *Hungarian Studies,* no. 2: 37–41.

14. "The Transatlantic Duel: Hitler vs. Roosevelt." *American Heritage,* December: 70–77.

1992

1. "America and Russia, Americans and Russians." *American Heritage,* February/March: 64–73.

    a. Reprinted in *New Directions for American History*, vol. 2, edited by Robert James Maddox, 230–35. Guilford, CT: Dushkin Publishing Group, 1993.

2. "The Restaurant Time Forgot." *Town and Country,* May: 68ff.

3. "A párviadal." Excerpts from the Hungarian edition of *The Duel. Nagyvilág*, May: 675–95.
4. "The Patriotic Impulse." Acceptance speech for the Ingersoll Award (1991). *Chronicles*, July: 18–20.
    a. Reprinted as "The Patriotic Identity." In *Immigration and the American Identity: Selections from* Chronicles, *1985–1995*, edited by The Rockford Institute, 197–202. Rockford, IL: The Rockford Institute, 1995.
5. "Finland Vindicated." *Foreign Affairs* (Fall): 50–63.
    a. Translated into Hungarian as "A megörzött Finnország." *Európai Szemle*, no. 1 (1993): 101–10.
6. "American History: The Terminological Problem." *American Scholar* (Winter): 17–32.
    a. Pursuant correspondence: (Summer): 634–36.
    b. Translated into Hungarian as "Amerikai történelem, A terminológiai probléma." *Világosság*, no. 6: 409–19.
7. "Christians and the Temptations of Nationalism." Excerpt from *The End of the Twentieth Century. New Oxford Review*, November: 12–17.

1993

1. "Henry Adams and the European Tradition of the Philosophy of History." In *Henry Adams and His World*, edited by David R. Contosta and Robert Muccigrosso, 322–24. Philadelphia: The American Philosophical Society.
2. "Western Civilization/European/Christian: What Did They Mean 500 Years Ago? What Do They Mean Today?" *Providence: Studies in Western Civilization* (Summer): 429–37.
3. "History: The Bearer of Culture." In *Studiosorum Speculum: Studies in Honor of Louis J. Léka, O. Cist*, edited by Francis R. Swietek and John R. Sommerfeldt, 263–72. Kalamazoo, MI: Cistercian Publications.
4. "Adenauers Deutschland zwischen Ost und West." In *Nach–Denken: Über Konrad Adenauer und seine Politik*, by Haus der Geschichte der Bundesrepublik Deutschland, 64–74. Bonn: Bouvier, 64–74.
5. "Hitler és Magyarország: A kutatás megválaszolandó kérdései." After: "Jodl vezérörnagy feljegyzései az 1944. március 19 és október 15 események elökészitéséröl." *Századok*, nos. 5 and 6: 750–60.
6. "The End of the Twentieth Century: A Historian's Reflection." *Harper's*, January: 39–58.
7. "History, Wild History." *New York Times*, January 8: sec. A, 25.
    a. Reprinted in *Toronto Globe and Mail*, January 18.
8. "Our Seven Deadly Sins of Misdiagnosis." *Arizona Republic*, January 17: sec. C, 1.
9. "Letter from the Baltics: Cold Comfort." *Chronicles*, February: 39–42.
    a. Corrections in *Chronicles*, June: 4.
10. "Prime Time in Budapest." *Los Angeles Times Magazine*, March 7: 36ff.
11. "Herbert Hoover Meets Adolf Hitler." *American Scholar* (Spring): 235–38.
    a. Pursuant correspondence: (Fall): 634–36.

12. "Atom Smasher Is Super Nonsense." *New York Times,* June 17, sec. A, 25.
13. "Philadelphia: A City of Neighborhoods." *Welcome, America* (Philadelphia Convention Center), June 25–July 5.
14. "How Certain Foreigners Saw New York." *City Journal* (Autumn): 104–09.
15. "Churchill és Magyarország." Excerpt from the Hungarian edition of *The Duel. Magyar Nemzet,* September 4.
16. "Horthy Miklós, 1868–1957." *Magyar Hirlap,* September 4.
17. "1918." *American Heritage,* November: 46–51.
18. "Zermatt: Little Town under a Big Mountain." *New York Times,* November 14, Sophisticated Traveler section, 22ff.
19. "Two Worlds." Excerpt from *The End of the Twentieth Century. Hungarian Quarterly* (Winter): 76–93.

1994

1. "Barcza György irott hagyatéka." In *Barcza György: Diplomata emlékeim, 1911–1945,* vol. 2. Budapest: Európa-Historia, 239–43.
2. "An Exceptional Mind, an Exceptional Friend." In *The Unbought Grace of Life: Essays in Honor of Russell Kirk,* edited by James E. Person, 51–54. Peru, IL: Sherwood Sugden, 1994.
3. "Kérdések a sajtószabadság és a demokrácia történelméröl." *Magyar Hirlap,* January 4.
4. "Oroszország a határvidék." Hungarian translations of excerpts from *The End of the Twentieth Century. Nagyvilág,* no. 4: 338–49.
5. "Tiger, Tigre: The perils of translation." *Chronicles,* April: 48.
6. "Benito Mussolini." *New York Times Magazine,* July 24: 14–17.
7. "Revising the Twentieth Century." *American Heritage,* September: 83–89.
   a. Translated into Hungarian as "A huszadik század reviziója." *Világosság,* no. 6, 1995: 63–70.
8. "To Hell with Culture." *Chronicles,* September: 16–19.
   a. Translated into Hungarian as "Pokolba a kulturával " *Európai Szemle,* no. 1, 1995: 11–19.
   b. Reprinted in *Chronicles,* July 2001, 13–15.
9. "Éhes farkas a nyáj között." *Népszabadság,* November 5.
   a. Also published as "Magyarország és a nagyhatalmak 1945–ben." In *Nagy Ferenc miniszterelnök,* edited by István Csicsery-Rónay, 135–38. Budapest: Occidental Press, 1995.

1995

1. "The Meaning of World War II." In *The Americana Annual, 1995: An Encyclopedia of the Events of 1994,* a yearbook of *Encyclopedia Americana,* 567–72. Danbury, CT: Grolier, 567–72.
2. "Off to Off-Season France." *Los Angeles Times,* January 22: sec. L, 1.

3. "Reason and Unreason in Civil Defense." *International Journal of Politics, Culture and Society* (Spring): 507–10.
4. "Neither the Wilderness nor the Shopping Mall." *New Oxford Review*, April: 6–8.
5. "Letter from Normandy." *American Scholar* (Summer): 359–70.

1996

1. Excerpts from *George F. Kennan and the Origins of Containment, 1944–1946: The Kennan-Lukacs Correspondence. Külpolitika*, 106–9.
2. "Our Enemy, the State?" *Wilson Quarterly* (Spring): 108–16.
3. "Phoenixville Needs a Rebuilding of a Small Town Atmosphere—Not a New Mall." *Phoenix* (Phoenixville, PA), May 31: sec. A, 4.
4. "Only in Hungary: The Owl's Castle." *Saveur*, May/June: 26.
5. "Varga Bela életútjáról, halála után egy évvel." *Magyar Nemzet*, November.
6. "A Spa for All Seasons." *New York Times Magazine*, November 10: Sophisticated Traveler section, 54ff.
7. "Goodbye (and Hello) to All That." *Newsday*, December 29: sec. A, 39.

1997

1. "Fear and Hatred." *American Scholar* (Summer): 437–41.
     a. Translated into Hungarian as "Félelem és gyülölet." *Korunk* (Cluj) no. 10: 111–16.
2. "Churchill the Visionary." The Fourteenth Crosby Kemper Lecture, Winston Churchill Memorial, Westminster College, Fulton, Missouri, April 13.
3. "A vallás és a történettudomány." *Vigilia* (Budapest), May: 384–90. Also: Interview with John Lukacs, 330–45.
4. "The Idea that Remade Europe." *Washington Post*, May 25, sec. C, 3.
5. "Moral und die Kunst des Möglichen: Betrachtungen eines amerikanischen Historikers zur Schweiz." *Neue Zürcher Zeitung*, July 31.
     a. Translated into English as "Morality and the Art of the Possible." *Swiss Review of World Affairs* (October): 28–30.
6. Excerpts from *A Thread of Years*, with a special introduction. *Hungarian Quarterly* (Autumn): 13–29.
7. "To Hell with College." *Chronicles*, September: 14–17.
8. "The Folly of Higher Education." *Arizona Republic*, September 14, sec. H, 1–3.

1998

1. "Conservatives Also Oppose Development that Destroys Farms and Neighborhoods." *Phoenix* (Phoenixville, PA), January 23: sec. A, 4.
2. "The Texture of Time." Excerpt from *A Thread of Years. American Heritage*, February/March, 68–72.
3. "A rövid évszázad után." *Magyar Hirlap*, March 28.

4. "The Meaning of '98." *American Heritage,* May/June: 72–80.
5. Excerpts from *A történelmi Hitler. Népszabadság,* June 6.
6. "Vallomások Budapeströl." *Uj Magyar Épitömüvészet,* no. 5: 13–14.
7. "Dwight Macdonald." *Chronicles,* November: 14–16.
8. "Teaching American History." *American Scholar* (Winter): 100–01.

1999

1. "Der Zweite Weltkrieg: In Schutt und Asche." In *Spiegel des 20. Jahrhunderts,* edited by Dieter Wild, 175–86. Hamburg: Spiegel–Buchverlag.
   a. Der Zweite Weltkrieg: In Schutt und Asche." *Der Spiegel,* January 25: 116–25.
2. "Historical Revisionism about the Origins of the Wars of the Twentieth Century." In *War, Resistance and Intelligence: Essays in Honor of M. R. D. Foot,* edited by K. G. Robertson, 71–82. Barnsley: Leo Cooper/Pen and Sword Books.
3. "The Reality of Written Words." *Chronicles,* January: 43–45.
4. "A roved évszázad után." *Forrás,* January: 6–9.
5. "*Évek...*" Excerpts from Hungarian translation of *A Thread of Years. Nagyvilág,* March/April: 216, 245.
6. "The Anderson Cemetery on Valley Park Road." *Schuylkill Township News* (Chester County, PA), Spring: 3.
7. "The Poverty of Anti–Communism." With responses from Robert Conquest, William F. Buckley Jr., and Nathan Glazer. *National Interest* (Spring): 75–86.
   a. Author's responses to Conquest, Buckley, and Glazer: (Summer): 149.
8. "Magyarország a hazám, Amerika az otthonom." *Magyar Nemzet,* June 5.
9. "Erik von Kuehnelt–Lehddin: A Memoir." *Intercollegiate Review* (Fall): 34–36.
10. "Austria." *New York Times Magazine,* November 21, Sophisticated Traveler section, 14–16.

2000

1. "Az Európa–fogalom kialakulàsa és fejlödése: Magyarorszàg helye Európàban." In *A hid tulsó oldalan. Tanulmányok Kelet–Közép Európáról,* edited by Bàn D. András, 9–43. Budapest: Osiris.
2. "1849: az európai forradalmak kora lezárult." *Nagyvilág* (Budapest), nos. 1 and 2: 90–96.
   a. Reprinted in *Magyar Nemzet* (Budapest), February 26: 7.
3. "The Trolley Park at Valley Forge." *Schuylkill Township News* (Chester County, PA), Spring: 3.
4. "The Price of Defending Hitler: A Historian Explains Why a Leading Voice of 'Holocaust Denial' Lost His Libel Case." *Newsweek,* April 24: 4.
5. "Elian Editorial Was Right on the Mark." *Phoenix* (Phoenixville, PA), May 1, sec. A, 4.
6. "Magyarország a huszadik században." *Magyar Nemzet* (Budapest), July 8.

7. "The Tragedy of Two Hungarian Prime Ministers." *Hungarian Quarterly* (Budapest), (Autumn): 77–83.
8. "The Pickering Resevoir." *Schuylkill Township News* (Chester County, PA), Autumn: 3.

2001

1. "The Great Gatsby? Yes, a Historical Novel." In *Novel History: Historians and Novelists Confront America's Past (and Each Other)*, edited by Mark C. Carnes, 235–58. New York: Simon and Schuster.
2. "Ëgy borivó vallomásai." In *Alibi hat h napra*, edited by Alexander Bródy, 9–13. Budapest: Alibi Kiado, 2001.
3. "The Election of Theodore Roosevelt, 1912." In *What If? Eminent Historians Imagine What Might Have Been*, edited by Robert Cowley, 181–94. New York: Putnam.
   a. Paperbound edition: 2002.
4. "Magyar Katolikovok és a zsidókérdés." *Vigilia*, no. 9.
5. "Brandy Old and Great: Armagnac Is Making a Comeback . . ." *Saveur*, January/February: 27–29. (Article badly mangled by editors.)
6. "The Population History of Schuylkill Township." *Schuylkill Township News* (Chester County, PA), Spring: 3.
7. "America's Venice." *American Heritage*, April: 42–49.
8. "Accumulating New Wealth." Commencement address delivered at Stonehill College. *Stonehill Alumni Magazine*, May 22: 33.
9. "Fény Keletröl. Húsvet Varsóban." Excerpts from the Hungarian translation of *Destinations Past. Nagyvilág*, no. 6: 879–90.
10. "Churchill the Visionary." Address at the Churchill Society for the Advancement of Parliamentary Democracy, Toronto, Canada, November 28, 2000. Published as pamphlet.

2002

1. "The Fifties: Another View: Revising the Eisenhower Era." *Harper's*, January: 64–70.
2. "It's the End of the Modern Age." Excerpt from chapter one of *At the End of an Age. Chronicle of Higher Education*, April 26, sec. B, 7–11.
3. "Mechanic." *American Scholar* (Winter): 107–10.
4. "The Old Pickering Schoolhouse." *Schuylkill Township News* (Chester County, PA), Spring: 3.
5. "Párt, nemzet, nép." *Népszabadság* (Budapest), April 13: 25.
6. "The Copenhagen Question: Why Did the Nazis Drop the A-Bomb?" *Daily Telegraph* (London), June 12: 18.
7. "Popular and Professional History." *Historically Speaking*, April: 2–5.
8. "The Universality of National Socialism." *Totalitarian Movements and Political Religions* (London) (Summer): 107–21.

a. Translated into Hungarian as "A nemzetiszocializmus egyetemes jellege." *Klió*, no. 1, 2003: 8–21.

9. "Education, Schooling, Learning: To Hell with Communications." *Chronicles*, September: 17–18.

10. "Hitler's War Years." In *One of Freedom's Finest Hours: Statesmanship and Soldiership in World War II*, edited by Joseph H. Alexander and Larry P. Arnn, 119–28. Hillsdale, MI: Hillsdale College Press.

11. "The Churchill-Roosevelt Forgeries." *American Heritage*, November/December: 65–67.

12. "Menton: Quiet Days and Silent Nights." *New York Times*, November 17, Sophisticated Traveler section, 40–44, 65, 72.

13. Summary of lecture, "The Condition of History." In *Aktuellt om Historia 2002: De svenska historiedagarna í Göteborg 5–7 Oktober 2001*, edited by Göran Olsson, 13–16.

14. "The Obsolescence of the American Intellectual." *Chronicle of Higher Education* October 4: sec. B, 7–10.

2003

1. "Egy någy államferfi érdeklödése Magyarorszá iránt." *Kritika*, February: 29–31.

2. "What *Is* History?" *Historically Speaking*, February: 9–12.

a. Translated into Hungarian as "Mi a történelem." *Klió*, no. 3, 3–10.

3. "Historians and the Cold War." In *The Cold War: Opening Shots 1945–1950*. Lexington, VA: Virginia Military Institute, 35–43.

4. "A Senseless Salute." *New York Times*, April 14, sec. A, 19.

a. Reprinted in *International Herald Tribune*, April 16: 9.

b. Reprinted in *Neue Zürcher Zeitung*, May 4: 22.

c. Reprinted in *Válasz* (Budapest), April 25.

d. Reprinted in *Hintergrund*, May 4: 22.

5. "Fürodökádakról." *Alibi*, no. 4: 95–98.

6. "Stella. De Mégis . . . ." *Alibi*, no. 5: 10–13.

7. "No Pearl Harbor? FDR Delays the War." In *What Ifs? of American History: Eminent Historians Imagine What Might Have Been*, edited by Robert Cowley, 179–88. New York: G. P. Putnam.

8. "A Final Chapter on Churchill." *Chronicle Review*, October 24, sec. B, 7–10.

Part III: Reviews

1948

1. Review of *Christianity and America*, by John J. Meng and Emro Joseph Gergely. *Liturgical Arts*, August: 126.
2. Review of *Kossuth Lajos a reformkorban*, by Domokos Kosáry. *Journal of Modern History* (December): 347–48.

1949

1. Review of *The Cardinal's Story*, by Stephen K. Swift. Under the pseudonym "Luke Ungern." *Thought*, March: 571–72.
2. Review of *Mezőgazdaság és agrártársadalom Magyarországon*, by Gyula Mérei. *Journal of Central European Affairs* (January): 425–26.
3. Review of *Forradalom után*, by Gyula Szekfü. *American Slavic and East European Review* (February): 73–75.
4. Review of *Chronology of the Second World War*, by the Royal Institute of International Affairs. *Journal of Modern History* (March): 69.
5. Review of *Mindszenty—The True Story of the Heroic Cardinal of Hungary*, by Nicholas Boer. *Philadelphia Catholic Standard and Times*, July 15: 8.
6. Review of *Immigrant Life in New York City, 1825–1863*, by Robert Ernst. *Pennsylvania Magazine of History and Biography*, October: 525–26.

1950

1. Review of *Vorspiel zum Krieg im Osten*, by Grigore Gafencu. *Journal of Central European Affairs*: 219–21.
2. Review of four books by and about Cardinal Mindszenty. Under the pseudonym "Luke Ungern." *Thought*: 681–83.

1951

1. Review of *La guerre germano-soviétique 1941–1945*, by A. Guillaume. *American Slavic and East European Review* (December): 308–10.

1953

1. Review of *A House on Bryanston Square*, by Algernon Cecil. *Commonweal*, February 27: 530.
2. Review of *The Genius of American Politics*, by Daniel J. Boorstin. *Commonweal*, July 24: 397–98.
3. Review of *Soviet Imperialism: Its Origin and Tactics*, edited by Waldemar Gurian. *Commonweal*, July 31: 426.
4. Review of *Beyond Containment*, by William Henry Chamberlain. *Commonweal*, October 16: 43.

1954

1. Review of *Une mancata intesa italo-sovietica nel 1940 e 1941*, by Mario Toscano. *American Historical Review* (January): 413.
2. Review of *Challenge in Eastern Europe*, edited by C. E. Black. *Catholic Historical Review* (January): 58–59.
3. Review of *Triumph and Tragedy: The Second World War*, vol. 6, by Winston Churchill. *Commonweal*, January 1: 335–36.
4. Review of *Queen Victoria and Her Prime Ministers*, by Algernon Cecil. *Commonweal*, January 8: 358–59.
5. Review of *World Power in the Balance*, by Tibor Mende. *Commonweal*, March 5: 562–63.
6. Review of *Melbourne*, by Lord David Cecil. *Commonweal*, December 10: 293–94.

1955

1. Review of *A Program for Conservatives*, by Russell Kirk. *Social Order*, May: 231–32.

1956

1. Review of *Czartoryski and European Unity, 1770–1861*, by M. Kukiel. *Catholic Historical Review* (April): 74–75.

1957

1. Review of *Alexis de Tocqueville: The Critical Years, 1848–1851*, by Edward Gargan *The Journal of Modern History* (June): 138–39.
2. Review of *Ouevres complètes*, by Alexis de Tocqueville, edited by J. P. Mayer, André Jardin, and Gustave Rudler. Paris: Gallimard: 1952–. (Review covers Tomb 1, *De la démocratie en Amérique*, Tomb 2, *L'Ancien régime et la révolution*, including *Fragments et notes inedited sur la revolution*, and Tomb 6, *Correspondence anglaise*.) *Journal of Modern History* (September): 280–84.

1958

1. Review of *On the Philosophy of History*, by Jacques Maritain. *National Review*, January 4: 20–21.
2. Review of *Philadelphia Gentlemen: The Making of a National Upper Class*, by E. Digby Baltzell. *National Review*, April 19: 380–81.
3. Review of *Winston Churchill and the Second Front, 1940–43*, by Trumbull Higgins. *New Leader*, May 12: 21–22.
4. Review of *Meinungsforschung und repräsentative Demokratie*, by Wilhelm Hennis. *Journal of Modern History* (September): 271.

1959

1. Review of *Ouevres complètes*, by Alexis de Tocqueville, edited by J. P. Mayer, André Jardin, Maurice Degros, et al. Paris: Gallimard: 1952–. (Review covers Tomb 5, vol.1, *Voyages en Sicile et aux États-Unis*; and vol. 2, *Voyages en Angleterre, Irlande, Suisse, et Algerie*); Also reviewed is: *Alexis de Tocqueville's Amerikabild*, by Bernhard Fabian. Heidelberg: C. Winter, 1957. *Journal of Modern History* (March): 57–60.

1960

1. Review of *Comte de Gobineau–Mère Benedicte de Gobineau: Correspondence, 1872–1883*, edited by A. B. Duff and R. Rancoeur. *Catholic Historical Review* (January): 473–75.
2. Review of *Alexis de Tocqueville in the Chamber of Deputies: His Views on Foreign and Colonial Policy*, by Sister Mary Lawlor. *Review of Politics* (April): 284–86.
3. Review of *Ouevres complètes*, by Alexis de Tocqueville, edited by J. P. Mayer, André Jardin, Maurice Degros, et al. Paris: Gallimard, 1952–. (Review covers Tomb 9, *Correspondence de Alexis de Tocqueville et d'Arthur de Gobineau*.) *Journal of Modern History* (September): 296–97.

1962

1. Review of *Bernanos—His Political Thought and Prophecy*, by Thomas Molnar. *Dokumente* (Cologne), April: 151–52.

1963

1. Review of *The French Army: A Military-Political History*, by Paul Marie de la Gorce and *Dare Call It Treason*, by Richard M. Watt. *New York Review of Books*, June 1: 36–38.
2. Review of *Tocqueville and the Old Regime*, by Richard Herr. *Catholic Historical Review* (January): 546–47.
3. Review of *German Catholics and Hitler's Wars*, by Gordon Zahn. *Review of Politics* (April): 241–43.

1964

1. Review of *The End of Alliance*, by Ronald Steel and *The Politics of the Atlantic Alliance*, by Alvin J. Cottrell and James E. Dougherty. *Worldview*, July/August: 13–15.

2. Review of *The Fall of the House of Hapsburg*, by Edward Crankshaw and *The Anschluss*, by Gordon Brook-Shepherd. *Review of Politics* (October): 547–51.

1965

1. Review of *Pétain et de Gaulle*, by J. R. Tournoux. *Die Zeit* (Hamburg), March 12: 43.

2. Review of *The Historian and History*, by Page Smith. *Catholic Historical Review* (April): 65–67.

3. Review of *Power at the Pentagon*, by Jack Raymond. *Die Zeit* (Hamburg), May 7: 30.

1966

1. Review of *Under Their Vine and Fig Tree: Travels through America in 1797–1799, 1805, with Some Further Account of Life in New Jersey*, by Julian Ursyn Niemcewicz, edited and translated by M. J. E. Budka. *Pennsylvania Magazine of History and Biography*, January: 90–91.

2. Review of *Letters of Oswald Spengler, 1913–1936*. *New York Times Book Review*, March 6: 6.

1967

1. Review of *Mussolini il revoluzionario, 1883–1920*, by Renzo De Felice. *American Historical Review* (April): 1027–28.

2. Review of *The War Years, 1939–1945*, vol. 2, *Diaries and Letters*, by Harold Nicolson. *Saturday Review*, June 17: 27–28.

3. Review of *An Introduction to Contemporary History*, by Geoffrey Barraclough. *Catholic Historical Review* (October): 432–33.

4. Review of *In Search of the Modern World*, by Robert Sinai. *New York Times Book Review*, October 22: 22–24.

5. Review of *Memoirs, 1925–1950*, by George F. Kennan. *New Republic*, October 28: 28–31.

6. Review of *After Victory: Churchill, Roosevelt, Stalin and the Making of Peace*, by William L. Neumann. *Progressive*, December: 42–44.

1968

1. Review of *Säkularisierung: Geschichte eines ideenpolitischen Begriffs*, by Hermann Lübbe. *Catholic Historical Review* (January): 731–32.

2. Review of *Three Faces of Fascism: Action Française, Italian Fascism, National Socialism,* by Ernst Nolte. *Catholic Historical Review* (October): 521.
3. Review of *Der Marschall. Pétain zwischen Kollaboration und Resistance,* by Pierre Bourget. *Die Zeit* (Hamburg), October 18.
4. Review of *History of the Cold War: From the October Revolution to the Korean War, 1917–1950,* by André Fontaine. *Interplay: The Magazine of International Affairs,* November: 54–55.

1969

1. Review of *The Fate of the Revolution: Interpretations of Soviet History: The Impact of the Russian Revolution, 1917–1967,* by Walter Laqueur. Also reviewed is *Revolutionary Russia: A Symposium,* edited by Richard Pipes. *Problems of Communism* (January/February): 35–37.
2. Review of *Why France Fell,* by Guy Chapman and *To Lose a Battle,* by Alistair Horne. *Commonweal,* August 22: 520–21.

1971

1. Review of *The Onset of the Cold War, 1945–1950,* by Herbert Feis. *National Review,* February 9: 152–53.
2. Review of *The Danube Swabians,* by G. C. Paikert. *Catholic Historical Review* (April): 144–46.
3. Review of *Ten Years After: The Hungarian Revolution in the Perspective of History,* edited by Tamás Aczél. *Catholic Historical Review* (July): 357.

1972

1. Review of *The Nature of Civilizations,* by Matthew Melko and *Timeless Problems in History,* by Bernard Norling. *American Historical Review* (October): 1083.
2. Review of *The Coming of Age,* by Simone de Beauvoir. *Triumph,* December: 37.

1973

1. Review of *Timeless Problems in History,* by Bernard Norling. *Catholic Historical Review* (July): 304–05.
2. Review of *Aid to Russia, 1941–1946: Strategy, Diplomacy, and the Origins of the Cold War,* by George C. Herring. *History: Reviews of New Books,* August: 197.
3. Review of *Dilemmas of Democracy: Tocqueville and Modernization,* by Seymour Drescher. *Catholic Historical Review* (October): 428–29.

1974

1. Review of *Fél évszázad,* by Paul Auer. *East Central Europe* 1: 111.

2. Review of *Has the Catholic Church Gone Mad?* by John Eppstein. *Christian Scholars Review* 4, no. 2: 156–57.
3. "The Diplomacy of the Holy See during World War II." Review-article of the series *Actes et documents du Saint Siège relatifs à la Seconde Guerre Mondial*, edited by Pierre Blet, Robert A. Graham, Angelo Martini, and Burkhart Schneider. Vatican City: Libreria editrice vaticana, 1965–1967. (Review covers vol. 6, *Le Saint Siège et les victims de la guerre, Mars 1939–Décembre 1940*, and vol. 7, *Le Saint Siège et la guerre mondiale, Novembre 1942—Décembre 1943. Catholic Historical Review* (July): 271–78. (See also related entries in Reviews: 1976, 1979, 1983.)
4. Review of *Aneurin Bevan: A Biography*, vol. 2, 1945–1960, by Michael Foot. *History: Reviews of New Books*, August: 231.
5. Review of *Race to Pearl Harbor: The Failure of the Second London Conference and the Onset of World War II*, by Stephen E. Pelz. *History: Reviews of New Books*, November/December: 14.

1975

1. Review of *Another Part of the Wood: A Self-Portrait*, by Kenneth Clark. *Philadelphia Sunday Bulletin*, May 18, sec. 4.
2. Review-essay of *Clio and the Doctors*, by Jacques Barzun. *Salmagundi* (Summer): 93–106.

1976

1. Review of *In Search of Europe*, by Guido Piovene. *New York Times Book Review*, February 22: 2ff.
2. Review of *The Complete Works of Saki. New York Times Book Review*, March 28: 6ff.
3. Review of *Uncle of Europe: The Social and Diplomatic Life of Edward VII*, by Gordon Brook-Shepherd. *National Review*, May 28: 572–73.
4. Review-article of *Actes et Documents du Saint Siège relatifs à la Seconde Guerre Mondiale*, edited by Pierre Blet, Robert A. Graham, Angelo Martini, and Burkhart Schneider. Vatican City: Libreria editrice vaticana, 1965–1967. (Review covers vol. 8, *Le Saint Siège et les victims de la guerre. Janvier 1941-Décembre 1942*). *Catholic Historical Review* (October): 667–68.
5. Review of *The Damnable Question: One Hundred and Twenty Years of Anglo-Irish Conflict*, by George Dangerfield. *National Review*, November 12: 1244–45.

1977

1. Review-essay of *Histoire et historiens: Une mutation idéologique des historiens français, 1865–1885*, by Charles-Oliver Carbonell. *Salmagundi* (Spring): 155–60.
2. Review of *Three French Writers and the Great War: Studies in the Rise of Communism and Fascism*, by Frank Field. *New Oxford Review*, May: 21–22.
3. Review of *Hitler's War*, by David Irving. *National Review*, August 19: 946–50.

1978

1. Review of *Interpretations of Fascism*, by Renzo de Felice. *New Oxford Review*, May: 21.
2. Review of *Final Entries 1945: The Diaries of Joseph Goebbels*, edited by Hugh Trevor-Roper. *National Review*, December 8: 50–51.

1979

1. Review-article of *Actes et Documents du Saint Siège relatifs à la Seconde Guerre Mondiale*, edited by Pierre Blet, Robert A. Graham, Angelo Martini, and Burkhart Schneider. Vatican City: Libreria editrice vaticana, 1965–1967. (Review covers vol. 9, *Le Saint Siège et les victims de la guerre, Janvier 1941–Décembre 1943*.) *Catholic Historical Review* (January): 92–94.
2. Review of *Adventures of a Bystander*, by Peter F. Drucker. *American Spectator*, September: 34.
3. Review of *The Old Patagonian Express: By Train through the Americas*, by Paul Theroux. *National Review*, October 26: 1372–74.
4. Review of *White House Years*, by Henry Kissinger. *Philadelphia Inquirer*, November 18, sec. I, 14.

1980

1. Review of *The Advent of War, 1939–1940*, by Roy Douglas. *American Historical Review* (February): 117.
2. Review of *Arabia*, by Jonathan Raban. *National Review*, June 27: 792–93.
3. Review of *Empire as a Way of Life*, by William Appleman Williams. *New Republic*, October 11: 31–33.
4. Review of *Fire in the Minds of Men: Origins of the Revolutionary Faith*, by James H. Billington. *National Review*, November 28: 1465.

1981

1. Review of *The Letters of Evelyn Waugh*, edited by Mark Amory. *National Review*, January 23: 41–44.
2. Review of *The War between the Generals: Inside the Allied High Command*, by David Irving. *New York Times Sunday Book Review*, March 8: 12–13, 27.
3. Review of *Off the Record: The Private Papers of Harry S. Truman*, by Robert H. Ferrell. *Philadelphia Inquirer Sunday Book Review*.
4. Review of *Monty: The Making of a General*, by Nigel Hamilton. *Business Week*, September 28: 15–17.
5. Review of *The Politics of Genocide: The Holocaust in Hungary*, vols. 1 and 2, by Randolph B. Braham. *History: Reviews of New Books*, October: 22–23.
6. "History with a Difference." Review of *God's Fifth Column: The Biography of an Age, 1880–1940*, by William Gerhardie. *New York Times Sunday Book Review*, November 29: 9.

1982

1. "Galbraith Unhooked." *American Spectator,* February: 29–44. (Correspondence about Sidney Hook's October 1981 article on *A Life in Our Times: Memoirs,* by John Kenneth Galbraith, followed by Hook's reply to Lukacs.)

1983

1. Review-article of *Actes et Documents du Saint Siège relatifs à la Seconde Guerre mondiale,* edited by Pierre Blet, Robert A. Graham, Angelo Martini, and Burkhart Schneider. Vatican City: Libreria editrice vaticana, 1965–1967. (Review covers vol. 10, *Le Saint Siège et les victimes de la guerre: Janvier 1944–Juillet 1945.*) *Catholic Historical Review* (January): 81–83.
2. Review of *Growing Up,* by Russell Baker. *National Review,* March 18: 331–32.
3. Review of *In War's Dark Shadow—The Russians before the Great War,* by W. Bruce Lincoln. *Detroit News,* May 18: sec. A, 13.
4. Review-article of *Actes et Documents du Saint Siège relatifs à la Seconde Guerre mondiale,* edited by Pierre Blet, Robert A. Graham, Angelo Martini, and Burkhart Schneider. Vatican City: Libreria editrice vaticana, 1965–1967. (Review covers vol. 11, *Le Saint Siège et les victimes de la guerre: Janvier 1944–Mai 1945.*) *Catholic Historical Review* (July): 414–19.
5. Review of *Like It Was: The Diaries of Malcolm Muggeridge,* by Malcolm Muggeridge. *New Republic,* July 18–25: 37–39.

1984

1. Review of *The Vatican and Hungary, 1846–1878: Reports and Correspondence on Hungary of the Apostolic Nuncios in Vienna,* by Lajos Lukács. *Catholic Historical Review* (July): 496–97.
2. Review of *At Dawn We Slept: The Untold Story of Pearl Harbor,* by Gordon W. Prange; *Infamy: Pearl Harbor and Its Aftermath,* by John Toland; *The Pacific War,* by John Costello; and *The American Magic: Codes, Ciphers and the Defeat of Japan,* by Ronald Lewin. *National Review,* July 9: 840–42.
3. Review of *Vita: A Biography of Vita Sackville-West,* by Victoria Glendenning. *National Review,* September 21: 50–52.
4. Review of *The Past Recaptured: Great Historians and the History of History,* by M. A. Fitzsimons. *Review of Politics* (October): 607–09.
5. Review of *One More Day's Journey,* by Allen B. Ballard. *Philadelphia,* December: 119–20.

1985

1. Review of *Revisionism and Empire: Socialist Imperialism in Germany, 1897–1915,* by Roger Fletcher. *History: Reviews of New Books,* January: 67.

2. Review of *How Democracies Perish*, by Jean-François Revel. *Philadelphia Inquirer*, January 27: sec. P, 1, 6.
3. Review of *Before the Trumpet: Young Franklin Roosevelt 1882–1905*, by Geoffrey C. Ward. *Philadelphia Inquirer*, May 26: sec. P, 1.
4. Review of *Between Russia and the West: Hungary and the Illusions of Peacemaking, 1945–1947*, by Stephen D. Kertesz. *National Review*, May 31: 52–53.
5. Review of *Harold Nicolson*, by James Lees-Milne. *New Yorker*, September 2: 82–86.
6. Review of *Churchill and Roosevelt: The Complete Correspondence*, edited by Warren F. Kimball. *New Yorker*, September 16: 114–22.
7. Review of *The Liberal Mind in a Conservative Age: American Intellectuals in the 1940s and 1950s*, by Richard H. Pells. *Chronicles of Culture*, October: 8–10.

1986

1. Review of *Vichy France and the Resistance: Culture and Ideology*, edited by H. R. Kedward and Roger Austin. *History: Reviews of New Books*, January/February: 79–80.
2. Review of *Son of the Morning Star*, by Evan S. Connell. *Chronicles*, May: 31–40.
3. Review of *Sacco and Vanzetti: The Case Resolved*, by Francis Russell. *National Review*, May 23: 42.
4. Review of *Monte Cassino*, edited by David Hapgood and David Richardson. *Catholic Historical Review* (July): 471.
5. Review of *Alexis de Tocqueville: Selected Letters on Politics and Society*, edited by Roger Boesche. *Chronicles*, September: 29–30.
6. Review of *Home: A Short History of an Idea*, by Witold Rybczynski. *New Yorker*, September 1: 96–99.
7. Review of *Philadelphia on the River*, by Philip Chadwick Foster Smith. *Pennsylvania Magazine of History and Biography*, October: 585.
8. Review of *Forgotten Allies: The Military Contribution of the Colonies, Exiled Governments, and Lesser Powers to the Allied Victory in World War II*, by J. Lee Ready. *American Historical Review* (October): 885.

1987

1. Review of *Passage through Armageddon: The Russians in War and Revolution, 1914–1918*, by W. Bruce Lincoln. *World and I*, January: 434–48.
2. Review of *Pio XII*, edited by Andrea Riccardi. *Catholic Historical Review* (January): 120–21.
3. Review of *The Cycles of American History*, by Arthur M. Schlesinger Jr. *Philadelphia Inquirer*, January 11: sec. P, 7.
4. Review of *István Tisza: The Liberal Vision and Conservative Statecraft of a Magyar Nationalist*, by Gábor Vermes. *Catholic Historical Review* (October): 674–75.

1988

1. Review of *The Tenants of Time*, by Thomas Flanagan. *World and I,* June: 441–44.
2. Review of *Die Tagebücher von Joseph Goebbels: Sämtliche Fragmente*, vols. 1–4, 1924–1941, edited by Elke Fröhlich. *New York Review of Books,* July 21: 14–17.
3. Review of *Catholics, the State, and the European Radical Right, 1919–1945*, by Richard J. Wolff and Jorg K. Hoensch. *Catholic Historical Review* (October): 645–46.
4. Review of *Tocqueville: A Biography*, by André Jardin. *New Yorker,* November 14: 136–40.
5. Review of *A Certain Climate*, by Paul Horgan. *National Review,* November 25: 47–48.

1989

1. Review of *La Romania nella diplomazia Vaticana*, by Ion Dimitriu-Snagov. *Catholic Historical Review* (April): 343.
2. Review of *Citizens*, by Simon Schama. *National Review,* July 1: 48–50.
3. Review of *The Danube*, by Claudio Magris. *Boston Sunday Globe,* September 24: sec. B, 106–07.

1990

1. Review of *Domenico Tardini,1888–1961: L'azione della Santa Sede nella crisi fra le due guerre*, by Carlo Felice Casula. *Catholic Historical Review* (April): 396–97.
2. Review of *Threshold of War: Franklin D. Roosevelt and American Entry into World War II*, by Waldo Heinrichs; *Wind over Sand: The Diplomacy of Franklin D. Roosevelt*, by Frederick W. Marks III; *Roosevelt and Stalin: The Failed Courtship*, by Robert Nisbet; and *From War to Cold War: The Education of Harry S. Truman*, by Robert James Maddox. *Virginia Quarterly Review* (Summer): 547–64.

1991

1. Review of *The Churchill-Eisenhower Correspondence, 1953–1955*, edited by Peter G. Boyle. *New York Times Book Review,* February 10: 3–5.
2. Review of *Reworking the Past: Hitler, the Holocaust, and the Historians' Debate*, edited by Peter Baldwin. *History: Reviews of New Books,* Summer: 174.
3. Review of *Stalin: Triumph and Tragedy*, by Dmitri Volkogonov and *Stalin, Breaker of Nations*, by Robert Conquest. *Boston Globe,* November 10, sec. A, 16.

1992

1. Review of *Bethlen István. Politikai életrajz*, by Ignác Romsics. *New Hungarian Quarterly* (Autumn): 137–39. Hungarian version in *Századok* (1992): 495–96.
2. Review of *Hitler and Stalin: Parallel Lives*, by Alan Bullock. *Philadelphia Inquirer,* March 29.

3. Review of *Church History in the Age of Uncertainty: Historiographical Patterns in the United States, 1906–1990*, by Henry Warner Bowden. *Catholic Historical Review*, (October): 689–90.
4. Review of *The End of History and the Last Man*, by Francis Fukuyama and *The Democracy Trap: Pitfalls of the Post–Cold War World*, by Graham E. Fuller. *Chronicles*, December: 39–40.

1993

1. Review of *Geschichte der Kirche Osteuropas im 20. Jahrhundert*, by Gabriel Andriányi. *Catholic Historical Review* (January): 143–44.
2. Review of *A Historian and His World: A Life of Christopher Dawson*, by Christina Scott. *Intercollegiate Review* (Spring): 50–52.
3. Review of *Out of Control: Global Turmoil on the Eve of the 21st Century*, by Zbigniew Brzezinski. *Washington Post Book World*, May 16: 9.
4. Review of *Összetört cimerek. A Magyar arisz-tokrácia és az 1945 utáni megpróbáltatások*, by János Gudenus-László Szentirmay. *Hungarian Quarterly* (Summer): 131–34.
5. Review of *Heisenberg's War: The Secret History of the German Bomb*, by Thomas Powers. *Philadelphia Inquirer*, 13 June: sec. H, 2.
6. Review of *Churchill: The End of Glory: A Political Biography*, by John Charmley. *Washington Post Book World*, August 22: 8.

1994

1. Review of *Fra Istanbul, Atene e la Guerra. La missione di A. G. Roncalli, 1935–1944*, by Alberto Melloni. *Catholic Historical Review* (April): 392–93.
2. Review of *The Wrath of Nations: Civilization and the Furies of Nationalism*, by William Pfaff. *Freedom Review*, February: 78–79.

1995

1. Review of *The First World War: A Complete History*, by Martin Gilbert and *The Origins of War*, by Donald Kagan. *Los Angeles Times Book Review*, January 22: 1.

1996

1. Review of *Anecdotage: A Summation*, by Gregor von Rezzori. *Washington Post Book World*, April 7: 11–12.
2. Review of *Stalin's Letters to Molotov, 1925–1936*, edited by Lars T. Lih, Oleg V. Naumov, and Oleg V. Khlevniuk. *Chronicles*, March: 36–37.
3. Review of *Die amerikanische Besetzung Deutschlands*, by Klaus-Dietmar Henke. *Review of Politics* (Fall): 840–45.

1997

1. Review of *The Unconscious Civilization*, by John Ralston Saul. *Washington Post Book World*, February 2: 8. Pursuant correspondence: March 2: 15.
2. Review of *The Transformation of European Politics, 1763–1848*, by Paul W. Schroeder. *Continuity* (Spring): 121–24.
3. Review of *André Malraux: A Biography*, by Curtis Cate. *Chronicles*, October: 42–44.

1998

1. Review of *Napoleon: A Biography*, by Frank McLynn. *Guardian* (London), February 19: 12.
2. Review of *The Historical Present: Uses and Abuses of the Past*, by Edwin M. Yoder Jr. *Los Angeles Times Book Review*, April 26: 12.
3. Review of *Faust's Metropolis: A History of Berlin*, by Alexandra Ritchie, and *Berlin and Its Culture: A Historical Portrait*, by Ronald Taylor. *Los Angeles Times Book Review*, May 10: 4.
4. Review of *The Dying President: Franklin D. Roosevelt, 1944–1945*, by Robert H. Ferrell. *Los Angeles Times Book Review*, July 26: 9.
5. Review of *Hitler, 1889–1936: Hubris*, by Ian Kershaw. *Spectator* (London), September 19: 39–40.
6. Review of *American Catholic*, by Charles R. Morris. *Pennsylvania History* (Winter): 97–98.

1999

1. Review of *Säkularisierung, Dechristianisierung, Rechristianisierung im neuzeitlichen Europa: Bilanz und Perspektiven der Forschung*, edited by Hartmut Lehmann. *Catholic Historical Review* (January): 81–82.
2. Review of *Secrecy: The American Experience*, by Daniel Patrick Moynihan. *Los Angeles Times Book Review*, January 3: 7.
3. Review of *The Pity of War*, by Niall Ferguson. *Wall Street Journal*, April 14: sec. A, 24.
4. Review of *Anglomania*, by Ian Buruma. *Los Angeles Times Book Review*, June 6: 2.
5. Review of *Hitler's Vienna: A Dictator's Apprenticeship*, by Brigitte Hamann. *Spectator* (London) July 3: 31–32.
6. Review of *The Passing of an Illusion: The Idea of Communism in the Twentieth Century*, by François Furet. *Boston Sunday Globe*, July 4: F3.
7. Review of *Grand Delusion: Stalin and the German Invasion of Russia*, by Gabriel Gorodetsky. *New Republic*, November 15: 47–50.
    a. Translated into Hungarian in *Klió*, no. 3.
8. Review of *Hitler's Pope*, by John Cornwell. *National Review*, November 22: 59–61.

2000

1. Review of *A Republic, Not an Empire: Reclaiming America's Destiny,* by Patrick J. Buchanan. *Chronicles,* January: 29.
2. Review of *Arthur Koestler: The Homeless Mind,* by David Cesarani. *Los Angeles Times Book Review,* January 9: 9.
   a. Translated into Hungarian as *A nyugtalan ember. Magyar Nemzet* (Budapest), March 14.
3. Review of *Holy Madness: Romantics, Patriots and Revolutionaries, 1776–1871,* by Adam Zamoyski. *Times* (London), February 3: 46.
4. Review of *Copenhagen,* by Michael Frayn. *Los Angeles Times Book Review,* May 12: 6.
   a. Translated into Hungarian as *Heisenberg és Bohr. Világosság* (Budapest), November/December.
5. Review of *Churchill and Appeasement,* by R. A. C. Parker. *Spectator* (London), July 22: 32–33.
6. Review of *Hitler, 1936–1945: Nemesis,* by Ian Kershaw. *Guardian* (London), October 7: 8.
7. Review of *The Third Reich: A New History,* by Michael Burleigh. *National Interest* (Winter): 103–06.

2001

1. Review of *Constantine's Sword: The Church and Jews—A History,* by James Carroll. *Inside the Vatican,* March/April: 50–51.
2. Review of *Lord Acton,* by Roland Hill. *Los Angeles Times Book Review,* April 8: 1.
   a. Translated into Hungarian in *Klió,* no. 3, 2001.
3. Review of *Churchill: A Biography,* by Roy Jenkins; *Churchill: A Study in Greatness,* by Geoffrey Best; and *War Diaries, 1939–1945,* by Field Marshall Lord Alanbrooke. *Los Angeles Times Book Review,* November 18: 1.
4. Review of *The World since 1945: An International History,* by P. M. H. Bell. *National Interest* (Fall): 140–42.
5. Review of *Churchill: A Biography,* by Roy Jenkins. *Spectator* (London), October 13: 48–49.
6. Review of *Huszezeregy Ejszaka,* by Alexander Brody. *Magyar Hirlap,* November 29.

2002

1. Review of *A Moral Temper: The Letters of Dwight Macdonald,* by Michael Wreszin. *Chronicles,* February: 32–33.
2. Review of *The American Line: 1871–1902,* by William Henry Flayhart. *Pennsylvania History* (Winter): 102–04.
3. Review of *Crowd Culture,* by Bernard Iddings Bell. *University Bookman* (Fall): 5–7.

4. Review of *Alamein*, by Jon Latimer; *Alamein*, by Stephen Bungay; *Alamein: War without Hate*, by John Bierman and Colin Smith; and *An Army at Dawn*, by Rick Atkinson. *Los Angeles Times Book Review*, November 24: 11–12.

5. Review of *Napoleon and Wellington*, by Andrew Roberts. *Los Angeles Times Book Review*, December 22: 8.

2003

1. Review of *The Conquerers*, by Michael Beschloss. *Los Angeles Times Book Review*, January 26: sec. R, 4.

2. Review of *Churchill's Cold War: Politics of Personal Diplomacy*, by Klaus Larres. *New Republic*, January 13: 35–38.

    a. Translated into Hungarian in *Klió*, no. 2: 90–97.

3. Review of *Amsterdam*, by Geert Mak. *Journal of the Historical Society* (Spring): 221–22.

4. Review of *The Culture of Defeat*, by Wolfgang Schivelbusch. *Los Angeles Times Book Review*, August 3: 11.

5. Review of *Pattern and Repertoire in History*, by Bertrand Roehner and Tony Syme. *Historically Speaking*, September: 35–38.

6. Review of *The Hungarians: A Thousand Years of Victory in Defeat*, by Paul Levandi. *National Interest* (Fall): 125–27.

Part IV: Miscellaneous

1948

1. Letter. *New York Times Magazine,* 12 September: 2.

1949

1. Letter. *New York Times,* 29 April.

1950

1. Study Group Reports, U.S.-U.S.S.R. Relations ("Minority Opinion"). *World Affairs Councilor,* Philadelphia, August: 4–5.

1951

1. "Kremlin's Rulers Not Superhuman When Heat Is On." *Saturday Evening Post,* May 19: 10, 12.

1953

1. Letter. *Commonweal,* September: 539.
2. Contribution to section titled "Critics' Choice for Christmas." *Commonweal,* December 4: 241–42.

1954

1. Letter. *Uj Hungária,* September 17.
2. Letter. *Commonweal,* November 12: 68–69.
3. "An Autumnal Mood." Review of *Melbourne,* by Lord David Cecil. Contribution to section titled "Critics' Choice for Christmas." *Commonweal,* December 10: 293–94.

1955

1. Letter. *U.S. Naval Institute Proceedings,* February: 213.
2. Letter. *Reporter,* February 10: 6.

1956

1. Contribution to the Loyola Toynbee Symposium. *Mid-America*, April: 73.

1957

1. "An Examination of the Correspondence between Alexis de Tocqueville, Arthur de Gobineau, and Nicholas Khanikov." *American Philosophical Society: Year Book 1957*. Summary of Grant no. 1929 (1955): 333–34.
2. Poem: "The French in Cyprus, 1956." *Commentary*, January: 71.

1958

1. Letter. *Commentary*, April: 352.

1959

1. Tocqueville Centenary: Program and Summary. April 13–14: 959.

1961

1. Letter: "Comment on Tocqueville Article." *French Historical Studies* (Spring): 123–25.
2. Letter. "Answering Professor Hook." *East Europe* 10, no. 10 (October): 39, 51. Reply to Sidney Hook's review of *A History of the Cold War*, in *East Europe* 10, no. 8 (August): 19.
3. Contributions to "The Communist Bloc—How United Is It?" and "A Bridge to Freedom," *East Europe* 10, no. 11 (November): 4, 7, 33–34.
4. Letter: "Haffner on Germany." *Encounter*, December: 93–94.

1962

1. Letter. *Encounter*, November: 94.
2. Correspondence. *American Political Science Review*, March: 141–42.

1963

1. "Father Lynch: A Memoir." *Fournier News*, November 20: 3.

1966

1. Letter. *Daily Republican* (Phoenixville, PA), January, sec. A, 4.
2. "Várhatunk-e változást a nemzetközi politikában és Magyarországon 1966–ban?" Roundtable, New York, March 11.
3. Letter. *Daily Republican* (Phoenixville, PA), November 4, sec. A, 4.

Bibliography

1967

1. Letter. *Daily Republican* (Phoenixville, PA), sec. A, 4.

1968

1. Letter: "The Bolsheviks—50 Years After." *New York Times Magazine,* January 7: 112–13.

1969

1. Letter: "Patriot or Nationalist?" *New York Times,* November 9: sec. E, 15.
2. Letter. *LaSalle Collegian,* November 25: 14.

1970

1. Letter. *Commentary,* June: 25.

1973

1. Author-Reviewers symposia: "*The Passing of the Modern Age.*" Peter A. Bertocci, Richard L. Morrill—Author's Response, John Lukacs. *Philosophy Forum* 12: 2–14.

1975

1. Interview. *Philadelphia Inquirer,* March 2: sec. H, 8.

1976

1. Letter. *Horizon,* Autumn: 110.
2. Letter. *Commentary,* November: 27–29
3. Interview. *Today's Post* (King of Prussia, PA), November 2.
4. Interview: "Prophet of the Past." *Washington Post,* December 31: sec. C, 1–2.

1977

1. Christmas book recommendations. *American Spectator,* December: 27–28.

1978

1. "C. A. Macartney." In *Austrian History Yearbook*, vol. 14, by the American Historical Association Conference Group for Central European History, 435–36. New York/Oxford: Berghahn Books.
2. Franco-American Symposium: "Images of the Two Peoples: Visions of France and America." *Mid-America,* April: 5–12.

1980

1. Obituary: "Ross Hoffman, R.I.P." *National Review,* March 7: 268–69.
2. Letter: "Wallenberg and the Jews of Hungary. Keeping Up with Friends Schlesinger and Liberalism." *New York Times Magazine,* May 4: 36.

1982

1. Letter. *American Spectator,* March: 41.
2. Remarks at symposium: "Tokyo Colloquium." Yomiuri Research Institute, Tokyo, September: 63–75. Also in *Daily Yomiuri,* October: 11–15.

1983

1. Interview. *La Nazione* (Florence), November 26.

1984

1. Response to Sniegoski review. *Continuity,* 105–06.
2. Interview. *Schuylkill Bugle* 1: 4.
3. Letter. *Evening Phoenix* (Phoenixville, PA),February 1.
4. Interview. *U.S. News and World Report,* August 13: 70.
5. Letter: "What Makes Our Candidates?" *Harper's,* September: 6–7.
6. "I Wish I'd Been There." *American Heritage,* December: 38.

1985

1. Excerpts from previous writings. *Raleigh (NC) Reporter,* March 2, April 13, May 11, May 25, and June 8.
2. "The Best Place to Live." *Philadelphia,* April: 144.
3. Contribution to section titled "Guide to Summer Reading." *Philadelphia,* July: 162.
4. Interview. *Kanadai Magyarság,* July 6.
5. Quip. *New Yorker,* August 5: 67.
6. Letter: "We Are Not the World." *National Review,* November 29: 4.

1986

1. "Churchill y Roosevelt." *La Prensa* (Buenos Aires), January 21. Same in *El Universal* (Caracas), January 24; *Tempo* (Lisbon), January 31–February 8; *Lauh-Kunj* (Jamshepdpur), February 8; *Janta* (Mirzapur), January 23; *Bharat-Ratna-Kesatri,* January 29; *Basti-Khi-Awaz,* February 2; *La Estrella de Panama,* January 22; *Adarsh-Bani,* January 25; *Nainpur-Times,* January 27; *Mai-Rastra,* January 24; *Rampur-Ki-Pukar,* January 26; *Madhya-Yug,* Banda, January 23; *Rashtra-Vhin* (Gorakhpur), January 20.

2. "Orwell's Legacy: A Discussion with John Lukacs, Edward Said and Gerald Graff." *Salmagundi* (Spring/Summer): 121–28.
3. "The Intellectual in Power: A Discussion with Conor Cruise O'Brien and John Lukacs." *Salmagundi* (Spring/Summer): 257–66.

1987

1. Letter: "Schlafly's America." *Harper's,* January: 7.
2. Contribution to "Symposium on Humane Socialism and Traditional Conservatism." *New Oxford Review,* October: 8.

1988

1. Contribution to roundtable: "Best and Worst in the Reagan Administration." *Wall Street Journal,* April 6: 25.
2. Interview. *Pittsburgh Tribune-Review,* April 24.
3. "American." In "Most Overrated/Most Underrated" symposium. *American Heritage,* July/August: 58.

1989

1. Conversation with Bill Moyers (televised, 1988). In *A World of Ideas: Conversations with Thoughtful Men and Women about America Today and the Ideas Shaping Our Future,* edited by Bill D. Moyers and Betty Sue Flowers. New York: Doubleday: 434–46. Also paperbound edition, 1989.
2. Letter. *Evening Phoenix* (Phoenixville, PA) April 3: sec. A.
3. Interview. *Philadelphia Inquirer,* April 30: sec. M, 11.
4. Interview. *Philadelphia Catholic Standard and Times,* May 25.
5. Interview: "Neighbors." *Philadelphia Inquirer,* June 4.
6. Summary of remarks at the Second International Conference on International Relations, University of Paris, September 26–30, 1989. *Newsletter of the American Committee on the History of the Second World War,* Autumn: 6–9.
7. Interview. *168 óra,* August 29.
8. "Enough for One Life." *American Heritage,* December: 76.

1990

1. Interview. *Mozgó Világ,* no. 2: 3–7.
2. Letter. *Evening Phoenix* (Phoenixville, PA), January 10: sec. A.
3. Correspondence. *New Oxford Review* (March): 6–8.
4. "Regret and Promise." Contribution to symposium titled "Christianity in Sight of the Third Millennium. *Modern Age* (Summer): 165–68.
5. Interview: "Now for an Opposing Point of View." *Philadelphia,* June: 57–60.
6. Contribution to roundtable: "The Pros and Cons of Immigration." *Chronicles,* July: 15–16.

7. Interview. *Chestnut Hill Local* (Philadelphia), December 27.

1991

1. "History of Schuylkill Township." Schuylkill Township Directory (Chester County, PA).
2. "Current Wisdom." Excerpt from "Berlin Letter." *American Spectator,* April: 43.
3. Interview. *Kurir,* May 2.
4. Interview. *168 óra,* June 4.
5. Letter: "Real Differences in Schuylkill." *Evening Phoenix* (Phoenixville, PA), October 31: sec. A.

1992

1. "A Harper's Magazine Dictionary of Words that Don't Exist but Ought to." Contribution to *In a Word,* edited by Jack Hitt, 21. New York: Dell Publishing.
2. "Appreciating John Lukacs," by Robert H. Ferrell. (Includes sentences from an interview.) *Review of Politics* (Spring): 1–8.
3. Contribution to roundtable: "My Favorite Historical Novel." *American Heritage,* October: 94. Pursuant correspondence: December: 8–9.
4. Letter. *American Heritage,* December: 8–9.

1993

1. Foreword to *As I Saw It: The Tragedy of Hungary,* by Géza Lakatos, i–iii. Englewood, NJ: Universe Publishing.
2. Interview. *Europeo* (Milan/Rome), January 29: 27–29.
3. Reply to letter. *New Oxford Review,* January/February: 6–7.
4. Interview. *Morning Call Magazine* (Allentown, PA), May 3.
5. Interview. *Arkansas Democrat-Gazette* (Little Rock, AR), May 30.
6. Interview. *Washington Times: Insight on the News,* July 5: 14–17.
7. Interview. *Philadelphia Inquirer,* August 5.
8. Quoted in On the Scene: "No Tidal Wave," by Donald Kirk. *National Review,* August 9: 26.
9. Interview. *Magyar Nemzet,* October 16.
10. Interview. *168 óra,* October 19.

1994

1. Excerpts from previous writings. *Raleigh (NC) Reporter,* February 26, March 12, March 26, April 23, May 7, May 21, June 4, June 18, July 2, July 16, July 30, September 24, October 8, October 22, November 5, November 19, December 3, December 17, and December 31.
2. Interview. *Beszélö,* January 26.
3. Interview. *Magyar Hirlap,* May 14.

4. Interview. *Népszabadság,* June 11.
5. "A Conversation with John Lukacs" and "Tributes to John Lukacs." (Includes tributes by E. Digby Baltzell, Jacques Barzun, and Robert Maddox.) *Pennsylvania History,* July: 271–87.
6. Interview. *Dagens Nyheter,* Stockholm, September 2.
7. Interview. *Het Parool,* Amsterdam, December 3.
8. "Hitler forutság kalla kriget." *Svenska Dagbladet,* Stockholm, December 3.

1995

1. Foreword to *Villanova University: 1842–1992,* by David R. Contosta, xiii–xiv. State College, PA: Pennsylvania State University Press.
2. Interview: "Szindbád Phoenixvilleben." In *Csodák pedig vannak. 12 amerikai karrier,* by György Bolgár and Erzsébet Fazekas, 69–81. Budapest: Lettera Works.
3. Interview. *Uj Magyarország,* January 16.
4. Interview. *Magyar Nemzet,* January 17.
5. Excerpts from previous writings. *Raleigh (NC) Reporter,* January 14, January 28, and February 11.

1996

1. Contribution to roundtable: "The Responsibility of Intellectuals." In *The New Salmagundi Reader,* edited by Robert Boyers and Peggy Boyers, 453ff. Syracuse, NY: Syracuse University Press.
2. "Thassy Jenö. Egy korkép." Introduction to vol. 1 of *Veszélyes vidék: visszaemlékezések,* an autobiography of Jenö Thassy. Budapest: Pesti Szalon.
3. "The Reader Replies." *American Scholar* (Summer): 478.
4. Interview: *Népszabadság,* June 26.
5. Excerpts of previous writings. *Raleigh (NC) Reporter,* September 10–October 8.
6. Interview. *Népszava,* December 11.
7. Interview. *Magyar Nemzer,* December 21.

1997

1. Introduction to *Sunflower,* by Gyula Krúdy, translated by John Bátki, 5–22. Budapest: Corvina. (Introduction is largely a reprint of an essay that appeared in the *New Yorker,* December 1, 1986.)
2. "Képek és különbözöségeik." In *Magyarország 2000, Magyarország képe a nagyvilágban,* edited by Gyula Keszthelyi, 153–55. Budapest: Osiris.
3. Interview. *Phoenix* (Phoenixville, PA), January 27: sec. A.
4. Obituary: "Recalling the Life of William H. Reeves III." *Phoenix* (Phoenixville, PA), May 16: sec. A.
5. Reprints of various writings. *Raleigh (NC)Reporter,* September 6, September 20, August 23, October 4, October 18, November 1, November 15, November 29, and December 13.

1998

1. "Erösiteni az önbizalmat." In *III. Magyarország 2000*, edited by Attila Komlós, 580–81. Budapest: Pan Press.
2. Interview. *Népszabadság*, January 31.
3. Interview. *Penn History Review* (Spring): 105–08.
4. Interview. *Kurir*, June.
5. Interview. *Szentendre/Castrum*, June 23.
6. Contribution to roundtable: "America: Triumphant or Troubled?" *American Enterprise*, July/August: 63–64.
7. Letter (concerning Gar Alperovitz and Harry Truman). *Los Angeles Times Book Review*, August 23: 10.
8. Interview. *Svenska Dagbladet*, Stockholm, October 25.

1999

1. Interview. *Demokrata*, no. 25.
2. Interview: "Messze még az egyesult Európa." *Magyar Nemzet*, March 13.
3. "Best Mistake (By Accident)." *New York Times Magazine*, April 18: 134–35.
4. "Ideas." In "Most Overrated; Most Underrated" symposium: *American Heritage*, June: 65.
5. Interview: "Isten görbe vonalakkal ir egyenest." *Népszabadság*, June 19.
6. Interview: *Heti Studentexpressz*, June 22.
7. Interview: *Könyvhét*, July.
8. Contribution to roundtable: "New People, New Century." *Chronicles*, August: 15–16.
9. Letter. *Phoenix* (Phoenixville, PA), August 10: sec. A.
10. Letter: "The Reader Replies: Is the Universe Designed?" *American Scholar* (Fall): 153.
11. Contribution to "Forgotten Treasures: A Symposium." *Los Angeles Times Book Review*, December 26: 5.

2000

1. Introductory essay to *Krúdy's Chronicles: Turn-of-the-Century Hungary in Gyula Krúdy's Journalism*, edited and translated by John Bátki. Budapest: Central European University Press.
2. Interview. *Népszabadság*, Budapest, January 29.
3. Interview: "Judging Pius XII." *Inside the Vatican*, February: 62.
4. Letter: "Let Residents Run the Roads." *Phoenix* (Phoenixville, PA), February 17: sec. A.
5. "Churchill vs. Hitler: The Duel: The Battle of Minds that Changed History." Consultant and partial writer to television program. *BBC Fourth Programme*, May 8.
6. Interview. *Debrecen*, May 31.

7. Interview. "A történelemnek nincs szaknyelve." *Hajdu Bihari Napló,* June 7.
8. Interview. "A tömeqek demokrácaja." *18 6ra,* Budapest, July.
9. Interview: "Vegetables Don't Have a History: A Conversation with Historian John Lukacs," by Donald A. Yerxa and Karl W. Giberson. *Books and Culture,* July/August: 14–15.
10. "Lukacs Speaks at First Curti Lecture." *Badger Herald* (Madison, WI), October 24.
11. Interview: "Nem kerül erös kézbe az amerikai kormányrúd." *Magyar Hirlap,* Budapest, November 13.

2001

1. Aphorisms. In *Huszezeregy éjszaka,* edited by Alexander Brody.
2. "Hitler." In *Encyclopedia Britannica,* 15th revised edition, vol. 20, 627–29.
3. "1849: Az europai forradalmak kora lezárult." *Petöfi Irodalmi Múszeum.*
4. Interview. *Fides et Historia* (Winter/Spring): 130–36.
5. Interview. *Enterprise,* May 21.
6. Interview. *Heti Válasz,* June 29.
7. Interview. *Népszáva,* July 7.
8. Interview. *Magyar Hirlap,* July 27.
9. "Nézem a hazámat. Beszélgetés John Lukacs (Lukács Janós) Amerikában élö történésszel." *Népszabadság,* August 25.
10. Interview. *Magyar Nemzet,* September 15.
11. Interview: "Lessons in History," by Laura Fording. *Newsweek.* Newsweek Web Exclusive. September 21. http://www.msnbc.msn.com/id/3668484/site/newsweek.
12. Obituary: "Bán András halálára." *Népszabadság,* October 1.
13. Interview. *Philadelphia Inquirer,* October 7: sec. H, 1, 7.
14. Quoted in "Man of the Hour: How Should a Leader Lead?" in *People Weekly,* by Alex Tresniowski, Mina Biddle, Molly Fahner, et al. November 12: 141ff.
15. "The Structure of History Is Changing." In "This New War" symposium. *American Heritage,* December: 29.
16. Excerpt of lecture at the Hungarian Embassy (October). *Magyar Nemzet,* December 14.

2002

1. "New Insight on Churchill's View of Hungary." *Budapest Sun,* June 13–19.
2. Interview. *Hetek,* June 14.
3. Interview. *Magyar Nemzet,* June 15.
4. Interview. *Népszabadság.* July 6.
5. Quote. *Merriam Webster's Collegiate Dictionary,* 10th edition: 417.
6. Interview. *Prime Time Magazine* (Bucks County, PA), September.
7. Interview. *O Estado de S. Paulo,* October 6.

2003

1. "History in the Democratic Age: Historian John Lukacs Talks with Chairman Bruce Cole." *Humanities* (January/February): 6–9, 49–50.
2. Letter. *New York Times*, April 25: sec. A, 30.
3. "Philosopher." In "Most Overrated/Most Underrated" symposium. *American Heritage*, October: 47.

Notes ❋❋❋

Preface

1. José Ortega y Gasset, *History as a System and Other Essays toward a Philosophy of History,* trans. by Helene Weyl (New York, 1961), 217. Italics in the original.

2. C. G. Jung, *Memories, Dreams, Reflections,* trans. by Richard and Clara Winston (New York, 1989), 236.

3. Ortega y Gasset, *History as a System,* 218.

4. John Lukacs, *At the End of an Age* (New Haven, CT, 2002), 59.

5. Benedetto Croce, *History: Its Theory and Practice,* trans. by Douglas Ainslie (New York, 1921), 11–15.

6. E. H. Carr, *What Is History?* (New York, 1961), 111.

7. Lukacs, *At the End of an Age,* 53–56.

8. Leopold von Ranke, "Fragment From The 1830's," in Fritz Stern, ed., *The Varieties of History from Voltaire to the Present* (New York, 1973), 59.

9. Leopold von Ranke, "Histories of the Latin and Germanic Nations from 1494–1514," in Stern, ed., *The Varieties of History from Voltaire to the Present,* 58.

10. John Bagnell Bury, "The Science of History," in Stern, ed., *The Varieties of History from Voltaire to the Present,* 211, 219.

11. John Lukacs, *Remembered Past: John Lukacs on History, Historians, and Historical Knowledge— A Reader,* ed. by Mark G. Malvasi and Jeffrey O. Nelson (Wilmington. DE, 2005), 175.

12. Lukacs, *At the End of an Age,* 58.

13. Raymond Aron, *Introduction to the Philosophy of History: An Essay on the Limits of Historical Objectivity,* trans. by George J. Irwin (Boston, 1961), 47. Italics in the original.

14. John Lukacs, *Historical Consciousness: The Remembered Past* (New Brunswick, NJ, 1994), 31.

15. Norman Kemp Smith, ed., *Descartes' Philosophical Writings* (New York, 1958), 131.

16. Lukacs, *Historical Consciousness,* 266.

17. Ibid., 31. Italics in the original.

18. Lukacs, *At the End of an Age,* 160–61, 150.

19. Lukacs, *Historical Consciousness,* 289.

20. Ibid., 268.

21. Lukacs, *At The End of an Age,* 206.

22. Ibid., 210.

23. Blaise Pascal, *Pensées,* trans. by W. F. Trotter (New York, 1958), 346–47, 97.

24. Lukacs, *At the End of an Age,* 204. Italics in the original.

25. Johan Huizinga, "The Task of Cultural History," in *Men and Ideas*, trans. by James S. Holmes and Hans van Marle (New York, 1959), 53.

26. R. G. Collingwood, *The Idea of History* (London, 1977), 215.

27. H. Stuart Hughes, *History as Art and Science: Two Vistas on the Past* (Chicago, 1975), 99.

28. Lukacs, *At the End of an Age*, 70; see also Lukacs, *Historical Consciousness*, 229.

29. Lukacs, *At the End of an Age*, 141.

30. Quoted in Harold C. Raley, *José Ortega y Gasset: Philosopher of European Unity* (Tuscaloosa, AL, 1971), 21.

31. Lukacs, *At the End of an Age*, 75.

32. Ibid., 214.

33. Marc Bloch, *The Historian's Craft*, trans. by Peter Putnam (New York, 1953), 4–5.

34. Lukacs, *At the End of an Age*, 223. Italics in the original.

35. Ibid., 184, 222.

36. Ibid., 183.

37. Ibid., 77.

38. Lukacs, *Historical Consciousness*, 236.

39. John Lukacs, *Confessions of an Original Sinner* (New York, 1990), xiv.

40. Ibid., 4.

41. John Lukacs, *A Thread of Years* (New Haven, CT, 1998), 477, 8.

42. John Lukacs, *Five Days in London, May 1940* (New Haven, CT, 1999), 219.

43. Lukacs, *Confessions of an Original Sinner*, 271.

I. The Problem of Historical Knowledge

❀ ❀ ❀

1. The Presence of Historical Thinking

1. This kind of association is of course part and parcel of the bureaucratization of entire societies. Yet there are historians who are not thus employed, who are not professors of history. They write history books on their own, which are published. When people know this, their inclination is to identify such a person as an amateur historian; but, more probably, as a *writer*.

There is nothing very wrong with this. A historian who cannot or does not write well cannot be much of a historian; moreover, the historian's instrument is everyday language, dependent on words that are more than the mere packaging of "facts." However, I must recount an amusing, and perhaps not altogether pleasing, experience during a coffee break at a scholarly conference where I had given a paper that was perhaps more fluent and easy than some of the others. I overheard someone answering a question about who I was: "He is a historian; but he is really a writer." There was something slightly deprecatory in this statement. (Such is the professionalization of historianship now in the United States. There are other countries and other languages where, even now, such a statement would not be deprecatory.)

2. The first edition of the *Dictionary of the French Academy*, published in 1694, defined history

as the "narration of actions and of matters worth remembering." The eighth edition, in 1935, said much the same: "the account of acts, of events, of matters worth remembering." *Dignes de mémoire!* Worth remembering! What nonsense this is! Is the historian the kind of person whose training qualifies him to tell ordinary people what is worth remembering, to label, or to authenticate persons or events as if they were fossil fish or pieces of rock? Is there such a thing as a person and another such as a historical person? Every event is a historical event; every source is a historical source; every person is a historical person.

3. Johann Wolfgang von Goethe, *Theory of Colours* (London, 1840), xvii, xxiv.

4. William James, *Memories and Studies* (New York, 1911), 312–13.

5. Cited in Nancy C. Struever, *The Language of History in the Renaissance* (Princeton, NJ, 1970), 51. Also Ibid., 70: Alberti's friend, Coluccio Salutati: "Eloquence is difficult, but history is even more difficult."

6. "*L'histoire digne de ce nom doit estre générale.*" From George Huppert, *The Idea of Perfect History: Historical Erudition and Historical Philosophy in Renaissance France* (Urbana, IL, 1970). A very impressive work, proving what I overlooked in *Historical Consciousness,* where I situated the crystallization of modern historical consciousness largely in the seventeenth century, not earlier. (Huppert, 182: "In sum, then, the French prelude to modern historiography was more than a prelude, it was a stunning first act, full of consequences.") Huppert, 166: "Here then is historical-mindedness—historicism, if you will—solidly established in the mental habits of a handful of scholars in the sixteenth century. Neither Locke's psychology nor the scientific revolution seem to have been prerequisites for the growth of a sense of history as we understand it. This state of mind existed in all of its essentials before 1660. It disappeared again—or at least it was weakened and suppressed—in the course of the next century, precisely during the time when science and Cartesian rationalism became important features of European culture." It was more than a historical oddity.

7. Aileen Kelly, *View From the Other Shore* (New Haven, CT, 1999), 210.

8. Consider what happens when we are concerned or worried about someone who is dear to us. Can we separate our concerns for her from how that concern affects (and will affect) us? There *may* be an imbalance of these two concerns; between our thinking *mostly* about her and our thinking *mostly* about how her situation affects or will affect us. But *in any case,* these concerns are inseparable: both "objectivity" (an exclusive concentration only on her condition) and "subjectivity" (an exclusive concentration only on my condition) are impossible. Our consciousness and our knowledge (and our concern and our expectations) are participatory, and thus inseparable.

Simone Weil: "I used to believe, with regard to any problem whatever, that to know was to solve the problem; now I realize that it means to know how the problem concerns me."

9. Johan Huizinga, *Men and Ideas: History, the Middle Ages, the Renaissance.* I chose this passage for the epigraph, and motto, of one of my books, *The Duel* (New York, 1990). The relative success of this book and of the related *Five Days in London: 24–28 May 1940* (New Haven, CT, 1999), was, I am convinced, largely the result of the fascination of readers in reading how close Hitler came at that time to winning the war, and how Churchill was able to deflect him: in other words, in reading of the existence of a potentiality inherent in, and inseparable from, the actuality of those times.

10. One characteristic of Christianity is the condition that it says little about the *motives* of evil, while it says plenty about how evil exists and comes into existence.

11. Peter Burke, *Vico* (Oxford, 1985), 78.
12. The great German historian Theodor Mommsen, more than one hundred years ago: "History is one of those academic subjects which cannot be directly acquired through precept and learning. For that, history is in some measure too easy and in some measure too difficult. The elements of the historical discipline cannot be learned, for every man is endowed with them." The great Jakob Burckhardt, one hundred years ago: history has no method, except one: *bisogna saper leggere*—you must know how to read.
13. Sociological: scientific, pretending to be *definitive*. Sociographical: *descriptive*, with an appeal to our retrospective and imaginative understanding.
14. Carr's is a twentieth-century, an automobile-age version, of Tolstoy's nineteenth-century nonsense of History as a Locomotive. Both Tolstoy and Carr deny free will. Moreover, the important thing is where the driver is going and not, as Tolstoy declared, the mechanism of the locomotive; the important question is "What is Carr driving at?" and not "What make is this Carr?"
15. Besides, Carr cannot quite detach himself from the terminology of Objectivity. "It does not follow," he writes, "that, because a mountain appears to take on different angles of vision, it has objectively no shape at all or an infinity of shapes." But the more objective our concept of the shape of the mountain, the more abstract that mountain becomes. For the existence of the mountain was meaningless until men appeared on the scene, and saw it, and eventually called it a mountain. (Much later they conceived it as an objective fact.) Ortega y Gasset in *The Modern Theme* (New York, 1923, trans. 1933): "Perspective is one of the components of reality. Far from being its deformation it is its organization. A reality which would remain always the same when seen from different points is an absurdity."
16. People do not *have* ideas. They *choose* them.
17. Every philosophy of idealities is also inevitably a historical phenomenon.
18. The fine Hungarian writer Dezsó Kosztolányi (about the absurdity of an international language): "Knife. Yes, someone may tell me that *couteau, coltello, Messer* do not quite correspond to 'knife.' But no one can tell me that knife is not a knife." Confucius: "When words lose their meaning people lose their freedom"—very true. (Yet in Chinese "country," "state," "nation" are one word....)
19. Owen Chadwick, in *Catholicism and History: The Opening of the Vatican Archives* (Cambridge, 1978), 2: "Modern history is sometimes called loosely 'scientific history.'" Page 44: "All historical events remain in part mysterious."
20. Are we ineluctably involved with history in *thinking* the truth? Yes, because thinking, "cognition," is almost always the result of re-cognition. But all of us experience occasional and mysterious stabs of truth that are *more* than recognitions.
21. Owen Barfield, *History, Guilt, and Habit* (Middletown, CT, 1979), 74. I consider this—so often hardly recognized—English writer (1898–1998) as one of the greatest, and surely one of the profoundest and clearest (a rare combination!) thinkers in the twentieth century. I am not alone in this. So had his friend C. S. Lewis considered Barfield (also T. S. Eliot at least on one occasion).
22. This widespread appetite for history exists when no such widespread appetite for science exists. Yet it is science that has produced its most wondrous and hardly imaginable applications during the twentieth century. In the 1920s Henry Ford declared, "History is bunk," and Herbert Hoover's Secretary of Commerce said: "Tradition is the enemy of progress." No "conservatives" or even "liberals" think that way now

23. "All kinds of writers have been trying this (Upton Sinclair, Dos Passos, Irwin Shaw, Styron, Doctorow, Mailer, Sontag, De Lillo, Vidal, Pynchon in this country, many others abroad . . .). What is significant is that these novelists are, all, interested in history. What they have been doing is the reverse of the historical novel, where history was the colorful background. For these twentieth-century novelists history is the foreground, since it attracts them. But most of these authors don't really know that, which is why their works are flawed: for they illegitimately, and sometimes dishonestly, mix up history and fiction. So they include and twist and deform and attribute thoughts and words and acts to historical figures—Lincoln, Wilson, Roosevelt, Kennedy—who actually existed. That is illegitimate, since it produces untruths—no matter that some academic historians may say it serves salutary purposes, as it introduces all kinds of people to history, after all. They are wrong. What they ought to recognize, rather, is the untrammeled spreading of a historical consciousness whereby it is indeed possible that in the future the novel may be entirely absorbed by history, rather than the contrary." From the introduction of my *A Thread of Years* (New Haven, CT, 1998).

24. In Kevin Starr's review of a biography of Randolph Hearst (by David Nasaw, in the *Los Angeles Times Book Review,* June 18, 2000)—which I read on the very day when I first composed these pages. "Coincidences are spiritual puns. . . ."

25. János Pilinszky: "The novel is the only real genre (perhaps the drama is, too, but only to an extent) the subject of which is *time.* No other form of art can deal with that, and yet it is the driving force of the novel. And therefore I regret when the novel in the twentieth century begins to move toward poetry." (Note that this was written by a poet.)

26. Thomas Hardy, "Candour in English Fiction," quoted in J. Korg, *George Gissing: A Critical Biography* (Seattle, 1979), 261.

27. From my *Historical Consciousness* (New York, 1984 edition), 341. Earlier (New York, 1968 edition) I wrote "that the Western world has yet to see the appearance of a truly classic historian, a historian Dante, a historian Shakespeare." "To this I shall add, eighteen years later, that I have grown more certain of this every year: that sooner or later someone, with all the natural ease of genius, will suddenly reveal to us a new kind of history for which there will have been hardly any precedent. I am no prophet, and historian enough to despise prognostication, but here I am somehow compelled to speculate that this might occur in the twenty-first century, and perhaps even sooner than that."

28. Of course I have not been alone in this. Here are a few random samples. Owen Barfield around 1980: "The Western outlook emphasizes the importance of *history* and pays an ever increasing attention to it. . . . There is a new concept of *history* in the air, a new feeling of its true significance. We have witnessed the dim dawning of a sense that history is to be grasped as something substantial to the being of man, as an 'existential encounter.'" (Barfield wrote this around the time when slogans about "post-historic man" and "the end of history" became current.) The epigrammatic Ortega y Gasset a generation earlier: "History is not only seeing, it is thinking what has been seen. And in one sense or another, thinking is always construction." "I am a man who truly loves the past. Traditionalists, on the other hand, do not love it; they want it to be not past but present." "Man is not a *res cogitans* but a *res dramatica.* He does not exist because he thinks, but, on the contrary, he thinks because he exists." "In short, man has no nature, but instead he has . . . history." "The dawning of a new age of historical reason." The historian Johan Huizinga (1935): "Historical thinking has entered our very blood."

2. About Historical Factors, or the Hierarchy of Powers

1. Perhaps it may be said that we remember "portions" of the past: whereas, whenever we think that we ought to reconstruct something historically, what we are striving for is the mental reconstruction of a certain "period."

2. Regarding inflation: In 1919 the dollar was worth dozens of German marks, in 1923 billions, in 1924 four or five. Leaving aside the point of the "old" and the "new" Reichsmark, not only does the wild extreme of 1923 give us a fantastically distorted picture of the— admittedly difficult—state of the German national economy in that year, but also, no serious historian will say that Germany was weaker in 1923 than she was in 1919. Moreover, while it is true that the German inflation was a very serious thing, and that it was involved with many disastrous social, political, and cultural consequences, in retrospect it seems that neither the inflation of the early Twenties nor the depression of the early Thirties fundamentally deflected the course of German history after World War I; with or without inflation, with or without depression, the recovery of German national power and of German national confidence is discernible after 1920. I am not saying that these economic catastrophes made no difference at all: I am only saying that they made less difference than what we have been accustomed to think. (Consider, too, the experiences of France in the 1790s, the United States in the 1770s, Greece in the 1940s; these disastrous inflations harmed these nations relatively little in the long run; their power and prestige and prosperity rose steeply after these chastening experiences.)

3. In his *Neue Wege der Sozialgeschichte* Otto Brunner made a very important distinction between the older "household" economics and the newer accounting-economics.

4. During the nineteenth century the principal productions of bureaucracies were verbal formulations. In the second half of the twentieth century they prove themselves by producing more and more "data."

5. A. J. P. Taylor wrote about England after World War I that the national debt "did not diminish the wealth of the community at all, just as an individual does not impoverish himself by transferring some of his money to a No. 2 account. The war had been paid for while it was being waged, and the Debt was a book-keeping transaction, its only real cost to the community being the salaries of the clerks who handled it. Its significance was purely social. . . ."

   Another chestnut that journalists cannot seem to do without is that of a nation, or an economy, "on the verge of total bankruptcy." Nothing like this ever happens. Not in Rhodesia; not in Indonesia; not in Egypt.

6. Aristotle: "The acquisition of money in excess of natural requirements is incompatible with economic activity."

7. Beginning with demography. For demographic data (but not demographic projections) are perhaps the richest mine for the modern historian, for two reasons at least: first, because the records of such things as birth, death, marriage are seldom disputable, they are closest to the nineteenth-century ideal of Solid Facts; second, because the transmission of life and the choices of people for their habitations involve the basic phenomena of all historical life. The fluctuations of the rate of birth, marriage, illegitimacy, suicide, divorce, of the movements of populations are, or rather ought to be, of central interest to the historian, even though the causalities that they involve may be extremely complex and profound, discernible only with great difficulty. The relationship between birth rates and material conditions is, for example, very different from what sociological "rea-

son" suggests. Why is the birth rate so high in the Soviet Union, with its chronic and miserable conditions of housing? Is there any relationship between the decline of the birth rate in Western Europe and the introduction of contraceptive devices? Not very much; the birth rate dropped in these countries decades before the manufacture of contraceptives began.

8. There is, for example, widespread confusion of status with function; and, as Professor Cobban writes ("The Vocabulary of Social History"), "function [is] interpreted in a single and restricted sense. An official, because he lives on a salary and has no share in the ownership of the means of production, is a wage-earner and therefore a proletarian; a poor shopkeeper, or even a peddler, is a capitalist. This is to ignore their level of remuneration, the way people live, and—most important of all—the way they feel. . . ."

9. This is why even such an otherwise interesting social history of England between the wars as *The Long Week-End,* by Robert Graves and Alan Hodge, with its journalistic *petite histoire* and coterie gossip, is often defective.

10. The history of certain minorities may be significant: but this significance resides in their quality (Spanish Jews, Huguenot minorites in exile and in France, etc.); as Américo Castro said, the importance of the Hispano-Hebrews (about 4 percent of the Iberian population in the fifteenth century) "consisted in the quality of their work and not in their numbers."

11. I remember hearing Edward R. Murrow refer to Joseph McCarthy in 1954 as someone "to the right of Louis XIV." Thereupon I had to turn the radio off.

12. On April 17, 1788, Louis XVI referred to the *parlements* as "an aristocracy of magistrates." "Consider," Tocqueville jotted down in one of his notes, "how furiously they react to this word! . . . The word 'aristocrat' is often employed afterwards but for the first time in this [bad] sense. . . . What is the hidden power in that democratic element of the nation that these people who do not *see* at all clearly, confusedly *feel* that the most effective blow the King could score now [1788] is to call his adversaries *aristocrats.*"

13. The argument that the general view of history professed by a twentieth-century research historian, such as Namier, is necessarily deeper than that of Seeley's, is, therefore, not indisputable. ("English history," Seeley wrote, "always tends to shrink into mere Parliamentary history; and there is scarcely a great English historian who does not sink somewhat below himself in the treatment of foreign relations.")

14. Captain John Smith in the *Generall Historie of Virginia:* "for as Geographie without Historie seemeth a Carkasse without motion, so Historie without Geographie wandereth as a Vagrant without a certaine habitation."

15. Hence the increasing importance of the "field" of human geography, and of historical geography (see Lucien Febvre, *A Geographical Introduction to History* (1924), a pioneer work).

16. This unusual but incisive view of the Bolshevik Revolution having been part of a deep-seated reaction of the Russian people against their cosmopolitan and Francophile upper classes was glimpsed, too, by such disparate people as Georges Sorel and Winston Churchill. In his *Reflections on Violence* Sorel wrote (1919): "When the time comes to evaluate present-day events with historical impartiality, it will be recognized that Bolshevism owed a good part of its power to the fact that the masses regarded it as a protest against an oligarchy whose greatest concern had been not to appear Russian. . . ." In *The World Crisis* (1929) Churchill suggested that the Western Allies' failure to push the Dardanelles campaign through exacerbated the suspicions of the Russian masses against England and facilitated the coming of the revolution.

17. Conversely, the Anglophile (and sometimes Francophile) sympathies of American humanist intellectuals in our times represented, too, something more than ideological preferences: they reflected historical inclinations toward certain cultural prototypes, since many of these people saw in Britain and in France still partial representatives of the ideas and culture of the Enlightenment; on the other hand the Germanophile (and often Hispanophile) sympathies of many American "conservatives" reflected not merely hidden sympathies for Hitler or Adenauer or Franco but their inclinations toward romantic, neo-medieval, and generally anti-Enlightenment cultural tendencies.

18. The history of this 1931–36 period furnishes one of the arguments why Nazis should not be simply called fascists, since the two were opponents then, with different ideas.

19. This last Catholic chancellor of an independent Austria could not liberate himself from the notion of a "German" Austria; and traces of his admiration for Germany appear even in his diaries jotted down during his imprisonment by the Germans.

20. What he meant by the "last refuge of scoundrels" was what we mean by nationalism nowadays. Boswell: Johnson "did not mean a real and generous love of our country, but that pretended patriotism which so many . . . have made a cloak of self-interest.

21. Harold Nicolson in his 1937 Rede Lectures (*The Meaning of Prestige*): for the German, "his personal honour becomes fused with his national honour, and the resultant form of [nationalism] is far more inflammable than that old warm blanket which patriotism is with us." It is perhaps symptomatic that some of these distinctions have been expressed best by certain writers rather than by political theorists and, moreover, by patriotic rather than internationalist intellectuals, who comprehended the historic origins of national consciousness: for the condition that Germany, unlike England, became a unified national state only relatively late in history may explain much of the peculiarly distasteful character of modern German nationalism.

22. The true patriot, on the other hand, is often the kind of thinking person who is bitterly critical of, because he is deeply concerned with, the faults of his own people.

23. Huizinga (1933): "Why do some intellectuals expect a concord of nations only through a melting down of national characteristics?" "Why this deep scepticism against a harmonious accord?"

24. Also, Christopher Dawson: the racialists are wrong in believing that "culture is the result of predetermined racial inheritance. On the contrary, it would be more true to say that race is the product of culture, and that the differentiation of racial types represents the culmination of an age-long process of cultural segregation and specialization . . ." especially among primitive peoples.

25. It is significant that the two historians who perceived and, as E. H. Carr, too, noted, "emphasized most strongly the continuity of the French Revolution with previous régimes" were Tocqueville, who was Foreign Minister in 1849, and Albert Sorel, the diplomatic historian.

26. This is why, for example, A. J. P. Taylor's *The Origins of the Second World War* is defective in one of its main arguments. Taylor explains the origins of the war in terms of *Realpolitik*, but his concept of *Realpolitik* is too narrow: he treats history as if it consisted of the relations of states, and of states with more-or-less identical reactions: he ignores the effects of certain national tendencies. For example he says that in the 1930s the Poles were just as anti-Semitic as were the Germans: but he overlooks the condition that the Poles and the Germans were anti-Semitic in different ways, and that they pursued their national interests in different ways. Pilsudski was a nationalist dictator, as indeed was Hitler: but he was a different kind of nationalist dictator.

27. Esmé Wingfield-Stratford: "It is only too facile a biographical lead to refer every thing to [Disraeli's] Jewish descent, but the popular conception of a Jew is, in fact, one that fits him a great deal less than Gladstone—since he was, as a man and a statesman, rather deficient than otherwise in the money sense—an out-and-out Romantic of the Byron, D'Orsay tradition; moreover, one who could have been described, throughout his career, as positively drunken with the love of his adopted country, a patriot of patriots. Where, then, it may be asked, does the Jew in Disraeli come in? And I would answer—in the quality of his patriotism. He loved England—but not quite in the English way."

28. The condition that within the United States the Catholic population increased in its numbers and influence was an important element in the popular development of anti-communism as *the* American national ideology in the 1950s. On the other hand, the relative absence of a deep-seated Russophobia—as distinct from anticommunism—among Americans, as well as the Russian people's liking for Americans, were no less important factors in keeping the "Cold War" "cold" in the Fifties, and in the general improvement of the relations of the two states later.

3. History and Physics

1. This word "elegance" is my only quibble with this excellent and eloquent passage (Banesh Hoffmann, *The Strange Story of the Quantum: An Account for the General Reader of the Growth of the Ideas Underlying Our Present Atomic Knowledge* (New York, 1947). *Elegance* derives from *discrimination; choice*. It is the *esprit de géometrie* that mistakes symmetry for elegance (not to speak of the condition that asymmetry, suggesting movement, is more dynamic than is symmetry).

2. For example, by the maverick old American historian James C. Malin (whose writings must, however, be read with great caution, even if with great sympathy); by the thoughtful paper of the Austrian Hugo Hantsch ("Zur Methodik der neueren Geschichte," 1952), by Diana Spearman, *Democracy in England* (New York, 1957); Reinhold Schneider, *Wesen und Verwaltung der Macht* (1954).

3. Heisenberg: "One can never simultaneously know with perfect accuracy both of those two important factors which determine the movement of one of these smallest [atomic] particles—its position and its velocity." Also: "It is impossible to determine accurately *both* the position and the direction and the speed of a particle *at the same instant*. If we determine experimentally its exact position at any given moment, its movement is disturbed to such a degree by that very experiment that we shall then be unable to find it at all. And, conversely, if we are able to measure exactly the velocity of a particle, the picture of its position becomes totally blurred."

4. Not only in quantum but in relativity concepts, too, "simultaneity" is, for example, inadequate; if two persons saw two things far apart happen at the same time, they might not find that the things happened at the same time. It is true that in relativity situations this happens only in extreme circumstances. But the significance of this physically demonstrable discovery is decisive: as Louis de Broglie said, too, it is philosophical as well as scientific.

5. Niels Bohr: In biology we are concerned with "manifestations of possibilities in that nature to which we belong rather than with outcomes of experiments which we can ourselves perform."

6. But already Goethe in his *Theory of Colours*: "What is there exact in mathematics except its own exactitude?"

7. Heisenberg: "It would not be fundamentally unimaginable that, for example, a future extension of mathematical logic might give a certain meaning to the statement that in exceptional cases $2 \times 2 = 5$, and it might even be possible that this extended mathematics would be of use in calculations in the field of economics."

8. For example, the so-called irrational numbers, which are both odd and even numbers at the same time; or the square root of 2, which cannot be fixed or measured.

9. Heisenberg: "The use of the concept of causality for describing the law of cause and effect is of relatively recent origin. In previous philosophies the word *causa* had a very much more general [meaning]. . . . [Already] Kant used the word 'causality' in a nineteenth-century sense. . . ." Kant was convinced that his concept of causality would be "the basis of any future metaphysics called Science," but he has been proven wrong; and, as Heisenberg says, "it is interesting to see where his arguments have been wrong. . . . We know the foregoing event. But not quite accurately. We know the forces in the atomic nucleus that are responsible for the emission of the alpha particle. But this knowledge contains the uncertainty which is brought about by the interaction between the nucleus and the rest of the world. If we wanted to know why the alpha particle was emitted at that particular time, we would have to know the microscopic structure of the whole world including ourselves, and that is impossible. Therefore, Kant's arguments for the *a priori* character of the law of causality no longer apply."

10. De Broglie (1939): "Even the notions of causality and of individuality have had to undergo a fresh scrutiny, and it seems certain that this major crisis, affecting the guiding principles of our physical concepts, will be the source of philosophical consequences which cannot yet be clearly perceived." Banesh Hoffmann: These are "hard, uncompromising, and at present inescapable facts of experiment and bitter experience . . . directly opposed" to the Newtonian way of scientific thinking.

11. This recognition corresponds, significantly, with certain philosophical principles first proposed by Dilthey. H. A. Hodges, *Wilhelm Dilthey: An Introduction* (London, 1944): "Philosophers have devoted endless trouble to discussing how we come to be aware of physical objects and how far subjective elements enter into our experience of them. They have talked as if our world consisted entirely of such objects, and as if the knowledge of them were our chief intellectual concern. Yet the most significant of our experiences lies in our relations with other people"—that is, when two microcosms meet—"and the nature and the extent of the knowledge which we have of other people is a question of equal importance with"—I would say that it is a question of *superior* importance to— "the first. Dilthey is the first philosopher in any country to tackle the question seriously and systematically, and his work has started a new movement in German thought. . . ."

12. Heisenberg in *Planck's Discovery and the Philosophical Problems of Atomic Physics*: "There are large areas of phenomena that cannot even be approximately described by the concepts of classical physics. . . . The science of nature does not deal with nature itself but in fact with the *science* of nature as man thinks and describes it. This does not introduce an element of subjectivity into natural science. We do not by any means pretend that occurrences in the universe depend on our observations, but we point out that natural science stands between nature and man and that we cannot renounce the use of man's intuition or innate conceptions."

13. Ernst Cassirer: "There is in the Cartesian mind a kind of natural distrust, almost an antipathy, for history."

14. Galileo (like Descartes): "The book of nature is written in the language of mathematics." This statement would have seemed revolutionary (and perhaps even nonsensical) to, say, Machiavelli, a century before Galileo; it became dogma a century or so after Galileo; and now, three centuries later, it is becoming nonsense again. The absolutist Hobbes on mathematical geometry: "the only science that it hath pleased God hitherto to bestow upon mankind." Spinoza: "If mathematics did not exist, man would not know what truth is." No: if man did not exist, there would be no mathematics (and if truth did not exist, there would be no man). All of this at the beginning of the Modern Age. Now compare these statements to Kierkegaard's, prophet near its end: "Numbers are the negation of truth."

15. Novalis: "Man is the Messiah of Nature," a forerunner to Weizsaecker's ". . . man is earlier than natural science." Heisenberg: Man must resign himself to the condition "that his Science is but a link in the infinite chain of man's argument with nature, and that it cannot singly speak of nature 'in itself.'"

16. See, for example, his summary in *The Physicist's Conception of Nature*: "1. Modern science, in its beginnings, was characterized by a conscious modesty, it made statements about strictly limited relations that *are only valid within the framework of these limitations. 2. This modesty was largely lost during the nineteenth century.* [His italics.] Physical knowledge was considered to make assertions about nature as a whole. Physics wished to turn philosopher, and the demand was voiced from many quarters that all true philosophers must be scientific. 3. Today physics is undergoing a basic change, the most characteristic trait of which is a return to its original self-limitation. 4. The philosophic content of a science is only preserved if science is conscious of its limits. . . ."

17. For example, Ortega in 1923: "In the introduction to my first *Espectador,* which appeared in January 1916, when nothing had yet been published on the general theory of relativity [Einstein's first publication on his recent discovery, *Die Grundlagen der allgemeinen Relativitaetstheorie* was published in that year] I put forward a brief exposition of the doctrine of perspective, giving it a range of reference ample enough to transcend physics and include all reality. I mention this fact to show the extent to which a similar cast of thought is a sign of the times."

18. Valéry: "A drop of wine falling into water barely colors it, and tends to disappear after showing as a pink cloud. That is the physical fact. But suppose now that some time after it has vanished, we should see, here and there in our glass—which seemed once more to hold *pure* water—drops of wine forming, dark and *pure*—what a surprise! . . . This phenomenon of Cana is not impossible in intellectual and social physics. . . ."

19. It would be interesting to know whether Planck's choice of the word *quantum* may not have had something to do with the high intellectual currency of this word at that time in Germany. (Nietzsche in *The Will to Power:* "Quanta of power alone determine rank and distinguish rank. . . .")

20. In 1930, at the Bruxelles-Solvay Congress of International Physics, Einstein, refusing to admit the Heisenberg uncertainty principle, suffered a humiliating defeat, which was administered by Bohr. I am not saying that this was a political event. I am saying that this event, and the time of its occurrence, has a significance in the general cultural history of Europe, involving politics to some extent. For there is a certain correspondence between Einstein's defeat in 1930 and the failure of German Marxism, with its interpretation of Economic Man, at that very historical moment. They were both failures of the deterministic thinking of the nineteenth century; and, in view of more universal historical developments of that time, it is at least significant that this happened in 1930. (On

the more vulgar level of mass political beliefs it is true what Klaus Mehnert wrote in 1951: "The German people's journey from Liebknecht to Hitler, and the Russian people's journey from Lenin to Stalin, were parallel performances of the same process. In both cases ... the journey was one from dialectic to magic. ...")

21. Perhaps it is not fanciful to outline the following correspondences:

    1894–1905: Beginning of the breakup of the Newtonian universe, of the Bourgeois Age, of the European political system in the world.

    1926–32: Indeterminacy in physics and in mathematics; neo-idealism and Fascism in Europe; even Russia moves away from internationalism, and the United States from nineteenth-century liberal capitalism.

    1941–45: Manufacture of the first atom bomb; end of the European Age; the United States and the Soviet Union rule Europe and most of the world.

    1955–: Scattered re-recognitions of a postmodern universe; the American-Soviet atomic monopoly nearing its end; Russian and American influence weakening in Europe.

22. The Swiss philosophical writer Peter Duerrenmatt (not to be confused with the dramatist) in 1960: "In the last resort, the European resistance was conservative. A kind of conservative attitude ... has contributed to the fact that the politics of Europe after 1945 have been something more than merely successful experiments in economic and social life." "The question whether Europe will survive depends on the strength or on the weakness of its peoples' will to exist."

23. Jacques Barzun in *Darwin, Marx, Wagner: Critique of a Heritage* (Boston, 1941; Chicago, 1981): "No greater mistake can be made than to consider Nietzsche's break with Wagner a personal quarrel resulting from a difference of opinion about music. It is much more. It is the first critical repudiation of the second half of the nineteenth century by a herald of the twentieth." But: "... the general public of our century has never departed from the Darwinian faith that the scientist is the man to do it." Also: "... what physicists have learned from the history of their science has not yet been learned by the biologists"— and let me add that this is as true today as when this was written more than a quarter-century ago—"which accounts for the curious fact that while some physicists are becoming a new sort of 'vitalists,' most biologists are still for the most part mechanists— like the ordinary man."

24. "Future generations may well call our era the Age of Einstein. ..."—Jeremy Bernstein in a slick review-article on the history of quantum physics in the *New Yorker*, April 19, 1966. Einstein: "I believe in Spinoza's God who reveals himself in the orderly harmony of what exists, not in a God who concerns himself with the fates and actions of human beings." (What could be less humanist than this?) Quoted by Felix Gilbert, "Einstein und das Europa seiner Zeit" in *Historiche Zeitschrift* 233 (1981), 10, from Banesh Hoffmann-Helen Dukas, *Albert Einstein, Creator and Rebel*—Einstein's most detailed biography (New York, 1972), 95. In this article, respectful and sympathetic of Einstein, Gilbert remarks Einstein's "lacking interest in anything that is changeable and passing, his rejection of history," 11—very much like Descartes and unlike Heisenberg.

25. "The European Spirit and the World of Machines" in *Last Essays*. Also: "The democracies have been decomposing, too, but some decompose more quickly than others. They have been decomposing into bureaucracies, suffering from it as a diabetic does from sugar, at the expense of his own substance. In the most advanced cases, this bureaucracy itself decomposes into its most degraded form, police bureaucracy. At the end of this evolution, all that is left of the state is the police. ..."

26. It is perhaps significant that this social Darwinist and Teutonophile public figure was also the first president of the American Historical Association.

27. Kepler: "The purpose of the world and of all creation is man. I believe that it is for this very reason that God chose the earth, designed as it is for bearing and nourishing the Creator's true image, for revolving among the planets. . . ." But Sir George Clark about Newton: "In 1698 the English parliament, of which Sir Isaac Newton had been and was again to be a member, passed an Act which made it a penal offense to deny the divinity of Christ. After Newton's death it was found from his unpublished papers that he himself did not believe in the doctrine of the Trinity as he understood it; but the fact was not clearly published until the twentieth century."

28. Planck: "For religion, the idea of God is at the beginning; for science the idea of God is at the end." Ellen Juhnke during the discussion after Heisenberg's 1958 lecture on Planck: "Is it not an extraordinary thing to see such syntheses being outlined in our atomic and atomized era?"

29. Voltaire thought that the most important person in modern history was Newton. So did Marx. Yet Marx's contemporary Tocqueville, a century after Voltaire and a century before Heisenberg (1858): "A hypothesis which permits the prediction of certain effects that always reoccur under the same conditions does, *in its way* [my italics], amount to a demonstrable truth. Even the Newtonian system has no more than such a foundation."

30. Burckhardt circa 1875: "Is the tendency of Europe still a rising or a falling one? This can never be decided through calculations. Its peoples are, still, not exhausted in a physical sense, and in a spiritual and moral sense one must always reckon with the existence of still invisible forces. Even now."

   Christopher Dawson circa 1955: "Neither Christianity nor humanism is dead. They still possess an infinite capacity of spiritual regeneration and cultural renaissance. What is passing away is the utopian idealism which was the original inspiration of all the revolutionary ideologies. Now that they have been brought down from the clouds to solid earth they have gained temporal power, but they have lost their old appeal. In so far as they continue to press their total claim to man's spiritual allegiance, they must inevitably drive civilization further and further toward nihilism and self-destruction.

   "The vital task of Europe at the present time is to resist this tendency and to recover and fortify the two great spiritual traditions which are the roots of its culture. This is a difficult task, and one which cannot be achieved without great moral and intellectual efforts. But it is by no means an impossible task, and since Europe was the original creator of the ideologies, she has a special responsibility and a special opportunity for finding a solution to the problems which the ideologies have raised."

31. 1951, 1957 ("The Past and Future of Modern Man"). But already in the 1930s in "History as a System": "Physical science can throw no clear light on the human element. Very well. This means simply that we must shake ourselves free, radically free, from the physical approach to the human element. Let us instead accept this in all its spontaneity, just as we see it and come upon it. In other words, the collapse of physical reason leaves the way clear for vital, historical reason." (I read this in 1959.)

4. Polite Letters and Clio's Fashions

1. T. O'Raifeartaigh, ed., *The Royal Irish Academy: A Bicentennial History, 1785–1985* (Dublin: The Royal Irish Academy, 1985). This essay was first delivered as a Royal Irish Academy Discourse on June 8, 1989.

2. Ibid., 9.

3. Ibid., 188.

4. Ibid., 195.

5. Jakob Burckhardt, *Briefe*, edited by Max Burckhardt (Basel: B. Schwabe, 1949–86), iv, 125, 169, 260. For further discussion, see John Lukacs, *Historical Consciousness*, 2nd ed. (New York: Schocken Books, 1985), 37, 98, 227–36.

6. For elaboration of this point, see Lukacs, *Historical Consciousness*, 108–14.

7. F. S. L. Lyons, *Culture and Anarchy in Ireland, 1890–1839* (Oxford: Oxford University Press, 1980), 1.

8. T. S. Eliot, *Notes towards the Definition of Culture* (London: Faber and Faber, 1948), 22.

9. Lyons, *Culture and Anarchy*, 22.

10. Angus McIntyre, *The Liberator* (London: Macmillan, 1965), 127–28.

11. Lyons, *Culture and Anarchy*, 22.

12. Ibid., 72.

13. C. P. Snow, *The Two Cultures and the Scientific Revolution* (Cambridge: Cambridge University Press, 1959).

14. José Ortega y Gasset, *Meditations on Don Quixote* (New York: Norton, 1961), 118.

15. Thomas Hardy, "Candour in English Fiction," in Thomas Hardy, *Personal Writings*, edited by Harold Orel (London: Macmillan, 1967), 127.

6. The Historiographical Problem of Belief and of Believers: Religious History in the Democratic Age

1. John Bossy, *The English Catholic Community, 1570–1850* (London, 1975), 5: "One of the ways of explaining the difference between this book and Mathew's is to notice that he spoke of his subject not as a community but as a minority.... A minority is by definition one of a pair; a community may be of several." (Reference to David Mathew, *Catholicism in England. The Portrait of a Minority: Its Culture and Tradition* (London, 1948). Also, 183: "We are not trying to calculate a body of opinion, but membership in a community; and I should define community membership in this case as meaning habitual, though in view of physical difficulties not necessarily very frequent, resort to the services of a priest...."

2. Address to the *Institut Français* in South Kensington as cited in John Lukacs, *Historical Consciousness* (New York, 1968), 344.

3. Probably also true of much of Europe but not necessarily of the United States at the time.

4. L. C. B. Seaman, *Victorian England: Aspects of English and Imperial History, 1837–1901* (London, 1976), 20–21.

5. *Catholic Historical Review* 62 (October 1976), 641

6. *Actes et documents du Saint Siège relatifs à la seconde guerre mondiale*, vol. 9 (Vatican City, 1975), 93.

7. Julian Marías, *Generations: A Historical Method* (Tuscaloosa, AL, 1972), 178.

8. *Catholic Historical Review* 61 (April 1975), 183.

9. *On History* (1830), as reprinted in F. Stern (ed.), *The Varieties of History* (New York, 1973), 99.

10. David Cecil, *The Stricken Deer: Life of William Cowper* (London, 1929), 16.

11. José Ortega y Gasset, *Obras Completas*, vol. 1 (Madrid, 1966), 369–70.

12. Marías, *Generations*, 7–8.

13. Cochrane, *Catholic Historical Review* 61 (April 1975), 185.

7. What *Is* History?

1. It may be significant that the publication of *What Is History?* in 1961 nearly coincided with an intellectually even more successful—but infinitely more poorly conceived, written, and thought out—book in 1962, Thomas Kuhn's *The Structure of Scientific Revolutions* (Chicago, 1962). Kuhn arrived at the conclusion that, Eureka!, science is but the product of scientists (e.g., Carr: "before you study the history, study the historian"; Kuhn: science "is the result of a consensus of the scientific community"). At least Carr spared the world from producing new and repulsive terms such as Kuhn's "paradigm shifts."

II. Historians Reviewed

❁ ❁ ❁

14. Jacques Barzun

1. The prototypical expression of this reasoning was written by the two leading American Progressives, Robinson and Beard, in their prospectus for "The New History" (1912: the very central year in the history of American Progressivism, the date in itself a symptom). Engagingly presented, democratic and optimistic, though essentially shallow, its basic arguments have been repeated and repeated, with decreasing cogency and increasing verbiage, during the following sixty or more years. The second wave of social-scientism came in the wake of the New Deal. Its most ludicrous manifestation was the attempt of the Social Science Research Council to scientize history, by means of the once celebrated *Social Science Research Council Bulletin 54*. In the early 1940s the Council spent a very large amount of money on the most outstanding (that is, best-known) American historians and philosophers, who would "solve" the problem of history by writing foolproof and leak-proof "definitions" of its "categories." The result resembled the efforts of Freudian psychoanalysts struggling with a hydrocephalic infant in the delivery room. (The grotesque nature of this effort escaped some of the humorless younger historians, such as John Higham, who as late as 1965 summarized it in a volume, with the modest title *History,* in a series modestly entitled "Humanistic Scholarship in America," thus: "The Social Science Research Council was looking for some concerted strategy to bring history into closer relation to the other sciences." "Concerted strategy" is good.) The third wave of social-scientism began after 1960, about which phenomenon see the rest of this essay.
2. Another, related, reason for this Atlantic convergence was the presence and influence of certain distinguished refugee scholars in American colleges and universities who had brought with themselves a considerable amount of intellectual baggage from Europe. Yet another was the impression, around the time of the formation of NATO, that an Atlantic civilization existed, indeed, that it was in full development. Another cause was the generally liberal-conservative—that is, determinedly anti-totalitarian—atmosphere that governed intellectual discourse in the West after the defeat of Fascism and during

the disillusionment with communism, again approximately from 1947 to the early 1960s. A prototypical example of the best of these tendencies, as reflected in their attitude to history, may be found in the thoughtful Introduction by Fritz Stern (himself a young German refugee) to his selection, *The Varieties of History* (New York, 1956). In the introductory note to the second edition of this, deservedly successful, anthology, published in 1970, Stern contented himself by saying that there had developed a crisis within the historical profession, but beyond that he chose to say nothing.

3. Example: In 1950 most of the articles in the *American Political Science Review* were still readable—by which I mean that they could be read by anyone without an acquaintance with a specialized jargon-vocabulary or with mathematical symbols; by 1965 most of them weren't. The first unreadable articles in historical journals, including the *American Historical Review*, began to appear after 1970.

4. The so-called "wave" of New Left revisionism was but an example of this. The revisionists simply (or, rather, primitively) projected the actual disillusionment with American involvement in the Vietnam War into American involvement in the so-called Cold War, twenty years earlier. That their research was usually incompetent, selective, and dishonest is beside the point. My point is that the appearance of this kind of revisionism around 1965 was neatly predictable—whereby the revisionists have not really been revisionists. They have not corrected or revised attitudes popular among intellectuals. To the contrary: they have applied popular attitudes of the present to related subjects of the past

5. Except that it is not diagnosis. It is the categorical attribution of motives—of "drives" over which the person has little or no influence; i.e. he is psychobiologically determined.

6. As Barzun points out in *Clio* (Chicago, 1974), as early as 1913 the New England historian Preserved Smith had written in an essay a kind of psychoanalytic study of Luther. The attraction of psychoanalysis, and especially of Freudianism, for the Puritan, and especially for the New England, mind is an important subject in itself (part and parcel of the attraction that Germanic forms of thinking have for the New England mind), which still awaits its master historian.

7. There is one other matter about which this writer feels compelled to argue with Barzun, for whom otherwise he professes his friendship and his respect. Barzun argues cogently that, contrary to Langer's asseverations, the psychologists were not pioneers in discovering men's motives, since this is what historians had been doing, at least since Herodotus: but Barzun is curiously unclear about the essential difference between motives and purposes. He is very right in pointing out something that few historians have considered (this writer attempted to do so, in *Historical Consciousness*, chapter 4: that even criminal law "is content to proceed without proof of motive" and that experienced judges and trial lawyers will say that "it is always dangerous to impute motives to any man in regard to anything he says or does." (As Dr. Johnson said: intentions must be gathered from acts.) But, again, Barzun stops here. What he ought to remark is that the attribution of motives—a practice spurred on by modern psychology—is one of the principal symptoms of pestilential arrogance and ignorance in the twentieth century. The title of his chapter, "The Motives behind the Purpose," is confusing: for it is not only the motive which is "behind" the purpose; the purpose is also "ahead" of the motive. Motive means a push from the past, imputing a determinism according to which every human act or thought or desire is no more than a reaction (Freud, like Einstein, was incapable of freeing his mind from nineteenth-century concepts of mechanical causality); whereas purpose imputes the far more complex, but also far more humanly discernible, pull of

the future, involving such essential functions of the human mind as imagination and aspiration.

8. Barzun also implies (152, 155) that the appeal of science to the modern student has remained universal, dominant, and strong. This does not seem to be the case. The very rigorousness of disciplines such as physics or chemistry deters students; the number of majors in the natural sciences has been declining for years. At least during the late 1960s crowds of students have been drifting away from history and away from other humanities into sociology, political science, psychology, etc.—not toward the natural sciences.

9. Consider, too, that *Clio and the Doctors* (a short book, extending the argument of an already published article) received a first-page review in the *New York Times Book Review,* and reviews in a large variety of magazines and journals; that in 1971 the *New York Times* daily edition reported at length about a conference on psychohistory; that in 1963 the *New Yorker* magazine ran a series of long articles by Ved Mehta on certain latter-day philosophers of history. Such disputes dealing with the nature of historical knowledge would not have attracted the attention of editors of the American popular press, including the *New York Times* or the *New Yorker,* fifty years ago.

10. In doing this, he unwittingly plays into the hands of the very people whom he otherwise disdains. See, for examples, the sociologist Herbert J. Gans, "Some Comments on the History of Italian Migration and on the Nature of Historical Research" in the *International Migration Review* (Summer 1967), 8–9. Gans writes: "To put it more bluntly, in a period like the present, in which psychology, sociology, and anthropology, economic, political sciences, and other sciences are flourishing as never before"—"flourishing" is good—"descriptive history is not enough; it cannot compete with the other social sciences. . . ." [For a while] "descriptive history can survive, but when the social sciences apply their superior methodology"—"their superior methodology" is even better—"to questions of change, development or process, then I suspect descriptive history will lose out. Consequently, history must become as analytic and as sophisticated in its methods and concepts as the other social sciences, or else it may disappear from the scene altogether." [But] "[i]f historical researchers play it right, history could become *the* dynamic social science par excellence, synthesizing the methods and concepts of all the individual disciplines. At that point, I might be one of the first to migrate from sociology into history." God protect the immigrant.

11. Three eminent scientists in 1968: C. H. Waddington: "There is something oppressive in the thought that such implausible systems as either logical positivism or Skinnerism could become fashionable." J. R. Smythies: "Could I suggest that Professor Waddington's question might provide the subject for another symposium—it is a vitally important question. Which are the organized forces in society that are suppressing meaning by devious and often unconscious means?" Paul Weiss: "There is a tendency to suppress not only meaning, but also the freedom of expression—these two problems are linked. . . ." See *Beyond Reductionism: New Perspectives in the Life Sciences* (The Alpbach Symposium), Koestler and Smythies, eds. (New York, 1970), 418–19.

12. Read any recent book by Arthur Koestler, this supremely talented cultural journalist and amateur thinker and popularizer of scientific discoveries: they are full of eloquent statements and proofs to the effect that nineteenth-century scientism is as dead as the dodo. Yet somehow *existentially* Koestler does not come to terms with the main issue, since he claims to deal with what mind does to man, instead of asking the other question, what men do to their minds.

13. This is the only thing which has changed—and then only slightly—during the last fifty

years, for otherwise everything in these paragraphs is as true as when they were written, in 1926. The reason for this is relatively simple: the Americanization of life in Europe has eventually affected even certain forms of intellectual life on the continent. In other words, Europe is caught up by the same kind of low-grade infection of feverishness and stagnation that characterizes intellectual life in modern democracy.

14. Huizinga, *America: A Dutch Historian's View from Afar and Near,* H. H. Rowa trans. (New York, 1974), 320–22.

15. *Democracy in America* (Bowen-Bradley edition, New York, 1945), vol. 2, 276–78.

16. He has dealt with some of these phenomena not only in the *House of Intellect* but in *Darwin, Marx, Wagner,* already thirty-five years ago, in the last chapters of which he did not merely say that "historians and social scientists ... make a show of aping science and have pilfered its vocabulary without excuse" but, going further, said: "To reverse such ingrained habits of thought and work can not be done in an instant. It will take as much work and a very different kind of thought in a fresh direction. But the difficulty of the task should only spur our efforts in the one realm which we have under some sort of immediate control: our minds. Failing this, the possibilities which Henry Adams foresaw seem likely to come true all at once: cynical pessimism among the leaders of mankind; a vast revival of semi-religious superstition; a brutish dictatorship by capital or labor." *Darwin, Marx, Wagner* (New York, 1958), 361–62.

17. As Bruce Catton wrote in his review-essay of Fogel and Engerman, *Time on the Cross: The Economics of American Negro Slavery* in *American Heritage* (December 1974): "A great breakthrough in history cliometrics is not; but it *is* a breakthrough in the field of publicity."

18. And this is, of course, part and parcel of the intellectualization of life of which we find evidences far beyond the circles of professional intellectuals. For example: for the first time in centuries millions of people think that to be caught with wrong opinions is worse than to be caught with bad taste.

15. Charles-Olivier Carbonell

1. Carbonell is neither a specialist nor a generalist idea-monger: but he has read *everything* that had been printed about history in France during a period of twenty years. This is in itself an extraordinary achievement. Such an exhaustive study is indeed rare nowadays, for many reasons, including the accumulation of the quantity of material. In this respect there is a certain similarity between Carbonell's achievement and that of René Rémond, who fifteen years ago published a monumental study on the image of the United States in French opinion from 1815 to 1852. Rémond's methodology is more impressive than Carbonell's, but the two have this in common: they literally exhausted *all* of the printed evidence of a certain period. After 1880 the ideal of the German-inspired scientific model of historiography, the monographic practice, according to which the trained historical researcher must exhaust *all* of the documentation and of the literature pertaining to his topic, was becoming less and less possible because of the oceanic rise of printed and bureaucratic materials, especially in Western Europe and in the United States.

2. This is odd, when one of his preceptors, whom he justly admires, is Henri-Irénée Marrou, whose superb book, *De la connaissance historique,* succeeded in doing just that.

16. David Irving

1. They were the counterparts of those people who, during the same period, passed from extreme interventionism to isolationism: extreme proponents of the destruction of Germany, they objected to any American action opposing Soviet Russia or communist China.

21. Henry Adams

1. Henry Adams, *The Education of Henry Adams* (Boston, 1918), 455.
2. Example: Adams's review of a text of French history written by Kitchin, an unfortunate English historian: Kitchin "again hops away to another branch of the subject, and chirrups about 'the page in my lady's bower,' and the other commonplaces of chivalry. In comparison with such fine writing, the French series of historical textbooks . . . rise to the dignity of historical monuments. Mr. Kitchen could not do better in a new edition than to omit the whole chapter on feudalism and substitute for it a simple translation of that of the *Moyen Age* by M. Duruy."
3. Brooks Adams, "The Heritage of Henry Adams," in *The Degradation of the Democratic Dogma* (Boston, 1919), 96.
4. Ernest Samuels, *Henry Adams: The Major Phase* (Cambridge, MA, 1964), 144.
5. An example is Tolstoy, no matter how Isaiah Berlin tried to explain this away (in *The Hedgehog and the Fox,* 1954).
6. Samuels, 255.
7. Ibid., 215.
8. Example: "Assuming that there was in existence such a universe and such a benevolent God with whom he could covenant, Mr. [John Quincy] Adams went on to explain as a scientific fact that a volume of energy lay stored within the United States, which as an administrator he could have developed, had he been able to work at leisure and had he been supported by his Creator." Or: "Like Moses, and a host of other idealists and reformers, John Quincy Adams had dreamed that, by his interpretation of the divine thought, as manifested in nature, he could covenant with God, and thus regenerate mankind. He knew that he had kept his part of the covenant, even too well. In return, when it came to the test, God had abandoned him and had made Jackson triumph."
9. That is: in the universe Scientific Laws came first, and God thereafter.
10. *The Education of Henry Adams,* 305.
11. Ibid., 382.
12. *American Historical Review,* October 1895. "Count Edward de Crillon," cited by Samuels, 150–51.
13. William Jordy, *Henry Adams, Scientific Historian* (New Haven, CT, 1952), 16.
14. But there are traces of Adams's scientism in the *History,* too, especially in volume 4. Example: George Washington "conceived the principle that a consolidated community which should have the energy to cohere must be the product of a social system resting on converging highways" (a statement worthy of a spokesman for the Teamsters). Or, also in volume 4, about Fulton's steamship: "Compared with such a step in progress, the medieval barbarisms of Napoleon and Spencer Perceval signified little more . . . than the doings of Achilles and Agamemnon." (An odd coincidence! In September 1939 Alexander Sachs, a New York banker, convinced Franklin Roosevelt to go ahead with Einstein's proposal to build an atom bomb with the argument that Napoleon had lost his bid for world domination because he had rejected Fulton's proposal to build a fleet of steam-

ships with which he could have invaded England. The argument was complete non-sense: yet its eventual result was the atom bomb.)

15. Samuels, 209.

16. "The Tendency of History," Adams's communication to the American Historical Association in 1894, cited by Samuels, 127.

17. Ibid., 124.

18. "A Letter to American Teachers of History," 1910, Ibid., 142, 146, 195, 234. (A sort of forerunner of C. P. Snow's fatuous and celebrated thesis about *The Two Cultures.* There is only one culture.)

19. Samuels, viii.

20. Ibid., 83–84.

21. Ibid., 321.

22. Brooks, *Heritage,* 89.

23. Ibid., 98.

24. Samuels, 28.

25. Brooks, 10

26. Samuels, 204–05.

27. Brooks, 89.

28. "The Rule of Phase Applied to History," in *Degradation of the Democratic Dogma,* 308.

27. Michael Burleigh

1. Including the United States, where—in European terms—it could be said that the difference between Republicans and Democrats was (and still is) that the former have been more nationalist than socialist; the latter more socialist than nationalist. (The same applies to the older categories of American Populists and American Progressives.)

2. Czarist Russia, Batista's Cuba, and the Shah's Persia were police states; but they were not totalitarian

30. Winston Churchill

1. J. H. Plumb, "The Historian," in *Churchill Revised: A Critical Assessment* (New York, 1969), 143.

2. Robert Blake, "Winston Churchill as Historian," lecture in 1990 at the University of Texas, rpt. in W. Roger Louis, ed., *Adventures with Britannia: Personalities, Politics, and Culture in Britain* (Austin, TX, 1995). Victor Feske, *From Belloc to Churchill: Private Scholars, Public Culture, and the Crisis of British Liberalism, 1900–1939* (Chapel Hill, NC, 1996). John Ramsden, "That Will Depend on Who Writes the History: Winston Churchill as His Own Historian," Queen Mary and Westfield College (London, 1996). David Reynolds, "Churchill's Writing of History: Appeasement, Autobiography, and *The Gathering Storm,*" in *Transactions of the Royal Historical Society,* series 6, vol. 11 (Cambridge, 2001), 221–47.

3. Veronica Wedgwood's excellent formulation: "History is an art—like all the other sciences." I think Churchill would have agreed.

4. Randolph Churchill, *Winston S. Churchill* (London, 1965) vol. 1, 327–28.

5. One example, his letter to his wife from Lourdes: "a monument to the *bêuse humaine.*" R. Churchill, *Winston S. Churchill* (London, 1967), vol. 2, 436.

6. His visit to Belfast, after his violent pro-Ulster speeches, was followed by a riot at which at least twenty-five people (mostly Catholics) were killed and hundreds injured.

7. He was well paid for this book. It is interesting to note that his literary agent was Frank Harris, the same Harris who later became famous for his crudely sexual autobiography.

8. A stunning example: In 1887 Joseph Chamberlain wrote a conciliatory letter to Lord Randolph Churchill which included a Latin phrase: "*Ira amantium redintegratio amoris*" (loose translation: love between us will be stronger after our quarrel). More than forty years after Churchill had read and printed this letter (vol. 2, 347) he used the same phrase in a message to Franklin Roosevelt in 1945.

9. Maurice Ashley, *Churchill as Historian* (New York, 1968), 4.

10. Winston Churchill, *Marlborough: His Life and Times,* 2 vols. (London, 1967).

11. Malcolm V. Hay, *Winston Churchill and James II of England* (London, 1936), 8, 62.

12. Cf. his portrait of Hitler.

13. See also Robin Prior, *Churchill's World Crisis as History* (London, 1983).

14. Ramsden, "That Will Depend on Who Writes the History," 14. Ramsden also notes that in February 1938 Churchill signed a letter of confidence, assuring Chamberlain of his support—contrary to the impression a reader receives from *The Gathering Storm.*

15. Plumb, "The Historian," 166.

16. Generally speaking, the last two volumes of *A History of the English-Speaking Peoples* are better than the first two. Churchill was not unduly interested in the Middle Ages.

17. Ashley, *Churchill as Historian,* 230–31.

18. Reynolds, "Churchill's Writing of History," 247.

19. A. L. Rowse, *The End of an Epoch: Reflections on Contemporary History* (London, 1947), 282–83; E. H. Carr, *What Is History?* (New York, 1962), 54.

20. Plumb, "The Historian," 142, 155.

21. About this half-truth see John Lukacs, *At the End of an Age* (New Haven, CT, 2002), 68, 69.

22. Roy Jenkins, *Churchill* (New York, 2001), 3.

23. Plumb, "The Historian," 142, 134, 151, 153, 155, 137, 167; Ashley, *Churchill as Historian,* 231.

24. Churchill (in 1899!), cited by Ashley, *Churchill as Historian,* 47.

25. Frederick Woods, *A Bibliography of the Works of Sir Winston Churchill,* 2 rev. ed. (London, 1975). An extensive bibliography, prepared by Ronald I. Cohen (Manotick, Ontario), is to be published soon. Cf. also Eric Stainbaugh, *Winston Churchill, a Reference Guide* (Boston, 1985).

III. Dissenting Opinions

❊ ❊ ❊

33. E. L. Doctorow

1. Or like Truman Capote when he, with a surprising lack of imagination, called *In Cold Blood* "a nonfiction novel."

2. He may have. Both *The Mauve Decade* and *Ragtime* end with a parade—the last paragraph in the former, the last sentence in the latter, an ironic snippet that Thomas Beer could

have used: "And Harry K. Thaw, having obtained his release from the insane asylum, marched annually at Newport in the Armistice Day parade."

3. The same thing seems true of Erica Jong, the woman pornographer. Her problem, too, is her Jewishness rather than her sex—but, unlike Roth, she does not *know* (or, perhaps, she does not wish to admit) this.

4. To trace the pedigree of the background even further: many of the madams of the New Orleans and St. Louis bordellos were Central European immigrants.

5. His attitude to professional history is ambiguous. *Ragtime* is full of arch little phrases, representing flashbacks to an earlier, illusory kind of history writing: "At this time in our history ..." "There was in these days in our history ..." "Many historians have studied this phenomenon ..." The irony is heavy-handed and ambiguous. This habit carries over from *The Book of Daniel*, where Doctorow found it necessary to incorporate long passages or interpretations of the origins of the Cold War from the writings of the Cold War revisionists (most of them third-rate historians).

6. His first published novel was a Western.

36. Tom Wolfe

1. The fraudulent character of the phenomenon of Radical Chic (as well as of Conservative Chic) may be seen from the following: The peak of Radical Chic in New York, the welcoming of Black Panthers and "revolutionaries" in certain places of the Upper East Side and Central Park West, occurred *at the same time* when, for the first time in the city's history, the fear of the presence of black criminality had penetrated those very same portions of New York. Thus Conservative Chic reaches its peak at the very time when the last vestiges of truly conservative behavior and traditional manners are vanishing from the American scene.

IV. Places and Times

❀ ❀ ❀

43. Budapest 1900: Colors, Words, Sounds

1. No longer. It was sold for $60,000 in 1988, after Wanamaker's had been bought by a conglomerate.

2. Two generations later a biographer of Munkácsy (Géza Perneczy) compared the launching of "Christ before Pilate" to a Hollywood super-production. An American art historian (John Maass) wrote about Munkácsy's American tour that Sedlmayer "anticipated ... publicity methods of the American film industry, including the 'personal appearance tour of the star. ... Scenes in biblical films like 'The Robe' (1953) and 'Barabbas' (1962) are strikingly similar to 'Christ before Pilate.'"

3. Sedlmayer may have done worse damage to his reputation. Not only malicious critics but all kinds of people found it distasteful when Sedlmayer showed "The Dying Mozart" against a musical accompaniment, or when he sold tickets for the showings of the "Christ before Pilate" tour, a new practice at the time.

4. Perneczy, 51. "This funeral was the last Munkácsy super-production, with all of the grotesque exaggerations of eclecticism, produced for a public avid for entertainment, festivities and impressive theatrics. . . . An honest and detached study should show us Munkácsy's great pictorial talents—and also that his faults and mistaken directions corresponded with the errors and mistaken ways of his nation."

5. When Theodore Roosevelt came to Budapest in 1910 he said that his desire to see Hungary had been kindled by his reading of Mikszáth's novel *Szent Péteresernyője* (*Saint Peter's Umbrella*), translated into English in 1901.

6. The only other writer of considerable stature born in Budapest was the brilliant literary critic Jenő Péterfy, who was also a musicologist and thoroughly bilingual (his occasional German essays were a masterpiece of style). A nervous and profound man, inclined to depressions, he killed himself in 1899.

7. Kóbor's title may also have been influenced by Zola's *Paris*, also published in 1896.

8. One of the weaker portions of *The Happy Generation* consists of its young protagonist's love affair during a year spent in a Swiss tuberculosis sanatorium, amidst men and women from many nations—the obvious influence of *The Magic Mountain*.

9. He actually says "happy" (*boldog*) but somehow that English word is not quite appropriate here or, indeed, in the book title. Perhaps it should be "blessed."

10. With the new century, even Magyar spelling changed. In 1900 the Hungarian Academy of Sciences, after serious discussions and study, declared that the old Hungarian usage of the double consonant *cz* must give way to the more modern *c* (both corresponding to the sound *ts* in English).

11.   *Comme de longs echos qui de loin se confondent*
      Dans use ténébreuse et profonde unite
      Vaste comme la nuit et comme la claret
      Les parfums, les couleurs et les lons se répondent . . .
    Urbane Hungarian poetry has always been influenced by French poetry, and perhaps especially around 1900. Baudelaire's *Correspondances* and Rimbaud's *Voyelles* had, for example, a great influence on the poet and novelist Dezső Kosztolányi, whose tour de force poem "Ilona," a poem playing with the vowels of that Magyar female name, surpasses *Voyelles* in its directness and in the beauty of its music.

44. Philadelphia 1950

1. They had some reasons for this on the state level: in November 1950 the third-rate Republican machine politician John S. Fine beat Richardson Dilworth, the reformer liberal Democrat, for the governorship; and Senator Francis J. Myers, the Democratic majority Whip in the United States Senate was also defeated by James H. Duff, a pro-Eisenhower Republican.

2. There was an exception to this time lag on the state level: in 1934 the Democrats won the governorship, losing it again in 1938. The governor of the Pennsylvania New Deal was George H. Earle III, a former independent Republican, friend of Franklin Roosevelt

and of William Bullitt, with whom he had much in common, including a flair for foreign policy and high living.

3. In the Philadelphia (or, rather, southeastern Pennsylvania) novel of Joseph Hergesheimer, *Three Black Pennys* (New York, 1917), 181–82, a Philadelphia lawyer's office circa 1860: "The lawyer's private chamber was bare, with snowy paneling and mahogany, the high somber shelves of a calf-bound law library, a ponderous cabriolet table, sturdy, rush-seated Dutch chairs, and a Franklin stove with slender brass capitals and shining hood."

4. Ibid., 54.

5. *A Casual Past* (New York, 1961), 89–90.

6. *Our Philadelphia* (London, 1914), 111–12.

7. *Philadelphia: Portrait of an American City* (Harrisburg, PA, 1975), 299.

8. *Democracy in America* (Mayer, ed.), vol. 1, 245.

9. Two squares further on, Paul Cret built the small Rodin Museum, donated by a civic-minded Jewish merchant of great wealth.

10. They were not built until the late 1930s. Two decades later they—and the Art Museum—were allowed to be overshadowed by two of the most monstrous apartment buildings ever to disfigure the skyline and physiognomy of Philadelphia—or perhaps of any great city.

11. Broad Street Station itself, a high-turreted Victorian skyscraper of a terminus, was demolished in 1952; the Philadelphia Orchestra was brought to the platform to play for the last train pulling away, a sentimental and appropriate Philadelphian gesture.

12. It is to be boarded up, for good (1980).

13. An old Philadelphian—meaning someone distinct from, but not less respectable than, an Old Philadelphian.

14. There was a loss inherent in the categorical set of regulations. Many of the interesting (and not only the decrepit) Victorian houses and warehouses, built after 1840, were condemned in the redevelopment process. The result was that of attractive rows of buildings with a touch of artificiality in their regimented rows, architectural prospects of unbroken uniformity, often beautifully rebuilt and re-set, but also devoid of the rich variety that marks the prospects of a traditional, as distinct from a reconstructed, town.

15. The New York Yankees blasted them out of the World Series: 4–0.

16. From his essay "Society," in *The Selected Writings of John Jay Chapman*, Jacques Barzun, ed. (New York, 1957), 244–46.

17. He received the Bok award in 1951.

18. All respect, therefore, is due to the survivors of the great and old Philadelphia tradition of painter craftsmen, such as Francis Speight, who knew that a painter's paradise consists in his object and not in his subject. "Despite the evident poverty of the working-class neighborhoods he so often depicted, Speight's paintings convey little of the sharp social comment characteristic of certain of his contemporaries during the 1930s and 1940s, who saw every factory or shanty as a symbol of the need for social and economic reform. Nevertheless, an exhibition of his work that perhaps made Speight happiest was held in a vacant store on Manayunk's Main Street in the 1930s and attended by the inhabitants of those very houses he loved to paint. Their pleased recognition of their own homes or a neighbor's backyard must have meant as much, if not more to him than the impressive prizes he received in numerous exhibitions at major museums"—except for the syntax of the last sentence, very true. *Philadelphia: Three Centuries of American Art* (Philadelphia, 1976), 149.

19. In Struthers Burt's Philadelphia novel, *Along These Streets* (Philadelphia, 1942), the hero

is a young Old Philadelphian archaeologist; his pallid passions and extreme sensitivities are revealing. It is a period illustration, an unwitting representation of how certain parochial attitudes and longings of an earlier generation typical, say, of American gentility around 1910, would survive in their descendants thirty years later.

20. Example: The proverbial *tomahto*, in Philadelphia, less nasal and more throaty than in New York or New England. On a different level, a lower-middle-class Philadelphia diction included a flat, twangy, semi-nasal *a*: "aysk" and "mayd" for *ask* and *mad*.

21. In a cosseted institution on the Main Line a victim of the Cold War chose to die that day. Biserka Krnjevic, a graduate student at Bryn Mawr College, was the daughter of a father who lived in London, a minister in the former Yugoslav royalist exile government, long abandoned by its Anglo-American allies. On a Sunday afternoon, that cruelest day for lonely people in Philadelphia, on a shiny cold April day, that proverbially cruelest month of the wasteland years, she found some rat poison, smeared it on her cookies, drank her tea, and died. The *Inquirer* next day: "According to Sgt. James Smyth, of the Lower Merion Township detectives, Miss Krnjevic was suffering from a simple case of homesickness."

22. Two standard features in its magazine in 1950: *Confident Living* by the Reverend Norman Vincent Peale ("How to Pray about a Problem." "Find Fellowship and Partnership in Your Prayers"). *FBI Girl* by Rupert Hughes ("A Beautiful FBI Fingerprint Clerk Helps Her Fiancé Uncover a Vicious Plot of International Intrigue").

23. He had Philadelphia connections: his wife was a Philadelphia Quaker.

24. Philadelphia had a larger proportion of Ukrainians than any other large city in the United States.

25. The Irish in Philadelphia, as also elsewhere, were less anti-British during the Second World War than they had been during the First, but the relentless preoccupation of the Catholic hierarchy with communism made many of them particularly receptive and attuned to the propaganda of anticommunism.

26. Title of an editorial in the *Philadelphia Bulletin*, July 1954, exasperated by the flood of McCarthyite letters to the editor: "What happened to the People in Philadelphia?" In 1951 the modest and well-known restaurant The Russian Inn on Locust Street was renamed The Inn. (In the 1960s its original name was restored. It no longer exists.)

27. The history of the appeal of militarism and nationalism in Philadelphia—in contrast to the old Quaker traditions of the city—still awaits its historian. In 1915: "Almost everybody who hasn't got a son or brother . . . is lying awake nights for fear peace may break out." Bullitt, *It's Not Done*, 223.

28. Until about 1960 real estate advertisements in Philadelphia newspapers would often indicate the location of houses for sale in certain neighborhoods by printing the name of the parish first.

   After the election of the first Irish-American president, much of this particular Irishness began to dissolve. There are no particularly Irish neighborhoods in Philadelphia now. In a middle-class Catholic college, such as Chestnut Hill, the great majority of the students was Irish from its beginning; since 1966, students with Irish or English family names have been in a minority. John Lukacs, *A Sketch of the History of Chestnut Hill College, 1924–1974* (Philadelphia, 1975, privately printed), 24–27. Much more important is Dennis Clark, *The Irish in Philadelphia* (Philadelphia, 1973).

29. The history of the Kelly family is interesting. John B. Kelly was one of ten children of an immigrant. In 1920 and in 1924 he won gold medals at the Olympic Games; he was the world's undisputed champion oarsman. Yet in 1920 the gentleman stewards of the Henley Sculls in England had scratched him from the race; his presence was disputable, he had

been a bricklayer. He made much money and ran for mayor as a Democrat in 1935; the Republican machine stole the election. His brother George was a fine playwright who had moved to New York. In the 1940s, John B. Kelly Jr. won the Diamond Sculls at Henley twice, sporting his father's old green sculling cap. (Another twenty years later he became a fixture of what passes for café society in Philadelphia.) When Grace Kelly visited her family after her sensational engagement to the Prince-Ruler of Monaco, the Irish of their neighborhood pretended to be uninterested.

30. From a television interview: Groucho Marx: "Well, how do you explain so many singers coming from one section of [Philly]? Is it because they don't produce any ballplayers there?" Frankie Avalon: "I'll tell you what. Y'know, before, mothers used to meet on the street and they used to say, uh, 'How's your son doin'?' and they'd say, 'Fine.' But now they meet on the streets and they say, 'How's your son's record doing?' 'Cause everybody's recording in South Philadelphia." Groucho: "Well, it was like that where I came from. My mother would say to another, 'How's your son's record?'" *The Secret Word Is Groucho* (New York, 1976), 190–91.

31. The most magnificent of these palaces, the Stotesburys' "Whitemarsh Hall," was occupied by its owners for hardly more than fifteen years. Its ruins still stand, abjectly and thoroughly vandalized.

32. I have seen some of them, with the grass growing rank, the mansions shut down, except perhaps for a gatehouse or a modern refectory and, once more, the wrought-iron gates locked save for a few hours of the day. By 1970 there were few young Catholics who had chosen the life of a religious; the number of vocations dropped precipitously, and the various orders chose to close down large portions of their novitiates or scholasticates. They, too, decided that they could no longer afford this kind of upkeep. With their increasing worldliness, bureaucracy had deeply penetrated into their thinking; they were ready to listen to management "experts" and to consider the offers of "developers." And so, in many instances, the occupation of these once grand premises by the new Catholic peoples was transitory; the latter, with all of their demonstrable vitality, were not impervious to that strange atrophy of the will, to the fatalism and the impermanence that may be the eternal Indian curse on the American land.

33. Certain indicators of inflation had actually dropped. The expenses of the Philadelphia General Hospital, one of the largest items in the city budget, were lower in 1949 than in 1948 (so was the number of patients admitted: 25, 273 in 1948, 23,273 in 1949). The real estate rates remained constant: $1.70 for the public schools, and $1.27 ½ per $100 of assessments.

34. Perhaps some of this was—literally—in the air. Even the weather was changing. Recall the crisp Philadelphia winters during the nineteenth century, when the Schuylkill and even the Delaware often froze over, and were skatable. Now the weather was getting warmer and damper. During the eighty years before 1950, ten of the twelve coldest months occurred between 1871 and 1900, and nine of the twelve hottest months between 1925 and 1950. In 1899 and 1900, 76 inches of snow had fallen on Philadelphia; in 1949 and 1950, 22.8.

35. The sale of ice cream on Sundays was allowed anew in 1922, the sale of gasoline on Sundays in 1926, baseball and football (after 2 p.m.) in 1933, movies in 1935. As late as 1950 there was no midnight Mass on Christmas Eve for the Catholics in Philadelphia; Cardinal Dougherty, a teetotaler, had forbidden it, lest some of the people in Philadelphia be scandalized during Holy Night by the eventual sight of unseemly alcoholic merriment.

36. This is judiciously set forth in Nicholas B. Wainwright, *History of the Philadelphia National Bank: A Century and a Half of Philadelphia Banking* (Philadelphia, 1953), especially 198 ff.
37. Owen Wister in *Monopolis* (Wister MSS., Box 83), 24: "Allusions to the Railroad were generally made with that bating of the voice observable in the godly as they approach the church-door on the Sabbath." As late as 1950, Fiske Kimball would refer to it as "the Valhalla."
38. *England Your England* (London, 1959), 229.
39. Wister MSS., Box 83, 21.

50. Hitler's Birthplace

1. His companion and wife, Eva Braun, was born in Simbach. She killed herself together with him, a few hours after they had been officially married in the bunker.

V. Some Twentieth-Century Questions

❁ ❁ ❁

51. Questions about Pius XII

1. It is, of course, both absurd and dishonest to say, as some American critics have said, that Hochhuth wished to shift the burden of responsibility from his fellow countrymen to the Pope. He did nothing of the sort.
2. To some extent his attitude toward Germany was typical of the attitudes of the Vatican, and of the "Black," that is, papal aristocracy of Rome during the first years of the World War. They sympathized with the Central Powers rather than the Allies (according to a dispatch from the Bavarian Minister in Rome, Pius X was supposed to have said in 1914 that the war Austria-Hungary was fighting against Serbia was a just war). There were various reasons for this at that time: the principal one was the association of the Western Allies, and especially of France, with laicism, secularism, liberalism, anti-clericalism.
3. Excerpt from "Les journals de Jean XXIII" in *Paris-Match*. I am leaving aside the intriguing speculation that, had Pius XII adopted some of John XXIII's attitudes toward the Soviets *already during the war*, certain of the evils done to the Church in Eastern Europe might have been avoided: for, after all, Stalin was a realist rather than a doctrinaire atheist: he clamped down on the Catholic churches of Eastern Europe (but not on the Orthodox ones) not because they were Catholic but because he saw in them the inevitable allies of anticommunism, of Western capitalism, and of the United States.
4. Marx is on the Index; *Mein Kampf* is not. The Pope did not encourage resistance to the Hitler government; after the Soviet suppression of the Hungarian Rising in 1956 he pronounced an allocution justifying armed resistance under certain circumstances.

5. "The Pope received me in his study with the dignity and informality which he can so happily combine. We had no lack of topics for conversation. The one that bulked the largest at this audience ... was the danger of Communism. I have always had the greatest dislike of it; and should I ever have the honour of another audience with the Supreme Pontiff I should not hesitate to recur to the subject."

The reminiscences of the very different *War Memoirs* of General de Gaulle are, in some respects, similar. He, too, was received by Pius XII after the liberation of Rome. "It was towards Germany, which in many respects was particularly dear to him, that his chief solicitude tended at this time. 'Those wretched people,' he said several times. 'How they will suffer!'" There are two curious coincidences. The first is that the Pope spoke these, otherwise unexceptionable and charitable, words on June 30, 1944, during the very week when the Auschwitz ovens reached the peak of their human consumption. The second is that there was one other statesman who revealed, surprisingly, a kind of sympathy for Hitler to de Gaulle. "The poor wretch!" said Stalin about Hitler to de Gaulle in December 1944.

6. The worst example of these is the Pope's monologue about the financial interests of the Vatican, in Act Four.

7. *Die Welt,* April 6, 1963. (See also Hochhuth's answer in the same number.)

8. This is what Eichmann's negotiations with certain Jews in Hungary involved. The British refused to go along with this; indeed, to some extent, they sabotaged the "deal" for higher political reasons: they were aware that behind the Eichmann proposal lurked the calculations of high German political strategy, of eventually splitting the Allies and Russia. (It seems that these considerations may have had something to do with the assassination of Lord Moyne by Jewish terrorists in late 1944.)

9. It is significant that, with few exceptions, there has been very little criticism of Pius and of the Vatican by Jews before Hochhuth, a Protestant, was to raise the dramatic question.

10. Among the pre-Christians I include the Jews of Europe: for I believe that a stronger papal policy during the war, while it may or may not have saved Jewish lives, would have led to a great movement of Jewish conversions after the war.

11. Görres, the intellectual hero of nineteenth-century German Catholicism, in 1814 called for the burning down of Strasbourg: "leave only the Cathedral! show the vengeance of the German peoples!"

53. Questions about Roosevelt and the Second World War

1. " ... without allowing too much danger to ourselves." Right-wing revisionists and critics of Roosevelt often cite this phrase, omitting these last seven words as well as how Roosevelt preceded it: ("the Japanese are notorious for attacking without warning and the question was what we should do?"). Many historians, too, overlooked that Roosevelt had said this on the day *before* the modus vivendi was cancelled. Heinrichs, on the other hand, fails to mention Roosevelt's now well-documented plan of a few days later, the sending of an American vessel across the path of the Japanese fleet moving southward, for the purpose of creating an incident.

2. Nisbet is not the only one among conservatives and neoconservatives whose hero is Robert A. Taft: "The victory of Communism would be far more dangerous to the United States than the victory of Fascism. . . . It is a greater danger . . . because it is a false philosophy which appeals to many. Fascism is a false philosophy which appeals to very

few indeed." Taft declared this in December 1941, when Hitler ruled most of Europe and when his armies were approaching suburbs of Moscow—a few days before Pearl Harbor.

54. Revising Joseph Goebbels

1. See Irene H. Gring, "Dr. Joseph Goebbels: Portrait of a Pioneer in Microfiche," in *Journal of Information and Image Management* (August 1984).
2. Helmet Heiber, *Goebbels: A Biography*, translated by John K. Dickinson (New York, 1983).
3. Published in 1987 in New York by Amok Press, in an excellent translation by Joachim Neugroschel.
4. There are, of course, many minor exceptions to this. One telling detail: from his discussions of the lamentable anti-Jewish movies (to the productions of which Goebbels devoted an extraordinary amount of energy and time) it appears that their directors and chief actors were as enthusiastic as he was. In their self-serving autobiographies, published in the 1960s, the actor Veit Harlan and Goebbels's film producer Fritz Hippler claimed that they had been reluctant and forced by Goebbels. This now seems to be wholly untrue.
5. More interesting than these introductory summaries are some of Goebbels's instructions to his staff that were retrieved and published in 1966 by Willi A. Boelcke (*Kriegspropaganda 1939–1941*). One should, however, consider at least that The Chronicler of the Reich, writing for posterity, *may* have—I am not saying that he *had*—chosen to exclude certain secretive details that would conflict with a more or less official version of how some of its great decisions were made. But this is not more than a possibility, and not an altogether plausible one.

55. Hitler: The Historical Problem

1. All of the following quotes from Geyl are from the preface of his *Napoleon: For and Against* (New Haven, CT, and London, 1949), 7–11.
2. His original essay about Napoleon was to be printed in a Dutch monthly review in June 1940. "After the capitulation, in May, the manuscript was returned to me, still marked with an instruction to the printer to be quick, and without a word of explanation. No explanation was needed for me to understand that, although I had not written a single word in it about Hitler and National Socialism, the parallel with our own times had seemed to the editor a little too pointed in the new circumstances." During the above-mentioned lectures in Rotterdam, "occasional bursts of laughter showed the audience to be equally alive to the parallel."
3. But not only Germans. "One can see"—and the spectacle is not a pretty one—Frenchmen "licking the hand that had chastised them": a hand that not only chastised but subjugated and sometimes tortured them, a hand not one of their own but of their national enemy, who had little more than contempt for them. One of their brilliant intellectuals, Robert Brasillach, dared to put it in one phrase during his trial in 1945: "We slept with the Germans; and we liked some of it." (Was it because of this phrase that General de Gaulle,

despite the requests of many intellectuals, refused to commute Brasillach's death sentence? Perhaps.) One positive consequence of World War II was the disappearance of Franco-German enmity, indeed, the subsequent reconciliation and alliance of the two nations and states. But there has been a less edifying consequence: a French sense of inferiority—not merely a political but also a cultural sense of inferiority—to things German. This includes their—sometimes outspoken—admiration for the Third Reich and for some of its representatives. The phenomenon of Le Pen and his millions of followers is something that was foreseen by the French "collaborationists" such as Brasillach and others, who were collaborationists not only with Germany but with Hitlerism. To this we may add the cult of Ernst Jünger, Carl Schmitt, Martin Heidegger, and others—not Nazis but believers in German superiority. In no other country have they become as respected and admired by intellectuals as they now are in France.

4. Let us recall, for example, that Napoleon entered Moscow and Hitler did not; also that the former arrived there a mere ten weeks after having crossed the Russian frontier; getting to the outskirts of Moscow took Hitler's mechanized armies five months. But then, Hitler survived his first winter in Russia, after which his armies began to advance again into its depths, whereas Napoleon suffered a catastrophe and withdrew from Russia in less than three months.

5. A strange coincidence not noted by other historians: It was in Hitler's birthplace, Braunau, that in 1810 Napoleon's new bride, the Archduchess Marie Louise, was festively transferred from her Austrian to her French entourage. During his campaigns against Austria in 1805 and again in 1809, Napoleon spent the night in that frontier town—in the same Haus Schüdl (and presumably in the same second-story rooms) where seventy years later Hitler's father came to live. (It is a well-proportioned building on the south side of the large market square.)

6. A book remains to be written about Hitler's expressed views of other nations and nationalities, which were in many instances varied or changing rather than constant and uniform. There is, for example, place for a serious study of his attitude toward Britain and the British people, which was more complicated than the sometimes overused cliché of a love-hate relationship. However, what is striking is the evidence of Hitler's hatefulness toward people who dared to oppose or defy him. Thus his occasional expressions of respect or even admiration for the people disappeared and gave way to expressions of a contemptuous hatred as the war went on and neared its end. Not dissimilar was his treatment of Poland and the Poles, about whom he uttered few disparaging remarks before 1939 but whose defiance—leading to the outbreak of the war in 1939—made him impose cruelties on them unparalleled anywhere except in his treatment of Jews. We find nothing similar in the reactions of Napoleon or even Stalin, who on occasion showed some respect for the bravery of his opponents.

7. Joachim Fest in *Adolf Hitler: Eine Biographie* (Berlin, 1973; new edition, with new introduction, 1995), 309, is convincing that Hitler's "entire intellectual and emotional system" seemed to have been dominated by a fundamental element of "Angst" (*Angsterlebnis*). This, among other matters, also differentiates Hitler from the young Mussolini, who resembled the early Bonaparte rather than Hitler.

8. On one occasion in 1940 Hitler was supposed to have said that he would impose his victorious peace treaty at Münster in Westphalia, thus putting an end to the European state system that had been established there in 1648.

9. Cited by Mathieu Molé in 1842, receiving Tocqueville in the Académie Française; also by François Furet, *Revolutionary France 1770–1880* (Oxford, 1988), 260–70.

10. Stendhal, *Vie de Napoléon*, 1837: "The greatest man the world has ever seen since Caesar." And: "The more becomes known of the truth, the greater Napoleon will be" (a belief often repeated by Hitler's admirers).

11. One tendency that they have in common with Napoleon's more circumspect—or partial—defenders is their attribution to the British of cruel design.

12. Chateaubriand in *Memoirs d'outre-tombe*, cited by Geyl: "For there is no gain-saying the fact that this subjugator has remained popular with a nation which once made it a point of honor to raise altars to independence and equality. . . . The miracles wrought by his arms have bewitched our youth and have taught it to worship brute force. . . ." To this add Aulard's recognition of the loyalty of the Parisian working class to Napoleon—not unlike the loyalty of most German industrial workers to Hitler against their country. (Jacques Bainville, for example, in the case of the former; Andreas Hillgruber in the case of the latter.)

13. Consider a comparison between the way Napoleon and Hitler respectively treated the Pope. The latter was more circumspect than the former. (But this had much to do with the fact that popes had greater prestige—and influence—in the mid-twentieth century than at the beginning of the nineteenth.) Napoleon learned, too late, that *Qui mange du Pape en meurt*; Hitler knew that only too well. One interesting detail: When Napoleon's envoy to Rome asked the Emperor how to treat the Pope, Napoleon said, "Treat him as if he had two hundred thousand men." (Albert Vandal, cited by Geyl, 230.) That is the origin of the witticism wrongly attributed to Stalin in 1935: "How many divisions has the Pope?" (A canard.)

14. Also Lefebvre, cited in Geyl, 424: "There has remained in [Napoleon] something of the uprooted person. Also of the man torn from his class: he is not entirely a nobleman nor entirely of the people." The first sentence is applicable to Hitler, even though we have noted their different personal characteristics and temperaments.

15. Lanfrey—a critic, not a eulogist of Napoleon, ranked among the "Against" by Geyl, 104: ". . . noted that Napoleon's order, in spite of its severity, remains general and leaves something to the initiative of his subordinates. He has no doubt that this was intentional, and indeed, did not the Emperor wash his hands of the whole business afterwards?" That Hitler didn't do. Napoleon, at least, chose to cover up in writing. In a letter to Cambacères, quoted by Lanfrey, he goes even further: "'The Pope was removed from Rome without my orders and against my wishes.' It is surprising, if that is the case, that he acquiesced in the accomplished fact. But indeed it is a flagrant untruth. It is all part of the system. In the Enghien affair he sheltered behind the alleged overhasty action of Savary. In the case of Spain it was Murat. And now it was Miollis, the Governor of Rome, who had to bear the discredit of a deed which Napoleon had undoubtedly wished done." To this Geyl adds a telling footnote: "One could make a comparison here with Queen Elizabeth, who was also very ready to saddle her servants with the blame in difficult situations. The best known, but certainly not the only example, is that of her rage against Davison, on the pretext that he had given the order for the execution of Mary Queen of Scots without her authority."

16. Consider, too, Napoleon's recorded musings—his "pièces justificatives"—at St. Helena, where, among other things, he predicted the rise of the United States and Russia and the necessity for France of friendship with England. Nothing like this with Hitler. *Avec et après moi le déluge*: improperly attributed to a French monarch but appropriate, in spirit, to Hitler.

17. However, we must keep in mind that the German words for "science" and "scientific"—

Wissenschaft and *wissenschaftlich*—are broader than our contemporary English usage of them. They include both "science" and "knowledge."

18. Veronica Wedgwood's *bon mot*: "History is an art—like all the other sciences."

19. Was Napoleon the peak figure of the nineteenth century? No—he was the unexpected culmination of the eighteenth.

20. "Of persons" only "d. 'The Great,' following a proper name [as] merely an honourable epithet, appended as a title to the names of certain historical persons, chiefly monarchs, implying . . . that the person so designated . . . ranks among the great men of history."

21. An example was Speer's monumental model of a future central Berlin (1940), in which he included Hitler's own 1925 design of a triumphal arch. It was fitted within the proportions of that monumental design but otherwise its style was unfitting, very different from Speer's modern neoclassicism, and utterly inferior both to the Arc de Triomphe and to the Arc du Carrousel.

Sebastian Haffner, *The Meaning of Hitler* (New York, 1979), 45: Unlike Napoleon, "Hitler did not create any state edifice, and his achievements, which for ten years overwhelmed the Germans and made the world hold its breath, have proved ephemeral and have left no trace, not only because they ended in disaster but because they were never designed for endurance." (Not quite: Hitler often insisted to Speer and others that his buildings must be constructed of granite, "lasting four hundred years.") "As a star performer, Hitler probably ranks even higher than Napoleon. But one thing he never was— a statesman." (Arguable.)

22. Vappu Tallgren, *Hitler und die Helden. Heroismus und Weltanschauung* (Helsinki, 1981), 258 (much praised by Zitelmann). Tallgren—in my opinion, convincingly—emphasizes the influence of Karl May's German-Indian "westerns" on Hitler.

23. Percy Ernst Schramm, *Hitler: The Man and Military Leader* (Chicago, 1971), 183: "The difficulty is that language offers no negative equivalents to 'hero' and 'genius.' Whoever is concerned that we may be possibly giving Hitler more than his due by seeking adequate terms for him misses the point."

24. It is not only that *The Great Dictator* is one of Chaplin's worst films. (Alan Bullock, *Hitler: A Study in Tyranny* [London, 1952; revised ed., 1962], 805: "Chaplin's brilliant [?] caricature in *The Great Dictator.*") See also Chaplin, *My Autobiography* (London, 1964), 316: Hitler: "a baggy-pants comic. . . .The face was obscenely comic—a bad imitation of me [!] with its absurd moustache . . . and disgusting, thin little mouth. I could not take Hitler seriously . . . his hands claw-like haranguing the crowd . . . one up and another down, like a cricketer about to bowl . . . [or] hands clenched in front of him as though lifting an imaginary dumb-bell. The salute with the hand thrown back over the shoulder, the palm upwards, made me want to put a tray of dirty dishes on it. "'This is a nut,' I thought. . . .'" (Another famous personage who underestimated and dismissed Hitler was Einstein.)

25. Examples from Lewis's *Hitler*, 1931 (reprinted in New York, 1972, not easily available in most libraries): "the Communists help the police to beat and shoot the Nazis" (16). The Nazis are "clean and law-abiding" (19). "Whereas the Communist is invariably armed, the Nazi has only his fists or sticks to defend himself with, owing to the discrimination of the Republican police authorities" (28). Hitler: "An asceticism not without nobility" (31). "In setting about to expound the doctrine of Hitlerism, it rapidly becomes apparent that it is rather *a person* than *a doctrine* with which we are dealing." England "is married to Jews," but (42): "still allow a little *Blutgefühl* to have its way (a blood-feeling toward this other mind and body like your own)—in favor of this brave and unhappy impoverished kinsman." "I do not think that if Hitler had his way he would bring the fire and the sword

across otherwise peaceful frontiers" (49). "Hitler *is* a very different person from Mussolini, Pilsudski, or Primo da Rivera" (51). In 1939 Lewis wrote *The Hitler Cult*—now very critical of Hitler, with some insights: "He disdains democracy and all its works. Yet he himself, as a demagogue, hanging upon the emotional suffrage of the masses, is a typical democratic statesman—and this in spite of the fact that the agreeable laissez-faire of Western democracy had passed over, with him, into a demagogic despotism."

26. The title of Lothar Burchardt's *Hitler und die historische Grösse* (Konstanz, 1979) is promising, but the book does not really deal with the idea or with qualifications of "greatness."

27. Irving, of course, has no such hesitations; in his foreword to *Hitler's War* (New York, 1977), xxiii, he suggests the epithet "Hitler the Great," citing Jodl in Nuremberg: "I blame his humble origins, but then I remember how many peasants' sons have been blessed by History with the name 'great.'" Jodl, too (International Military Tribunal [documents], xv, 602, cited by Werner Maser, *Adolf Hitler: Legende, Mythos, Wirklichkeit* [Munich, 1971], 195): Hitler was "no charlatan, but a gigantic personality, at the end acquiring an infernal kind of greatness, but greatness he possessed undoubtedly. . . ." Doenitz, also at Nuremberg: "Hitler was a great military leader: despite the defeat at Carthage the people admired Hannibal. . . . And despite our German defeat the people still admire Hitler. . . ."

28. Haffner, *The Meaning of Hitler,* 40. See also another unexceptionable anti-Hitlerian, Golo Mann, cited in Günther Scholdt, *Autoren über Hitler* (Bonn, 1993), 18: Hitler "changed everything. . . . Hitler alone could achieve what he had planned, to build a popular movement and then keep it under his control. He proved himself far superior [*turmhoch*] to all of his rivals, opponents within the Party on occasion, as well as to the conservative holders of his stirrup [*Steigbügelhalter*]. Hatred of Jews was *his* passion; the war was *his* enterprise from the beginning, from 1933 to 1945. The will to prove that Germany could have won the war of 1914 if he had commanded it then, if he had waged that war with the right means to the right ends, this remains the source of his entire, unbelievable, disastrous adventure. 'Then it was the Kaiser, now it is I.' In the modern history of Europe I find no one who had affected events so decisively and so destructively, even more than had Napoleon."

29. Fest, *Adolf Hitler,* 17, 189. Karl-Dietrich Erdmann "solves" the problem (or, rather, unsolves it) by a dual adjective: "the impenetrable darkness of his person . . . his diabolical world-historical greatness" (in Gebhardt, ed., *Handbuch der Geschichte. Die Zeir der Weltkriege,* vol. 2, Stuttgart, 1976). Bullock's conclusion is somewhat better (Bullock, *Hitler,* 806): "The fact that his career ended in failure, and that his defeat was preeminently due to his own mistakes, does not by itself detract from Hitler's claim to greatness. The flaw lies deeper. For those remarkable powers were combined with an ugly and strident egotism, a moral and intellectual cretinism. [*Not a mot juste.*] The passions which ruled Hitler's mind were ignoble: hatred, resentment, the lust to dominate, and, where he could not dominate, to destroy."

30. Schramm, *Hitler,* 12. "By comparison, the autocracy of previous despots seems almost timorous and halting." Görlitz-Quint in Walter Görlitz and Herbert A. Quint (both pseudonyms), *Adolf Hitler: Eine Biographie* (Stuttgart, 1952), 234: "In any case there is no leading figure in German history comparable to him." Also 628: "We consciously avoid the word 'great' because 'great' suggests a connection to ethical value."

31. Schramm, *Hitler,* 123. In this respect Schramm's view accords with that of the otherwise different Heer. Schramm, *Hitler,* 182–83: "Anyone who speaks of him as satanic or infer-

nal is, in effect, making a theological statement. Whoever calls him a 'demon' is ulti-mately reserving judgment about the nature of his acts."

32. On April 6, 1938, in Salzburg he said: "I think that the times in which I lead Germany are historical times of German greatness. . . . I believe that the future and German history will confirm that in the times of my leadership I achieved the highest benefits for the German people." (Deuerlein, 133.)

33. It saved Churchill from a difficult and perhaps embarrassing problem. "At any time in the last few months of the war he could have flown to England and surrendered himself, saying: 'Do what you will with me, but spare my misguided people.'" (Churchill, *The Second World War*, vol. 6, *Triumph and Tragedy*, 673.) Would that embarrassment have been due to Hitler's "greatness"? No: it would have been merely political. (Churchill respected Napoleon but not Hitler.) That embarrassment—together with thoughtlessness—among the Allies also marked the fate of Mussolini in 1943, when they (or the Italian royal government) made no effort to deliver Mussolini to the Allies or even to take him south with the royal government. He remained on the Gran Sasso for nine days after the sign-ing of the Italian surrender, four days after its public announcement and the flight of the king and the government from Rome to the south. No provision was made in the armi-stice instrument for the surrender of Mussolini.

34. Samuel Johnson about Charles XII of Sweden, in *The Vanity of Human Wishes*. Fest, in his conclusion, 1029: "In a variation on a phrase of Schopenhauer whom he [Hitler] in his way respected it may be said that he taught something to the world that the world shall never again forget."

35. Lukacs, *Historical Consciousness* (New York, 1968; extended ed., 1994), 93: "Its survival depends on the coagulating consensus of civilized tradition, and on authentic responses to quality; but that is a long-range consensus, formed by the historical thinking of gen-erations and confirmed by existential experience. For it is in the long run that, somehow, truth may survive—through the decay of untruth."

36. Haffner gives a telling summary of this (*The Meaning of Hitler*, 100–01): "Today's world, whether we like it or not, is the work of Hitler. Without Hitler there would have been no partition of Germany and Europe; without Hitler there would be no Americans and Russians in Berlin; without Hitler there would be no Israel; without Hitler there would be no decolonisation, at least not such a rapid one; there would be no Asian, Arab, or Black African emancipation, and no diminution of European pre-eminence. Or, more accurately, there would be none of all this without Hitler's mistakes. He certainly did not want any of it."

"One has to go back a long way in history—perhaps to Alexander the Great—to find a man who, in a below-average short span of life, transformed the world so fundamen-tally and lastingly as Hitler. But what one would not find in the whole of world history is a man who, with an unparalleled and gigantic effort, achieved, as Hitler did, the exact opposite of what he had hoped to achieve."

37. This is but a brief statement of what is summarized at somewhat greater length in Lukacs, *The Last European War, 1939–1941* (New York, 1976), especially 6–7 and 519–27.

38. Two random examples of an, alas, wholehearted belief in this deterministic idealism by two of his generals. Jodl on November 7, 1943: "We will win because we must win, for otherwise world history will have lost its meaning." Field Marshal Model on March 29, 1945: "In our struggle for the ideals [*Ideenwelt*] of National Socialism . . . it is a math-ematical certainty [!] that we will win, as long as our belief and will remains unbroken." Cited by Manfred Messerschmitt, "Die Wehrmacht in der Endphase. Realität and Perzeption," *Aus Politik und Zeitgeschichte*, August 4, 1989, 37–38.

39. Owen Chadwick, *The Secularization of the European Mind in the Nineteenth Century* (Cambridge, 1991), 73.

40. For the last time, he was a populist nationalist, not a traditional patriot. He knew better than most people that the true opposite of nationalism, with its cult of the people, is not so much a modern internationalism as a traditional patriotism, with its love for the land and for its history.

41. Schramm, *Hitler,* 107. Consider, too, Perón's (a National Socialist prototype) successful assumption of power in Argentina in October 1945, a few months after Hitler's death. Apart from its significance, the importance of that must not be overestimated, in view of the Latin American tendency to emulate other revolutions after a time span of many years: Bolívar and San Martín twenty or thirty years after Washington, Castro fifteen years after 1945, and so on.

42. *Historikerstreit* (Piper, ed.; Munich, 1987), 149. Consider also the tendency of the press and of commentators all over the Western world: their extreme sensitivity to every manifestation suggesting the appearance of so-called right-wing political phenomena anywhere. That sensitivity is not comparable to anxieties about a resurgence of the extreme Left. This is not simply attributable to "political correctness" (a stupid term): It reflects an anxiety about the mass appeal of extreme nationalism in the age of mass democracy. But here a historical, or, rather, a political comparison may be in order. It is generally accepted that Hitler's breakthrough came in September 1930, with the sudden 18 percent of the vote the National Socialists won in that year's German elections. In our day we may find that in many countries of the Western world so-called right-wing movements (Le Pen in France, the neo-fascists in Italy, Haider in Austria, perhaps Buchanan, too, in the United States) may count on a 12 to 20 percent support among the electorate . . . but not in Germany. There, in 1930, the National Socialists gained respectability because of their nationalism, the decisive element in Hitler's coming to power. A concerted opposition to that did not exist. This is not so today. History does not repeat itself. Still we must not eschew the possibility that in the future, as in the past, "hard" minorities may achieve important inroads into "soft majorities."

43. Symbols matter; or at least they tell us something. The flag of the party and then of the Third Reich, the swastika in a red field, was Hitler's own, brilliant design. Yet he would have done better—probably in both the short and the long run—if he had kept the black-white-red flag of the imperial Reich. (Next to the swastika flag it survived in Germany until about 1935; and January 18, the birthday of the Second Reich, remained a day of public celebration during the Third.) But now the swastika flag, like the Third Reich, is only an episode, and the republican-democratic black-red-gold flag has outlasted even the forty-seven years of the black-white-red one.

44. Conversely, the crucial phase of the nineteenth century (1815 to 1914) was *not* its first one-third (1815 to 1848), which was (as Napoleon had foreseen) a continuation of the appeal of the French and other European revolutions. After 1849, the period of repeated revolutions was succeeded by a period of wars (which Bismarck had correctly foreseen), which was much more decisive; in spite of the recognition of Marx, the struggle of nations succeeded the struggle of classes. *That* period ended in 1945.

45. Ernst Deuerlein in a trenchant conclusion, 143, correctly put it: "Meanwhile he had become a global political phenomenon—an object not only of hate but of hope (for many)." Fest, *Hitler,* 148: Hitler's "superiority over many of his opponents and competitors had much to do with his grasp of the essence of a world crisis of which he himself was the symptom." In *Hitler,* 569, Fest cites the Austrian writer Robert Musil in 1933,

who also admitted that his resistance is bereft of alternatives: he cannot think that the old or an even older order might return and replace this new kind of a revolutionary order. "What explains this feeling is that National Socialism has its destiny and its hour, that it is not a whirl [*Wirbel*] but a phase of history." A general statement by Eberhard Jäckel in *Hitler in History* (Hanover, NH, 1984), 43: "[Hitler] undoubtedly developed a program of his own, individually and alone, but his program must have coincided with the deeper tendencies and ambitions of his country and of his time. We may not be able to explain this, and yet we have to recognize it. Was he an author or an executor, a producer or a product? Was he so successful for a long time as an author because he was executing deeper tendencies? Or had he simply a better understanding than most of his contemporaries of the requirements and the possibilities of his time? These are fundamental questions about not only the role of the individual in history but also about historical understanding in general." (These generalizations of Jäckel's are too categorical and somewhat pedestrian in their expressions; moreover, they are not only applicable to Hitler.)

46. Again Deuerlein, in a trenchant conclusion of his small book (*Hitler: Eine politische Biographie,* Munich, 1969, 170): There is plenty of proof that "the historical appearance of Hitler was not only a problem of his person alone, but in a much wider sense that of his environment, of the German and also the extra-German world—a fact that explains why the preoccupation with Hitler has not come to an end after his death, and at the same time directing our attention to its obstacles and difficulties." Bullock, *Hitler,* 808: "Hitler, indeed, was a European, no less than a German phenomenon. The conditions and the state of mind which he exploited ... were not confined to his own country, although they were more strongly marked in Germany than anywhere else. Hitler's idiom was German, but the thoughts and emotions to which he gave expression have a more universal currency."

47. Gerhard Schreiber, *Hitler: Interpretationen 1923–1983* (2nd, extended ed., Darmstadt, 1988), 332. A long but essentially uninspiring attempt (in reality not much more than a bibliographical disquisition) was made by Klaus Hildebrand in *Historische Zeitschrift,* 583–632, "Hitlers Ort in der Geschichte des preussisch-deutschen National-states." In 1988 the neoconservative Michael Stürmer wrote that Germany "today is a land without history." In some ways the opposite is true. Maser in his conclusion of *Adolf Hitler* was proved wrong (439): "Only when West and East Germany are unified will Adolf Hitler, the all-German trauma, be finally superseded." It did not happen thus.

48. Friedrich Heer, *Der Glaube des Adolf Hitler: Anatomie einer politischen Religiosität* (Munich, 1968), 535–36.

49. This is much more profound than Graham Greene: "The greatest saints have been men with more than a normal capacity for evil, and the most vicious men have sometimes narrowly evaded sanctity." (Cited in John Toland's foreword to his *Adolf Hitler* (New York, 1977), xiii, where he wriggles around the question of Hitler's "greatness.")

50. In this respect we ought to, again, reject the "demonization" of Hitler, or the temptation to attribute to him the qualities of being "diabolical" or "satanic." To the contrary, we can see elements in his career that bear an uncanny reminder of what St. John of the Apocalypse predicted as the Antichrist. The Antichrist will not be horrid and devilish, incarnating some kind of frightful monster—hence recognizable immediately. He will not seem to be anti-Christian. He will be smiling, generous, popular, an idol, adored by masses of people because of the sunny prosperity he seems to have brought, a false father (or husband) to his people. Save for a small minority, Christians will believe in

him and follow him. Like the Jews at the time of the First Coming, Christians at the time of the Antichrist—that is, before the Second Coming—will divide. Before the end of the world the superficial Christians will follow the Antichrist, and only a small minority will recognize his awful portents. Well, Hitler did not bring about the end of the world, but there was a time—not yet the time of the mass murders but the time of the Third Reich in the 1930s—when some of St. John's prophecies about the Antichrist accorded with this appearance and his appeal. And it may not be unreasonable to imagine that in the coming age of the masses he was but the first of Antichrist-like popular figures.

In 1933 Joseph Roth wrote: "The Third Reich is now a country of Hell." No: but it did have some of the features of a nation led by an Antichrist. (Already in 1923 some of Hitler's followers had compared his life to that of Christ: thirty years of obscurity and then suddenly three years of a shining revelation.) Carl Jung: "Hitler's power is not political; it is magic." Also Lukacs (*The Last European War*, 524, note 194, and *Historical Consciousness*, 298). Klaus Mehnert in 1951: "The German people's journey from Liebknecht to Hitler and the Russian people's journey from Lenin to Stalin.... In both cases ... the journey was one from dialectic to magic." An exaggeration of a generalization; but not without some substance.

51. During World War I, many Germans held the belief that German "Kultur" was infinitely superior to the English "Zivilisation." Of course there are national and linguistic problems here. Consider "Sebastian" in *The Edwardians*, at their elegant house parties in 1906: "... sometimes so vehemently did he deprecate them, sometimes he thought that they had mastered the problem of civilisation more truly than the Greeks or Romans." This would be unintelligible to many Germans, while the substitution of the word "culture" for "civilization" in such a sentence would be senseless in English.

52. Cited in Peter Adam, *The Art of the Third Reich* (New York, 1992), 129.

53. Speer in prison already in 1947: Hitler's war has shown "the vulnerability of modern civilization, built up during centuries. We know now that we live in a building that is not immune to earthquakes ... if the automation of progress leads to a further dehumanization [*Entpersönlichung*] of people, depriving them of responsibility even more. [In the] decisive years of my life I have served technology, blinded to its possibilities. In the end I am skeptical about it." This is the opposite of Spenglerianism.

54. The Middle Ages is a misnomer, too, because the term suggests a position in the "middle," between Ancient and Modern. But there is a difference, because of our historical consciousness: People during and at the end of the Middle Ages did *not* know that they lived in the Middle Ages, whereas we know that we have been living in the Modern Age, and that we are near the end of it.

55. We must recognize, too, that in an essential way he belonged to his age, for in his own way, he believed in Progress—unable and unwilling to recognize that the grave task before civilization now is a necessary rethinking of the entire meaning of Progress (a term that Tocqueville abhorred, but Hitler did not.)

56. The Poverty of Anticommunism

1. One—possible—exception: the suicide of General Akhromaev, former Soviet chief of staff; but it is reasonable to conclude that he killed himself not because of the end of Communism but because of the collapse of the Russian military empire.

2. See my introduction to *Tocqueville: The European Revolution and Correspondence with Gobineau* (New York, 1959).
3. I have written about this before. See, for example, the chapter entitled "Anti-Anti" in *Confessions of an Original Sinner* (New York, 1990).

57. The Problem of American Conservatism

1. Example: an American of older native stock will usually prefer to assert that this or that ancestor of his was a radical, since somehow this will sound better (and even socially preferable) than to say that his ancestor had been a conservative. The same thing holds for the reputation of an occasional American Indian ancestor (except perhaps among the lower class of white people in the South). It is the immigrant who—sometimes fraudulently—will claim that this or that of his European ancestors was an aristocrat.
2. An Illinois newspaper in 1859, cited in Edgar Lee Masters, *Lincoln, the Man* (New York, 1931), 215.
3. And to Redskins and Palefaces. Hemingway was a modern American Redskin of sorts: but he enjoyed that image especially against a European background. In this respect he was but a successor of that other public relations American, Benjamin Franklin, who wore his coonskin cap not in Philadelphia but in Paris.
4. Anne Morrow Lindbergh, *War Within and Without: Diaries and Letters of Anne Morrow Lindbergh 1939–1944* (New York, 1980), 189–90.
5. In 1940–41 John F. Kennedy was a secret contributor to America First; in 1950 he gave financial support to Richard Nixon against the latter's liberal opponent in California; as late as 1955 he chose not to take a stand, and preferred not to vote, against McCarthy; but in 1960 he ran, and won, his campaign for the American presidency as an internationalist; and by the time of his death the entire Kennedy clan had associated themselves with certain liberal causes while they incurred the opposition and the occasional wrath of conservatives. Much of this was due to the Kennedys' political opportunism and to the then still prevalent American phenomenon of becoming more liberal as one moves up with the social and intellectual and institutional establishment. (This liberalization was taking place among the Irish-American population at large: with their rise in American society many of their bitter memories and old animosities were vanishing from their minds.)
6. Between 1935 and 1945 a host of such intellectuals: Max Eastman, John Dos Passos, Charles A. Beard, Harry Elmer Barnes, H. L. Mencken—this list is not at all complete—had become postliberals. In this respect they were "antennae of the race," forerunners of a national development, in some cases in extreme forms. Harry Elmer Barnes, an intellectual debunker in the Twenties, Darwinist, and bitter enemy of religion (*The Twilight of Christianity*, 1929) became a defender of Hitler; the Nietzscheite Mencken became an acrid opponent of Roosevelt; Beard became a nationalist isolationist and saw Roosevelt's foreign policy as a conspiracy, etc. All of this had a significance beyond mundane politics, a significance that went beyond the usual appeal of conspiracy theories to embittered intellectuals whose cause does not prevail. This significance resides in the fact that for at least fifty years most conversions among American intellectuals went from Left to Right—as in Russia during the nineteenth century, where despite the overall (and, as I wrote above, ultimately deceptive) triumph of the Westernizers, the few sig-

nificant conversions (e.g., Dostoyevsky) had gone in one direction, from Westernizer to Slavophile, from liberal to conservative, from cosmopolitan to nationalist.

7. Speech in Des Moines, Iowa, October 1941.

8. In an article in the *New York Times Magazine* (December 28, 1980) about the American neoconservative movement, all of the six intellectuals described therein (Kristol, Lipset, Podhoretz, Gershman, Decter, Hook) were Jews, and at least two of them former Trotskyites.

9. *Harper's,* April 1955.

10. December 15, 1953.

11. As late as the 1950s the *New York Times* was sponsoring an annual mock United Nations Assembly composed of ten- to twelve-year old American children.

12. For about three decades before 1965 the Liberal Party in New York was an important municipal political force whose endorsement was eagerly sought by candidates. By 1970 the Conservative Party replaced it to such an extent that no Republican (and, on occasion, not even a Democratic) candidate in New York City could hope to be successful without Conservative support.

13. Bill Buckley started out as an isolationist: as late as 1950 he was suspicious of the Yalie types who made up the CIA and its forerunner, the OSS. Twenty years later the hero of his ideological thrillers was a CIA agent out of Yale, an amoral American James Bond.

14. "Tradition is the enemy of progress." This was not a statement by a liberal or an intellectual. It was stated in 1928 by Julius A. Klein, Herbert Hoover's assistant secretary of commerce, with enthusiastic approval by the Great Engineer (who was himself a Wilsonian and a progressive). In 1960 the neoconservative Seymour Martin Lipset wrote: "The growth of large organizations may actually have the more important consequences of providing new sources of continued freedom and more opportunity to innovate." *Political Man* (New York, 1960), 414, cited by Samuel P. Huntington, *American Politics: The Promise of Disharmony* (Cambridge, MA, 1981), 170.

15. The belief that the United States is not only the greatest country in the world but that it represents the culmination of the entire history of mankind was still dearly held by millions of Americans, including (from all evidence) Ronald Reagan: but this did not mean that they, or he, were old-fashioned or conservative, except in a very limited and unhistorical sense. This kind of shortsighted and self-congratulatory inclination was, alas, only too evident among conservative intellectuals, too—as, for example, in the incredible statement of Michael Novak (*National Review,* September 16, 1983): ". . . the American people are, by every test of fact, the most religious on this planet."

58. The Elective Monarchy

1. In his *Histoire des Français,* esp.1. Robert H. Ferrell, ed., *Off the Record: The Private Papers of Harry S. Truman* (New York, 1980).

2. Hoover was the last president who composed most of his speeches; Truman was the last president who wrote at least some of them.

3. During the crucial election campaign of 1932 less was spent than in 1928. The reported (that is, very much underestimated) expenditures on presidential campaigns rose eightfold in twenty years, from $5 million in 1948 to more than $40 million in 1968. In 1980 the major candidates reported that they had spent $73 million on the campaign, whereof

more than $63 million was covered by the public financing provisions of the Federal Election Campaign Act as amended in 1974.

4. Except for Tocqueville, who foresaw that the result of popular rule would not be extremism but conformism with long periods of intellectual stagnation.

5. These quotes are from my chapter on Penrose in *Philadelphia 1900–1950: Patricians and Philistines* (New York, 1981), 56–60.

6. "The reformers' attacks on the politicians of today are peculiarly unjust. By management and not by statesmanship are questions generally decided in the Legislatures.... When management is all that is essential, have we a right to be disappointed if Van Buren is not Webster?" cited in John Lukacs, *Philadelphia 1900–1950: Patricians and Philistines* (New York, 1981), 57–58.

7. Dickens, in *Hard Times,* attacked the "national dustmen," that is, members of Parliament, for their "abstraction called a People."

8. Walter Bagehot (1869): "The middle-classes—the ordinary majority of educated men, are in the present day the despotic power in England. 'Public opinion,' nowadays, is the opinion of the bald-headed men at the back of the omnibus." There was a corresponding American linguistic usage. Before 1918 the phrase "men in the cars" (that is, in the streetcars) was the equivalent of the later "man in the street."

9. By 1789, he said, the ruling people had learned "that opinion makes and changes the world—as the traditional authorities had become too feeble to put obstacles in its way, and as they themselves had begun trafficking with some of its features.... But today the success of the press lies more in the general levelling of views than in its direct function. ... [O]ften the press shrieks so loud *because* people no longer listen...."

10. "So far as their extent goes, we may venture to say that public opinion is usually smaller than the majority, which, in turn, is smaller than popular sentiment; but, so far as their articulateness goes, public opinion is often more important than either the majority or than popular sentiment." John Lukacs, *Historical Consciousness* (New York, 1968 and 1984), 82.

11. There was also the Indian element of war slogans. George Bancroft, in his *History of the United States* (New York, 1880), vol. II, 113, about Indians: "Anyone who, on chanting the war-song, could obtain volunteer followers, became a war-chief." (The caucus was another Indian term and practice in American politics; so was Tammany.)

12. The English historian Maitland in 1898: "One of the great books that remains to be written is the History of the Majority. Our habit of treating the voice of a majority as equivalent to the voice of an all is so deeply engrained that we hardly think that it has a history."

13. George Kennan: "I ... suspect that what purports to be public opinion in most countries that consider themselves to have popular government is often not really the consensus of the feelings of the mass of people at all but rather the expression of the interests of special highly vocal minorities—politicians, commentators, and publicity-seekers of all sorts: people who live by their ability to draw attention to themselves...."

14. In 1893 a huge Department of Publicity at the Chicago Columbian Exposition was in charge of editing all of the printed material; its approval was required for every pamphlet, no matter of what organization.

15. Harding's majority was impressive; yet the politicians' expectations for the feminine vote (in 1920, for the first time, all American women had been enfranchised) may have been exaggerated. The total number of voters among the eligible was less than 50 percent in 1920 (it was 61 percent in 1916).

16. Van Wyck Brooks, *America's Coming-of-Age* (New York, 1915), 79–80.
17. Jules Abeis, *In the Time of Silent Cal* (New York, 1969), 29.
18. There's still another fine Coolidge portrait; in it he holds up—without discernible en-thusiasm—a distinctly antiquated fish which he has supposedly just landed; it is bent at an alarming angle, *rigor mortis* having long since set in. (Told me by Geoffrey C. Ward.) This was the Coolidge who said in 1926 in a speech to the American Association of Advertising Agencies, "There can be no permanent basis for advertising except the rep-resentation of the exact truth."
19. The *Reporter,* March 19, 1959: "When an Army colonel was court-martialed in 1957 for leaking to the press information about the Army missile Jupiter, Dr. Wernher von Braun, head of the Army Missile Program, testified in his defense: 'The Jupiter involves several million dollars of the taxpayers' money. One hundred per cent security would mean no information for the public, no money for the Army, no Jupiter. . . .'"
20. One example of this is the "hurrying on" of an event (often desired by the reporter himself) by publicizing it, as in the case of a presidential appointment or decision, with the hope that this kind of publicity will tilt the balance and make it difficult for the president to withhold or to change the appointment or the decision in question. In other words, the "reporting" of an event sometimes precedes, and not follows, the "event" itself.
21. During the Kennedy presidency there was some talk about the establishment of a simple electronic device in every American home whereby a president could, in a matter of seconds, ascertain the preferences of the American people on a single alternative or question.
22. This essential condition of predetermined alternatives governs, of course, the most ex-tensive and "sophisticated" public-opinion questionnaire as much as the choice of two soap cartons or two presidential candidates—because the questions to which the an-swers are being solicited have been determined and asked by the researchers themselves and because the answers have been formulated by them, usually in the form of two or more alternatives that can be mechanically counted and computed. They have, thus, nothing to do with either the intensity or authenticity or with the possible range of choices (not to speak of opinions) by the person who does the "answering." One may ascertain the number of certain limited, and preformulated, choices: one cannot really "measure" opinions and sentiments. It is wrong to coax people in order to elicit prefor-mulated opinions and fictious choices, just as it is wrong to berate a child with questions that he never asked himself; the more the child is forced to answer prematurely, the less he will know himself.
23. We can see its effects not only in literary but also in academic life, where the chances of promotion of the most popular (for whatever reasons) teacher had become decidedly secondary to those of his colleagues who were "publishing" (no matter what) *and* who were publicly visible through their publicized attendances at meetings, conferences, committees, conventions. The ideal of privacy in the ivory tower was gone—together with its no less illusory successor, the Democratic Teacher.
24. A few days later Coolidge's attorney general, Harry M. Daugherty, told him that Coolidge's father had no authority to swear in a federal official. Several days later Coolidge took a new oath in the White House, administered by Justice Hoehling of the Supreme Court of the District of Columbia. This was not told to the nation. That Daugherty turned out to be a crook is telling. His cramped insistence on constitutional exactness reminds one of the gamblers and mobsters who put their hands on their hearts and whose eyes are

filmed over by tears when the national anthem is played before the—sometimes fixed—prizefight.

25. Fred I. Greenstein, "Change and Continuity in the Presidency," in *The New American Political System,* A. King, ed. (Washington, DC, 1975), 46–47.

26. In Nixon's memoirs *(RN: The Memoirs of Richard Nixon,* New York, 1978), 1017, June 1974: "We must have gotten some lift from the trip [to the Middle East] although it seems almost impossible to break through the polls"—whatever that meant.

27. Sidney Blumenthal, "Marketing the President" in *New York Times Magazine,* September 13, 1981.

28. Ibid. "The President's strategists are at the center of the new political age. At the end of the day, they become spectators, seeing their performance tested by the contents of the television news program. For the Reagan White House, every night is election night on television. How an Administration action is placed and portrayed in the network news often determines what initiatives the President will take the next day.

"Gergen's office desk faces a television set, on top of which are stacked a dozen newspapers, mostly unread. Like other important White House officials, Gergen has a special hookup, so that he receives a broadcast of the CBS Evening News from Baltimore a half-hour earlier than it is shown in Washington. On a recent occasion, he turned the set on by remote control, saying, 'Let's see how Casey's playing.' Allegations of financial wrongdoing on the part of William J. Casey, the new Director of Central Intelligence, had not been good news for the Administration. That night, the lead news item was about Britain. 'Good!' Gergen exclaimed."

29. As late as 1941 Admiral Leahy reported from Vichy to President Roosevelt, "The radical de Gaullists whom I have met do not seem to have the stability, intelligence, and *popular standing* [my italics] in their communities that should be necessary to succeed in their announced purpose." This writer remembers a sign in 1958 on the Nantucket beaches put there by the Yankee selectmen of that community concerning local regulations of bathing suits: "On Nantucket Island bikini-style suits are not popular." This usage of "popular" has disappeared since that time.

30. 1941: 62; 1954: 250; 1960: 355. Even more White House employees are statistically concealed under other headings of bureaus. The 600 mark was first reached by the Nixon White House in 1970. Jimmy Carter tried to cut back the number of full-time employees, yet the staff of Rosalynn Carter *alone* was one half as large as Roosevelt's at the height of the Second World War.

31. Greenstein, op. cit., 51.

32. We have seen that in 1972 President Nixon found it proper to divide his State of the Union address into two parts, the second called "The State of the World"—at a time when American influence in the world was declining. In December 1981, after the Polish military coup d'état, President Reagan announced that he had called the pope on the telephone—this at a time when the American ability to actively influence the situation in Poland existed not at all.

33. *The Civilization of the Renaissance in Italy* (New York, 1954), 321.

59. The Bourgeois Interior

1. In his *Histoire des Français,* esp. vol. 2 (Paris, 1951).

2. Dutourd, *Le fond et la forme,* I (Paris, 1958), 22–25.

3. (Paris, 1967), 10.
4. Ibid., 12.
5. Philippe Ariès, *Centuries of Childhood* (London, 1961), 346–47.
6. Ibid., 394.
7. Ibid., 384: "It may be that the family was weakened at the time of the Germanic invasions, yet it would be vain to deny the existence of a family life in the Middle Ages. But the family existed in silence; it did not awaken feelings strong enough to inspire poet or artist. We must recognize the importance of this silence: not much value was placed on the family. Similarly we must admit the significance of the iconographic blossoming which after the fifteenth and especially the sixteenth century followed this long period of obscurity: the birth and development of the concept of the family."
8. Ibid., 404
9. Ibid., 414–15.

VI. Reading, Writing, and Teaching History

❊ ❊ ❊

61. Teaching

1. One of these was directed to a master of one of the colleges at Yale, where I had an embarrassing experience. This kind, genial, and cultured man had expected to receive a European scholar of respectable age and stature, putting him up in a suite where, the night before, a trustee of the university, a famous United States senator, had stayed. Instead, he found himself face-to-face with a callow and nervous and unnecessarily voluble young man of twenty-three. He had also arranged a dinner with the principal fellows and professors, during which I babbled unnecessarily and made an ill-prepared little speech. I spent my last dollars on a bouquet of flowers that I sent to Professor and Mrs. French, and slunk down in the seat of the train to New York with the seasick knowledge of having given the unavoidable impression of an importunate fraud.

2. The first one was that of a translator (French-English) in a firm that was engaged in the rebuilding and selling of ships. Years later I learned that the owners and the chief naval architect of this firm had been engaged in an enormous fraud: they had been buying Liberty ships built during the war and which the U.S. government sold cheaply with the provision that they were not to be resold to foreigners; what this firm did was to redesign and rebuild portions of these ships so that they could be sold under false names. My second job did not last long: the employer, an importer of Oriental rugs, wanted me to accompany him on his public-speaking engagements, since he belonged to an organization devoted to the perfection of public speaking, no matter on what topic. He also wanted me to consider marrying his daughter, a moon-faced and sloe-eyed, sad and kind Levantine girl. My third job, like the first, was due to my knowledge of languages. The owners of this firm were horrified on learning that I was interested in teaching and writing. They had begun to train me in the intricacies of importing and exporting inter-

national wax. Consequently and disingenuously, I kept silent about the fact that, come September, I was off to Philadelphia in the morning.

3. Example: the extreme—and I mean extreme—attention that American students pay to their teachers' clothing.

4. Consider this *excursus* beyond teaching. Consider that by calling a newly met person by his first name you have actually reduced his individuality. He is now only one of a million Joes or one of ten thousand Josephines. His connection with his family name, with his ancestors, and with his provenance has been severed. Alas, this is but one illustration of how the exaggeration of democracy inevitably leads to the degradation of human dignity.

5. Cars! Cars! One day a student accompanied me to the parking lot. He said, "We are all wondering what kind of car you drive." ??? "We thought it must be a Mercedes or a Bug." I was driving a Pontiac convertible then. Whether he was disappointed or not I did not know.

6. Occasionally, I would berate them with a somewhat vulgar simile. "With you," I would say, "it is not only a matter of in one ear and out another. That wouldn't be so bad because anything going in one ear and out another means that it is passing through your brain, so that some of it will stick. That is the mystery of learning, you know. Think of the very best book you have ever read. How much can you remember of it? Perhaps 1 percent. But this doesn't mean that the other 99 percent is lost. Yet with you it is not even in one ear because those ears and heads of yours are stuffed with all kinds of things: moldy phrases, bits of cheap information, old Kleenexes. Instead of drilling a hole in thick heads and pouring in new stuff through a funnel, what a teacher must now do first is to use something like a vacuum cleaner. I must unteach you while I teach you." At least I said *while*, not *before*, aware that unteaching and teaching are simultaneous.

7. When my first wife graduated from Springside School in 1944, one of the three top Philadelphia private girls' schools at the time, she was one of three of a class of about thirty who chose to go on to college: "brains"; the rest were "coming out," debutantes. I doubt whether there was a single Springside graduate twenty years later who wasn't trying to get into college—any college.

8. One exception was my professorship at the University of Toulouse, in France, where my students were singularly uncharitable of my halting—no, of my inadequate—knowledge of the French subjunctive, while they were appreciative, en masse, of my hazardous, and possibly even impertinent, attempts at wit.

9. Example: Numerous American intellectuals and academics kept telling me, early in my American years, that to understand America I ought to read the short story by Shirley Jackson, "The Lottery," written in 1948. In this dreadful tale the villagers take great pleasure in having a yearly fête, during which they select one of their own and stone him to death—the villagers being ordinary Americans, presumably New Englanders, people of this most advanced democracy enlightening the world. What struck me was how this story, incarnating a hatred and fear of The People, has been devoured and admired by the people who were votaries of Progressivism, the Left, Liberalism, Adlai Stevenson, etc.

10. Most, but not all. It was there that I met a Norwegian physicist, Professor Torger Holtsmark, whose truly exceptional integrity and scientific purpose were, and remained, a starry event in my life, maturing to an enduring friendship. So my going there was worthwhile after all.

62. Writing

1. "Dreams are the outcomes of memories, not of the subconscious. This separation of memory from the subconscious is the task for a genius of the future." (Diary, July 28, 1983.)

2. In 1933 A. L. Rowse wrote in *The End of an Epoch* that Churchill, "unlike Trotsky," had "no philosophy of history." This was cited and repeated in 1961 by W. H. Carr in *What Is History?* It is absolute nonsense. What these celebrated British panjandrums failed to see was that Churchill possessed something far more important than a systematic philosophy of history (about which Burckhardt had written that a philosophy of history is a contradiction per se); Churchill had a profound sense of history, a historical philosophy. The Trotsky example is very telling. Trotsky *did* have a philosophy of history; but that did him no good, and I do not mean only his political career. His writings in exile show that his understanding of the historical realities of his time was woefully cramped and wrong. Also, there exisits a portrait that Churchill limned of Trotsky in *Great Contemporaries*, where in a few sentences he sketched the conflict between Trotsky and Stalin: the essential elements in the fall of Trotsky and the rise of Stalin (including suggestive statements of what Stalin's rule meant and where it was to lead). The statements are astonishingly acute and even prophetic, especially when we consider that Churchill wrote this in the early 1930s. They are also more correct and insightful than the gist of Carr's many volumes dealing with the same problem and topic and period—of the Carr who was not an inconsiderable but a very knowledgeable historian, devoting decades of his life to the study and writing of the history of Soviet Russia.

3. That important thing is Churchill's recognition that the decisive turning point in Hitler's life came in 1918–19 and not before 1914, in Munich and not in Vienna. This is contrary to the even now accepted opinion; and contrary, too, to Hitler's own self-serving argument in *Mein Kampf*, according to which the crystallization of his political ideology happened during his Vienna years, and not in Munich later.

4. One result of this obsession with connections is my habit of writing long footnotes on the bottom of too many pages in my books. These footnotes are illustrative and explanatory, not only referential. They are the results of my compulsion to tell something significant, or at least interesting, to my readers that would otherwise disturb and unduly crowd a paragraph of the main text. (They surely disturb and unduly crowd the appearance of the printed page.)

5. And perhaps, moving from the sublime to the ridiculous, as when Nathanael West named his protagonist Lemuel Pitkin in *A Cool Million*. Within that name are condensed the late twenties in a Far Western Civilization, with their compound of arid biblical leftovers *and* Hollywood, the era of Coolidge and of Louis B. Mayer, by now embedded in the historical evolution of the United States.

6. There was, too, my call at the house of a charming and harebrained descendant of one of my subjects, who produced, without a moment of hesitation, a very large black leather chest containing her illustrious forbear's remnant papers. The chest served as a wondrous footrest in my library for a number of years—I had some difficulty in returning it to its elusive proprietress. The papers, alas, were not especially valuable; they were the papers of a man who had written, among other things: "I never wrote a letter to a woman you couldn't chill beer on."

7. They were an essay-review of James Lees-Milne's two-volume biography of Harold Nicolson; of the three-volume edition of the complete Churchill-Roosevelt correspondence; of Witold Rybczynski's beautiful book *Home*; my three articles were an account

of the Gotthard Walk, a thirteen-day trek across Switzerland with my daughter; of a visit to the ruins of Dresden and its rebuilt opera; and a profile of Gyula Krúdy.

8. Of course I am not alone in this predicament. David McCullough, who is a very good American historian, wrote the finest history of the building of the Panama Canal: *The Path Between the Seas.* In a widely adopted and most remunerative American history textbook by Harvard professors Freidel and Brinkley, this work appears in the bibliography in these words: "A lucid popular history of the building of the canal." What do they mean by "popular"? Here is an example of the, perhaps unwitting, petty snobbery of the professional guild. McCullough's references and his bibliography alone show that he did all of the research and the homework of a first-rate professional historian—and then some.

9. This first public speech of mine in my native city after thirty-seven years was a sentimental occasion. It also happened on the one hundredth birthday of my father; and in a district of the city that my father had loved, studied, and once filmed with amateur dedication. It was a fine sunny morning; but my appearance was not sufficiently elegant. Having misplaced my glasses, I was dependent on the glasses borrowed from a friend, which in turn depended dejectedly from my nose.

10. There is, too, a fortunate conjunction. English and Magyar, no matter how different, have certain salutary tendencies in common. The rhythm, the grammar, the syntax, the very rhetoric of the Magyar language are very different from English; but both Magyar and English have the great virtue of directness. Magyar, like English, is a very descriptive and at times surprisingly onomatopoeic language. It is uncomfortable with anything abstract, and it eschews the passive tense, like English and unlike German.

11. But even in prose I run across English sentences that make me fully aware of my foreignness. "His smile, he saw, would have been pleasant if it had ever got up into his eyes as well." I could not have written this.

12. Simone Weil (1942): "The relation of the sign to the thing signified is being destroyed, the game of exchanges between signs is being multiplied of itself and for itself. And the increasing complication demands that there should be signs for signs. . . . As collective thought cannot exist as thought, it passes into things (signs, machines . . .). Hence the paradox: It is the thing which thinks, and the man who is reduced to the state of a thing." Bernanos (1946): "Between those who think that a civilization is a victory for man in the struggle against the determinism of things . . . and those who want to make of man a thing among things, there is no possible scheme of reconciliation."

13. Diary, July 11, 1980: "Suddenly the thought comes to me: no work of art is ever *finished.* I am not only thinking of the fact that the pigment decays, etc., or that a cathedral must be forever cleaned and restored, or that it changes when a city grows up around it, etc. I am thinking of the condition that it is not separate from the rest of the universe, and from the human beings who will come into contact with it centuries after its creation."
But (1988): I am not certain that my writing is "art."

63. What Is Happening to History?

1. Readers interested in more detailed illustrations of this argument may find them in my articles in *Salmagundi* (Summer 1975; Fall/Winter 1975–76) and in *Historical Consciousness* (New York, 1968), especially pages 114–27.

2. This is, after all, what happens when freshmen coming into our colleges are choosing their majors. During thirty years of teaching, one of the mysteries that I have not been able to comprehend is the process whereby these children "select" their majors. I do not know how they go about it; I doubt that they know themselves. What I know is that when they are told that history does not "pay," they will act accordingly. This is one of the problems that all college teachers in the humanities have now to face. The other, greater, problem is with the few who choose to be history majors, with the now immense gaps of historical knowledge with which these youngsters appear in the classroom, facing the first history course in their lives.

   On the other hand, an encouraging fact, which suggests that not all of the interests and choices of young people are governed by the ebb and flow of fads: my colleagues tell me that during the last ten years the percentage of students taking history courses that they were not required to take has remained constant. In some of the institutions with which I am familiar this percentage is higher than in any other field of non-required courses.

66. Agnes Repplier, Writer and Essayist

1. Her Repplier grandfather was Alsatian. She preferred to think of him as having come from Lorraine. Yet she refused to Frenchify the pronunciation of the family name, which was (and remains) Reppli*er* not Repplié.
2. Emma Repplier Witmer (Mrs. Lightner Witmer), *Agnes Repplier, a Memoir* (1957) (hereafter Witmer), 17.
3. "Until I had mastered print, my memory was abnormally retentive. There was nothing to disturb its hold. My mother taught me *viva voce* a quantity of English verse, sometimes simple as befitted my intelligence, sometimes meaningless, but none the less pleasant to the ear. I regret to say that I was permitted and encouraged to repeat these poems to visitors. Why they ever returned to the house I cannot imagine. Perhaps they never did." Agnes Repplier, *Eight Decades* (New York, 1937), 6.
4. "Possibly because of the recent anti-Catholic riots, it had been constructed mainly after sundown by candlelight, and the pointing wavered in perpetual sympathy with what had been the workmen's unsteady illumination." George Stewart Stokes, *Agnes Repplier* (Philadelphia, 1949) (hereafter Stokes), 20.
5. Witmer, 23.
6. She was supposed to have been caught smoking, but we cannot be sure. She was, in any event, a smoking addict during the next eighty years.
7. Her niece: "Judging from my own later experience, a new pupil was practically certain to be asked three questions by her classmates, 'Where do you live?' 'What does your father do?' 'What church do you go to?' Depending on the answers, you were apt to be graded socially." Witmer, 28–29. Agnes's grades were low.
8. One day Miss Irwin asked her something in class. "I'm sorry," Agnes replied, "I forget." "You have a tenacious memory," Miss Irwin said, "and you have no business forgetting anything." Stokes, 35.
9. "My aunt was over eighty when she told me of this incident, but there was no emotion in her voice, neither anger nor resentment. The years had erased all passion, but the words remained fresh and indestructible." Witmer, 35.

10. Ibid.

11. She was born on North 11th Street. They moved to 2005 Chestnut Street when she was seven or eight, and to 4015 Locust Street when she was twenty-one.

12. The youngest son, John (for whom his mother seemed to have cherished a, for her, unusual affection), a handsome and preternaturally clever child, perished of the croup at the age of four. Another son, Louis, afflicted by partial paralysis, would remain the burdensome responsibility of his sisters until his death at the age of seventy-five.

13. Stokes, 47.

14. Witmer, 7.

15. *Eight Decades,* 9.

16. Quoted by Stokes, 59.

17. April 1886: "Children, Past and Present."

18. Agnes's father had two sons from his first marriage. At the age of sixteen George Repplier ran away from home, where his stepmother had been cold and hostile to him. He fled to South America. Fifteen years later he returned to Philadelphia. He asked his father to come to his wedding in Savannah, where he was about to marry a divorced woman in a civil ceremony. The plan was torpedoed by his stepmother, and the link between the two families was broken. Thirteen years later Agnes, "immediately after her mother's death, and while still in deep mourning . . . appeared suddenly and without warning in my parents' home in New York. Her purpose was to make peace and offer amity, and the success of her mission brought to me, a little girl of five, the rarest of gifts, her life-long friendship and love." Witmer, 35.

19. "The chair of the American Essay is in Philadelphia, on Clinton Street in the old city. It has been gloriously occupied for forty years by Agnes Repplier who is at present denied the title of professor emeritus, even though she were ready for it, since there is no worthy successor." Mary Ellen Chase, "The Dean of American Essayists," *Commonweal,* August 18, 1933.

20. Stokes, 217–18.

21. "In different ways, though proud of her achievements, the sister and brother resented her constant engagements and growing fame. These three ill-assorted characters . . ." Witmer, 118. Agnes to Harrison Morris: "'The Reppliers,' like the Jameses or the Robinsons, sets my teeth on edge."

22. To Harrison Morris: "I can only work in the morning and for three or four hours. Then I grow tired and stupid. The pleasure is gone, and I have to stop. So I don't accomplish a great deal, try as I may. Neither do I work with ease, but with infinite painstaking." Stokes, 116.

23. Houghton Mifflin, her first publisher, was uninspired and niggardly with her first collection of essays (*Books and Men:* a singularly dull title) in 1888; Miss Repplier had to pay some of the costs of the first printing. In October 1888 she wrote: "My copies of the essays have just arrived: neat quakerish little books with an air of deprecating modesty about them that forcibly suggests the most remote corner of the bookseller's shelf. I can see them already shrinking bashfully into their appointed nooks and powdering their little gray heads with the dust of the undisturbed." Reprintings followed swiftly. Her diffidence was unwarranted.

24. Agnes Repplier, *Points of Friction* (1920), 93.

25. Agnes Repplier, *Essays in Idleness* (1893), 115.

26. Ibid., 117.

27. Ibid., 116.

28. Ibid., 94–95. "Dr Johnson," she wrote elsewhere, "whose name is a tonic for the morally debilitated . . ." *Points of Friction,* 217.

29. *Points of Friction,* 154–55.

30. Witmer, 88.

31. "But of what earthly good or pleasure is a book which is read only once? It is like an acquaintance whom one never meets again, or a picture never seen a second time." *Eight Decades,* 5.

32. "For myself, I confess that the last twenty-five years of the eighteenth century and the first twenty-five years of the nineteenth make up my chosen period, and that my motive for so choosing is contemptible. It was not a time distinguished—in England at least—for wit and wisdom, for public virtues or for private charm; but it *was* a time when literary reputations were so cheaply gained that nobody needed to despair of one." Agnes Repplier, *A Happy Half-Century, and Other Essays* (Boston, 1908), 1–2.

"Like the fabled Caliph who stood by the Sultan's throne, translating the flowers of Persian speech into comprehensible and unflattering truths, so Dr Johnson stands undeceived in this pleasant half-century of pretence, translating its ornate nonsense into language we can too readily understand.

"But how comfortable and how comforting the pretence must have been, and how kindly tolerant all the pretenders were to one another! If, in those happy days, you wrote an essay on 'The Harmony of Numbers and Versification,' you unhesitatingly asked your friends to come and have it read aloud to them: and your friends—instead of leaving town next day—came, and listened, and called it a 'Miltonic evening.'" Ibid., 11–12.

33. Writing about the inane Mrs. Chapone, an English educationist during the "happy half-century": "A firm insistence upon admitted truths, a loving presentation of the obvious, a generous championship of those sweet commonplaces we all deem dignified and safe . . ." Ibid., 122. Elsewhere: "Alas for those who succeed, as Montaigne observed, in giving to their harmless opinions a false air of importance." Agnes Repplier, *Points of View* (Boston, 1891), 99.

34. Witmer, 77.

35. Ibid., 49.

36. *Points of Friction,* 93. She had gone to Camden with her friend Harrison Morris. Whitman was rather dirty and offered his guests whiskey in a tooth mug. His own diary does not improve upon this impression: "My friend, Harrison Morris, brought Agnes Repplier, a nice young critter, to see me." Ibid., 101.

37. Ibid., 252, 248.

38. Ibid., 146.

39. *Eight Decades,* 861. Still, on another occasion she wrote that "the Englishman who complained that he could not look out of his window in Rome without seeing the sun, had a legitimate grievance (we all know what it is to sigh for grey skies, and for the unutterable rest they bring); but if we want Rome, we must take her sunshine, along with her fleas and her Church. Accepted philosophically, they need not mar our infinite content."

40. Agnes Repplier, *Counter-Currents* (1916), 281.

41. *Points of Friction,* 150.

42. Ibid., 158–59. She may have meant Dickens: "Readers of Dickens (which ought to mean all men and women who mastered the English alphabet) . . ." *Happy Half-Century,* 217.

43. *Essays in Idleness,* 85.

44. Ibid., 120.

45. Agnes Repplier, *Compromises* (Boston and New York, 1904), 50.

46. *Happy Half-Century,* 176.

47. *Essays in Idleness,* 181.

48. *Happy Half-Century,* 79–80. I know but one example (a not altogether incontestable one) in which Miss Agnes allowed herself a touch of earthly humor. She was writing about the monumentally silly Mrs. Barbauld, another female educationist of the eighteenth century. "This pregnant sentence ... occurs in a chapter of advice to young girls: 'An ass is much better adapted than a horse to show off a young lady.'" Ibid., 5.

49. In the superb essay "Books That Have Hindered Me." *Points of View,* 71. Also: ". . . if the experience of mankind teaches anything, it is that vital convictions are not at the mercy of eloquence." *Eight Decades,* 267.

50. *Points of View,* 1

51. Ibid., 8.

52. Agnes Repplier, *Americans and Others* (Boston and New York, 1912), 245–46.

53. *Eight Decades,* 62–63

54. *Compromises,* 55. "The Cardinal de Rohan had all his kitchen utensils of solid sliver, which must have given as much satisfaction to his cooks as did Nero's golden fishing-hooks to the fish he caught with them," Agnes Repplier, *In the Dozy Hours, and Other Papers* (Boston and New York, 1894), 117.

55. *Eight Decades,* 302.

56. *Essays in Idleness,* 42.

57. *In the Dozy Hours,* 95.

58. *Eight Decades,* 106.

59. Even so, these lines penned more than fifty years ago ring ever more true: "Professional men, doctors and dentists especially, delight in living in the suburbs, so that those who need their services cannot reach them. The doctor escapes from his patients, who may fall ill on Saturday, and die on Sunday, without troubling him. The dentist is happy in that he can play golf all Saturday and Sunday while his patients agonize in town. Only the undertaker, man's final servitor, stands staunchly by his guns." *Eight Decades,* 118.

60. Ibid., 105. "They talk with serious fervour about Nature, when the whole of their landed estate is less than one of the back yards in which the town dwellers of my youth grew giant rosebushes that bloomed brilliantly in the mild city air." Ibid.,109.

61. Ibid., 103. But William Penn said: "The country life is to be preferred, for there we see the works of God, but in cities little else than the works of men." (*Reflexions and Maxims,* no. 220).

62. *Compromises,* 5.

63. Ibid., 7.

64. Ibid., 6.

65. James wrote to Gosse that he liked Agnes Repplier for her "bravery and (almost) brilliancy." Around that time she wrote in her essay on conversation: "We realize how far the spirit of lecture had intruded upon the spirit of conversation forty years ago, when Mr. Bagehot admitted that, with good modern talkers, 'the effect seems to be produced by that which is stated, and not by the manner in which it is stated'—a reversal of ancient rules." *Compromises,* 4.

66. *A Book of Famous Verse* (Boston, 1892), edited by Agnes Repplier.

67. *Essays in Idleness,* 186.

68. *Points of Friction,* 73–74.

69. *Compromises,* 166.

70. *Points of View,* 117.

71. *Americans and Others,* 160.

72. *Compromises,* 39–40.

73. Ibid., 145.

74. Example: "Judge Peters enjoyed an enviable reputation as a wit, and some of his pleasantries have come floating down to us in cold unsympathetic print, illustrating, as a captious biographer expresses it, 'the great difference between hearing a joke and reading one.' The Indians, whose councils he occasionally attended, and who are not a humorous race, christened him the Talking Bird. It is a pity ever to waste wit upon Indians." Agnes Repplier, *Philadelphia: The Place and the People* (New York, 1898), 163. She could write with wit and detachment about the saddest of events in her native city, the anti-Catholic Know-Nothing riots of the 1840s: "They stretched ropes across the darkening streets to obstruct the passage of the cavalry. It was picturesque, and exceedingly like Perugia in the Middle Ages, when the Baglioni and their rivals fought in the great square of the Cathedral; but it was not at all like Penn's City of Peace, which he had founded as an asylum of the oppressed, where no sword was to be drawn, and no man persecuted for his creed." Ibid., 353.

75. *Life:* a literary and humorous magazine, not the picture magazine of the mid-twentieth century.

76. *Points of Friction,* 7, 10. "We can know nothing of any nation unless we know its history."

77. "It was not possible for a child who had lived in spirit with Saint Genevieve to be indifferent to the siege of Paris in 1870. It is not possible for a child who has lived in spirit with Jeanne d'Arc to be indifferent to the destruction of Rheims Cathedral in 1914," *Points of Friction,* 25–26.

78. "... even a conservative American, if such anomaly exists ..." *In the Dozy Hours,* 101.

79. *Points of Friction,* 102.

80. Ibid., 99.

81. *Counter-Currents,* 32. "A moderate knowledge of history—which, though discouraging, is also enlightening—might prove serviceable to all the enthusiasts who are engaged in making over the world. Many of them (in this country, at least) talk and write as if nothing in particular had happened between the Deluge and the Civil War." Ibid., 21.

82. *Points of Friction,* 97–98.

83. Ibid., 122–23.

84. *Counter-Currents,* 137. "Great events, however lamentable, must be looked at greatly." Ibid., 105.

85. *Americans and Others,* 142.

86. Ibid., 72.

87. *Points of View,* 139.

88. *Points of Friction,* 109.

89. *Points of View,* 147.

90. *Eight Decades,* 60.

91. Ibid., 75.

92. Ibid., 86–87. About the "painful and precocious" diary of "young Nathaniel Mather, who happily died before reaching manhood, but not before he had scaled the heights of self-esteem, and sounded the depths of despair. When a boy, a real human boy, laments and bewails in his journal that he whittled a stick upon the Sabbath Day, 'and, for fear of being seen, did it behind the door, a great reproach of God, and a specimen of that atheism I brought into the world with me'—we recognize the fearful possibilities of untempered sanctimony." Agnes Repplier, *Varia* (Boston, 1897), 36.

93. From "Books That Have Hindered Me": "The last work to injure me seriously as a girl, and to root up the good seed sown in long years of righteous education, was *Uncle Tom's Cabin*, which I read from cover to cover with the innocent credulity of youth; and, when I had finished, the awful conviction forced itself upon me that the Thirteenth Amendment was a ghastly error, and that the war had been fought in vain. Slavery, which had seemed to me before undeviatingly wicked, now shone in a new and alluring light. All things must be judged by their results: and if the result of slavery was to produce a race so infinitely superior to common humanity; if it bred strong, capable, self-restraining men like George, beautiful, courageous, tender-hearted women like Eliza, visions of innocent loveliness like Emmeline, marvels of acute intelligence like Cassy, children of surpassing precocity and charm like little Harry, mothers and wives of patient, simple goodness like Aunt Chloe, and, finally, models of all known chivalry and virtue like Uncle Tom himself—then slavery was the most ennobling institution in the world, and we had committed a grievous crime in degrading a whole heroic race to our narrower, viler level. It was but too apparent, even to my immature mind, that the negroes whom I knew, or knew about, were very little better than white people; that they shared in all the manifold failings of humanity, and were not marked by any higher intelligence than their Caucasian neighbors. Even in the matters of physical beauty and mechanical ingenuity there had been plainly some degeneracy, some falling off from the high standard of old slavery days. Reluctantly I concluded that what had seemed so right had all been wrong indeed, and that the only people who stood preeminent for virtue, intellect, and nobility had been destroyed by our rash act, had sunk under the enervating influence of freedom to a range of lower feeling, to baser aspirations and content. It was the greatest shock of all, and the last." *Points of View*, 75–76.

94. About John Fiske, the greatly respected Boston historian: "He cannot for a moment forget how much better he knows; and instead of an indulgent smile at the delightful follies of our ancestors, we detect here and there through his very valuable pages something unpleasantly like a sneer." *Books and Men*, 58–59. "Longfellow wrote a 'Drinking Song' to water which achieved humour without aspiring to it, and Dr. Holmes wrote a teetotaler's adaptation of a drinking song, which aspired to humour without achieving it." *Points of Friction*, 206.

95. Agnes Repplier, *Books and Men* (Boston, 1890), 119.

96. *Points of View*, 105.

97. Witmer, 257.

98. *Points of View*, 3.

99. Ibid., 118–19.

100. *Counter-Currents*, 136.

101. She instinctively understood the connection between the utilitarianism of a Franklin and the sentimentalism of the Brownings, a century later. She cited "the robust statement of Benjamin Franklin: 'I approved, for my part, the amusing one's self now and then with poetry, so far as to improve one's language, but no farther.' What a delicious picture is presented to our fancy of a nineteenth-century Franklin amusing himself and improving his language by an occasional study of 'Sordello.'" *Eight Decades*, 127.

102. *Compromises*, 128.

103. Ibid., 151.

104. *Eight Decades*, 81.

105. *Points of Friction*, 6.

106. Ibid., 75–76.

107. Ibid., 115.

108. *In the Dozy Hours,* 50.
109. Ibid., 53–54. Reminiscing about her convent days: "The very bareness of our surroundings, the absence of all appliances for play, flung us back unreservedly upon the illimit-
able resources of invention." Agnes Repplier, *In Our Convent Days* (Boston and New
York, 1905), 148.
110. Agnes Repplier, *Under Dispute* (Boston and New York, 1923), 303–04.
111. *Eight Decades,* 253.
112. From her address to the English-Speaking Union (Witmer, 116). When she first set foot
in England: "After French, Dutch, German, Flemish, to say nothing of American, the
mother tongue was made doubly blessed by being so sweetly spoken. . . . The charming
intonations of the English fill me with wonder and regret. Why can't I speak in that
way?" Stokes, 100. Later she would qualify her unconditional admiration for English
speech, and for certain English characteristics. Throughout her life, however, she determined to spell certain words in the English way: "fervour," "harbour," "humour," etc.
(She must have had a recurrence of trouble with proofreaders.)
113. She preferred the English to the Irish people, as she preferred the King James Bible to
the Douay. Around 1600 the English tongue "had reached its first splendour, with the
tenderness, vigor, and warmth of a language fresh from the mint. If all other English
were to be blotted out from the world, the King James Bible would preserve intact its
beauty and its power." Witmer, 148. (What would she say today?)
114. She had a fine correspondence with Andrew Lang, the eccentric critic and essayist,
whose letters to her were full of unexpected small delights. When she finally met Lang
in London she found him "sulky, and irresistibly charming; tall, lean, grey and very
handsome." Stokes, 119. He was lean and gray indeed. On one occasion he asked Agnes
Repplier to pay for their tea. At the end of her visit he bade her goodbye and never wrote
to her again.
115. In 1914 she composed a pamphlet, together with J. William White, entitled: "Germany
and Democracy, the Real Issue, the Views of Two Average Americans, a reply to Doctor
Dernburg." (Dr. Dernburg had presented the case for Germany in the *Saturday Evening
Post.*) The pamphlet was subsequently republished in England, France, and Holland. "In
good truth," she wrote, "*all* German apologists, writing to enlist the sympathy of Americans, should be made to understand the value of an understatement. If they would claim
a little less, we could believe a great deal more. . . ." Stokes, 175.
116. As early as 1902 she wrote: "There is a power of universal mastery about the traveling
Teuton which affronts our feebler souls. We cannot cope with him; we stand defeated at
every turn by his restless determination to secure the best. The windows of the railway
carriages, the little sunny tables in the hotel dining-rooms, the back seats—commanding the view—of the Swiss *funiculaires;* all these strong positions he occupies at once
with the strategical genius of a great military nation. No weak concern for other people's
comfort mars the simple straightforwardness of his plans, nor interferes with their prompt
and masterly execution. Amid the confusion and misery of French and Italian railway
stations, he plays a conqueror's part, commanding the services of the porters, and marching off triumphantly with his innumerable pieces of hand luggage, while his fellow tourists clamour helplessly for aid. 'The Germans are a rude, unmannered race, but active
and expert where their personal advantages are concerned,' wrote the observant Froissart
many years ago. He could say neither more nor less were he traveling over the Continent to day." *Compromises,* 187–88.
    But, then, she also wrote: "'Potter hates Potter, and Poet hates Poet,'—so runs the

wisdom of the ancients—but tourist hates tourist with a cordial Christian animosity that casts all Pagan prejudices in the shade." Ibid., 185.

117. *Books and Men,* 189.

118. Witmer, 92.

119. Her then young admirer, Constance O'Hara, told about a Monsignor Kieran who "preached a fine sermon . . . rich with classical allusions and splendid imagery that got off the subject only once or twice when he thundered at the French for their anti-clericalism. He always got that in—despite Agnes Repplier, the bluestocking, looking at him coldly from her pew, and thinking no doubt scornful thoughts about Irish Catholics." Constance O'Hara, *Heaven Was Not Enough* (Philadelphia, 1955), 41–42.

120. "When the news of the Belgian campaign sickened the heart of humanity, more than one voice was raised to say that England had, by her treatment of militant suffragists (a treatment so feeble, so wavering, so irascible, and so soft-hearted that it would not have crushed a rebellious snail), forfeited her right to protest against the dishonouring of Belgian women." *Points of Friction,* 141–48. "The only agreeable thing to be recorded in connection with Europe's sudden and disastrous war is the fact that people stopped talking about women, and began to talk about men." *Cross-Currents,* 98.

121. *Points of Friction,* 143.

122. *Cross-Currents,* 71.

123. Husband of Agnes Repplier's childhood friend Elizabeth Robins, a painter, engraver, and etcher of considerable talent: a large and saturnine man, wishing to combine throughout his life the attributes of artist and aristocrat, with indifferent success.

124. Stokes, 188.

125. *Cross-Currents,* 291–92.

126. *Points of Friction,* 24–25.

127. *Cross-Currents,* 1.

128. Ibid., 67.

129. *In the Dozy Hours,* 105. Apollinaris: a mineral water.

130. Agnes Repplier, *In Pursuit of Laughter* (Boston, 1936), 180. Twenty years earlier she wrote: "When Mr. Carnegie thanked God (through the medium of the newspapers) that he lived in a brotherhood of nations—'forty-eight nations in one Union,'—he forgot that these forty-eight nations, or at least thirty-eight of them, were not always a brotherhood. Nor was the family tie preserved by moral suasion. What we of the North did was to beat our brothers over the head until they consented to be brotherly. And some three hundred thousand of them died of grievous wounds and fevers rather than love us as they should." *Cross-Currents,* 65–66.

131. Agnes Repplier, *To Think of Tea!* (Boston, 1932), 79.

132. *Eight Decades,* 240.

133. In 1919 she wrote: "If the principles of conservatism are based on firm supports, on a recognition of values, a sense of measure and proportion, a due regard for order—its prejudices are indefensible. The wise conservative does not attempt to defend them; he only clings to them more lovingly under attack. He recognizes triumphant science in the telephone and the talking machine, and his wish to escape these benefactions is but a humble confession of unworthiness. He would be glad if scientists, hitherto occupied with preserving and disseminating sound, would turn their attention to suppressing it, would collect noise as an ashman collects rubbish, and dump it in some only place, thus preserving the sanity of the world." *Points of Friction,* 100.

134. *Under Dispute,* 75.

135. Witmer, 159.

136. Ibid., 158, 157.

137. Agnes Repplier, *Times and Tendencies* (Boston and New York, 1931), 35.

138. *Under Dispute,* 83. She admired this quality in others, watching them with a gimlet eye. "Mr Philip Guedalla, whose charm as a historian lies in his happy detachment—for the time—from the prejudices of his day ..." *Times and Tendencies,* 39.

139. *Points of Friction,* 72.

140. 1931: "A young Englishman, teaching in an American school, said that what struck him most sharply about American boys was their docility. He did not mean by this their readiness to do what they were told, but their readiness to think as they were told, in other words, to permit him to do their thinking for them." *Times and Tendencies,* 305–06.

141. *Points of Friction,* 78–79.

142. "I do strive to think well of my fellow man, but no amount of striving can give me confidence in the wisdom of a Congressional vote." Witmer, 160.

143. *Points of Friction,* 74–75. Thirty years earlier she wrote: "It is an interesting circumstance in the lives of those persons who are called either heretics or reformers, according to the mental attitudes or antecedent prejudices of their critics, that they always begin by hinting their views with equal modesty and moderation. It is only when rubbed sore by friction, when hard driven and half spent, that they venture into the open, and define their positions before the world in all their bald malignity." *Points of View,* 136. In 1892: "... the sanguine socialist of to-day, who dreams of preparing for all of us a lifetime of unbroken ennui." *Essays in Idleness,* 167.

144. *Points of Friction,* 106.

145. Ibid., 241.

146. *Americans and Others,* 47–48. Her appreciation for American humor was not restricted to such odd samples of *esprit* from the upper classes: "the indolent and luminous genius of Mr. Dooley has widened our mental horizon. Mr. Dooley is a philosopher, but his is the philosophy of the looker-in, of that genuine unconcern which finds Saint George and the dragon to be both a trifle ridiculous." Ibid., 49–50.

147. *Times and Tendencies,* 225.

148. In a letter to Harrison Morris, 1912: "You know everything and everybody. Please tell me what is the American Social Science Association, of which I have been asked to become a member. It has dues and gives medals. Shall I accept?" She adds a postcript: "I see by looking again at the card, the name of the thing is the National Institute of Social Sciences. What are social sciences?"

149. *Points of Friction,* 160–61.

150. She did not, like Edith Sitwell, wear eccentric and Gothic costumes; she had, however, a predilection for Turkish rings.

151. "Real biting poverty, which withers lesser evils with its deadly breath ..." *Essays in Idleness,* 144. Fortunately enough, this was not her experience. Her mother left a small inheritance. As early as the year 1887 she earned by her writings more than $1,000, a small but respectable sum for a writer in those days.

152. She wrote in the rubric of her passport: "Face, broad; Complexion, sallow; Mouth, too large." Stokes, 122. She was unduly conscious of what she considered the inadequacies of her looks. Her mouth was beautifully shaped.

153. About her trials on the lecturing circuit she wrote to Mrs. Schuyler Warren (see below) in April 1914: "Boston is even more mad about prostitutes than Philadelphia and New York. She talks about little else, tells blood-curdling stories, which bear every evidence

of ripe invention, and the Dedham Club at which I lectured had actually had a real live 'white slave' (at least she claimed to be one, but she may have been only bragging) to address them last month. Now how can a respectable old lady like myself compete with such an attraction!..." Ibid., 172.

154. At that time she lived but a few houses away from Penrose, with whom she had very little in common. On Chestnut Street (2035) she lived but a few doors from the house (2005) where she had lived as a child.

155. In 1931 a college girl asked for an interview with "Miss Repplier of Clinton Street." "Our glance wanders momentarily through the lace-curtained windows. Again there is that feeling of time gone backward. A black carriage, proud with metal trappings, is passing. A coachman, resplendent in white cord breeches, black coat and cockaded top-hat. A fine sleek horse stepping daintily—Clinton Street, perhaps the only thorough-fare in Philadelphia where a horse and carriage is not an anachronism, but a common-place." J. O'K. in the *Grackle,* the literary magazine of Chestnut Hill College, fall 1931. The writer probably did not know that Agnes Repplier, who disliked automobiles, was one of the very last Philadelphians to hire a horse-drawn carriage from a livery stable, as late as the early 1930s.

156. In 1893 she had written: "It is a painful thing, at best, to live up to one's bricabrac if one has any; but to live up to the bricabrac of many lands and of many centuries is a strain which no wise man would dream of inflicting upon his constitution." *In the Dozy Hours,* 113.

157. I like the Acorn Club," she said on one occasion. "They never do anything."

158. There was a Browning Society: "We encouraged each other in mediocrity." Yet this society "endeavoured to keep letters alive, which was certainly a noble enterprise, even if in Philadelphia it was much like keeping a selection of corpses moving about." Stokes, 101. She was a founding member of the Contemporary Club in 1886.

159. His "astoundingly prudish wife" was not an asset during their gatherings. Agnes Repplier to A. Edward Newton, May 10, 1930 (ALS in Princeton University Library).

160. To cover the upper portion of a thin scar Agnes Repplier wore a black, sometimes velvet choker for the rest of her life. It became her very well.

161. That year she dined with White and Theodore Roosevelt. "Heavenly! There were seven men. I was the only woman." Witmer, 111.

162. "Cornelia Frothingham was ill for ten weeks with a nervous collapse, all the more serious because it had no cause." Agnes Repplier to Mrs. Wilson Farrand, Easter Monday 1913 (ALS in Princeton University Library).

163. If Miss Repplier could be deaf to the unwitting language of music, Miss Wister could on occasion be deaf to the unwitting humor of words. She gave a sherry party in honor of Marcel Tabuteau, the famous oboist of the Philadelphia Orchestra. She proposed a toast: "For years," she said, "he delighted me every Friday afternoon with his little in-strument."

164. One of the few examples: when visiting Clarens, Switzerland, with Cornelia Frothingham, she wrote (in 1902): "We want to live here together." Stokes, 146.

165. Her friend Agnes Irwin on Eliot of Harvard: "Wherever he is, he lowers the tempera-ture."

166. Agnes Repplier, *The Fireside Sphinx* (Boston, 1901), 301. About the Westminster cats in London: their bad behavior "has given rise to the pleasant legend of a country house whither these rakish animals retire for nights of gay festivity, and whence they return in the early morning, jaded, repentant, and forlorn." *Essays in Idleness,* 23.

167. *Compromises,* 51.

168. Her friends "gave her so much, [but] they were not able to give her what she craved most. Once she said with strong feeling. 'I never have been first with anyone.'" Witmer, 107.

169. *Compromises,* 184.

170. *Eight Decades,* 59.

171. Ibid., 54.

172. *Points of Friction,* 192.

173. *Varia,* 28.

174. *In the Dozy Hours,* 72.

175. *Points of Friction,* 167. "'*Qui veut faire l'ange fait la bête,*' said Pascal; and the Michigan angel is a danger signal.... No sane woman believes that women, as a body, will vote more honestly than men; but no sane man believes that they will vote less honestly. They are neither 'the gateway to hell,' as Tertullian pointed out, nor the builders of Sir Rabindranath Tagore's 'spiritual civilization.' They are neither the repositories of wisdom, nor the final word of folly." Ibid., 201–02. "'God help women when they have only their rights!' exclaimed a brilliant American lawyer; but it is in the 'only' that all savour lies. Rights and privileges are incompatible. Emancipation implies the sacrifice of immunity, the acceptance of obligation. It heralds the reign of sober and disillusioning experience. Women, as M. Faguet reminds us, are only the equals of men; a truth which was simply phrased in the old Cornish adage, 'Lads are as good as wenches when they are washed.'" Ibid., 202–03.

176. *Points of Friction,* 82.

177. *Cross-Currents,* 123.

178. *Points of Friction,* 183.

179. *Essays in Idleness,* 164.

180. Witmer, 90.

181. She found independence attractive in every sense. It attracted her to cats, about which she wrote (too often for my taste: at least three essays, and an entire book): she liked the dormant savage energy beneath their lazy composture, and their total absence of docile loyalties.

182. In 1931: "Linguistic idiosyncrasies are social idiosyncrasies. I thought of this when I heard an American prelate, a man of learning and piety, allude in a sermon 'to the most important and influential of the saints and martyrs.' It sounded aggressively modern. 'Powerful' is a word well-fitted to the Church Triumphant.... But 'important' has a bustling accent, and an 'influential' martyr suggests a heavenly banking-house." *Times and Tendencies,* 222–23.

183. "The one Catholic who made me feel better about the situation was Miss Agnes Repplier. She was Philadelphia—and it was her co-religionists who rejected this witty and wonderful woman, not the inner circle where she was a fêted and sought-after personage. When I was a child she had an apartment with her brother Louis and her sister Mary at Twenty-first and Pine Streets. She was a slight woman with keen grey eyes behind nose-glasses that gave her a Pecksniffian expression and she had then a nervous jerk to her head." O'Hara, 110

184. In 1919 Archbishop Dougherty removed Msgr. Drumgoole from St. Charles Seminary to the rectorate of a workingman's parish, St. Gregory's. "The good and devout people, most of whom worked on the Pennsylvania Railroad, were astounded at their new Rector, and soon indignant. Archbishop Dougherty had exposed a congregation of hard-

working people to one of the most brilliant men in the Church. They yearned for the comfortable mugginess of the religion they knew, and Monsignor Drumgoole, with his assistant Father Edward Hawks, the converted Anglican, made it a dazzling, golden thing. It was perhaps as well the Monsignor Sigourney Fay, another converted Anglican, died the year before Monsignor Drumgoole became Rector of St. Gregory's, for Father Fay was something of an aesthete, a lover of epigrams, and, devoted to Monsignor Drumgoole, would often have been in residence at St. Gregory's. The puritanical Archbishop would have something to think about, since Monsignor Fay, a close friend of Cardinal Gibbons, was not sparing with the perfume he used. He achieved a brief fame as Father Darcy in Scott Fitzgerald's *This Side of Paradise,* the novel that heralded the arrival of the twenties." Ibid., 132.

185. *Eight Decades,* 265.

186. *Cross-Currents,* 145.

187. "... our great-grandfathers, who were assuredly not a tender-hearted race ... cried right heartily over poems, and novels, and pictures, and plays, and scenery, and everything, in short, that their great-grandsons would not now consider as worthy of emotion." *Books and Men,* 113.

188. She said often that she did not expect most of her writings to survive. On October 18, 1930, she wrote to A. Edward Newton about her *Essays in Miniature.* "... a horrid little book" (ALS in Princeton University Library).

189. The first Philadelphia Award, carrying $10,000, established by Edward W. Bok, was accorded to Cornelius McGillicuddy (Connie Mack), the manager of the Philadelphia Athletics baseball team.

190. *Philadelphia: The Place and the People,* 390–91.

191. She was vexed by the public celebrity of a distant cousin, who had become a society reporter on the *Evening Ledger.* "Agnes Repplier Junior, who often dispensed with the youthful appendage, was a comely, amiable young woman, not particularly intelligent, and as it turned out, not averse to reaping a little advantage from the hazards of mistaken identity." Witmer, 123. Her marriage eliminated this vexation.

192. Between 1912 and 1916 she lost many of her closest friends: Furness, Mitchell, the Irwin sisters, and Dr. White.

193. *Under Dispute* (Boston, 1924) and *Times and Tendencies* contain some of her best writing, to wit, "The Unconscious Humour of the Movies" in the latter.

194. *In Pursuit of Laughter,* 191.

195. *Père Marquette* (Garden City, NY, 1929), *Mère Marie of the Ursulines* (Garden City, NY, 1931), *Junípero Serra* (1933).

196. *In Pursuit of Laughter,* 221.

197. "The Happiness of Writing an Autobiography": "... even the titles of certain autobiographical works are saturated with self-appreciation. We can see the august simper with which a great lady in the days of Charles the Second headed her manuscript: 'A True Relation of the Birth, Breeding and Life of Margaret Cavendish, Duchess of Newcastle. Written by Herself.' Mr. Theodore Dreiser's *A Book about Myself* sounds like nothing but a loud human purr. The intimate wording of *Margot Asquith, an Autobiography* gives the key to all the cheerful confidences that follow. Never before or since has any book been so much relished by its author. She makes no foolish pretence of concealing the pleasure that it gives her; but passes on with radiant satisfaction from episode to episode, extracting from each in turn its full and flattering significance. The volumes are as devoid of revelations as of reticence. If at times they resemble the dance of the seven veils, the

reader is invariably reassured when the last veil has been whisked aside, and he sees there is nothing behind it." *Under Dispute,* 90–91.

198. Witmer, 164.

199. Ibid., 170.

67. A Student's Guide to the Study of History

1. Note, already at this point, that *descriptions* are more telling than are *definitions.* For such is the nature of human language and of human thinking. Try to "define" such things as "beauty" or "truth" or "straight." We all know what they are—without their definitions. Yes, "straight is the shortest possible distance between two points." A child does not know that definition, but he knows what *straight* is. Definitions are the sometimes necessary, surely in natural-scientific matters, instruments for accuracy. But historical knowledge is marked by the aim of understanding, even more than of accuracy, though not necessarily at the expense of the latter. History is always *descriptive*—and, by necessity, never *definitive.*

2. It is not only the *quantity* but the *quality* of your past that changes. Suppose that something happened to you today, something bothersome, of which you can remember the smallest details. A few years pass. You recall that day—forgetting many of its details—and may say to yourself: "Why was I so upset about *that?*" (Or: "Why had I not noticed *that* then?") The *quantity* of details of that day has waned; but the *quality* of your understanding of what had happened increased.

3. Two examples: (1) Someone gives you an address or a telephone number, which is 1776. An added piece of your knowledge but also something that *eases* your mind: it is easier to remember, since you *already* know the number 1776. (2) Psychoanalysis, when it is reasonably applied (which is not always the case), may *ease* the patient's mind by making him recall, on a conscious level, something that he had suppressed or forgotten: a welcome *addition* to his consciousness. (In other words, the very opposite of the case of a pebble in our shoe: we know that it is a pebble, and we want to throw it away.)

4. The last presidents who wrote—some of—their own speeches, and who signed—most of—their letters and documents by hand, with a fountain pen, were Franklin Roosevelt and Harry Truman.

5. Note that the word *legend* originally meant "something that ought to be read." (The history of words—their original meaning, their eventual changes—is often the surest key to the history of human thought, for there is no thinking without words. "In the Beginning Was the Word"—not the number, or the image.)

6. Note: there can be no good historian who cannot write well. That is not simply a matter of style. Writing well means thinking well. If you cannot tell a story clearly, this means that it is not really clear in your own mind.

7. We have to be careful with this phrase. In this matter—perhaps only in this matter—we have become more sophisticated than Thucydides. A very similar and oft-cited sentence was that by the fine American philosopher George Santayana: "Those who do not know history are condemned to repeat it." This is a poetic formulation, full and rich in meaning, while not definitely precise. We are not "condemned" to repeat our mistakes: repeating them, we condemn ourselves. More important, history does not exactly repeat itself, but historical circumstances, and human inclinations, do. This happens not

only because of the passage of time, but also because of God's miraculous creation to the effect that no two human beings are ever exactly the same. When we say that someone "makes the same mistakes over and over again" this may be largely so, but those mistakes are never *exactly* the same ones. As another great Greek thinker said, time is like a river (and we may say, life is a pilgrimage) in which no one can ever put his foot in the same place.

8. Throughout his life, Harry S. Truman remembered having read him in high school—our last president with such a classical education or, rather, with a *memory* of a classical education.

9. *When!* That is something that you must *always* keep in mind. Yes, history is more than a list of dates; but *when* something happened (or someone lived) may be the most important component of their reality. As a matter of fact, it is indispensable. Julian Marías (a Spanish philosopher) wrote: "We cannot understand the meaning of what a man says unless we know *when* he said it and *when* he lived. Until quite recently, one could read a book or contemplate a painting without knowing the exact period during which it was brought into being.... Today ... all undated reality seems vague and invalid, having the insubstantial form of a ghost."

10. So it is conceivable that after a long disappearance of book printing and book reading, hundreds of years from now more people may actually print and buy and read books—Shakespeare's sonnets or Balzac's novels, for example—than do now.

11. This is worth keeping in mind, especially nowadays. The Renaissance began, in many ways, with an emulation of Greek and Roman forms of art, especially painting, sculpture, and architecture; then the Renaissance craftsmen went on, far beyond emulation, achieving masterpieces of their own. For all art, indeed, all human creation (including the writing of history), must *begin* with emulation, with a wish to imitate the finished achievements of great masters.

12. Surely we do not expect to see George Washington represented as riding in an automobile. That is an *anachronism*—according to the dictionary, "anything existing or represented out of date"—a word that first appeared in English only about three centuries ago.

13. A definite symptom of our present consciousness of history is our knowledge that we live at the end, or near the end, of an age. (A phrase such as "It's like the end of the Roman empire" may be understood or even spoken by many an unschooled man or woman today, when confronted with a particularly ugly example of moral decay.) The Romans of the fourth or fifth centuries AD knew that many things had gone wrong and that matters were so much better in the time of their grandparents, but none of them thought that what was happening to them was something like what had happened to the Assyrians or Egyptians or Greeks.

14. Consider the estimable knowledge of ancient history by our founders, who used much of that knowledge in mulling over the drafting of the new Constitution of the United States.

15. The view that the great cathedral of history is being built brick by brick by historians, some of them filling gaps and forming pillars, while the majority of them add their small bricks in the form of monographs (a monograph is a work dealing with a single subject) or even monographic doctoral dissertations, is not entirely a wrong one—but we must recognize that the greatest of cathedrals are never finished; they are in constant need of cleaning and of refurbishing, indeed, of all kinds of repairs—and also that every generation may see them differently.

16. One of the significant developments of the twentieth century has been the appearance of historians and of the Western methods of historical research among peoples who had been previously unacquainted with them. For, until very recently, history has been a particularly Western form of inquiry and of exposition. The richest chronicles of Indian or Chinese or Japanese culture are legends and chronicles, not histories: they are devoid of the critical sense of a Thucydides. (One exception is the Arab Ibn Khaldoon.) As late as a century ago, a Japanese or Chinese or Indian wishing to read something fairly accurate and particular of the recent history of his country had to rely on histories of his country written by European or English or American historians. This is no longer so.

17. No matter how detailed and assiduous, your research will never be complete. The nineteenth-century monographic ideal was that certifiable historian who, having read every document and every writing relating to his topic, is able to produce a *complete* and *definitive* history of it. This is no longer possible—because of the possibility that new documents, new treatments, and more publications about his topic, many in different places and languages of the world, may yet appear. (Of course some histories are more "definitive" than others. But never absolutely so.)

18. Note this word: historiography. Its literal meaning: the writing of history. Thus, strictly speaking, a PhD in history should really be a PhD in historiography. But no: because in our minds and languages, *historiography* and *history* and *story* overlap. (In the Latin languages, for example, *story* and *history* are the same words.) Yes, because history essentially means telling a story, being (as we saw at the beginning of this essay) descriptive, rather than definitive, while historiography is the study of what others have written about this or that historical topic.

   Allow me to give a personal example. My recent (1997) book *The Hitler of History* is a critical study of the historians and biographers who have written about Hitler. But it is, inevitably, a study of Hitler himself, too. Thus (a) it is both a historiographical and a historical work; and (b) its main subject is that of problems, rather than that of periods— but the latter is true of much history, always.

19. Keep in mind that just as a small book or painting or sculpture or building is not necessarily inferior to large ones, a research paper with an impressive number of footnotes is not necessarily better than one with few footnotes (or even with none).

20. In our colleges and universities, too, the requirements and sometimes the very content of historical study have declined. This includes the tendency to emphasize what is sometimes inadequately called "social history," at times amounting to hardly more than a retrospective and shortsighted sociologizing, something that inspires little interest in students.

21. In the 1920s, Henry Ford proclaimed, "History is bunk," and Herbert Hoover's Secretary of Commerce said, "Tradition is the enemy of Progress." No "conservatives" (or even "liberals") think that way now.

22. Perhaps the Greeks sensed that, too: for them, Memory was the mother of all the Muses.

23. *The Varieties of History* (New York, 1956; revised 1973), edited by Fritz Stern, is another excellent book to have. It deals with the various writings of historians about history itself. Strictly speaking, its contents deal with the varieties of historiography.

24. The French writer Guy de Maupassant (1850–93) said: The aim of the realistic novel "is not to tell a story, to amuse us or to appeal to our feelings, but to compel us to reflect, and to understand the darker and deeper meaning of events."

25. A frivolous remark. Look at the dates of these ancient historians, at a time when the human life span was about forty years long. There is this tendency for historians to live

for a remarkably long time! Of course there are exceptions. But there is no exception to the rule that no good history was ever written by an immature person!

26. Livy was not alone in this. All great historians incline to such a recognition, through all ages. His forerunner Dionysius Halicarnassus (first century BC), a Greek philosopher said: "History is philosophy, teaching by example." This was repeated by Lord Bolingbroke, the English statesman, word for word in the early eighteenth century.

Index ✿✿✿

❦ C ❦

❀ F ❀

❀ G ❀

❈ H ❈

❧ K ❧

❧ O ❧

❧ P ❧

382, 497, 557, 581–82
Pauli, Wolfgang, 60, 75
Peace of Amiens, 144
Pearl Harbor, Japanese attack on, 112, 146,
    192, 265, 416, 528, 536, 569, 666
Pederson, Susan, 134
Péguy, Charles, 74, 77, 347, 498, 663
Peking, 608, 713
Pells, Richard H., 334
Penn, William, 291, 435, 745
Pennell, Elizabeth Robins, 414, 729, 755
Pennell, Joseph, 748, 755
Pennsylvania, 428, 521
Penrose, Boies, 432, 591–92
Pepper, George Wharton, 413, 414, 415,
    416, 432
Perkins, Maxwell, 722
Perón, Juan Domingo, 34, 579, 602
Perret, Geoffrey, 365
Persian Wars (Herodotus), 778
Pétain, Henri Philippe, 358, 481, 510, 528,
    657
Peter I, the Great (Tsar of Russia), 552
Philadelphia, 83, 341, 367, 391, 392, 395,
    411–33, 528, 591, 607, 628, 643, 644,
    668–69, 672, 692, 701, 702, 703, 704,
    706, 707, 714, 727, 728, 731, 733,
    735, 737, 739, 740, 745, 746, 748,
    752, 755, 756, 759, 760, 761, 763
Philadelphia: Patricians and Philistines, 1900–
    1950 (J. Lukacs), 668–69
Philadelphia: The Place and the People
    (Repplier), 741
Philadelphia Centennial Exposition, 446,
    692
Philadelphia Inquirer, 411, 423–24
Philadelphia Redevelopment Authority,
    419, 420
Philip II (King of Spain), 735
Phillips, Wendell, 573
physics, history of, 58–65, 68, 74–75, 77–
    79, 81, 379; nature of, 58–59, 62, 68–
    69, 75
Physics and Philosophy (Heisenberg), 60, 62–
    63
Physicist's Conception of Nature (Heisenberg),
    62, 68
Picasso, Pablo, 85, 136

pictorialization, 595–97, 606, 609, 612,
    642–43, 682, 690
Pieper, Joseph, 663
Pierce, Franklin, 588
Pierre et Jean (Maupassant), 20
Pilate, Pontius, 16
Pilgrim's Way (Buchan), 677
Pilnszky, János, 4, 682
Pinchot, Gifford, 305
Pirandello, Luigi, 709
Pirenne, Henri, 618, 780
Pissarro, Camille, 85, 259
Pius IX, 88, 277, 278
Pius XI, 500, 509, 516
Pius XII, 124, 125, 483, 507, 509–16, 559
Plamenatz, John, 41
Planck, Max, 59, 74, 77
Platen, August von, 204
Plato, 321, 464, 661
Playboy, 584
Pliny the Elder, 779
Pliny the Younger, 779
Plowden, Pamela (Lady Lytton), 281
Plumb, J. H., 283, 293, 294–95
Plutarch, 768–69, 779
Podhoretz, Norman, 333
Pol Pot, 333, 570
Poland, 37, 52, 265, 332, 425, 438, 460,
    478–79, 555, 562
Polanyi, Michael, 647
Poling, Daniel, 412
Polish Revolution (1956), 564
Politics of War (Kolko), 146
Polk, James K., 157
Pollock, Jackson, 85
Polybius, 768, 779
Popalo d'Italia, 108
Popelinère, Henri Voisin de la, 7
populists, 110, 111–12, 114, 148–49, 592
Porter, Cole, 426
Portnoy's Complaint (Roth), 315
Portrait of a Marriage (N. Nicolson), 231
positivism, 76, 77, 78, 378
Potsdam Conference, 534, 563
Pound, Ezra, 338, 582
Poussin, Nicholas, 769
Powell, Anthony, 472
Power, Eileen, 26, 780

About the Author and Editors ❊❊❊

Born in Budapest in 1924, JOHN LUKACS came to the United States in 1946. Until his retirement, he taught history at Chestnut Hill College near Philadelphia. He also held visiting professorships at Columbia, Johns Hopkins, Tufts, and the University of Pennsylvania. A prolific writer, Lukacs's best-known works include *The Duel, Five Days in London, The End of the Twentieth Century and the End of the Modern Age, A Thread of Years,* and *Historical Consciousness.*

MARK G. MALVASI is the author of more than forty essays, editorials, and reviews and has published two books: *The Unregenerate South: The Agrarian Thought of John Crowe Ransom, Allen Tate, and Donald Davidson,* and *Slavery in the Western Hemisphere, c. 1500–1888.* Since 1992, Malvasi has taught at Randolph-Macon College in Ashland, Virginia.

JEFFREY O. NELSON is vice president, publications, at the Intercollegiate Studies Institute. He is the editor of the *University Bookman* and has edited two book collections: *Redeeming the Time,* by Russell Kirk, and *Perfect Sowing: Reflections of a Bookman,* by Henry Regnery. He is also coeditor of *American Conservatism: An Encyclopedia.*